MW01675444

The CQ 1994 Amateur Radio Almanac

First Edition

Edited By Doug Grant, K1DG

CQ Communications, Inc.

Library of Congress Catalog Card Number 93-074224
ISBN 0-943016-06-1

Editor: Doug Grant, K1DG
Managing Editor: Edith Lennon
Assistant Editor: Charlie Morrison, WZ1R
Editorial Assistant: Nancy Barry

Published by CQ Communications, Inc.
76 North Broadway
Hicksville, NY 11801 USA

Printed in the United States of America

Copyright 1993 by CQ Communications, Inc.

All rights reserved. No part of this book may be used or reproduced in any form, or stored in a database or retrieval system without the express written permission of the publisher. Making copies of editorial or pictorial content in any manner except for an individual's own personal use is prohibited, and is in violation of United States copyright laws.

While every precaution has been taken in the preparation of this book, the editor and publisher assume no responsibility for errors or omissions. Neither the editor nor the publisher shall be liable to the purchaser or any other person or entity with respect to liability, loss, or damage caused or alleged to have been caused directly or indirectly by this book or the contents contained herein.

About the Editors...

Doug Grant, K1DG, was originally licensed in 1967 as WN1ICD. He holds the Amateur Extra Class license and has been active in nearly every facet of amateur radio at one time or another. He is best-known for his accomplishments as a contest operator and has held several world and national records in both single-operator and multi-operator categories. He holds DXCC on six bands, has worked all current DXCC countries, and has held reciprocal callsigns in a dozen countries. Doug maintains a competitive contest station in Windham, New Hampshire, where he lives with his wife, Karen, and their two children. He is a Life Member of ARRL, past member and Chairman of the ARRL Contest Advisory Committee, and a member of the CQ Contest Committee.

Edith Lennon has been a writer and editor for a variety of technical and other publications for over 10 years. She is the Editor of CQ's *Equipment Buyer's Guide* and *Beginner's Guide to Amateur Radio* and is involved in several special projects at CQ as well. Edith is also a free-lance travel writer and is currently studying for her first Amateur Radio license.

Charlie Morrison, WZ1R, was first licensed in 1977 as WB2RNT and in 1986 became KD2SX. Charlie discovered ham radio contesting as an SWL in 1976, and has since participated in contests under 35 different callsigns, achieving several W1 area and section single-operator and multi-operator contest records. Charlie is a member of the Yankee Clipper Contest Club, and has 300 countries confirmed, as well as WAC, WAS, and WAZ. He is very interested in radio wave propagation and antennas, and enjoys DXing—he met his wife while on a DXpedition in 1986. He currently lives in Pawtucket, Rhode Island with his wife, Yvonne, and their two children.

Nancy Barry has been an editor at CQ Communications, Inc. for over three years. She is currently the Assistant Editor of *Communications Quarterly*, the *Equipment Buyer's Guide*, the *Beginner's Guide to Amateur Radio*, and the *Popular Communications Communications Guide*.

Dedications

To my wife, Karen, and our kids, who missed out on a lot of weekends and bedtime stories in 1993; and to my parents, who never quite understood what this hobby was all about, but supported me anyway. *—Doug Grant, K1DG*

To Diego, who keeps teaching me without making me feel like a student; to my wife, Yvonne, who has put up with this crazy hobby since she met me; and to our children Rick and Lindsay, who are my joys; and to Mom and Dad.

—Charlie Morrison, WZ1R

CONTENTS

PREFACE TO THE FIRST EDITION

Radio amateurs are pack rats by nature. We save all sorts of miscellaneous parts, books, and useless equipment in the belief that we will someday have a need for all this junk. There's something else we all tend to collect: information. Hams can often recite the model numbers of every piece of equipment they've ever owned. Many can amaze their friends with an astonishing command of obscure geographical trivia, based on years of chasing rare DXCC countries. The simple task of learning enough radio regulations to pass the license exam shows an interest in collecting information.

This book represents a collection of data and information that a lot of hams know is "out there," and would like to have. Ever wonder how many hams there are in your town? Which towns have the most hams in them? Or which celebrities and famous people hold ham licenses besides Barry Goldwater? It's in here—all of that and more. What was the call of the world's fastest CW operator? It's in here. How about the full text of the FCC's landmark PRB-1 ruling? Or the complete, up-to-date version of FCC Part 97? It's in here. What CQ zone is Pratas in?

Like most almanacs, there is also a summary of the Amateur Radio news stories of the past year. Items of real interest like the new rules regarding business communications (97.113). And some historical perspective, like a news roundup of Amateur Radio events of 25, 50, and 75 years ago. For example, do you know why 1919 was the most important year in the history of this hobby? Or when the first World Wide DX Contest was held?

The idea for this project originated with Dick Ross, K2MGA, Publisher of *CQ Magazine*. John Dorr, K1AR, asked me what I thought of the concept of an Almanac of Amateur Radio. I replied that I would probably buy one, if it had enough interesting material in it. Then he asked me what sort of material I'd like to see included. I jotted down a few notes and sent them to John. A few days later, he called and asked if I'd be interested in editing the book. By then, I was hooked and he knew it.

When most people use an Almanac, it's usually to look up one specific thing. Then they generally find themselves turning the pages, discovering all sorts of obscure but interesting facts about history, sports, geography, etc. When I thought about an Amateur Radio Almanac, I began thinking about radio-related equivalents to the topics usually found in Almanacs. When I was done with the final outline, I found myself staring at an intimidating list of data to be collected and assembled into a book, and wondering how it would ever all come together.

Fortunately, help was available in the person of Charlie ("Wiz") Morrison, WZ1R, who became Assistant Editor, and spent endless hours compiling contest statistics and records, verifying data in the library, and tracking down information sources around the world.

Nearly everyone we asked for information was cooperative, and supplied everything we requested and more. Without their generous support, this book would not have been possible. The contributions of the following are hereby gratefully acknowledged: W5YI, VP2ML, K1TR, W1JR, K1MEM, K1AR, W9TO, N6OQZ, N8BJQ, K3EST, N5KR, W3ASK, W6ISQ, K1BV, W3INK, K5ZC, AK1A, NV6Z, K1MM, NX1G, W2JGR, W1IMQ, DL2DN, OH1BR, KC1F, K1RT, K1GPJ, K1TOL, K8GL, NT2X, ON4HW, AD1C, K1DAT, KD6GGD, KD3FU, AA3DI, NX1L of the IARU, Roger Clark of the NTIA. The assistance of K1ZZ, AA2Z, K5FUV, and other staffers at the ARRL was invaluable. Additional assistance was provided by Eric Kihn of the National Geophysical Data Center. One contributor requested anonymity, but this close friend provided the maximum amount of inspiration imaginable.

Further credit is due to Managing Editor Edith Lennon and the CQ production staff, who somehow turned an enormous collection of data into a book.

Our hope is that you will pick up this book from time to time to look something up, and then find yourself jumping from page to page, unable to put it down. And you'll probably think of something that we forgot to include. Don't worry—if you fill out the card inside the back cover with the subject material you want, we'll try to get it for next year's edition.

And while we did our best to verify all the information, we recognize that errors may have crept in. Use the card to correct those for us, too. We'll acknowledge your contributions in the next edition.

73,

Doug

Doug Grant, K1DG
Editor-in-Chief

THE YEAR IN REVIEW, 1993
(September 1992 — August 1993)

Like the weather, if you don't like the current state of Amateur Radio, just wait a while. It will change! Our hobby is entirely regulated by local, state, federal and international law. And regulators like to do just that. Regulate. It has a massive impact on the hobby! Here are what we feel are the major stories of 1993.

Continued Success of the Code Free Technician Class

One Ham in Three Is a Technician

Up until February 14, 1991 (Valentine's Day, no less) the usual way into ham radio in the United States was via the Novice Class which required telegraphy proficiency at 5 words-per-minute. Now there are two entry paths into the Amateur Radio hobby. Today's ham can either begin the traditional way as a Novice (which requires passing a 30 question multiple choice written examination and a 5 wpm code test) or you can pass an additional (25 question) exam instead of learning the code. By passing two written tests you start as a Technician Class amateur. Technicians get to use all spectrum above 30 MHz - including the VHF 2-meter ham band used for voice and computer-to-computer packet radio. Two meters is the ham's social chat line and the most popular band in Amateur Radio.

There can be no doubt that most newcomers today are opting for the Technician route into ham radio. When the No-code Technician Class began, one amateur in four was a Technician. Today, one amateur in three is a Tech. We have added more than 100,000 new Technicians to ham radio since 1991. Or to put it a different way, 80% of the total growth in Amateur Radio is due to establishing the No-Code Technician Class as an alternate way into ham radio.

The big question in code-free hamming was, would interest wear off after the first influx of new operators. The answer is a resounding "No!" The first year of "No Code" saw more than 48,000 newcomers to Amateur Radio. Another 42,500 joined the second year. Compare this with the 18,800 average number of ham operator beginners for the five year period previous!

At the present growth rate, the Amateur Service will grow to more than 1 million licensees by 1999 - with more than 600,000 being from the Technician Class.

"No Business" Rule Changed

New Permissible Amateur Communications

This proceeding got its start more than two years ago when the FCC suggested permitting "other than regular" amateur communications on the ham bands to "provide greater flexibility to transmit communications for public service projects and personal matters."

Historically, amateurs have been restricted to emergency, technical and non-business communications. But the Commission has been overwhelmed in recent years with many requests from the amateur community to deviate from 97.113. Basically that rule bans all commercial communications of any type.

The restrictions were designed to protect the noncommercial character of the Amateur Service and ensure its basis and purpose, that is, as a reservoir of volunteer communicators, technicians and electronics experts dedicated to advancing the radio art, to provide public service communications particularly in times of emergencies, and to enhance international goodwill.

Ham radio was never intended to be a communications service to assist public safety and other government agencies...or for such things as logistical support for parades and other events, classroom instruction, ordering supplies for remotely located organizations, supplying news to the media, selling ham gear, rebroadcasting nonamateur communications...or for expediting the personal and club business of ham operators. In fact these communications are specifically outlawed from the ham bands. Still, the FCC gets dozens of requests to permit this type information to be handled on amateur frequencies.

In trying to find a way to accommodate the steady stream of these requests, the FCC initially thought that perhaps a system of communications priorities might allow amateurs to more fully participate in non-amateur communications. Initially, three types or levels of amateur communications were suggested; Priority, Primary and Secondary.

Those communications which involve emergencies and disasters where the safety of life and property are at stake would be "Priority." Primary communications would be the currently authorized amateur communications. The transporting of all other non-amateur information would be Secondary.

The FCC also remarked that perhaps amateurs might even be permitted to discuss any type of personal and business communications on the ham bands as long as their communications service was not sold.

They listed three possible exceptions: Morse code practice and information bulletins where the operator might be compensated as an employee, and classroom instruction where the teacher was paid.

The challenge was how to write a simple, easy-to-understand rule that allows an expansion of amateur communications without throwing open ham frequencies to those who would exploit them commercially. The Commission asked for recommendations from the American Radio Relay League.

The ARRL responded by agreeing that the FCC should indeed relax the no-business communications rule and legalize more types of communications. They suggested that amateur radio operators should be permitted to conduct communications for themselves or for others that "...could reasonably be furnished alternatively through other radio services" as long as they did not do so "...on a regular basis."

The League also felt that all "...communications for hire or for material compensation direct or indirect, paid or promised" except classroom instruction, telegraphy practice and information bulletins should be outlawed. Surprisingly, the League's proposal did not address the use of ham radio spectrum for personal business use ...a key component of what was to become the FCC's proposal for new permissible communications on the ham bands. The Commission repeatedly mentioned the possibility of using amateur radio to conduct personal business—such as for ordering a pizza or making a hotel reservation - on the amateur air waves!

The ARRL did not define what "on a regular basis" meant except to say that a "...degree of rigidity ...does not properly belong in the content rules for the Amateur Radio Service." In August 1993, the Federal Communications Commission basically adopted the ARRL proposal. Any amateur-to-amateur and personal business communications are now permitted unless:

(a.) Specifically prohibited. These include:

1. Music (except incidental space shuttle music);
2. Communications facilitating a criminal act;
3. Messages obscured by codes or ciphers;
4. Obscene or indecent words or language; and
5. False or deceptive messages, signals or identification.

(b.) Transmissions for compensation. The following exceptions apply:

1. Morse code practice and information bulletins (special criteria);
2. Classroom teachers using ham radio in the classroom.

(c.) Transmissions for the pecuniary benefit of station control operator or his or her employer.

The following communications are permitted, but not "...on a regular basis" which was not further defined by the FCC:

1. Communications which could reasonably be furnished through other radio services;
2. Notices concerning sale or trade of amateur station apparatus; and
3. Retransmissions of Government provided space shuttle, propagation and weather forecast broadcasts.

The Commission has now established a 4-part test that amateurs will have to use in deciding whether or not they should transmit a particular communication. That test is:

(1) whether the communications are for hire or material compensation;

(2) does the control operator or;

(3) his employer have a pecuniary interest in the communication, and;

(4) is it specifically prohibited.

If the control operator determines that he is not on the wrong side of one of those standards, then it is up to them to decide whether or not to transmit that message. And "Yes", it is now legal to order a pizza on the ham bands through an amateur-to-telephone link (commonly known as an auto-patch.) Personal business transactions on the ham bands in which the ham operator or his employer do not benefit are now legal.

The new permissible/prohibited Amateur Service communications guidelines went into effect on September 12, 1993.

Folding the Novice Class into the VEC System

The FCC is very pleased with the way that the Volunteer-Examiner Coordinator (VEC) program has been going. It is the VEC System that provides the ham operator license examinations. Up until 1984, the FCC spent hundreds of thousands of dollars maintaining and conducting the Amateur Service's license examination program. The government said at the time that it was costing them $7.26 to administer a ham exam to a person. Using that figure, it would have cost the Government nearly a million dollars to examine applicants for ham tickets last year. Under the VEC System, this cost is shifted away from the taxpayer.

Up until recently, there were actually two examination programs in the Amateur Service. Beginning "Novices" had been tested informally by two volunteer examiners for decades. The Technician through Amateur Extra Class, however, are tested under the newer VEC System which uses teams of three accredited volunteer examiners (VEs) to conduct the examinations. The VEs are managed by a volunteer-examiner coordinator (VEC) who acts as the link between the FCC and the volunteer testing community. They also develop all of the examination questions—including those for the Novice class. Since all VEC System examination teams are known, it is a relatively simple administrative job to keep the VE teams up-to-date.

More than a year ago, the American Radio Relay League's ARRL-VEC and the W5YI-VEC which together account for 85% of all VEC testing asked the FCC to also include Novice Class testing under the VEC System. For one thing, errors are less frequent in the VEC System while Novice applications have an error rate approaching 10%. Error handling is not only costly to the Government but they slow down license issuance since the applications must be returned for correction.

The data on the Novice system is also incomplete since the FCC has no idea how many people fail the exam, unlike the VEC System where the passing rate is closely monitored as one of its vital signs. Having only one testing system would also simplify the application Form 610 by eliminating the separate certification section and Novice instructions. And the safeguards in the VEC System minimize the potential for fraud.

The single biggest advantage, however, is that the Novice level volunteer examiner will be kept current on test questions and procedures since their identities will be known. Such was not the case previously.

Shortly after the joint proposal, the FCC adopted a Notice of Proposed Rulemaking which looked toward consolidating the two testing programs. "Our experience with the VEC System and with the current Novice examination system indicates that the VEC System is the superior system," the FCC said. "The informal ad hoc Novice system is inefficient and susceptible to various irregularities." The Commission pointed out that all Novice examinations are currently being administered in the VEC System as a part of other classes of operator licenses.

The FCC proposed to include the responsibility for the preparation and administration of Novice Class operator license examinations under the VEC System with the same conditions that apply to the four higher classes of licenses. These conditions include requiring each VE to be accredited by a VEC, three VEs for the administration of an examination, coordination by a VEC of each examination session, issuance of a Certificate of Successful Completion of Examination (CSCE) to every examine who scores a passing grade on an examination element and expense reimbursement (a test fee) authorized to the testing community.

The W5YI-VEC also suggested that General Class VEs be authorized to conduct Technician Class examinations since this examination requires more examiners and would more positively impact the General Class VE - some of whom might feel they are losing testing privileges.

On May 3, 1993, the FCC Commissioners agreed to place Novice Class operator license examinations in the VEC System. The use of General Class licensees to serve as VE's for the Novice and Technician Class was also approved. The new rules went into effect on July 1, 1993. There is now only one examination program in the Amateur Service, the VEC System.

New Novice and Technician Question Pools

Element 2 and 3(A) Revised

97.523 of the Amateur Service rules require that "All VECs must cooperate in maintaining one question pool for each written examination element. These question pools must contain at least ten times the number of questions required for a single examination. Each question pool must be published and made available to the public prior to its use for making a question set." The VECs Question Pool Committee began reviewing all Element 2 (Novice) and Element 3A (Technician) examination questions during the summer of 1992.

All examination questions and multiple choices for all five written Amateur Radio operator license tests are revised on a four year cycle. The amateur community participates in this process by submitting their recommendations for examination topics and questions. Novice and Technician are reviewed together since they are the sole requirement for the new no-code Technician license. Volunteer examiners must begin using the new questions in their examinations every July 1st.

The Question Pool Committee determined and released the new Element 2 and Element 3A question pools into the public domain on December 1992. They contain approximately 10% less questions than the previous versions. There were 695 questions in the previous pools; only 645 in the current set.

A list of all questions in the new Element 2 and 3A pools appears in this Almanac, courtesy of The W5YI Group.

All license preparation publishers agreed to have their new Codeless Technician study manuals available in the publishing marketplace during May 1993. The newly revised Element 2 and 3(A) question pools began showing up in all Novice and Technician written examinations administered after June 30, 1993. All VECs and VEs use exactly the same word-for-word questions, multiple choices and answers.

The next question pool to be revised will be the General Class. The VEC's Question Pool Committee has been working on these questions and a new Element 3B question pool will be released by year end 1993. The new General Class questions must be used in all examinations effective July 1, 1994. Newly revised Advanced Class questions take effect on July 1, 1995; Amateur Extra Class on July 1, 1996.

Privatization of Commercial Radio Operator Examinations

Because of budgetary constraints, the FCC asked for and received legislation authorizing it to delegate the examination of commercial radio operators to non-government organizations. Currently, there are six types of commercial radio licenses and two types of endorsements. In addition, there are two new commercial licenses; the Global Maritime Distress and Safety System Radio Operator's and Maintainer's license.

Actually this proceeding started in the Field Operations Bureau (FOB) since it was they who administered the examinations. Last year, the responsibility for Commercial Radio Operator examinations was transferred to the Private Radio Bureau and PRB has now assumed control of the rulemaking. The Notice of Proposed Rulemaking asked the public for their views on how such a private sector program should be structured.

During early 1993, the FCC issued a Report and Order transferring the handling of all future Commercial Radio Operator license examinations to the private sector. Basically, the FCC's Commercial Radio Operator license testing program will be handled in much the same fashion as the successful VEC System in the Amateur Service. That is, examinations will be constructed by selecting questions from a large bank of publicly known questions.

To get the program going, the FCC solicited potential test questions from interested parties and received over 2,200 potential question pool candidates from many different groups. Eventually there will be seven different question sets. Both the questions and multiple choices being released to the public.

The first two pools made available are the Element 1 (Basic radio law and radiotelephone operating practices which every maritime operator should be familiar with) and Element 3 (Electronic fundamentals and techniques.) These two pools contain nearly 900 questions. The questions, multiple choices and answers were released to the public during September 1993. The other question pools will follow in the coming six month period.

Passing Elements 1 and 3 (the pass mark is 75% answered correct) will yield a General Radiotelephone Operator License (GROL) to the applicant. The GROL, (which was previously known as the First Class Radiotelephone) is the most popular of all commercial radio operator licenses. The Element 1 examination contains 24 questions, Element 3: 76, for a total of 100 questions. The applicant must answer 18 Element 1 and 57 Element 3 correctly.

The General Radiotelephone Operator License is required to adjust, maintain or internally repair transmitters in the aviation, maritime and international fixed public radio services. It also permits operation of high powered maritime radio stations and pleasure vessels operating at more than 1,000 watts. Many companies also require the GROL as an indication of technical proficiency in communications and electronics.

The FCC's new Commercial Radio Operator testing program is directed by private groups known as Commercial Operator Licensing Examination Managers (COLEMs.)

Examination managers are responsible for recruiting examiners, establishing testing centers, announcing examination sessions, and preparing, administering, grading, and notifying applicants of passed examinations. A "Proof of Passing" certificate (PPC) issued by the COLEM or his representative to examinees certifies the examinee's qualifications.

Nine different organizations were certified by the FCC as COLEMs last summer from more than 60 groups that applied. Those selected are NABER (National Association of Business and Educational Radio, Inc., (ISCET) International Society of Certified Electronic Technicians, Elkins Institute, Sylvan Learning Systems, Sea School, Inc., Drake Training and Technology, ETAI (Electronic Technicians Association International), NARTE (the National Association of Radio and Telecommunications Engineers, Inc.) and NRE (National Radio Examiners.) NRE, a division of The W5YI Group, Inc., was the only COLEM chosen by the FCC that also administers Amateur Service examinations.

Each COLEM has now entered into a Memorandum of Agreement with the Government and the FCC has put out a Public Notice announcing the new commercial radio operator license examination program. Applicants wishing to take a Commercial Radio Operator examination are asked to contact a COLEM. Of interest to ham radio operators is that Amateur Extra class operators are automatically given credit for the telegraphy portion of the Second Class Radiotelegraph Operator Certificate without examination.

Special Personal and Club Station Callsigns

According the FCC, the most asked question is "How can I get a specific call sign?" As it is now, you can change your call sign but you can not get a specific combination. It now appears that this is all about to change! The FCC has not issued club and military recreation ham station call signs since 1978. Special station call signs have not been available since the mid-1970's when Extra Class amateurs were permitted to select an available station call.

In 1989, the FCC terminated a proceeding that looked into whether a custom-assigned callsign system could be established using private sector support. The FCC concluded that such a system would be too costly. Some hams offered to pay for callsigns, but the FCC did not have authority to charge a fee for the this service.

In the Telecommunications Act of 1992, Congress authorized the FCC to use the uncompensated and unreimbursed services of amateur radio organizations who have tax exempt status under Sec. 501(c)3 of the Internal Revenue Service code to provide club and military recreation call signs. Several amateur organizations applied to become club call sign administrators. The ARRL asked that they be designated as the exclusive club and military recreational station call sign administrator.

This past summer, Congress surprised the amateur community by including a provision for "vanity" amateur station call signs in President Clinton's much publicized Deficit Reduction Plan. The legislation authorizes the Federal Communications Commission to issue unique amateur station call signs at a cost of $7.00 per year to the general ham radio population. This action was largely the result of a single amateur (Jim Wills, N5HCT, of Tyler, TX) who told his congressman that amateurs were indeed willing to pay for a special call sign. It came at an opportune time since the Clinton administration was looking for ways to generate revenue. Clinton signed the legislation into law on August 10th. The Commission now has the authority to charge for special ham call signs.

The FCC is in the process of bringing a new computer system on-line at their Gettysburg, PA, licensing facility. And it is being programmed to issue distinctive "vanity" call signs. These special call signs will be in addition to the current Group A, B, C and D call sign system adopted in 1978. That system permits higher class amateurs to qualify for shorter - and theoretically more desirable - amateur radio station call signs by upgrading their license class. That plan provides for 7 prefix blocks, 93 prefixes (AA-AL, K, KA-KZ, N, NA-NZ, W, WA-WZ), 5 format arrangements (1x2, 1x3, 2x1, 2x2 and 2x3) in each of the 10 Amateur Service regions. Although a total of 14,888,860 combinations are possible, only 4% of the available call signs are currently assigned.

The FCC has said that it could be possible in the future - maybe as early as 1994—to obtain any unassigned call sign, "will" call signs to heirs or friends ...or retire a callsign permanently. An applicant would list up to five call signs and the first available call would be assigned. And there could be two types of "reserved" calls. First, upon notification, a current holder of a call sign could reserve his/her call for assignment only to a designated club station or to a designated person upon that person becoming eligible for a call sign in that group. Second, anyone—amateur or non-amateur—could reserve any available call sign. This reserved call sign would be available for assignment only to a designated club station or to a designated person, including the person making the reservation upon that person becoming eligible for a call sign in that group.

Since the FCC now has authority to issue "vanity" station call signs, the earlier authorized special club and military call sign program has been put on "hold." It is now anticipated that the FCC will now handle all issuance of special call signs rather than use the previously proposed Call Sign Administrators from the private sector.

The FCC is also considering a system that would allow new hams to become control operators immediately after passing the required examinations. The current system requires a wait of two or three months for the first call sign to arrive! The "instant authorization" would utilize a temporary call sign from the WZ-by-3 letter call sign block. A new Amateur would simply use his initials and the appropriate license class identifier indicating that he/she has qualified for a specific amateur license class.

Electronic amateur operator/station application filing should also be in place in 1994. VEC's, using a PC, will be able to file Form 610 applications over the phone lines with the FCC in Gettysburg, PA. It is anticipated that with electronic filing, ham licenses could be issued in as little as a week or less.

Packet Message Forwarding

Early in 1991, several hams were cited for unknowingly and automatically retransmitting an anti-war packet message supposedly originated by another politically active ham. The message urged amateurs to vote against the Persian Gulf war by telephoning "900-44-NO WAR" to tell President Bush "NO WAR." It wound its way through several packet stations before being killed.

The Commission believed that the message was a prohibited communication in that it advanced the business interests of "The Coalition to Stop U.S. Intervention in the Middle East." Furthermore, "900" phone calls almost always generate revenue which presented the likelihood that this also might be a fund raising scheme being promoted on the ham bands.

The FCC action faulting amateurs for automatically retransmitting questionable messages they did not originate caused immediate havoc in the ham community. Under the current rules each amateur licensee is fully responsible for assuring that the contents of every transmission from his or her station complies with the rules. Many said the amateur high-speed packet network would have to shut down since there was no way thousands of messages passing through a mail switch could be reviewed by a human control operator one by one.

The Commission now agrees that message screening of automatic data systems is difficult and diminishes the advantage of high speed. It has now issued a Notice of Proposed Rulemaking that would establish a compliance policy of holding the licensee of the station originating a message and the licensee of the first forwarding station accountable for the transmission of prohibited communications.

Under this approach, amateurs that only retransmit messages within a high speed message forwarding system would not be responsible for the messages they forward or their stations retransmit unwittingly. At press time, the proceeding had gone through the Notice and Comment period and a final Report and Order is expected shortly.

Licensing of Visiting Foreign Amateurs

This rulemaking suggests a novel licensing scheme whereby all foreign licensed amateur radio operators temporarily visiting the United States would be able to operate their amateur radios for up to 60 days. It would more or less replace the current reciprocal licensing procedure.

The FCC issues about 2100 one-year reciprocal permits annually to amateurs from the country whose governments have signed reciprocal agreements with the United States. The only way a ham from a country that does not have the reciprocal agreement can get on the air in the United States or its possessions is to pass the exams. Both of these procedures are time consuming.

A new rule being considered would complete the whole process during one quick visit to a VEC System exam session. It would work like this: VE teams would determine the extent of a foreign hams operating privileges and determine how this most closely corresponds with U.S. privileges. A 20 question multiple-choice test on FCC rules and regulations (pass rate: 90%) would then be administered to the visiting foreign amateur. A CSCE (Certificate of Successful Completion of Examination) issued by a VE team would validate immediate 60 day operation. The VECs would keep track of these authorizations by maintaining a database of all 60-day temporary operating permits.

Comments closed on this NPRM some time ago and final FCC action is expected shortly. Some of the comments indicate that VE teams might have a difficult time deciphering the operating privileges granted by a foreign ham ticket most of which are in an unfamiliar language. On the other hand, hundreds of reciprocal operating permits are currently issued to foreign amateurs annually by the Commission.

The FCC in Gettysburg also has the same problem but manages to issue the permit anyway. Even if a foreign license can not be fully understood, the FCC has a Part 97 regulation that covers the situation. The rules governing reciprocal licenses (Part 97.107) state that the "...operating terms and conditions [of a reciprocal permit are those] issued by the alien's government ...not to exceed the privileges of an Amateur Extra Class operator license".

The FCC staff has finished their work on this proceeding and a Report and Order adopting the measure in some form is expected. The ARRL is on record as opposing the procedure. They would rather see the United States work toward a common licensing program of radio amateurs throughout the world.

Automatic Control of HF Packet

Several amateur stations have been operating high frequency digital communications under a Special Temporary Operating Authority (STA) for more than five years! The one year authority has been extended five times. The American Radio Relay League has now proposed permanent rules governing HF data operation under automatic control.

The current rules do not permit automatic networking below 50 MHz and third party traffic must use the AX.25 packet protocol. The big concern about HF packet is the potential for "robot" stations to interfere with HF ham band operation. HF packet appears to work well and "tons" of messages move along the network.

It is generally agreed that any HF packet operation should be conducted on specific subbands rather than being allowed on entire bands. A compromise plan to permit semi-automatic control was criticized as unworkable and unacceptable by HF packeteers.

An IARU (International Amateur Radio Union) Region 2 General Assembly meeting produced an HF band plan which provided for automatically controlled data communications. These segments include all bands between 80 and 10 meters and provide for all digital modes including new Clover and Pactor systems. Any HF data operation outside these segments must be under local control

With respect to HF data transmissions, the League is now recommending that: "Consistent with the frequency privileges and other operating limitations applicable to the license class of the operator, any amateur station may be operated under automatic control using any accepted protocol for data transmission within the following frequency segments: 28.120–28.189 MHz, 24.925–24.930 MHz, 21.090–21.100 MHz, 18.105–18.110 MHz, 14.095–14.0995 MHz, 14.1005–14.112 MHz, 10.140–10.150 MHz, 7.100–7.105 MHz and 3.620–3.635 MHz. Such stations should be equipped with means to limit transmissions to no more than five minutes in the event of an equipment malfunction or interruption of contact with another station. Third party communications may be transmitted under automatic control using any authorized emission code, provided that the retransmitted messages must originate at a station that is being locally or remotely controlled. HF data operation should be permitted outside these specified subbands as per current rules, but only under local (or remote) control."

Dealers Cited for Marketing Expanded Coverage Radios

Three Los Angeles area amateur radio equipment dealers received Notices of Apparent Liability (NAL's) in the amount of $7,000 each for marketing a well-known compact HF transceiver (specifically, the Kenwood TS-50S) which could be "...operated on frequencies not authorized for amateur radio use." The dealers were investigated by engineers from the FCC's Cerritos, California, field office between March 8 and 10, 1993, in response to a complaint lodged against the manufacturer (the FCC did not identify the party that complained). Each of the dealers were ordered to either pay the fine or to "...file a written response showing why the forfeiture should be reduced or not imposed...."

The violations cited by the FCC involved equipment that was not properly type accepted (approved) as required prior to marketing to the public. A sales brochure initially distributed to the manufacturer's dealer network and the public showed operating ranges of the radio to be significantly above and below the authorized U.S. ham bands. While the manufacturer later had the flyers reprinted to show operation only on authorized amateur spectrum, the FCC said it confirmed the radios would operate outside the ham bands.

Even though the FCC visited the three amateur radio equipment dealers in early March, the NAL's were not issued by J.R. Zoulek, Engineer-in-Charge of the Los Angeles field office until July 2nd. Zoulek said that, for the most part, amateur transceivers that have the capability to transmit on other than amateur spectrum must be approved (type accepted) by the FCC. He said there were exceptions, ...such as spectrum assigned to the U.S. Government.

The 27.5 to 28.0 MHz band is partially allocated to the Land Mobile (Business Radio) Service and Part 90.203 (a) and (b) of the FCC Rules cover the land mobile service type acceptance requirements. A radio that is capable of transmitting on spectrum that requires type acceptance must be approved by the Commission. Amateur transceivers that just transmit on amateur frequencies are not required to be FCC approved.

The FCC citation was issued based on a 1987 Public Notice entitled "Extended Coverage Transceivers in the Amateur Service." This bulletin said that "The Commission has noted that a number of transceivers marketed for use in the ARS are also capable of transmitting in the adjacent bands allocated to other radio services, such as the Private Land Mobile Radio Services and the Maritime Services. Some manufacturers are offering conversion kits to permit their transmitters and receivers to be modified so that they can operate in a similar manner.

The manufacturers and users of such devices are reminded that transmitters intended for operation on frequencies allocated to most of the licensed services, e.g., the Private Land Mobile Radio Services, Maritime Services, etc., must be type accepted by the Commission for the particular radio service in which they are intended to operate prior to the marketing or use of such devices. Transmitters used in the ARS, as well as transmitters used by the Civil Air Patrol (CAP) and the Military Affiliate Radio System (MARS) must comply with the applicable standards but are not required to be type accepted.

It is a violation of the Commissions regulations to: (1) market an Amateur Radio Service (ARS) transmitter that is intended to operate, also, on frequency bands outside of the ARS, CAP, or MARS bands without a grant of equipment authorization required for the radio service(s) in which the transmitter operates; (2) market or operate a transmitter that requires a grant of equipment authorization but for which no grant has been issued; or (3) transmit on a frequency allocated to a licensed service without the appropriate commission-issued station license."

Zoulek said there were several frequency bands at issue, not just the so-called "freeband" between 27.5 MHz and the bottom of the amateur ten meter band. He said he was especially concerned about interference to public safety frequencies. "The radio regulations are written as a scheme to encourage people to transmit in an orderly fashion. And if people would abide by the Rules, then we would not have any problems."

Contributed by Frederick O. Maia, W5YI

FCC ACTIONS OF INTEREST TO AMATEURS (September 1992 - August 1993)

One of the biggest changes to the rules covering amateur radio occurred in August 1993, when the FCC modified the rules relating to use of amateur radio for business communications.

The following is the text of the 1993 change to FCC rule 97.113:

97.113 Prohibited Transmissions.

(a) No amateur station shall transmit:

(1) Communications specifically prohibited elsewhere in this Part:

(2) Communications for hire or for material compensation, direct or indirect, paid or promised, except as otherwise provided in these rules;

(3) Communications in which the station licensee or control operator has a pecuniary interest, including communications on behalf of an employer. Amateur operators may, however, notify other amateur operators of the availability for sale or trade, of apparatus normally used in an amateur station, provided that such activity is not conducted on a regular basis;

(4) Music using a phone emission except as specifically provided elsewhere in this Section; Communications intended to facilitate a criminal act; Messages in codes or ciphers intended to obscure the meaning thereof, except as otherwise provided herein; Obscene or indecent words or language; or false or deceptive messages, signals, or identification;

(5) Communications, on a regular basis, which could reasonably be furnished alternatively through other radio services.

(b) An amateur station shall not engage in any form of broadcasting, nor may an amateur station transmit one-way communications except as specifically provided in these rules; nor shall an amateur station engage in any activity related to program production or newsgathering for broadcasting purposes, except that communications directly related to the immediate safety of human life or the protection of property may be provided by amateur stations to broadcasters for dissemination to the public where no other means of communication is reasonably available before or at the time of the event.

(c) A control operator may accept compensation as an incident of a teaching position during periods of time when an amateur station is used by that teacher as a part of classroom instruction at an educational institution.

(d) A control operator of a club station may accept compensation for the periods of time when the station is transmitting telegraphy practice or information bulletins, provided that the station transmits such telegraphy practice and bulletins for at least 40 hours per week; schedules operations on at least six amateur service MF and HF bands using reasonable measures to maximize coverage; where the schedule of normal operating times and frequencies is published at least 30 days in advance of the actual transmissions; and where the control operator does not accept any direct or indirect compensation for any other service as a control operator.

(e) No station shall retransmit programs or signals emanating from any type of radio station other than an amateur station, except propagation and weather forecast information intended for use by the general public and originated from United States Government stations, and communications, including incidental music, originating on United States Government frequencies between a space shuttle and its associated Earth stations. Prior approval for shuttle retransmissions must be obtained from the National Aeronautics and Space Administration. Such retransmissions must be for the exclusive use of amateur operators. Propagation, weather forecasts, and shuttle retransmissions may not be conducted on a regular basis, but only occasionally, as an incident of normal amateur radio communications.

(f) No amateur station, except an auxiliary, repeater or space station, may automatically retransmit the radio signals of other amateur stations.

222 and 1240 MHz Band Changes

The FCC proposed several changes in the 222 and 1240 MHz amateur bands. The first would establish a small new subband in the 222-MHz band, where repeater stations would be prohibited in order to enhance weak-signal communications and experimentation.

The second proposal would allow Novice Class licensees access to the entire 222-225 MHz amateur band.

The third proposal would allow Novice Class operators to be licensees and control operators of repeaters in the 222-225 MHz band and in the 1270-1295 MHz Novice subband of the 1240-1300 MHz band.

The "weak signal" proposal was made by the ARRL in November, 1991, following the reassignment of 220-222 MHz to commercial interests (see January, 1992 *QST*, page 73, and April, 1992 *QST*, page 62). The League suggested a 150-kHz subband at 222.00-222.15 MHz for such weak signal work. The ARRL at that time also requested expansion of Novice operating privileges to include the entire 222-MHz band, in order to establish a common meeting ground where Novices could sample other modes of amateur operation in addition to repeaters.

The proposed changes in Novice repeater licensee and control operator privileges came as the result of petitioner Michael C. Trahos, who argued that the amateur service should follow the General Mobile Radio Service and the Private Land Mobile Radio Services, where user licensees may also be licensees of repeaters without being required to pass any additional examination.

The Commission said it believed there was merit in the petitions of both the ARRL and Trahos, and asked for comments on the proposed rule changes in PR Docket 92-289.

219-220 MHz Band Proposed

The FCC proposed in ET Docket 93-40 to establish a secondary allocation for the amateur service in the 219-220 MHz band to be used for amateur auxiliary station (point-to-point) packet backbone networks and other amateur point-to-point fixed communications. The Commission also proposed operating limits and other measures to ensure that such amateur operations do not cause interference to primary operations in and adjacent to the 219-220 MHz band.

The FCC noted that these systems can be used in times of emergency when other communications facilities are out of service or too overloaded to efficiently carry a large volume of messages, and that amateurs plan to use wideband backbone packet radio networks to provide intercity links of their local packet radio systems.

The Commission is proposing to authorize amateur wideband packet point-to-point communications and other point-to-point fixed communications on a secondary basis in the 219-220 MHz band. The Commission said it believes this will foster technological experimentation and innovation, particularly with higher data rates, and facilitate the construction of a nationwide packet data backbone network. The Commission expects that this action will relieve congestion in the 222-225 MHz band in certain geographic areas. The Commission said the amateurs' ability to perform interference analysis, the directional nature of the proposed services, and the secondary status of this proposed allocation should adequately protect all primary and existing secondary operations in and adjacent to the 219-220 MHz band.

The FCC later issued a Notice of Proposed Rule Making to create a new shared band for amateurs at 219-220 MHz. In RM-7747 the Commission would allocate 219-220 MHz to amateurs on a secondary basis for amateur for point-to-point fixed communications.

The FCC said the new allocation would help alleviate crowding in the 222-225 MHz band and would facilitate establishment of regional and nationwide backbone networks for amateur packet communications.

The FCC proposed requirements to ensure that secondary use of the 219-220 MHz band by amateurs does not interfere with primary and existing secondary licensees in this and adjacent bands.

The FCC cited several commenters who supported the League's request, as well as one opposing it. The Association for Maximum Service Television (MSTV) said that no amateur operations should be allowed in the 216-220 MHz range because of a potential for interference to TV channel 13 (at 210-216 MHz).

The FCC said that amateur access to the 216-219 MHz range is not feasible because of potential interference to other point-to-point services, and to TV channel 13. The FCC said that amateurs do have the technical expertise to design their packet systems to operate in the 219-220 MHz band without interference to other services.

The FCC also agreed that power limits suggested by the ARRL in its petition (25 watts PEP for Novices, 50 watts PEP for all others) "are appropriate and reasonable," but are not proposing Novices be permitted to operate at 219-220 MHz.

The FCC proposed a notification system to prevent interference by amateur stations to stations in the Automated Maritime Telecommunications Systems (AMTS) and in some cases to require written permission from such AMTS stations.

Finally, amateur operation in the 219-220 MHz band would be limited to 56 kilobauds and a maximum bandwidth of 100 kHz, although the FCC requested comments on relaxing the 56-kB limit.

449 MHz Wind-Profiler Radars

The FCC on March 10, 1993 agreed to issue a Notice of Proposed Rule Making and Notice of Inquiry on the subject of wind profiler radars (ET Docket 93-59). The NPRM and NOI were issued on April 1, 1993.

The FCC proposed to allocate the 448-450 MHz band on a primary basis to wind profiler radar systems (wind profilers) and requests comment on whether wind profilers also should be accommodated on a secondary basis in the 915 MHz band, as proposed by Radian Corporation, or in some other frequency band.

Based on a study by the National Telecommunications and Information Administration (NTIA), the FCC called for comment on whether potential interference between 449-MHz amateur and wind profiler operations could be alleviated by using RF screens or by altering repeater antenna radiation patterns.

The FCC also said it will consider zones around wind profilers in which amateur transmitters would be prohibited. The FCC says that since 449-MHz wind profilers are planned primarily for rural areas, it expects few amateur operations to be disrupted.

The FCC also said it is not proposing to change amateurs' secondary status in the 448-450 MHz range, since amateurs already are required to protect against interference to government services with which it already shares that spectrum.

As for the inquiry into 915 MHz wind profilers, the FCC called for technical information and says it will consider the proposal "with other existing and proposed uses."

902-928 MHz Band

The FCC proposed new rules in PR Docket 93-61 to allow greater use of the 902-928 MHz band for so-called automatic vehicle monitoring systems. The proposed new rules would replace interim rules adopted in 1974.

An FCC news release said,

> The Commission proposed to expand the service to encompass location of all objects, animate and inanimate, and to allow licensees to provide service on a private carrier basis to individuals, the Federal Government, and Part 90 eligibles. The Commission also proposed to rename the AVM service as the Location and Monitoring Service (LMS) and to define LMS as the use of non-voice signalling methods from and to radio units to make known the location of such units.
>
> Comments are requested on this proposal and on whether LMS systems and other entities currently occupying the 902-928 MHz band will be capable of handling any increased congestion.
>
> In the 902-928 MHz band, the Commission proposed that wide-band and narrow-band LMS systems not be licensed on the same spectrum. The Commission proposed the wide-band LMS systems be licensed on the 904-912 and 918-926 MHz bands and the narrow-band LMS systems be licensed on the 902-904, 912-918, and 926-928 MHz bands. The Commission believes that wide-band systems are capable of operating in a shared environment, with cooperation among the various licensees, but solicits comments on the need and desirability of providing for exclusivity for some period of time....

Amateurs currently share this band with government radiolocation, fixed, and mobile services. The FCC noted that interference from all of these services, including amateur, to the expanded LMS systems is possible.

The FCC also asked for comments from potential LMS users on whether,

> ...they believe it possible to establish reliable LMS systems considering the number and diversity of other users of this band. If not, commenters should offer potential solutions, such as removing Part 15 users and amateur operations from the band, restricting where such users could operate in the band, or placing stricter limitations on the operations in this band.

RF Effects Guidelines

The FCC released a Notice of Proposed Rule Making to update guidelines and methods used for evaluating the environmental effects of radiofrequency radiation, based on new RF exposure standards adopted by the American National Standards Institute, in conjunction with the Institute of Electronic and Electrical Engineers, in 1992.

In 1985 the FCC adopted 1982 ANSI guidelines, which resulted in some transmitting facilities being required to prepare an Environmental Assessment if they would expose humans to RF levels greater than those recommended by the guidelines. Under the 1985 guidelines many low-power, intermittent, or normally inaccessible RF facilities were excluded from the FCC's rules, including Amateur Radio stations.

The new, 1992 ANSI guidelines in many respects are more restrictive in the amount of RF permitted and they also extend the frequency range under consideration from 3 kHz to 300 GHz. The new guidelines also specify two sets of exposure recommendations, one for "controlled environments" (usually involving workers) and one for "uncontrolled environments" (usually involving the general public).

Hand-held devices are treated for the first time in the new ANSI guidelines. The 1982 guidelines included exclusions for devices that did not exceed a "specific absorption rate" (SAR) or whose input was 7 watts or less. The 1992 guidelines also contain low-power exclusions, but they are more stringent and could require manufacturers to demonstrate compliance with SAR requirements.

More Power Denied

The FCC has denied a request for a waiver of the amateur 1,500 watt power output limitation. Dale Gagnon, KW1I, of Bowe, NH, had asked for the waiver earlier, as well as a reconsideration of the FCC's original denial. The FCC said that Gagnon's latest request for a waiver "has not shown that his circumstances are unique nor has he presented any facts that would warrant a waiver."

Gagnon wanted the waiver for his own use, to legally operate on AM at a PEP power more than 1,500 watts output.

Electronic Filings

The FCC on April 1 changed its rules to allow for the eventual "electronic" filing of license applications in the private radio services. Currently all license applications must include a handwritten signature. Last October, Congress amended the Communications Act of 1934 to allow electronic filing of applications, applications signed "in any manner or form, including by electronic means, as the Commission may prescribe by regulation."

Any changes to come will only be after the FCC has established procedures for electronic filing; for now amateurs, and all others, are still bound by the handwritten signature requirement.

HF Digital Rules

The FCC issued a Public Notice on the ARRL proposal for rule making regarding digital rules for the amateur high frequency bands. The proceeding, which bears the file number RM-8218, originated with submission of a request by the League on February 1, 1993. A synopsis appears on page 82, *QST* for March, 1993.

30 Meter Petition Denied

The FCC has denied a petition to grant Novice and Morse code certified Technician class licensees access to the amateur 30 meter band. The petition, by William G. Welsh, W6DDB, asked that such licensees be allowed CW operation from 10.1 to 10.15 MHz.

Welsh argued that the 40, 15, and 10 meter bands currently occupied by Novices and Technicians are becoming less useful due to changing sunspot conditions and interference from shortwave broadcast stations. He also said that the longer antennas needed for operation on 80 meters limited the appeal of that band for Novices and Technicians.

The FCC said that in opening the 30 meter band to the Amateur Service in 1985 it had not included Novices and Technicians in order to promote an acceptable balance between licensing incentives and operating privileges. It followed the same guideline in the opening of the 17 meter band in 1989; thus, this petition for rule making was repetitive, the FCC said.

Scanner Ban

Effective April 26, 1993, the FCC banned the importation and sale of radio scanners capable of receiving cellular telephone transmissions (ET Docket 93-1).

While the FCC denied an ARRL request for specific wording that bona fide amateur equipment be exempted from the new rules, the Commission did agree to modify its proposed rule on converters so that it applies only to converters "designed or marketed for use with scanning receivers."

The new regulations change Parts 2 and 15 of the FCC Rules to prohibit the manufacture or importation of radio scanners capable of receiving frequencies allocated to the Domestic Public Cellular Radio Telecommunications Service (presently, 824-849 and 869-984 MHz).

The FCC's new rules, in addition to the anticipated banning of scanners capable of tuning cellular telephone frequencies (or of being easily modified to do so), also prohibit frequency converters that either convert or are easily modified to convert cellular frequencies to other frequencies outside the cellular band that are easily received by most scanners.

It is possible that commercial manufacturers may file petitions for reconsideration, particularly for clarification of the "readily modified" definition.

Changes in FCC rules regarding radio scanners capable of receiving cellular telephone transmissions will be implemented over the next year.

Effective with the adoption of the new FCC Part 15 rules on April 26, 1993, the Commission will not grant equipment authorization for receivers that do not comply with the new provisions of Part 15.121. These new provisions do not prohibit the sale or use of authorized receivers manufactured in the U.S., or imported into the U.S., prior to April 26, 1994.

In addition, the manufacture or importation of scanning receivers, and frequency converters designed or marketed for use with scanning receivers, that do not comply with the new provisions in Part 15.121, must cease by April 26, 1994.

FCC Fines are Fine

A federal court judge in Washington, D.C., decided in favor of the FCC in a lawsuit brought by Action for Children's Television and 20 other broadcasting and public-interest organizations, challenging the FCC's monetary forfeiture procedures in indecency cases. The ARRL had filed a friend-of-the-court brief to protect the interests of radio amateurs in effective FCC enforcement.

On May 18, 1993, U.S. District Judge Royce C. Lamberth granted an FCC motion to dismiss the plaintiffs' request that all indecency forfeiture proceedings currently before the FCC be dismissed; as well as a Commission motion to dismiss the major complainants in the lawsuit for "lack of standing."

In addition, Judge Lamberth granted the FCC's motion to dismiss the two other major points sought by the plaintiffs:

1. To find that the review procedures now used by the FCC cannot constitutionally be used to adjudicate alleged indecency violations under federal law; and
2. To enjoin the FCC from initiating or conducting forfeiture proceedings for alleged violations of federal law concerning indecency.

The court did deny the FCC's motion to dismiss a constitutional claim by Infinity Broadcasting Corp. arising from a 1990 Notice of Apparent Liability.

The entire case was ordered dismissed.

License Fees Rejected

Several items of interest to radio amateurs are related to the Omnibus Budget Reconciliation Act (H.R. 2264).

One draft version of the bill would have imposed an annual regulatory fee on every licensed ham in the U.S. Through efforts by the ARRL's Washington representatives, the Act, *minus* the fee for Amateurs, was reported out of the Budget Reconciliation Conference Committee and passed by the House and Senate.

Amateurs also moved a step closer to being able to obtain specific callsigns. The budget bill includes a provision for the FCC to charge a special processing fee for "Amateur vanity callsigns."

The conference also accepted, as proposed, language in the Senate's Emerging Telecommunications Technology Act requiring the Secretary of Commerce to seek to avoid excessive disruption of existing use of shared Federal/Amateur Radio frequencies.

Restructuring Denied

The FCC denied a petition by Scott Leyshon, WA2EQF, to eliminate written examinations for amateur operator licenses. At the same time the Commission denied a petition by Vincent Biancomano, WB2EZG, which, although it did not advocate a "no written test" license, did, the FCC said, concur in all other respects with Leyshon's proposal.

Leyshon's petition, filed April 19, 1993, argued that current written examinations place a premium on FCC rules over technical content. No comments were received on his petition.

Biancomano's petition, like Leyshon's, was characterized by the FCC as proposing that the Commission state a goal of the amateur service as being either a technical or a non-technical service.

The FCC said that of the 170 questions that appear on examinations for amateur operator licenses, only (their word) 46 concern rules and operating procedures, while 124 concern "contemporary technical matters." The Commission said it did not believe that present examinations place an unjustified premium on rules.

The FCC said that amateurs have over the years expressed the view that they agree with the current statement of the purposes of Amateur Radio, as found in the FCC Rules, and the FCC agreed.

FCC Unveils New Fines

The FCC has issued a new schedule of suggested base amounts

for monetary fines, with some reductions and some increases.

Fines in the Amateur Radio Service have been more numerous since a 1991 Commission policy statement which outlined standards for assessing forfeitures. Most have been for amateur band operation by unlicensed persons, for indecent language, and for malicious and willful interference with other amateurs.

The FCC said that the new schedule still allows it leeway in adjusting forfeiture amounts up or down depending on circumstances. It also said that a "significant change" is to "allow a presumption of diminished ability to pay in certain services for individuals."

The typical monetary forfeiture assessed for amateur band violations under the 1991 guidelines has been $2,000.

The National Association of Broadcasters, which challenged the 1991 fine schedule saying it had not been subject to public comment, noted that the new schedule is also not subject to public comment.

Local, State Law Relief

The FCC has granted, in part, a motion by the ARRL for a declaratory ruling asking the Commission to preempt certain state statutes and local ordinances affecting transceivers used by amateurs.

The laws addressed (in PR Docket 91-36) prohibit the possession of such transceivers if they are capable of receiving on certain frequencies other than amateur bands.

The ARRL said that amateur transceivers typically allow for incidental reception of frequencies adjacent to amateur bands in order to ensure adequate performance within the amateur bands. The League also said that amateurs have special needs for out-of-band reception, a fact the marketplace long has recognized by offering transceivers to accommodate those needs.

The FCC said that state and local laws that make possession of amateur transceivers in vehicles or elsewhere illegal merely because they can receive certain frequencies, the reception of which is not precluded by federal law, are preempted by federal law. The Commission said that such local and state laws are inconsistent with the federal laws that promote and facilitate Amateur Radio.

The Commission's action was August 20 and released August 25.

(Much of the preceding section originally appeared in ARRL Bulletins, provided courtesy of ARRL)

FCC ENFORCEMENT ACTIONS OF INTEREST TO AMATEURS (September 1992 - August 1993)

KA4URC

On September 23, 1992, the Commission announced a Notice of Apparent Liability (NAL) for 2,000 dollars had been sent to Allen Burton, KA4URC, of Hornbeak, TN, alleged for willful violation of FCC Rule 97.113(d), which prohibits transmission of indecent words and language on Amateur Radio stations.

Burton, 60, is a General class licensee. According to the NAL, on the afternoon of June 29, 1992, the Commission's Kingsville, TX office monitored a conversation on 14.300 MHz which included KA4URC. "We find," the NAL said, "that the words and language transmitted are indecent within the meaning of Section 97.113(d) and prevailing Supreme Court and Commission precedent.

"We find that the transmissions describe sexual acts and organs in a patently offensive manner and go well beyond what an average adult person in any community would consider to be worthy of protection," the Commission said.

The NAL said one of the Commission's goals is to "protect children from exposure to sexually explicit communications over the airwaves," and noted here that "the transmissions were made in the summertime in the afternoon when there is a real likelihood that children are listening." An ARRL survey of young radio amateurs was used as corroboration.

Burton was fined less than the $5,000 that Commission guidelines would have allowed because it was his first offense and because he is an individual rather than a corporation (such as a broadcast radio or television station). Burton was given 30 days in which to pay the fine or to explain why it should be reduced or not imposed.

According to the FCC, Burton apologized for the incident and said he could not afford to pay the $2,000 forfeiture. The Commission on November 23, 1992 announced that since federal law "directs the FCC to consider ability to pay when imposing monetary forfeitures," it was reducing the fine to $200. "If in the future," the Commission told Burton, "you repeat the same violations, however, the FCC may impose a substantially higher monetary forfeiture."

KC6TYR

Roy L. Eyman II, KC6TYR, was sentenced to three years supervised probation and 250 hours of community service for transmitting on a tactical operations radio channel of the San Diego police department. Eyman, 22, also was ordered to deprogram his amateur radio equipment of all public safety frequencies, according to an FCC press release.

The FCC's San Diego office said that on September 16, 1991, Eyman was transmitting music on a San Diego Police Department tactical operations channel. At the time a police sergeant who also is an Amateur Radio operator heard the interference and used a hand-held transceiver to direction-find the source of the interfering signal, the FCC said.

The officer "heard the music over his Amateur Radio hand-held unit as well as hearing it aurally originating from Mr. Eyman's vehicle," the FCC said. "The sergeant then seized Mr. Eyman's amateur radio equipment."

The maximum penalty for unlicensed operation in a first conviction is a fine of up to $100,000 or imprisonment of up to one year, or both.

The sentence was handed down by a U.S. magistrate in an out-of-court settlement, the FCC said.

WB4PVK

The FCC suspended the amateur and commercial operator licenses of Thomas M. Haynie, WB4PVK, as well as revoked his amateur station license.

In September, 1990, Haynie, of Virginia Beach, VA, was convicted of deliberately causing interference to a communications satellite (a felony) as well as of a criminal violation for the unauthorized operation of a satellite transmitter. He received a suspended sentence, a $1,000 fine, and was ordered to perform 50 hours of public service work. The conviction was upheld by an appeals court in August, 1991.

On July 31, 1992, the FCC ordered the license suspensions and revocation, and notified Haynie of his right to a hearing on the suspension orders. Haynie responded with a letter to the FCC Private Radio Bureau, in which he did not ask for reconsideration of the suspension of his commercial license but did argue for retaining his amateur Advanced class operator and station licenses.

According to the FCC, Haynie made several arguments in support of his request, saying that he is not a habitual offender, that since his conviction he has not violated any FCC rules, and that his conviction was not Amateur Radio-related.

Haynie also said that he has properly operated his amateur station for more than 25 years and that he obtained his license at "an early age, cherishes it dearly," and would do everything in his power to adhere to the rules in the future. He also argued that revocation of his station license would not be in the best interests of the public because of the role amateur operators can play during times of disaster.

The FCC found Haynie's arguments "unpersuasive," calling his interfering with a communications satellite "egregious conduct," and affirmed the operator license suspensions for their remaining terms, as well as revocation of his WB4PVK station license.

KG5WS

In another case, Richard C. Bortner, KG5WS, of Zapata, TX, in October 1992 was ordered to show cause why his license should not be revoked. Bortner had failed to respond to correspondence from the Commission in June and August of 1992, in which he was accused of fraud in the obtaining of his amateur license.

On November 10, 1993, the Commission withdrew the Order to Show Cause in view of on-going proceedings in the case. However, the termination "pertains only to the licensee's previous failure to reply to Commission correspondence," the FCC said, "and does not restrict the Field Operations Bureau from reasserting the original enforcement action against the licensee based on the underlying violation."

WB2OTK

The FCC's Kingsville, TX office issued a Notice of Apparent Liability for $10,500 to Richard L. Whiten, WB2OTK, 46, of Taylors, SC. Whiten was cited for "willful and malicious interfering transmissions" monitored by the FCC on September 26, 1992, on 14314.7 kHz.

Whiten, a General class licensee, was issued the NAL two days later. In his reply to the FCC he did not, according to the Commission, dispute making the transmissions, but he "denied that his signals constituted willful, malicious interference, because, he says in his letter, if he truly wanted to willfully and maliciously interfere he could have done so to such an extent that communications between other amateur radio operators would have been impossible; that his comments were not disruptive; that his statements were innocuous, that he was recognized and spoken to by the other amateur operators, and that he was the victim of entrapment by the other operators."

The FCC did not accept this argument, and noted that Whiten already had received two previous NALs, on January 28, 1991 and July 12, 1991, for the same rules violation.

The FCC's "base amount" fine for willful interference is $7,000; in this case the fine was raised 50 per cent "in view of Mr. Whiten's repeated violations."

On January 14, 1993, the FCC issued a Notice of Apparent Liability for $2,000 to William A. Moskowitz, KA3HSZ, of Plano, TX. The FCC said its Vero Beach, FL office monitored Moskowitz on November 26, 1992, and during a 17-minute period observed him changing operating frequency twice, in the vicinity of 14.313 MHz, "in order to interfere with on-going communications." "The violation was willful," the FCC said.

The FCC said "we are treating this as a minor violation," and that because Moskowitz is an individual, because of the nature of the violation, and because it is a first offense, the Commission set the fine at $2,000. The FCC's base forfeiture for malicious interference is $7,000.

Moskowitz was given the usual 30 days to pay the fine or to appeal it.

NS3K

Jorge Mestre, NS3K, of Fairfax VA, pleaded guilty on February 12, 1993 to knowingly and willfully communicating a false distress signal, resulting in the U.S. Coast Guard launching a major search and rescue operation on August 7, 1992.

The FCC used direction finding data, detailed signal analysis of the transmissions, and other information to identify Mestre's station as the source of the false distress messages. Mestre is also suspected of having been involved in at least three additional false distress cases in the last few years.

Mestre agreed to surrender his Extra class amateur radio license, dispose of his amateur radio equipment within 60 days, and make immediate restitution of $50,000 to the U.S. Coast Guard.

At sentencing in U.S. District Court in Alexandria, VA. in May 1993, Mestre was given one-year probation on condition of his serving 60 days home confinement, ordered to perform 200 hours of community service, and to pay a $50 special assessment.

Mestre could have received a fine of up to $250,000 and up to six years imprisonment.

Cable TV Systems Monitored

In May 1993, the FCC announced the results of a recent project to enforce its cable television leakage standards. In March, 1993, the Commission's Enforcement Division focused on cable systems which could pose a danger to public service radio communications, such as aeronautical.

According to the Commission, the March sweep included monitoring 321 cable TV systems, visiting eight systems to "discuss operator measurements," and the closing down of one system for violating the FCC's Cumulative Leakage Index (CLI) limit. This project was in addition to the FCC's ongoing monitoring by its field offices nationwide.

In addition, the FCC sent letters to 1,550 cable TV operators, issued 112 complimentary letters to "clean" systems, and issued 73 violation letters. The effort was directed at all areas of the country, the Commission said.

The system, which was closed, was found to have a small number of significant leaks, according to the FCC's Jeffrey Young. Most system violations of the CLI are due to the additive effect of a large number of small leaks, Young said.

The FCC plans another monitoring project later this year, on a random basis, to gauge the effect of its enforcement and education efforts, Young said.

K3CQR

In August, 1993, the FCC fined William P. Irwin, K3CQR, $2,000. The Commission's Vero Beach, FL office said Irwin, 51, of De Bary, FL, was found causing "willful and malicious interference" on or near 14.313 MHz over a period of months.

Irwin, a General class licensee, was issued a Notice of Apparent Liability for $2,000. He was found and identified by the FCC on July 22, 1993, while he was operating from his residence, the FCC said in a release. The FCC inspected Irwin's station the next day. Irwin had identified himself on the air as "Raincoat Charlie," and had vowed on the air that "the Commission would never find him," the FCC said.

Robert McKinney, Engineer-in-Charge at the FCC's Vero Beach office said, "Some amateurs, it seems, have lost sight of the concepts 'good amateur practice' and 'enhance international good will' embodied in the purpose of the service. Mr. Irwin's sole purpose for being on the air appeared to many to be to harass and ridicule other amateurs in a particularly vulgar way.

"It is widely known," McKinney said, "that budget restraints limit the Commission's enforcement efforts; but blatant, repeated violations such as these will not be tolerated or go unpunished."

McKinney also said, however, that "It should be pointed out that a considerable number of concerned amateurs cooperated in the investigation. We appreciate the efforts of these amateurs as a community willing to take responsibility for being self-policing."

WA4D

Michael E. Whatley, WA4D, was hit with an FCC Notice of Monetary Forfeiture for $2,000. The Commission denied a request from Whatley that it reconsider the Notice of Apparent Liability it issued to him in November, 1992.

Whatley was accused of willful and malicious interference based on FCC monitoring on 7257 and 7258 kHz in late 1992. According to the FCC, Whatley asked the FCC's Field Operations Bureau for copies of recordings of the transmissions in question and also requested a 30-day extension in which to respond to the NAL.

The FOB said it granted Whatley the extension and provided him with both the tape and a transcript of it.

Whatley then argued that other amateur operators were interfering with *his* transmissions, that the transcripts are incomplete (not reflecting all communications which were recorded on tape), and that the parties to other communications on the band ignored his attempt to "compromise."

On August 20, the FCC announced the monetary forfeiture order, the FOB saying, "We have reviewed the record and affirm our initial findings."

The FCC said it was not persuaded by Whatley's arguments, and "further, Mr. Whatley's actions and communications indicate hostility towards the net members [on 7255 kHz] that were communicating, and do not support his claim that he intended to be conciliatory."

Although the base forfeiture amount for malicious interference is $7,000, the FCC set the fine against Whatley at $2,000 because he is an individual and has no record of prior violations.

Whatley was given 30 days to pay the fine.

(The preceding section compiled from contributions by ARRL and W5YI)

75 YEARS AGO IN AMATEUR RADIO—1919

The year 1919 was probably the single most important year in the history of Amateur Radio. It can be said that the efforts of a select few men saved the hobby from extinction.

World War I ended on November 11, 1918. During the war, amateur radio had been closed down, and the following letter was sent to all known radio amateurs in April 1917:

> To all Radio Experimenters,
>
> Sirs:
>
> By virtue of the authority given the President of the United States by an Act of Congress, approved August 13, 1912, entitled "An Act to Regulate Radio Communication," and of all other authority vested in him, and in pursuance of an order issued by the President of the United States, I hereby direct the immediate closing of all stations for radio communications, both transmitting and receiving, owned or operated by you. In order fully to carry this order into effect, I direct that the antennae and all aerial wires be immediately lowered to the ground, and that all radio apparatus both for transmitting and receiving be disconnected from both the antennae and ground circuits and that it otherwise be rendered inoperative both for transmitting and receiving until this order is revoked. Immediate compliance with this order is insisted upon and will be strictly enforced. Please report on the enclosed blank your compliance with this order; a failure to return such blanks promptly will lead to a rigid investigation.
>
> Lieutenant, U.S. Navy,
> District Communication
> Superintendent.

QST was published for a few months after this order was issued. Since many of the ARRL members were called into the armed forces as radio operators, however, ARRL membership declined. Since nobody could operate, there was no need for equipment and advertising revenues dried up predictably. The last issue of *QST* in 1917 was published in September, and no issues were published in 1918.

After the Armistice, Representative Alexander of Missouri introduced a bill in Congress, H.R. 13159, that would have given the Secretary of the Navy sole control of all radio in the United States. A companion bill, S.5038, was also introduced in the Senate. Similar bills had been debated prior to and during the War, but now the amateurs mobilized. Delegates from the ARRL, the Wireless Association of Pennsylvania, the Hoosier Radio Club, the South Jersey Radio Association, and the Baltimore Radio Association attended the hearing on these bills. A letter-writing campaign was also mounted, and family members of known amateurs were urged to write their representatives. These efforts paid off—the bills never got out of committee.

In February 1919, the ARRL Board of Directors met to determine the fate of the League. The picture was pretty bleak: all memberships had lapsed, the ARRL treasury contained a mere $33, and *QST* was owned by Lt. C.D. Tuska, the Secretary of the ARRL. Although there were essentially no assets, the ARRL Board voted to purchase QST from Tuska for $4,700, including payment of outstanding printing bills. At the March 29, 1919 ARRL Board meeting in New York, the 11 men present (Hiram Percy Maxim, A. A. Hebert, Lt. C. D. Tuska, Radio Gunner R. H. G. Matthews, J. O. Smith, Lt. V. F. Camp, H. L. Stanley, W. S. Browne, Lt. K. B. Warner, A. F. Clough, and H. E. Nichols) contributed a total of $100 to permit the ARRL to print a six-page "midget issue" of *QST*. The goal of this issue was to alert the former members of the ARRL that the organization was indeed alive and attempting to get itself and amateur radio running again. The last page of this issue contained an appeal from Hiram Percy Maxim himself for members to purchase ARRL bonds. The Board had decided that a loan totaling $7,500 would be sufficient to purchase *QST*, pay off old debts, hire a paid Secretary, establish a headquarters office, reorganize the old members, and attract new members from the newly-trained pool of ex-military radio operators.

The midget issue was a success, and, in June 1919, a full-size issue (all of 32 pages) of *QST* was published.

On April 12, 1919, the Navy Department removed the ban on amateur receiving stations, while maintaining the prohibition on transmitting until the President officially announced that a state of peace existed. This meant that a lot of frustrated amateurs were piecing their receivers and antennas back together and tuning around trying to find something to copy. Fortunately, several military and commercial traffic stations were on the air and provided some satisfaction to the hams.

In July 1919, the Secretary of the Navy wrote to the President of the Senate urging that the Navy be awarded sole jurisdiction over international and oceanic radio operation. As a result, the Poindexter bill, S.4038, was introduced. Fortunately, by that time, numerous other parties had taken an interest in commercial use of the airwaves and sufficient opposition arose to kill the bill.

Amateurs grew impatient waiting for permission to transmit to be granted. A group from the ARRL went to Washington and called upon the Honorable William Stedman Greene who was a 21-year veteran of Congress from Massachusetts and the Chairman of the House Committee on the Merchant Marine and Fisheries. Greene introduced a resolution in Congress asking the Department of the Navy why Amateur Radio transmitting was still prohibited. A month or so passed with no action, and Greene introduced the following Joint Resolution, H. J. Res. 217:

> Joint Resolution, to direct the Secretary of the Navy to remove the restrictions on the use and operation of amateur radio stations throughout the United States. Resolved by the Senate and House of Representatives of the United States of America in Congress assembled, that the Secretary of the Navy be, and he is hereby, directed to remove the restrictions now existing on the use and operation of amateur radio stations throughout the United States.

On September 26, 1919, the Navy complied with the order. The Bureau of Navigation of the Department of Commerce was once again given the responsibility for setting up a procedure for issuing licenses, since all previously-issued licenses had expired during the war. Slowly, but surely, licenses were issued, and amateurs began transmitting once again.

At this point, wireless communications was still in its infancy: equipment was crude, primarily using spark-gap transmitters and wavelengths of 200 to 10,000 meters (corresponding to frequencies of 30 kHz to 1500 kHz). Modern amateurs will instantly realize that these low frequencies will only propagate over relatively short distances, so sending a message across the continent required a number of "relay" points. The goal of the American Radio Relay League , therefore, was to establish a network of relay stations, organized such that messages could be communicated by wireless over a long distance. Ragchewing, contests, DX chasing for awards—none of these was part of the amateur radio hobby of 1919.

As *QST* pointed out in the November 1919 issue's editorial,

> ...Up to the time we amateurs began relay work, the limit which one could transmit intelligence without either paying tribute either to the Government or the Western Union or the Postal Telegraph Company, was the distance one's voice would carry.

The ARRL wanted to provide an alternative message transmission service, free of cost. On December 4, 1919, a message was originated in California by the Seefred Brothers, operators of station 6EA. It was relayed to "LF" in Roswell, NM, then to 9BT and 8DA in Salem, OH, who relayed the message directly to H. P. Maxim, 1AW. Later that evening, 1AW originated a reply, sent via 9ZN, through LF, and then to 6EA. This relay took several hours to complete. While faster relays had been accomplished before the war, this was the first successful post-war relay.

The *QST* advertisements of late 1919 show a huge number of new radio parts manufacturers and distributors turning up. Nearly all those companies now belong to history, however. The products advertised included DeForest tubes and receivers, Marconi vacuum tubes, rotary quenched spark gaps from Benwood (is this where Kenwood got the idea for their name?), Murdock headphones, and a marble-base "Navy-type" telegraph key offered from the Radio Apparatus catalog of Sears, Roebuck, & Company!

50 YEARS AGO IN AMATEUR RADIO—1944

The year 1944 was another important milestone in the history of amateur radio. During World War II, U. S. amateurs were not allowed to transmit, except as part of a civilian defense organization known as the War Emergency Radio Service (WERS). The FCC issued a notice on December 8, 1941, reading,

> All amateur licensees are hereby notified that the Commission has ordered the immediate suspension of all amateur radio operation in the continental United States, its territories and possessions. Under this action, all amateur radio operation in the continental United States, its territories and possessions is prohibited until further notice. In any instances where amateur radio is deemed to be required in connection with the national defense, appropriate authorization to engage in such operation will be issued but only upon application by a duly authorized federal, state, or local official made to the Defense Communications Board.

It was the last part of that statement that kept the door open for hams to keep on the air during the war. This was in sharp contrast to the rules imposed during WWI when physically dismantling all equipment and antennas was required. The WERS was established, with select hams (and some non-hams) chosen to organize communications in various cities, and eventually operated in 36 states. Communications were conducted in the 112 MHz band (2 1/2 meters). Never heard of that band? The VHF ham bands at the time were all harmonically-related, just as the HF bands were. The VHF bands were 5 meters (56-60 MHz), 2 1/2 meters (112-116 MHz), and 1 1/4 meters (224-230 MHz). Additionally, amateurs were authorized to use all frequencies above 300 MHz for experimentation.

The FCC continued to administer and regulate the amateur service, graciously allowing automatic extension of amateur licenses during the war period—provided that the operator provided fingerprints and proof of citizenship!

QST was the only completely amateur radio-oriented magazine of the time. *RADIO* had turned more to the engineering and technical side of radio, and coverage of amateur radio was minimal. *QST* articles were devoted to construction of 112-MHz WERS equipment and antennas, news of hams involved in war activities (including recognition of hams who were prisoners of war, missing in action, or killed in action in the war), new technologies like television and light-wave communications, and basic technical articles about tube amplifier design, antenna matching, even basic engineering math. Many more articles were authored by professional engineers than are found in today's amateur magazines as the ARRL sought technical articles of interest to the off-the-air hams of the day. Additionally, each issue of *QST* declared that it complied with the "Code of Wartime Practices for the American Press" and that all material had been reviewed by the U.S. Office of Censorship.

The editorial of the June 1944 *QST* issue described the national benefits of an amateur radio service in times of war. Five areas were spelled out. First, amateurs provided a ready-trained pool of personnel for communications, research and industrial work. Second, the existence of a manufacturing infrastructure for amateur communications equipment could be easily adapted to wartime production. Third, the actual amateur stations could be pressed into service for activities such as WERS, training schools, and laboratories. Fourth, hams could serve as teachers in the vast number of training programs that supported the operating and technical needs of the war effort. The technical literature used by amateurs also turned out to be some of the most useful in that training. Last, the existence of spectrum space for the amateurs meant that the military had ready access to frequencies without having to displace other services. By shutting down the hams in times of war, the military could take over those bands. The implication, of course, was that the hams would get them back when the war was over.

The ARRL Field Organization was slightly different in 1944. There were 72 Sections, and that number included Sections that no longer exist today, such as the Philippines and Cuba.

The August *QST* reported in a short article that AT&T had been granted a construction permit to erect a chain of "automatic relay stations" from Boston to New York, operating on wavelengths between 2 1/2 and 15 centimeters (1900 MHz to 12,500 MHz). These were the highest frequencies ever licensed. The editorial in September 1944 *QST* issue fantasized that someday amateurs could erect a similar network of "relay" stations to extend the range of VHF stations, which were expected to have ranges similar to the spark-gap rigs of long ago. Both star and ring topologies were envisioned for a nationwide intercity automatic relay network. Although only phone and CW were envisioned as the communications modes, the concept is not far afield from the emerging amateur packet data network of the 1990s!

In late 1944, the Allies were gaining the upper hand in the war, and the FCC began preparing for post-war frequency allocations. On September 28, 1944, the first of many hearings was held by the FCC and the Radio Technical Planning Board (RTPB, an industry group of which ARRL was a member society) to determine which services would get which bands.

The band assignments for amateur radio in the United States before the war had been as follows:

1.750 to 2.050 MHz
3.500 to 4.000 MHz
7.000 to 7.300 MHz
14.000 to 14.400 MHz
28.000 to 30.000 MHz
56.000 to 60.000 MHz
112.000 to 116.000 MHz
224.000 to 230.000 MHz
400.000 to 401.000 MHz
and shared rights above 300.000 MHz

The league filed testimony with both the FCC and RTPB arguing for retention of most of the existing allocations on the basis of international agreements, and for the need to relocate other services if the amateur allocations were moved. It also argued against "channelizing" amateur operations as was envisioned for the television and similar broadcasting services. The ARRL requested the same allocations below 60 MHz as before the war, with the addition of one band at 21.000 to 22.000 MHz.

One of the most interesting discussions concerned allocation of frequency bands above 60 MHz. The demand for VHF spectrum space was driven by the needs of the fledgling television broadcasters. The ARRL requested assignments at the following frequencies:

112 to 116 MHz
224 to 230 MHz
448 to 480 MHz
896 to 960 MHz
1792 to 1920 MHz
3584 to 3840 MHz
7168 to 7680 MHz
14336 to 15360 MHz
28672 to 30720 MHz
and shared rights above 30720 MHz.

The rather unusual numbers were not derived completely arbitrarily. The ARRL calculated that the bands from 28 to 30 MHz and 56 to 60 MHz each represented bandwidths of 7.14 percent of that particular frequency octave. Thus, the League argued, amateurs should be entitled to the same percentage of the octave at which each band would begin.

The League than learned which bands the military was going to request. A compromise set of amateur allocations was prepared and submitted requesting the following allocations in the VHF/UHF range:

144 to 148 MHz

218 to 225 MHz
420 to 460 MHz
840 to 900 MHz
1125 to 1225 MHz
2500 to 2700 MHz
5200 to 5750 MHz
10000 to 10500 MHz
21000 to 22000 MHz
and shared rights above 30000 MHz.

The RTPB recommended moving the 10-meter band from the original 28-30 MHz band to 27-29 MHz and the 56-60 MHz band to 58-60 MHz. The ARRL filed comments in opposition to these elements of the proposed frequency re-allocations, breaking with the RTPB's recommendations. Editorial comments in *QST* noted that much of the spectrum in discussion was deemed entirely useless, since nobody had yet figured out how to transmit or receive signals at those high frequencies. It was obvious that the ARRL staffers recalled an earlier (1920s) exercise in spectrum allocation. In those days, it was believed that all wavelengths shorter than 200 meters (frequencies above 1.5 MHz) were useless. As a result, those "useless" bands were given to amateur radio, while commercial and military users were given the longer wavelengths. The hams soon realized that long-distance communications could be readily accomplished with the shorter wavelengths, primarily through experimentation and sheer luck. In the 1945 spectrum-allocation debate, the ARRL fully expected that the hams would once again be given the "useless" spectrum, and wanted hams to be ready to make the best of these new bands. Indeed, the editorial in December *QST* encouraged hams to give serious thought to experimentation in the VHF/UHF spectrum after the resumption of amateur radio, rather than merely returning to the pre-war DX chasing on 80, 40, and 20 meters.

In January 1944, an obscure seven-year tradition died in *QST* advertising. The National Radio Company of Malden, MA had every year taken out a "Happy New Year" advertisement in *QST* and manually affixed a National Tuberculosis Society Christmas Seal to the page. The January 1944 ad carried an apology, stating that the necessary "girl-power" was needed elsewhere, and a donation equal to the price of 60,000 Christmas Seals had been made instead.

The other advertisements of that year were very different from current *QST* ads. The prominent manufacturers of the day (Hallicrafters, Collins, Hammarlund, Meissner, National, and others) touted their support of the war effort and the superiority of their radios being used in the military. Sensing that the war would be over soon, Hallicrafters launched a campaign soliciting letters from *QST* readers who were servicemen, asking them to relate their experiences with Hallicrafters' military gear and offering a $100 prize for the best letter. This would give Hallicrafters a head start on testimonials to use in advertising after the war, as well as a known base of loyal customers. At the time, none of the manufacturers actually offered equipment for sale, since most radio production was devoted to equipment to aid the war effort. Advertisers paid higher-than-normal rates for smaller ad space in *QST* during 1944 as a show of support for the ARRL and to "allow an editorially-adequate" *QST* to be published.

25 YEARS AGO IN AMATEUR RADIO—1969

Amateur Radio was on the threshold of becoming the hobby we know today in 1969. Regulatory and technological changes were afoot that would change the hobby forever.

The controversial modification to the structure of the Amateur Radio Service known as "Incentive Licensing," which was announced in August 1967, first took effect on November 22, 1968. In this "Act I" phase, certain segments of the HF amateur bands were assigned to the exclusive use of Advanced and Extra class licensees. Prior to 1968, all General class and higher licensees were allowed to use the same frequencies, and the Advanced and Extra class licenses conferred no additional privileges to their holders. Consequently, a very small percentage of hams held the higher class licenses.

In a May 1969 speech by William Grenfell, W4GF, Chief of the Rules and Standards Branch, Amateur & Citizens Radio Division, FCC (given at the New England Division ARRL Convention in Boston, MA), the goal of incentive licensing was described as an effort to improve the "quality" of the amateur service. There was concern about the lack of growth in amateur radio in the 1960s. Total U.S. ham census was 86,662 on July 1, 1950, and grew 9-10% per year through July 1960 when it reached 212,107. The rate of growth slowed to 4-5% per year thereafter. The total as of July 1964 was 256,237. From July 1964 to mid-1969, the total wavered between 256,000 and 262,000, with no trend up or down. A $4 license fee had been imposed in 1964, and, in 1965, the geographic area for which the Conditional class license (no longer issued, this had been available to those amateurs living too far from an FCC examination point to travel for the test) could be used was reduced—some speculated that these two events were responsible for the stagnation of the hobby. Grenfell suggested that the main reason was actually either saturation or "hobby competition"; in other words, there were too many alternatives for leisure-time activities.

Throughout 1969, all the ham magazines were filled with editorials and letters alternately praising or condemning the incentive licensing system and/or the ARRL's role in the program. The band segments in Act I included exclusive Extra-class CW segments 25 kHz wide in the 80-15 meter bands, and several exclusive Extra and Extra/Advanced bands on phone. The original plan was for Act II to take effect on November 22, 1969, further extending the exclusive subbands (to 50 kHz on CW, for example). Several petitions were filed with the FCC during 1969, mostly suggesting that the exclusive bands be maintained at 25 kHz width. On September 24, 1969, the FCC announced the new allocations as follows:

Extra Class Only
CW: 3500-3525, 7000-7025, 14000-14025, 21000-21025
Phone: 3800-3825, 21250-21275

Extra/Advanced Only
Phone: 3825-3900, 7200-7250, 14200-14275, 21275-21350, 50000-50100

Technician
50.1-54.0, 145-147, all above 220 MHz

Later in the year, the ARRL petitioned the FCC to expand Technician license privileges to include the whole 2-meter band (not just 145-147 MHz) and part of 10 meters.

Novice privileges remained essentially unchanged, with a two-year, non-renewable term and privileges in the 80, 40, 15, and 2-meter bands, with 75 watts maximum input power and crystal control only (no VFO or synthesizers). The only significant change to the Novice license was that a holder whose license had expired was eligible to acquire another Novice license after a one-year waiting period. Waiting periods seemed fashionable in those days—an applicant for an Extra class license had to hold a General or higher class license for at least two years before applying!

The FCC denied a request to modify the rules for power measurement to be output-based instead of input-based. The General and higher license classes were permitted 1000 watts maximum DC input power.

FM repeaters were just starting out, with about 200 open machines active in the U.S. and Canada. Almost half were on the 146.34/146.94 pair! The growth of repeaters was in part held back by FCC rules requiring a control operator to always monitor an amateur transmitter—this included repeaters! There were no provisions in the FCC rules for unattended operation; in fact, there was no mention of repeaters in Part 97 at all!

The FCC rules on station identification were modified to require that calls of both stations be transmitted only at the end of the contact; previously, both callsigns were required in every transmission.

The FCC approved new tariffs for AT&T for direct connection of customer-owned equipment to the network, effective 1 January 1969, as a consequence of the "Carterfone" decision of 1968. Prior to that decision, it was not permitted to connect non-Bell equipment to the telephone network, thus making phone patches technically illegal. This changed in 1969, and numerous construction articles appeared on how to build a phone patch. It is not clear how many hams notified their local phone company that they had attached these boxes to their phones, or how many paid the 50-cent-per month tariff.

Also that year, Senator Barry Goldwater introduced Senate Joint Resolution 27, later known as S. 1466, to reduce the waiting period (another one!) for immigrants from five years to one before they could become eligible for an amateur license. And David Packard of Hewlett-Packard (ex-W9DRV) was named Deputy Secretary of Defense in the Nixon Administration.

On the international front, Indonesia and Thailand changed their rules in 1969 to allow their hams to contact hams in other countries. Cambodia and Vietnam still banned outside communications. The USSR announced that foreign visitors could be granted permission to operate. The International Amateur Radio Union (IARU) admitted national societies from Mauritius and Surinam, bringing the IARU membership to 80 countries.

Ansel "Grid" Gridley, W4GJO, of Sarasota, FL, was sued for one million dollars by his next-door neighbor who alleged TVI. The neighbor, Mr. Lee H. Eggers, owner of Dixie Lee's Bar and Package Store, had experienced TVI and RFI for 10 years and had complained twice (both times the TVI was cured by high-pass filters on the TV sets). He apparently did not want filters installed on his new color TV set, however, but wanted to watch TV stations located 50, 65, and 100 miles away. An FCC investigation found that a mast-mounted pre-amp was the main cause of the TVI—Gridley's station was given a clean bill of health by the FCC. Mr. Eggers ran a series of advertisements in the local newspaper, in which he editorialized on the "electronic invasion of privacy" being committed by his neighbor. Gridley countersued.

A hearing was held on January 8, 1969, and the presiding judge requested more information from both sides. The case was ultimately settled later in the year, with Eggers and Gridley agreeing to drop their suits against each other. The cases were dismissed "with prejudice" (meaning the same matters could not again be brought into court). Gridley was not required to pay any damages.

On March 3, 1969, the Radio Amateur Satellite Corporation (AMSAT) was formed. George Jacobs, W3ASK, suggested at a meeting of the Comsat Corporation Amateur Radio Club in January 1969 that a D.C.-area group could actually design, construct, and test satellites to continue Project OSCAR (Orbiting Satellite Carrying Amateur Radio). The response was enthusiastic, and the original members came from several other area clubs, including Comsat, Johns Hopkins University Applied Physics Laboratory, IBM Federal Systems Division, Aeronautical Radio, Inc., Communications & Systems, and NASA Goddard Space Flight Center. Construction and testing of Australis-OSCAR 5 continued through the year, building on the work begun by a group in Australia. At year-end, NASA had agreed to launch AO-5 as a secondary payload on the TIROS-M mission, scheduled for early 1970. AO-5 was finally launched on January 23, 1970 at 13:50 GMT.

Operation on other specialized modes was being raised to new levels in 1969. The first U.S.-Europe Slow-scan TV contact was completed between SMØBUO and W8SH on 28.7 MHz. RTTY was growing in popularity. AFSK was becoming practical, but only if the SSB rig had good enough carrier and unwanted-sideband suppression (many didn't).

Moonbounce was very much in the news of 1969. The first 144 MHz EME contact on SSB using amateur antennas took place between K6MYC and KØMQS on January 10, 1969. K6MYC used a 160-element collinear array, and KØMQS used an eight-wire rhombic stack, 700 feet long. WB6IOM and G3LTF made an audible two-way QSO on 1296 MHz EME—a distance record of 5,492 miles. Previous work was limited to strip-chart recordings of signals. SM7BAE and ZL1AZR succeeded in a two-way moonbounce QSO on March 4 for a distance of 11,370 miles, a new record. W4HHK copied signals from W3GKP on 2304 MHz off the moon. W3GKP used 275 W to a 28-foot dish. He had previously (March 1953) transmitted the first amateur signal ever bounced off the moon.

The ARRL started the 5BDXCC program on January 1, 1969. On March 11, W4QCW (now W4DR) worked his 100th country on 80 meters. Getting the cards took a while, but by September he had 5BDXCC #1. The next stations to qualify were DL7AA, W1EVT (now NY1N), W8GZ, and W8BT (now W8AH). The program was considered so successful that the ARRL decided to institute a 5BWAS Award, with a start date of 1 January 1970.

The ARRL Board of Directors appointed the first two Advisory Committees to deal with specialized aspects of Amateur Radio. Specifically, these were the Contest and VHF Repeater Advisory Committees. WØCXW was the first VRAC Chairman; W6CUF (now W6CF) was the first CAC Chairman.

In 1969, the ARRL officially adopted the ICAO Phonetic Alphabet (Alfa-Bravo-Charlie-Delta, etc.), replacing the WWII vintage Joint-Army-Navy version (Adam-Baker-Charlie-David, etc.).

The first-ever ham radio movie ("Ham's Wide World") premiered at the Des Moines, IA ARRL National convention in June 1969. It starred Barry Goldwater, K7UGA, Arthur Godfrey, K4LIB, and Bill Leonard, W2SKE, of CBS. It was produced by Dave Bell, W6AQ.

Several interesting nets became active in the 40-meter phone band during 1969. The East Coast Amateur Radio Service on 7255 kHz (ECARS), and the corresponding Midwest and West Coast nets (MIDCARS on 7258 and WCARS on 7255, respectively) were providing "Instant Service" net operations for mobile operators and natural disaster victims. Some amateurs objected to these nets "owning" these frequencies "all day, every day," but they provided a valuable service and became very popular.

The U.S. Coast Guard announced that it would once again allow visitors to Navassa Island. No permission had been granted for amateur operation since 1958. One unauthorized DXpedition in 1966 had reinforced the Coast Guard's no-visit policy. By 1969, Navassa was at the top of the "Most-Needed Countries" survey. When permission was granted, a group consisting of W4QCW (now W4DR), KV4FZ, K4IA, K4FU, W4DQS, W4KET, K4CAH, W4PJG, W4USQ, and WA4HTR activated K4IA/KC4 in June for 11,000 QSOs in 72 hours on Navassa. December 1969 *QST* also carried the story of the 1928 K4NI Navassa operation by W3BBF, then a radio operator and lighthouse keeper on the island.

There were a few other special operations of note in 1969. The HKØTU Malpelo Island DXpedition yielded 8000 QSOs in three days. Norwegian explorer Thor Heyerdahl sailed a papyrus-reed raft from Europe to the Caribbean—the callsign LI2B was used on the amateur bands. GB2HRH operated from the investiture of His Royal Highness the Prince of Wales on July 1, 1969.

Bonin & Volcano Islands and Marcus Island reverted to Japanese sovereignty, losing the KG6I and KA1 prefixes, and were renamed Ogasawara and Minami Torishima, prefix JD1.

The technology of amateur radio was also changing fast in 1969. At the beginning of the year, construction articles in ham magazines were almost all tube-based projects, such as *QST's* "Building a Novice Rig from an Old TV Set" (75 watts crystal-controlled on 80, 40, and 15 meters). By the end of the year, nearly all construction projects were transistor-based. One example, from the August 1969 *QST*, was an 8-watt, solid-state, 2-meter transmitter! A few projects even used some simple ICs (most ICs made in 1969 were pretty simple). It seemed that everybody wanted to design an electronic keyer with RTL logic!

Antenna innovations included the Delta Loop beam, first introduced in January 1969 *QST* by Harry Habig, K8ANV (although the article refers to a previous mention of triangular elements by W6DL in April 1968 *QST*'s "Technical Correspondence"). The TH6DXX antenna was unveiled by HyGain. W6KPC described a square array of four 6-element, 10-meter Yagis dubbed the "Quartet," and similar to the "H-frame" arrays used commonly on VHF. The cover of the February 1969 *CQ* shows the 12-element, 20-meter yagi on a 152-foot boom at WA6ZZK—perhaps it didn't qualify as innovation, but it sure was big!

The equipment of 1969 included innovations now considered standard (and a few that have recently been re-discovered!). The biggest product announcement was the Signal/One CX-7 "Integrated station." This state-of-the-art transceiver was much more than just a transceiver—it was the first amateur rig with electronic digital readout to 100 Hz, dual VFOs, with dual-receive capability, built-in CW keyer, full break-in, 300 watt input, and coverage from 10 through 160 meters (few rigs of that era included any of those features). It carried a price tag of $1,595—remember, those are 1969 dollars! With this introduction, Signal/One claimed the high ground in the market, displacing Collins in features and price! However, the Collins S Line remained the standard of comparison for performance and reliability at the high-priced end of the market.

Hallicrafters announced the SR400 transceiver which could provide dual-receive with an external VFO. Drake offered the "4B-line" at $879, the TR-4 transceiver, and the beginner's 2-B receiver, 2-NT transmitter for a total of $378. Heathkit offered the HW-100 at $250, and the higher-priced SB Series; they also introduced the SB-220 2 kW amplifier for $349.95.

Several manufacturers took advantage of the inexpensive horizontal sweep tubes developed for color TV applications and used them in new transceivers with high-power output stages. National Radio offered the NCX-500, a 500-watt, five-band transceiver, and followed it in September 1969 with the NCX-1000, a 1-kW HF transceiver priced at $995. Swan offered the 500C ($565, less power supply), the Model 260 ($395), and later the 270 at $525. These two latter models were complete with built-in AC power supply. World Radio labs offered the Galaxy GT550 at $449.

Yaesu introduced the FTDX-400 at $600, and became the first Japanese manufacturer to market HF equipment in the U.S.

Heath introduced the HW-17 2-meter AM mobile transceiver. It required a separate DC supply, and included 15 transistors, 18 diodes, and three tubes. It could accept up to four crystals and an external VFO. It did not transmit FM.

Inoue Communications (now ICOM) introduced the FDFM-2, one of the first dedicated amateur 2-meter FM rigs. Most hams operating on VHF FM did so with used commercial equipment, mostly made by Motorola and General Electric. The Galaxy FM-210 was the first U.S.-made amateur two-meter FM rig.

In December 1969, Drake announced the SPR-4 all-solid-state (a first) communications receiver at $379.00. Ten-Tec announced its PM-1, a two-watt 80/40/15 meter transceiver for $49.95.

Hy-Gain introduced the "Afterburner" amplifier with 3.5 watts in, 80 watts out for 10 and 6 meters. No mention was made of the likely ability to use this product on 11 meters.

The first CW keyboard (Pickering KB-1) was announced in September at a price of $265.00, or slightly more than a new HW-100 transceiver.

Eimac announced the 3-500Z. It quickly became the tube of choice in "legal-limit" amplifiers. The magazines of 1969 also carried numerous RCA advertisements for receiving tubes, the Receiving Tube Manual, various new transistors (such as the 40673 dual-gate MOSFET), and small construction projects using their new components.

Where there had been only one major magazine in the U.S. in 1919 and 1945, there were four by 1969: *QST*, *CQ Amateur Radio*, *73*, and *Ham Radio*. *QST*'s cover price was $.75; annual ARRL membership was $6.50 (including a subscription to *QST*). Ms. Kayla Bloom, W1EMV, left *73* magazine after 22 months as editor to marry K4MWS. Wayne Greene, W2NSD, resumed editorial duties.

Several noteworthy hams passed away in 1969. Herbert Hoover, Jr., W6ZH/K6ZH, died July 9, 1969. He was president of ARRL and IARU from 1962 to 1966. His father was President Herbert Hoover.

VHF/UHF pioneer John Chambers, W6NLZ, died in October 1969. His work with KH6UK resulted in long-standing terrestrial distance records on 144, 220, and 432 MHz. Another noted VHFer, W5MCC, was shot to death in the front yard of his home in a dispute, which was in part related to a TVI complaint.

Leon Deloy, ex-8AB of Nice, France, also died in 1969. He was at the eastern end of the first transatlantic amateur QSO on November 27, 1923 (ARRL Traffic Manager Fred Schnell, 1MO, was at the western end). Other noteworthy events of 1969 included the Apollo 11 landing on the moon, Richard Nixon's inaugural, the first flight of the Concorde jet airplane, and a concert in New York called the Woodstock Music Festival.

COUNTRIES THAT SHARE THIRD-PARTY TRAFFIC AGREEMENTS WITH THE U.S.

V2	Antigua/Barbuda
LU	Argentina
VK	Australia
V3	Belize
CP	Bolivia
PY	Brazil
VE	Canada
CE	Chile
HK	Colombia
D6	Comoros
TI	Costa Rica
CO	Cuba
HI	Dominican Republic
J7	Dominica
HC	Ecuador
YS	El Salvador
V6	Federated States of Micronesia
C5	Gambia
9G	Ghana
J3	Grenada
TG	Guatemala
8R	Guyana
HH	Haiti
HR	Honduras
4X	Israel
6Y	Jamaica
JY	Jordan
EL	Liberia
V7	Marshall Islands**
XE	Mexico
YN	Nicaragua
HP	Panama
ZP	Paraguay
OA	Peru
DU	Philippines
V4	St. Christopher/Nevis
J6	St. Lucia
J8	St. Vincent
9L	Sierra Leone
3DA	Swaziland
9Y	Trinidad/Tobago
GB	United Kingdom *
CX	Uruguay
YV	Venezuela
4U1ITU - ITU,	Geneva
4U1VIC - VIC,	Vienna

* Limited to special-event stations with callsign prefix GB (GB3 excluded) and informally to stations on Pitcairn Island (VR6).

** The Marshall Islands are independent, but the FCC currently honors the previous agreement until a formal agreement can be made.

NOTE: U.S. licensed amateurs may operate in the following US territories under their FCC license: The Northern Marianas Islands, Guam, Johnston Island, Midway Island, Kure Island, American Samoa, Wake Island, Wilkes Island, Peale Island, the U.S. Virgin Islands, and Palau.

COUNTRIES THAT SHARE RECIPROCAL OPERATING/LICENSING AGREEMENTS WITH THE U.S.

V2	Antigua/Barbuda
LU	Argentina
VK	Australia
OE	Austria
C6	Bahamas
8P	Barbados
ON	Belgium
V3	Belize
CP	Bolivia
A2	Botswana
PY	Brazil
VE	Canada
CE	Chile
HK	Colombia
TI	Costa Rica
5B	Cyprus
OZ	Denmark(incl.Greenland)
HI	Dominican Republic
J7	Dominica
HC	Ecuador
YS	El Salvador
V6	Federated States of Micronesia
3D	Fiji
OH	Finland
F	France*
DL	Germany
SV	Greece
J3	Grenada
TG	Guatemala
8R	Guyana
HH	Haiti
HR	Honduras
VS	Hong Kong
TF	Iceland
VU	India
YB	Indonesia
EI	Ireland
4X	Israel
I	Italy
6Y	Jamaica
JA	Japan
JY	Jordan
T3	Kiribati
9K	Kuwait
EL	Liberia
LX	Luxembourg
V7	Marshall Islands**
XE	Mexico
3A	Monaco
PA	Netherlands
PJ	Neth. Antilles
YN	Nicaragua
LA	Norway
HP	Panama
P2	Papua New Guinea
ZP	Paraguay
OA	Peru
DU	Philippines
CT	Portugal
J6	St. Lucia
J8	St. Vincent/Grenadines
S7	Seychelles
9L	Sierra Leone
H4	Solomon Island
ZS	South Africa
EA	Spain
PZ	Suriname
SM	Sweden
HB	Switzerland
HS	Thailand
9Y	Trinidad/Tobago
T2	Tuvalu
G	United Kingdom***
CX	Uruguay
YV	Venezuela
YU	Yugoslavia
ZL	New Zealand

* Including French Guiana, French Polynesia, Guadeloupe,

Amsterdam Island, Saint-Paul Island, Crozet Island, Kerguelen Island, Martinique, New Caledonia, Reunion, St. Pierre and Miquelon, and Wallis and Futuna Islands

** The Marshall Islands are independent, but the FCC currently honors the previous reciprocal and third party agreements until formal agreements can be made.

*** Including Bermuda, British Virgin Islands, Cayman Islands, Falkland Islands, South Georgia Islands, Gibraltar, Montserrat, St. Helena, Gough Island, Tristan Da Cuhna Island, and the Turks and Caicos Islands

NOTES:
1. An automatic reciprocal agreement exists between the U.S. and Canada, so there is no need to apply for a permit. Simply sign your U.S. call followed by a slantbar and the Canadian letter/number identifier.
2. U.S. licensed amateurs may also operate in the following U.S. territories under their FCC license: The Northern Marianas Islands, Guam, Johnston Island, Midway Island, Kure Island, American Samoa, Wake Island, Wilkes Island, Peale Island, the U.S. Virgin Islands, and Palau.

FCC QUESTION POOL 2

The questions in Question Pool 2 are used for the Novice Class License examination. The Novice questions were revised in 1992-1993. The questions listed here became effective July 1, 1993, and will be used until June 30, 1997.

The letter in parentheses indicate the correct answer for each questions.

Subelement N1, Commission's Rules: 10 Exam Questions, 10 Groups

N1A Basis and Purpose of Amateur Service and Definitions.

N1A01 (A) [97]
What document contains the rules and regulations for the amateur service in the US?
A. Part 97 of Title 47 CFR (Code of Federal Regulations)
B. The Communications Act of 1934 (as amended)
C. The Radio Amateur's Handbook
D. The minutes of the International Telecommunication Union meetings

N1A02 (B) [97]
Who makes and enforces the rules and regulations of the amateur service in the US?
A. The Congress of the United States
B. The Federal Communications Commission (FCC)
C. The Volunteer Examiner Coordinators (VECs)
D. The Federal Bureau of Investigation (FBI)

N1A03 (A) [97]
Which three topics are part of the rules and regulations of the amateur service?
A. Station operation standards, technical standards, emergency communications
B. Notice of Violation, common operating procedures, antenna lengths
C. Frequency band plans, repeater locations, Ohm's law
D. Station construction standards, FCC approved radios, FCC approved antennas

N1A04 (D) [97]
Which of these topics is NOT part of the rules and regulations of the amateur service?
A. Qualifying examination systems
B. Technical standards
C. Providing emergency communications
D. Station construction standards

N1A05 (A) [97.1]
What are three reasons that the amateur service exists?
A. To recognize the value of emergency communications, advance the radio art, and improve communication and technical skills
B. To learn about business communications, increase testing by trained technicians, and improve amateur communications
C. To preserve old radio techniques, maintain a pool of people familiar with early tube-type equipment, and improve tube radios
D. To improve patriotism, preserve nationalism, and promote world peace

N1A06 (D) [97.1]
What are two of the five purposes for the amateur service?
A. To protect historical radio data, and help the public understand radio history
B. To help foreign countries improve communication and technical skills, and encourage visits from foreign hams
C. To modernize radio schematic drawings, and increase the pool of electrical drafting people
D. To increase the number of trained radio operators and electronics experts, and improve international goodwill

N1A07 (B) [97.3a1]
What is the definition of an amateur operator?
A. A person who has not received any training in radio operations
B. A person who has a written authorization to be the control operator of an amateur station
C. A person who has very little practice operating a radio station
D. A person who is in training to become the control operator of a radio station

N1A08 (C) [97.3a4]
What is the definition of the amateur service?
A. A private radio service used for profit and public benefit
B. A public radio service for US citizens which requires no exam
C. A personal radio service used for self-training, communication, and technical studies
D. A private radio service used for self-training of radio announcers and technicians

N1A09 (D) [97.3a5]
What is the definition of an amateur station?
A. A station in a public radio service used for radiocommunications
B. A station using radiocommunications for a commercial purpose
C. A station using equipment for training new radiocommunications operators
D. A station in an Amateur Radio service used for radiocommunications

N1A10 (C) [97.3a11]
What is the definition of a control operator of an amateur station?
A. Anyone who operates the controls of the station
B. Anyone who is responsible for the station's equipment
C. Any licensed amateur operator who is responsible for the station's transmissions
D. The amateur operator with the highest class of license who is near the controls of the station

N1A11 (C) [97.513a]
What is a Volunteer Examiner (VE)?
A. An amateur who volunteers to check amateur teaching manuals
B. An amateur who volunteers to teach amateur classes
C. An amateur who volunteers to test others for amateur licenses
D. An amateur who volunteers to examine amateur station equipment

N1B Station/Operator License.

N1B01 (D) [97.5a]
Which one of these must you have an amateur license to do?
A. Transmit on public-service frequencies
B. Retransmit shortwave broadcasts

C. Repair broadcast station equipment
D. Transmit on amateur service frequencies

N1B02 (B) [97.5a]
What does an amateur license allow you to control?
A. A shortwave-broadcast station's transmissions
B. An amateur station's transmissions
C. Non-commercial FM broadcast transmissions
D. Any type of transmitter, as long as it is used for non-commercial transmissions

N1B03 (C) [97.5a]
What allows someone to operate an amateur station in the US?
A. An FCC operator's training permit for a licensed radio station
B. An FCC Form 610 together with a license examination fee
C. An FCC amateur operator/primary station license
D. An FCC Certificate of Successful Completion of Amateur Training

N1B04 (B) [97.5d]
Where does a US amateur license allow you to operate?
A. Anywhere in the world
B. Wherever the amateur service is regulated by the FCC
C. Within 50 km of your primary station location
D. Only at your primary station location

N1B05 (C) [97.5e]
If you have a Novice license, how many transmitters may you control in your station at the same time?
A. Only one at a time
B. Only one at a time, except for emergency communications
C. Any number
D. Any number, as long as they are transmitting on different bands

N1B06 (A) [97.5e]
What document must you keep at your amateur station?
A. A copy of your written authorization for an amateur station
B. A copy of the Rules and Regulations of the Amateur Service (Part 97)
C. A copy of the Amateur Radio Handbook for instant reference
D. A chart of the frequencies allowed for your class of license

N1B07 (C) [97.7]
Which one of the following does not allow a person to control a US amateur station?
A. An operator/primary station license from the FCC
B. A reciprocal permit for alien amateur licensee from the FCC
C. An amateur service license from any government which is a member of the European Community (EC)
D. An amateur service license from the Government of Canada, if it is held by a Canadian citizen

N1B08 (D) [97.9a]
What are the five US amateur operator license classes?
A. Novice, Communicator, General, Advanced, Amateur Extra
B. Novice, Technician, General, Advanced, Expert
C. Novice, Communicator, General, Amateur, Extra
D. Novice, Technician, General, Advanced, Amateur Extra

N1B09 (A) [97.9]
What does the FCC consider to be the first two classes of US amateur operator licenses (one of which most new amateurs initially hold)?
A. Novice and Technician
B. CB and Communicator
C. Novice and General
D. CB and Novice

N1B10 (B) [97.9]
What must you have with you when you are the control operator of an amateur station?
A. A copy of the Rules and Regulations of the Amateur Service (Part 97)
B. The original or a photocopy of your amateur license
C. A list of countries which allow third-party communications from the US
D. A chart of the frequencies allowed for your class of license

N1B11 (D) [97.501d]
Which US amateur license has no Morse code requirements?
A. Amateur Extra
B. Advanced
C. General
D. Technician

N1C Novice Control Operator Frequency Privileges.

N1C01 (B) [97.301e]
What are the frequency limits of the 80-meter Novice band?
A. 3500 - 4000 kHz
B. 3675 - 3725 kHz
C. 7100 - 7150 kHz
D. 7000 - 7300 kHz

N1C02 (C) [97.301e]
What are the frequency limits of the 40-meter Novice band (ITU Region 2)?
A. 3500 - 4000 kHz
B. 3700 - 3750 kHz
C. 7100 - 7150 kHz
D. 7000 - 7300 kHz

N1C03 (A) [97.301e]
What are the frequency limits of the 15-meter Novice band?
A. 21.100 - 21.200 Mhz
B. 21.000 - 21.450 MHz
C. 28.000 - 29.700 MHz
D. 28.100 - 28.200 MHz

N1C04 (C) [97.301e]
What are the frequency limits of the 10-meter Novice band?
A. 28.000 - 28.500 MHz
B. 28.100 - 29.500 MHz
C. 28.100 - 28.500 MHz
D. 29.100 - 29.500 MHz

N1C05 (B) [97.301f]
What are the frequency limits of the 1.25-meter Novice band (ITU Region 2)?
A. 225.0 - 230.5 Mhz
B. 222.1 - 223.91 MHz
C. 224.1 - 225.1 MHz
D. 222 - 225 MHz

N1C06 (C) [97.301f]
What are the frequency limits of the 23-centimeter Novice band?
A. 1260 - 1270 MHz
B. 1240 - 1300 MHz
C. 1270 - 1295 MHz
D. 1240 - 1246 MHz

N1C07 (A) [97.301e]
If you are operating on 3700 kHz, in what amateur band are you operating?
A. 80 meters
B. 40 meters
C. 15 meters
D. 10 meters

N1C08 (B) [97.301e]
If you are operating on 7125 kHz, in what amateur band are you operating?
A. 80 meters
B. 40 meters
C. 15 meters
D. 10 meters

N1C09 (C) [97.301e]
If you are operating on 21.150 MHz, in what amateur band are you operating?
A. 80 meters
B. 40 meters

C. 15 meters
D. 10 meters

N1C10 (D) [97.301e]
If you are operating on 28.150 MHz, in what amateur band are you operating?
A. 80 meters
B. 40 meters
C. 15 meters
D. 10 meters

N1C11 (D) [97.301f]
If you are operating on 223 MHz, in what amateur band are you operating?
A. 15 meters
B. 10 meters
C. 2 meters
D. 1.25 meters

N1D Novice Eligibility, Exam Elements, Mailing Addresses, US Call Sign Assignment and Life of License.

N1D01 (A) [97.5d1]
Who can become an amateur licensee in the US?
A. Anyone except a representative of a foreign government
B. Only a citizen of the United States
C. Anyone except an employee of the US government
D. Anyone

N1D02 (D) [no ref]
What age must you be to hold an amateur license?
A. 14 years or older
B. 18 years or older
C. 70 years or younger
D. There are no age limits

N1D03 (C) [97.501e]
What minimum examinations must you pass for a Novice amateur license?
A. A written exam, Element 1(A); and a 5 WPM code exam, Element 2(A)
B. A 5 WPM code exam, Element 1(A); and a written exam, Element 3(A)
C. A 5 WPM code exam, Element 1(A); and a written exam, Element 2
D. A written exam, Element 2; and a 5 WPM code exam, Element 4

N1D04 (B) [97.21]
Why must an amateur operator have a current US Postal mailing address?
A. So the FCC has a record of the location of each amateur station
B. To follow the FCC rules and so the licensee can receive mail from the FCC
C. So the FCC can send license-renewal notices
D. So the FCC can publish a call-sign directory

N1D05 (D) [97.27]
What must you do to replace your license if it is lost, mutilated or destroyed?
A. Nothing; no replacement is needed
B. Send a change of address to the FCC using a current FCC Form 610
C. Retake all examination elements for your license
D. Request a new one from the FCC, explaining what happened to the original

N1D06 (B) [97.19]
What must you do to notify the FCC if your mailing address changes?
A. Fill out an FCC Form 610 using your new address, attach a copy of your license, and mail it to your local FCC Field Office
B. Fill out an FCC Form 610 using your new address, attach a copy of your license, and mail it to the FCC office in Gettysburg, PA
C. Call your local FCC Field Office and give them your new address over the phone
D. Call the FCC office in Gettysburg, PA, and give them your new address over the phone

N1D07 (C) [no ref]
Which of the following call signs is a valid US amateur call?
A. UA4HAK
B. KBL7766
C. KA9OLS
D. BY7HY

N1D08 (B) [no ref]
What letters must be used for the first letter in US amateur call signs?
A. K, N, U and W
B. A, K, N and W
C. A, B, C and D
D. A, N, V and W

N1D09 (D) [no ref]
What numbers are normally used in US amateur call signs?
A. Any two-digit number, 10 through 99
B. Any two-digit number, 22 through 45
C. A single digit, 1 though 9
D. A single digit, 0 through 9

N1D10 (C) [97.23]
For how many years is an amateur license normally issued?
A. 2
B. 5
C. 10
D. 15

N1D11 (A) [97.19c]
How soon before your license expires should you send the FCC a completed 610 for a renewal?
A. 60 to 90 days
B. within 21 days of the expiration date
C. 6 to 9 months
D. 6 months to a year

N1E Novice Control Operator Emission Privileges.

N1E01 (A) [97.305/.307f9]
What emission types are Novice control operators allowed to use in the 80-meter band?
A. CW only
B. Data only
C. RTTY only
D. Phone only

N1E02 (A) [97.305/307f9]
What emission types are Novice control operators allowed to use in the 40-meter band?
A. CW only
B. Data only
C. RTTY only
D. Phone only

N1E03 (A) [97.305/307f9]
What emission types are Novice control operators allowed to use in the 15-meter band?
A. CW only
B. Data only
C. RTTY only
D. Phone only

N1E04 (D) [97.305/307f9]
What emission types are Novice control operators allowed to use from 3675 to 3725 kHz?
A. Phone only
B. Image only
C. Data only
D. CW only

N1E05 (D) [97.305/307f9]
What emission types are Novice control operators allowed to use from 7100 to 7150 kHz in ITU Region 2?
A. CW and data
B. Phone
C. Data only
D. CW only

N1E06 (D) [97.305/307f9]
What emission types are Novice control operators allowed to use on frequencies from 21.1 to 21.2 MHz?
A. CW and data
B. CW and phone
C. Data only
D. CW only

N1E07 (C) [97.305]
What emission types are Novice control operators allowed to use on frequencies from 28.1 to 28.3 MHz?
A. All authorized amateur emission privileges
B. Data or phone
C. CW, RTTY and data
D. CW and phone

N1E08 (C) [97.305/307f10]
What emission types are Novice control operators allowed to use on frequencies from 28.3 to 28.5 MHz?
A. All authorized amateur emission privileges
B. CW and data
C. CW and single-sideband phone
D. Data and phone

N1E09 (D) [97.305]
What emission types are Novice control operators allowed to use on the amateur 1.25-meter band in ITU Region 2?
A. CW and phone
B. CW and data
C. Data and phone
D. All amateur emission privileges authorized for use on the band

N1E10 (D) [97.305]
What emission types are Novice control operators allowed to use on the amateur 23-centimeter band?
A. Data and phone
B. CW and data
C. CW and phone
D. All amateur emission privileges authorized for use on the band

N1E11 (D) [97.305/.307f10]
On what HF frequencies may Novice control operators use single-sideband (SSB) phone?
A. 3700 - 3750 kHz
B. 7100 - 7150 kHz
C. 21100 - 21200 kHz
D. 28300 - 28500 kHz

N1E12 (C) [97.305]
On what frequencies in ITU Region 2 may Novice control operators use FM phone?
A. 28.3 - 28.5 MHz
B. 144.0 - 148.0 MHz
C. 222.1 - 223.91 MHz
D. 1240 - 1270 MHz

N1E13 (B) [97.301e/.305]
On what frequencies in the 10-meter band may Novice control operators use RTTY?
A. 28.0 - 28.3 MHz
B. 28.1 - 28.3 MHz
C. 28.0 - 29.3 MHz
D. 29.1 - 29.3 MHz

N1E14 (B) [97.301e/.305]
On what frequencies in the 10-meter band may Novice control operators use data emissions?
A. 28.0 - 28.3 MHz
B. 28.1 - 28.3 MHz
C. 28.0 - 29.3 MHz
D. 29.1 - 29.3 MHz

N1F Transmitter Power on Novice Subbands and Digital Communications [Limited to Concepts Only].

N1F01 (D) [97.313a]
What amount of transmitter power must amateur stations use at all times?
A. 25 watts PEP output
B. 250 watts PEP output
C. 1500 watts PEP output
D. The minimum legal power necessary to communicate

N1F02 (C) [97.313c1]
What is the most transmitter power an amateur station may use on 3700 kHz?
A. 5 watts PEP output
B. 25 watts PEP output
C. 200 watts PEP output
D. 1500 watts PEP output

N1F03 (C) [97.313c1]
What is the most transmitter power an amateur station may use on 7125 kHz?
A. 5 watts PEP output
B. 25 watts PEP output
C. 200 watts PEP output
D. 1500 watts PEP output

N1F04 (C) [97.313c1]
What is the most transmitter power an amateur station may use on 21.125 MHz?
A. 5 watts PEP output
B. 25 watts PEP output
C. 200 watts PEP output
D. 1500 watts PEP output

N1F05 (C) [97.313c2]
What is the most transmitter power a Novice station may use on 28.125 MHz?
A. 5 watts PEP output
B. 25 watts PEP output
C. 200 watts PEP output
D. 1500 watts PEP output

N1F06 (C) [97.313c2]
What is the most transmitter power a Novice station may use on the 10-meter band?
A. 5 watts PEP output
B. 25 watts PEP output
C. 200 watts PEP output
D. 1500 watts PEP output

N1F07 (B) [97.313d]
What is the most transmitter power a Novice station may use on the 1.25-meter band?
A. 5 watts PEP output
B. 25 watts PEP output
C. 200 watts PEP output
D. 1500 watts PEP output

N1F08 (A) [97.313e]
What is the most transmitter power a Novice station may use on the 23-centimeter band?
A. 5 watts PEP output
B. 25 watts PEP output
C. 200 watts PEP output
D. 1500 watts PEP output

N1F09 (A) [97.313c]
On which bands may a Novice station use up to 200 watts PEP output power?
A. 80, 40, 15, and 10 meters
B. 80, 40, 20, and 10 meters

C. 1.25 meters
D. 23 centimeters

N1F10 (C) [97.313d]
On which bands must a Novice station use no more than 25 watts PEP output power?
A. 80, 40, 15, and 10 meters
B. 80, 40, 20, and 10 meters
C. 1.25 meters
D. 23 centimeters

N1F11 (D) [97.313e]
On which bands must a Novice station use no more than 5 watts PEP output power?
A. 80, 40, 15, and 10 meters
B. 80, 40, 20, and 10 meters
C. 1.25 meters
D. 23 centimeters

N1G Responsibility of Licensee, Control Operator Requirements.

N1G01 (D) [97.3a11]
If you allow another amateur to be responsible for the transmissions from your station, what is the other operator called?
A. An auxiliary operator
B. The operations coordinator
C. A third-party operator
D. A control operator

N1G02 (C) [97.103a]
Who is responsible for the proper operation of an amateur station?
A. Only the control operator
B. Only the station licensee
C. Both the control operator and the station licensee
D. The person who owns the station equipment

N1G03 (A) [97.103a]
If you transmit from another amateur's station, who is responsible for its proper operation?
A. Both of you
B. The other amateur (the station licensee)
C. You, the control operator
D. The station licensee, unless the station records show that you were the control operator at the time

N1G04 (D) [97.103a]
What is your responsibility as a station licensee?
A. You must allow another amateur to operate your station upon request
B. You must be present whenever the station is operated
C. You must notify the FCC if another amateur acts as the control operator
D. You are responsible for the proper operation of the station in accordance with the FCC rules

N1G05 (C) [97.103b]
Who may be the control operator of an amateur station?
A. Any person over 21 years of age
B. Any person over 21 years of age with a General class license or higher
C. Any licensed amateur chosen by the station licensee
D. Any licensed amateur with a Technician class license or higher

N1G06 (B) [97.103]
If another amateur transmits from your station, which of these is NOT true?
A. You must first give permission for the other amateur to use your station
B. You must keep the call sign of the other amateur, together with the time and date of transmissions, in your station records
C. The FCC will think that you are the station's control operator unless your station records show that you were not
D. Both of you are equally responsible for the proper operation of the station

N1G07 (A) [97.105b]
If you let another amateur with a higher class license than yours control your station, what operating privileges are allowed?
A. Any privileges allowed by the higher license
B. Only the privileges allowed by your license
C. All the emission privileges of the higher license, but only the frequency privileges of your license
D. All the frequency privileges of the higher license, but only the emission privileges of your license

N1G08 (B) [97.105b]
If you are the control operator at the station of another amateur who has a higher class license than yours, what operating privileges are you allowed?
A. Any privileges allowed by the higher license
B. Only the privileges allowed by your license
C. All the emission privileges of the higher license, but only the frequency privileges of your license
D. All the frequency privileges of the higher license, but only the emission privileges of your license

N1G09 (C) [97.7]
When must an amateur station have a control operator?
A. Only when training another amateur
B. Whenever the station receiver is operated
C. Whenever the station is transmitting
D. A control operator is not needed

N1G10 (A) [97.109b]
When a Novice station is transmitting, where must its control operator be?
A. At the station's control point
B. Anywhere in the same building as the transmitter
C. At the station's entrance, to control entry to the room
D. Anywhere within 50 km of the station location

N1G11 (B) [97.109b]
Why can't unlicensed persons in your family transmit using your amateur station if they are alone with your equipment?
A. They must not use your equipment without your permission
B. They must be licensed before they are allowed to be control operators
C. They must first know how to use the right abbreviations and Q signals
D. They must first know the right frequencies and emissions for transmitting

N1H Station Identification, Points of Communication and Operation, and Business Communications.

N1H01 (D) [97.5a]
When may you operate your amateur station somewhere in the US besides the location listed on your license?
A. Only during times of emergency
B. Only after giving proper notice to the FCC
C. During an emergency or an FCC-approved emergency practice
D. Whenever you want to

N1H02 (C) [97.111]
With which non-amateur stations is a US amateur station allowed to communicate?
A. No non-amateur stations
B. All non-amateur stations
C. Only those authorized by the FCC
D. Only those who use international Morse code

N1H03 (A) [97.113a]
When are communications for business allowed in the amateur service?
A. Only if they are for the safety of human life or immediate protection of property
B. There are no rules against business communications
C. No business communications are ever allowed
D. Business communications are allowed between the hours of 9 AM to 5 PM, weekdays

N1H04 (A) [97.113a]
Which of the following CANNOT be discussed on an amateur club net?
A. Business planning
B. Recreation planning
C. Code practice planning
D. Emergency planning

N1H05 (B) [97.113a]
If you wanted to join a radio club, would you be allowed to send a message to them via amateur radio requesting an application?
A. Yes, if the club is a not-for-profit organization
B. No. This would facilitate the commercial affairs of the club
C. Yes, but only during normal business hours, between 9 AM and 5 PM, weekdays
D. Yes, since there are no rules against business communications in the amateur service

N1H06 (C) [97.119a]
How often must an amateur station be identified?
A. At the beginning of a contact and at least every ten minutes after that
B. At least once during each transmission
C. At least every ten minutes during and at the end of a contact
D. At the beginning and end of each transmission

N1H07 (B) [97.119a]
What do you transmit to identify your amateur station?
A. Your "handle"
B. Your call sign
C. Your first name and your location
D. Your full name

N1H08 (A) [97.119a]
What identification, if any, is required when two amateur stations begin communications?
A. No identification is required
B. One of the stations must give both stations' call signs
C. Each station must transmit its own call sign
D. Both stations must transmit both call signs

N1H09 (C) [97.119a]
What identification, if any, is required when two amateur stations end communications?
A. No identification is required
B. One of the stations must transmit both stations' call signs
C. Each station must transmit its own call sign
D. Both stations must transmit both call signs

N1H10 (B) [97.115c]
Besides normal identification, what else must a US station do when sending third-party communications internationally?
A. The US station must transmit its own call sign at the beginning of each communication, and at least every ten minutes after that
B. The US station must transmit both call signs at the end of each communication
C. The US station must transmit its own call sign at the beginning of each communication, and at least every five minutes after that
D. Each station must transmit its own call sign at the end of each communication, and at least every five minutes after that

N1H11 (B) [97.119a]
What is the longest period of time an amateur station can operate without transmitting its call sign?
A. 5 minutes
B. 10 minutes
C. 15 minutes
D. 20 minutes

N1I International and Space Communications, Authorized and Prohibited Transmissions.

N1I01 (A) [97.3a39]
What is the definition of third-party communications?
A. A message sent between two amateur stations for someone else
B. Public service communications for a political party
C. Any messages sent by amateur stations
D. A three-minute transmission to another amateur

N1I02 (D) [97.111a1]
When are you allowed to communicate with an amateur in a foreign country?
A. Only when the foreign amateur uses English
B. Only when you have permission from the FCC
C. Only when a third-party agreement exists between the US and the foreign country
D. At any time, unless it is not allowed by either government

N1I03 (C) [97.3a36]
What is an amateur space station?
A. An amateur station operated on an unused frequency
B. An amateur station awaiting its new call letters from the FCC
C. An amateur station located more than 50 kilometers above the Earth's surface
D. An amateur station that communicates with Space Shuttles

N1I04 (B) [New 97.207a per FCC 92-310]
Who may be the licensee of an amateur space station?
A. An amateur holding an Amateur Extra class operator license
B. Any licensed amateur operator
C. Anyone designated by the commander of the spacecraft
D. No one unless specifically authorized by the government

N1I05 (D) [97.113b]
When may someone be paid to transmit messages from an amateur station?
A. Only if he or she works for a public service agency such as the Red Cross
B. Under no circumstances
C. Only if he or she reports all such payments to the IRS
D. Only if he or she works for a club station and special requirements are met

N1I06 (A) [97.113c]
When is an amateur allowed to broadcast information to the general public?
A. Never
B. Only when the operator is being paid
C. Only when broadcasts last less than 1 hour
D. Only when broadcasts last longer than 15 minutes

N1I07 (A) [97.113d]
When is an amateur station permitted to transmit music?
A. Never
B. Only if the music played produces no spurious emissions
C. Only if it is used to jam an illegal transmission
D. Only if it is above 1280 MHz

N1I08 (C) [97.113d]
When is the use of codes or ciphers allowed to hide the meaning of an amateur message?
A. Only during contests
B. Only during nationally declared emergencies
C. Never, except when special requirements are met
D. Only on frequencies above 1280 MHz

N1I09 (B) [97.3a42]
What is a "third-party" in amateur communications?
A. An amateur station that breaks in to talk
B. A person who is sent a message by amateur communications other than a control operator who handles the message
C. A shortwave listener who monitors amateur communications
D. An unlicensed control operator

N1I10 (A) [97.115a2]
If you are allowing a non-amateur friend to use your station to talk to someone in the US, and a foreign station breaks in to talk to your friend, what should you do?
A. Have your friend wait until you find out if the US has a third-party agreement with the foreign station's government

B. Stop all discussions and quickly sign off
C. Since you can talk to any foreign amateurs, your friend may keep talking as long as you are the control operator
D. Report the incident to the foreign amateur's government

N1I11 (D) [97.115a2]
When are you allowed to transmit a message to a station in a foreign country for a third party?
A. Anytime
B. Never
C. Anytime, unless there is a third-party agreement between the US and the foreign government
D. If there is a third-party agreement with the US government, or if the third party could be the control operator

N1J False Signals or Unidentified Communications and Malicious Interference.

N1J01 (B) [97.3a21]
What is a transmission called that disturbs other communications?
A. Interrupted CW
B. Harmful interference
C. Transponder signals
D. Unidentified transmissions

N1J02 (B) [97.3a21]
Why is transmitting on a police frequency as a "joke" called harmful interference that deserves a large penalty?
A. It annoys everyone who listens
B. It blocks police calls which might be an emergency and interrupts police communications
C. It is in bad taste to communicate with non-amateurs, even as a joke
D. It is poor amateur practice to transmit outside the amateur bands

N1J03 (C) [97.101d]
When may you deliberately interfere with another station's communications?
A. Only if the station is operating illegally
B. Only if the station begins transmitting on a frequency you are using
C. Never
D. You may expect, and cause, deliberate interference because it can't be helped during crowded band conditions

N1J04 (A) [97.113d]
When may false or deceptive amateur signals or communications be transmitted?
A. Never
B. When operating a beacon transmitter in a "fox hunt" exercise
C. When playing a harmless "practical joke"
D. When you need to hide the meaning of a message for secrecy

N1J05 (C) [97.113d]
If an amateur pretends there is an emergency and transmits the word "MAYDAY," what is this called?
A. A traditional greeting in May
B. An emergency test transmission
C. False or deceptive signals
D. Nothing special; "MAYDAY" has no meaning in an emergency

N1J06 (C) [97.119a]
When may an amateur transmit unidentified communications?
A. Only for brief tests not meant as messages
B. Only if it does not interfere with others
C. Never, except to contol a model craft
D. Only for two-way or third-party communications

N1J07 (A) [97.119a]
What is an amateur communication called that does not have the required station identification?
A. Unidentified communications or signals
B. Reluctance modulation
C. Test emission
D. Tactical communication

N1J08 (D) [97.405a]
If you hear a voice distress signal on a frequency outside of your license privileges, what are you allowed to do to help the station in distress?
A. You are NOT allowed to help because the frequency of the signal is outside your privileges
B. You are allowed to help only if you keep your signals within the nearest frequency band of your privileges
C. You are allowed to help on a frequency outside your privileges only if you use international Morse code
D. You are allowed to help on a frequency outside your privileges in any way possible

N1J09 (D) [97.119a]
If you answer someone on the air without giving your call sign, what type communication have you just conducted?
A. Test transmission
B. Tactical signal
C. Packet communication
D. Unidentified communication

N1J10 (C) [97.403]
When may you use your amateur station to transmit an "SOS" or "MAYDAY"?
A. Never
B. Only at specific times (at 15 and 30 minutes after the hour)
C. In a life or property threatening emergency
D. When the National Weather Service has announced a severe weather watch

N1J11 (B) [97.405a]
When may you send a distress signal on any frequency?
A. Never
B. In a life or property threatening emergency
C. Only at specific times (at 15 and 30 minutes after the hour)
D. When the National Weather Service has announced a severe weather watch

Subelement N2, Operating Procedures: 2 Exam Questions, 2 Groups

N2A Choosing a Frequency for Tune-Up, Operating or Emergencies; Understanding the Morse Code; RST Signal Reports; Q Signals; Voice Communications and Phonetics.

N2A01 (A)
What should you do before you transmit on any frequency?
A. Listen to make sure others are not using the frequency
B. Listen to make sure that someone will be able to hear you
C. Check your antenna for resonance at the selected frequency
D. Make sure the SWR on your antenna feed line is high enough

N2A02 (D)
If you make contact with another station and your signal is extremely strong and perfectly readable, what adjustment might you make to your transmitter?
A. Turn on your speech processor
B. Reduce you SWR
C. Continue with your contact, making no changes
D. Turn down your power output to the minimum necessary

N2A03 (C)
What is one way to shorten transmitter tune-up time on the air to cut down on interference?
A. Use a random wire antenna
B. Tune up on 40 meters first, then switch to the desired band
C. Tune the transmitter into a dummy load
D. Use twin lead instead of coaxial-cable feed lines

N2A04 (D)
If you are in contact with another station and you hear an emergency call for help on your frequency, what should you do?
A. Tell the calling station that the frequency is in use

B. Direct the calling station to the nearest emergency net frequency
C. Call your local Civil Preparedness Office and inform them of the emergency
D. Stop your QSO immediately and take the emergency call

N2A05 (B)
What is the correct way to call CQ when using Morse code?
A. Send the letters "CQ" three times, followed by "DE," followed by your call sign sent once
B. Send the letters "CQ" three times, followed by "DE," followed by your call sign sent three times
C. Send the letters "CQ" ten times, followed by "DE," followed by your call sign sent once
D. Send the letters "CQ" over and over

N2A06 (B)
How should you answer a Morse code CQ call?
A. Send your call sign four times
B. Send the other station's call sign twice, followed by "DE," followed by your call sign twice
C. Send the other station's call sign once, followed by "DE," followed by your call sign four times
D. Send your call sign followed by your name, station location and a signal report

N2A07 (C)
At what speed should a Morse code CQ call be transmitted?
A. Only speeds below five WPM
B. The highest speed your keyer will operate
C. Any speed at which you can reliably receive
D. The highest speed at which you can control the keyer

N2A08 (D)
What is the meaning of the procedural signal "CQ"?
A. "Call on the quarter hour"
B. "New antenna is being tested" (no station should answer)
C. "Only the called station should transmit"
D. "Calling any station"

N2A09 (A)
What is the meaning of the procedural signal "DE"?
A. "From" or "this is," as in "W9NGT DE N9BTT"
B. "Directional Emissions" from your antenna
C. "Received all correctly"
D. "Calling any station"

N2A10 (A)
What is the meaning of the procedural signal "K"?
A. "Any station transmit"
B. "All received correctly"
C. "End of message"
D. "Called station only transmit"

N2A11 (B)
What is meant by the term "DX"?
A. Best regards
B. Distant station
C. Calling any station
D. Go ahead

N2A12 (B)
What is the meaning of the term "73"?
A. Long distance
B. Best regards
C. Love and kisses
D. Go ahead

N2A13 (C)
What are RST signal reports?
A. A short way to describe ionospheric conditions
B. A short way to describe transmitter power
C. A short way to describe signal reception
D. A short way to describe sunspot activity

N2A14 (D)
What does RST mean in a signal report?
A. Recovery, signal strength, tempo
B. Recovery, signal speed, tone
C. Readability, signal speed, tempo
D. Readability, signal strength, tone

N2A15 (B)
What is one meaning of the Q signal "QRS"?
A. Interference from static
B. Send more slowly
C. Send RST report
D. Radio station location is

N2A16 (D)
What is one meaning of the Q signal "QTH"?
A. Time here is
B. My name is
C. Stop sending
D. My location is

N2A17 (C)
What is a QSL card?
A. A letter or postcard from an amateur pen pal
B. A Notice of Violation from the FCC
C. A written proof of communication between two amateurs
D. A postcard reminding you when your license will expire

N2A18 (C)
What is the correct way to call CQ when using voice?
A. Say "CQ" once, followed by "this is," followed by your call sign spoken three times
B. Say "CQ" at least five times, followed by "this is," followed by your call sign spoken once
C. Say "CQ" three times, followed by "this is," followed by your call sign spoken three times
D. Say "CQ" at least ten times, followed by "this is," followed by your call sign spoken once

N2A19 (D)
How should you answer a voice CQ call?
A. Say the other station's call sign at least ten times, followed by "this is," then your call sign at least twice
B. Say the other station's call sign at least five times phonetically, followed by "this is," then your call sign at least once
C. Say the other station's call sign at least three times, followed by "this is," then your call sign at least five times phonetically
D. Say the other station's call sign once, followed by "this is," then your call sign given phonetically

N2A20 (A)
To make your call sign better understood when using voice transmissions, what should you do?
A. Use Standard International Phonetics for each letter of your call
B. Use any words which start with the same letters as your call sign for each letter of your call
C. Talk louder
D. Turn up your microphone gain

N2B Radio Teleprinting, Packet, Repeater Operating Procedures, Special Operations.

N2B01 (B)
What is the correct way to call CQ when using RTTY?
A. Send the letters "CQ" three times, followed by "DE," followed by your call sign sent once
B. Send the letters "CQ" three to six times, followed by "DE," followed by your call sign sent three times
C. Send the letters "CQ" ten times, followed by the procedural signal "DE", followed by your call sent one time
D. Send the letters "CQ" over and over

N2B02 (B)
What speed should you use when answering a CQ call using RTTY?
A. Half the speed of the received signal

B. The same speed as the received signal
C. Twice the speed of the received signal
D. Any speed, since RTTY systems adjust to any signal speed

N2B03 (C)
What does "connected" mean in a packet-radio link?
A. A telephone link is working between two stations
B. A message has reached an amateur station for local delivery
C. A transmitting station is sending data to only one receiving station; it replies that the data is being received correctly
D. A transmitting and receiving station are using a digipeater, so no other contacts can take place until they are finished

N2B04 (D)
What does "monitoring" mean on a packet-radio frequency?
A. The FCC is copying all messages
B. A member of the Amateur Auxiliary to the FCC's Field Operations Bureau is copying all messages
C. A receiving station is displaying all messages sent to it, and replying that the messages are being received correctly
D. A receiving station is displaying messages that may not be sent to it, and is not replying to any message

N2B05 (A)
What is a digipeater?
A. A packet-radio station that retransmits only data that is marked to be retransmitted
B. A packet-radio station that retransmits any data that it receives
C. A repeater that changes audio signals to digital data
D. A repeater built using only digital electronics parts

N2B06 (B)
What does "network" mean in packet radio?
A. A way of connecting terminal-node controllers by telephone so data can be sent over long distances
B. A way of connecting packet-radio stations so data can be sent over long distances
C. The wiring connections on a terminal-node controller board
D. The programming in a terminal-node controller that rejects other callers if a station is already connected

N2B07 (A)
What is simplex operation?
A. Transmitting and receiving on the same frequency
B. Transmitting and receiving over a wide area
C. Transmitting on one frequency and receiving on another
D. Transmitting one-way communications

N2B08 (B)
When should you use simplex operation instead of a repeater?
A. When the most reliable communications are needed
B. When a contact is possible without using a repeater
C. When an emergency telephone call is needed
D. When you are traveling and need some local information

N2B09 (C)
What is a good way to make contact on a repeater?
A. Say the call sign of the station you want to contact three times
B. Say the other operator's name, then your call sign three times
C. Say the call sign of the station you want to contact, then your call sign
D. Say, "Breaker, breaker," then your call sign

N2B10 (A)
When using a repeater to communicate, what do you need to know about the repeater besides its output frequency?
A. Its input frequency
B. Its call sign
C. Its power level
D. Whether or not it has a phone patch

N2B11 (D)
What is the main purpose of a repeater?
A. To make local information available 24 hours a day
B. To link amateur stations with the telephone system
C. To retransmit NOAA weather information during severe storm warnings
D. To increase the range of portable and mobile stations

N2B12 (A)
What does it mean to say that a repeater has an input and an output frequency?
A. The repeater receives on one frequency and transmits on another
B. The repeater offers a choice of operating frequency, in case one is busy
C. One frequency is used to control the repeater and another is used to retransmit received signals
D. The repeater must receive an access code on one frequency before retransmitting received signals

N2B13 (C)
What is an autopatch?
A. Something that automatically selects the strongest signal to be repeated
B. A device which connects a mobile station to the next repeater if it moves out of range of the first
C. A device that allows repeater users to make telephone calls from their stations
D. A device which locks other stations out of a repeater when there is an important conversation in progress

N2B14 (D)
What is the purpose of a repeater time-out timer?
A. It lets a repeater have a rest period after heavy use
B. It logs repeater transmit time to predict when a repeater will fail
C. It tells how long someone has been using a repeater
D. It limits the amount of time someone can transmit on a repeater

N2B15 (B)
What is a CTCSS (or PL) tone?
A. A special signal used for telecommand control of model craft
B. A sub-audible tone added to a carrier which may cause a receiver to accept a signal
C. A tone used by repeaters to mark the end of a transmission
D. A special signal used for telemetry between amateur space stations and Earth stations

Subelement N3, Radio Wave Propagation: 1 Exam Question, 1 Group

N3A Radio Wave Propagation, Line of Sight, Ground Wave, Sky wave, Sunspots and the Sunspot Cycle, Reflection of VHF/UHF Signals.

N3A01 (A)
When a signal travels in a straight line from one antenna to another, what is this called?
A. Line-of-sight propagation
B. Straight-line propagation
C. Knife-edge diffraction
D. Tunnel propagation

N3A02 (C)
What type of propagation usually occurs from one hand held VHF transceiver to another nearby?
A. Tunnel propagation
B. Sky-wave propagation
C. Line-of-sight propagation
D. Auroral propagation

N3A03 (B)
How do VHF and UHF radio waves usually travel from a transmitting antenna to a receiving antenna?
A. They bend through the ionosphere
B. They go in a straight line
C. They wander in any direction
D. They move in a circle going either east or west from the transmitter

N3A04 (C)
What can happen to VHF or UHF signals going towards a metal-framed building?
A. They will go around the building
B. They can be bent by the ionosphere
C. They can be easily reflected by the building
D. They are sometimes scattered in the ectosphere

N3A05 (D)
When a signal travels along the surface of the Earth, what is this called?
A. Sky-wave propagation
B. Knife-edge diffraction
C. E-region propagation
D. Ground-wave propagation

N3A06 (B)
How does the range of sky-wave propagation compare to ground-wave propagation?
A. It is much shorter
B. It is much longer
C. It is about the same
D. It depends on the weather

N3A07 (A)
When a signal is returned to earth by the ionosphere, what is this called?
A. Sky-wave propagation
B. Earth-moon-earth propagation
C. Ground-wave propagation
D. Tropospheric propagation

N3A08 (C)
What is the usual cause of sky-wave propagation?
A. Signals are reflected by a mountain
B. Signals are reflected by the moon
C. Signals are bent back to earth by the ionosphere
D. Signals are repeated by a repeater

N3A09 (C)
What is a skip zone?
A. An area covered by ground-wave propagation
B. An area covered by sky-wave propagation
C. An area which is too far away for ground-wave propagation, but too close for sky-wave propagation
D. An area which is too far away for ground-wave or sky-wave propagation

N3A10 (A)
What are the regions of ionized gases high above the earth called?
A. The ionosphere
B. The troposphere
C. The gas region
D. The ion zone

N3A11 (A)
How do sunspots change the ionization of the atmosphere?
A. The more sunspots there are, the greater the ionization
B. The more sunspots there are, the less the ionization
C. Unless there are sunspots, the ionization is zero
D. They have no effect

N3A12 (C)
How long is an average sunspot cycle?
A. 2 years
B. 5 years
C. 11 years
D. 17 years

Subelement N4, Amateur Radio Practices: 4 Exam Questions, 4 Groups

N4A Unauthorized Use Prevention, Lightning Protection, and Station Grounding.

N4A01 (B)
How could you best keep unauthorized persons from using your amateur station at home?
A. Use a carrier-operated relay in the main power line
B. Use a key-operated on/off switch in the main power line
C. Put a "Danger - High Voltage" sign in the station
D. Put fuses in the main power line

N4A02 (A)
How could you best keep unauthorized persons from using a mobile amateur station in your car?
A. Disconnect the microphone when you are not using it
B. Put a "do not touch" sign on the radio
C. Turn the radio off when you are not using it
D. Tune the radio to an unused frequency when you are done using it

N4A03 (A)
Why would you use a key-operated on/off switch in the main power line of your station?
A. To keep unauthorized persons from using your station
B. For safety, in case the main fuses fail
C. To keep the power company from turning off your electricity during an emergency
D. For safety, to turn off the station in the event of an emergency

N4A04 (D)
Why should you ground all antenna and rotator cables when your amateur station is not in use?
A. To lock the antenna system in one position
B. To avoid radio frequency interference
C. To save electricity
D. To protect the station and building from lightning damage

N4A05 (C)
How can an antenna system best be protected from lightning damage?
A. Install a balun at the antenna feed point
B. Install an RF choke in the antenna feed line
C. Ground all antennas when they are not in use
D. Install a fuse in the antenna feed line

N4A06 (D)
How can amateur station equipment best be protected from lightning damage?
A. Use heavy insulation on the wiring
B. Never turn off the equipment
C. Disconnect the ground system from all radios
D. Disconnect all equipment from the power lines and antenna cables

N4A07 (B)
For best protection from electrical shock, what should be grounded in an amateur station?
A. The power supply primary
B. All station equipment
C. The antenna feed line
D. The AC power mains

N4A08 (A)
What is usually a good indoor grounding point for an amateur station?
A. A metallic cold water pipe
B. A plastic cold water pipe
C. A window screen
D. A metallic natural gas pipe

N4A09 (C)
Where should you connect the chassis of each piece of your station equipment to best protect against electrical shock?
A. To insulated shock mounts
B. To the antenna
C. To a good ground connection
D. To a circuit breaker

N4A10 (B)
Which of these materials is best for a ground rod driven into the earth?
A. Hard plastic
B. Copper or copper-clad steel
C. Iron or steel
D. Fiberglass

N4A11 (C)
If you ground your station equipment to a ground rod driven into the earth, what is the shortest length the rod should be?
A. 4 feet
B. 6 feet
C. 8 feet
D. 10 feet

N4B Radio Frequency Safety Precautions, Safety Interlocks, Antenna Installation Safety Procedures.

N4B01 (B)
What should you do for safety when operating at 1270 MHz?
A. Make sure that an RF leakage filter is installed at the antenna feed point
B. Keep antenna away from your eyes when RF is applied
C. Make sure the standing wave ratio is low before you conduct a test
D. Never use a shielded horizontally polarized antenna

N4B02 (A)
What should you do for safety if you put up a UHF transmitting antenna?
A. Make sure the antenna will be in a place where no one can get near it when you are transmitting
B. Make sure that RF field screens are in place
C. Make sure the antenna is near the ground to keep its RF energy pointing in the correct direction
D. Make sure you connect an RF leakage filter at the antenna feed point

N4B03 (C)
What should you do for safety before removing the shielding on a UHF power amplifier?
A. Make sure all RF screens are in place at the antenna feed line
B. Make sure the antenna feed line is properly grounded
C. Make sure the amplifier cannot accidentally be turned on
D. Make sure that RF leakage filters are connected

N4B04 (A)
Why should you use only good quality coaxial cable and connectors for a UHF antenna system?
A. To keep RF loss low
B. To keep television interference high
C. To keep the power going to your antenna system from getting too high
D. To keep the standing wave ratio of your antenna system high

N4B05 (B)
Why should you make sure the antenna of a hand held transceiver is not close to your head when transmitting?
A. To help the antenna radiate energy equally in all directions
B. To reduce your exposure the radio-frequency energy
C. To use your body to reflect the signal in one direction
D. To keep static charges from building up

N4B06 (D)
Microwave oven radiation is similar to what type of amateur station RF radiation?
A. Signals in the 3.5 MHz range
B. Signals in the 21 MHz range
C. Signals in the 50 MHz range
D. Signals in the 1270 MHz range

N4B07 (D)
Why would there be a switch in a high-voltage power supply to turn off the power if its cabinet is opened?
A. To keep dangerous RF radiation from leaking out through an open cabinet
B. To keep dangerous RF radiation from coming in through an open cabinet
C. To turn the power supply off when it is not being used
D. To keep anyone opening the cabinet from getting shocked by dangerous high voltages

N4B08 (D)
What kind of safety equipment should you wear if you are working on an antenna tower?
A. A grounding chain
B. A reflective vest of approved color
C. A flashing red, yellow or white light
D. A carefully inspected safety belt, hard hat and safety glasses

N4B09 (D)
Why should you wear a safety belt if you are working on an antenna tower?
A. To safely hold your tools so they don't fall and injure someone on the ground
B. To keep the tower from becoming unbalanced while you are working
C. To safely bring any tools you might use up and down the tower
D. To prevent you from accidentally falling

N4B10 (A)
For safety, how high should you place a horizontal wire antenna?
A. High enough so that no one can touch any part of it from the ground
B. As close to the ground as possible
C. Just high enough so you can easily reach it for adjustments or repairs
D. Above high-voltage electrical lines

N4B11 (C)
Why should you wear a hard hat if you are on the ground helping someone work on an antenna tower?
A. So you won't be hurt if the tower should accidentally fall
B. To keep RF energy away from your head during antenna testing
C. To protect your head from something dropped from the tower
D. So someone passing by will know that work is being done on the tower and will stay away

N4C SWR Meaning and Measurements.

N4C01 (C)
What instrument is used to measure standing wave ratio?
A. An ohmmeter
B. An ammeter
C. An SWR meter
D. A current bridge

N4C02 (D)
What instrument is used to measure the relative impedance match between an antenna and its feed line?
A. An ammeter
B. An ohmmeter
C. A voltmeter
D. An SWR meter

N4C03 (A)
Where would you connect an SWR meter to measure standing wave ratio?
A. Between the feed line and the antenna
B. Between the transmitter and the power supply
C. Between the transmitter and the receiver
D. Between the transmitter and the ground

N4C04 (B)
What does an SWR reading of 1:1 mean?
A. An antenna for another frequency band is probably connected
B. The best impedance match has been attained
C. No power is going to the antenna
D. The SWR meter is broken

N4C05 (C)
What does an SWR reading of less than 1.5:1 mean?
A. An impedance match which is too low
B. An impedance mismatch; something may be wrong with the antenna system
C. A fairly good impedance match
D. An antenna gain of 1.5

N4C06 (D)
What does an SWR reading of 4:1 mean?
A. An impedance match which is too low
B. An impedance match which is good, but not the best
C. An antenna gain of 4
D. An impedance mismatch; something may be wrong with the antenna system

N4C07 (A)
What kind of SWR reading may mean poor electrical contact between parts of an antenna system?
A. A jumpy reading
B. A very low reading
C. No reading at all
D. A negative reading

N4C08 (A)
What does a very high SWR reading mean?
A. The antenna is the wrong length, or there may be an open or shorted connection somewhere in the feed line
B. The signals coming from the antenna are unusually strong, which means very good radio conditions
C. The transmitter is putting out more power than normal, showing that it is about to go bad
D. There is a large amount of solar radiation, which means very poor radio conditions

N4C09 (B)
If an SWR reading at the low frequency end of an amateur band is 2.5:1, and is 5:1 at the high frequency end of the same band, what does this tell you about your 1/2-wavelength dipole antenna?
A. The antenna is broadbanded
B. The antenna is too long for operation on the band
C. The antenna is too short for operation on the band
D. The antenna is just right for operation on the band

N4C10 (C)
If an SWR reading at the low frequency end of an amateur band is 5:1, and 2.5:1 at the high frequency end of the same band, what does this tell you about your 1/2-wavelength dipole antenna?
A. The antenna is broadbanded
B. The antenna is too long for operation on the band
C. The antenna is too short for operation on the band
D. The antenna is just right for operation on the band

N4C11 (A)
If you use a 3-30 MHz RF-power meter at UHF frequencies, how accurate will its readings be?
A. They may not be accurate at all
B. They will be accurate enough to get by
C. They will be accurate but the readings must be divided by two
D. They will be accurate but the readings must be multiplied by two

N4D RFI and its Complications.

N4D01 (C)
What is meant by receiver overload?
A. Too much voltage from the power supply
B. Too much current from the power supply
C. Interference caused by strong signals from a nearby transmitter
D. Interference caused by turning the volume up too high

N4D02 (B)
What is one way to tell if radio-frequency interference to a receiver is caused by front-end overload?
A. If connecting a low-pass filter to the transmitter greatly cuts down the interference
B. If the interference is about the same no matter what frequency is used for the transmitter
C. If connecting a low-pass filter to the receiver greatly cuts down the interference
D. If grounding the receiver makes the problem worse

N4D03 (C)
If your neighbor reports television interference whenever you are transmitting from your amateur station, no matter what frequency band you use, what is probably the cause of the interference?
A. Too little transmitter harmonic suppression
B. Receiver VR tube discharge
C. Receiver overload
D. Incorrect antenna length

N4D04 (D)
If your neighbor reports television interference on one or two channels only when you are transmitting on the 15-meter band, what is probably the cause of the interference?
A. Too much low-pass filtering on the transmitter
B. De-ionization of the ionosphere near your neighbor's TV antenna
C. TV receiver front-end overload
D. Harmonic radiation from your transmitter

N4D05 (B)
What type of filter should be connected to a TV receiver as the first step in trying to prevent RF overload from an amateur HF station transmission?
A. Low-pass
B. High-pass
C. Band pass
D. Notch

N4D06 (B)
What type of filter might be connected to an amateur HF transmitter to cut down on harmonic radiation?
A. A key-click filter
B. A low-pass filter
C. A high-pass filter
D. A CW filter

N4D07 (A)
What is meant by harmonic radiation?
A. Unwanted signals at frequencies which are multiples of the fundamental (chosen) frequency
B. Unwanted signals that are combined with a 60-Hz hum
C. Unwanted signals caused by sympathetic vibrations from a nearby transmitter
D. Signals which cause skip propagation to occur

N4D08 (A)
Why is harmonic radiation from an amateur station not wanted?
A. It may cause interference to other stations and may result in out-of-band signals
B. It uses large amounts of electric power
C. It may cause sympathetic vibrations in nearby transmitters
D. It may cause auroras in the air

N4D09 (A)
What type of interference may come from a multi-band antenna connected to a poorly tuned transmitter?
A. Harmonic radiation
B. Auroral distortion
C. Parasitic excitation
D. Intermodulation

N4D10 (C)
What is the main purpose of shielding in a transmitter?
A. It gives the low-pass filter a solid support
B. It helps the sound quality of transmitters
C. It prevents unwanted RF radiation
D. It helps keep electronic parts warmer and more stable

N4D11 (A)
If you are told that your amateur station is causing television interference, what should you do?
A. First make sure that your station is operating properly, and that it does not cause interference to your own television
B. Immediately turn off your transmitter and contact the nearest FCC office for assistance
C. Connect a high-pass filter to the transmitter output and a low-pass filter to the antenna-input terminals of the television
D. Continue operating normally, because you have no reason to worry about the interference

Subelement N5, Electrical Principles: 4 Exam Questions, 4 Groups

N5A Metric Prefixes (i.e. Pico, Micro, Milli, Centi, Kilo, Mega, Giga).

N5A01 (B)
If a dial marked in kilohertz shows a reading of 7125 kHz, what would it show if it were marked in megahertz?
A. 0.007125 MHz
B. 7.125 MHz
C. 71.25 MHz
D. 7,125,000 MHz

N5A02 (C)
If a dial marked in megahertz shows a reading of 3.525 MHz, what would it show if it were marked in kilohertz?
A. 0.003525 kHz
B. 35.25 kHz
C. 3525 kHz
D. 3,525,000 kHz

N5A03 (D)
If a dial marked in kilohertz shows a reading of 3725 kHz, what would it show if it were marked in hertz?
A. 3,725 Hz
B. 37.25 Hz
C. 3,725 Hz
D. 3,725,000 Hz

N5A04 (B)
How long is an antenna that is 400 centimeters long?
A. 0.0004 meters
B. 4 meters
C. 40 meters
D. 40,000 meters

N5A05 (C)
If an ammeter marked in amperes is used to measure a 3000-milliampere current, what reading would it show?
A. 0.003 amperes
B. 0.3 amperes
C. 3 amperes
D. 3,000,000 amperes

N5A06 (C)
If a voltmeter marked in volts is used to measure a 3500-millivolt potential, what reading would it show?
A. 0.35 volts
B. 3.5 volts
C. 35 volts
D. 350 volts

N5A07 (B)
How many farads is 500,000 microfarads?
A. 0.0005 farads
B. 0.5 farads
C. 500 farads
D. 500,000,000 farads

N5A08 (B)
How many microfarads is 1,000,000 picofarads?
A. 0.001 microfarads
B. 1 microfarad
C. 1,000 microfarads
D. 1,000,000,000 microfarads

N5A09 (C)
How many hertz are in a kilohertz?
A. 10
B. 100
C. 1000
D. 1000000

N5A10 (C)
How many kilohertz are in a megahertz?
A. 10
B. 100
C. 1000
D. 1000000

N5A11 (B)
If you have a hand held transceiver which puts out 500 milliwatts, how many watts would this be?
A. 0.02
B. 0.5
C. 5
D. 50

N5B Concepts of current, voltage, conductor, insulator, resistance, and the measurements thereof.

N5B01 (D)
What is the flow of electrons in an electric circuit called?
A. Voltage
B. Resistance
C. Capacitance
D. Current

N5B02 (C)
What is the basic unit of electric current?
A. The volt
B. The watt
C. The ampere
D. The ohm

N5B03 (B)
What is the pressure that forces electrons to flow through a circuit?
A. Magnetomotive force, or inductance
B. Electromotive force, or voltage
C. Farad force, or capacitance
D. Thermal force, or heat

N5B04 (A)
What is the basic unit of voltage?
A. The volt
B. The watt
C. The ampere
D. The ohm

N5B05 (A)
How much voltage does an automobile battery usually supply?
A. About 12 volts
B. About 30 volts
C. About 120 volts
D. About 240 volts

N5B06 (C)
How much voltage does a wall outlet usually supply (in the US)?
A. About 12 volts
B. About 30 volts
C. About 120 volts
D. About 480 volts

N5B07 (C)
What are three good electrical conductors?
A. Copper, gold, mica

B. Gold, silver, wood
C. Gold, silver, aluminum
D. Copper, aluminum, paper

N5B08 (A)
What are four good electrical insulators?
A. Glass, air, plastic, porcelain
B. Glass, wood, copper, porcelain
C. Paper, glass, air, aluminum
D. Plastic, rubber, wood, carbon

N5B09 (B)
What does an electrical insulator do?
A. It lets electricity flow through it in one direction
B. It does not let electricity flow through it
C. It lets electricity flow through it when light shines on it
D. It lets electricity flow through it

N5B10 (D)
What limits the amount of current that flows through a circuit if the voltage stays the same?
A. Reliance
B. Reactance
C. Saturation
D. Resistance

N5B11 (D)
What is the basic unit of resistance?
A. The volt
B. The watt
C. The ampere
D. The ohm

N5C Ohm's Law (Any Calculations Will Be Kept to a Very Low Level—No Fractions or Decimals) and the Concepts of Energy and Power, and Open and Short Circuits.

N5C01 (A)
What formula shows how voltage, current and resistance relate to each other in an electric circuit?
A. Ohm's Law
B. Kirchhoff's Law
C. Ampere's Law
D. Tesla's Law

N5C02 (C)
If a current of 2 amperes flows through a 50-ohm resistor, what is the voltage across the resistor?
A. 25 volts
B. 52 volts
C. 100 volts
D. 200 volts

N5C03 (B)
If a 100-ohm resistor is connected to 200 volts, what is the current through the resistor?
A. 1/2 ampere
B. 2 amperes
C. 300 amperes
D. 20000 amperes

N5C04 (A)
If a current of 3 amperes flows through a resistor connected to 90 volts, what is the resistance?
A. 30 ohms
B. 93 ohms
C. 270 ohms
D. 1/30 ohm

N5C05 (C)
What is the word used to describe how fast electrical energy is used?
A. Resistance
B. Current
C. Power
D. Voltage

N5C06 (C)
If you have light bulbs marked 60 watts, 75 watts and 100 watts, which one will use electrical energy the fastest?
A. The 60 watt bulb
B. The 75 watt bulb
C. The 100 watt bulb
D. They will all be the same

N5C07 (B)
What is the basic unit of electrical power?
A. The ohm
B. The watt
C. The volt
D. The ampere

N5C08 (C)
Which electrical circuit can have no current?
A. A closed circuit
B. A short circuit
C. An open circuit
D. A complete circuit

N5C09 (D)
Which electrical circuit uses too much current?
A. An open circuit
B. A dead circuit
C. A closed circuit
D. A short circuit

N5C10 (B)
What is the name of a current that flows only in one direction?
A. An alternating current
B. A direct current
C. A normal current
D. A smooth current

N5C11 (A)
What is the name of a current that flows back and forth, first in one direction, then in the opposite direction?
A. An alternating current
B. A direct current
C. A rough current
D. A reversing current

N5D Concepts of Frequency, Including AC vs. DC, Frequency Units, AF vs. RF and Wavelength.

N5D01 (D)
What term means the number of times per second that an alternating current flows back and forth?
A. Pulse rate
B. Speed
C. Wavelength
D. Frequency

N5D02 (A)
What is the basic unit of frequency?
A. The hertz
B. The watt
C. The ampere
D. The ohm

N5D03 (B)
What frequency can humans hear?
A. 0 - 20 Hz
B. 20 - 20,000 Hz
C. 200 - 200,000 Hz
D. 10,000 - 30,000 Hz

N5D04 (B)
Why do we call signals in the range 20 Hz to 20,000 Hz audio frequencies?
A. Because the human ear cannot sense anything in this range
B. Because the human ear can sense sounds in this range
C. Because this range is too low for radio energy
D. Because the human ear can sense radio waves in this range

N5D05 (C)
What is the lowest frequency of electrical energy that is usually known as a radio frequency?
A. 20 Hz
B. 2,000 Hz
C. 20,000 Hz
D. 1,000,000 Hz

N5D06 (B)
Electrical energy at a frequency of 7125 kHz is in what frequency range?
A. Audio
B. Radio
C. Hyper
D. Super-high

N5D07 (C)
If a radio wave makes 3,725,000 cycles in one second, what does this mean?
A. The radio wave's voltage is 3,725 kilovolts
B. The radio wave's wavelength is 3,725 kilometers
C. The radio wave's frequency is 3,725 kilohertz
D. The radio wave's speed is 3,725 kilometers per second

N5D08 (C)
What is the name for the distance an AC signal travels during one complete cycle?
A. Wave speed
B. Waveform
C. Wavelength
D. Wave spread

N5D09 (A)
What happens to a signal's wavelength as its frequency increases?
A. It gets shorter
B. It gets longer
C. It stays the same
D. It disappears

N5D10 (A)
What happens to a signal's frequency as its wavelength gets longer?
A. It goes down
B. It goes up
C. It stays the same
D. It disappears

N5D11 (B)
What does 60 hertz (Hz) mean?
A. 6000 cycles per second
B. 60 cycles per second
C. 6000 meters per second
D. 60 meters per second

Subelement N6, Circuit Components: 2 Exam Questions, 2 Groups

N6A Electrical Function and/or Schematic Representation of Resistor, Switch, Fuse, or Battery.

N6A01 (B)
What can a single-pole, double-throw switch do?
A. It can switch one input to one output
B. It can switch one input to either of two outputs
C. It can switch two inputs at the same time, one input to either of two outputs, and the other input to either of two outputs
D. It can switch two inputs at the same time, one input to one output, and the other input to another output

N6A02 (D)
What can a double-pole, single-throw switch do?
A. It can switch one input to one output
B. It can switch one input to either of two outputs
C. It can switch two inputs at the same time, one input to either of two outputs, and the other input to either of two outputs
D. It can switch two inputs at the same time, one input to one output, and the other input to the other output

N6A03 (A)
Which component has a positive and a negative side?
A. A battery
B. A potentiometer
C. A fuse
D. A resistor

N6A04 (B)
Which component has a value that can be changed?
A. A single-cell battery
B. A potentiometer
C. A fuse
D. A resistor

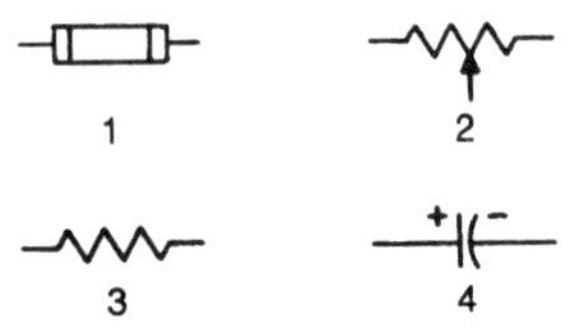

Figure N6–1

N6A05 (B)
In Figure N6-1 which symbol represents a variable resistor or potentiometer?
A. Symbol 1
B. Symbol 2
C. Symbol 3
D. Symbol 4

N6A06 (C)
In Figure N6-1 which symbol represents a fixed resistor?
A. Symbol 1
B. Symbol 2
C. Symbol 3
D. Symbol 4

N6A07 (A)
In Figure N6-1 which symbol represents a fuse?
A. Symbol 1
B. Symbol 2
C. Symbol 3
D. Symbol 4

N6A08 (D)
In Figure N6-1 which symbol represents a single-cell battery?
A. Symbol 1
B. Symbol 2
C. Symbol 3
D. Symbol 4

N6A09 (A)
In Figure N6-2 which symbol represents a single-pole, single-throw switch?
A. Symbol 1
B. Symbol 2
C. Symbol 3
D. Symbol 4

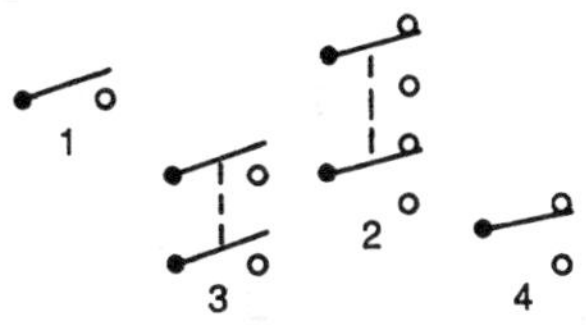

Figure N6–2

N6A10 (D)
In Figure N6-2 which symbol represents a single-pole, double-throw switch?
A. Symbol 1
B. Symbol 2
C. Symbol 3
D. Symbol 4

N6A11 (C)
In Figure N6-2 which symbol represents a double-pole, single-throw switch?
A. Symbol 1
B. Symbol 2
C. Symbol 3
D. Symbol 4

N6A12 (B)
In Figure N6-2 which symbol represents a double-pole, double-throw switch?
A. Symbol 1
B. Symbol 2
C. Symbol 3
D. Symbol 4

N6B Electrical function and/or schematic representation of a ground, antenna, transistor, or a triode vacuum tube.

N6B01 (A)
Which component can amplify a small signal using low voltages?
A. A PNP transistor
B. A variable resistor
C. An electrolytic capacitor
D. A multiple-cell battery

N6B02 (B)
Which component conducts electricity from a negative emitter to a positive collector when its base voltage is made positive?
A. A variable resistor
B. An NPN transistor
C. A triode vacuum tube
D. A multiple-cell battery

N6B03 (A)
Which component is used to radiate radio energy?
A. An antenna
B. An earth ground
C. A chassis ground
D. A potentiometer

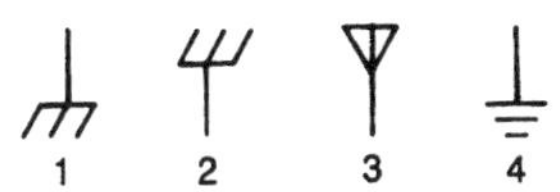

Figure N6–3

N6B04 (D)
In Figure N6-3 which symbol represents an earth ground?
A. Symbol 1
B. Symbol 2
C. Symbol 3
D. Symbol 4

N6B05 (A)
In Figure N6-3 which symbol represents a chassis ground?
A. Symbol 1
B. Symbol 2
C. Symbol 3
D. Symbol 4

N6B06 (C)
In Figure N6-3 which symbol represents an antenna?
A. Symbol 1
B. Symbol 2
C. Symbol 3
D. Symbol 4

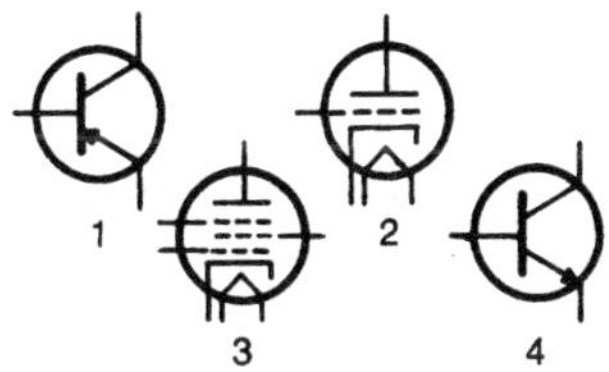

Figure N6–4

N6B07 (D)
In Figure N6-4 which symbol represents an NPN transistor?
A. Symbol 1
B. Symbol 2
C. Symbol 3
D. Symbol 4

N6B08 (A)
In Figure N6-4 which symbol represents a PNP transistor?
A. Symbol 1
B. Symbol 2
C. Symbol 3
D. Symbol 4

N6B09 (B)
In Figure N6-4 which symbol represents a triode vacuum tube?
A. Symbol 1
B. Symbol 2
C. Symbol 3
D. Symbol 4

N6B10 (A)
What is one reason a triode vacuum tube might be used instead of a transistor in a circuit?
A. It handles higher power
B. It uses lower voltages
C. It uses less current
D. It is much smaller

N6B11 (C)
Which component can amplify a small signal but must use high voltages?
A. A transistor
B. An electrolytic capacitor
C. A vacuum tube
D. A multiple-cell battery

Subelement N7, Practical Circuits: 2 Exam Questions, 2 Groups

N7A Functional Layout of Transmitter, Transceiver, Receiver, Power Supply, Antenna, Antenna Switch, Antenna Feed Line Impedance Matching Device, SWR Meter.

N7A01 (B)
What would you connect to your transceiver if you wanted to switch it between more than one type of antenna?
A. A terminal-node switch
B. An antenna switch
C. A telegraph key switch
D. A high-pass filter

N7A02 (C)
What device might allow use of an antenna on a band it was not designed for?
A. An SWR meter
B. A low-pass filter
C. An antenna tuner
D. A high-pass filter

N7A03 (D)
What connects your transceiver to your antenna?
A. A dummy load
B. A ground wire
C. The power cord
D. A feed line

N7A04 (B)
What might you connect between your transceiver and an antenna switch connected to several types of antennas?
A. A high-pass filter
B. An SWR meter
C. A key click filter
D. A mixer

N7A05 (D)
If your SWR meter is connected to an antenna tuner on one side, what would you connect to the other side of it?
A. A power supply
B. An antenna
C. An antenna switch
D. A transceiver

N7A06 (D)
Which of these should never be connected to the output of a transceiver?
A. An antenna switch
B. An SWR meter
C. An antenna
D. A receiver

N7A07 (A)
If your mobile transceiver works in your car but not in your home, what should you check first?
A. The power supply
B. The speaker
C. The microphone
D. The SWR meter

N7A08 (A)
What does an antenna tuner do?
A. It matches a transceiver to a mismatched antenna system
B. It helps a receiver automatically tune in stations that are far away
C. It switches an antenna system to a transceiver when sending, and to a receiver when listening
D. It switches a transceiver between different kinds of antennas connected to one feed line

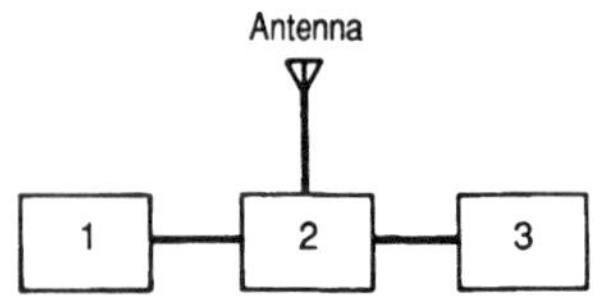

Figure N7–1

N7A09 (B)
In Figure N7-1, if block 1 is a transceiver and block 3 is a dummy antenna what is block 2?
A. A terminal-node switch
B. An antenna switch
C. A telegraph key switch
D. A high-pass filter

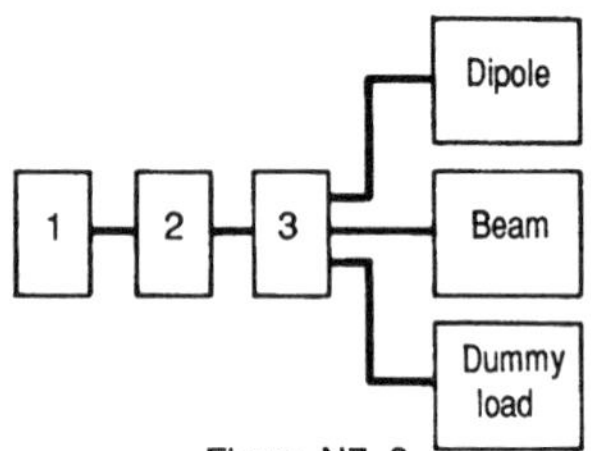

Figure N7–2

N7A10 (A)
In Figure N7-2, if block 2 is an SWR meter and block 3 is an antenna switch, what is block 1?
A. A transceiver
B. A high-pass filter
C. An antenna tuner
D. A modem

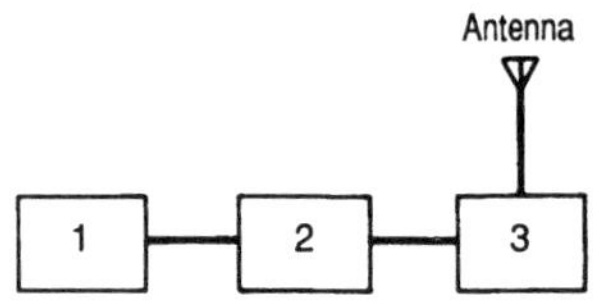

Figure N7–3

N7A11 (B)
In Figure N7-3, if block 1 is a transceiver and block 2 is an SWR meter, what is block 3?
A. An antenna switch
B. An antenna tuner
C. A key-click filter
D. A terminal-node controller

N7A12 (C)
What device converts household current to 12 VDC?
A. A catalytic converter
B. A low-pass filter
C. A power supply
D. An RS-232 interface

N7A13 (C)
Which of these usually needs a heavy-duty power supply?
A. An SWR meter
B. A receiver
C. A transceiver
D. An antenna switch

N7B Station layout and accessories for telegraphy, radiotelephone, radioteleprinter or packet

N7B01 (B)
What would you connect to a transceiver to send Morse code?
A. A terminal-node controller
B. A telegraph key
C. An SWR meter
D. An antenna switch

N7B02 (C)
Where would you connect a telegraph key to send Morse code?
A. To a power supply
B. To an antenna switch
C. To a transceiver
D. To an antenna

N7B03 (B)
What do many amateurs use to help form good Morse code characters?
A. A key-operated on/off switch
B. An electronic keyer
C. A key-click filter
D. A DTMF keypad

N7B04 (C)
Where would you connect a microphone for voice operation?
A. To a power supply
B. To an antenna switch
C. To a transceiver
D. To an antenna

N7B05 (D)
What would you connect to a transceiver for voice operation?
A. A splatter filter
B. A terminal-voice controller
C. A receiver audio filter
D. A microphone

N7B06 (A)
What would you connect to a transceiver for RTTY operation?
A. A modem and a teleprinter or computer system
B. A computer, a printer and a RTTY refresh unit
C. A terminal voice controller
D. A modem, a monitor and a DTMF keypad

N7B07 (C)
What would you connect between a transceiver and a computer system or teleprinter for RTTY operation?
A. An RS-232 interface
B. A DTMF keypad
C. A modem
D. A terminal-network controller

N7B08 (A)
What would you connect between a computer system and a transceiver for packet-radio operation?
A. A terminal-node controller
B. A DTMF keypad
C. An SWR bridge
D. An antenna tuner

N7B09 (C)
Where would you connect a terminal-node controller for packet-radio operation?
A. Between your antenna and transceiver
B. Between your computer and monitor
C. Between your computer and transceiver
D. Between your keyboard and computer

N7B10 (D)
In RTTY operation, what equipment connects to a modem?
A. A DTMF keypad, a monitor and a transceiver
B. A DTMF microphone, a monitor and a transceiver
C. A transceiver and a terminal-network controller
D. A transceiver and a teleprinter or computer system

N7B11 (B)
In packet-radio operation, what equipment connects to a terminal-node controller?
A. A transceiver and a modem
B. A transceiver and a terminal or computer system
C. A DTMF keypad, a monitor and a transceiver
D. A DTMF microphone, a monitor and a transceiver

Subelement N8, Signals and Emissions: 2 Exam Questions, 2 Groups

N8A Emission Types, Key Clicks, Chirps or Superimposed Hum.

N8A01 (B)
How is CW usually transmitted?
A. By frequency-shift keying an RF signal
B. By on/off keying an RF signal
C. By audio-frequency-shift keying an oscillator tone
D. By on/off keying an audio-frequency signal

N8A02 (A)
How is RTTY usually transmitted?
A. By frequency-shift keying an RF signal
B. By on/off keying an RF signal
C. By digital pulse-code keying of an unmodulated carrier
D. By on/off keying an audio-frequency signal

N8A03 (C)
What is the name for international Morse code emissions?
A. RTTY
B. Data
C. CW
D. Phone

N8A04 (A)
What is the name for narrow-band direct-printing telegraphy emissions?
A. RTTY
B. Data
C. CW
D. Phone

N8A05 (B)
What is the name for packet-radio emissions?
A. RTTY
B. Data
C. CW
D. Phone

N8A06 (D)
What is the name for voice emissions?
A. RTTY
B. Data
C. CW
D. Phone

N8A07 (D)
How can you prevent key clicks?
A. By sending CW more slowly
B. By increasing power
C. By using a better power supply
D. By using a key-click filter

N8A08 (C)
What does chirp mean?
A. An overload in a receiver's audio circuit whenever CW is received
B. A high-pitched tone which is received along with a CW signal
C. A small change in a transmitter's frequency each time it is keyed
D. A slow change in transmitter frequency as the circuit warms up

N8A09 (D)
What can be done to keep a CW transmitter from chirping?
A. Add a low-pass filter
B. Use an RF amplifier
C. Keep the power supply current very steady
D. Keep the power supply voltages very steady

N8A10 (D)
What may cause a buzzing or hum in the signal of an HF transmitter?
A. Using an antenna which is the wrong length
B. Energy from another transmitter
C. Bad design of the transmitter's RF power output circuit
D. A bad filter capacitor in the transmitter's power supply

N8A11 (A)
Which sideband is commonly used for 10-meter phone operation?
A. Uppper-sideband
B. Lower-sideband
C. Amplitude-compandored sideband
D. Double-sideband

N8B Harmonics and unwanted signals, equipment and adjustments to help reduce interference to others.

N8B01 (C)
How does the frequency of a harmonic compare to the desired transmitting frequency?
A. It is slightly more than the desired frequency
B. It is slightly less than the desired frequency
C. It is exactly two, or three, or more times the desired frequency
D. It is much less than the desired frequency

N8B02 (A)
What is the fourth harmonic of a 7160-kHz signal?
A. 28,640 kHz
B. 35,800 kHz
C. 28,160 kHz
D. 1790 kHz

N8B03 (C)
If you are told your station was heard on 21,375 kHz, but at the time you were operating on 7125 kHz, what is one reason this could happen?
A. Your transmitter's power-supply filter capacitor was bad
B. You were sending CW too fast
C. Your transmitter was radiating harmonic signals
D. Your transmitter's power-supply filter choke was bad

N8B04 (D)
If someone tells you that signals from your hand held transceiver are interfering with other signals on a frequency near yours, what may be the cause?
A. You may need a power amplifier for your hand held
B. Your hand held may have chirp from weak batteries
C. You may need to turn the volume up on your hand held
D. Your hand held may be transmitting spurious emissions

N8B05 (D)
If your transmitter sends signals outside the band where it is transmitting, what is this called?
A. Off-frequency emissions
B. Transmitter chirping
C. Side tones
D. Spurious emissions

N8B06 (A)
What problem may occur if your transmitter is operated without the cover and other shielding in place?
A. It may transmit spurious emissions
B. It may transmit a chirpy signal
C. It may transmit a weak signal
D. It may interfere with other stations operating near its frequency

N8B07 (B)
What may happen if an SSB transmitter is operated with the microphone gain set too high?
A. It may cause digital interference to computer equipment
B. It may cause splatter interference to other stations operating near its frequency
C. It may cause atmospheric interference in the air around the antenna
D. It may cause interference to other stations operating on a higher frequency band

N8B08 (B)
What may happen if an SSB transmitter is operated with too much speech processing?
A. It may cause digital interference to computer equipment
B. It may cause splatter interference to other stations operating near its frequency
C. It may cause atmospheric interference in the air around the antenna
D. It may cause interference to other stations operating on a higher frequency band

N8B09 (B)
What may happen if an FM transmitter is operated with the microphone gain or deviation control set too high?
A. It may cause digital interference to computer equipment
B. It may cause interference to other stations operating near its frequency
C. It may cause atmospheric interference in the air around the antenna
D. It may cause interference to other stations operating on a higher frequency band

N8B10 (B)
What may your FM hand held or mobile transceiver do if you shout into its microphone?
A. It may cause digital interference to computer equipment
B. It may cause interference to other stations operating near its frequency
C. It may cause atmospheric interference in the air around the antenna
D. It may cause interference to other stations operating on a higher frequency band

N8B11 (D)
What can you do if you are told your FM hand held or mobile transceiver is over deviating?
A. Talk louder into the microphone
B. Let the transceiver cool off
C. Change to a higher power level
D. Talk further away from the microphone

Subelement N9 - Antennas and Feed Lines: 3 exam questions - 3 groups

N9A Wavelength vs antenna length.

N9A01 (D)
How do you calculate the length (in feet) of a half-wavelength dipole antenna?
A. Divide 150 by the antenna's operating frequency (in MHz) [150\f(in MHz)]
B. Divide 234 by the antenna's operating frequency (in MHz) [234\f (in MHz)]
C. Divide 300 by the antenna's operating frequency (in MHz) [300\f (in MHz)]
D. Divide 468 by the antenna's operating frequency (in MHz) [468\f (in MHz)]

N9A02 (B)
How do you calculate the length (in feet) of a quarter-wavelength vertical antenna?
A. Divide 150 by the antenna's operating frequency (in MHz) [150\f (in MHz)]
B. Divide 234 by the antenna's operating frequency (in MHz) [234\f (in MHz)]
C. Divide 300 by the antenna's operating frequency (in MHz) [300\f (in MHz)]
D. Divide 468 by the antenna's operating frequency (in MHz) [468\f (in MHz)]

N9A03 (A)
If you made a half-wavelength dipole antenna for 3725 kHz, how long would it be (to the nearest foot)?
A. 126 ft
B. 81 ft
C. 63 ft
D. 40 ft

N9A04 (C)
If you made a half-wavelength dipole antenna for 28.150 MHz, how long would it be (to the nearest foot)?
A. 22 ft
B. 11 ft
C. 17 ft
D. 34 ft

N9A05 (D)
If you made a quarter-wavelength vertical antenna for 7125 kHz, how long would it be (to the nearest foot)?
A. 11 ft
B. 16 ft
C. 21 ft
D. 33 ft

N9A06 (B)
If you made a quarter-wavelength vertical antenna for 21.125 MHz, how long would it be (to the nearest foot)?
A. 7 ft
B. 11 ft
C. 14 ft
D. 22 ft

N9A07 (C)
If you made a half-wavelength vertical antenna for 223 MHz, how long would it be (to the nearest inch)?
A. 112 inches
B. 50 inches
C. 25 inches
D. 12 inches

N9A08 (A)
If an antenna is made longer, what happens to its resonant frequency?
A. It decreases
B. It increases
C. It stays the same
D. It disappears

N9A09 (B)
If an antenna is made shorter, what happens to its resonant frequency?
A. It decreases
B. It increases
C. It stays the same
D. It disappears

N9A10 (A)
How could you lower the resonant frequency of a dipole antenna?
A. Lengthen the antenna
B. Shorten the antenna
C. Use less feed line
D. Use a smaller size feed line

N9A11 (B)
How could you raise the resonant frequency of a dipole antenna?
A. Lengthen the antenna
B. Shorten the antenna
C. Use more feed line
D. Use a larger size feed line

N9B Yagi parts, concept of directional antennas, and safety near antennas.

N9B01 (B)
In what direction does a Yagi antenna send out radio energy?
A. It goes out equally in all directions
B. Most of it goes in one direction
C. Most of it goes equally in two opposite directions
D. Most of it is aimed high into the air

N9B02 (C)
About how long is the driven element of a Yagi antenna?
A. 1/4 wavelength
B. 1/3 wavelength
C. 1/2 wavelength
D. 1 wavelength

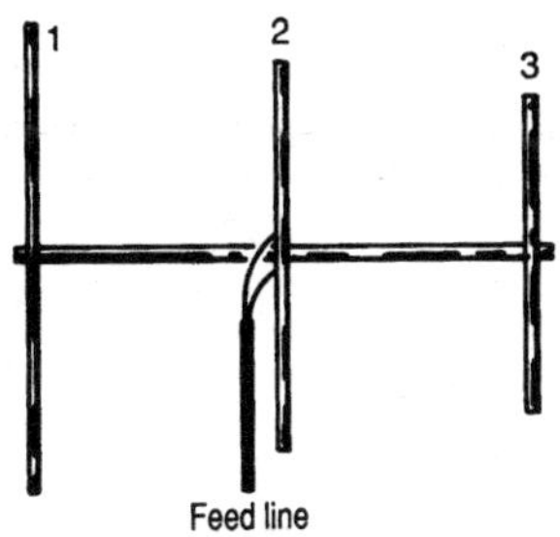

Figure N9–1

N9B03 (D)
In Figure N9-1, what is the name of element 2 of the Yagi antenna?
A. Director
B. Reflector
C. Boom
D. Driven element

N9B04 (A)
In Figure N9-1, what is the name of element 3 of the Yagi antenna?
A. Director
B. Reflector
C. Boom
D. Driven element

N9B05 (B)
In Figure N9-1, what is the name of element 1 of the Yagi antenna?
A. Director
B. Reflector
C. Boom
D. Driven element

N9B06 (B)
Looking at the Yagi antenna in Figure N9-1, in which direction on the page would it send most of its radio energy?
A. Left
B. Right

C. Top
D. Bottom

N9B07 (B)
Why is a 5/8-wavelength vertical antenna better than a 1/4-wavelength vertical antenna for VHF or UHF mobile operations?
A. A 5/8-wavelength antenna can handle more power
B. A 5/8-wavelength antenna has more gain
C. A 5/8-wavelength antenna has less corona loss
D. A 5/8-wavelength antenna is easier to install on a car

N9B08 (C)
In what direction does a vertical antenna send out radio energy?
A. Most of it goes in two opposite directions
B. Most of it goes high into the air
C. Most of it goes equally in all horizontal directions
D. Most of it goes in one direction

N9B09 (C)
If the ends of a half-wave dipole antenna point east and west, which way would the antenna send out radio energy?
A. Equally in all directions
B. Mostly up and down
C. Mostly north and south
D. Mostly east and west

N9B10 (A)
How should you hold the antenna of a hand held transceiver while you are transmitting?
A. Away from your head and away from others
B. Pointed towards the station you are contacting
C. Pointed away from the station you are contacting
D. Pointed down to bounce the signal off the ground

N9B11 (B)
Why should your outside antennas be high enough so that no one can touch them while you are transmitting?
A. Touching the antenna might cause television interference
B. Touching the antenna might cause RF burns
C. Touching the antenna might radiate harmonics
D. Touching the antenna might reflect the signal back to the transmitter and cause damage

N9C Feed lines, baluns and polarization via element orientation.

N9C01 (D)
What is a coaxial cable?
A. Two wires side-by-side in a plastic ribbon
B. Two wires side-by-side held apart by insulating rods
C. Two wires twisted around each other in a spiral
D. A center wire inside an insulating material covered by a metal sleeve or shield

N9C02 (B)
Why does coaxial cable make a good antenna feed line?
A. You can make it at home, and its impedance matches most amateur antennas
B. It is weatherproof, and its impedance matches most amateur antennas
C. It is weatherproof, and its impedance is higher than that of most amateur antennas
D. It can be used near metal objects, and its impedance is higher than that of most amateur antennas

N9C03 (B)
Which kind of antenna feed line can carry radio energy very well even if it is buried in the ground?
A. Twin lead
B. Coaxial cable
C. Parallel conductor
D. Twisted pair

N9C04 (A)
What is the best antenna feed line to use if it must be put near grounded metal objects?
A. Coaxial cable
B. Twin lead
C. Twisted pair
D. Ladder-line

N9C05 (B)
What is parallel-conductor feed line?
A. Two wires twisted around each other in a spiral
B. Two wires side-by-side held apart by insulating rods
C. A center wire inside an insulating material which is covered by a metal sleeve or shield
D. A metal pipe which is as wide or slightly wider than a wavelength of the signal it carries

N9C06 (D)
What are some reasons to use parallel-conductor feed line?
A. It has low impedance, and will operate with a high SWR
B. It will operate with a high SWR, and it works well when tied down to metal objects
C. It has a low impedance, and has less loss than coaxial cable
D. It will operate with a high SWR, and has less loss than coaxial cable

N9C07 (A)
What are some reasons not to use parallel-conductor feed line?
A. It does not work well when tied down to metal objects, and you must use an impedance matching device with your transceiver
B. It is difficult to make at home, and it does not work very well with a high SWR
C. It does not work well when tied down to metal objects, and it cannot operate under high power
D. You must use an impedance matching device with your transceiver, and it does not work very well with a high SWR

N9C08 (B)
What kind of antenna feed line is made of two conductors held apart by insulated rods?
A. Coaxial cable
B. Open-conductor ladder line
C. Twin lead in a plastic ribbon
D. Twisted pair

N9C09 (C)
What would you use to connect a coaxial cable of 50-ohms impedance to an antenna of 35-ohms impedance?
A. A terminating resistor
B. An SWR meter
C. An impedance matching device
D. A low-pass filter

N9C10 (D)
What does balun mean?
A. Balanced antenna network
B. Balanced unloader
C. Balanced unmodulator
D. Balanced to unbalanced

N9C11 (A)
Where would you install a balun to feed a dipole antenna with 50-ohm coaxial cable?
A. Between the coaxial cable and the antenna
B. Between the transmitter and the coaxial cable
C. Between the antenna and the ground
D. Between the coaxial cable and the ground

FCC QUESTION POOL 3A

The questions in Question Pool 2 are used for the Technician Class License examination. The Technician questions were revised in 1992-1993. The questions listed here became effective July 1, 1993, and will be used until June 30, 1997.

The letter in parentheses indicates the correct answer for each question.

Subelement T1, Commission's Rules: 5 Exam Questions, 5 Groups

T1A, Station control, frequency privileges authorized to the Technician class control operator, term of licenses, grace periods and modifications of licenses.

T1A01 (D) [97.3a12]
What is the control point of an amateur station?
A. The on/off switch of the transmitter
B. The input/output port of a packet controller
C. The variable frequency oscillator of a transmitter
D. The location at which the control operator function is performed

T1A02 (B) [97.3a12]
What is the term for the location at which the control operator function is performed?
A. The operating desk
B. The control point
C. The station location
D. The manual control location

T1A03 (A) [97.19a/b]
What must you do to renew or change your operator/primary station license?
A. Properly fill out FCC Form 610 and send it to the FCC in Gettysburg, PA
B. Properly fill out FCC Form 610 and send it to the nearest FCC field office
C. Properly fill out FCC form 610 and send it to the FCC in Washington, DC
D. An amateur license never needs changing or renewing

T1A04 (A) [97.19c]
What is the "grace period" during which the FCC will renew an expired 10-year license?
A. 2 years
B. 5 years
C. 10 years
D. There is no grace period

T1A05 (C) [97.301/305e]
Which of the following frequencies may a Technician operator who has passed a Morse code test use?
A. 7.1 – 7.2 MHz
B. 14.1 – 14.2 MHz
C. 21.1 – 21.2 MHz
D. 28.1 – 29.2 MHz

T1A06 (C) [97.301a]
Which operator licenses authorize privileges on 52.525 MHz?
A. Extra, Advanced only
B. Extra, Advanced, General only
C. Extra, Advanced, General, Technician only
D. Extra, Advanced, General, Technician, Novice

T1A07 (B) [97.301a]
Which operator licenses authorize privileges on 146.52 MHz?
A. Extra, Advanced, General, Technician, Novice
B. Extra, Advanced, General, Technician only
C. Extra, Advanced, General only
D. Extra, Advanced only

T1A08 (A) [97.301a]
Which operator licenses authorize privileges on 223.50 MHz?
A. Extra, Advanced, General, Technician, Novice
B. Extra, Advanced, General, Technician only
C. Extra, Advanced, General only
D. Extra, Advanced only

T1A09 (B) [97.301a]
Which operator licenses authorize privileges on 446.0 MHz?
A. Extra, Advanced, General, Technician, Novice
B. Extra, Advanced, General, Technician only
C. Extra, Advanced, General only
D. Extra, Advanced only

T1A10 (D) [97.301e]
In addition to passing the Technician written examination (Elements 2 and 3A), what must you do before you are allowed to use amateur frequencies below 30 MHz?
A. Nothing special is needed; all Technicians may use the HF bands at any time
B. You must notify the FCC that you intend to operate on the HF bands
C. You must attend a class to learn about HF communications
D. You must pass a Morse code test (either Element 1A, 1B or 1C)

T1A11 (C) [97.301e]
If you are a Technician licensee, what must you have to prove that you are authorized to use the Novice amateur frequencies below 30 MHz?
A. A certificate from the FCC showing that you have notified them that you will be using the HF bands
B. A certificate from an instructor showing that you have attended a class in HF communications
C. Written proof of having passed a Morse code test
D. No special proof is required before using the HF bands

T1B Emission privileges for Technician class control operator, frequency selection and sharing, transmitter power.

T1B01 (C) [97.3b6]
At what point in your station is transceiver power measured?
A. At the power supply terminals inside the transmitter or amplifier
B. At the final amplifier input terminals inside the transmitter or amplifier
C. At the antenna terminals of the transmitter or amplifier
D. On the antenna itself, after the feed line

T1B02 (D) [97.3b6]
What is the term for the average power supplied to an antenna transmission line during one RF cycle at the crest of the modulation envelope?
A. Peak transmitter power
B. Peak output power
C. Average radio-frequency power
D. Peak envelope power

T1B03 (B) [97.203c]
What is the maximum transmitting power permitted an amateur station in beacon operation?
A. 10 watts PEP output
B. 100 watts PEP output
C. 500 watts PEP output
D. 1500 watts PEP output

T1B04 (C) [97.303]
If the FCC rules say that the amateur service is a secondary user of a frequency band, and another service is a primary user, what does this mean?
A. Nothing special; all users of a frequency band have equal rights to operate
B. Amateurs are only allowed to use the frequency band during emergencies
C. Amateurs are allowed to use the frequency band only if they do not cause harmful interference to primary users

D. Amateurs must increase transmitter power to overcome any interference caused by primary users

T1B05 (D) [97.303]
If you are using a frequency within a band assigned to the amateur service on a secondary basis, and a station assigned to the primary service on that band causes interference, what action should you take?
A. Notify the FCC's regional Engineer in Charge of the interference
B. Increase your transmitter's power to overcome the interference
C. Attempt to contact the station and request that it stop the interference
D. Change frequencies; you may be causing harmful interference to the other station, in violation of FCC rules

T1B06 (C) [97.303a]
What rule applies if two amateur stations want to use the same frequency?
A. The station operator with a lesser class of license must yield the frequency to a higher class licensee
B. The station operator with a lower power output must yield the frequency to the station with a higher power output
C. Both station operators have an equal right to operate on the frequency
D. Station operators in ITU Regions 1 and 3 must yield the frequency to stations in ITU Region 2

T1B07 (A) [97.305a]
What emission type may always be used for station identification, regardless of the transmitting frequency?
A. CW
B. RTTY
C. MCW
D. Phone

T1B08 (B) [97.305c]
On what frequencies within the 6-meter band may phone emissions be transmitted?
A. 50.0 – 54.0 MHz only
B. 50.1 – 54.0 MHz only
C. 51.0 – 54.0 MHz only
D. 52.0 – 54.0 MHz only

T1B09 (A) [97.305c]
On what frequencies within the 2-meter band may image emissions be transmitted?
A. 144.1 – 148.0 MHz only
B. 146.0 – 148.0 MHz only
C. 144.0 – 148.0 MHz only
D. 146.0 – 147.0 MHz only

T1B10 (D) [97.313b]
What is the maximum transmitting power permitted an amateur station on 146.52 MHz?
A. 200 watts PEP output
B. 500 watts ERP
C. 1000 watts DC input
D. 1500 watts PEP output

T1B11 (A) [97.209b2]
Which band may NOT be used by Earth stations for satellite communications?
A. 6 meters
B. 2 meters
C. 70 centimeters
D. 23 centimeters

T1C Digital communications, station identification, ID with CSCE.

T1C01 (A) [97.119e1]
If you are a Novice licensee with a Certificate of Successful Completion of Examination (CSCE) for Technician privileges, how do you identify your station when transmitting on 146.34 MHz?
A. You must give your call sign, followed by any suitable word that denotes the slant mark and the identifier "KT"
B. You may not operate on 146.34 until your new license arrives
C. No special form of identification is needed
D. You must give your call sign and the location of the VE examination where you obtained the CSCE

T1C02 (C) [97.307f3/4]
What is the maximum frequency shift permitted for RTTY or data transmissions below 50 MHz?
A. 0.1 kHz
B. 0.5 kHz
C. 1 kHz
D. 5 kHz

T1C03 (D) [97.307]
What is the maximum frequency shift permitted for RTTY or data transmissions above 50 MHz?
A. 0.1 kHz or the sending speed, in bauds, whichever is greater
B. 0.5 kHz or the sending speed, in bauds, whichever is greater
C. 5 kHz or the sending speed, in bauds, whichever is greater
D. The FCC rules do not specify a maximum frequency shift above 50 MHz

T1C04 (B) [97.307f4]
What is the maximum symbol rate permitted for packet transmissions on the 10-meter band?
A. 300 bauds
B. 1200 bauds
C. 19.6 kilobauds
D. 56 kilobauds

T1C05 (C) [97.307f5]
What is the maximum symbol rate permitted for packet transmissions on the 2-meter band?
A. 300 bauds
B. 1200 bauds
C. 19.6 kilobauds
D. 56 kilobauds

T1C06 (C) [97.307f4]
What is the maximum symbol rate permitted for RTTY or data transmissions between 28 and 50 MHz?
A. 56 kilobauds
B. 19.6 kilobauds
C. 1200 bauds
D. 300 bauds

T1C07 (B) [97.307f5]
What is the maximum symbol rate permitted for RTTY or data transmissions between 50 and 222 MHz?
A. 56 kilobauds
B. 19.6 kilobauds
C. 1200 bauds
D. 300 bauds

T1C08 (A) [97.307f5]
What is the maximum authorized bandwidth of RTTY, data or multiplexed emissions using an unspecified digital code within the frequency range of 50 to 222 MHz?
A. 20 kHz
B. 50 kHz
C. The total bandwidth shall not exceed that of a single-sideband phone emission
D. The total bandwidth shall not exceed 10 times that of a CW emission

T1C09 (D) [97.307f6]
What is the maximum symbol rate permitted for RTTY or data transmissions above 222 MHz?
A. 300 bauds
B. 1200 bauds
C. 19.6 kilobauds
D. 56 kilobauds

T1C10 (B) [97.307f6]
What is the maximum authorized bandwidth of RTTY, data or multiplexed emissions using an unspecified digital code within the frequency range of 222 to 450 MHz?
A. 50 kHz
B. 100 kHz
C. 150 kHz
D. 200 kHz

T1C11 (C) [97.307f6]
What is the maximum authorized bandwidth of RTTY, data or multiplexed emissions using an unspecified digital code within the 70 cm amateur band?
A. 300 kHz
B. 200 kHz
C. 100 kHz
D. 50 kHz

T1D Correct language, phonetics, beacons and radio control of model craft and vehicles.

T1D01 (A) [97.3a9]
What is an amateur station called which transmits communications for the purpose of observation of propagation and reception?
A. A beacon
B. A repeater
C. An auxiliary station
D. A radio control station

T1D02 (B) [97.119b1]
What is the fastest code speed a repeater may use for automatic identification?
A. 13 words per minute
B. 20 words per minute
C. 25 words per minute
D. There is no limitation

T1D03 (C) [97.119b2]
If you are using a language besides English to make a contact, what language must you use when identifying your station?
A. The language being used for the contact
B. The language being used for the contact, providing the US has a third-party communications agreement with that country
C. English
D. Any language of a country which is a member of the International Telecommunication Union

T1D04 (C) [97.119b2]
What do the FCC rules suggest you use as an aid for correct station identification when using phone?
A. A speech compressor
B. Q signals
C. A phonetic alphabet
D. Unique words of your choice

T1D05 (B) [97.203a]
What minimum class of amateur license must you hold to operate a beacon station?
A. Novice
B. Technician
C. General
D. Amateur Extra

T1D06 (A) [97.205c]
If a repeater is causing harmful interference to another repeater and a frequency coordinator has recommended the operation of one station only, who is responsible for resolving the interference?
A. The licensee of the unrecommended repeater
B. Both repeater licensees
C. The licensee of the recommended repeater
D. The frequency coordinator

T1D07 (D) [97.205c]
If a repeater is causing harmful interference to another amateur repeater and a frequency coordinator has recommended the operation of both stations, who is responsible for resolving the interference?
A. The licensee of the repeater which has been recommended for the longest period of time
B. The licensee of the repeater which has been recommended the most recently
C. The frequency coordinator
D. Both repeater licensees

T1D08 (A) [97.205c]
If a repeater is causing harmful interference to another repeater and a frequency coordinator has NOT recommended either station, who is primarily responsible for resolving the interference?
A. Both repeater licensees
B. The licensee of the repeater which has been in operation for the longest period of time
C. The licensee of the repeater which has been in operation for the shortest period of time
D. The frequency coordinator

T1D09 (C) [97.215a]
What minimum information must be on a label affixed to a transmitter used for telecommand (control) of model craft?
A. Station call sign
B. Station call sign and the station licensee's name
C. Station call sign and the station licensee's name and address
D. Station call sign and the station licensee's class of license

T1D10 (D) [97.215a]
What are the station identification requirements for an amateur transmitter used for telecommand (control) of model craft?
A. Once every ten minutes
B. Once every ten minutes, and at the beginning and end of each transmission
C. At the beginning and end of each transmission
D. Station identification is not required if the transmitter is labeled with the station licensee's name, address and call sign

T1D11 (B) [97.215c]
What is the maximum transmitter power an amateur station is allowed when used for telecommand (control) of model craft?
A. One milliwatt
B. One watt
C. Two watts
D. Three watts

T1E Emergency communications; broadcasting; permissible one-way, satellite and third party communication; indecent and profane language.

T1E01 (A) [97.3a10]
What is meant by the term broadcasting?
A. Transmissions intended for reception by the general public, either direct or relayed
B. Retransmission by automatic means of programs or signals from non-amateur stations
C. One-way radio communications, regardless of purpose or content
D. One-way or two-way radio communications between two or more stations

T1E02 (B) [97.3a10]
Which of the following one-way communications may not be transmitted in the amateur service?
A. Telecommands to model craft
B. Broadcasts intended for the general public
C. Brief transmissions to make adjustments to the station
D. Morse code practice

T1E03 (D) [97.113b]
What kind of payment is allowed for third-party messages sent by an amateur station?
A. Any amount agreed upon in advance
B. Donation of equipment repairs
C. Donation of amateur equipment
D. No payment of any kind is allowed

T1E04 (B) [97.113d]
When may you send obscene words from your amateur station?
A. Only when they do not cause interference to other communications
B. Never; obscene words are prohibited in amateur transmissions
C. Only when they are not retransmitted through a repeater
D. Any time, but there is an unwritten rule among amateurs that they should not be used on the air

T1E05 (D) [97.113d]
When may you send indecent words from your amateur station?
A. Only when they do not cause interference to other communications
B. Only when they are not retransmitted through a repeater
C. Any time, but there is an unwritten rule among amateurs that they should not be used on the air
D. Never; indecent words are prohibited in amateur transmissions

T1E06 (C) [97.113d]
When may you send profane words from your amateur station?
A. Only when they do not cause interference to other communications
B. Only when they are not retransmitted through a repeater
C. Never; profane words are prohibited in amateur transmissions
D. Any time, but there is an unwritten rule among amateurs that they should not be used on the air

T1E07 (C) [97.113e]
If you wanted to use your amateur station to retransmit communications between a space shuttle and its associated Earth stations, what agency must first give its approval?
A. The FCC in Washington, DC
B. The office of your local FCC Engineer In Charge (EIC)
C. The National Aeronautics and Space Administration
D. The Department of Defense

T1E08 (D) [97.115a2]
When are third-party messages allowed to be sent to a foreign country?
A. When sent by agreement of both control operators
B. When the third party speaks to a relative
C. They are not allowed under any circumstances
D. When the US has a third-party agreement with the foreign country or the third party is qualified to be a control operator

T1E09 (A) [97.115b1]
If you let an unlicensed third party use your amateur station, what must you do at your station's control point?
A. You must continuously monitor and supervise the third party's participation
B. You must monitor and supervise the communication only if contacts are made in countries which have no third-party communications agreement with the US
C. You must monitor and supervise the communication only if contacts are made on frequencies below 30 MHz
D. You must key the transmitter and make the station identification

T1E10 (A) [97.401a]
If a disaster disrupts normal communication systems in an area where the amateur service is regulated by the FCC, what kinds of transmissions may stations make?
A. Those which are necessary to meet essential communication needs and facilitate relief actions
B. Those which allow a commercial business to continue to operate in the affected area
C. Those for which material compensation has been paid to the amateur operator for delivery into the affected area
D. Those which are to be used for program production or newsgathering for broadcasting purposes

T1E11 (C) [97.401c]
What information is included in an FCC declaration of a temporary state of communication emergency?
A. A list of organizations authorized to use radio communications in the affected area
B. A list of amateur frequency bands to be used in the affected area
C. Any special conditions and special rules to be observed during the emergency
D. An operating schedule for authorized amateur emergency stations

Subelement T2, Operating Procedures: 3 Exam Questions, 3 Groups

T2A Repeater operation, courteous operation

T2A01 (B)
How do you call another station on a repeater if you know the station's call sign?
A. Say "break, break 79," then say the station's call sign
B. Say the station's call sign, then identify your own station
C. Say "CQ" three times, then say the station's call sign
D. Wait for the station to call "CQ," then answer it

T2A02 (C)
Why should you pause briefly between transmissions when using a repeater?
A. To check the SWR of the repeater
B. To reach for pencil and paper for third-party communications
C. To listen for anyone wanting to break in
D. To dial up the repeater's autopatch

T2A03 (A)
Why should you keep transmissions short when using a repeater?
A. A long transmission may prevent someone with an emergency from using the repeater
B. To see if the receiving station operator is still awake
C. To give any listening non-hams a chance to respond
D. To keep long distance charges down

T2A04 (D)
What is the proper way to break into a conversation on a repeater?
A. Wait for the end of a transmission and start calling the desired party
B. Shout, "break, break!" to show that you're eager to join the conversation
C. Turn on an amplifier and override whoever is talking
D. Say your call sign during a break between transmissions

T2A05 (B)
What is the purpose of repeater operation?
A. To cut your power bill by using someone else's higher power system
B. To help mobile and low-power stations extend their usable range
C. To transmit signals for observing propagation and reception
D. To make calls to stores more than 50 miles away

T2A06 (B)
What causes a repeater to "time out"?
A. The repeater's battery supply runs out
B. Someone's transmission goes on longer than the repeater allows
C. The repeater gets too hot and stops transmitting until its circuitry cools off
D. Something is wrong with the repeater

T2A07 (D)
During commuting rush hours, which type of repeater operation should be discouraged?
A. Mobile stations
B. Low-power stations
C. Highway traffic information nets
D. Third-party communications nets

T2A08 (B)
What is a courtesy tone (used in repeater operations)?
A. A sound used to identify the repeater
B. A sound used to indicate when a transmission is complete
C. A sound used to indicate that a message is waiting for someone
D. A sound used to activate a receiver in case of severe weather

T2A09 (A)
What is the meaning of: "Your signal is full quieting..."?
A. Your signal is strong enough to overcome all receiver noise
B. Your signal has no spurious sounds
C. Your signal is not strong enough to be received
D. Your signal is being received, but no audio is being heard

T2A10 (C)
How should you give a signal report over a repeater?
A. Say what your receiver's S-meter reads
B. Always say: "Your signal report is five five..."
C. Say the amount of signal quieting into the repeater
D. Try to imitate the sound quality you are receiving

T2A11 (A)
What is a repeater called which is available for anyone to use?
A. An open repeater
B. A closed repeater
C. An autopatch repeater
D. A private repeater

T2A12 (A)
What is the usual input/output frequency separation for repeaters in the 2-meter band?
A. 600 kHz
B. 1.0 MHz
C. 1.6 MHz
D. 5.0 MHz

T2A13 (C)
What is the usual input/output frequency separation for repeaters in the 1.25-meter band?
A. 600 kHz
B. 1.0 MHz
C. 1.6 MHz
D. 5.0 MHz

T2A14 (D)
What is the usual input/output frequency separation for repeaters in the 70-centimeter band?
A. 600 kHz
B. 1.0 MHz
C. 1.6 MHz
D. 5.0 MHz

T2A15 (A)
Why should local amateur communications use VHF and UHF frequencies instead of HF frequencies?
A. To minimize interference on HF bands capable of long distance communication
B. Because greater output power is permitted on VHF and UHF
C. Because HF transmissions are not propagated locally
D. Because signals are louder on VHF and UHF frequencies

T2A16 (A)
How might you join a closed repeater system?
A. Contact the control operator and ask to join
B. Use the repeater until told not to
C. Use simplex on the repeater input until told not to
D. Write the FCC and report the closed condition

T2A17 (B)
How can on-the-air interference be minimized during a lengthy transmitter testing or loading up procedure?
A. Choose an unoccupied frequency
B. Use a dummy load
C. Use a non-resonant antenna
D. Use a resonant antenna that requires no loading-up procedure

T2A18 (C)
What is the proper way to ask someone their location when using a repeater?
A. What is your QTH
B. What is your 20
C. Where are you
D. Locations are not normally told by radio

T2B Simplex operations, Q signals, RST signal reporting, repeater frequency coordination.

T2B01 (C)
Why should simplex be used where possible, instead of using a repeater?
A. Signal range will be increased
B. Long distance toll charges will be avoided
C. The repeater will not be tied up unnecessarily
D. Your antenna's effectiveness will be better tested

T2B02 (A)
If you are talking to a station using a repeater, how would you find out if you could communicate using simplex instead?
A. See if you can clearly receive the station on the repeater's input frequency
B. See if you can clearly receive the station on a lower frequency band
C. See if you can clearly receive a more distant repeater
D. See if a third station can clearly receive both of you

T2B03 (C)
If you are operating simplex on a repeater frequency, why would it be good amateur practice to change to another frequency?
A. The repeater's output power may ruin your station's receiver
B. There are more repeater operators than simplex operators
C. Changing the repeater's frequency is not practical
D. Changing the repeater's frequency requires the authorization of the FCC

T2B04 (D)
What is a repeater frequency coordinator?
A. Someone who organizes the assembly of a repeater station
B. Someone who provides advice on what kind of repeater to buy
C. The person whose call sign is used for a repeater's identification
D. A person or group that recommends frequencies for repeater usage

T2B05 (C)
What is the proper Q signal to use to see if a frequency is in use before transmitting on CW?
A. QRV?
B. QRU?
C. QRL?
D. QRZ?

T2B06 (A)
What is one meaning of the Q signal "QSY"?
A. Change frequency
B. Send more slowly
C. Send faster
D. Use more power

T2B07 (B)
What is one meaning of the Q signal "QSO"?
A. A contact is confirmed
B. A conversation is in progress
C. A contact is ending
D. A conversation is desired

T2B08 (B)
What is the proper Q signal to use to ask if someone is calling you on CW?
A. QSL?
B. QRZ?
C. QRL?
D. QRT?

T2B09 (A)
What is the meaning of: "Your signal report is five seven..."?
A. Your signal is perfectly readable and moderately strong

B. Your signal is perfectly readable, but weak
C. Your signal is readable with considerable difficulty
D. Your signal is perfectly readable with near pure tone

T2B10 (C)
What is the meaning of: "Your signal report is three three..."?
A. The contact is serial number thirty-three
B. The station is located at latitude 33 degrees
C. Your signal is readable with considerable difficulty and weak in strength
D. Your signal is unreadable, very weak in strength

T2B11 (D)
What is the meaning of: "Your signal report is five nine plus 20 dB..."?
A. Your signal strength has increased by a factor of 100
B. Repeat your transmission on a frequency 20 kHz higher
C. The bandwidth of your signal is 20 decibels above linearity
D. A relative signal-strength meter reading is 20 decibels greater than strength 9

T2C Distress calling and emergency drills and communications – operations and equipment, Radio Amateur Civil Emergency Service (RACES)

T2C01 (A)
What is the proper distress call to use when operating phone?
A. Say "MAYDAY" several times
B. Say "HELP" several times
C. Say "EMERGENCY" several times
D. Say "SOS" several times

T2C02 (D)
What is the proper distress call to use when operating CW?
A. MAYDAY
B. QRRR
C. QRZ
D. SOS

T2C03 (A)
What is the proper way to interrupt a repeater conversation to signal a distress call?
A. Say "BREAK" twice, then your call sign
B. Say "HELP" as many times as it takes to get someone to answer
C. Say "SOS," then your call sign
D. Say "EMERGENCY" three times

T2C04 (C)
With what organization must you register before you can participate in RACES drills?
A. A local Amateur Radio club
B. A local racing organization
C. The responsible civil defense organization
D. The Federal Communications Commission

T2C05 (A)
What is the maximum number of hours allowed per week for RACES drills?
A. One
B. Six, but not more than one hour per day
C. Eight
D. As many hours as you want

T2C06 (D)
How must you identify messages sent during a RACES drill?
A. As emergency messages
B. As amateur traffic
C. As official government messages
D. As drill or test messages

T2C07 (B)
What is one reason for using tactical call signs such as "command post" or "weather center" during an emergency?
A. They keep the general public informed about what is going on
B. They are more efficient and help coordinate public-service communications
C. They are required by the FCC
D. They increase goodwill between amateurs

T2C08 (D)
What type of messages concerning a person's well-being are sent into or out of a disaster area?
A. Routine traffic
B. Tactical traffic
C. Formal message traffic
D. Health and Welfare traffic

T2C09 (B)
What are messages called which are sent into or out of a disaster area concerning the immediate safety of human life?
A. Tactical traffic
B. Emergency traffic
C. Formal message traffic
D. Health and Welfare traffic

T2C10 (B)
Why is it a good idea to have a way to operate your amateur station without using commercial AC power lines?
A. So you may use your station while mobile
B. So you may provide communications in an emergency
C. So you may operate in contests where AC power is not allowed
D. So you will comply with the FCC rules

T2C11 (C)
What is the most important accessory to have for a hand held radio in an emergency?
A. An extra antenna
B. A portable amplifier
C. Several sets of charged batteries
D. A microphone headset for hands-free operation

T2C12 (C)
Which type of antenna would be a good choice as part of a portable HF amateur station that could be set up in case of an emergency?
A. A three-element quad
B. A three-element Yagi
C. A dipole
D. A parabolic dish

Subelement T3, Radio Wave Propagation: 3 Exam Questions, 3 Groups

T3A, Ionosphere, Ionospheric regions, solar radiation.

T3A01 (A)
What is the ionosphere?
A. A area of the outer atmosphere where enough ions and free electrons exist to propagate radio waves
B. A area between two air masses of different temperature and humidity, along which radio waves can travel
C. An ionized path in the atmosphere where lightning has struck
D. An area of the atmosphere where weather takes place

T3A02 (D)
What is the name of the area that makes long-distance radio communications possible by bending radio waves?
A. Troposphere
B. Stratosphere
C. Magnetosphere
D. Ionosphere

T3A03 (A)
What causes the ionosphere to form?
A. Solar radiation ionizing the outer atmosphere
B. Temperature changes ionizing the outer atmosphere
C. Lightning ionizing the outer atmosphere
D. Release of fluorocarbons into the atmosphere

T3A04 (C)
What type of solar radiation is most responsible for ionization in the outer atmosphere?
A. Thermal
B. Ionized particle
C. Ultraviolet
D. Microwave

T3A05 (A)
Which ionospheric region limits daytime radio communications on the 80-meter band to short distances?
A. D region
B. E region
C. F1 region
D. F2 region

T3A06 (B)
Which ionospheric region is closest to the earth?
A. The A region
B. The D region
C. The E region
D. The F region

T3A07 (B)
Which ionospheric region most affects sky-wave propagation on the 6-meter band?
A. The D region
B. The E region
C. The F1 region
D. The F2 region

T3A08 (A)
Which region of the ionosphere is the least useful for long-distance radio wave propagation?
A. The D region
B. The E region
C. The F1 region
D. The F2 region

T3A09 (D)
Which region of the ionosphere is mainly responsible for long-distance sky-wave radio communications?
A. D region
B. E region
C. F1 region
D. F2 region

T3A10 (B)
What two sub-regions of ionosphere exist only in the daytime?
A. Troposphere and stratosphere
B. F1 and F2
C. Electrostatic and electromagnetic
D. D and E

T3A11 (C)
Which two daytime ionospheric regions combine into one region at night?
A. E and F1
B. D and E
C. F1 and F2
D. E1 and E2

T3B Ionospheric absorption, causes and variation, maximum usable frequency.

T3B01 (D)
Which region of the ionosphere is mainly responsible for absorbing radio signals during the daytime?
A. The F2 region
B. The F1 region
C. The E region
D. The D region

T3B02 (B)
When does ionospheric absorption of radio signals occur?
A. When tropospheric ducting occurs
B. When long wavelength signals enter the D region
C. When signals travel to the F region
D. When a temperature inversion occurs

T3B03 (A)
What effect does the D region of the ionosphere have on lower-frequency HF signals in the daytime?
A. It absorbs the signals
B. It bends the radio waves out into space
C. It refracts the radio waves back to earth
D. It has little or no effect on 80-meter radio waves

T3B04 (B)
What causes the ionosphere to absorb radio waves?
A. The weather below the ionosphere
B. The ionization of the D region
C. The presence of ionized clouds in the E region
D. The splitting of the F region

T3B05 (D)
What is the condition of the ionosphere just before local sunrise?
A. Atmospheric attenuation is at a maximum
B. The D region is above the E region
C. The E region is above the F region
D. Ionization is at a minimum

T3B06 (C)
When is the ionosphere most ionized?
A. Dusk
B. Midnight
C. Midday
D. Dawn

T3B07 (A)
When is the ionosphere least ionized?
A. Shortly before dawn
B. Just after noon
C. Just after dusk
D. Shortly before midnight

T3B08 (B)
When is the E region most ionized?
A. Dawn
B. Midday
C. Dusk
D. Midnight

T3B09 (A)
What happens to signals higher in frequency than the critical frequency?
A. They pass through the ionosphere
B. They are absorbed by the ionosphere
C. Their frequency is changed by the ionosphere to be below the maximum usable frequency
D. They are reflected back to their source

T3B10 (C)
What causes the maximum usable frequency to vary?
A. The temperature of the ionosphere
B. The speed of the winds in the upper atmosphere
C. The amount of radiation received from the sun, mainly ultraviolet
D. The type of weather just below the ionosphere

T3B11 (A)
What does maximum usable frequency mean?
A. The highest frequency signal that is bent back to the earth
B. The lowest frequency signal that is bent back to the earth
C. The highest frequency signal that is most absorbed by the ionosphere
D. The lowest frequency signal that is most absorbed by the ionosphere

T3C Propagation, including ionospheric, tropospheric, line-of-sight scatter propagation, and Maximum Usable Frequency.

T3C01 (C)
What kind of propagation would best be used by two stations within each other's skip zone on a certain frequency?
A. Ground-wave
B. Sky-wave
C. Scatter-mode
D. Ducting

T3C02 (C)
If you are receiving a weak and distorted signal from a distant station on a frequency close to the maximum usable frequency, what type of propagation is probably occurring?
A. Ducting
B. Line-of-sight
C. Scatter
D. Ground-wave

T3C03 (B)
How are VHF signals propagated within the range of the visible horizon?
A. By sky wave
B. By direct wave
C. By plane wave
D. By geometric wave

T3C04 (C)
Ducting occurs in which region of the atmosphere?
A. F2
B. Ectosphere
C. Troposphere
D. Stratosphere

T3C05 (A)
What effect does tropospheric bending have on 2-meter radio waves?
A. It lets you contact stations farther away
B. It causes them to travel shorter distances
C. It garbles the signal
D. It reverses the sideband of the signal

T3C06 (D)
What causes tropospheric ducting of radio waves?
A. A very low pressure area
B. An aurora to the north
C. Lightning between the transmitting and receiving stations
D. A temperature inversion

T3C07 (B)
What causes VHF radio waves to be propagated several hundred miles over oceans?
A. A polar air mass
B. A widespread temperature inversion
C. An overcast of cirriform clouds
D. A high-pressure zone

T3C08 (D)
In what frequency range does tropospheric ducting most often occur?
A. SW
B. MF
C. HF
D. VHF

T3C09 (D)
In what frequency range does sky-wave propagation least often occur?
A. LF
B. MF
C. HF
D. VHF

T3C10 (A)
What weather condition may cause tropospheric ducting?
A. A stable high-pressure system
B. An unstable low-pressure system
C. A series of low-pressure waves
D. Periods of heavy rainfall

T3C11 (D)
What band conditions might indicate long-range skip on the 6-meter and 2-meter bands?
A. Noise on the 80-meter band
B. The absence of signals on the 10-meter band
C. Very long-range skip on the 10-meter band
D. Strong signals on the 10-meter band from stations about 500-600 miles away

Subelement T4, Amateur Radio Practices: 4 Exam Questions, 4 groups

T4A Electrical wiring, including switch location, dangerous voltages and currents.

T4A01 (C)
Where should the green wire in a three-wire AC line cord be connected in a power supply?
A. To the fuse
B. To the "hot" side of the power switch
C. To the chassis
D. To the white wire

T4A02 (D)
Where should the black (or red) wire in a three-wire AC line cord be connected in a power supply?
A. To the white wire
B. To the green wire
C. To the chassis
D. To the fuse

T4A03 (B)
Where should the white wire in a three-wire AC line cord be connected in a power supply?
A. To the side of the power transformer's primary winding that has a fuse
B. To the side of the power transformer's primary winding that does not have a fuse
C. To the chassis
D. To the black wire

T4A04 (D)
What document is used by almost every US city as the basis for electrical safety requirements for power wiring and antennas?
A. The Code of Federal Regulations
B. The Proceedings of the IEEE
C. The ITU Radio Regulations
D. The National Electrical Code

T4A05 (C)
What document would you use to see if you comply with standard electrical safety rules when building an amateur antenna?
A. The Code of Federal Regulations
B. The Proceedings of the IEEE
C. The National Electrical Code
D. The ITU Radio Regulations

T4A06 (D)
Where should fuses be connected on a mobile transceiver's DC power cable?
A. Between the red and black wires
B. In series with just the black wire
C. In series with just the red wire
D. In series with both the red and black wires

T4A07 (B)
Why is the retaining screw in one terminal of a wall outlet made of brass while the other one is silver colored?
A. To prevent corrosion

B. To indicate correct wiring polarity
C. To better conduct current
D. To reduce skin effect

T4A08 (A)
How much electrical current flowing through the human body is usually fatal?
A. As little as 1/10 of an ampere
B. Approximately 10 amperes
C. More than 20 amperes
D. Current flow through the human body is never fatal

T4A09 (A)
Which body organ can be fatally affected by a very small amount of electrical current?
A. The heart
B. The brain
C. The liver
D. The lungs

T4A10 (A)
How much electrical current flowing through the human body is usually painful?
A. As little as 1/500 of an ampere
B. Approximately 10 amperes
C. More than 20 amperes
D. Current flow through the human body is never painful

T4A11 (A)
What is the minimum voltage which is usually dangerous to humans?
A. 30 volts
B. 100 volts
C. 1000 volts
D. 2000 volts

T4A12 (C)
Where should the main power switch for a high-voltage power supply be located?
A. Inside the cabinet, to kill the power if the cabinet is opened
B. On the back side of the cabinet, out of sight
C. Anywhere that can be seen and reached easily
D. A high voltage power supply should not be switch-operated

T4A13 (B)
What precaution should you take when leaning over a power amplifier?
A. Take your shoes off
B. Watch out for loose jewelry contacting high voltage
C. Shield your face from the heat produced by the power supply
D. Watch out for sharp edges which may snag your clothing

T4A14 (C)
What is an important safety rule concerning the main electrical box in your home?
A. Make sure the door cannot be opened easily
B. Make sure something is placed in front of the door so no one will be able to get to it easily
C. Make sure others in your home know where it is and how to shut off the electricity
D. Warn others in your home never to touch the switches, even in an emergency

T4A15 (B)
What should you do if you discover someone who is being burned by high voltage?
A. Run from the area so you won't be burned too
B. Turn off the power, call for emergency help and give CPR if needed
C. Immediately drag the person away from the high voltage
D. Wait for a few minutes to see if the person can get away from the high voltage on their own, then try to help

T4B Meters, including volt, amp, multi, peak-reading, RF watt and placement, and ratings of fuses and switches.

T4B01 (B)
How is a voltmeter usually connected to a circuit under test?
A. In series with the circuit
B. In parallel with the circuit
C. In quadrature with the circuit
D. In phase with the circuit

T4B02 (C)
How can the range of a voltmeter be increased?
A. By adding resistance in series with the circuit under test
B. By adding resistance in parallel with the circuit under test
C. By adding resistance in series with the meter, between the meter and the circuit under test
D. By adding resistance in parallel with the meter, between the meter and the circuit under test

T4B03 (A)
What happens inside a voltmeter when you switch it from a lower to a higher voltage range?
A. Resistance is added in series with the meter
B. Resistance is added in parallel with the meter
C. Resistance is reduced in series with the meter
D. Resistance is reduced in parallel with the meter

T4B04 (A)
How is an ammeter usually connected to a circuit under test?
A. In series with the circuit
B. In parallel with the circuit
C. In quadrature with the circuit
D. In phase with the circuit

T4B05 (D)
How can the range of an ammeter be increased?
A. By adding resistance in series with the circuit under test
B. By adding resistance in parallel with the circuit under test
C. By adding resistance in series with the meter
D. By adding resistance in parallel with the meter

T4B06 (D)
What does a multimeter measure?
A. SWR and power
B. Resistance, capacitance and inductance
C. Resistance and reactance
D. Voltage, current and resistance

T4B07 (A)
Where should an RF wattmeter be connected for the most accurate readings of transmitter output power?
A. At the transmitter output connector
B. At the antenna feed point
C. One-half wavelength from the transmitter output
D. One-half wavelength from the antenna feed point

T4B08 (B)
At what line impedance do most RF wattmeters usually operate?
A. 25 ohms
B. 50 ohms
C. 100 ohms
D. 300 ohms

T4B09 (A)
What does a directional wattmeter measure?
A. Forward and reflected power
B. The directional pattern of an antenna
C. The energy used by a transmitter
D. Thermal heating in a load resistor

T4B10 (B)
If a directional RF wattmeter reads 90 watts forward power and 10 watts reflected power, what is the actual transmitter output power?
A. 10 watts

B. 80 watts
C. 90 watts
D. 100 watts

T4B11 (C)
If a directional RF wattmeter reads 96 watts forward power and 4 watts reflected power, what is the actual transmitter output power?
A. 80 watts
B. 88 watts
C. 92 watts
D. 100 watts

T4C Marker generator, crystal calibrator, signal generators and impedance-match indicator.

T4C01 (A)
What is a marker generator?
A. A high-stability oscillator that generates reference signals at exact frequency intervals
B. A low-stability oscillator that "sweeps" through a range of frequencies
C. A low-stability oscillator used to inject a signal into a circuit under test
D. A high-stability oscillator which can produce a wide range of frequencies and amplitudes

T4C02 (A)
How is a marker generator used?
A. To calibrate the tuning dial on a receiver
B. To calibrate the volume control on a receiver
C. To test the amplitude linearity of a transmitter
D. To test the frequency deviation of a transmitter

T4C03 (D)
What device is used to inject a frequency calibration signal into a receiver?
A. A calibrated voltmeter
B. A calibrated oscilloscope
C. A calibrated wavemeter
D. A crystal calibrator

T4C04 (B)
What frequency standard may be used to calibrate the tuning dial of a receiver?
A. A calibrated voltmeter
B. Signals from WWV and WWVH
C. A deviation meter
D. A sweep generator

T4C05 (C)
How might you check the accuracy of your receiver's tuning dial?
A. Tune to the frequency of a shortwave broadcasting station
B. Tune to a popular amateur net frequency
C. Tune to one of the frequencies of station WWV or WWVH
D. Tune to another amateur station and ask what frequency the operator is using

T4C06 (C)
What device produces a stable, low-level signal that can be set to a desired frequency?
A. A wavemeter
B. A reflectometer
C. A signal generator
D. An oscilloscope

T4C07 (B)
What is an RF signal generator used for?
A. Measuring RF signal amplitudes
B. Aligning tuned circuits
C. Adjusting transmitter impedance-matching networks
D. Measuring transmission line impedances

T4C08 (D)
What device can measure an impedance mismatch in your antenna system?
A. A field-strength meter
B. An ammeter
C. A wavemeter
D. A reflectometer

T4C09 (A)
Where should a reflectometer be connected for best accuracy when reading the impedance match between an antenna and its feed line?
A. At the antenna feed point
B. At the transmitter output connector
C. At the midpoint of the feed line
D. Anywhere along the feed line

T4C10 (A)
If you use a 3-30 MHz RF power meter for VHF, how accurate will its readings be?
A. They will not be accurate
B. They will be accurate enough to get by
C. If it properly calibrates to full scale in the set position, they may be accurate
D. They will be accurate providing the readings are multiplied by 4.5

T4C11 (C)
If you use a 3-30 MHz SWR meter for VHF, how accurate will its readings be?
A. They will not be accurate
B. They will be accurate enough to get by
C. If it properly calibrates to full scale in the set position, they may be accurate
D. They will be accurate providing the readings are multiplied by 4.5

T4D Dummy antennas, S-meter, exposure of the human body to RF.

T4D01 (D)
What device should be connected to a transmitter's output when you are making transmitter adjustments?
A. A multimeter
B. A reflectometer
C. A receiver
D. A dummy antenna

T4D02 (B)
What is a dummy antenna?
A. An nondirectional transmitting antenna
B. A nonradiating load for a transmitter
C. An antenna used as a reference for gain measurements
D. A flexible antenna usually used on hand held transceivers

T4D03 (C)
What is the main component of a dummy antenna?
A. A wire-wound resistor
B. An iron-core coil
C. A noninductive resistor
D. An air-core coil

T4D04 (B)
What device is used in place of an antenna during transmitter tests so that no signal is radiated?
A. An antenna matcher
B. A dummy antenna
C. A low-pass filter
D. A decoupling resistor

T4D05 (A)
Why would you use a dummy antenna?
A. For off-the-air transmitter testing
B. To reduce output power
C. To give comparative signal reports
D. To allow antenna tuning without causing interference

T4D06 (A)
What minimum rating should a dummy antenna have for use with a 100-watt single-sideband phone transmitter?
A. 100 watts continuous

B. 141 watts continuous
C. 175 watts continuous
D. 200 watts continuous

T4D07 (D)
Why might a dummy antenna get warm when in use?
A. Because it stores electric current
B. Because it stores radio waves
C. Because it absorbs static electricity
D. Because it changes RF energy into heat

T4D08 (A)
What is used to measure relative signal strength in a receiver?
A. An S meter
B. An RST meter
C. A signal deviation meter
D. An SSB meter

T4D09 (B)
How can exposure to a large amount of RF energy affect body tissue?
A. It causes radiation poisoning
B. It heats the tissue
C. It paralyzes the tissue
D. It produces genetic changes in the tissue

T4D10 (A)
Which body organ is the most likely to be damaged from the heating effects of RF radiation?
A. Eyes
B. Hands
C. Heart
D. Liver

T4D11 (D)
What organization has published safety guidelines for the maximum limits of RF energy near the human body?
A. The Institute of Electrical and Electronics Engineers (IEEE)
B. The Federal Communications Commission (FCC)
C. The Environmental Protection Agency (EPA)
D. The American National Standards Institute (ANSI)

T4D12 (B)
What is the purpose of the ANSI RF protection guide?
A. It lists all RF frequency allocations for interference protection
B. It gives RF exposure limits for the human body
C. It sets transmitter power limits for interference protection
D. It sets antenna height limits for aircraft protection

T4D13 (D)
According to the ANSI RF protection guide, what frequencies cause us the greatest risk from RF energy?
A. 3 to 30 MHz
B. 300 to 3000 MHz
C. Above 1500 MHz
D. 30 to 300 MHz

T4D14 (D)
Why is the limit of exposure to RF the lowest in the frequency range of 30 MHz to 300 MHz, according to the ANSI RF protection guide?
A. There are more transmitters operating in this range
B. There are fewer transmitters operating in this range
C. Most transmissions in this range are for a longer time
D. The human body absorbs RF energy the most in this range

T4D15 (B)
According to the ANSI RF protection guide, what is the maximum safe power output to the antenna of a hand held VHF or UHF radio?
A. 125 milliwatts
B. 7 watts
C. 10 watts
D. 25 watts

T4D16 (C)
After you have opened a VHF power amplifier to make internal tuning adjustments, what should you do before you turn the amplifier on?
A. Remove all amplifier shielding to ensure maximum cooling
B. Make sure that the power interlock switch is bypassed so you can test the amplifier
C. Be certain all amplifier shielding is fastened in place
D. Be certain no antenna is attached so that you will not cause any interference

Subelement T5, Electrical Principles: 2 Exam Questions, 2 groups

T5A Definition of resistance, inductance, and capacitance and unit of measurement, calculation of values in series and parallel.

T5A01 (D)
What does resistance do in an electric circuit?
A. It stores energy in a magnetic field
B. It stores energy in an electric field
C. It provides electrons by a chemical reaction
D. It opposes the flow of electrons

T5A02 (D)
What is the ability to store energy in a magnetic field called?
A. Admittance
B. Capacitance
C. Resistance
D. Inductance

T5A03 (C)
What is the basic unit of inductance?
A. The coulomb
B. The farad
C. The henry
D. The ohm

T5A04 (C)
What is a henry?
A. The basic unit of admittance
B. The basic unit of capacitance
C. The basic unit of inductance
D. The basic unit of resistance

T5A05 (D)
What is the ability to store energy in an electric field called?
A. Inductance
B. Resistance
C. Tolerance
D. Capacitance

T5A06 (A)
What is the basic unit of capacitance?
A. The farad
B. The ohm
C. The volt
D. The henry

T5A07 (B)
What is a farad?
A. The basic unit of resistance
B. The basic unit of capacitance
C. The basic unit of inductance
D. The basic unit of admittance

T5A08 (B)
If two equal-value inductors are connected in series, what is their total inductance?
A. Half the value of one inductor
B. Twice the value of one inductor
C. The same as the value of either inductor
D. The value of one inductor times the value of the other

T5A09 (A)
If two equal-value inductors are connected in parallel, what is their total inductance?
A. Half the value of one inductor
B. Twice the value of one inductor
C. The same as the value of either inductor
D. The value of one inductor times the value of the other

T5A10 (C)
If two equal-value capacitors are connected in series, what is their total capacitance?
A. Twice the value of one capacitor
B. The same as the value of either capacitor
C. Half the value of either capacitor
D. The value of one capacitor times the value of the other

T5A11 (A)
If two equal-value capacitors are connected in parallel, what is their total capacitance?
A. Twice the value of one capacitor
B. Half the value of one capacitor
C. The same as the value of either capacitor
D. The value of one capacitor times the value of the other

T5B Ohm's Law.

T5B01 (D)
Ohm's Law describes the mathematical relationship between what three electrical quantities?
A. Resistance, voltage and power
B. Current, resistance and power
C. Current, voltage and power
D. Resistance, current and voltage

T5B02 (C)
How is the current in a DC circuit calculated when the voltage and resistance are known?
A. I = R x E [current equals resistance multiplied by voltage]
B. I = R / E [current equals resistance divided by voltage]
C. I = E / R [current equals voltage divided by resistance]
D. I = P / E [current equals power divided by voltage]

T5B03 (B)
How is the resistance in a DC circuit calculated when the voltage and current are known?
A. R = I / E [resistance equals current divided by voltage]
B. R = E / I [resistance equals voltage divided by current]
C. R = I x E [resistance equals current multiplied by voltage]
D. R = P / E [resistance equals power divided by voltage]

T5B04 (C)
How is the voltage in a DC circuit calculated when the current and resistance are known?
A. E = I / R [voltage equals current divided by resistance]
B. E = R / I [voltage equals resistance divided by current]
C. E = I x R [voltage equals current multiplied by resistance]
D. E = P / I [voltage equals power divided by current]

T5B05 (D)
If a 12-volt battery supplies 0.25 ampere to a circuit, what is the circuit's resistance?
A. 0.25 ohm
B. 3 ohm
C. 12 ohms
D. 48 ohms

T5B06 (D)
If a 12-volt battery supplies 0.15 ampere to a circuit, what is the circuit's resistance?
A. 0.15 ohm
B. 1.8 ohm
C. 12 ohms
D. 80 ohms

T5B07 (B)
If a 4800-ohm resistor is connected to 120 volts, approximately how much current will flow through it?
A. 4 A
B. 25 mA
C. 25 A
D. 40 MA

T5B08 (D)
If a 48000-ohm resistor is connected to 120 volts, approximately how much current will flow through it?
A. 400 A
B. 40 A
C. 25 mA
D. 2.5 mA

T5B09 (A)
If a 4800-ohm resistor is connected to 12 volts, approximately how much current will flow through it?
A. 2.5 mA
B. 25 mA
C. 40 A
D. 400 A

T5B10 (A)
If a 48000-ohm resistor is connected to 12 volts, approximately how much current will flow through it?
A. 250 μA
B. 250 mA
C. 4000 mA
D. 4000 A

T5B11 (A)
If you know the voltage and current supplied to a circuit, what formula would you use to calculate the circuit's resistance?
A. Ohm's law
B. Tesla's law
C. Ampere's law
D. Kirchoff's law

Subelement T6, Circuit Components: 2 Exam Questions, 2 Groups

T6A Resistors, construction types, variable and fixed, color code, power ratings, schematic symbols.

T6A01 (B)
What are the most common resistor types?
A. Plastic and porcelain
B. Film and wire-wound
C. Electrolytic and metal-film
D. Iron core and brass core

T6A02 (C)
What does a variable resistor or potentiometer do?
A. Its resistance changes when AC is applied to it
B. It transforms a variable voltage into a constant voltage
C. Its resistance changes when its slide or contact is moved
D. Its resistance changes when it is heated

T6A03 (B)
How do you find a resistor's tolerance rating?
A. By using a voltmeter
B. By reading the resistor's color code
C. By using Thevenin's theorem for resistors
D. By reading its Baudot code

T6A04 (A)
What do the first three color bands on a resistor indicate?
A. The value of the resistor in ohms
B. The resistance tolerance in percent
C. The power rating in watts
D. The resistance material

T6A05 (B)
What does the fourth color band on a resistor indicate?
A. The value of the resistor in ohms
B. The resistance tolerance in percent
C. The power rating in watts
D. The resistance material

T6A06 (A)
Why do resistors sometimes get hot when in use?
A. Some electrical energy passing through them is lost as heat
B. Their reactance makes them heat up
C. Hotter circuit components nearby heat them up
D. They absorb magnetic energy which makes them hot

T6A07 (C)
Why would a large size resistor be used instead of a smaller one of the same resistance?
A. For better response time
B. For a higher current gain
C. For greater power dissipation
D. For less impedance in the circuit

T6A08 (C)
What are the possible values of a 100-ohm resistor with a 10% tolerance?
A. 90 to 100 ohms
B. 10 to 100 ohms
C. 90 to 110 ohms
D. 80 to 120 ohms

T6A09 (B)
How do you find a resistor's value?
A. By using a voltmeter
B. By using the resistor's color code
C. By using Thevenin's therom for resistors
D. By using the Baudot code

T6A10 (A)
Which tolerance rating would a high-quality resistor have?
A. 0.1%
B. 5%
C. 10%
D. 20%

T6A11 (D)
Which tolerance rating would a low-quality resistor have?
A. 0.1%
B. 5%
C. 10%
D. 20%

T6B Schematic symbols – inductors and capacitors, construction of variable and fixed, factors affecting inductance and capacitance, capacitor construction.

T6B01 (D)
What is an inductor core?
A. The place where a coil is tapped for resonance
B. A tight coil of wire used in a transformer
C. Insulating material placed between the wires of a transformer
D. The place inside an inductor where its magnetic field is concentrated

T6B02 (C)
What does an inductor do?
A. It stores a charge electrostatically and opposes a change in voltage
B. It stores a charge electrochemically and opposes a change in current
C. It stores a charge electromagnetically and opposes a change in current
D. It stores a charge electromechanically and opposes a change in voltage

T6B03 (D)
What determines the inductance of a coil?
A. The core material, the core diameter, the length of the coil and whether the coil is mounted horizontally or vertically
B. The core diameter, the number of turns of wire used to wind the coil and the type of metal used for the wire
C. The core material, the number of turns used to wind the core and the frequency of the current through the coil
D. The core material, the core diameter, the length of the coil and the number of turns of wire used to wind the coil

T6B04 (A)
As an iron core is inserted in a coil, what happens to the coil's inductance?
A. It increases
B. It decreases
C. It stays the same
D. It disappears

T6B05 (A)
What can happen if you tune a ferrite-core coil with a metal tool?
A. The metal tool can change the coil's inductance and cause you to tune the coil incorrectly
B. The metal tool can become magnetized so much that you might not be able to remove it from the coil
C. The metal tool can pick up enough magnetic energy to become very hot
D. The metal tool can pick up enough magnetic energy to become a shock hazard

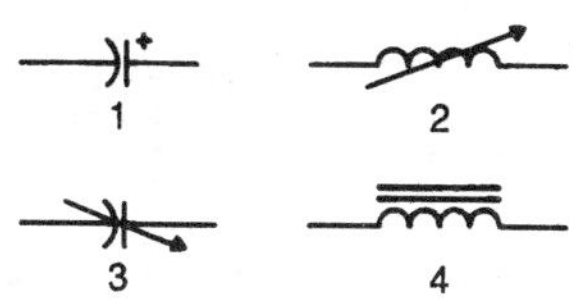

Figure T6–1

T6B06 (B)
In Figure T6-1 which symbol represents an adjustable inductor?
A. Symbol 1
B. Symbol 2
C. Symbol 3
D. Symbol 4

T6B07 (D)
In Figure T6-1 which symbol represents an iron-core inductor?
A. Symbol 1
B. Symbol 2
C. Symbol 3
D. Symbol 4

T6B08 (D)
In Figure T6-1 which symbol represents an inductor wound over a toroidal
core?
A. Symbol 1
B. Symbol 2
C. Symbol 3
D. Symbol 4

T6B09 (A)
In Figure T6-1 which symbol represents an electrolytic capacitor?
A. Symbol 1
B. Symbol 2
C. Symbol 3
D. Symbol 4

T6B10 (C)
In Figure T6-1 which symbol represents a variable capacitor?
A. Symbol 1
B. Symbol 2
C. Symbol 3
D. Symbol 4

T6B11 (C)
What describes a capacitor?
A. Two or more layers of silicon material with an insulating material between them
B. The wire used in the winding and the core material
C. Two or more conductive plates with an insulating material between them
D. Two or more insulating plates with a conductive material between them

T6B12 (B)
What does a capacitor do?
A. It stores a charge electrochemically and opposes a change in current
B. It stores a charge electrostatically and opposes a change in voltage
C. It stores a charge electromagnetically and opposes a change in current
D. It stores a charge electromechanically and opposes a change in voltage

T6B13 (A)
What determines the capacitance of a capacitor?
A. The material between the plates, the area of one side of one plate, the number of plates and the spacing between the plates
B. The material between the plates, the number of plates and the size of the wires connected to the plates
C. The number of plates, the spacing between the plates and whether the dielectric material is N type or P type
D. The material between the plates, the area of one plate, the number of plates and the material used for the protective coating

T6B14 (B)
As the plate area of a capacitor is increased, what happens to its capacitance?
A. It decreases
B. It increases
C. It stays the same
D. It disappears

Subelement T7, Practical Circuits: 1 Exam Question,1 Group

T7A Practical circuits.

T7A01 (C)
Why do modern HF transmitters have a built-in low-pass filter in their RF output circuits?
A. To reduce RF energy below a cutoff point
B. To reduce low-frequency interference to other amateurs
C. To reduce harmonic radiation
D. To reduce fundamental radiation

T7A02 (A)
What circuit blocks RF energy above and below a certain limit?
A. A band-pass filter
B. A high-pass filter
C. An input filter
D. A low-pass filter

T7A03 (A)
What type of filter is used in the IF section of receivers to block energy outside a certain frequency range?
A. A band-pass filter
B. A high-pass filter
C. An input filter
D. A low-pass filter

T7A04 (C)
What circuit is found in all types of receivers?
A. An audio filter
B. A beat-frequency oscillator
C. A detector
D. An RF amplifier

T7A05 (D)
What circuit has a variable-frequency oscillator connected to a driver and a power amplifier?
A. A packet-radio transmitter
B. A crystal-controlled transmitter
C. A single-sideband transmitter
D. A VFO-controlled transmitter

T7A06 (B)
What circuit combines signals from an IF amplifier stage and a beat-frequency oscillator (BFO), to produce an audio signal?
A. An AGC circuit
B. A detector circuit
C. A power supply circuit
D. A VFO circuit

T7A07 (D)
What circuit uses a limiter and a frequency discriminator to produce an audio signal?
A. A double-conversion receiver
B. A variable-frequency oscillator
C. A superheterodyne receiver
D. A FM receiver

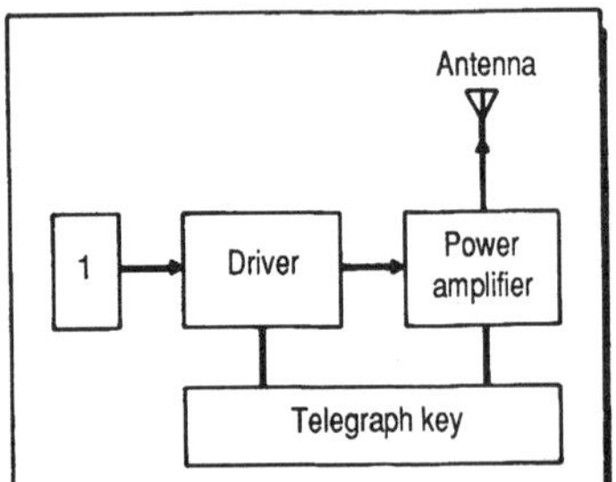

Figure T7–1

T7A08 (D)
What circuit is pictured in Figure T7-1 if block 1 is a variable-frequency oscillator?
A. A packet-radio transmitter
B. A crystal-controlled transmitter
C. A single-sideband transmitter
D. A VFO-controlled transmitter

Figure T7–2
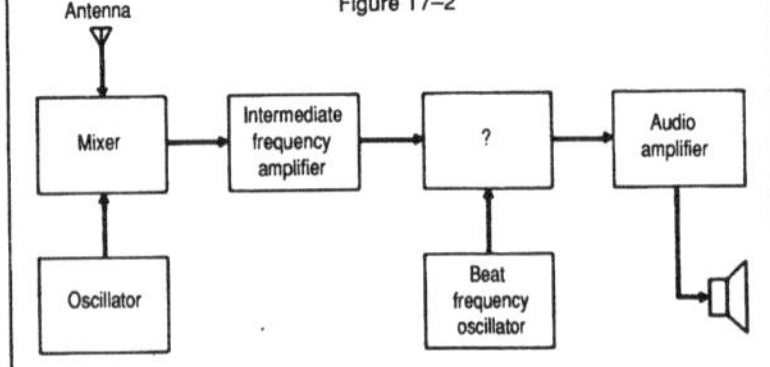

T7A09 (B)
What is the unlabeled block in Figure T7-2?
A. An AGC circuit
B. A detector

C. A power supply
D. A VFO circuit

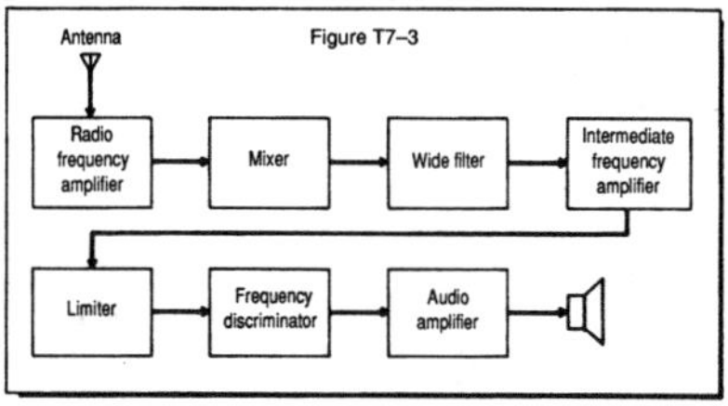

T7A10 (D)
What circuit is pictured in Figure T7-3?
A. A double-conversion receiver
B. A variable-frequency oscillator
C. A superheterodyne receiver
D. An FM receiver

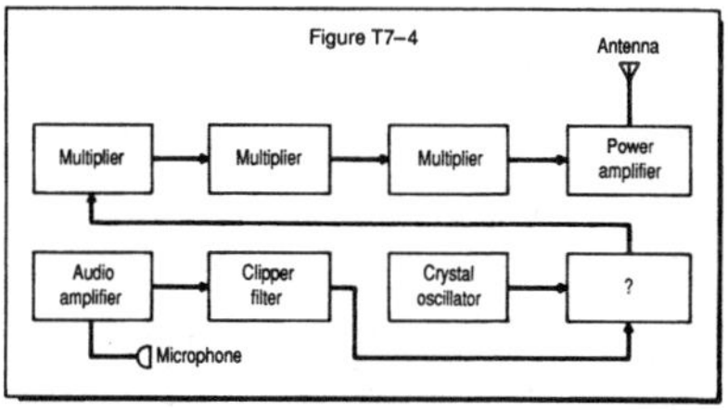

T7A11 (C)
What is the unlabeled block in Figure T7-4?
A. A band-pass filter
B. A crystal oscillator
C. A reactance modulator
D. A rectifier modulator

Subelement T8, Signals and Emissions: 2 Exam Questions, 2 groups

T8A Definition of modulation and emission types.

T8A01 (B)
What is the name for unmodulated carrier wave emissions?
A. Phone
B. Test
C. CW
D. RTTY

T8A02 (C)
What is the name for Morse code emissions produced by switching a transmitter's output on and off?
A. Phone
B. Test
C. CW
D. RTTY

T8A03 (B)
What is RTTY?
A. Amplitude-keyed telegraphy
B. Frequency-shift-keyed telegraphy
C. Frequency-modulated telephony
D. Phase-modulated telephony

T8A04 (B)
What is the name for packet-radio emissions?
A. CW
B. Data
C. Phone
D. RTTY

T8A05 (D)
How is tone-modulated Morse code produced?
A. By feeding a microphone's audio signal into an FM transmitter
B. By feeding an on/off keyed audio tone into a CW transmitter
C. By on/off keying of a carrier
D. By feeding an on/off keyed audio tone into a transmitter

T8A06 (D)
What is the name of the voice emission most used on VHF/UHF repeaters?
A. Single-sideband phone
B. Pulse-modulated phone
C. Slow-scan phone
D. Frequency modulated phone

T8A07 (A)
What is the name of the voice emission most used on amateur HF bands?
A. Single-sideband phone
B. Pulse-modulated phone
C. Slow-scan phone
D. Frequency modulated phone

T8A08 (A)
What is meant by the upper-sideband (USB)?
A. The part of a single-sideband signal which is above the carrier frequency
B. The part of a single-sideband signal which is below the carrier frequency
C. Any frequency above 10 MHz
D. The carrier frequency of a single-sideband signal

T8A09 (D)
What emissions are produced by a transmitter using a reactance modulator?
A. CW
B. Test
C. Single-sideband, suppressed-carrier phone
D. Phase-modulated phone

T8A10 (C)
What other emission does phase modulation most resemble?
A. Amplitude modulation
B. Pulse modulation
C. Frequency modulation
D. Single-sideband modulation

T8A11 (B)
What is the name for emissions produced by an on/off keyed audio tone?
A. RTTY
B. MCW
C. CW
D. Phone

T8B RF carrier, modulation, bandwidth and deviation.

T8B01 (A)
What is another name for a constant-amplitude radio-frequency signal?
A. An RF carrier
B. An AF carrier
C. A sideband carrier
D. A subcarrier

T8B02 (A)
What is modulation?
A. Varying a radio wave in some way to send information
B. Receiving audio information from a signal
C. Increasing the power of a transmitter
D. Suppressing the carrier in a single-sideband transmitter

T8B03 (A)
What kind of emission would your FM transmitter produce if its microphone failed to work?
A. An unmodulated carrier
B. A phase-modulated carrier
C. An amplitude-modulated carrier
D. A frequency-modulated carrier

T8B04 (B)
How would you modulate a 2-meter FM transceiver to produce packet-radio emissions?
A. Connect a terminal-node-controller to interrupt the transceiver's carrier wave
B. Connect a terminal-node-controller to the transceiver's microphone input
C. Connect a keyboard to the transceiver's microphone input
D. Connect a DTMF key pad to the transceiver's microphone input

T8B05 (C)
Why is FM voice best for local VHF/UHF radio communications?
A. The carrier is not detectable
B. It is more resistant to distortion caused by reflected signals
C. It has high-fidelity audio which can be understood even when the signal is somewhat weak
D. Its RF carrier stays on frequency better than the AM modes

T8B06 (D)
Why do many radio receivers have several IF filters of different bandwidths that can be selected by the operator?
A. Because some frequency bands are wider than others
B. Because different bandwidths help increase the receiver sensitivity
C. Because different bandwidths improve S-meter readings
D. Because some emission types need a wider bandwidth than others to be received properly

T8B07 (C)
Which list of emission types is in order from the narrowest bandwidth to the widest bandwidth?
A. RTTY, CW, SSB voice, FM voice
B. CW, FM voice, RTTY, SSB voice
C. CW, RTTY, SSB voice, FM voice
D. CW, SSB voice, RTTY, FM voice

T8B08 (D)
What is the usual bandwidth of a single-sideband amateur signal?
A. 1 kHz
B. 2 kHz
C. Between 3 and 6 kHz
D. Between 2 and 3 kHz

T8B09 (C)
What is the usual bandwidth of a frequency-modulated amateur signal?
A. Less than 5 kHz
B. Between 5 and 10 kHz
C. Between 10 and 20 kHz
D. Greater than 20 kHz

T8B10 (B)
What is the result of overdeviation in an FM transmitter?
A. Increased transmitter power
B. Out-of-channel emissions
C. Increased transmitter range
D. Poor carrier suppression

T8B11 (C)
What causes splatter interference?
A. Keying a transmitter too fast
B. Signals from a transmitter's output circuit are being sent back to its input circuit
C. Overmodulation of a transmitter
D. The transmitting antenna is the wrong length

Subelement T9, Antennas and Feed Lines: 3 Exam Questions, 3 Groups

T9A Parasitic beam and non-directional antennas.

T9A01 (C)
What is a directional antenna?
A. An antenna which sends and receives radio energy equally well in all directions
B. An antenna that cannot send and receive radio energy by sky-wave or skip propagation
C. An antenna which sends and receives radio energy mainly in one direction
D. An antenna which sends and receives radio energy equally well in two opposite directions

T9A02 (A)
How is a Yagi antenna constructed?
A. Two or more straight, parallel elements are fixed in line with each other
B. Two or more square or circular loops are fixed in line with each other
C. Two or more square or circular loops are stacked inside each other
D. A straight element is fixed in the center of three or more elements which angle toward the ground

T9A03 (C)
What type of beam antenna uses two or more straight elements arranged in line with each other?
A. A delta loop antenna
B. A quad antenna
C. A Yagi antenna
D. A Zepp antenna

T9A04 (B)
How many directly driven elements do most beam antennas have?
A. None
B. One
C. Two
D. Three

T9A05 (A)
What is a parasitic beam antenna?
A. An antenna where some elements obtain their radio energy by induction or radiation from a driven element
B. An antenna where wave traps are used to magnetically couple the elements
C. An antenna where all elements are driven by direct connection to the feed line
D. An antenna where the driven element obtains its radio energy by induction or radiation from director elements

T9A06 (D)
What are the parasitic elements of a Yagi antenna?
A. The driven element and any reflectors
B. The director and the driven element
C. Only the reflectors (if any)
D. Any directors or any reflectors

T9A07 (B)
What is a cubical quad antenna?
A. Four straight, parallel elements in line with each other, each approximately 1/2-electrical wavelength long
B. Two or more parallel four-sided wire loops, each approximately one-electrical wavelength long
C. A vertical conductor 1/4-electrical wavelength high, fed at the bottom
D. A center-fed wire 1/2-electrical wavelength long

T9A08 (A)
What is a delta loop antenna?
A. A type of cubical quad antenna, except with triangular elements rather than square
B. A large copper ring or wire loop, used in direction finding
C. An antenna system made of three vertical antennas, arranged in a triangular shape
D. An antenna made from several triangular coils of wire on an insulating form

T9A09 (D)
What type of non-directional antenna is easy to make at home and works well outdoors?
A. A Yagi
B. A delta loop
C. A cubical quad
D. A ground plane

T9A10 (D)
What type of antenna is made when a magnetic-base whip antenna is placed on the roof of a car?
A. A Yagi
B. A delta loop
C. A cubical quad
D. A ground plane

T9A11 (A)
If a magnetic-base whip antenna is placed on the roof of a car, in what direction does it send out radio energy?
A. It goes out equally well in all horizontal directions
B. Most of it goes in one direction
C. Most of it goes equally in two opposite directions
D. Most of it is aimed high into the air

T9B Polarization, impedance matching and SWR, feed lines, balanced vs unbalanced (including baluns).

T9B01 (B)
What does horizontal wave polarization mean?
A. The magnetic lines of force of a radio wave are parallel to the earth's surface
B. The electric lines of force of a radio wave are parallel to the earth's surface
C. The electric lines of force of a radio wave are perpendicular to the earth's surface
D. The electric and magnetic lines of force of a radio wave are perpendicular to the earth's surface

T9B02 (C)
What does vertical wave polarization mean?
A. The electric lines of force of a radio wave are parallel to the earth's surface
B. The magnetic lines of force of a radio wave are perpendicular to the earth's surface
C. The electric lines of force of a radio wave are perpendicular to the earth's surface
D. The electric and magnetic lines of force of a radio wave are parallel to the earth's surface

T9B03 (C)
What electromagnetic-wave polarization does a Yagi antenna have when its elements are parallel to the earth's surface?
A. Circular
B. Helical
C. Horizontal
D. Vertical

T9B04 (D)
What electromagnetic-wave polarization does a half-wavelength antenna have when it is perpendicular to the earth's surface?
A. Circular
B. Horizontal
C. Parabolical
D. Vertical

T9B05 (D)
What electromagnetic-wave polarization does most man-made electrical noise have in the HF and VHF spectrum?
A. Horizontal
B. Left-hand circular
C. Right-hand circular
D. Vertical

T9B06 (D)
What does standing-wave ratio mean?
A. The ratio of maximum to minimum inductances on a feed line
B. The ratio of maximum to minimum resistances on a feed line
C. The ratio of maximum to minimum impedances on a feed line
D. The ratio of maximum to minimum voltages on a feed line

T9B07 (A)
What does forward power mean?
A. The power traveling from the transmitter to the antenna
B. The power radiated from the top of an antenna system
C. The power produced during the positive half of an RF cycle
D. The power used to drive a linear amplifier

T9B08 (B)
What does reflected power mean?
A. The power radiated down to the ground from an antenna
B. The power returned to a transmitter from an antenna
C. The power produced during the negative half of an RF cycle
D. The power returned to an antenna by buildings and trees

T9B09 (C)
What happens to radio energy when it is sent through a poor quality coaxial cable?
A. It causes spurious emissions
B. It is returned to the transmitter's chassis ground
C. It is converted to heat in the cable
D. It causes interference to other stations near the transmitting frequency

T9B10 (C)
What is an unbalanced line?
A. Feed line with neither conductor connected to ground
B. Feed line with both conductors connected to ground
C. Feed line with one conductor connected to ground
D. Feed line with both conductors connected to each other

T9B11 (A)
What device can be installed to feed a balanced antenna with an unbalanced feed line?
A. A balun
B. A loading coil
C. A triaxial transformer
D. A wavetrap

T9C Line losses by line type, length and frequency, RF safety.

T9C01 (B)
What common connector usually joins RG-213 coaxial cable to an HF transceiver?
A. An F-type cable connector
B. A PL-259 connector
C. A banana plug connector
D. A binding post connector

T9C02 (A)
What common connector usually joins a hand held transceiver to its antenna?
A. A BNC connector
B. A PL-259 connector
C. An F-type cable connector
D. A binding post connector

T9C03 (B)
Which of these common connectors has the lowest loss at UHF?
A. An F-type cable connector
B. A type-N connector
C. A BNC connector
D. A PL-259 connector

T9C04 (A)
If you install a 6-meter Yagi antenna on a tower 150 feet from your transmitter, which of the following feed lines is best?
A. RG-213
B. RG-58
C. RG-59
D. RG-174

T9C05 (C)
If you have a transmitter and an antenna which are 50 feet apart, but are connected by 200 feet of RG-58 coaxial cable, what should be done to reduce feed line loss?
A. Cut off the excess cable so the feed line is an even number of wavelengths long
B. Cut off the excess cable so the feed line is an odd number of wavelengths long
C. Cut off the excess cable
D. Roll the excess cable into a coil which is as small as possible

T9C06 (B)
As the length of a feed line is changed, what happens to signal loss?
A. Signal loss is the same for any length of feed line
B. Signal loss increases as length increases
C. Signal loss decreases as length increases
D. Signal loss is the least when the length is the same as the signal's wavelength

T9C07 (B)
As the frequency of a signal is changed, what happens to signal loss in a feed line?
A. Signal loss is the same for any frequency
B. Signal loss increases with increasing frequency
C. Signal loss increases with decreasing frequency
D. Signal loss is the least when the signal's wavelength is the same as the feedline's length

T9C08 (D)
If your antenna feed line gets hot when you are transmitting, what might this mean?
A. You should transmit using less power
B. The conductors in the feed line are not insulated very well
C. The feed line is too long
D. The SWR may be too high, or the feed line loss may be high

T9C09 (D)
Why should you make sure that no one can touch an open-wire feed line while
you are transmitting with it?
A. Because contact might cause a short circuit and damage the transmitter
B. Because contact might break the feed line
C. Because contact might cause spurious emissions
D. Because high-voltage radio energy might burn the person

T9C10 (C)
For RF safety, what is the best thing to do with your transmitting antennas?
A. Use vertical polarization
B. Use horizontal polarization
C. Mount the antennas where no one can come near them
D. Mount the antenna close to the ground

T9C11 (A)
Why should you regularly clean, tighten and re-solder all antenna connectors?
A. To help keep their resistance at a minimum
B. To keep them looking nice
C. To keep them from getting stuck in place
D. To increase their capacitance

FCC FIELD OPERATIONS BUREAU (FOB) FIELD SERVICE BOUNDARIES (BY STATE)

State	County	Office
ALABAMA	All	ATLANTA
ALASKA	All	ANCHORAGE
AMERICAN SAMOA	All	HONOLULU
ARIZONA	All except La Paz and Yuma	DOUGLAS
	La Paz and Yuma	SAN DIEGO
ARKANSAS	All	NEW ORLEANS
CALIFORNIA	Alpine, Amador, Calaveras, Inyo, Mono, San Joaquin, Stanislaus and Tuolumne	LIVERMORE
	Kern, Los Angeles, Orange, San Bernardino, San Luis Obispo, Santa Barbara and Ventura	LOS ANGELES
	Imperial, Riverside, San Diego	SAN DIEGO
	Alameda, Butte, Colusa, Contra Costa, Del Norte, El Dorado, Fresno, Glenn, Humboldt, Kings, Lake, Lassen, Madera, Marin, Mariposa, Mendocino, Merced, Modoc, Monterey, Napa, Nevada, Placer, Plumas, Sacramento, San Benito, San Francisco, San Mateo, Santa Clara, Santa Cruz, Shasta, Sierra, Siskiyou, Solano, Sonoma, Sutter, Tehama, Trinity, Tulare, Yolo and Yuba	SAN FRANCISCO
COLORADO	All	DENVER
CONNECTICUT	All	BOSTON
DELAWARE	Kent, Sussex, New Castle (below C & D Canal)	BALTIMORE
	New Castle (above C & D Canal)	PHILADELPHIA

DISTRICT OF COLUMBIA	All	BALTIMORE
FLORIDA	Escambia and Santa Rosa	ATLANTA
	Broward, Collier, Dade, Hendry, Lee, Monroe, Palm Beach	MIAMI
	Brevard, Flagler, Indian River, Martin, Okeechobee, Orange, Osceola, St. Lucie, Seminole, Volusia	VERO BEACH
	Duval with assistance from Vero Beach plus all counties not covered by Miami or Vero Beach.	TAMPA
GEORGIA	All	ATLANTA
GUAM	All	HONOLULU
HAWAII	All	HONOLULU
IDAHO	Benewah, Bonner, Boundary, Clearwater, Idaho, Kootenai, Latah, Lewis, Nez Perce, Shosone.	SEATTLE
	All others	PORTLAND
ILLINOIS	All	CHICAGO
INDIANA	Allen, De Kalb, Elkhart, Fulton, Kosciusko, La Grange, Marshall, Noble, St. Joseph, Steuben, Whitley	ALLEGAN
	All others	CHICAGO
IOWA	All	KANSAS CITY
KANSAS	All	KANSAS CITY
KENTUCKY	Bath, Bell, Boone, Bourbon, Boyd, Bracken, Breathitt, Campbell, Carter, Clark, Clay, Elliott, Estill, Fayette, Fleming, Floyd, Franklin, Gallatin, Garrard, Grant, Greenup, Harlan, Harrison, Jackson, Jessamine, Johnson, Kenton, Knox, Knott, Larel, Lawrence, Lee, Leslie, Letcher, Lewis, Lincoln, Madison, Magoffin, Martin, Mason, McCreary, Menifee, Montgomery, Morgan, Nicholas, Owen, Ownsley, Pendleton, Perry, Pike, Powell, Pulaski, Robertson, Rockcastle, Rowan, Wayne, Whitley, Wolfe, Woodford, Scott.	DETROIT
	All others	CHICAGO
LOUISIANA	All	NEW ORLEANS
MAINE	York and Cumberland	BOSTON
	All others	BELFAST
MARIANA ISLANDS	All	HONOLULU
MARYLAND	All	BALTIMORE
MASSACHUSETTS	All	BOSTON
MICHIGAN	Allegan, Antrim, Barry, Benzie, Berrien, Branch, Calhoun, Cass, Charlevoix, Clare, Eaton, Grand Traverse, Ionia, Isabella, Kalamazoo, Kalkaska, Kent, Lake, Leelanau, Manistee, Mason, Mecosta, Missaukee, Montcalm,	ALLEGAN

	Muskegon, Newaygo, Oceana, Osceola, Ottawa, St. Joseph, Van Buren, Wexfor.	
	Alger, Baraga, Delta, Dickinson, Gogebic, Houghton, Iron, Keweenaw, Marquette, Menominee, Ontonagon, Schoolcraft	ST. PAUL
	All others	DETROIT
MIDWAY ISLANDS	All	HONOLULU
MINNESOTA	All	ST. PAUL
MISSISSIPPI	All	NEW ORLEANS
MISSOURI	All	KANSAS CITY
MONTANA	All	SEATTLE
NEBRASKA	All	GRAND ISLAND
NEVADA	All	LIVERMORE
NEW HAMPSHIRE	Coos	BELFAST
	All others	BOSTON
NEW JERSEY	Bergen, Essex, Hudson, Hunterdon, Mercer, Middlesex, Monmouth, Morris, Passaic, Somerset, Sussex, Union, Warren.	NEW YORK
	Atlantic, Burlington, Camden, Cape May, Cumberland, Gloucester, Ocean, and Salem.	PHILADELPHIA
NEW MEXICO	All	DENVER
NEW YORK	Allegany, Broome, Cattaraugus, Cayuga, Chautaugua, Chemung, Chenango, Clinton, Cortland, Erie, Essex, Franklin, Fulton, Genesee, Hamilton, Herkimer, Jefferson, Lewis, Livingston, Madison, Monroe, Montgomery, Niagra, Oneida, Onondaga, Ontario, Orleans, Oswego, Otsego, St. Lawrence, Saratoga, Schoharie, Schuyler, Steuben, Tioga, Tomkins, Warren, Washington, Wayne, Wyoming, and Yates.	BUFFALO
	Albany, Bronx, Columbia, Delaware, Dutchess, Greene, Kings, Nassau, New York, Orange, Putnam, Queens, Rensselaer, Richmond, Rockland, Schenectady, Suffolk, Sullivan, Ulster, Westchester.	NEW YORK
NORTH CAROLINA	All	NORFOLK
NORTH DAKOTA	All	ST. PAUL
OKLAHOMA	All	DALLAS
OHIO	All	DETROIT
OREGON	All	PORTLAND
PACIFIC TRUST TERRITORIES & COMMONWEALTH	All	HONOLULU

PENNSYLVANIA	All	PHILADELPHIA
PUERTO RICO	All	SAN JUAN
RHODE ISLAND	All	BOSTON
SOUTH CAROLINA	All	ATLANTA
SOUTH DAKOTA	All	DENVER
SWAINS ISLAND	All	HONOLULU
TENNESSEE	All	ATLANTA
TEXAS	Aransas, Atascosa, Bandera, Bee, Brooks, Calhoun, Cameron, Dimmit, Duval, Edwards, Frio, Goliad, Hidalgo, Jim Hogg, Jim Wells, Karnes, Kenedy, Kinney, Kleberg, La Salle, Live Oak, Maverick, McMullen, Medina, Nueces, Real, Refugio, San Patricio, Starr, Uvalde, Val Verde, Webb, Willacy, Wilson, Zapata and Zavala.	KINGSVILLE
	Angelina, Austin, Bastrop, Bexar, Blanco, Brazoria, Brazos, Burleson, Caldwell, Chambers, Colorado, Comal, De Witt, Fayette, Fort Bend, Galveston, Gillespie, Gonzales, Grimes, Guadalupe, Hardin, Harris, Hays, Jackson, Jasper, Jefferson, Kendall, Kerr, Lavaca, Lee, Liberty, Madison, Matagorda, Montgomery, Nacogdoches, Newton, Orange, Polk, Sabine, San Augustine, San Jacinto, Travis, Trinity, Tyler, Victoria, Walker, Waller, Washington, Wharton, and Williamson.	HOUSTON
	All others	DALLAS
UTAH	Emery, Garfield, Grand, Kane, Piute, San Juan, Sevier and Wayne.	DOUGLAS
	All others	LIVERMORE
VERMONT	All	BOSTON
VIRGIN ISLANDS	All	SAN JUAN
VIRGINIA	Arlington, Fairfax, Loudoun, Prince WIlliam.	BALTIMORE
	All others	NORFOLK
WAKE ISLAND	All	HONOLULU
WASHINGTON	Clark, Cowlitz, Klickitat, Skamania, and Wahkiakum	PORTLAND
	Whatcom, San Juan, Skagit	FERNDALE
	All others	SEATTLE
WEST VIRGINIA	All	BALTIMORE
WISCONSIN	Brown, Calumet, Columbia, Crawford, Dane, Dodge, Door, Fond du'Lac, Grant, Green, Iowa, Jefferson, Kenosha, Kewaunee, LaFayette, Manitowoc, Milwaukee, Outagamie, Ozaukee, Racine, Richland, Rock, Sauk, Sheboygan, Walworth, Washington, Waukesha, Winnebago.	CHICAGO
	All others	ST. PAUL
WYOMING	All	DENVER

FCC OFFICE ADDRESSES

ALASKA, Anchorage Office
Federal Communications Commission
6721 West Raspberry Road
Anchorage, Alaska 99502
Phone: (907) 243-2153

*ARIZONA, Douglas Office
Federal Communications Commission
P.O. Box 6
Douglas, Arizona 85608
Phone: (602) 364-8414

CALIFORNIA, San Diego Office
Federal Communications Commission
4542 Ruffner Street
Room 370
San Diego, California 92111-2216
Phone: (619) 557-5478

*CALIFORNIA, Livermore Office
Federal Communications Commission
P.O. Box 311
Livermore, California 94551-0311
Phone: (415) 447-3614

CALIFORNIA, Los Angeles Office
Federal Communications Commission
Cerritos Corporate Tower
18000 Studebaker Road, Room 660
Cerritos, California 90701
Phone: (213) 809-2096

CALIFORNIA, San Francisco Office
Federal Communications Commission
424 Customhouse
555 Battery Street
San Francisco, California 94111
Phone: (415) 705-1101

COLORADO, Denver Office
Federal Communications Commission
12477 West Cedar Drive
Denver, Colorado 80228
Phone: (303) 236-8026

*FLORIDA, Vero Beach Office
Federal Communications Commission
P.O. Box 1730
Vero Beach, Florida 32961-1730
Phone: (407) 778-3755

FLORIDA, Miami Office
Federal Communications Commission
Rochester Building, Room 310
8390 N.W. 53rd Street
Miami, Florida 33166
Phone: (305) 526-7420

FLORIDA, Tampa Office
Federal Communications Commission
Room 1215
2203 N. Lois Avenue
Tampa, Florida 33607-2356
Phone: (813) 228-2872

GEORGIA, Atlanta Office
Federal Communications Commission
Massell Building, Room 440
1365 Peachtree Street, N.E.
Atlanta, Georgia 30309
Phone: (404) 347-2631

*GEORGIA, Powder Springs Office
Federal Communications Commission
P.O. Box 85
Powder Springs, Georgia 30073
Phone: (404) 943-5420

HAWAII, Honolulu Office
Federal Communications Commission
P.O. Box 1030
Waipahu, Hawaii 96797
Phone: (808) 677-3318

ILLINOIS, Chicago Office
Federal Communications Commission
Park Ridge Office Center, Rm 306
1550 Northwest Highway
Park Ridge, Illinois 60068
Phone: (312) 353-0195

LOUISIANA, New Orleans Office
Federal Communications Commission
800 West Commerce Rd,. Room 505
New Orleans, Louisiana 70123
Phone: (504) 589-2095

*MAINE, Belfast Office
Federal Communications Commission
P.O. Box 470
Belfast, Maine 04915
Phone: (207) 338-4088

*MARYLAND, Baltimore Office
Federal Communications Commission
1017 Federal Building
31 Hopkins Plaza
Baltimore, Maryland 21201
Phone: (301) 962-2729

*MARYLAND, Laurel Office
Federal Communications Commission
P.O. Box 250
Columbia, Maryland 21045
Phone: (301) 725-3474

MASSACHUSETTS, Boston Office
Federal Communications Commission
NFPA Building
1 Batterymarch Park
Quincy, Massachusetts 02169
Phone: (617) 770-4023

*MICHIGAN, Allegan Office
Federal Communications Commission
P.O. Box 89
Allegan, Michigan 49010
Phone: (616) 673-2063

MICHIGAN, Detroit Office
Federal Communications Commission
24897 Hathaway Street
Farmington Hills, Michigan 48331-4361
Phone: (313) 226-6078

MINNESOTA, Street Paul Office
Federal Communications Commission
693 Federal Building & US Courthouse
316 North Robert Street
St. Paul, Minnesota 55101
Phone: (612) 290-3819

MISSOURI, Kansas City Office
Federal Communications Commission
Brywood Office Tower, Room 320
8800 East 63rd Street

Kansas City, Missouri 64133
Phone: (816) 926-5111

*NEBRASKA, Grand Island Office
Federal Communications Commission
P.O. Box 1588
Grand Island, Nebraska 68802
Phone: (308) 382-4296

NEW YORK, Buffalo Office
Federal Communications Commission
1307 Federal Building
111 West Huron Street
Buffalo, New York 14202
Phone: (716) 846-4511

NEW YORK, New York Office
Federal Communications Commission
201 Varick Street
New York, New York 10014-4870
Phone: (212) 620-3437

OREGON, Portland Office
Federal Communications Commission
1782 Federal Office Building
1220 S.W. 3rd Avenue
Portland, Oregon 97204
Phone: (503) 326-4114

PENNSYLVANIA, Philadelphia Office.
Federal Communications Commission
One Oxford Valley Office Building
2300 East Lincoln Highway
Room 404
Langhorne, Pennsylvania 19047
Phone: (215) 752-1324

PUERTO RICO, San Juan Office
Federal Communications Commission
747 Federal Building
Hato Rey, Puerto Rico 009118-2251
Phone: (809) 766-5567

TEXAS, Dallas Office
Federal Communications Commission
9330 LBJ Expressway, Room 1170
Dallas, Texas 75243
Phone: (214) 767-4827

TEXAS, Houston Office
Federal Communications Commission
1225 North Loop West, Rm 900
Houston Texas 77008
Phone: (713) 229-2748

*TEXAS, Kingsville Office
Federal Communications Commission
P.O. Box 632
Kingsville, Texas 78363-0632
Phone: (512) 592-2531

VIRGINIA, Norfolk Office
Federal Communications Commission
1200 Communications Circle
Virginia Beach, Virginia 23455-3725
Phone: (804) 441-6472

*WASHINGTON, Ferndale Office
Federal Communications Commission
1330 Loomis Trail Road
Custer, Washington 98240
Phone: (206) 354-4892

WASHINGTON, Seattle Office
Federal Communications Commission
One Newport, Room 414
3605 132nd Avenue, S.E.
Bellevue, Washington 98006
Phone: (206) 764-3324

*Licenses not available at * locations
10/10/89, List Courtesy FCC

U.S. VOLUNTEER-EXAMINER COORDINATORS IN THE AMATEUR SERVICE

Anchorage Amateur Radio Club, 2628 Turnagain Parkway, Anchorage, AK 99517; (907) 786-8121 (Day), (907) 243-2221 (Night), (907) 276-5121, (907) 274-5546

ARRL/VEC*, 25 Main Street, Newington, CT 06111-1492; (203) 666-1541, (208) 665-7531 (FAX)

Central Alabama VEC, Inc., 1215 Dale Drive SE, Huntsville, AL 35801-2031; (205) 536-3904

Charlotte VEC, 227 Bennett Lane, Charlotte, NC 28213-6719, (704) 596-2168

Golden Empire Amateur Radio Society, P.O. Box 508, Chico, CA 95927-0508; (916) 342-1180

Great Lakes Amateur Radio Club VEC, Inc., 3040 Harrison St., Glenview, IL 60025-0273; (708) 486-8019

Greater Los Angeles Amateur Radio Group, 9737 Noble Avenue, North Hills, CA 91343-2403; (818) 892-2068, (818) 892-9855

Jefferson Amateur Radio Club, P.O. Box 24368, New Orleans, LA 70184-4368

Koolau Amateur Radio Club, 45-529 Nakuluai Street, Kaneohe, HI 96744-2224; (808) 235-4132

Laurel Amateur Radio Club, Inc., P.O. Box 3039, Laurel, MD 20709-0039; (301) 572-5124 (0900-2100; (301) 317-7819

The Milwaukee Radio Amateurs Club, Inc., 1737 N. 116th Street, Wauwatosa, WI 53226-3003; (414) 774-6999

Mountain Amateur Radio Club, P.O. Box 10, Burlington, WV 26710-0010; (304) 289-3576, (301) 724-0674

PHD Amateur Radio Association, Inc., P.O. Box 11, Liberty, MO 64068-0011; (816) 781-7313

Sandarc-VEC, P.O. Box 2446, La Mesa, CA 91943-2446; (619) 465-3926

Sunnyvale VEC Amateur Radio Club, P.O. Box 60307, Sunnyvale, CA 94088-0307; (408) 255-9000 (24 hours)

Triad Emergency Amateur Radio Club, 3504 Stonehurst Place, High Point, NC 27265-2106; (919) 841-7576

Western Carolina Amateur Radio Society VEC, Inc., 5833 Clinton Hwy., Suite 203, Knoxville, TN 37912-2545; (615) 688-7771, (615) 689-7062 (FAX)

W5YI-VEC*, P.O. Box 565101, Dallas, TX 75356-5101; (817) 461-6443, (817) 548-9594 (FAX)

*This VEC regularly offers monthly exams in all parts of the country.

FCC PART 97

The rules governing all telecommunication services in the United States are contained in Title 47 of the Code of Federal Regulations. The entire text is published in five volumes, containing Parts 0-19, 20-39, 40-69, 70-79, and 80 to End. The published version of Title 47 is revised yearly, with regulations current as of October of that year. Any volume (or all five) can be purchased by contacting the Superintendent of Documents, U.S. Government Printing Office, Washington, DC, 20402, telephone (202) 783-3238. Each volume costs approximately $25, and credit cards are accepted.

From time to time, rules are changed. Since they often become effective before the next printing of the appropriate Title of the CFR, a monthly List of Sections Affected (LSA) is also published by the Government. Subscriptions are available to this publication for $21 per year, but be advised that it is only a list of changes to all 50 Titles of the U.S. Code (which documents all the rules and regulations administered by the Executive departments and agencies of the Federal Government). The LSA indicates which page of the Federal Register contains the complete text of any changed rule. The Federal Register is published daily (with a monthly index and Reader Aids section). Subscriptions are also available to the Federal Register, but be advised that it contains approximately 150 pages per day. Fortunately, most large libraries subscribe to both the LSA and the Federal Register, making it relatively easy to find the exact wording of a particular rule regarding amateur radio (or anything else regulated by the Government).

Part 97 (referred to as 47 CFR 97) contains all the rules relating to Amateur Radio in the U.S. The most current available version is presented here in its entirety, courtesy of The W5YI Group.

RULES AND REGULATIONS

Part 97 *Amateur Radio Service*

FEDERAL COMMUNICATIONS COMMISSION

PART 97 — AMATEUR RADIO SERVICE

Subpart A—General Provisions

§ 97.1 Basis and purpose.

The rules and regulations in this Part are designed to provide an amateur radio service having a fundamental purpose as expressed in the following principles:

(a) Recognition and enhancement of the value of the amateur service to the public as a voluntary noncommercial communication service, particularly with respect to providing emergency communications.

(b) Continuation and extension of the amateur's proven ability to contribute to the advancement of the radio art.

(c) Encouragement and improvement of the amateur service through rules which provide for advancing skills in both the communication and technical phases of the art.

(d) Expansion of the existing reservoir within the amateur radio service of trained operators, technicians and electronics experts.

(e) Continuation and extension of the amateur's unique ability to enhance international goodwill.

§ 97.3 Definitions.

(a) The definitions of terms used in Part 97 are:

(1) *Amateur operator.* A person holding a written authorization to be the control operator of an amateur station.

(2) *Amateur radio services.* The amateur service, the amateur-satellite service and the Radio Amateur Civil Emergency Service.

(3) *Amateur-satellite service.* A radiocommunication service using stations on Earth satellites for the same purpose as those of the amateur service.

(4) *Amateur service.* A radiocommunication service for the purpose of self-training, intercommunication and technical investigations carried out by amateurs, that is, duly authorized persons interested in radio technique solely with a personal aim and without pecuniary interest.

(5) *Amateur station.* A station in an amateur radio service consist-

ing of the apparatus necessary for carrying on radiocommunications.

(6) *Automatic control.* The use of devices and procedures for control of a station when it is transmitting so that compliance with the FCC Rules is achieved without the control operator being present at a control point.

(7) *Auxiliary station.* An amateur station transmitting communications point-to-point within a system of cooperating amateur stations.

(8) *Bandwidth.* The width of a frequency band outside of which the mean power of the transmitted signal is attenuated at least 26 dB below the mean power of the transmitted signal within the band.

(9) *Beacon.* An amateur station transmitting communications for the purposes of observation of propagation and reception or other related experimental activities.

(10) *Broadcasting.* Transmissions intended for reception by the general public, either direct or relayed.

(11) *Control operator.* An amateur operator designated by the licensee of a station to be responsible for the transmissions from that station to assure compliance with the FCC Rules.

(12) *Control point.* The location at which the control operator function is performed.

(13) *CSCE.* Certificate of Successful Completion of Examination.

(14) *Earth station.* An amateur station located on, or within 50 km of the Earth's surface intended for communications with space stations or with other Earth stations by means of one or more other objects in space.

(15) *EIC.* Engineer in Charge of an FCC Field Facility.

(16) *External RF power amplifier.* A device capable of increasing power output when used in conjunction with, but not an integral part of, a transmitter.

(17) *External RF power amplifier kit.* A number of electronic parts, which, when assembled, is an external RF power amplifier, even if additional parts are required to complete assembly.

(18) *FAA.* Federal Aviation Administration.

(19) *FCC.* Federal Communications Commission.

(20) *Frequency coordinator.* An entity, recognized in a local or regional area by amateur operators whose stations are eligible to be auxiliary or repeater stations, that recommends transmit/receive channels and associated operating and technical parameters for such stations in order to avoid or minimize potential interference.

(21) *Harmful interference.* Interference which endangers the functioning of a radionavigation service or of other safety services or seriously degrades, obstructs or repeatedly interrupts a radiocommunication service operating in accordance with the Radio Regulations.

(22) *Indicator.* Words, letters or numerals appended to and separated from the call sign during the station identification.

(23) *Information bulletin.* A message directed only to amateur operators consisting solely of subject matter of direct interest to the amateur service.

(24) *International Morse code.* A dot-dash code as defined in International Telegraph and Telephone Consultative Committee (CCITT) Recommendation F.1 (1984), Division B. I. Morse code.

(25) *ITU.* International Telecommunication Union.

(26) *Line A.* Begins at Aberdeen, WA, running by great circle arc to the intersection of 48°N, 120°W, thence along parallel 48°N, to the intersection of 95°W, thence by great circle arc through the southernmost point of Duluth, MN, thence by great circle arc to 45°N, 85°W, thence southward along meridian 85°W, to its intersection with parallel 41°N, thence along parallel 41°N, to its intersection with meridian 82°W, thence by great circle arc through the southernmost point of Bangor, ME, thence by great circle arc through the southernmost point of Searsport, ME, at which point it terminates.

(27) *Local control.* The use of a control operator who directly manipulates the operating adjustments in the station to achieve compliance with the FCC Rules.

(28) *National Radio Quiet Zone.* The area in Maryland, Virginia and West Virginia bounded by 39° 15'N on the north, 78° 30'W on the east, 37° 30'N on the south and 80° 30'W on the west.

(29) *Physician.* For the purposes of this Part, a person who is licensed to practice in a place where the amateur service is regulated by the FCC, as either a Doctor of Medicine (M.D.) or a Doctor of Osteopathy (D.O.).

(30) *Question pool.* All current examination questions for a designated written examination element.

(31) *Question set.* A series of examination questions on a given examination selected from the question pool.

(32) *Radio Regulations.* The latest ITU *Radio Regulations* to which the United States is a party.

(33) *RACES* (Radio Amateur Civil Emergency Service). A radio service using amateur stations for civil defense communications during periods of local, regional or national civil emergencies.

(34) *Remote control.* The use of a control operator who indirectly manipulates the operating adjustments in the station through a control link to achieve compliance with the FCC Rules.

(35) *Repeater.* An amateur station that automatically retransmits the signals of other stations.

(36) *Space station.* An amateur station located more than 50 km above the Earth's surface.

(37) *Space telemetry.* A one-way transmission from a space station of measurements made from the measuring instruments in a spacecraft, including those relating to the functioning of the spacecraft.

(38) *Spurious emission.* An emission, on frequencies outside the necessary bandwidth of a transmission, the level of which may be reduced without affecting the information being transmitted.

(39) *Telecommand.* A one-way transmission to initiate, modify, or terminate functions of a device at a distance.

(40) *Telecommand station.* An amateur station that transmits communications to initiate, modify or terminate functions of a space station.

(41) *Telemetry.* A one-way transmission of measurements at a distance from the measuring instrument.

(42) *Third party communications.* A message from the control operator (first party) of an amateur station to another amateur station control operator (second party) on behalf of another person (third party).

(43) *VE.* Volunteer Examiner.

(44) *VEC.* Volunteer-Examiner Coordinator.

(b) The definitions of technical symbols used in this Part are:

(1) *EHF* (Extremely High Frequency). The frequency range 30-300 GHz.

(2) *HF* (High Frequency). The frequency range 3-30 MHz.

(3) *Hz.* Hertz.

(4) *m.* Meters.

(5) *MF* (Medium Frequency). The frequency range 300-3000 kHz.

(6) *PEP* (Peak Envelope Power). The average power supplied to the antenna transmission line by a transmitter during one RF cycle at the crest of the modulation envelope taken under normal operating conditions.

(7) *RF.* Radio Frequency.

(8) *SHF* (Super-High Frequency). The frequency range 3-30 GHz.

(9) *UHF* (Ultra-High Frequency). The frequency range 300-3000 MHz.

(10) *VHF* (Very-High Frequency). The frequency range 30 -300 MHz.

(11) *W.* Watts.

(c) The following terms are used in this Part to indicate emission types. Refer to §2.201 of the FCC Rules, *Emission, modulation and transmission characteristics,* for information on emission type designators.

(1) *CW.* International Morse code telegraphy emissions having designators with A, C, H, J or R as the first symbol; 1 as the second symbol; A or B as the third symbol; and emissions J2A and J2B.

(2) *Data.* Telemetry, telecommand and computer communications emissions having designators with A, C, D, F, G, H, J or R as the first symbol; 1 as the second symbol; D as the third symbol; and emission J2D. Only a digital code of a type specifically authorized in this Part may be transmitted.

(3) *Image.* Facsimile and television emissions having designators with A, C, D, F, G, H, J or R as the first symbol; 1, 2 or 3 as the second symbol; C or F as the third symbol; and emissions having B as the first symbol; 7, 8 or 9 as the second symbol; W as the third symbol.

(4) *MCW.* Tone-modulated international Morse code telegraphy

emissions having designators with A, C, D, F, G, H or R as the first symbol; 2 as the second symbol; A or B as the third symbol.

(5) *Phone*. Speech and other sound emissions having designators with A, C, D, F, G, H, J or R as the first symbol; 1, 2 or 3 as the second symbol; E as the third symbol. Also speech emissions having B as the first symbol; 7, 8 or 9 as the second symbol; E as the third symbol. MCW for the purpose of performing the station identification procedure, or for providing telegraphy practice interspersed with speech. Incidental tones for the purpose of selective calling or alerting or to control the level of a demodulated signal may also be considered phone.

(6) *Pulse*. Emissions having designators with K, L, M, P, Q, V or W as the first symbol; 0, 1, 2, 3, 7, 8, 9 or X as the second symbol; A, B, C, D, E, F, N, W or X as the third symbol.

(7) *RTTY*. Narrow-band direct-printing telegraphy emissions having designators with A, C, D, F, G, H, J or R as the first symbol; 1 as the second symbol; B as the third symbol; and emission J2B. Only a digital code of a type specifically authorized in this Part may be transmitted.

(8) *SS*. Spread-spectrum emissions using bandwidth-expansion modulation emissions having designators with A, C, D, F, G, H, J or R as the first symbol; X as the second symbol; X as the third symbol. Only a SS emission of a type specifically authorized in this Part may be transmitted.

(9) *Test*. Emissions containing no information having the designators with N as the third symbol. Test does not include pulse emissions with no information or modulation unless pulse emissions are also authorized in the frequency band.

§ 97.5 Station license required.

(a) When a station is transmitting on any amateur service frequency from a geographic location within 50 km of the Earth's surface where the amateur service is regulated by the FCC, the person having physical control of the apparatus must hold an FCC-issued written authorization for an amateur station.

(b) When a station is transmitting on any amateur service frequency from a location within 50 km of the Earth's surface and aboard any vessel or craft that is documented or registered in the United States, the person having physical control of the apparatus must hold an FCC-issued written authorization for an amateur station.

(c) When a station is transmitting on any amateur-satellite service frequency from a location more than 50 km above the Earth's surface aboard any craft that is documented or registered in the United States, the person having physical control of the apparatus must hold an FCC-issued written authorization for an amateur station.

(d) The types of written authorizations that permit amateur station operation where the amateur service is regulated by the FCC are:

(1) An operator/primary station license (FCC Form 660) issued to the person by the FCC. A primary station license is issued only to a person, together with an operator license on the same document. Every amateur operator licensed by the FCC must have one, but only one, primary station license. Except a representative of a foreign government, any person who qualifies by examination is eligible to apply for an operator/primary station license.

(2) A club station license (FCC Form 660) issued to the person by the FCC. A club station license is issued only to the person who is the license trustee designated by an officer of the club. The trustee must hold an FCC-issued Amateur Extra, Advanced, General, or Technician operator license. The club must be composed of at least two persons and must have a name, a document of organization, management and a primary purpose devoted to amateur service activities consistent with this Part.

(3) A military recreation station license (FCC Form 660) issued to the person by the FCC. A military recreation station license is issued only to the person who is the license custodian designated by the official in charge of the United States military recreational premises where the station is situated. The custodian must not be a representative of a foreign government. The custodian need not hold an amateur operator license.

(4) A RACES station license (FCC Form 660) issued to the person by the FCC. A RACES station license is issued only to the person who is the license custodian designated by the official responsible for the governmental agency served by that civil defense organization. The custodian must not be a representative of a foreign government. The custodian must be the civil defense official responsible for coordination of all civil defense activities in the area concerned. The custodian need not hold an amateur operator license.

(5) A reciprocal permit for alien amateur licensee (FCC Form 610-AL) issued to the person by the FCC. A reciprocal permit for alien amateur licensee is issued only to a person who is a citizen of a country with which the United States has arrangements to grant reciprocal operating permits to visiting alien amateur operators. The person must be a citizen of the same country that issued the amateur service license. No person who is a citizen of the United States, regardless of any other citizenship also held, is eligible for a reciprocal permit for alien amateur licensee. No person holding an FCC-issued amateur service license will be issued a reciprocal permit for alien amateur licensee.

(6) An amateur service license issued to the person by the Government of Canada. The person must be a Canadian citizen.

(e) The written authorization for an amateur station authorizes the use in accordance with the FCC Rules of all transmitting apparatus under the physical control of the station licensee at points where the amateur service is regulated by the FCC. The original written authorization document or a photocopy thereof must be retained at the station.

§ 97.7 Control operator required.

When transmitting, each amateur station must have a control operator. Only a person holding one of the following documents may be the control operator of a station:

(a) An operator/primary station license (FCC Form 660) issued to the person by the FCC.

(b) A reciprocal permit for alien amateur licensee (FCC Form 610-AL) issued to the person by the FCC.

(c) An amateur service license issued to a Canadian citizen by the Government of Canada.

§ 97.9 Operator license.

(a) There are 5 classes of operator licenses: Novice, Technician, General, Advanced and Amateur Extra. An operator license authorizes the holder to be the control operator of a station with the privileges of the operator class specified on the license. The license document or a photocopy thereof must be in the personal possession of the licensee at all times when the person is the control operator of a station.

(b) A person holding a Novice, Technician, General or Advanced Class operator license who has properly filed with the FCC an application for a higher operator class which has not yet been acted upon, and who holds a CSCE indicating that the person completed the necessary examinations within the previous 365 days is authorized to exercise the rights and privileges of the higher operator class.

§ 97.11 Stations aboard ships or aircraft.

(a) The installation and operation of an amateur station on a ship or aircraft must be approved by the master of the ship or pilot in command of the aircraft.

(b) The station must be separate from and independent of all other radio apparatus installed on the ship or aircraft, except a common antenna may be shared with a voluntary ship radio installation. The station's transmissions must not cause interference to any other apparatus installed on the ship or aircraft.

(c) The station must not constitute a hazard to the safety of life or property. For a station aboard an aircraft, the apparatus shall not be operated while the aircraft is operating under Instrument Flight Rules, as defined by the FAA, unless the station has been found to comply with all applicable FAA Rules.

§ 97.13 Restrictions on station location.

(a) Before placing an amateur station on land of environmental importance or that is significant in American history, architecture or culture, the licensee may be required to take certain actions prescribed by §§1.1301-1.1319 of the FCC Rules.

(b) A station within 1600 m (1 mile) of an FCC monitoring facility must protect that facility from harmful interference. Failure to do so could result in imposition of operating restrictions upon the amateur station by an EIC pursuant to §97.121 of this Part. Geographical coordinates of the facilities that require protection are listed in §0.121(c) of the FCC Rules.

§ 97.15 Station antenna structures.

(a) Unless the amateur station licensee has received prior approval from the FCC, no antenna structure, including the radiating elements, tower, supports and all appurtenances, may be higher than 61 m (200 feet) above ground level at its site.

(b) Unless the amateur station licensee has received prior approval from the FCC, no antenna structure, at an airport or heliport that is available for public use and is listed in the *Airport Directory* of the current *Airman's Information Manual* or in either the *Alaska* or *Pacific Airman's Guide and Chart Supplement*; or at an airport or heliport under construction that is the subject of a notice or proposal on file with the FAA, and except for military airports, it is clearly indicated that the airport will be available for public use; or at an airport or heliport that is operated by the armed forces of the United States; or at a place near any of these airports or heliports, may be higher than:

(1) 1 m above the airport elevation for each 100 m from the nearest runway longer than 1 km within 6.1 km of the antenna structure.

(2) 2 m above the airport elevation for each 100 m from the nearest runway shorter than 1 km within 3.1 km of the antenna structure.

(3) 4 m above the airport elevation for each 100 m from the nearest landing pad within 1.5 km of the antenna structure.

(c) An amateur station antenna structure no higher than 6.1 m (20 feet) above ground level at its site or no higher than 6.1 m above any natural object or existing manmade structure, other than an antenna structure, is exempt from the requirements of paragraphs (a) and (b) of this Section.

(d) Further details as to whether an aeronautical study and/or obstruction marking and lighting may be required, and specifications for obstruction marking and lighting, are contained in Part 17 of the FCC Rules, *Construction, Marking, and Lighting of Antenna Structures*. To request approval to place an antenna structure higher than the limits specified in paragraphs (a), (b), and (c) of this Section, the licensee must notify the FAA on FAA Form 7460-1 and the FCC on FCC Form 854.

(e) Except as otherwise provided herein, a station antenna structure may be erected at heights and dimensions sufficient to accommodate amateur service communications. [State and local regulation of a station antenna structure must not preclude amateur service communications. Rather, it must reasonably accommodate such communications and must constitute the minimum practicable regulation to accomplish the state or local authority's legitimate purpose. *See* PRB-1, 101 FCC 2d 952 (1985) *for details.*]

§ 97.17 Application for new license.

(a) Any qualified person is eligible to apply for an amateur service license.

(b) Each application for a new operator/primary station license must be made on FCC Form 610. Each application for a reciprocal permit for alien amateur licensee must be made on FCC Form 610-A. Each application for a new amateur service club or military recreation station license must be made on FCC Form 610-B. No new license for a RACES station will be issued.

(c) Each application for a new operator/primary station license and each application involving a change in operator class must be submitted to the VEs administering the qualifying examination.

(d) Any qualified person is eligible to apply for a reciprocal permit for alien amateur licensee. The application must be submitted to the FCC, 1270 Fairfield Road, Gettysburg, PA 17325-7245.

(e) No person shall obtain or attempt to obtain, or assist another person to obtain or attempt to obtain, an operator license or reciprocal permit for alien amateur licensee by fraudulent means.

(f) A call sign will be assigned systematically to each primary station. The FCC will issue public announcements detailing the policies and procedures of the primary station call sign assignment system. The FCC will not grant any request for a specific call sign.

(g) Each application for a new amateur service club or military recreation station license must be submitted to a club and military recreation station call sign administrator.

§ 97.19 Application for a renewed or modified license.

(a) Each application for a renewed or modified operator/primary station license must be made on FCC Form 610. Each application for a renewed or modified RACES station license must be made on FCC Form 610-B. A reciprocal permit for alien amateur licensee is not renewable. A new reciprocal permit may be issued upon proper application.

(b) Each application for a renewed or modified amateur service license must be accompanied by a photocopy of the license document or the original document, unless it has been lost, mutilated or destroyed. Each application for a modified operator license involving a change in operator class must be submitted to the VEs administering the qualifying examination. Each application for a modified or renewed amateur service club or military recreation station license must be made on FCC Form 610-B and submitted to the club and military recreation station call sign administrator that provided it. All other applications must be submitted to: FCC, 1270 Fairfield Road, Gettysburg, PA 17325-7245.

(c) When the licensee has submitted a timely application for renewal of an unexpired license (between 60 and 90 days prior to the end of the license term is recommended), the licensee may continue to operate until the disposition of the application has been determined. If a license expires, application for renewal may be made during a grace period of 2 years after the expiration date. During this grace period, the expired license is not valid. A license renewed during the grace period must be dated as of the date of the renewal.

§ 97.21 Mailing address and station location.

Each application for an amateur service license and each application for a reciprocal permit for alien amateur licensee must show a mailing address and a station location (the addresses may be the same) in an area where the amateur service is regulated by the FCC. The mailing address must be one where the licensee can receive mail delivery by the United States Postal Service. The station location must be a place where a station can be physically located. (A post office box whether provided by the United States Postal Service or by any other party, a rural or highway contract route designation and box number, and general delivery are unsuitable as a station location.)

§ 97.23 License term.

(a) An amateur service license is normally issued for a 10-year term.

(b) A reciprocal permit for alien amateur licensee is normally issued for a 1-year term.

§ 97.25 FCC modification of station license.

(a) The FCC may modify a station license, either for a limited time or for the duration of the term thereof, if it determines:

(1) That such action will promote the public interest, convenience and necessity; or

(2) That such action will promote fuller compliance with the provisions of the Communications Act of 1934, as amended, or of any treaty ratified by the United States.

(b) When the FCC makes such a determination, it will issue an order of modification. The order will not become final until the licensee is notified in writing of the proposed action and the grounds and reasons therefor. The licensee will be given reasonable opportunity of no less than 30 days to protest the modification; except that, where safety of life or property is involved, a shorter period of notice may be provided. Any protest by a licensee of an FCC order of modification will be handled in accordance with the provisions of 47 U.S.C. §316.

§ 97.27 Replacement license.

Each licensee or permittee whose original document is lost, mutilated or destroyed must request a replacement. The request must be made to: FCC, 1270 Fairfield Road, Gettysburg, PA 17325-7245. A statement of how the document was lost, mutilated or destroyed must be attached to the request. A replacement license must bear the same expiration date as the license that it replaces.

§ 97.29 Club and military recreation station call sign administration.

No organization may serve as an amateur service club and military recreation station call sign administrator unless it has entered into a written agreement with the FCC. The FCC will issue public announcements listing the club and military recreation station call sign administrators. Each club and military recreation station call sign administrator must abide by the terms of the agreement. Each club and military recreation station call sign administrator must:

(a) Be an organization that has tax-exempt status under Section 501(c)(3) of the Internal Revenue Code of 1986 and that exists for the purpose of furthering the amateur service;

(b) Be an organization whose membership includes at least one percent of the amateur operators licensed by the FCC;

(c) Be capable of serving as a club and military recreation call sign administrator in all places where the amateur service is regulated by the FCC;

(d) Accept and process all properly-completed license application Forms 610-B received from qualified club and military recreation station license trustees or custodians and submit them to: FCC, 1270 Fairfield Road, Gettysburg, PA 17325-7245;

(e) Not charge the applicants any fee or accept any form of reimbursement for services provided as an amateur service club and military recreation station call sign administrator;

(f) Accept and process applications from applicants for club or military recreation station licenses, under §§97.5(d)(2) and (3) of this Part, without regard to race, sex, religion, national origin or membership (or lack thereof) in any amateur service organization;

(g) Provide the FCC with a license document, including the unique station call sign, ready for endorsement and mailing within 10 days of receipt of a properly-completed application for a club or military recreation station license;

(h) Provide the FCC each month, in a format specified by the FCC, a data file of license documents processed during that month;

(i) Issue public announcements detailing the policies and procedures of the club and military recreation station call sign assignment system;

(j) Accept and respond to inquiries concerning club and military recreation station applications and license matters;

(k) Provide the FCC with a plan for processing applications for modified or renewed amateur service club or military recreation station licenses in the event that the organization ceases to function as a club and military recreation station call sign administrator.

Subpart B—Station Operation Standards

§ 97.101 General standards.

(a) In all respects not specifically covered by FCC Rules each amateur station must be operated in accordance with good engineering and good amateur practice.

(b) Each station licensee and each control operator must cooperate in selecting transmitting channels and in making the most effective use of the amateur service frequencies. No frequency will be assigned for the exclusive use of any station.

(c) At all times and on all frequencies, each control operator must give priority to stations providing emergency communications, except to stations transmitting communications for training drills and tests in RACES.

(d) No amateur operator shall willfully or maliciously interfere with or cause interference to any radio communication or signal.

§ 97.103 Station licensee responsibilities.

(a) The station licensee is responsible for the proper operation of the station in accordance with the FCC Rules. When the control operator is a different amateur operator than the station licensee, both persons are equally responsible for proper operation of the station.

(b) The station licensee must designate the station control operator. The FCC will presume that the station licensee is also the control operator, unless documentation to the contrary is in the station records.

(c) The station licensee must make the station and the station records available for inspection upon request by an FCC representative. When deemed necessary by an EIC to assure compliance with the FCC Rules, the station licensee must maintain a record of station operations containing such items of information as the EIC may require in accord with §0.314(x) of the FCC Rules.

§ 97.105 Control operator duties.

(a) The control operator must ensure the immediate proper operation of the station, regardless of the type of control.

(b) A station may only be operated in the manner and to the extent permitted by the privileges authorized for the class of operator license held by the control operator.

§ 97.107 Alien control operator privileges.

(a) The privileges available to a control operator holding an amateur service license issued by the Government of Canada are:

(1) The terms of the *Convention Between the United States and Canada (TIAS No. 2508) Relating to the Operation by Citizens of Either Country of Certain Radio Equipment or Stations in the Other Country;*

(2) The operating terms and conditions of the amateur service license issued by the Government of Canada; and

(3) The applicable provisions of the FCC Rules, but not to exceed the control operator privileges of an FCC-issued Amateur Extra Class operator license.

(b) The privileges available to a control operator holding an FCC-issued reciprocal permit for alien amateur licensee are:

(1) The terms of the agreement between the alien's government and the United States;

(2) The operating terms and conditions of the amateur service license issued by the alien's government;

(3) The applicable provisions of the FCC Rules, but not to exceed the control operator privileges of an FCC-issued Amateur Extra Class operator license; and

(4) None, if the holder of the reciprocal permit has obtained an FCC-issued operator/primary station license.

(c) At any time the FCC may, in its discretion, modify, suspend, or cancel the amateur service privileges within or over any area where radio services are regulated by the FCC of any Canadian amateur service licensee or alien reciprocal permittee.

§ 97.109 Station control.

(a) Each amateur station must have at least one control point.

(b) When a station is being locally controlled, the control operator must be at the control point. Any station may be locally controlled.

(c) When a station is being remotely controlled, the control operator must be at the control point. Any station may be remotely controlled.

(d) When a station is being automatically controlled, the control operator need not be at the control point. Only stations transmitting RTTY or data emissions on the 6 m or shorter wavelength bands, and stations specifically designated elsewhere in this Part may be automatically controlled. Automatic control must cease upon notification by an EIC that the station is transmitting improperly or causing harmful interference to other stations. Automatic control must not be resumed without prior approval of the EIC.

(e) No station may be automatically controlled while transmitting third-party communications, except a station retransmitting digital packet radio communications on the 6 m and shorter wavelength bands. Such stations must be using the American Radio Relay League, Inc. *AX.25 Amateur Packet-Radio Link-Layer Protocol, Version 2.0,* October 1984 (or compatible), which is available from the American Radio Relay League, Inc., 225 Main Street, Newington, Connecticut, 06111. The retransmitted messages must originate at a station that is being locally or remotely controlled.

§ 97.111 Authorized transmissions.

(a) An amateur station may transmit the following types of two-way communications:

(1) Transmissions necessary to exchange messages with other stations in the amateur service, except those in any country whose administration has given notice that it objects to such communications. The FCC will issue public notices of current arrangements

for international communications;

(2) Transmissions necessary to exchange messages with a station in another FCC-regulated service while providing emergency communications;

(3) Transmissions necessary to exchange messages with a United States government station, necessary to providing communications in RACES; and

(4) Transmissions necessary to exchange messages with a station in a service not regulated by the FCC, but authorized by the FCC to communicate with amateur stations. An amateur station may exchange messages with a participating United States military station during an Armed Forces Day Communications Test.

(b) In addition to one-way transmissions specifically authorized elsewhere in this Part, an amateur station may transmit the following types of one-way communications:

(1) Brief transmissions necessary to make adjustments to the station;

(2) Brief transmissions necessary to establishing two-way communications with other stations;

(3) Telecommand;

(4) Transmissions necessary to providing emergency communications;

(5) Transmissions necessary to assisting persons learning, or improving proficiency in, the international Morse code;

(6) Transmissions necessary to disseminate information bulletins; and

(7) Transmissions of telemetry.

§ 97.113 Prohibited transmissions.

(a) No amateur station shall transmit:

(1) Communications specifically prohibited elsewhere in the Part:

(2) Communications for hire or for material compensation, direct or indirect, paid or promised, except as otherwise provided in these rules:

(3) Communications in which the station licensee or control operator has a pecuniary interest, including communications on behalf of an employer. Amateur operators may, however, notify other amateur operators of the availability for sale or trade of apparatus normally used in an amateur station, provided that such activity is not conducted on a regular basis.

(4) Music using a phone emission except as specifically provided elsewhere in this Section; communications intended to facilitate a criminal act; messages in codes or ciphers intended to obscure the meaning thereof, except as otherwise provided herein; obscene or indecent words or language; or false or deceptive messages, signals or identification.

(5) Communications, on a regular basis, which could reasonably be furnished through other radio services.

(b) An amateur station shall not engage in any form of broadcasting, nor may an amateur station transmit one-way communications except as specifically provided in these rules; nor shall an amateur station engage in any activity related to program production or newsgathering for broadcasting purposes, except that communications directly related to the immediate safety of human life or the protection of property may be provided by amateur stations to broadcasters for dissemination to the public where no other means of communication is reasonably available before or at the time of the event.

(c) A control operator may accept compensation as an incident of a teaching position during periods of time when an amateur station is used by that teacher as a part of classroom instruction at an educational institution.

(d) The control operator of a club station may accept compensation for the periods of time when the station is transmitting telegraphy practice or information bulletins, provided that the station transmits such telegraphy practice and bulletins for at least 40 hours per week; schedules operations on at least six amateur service MF and HF bands using reasonable measures to maximize coverage; where the schedule of normal operating times and frequencies is published at least 30 days in advance of the actual transmissions; and where the control operator does not accept any direct or indirect compensation for any other service as a control operator.

(e) No station shall retransmit programs or signals emanating from any type of radio station other than an amateur station, except propagation and weather forecast information intended for use by the general public and originated from United States Government stations and communications, including incidental music originating on United States Government frequencies between a space shuttle and its associated Earth stations. Prior approval for shuttle retransmissions must be obtained from the National Aeronautics and Space Administration. Such retransmissions must be for the exclusive use of amateur operators. Propagation, weather forecasts, and shuttle retransmissions may not be conducted on a regular basis, but only occasionally, as an incident of normal amateur radio communications.

(f) No amateur station, except an auxiliary, repeater or space station, may automatically retransmit the radio signals of other amateur stations.

§ 97.115 Third party communications.

(a) An amateur station may transmit messages for a third party to:

(1) Any station within the jurisdiction of the United States;

(2) Any station within the jurisdiction of any foreign government whose administration has made arrangements with the United States to allow amateur stations to be used for transmitting international communications on behalf of third parties. No station shall transmit messages for a third party to any station within the jurisdiction of any foreign government whose administration has not made such an arrangement. This prohibition does not apply to a message for any third party who is eligible to be a control operator of the station.

(b) The third party may participate in stating the message where:

(1) The control operator is present at the control point and is continuously monitoring and supervising the third party's participation; and

(2) The third party is not a prior amateur service licensee whose license was revoked; suspended for less than the balance of the license term and the suspension is still in effect; suspended for the balance of the license term and relicensing has not taken place; or surrendered for cancellation following notice of revocation, suspension or monetary forfeiture proceedings. The third party may not be the subject of a cease and desist order which relates to amateur service operation and which is still in effect.

(c) At the end of an exchange of international third party communications, the station must also transmit in the station identification procedure the call sign of the station with which a third party message was exchanged.

§ 97.117 International communications.

Transmissions to a different country, where permitted, shall be made in plain language and shall be limited to messages of a technical nature relating to tests, and, to remarks of a personal character for which, by reason of their unimportance, recourse to the public telecommunications service is not justified.

§ 97.119 Station identification.

(a) Each amateur station, except a space station or telecommand station, must transmit its assigned call sign on its transmitting channel at the end of each communication, and at least every 10 minutes during a communication, for the purpose of clearly making the source of the transmissions from the station known to those receiving the transmissions. No station may transmit unidentified communications or signals, or transmit as the station call sign, any call sign not authorized to the station.

(b) The call sign must be transmitted with an emission authorized for the transmitting channel in one of the following ways:

(1) By a CW emission. When keyed by an automatic device used only for identification, the speed must not exceed 20 words per minute;

(2) By a phone emission in the English language. Use of a phonetic alphabet as an aid for correct station identification is encouraged;

(3) By a RTTY emission using a specified digital code when all or part of the communications are transmitted by a RTTY or data emission;

(4) By an image emission conforming to the applicable transmission standards, either color or monochrome, of §73.682(a) of the FCC Rules when all or part of the communications are transmitted in the same image emission; or

(5) By a CW or phone emission during SS emission transmission on a narrow bandwidth frequency segment. Alternatively, by the changing of one or more parameters of the emission so that a conventional CW or phone emission receiver can be used to determine the station call sign.

(c) An indicator may be included with the call sign. It must be separated from the call sign by the slant mark or by any suitable word that denotes the slant mark. If the indicator is self-assigned, it must be included after the call sign and must not conflict with any other indicator specified by the FCC Rules or with any prefix assigned to another country.

(d) When the operator license class held by the control operator exceeds that of the station licensee, an indicator consisting of the call sign assigned to the control operator's station must be included after the call sign.

(e) When the control operator is a person who is exercising the rights and privileges authorized by §97.9(b) of this Part, an indicator must be included after the call sign as follows:

(1) For a control operator who has requested a license modification from Novice Class to Technician Class: KT;

(2) For a control operator who has requested a license modification from Novice or Technician Class to General Class: AG;

(3) For a control operator who has requested a license modification from Novice, Technician or General Class to Advanced Class: AA;

(4) For a control operator who has requested a license modification from Novice, Technician, General or Advanced Class to Amateur Extra Class: AE.

(f) When the station is transmitting under the authority of a reciprocal permit for alien amateur licensee, an indicator consisting of the appropriate letter-numeral designating the station location must be included before the call sign issued to the station by the licensing country. When the station is transmitting under the authority of an amateur service license issued by the Government of Canada, a station location indicator must be included after the call sign. At least once during each intercommunication, the identification announcement must include the geographical location as nearly as possible by city and state, commonwealth or possession.

§ 97.121 Restricted operation.

(a) If the operation of an amateur station causes general interference to the reception of transmissions from stations operating in the domestic broadcast service when receivers of good engineering design, including adequate selectivity characteristics, are used to receive such transmissions, and this fact is made known to the amateur station licensee, the amateur station shall not be operated during the hours from 8 p.m. to 10:30 p.m., local time, and on Sunday for the additional period from 10:30 a.m. until 1 p.m., local time, upon the frequency or frequencies used when the interference is created.

(b) In general, such steps as may be necessary to minimize interference to stations operating in other services may be required after investigation by the FCC.

Subpart C—Special Operations

§ 97.201 Auxiliary station.

(a) Any amateur station licensed to a holder of a Technician, General, Advanced or Amateur Extra Class operator license may be an auxiliary station. A holder of a Technician, General, Advanced or Amateur Extra Class operator license may be the control operator of an auxiliary station, subject to the privileges of the class of operator license held.

(b) An auxiliary station may transmit only on the 1.25 m and shorter wavelength bands, except the 431-433 MHz and 435-438 MHz segments.

(c) Where an auxiliary station causes harmful interference to another auxiliary station, the licensees are equally and fully responsible for resolving the interference unless one station's operation is recommended by a frequency coordinator and the other station's is not. In that case, the licensee of the non-coordinated auxiliary station has primary responsibility to resolve the interference.

(d) An auxiliary station may be automatically controlled.

(e) An auxiliary station may transmit one-way communications.

§ 97.203 Beacon Station.

(a) Any amateur station licensed to a holder of a Technician, General, Advanced or Amateur Extra Class operator license may be a beacon. A holder of a Technician, General, Advanced or Amateur Extra Class operator license may be the control operator of a beacon, subject to the privileges of the class of operator license held.

(b) A beacon must not concurrently transmit on more than 1 channel in the same amateur service frequency band, from the same station location.

(c) The transmitter power of a beacon must not exceed 100 W.

(d) A beacon may be automatically controlled while it is transmitting on the 28.20-28.30 MHz, 50.06-50.08 MHz, 144.275-144.300 MHz, 222.05-222.06 MHz or 432.300-432.400 MHz segments, or on the 33 cm and shorter wavelength bands.

(e) Before establishing an automatically controlled beacon in the National Radio Quiet Zone or before changing the transmitting frequency, transmitter power, antenna height or directivity, the station licensee must give written notification thereof to the Interference Office, National Radio Astronomy Observatory, P.O. Box 2, Green Bank, WV 24944.

(1) The notification must include the geographical coordinates of the antenna, antenna ground elevation above mean sea level (AMSL), antenna center of radiation above ground level (AGL), antenna directivity, proposed frequency, type of emission, and transmitter power.

(2) If an objection to the proposed operation is received by the FCC from the National Radio Astronomy Observatory at Green Bank, Pocahontas County, WV, for itself or on behalf of the Naval Research Laboratory at Sugar Grove, Pendleton County, WV, within 20 days from the date of notification, the FCC will consider all aspects of the problem and take whatever action is deemed appropriate.

(f) A beacon must cease transmissions upon notification by an EIC that the station is operating improperly or causing undue interference to other operations. The beacon may not resume transmitting without prior approval of the EIC.

(g) A beacon may transmit one-way communications.

§ 97.205 Repeater station.

(a) Any amateur station licensed to a holder of a Technician, General, Advanced or Amateur Extra Class operator license may be a repeater. A holder of a Technician, General, Advanced or Amateur Extra Class operator license may be the control operator of a repeater, subject to the privileges of the class of operator license held.

(b) A repeater may receive and retransmit only on the 10 m and shorter wavelength frequency bands except the 28.0-29.5 MHz, 50.0-51.0 MHz, 144.0-144.5 MHz, 145.5-146.0 MHz, 431.0-433.0 MHz and 435.0-438.0 MHz segments.

(c) Where the transmissions of a repeater cause harmful interference to another repeater, the two station licensees are equally and fully responsible for resolving the interference unless the operation of one station is recommended by a frequency coordinator and the operation of the other station is not. In that case, the licensee of the non-coordinated repeater has primary responsibility to resolve the interference.

(d) A repeater may be automatically controlled.

(e) Ancillary functions of a repeater that are available to users on the input channel are not considered remotely controlled functions of the station. Limiting the use of a repeater to only certain user stations is permissible.

(f) Before establishing a repeater in the National Radio Quiet Zone or before changing the transmitting frequency, transmitter power, antenna height or directivity, or the location of an existing repeater, the station licensee must give written notification thereof to the Interference Office, National Radio Astronomy Observatory, P.O. Box 2, Green Bank, WV 24944.

(1) The notification must include the geographical coordinates of the station antenna, antenna ground elevation above mean sea level (AMSL), antenna center of radiation above ground level (AGL), antenna directivity, proposed frequency, type of emission, and transmitter power.

(2) If an objection to the proposed operation is received by the FCC from the National Radio Astronomy Observatory at Green Bank, Pocahontas County, WV, for itself or on behalf of the Naval Research Laboratory at Sugar Grove, Pendleton County, WV, within 20 days from the date of notification, the FCC will consider all aspects of the problem and take whatever action is deemed appropriate.

§ 97.207 Space station.

(a) Any amateur station may be a space station. A holder of any class operator license may be the control operator of a space station, subject to the privileges of the class of operator license held by the control operator.

(b) A space station must be capable of effecting a cessation of transmissions by telecommand whenever such cessation is ordered by the FCC.

(c) The following frequency bands and segments are authorized to space stations:

(1) The 17 m, 15 m, 12 m, and 10 m bands, 6 mm, 4 mm, 2 mm and 1 mm bands; and

(2) The 7.0-7.1 MHz, 14.00-14.25 MHz, 144-146 MHz, 435-438 MHz, 1260-1270 MHz, and 2400-2450 MHz, 3.40-3.41 GHz, 5.83-5.85 GHz, 10.45-10.50 GHz and 24.00-24.05 GHz segments.

(d) A space station may automatically retransmit the radio signals of Earth stations and other space stations.

(e) A space station may transmit one-way communications.

(f) Space telemetry tramsmissions may consist of specially coded messages intended to facilitate communications or related to the function of the spacecraft.

(g) The licensee of each space station must give two written, pre-space station notifications to the Private Radio Bureau, FCC, Washington, DC 20554. Each notification must be in accord with the provisions of Articles 11 and 13 of the Radio Regulations.

(1) The first notification is required no less than 27 months prior to initiating space station transmissions and must specify the information required by Appendix 4 and Resolution No. 642 of the Radio Regulations.

(2) The second notification is required no less than 5 months prior to initiating space station transmissions and must specify the information required by Appendix 3 and Resolution No. 642 of the Radio Regulations.

(h) The licensee of each space station must give a written, in-space station notification to the Private Radio Bureau, FCC, Washington, DC 20554, no later than 7 days following initiation of space station transmissions. The notification must update the information contained in the pre-space notification.

(i) The licensee of each space station must give a written, post-space station notification to the Private Radio Bureau, FCC, Washington, DC 20554, no later than 3 months after termination of the space station transmissions. When the termination is ordered by the FCC, notification is required no later than 24 hours after termination.

§ 97.209 Earth station.

(a) Any amateur station may be an Earth station. A holder of any class operator license may be the control operator of an Earth station, subject to the privileges of the class of operator license held by the control operator.

(b) The following frequency bands and segments are authorized to Earth stations:

(1) The 17 m, 15 m, 12 m and 10 m bands, 6 mm, 4 mm, 2 mm and 1 mm bands; and

(2) The 7.0-7.1 MHz, 14.00-14.25 MHz, 144-146 MHz, 435-438 MHz, 1260-1270 MHz and 2400-2450 MHz, 3.40-3.41 GHz, 5.65-5.67 GHz, 10.45-10.50 GHz and 24.00-24.05 GHz segments.

§ 97.211 Space telecommand station.

(a) Any amateur station designated by the licensee of a space station is eligible to transmit as a telecommand station for that space station, subject to the privileges of the class of operator license held by the control operator.

(b) A telecommand station may transmit special codes intended to obscure the meaning of telecommand messages to the station in space operation.

(c) The following frequency bands and segments are authorized to telecommand stations:

(1) The 17 m, 15 m, 12 m and 10 m bands, 6 mm, 4 mm, 2 mm and 1 mm bands; and

(2) The 7.0-7.1 MHz, 14.00-14.25 MHz, 144-146 MHz, 435-438 MHz, 1260-1270 MHz and 2400-2450 MHz, 3.40-3.41 GHz, 5.65-5.67 GHz, 10.45-10.50 GHz and 24.00-24.05 GHz segments.

(d) A telecommand station may transmit one-way communications.

§ 97.213 Telecommand of an amateur station.

An amateur station on or within 50 km of the Earth's surface may be under telecommand where:

(a) There is a radio or wireline control link between the control point and the station sufficient for the control operator to perform his/her duties. If radio, the control link must use an auxiliary station. A control link using a fiber optic cable or another telecommunication service is considered a wireline.

(b) Provisions are incorporated to limit transmission by the station to a period of no more than 3 minutes in the event of malfunction in the control link.

(c) The station is protected against making, willfully or negligently, unauthorized transmissions.

(d) A photocopy of the station license and a label with the name, address, and telephone number of the station licensee and at least one designated control operator is posted in a conspicuous place at the station location.

§ 97.215 Telecommand of model craft.

An amateur station transmitting signals to control a model craft may be operated as follows:

(a) The station identification procedure is not required for transmissions directed only to the model craft, provided that a label indicating the station call sign and the station licensee's name and address is affixed to the station transmitter.

(b) The control signals are not considered codes or ciphers intended to obscure the meaning of the communication.

(c) The transmitter power must not exceed 1 W.

§ 97.216 Telemetry.

Telemetry transmitted by an amateur station on or within 50 km of the Earth's surface is not considered to be codes or ciphers intended to obscure the meaning of communications.

Subpart D—Technical Standards

§ 97.301 Authorized frequency bands.

The following transmitting frequency bands are available to an amateur station located within 50 km of the Earth's surface, within the specified ITU Region and outside any area where the amateur service is regulated by any authority other than the FCC.

§ 97.303 Frequency sharing requirements.

The following is a summary of the frequency sharing requirements that apply to amateur station transmissions on the frequency bands specified in §97.301 of this Part. (For each ITU Region, each frequency band allocated to the amateur service is designated as either a secondary service or a primary service. A station in a secondary service must not cause harmful interference to, and must accept interference from, stations in a primary service. See §§2.105 and 2.106 of the FCC Rules, *United States Table of Frequency Allocations* for complete requirements.)

(a) Where, in adjacent ITU Regions or Subregions, a band of frequencies is allocated to different services of the same category, the basic principle is the equality of right to operate. The stations of each service in one region must operate so as not to cause harmful interference to services in the other Regions or Subregions. (*See* ITU *Radio Regulations*, No. 346 (Geneva, 1979).)

(b) No amateur station transmitting in the 1900-2000 kHz seg-

(a) For a station having a control operator holding a Technician, General, Advanced or Amateur Extra Class operator license:

Wavelength band	ITU Region 1	ITU Region 2	ITU Region 3	Sharing requirements See §97.303, Paragraph:
VHF	MHz	MHz	MHz	
6 m	—	50-54	50-54	(a)
2 m	144-146	144-148	144-148	(a)
1.25 m	—	222-225	—	(a)
UHF	MHz	MHz	MHz	
70 cm	430-440	420-450	420-450	(a), (b), (f)
33 cm	—	902-928	—	(a), (b), (g)
23 cm	1240-1300	1240-1300	1240-1300	(h), (i)
13 cm	2300-2310	2300-2310	2300-2310	(a), (b), (j)
-do-	2390-2450	2390-2450	2390-2450	(a), (b), (j)
SHF	GHz	GHz	GHz	
9 cm	—	3.3-3.5	3.3-3.5	(a), (b), (k), (l)
5 cm	5.650-5.850	5.650-5.925	5.650-5.850	(a), (b), (m)
3 cm	10.00-10.50	10.00-10.50	10.00-10.50	(a), (b), (c), (i), (n)
1.2 cm	24.00-24.25	24.00-24.25	24.00-24.25	(a), (b), (h), (o)
EHF	GHz	GHz	GHz	
6 mm	47.0-47.2	47.0-47.2	47.0-47.2	
4 mm	75.5-81.0	75.5-81.0	75.5-81.0	(b), (c), (h)
2.5 mm	119.98-120.02	119.98-120.02	119.98-120.02	(k), (p)
2 mm	142-149	142-149	142-149	(b), (c), (h), (k)
1 mm	241-250	241-250	241-250	(b), (c), (h), (q)
—	above 300	above 300	above 300	(k)

(b) For a station having a control operator holding an Amateur Extra Class operator license:

Wavelength band	ITU Region 1	ITU Region 2	ITU Region 3	Sharing requirements See §97.303, Paragraph:
MF	kHz	kHz	kHz	
160 m	1810-1850	1800-2000	1800-2000	(a), (b), (c)
HF	MHz	MHz	MHz	
80 m	3.50-3.75	3.50-3.75	3.50-3.75	(a)
75 m	3.75-3.80	3.75-4.00	3.75-3.90	(a)
40 m	7.0-7.1	7.0-7.3	7.0-7.1	(a)
30 m	10.10-10.15	10.10-10.15	10.10-10.15	(d)
20 m	14.00-14.35	14.00-14.35	14.00-14.35	
17 m	18.068-18.168	18.068-18.168	18.068-18.168	
15 m	21.00-21.45	21.00-21.45	21.00-21.45	
12 m	24.89-24.99	24.89-24.99	24.89-24.99	
10 m	28.0-29.7	28.0-29.7	28.0-29.7	

(c) For a station having a control operator holding an Advanced Class operator license:

Wavelength band	ITU Region 1	ITU Region 2	ITU Region 3	Sharing requirements See §97.303, Paragraph:
MF	kHz	kHz	kHz	
160 m	1810-1850	1800-2000	1800-2000	(a), (b), (c)
HF	MHz	MHz	MHz	
80 m	3.525-3.750	3.525-3.750	3.525-3.750	(a)
75 m	3.775-3.800	3.775-4.000	3.775-3.900	(a)
40 m	7.025-7.100	7.025-7.300	7.025-7.100	(a)
30 m	10.10-10.15	10.10-10.15	10.10-10.15	(d)
20 m	14.025-14.150	14.025-14.150	14.025-14.150	
-do-	14.175-14.350	14.175-14.350	14.175-14.350	
17 m	18.068-18.168	18.068-18.168	18.068-18.168	
15 m	21.025-21.200	21.025-21.200	21.025-21.200	
-do-	21.225-21.450	21.225-21.450	21.225-21.450	
12 m	24.89-24.99	24.89-24.99	24.89-24.99	
10 m	28.0-29.7	28.0-29.7	28.0-29.7	

(d) For a station having a control operator holding a General Class operator license:

Wavelength band	ITU Region 1	ITU Region 2	ITU Region 3	Sharing requirements See §97.303, Paragraph:
MF	kHz	kHz	kHz	
160 m	1810-1850	1800-2000	1800-2000	(a), (b), (c)
HF	MHz	MHz	MHz	
80 m	3.525-3.750	3.525-3.750	3.525-3.750	(a)
75 m	—	3.85-4.00	3.85-3.90	(a)
40 m	7.025-7.100	7.025-7.150	7.025-7.100	(a)
-do-	—	7.225-7.300	—	(a)
30 m	10.10-10.15	10.10-10.15	10.10-10.15	(d)
20 m	14.025-14.150	14.025-14.150	14.025-14.150	
-do-	14.225-14.350	14.225-14.350	14.225-14.350	
17 m	18.068-18.168	18.068-18.168	18.068-18.168	
15 m	21.025-21.200	21.025-21.200	21.025-21.200	
-do-	21.30-21.45	21.30-21.45	21.30-21.45	
12 m	24.89-24.99	24.89-24.99	24.89-24.99	
10 m	28.0-29.7	28.0-29.7	28.0-29.7	

(e) For a station having a control operator holding a Novice Class operator license, or a Technician Class operator license plus a CSCE indicating that the person passed element 1(A), 1(B) or 1(C), or a Technician Class operator license issued before February 14, 1991:

Wavelength band	ITU Region 1	ITU Region 2	ITU Region 3	Sharing requirements See §97.303, Paragraph:
HF	MHz	MHz	MHz	
80 m	3.675-3.725	3.675-3.725	3.675-3.725	(a)
40 m	7.050-7.075	7.10-7.15	7.050-7.075	(a)
15 m	21.10-21.20	21.10-21.20	21.10-21.20	
10 m	28.1-28.5	28.1-28.5	28.1-28.5	

(f) For a station having a control operator holding a Novice Class operator license:

Wavelength band	ITU Region 1	ITU Region 2	ITU Region 3	Sharing requirements See §97.303, Paragraph:
VHF	MHz	MHz	MHz	
1.25 m	—	222.10-223.91	—	(a)
UHF	MHz	MHz	MHz	
23 cm	1270-1295	1270-1295	1270-1295	(i)

ment, the 70 cm band, the 33 cm band, the 13 cm band, the 9 cm band, the 5 cm band, the 3 cm band, the 24.05-24.25 GHz segment, the 76-81 GHz segment, the 144-149 GHz segment and the 241-248 GHz segment shall cause harmful interference to, nor is protected from interference due to the operation of, the Government radiolocation service.

(c) No amateur station transmitting in the 1900-2000 kHz segment, the 3 cm band, the 76-81 GHz segment, the 144-149 GHz segment and the 241-248 GHz segment shall cause harmful interference to, nor is protected from interference due to the operation of, stations in the non-Government radiolocation service.

(d) No amateur station transmitting in the 30 meter band shall cause harmful interference to stations authorized by other nations in the fixed service. The licensee of the amateur station must make all necessary adjustments, including termination of transmissions, if harmful interference is caused.

(e) (Removed per Report and Order, PR Docket No. 89-552, dated March 14, 1991.)

(f) In the 70 cm band:

(1) No amateur station shall transmit from north of Line A in the 420-430 MHz segment.

(2) The 420-430 MHz segment is allocated to the amateur service in the United States on a secondary basis, and is allocated in the fixed and mobile (except aeronautical mobile) services in the International Table of allocations on a primary basis. No amateur station transmitting in this band shall cause harmful interference to, nor is protected from interference due to the operation of, stations authorized by other nations in the fixed and mobile (except aeronautical mobile) services.

(3) The 430-440 MHz segment is allocated to the amateur service on a secondary basis in ITU Regions 2 and 3. No amateur station transmitting in this band in ITU Regions 2 and 3 shall cause harmful interference to, nor is protected from interference due to the operation of, stations authorized by other nations in the radiolocation service. In ITU Region 1, the 430-440 MHz segment is allocated to the amateur service on a co-primary basis with the radiolocation service. As between these two services in this band in ITU Region 1, the basic principle that applies is the equality of right to operate. Amateur stations authorized by the United States and radiolocation stations authorized by other nations in ITU Region 1 shall operate so as not to cause harmful interference to each other.

(4) No amateur station transmitting in the 449.75-450.25 MHz segment shall cause interference to, nor is protected from interference due to the operation of stations in, the space operation service and the space research service or Government or non-Government stations for space telecommand.

(g) In the 33 cm band:

(1) No amateur station shall transmit from within the States of Colorado and Wyoming, bounded on the south by latitude 39°N, on the north by latitude 42°N, on the east by longitude 105° W, and on the west by longitude 108° W. This band is allocated on a secondary basis to the amateur service subject to not causing harmful interference to, and not receiving protection from any interference due to the operation of, industrial, scientific and medical devices, automatic vehicle monitoring systems or Government stations authorized in this band.

(2) No amateur station shall transmit from those portions of the States of Texas and New Mexico bounded on the south by latitude 31° 41' N, on the north by latitude 34° 30' N, on the east by longitude 104° 11' W, and on the west by longitude 107° 30' W.

(h) No amateur station transmitting in the 23 cm band, the 3 cm band, the 24.05-24.25 GHz segment, the 76-81 GHz segment, the 144-149 GHz segment and the 241-248 GHz segment shall cause harmful interference to, nor is protected from interference due to the operation of, stations authorized by other nations in the radiolocation service.

(i) In the 1240-1260 MHz segment, no amateur station shall cause harmful interference to, nor is protected from interference due to the operation of, stations in the radionavigation-satellite service, the aeronautical radionavigation service, or the radiolocation service.

(j) In the 13 cm band:

(1) The amateur service is allocated on a secondary basis in all ITU Regions. In ITU Region 1, no amateur station shall cause harmful interference to, and is not protected from interference due to the operation of, stations authorized by other nations in the fixed service. In ITU Regions 2 and 3, no station shall cause harmful interference to, and is not protected from interference due to the operation of, stations authorized by other nations in the fixed, mobile and radiolocation services.

(2) In the United States, the 2300-2310 MHz segment is allocated to the amateur service on a co-secondary basis with the Government fixed and mobile services. In this segment, the fixed and mobile services must not cause harmful interference to the amateur service. No amateur station transmitting in the 2400-2450 MHz segment is protected from interference due to the operation of industrial, scientific and medical devices on 2450 MHz.

(k) No amateur station transmitting in the 3.332-3.339 GHz and 3.3458-3525 GHz segments, the 2.5 mm band, the 144.68-144.98 GHz, 145.45-145.75 GHz and 146.82-147.12 GHz segments and the 343-348 GHz segment shall cause harmful interference to stations in the radio astronomy service. No amateur station transmitting in the 300-302 GHz, 324-326 GHz, 345-347 GHz, 363-365 GHz and 379-381 GHz segments shall cause harmful interference to stations in the space research service (passive) or Earth exploration-satellite service (passive).

(l) In the 9 cm band:

(1) In ITU Regions 2 and 3, the band is allocated to the amateur service on a secondary basis.

(2) In the United States, the band is allocated to the amateur service on a co-secondary basis with the non-Government radiolocation service.

(3) In the 3.3-3.4 GHz segment, no amateur station shall cause harmful interference to, nor is protected from interference due to the operation of, stations authorized by other nations in the radiolocation service.

(4) In the 3.4-3.5 GHz segment, no amateur station shall cause harmful interference to, nor is protected from interference due to the operation of, stations authorized by other nations in the fixed and fixed-satellite service.

(m) In the 5 cm band:

(1) In the 5.650-5.725 GHz segment, the amateur service is allocated in all ITU Regions on a co-secondary basis with the space research (deep space) service.

(2) In the 5.725-5.850 GHz segment, the amateur service is allocated in all ITU Regions on a secondary basis. No amateur station shall cause harmful interference to, nor is protected from interference due to the operation of, stations authorized by other nations in the fixed-satellite service in ITU Region 1.

(3) No amateur station transmitting in the 5.725-5.875 GHz segment is protected from interference due to the operation of industrial, scientific and medical devices operating on 5.8 GHz.

(4) In the 5.650-5.850 GHz segment, no amateur station shall cause harmful interference to, nor is protected from interference due to the operation of, stations authorized by other nations in the radiolocation service.

(5) In the 5.850-5.925 GHz segment, the amateur service is allocated in ITU Region 2 on a co-secondary basis with the radiolocation service. In the United States, the segment is allocated to the amateur service on a secondary basis to the non-Government fixed-satellite service. No amateur station shall cause harmful interference to, nor is protected from interference due to the operation of, stations authorized by other nations in the fixed, fixed-satellite and mobile services. No amateur station shall cause harmful interference to, nor is protected from interference due to the operation of, stations in the non-Government fixed-satellite service.

(n) In the 3 cm band:

(1) In the United States, the 3 cm band is allocated to the amateur service on a co-secondary basis with the non-government radiolocation service.

(2)In the 10.00-10.45 GHz segment in ITU Regions 1 and 3, no amateur station shall cause interference to, nor is protected from interference due to the operation of, stations authorized by other nations in the fixed and mobile services.

(o) No amateur station transmitting in the 1.2 cm band is protected from interference due to the operation of industrial, scientific and medical devices on 24.125 GHz. In the United States, the 24.05-24.25 GHz segment is allocated to the amateur service on a co-secondary basis with the non-government radiolocation and Government and non-government Earth exploration-satellite (active) services.

(p) The 2.5 mm band is allocated to the amateur service on a secondary basis. No amateur station transmitting in this band shall cause harmful interference to, nor is protected from interference due to the operation of, stations in the fixed, inter-satellite and mobile services.

(q) No amateur station transmitting in the 244-246 GHz segment of the 1 mm band is protected from interference due to the operation of industrial, scientific and medical devices on 245 GHz.

§ 97.305 Authorized emission types.

(a) An amateur station may transmit a CW emission on any frequency authorized to the control operator.

(b) A station may transmit a test emission on any frequency authorized to the control operator for brief periods for experimental purposes, except that no pulse modulation emission may be transmitted on any frequency where pulse is not specifically authorized.

(c) A station may transmit the following emission types on the frequencies indicated, as authorized to the control operator, subject to the standards specified in §97.307(f) of this Part.

§ 97.307 Emission standards.

(a) No amateur station transmission shall occupy more bandwidth than necessary for the information rate and emission type being transmitted, in accordance with good amateur practice.

(b) Emissions resulting from modulation must be confined to the band or segment available to the control operator. Emissions outside the necessary bandwidth must not cause splatter or keyclick interference to operations on adjacent frequencies.

(c) All spurious emissions from a station transmitter must be reduced to the greatest extent practicable. If any spurious emission, including chassis or power line radiation, causes harmful interference to the reception of another radio station, the licensee of the interfering amateur station is required to take steps to eliminate the interference, in accordance with good engineering practice.

(d) The mean power of any spurious emission from a station transmitter or external RF power amplifier transmitting on a frequency below 30 MHz must not exceed 50 mW and must be at least 40 dB below the mean power of the fundamental emission. For a transmitter of mean power less than 5 W, the attenuation must be at least 30 dB. A transmitter built before April, 15, 1977, or first marketed before January 1, 1978, is exempt from this requirement.

(e) The mean power of any spurious emission from a station

Wavelength band	Frequencies authorized	Emission types	Standards See §97.307(f), Paragraph:
MF:			
160 m	Entire band	RTTY, data	(3)
-do-	Entire band	Phone, image	(1), (2)
HF:			
80 m	Entire band	RTTY, data	(3), (9)
75 m	Entire band	Phone, image	(1), (2)
40 m	7.000-7.100 MHz	RTTY, data	(3), (9)
-do-	7.075-7.100 MHz	Phone, image	(1), (2), (9), (11)
-do-	7.100-7.150 MHz	RTTY, data(3), (9)	
-do-	7.150-7.300 MHz	Phone, image(1), (2)	
30 m	Entire band	RTTY, data	(3)
20 m	14.00-14.15 Mhz	RTTY, data	(3)
-do-	14.15-14.35 Mhz	Phone, image	(1), (2)
17 m	18.068-18.110 MHz	RTTY, data	(3)
-do-	18.110-18.168 MHz	Phone, image	(1), (2)
15 m	21.0-21.2 MHz	RTTY, data	(3), (9)
-do-	21.20-21.45 MHz	Phone, image	(1), (2)
12 m	24.89-24.93 MHz	RTTY, data	(3)
-do-	24.93-24.99 MHz	Phone, image	(1), (2)
10 m	28.0-28.3 MHz	RTTY, data	(4)
-do-	28.3-28.5 MHz	Phone, image	(1), (2), (10)
-do-	28.5-29.0 MHz	Phone, image	(1), (2)
-do-	29.0-29.7 MHz	Phone, image	(2)
VHF:			
6 m	50.1-51.0 MHz	MCW, phone, image, RTTY, data	(2),(5)
-do-	51.0-54.0 MHz	MCW, phone, image, RTTY, data, test	(2), (5), (8)
2 m	144.1-148.0 MHz	MCW, phone, image, RTTY, data, test	(2), (5), (8)
1.25 m	Entire band	MCW, phone, image, RTTY, data, test	(2), (6), (8)
UHF:			
70 cm	Entire band	MCW, phone, image, RTTY, data, SS, test	(6), (8)
33 cm	Entire band	MCW, phone, image, RTTY, data, SS, test, pulse	(7), (8), (12)
23 cm	Entire band	MCW, phone, image, RTTY, data, SS, test	(7), (8), (12)
13 cm	Entire band	MCW, phone, image, RTTY, data, SS, test, pulse	(7), (8), (12)
SHF:			
9 cm	Entire band	MCW, phone, image, RTTY, data, SS, test, pulse	(7), (8), (12)
5 cm	Entire band	MCW, phone, image, RTTY, data, SS, test, pulse	(7), (8), (12)
3 cm	Entire band	MCW, phone, image, RTTY, data, SS, test	(7), (8), (12)
1.2 cm	Entire band	MCW, phone, image, RTTY, data, SS, test, pulse	(7), (8), (12)
EHF:			
6 mm	Entire band	MCW, phone, image, RTTY, data, SS, test, pulse	(7), (8), (12)
4 mm	Entire band	MCW, phone, image, RTTY, data, SS, test, pulse	(7), (8), (12)
2.5 mm	Entire band	MCW, phone, image, RTTY, data, SS, test, pulse	(7), (8), (12)
2 mm	Entire band	MCW, phone, image, RTTY, data, SS, test, pulse	(7), (8), (12)
1 mm	Entire band	MCW, phone, image, RTTY, data, SS, test, pulse	(7), (8), (12)
—	Above 300 GHz	MCW, phone, image, RTTY, data, SS, test, pulse	(7), (8), (12)

transmitter or external RF power amplifier transmitting on a frequency between 30-225 MHz must be at least 60 dB below the mean power of the fundamental. For a transmitter having a mean power of 25 W or less, the mean power of any spurious emission supplied to the antenna transmission line must not exceed 25 uW and must be at least 40 dB below the mean power of the fundamental emission, but need not be reduced below the power of 10 uW. A transmitter built before April 15, 1977, or first marketed before January 1, 1978, is exempt from this requirement.

(f) The following standards and limitations apply to transmissions on the frequencies specified in §97.305(c) of this Part.

(1) No angle-modulated emission may have a modulation index greater than 1 at the highest modulation frequency.

(2) No non-phone emission shall exceed the bandwidth of a communications quality phone emission of the same modulation type. The total bandwidth of an independent sideband emission (having B as the first symbol), or a multiplexed image and phone emission, shall not exceed that of a communications quality A3E emission.

(3) Only a RTTY or data emission using a specified digital code listed in §97.309(a) of this Part may be transmitted. The symbol rate must not exceed 300 bauds, or for frequency-shift keying, the frequency shift between mark and space must not exceed 1 kHz.

(4) Only a RTTY or data emission using a specified digital code listed in §97.309(a) of this Part may be transmitted. The symbol rate must not exceed 1200 bauds, or for frequency-shift keying, the frequency shift between mark and space must not exceed 1 kHz.

(5) A RTTY, data or multiplexed emission using a specified digital code listed in §97.309(a) of this Part may be transmitted. The symbol rate must not exceed 19.6 kilobauds. A RTTY, data or multiplexed emission using an unspecified digital code under the limitations listed in §97.309(b) of this Part also may be transmitted. The authorized bandwidth is 20 kHz.

(6) A RTTY, data or multiplexed emission using a specified dig-

ital code listed in §97.309(a) of this Part may be transmitted. The symbol rate must not exceed 56 kilobauds. A RTTY, data or multiplexed emission using an unspecified digital code under the limitations listed in §97.309(b) of this Part also may be transmitted. The authorized bandwidth is 100 kHz.

(7) A RTTY, data or multiplexed emission using a specified digital code listed in §97.309(a) of this Part or an unspecified digital code under the limitations listed in §97.309(b) of this Part may be transmitted.

(8) A RTTY or data emission having designators with A, B, C, D, E, F, G, H, J or R as the first symbol; 1, 2, 7 or 9 as the second symbol; and D or W as the third symbol is also authorized.

(9) A station having a control operator holding a Novice or Technician Class operator license may only transmit a CW emission using the international Morse code.

(10) A station having a control operator holding a Novice or Technician Class operator license may only transmit a CW emission using the international Morse code or phone emissions J3E and R3E.

(11) Phone and image emissions may be transmitted only by stations located in ITU Regions 1 and 3, and by stations located within ITU Region 2 that are west of 130° West longitude or south of 20° North latitude.

(12) Emission F8E may be transmitted.

§ 97.309 RTTY and data emission codes.

(a) Where authorized by §§97.305(c) and 97.307(f) of this Part, an amateur station may transmit a RTTY or data emission using the following specified digital codes:

(1) The 5-unit, start-stop, International Telegraph Alphabet No. 2, code defined in International Telegraph and Telephone Consultative Committee Recommendation F.1, Division C (commonly known as Baudot).

(2) The 7-unit code specified in International Radio Consultative Committee Recommendation CCIR 476-2 (1978), 476-3 (1982), 476-4 (1986) or 625 (1986) (commonly known as AMTOR).

(3) The 7-unit code defined in American National Standards Institute X3.4-1977 or International Alphabet No. 5 defined in International Telegraph and Telephone Consultative Committee Recommendation T.50 or in International Organization for Standardization, International Standard ISO 646 (1983), and extensions as provided for in CCITT Recommendation T.61 (Malaga-Torremolinos, 1984) (commonly known as ASCII).

(b) Where authorized by §§97.305(c) and 97.307(f) of this Part, a station may transmit a RTTY or data emission using an unspecified digital code, except to a station in a country with which the United States does not have an agreement permitting the code to be used. RTTY and data emissions using unspecified digital codes must not be transmitted for the purpose of obscuring the meaning of any communication. When deemed necessary by an EIC to assure compliance with the FCC Rules, a station must:

(1) Cease the transmission using the unspecified digital code;

(2) Restrict transmissions of any digital code to the extent instructed;

(3) Maintain a record, convertible to the original information, of all digital communications transmitted.

§ 97.311 SS emission types.

(a) SS emission transmissions by an amateur station are authorized only for communications between points within areas where the amateur service is regulated by the FCC. SS emission transmissions must not be used for the purpose of obscuring the meaning of any communication.

(b) Stations transmitting SS emission must not cause harmful interference to stations employing other authorized emissions, and must accept all interference caused by stations employing other authorized emissions. For the purposes of this paragraph, unintended triggering of carrier operated repeaters is not considered to be harmful interference.

(c) Only the following types of SS emission transmissions are authorized (hybrid SS emissions transmissions involving both spreading techniques are prohibited):

(1) Frequency hopping where the carrier of the transmitted signal is modulated with unciphered information and changes frequency at fixed intervals under the direction of a high speed code sequence.

(2) Direct sequence where the information is modulo-2 added to a high speed code sequence. The combined information and code are then used to modulate the RF carrier. The high speed code sequence dominates the modulation function, and is the direct cause of the wide spreading of the transmitted signal.

(d) The only spreading sequences that are authorized are from the output of one binary linear feedback shift register (which may be implemented in hardware or software).

(1) Only the following sets of connections may be used:

Number of stages in shift register	Taps used in feedback
7	7, 1
13	13, 4, 3, 1
19	19, 5, 2, 1

(2) The shift register must not be reset other than by its feedback during an individual transmission. The shift register output sequence must be used without alteration.

(3) The output of the last stage of the binary linear feedback shift register must be used as follows:

(i) For frequency hopping transmissions using x frequencies, n consecutive bits from the shift register must be used to select the next frequency from a list of frequencies sorted in ascending order. Each consecutive frequency must be selected by a consecutive block of n bits. (Where n is the smallest integer greater than $\log_2 x$.)

(ii) For direct sequence transmissions using m-ary modulation, consecutive blocks of $\log_2 m$ bits from the shift register must be used to select the transmitted signal during each interval.

(e) The station records must document all SS emission transmissions and must be retained for a period of 1 year following the last entry. The station records must include sufficient information to enable the FCC, using the information contained therein, to demodulate all transmissions. The station records must contain at least the following:

(1) A technical description of the transmitted signal;

(2) Pertinent parameters describing the transmitted signal including the frequency or frequencies of operation and, where applicable, the chip rate, the code rate, the spreading function, the transmission protocol(s) including the method of achieving synchronization, and the modulation type;

(3) A general description of the type of information being conveyed, (voice, text, memory dump, facsimile, television, etc.);

(4) The method and, if applicable, the frequency or frequencies used for station identification; and

(5) The date of beginning and the date of ending use of each type of transmitted signal.

(f) When deemed necessary by an EIC to assure compliance with this Part, a station licensee must:

(1) Cease SS emission transmissions;

(2) Restrict SS emission transmissions to the extent instructed; and

(3) Maintain a record, convertible to the original information (voice, text, image, etc.) of all spread spectrum communications transmitted.

(g) The transmitter power must not exceed 100 W.

§ 97.313 Transmitter power standards.

(a) An amateur station must use the minimum power necessary to carry out the desired communications.

(b) No station may transmit with a transmitter power exceeding 1.5 kW PEP.

(c) No station may transmit with a transmitter power exceeding 200 W PEP on:

(1) The 3.675-3.725 MHz, 7.10-7.15 MHz, 10.10-10.15 MHz and 21.1-21.2 MHz segments;

(2) The 28.1-28.5 MHz segment when the control operator is a Novice or Technician operator; or

(3) The 7.050-7.075 MHz segment when the station is within ITU Regions 1 or 3.

(d) No station may transmit with a transmitter power exceeding 25 W PEP on the VHF 1.25 m band when the control operator is a

Novice operator.

(e) No station may transmit with a transmitter power exceeding 5 W PEP on the UHF 23 cm band when the control operator is a Novice operator.

(f) No station may transmit with a transmitter power exceeding 50 W PEP on the UHF 70 cm band from an area specified in footnote US7 to §2.106 of the FCC Rules, unless expressly authorized by the FCC after mutual agreement, on a case-by-case basis, between the EIC of the applicable field facility and the military area frequency coordinator at the applicable military base. An Earth station or telecommand station, however, may transmit on the 435-438 MHz segment with a maximum of 611 W effective radiated power (1 kW equivalent isotropically radiated power) without the authorization otherwise required. The transmitting antenna elevation angle between the lower half-power (-3 dB relative to the peak or antenna bore sight) point and the horizon must always be greater than 10°.

(g) No station may transmit with a transmitter power exceeding 50 W PEP on the 33 cm band from within 241 km of the boundaries of the White Sands Missile Range. Its boundaries are those portions of Texas and New Mexico bounded on the south by latitude 31° 41' North, on the east by longitude 104° 11' West, on the north by latitude 34° 30' North, and on the west by longitude 107° 30' West.

§ 97.315 Type acceptance of external RF power amplifiers.

(a) No more than 1 unit of 1 model of an external RF power amplifier capable of operation below 144 MHz may be constructed or modified during any calendar year by an amateur operator for use at a station without a grant of type acceptance. No amplifier capable of operation below 144 MHz may be constructed or modified by a non-amateur operator without a grant of type acceptance from the FCC.

(b) Any external RF power amplifier or external RF power amplifier kit (see §2.815 of the FCC Rules), manufactured, imported or modified for use in a station or attached at any station must be type accepted for use in the amateur service in accordance with Subpart J of Part 2 of the FCC Rules. This requirement does not apply if one or more of the following conditions are met:

(1) The amplifier is not capable of operation on frequencies below 144 MHz. For the purpose of this part, an amplifier will be deemed to be incapable of operation below 144 MHz if it is not capable of being easily modified to increase its amplification characteristics below 120 MHz and either:

(i) The mean output power of the amplifier decreases, as frequency decreases from 144 MHz, to a point where 0 dB or less gain is exhibited at 120 MHz; or

(ii) The amplifier is not capable of amplifying signals below 120 MHz even for brief periods without sustaining permanent damage to its amplification circuitry.

(2) The amplifier was manufactured before April 28, 1978, and has been issued a marketing waiver by the FCC, or the amplifier was purchased before April 28, 1978, by an amateur operator for use at that amateur operator's station.

(3) The amplifier was:

(i) Constructed by the licensee, not from an external RF power amplifier kit, for use at the licensee's station; or

(ii) Modified by the licensee for use at the licensee's station.

(4) The amplifier is sold by an amateur operator to another amateur operator or to a dealer.

(5) The amplifier is purchased in used condition by an equipment dealer from an amateur operator and the amplifier is further sold to another amateur operator for use at that operator's station.

(c) A list of type accepted equipment may be inspected at FCC headquarters in Washington, DC, or at any FCC field location. Any external RF power amplifier appearing on this list as type accepted for use in the amateur service may be marketed for use in the amateur service.

§ 97.317 Standards for type acceptance of external RF power amplifiers.

(a) To receive a grant of type acceptance, the amplifier must satisfy the spurious emission standards of §97.307(d) or (e) of this Part, as applicable, when the amplifier is:

(1) Operated at its full output power;

(2) Placed in the "standby" or "off" positions, but still connected to the transmitter; and

(3) Driven with at least 50 W mean RF input power (unless a higher drive level is specified).

(b) To receive a grant of type acceptance, the amplifier must not be capable of operation on any frequency or frequencies between 24 MHz and 35 MHz. The amplifier will be deemed incapable of such operation if it:

(1) Exhibits no more than 6 dB gain between 24 MHz and 26 MHz and between 28 MHz and 35 MHz. (This gain will be determined by the ratio of the input RF driving signal (mean power measurement) to the mean RF output power of the amplifier); and

(2) Exhibits no amplification (0 dB gain) between 26 MHz and 28 MHz.

(c) Type acceptance may be denied when denial would prevent the use of these amplifiers in services other than the amateur service. The following features will result in dismissal or denial of an application for type acceptance:

(1) Any accessible wiring which, when altered, would permit operation of the amplifier in a manner contrary to the FCC Rules;

(2) Circuit boards or similar circuitry to facilitate the addition of components to change the amplifier's operating characteristics in a manner contrary to the FCC Rules;

(3)Instructions for operation or modification of the amplifier in a manner contrary to FCC Rules;

(4) Any internal or external controls or adjustments to facilitate operation of the amplifier in a manner contrary to the FCC Rules;

(5) Any internal RF sensing circuitry or any external switch, the purpose of which is to place the amplifier in the transmit mode;

(6) The incorporation of more gain in the amplifier than is necessary to operate in the amateur service; for purposes of this paragraph, the amplifier must:

(i) Not be capable of achieving designed output power when driven with less than 50 W mean RF input power;

(ii) Not be capable of amplifying the input RF driving signal by more than 15 dB, unless the amplifier has a designed transmitter power of less than 1.5 kW (in such a case, gain must be reduced by the same number of dB as the transmitter power relationship to 1.5 kW; This gain limitation is determined by the ratio of the input RF driving signal to the RF output power of the amplifier where both signals are expressed in peak envelope power or mean power);

(iii) Not exhibit more gain than permitted by paragraph (c)(6)(ii) of this Section when driven by an RF input signal of less than 50 W mean power; and

(iv) Be capable of sustained operation at its designed power level;

(7) Any attenuation of the input of the amplifier which, when removed or modified, would permit the amplifier to function at its designed transmitter power when driven by an RF frequency input signal of less than 50 W mean power; or

(8) Any other features designed to facilitate operation in a telecommunication service other than the Amateur Radio Services, such as the Citizens Band (CB) Radio Service.

Subpart E—Providing Emergency Communications

§ 97.401 Operation during a disaster.

(a) When normal communication systems are overloaded, damaged or disrupted because a disaster has occurred, or is likely to occur, in an area where the amateur service is regulated by the FCC, an amateur station may make transmissions necessary to meet essential communication needs and facilitate relief actions.

(b) When normal communication systems are overloaded, damaged or disrupted because a natural disaster has occurred, or is likely to occur, in an area where the amateur service is not regulated by the FCC, a station assisting in meeting essential communication needs and facilitating relief actions may do so only in accord with ITU Resolution No. 640 (Geneva, 1979). The 80 m, 75 m, 40 m, 30 m, 20 m, 17 m, 15 m, 12 m and 2 m bands may be used for these purposes.

(c) When a disaster disrupts normal communication systems in a particular area, the FCC may declare a temporary state of communication emergency. The declaration will set forth any special conditions and special rules to be observed by stations during the communication emergency. A request for a declaration of a temporary state of emergency should be directed to the EIC in the area concerned.

(d) A station in, or within 92.6 km, of Alaska may transmit emissions J3E and R3E on the channel at 5.1675 MHz for emergency communications. The channel must be shared with stations licensed in the Alaska-private fixed service. The transmitter power must not exceed 150 W.

§ 97.403 Safety of life and protection of property.

No provision of these rules prevents the use by an amateur station of any means of radiocommunication at its disposal to provide essential communication needs in connection with the immediate safety of human life and immediate protection of property when normal communication systems are not available.

§ 97.405 Station in distress.

(a) No provision of these rules prevents the use by an amateur station in distress of any means at its disposal to attract attention, make known its condition and location, and obtain assistance.

(b) No provision of these rules prevents the use by a station, in the exceptional circumstances described in paragraph (a), of any means of radiocommunications at its disposal to assist a station in distress.

§ 97.407 Radio Amateur Civil Emergency Service.

(a) No station may transmit in RACES unless it is an FCC-licensed primary, club, or military recreation station and it is certified by a civil defense organization as registered with that organization, or it is an FCC-licensed RACES station. No person may be the control operator of a RACES station, or may be the control operator of an amateur station transmitting in RACES unless that person holds an FCC-issued amateur operator license and is certified by a civil defense organization as enrolled in that organization.

(b) The frequency bands and segments and emissions authorized to the control operator are available to stations transmitting communications in RACES on a shared basis with the amateur service. In the event of an emergency which necessitates the invoking of the President's War Emergency Powers under the provisions of Section 706 of the Communications Act of 1934, as amended, 47 U.S.C. §606, RACES stations and amateur stations participating in RACES may only transmit on the following frequencies:

(1) The 1800-1825 kHz, 1975-2000 kHz, 3.50-3.55 MHz, 3.93-3.98 MHz, 3.984-4.000 MHz, 7.079-7.125 MHz, 7.245-7.255 MHz, 10.10-10.15 MHz, 14.047-14.053 MHz, 14.22-14.23 MHz, 14.331-14.350 MHz, 21.047-21.053 MHz, 21.228-21.267 MHz, 28.55-28.75 MHz, 29.237-29.273 MHz, 29.45-29.65 MHz, 50.35-50.75 MHz, 52-54 MHz, 144.50-145.71 MHz, 146-148 MHz, 2390-2450 MHz segments;

(2) The 1.25 m, 70 cm and 23 cm bands; and

(3) The channels at 3.997 MHz and 53.30 MHz may be used in emergency areas when required to make initial contact with a military unit and for communications with military stations on matters requiring coordination.

(c) A RACES station may only communicate with:

(1) Another RACES station;

(2) An amateur station registered with a civil defense organization;

(3) A United States Government station authorized by the responsible agency to communicate with RACES stations;

(4) A station in a service regulated by the FCC whenever such communication is authorized by the FCC.

(d) An amateur station registered with a civil defense organization may only communicate with:

(1) A RACES station licensed to the civil defense organization with which the amateur station is registered;

(2) The following stations upon authorization of the responsible civil defense official for the organization with which the amateur station is registered:

(i) A RACES station licensed to another civil defense organization;

(ii) An amateur station registered with the same or another civil defense organization;

(iii) A United States Government station authorized by the responsible agency to communicate with RACES stations; and

(iv) A station in a service regulated by the FCC whenever such communication is authorized by the FCC.

(e) All communications transmitted in RACES must be specifically authorized by the civil defense organization for the area served. Only civil defense communications of the following types may be transmitted:

(1) Messages concerning impending or actual conditions jeopardizing the public safety, or affecting the national defense or security during periods of local, regional or national civil emergencies;

(2) Messages directly concerning the immediate safety of life of individuals, the immediate protection of property, maintenance of law and order, alleviation of human suffering and need, and the combating of armed attack or sabotage;

(3) Messages directly concerning the accumulation and dissemination of public information or instructions to the civilian population essential to the activities of the civil defense organization or other authorized governmental or relief agencies; and

(4) Communications for RACES training drills and tests necessary to ensure the establishment and maintenance of orderly and efficient operation of the RACES as ordered by the responsible civil defense organization served. Such drills and tests may not exceed a total time of 1 hour per week. With the approval of the chief officer for emergency planning in the applicable State, Commonwealth, District or territory, however, such tests and drills may be conducted for a period not to exceed 72 hours no more than twice in any calendar year.

Subpart F—Qualifying Examination Systems

§ 97.501 Qualifying for an amateur operator license.

An applicant must pass an examination for the issuance of a new amateur operator license and for each change in operator class. Each applicant for the class of operator license specified below must pass, or otherwise receive examination credit for, the following examination elements:

(a) Amateur Extra Class operator: Elements 1(C), 2, 3(A), 3(B), 4(A) and 4(B);

(b) Advanced Class operator: Elements 1(B) or 1(C), 2, 3(A), 3(B) and 4(A);

(c) General Class operator: Elements 1(B) or 1(C), 2, 3(A) and 3(B);

(d) Technician Class operator: Elements 2 and 3(A);

(e) Novice Class operator: Elements 1(A) or 1(B) or 1(C), and 2.

§ 97.503 Element standards.

(a) A telegraphy examination must be sufficient to prove that the examinee has the ability to send correctly by hand and to receive correctly by ear texts in the international Morse code at not less than the prescribed speed, using all the letters of the alphabet, numerals 0-9, period, comma, question mark, slant mark and prosigns $\overline{AR}$, $\overline{BT}$ and $\overline{SK}$.

(1) Element 1(A): 5 words per minute;

(2) Element 1(B): 13 words per minute;

(3) Element 1(C): 20 words per minute.

(b) A written examination must be such as to prove that the examinee possesses the operational and technical qualifications required to perform properly the duties of an amateur service licensee. Each written examination must be comprised of a question set as follows:

(1) Element 2: 30 questions concerning the privileges of a Novice Class operator license. The minimum passing score is 22 questions answered correctly.

(2) Element 3(A): 25 questions concerning the additional privileges of a Technician Class operator license. The minimum passing score is 19 questions answered correctly.

(3) Element 3(B): 25 questions concerning the additional privileges of a General Class operator license. The minimum passing score is 19 questions answered correctly.

(4) Element 4(A): 50 questions concerning the additional privileges of an Advanced Class operator license. The minimum passing score is 37 questions answered correctly.

(5) Element 4(B): 40 questions concerning the additional privi-

leges of an Amateur Extra Class operator license. The minimum passing score is 30 questions answered correctly.

(c) The topics and number of questions required in each question set are listed below for the appropriate examination element:

§ 97.505 Element credit.

(a) The administering VEs must give credit as specified below to an examinee holding any of the following documents:

(1) An unexpired (or within the grace period) FCC-issued amateur operator license: The least elements required for the license held. For a Technician Class operator license issued before March 21, 1987, credit must also be given for Element 3(B).

(2) A CSCE: Each element the CSCE indicates the examinee passed within the previous 365 days.

(3) A photocopy of an FCC Form 610 which was submitted to the FCC indicating the examinee qualified for a Novice Class operator license within the previous 365 days: Elements 1(A) and 2.

(4) An unexpired (or expired less than 5 years) FCC-issued commercial radiotelegraph operator license or permit: Element 1(C).

(5) A current, or expired but within the grace period for renewal, Novice, Technician plus a CSCE indicating that the person passed element 1(A) or 1(B), Technician issued before February 14, 1991, General or Advanced Class operator license, and a Form 610 containing:

(i) A physician's certification stating that because the person is an individual with a severe handicap, the duration of which extends for more than 365 days beyond the date of certification, the person is unable to pass a 13 or 20 words per minute telegraphy examination; and

(ii) A release signed by the person permitting the disclosure to the FCC of medical information pertaining to the person's handicap: Element 1(C).

(b) No examination credit, except as herein provided, shall be allowed on the basis of holding or having held any other license.

§ 97.507 Preparing an examination.

(a) Each telegraphy message and each written question set administered to an examinee must be prepared by a VE holding an FCC-issued Amateur Extra Class operator license. A telegraphy message or written question set, however, may also be prepared for the following elements by a VE holding an FCC-issued operator license of the Class indicated:

(1) Element 3(B): Advanced Class operator.

(2) Elements 1(A) and 3(A): Advanced or General Class operator.

(3) Element 2: Advanced, General or Technician Class operator.

(b) Each question set administered to an examinee must utilize questions taken from the applicable question pool.

(c) Each telegraphy message and each written question set administered to an examinee for an amateur operator license must be prepared, or obtained from a supplier, by the administering VEs according to instructions from the coordinating VEC.

(d) A telegraphy examination must consist of a message sent in the international Morse code at no less than the prescribed speed for a minimum of 5 minutes. The message must contain each required telegraphy character at least once. No message known to the examinee may be administered in a telegraphy examination. Each 5 letters of the alphabet must be counted as 1 word. Each numeral, punctuation mark and prosign must be counted as 2 letters of the alphabet.

§ 97.509 Administering an examination.

(a) Each examination for an amateur operator license must be administered at a location and a time specified by the administering VEs. Each administering VE must be present and observe the examinee throughout the entire examination. The administering VEs are responsible for the proper conduct and necessary supervision of each examination. The administering VEs must immediately terminate the examination upon failure of the examinee to comply with their instructions.

(b) Each examinee must comply with the instructions given by the administering VEs.

(c) No examination that has been compromised shall be administered to any examinee. Neither the same telegraphy message nor the same question set may be readministered to the same examinee.

Topics	Element 2	3(A)	3(B)	4(A)	4(B)
(1) FCC rules for the amateur radio services	10	5	4	6	8
(2) Amateur station operating procedures	2	3	3	1	4
(3) Radio wave propagation characteristics of amateur service frequency bands	1	3	3	2	2
(4) Amateur radio practices	4	4	5	4	4
(5) Electrical principles as applied to amateurstation equipment	4	2	2	10	6
(6) Amateur station equipment circuit components	2	2	1	6	4
(7) Practical circuits employed in amateur station equipment	2	1	1	10	4
(8) Signals and emissions transmitted by amateur stations	2	2	2	6	4
(9) Amateur station antennas and feed lines	3	3	4	5	4

(d) Passing a telegraphy receiving examination is adequate proof of an examinee's ability to both send and receive telegraphy. The administering VEs, however, may also include a sending segment in a telegraphy examination.

(e) Upon completion of each examination element, the administering VEs must immediately grade the examinee's answers. The administering VEs are responsible for determining the correctness of the examinee's answers.

(f) When the examinee is credited for all examination elements required for the operator license sought, the administering VEs must certify on the examinee's application form that the applicant is qualified for the license and report the basis for the qualification.

(g) When the examinee does not score a passing grade on an examination element, the administering VEs must return the application form to the examinee and inform the examinee of the grade.

(h) The administering VEs must accommodate an examinee whose physical disabilities require a special examination procedure. The administering VEs may require a physician's certification indicating the nature of the disability before determining which, if any, special procedures must be used.

(i) The FCC may:

(1) Administer any examination element itself;

(2) Readminister any examination element previously administered by VEs, either itself or under the supervision of VEs designated by the FCC; or

(3) Cancel the operator and station licenses of any licensee who fails to appear for readministration of an examination when directed by the FCC, or who does not successfully complete any required element which is readministered. In an instance of such cancellation, the person will be issued operator and station licenses consistent with completed examination elements that have not been invalidated by not appearing for, or by failing, the examination upon readministration.

§ 97.511 Amateur operator license examination.

(a) Each session where an examination for an amateur operator license is administered must be coordinated by a VEC. Each administering VE must be accredited by the coordinating VEC.

(b) Each examination must be administered by 3 VEs, each of whom must hold an FCC-issued amateur operator license of the class specified below:

(1) For a Novice or Technician Class operator license examination, the administering VEs must hold Amateur Extra, Advanced, or General Class operator licenses; and

(2) For a General, Advanced or Amateur Extra Class operator

license examination, the administering VEs must hold Amateur Extra Class operator licenses.

(c) The administering VEs must make a public announcement before administering an examination for an amateur operator license. The number of candidates at any examination may be limited.

(d) The administering VEs must issue a CSCE to an examinee who scores a passing grade on an examination element.

(e) Within 10 days of the administration of a successful examination for an amateur operator license, the administering VEs must submit the application to the coordinating VEC. If telegraphy element credit is claimed under Section 97.505(a)(5), the physician's certification and the patient's release on the license application, Form 610, must be completed.

§ 97.515 Volunteer examiner requirements.

(a) Each administering VE must be at least 18 years of age.

(b) Any person who owns a significant interest in, or is an employee of, any company or other entity that is engaged in the manufacture or distribution of equipment used in connection with amateur station transmissions, or in the preparation or distribution of any publication used in preparation for obtaining amateur licenses, is ineligible to be an administering VE. An employee who does not normally communicate with that part of an entity engaged in the manufacture or distribution of such equipment, or in the preparation or distribution of any publication used in preparation for obtaining amateur operator licenses, is eligible to be an administering VE.

(c) No person may be a VE if that person's amateur station license or amateur operator license has ever been revoked or suspended.

(d) No VE may administer an examination to that VE's spouse, children, grandchildren, stepchildren, parents, grandparents, stepparents, brothers, sisters, stepbrothers, stepsisters, aunts, uncles, nieces, nephews and in-laws.

§ 97.517 Volunteer examiner conduct.

No VE may administer or certify any examination by fraudulent means or for monetary or other consideration including reimbursement in any amount in excess of that permitted. Violation of this provision may result in the revocation of the VE's amateur station license and the suspension of the VE's amateur operator license.

§ 97.519 Coordinating examination sessions.

(a) A VEC must coordinate the efforts of VEs in preparing and administering examinations.

(b) At the completion of each examination session coordinated, the coordinating VEC must collect the applications and test results from the administering VEs. The coordinating VEC must screen and forward all applications for qualified examinees within 10 days of their receipt from the administering VEs to: FCC, 1270 Fairfield Road, Gettysburg, PA 17325-7245.

(c) Each VEC must make any examination records available to the FCC, upon request.

§ 97.521 VEC qualifications.

No organization may serve as a VEC unless it has entered into a written agreement with the FCC. The VEC must abide by the terms of the agreement. In order to be eligible to be a VEC, the entity must:

(a) Be an organization that exists for the purpose of furthering the amateur service;

(b) Be capable of serving as a VEC in at least the VEC region (see Appendix 2) proposed;

(c) Agree to coordinate examinations for any class of amateur operator license;

(d) Agree to assure that, for any examination, every examinee qualified under these rules is registered without regard to race, sex, religion, national origin or membership (or lack thereof) in any amateur service organization;

(e) Not be engaged in the manufacture or distribution of equipment used in connection with amateur station transmissions, or in the preparation or distribution of any publication used in preparation for obtaining amateur licenses, unless a persuasive showing is made to the FCC that preventive measures have been taken to preclude any possible conflict of interest.

§ 97.523 Question pools.

All VECs must cooperate in maintaining one question pool for each written examination element. Each question pool must contain at least 10 times the number of questions required for a single examination. Each question pool must be published and made available to the public prior to its use for making a question set. Each question on each VEC question pool must be prepared by a VE holding the required FCC-issued operator license. See §97.507(a) of this Part.

§ 97.525 Accrediting VEs.

(a) No VEC may accredit a person as a VE if:

(1) The person does not meet minimum VE statutory qualifications or minimum qualifications as prescribed by this Part;

(2) The FCC does not accept the voluntary and uncompensated services of the person;

(3) The VEC determines that the person is not competent to perform the VE functions; or

(4) The VEC determines that questions of the person's integrity or honesty could compromise the examinations.

(b) Each VEC must seek a broad representation of amateur operators to be VEs. No VEC may discriminate in accrediting VEs on the basis of race, sex, religion or national origin; nor on the basis of membership (or lack thereof) in an amateur service organization; nor on the basis of the person accepting or declining to accept reimbursement.

§ 97.527 Reimbursement for expenses.

(a) VEs and VECs may be reimbursed by examinees for out-of-pocket expenses incurred in preparing, processing, administering or coordinating an examination for an amateur operator license.

(b) The maximum amount of reimbursement from any one examinee for any one examination at a particular session regardless of the number of examination elements taken must not exceed that announced by the FCC in a Public Notice. (The basis for the maximum fee is $4.00 for 1984, adjusted annually each January 1 thereafter for changes in the Department of Labor Consumer Price Index.)

(c) Each VE and each VEC accepting reimbursement must maintain records of out-of-pocket expenses and reimbursements for each examination session. Written certifications must be filed with the FCC each year that all expenses for the period from January 1 to December 31 of the preceding year for which reimbursement was obtained were necessarily and prudently incurred.

(d) The expense and reimbursement records must be retained by each VE and each VEC for 3 years and be made available to the FCC upon request.

(e) Each VE must forward the certification by January 15 of each year to the coordinating VEC for the examinations for which reimbursement was received. Each VEC must forward all such certifications and its own certification to the FCC on or before January 31 of each year.

(f) Each VEC must disaccredit any VE failing to provide the certification. The VEC must advise the FCC on January 31 of each year of any VE that it has disaccredited for this reason.

Appendix 1:

Places where the amateur service is regulated by the FCC.

In ITU Region 2, the amateur service is regulated by the FCC within the territorial limits of the 50 United States, District of Columbia, Caribbean Insular areas [Commonwealth of Puerto Rico, United States Virgin Islands (50 islets and cays) and Navassa Island], and Johnston Island (islets East, Johnston, North and Sand) and Midway Island (Islets Eastern and Sand) in the Pacific Insular areas.

In ITU Region 3, the amateur service is regulated by the FCC within the Pacific Insular territorial limits of American Samoa (seven islands), Baker Island, Commonwealth of Northern Marianna Islands, Guam Island, Howland Island, Jarvis Island,

Kingman Reef, Palmyra Island (more than 50 islets) and Wake Island (Islets Peale, Wake and Wilkes).

Appendix 2:

VEC Regions.

1. Connecticut, Maine, Massachusetts, New Hampshire, Rhode Island and Vermont.
2. New Jersey and New York.
3. Delaware, District of Columbia, Maryland and Pennsylvania
4. Alabama, Florida, Georgia, Kentucky, North Carolina, South Carolina, Tennessee and Virginia.
5. Arkansas, Louisiana, Mississippi, New Mexico, Oklahoma and Texas.
6. California.
7. Arizona, Idaho, Montana, Nevada, Oregon, Utah, Washington and Wyoming.
8. Michigan, Ohio and West Virginia.
9. Illinois, Indiana and Wisconsin.
10. Colorado, Iowa, Kansas, Minnesota, Missouri, Nebraska, North Dakota and South Dakota.
11. Alaska.
12. Caribbean Insular areas.
13. Hawaii and Pacific Insular areas.

PRB-1

Before the
Federal Communications Commission
Washington, DC 20554

FCC 85-506
36149

In the Matter of

Federal preemption of state and local regulations pertaining to Amateur radio facilities. PRB-1

MEMORANDUM OPINION AND ORDER

Adopted: September 16, 1985;
Released: September 19, 1985

By the Commission: Commissioner Rivera not participating.

Background

1. On July 16, 1984, the American Radio Relay League, Inc. (ARRL) filed a Request for Issuance of a Declaratory Ruling asking us to delineate the limitations of local zoning and other local and state regulatory authority over Federally-licensed radio facilities. Specifically, the ARRL wanted an explicit statement that would preempt all local ordinances which provably preclude or significantly inhibit effective, reliable amateur radio communications. The ARRL acknowledges that local authorities can regulate amateur installations to insure the safety and health of persons in the community, but believes that those regulations cannot be so restrictive that they preclude effective amateur communications.

2. Interested parties were advised that they could file comments in the matter[1]. With extension, comments were due on or before December 26, 1984[2], with reply comments due on or before January 25, 1985[3]. Over sixteen hundred comments were filed.

Local Ordinances

3. Conflicts between amateur operators regarding radio antennas and local authorities regarding restrictive ordinances are common. The amateur operator is governed by the regulations contained in Part 98 of our rules. Those rules do not limit the height of an amateur antenna but they require, for aviation safety reasons, that certain FAA notification and FCC approval procedures must be followed for antennas which exceed 200 feet in height above ground level or antennas which are to be erected near airports. Thus, under FCC rules some amateur antenna support structures require obstruction marking and lighting. On the other hand, local municipalities or governing bodies frequently enact regulations limiting antennas and their support structures in height and location, e.g. to side or rear yards, for health, safety or aesthetic considerations. These limiting regulations can result in conflict because the effectiveness of the communications that emanate from an amateur radio station are directly dependent upon the location and the height of the antenna. Amateur operators maintain that they are precluded from operating in certain bands allocated for their use if the height of their antennas is limited by a local ordinance.

4. Examples of restrictive local ordinances were submitted by several amateur operators in this proceeding. Stanley J. Cichy, San Diego, California, noted that in San Diego amateur radio antennas come under a structures ruling which limits building heights to 30 feet. Thus, antennas there are also limited to 30 feet. Alexander Vrenios, Mundelein, Illinois wrote that an ordinance of the Village of Mundelein provides that an antenna must be a distance from the property line that is equal to one and one-half times its height. In his case, he is limited to an antenna tower for his amateur station just over 53 feet in height.

5. John C. Chapman, an amateur living in Bloomington, Minnesota, commented that he was not able to obtain a building permit to install an amateur radio antenna exceeding 35 feet in height because the Bloomington city ordinance restricted "structures" heights to 35 feet. Mr. Chapman said that the ordinance, when written, undoubtedly applied to buildings but was now being applied to antennas in the absence of a specific ordinance regulating them. There were two options open to him if he wanted to engage in amateur communications. He could request a variance to the ordinance by way of a hearing before the City Council, or he could obtain affidavits from his neighbors swearing that they had no objection to the proposed antenna installation. He got the building permit after obtaining the cooperation of his neighbors. His concern, however, is that he had to get permission from several people before he could effectively engage in radio communications for which he had a valid FCC amateur license.

6. In addition to height restrictions, other limits are enacted by local jurisdictions—anti-climb devices on towers or fences around them; minimum distances from high voltage power lines; minimum distances of towers from property lines; and regulations pertaining to the structural soundness of the antenna installation. By and large, amateurs do not find these safety precautions objectionable. What they do object to are the sometimes prohibitive, non-refundable application filing fees to obtain a permit to erect an antenna installation and those provisions in ordinances which regulate antennas for purely aesthetic reasons. The amateurs contend, almost universally, that "beauty is in the eye of the beholder." They assert that an antenna installation is not more aesthetically displeasing than other objects that people keep on their property, e.g. motor homes, trailers, pick-up trucks, solar collectors and gardening equipment.

Restrictive Covenants

7. Amateur operators also oppose restrictions on their amateur operations which are contained in the deeds for their homes or in their apartment leases. Since these restrictive covenants are contractual agreements between private parties, they are not generally a matter of concern to the Commission. However, since some amateurs who commented in this proceeding provided us with examples of restrictive covenants, they are included for information. Mr. Eugene O. Thomas of Hollister, California included in his comments an extract of the Declaration of Covenants and Restrictions for Ridgemark Estates, County of San Benito, State of California. It provides:

> No antenna for transmission or reception of radio signals shall be erected outdoors for use by any dwelling unit except upon approval of the Directors. No radio or television signals or any other form of electromagnetic radiation shall be permitted to originate from any lot which may unreasonably interfere with the reception of television or radio signals upon any other lot.

Marshall Wilson, Jr. provided a copy of the restrictive covenant contained in deeds for the Bell Martin Addition #2, Irving, Texas. It is binding upon all of the owners or purchasers of the lots in the said addition, his or their heirs, executors, administrators or assigns. It reads:

> No antenna or tower shall be erected upon any lot for the purposes of radio operations.

William J. Hamilton resides in an apartment building in Gladstone, Missouri. He cites a clause in his lease prohibiting the erection of an antenna. He states that he has been forced to give up operating amateur radio equipment except a hand-held 2 meter (144–148 MHz) radio transceiver. He maintains that he should not be penalized just because he lives in an apartment.

Other restrictive covenants are less global in scope than those cited above. For example, Robert Webb purchased a home in Houston, Texas. His deed restriction prohibited "transmitting or receiving antennas extending above the roof line."

8. Amateur operators generally oppose restrictive covenants for several reasons. They maintain that such restrictions limit the places that they can reside if they want to pursue their hobby of amateur radio. Some state that they impinge on First Amendment rights of free speech. Others believe that a constitutional right is being abridged because, in their view, everyone has a right to access the airwaves regardless of where they live.

9. The contrary belief held by housing subdivision communities and condominium or homeowner's associations is that amateur radio installations constitute safety hazards, cause interference to other electronic equipment which may be operated in the home (televisions, radio, stereos) or are eyesores that detract from the aesthetic and tasteful appearance of the housing development or apartment complex. To counteract these negative consequences, the subdivisions and associations include in their deeds, leases or by-laws restrictions and limitations on the location and height of antennas or, in some cases, prohibit them altogether. The restrictive covenants are contained in the contractual agreement entered into at the time of the sale or lease of the property. Purchasers or lessees are free to choose whether they wish to reside where such restrictions on amateur antennas are in effect or settle elsewhere.

Supporting Comments

10. The Department of Defense (DOD) supported the ARRL and emphasized in its comments that continued success of existing national security and emergency preparedness telecommunications plans involving amateur stations would be severely diminished if state and local ordinances were allowed to prohibit the construction and usage of effective amateur transmission facilities. DOD utilizes volunteers in the Military Affiliate Radio Service (MARS)[4], Civil Air Patrol (CAP) and the Radio Amateur Civil Emergency Service (RACES). It points out that these volunteer communicators are operating radio equipment installed in their homes and that undue restrictions on antennas by local authorities adversely affect their efforts. DOD states that the responsiveness of these volunteer systems would be impaired if local ordinances interfere with the effectiveness of these important national telecommunication resources. DOD favors the issuance of a ruling that would set limits for local and state regulatory bodies when they are dealing with amateur stations.

11. Various chapters of the American Red Cross also came forward to support the ARRL's request for a preemptive ruling. The Red Cross works closely with amateur radio volunteers. It believes that without amateurs' dedicated support, disaster relief operations would significantly suffer and that its ability to serve disaster victims would be hampered. It feels that antenna height limitations that might be imposed by local bodies will negatively affect the service now rendered by the volunteers.

12. Cities and counties from various parts of the United States filed comments in support of the ARRL's request for a Federal preemption ruling. The comments from the Director of Civil Defense, Port Arthur, Texas are representative:

> The Amateur Radio Service plays a vital role with our Civil Defense program here in Port Arthur and the design of these antennas and towers lends greatly to our ability to communicate during times of disaster.
>
> We do not believe there should be any restrictions on the antennas and towers except for reasonable safety precautions. Tropical storms, hurricanes and tornadoes are a way of life here on the Texas Gulf Coast and good communications are absolutely essential when preparing for a hurricane and even more so, during recovery operations after the hurricane has past.

13. The Quarter Century Wireless Association took a strong stand in favor of the issuance of a declaratory ruling. It believes that Federal preemption is necessary so that there will be uniformity for all Amateur radio installations on private property throughout the United States.

14. In its comments, the ARRL argued that the Commission has the jurisdiction to preempt certain local land use regulations which frustrate or prohibit amateur radio communications. It said that the appropriate standard in preemption cases is not the extent of state and local interest in a given regulation, but rather the impact of that regulation on Federal goals. Its position is that Federal preemption is warranted whenever local governmental regulations relate adversely to the operational aspects of amateur communication. The ARRL maintains that localities routinely employ a variety of land use devices to preclude the installation of effective amateur antennas, including height restrictions, conditional use permits, building setbacks and dimensional limitations on antennas. It sees a declaratory ruling of Federal preemption as necessary to cause municipalities to accommodate amateur operator needs in land use planning efforts.

15. James C. O'Connell, an attorney who has represented several amateurs before local zoning authorities, said that requiring amateurs to seek variances or special use approval to erect reasonable antennas unduly restricts the operation of amateur stations. He suggested that the Commission preempt zoning ordinances which impose antenna height limits of less than 65 feet. He said that this height would represent a reasonable accommodation of the communication needs of most amateurs and the legitimate concerns of local zoning authorities.

Opposing Comments

16. The City of La Mesa, California has a zoning regulation which controls amateur antennas. Its comments reflected an attempt to reach a balanced view.

> This regulation has neither the intent, nor the effect, of precluding or inhibiting effective and reliable communications. Such antennas may be built as long as their construction does not unreasonably block views or constitute eyesores. The reasonable assumption is that there are always alternatives at a given site for different placement, and/or methods for aesthetic treatment. Thus, both public objectives of controlling land use for the public health, safety, and convenience, and providing an effective communications network, can be satisfied.

A blanket ruling to completely set aside local control, or a ruling which recognizes control only for the purpose of safety of antenna construction, would be contrary to...legitimate local control.

17. Comments from the county of San Diego state:

While we are aware of the benefits provided by amateur operators, we oppose the issuance of a preemption ruling which would elevate 'antenna effectiveness' to a position above all other considerations. We must, however, argue that the local government must have the ability to place reasonable limitations upon the placement and configuration of amateur radio transmitting and receiving antennas. Such ability is necessary to assure that the local decision-makers have the authority to protect the public health, safety and welfare of all citizens.

In conclusion, I would like to emphasize an important difference between your regulatory powers and that of local governments. Your Commission's approval of the preemptive requests would establish a 'national policy.' However, any regulation adopted by a local jurisdiction could be overturned by your Commission or a court if such regulation was determined to be unreasonable.

18. The City of Anderson, Indiana, summarized some of the problems that face local communities:

I am sympathetic to the concerns of these antenna owners and I understand that to gain the maximum reception from their devices, optimal location is necessary. However, the preservation of residential zoning districts as 'liveable' neighborhoods is jeopardized by placing these antennas in front yards of homes. Major problems of public safety have been encountered, particularly vision blockage for auto and pedestrian access. In addition, all communities are faced with various building lot sizes. Many building lots are so small that established setback requirements (in order to preserve adequate air and light) are vulnerable to the unregulated placement of these antennas.

...the exercise of preemptive authority by the FCC in granting this request would not be in the best interest of the general public.

19. The National Association of Counties (NACO), the American Planning Association (APA) and the National League of Cities (NLC) all opposed the issuance of an antenna preemption ruling. NACO emphasized that federal and state power must be viewed in harmony and warns that Federal intrusion into local concerns of health, safety and welfare could weaken the traditional police power exercised by the state and unduly interfere with the legitimate activities of the states. NLC believed that both Federal and local interests can be accommodated without preempting local authority to regulate the installation of amateur radio antennas. The APA said that the FCC should continue to leave the issue of regulating amateur antennas with the local government and with the state and Federal courts.

Discussion

20. When considering preemption, we must begin with two constitutional provisions. The tenth amendment provides that any powers which the constitution either does not delegate to the United States or does not prohibit the states from exercising are reserved to the states. These are the police powers of the states. The Supremacy Clause, however, provides that the constitution and the laws of the United States shall supersede any state law to the contrary. Article III, Section 2. Given these basic premises, state laws may be preempted in three ways: First, Congress may expressly preempt the state law. See Jones v. Rath Packing Co., 430 U.S. 519, 525 (1977). Or, Congress may indicate its intent to completely occupy a given field so that any state law encompassed within that field would implicitly be preempted. Such intent to preempt could be found in a congressional regulatory scheme that was so pervasive that it would be reasonable to assume that Congress did not intend to permit the states to supplement it. See Fidelity Federal Savings & Loan Ass'n v. de la Cuesta, 458 U.S. 141, 153 (1982). Finally, preemption may be warranted when state law conflicts with federal law. Such conflicts may occur when "compliance with both Federal and state regulations is a physical impossibility," Florida Lime & Avocado Growers, Inc. v. Paul, 373 U.S. 132, 142, 143 (1963), or when state law "stands as an obstacle to the accomplishment and execution of the full purposes and objectives of Congress," Hines v. Davidowitz, 312 U.S. 52, 67 (1941). Furthermore, federal regulations have the same preemptive effect as federal statutes. Fidelity Federal Savings & Loan Association v. de la Cuesta, supra.

21. The situation before us requires us to determine the extent to which state and local zoning regulations may conflict with federal policies concerning amateur radio operators.

22. Few matters coming before us present such a clear dichotomy of viewpoint as does the instant issue. The cities, counties, local communities and housing associations see an obligation to all of their citizens and try to address their concerns. This is accomplished through regulations, ordinances or covenants oriented toward the health, safety and general welfare of those they regulate. At the opposite pole are the individual amateur operators and their support groups who are troubled by local regulations which may inhibit the use of amateur stations or, in some instances, totally preclude amateur communications. Aligned with the operators are such entities as the Department of Defense, the American Red Cross and local civil defense and emergency organizations who have found in Amateur Radio a pool of skilled radio operators and a readily available backup network. In this situation, we believe it is appropriate to strike a balance between the federal interest in promoting amateur operations and the legitimate interests of local governments in regulating local zoning matters. The cornerstone on which we will predicate our decision is that a reasonable accommodation may be made between the two sides.

23. Preemption is primarily a function of the extent of the conflict between federal and state and local regulation. Thus, in considering whether our regulations or policies can tolerate a state regulation, we may consider such factors as the severity of the conflict and the reasons underlying the state's regulations. In this regard, we have previously recognized the legitimate and important state interests reflected in local zoning regulations. For example, in Earth Satellite Communications, Inc., 95 FCC 2d 1223 (1983), we recognized that

...countervailing state interests inhere in the present situation...For example, we do not wish to preclude a state or locality from exercising jurisdiction over certain elements of an SMATV operation that properly may fall within its authority, such as zoning or public safety and health, provided the regulation in question is not undertaken as a pretext for the actual purpose of frustrating achievement of the preeminent federal objective and so long as the non-federal regulation is applied in a nondiscriminatory manner.

24. Similarly, we recognize here that there are certain general state and local interests which may, in their even-handed application, legitimately affect amateur radio facilities. Nonetheless, there is also a strong federal interest in promoting amateur communications. Evidence of this interest may be found in the comprehensive set of rules that the Commission has adopted to regulate the amateur service.[5] Those rules set forth procedures for the licensing of stations and operators, frequency allocations, technical standards which amateur radio equipment must meet and operating practices which amateur operators must follow. We recognize the Amateur

radio service as a voluntary, noncommercial communication service, particularly with respect to providing emergency communications. Moreover, the amateur radio service provides a reservoir of trained operators, technicians and electronic experts who can be called on in times of national or local emergencies. By its nature, the Amateur Radio Service also provides the opportunity for individual operators to further international goodwill. Upon weighing these interests, we believe a limited preemption policy is warranted. State and local regulations that operate to preclude amateur communications in their communities are in direct conflict with federal objectives and must be preempted.

25. Because amateur station communications are only as effective as the antennas employed, antenna height restrictions directly affect the effectiveness of amateur communications. Some amateur antenna configurations require more substantial installations than others if they are to provide the amateur operator with the communications that he/she desires to engage in. For example, an antenna array for international amateur communications will differ from an antenna used to contact other amateur operators at shorter distances. We will not, however, specify any particular height limitation below which a local government may not regulate, nor will we suggest the precise language that must be contained in local ordinances, such as mechanisms for special exceptions, variances, or conditional use permits. Nevertheless, local regulations which involve placement, screening, or height of antennas based on health, safety, or aesthetic considerations must be crafted to accommodate reasonable amateur communications, and to represent the minimum practicable regulation to accomplish the local authority's legitimate purpose.[6]

26. Obviously, we do not have the staff or financial resources to review all state and local laws that affect amateur operations. We are confident, however, that state and local governments will endeavor to legislate in a manner that affords appropriate recognition to the important federal interest at stake here and thereby avoid unnecessary conflicts with federal policy, as well as time-consuming and expensive litigation in this area. Amateur operators who believe that local or state governments have been overreaching and thereby have precluded accomplishment of their legitimate communications goals, may, in addition, use this document to bring our policies to the attention of local tribunals and forums.

27. Accordingly, the Request for Declaratory Ruling filed July 16, 1984, by the American Radio Relay League, Inc., IS GRANTED to the extent indicated herein and, in all other respects, IS DENIED.

FEDERAL COMMUNICATIONS COMMISSION

William J. Tricarico

Secretary

Footnotes

1. Public Notice, August 30, 1984, Mimeo. No. 6299, 49 F.R. 36113, September 14, 1984.

2. Public Notice, December 19, 1984, Mimeo. No. 1498.

3. Order, November 8, 1984, Mimeo. No. 770.

4. MARS is solely under the auspices of the military which recruits volunteer amateur operators to render assistance to it. The Commission is not involved in the MARS program.

5. 47 CFR Part 97.

6. We reiterate that our ruling herein does not reach restrictive covenants in private contractual agreements. Such agreements are voluntarily entered into by the buyer or tenant when the agreement is executed and do not usually concern this Commission.

THE "CONSIDERATE OPERATOR'S FREQUENCY GUIDE"

Frequencies generally recognized for certain modes or activities (all frequencies are in MHz):

1.800–1.830	CW, RTTY and other narrowband modes
1.830–1.840	CW, RTTY and other narrowband modes, intercontinental QSOs only
1.840–1.850	CW, SSB, SSTV and other wideband modes, intercontinental QSOs only
1.840–2.000	CW, phone, SSTV and other wideband modes
3.590	RTTY DX
3.580–3.620	RTTY
3.620–3.635	Packet
3.790–3.800	DX window
3.845	SSTV
3.885	AM calling freq.
7.040	RTTY DX
7.080–7.100	RTTY
7.171	SSTV
7.290	AM
10.130–10.140	RTTY
10.140–10.150	Packet
14.070–14.095	RTTY
14.095–14.0995	Packet
14.100	NCDXF beacons
14.1005–14.112	Packet
14.230	SSTV
14.286	AM calling freq.
18.100–18.105	RTTY
18.105–18.110	Packet
21.070–21.090	RTTY
21.090–21.100	Packet
21.340	SSTV
24.920–24.925	RTTY
24.925–24.930	Packet
28.070–28.120	RTTY
28.120–28.189	Packet
28.190–28.225	Beacons
28.680	SSTV
29.000–29.200	AM
29.300–29.510	Satellite downlinks
29.520–29.580	Repeater inputs
29.600	FM simplex
29.620–29.680	Repeater outputs

Courtesy of ARRL

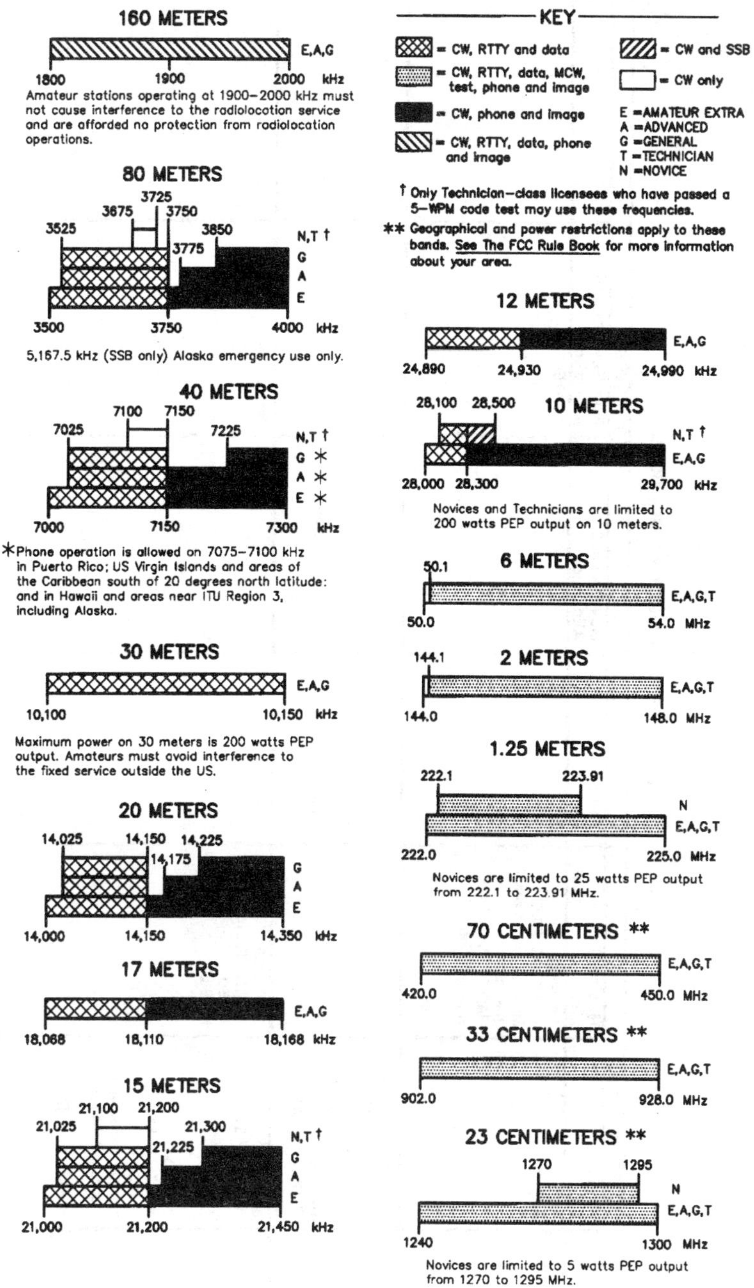

(Courtesy of ARRL)

TABLE OF FREQUENCY ALLOCATIONS

INTERNATIONAL			UNITED STATES			
Region 1 kHz	**Region 2 kHz**	**Region 3 kHz**	**Band kHz**	**Government Allocation**	**Non-Government Allocation**	**Remarks**
1800-1810 RADIOLOCATION 487 485 486 1810-1850 AMATEUR 490 491 492 493	1800-1850 AMATEUR	1800-2000 AMATEUR, FIXED MOBILE except aero-nautical mobile RADIONAVIGATION Radiolocation 489	1800-1900		AMATEUR	
1850-2000 FIXED,MOBILE except aeronautical mobile 484 488 495	1850-2000 AMATEUR, FIXED MOBILE except aero-nautical mobile RADIOLOCATION RADIONAVIGATION 494		1900-2000	RADIOLOCATION US290	RADIOLOCATION US290	
3500-3800 AMATEUR 510 FIXED MOBILE except aero-nautical mobile 484	3500-3750 AMATEUR 510 509 511 3750-4000 AMATEUR 510 FIXED MOBILE except aero-nautical mobile (R) 511 512 514 515	3500-3900 AMATEUR 510 FIXED MOBILE	3500-4000	510	AMATEUR 510	
3800-3900 FIXED AERONAUTICAL MOBILE (OR) LAND MOBILE						

INTERNATIONAL			UNITED STATES			
Region 1 kHz	**Region 2 kHz**	**Region 3 kHz**	**Band kHz**	**Government Allocation**	**Non-Government Allocation**	**Remarks**
3950-4000 FIXED BROADCASTING		3950-4000 FIXED BROADCASTING 516				
7000-7100 AMATEUR 510, AMATEUR-SATELLITE 526 527			7000-7100	510	AMATEUR AMATEUR-SATELLITE 510	
7100-7300 BROADCASTING	7100-7300 AMATEUR 510 528	7100-7300 BROADCASTING	7100-7300	510 528	AMATEUR 510 528	
10100-10150 FIXED Amateur 510			10100-10150	US247 510	AMATEUR US247 510	
14000-14250 AMATEUR 510 AMATEUR-SATELLITE			14000-14250	510	AMATEUR AMATEUR-SATELLITE 510	
14250-14350 AMATEUR 510 535			14250-14350	510	AMATEUR 510	
18068-18168 AMATEUR 510, AMATEUR-SATELLITE 537 538			18068-18168	510	AMATEUR AMATEUR-SATELLITE 510	
21000-21450 AMATEUR 510 AMATEUR-SATELLITE			21000-21450	510	AMATEUR AMATEUR-SATELLITE 510	
24890-24990 AMATEUR 510, AMATEUR-SATELLITE 542 543			24890-24990	510	AMATEUR AMATEUR-SATELLITE 510	
28-29.7 MHz AMATEUR, AMATEUR-SATELLITE			28-29.7		AMATEUR AMATEUR-SATELLITE	

INTERNATIONAL			UNITED STATES			
Region 1 **MHz**	**Region 2** **MHz**	**Region 3** **MHz**	**Band** **MHz**	**Government** **Allocation**	**Non-Government** **Allocation**	**Remarks**
47-68 BROADCASTING 553 554 555 559 561	50-54 AMATEUR 556 557 558 560		50-54		AMATEUR	
144-146 AMATEUR 510, AMATEUR-SATELLITE 605 606			144-146	510	AMATEUR AMATEUR-SATELLITE 510	
146-148 FIXED MOBILE except aeronautical mobile (R) 608	146-148 AMATEUR 607	146-148 AMATEUR FIXED MOBILE 607	146-148		AMATEUR	
	220-225 AMATEUR FIXED MOBILE Radiolocation 627		220-222	LAND MOBILE Radiolocation US243 627 G2	LAND MOBILE US243 627	The Channeling Plan for Land Mobile assignments in this band is shown in Section 4.3.15 of the NTIA Manual.
223-230 BROADCASTING Fixed Mobile 622 628 629 631 632 633 634 635		223-230 FIXED, MOBILE BROADCASTING AERONAUTICAL RADIONAVIGATION Radiolocation 636 637	222-225	Radiolocation US243 627 G2	AMATEUR US243 627	
	225-235 FIXED MOBILE					
420-430 FIXED, MOBILE except aeronautical mobile Radiolocation 651 652 653			420-450	RADIOLOCATION US7 US87 US217 US228 US230 664 668 G2 G8	Amateur US7 US87 US217 US228 US230 664 668 NG135	
	902-928 FIXED, Amateur Mobile except aeronaut-ical mobile Radiolocation 705 707 707A		902-928	RADIOLOCATION US215 US218 US267 US275 707 G11 G59	US215 US218 US267 US275 707	ISM 915 ± 13 MHz

INTERNATIONAL			UNITED STATES			
Region 1 MHz	**Region 2 MHz**	**Region 3 MHz**	**Band MHz**	**Government Allocation**	**Non-Government Allocation**	**Remarks**
1240-1260 RADIOLOCATION RADIONAVIGATION-SATELLITE (space-to-Earth) 710 Amateur 711 712 712A 713 714			1240-1300	RADIOLOCATION 664 713 714 G56	Amateur 664 713 714	
1260-1300 RADIOLOCATION Amateur 664 711 712A 713 714						
2300-2450 FIXED Amateur Mobile Radiolocation 664 743A 752	2300-2450 FIXED MOBILE RADIOLOCATION Amateur 664 751 752		2300-2310 2310-2390	RADIOLOCATION Fixed Mobile US253 G2 RADIOLOCATION MOBILE, Fixed US276 G2 G120	Amateur US253 MOBILE US276	
			2390-2450	RADIOLOCATION 664 752 G2	Amateur 664 752	ISM 2450 ± 50 MHz
3300-3400 RADIOLOCATION 778 779 780	3300-3400 RADIOLOCATION Amateur, Fixed, Mobile 778 780	3300-3400 RADIOLOCATION Amateur 778 779	3300-3500	RADIOLOCATION US108 664 778 G31	Amateur Radiolocation US108 664 778	
3400-3600 FIXED FIXED-SATELLITE (space-to-Earth) Mobile Radiolocation 781 782 785	3400-3500 FIXED FIXED-SATELLITE (space-to-Earth) Amateur, Mobile Radiolocation 784 664 783					
5650-5725 RADIOLOCATION Amateur, Space Research (Deep Space) 664 801 803 804 805			5650-5850	RADIOLOCATION 664 806 808 G2	Amateur 664 806 808	ISM 5800 ± 75 MHz

INTERNATIONAL			UNITED STATES			
Region 1 MHz	**Region 2 MHz**	**Region 3 MHz**	**Band MHz**	**Government Allocation**	**Non-Government Allocation**	**Remarks**
5725-5850 FIXED-SATELLITE (Earth-to-space) RADIOLOCATION Amateur 801 803 805 806 807 808	5725-5850 RADIOLOCATION Amateur 803 805 806 808					
5850-5925 FIXED FIXED-SATELLITE (Earth-to-space) MOBILE 806	5850-5925 FIXED FIXED-SATELLITE (Earth-to-space) MOBILE, Amateur Radiolocation 806	5850-5925 FIXED FIXED-SATELLITE (Earth-to-space) MOBILE Radiolocation 806	5850-5925	RADIOLOCATION US245 806 G2	FIXED-SATELLITE (Earth-to-space) Amateur US245 806	
10-10.45 GHZ FIXED, MOBILE RADIOLOCATION Amateur 828	10-10.45 RADIOLOCATION Amateur 828 829	10-10.45 FIXED, MOBILE RADIOLOCATION Amateur 828	10-10.45	RADIOLOCATION US58 US108 828 G32	Amateur Radiolocation US58 US108 828 NG42	
10.45-10.5 RADIOLOCATION Amateur, Amateur-Satellite 830			10.45-10.5	RADIOLOCATION US58 US108 G32	RADIOLOCATION Amateur Amateur-Satellite US58 US108 NG42 NG134	
24-24.05 AMATEUR, AMATEUR-SATELLITE 881			24-24.05	US211 811	AMATEUR AMATEUR-SATELLITE US211 881	
24.05-24.25 RADIOLOCATION Amateur Earth Exploration-Satellite (Active) 881			24.05-24.25	RADIOLOCATION Earth Exploration-Satellite (Active) US110 881 G59	Amateur Earth Exploration-Satellite (Active) Radiolocation US110 881	ISM 24.125 ± 125 MHz
47-47.2 AMATEUR, AMATEUR-SATELLITE			47-47.2		AMATEUR AMATEUR-SATELLITE	

INTERNATIONAL			UNITED STATES			
Region 1 GHz	Region 2 GHz	Region 3 GHz	Band GHz	Government Allocation	Non-Government Allocation	Remarks
75.5-76 AMATEUR, AMATEUR-SATELLITE			75.5-76		AMATEUR AMATEUR-SATELLITE	
76-81 RADIOLOCATION Amateur Amateur-Satellite 912			76-81	RADIOLOCATION 912	RADIOLOCATION Amateur Amateur-Satellite 912	
142-144 AMATEUR, AMATEUR-SATELLITE			142-144		AMATEUR AMATEUR-SATELLITE	
144-149 RADIOLOCATION Amateur, Amateur-Satellite 918			144-149	RADIOLOCATION 2241918	RADIOLOCATION Amateur Amateur-Satellite 918	
241-248 RADIOLOCATION, Amateur, Amateur-Satellite 922			241-248	RADIOLOCATION 922	RADIOLOCATION Amateur Amateur-Satellite 922	ISM 245 ± 1 GHz
248-250 AMATEUR, AMATEUR-SATELLITE			248-250		AMATEUR AMATEUR-SATELLITE	

Footnotes:

G2—In the bands 216-225, 420-450 (except as provided by US217), 890-902, 928-942, 1300-1400, 2300-2450, 2700-2900, 5650-5925, and 9000-9200 MHz, the Government radiolocation is limited to the military services.

G11—Government fixed and mobile radio services including low power radio control operations, are permitted in the band 902-928 MHz on a secondary basis.

G31—In the bands 3300-3500 MHz, the Government radiolocation is limited to the military services, except as provided by footnote US108.

G32—Except for weather radars on meteorological-satellites in the band 9975-10025 MHz and for Government survey operations (see footnote US108), Government radiolocation in the band 10000-10500 MHz is limited to the military services.

G56—Government radiolocation in the bands 1215-1300, 2900-3100, 5350-5650 and 9300-9500 MHz is primarily for the military services; however, limited secondary use is permitted by other Government agencies in support of experimentation and research programs. In addition, limited secondary use is permitted for surveyoperations in the band 2900-3100 MHz.

G59—In the bands 902-928 MHz, 3100-3300 MHz, 3500-3700 MHz, 5250-5350 MHz, 8500-9000 MHz, 9200-9300 MHz, 13.4-14.0 GHz, 15.7-17.7 GHz and 24.05-24.25 GHz, all Government non-military radiolocation shall be secondary to military radiolocation, except in the subband 15.7-16.2 GHz airport surface detection equipment (ASDE) is permitted on a co-equal basis subject to coordination with the military departments.

US7—In the band 420-450 MHz and within thefollowing areas, the peak envelope power output of a transmitter employed in the amateur service shall not exceed 50 watts, unless expressly authorized by the Commission after mutual agreement, on a case-by-case basis, between the Federal Communications Commission Engineer in Charge at the applicable district office and the military area frequency coordinator at the applicable military base. For areas (e) through (j), the appropriate military coordinator is located at Peterson AFB, CO.

(a) Those portions of Texas and New Mexico bounded on the south by latitude 31°45' North, on the east by 104°00' West, on the north by latitude 34°30' North, and on the west by longitude 107°30' West;

(b) The entire State of Florida including the Key West area and the areas enclosed within a 322 kilometer (200-mile) radius of Patrick Air Force Base, Florida (latitude 28°21' North, longitude 80°43' West), and within a 322 kilometer (200-mile) radius of Eglin Air Force Base, Florida (latitude 30°30' North, longitude 86°30' West);

(c) The entire State of Arizona;

(d) Those portions of California and Nevada south of latitude 37°10' North, and the areas enclosed within a 322 kilometer (200-mile) radius of the Pacific Missile Test Center, Point Mugu, California (latitude 34°09' North, longitude 119°11' West).

(e) In the State of Massachusetts within a 160-kilometer (100 mile) radius around locations at Otis Air Force Base, Massachusetts (latitude 41°45' North, longitude 70°32' West).

(f) In the State of California within a 240-kilometer (150 mile) radius around locations at Beale Air Force Base, California (latitude 39°08' North, longitude 121°26' West).

(g) In the State of Alaska within a 160 kilometer (100 mile) radius of Clear, Alaska (latitude 64 degrees, 17' North, longitude 149 degrees 10' West).

(h) In the State of North Dakota within a 160 kilometer (100 mile) radius of Concrete, North Dakota (latitude 48 degrees 43' North, longitude97 degrees 54' West).

(i) In the States of Alabama, Florida, Georgia and South Carolina within a 200 kilometer (124 mile) radius of Warner Robins Air Force Base, Georgia (latitude 32° 38' North, longitude 83° 35' West).

(j) In the State of Texas within a 200-kilometer (124 mile) radius of Goodfellow Air Force Base, Texas (latitude 31° 25' North, longitude 100° 24' West).

US58—In the band 10000-10500 MHz, pulsed emissions are prohibited, except for weather radars on board meteorological-satellites in the band 10000-10025 MHz. The amateur service and the non-Government radiolocation service, which shall not cause harmful interference to the Government radiolocation service, are the only non-Government services permitted in this band. The non-Government radiolocation service is limited to survey operations as specified in footnote US108.

US87—The frequency 450 MHz, with maximum emission bandwidth of 500 kHz, may be used by Government and non-Government stations for space telecommand at specific locations, subject to such conditions as may be applied on a case-by-case basis.

US108—Within the bands 3300-3500 MHz and 10000-10500 MHz, survey operations, using transmitters with a peak power not to exceed five watts into the antenna, may be authorized for Government and non-Government use on a secondary basis to other Government radiolocation operations.

US110—In the frequency bands 3100-3300 MHz, 3500-3700 MHz, 5250-5350 MHz, 8500-9000 MHz, 9200-9300 MHz, 9500-10000 MHz, 13.4-14.0 GHz, 15.7-17.3 GHz, 24.05-24.25 GHz and 33.4-36 GHz, the non-Government radiolocation service shall be secondary to the Government radiolocation service and to airborne doppler radars at 8800 MHz, and shall provide protection to airport surface detection equipment (ASDE) operating between 15.7-16.2 GHz.

US211—In the bands 1670-1690, 5000-5250 MHz, and 10.7-11.7, 15.1365-15.35, 15.4-15.7, 22.5-22.55, 24-24.05, 31.0-31.3, 31.8-32, 40.5-42.5, 84-86, 102-105, 116-126, 151-164, 176.5-182, 185-190, 231-235, 252-265 GHz, applicants for airborne or space station assignments are urged to take all practicable steps to protect radio astronomy observations in the adjacent bands from harmful interference; however, US74 applies.

US215—Emissions from microwave ovens manufactured on and after January 1, 1980, for operation on the frequency 915 MHz must be confined within the band 902-928 MHz. Emissions from microwave ovens manufactured prior to January 1, 1980, for operation on the frequency 915 MHz must be confined within the band 902-940 MHz. Radiocommunications services operating within the band 928-940 MHz must accept any harmful interference that may be experienced from the operation of microwave ovens manufactured before January 1, 1980.

US217—Pulse-ranging radiolocation systems may be authorized for Government and non-Government use in the 420-450 MHz band along the shorelines of Alaska and the contiguous 48 States. Spread spectrum radiolocation systems may be authorized in the 420-435 MHz portion of the band for operation within the contiguous 48 States and Alaska. Authorizations will be granted on a case-by-case basis; however, operations proposed to be located within the zones set forth in US228 should not expect to be accommodated. All stations operating in accordance with this provision will be secondary to stations operating in accordance with the Table of Frequency Allocations.

US218—The band segments 902-912 MHz and918-928 MHz are available for Automatic Vehicle Monitoring (AVM) Systems subject to not causing harmful interference to the operation of Government stations authorized in these bands. These systems must tolerate any interference from the operation of industrial, scientific, and medical (ISM) devices and the operation of Government stations authorized in these bands.

US228—Applicants of operation in the band 420 to 450 MHz under the provisions of US217 should not expect to be accommodated if

their area of service is within the following geographic areas:
(a) Those portions of Texas and New Mexico bounded on the south by latitude 31° 45' North, on the east by longitude 104° 00' West, on the north by latitude 34° 30' North, and on the West by longitude 107° 30' West.
(b) The entire State of Florida including the Key West area and the areas enclosed within a 322 kilometer (200-mile) radius of Patrick Air Force Base, Florida (latitude 28° 21' North, longitude 80° 43' West), and within a 322 kilometer (200-mile) radius of Eglin Air Force Base, Florida (Latitude 30° 30' North, Longitude 86° 30' West).
(c) The entire State of Arizona;
(d) Those portions of California and Nevada south of latitude 37° 10' North, and the areas enclosed within a 322 kilometer (200-mile) radius of the Pacific Missile Test Center, Point Mugu, California (latitude 34° 09' North, longitude 119° 11' West).
(e) In the State of Massachusetts within a 160-kilometer (100-mile) radius around locations at Otis Air Force Base, Massachusetts (latitude 41° 45' North, longitude 70° 32' West).
(f) In the State of California within a 240-kilometer (150-mile) radius around locations at Beale Air Force Base, California (latitude 39° 08' North, longitude 121° 26' West).
(g) In the State of Alaska within a 160 kilometer (100-mile) radius of Clear, Alaska (latitude 64 degrees, 17' North, longitude 149 degrees 10' West).
(h) In the State of North Dakota within a 160-kilometer (100-mile) radius of Concrete, North Dakota (latitude 48 degrees 43' North, longitude 97 degrees 54' West).
(i) In the States of Alabama, Florida, Georgia and South Carolina within a 200- kilometer (124-mile) radius of Warner Robins Air Force Base, Georgia (latitude 32° 38' North, longitude 83° 35' West).
(j) In the State of Texas within a 200-kilometer (124-mile) radius of Goodfellow Air Force Base, Texas (latitude 31° 25' North, longitude 100° 24' West).

US230—Non-government land mobile service is allocated on a primary basis in the bands 422.1875-425.4875 and 427.1875-429.9875 MHz within 80 kilometers (50 statute miles) of Detroit, MI, and Cleveland, OH, and in the bands 423.8125-425.4875 and 428.8125-429.9875 MHzwithin 80 kilometers (50 sta- tute miles) of Buffalo, NY.

US243—In the band 220-225 MHz, stations in the radiolocation service have priority until 1 January 1990.

US245—The Fixed-Satellite Service is limited to International inter-Continental systems and subject to case-by-case electromagnetic compatibility analysis.

US247—The band 10100-10150 kHz is allocated to the fixed service on a primary basis outside the United States and Possessions. Transmissions of stations in the amateur service shall not cause harmful interference to this fixed service use and stations in the amateur service shall make all necessary adjustments (including termination of transmission) if harmful interference is caused.

US253—In the band 2300-2310 MHz, the fixed and mobile services shall not cause harmful interference to the amateur service.

US267—In the band 902-928 MHz, amateur radio stations shall not operate within the States of Colorado and Wyoming, bounded by the area of: latitude 39° N to 42° N and longitude 103° W to 108° W.

US275—The band 902-928 MHz is allocated on a secondary basis to the amateur service subject to not causing harmful interference to the operations of Government stations authorized in this band or to the Automatic Vehicle Monitoring (AVM) systems. Stations in the amateur service must tolerate any interference from the operations of industrial, scientific and medical (ISM) devices, AVM systems, and the operations of Government stations authorized in this band. Further, the Amateur Service is prohibited in those portions of Texas and New Mexico bounded on the south by latitude 31° 41' North, on the east by longitude 104° 11' West, on the north by latitude 34° 30' North, and on the west by longitude 107° 30' West; in addition, outside this area but within 240 kilometers (150 miles) of these boundaries of White Sands Missile Range the service is restricted to a maximum transmitter peak envelope power output of 50 watts.

US276—Except as otherwise provided for herein, use of the band 2310-2390 MHz by the mobile service is limited to aeronautical telemetering and associated telecommand operations for flight testing of manned or unmanned aircraft, missiles or major components thereof. The following six frequencies are shared on a co-equal basis by Government and non-Government stations for telemetering and associated telecommand operations of expendable and re-usable launch vehicles whether or not such operations involve flight testing: 2312.5, 2332.5, 2352.5, 2364.5, 2370.5, and 2382.5 MHz. All other mobile telemetering uses shall be secondary to the above uses.

US290—In the band 1900-2000 kHz, amateur stations may continue to operate on a secondary basis to the Radiolocation Service, pending a decision as to their disposition through a future rule making proceeding in conjunction with implementation of the Standard Broadcasting Service in the 1625-1705 kHz band.

484—Some countries of Region 1 use radiodetermination systems in the bands 1606.5-1625 kHz,1635-1800 kHz, 1850-2160 kHz, 2194-2300 kHz, 2502-2850 kHz and 3500-3800 kHz. The establishment and operation of such systems are subject to agreement obtained under the procedures set forth in Article 14. The radiated mean power of these stations shall not exceed 50 W.

485—Additional allocation: in Angola, Bulgaria, Hungary, Mongolia, Nigeria, Poland, the German Democratic Republic, Chad, Czechoslovakia and the U.S.S.R., the bands 1625-1635 kHz, 1800-1810 kHz and 2160-2170 kHz are also allocated to the fixed and land mobile services on a primary basis subject to agreement obtained under the procedure set forth in Article 14.

486—In Region 1, in the bands 1625-1635 kHz, 1800-1810 kHz and 2160-2170 kHz (except in the countries listed in No. 485 and those listed in No. 499 for the band 2160-2170 kHz), existing stations in the fixed and mobile except aeronautical mobile, services (and stations of the aeronautical mobile (OR) service in the band 2160-2170 kHz) may continue to operate on a primary basis until satisfactory replacement assignments have been found and implemented in accordance with Resolution 38.

488—In the Federal Republic of Germany, Denmark, Finland, Hungary, Ireland, Israel, Jordan, Malta, Norway, Poland, the German Democratic Republic, the United Kingdom, Sweden, Czechoslovakia and the U.S.S.R., administrations may allocate up to 200 kHz to their amateur service in the bands 1715-1800 kHz and 1850-2000 kHz. However, when allocating the bands within this range to their amateur service, administrations shall, after prior consultations with administrations of neighboring countries, take such steps as may be necessary to prevent harmful interference from their amateur service to the fixed and mobile services of other countries. The meanpower of any amateur station shall not exceed 10 W.

489—In Region 3, the Loran system operates either on 1850 kHz or 1950 kHz, the bands occupied being 1825-1875 kHz and 1925-1975 kHz, respectively. Other services to which the band 1800-2000 kHz is allocated may use any frequency therein on condition that no harmful interference is caused to the Loran system operating on 1850 kHz or 1950 kHz.

490—Alternative allocation: in the Federal Republic of Germany, Angola, Austria, Belgium, Bulgaria, Cameroon, the Congo, Denmark, Egypt, Spain, Ethiopia, France, Greece, Italy, the Lebanon, Luxembourg, Malawi, the Netherlands, Portugal, Syria, the German Democratic Republic, Somalia, Tanzania, Tunisia, Turkey and the U.S.S.R., the band 1810-1830 kHz is allocated to the fixed and mobile, except aeronautical mobile, services on a primary basis.

491—Additional allocation: in Saudi Arabia, Iraq, Israel, Libya, Poland, Romania, Chad, Czechoslovakia, Togo and Yugoslavia, the band 1810-1830 kHz is also allocated to the fixed and mobile, except aeronautical mobile, services on a primary basis.

492—In Region 1, the use of the band 1810-1850 kHz by the amateur service is subject to the condition that satisfactory replacement assignments have been found and implemented in accordance with Resolution 38, for frequencies to all existing stations of the fixed and mobile, except aeronautical mobile, services operating in this band (except for the stations of the countries listed in Nos. 490, 491 and 493). On completion of satisfactory transfer, the authorization to use the band 1810-1830 kHz by the amateur service in countries situated totally or partially north of 40°N shall be given only after consultation with the countries mentioned in Nos. 490 and 491 to define the necessary steps to be taken to prevent harmful interference between amateur stations and stations of other services operating in accordance with Nos. 490 and 491.

493—Alternative allocation: in Burundi and Lesotho, the band 1810-1850 kHz is allocated to the fixed and mobile, except aeronautical mobile,services on a primary basis.

494—Alternative allocation: in Argentina, Bolivia, Chile, Mexico, Paraguay, Peru, Uruguay and Venezuela, the band 1850-2000 kHz is allocated to the fixed mobile, except aero-nautical mobile, radiolocation and radionavigation services on a primary basis.

495—In Region 1, in making assignments to stations in the fixed and mobile services in the bands 1850-2045 kHz, 2194-2498 kHz, 2502-2625 kHz and 2650-2850 kHz, administrations should bear in mind the special requirements of the maritime mobile service.

509—Additional allocation: in Honduras, Mexico, Peru and Venezuela, the band 3500-3750 kHz is also allocated to the fixed and mobile services on a primary basis.

510—For the use of the bands allocated to the amateur service at 3.5 MHz, 7.0 MHz, 10.1 MHz, 14.0 MHz, 18.068 MHz, 21.0 MHz, 24.89 MHz and 144 MHz in the event of natural disasters, see Resolution 640.

511—Additional allocation: in Brazil, the band 3700-4000 kHz is also allocated to the radiolocation service on a primary basis.

512—Alternative allocation: in Argentina, Bolivia, Chile, Ecuador, Paraguay, Peru and Uruguay, the band 3750-4000 kHz is allocated to the fixed andmobile, except aeronautical mobile, services on a primary basis.

513—Alternative allocation: in Botswana, Lesotho, Malawi, Mozambique, Namibia, South Africa, Swaziland, Zambia and Zimbabwe, the band 3900-3950 kHz is allocated to the broadcasting service on a primary basis. The use of this band by the broadcasting service is subject to agreement obtained under the procedure set forth in Article 14 with neighboring countries having services operating in accordance with the Table.

514—Additional allocation: in Canada, the band 3950-4000 kHz is also allocated to the broadcasting service on a primary basis. The power of broadcasting stations operating in this band shall not exceed that necessary for a national service within the frontier of this country and shall not cause harmful interference to other services operating in accordance with the Table.

515—Additional allocation: in Greenland, the band 3950-4000 kHz is also allocated to the broadcasting service on a primary basis. The power of the broadcasting stations operating in this band shall not exceed that necessary for a national service and shall in no case exceed 5 kW.

516—In Region 3, the stations of those services to which the band 3995-4005 kHz is allocated may transmit standard frequency and time signals.

526—Additional allocation: in Angola, Iraq, Kenya, Rwanda, Somalia and Togo, the band 7000-7050 kHz is also allocated to the fixed service on a primary basis.

527—Alternative allocation: in Egypt, Ethiopia, Guinea, Libya, Madagascar, Malawi and Tanzania, the band 7000-7050 kHz is allocated to the fixed service on a primary basis.

528—The use of the band 7 100-7 300 kHz in Region 2 by the amateur service shall not impose constraints on the broadcasting service intended for use within Region 1 and Region 3.

535—Additional allocation: in Afghanistan, China, the Ivory Coast, Iran and the U.S.S.R., the band 14 250-14 350 kHz is also allocated to the fixed service on a primary basis. Stations of the fixed service shall not use a radiated power exceeding 24 dBW.

537—The band 18 068-18 168 kHz is allocated tothe fixed service on a primary basis subject to the procedure described in Resolution 8. The use of this band by the amateur and amateur-satellite services shall be subject to the completion of satisfactory transfer of all assignments to stations in the fixed service operating in this band and recorded in the Master Register, in accordance with the procedure described in Resolution 8.

538—Additional allocation: in the U.S.S.R., the band 18 068-18 168 kHz is also allocated to the fixed service on a primary basis for use within the boundary of the U.S.S.R., with a peak envelope power not exceeding 1 kW.

542—Additional allocation: in Kenya, the band 23 600-24 900 kHz is also allocated to the meteorological aids service (radiosondes) on a primary basis.

543—The band 24 890-24 990 kHz is allocated to the fixed and land mobile services on a primary basis subject to the procedure described in Resolution 8. The use of this band by the amateur and amateur-satellite services shall be subject to the completion of the satisfactory transfer of all assignments to fixed and land mobile stations operating in this band and recorded in the Master Register, in accordance with the procedure described in Resolution 8.

556—Alternative allocation: in New Zealand, the band 50-51 MHz is allocated to the fixed, mobile and broadcasting services on a primary basis, the band 53-54 MHz is allocated to the fixed and mobile services on a primary basis.

557—Alternative allocation: in Afghanistan, Bangladesh, Brunei, India, Indonesia, Iran, Malaysia, Pakistan, Singapore and Thai-land, the band 50-54 MHz is allocated to the fixed, mobile and broadcasting services on a primary basis.

558—Additional allocation: in Australia, China and the Democratic People's Republic of Korea, the band 50-54 MHz is also allocated to the broadcasting service on a primary basis.

560—Additional allocation: in New Zealand, the band 51-53 MHz is also allocated to the fixed and mobile services on a primary basis.

605—Additional allocation: in Singapore, the band 144-145 MHz is also allocated to the fixed and mobile services on a primary basis. Such use is limited to systems in operation on or before 1 January 1980, which in any case shall cease by 31 December 1995.

606—Additional allocation: In China, the band 144-146 MHz is also allocated to the aeronautical mobile (OR) service on a secondary basis.

607—Alternative allocation: in Afghanistan, Bangladesh, Cuba, Guyana and India, the band 146-148 MHz is allocated to the fixed and mobile services on a primary basis.

608—Subject to agreement obtained under the procedure set forth in Article 14, the band 148-149.9 MHz may be used by the space operation service (Earth-to-space). The bandwidth of an individual transmission shall not exceed ± 25 kHz.

622—Different category of service: in the FederalRepublic of Germany, Austria, Belgium, Denmark, Spain, Finland, France, Israel, Italy, Liechtenstein, Luxembourg, Monaco, Norway, the Netherlands, Portugal, the United Kingdom, Sweden, Switzerland, and Yemen (P.D.R. of), the band 223-230 MHz is allocated to the land mobile service on a permitted basis (see No. 425). However, the stations of the land mobile service shall not cause harmful interference to, nor claim protection from, broadcasting stations, existing or planned, in countries other than those listed in this footnote.

627—In Region 2, the band 216-225 MHz is allocated to the radiolocation service on a primary basis until 1 January 1990. On and after 1 January 1990, no new stations in that service may be authorized. Stations authorized prior to 1 January 1990 may continue to operate on a secondary basis.

628—Additional allocation: in Somalia, the band 216-225 MHz is also allocated to the aero-nautical radionavigation service on a primary basis, subject to not causing harmful interference to existing or planned broad-casting services in other countries.

629—Additional allocation: in Oman, the United Kingdom and Turkey, the band 216-235 MHz is also allocated to the radiolocation service on a secondary basis.

631—Different category of service: in Spain and Portugal, the band 223-230 MHz is allocated to the fixed service on a permitted basis (see No. 425). Stations of this service shall not cause harmful interference to, or claim protection from, broadcasting stations of other countries, whether existing or planned, that operate in accordance with the Table.

632—Additional allocation: in Saudi Arabia, Bahrain, the United Arab Emirates, Israel, Jordan, Oman, Qatar and Syria, the band 223-235 MHz is also allocated to the aero-nautical radionavigation service on a permitted basis.

633—Additional allocation: in Spain and Portugal, the band 223-235 MHz is also allocated to the aeronautical radionavigation service on a permitted basis until 1 January 1990, subject to not causing harmful interference to existing or planned broadcasting stations in other countries.

634—Additional allocation: in Sweden, the band 223-235 MHz is also allocated to the aeronautical radionavigation service on a permitted basis until 1 January 1990, subject to agreement obtained under the procedure set forth in Article 14, and on condition that no harmful interference is caused to existing and planned broadcasting stations in other countries.

635—Alternative allocation: in Botswana, Lesotho, Namibia, South Africa, Swaziland and Zambia, the bands 223-238 MHz and 246-254 MHz are allocated to the broadcasting service on a primary basis subject to agreement obtained under the procedure set forth in Article 14.

636—Alternative allocation: in New Zealand, Western Samoa and the Niue and Cook Islands, the band 225-230 MHz is allocated to the fixed, mobile and aeronautical radio-navigation services on a primary basis.

637—Additional allocation: in China, the band225-235 MHz is also allocated to the radio astronomy service on a secondary basis.

651—Different category of service: in Australia, the United States, India, Japan and the United Kingdom, the allocation of the bands 420-430 MHz and 440-450 MHz to the radiolocation service is on a primary basis (see No. 425).

652—Additional allocation: in Australia, the United States, Jamaica and the Philippines, the bands 420-430 MHz and 440-450 MHz are also allocated to the amateur service on a secondary basis.

653—Additional allocation: in China, India, the German Democratic Republic, the United Kingdom and the U.S.S.R., the band 420-460 MHz is also allocated to the aero-nautical radionavigation service (radio altimeters) on a secondary basis.

654—Different category of service: in France, the allocation of the band 430-434 MHz to the amateur service is on a secondary basis (see No. 424).

655—Different category of service: in Denmark, Libya, Norway and Sweden, the allocation of the bands 430-432 MHz and 438-440 MHz to the radiolocation service is on a secondary basis (see No 424).

656—Alternative allocation: in Denmark, Norway and Sweden, the bands 430-432 MHz and 438-440 MHz are allocated to the fixed and mobile, except aeronautical mobile, services on a primary basis.

657—Additional allocation: in Finland, Libya and Yugoslavia, the bands 430-432 MHz and 438-440 MHz are also allocated to the fixed and mobile except aeronautical mobile, services on a primary basis.

658—Additional allocation: in Afghanistan, Algeria, Saudi Arabia, Bahrain, Bangladesh, Brunei, Burundi, Egypt, the United Arab Emirates, Ecuador, Ethiopia, Greece, Guinea, India, Indonesia, Iran, Iraq, Israel, Italy, Jordan, Kenya, Kuwait, the Lebanon, Libya, Liechtenstein, Malaysia, Malta, Nigeria, Oman, Pakistan, the Philippines, Qatar, Syria, Singapore, Somalia, Switzerland, Tanzania, Thailand and Togo, the band 430-440 MHz is also allocated to the fixed service on a primary basis and the bands 430-435 MHz and 438-440 MHz are also allocated to the mobile, except aeronautical mobile, service on a primary basis.

659—Additional allocation: in Angola, Bulgaria, Cameroon, the Congo, Gabon, Hungary, Mali, Mongolia, Niger, Poland, the German Democratic Republic, Romania, Rwanda, Chad, Czechoslovakia and the U.S.S.R., the band 430-440 MHz is also allocated to the fixed service on a primary basis.

660—Different category of service: in Argentina, Colombia, Costa Rica, Cuba, Guyana, Honduras, Panama and Venezuela, the allocation of the band 430-440 MHz to the amateur service is on aprimary basis (see No. 425).

660A—Additional allocation: in Mexico, the bands 430-435 MHz and 438-440 MHz are also allocated on a primary basis to the land mobile service, subject to agreement obtained under the procedure set forth in Article 14.

661—In Region 1, except in the countries mentioned in No. 662, the band 433.05-434.79 MHz (center frequency 433.92 MHz) is designated for industrial, scientific and medical (ISM) applications. The use of this frequency band for ISM applications shall be subject to special authorization by the administration concerned, in agreement with other administrations whose radio-communication services might be affected. In applying this provision, administrations shall have due regard to the latest relevant CCIR Recommendations.

662—In the Federal Republic of Germany, Austria, Liechtenstein, Portugal, Switzerland and Yugoslavia, the band 433.05-434.79 MHz (center frequency 433.92 MHz) is designated for industrial, scientific and medical (ISM) applications. Radiocommunication services of these countries operating within this band must accept harmful interference which may be caused by these applications. ISM equipment operating in this band is subject to the provisions of No. 1815.

663—Additional allocation: in Brazil, France and the French Overseas Departments in Region 2, and India, the band 433.75-434.25 MHz is also allocated to the space operation service (Earthto-space) on a primary basis until 1 January 1990, subject to agreement obtained under the procedure set forth in Article 14. After 1 January 1990, the band 433.75-434.25 MHz will be allocated in the same countries to the same service on a secondary basis.

664—In the bands 435-438 MHz, 1260-1270 MHz, 2400-2450 MHz, 3400-3410 MHz (in Regions 2 and 3 only) and 5650-5670 MHz, the amateur-satellite service may operate subject to not causing harmful interference to other services operating in accordance with the Table (see No. 435). Administrations authorizing such use shall ensure that any harmful interference caused by emissions from a station in the amateur-satelliteservice is immediately eliminated in accordance with the provisions of No. 2741. The use of the bands 1260-1270 MHz and 5650-5670 MHz by the amateur-satellite service is limited to the Earth-to-space direction.

665—Additional allocation: in Austria, the band 438-440 MHz is also allocated to the fixed and mobile, except aeronautical mobile, services on a primary basis.

668—Subject to agreement obtained under the procedure set forth in Article 14, the band
449.75-450.25 MHz may be used for the space operation service (Earth-to-space) and the space research service (Earth-to-space).

705—Different category of service: in the UnitedStates, the allocation of the band 890-942 MHz to the radiolocation service is on a primary basis (see No. 425) and subject to agreement obtained under the procedure set forth in Article 14.

707—In Region 2, the band 902-928 MHz (center frequency 915 MHz) is designated for industrial, scientific and medical (ISM) applications. Radiocommunication services operating within this band must accept harmful interference which may be caused by these applications. ISM equipment operating in this band is subject to the provisions of No. 1815.

707A—Different category of service: in Chile, the band 903-905 MHz is allocated to the mobile, except aeronautical mobile, service on a primary basis and is subject to agreement obtained under the procedure set forth in Article 14.

710—Use of the radionavigation-satellite service in the band 1 215-1 260 MHz shall be subject to the condition that no harmful interference is caused to the radionavigation service authorized under No. 712.

711—Additional allocation: in Afghanistan, Angola, Saudi Arabia, Bahrain, Bangladesh, Cameroon, China, the United Arab Emirates, Ethiopia, Guinea, Guyana, India, Indonesia, Iran, Iraq, Israel, Japan, Jordan, Kuwait, the Lebanon, Libya, Malawi, Morocco, Mozambique, Nepal, Nigeria, Oman, Pakistan, the Philippines, Qatar, Syria, Somalia, Sudan, Sri Lanka, Chad, Thailand, Togo and Yemen (P.D.R. of), the band 1215-1300 MHz is also allocated to the fixed and mobile services on a primary basis.

712—Additional allocation: in Algeria, the Federal Republic of Germany, Austria, Bahrain, Belgium, Benin, Burundi, Cameroon, China, Denmark, the United Arab Emirates, France, Greece, India, Iran, Iraq, Kenya, Liechtenstein, Luxembourg, Mali, Mauritania, Norway, Oman, Pakistan, the Netherlands, Portugal, Qatar, Senegal, Somalia, Sudan, Sri Lanka, Sweden, Switzerland, Tanzania, Turkey and Yugoslavia, the band 1 215-1 300 MHz is also allocated to the radionavigation service on a primary basis.

712A—Additional allocation: in Cuba, the band 1215-1300 MHz is also allocated to the radionavigation service on a primary basis subject to the agreement obtained under the procedure set forth in Article 14.

713—In the bands 1215-1300 MHz, 3100-3300 MHz, 5250-5350 MHz, 8550-8650 MHz, 9500-9800 MHz and 13.4-14.0 GHz, radiolocation stations installed on spacecraft may also be employed for the earth exploration-satellite and space research services on a secondary basis.

714—Additional allocation: in Canada and the United States, the bands 1240-1300 MHz and 1350-1370 MHz are also allocated to the aeronautical radionavigation service on a primary basis.

743A—Different category of service: in the Federal Republic of Germany, Austria, Denmark, Finland, Israel, Norway, the Netherlands, the United Kingdom, Switzerland, and Syria, in theband 1700-2450 MHz, in Sweden in the bands 1700-1710 MHz and 2290-2450 MHz and in Yugoslavia in the band 2300-2450 MHz, the allocation to the land mobile service is on a primary basis (see No. 425), subject to agreement obtained under the procedure set forth in Article 14.

751—In Australia, the United States and Papua New Guinea, the use of the band 2310-2390 MHz by the aeronautical mobile service for telemetry has priority over other uses by the mobile services.

752—The band 2 400-2 500 MHz (center frequency 2 450 MHz) is designated for industrial, scientific and medical (ISM) applications. Radio services operating within this band must accept harmful interference which may be caused by these applications. ISM equipment operating in this band is subject to the provisions of No. 1815.

778—In making assignments to stations of other services, administrations are urged to take all practicable steps to protect the spectral line observations of the radio astronomy service from harmful interference in the bands 3260-3267 MHz, 3332-3339 MHz, 3345.8-3352.5 MHz and 4825-4835 MHz. Emissions from space or airborne stations can be particularly serious sources of interference to the radio astronomy service (see Nos. 343 and 344 and Article 36).

779—Additional allocation: in Afghanistan, Saudi Arabia, Bahrain, Bangladesh, China, the Congo, the United Arab Emirates, India, Indonesia, Iran, Iraq, Israel, Japan, Kuwait, the Lebanon, Libya, Malaysia, Oman, Pakistan, Qatar, Syria, Singapore, Sri Lanka and Thailand, the band 3300-3400 MHz is also allocated to the fixed and mobile services on a primary basis. The countries bordering the Mediterranean shall not claim protection for their fixed and mobile services from the radiolocation service.

780—Additional allocation: in Bulgaria, Cuba, Hungary, Mongolia, Poland, the German Democratic Republic, Romania, Czechoslovakia and the U.S.S.R., the band 3300-3400 MHz is also allocated to the radio-navigation service on a primary basis.

781—Additional allocation: in the Federal Republic of Germany, Israel, Nigeria and the United Kingdom, the band 3 400-3 475 MHz is also allocated to the amateur service on a secondary basis.

782—Different category of service: in Austria, theallocation of the band 3 400-3 500 MHz to the radiolocation service is on a primary basis (see No. 425), subject to the agreement of the Administrations of the following countries: Hungary, Italy, the German Democratic Republic, Czechoslovakia and Yugoslavia. Such use is limited to ground-based stations. However, this Administration is urged to cease operations by 1985. After this date, this Administration shall take all practicable steps to protect the fixed-satellite service and coordination requirements shall not be imposed on the fixed-satellite service.

783—Different category of service: in Indonesia, Japan, Pakistan and Thailand, the allocation of the band 3 400-3 500 MHz to the mobile, except aeronautical mobile, service is on a primary basis (see No. 425).

785—In Denmark, Norway and the United Kingdom, the fixed, radiolocation and fixed-satellite services operate on a basis of equality of rights in the band 3 400-3 600 MHz. However, these Administrations operating radiolocation systems in this band are urged to cease operations by 1985. After this date, these Administrations shall take all practicable steps to protect the fixed-satellite service and coordination requirements shall not be imposed on the fixed-satellite service.

801—Additional allocation: in the United Kingdom, the band 5 470-5 850 MHz is also allocated to the land mobile service on a secondary basis. The power limits specified in Nos. 2502, 2505, 2506 and 2507 shall apply in the band 5 725-5 850 MHz.

803—Additional allocation: in Afghanistan, Saudi Arabia, Bahrain, Bangladesh, Cameroon, the Central African Republic, China, the Congo, the Republic of Korea, Egypt, the United Arab Emirates, Gabon, Guinea, India, Indonesia, Iran, Iraq, Israel, Japan, Jordan, Kuwait, the Lebanon, Libya, Madagascar, Malaysia, Malawi, Malta, Niger, Nigeria, Pakistan, the Philippines, Qatar, Syria, Singapore, Sri Lanka, Tanzania, Chad, Thailand and Yemen (P.D.R. of), the band 5 650-5 850 MHz is also allocated to the fixed and mobile services on a primary basis.

804—Different category of service: in Bulgaria, Cuba, Hungary, Mongolia, Poland, the German Democratic Republic, Czechoslovakia and the U.S.S.R., the allocation of the band 5 670-5 725 MHz to the space research service is on a primary basis (see No. 425).

805—Additional allocation: in Bulgaria, Cuba, Hungary, Mongolia, Poland, the German Democratic Republic, Czechoslovakia and the U.S.S.R., the band 5 670-5 850 MHz is alsoallocated to the fixed service on a primary basis.

806—The band 5 725-5 875 MHz (center frequency 5 800 MHz) is designated for industrial, scientific and medical (ISM) applications. Radiocommunication services operating within this band must accept harmful interference which may be caused by these applications. ISM equipment operating in this band is subject to the provisions of No. 1815. **807**—Additional allocation: in the Federal Republic of Germany and in Cameroon, the band 5 755-5 850 MHz is also allocated to the fixed service on a primary basis.

808—The band 5 830-5 850 MHz is also allocated in the amateur-satellite service (space-to-Earth) on a secondary basis.

811—Subject to agreement obtained under the procedure set forth in Article 14, the band 7 145-7 235 MHz may be used for Earth-to-space transmissions in the space research service. The use of the band 7 145-7 190 MHz is restricted to deep space; no emissions to deep space shall be effected in the band 7 190-7 235 MHz.

828—The band 9 975-10 025 MHz is also allocated to the meteorological-satellite service on a secondary basis for use by weather radars.

829—Additional allocation: in Costa Rica, Ecuador, Guatemala and Honduras, the band 10-10.45 GHz is also allocated to the fixed and mobile services on a primary basis.

830—Additional allocation: in the Federal Republic of Germany, Angola, China, Ecuador, Spain, Japan, Kenya, Morocco, Nigeria, Sweden, Tanzania and Thailand, the band 10.45-10.5 GHz is also allocated to the fixed and mobile services on a primary basis.

881—The band 24-24.25 GHz (center frequency 24.125 GHz) is designated for industrial, scientific and medical (ISM) applications. Radiocommunication services operating within this band must accept harmful interference which may be caused by these applications. ISM equipment operating in this band is subject to the provisions of No. 1815.

902—In the bands 43.5-47 GHz, 66-71 GHz, 95-100 GHz, 134-142 GHz, 190-200 GHz and 252-265 GHz, stations in the land mobile service may be operated subject to not causing harmful interference to the space radiocommunication services to which these bands are allocated (see No. 435).

903—In the bands 43.5-47 GHz, 66-71 GHz, 95-100 GHz, 134-142 GHz, 190-200 GHz and 252-265 GHz, satellite links connecting land stations at specified fixed points are also authorized when used in conjunction with the mobile-satellite service or the radionavigation-satellite service.

912—In the band 78-79 GHz radars located on space stations may be operated on a primary basis in the Earth exploration-satellite service and inthe space research service.

917—In the band 140.69-140.98 GHz all emissions from airborne stations, and from space stations in the space-to-Earth direction, are prohibited.

918—The bands 140.69-140.98 GHz, 144.68-144.98 GHz, 145.45-145.75 GHz and 146.82-147.12 GHz are also allocated to the radio astronomy service on a primary basis for spectral line observations. In making assignments to stations of other services to which the bands are allocated, administrations are urged to take all practicable steps to protect the radio astronomy service from harmful interference. Emissions from space or air-borne stations can be particularly serious sources of interference to the radio astronomy service (see Nos. 343 and 344 and Article 36).

922—The band 244-246 GHz (center frequency 245 GHz) is designated for industrial, scientific and medical (ISM) applications. The use of this frequency band for ISM applications shall be subject to special authorization by the administration concerned in agreement with other administrations whose radiocommunication services might be affected. In applying this provision administrations shall have due regard to the latest relevant CCIR Recommendations.

NG42—Non-Government stations in the radiolocation service shall not cause harmful interference to the amateur service.

NG134—In the band 10.45-10.5 GHz non-Government stations in the radiolocation service shall not cause harmful interference to the amateur and amateur-satellite services.

FCC EMISSION DESIGNATORS

Subpart C—Emissions

§ 2.201 Emission, modulation, and transmission characteristics.

The following system of designating emission, modulation, and transmission characters shall be employed.

(a) Emissions are designated according to their classification and their necessary bandwidth.

(b) A minimum of three symbols are used to describe the basic characteristics of radio waves. Emissions are classified and symbolized according to the following characteristics.

(1) First symbol—type of modulation of the main character;

(2) Second symbol—nature of signal(s) modulating the main carrier;

(3) Third symbol—type of information to be transmitted.

NOTE: A fourth and fifth symbol are provided for additional information and are shown in Appendix 6, part of the ITU Radio Regulations. Use of the fourth and fifth symbol is optional. Therefore, the symbols may be used as described in Appendix 6, but are not required by the Commission.

(c) First Symbol—types of modulation of the main carrier:

(1) Emission of an unmodulated carrier .... N

(2) Emission in which the main carrier is amplitude-modulated (including cases where sub-carriers are angle-modulated):

—Double-sidebanded .... A

—Single-sidebanded, full carrier .... H

—Single-sidebanded, reduced or variable level carrier .... R

—Single-banded, suppressed carrier .... J

—Independent sidebands .... B

—Vestigal sideband C

(3) Emission in which the main carrier is angle-modulated:

—Frequency modulation .... F

—Phase modulation .... G

NOTE: Whenever frequency modulation "F" is indicated, Phase modulation "G" is also acceptable.

(4) Emission in which the main carrier is amplitude and angle-modulated either simultaneously or in a pre-established sequence .... D

(5) Emission pulses:[1]

—Sequence of unmodulated pulses .... P

—A sequence of pulses:

—Modulated in amplitude .... K

—Modulated in width/duration L

—Modulated in position/phase .... M

—In which the carrier is angle-modulated during the period of the pulse .... Q

—Which is a combination of the foregoing or is produced by other means V

(6) Cases not covered above, in which an emission consists of the main carrier modulated, either simultaneously or in a pre-established sequence, in a combination of two or more of the following modes: amplitude, angle or pulse .... W

(7) Cases not otherwise covered X

[1] Emissions where the main carrier is directly modulated by a signal which has been coded into a quantized form (e.g. pulse code modulation) should be designated under (2) or (3).

(d) Second Symbol—nature of signal(s) modulating the main carrier:

(1) No modulating signal....................0
(2) A single channel containing quantized or digital information without the use of a modulating sub-carrier, excluding time-division multiplex....................1
(3) A single channel containing quantized or digital information with the use of a modulating sub-carrier, excluding time-division multiplex....................2
(4) A single channel containing analog information....................3
(5) Two or more channels containing quantized or digital information....................7
(6) Two or more channels containing analog information....................8
(7) Composite system with one or more channels containing quantized or digital information, together with one or more channels containing analog information....................9
(8) Cases not otherwise covered....................X

(e) Third Symbol—type of information to be transmitted:[2]

(1) No information transmitted....................N
(2) Telegraphy—for aural reception....................A
(3) Telegraphy—for automatic reception....................B
(4) Facsimile....................C
(5) Data transmission, telemetry, telecommand....................D
(6) Telephony (including sound broadcasting)....................E
(7) Television (video)....................F
(8) Combination of the above....................W
(9) Cases not otherwise covered....................X

(f) Type B emission: As an exception to the above principles, damped waves are symbolized in the Commission's rules and regulations as type B emission. The use of type B emissions is forbidden.
(g) Whenever the full designation of an emission is necessary, the symbol for that emission, as given above, shall be preceded by the necessary bandwidth of the emission as indicated in §2.202 (b)(1).
[49 FR 48697, Dec. 14, 1984]

[2] In this context the word "information" does not include information of a constant, unvarying nature such as is provided by standard frequency emissions, continuous wave and pulse radars, etc.

§ 2.202 Bandwidths.

(a) *Occupied bandwidth.* The frequency bandwidth such that, below its lower and above its upper frequency limits, the mean powers radiated are each equal to 0.5 percent of the total mean power radiated by a given emission. In some cases, for example multichannel frequency-division systems, the percentage of 0.5 percent may lead to certain difficulties in the practical application of the definitions of occupied and necessary bandwidth; in such cases a different percentage may prove useful.
(b) *Necessary bandwidth.* For a given class of emission, the minimum value of the occupied bandwidth sufficient to ensure the transmission of information at the rate and with the quality required for the system employed, under specific conditions. Emissions useful for the good functioning of the receiving equipment as, for example, the emission corresponding to the carrier of reduced carrier systems, shall be included in the necessary bandwidth.
(1) The necessary bandwidth shall be expressed by three numerals and one letter. The letter occupies the position of the decimal point and represents the unit of bandwidth. The first character shall be neither zero nor K, M, or G.
(2) Necessary bandwidths:

between 0.001 and 999 Hz shall be expressed in Hz (letter H);
between 1.00 and 999 kHz shall be expressed in kHz (letter K);
between 1.00 and 999 MHz shall be expressed in MHz (letter M);
between 1.00 and 999 GHz shall be expressed in GHz (letter G).

(3) Examples:
0.002 Hz—H002....................180.5 kHz—181K
0.1 Hz—H100....................180.7 kHz—181K
25.3 Hz—25H3....................1.25 MHz—1M25
400 Hz—400H....................2 MHz—2M00
2.4 kHz—2K40....................10 MHz—10M0
6 kHz—6K00....................202 MHz—202M
12.5 kHz—12K5....................5.65 GHz—5G65
180.4 kHz—180K

(c) The necessary bandwidth may be determined by one of the following methods:
(1) Use of the formulas included in the table, in paragraph (g) of this section, which also gives examples of necessary bandwidths and designation of corresponding emission;
(2) For frequency modulated radio systems which have a substantially linear relationship between the value of input voltage to the modulator and the resulting frequency deviation of the carrier and which carry either single sideband suppressed carrier frequency division multiplex speech channels or television, computation in accordance with provisions of paragraph (f) of this section and formulas and methods indicated in the table, in paragraph (g) of this section;
(3) Computation in accordance with Recommendations of the International Radio Consultative Committee (C.C.I.R.);
(4) Measurement in cases not covered by paragraph (c) (1), (2), or (3) of this section.
(d) The value so determined should be used when the full designation of an emission is required. However, the necessary bandwidth so determined is not the only characteristic of an emission to be considered in evaluating the interference that may be caused that emission.
(e) In the formulation of the table in paragraph (g) of this section, the following terms are employed:

B_n = Necessary bandwidth in hertz
B = Modulation rate in bauds
N = Maximum possible number of black plus white elements to be transmitted per second, in facsimile
M = Maximum modulation frequency in hertz
C = Sub-carrier frequency in hertz
D = Peak frequency deviation, i.e., half the difference between the maximum and minimum values of the instantaneous frequency. The instantaneous frequency in hertz is the time rate of change in phase in radians divided by 2
t = Pulse duration in seconds at half-amplitude
t_r = Pulse rise time in seconds between 10% and 90% of maximum amplitude
K = An overall numeric factor which varies according to the emission and which depends upon the allowable signal distortion
N_c = Number of baseband telephone channels in radio systems employing multi-channel multiplexing
P = Continuity pilot sub-carrier frequency (Hz) (continuos signal utilized to verify performance of frequency-division multiplex systems).

(f) Determination of values of *D* and B_n for systems specified in paragraph (c) (2) of this section:
(1) Determination of *D* in systems for multi-channel telephony:
(i) The rms value of the per-channel deviation for the system shall be specified. (In the case of systems employing preemphasis or phase modulation, this value of per-channel deviation shall be specified at the characteristic baseband frequency.)
(ii) The value of D is then calculated by multiplying the rms value of the per-channel deviation by the appropriate factors, as follows:

Number of message circuits	Multiplying factors	Limits of X (P_{avg} (dBmO))
More than 3, but less than 12	4.47 x [a factor specified by the equipment manufacturer or station licensee, subject to Commission approval].	
At least 12, but less than 60	$3.76 \text{ antilog } \frac{(X+2\log_{10} N_c)}{20}$	X: –2 to +2.6.
At least 60, but less than 240	$3.76 \text{ antilog } \frac{(X+4\log_{10} N_c)}{20}$	X: –5.6 to –1.0.
240 or more	$3.76 \text{ antilog } \frac{(X+10\log_{10} N_c)}{20}$	x: –19.6 to –15.0.

Where X represents the average power in a message circuit in dBmO; N_c is the number of circuits in the multiplexed message load; 3.76 corresponds to a peak load factor of 11.5 dB.

(2) The necessary bandwidth (B_n) normally is considered to be numerically equal to:
(i) $2M+2DK$, for systems having no continuity pilot subcarrier or having a continuity pilot subcarrier whose frequency is not the highest modulating the main carrier;
(ii) $2P+2DK$, for systems having a continuity pilot subcarrier whose frequency exceeds that of any other signal modulating the main carrier, unless the conditions set forth in paragraph (f)(3) of this section are met.
(3) As an exception to paragraph (f)(2)(ii) of this section, the necessary bandwidth (B_n) for such systems is numerically equal to $2P$ or $2M+2DK$, whichever is greater, provided the following conditions are met:
(i) The modulation index of the main carrier due to the continuity pilot subcarrier does not exceed 0.25, and
(ii) In a radio system of multichannel telephony, the rms frequency deviation of the main carrier due to the continuity pilot subcarrier does not exceed 70 percent of the rms value of the per-channel deviation, or , in a radio system for television, the rms deviation of the main carrier due to the pilot does not exceed 3.55 percent of the peak deviation of the main carrier.
(g) Table of necessary bandwidths:

Description of emission	Necessary bandwidth		Designation of emission
	Formula	Sample calculation	
I. NO MODULATING SIGNAL			
Continuous wave emission.			NON (zero)

II. AMPLITUDE MODULATION

1. Signal With Quantized or Digital Information

Continuous wave telegraphy.	B_n=BK, k=5 for fading circuits, K=3 for non-fading circuits	25 words per minute; B=20, K=5, Bandwidth: 100 Hz	100HA1A
Telegraphy by on-off keying of a tone modulated carrier.	B_n=BK+2M, K=5 for fading circuits, K=3 for non-fad ing circuits	25 words per minute; B=20, M=1000, K=5, Bandwidth: 2100 Hz=2.1 kHz	2K10A2A
Selective calling signal, single-sideband full carrier.	B_n=M	Maximum code frequency is: 2110 Hz, M=2110, Bandwidth: 2110 Hz=2.11 kHz.	2K11H2B
Direct-printing telegraphy using a frequency shifted modulating sub-carrier single-sideband suppressed carrier.	B_n=2M+2DK, M=B÷2	B=50, D=35 Hz (70 Hz shift), K=1.2, Bandwidth: 134 Hz.	134HJ2B
Telegraphy, single sideband reduced carrier.	B_n=central frequency+M+DK, M=B÷2	15 channels; highest central frequency is: 2805 Hz, B=100, D=42.5 Hz (85 Hz shift), K=0.7 Bandwidth: 2885 Hz=2.885 kHz	2K89R7B

2. Telephony (Commercial Quality)

Telephony double-sideband.	B_n=2M	M=3000, Bandwidth: 6000 Hz=6 kHz	6K00A3E
Telephony, single-sideband, full carrier.	B_n=2M	M=3000, Bandwidth: 3000 Hz=3 kHz	3K00H3E
Telephony, single-sideband suppressed carrier.	B_n=M–lowest modulation frequency	M=3000, lowest modulation frequency is 3000Hz, 2700 Hz Bandwidth: 2700 Hz=2.7 kHz	2K70J3E
Telephony with separate frequency modulated signal to control the level of demodulated speech signal, single-sideband, reduced carrier.	B_n=M	Maximum control frequency is 2990 Hz, M=2990, Bandwidth: 2990 Hz=2.99 kHz	2K99R3E
Telephony with privacy, single-sideband, suppressed carrier (two or more channels).	B_n=N_cM–lowest modulation frequency in the lowest channel	N_c=2, M=3000 lowest modulation frequency is 250 Hz, Bandwidth: 5750 Hz=5.75 kHz.	5K75J8E
Telephony, independent sideband (two or more channels).	B_n=sum of M for each sideband	2 channels, M=3000, Bandwidth: 6000 Hz=6 kHz	6K00B8E

3. Sound Broadcasting

Sound broadcasting, double sideband.	B_n=2M, M may vary between 4000 and 10000 depending on the quality desired	Speech and music, M=4000, Bandwidth: 8000 Hz=8 kHz	8K00A3E
Sound broadcasting, single-sideband reduced carrier (single channel).	B_n=M, M may vary between 4000 and 10000 depending on the quality desired	Speech and music, M=4000, Bandwidth: 4000 Hz=4 kHz	4K00R3E
Sound broadcasting, single-sideband, suppressed carrier.	B_n=M–lowest modulation frequency	Speech and music, M=4500, lowest modulation frequency= 50 Hz, Bandwidth: 4450 Hz=4.45 kHz	4K45J3E

4. Television

Television, vision and sound.	Refer to CCIR documents for the bandwidths of the commonly used television systems	Number of lines=525; Nominal video bandwidth, 4.2 MHz, Sound carrier relative to video carrier=4.5 MHz.	5M75C3F
		Total vision bandwidth: 5.75 MHz; FM aural bandwidth including guardbands: 250,000 Hz	250KF3E
		Total bandwidth: 6 MHz	6M25C3F

5. Facsimile

Analogue facsimile by sub-carrier frequency modulation of a single-sideband emission with reduced carrier.	B_n=C–N÷2+DK, K=1.1 (typically)	N=1100, corresponding to an index of cooperation of 352 and a cycler rotation speed of 60 rpm. Index of cooperation is the product of the drum diameter and number of lines per unit length C=1900, D=400 Hz, Bandwidth: 2.890 Hz+2.89 kHz	2K89R3C
Analogue facsimile; frequency modulation of an audio frequency sub-carrier which moduates the main carrier, single-sideband suppressed carrier.	B_n=2M+2DK, M=N/$_2$, K=1.1 (typically)	N=1100, D-400 Hz, Bandwidth: 1980 Hz=1.98 kHz	1K98J3C

6. Composite Emissions

Double-sideband, television relay.	B_n=2C+2M+2D	Video limited to 5 MHz, audio on 6.5 MHz frequency modulated sub-carrier deviation =50 kHz: C=6.5x10^6 D=50x10^3 Hz, M=15,000, Bandwidth: 13.13x10^6 Hz=13.13 MHz	13M2A8W
Double-sideband radio relay system.	B_n=2M	10 voice channels occupying baseband between 1 kHz and 164 kHz; M=164,000 bandwidth=328,000 Hz=328 kHz	328KA8E
Double-sideband emission of VOR with voice (VOR=VHF omnidirectional radio range).	B_n=2C_{max}+2M+2DK, K=1 (typically)	The main carrier is modulated by:—a 30 Hz sub-carrier—a carrier resulting from a 9960 Hz tone frequency modulated by a 30 Hz tone—a telephone channel—a 1020 Hz keyed tone for continual Morse identification. C_{max}=9960, M=30, D=480 Hz, Bandwidth: 20,940 Hz=20.94 kHz	20K9A9W
Independent sidebands; several telegraph channels together with several telephone channels.	B_n=sum of M for each sideband	Normally composite systems are operated in accordance with standardized channel arrangements (e.g. CCIR Rec. 348-2) 3 telephone channels require and 15 telegraphy channels require the bandwidth 12,000 Hz=12 kHz	12K0B9W

III-A. FREQUENCY MODULATION

1. Signal With Quantized or Digital Information

Telegraphy without error-correction (single-channel).	B_n=2M+2DK, M=B÷2, K=1.2 (typically)	B=100, D=85 Hz (170 Hz shift), Bandwidth: 304 Hz	304HF1B
Four-frequency duplex telegraphy.	B_n2M+2DK, B=Modulation rate in bands of the faster channel. If the channels are synchronized: M=B÷2, otherwise M=2B, K=1.1 (typically)	Spacing between adjacent frequencies= 400 Hz; Synchronized channels; B=100, M=50, D=600 Hz, Bandwidth: 1420 Hz= 1.42 kHz	1K42F7B

2. Telephony (Commercial Quality)

Commercial telephony	B_n=2M+2DK, K=1 (typically, but under conditions a higher value may be necessary)	For an average case of commercial telephony, M=3000, Bandwidth: 16,000 Hz=16 kHz	16K0F3E

3. Sound Broadcasting

Sound broadcasting	B_n=2M+2DK, K=1 (typically)	Monaural, D=75,000 Hz, M=15,000, Bandwidth: 18,000 Hz=180 kHz	180KF3E

4. Facsimile

Facsimile by direct frequency modulation of the carrier; black and white.	B_n=2M+2DK, M=N÷2, K=1.1 (typically)	N=1100 elements/sec; D=400 Hz, Bandwidth: 1980 Hz=1.98 kHz	1K98F1C
Analogue facsimile	B_n=2M+2DK, M=N÷2, K=1.1 (typically)	N=1100 elements/sec; D=400 Hz, Bandwidth: 1980 Hz=1.98 kHz	1K98F3C

5. Composite Emissions (See Table III-B)

Radio-relay system, frequencydivision multiplex.	B_n=2P+2DK, K=1	Microwave radio relay system specifications: 60 telephone channels occupying baseband between 60 and 300 kHz; rms per-channel deviation 200 kHz; pilot at 331 kHz produces 200 kHz rms deviation of main carrier. Computation of B_n:D=(200x10^3 3x3.76x1.19), Hz=0.895x10^6, P=0.331x10^6 Hz; Bandwidth: 2.452x10^6 Hz.	2M45F8E
Radio-relay system, frequency division multiplex.	B_n+2M+2DK, K=1	Microwave radio relay system specifications: 1200 telephone channels occupying base-band between 60 and 5564 kHz; rms per channel deviation 200 kHz; continuity pilot at 6199 kHz produces 140 kHz rms deviation of main carrier. Computation of B_n:D= (20^{0}x10^{3}x 3.76x3.63)=2.73x10^6, M=5.64x10^6 Hz; P=6.2x10^6 Hz; (2M+2DK<2P; Bandwidth 16.59x10^6 Hz	16M6F8E
Radio-relay system, frequency division multiplex.	B_n=2P	Microwave radio relay system specifications: Multiplex 600 telephone channels occupying baseband between 60 and 2540 kHz; continuity pilot at 8500 kHz produces 140 kHz rms deviation of main carrier. Computation of B_n:D=(200x10^{3}x3.76x2.565) = 1.93x 10^6 Hz; M=2.54x10^6 Hz; 2DK)$\leq$2P Bandwidth: 17x10^6 Hz	17M0F8E
Unmodulated pulse emission.	B_n=2K÷t, K depends upon the ratio of pulse rise time. Its value usually falls between 1 and 10 and in many cases it does not need to exceed 6	Primary Radar Range resolution: 150 m, K=1.5 (triangular pulse where t$\simeq$t$_r$, only components down to 27 dB from the strongest are considered). Then t=2 x range resolution ÷ velocity of light=2x150÷ 3x10^8=1x10^{-6} seconds, Bandwidth: 3x10^6 Hz=3 MHz	3M00P0N

6. Composite Emissions

Radio-relay system	B_n=2K÷t, K=1.6	Pulse position modulated by 36 voice channel baseband; pulse width at half amplitude=0.4 μs, Bandwidth: 8x10^6 Hz=8 MHz (Bandwidth independent of the number of voice channels)	8M00M7E

[28 FR 12465, Nov. 22, 1963, as amended at 37 FR 8883, May 2, 1972; 37 FR 9996, May 18, 1972; 48 FR 16492, Apr. 18, 1983; 49 FR 48698, Dec. 14, 1984]

Subpart D—Call Signs and Other Forms of Identifying Radio Transmissions

AUTHORITY: Secs. 4, 5, 303, 48 Stat., as amended, 1066, 1068, 1082; 47 U.S.C. 154, 155, 303.

§2.301 Station identification requirement.

Each station using radio frequencies shall identify its transmissions according to the procedures prescribed by the rules governing the class of station to which it belongs with a view to the elimination of harmful interference and the general enforcement of applicable radio treaties, conventions, regulations, arrangements and agreements in force, and the enforcement of the Communications Act of 1934, as amended, and the Commission's rules.

[34 FR 5104, Mar. 12, 1969]

§ 2.302 Call Signs.

The table which follows indicates the composition and blocks of international call signs available for assignment when such call signs are required by the rules pertaining to particular classes of stations. When stations operating in two or more classes are authorized to the same licensee for the same location, the Commission may elect to assign a separate call sign to each station in a different class. (In addition to the U.S. call sign allocations listed below, call sign blocks AAA through AEZ and ALA through ALZ have been assigned to the Department of the Army; call sign block AFA through AKZ has been assigned to the Department of the Air Force; and call sign block NAA through NZZ has been assigned jointly to the Department of the Navy and the U.S. Coast Guard.

Class of station	Composition of call sign	Call sign blocks
Coast (Class I) except for coast telephone in Alaska.	3 letters	KAA through KZZ. WAA through WZZ.
Coast (Classes II and III) and maritime radio-determination.	3 letters, 3 digits	KAA2ØØ through KZZ999. WAA2ØØ through WZZ999.
Coast telephone in Alaska	3 letters, 2 digits 3 letters, 3 digits (for stations assigned frequencies above 30 MHz).	KAA2Ø through KZZ99. WAA2Ø through WZZ99. WZZ2ØØ through WZZ999
Fixed	3 letters, 2 digits 3 letters, 3 digits (for stations assigned frequencies above 30 MHz).	KAA2Ø through KZZ99. WAA2Ø through WZZ99. WAA2ØØ through WZZ999.
Marine receiver test	3 letters, 3 digits, (plus general geographic location when required).	KAA2ØØ through KZZ999. WAA2ØØ through WZZ999.
Ship telegraph	4 letters[1]	KAAA through KZZZ. WAAA through WZZZ.
Ship telephone	2 letters, 4 digits or 3 letters, 4 digits[1].	WA2ØØØ through WZ9999, through WZZ9999.
Ship telegraph plus telephone	4 letters	KAAA through KZZZ. WAAA through WZZZ.
Ship radar	Same as ship telephone and/or telegraph call sign, or, if ship has no telephone or telegraph: 2 letters, 4 digits, or 3 letters, 4 digits.	WA2ØØØ through WZ9999, through WZZ9999.
Ship survival craft	Call sign of the parent ship followed by 2 digits.	KAAA2Ø through KZZZ99. WAAA2Ø through WZZZ99.
Cable repair ship marker buoy	Call sign of the parent ship followed by the letters "BT" and the identifying number of the buoy.	
Marine utility	2 letters, 4 digits	KA2ØØØ through KZ9999.
Shipyard mobile	2 letters, 4 digits	KA2ØØØ through KZ9999.
Aircraft telegraph	5 letters	KAAAA through KZZZZ. WAAAA through WZZZZ.

Aircraft telegraph and telephone	5 letters[2].	KAAAA through KZZZZ. WAAA through WZZZZ.
Aircraft telephone	5 letters[2] (whenever a call sign is assigned).	KAAAA through KZZZZ. WAAA through WZZZZ.
Aircraft survival craft	Whenever a call sign[2] is assigned, call sign of the parent aircraft followed by a single digit other than 0 or 1.	
Aeronautical	3 letters, 1 digit[2]	KAA2 through KZZ9. WAA2 through WZZ9.
Land mobile (base)	3 letters, 3 digits	KAA2ØØ through KZZ999. WAA2ØØ through WZZ999.
Land mobile (mobile telegraph)	4 letters, 1 digit	KAAA2 through KZZZ9. WAAA2 through WZZZ9
Land mobile (mobile telephone)	2 letters, 4 digits	KA2ØØØ through KZ9999. WA2ØØØ through WZ9999
Broadcasting (standard)	4 letters[3] (plus location of station)	KAAA through KZZZ. WAAA through WZZZ
Broadcasting (FM)	4 letters plus location of station)	KAAA through KZZZ. WAAA through WZZZ.
Broadcasting with suffix "FM"	6 letters[3] (plus location of station)	KAAA-FM through KZZZ-FM. WAAA-FM through WZZZ-FM.
Broadcasting (television)	4 letters (plus location of station)	KAAA through KZZZ. WAAA through WZZZ.
Broadcasting with suffix "TV"	6 letters[3] (plus location of station)	KAAA-TV through KZZZ-TV. WAAA-TV through WZZZ-TV.
Television broadcast translator	1 letter—output channel number—2 letters	KØ2AA through K83ZZ. WØ2AA through W83ZZ.
Disaster station, except U.S. Government	4 letters, 1 digit	KAAA2 through KZZZ9. WAAA2 through WZZZ9.
Experimental (letter "X" follows the digit)	2 letters, 1 digit, 3 letters	KA2XAA through KZ9XZZ. WA2XAA through WZ9XZZ.
Amateur (letter "X" may not follow digit)	1 letter, 1 digit, 1 letter[4]	K1A through KØZ. N1A through NØZ. W1A through WØZ.
Amateur	1 letter, 1 digit, 2 letters[4]	K1AA through KØZZ. N1AA through NØZZ. W1AA through WØZZ.
Do	1 letter, 1 digit, 3 letters[4]	K1AAA through KØZZZ. N1AAA through NØZZZ. W1AAA through WØZZZ.
Do	2 letters, 1 digit, 1 letter[4]	AA1A through ALØZ. KA1A through KZØZ. NA1A through NZØZ. WA1A through WZØZ.
Do	2 letters, 1 digit, 2 letters[4]	AA1AA through ALØZZ. KA1AA through KZØZZ. NA1AA through NZØZZ. WA1AA through WZØZZ.
Amateur (letter "X" may not follow digit)	2 letters, 1 digit, 3 letters[4]	AA1AAA through ALØZZZ. KA1AAA through KZØZZZ. NA1AAA through NZØZZZ. WA1AAA through WZØZZZ.
Standard frequency		WWV, WWVB through WWVI, WWVL, WWVS.

Personal radio	3 letters, 4 digits or 4 letters, 4 digits	KAAØØØ1 through KZZ9999, WAAØØØ1 through WPZ9999, KAAAØØØ1 through KZZZ9999.
Personal radio, temporary permit	3 letters, 5 digits	KAAØØØØØ through KZZ99999.
Personal radio in trust territories	1 letter, 4 digits	KØØØ1 through K9999.
Business radio temporary permit	2 letters, 7 digits	WT plus local telephone number.
Part 90 temporary permit	2 letters, 7 digits	WT plus local telephone number.
Part 90 conditional permit	2 letters, 7 digits	WT plus local telephone number.
General Mobile Radio Service, temporary permit	2 letters, 7 digits	WT plus business or residence telephone number.

NOTE: The symbol Ø indicates the digit zero.

[1] Ships with transmitter-equipped survival craft shall be assigned four letter call signs.

[2] See § 2.303.

[3] A letter call sign now authorized for and in continuous use by a licensee of a standard broadcasting station may continue to be used by that station. The same exception applies also to frequency modulation and television broadcasting stations using 5 letter call signs consisting of 3 letters with the suffix "FM" or "TV."

[4] Plus other identifying data as may be specified.

[34 FR 5104, Mar. 12, 1969; as amended at 54 50239, Dec. 5, 1989]

§ 2.303 Other forms of identification of stations.

a) The following table indicates forms of identification which may be used in lieu of call signs by the specified classes of stations. Such recognized means of identification may be one or more of the following: name of station, location of station, operating agency, official registration mark, flight identification number, selective call number or signal, selective call identification or signal, characteristic signal, characteristic of emission or other clearly distinguishing form of identification readily recognized internationally. Reference should be made to the appropriate part of the rules for complete information or identification procedures for each service.

Class of station	Identification, other than assigned call sign
Aircraft (U.S. registry) telephone	Registration number preceded by the type of the aircraft, or the radiotelephony designator of the aircraft operating agency followed by the flight identification number.
Aircraft (foreign registry) telephone	Foreign registry identification consisting of five characters. This may be preceded by the radiotelephony designator of the aircraft operating agency or it may be preceded by the type of aircraft.
Aeronautical	Name of the city, area, or airdrome served together with such additional identification as may be required.
Aircraft survival craft	Appropriate reference to parent aircraft, e.g., the air carrier parent aircraft flight number or identification, the aircraft registration number, the name of the air craft manufacturer, the name of the aircraft owner, or any other pertinent information.
Ship telegraph	When an official call sign is not yet assigned: Complete name of the ship and name of licensee. On 156.65 MHz: Name of ship. Digital selective call.
Ship telegraph	Digital selective call.
Public coast (radiotelephone) and Limited Coast (radiotelephone).	The approximate geographic location in a format approved by the Commission. Coast station identification number.
Public coast (radiotelegraph)	Coast station identification number.
Fixed	Geographic location. When an approved method of superimposed identification is used, QTT DE (abbreviated name and company or station).
Fixed: Rural subscriber service	Assigned telephone number.
Land mobile: Public safety, forestry conservation, highway maintenance, local government, shipyard, land transportation, and aviation services.	Name of station licensee (in abbreviated form if practicable), or location of station, or name of city, area, or facility served. Individual stations may be identified by additional digits following the more general identification.

Land mobile:Industrial service	Mobile unit cochannel with its base station: Unit identifier on file in the base sta tion records. Mobile unit not co-channel with its base station: Unit identifier on file in base station records and the assigned call sign of either the mobile or base station. Temporary base station: Unit designator in addition to base sta tion identification.
Land mobile: Domestic public and rural radio	Special mode unit designation assigned by licensee or by assigned telephone number.
Land mobile: Railroad radio service	Name of railroad, train number, caboose number, engine number, or name of fixed wayside station or such other number or name as may be specified for use of railroad employees to identify a specific fixed point or mobile unit. A rail road's abbreviated name or initial letters may be used where such are in gener al usage. Unit designators may be used in addition to the station identification to identify an individual unit or transmitter of a base station.
Land mobile: Broadcasting (remote pickup)	Identification of an associated broadcasting station.
Broadcasting (Emergency Broadcast System)	State and operational area identification.
Broadcasting (aural STL and intercity relay)	Call sign of the TV broadcasting station with which it is associated.
Broadcasting (television auxiliary)	Call sign of the TV broadcasting station with which it is licensed as an auxiliary, or call sign of the TV broadcasting station whose signals are being relayed, or by network identification.
Broadcasting (television booster)	Retransmission of the call sign of the primary station.
Disaster station	By radiotelephony: Name, location, or other designation of station when same as that of an associated station in some other service. Two or more separate units of a station operated at different locations are separately identified by the addition of a unit name, number, or other designation at the end of its autho rized means of identification.

(b) Digital selective calls will be authorized by the Commission and will be formed by groups of numbers (0 through 9), however, the first digit must be other than 0, as follows:
(1) Coast station identification number: 4 digits.
(2) Ship station selective call number: 5 digits.
(3) Predetermined group of ship stations: 5 digits.

(c) Ship stations operating under a temporary operating authority shall identify by a call sign consisting of the letter "K" followed by the vessel's Federal or State registration number, or a call sign consisting of the letters "KUS" followed by the vessel's documentation number. However, if the vessel has no registration number or documentation number, the call sign shall consist of the name of the vessel and the name of the licensee as they appear on the station application form.

[28 FR 12465, Nov. 22, 1963, as amended at 40 FR 57675, Dec. 11, 1975; 41 FR 44042, Oct. 6, 1976; 42 FR 31008, June 17, 1977; 44 FR 62284, Oct. 30, 1979]

Amateur Callsign Districts by Country

AA-AG, AH6, AI-AK, AL7, K, KA-KG, KH6, KI-KK, KL7, KM-KO, KQ-KZ, N, NA-NG, NH6, NI-NK, NL7, NM-NO, NQ-NZ, W, WA-WG, WH6, WI-WK, WL7, WM-WO, WQ-WZ United States of America

1 Maine (ME), New Hampshire (NH), Vermont (VT), Massachusetts (MA), Rhode Island (RI), Connecticut (CT)

2 New York (NY), New Jersey (NJ)

3 Pennsylvania (PA), Delaware (DE), Maryland (MD), District of Columbia (DC)

4 North Carolina (NC), South Carolina (SC), Georgia (GA), Tennessee (TN), Alabama (AL), Florida (FL), Kentucky (KY), Virginia (VA)

5 Mississippi (MS), Louisiana (LA), Arkansas (AR), Texas (TX), Oklahoma (OK), New Mexico (NM)

6 California (CA)

7 Nevada (NV), Utah (UT), Arizona (AZ), Oregon (OR), Washington (WA), Idaho (ID), Montana (MT), Wyoming (WY)

8 Michigan (MI), Ohio (OH), West Virginia (WV)

9 Illinois (IL), Indiana (IN), Wisonsin (WI)

Ø Colorado (CO), Iowa (IA), Kansas (KS), Minnesota (MN), Missouri (MO), Nebraska (NE), North Dakota (ND), South Dakota (SD)

AH6, KH6, NH6, WH6 Hawaii (HI)

AL7, KL7, NL7, WL7 Alaska (AK)

AZ See LU, LW, AZ

BG, BT, BW, BY, BZ China (People's Republic) (BG Private Stations, BT Special Calls, BW Reciprocal Licenses, BY Club Stations, BZ Individual Callsigns for Operators of Club Stations

1 Beijing

2A-I Heilongjiang

2J-Q Jilin

2R-Z Liaoning

3A-F Tianjin

3G-L Nei Monggol (Inner Mongolia) (Autonomous Region)

3M-S	Hebei
3T-Z	Shanxi
4A-I	Shanghai
4J-Q	Shandong
4R-Z	Jiangsu
5A-I	Zhejiang
5J-Q	Jiangxi
5R-Z	Fugian
6A-I	Henan
6J-Q	Anhui
6R-Z	Hubei
7A-I	Hunan
7J-Q	Guangxi (Autonomous Region), Hainan
7R-Z	Guangdong
8A-I	Sichuan
8J-Q	Guizhou
8R-Z	Yunnan
9A-F	Ningxia (Autonomous Region)
9G-L	Qinghai
9M-S	Shaanxi
9T-Z	Gansu
ØA-M	Xinjiang (Autonomous Region)
ØN-Z	Xizang (Tibet) (Autonomous Region)

BV	Taiwan
1	Ilan, Keelung Shi
2	Taipei, Taipei Shi
3	Hsinchu, Hsinchu Shi, Miaoli, Taoyuan
4	Nantou, Taichung, Taichung Shi
5	Changhwa, Chiayi, Chiayi Shi, Yunlin
6	Tainan, Tainan Shi
7	Kaohsiung, Kaohsiung Shi, Pingtung
8	Hualien, Taitung
9	Taiwanese Islands
Ø	Reciprocal Licenses

BW, BY, BZ	See BG, BT, BW, BY, BZ

CE, XQ	Chile
1	Antofagasta, Atacama, Tarapaca
2	Aconcagua, Coquimbo
3	Metropolitan
4	Maule, Liberador
5	Bio-Bio
6	Araucania
7	Aisen, Los Lagos
8	Magallanes
ØY	Easter Island
ØX	San Felix Island
ØX	San Ambrosio Island
ØZ	Juan-Fernandez Island

CL, CM, CO	Cuba
1	Pinar del Rio
2	Havana City
3	Havana
4	Isla de la Juventud
5	Matanzas
6	Cienfuegos, Sancti Spiritus, Villa Clara
7	Camaguey, Ciego de Avila
8	Granma, Guantanamo, Holguin, Las Tunas, Santiago de Cuba

CP	Bolivia
1	La Paz
2	Chuquisaca
3	Oruro
4	Potosi
5	Cochabamba
6	Santa Cruz
7	Tarija
8	Beni
9	Pando
Ø	Special Calls

CU	Azores
1	Santa Maria
2	Sao Miguel
3	Terceira
4	Graciosa
5	Sao Jorge
6	Pico
7	Faial
8	Flores
9	Corvo
Ø	Repeaters

CW-CX	
1–9	Uruguay
	The First Letter After the Number Designates:
A, B, C	Montevideo
D	Canelones
E	San Jose
F	Colonia
G	Soriano
H	Rio Negro
I	Paysandu
J	Salto
K	Artigas
L	Florida
M	Flores
N	Durazno
O	Tacuarembo
P	Rivera
R	Maldonado
S	Lavalleja
T	Rocha
U	Treinta y Tres
V	Cerro Largo
X	Special Calls
Z	Mobile Stations

DA–DD, DG–DH, DJ–DL, DP	Germany
DA1, 2, 4	Foreign Military personnel
DBØ	Club and relay stations
DB, DC, DD, DG	VHF License
DCØFA-DCØJZ	Reciprocal VHF license
DC7AA-DC7ZZ	West Berlin VHF license
DD6AAA-DD6ZZZ	West Berlin VHF license
DH	Class A license VHF + limited HF
DH7AAA-DH7ZZZ	Class A license, West Berlin
DF, DJ, DK, DL	Class B license
DL7AAA-DL7ZZZ	West Berlin Class B license
DBØ	Repeaters
DJØAAA-DJØZZZ	Reciprocal licenses
DFØ, DLØ, DKØ	Club Stations
DP	Stations outside Germany

Examples: DPØGVN Antarctica—Georg Von Neumeier Station; DP1MIR/DPØSL—Spacelab operations

Former East German licensees (Y2, Y3, etc. prefixes) are now being issued callsigns in the following blocks: DL1RAA-RZZ, DL2RAA-RZZ, DL6RAA-RZZ, DL6UAA-UZZ, DL6VAA-VZZ, DL7UAA-UZZ, DL7VAA-VZZ, and DF1YA-DF6YZ for Berlin.

EA, EB, EC, ED, EE, EF, EH	Spain (EB VHF Licenses, EC Novice Class, ED, EE, EF, EG, EH)

1	Asturias, Avila, Burgos, Cantabria, La Coruna, Leon, Lugo, Orense, Palencia, Pontevedra, Rioja, Salamanca, Segovia, Soria, Valladolid, Zamora
2	Alava, Guipuzcoa, Huesca, Navarra, Teruel, Vizcaya, Zaragoza
3	Barcelona, Gerona, Lerida, Tarragona
4	Badajoz, Caceres, Ciudad Real, Cuenca, Guadalajara, Madrid, Toledo
5	Albacete, Alicante, Castellon, Murcia, Valencia
6	Balearen
7	Almeria, Cadiz, Cordoba, Granada, Huelva, Jaen, Malaga, Sevilla
8	Kanarische Inseln
9	Ceuta and Mililla
Ø	–
EL	Liberia
1	Grand Bassa, Rivercess
2	Bomi, Federal District, Margibi, Montserrado
3	Grand Kru, Sinoe
4	Maryland
5	Lofa
6	Grand Gedeh
7	Bong
8	Nimba
9	Grand Cape Mount
Ø	Maritime Mobile Stations
ES	Estonia
1	Tallinn, Northern Islands
2	Harju Rajon
3	Haapsalu, Rapla, Paide
4	Kohtla-Jarve, Rakvere, Sillamae, Narva
5	Jogeva, Polca, Tartu
6	Valga, Voru
7	Viljandi
8	Parnu
9	Special Calls
Ø	Western Islands
HA, HG	Hungary
1	Gyor-Sopron, Vas, Zala
2	Komarom-Esztergom, Veszprem
3	Baranya, Somogy, Tolna
4	Fejer
5	Budapest (city)
6	Heves, Nograd
7	Pest, Jasz-Nagykun-Szolnok
8	Bacs-Kiskun, Bekes, Csongrad
9	Borsod-Abauj-Zemplen
Ø	Hajdu-Bihar, Szabolcs-Szatmar-Bereg
HC	Ecuador
1	Carchi, Imbabura, Pichincha
2	Guayas, Los Rios
3	El Oro, Loja
4	Esmeraldas, Manabi
5	Azuay, Canar, Chimborazo
6	Bolivar, Cotopaxi, Tungurahua
7	Morona-Santiago, Napo, Pastaza, Zamora
8	Galapagos Islands
9	Maritime Mobile Stations
Ø	Mobile Stations
HG	HA, HG
HI	Dominican Repulblic
1	Alto Velo-Island, Beata-Island
2	Catalina-Island, Catalinita-Island, Saona-Island
3	Duarte, Espaillat, La Vega, Puerto Plata, Salcedo, Sanchez Ramirez, Santiago
4	Dajabon, Monte Cristi, Santiago Rodriguez, Valverde
5	Bahoruco, Barahona, Independencia, Pedernales
6	Azua, La Estrelleta, San Juan
7	El Seibo, Hato Mayor, La Altagracia, La Romana, San Pedro de Macoris
8	Districto Nacional, Peravia, San Cristobal
9	Maria Trinidad Sanchez, Samana
HJ, HK	Colombia (HJ Novice Class)
1	Atlantico, Bolivar, Cordoba, Sucre
2	Cesar, Guajira, Magdalena, Norte de Santander
3	Cundinamarca, Meta, Vichada
4	Antioquia, Choco
5	Cauca, Valle del Cauca
6	Caldas, Huila, Quindio, Risaralda, Tolima
7	Arauca, Boyaca, Casanare, Santander
8	Caqueta, Narino, Putumayo
9	Amazonas, Guainia, Guaviare, Vaupes
Ø	Bajo Nuevo, San Andres-Island, Providencia-Archipelago Malpelo-Island, Roncador Cay, Serrana Bank
HL	Korea
1	Seoul
2	Kyonggi, Kangwon, Inchon
3	North-Chungchong, South-Chungchong
4	North-Cholla, South-Cholla, Cheju-Island
5	North-Kyongsang, South-Kyongsang, Pusan, Taegu
8	Mobile Stations
9	Reciprocal Licenses
Ø	Club Stations
HP	Panama
1	Panama
2	Colon, San Blas
3	Chiriqui
4	Bocas del Toro, Cocle
5	Herrera, Los Santos
6	Veraguas
7	Darien
8	Perlas-Archipelago
9	Maritime Mobile Stations
Ø	Coiba-Island
HR	Honduras
1	Comayagua, Distrito Central, Francisco Morazan
2	Cortes, La Paz, Yoro
3	Atlantida, Colon, El Paraiso, Gracias a Dios, Olancho
4	Choluteca, Valle
5	Copan, Intibuca, Lempira, Ocotepeque, Santa Barbara
6	Bahia-Island
I, IA-IZ	Italy
1	LIGUREE Genova (GE), Imperia (IM), La Spezia (SP), Savona (SV). PIEMONT Alessandria (AL), Asti (AT), Cuneo (CN), Novara (NO), Torino (TO), Vercelli (VC).
2	LOMBARDI Bergamo (BG), Brescia (BS), Como (CO), Cremona (CR), Milano (MI), Mantova (MN), PAVIA (PV), Sondrio (SO), Varese (VA).
3	VENIZIA Belluno (BL), Padova (PD), Rovigo (RO), Treviso (TV), Venezia (VE), Verona (VR), Vicenza (VI).
4	EMILIA-ROMAGNA Bologna (BO), Ferrara (FE), Forli (FO), Modena (MO), Parma (PR), Piacenza(PC), Ravenna (RA), Reggio Emilia (RE).
5	TOSCANA Arezzo (AR), Firenze (FI), Grosseto (GR), Livorno (LI), Lucca (LU),

Massa VCarrara (MS), Pisa (PI), Pistoia (PT), Siena (SI).

6 ABRUZZO
Chieti (CH), L'Aquila (AQ), Pescara(PE), Teramo (TE).
MARCHE Ancona (AN), Ascoli Piceno (AP), Macerata (MC), Pesaro (PS).

7 PUGLIA
Bari (BA), Brindisi (BR), Foggia (FG), Lecce (LE), Taranto (TA).
BASILICATA Matera (MT).

8 BASILACATA
Potenza (PZ).
CALABRIA Catanzaro (CZ), Cosenza (CS), Reggio Calabria (RC). CAMPANIA Avellino (AV), Benevento (BN), Caserta (CE), Napoli (NA), Salerno (SA). MOLISE Campobasso (CB), Isernia (IS).

Ø LATINA
Frosinone (FR), Latina (LT), Rieti (RI), Roma (ROMA), Viterbo (VT).
UMBRIA Perugia (PG), Terni (TR).

A2 Islands of Laco Maggiore.

A5 Toscani Islands.
Argentarlo, Capraia, Cerboli, Corallo, Corbella, Corbelli, Di liscoli, Di Vada, Elba, Falconcino, Formica di Burano, Formiche, Formiche di Grosseto, Formiche di Montecristo, Ogliera, Ortano, Palmarola, Pianosa, Porcelli, Remaiolo, Santa Lucia, Scoglietto, Scolglio d'Africa, Sedia di Paolina, Sparviero, Topi, Triglia.

BØ Latina Islands
Botte, Calzone Muto, Calzone Parroco, Cappello, Evangelista, Faraglioni, Faraglioni Madonna, Forcina, Fucile, Gavi, La Nave, Le Formiche, La Galere, Mezzogiorno, Monaco, Pallante, Palmarola, Piatti, Ponza, Ravia, Rosso, San Silverio, Santo Stefano, Scogliatelle, Scuncillo, Spaccapolpi, Suvace, Torre Astura, Venotene, Zannone.

C8 Neapolitan Islands.
A Penna, Camerota, Capri, Faraglioni, Gaiola, Isca, Ischia, Li Galli, Licosa, Monacone, Nisida, Procida, Revigliano, Santo Ianni, Scrupolo, Vervece, Vetara, Vivara.

D8 Calabrian Islands.
Cirella, Dino, Formicola, Ianni, Le Castelle, Licosa, Pietra Grande, San Leonardo, Scoglio Galera, Scoglio Iscra.

D9 Eolie Islands.
Alicudi, Basiluzzo, Bottaro, Canna, Dattilo, Faraglione, Filicudi, Formiche, Galera, Imeratr, Lipari, Lisca bianca, Lisca Nera, Montenassari, Nave Panarea, Panarea, Panarelli, Pietra del Bagno, Pietra Lunga, Pietra Menalda, Quaedri, Salina, Santa Palomba, Spinazzola, Stromboli, Strombolicchio, Vulcano.

E9 Ustican Islands.
Banco Apollo, Colombara, Medico, Ustica.

F9 Egadi Islands.
Asinelli, Cammello, Correnti, Faraglione, Favignana, Formica, Galeotta, Galera, Levanzo, Maraone, Marettimo, Porcelli, Preveto, Scherchi.

G9 Pelagie Islands.
Conigli, Lampedusa, Lampione, Linosa.

H9 Pantelleria Island.

J7 Cheradi Islands.
San Paolo, San Pietro.

J9 Sicilian Islands.
Bottazza, Ciclopi, Colombaia, Dei Porri, Delle Correnti, Delle Femmine, Dello Stagnone, Di Capo Passero, Di Patti, Di Pietra Patella, Dietro Isola, Due Fratelli, Formica, Grande di Marzameni, Iannuzzo, Isola Bella, La Scuola, Lachea, Le Pietre, Nere, Lunga, Mal Consiglio, Ognina, Ortigia, Piccola, San Biagio, San Pantaleo, Santa Maria, Scialandro, Scoglio di Brono, Tracino, Vendicari.

L3 Grado Islands.
Anfora, Ara Storta, Dei Belli, Dei Brusiari, Del Lovo, Gorgo, Grado, Gran Chiusa, Manzi, Marina di Macia, Martignano, Mezzano, Montaron, Morgo, Orbi, Pampiola, Panera, Ravaiarina, San Andrea, San Giuliano, San Pietro d'Oro, Santa Maria Barbana, Schiusa, Sian, Taglio Nuovo, Valerian, Villa Nova, Volpera, Volperossa.

IL3 Venezian Islands.
Buel del Lovo, Burano, Campalto, Campana, Carbonera, Crevan, Falconera, Le Certosa, La Cura, La Giudecca e Sacca Fisola, La Grazia, Lazzaretto Nuovo, Lazzaretto Vecchio, Le Vignole, lido, Lio Mazor, Lio Piccolo, Madonna del Monte, Mazzorbo, Monte del Oro, Motta del Cunigi, Motta San Lorenzo, Murano, Ottagono Alberoni, Pellestrina, Poveglia, Sacca Sessola, Salina, San Angelo di Polvere, San Ariano, SAn Biagio, San Clemente, San Cristina, San Cristoforo, San Erasmo, San Francesco del Desreto, San Giacamo in Paluo, San Giorgio in Alba, San Giorgio Maggiore, San Giuliano, San Lazzaro di Armeni, San Michele, San Secondo, San Servolo, Sant'Elena, Santo Spirito, Sette Soleri, Spignon, Tessera, Torcello, Torson, Trezze, Tronchetto, Val di Pozzo, Volpego.

L4 Adriatic Islands.
Albarella, Barone, Chioggia, Polesine, Scanno, Piallazza.

L7 Puglia Islands.
Cacio, Cavallo, Campi, Campo, Chianca, Del Capezzone, Della Malva, Due Sorelle, Fanciulla, Gallipoli, Giurlita, Grande, I Guaceto, I Pagliai, La Vecchia, Malva, Palombaro, Pazzi, Pedacine, Portonouvo, Sant'Andrea, Sant'Eufemia, Santo Emiliano, Scoglio Portonouvo, Tondo.

L7 Tremiti Islands.
Caprara, Cretaccio, Pianosa, San Domino, San Nicola.

MØ Cagliari Islands.
Campianna, Cavoli, Corno, Di Cala Vinagra. Il Catalano, Il Toro, La Vacca, Mal di Ventre, Meli, Pgliastra, Padiglioni, Pan di Zucchero, Piana di San Pietro, Piscadeddus, Proci, Quirra, Ratti, Rossa di Teulada, San Macario, San Pietro, Sant'Antioco, Sant'Elmo, Serpantara, Su Cardulinu, Su Giudeu, Tuaredda, Variglioni, Vitello.

MØ Sassarian Islands.
Asinara, Barca Sconcia, Bianca, Cana, Cappuccini, Coluccia, Corona Niedda, Dei Poeri, Della Bocca, Della Pelosa, Delli Nibani, Di Zui Paulo, Figarolo, Foradada, Gabbia, Giardinelli, Isolotto Rosso, Le Camere Le Soffi, Lepre, Maddalena Alghero, Manna, Marmorata, Molara, Molarotto, Monica, Mortorio, Mortoriotto, Pagliosa, Patron Fiaso, Pecora, Pedrami, Piana di Alghero, Piana di Paolo, Porri, Porritula, Portisco, Poveri, Proratola, Reulino, Rossa, Rossa di Alghero, Ruia, Scoglio Businco, Scoglio Forani, Scoglio Paganetto, Tavolara, Verde.

MØ Maddelena Islands.
Abbatoggia, Barattinelli di Fuore, Barettinelli, Barrenttini, Bisce, Budelli, Camize, Camize, Cana, Capicciolu, Caprera, Carpa, Cavalli, Chiesa, Corcelli, Degli Italiani, Giardinelli, La Presa, Maddalena, Monaci, Paduleddi, Piana, Porco, Porraggi, Ratino, Razzoli, Roma, Santa Maria, Santo Stefano, Spargi, Spargiottello, Spargiotto, Stramanari.

MØ Sardia Islands.
Brecconi, Corona Niedda, Dei Mucchi Bianchi, Dei Pedrami, Della Olgiastra, Delle Bisce, La

	Ghinghetta, Mangiabarche, Ottiolo, Pan di Zucchero, Peloso, Piana.
N3	TRIENT
	Bolzano (BZ), Trento (TN).
P1	Ligurian Islands.
	Bergeggi, Fercale, Gallinara, Palmaria, Tino, Tinetto.
SØ	SARDINIA
	Cagliari (CA), Nuoro (NU), Oristano (OR), Sassari (SS).
T9	SICILY
	Agrigento (AG), Caltanisetta (CL), Catania (CT), Enna (EN), Messina (ME), Palermo (PA), Ragusa (RG), Siracusa (SR), Trapani (TP).
V3	FRUILI-VENEZIA GIULIA
	Gorizia (GO), Pordenone (PN), Trieste (TS), Udine (UD).
W	VHF License
X1	AOSTATA
	Aostata (AO).

JA, JE, JF, JG, JH, JI, JJ, JK, JL, JM, JN, JO, JP, JQ, JR, JS, 7J, 7K, 7L, 7M, 7N, 8J	Japan (7J Reciprocal Licenses, 8J Sonderrufzeichen)
1	Chiba, Gumma, Ibaraki, Kanagawa, Saitama, Tochigi, Tokio, Yamanashi
2	Aichi, Gifu, Mie, Shizuoka
3	Hyogo, Kyoto, Nara, Osaka, Shiga, Wakayama
4	Hiroshima, Okayama, Shimane, Tottori, Yamaguchi
5	Ehime, Kagawa, Kochi, Tokushima
6	Fukuoka, Kagoshima, Kumamoto, Miyazaki, Nagasaki, Oita, Okinawa, Saga
7	Akita, Aomori, Fukushima, Iwate, Miyagi, Yamagata
8	Hokkaido
9	Fukui, Ishikawa, Toyama
Ø	Nagano, Niigata

JT	Mongolia
1A-G	Ulan Bator
1H-Z	Nalajch
2A-M	Dornod
2N-Z	Suchbatar
3A-M	Chentij
3N-Z	Dornogobi
4A-M	Omnogobi
4N-Z	Dungobi
5A-M	Selenge
5N-Z	Tow
6A-M	Archangaj
6N-Z	Oworchangaj
7A-M	Chowsgol
7N-Z	Bulgan
8A-M	Gobi-Altai
8N-Z	Bayan-Chongor
9A-M	Uws
9N-Z	Dzawchan
ØA-M	Bayan-Olgij
ØN-Z	Khowd

K, KA-KG, KI-KK, KM-KO, KQ-KZ	See AA-AG

LU, LW, AZ	Argentina (LW Novice Class, AZ Sonderrufzeichen)
	The First Letter After The Number Indicates The Region:
A, B, C	Buenos Aires (City)
D, E	Buenos Aires (Province)
F	Santa Fe
GA-GO	Chaco
GP-GZ	Formosa
H	Cordoba
I	Misiones
J	Entre Rios
K	Tucuman
L	Corrientes
M	Mendoza
N	Santiago del Estero
O	Salta
P	San Juan
Q	San Luis
R	Catamarca
S	La Rioja
T	Jujuy
U	La Pampa
V	Rio Negro
W	Chubut
XA-XO	Santa Cruz
XP-XZ	Tierra del Fuego
Y	Neuquen
LUØ	Mobile Stations

N, NA-NG, NI-NK, NM-NO, NQ-NZ	See AA-AG

OA	Peru
1	Lambayeque, Piura, Tumbes
2	Cajamarca, La Libertad
3	Ancash, Huanuco
4	Callao, Junin, Lima, Pasco
5	Apurimac, Ayacucho, Huancavelica, Ica
6	Arequipa, Moquegua, Tacna
7	Cuzco, Madre de Dios, Puno
8	Loreto, Ucayali
9	Amazonas, San Martin
Ø	Special Calls

OE	Austria
1	Wien
2	Salzburg
3	Niederosterreich
4	Burgenland
5	Oberosterreich
6	Steiermark
7	Tirol
8	Karnten
9	Vorarlberg
Ø	Special Calls
	First Letter After The Number:
X	Club Station Repeater, Beacon
Z	Reciprocal Licenses

OG, OH, OI	Finland (Military Stations)
1	Turku-Pori
2	Uusimaa
3	Hame
4	Mikkeli
5	Kymi
6	Keski-Suomi, Vaasa
7	Kuopio, Pohjois-Karjala
8	Oulu
9	Lappi (Lappland)
Ø	Aland Island
OJØ	Market Reef
	First Letter After The Number:
Z	Reciprocal Licenses

PJ	Netherlands Antilles
1	Special Calls
2	Curacao

4	Bonaire
5	St. Eustatius
6	Saba
7	St. Maarten
8	St. Eustatius, St. Maarten, Saba (Reciprocal Licenses & Special Calls
9	Bonaire, Curacao (Reciprocal Licenses & Special Calls)
Ø	Special Calls

PP, PQ, PR, PS, PT, PU, PV, PW, PY, ZV, ZW, ZX, XY, ZZ	Brazil (PU Novice Class, ZV-ZZ Sonderlandeskenner)
PP1, ZZ1	Espirito Santo
PP2, ZZ2	Goias
PP5, ZZ5	Santa Catarina
PP6, ZZ6	Sergipe
PP7, ZZ7	Alagoas
PP8, ZZ8A-G	Amazonas
PQ2, ZX2	Tocantins
PZ8, ZV8	Amapa
PR7, ZX7	Paraiba
PR8, ZX8	Maranhao
PS7, ZW7	Rio Grande do Norte
PS8, ZW8	Piaui
PT2, ZV2	Distrito Federal
PT7, ZV7	Ceara
PT8, ZZ8H-M	Acre
PT9, ZV9	Mato Grosso do Sul
PU1A-I	Espirito Santo
PU1J-Z	Rio de Janeiro
PU2A-E	Distrito Federal
PU2F-H	Goias
PU2I-J	Tocantins
PU2K-Z	Sao Paulo
PU3	Rio Grande do Sul
PU4	Minas Gerais
PU5A-L	Santa Catarina
PU5M-Z	Parana
PU6A-I	Sergipe
PU6J-Z	Bahia
PU7A-D	Alagoas
PU7E-H	Paraiba
PU7I-L	Rio Grande do Norte
PU7M-P	Ceara
PU7R-Z	Pernambuco
PU8A-C	Amazonas
PU8D-F	Rondonia
PU8G-I	Amapa
PU8J-L	Acre
PU8M-O	Maranhao
PU8P-S	Piaui
PU8T-V	Roraima
PU8W-Z	Para
PU9A-N	Mato Grosso do Sul
PU9O-Z	Mato Grosso
PUØ	(See PYØ)
PV8, ZZ8T-Z	Roraima
PW8, ZZ8N-S	Rondonia
PY1, ZY1	Rio de Janeiro
PY2, ZY2	Sao Paulo
PY3, ZY3	Rio Grande do Sol
PY4, ZY4	Minas Gerais
PY5, ZY5	Parana
PY6, ZY6	Bahia
PY7, ZY7	Pernambuco
PY8, ZY8	Para
PY9, ZY9	Mato Grosso
PYØ, ZWØ	Brazilian Islands
PYØF, PYØZF, ZYØ	Fernando de Noronha
PYØM, PYØZM, PYØ	Martim Vaz Island
PYØR, PYØZR, ZYØ	Rocas-Atoll
PYØS, PYØZS, ZYØ	St. Peter-and Paul-Island
PYØT, PYØZT, ZYØ	Trindade-Island
	First Letter After The Number:
Z	Reciprocal Licenses

PZ	Suriname
1	Paramaribo, Sipalwini
2	Nickerie
3	Coronie
4	Saramacca
5	Reciprocal Licenses
6	Para
7	Brokopondo
8	Commewijne
9	Marowijne
Ø	Special Calls

RA-RZ	See UA-UZ

SI, SJ, SK, SL, SM	Sweden (SK Club & Repeater Stations, SL Military Stations)
SI8	Market Reef
SJ9	Morokulien
SM1	Gotland
SM2	Norrbotten, Vasterbotten
SM3	Gavleborg, Jamtland, Vasternorrland
SM4	Kopparberg, Orebro, Varmland
SM5	Ostergotland, Sodermanland, Stockholm Lan, Uppsala, Vastmanland
SM6	Alvsborg, Goteborg/Bohus, Halland, Skaraborg
SM7	Blekinge, Jonkoping, Kalmar, Kristianstad, Kronoberg, Malmohus
SMØ	Stockhom City

SO, SP, SR	Polen (SO Reciprocal Licenses, SR Repeaters)
1	Koszalin, Slupsk, Szczecin
2	Bydgoszcz, Elblag, Gdansk, Torun, Wlocklawek
3	Gorzow, Wielkopolski, Kalisz, Konin, Leszno, Pila, Poznan, Zielona Gora
4	Bialystok, Lomza, Olsztyn, Suwalki
5	Ciechanow, Ostroleka, Plock, Siedlce, Warszawa
6	Jelenia Gora, Legnica, Opole, Walbrzych, Wroclaw
7	Kielce, Lodz, Piotrkow, Trybunalski, Radom, Sieradz, Skierniewice, Tarnobrzeg
8	Biala Podlaska, Chelm, Krosno, Lublin, Przemysl, Rzeszow, Zamosc
9	Bielsko Biala, Czestochowa, Katowice, Krakow, Nowy Sacz, Tarnow
Ø	Special Calls

SV	Greece
1	Central Greece, Euboa, Athens
2	Macedonia
3	Peloponnes
4	Thessalien
5	Dodecanese (Alimia, Arki, Astipalea, Chalki, Giali, Kalimnos, Karpathos, Kasos, Kos, Leros, Lipsos, Nisiros, Patmos, Pserimos, Rhodos, Saria, Simi, Tilos)
6	Epiros
7	East Macedonia, Thrace
8	Islands in Ionian Sea (Kefallenia, Korfu, Levkas, Zakynthos), Islands in Aegean Sea except Crete & Dodecancese Dodekanes) (Chios, Kykladen, Lesbos, Samos, Sporaden, Thasos)

9 Crete
Ø Reciprocal Licenses

TA, TB, TC Turkey
1 Edirne, Istanbul (European Sector), Kirklareli, Tekirdag
2 Ankara, Bilecik, Bolu, Eskisehir, Istanbul (Asian Sector), Kocaeli, Sakarya, Zonguldak
3 Balikesir, Bursa, Canakkale, Izmir, Manisa
4 Afyonkarahisar, Antalya, Aydin, Burdur, Denizli, Isparta, Kutahya, Mugla, Usak
5 Adana, Hatay, Icel, Konya, Nevsehir, Nigde
6 Amasya, Cankiri, Corum, Kastamonu, Kirsehir, Samsun, Sinop, Tokat, Yozgat
7 Erzincan, Giresun, Gumushane, Kayseri, Ordu, Sivas, Trabzon, Tunceli
8 Adiyaman, Bingol, Diyarbakir, Elazig, Gaziantep, Kahramanmaras, Malatya, Margin, Sanliurfa
9 Agri, Artvin, Bitlis, Erzurum, Hakkari, Kars, Mus, Rize, Siirt, Van
ØA-D Mediterranean Islands
ØE-L Aegean Islands
ØM-X Marmara Sea Islands
ØY-Z Black Sea Islands

TF Iceland
1 Arnessysla, Rangarvallasysla, West-Skaftafellssysla
2 Borgarfjardarsysla, Myrarsysla, Snaefells and Hnappadalssysla, Dalasysla
3 Kjosarsysla, Reykjavik, Kopavogskaupstadur, Garda- Kaupstadur, Hafnarfjardarbair, Seltjarnarnesskaupsta- dur
4 East and West-Bardastrandarsyslur, West and North Isafjardarsyslur, Starandasysla
5 Eyafjardarsysla, South and North Thingeyjarsyslur
6 North & South Mulasyslur, East Skaftafellssysla
7 Vestmannaeyjar-Islands
8 Gullbringusysla
9 West and East-Hunavatnssyslur, Skagafjardarsysla
Ø Unbewohnte Gebiete in Central Island

TG Guatemala
4 Chimaltenango, Escuintla, Santa Rosa, Solola, Suchitepequez
5 Huehuetenango, Quiche, totonicapan
6 Chiquimula, Jutiapa, Zacapa
7 Alta Verapaz, Izabal, Peten
8 Quetzaltenango, Retalhuleu, San Marcos
9 Baja Verapaz, El Progreso, Guatemala, Jalapa, Sacatepequez
Ø Special Calls

TI Costa Rica
1 Special Calls
2 San Jose
3 Cartago
4 Heredia
5 Alajuela
6 Limon
7 Guanacaste
8 Puntarenas
9 Cocos Island
Ø Special Calls

NOTE: *At press time, details of the new callsign systems of the former USSR republics are not available.*

VE, VO, VY Canada
VE1 Nova Scotia (NS), New Brunswick (NB)
VE2 Quebec (PQ)
VE3 Ontario (ON)
VE4 Manitoba (MB)
VE5 Saskatchewan (SK)
VE6 Alberta (AB)
VE7 British Columbia (BC)
VE8 Northwest Territories (NW)
VEØ
MAA-NZZ Maritime Mobile Stations
VO1 Newfoundland (NF)
VO2 Newfoundland (Labrador) (LB)
VY1 Yukon Territory (YK)
VY2 Prince Edward Island (PE)
VY9 Department of Communications Club Stations

VK Australia
1 Capital Territory
2 New South Wales
3 Victoria
4 Queensland
5 South Australia
6 Western Australia
7 Tasmania
8 Northern Territory
9C, 9NC Cocos (Keeling) Island
9L, 9NL Lord Howe Island
9M, 9NM Mellish Reef
9N, 9NN Norfolk Island
9W, 9NW Willis Island
9X, 9NX Christmas Island
Ø Macquarie, Heard Island

First letter after the number, if N or V, for 3 letter suffixes denotes novice class license

VO, VY SEE VE, VO, VY

V31, 2 Belize
The first letter after the number indicates the district
A, B Corozal
C, D Orange Walk
E-K Belize
L, M Stann Creek
N, O Cayo
P, Q Toledo

W, WA-WG, WI-WK, WM-WO, WQ-WZ See AA-AG

XE, XF Mexico
XE1 Colima, Distrito Federal, Guanajuato, Hidalgo, Jalisco, Mexico, Michoacan, Morelos, Nayarit, Puebla, Queretaro, Tlaxcala, Veracruz

XE2 Aguascalientes, Baja California Norte, Baja California Sur, Chihuahua, Coahuila, Durango, Nuevo Leon, San Luis Potosi, Sinaloa, Sonora, Tamaulipas, Zacatecas
XE3 Campeche, Chiapas, Guerrero, Oaxaca, Quintana Roo, Tabasco, Yucatan
XEØ Special Callsigns
XF1 Pacific Islands North of 20° Latitude
XF2 Islands in the Gulf of Mexico East of 90° Longitude
XF3 Caribbean Islands
XF4 (Revillagigedo-Inseln) Pacific Islands South of 20° Latitude, including Revillagigedo

XQ See CE, XQ

YB, YC, YD, YE, YF, YG, YH Indonesia
1 West-Java
2 Middle-Java
3 East-Java
4 South-Sumatra
5 West-Sumatra

6 North-Sumatra
7 Kalimantan (Borneo)
8 Sulawesi (Celebes), Molukken
9 Bali, Irian Jaya, Nusa Tenggara Barat, Nusa Tenggara Timur, Timor Timur
Ø Jakarta

YO Romania
2 Arad, Caras-Serverin, Hunedoara, Timis
3 Bucharest
4 Braila, Constanta, Galati, Tulcea, Vrancea
5 Alba, Bihor, Bistrita-Nasaud, Cluj, Maramures, Salaj, Satu Mare
6 Brasov, Covasna, Harghita, Mures, Sibiu
7 Arges, Dolj, Gorj, Mehedinti, Olt, Vilcea
8 Bacau, Botosani, lasi, Neamt, Suceava, Vaslui
9 Buzau, Calarasi, Dimbovita, Giurgiu, lalomita, Prahova, Teleorman
Ø Special Callsigns

YS El Salvador
1 San Salvador
2 Santa Ana
3 San Miguel
4 La Libertad
5 Chalatenango, Cuscatlan, La Paz
6 Cabanas, San Vicente, Usulutan
7 Sonsonate
8 Ahuachapan
9 La Union, Morazan

YV Venezuela
1 Falcon, Trujillo, Zulia
2 Barinas, Merida, Tachira
3 Lara, Portuguesa, Yaracuy
4 Aragua, Carabobo, Cojedes
5 Distrito Federal, Guarico, Miranda
6 Anzoategui, Bolivar
7 Nueva Esparta, Sucre
8 Delta Amacuro, Monagas
9 Amazonas, Apure
Ø Islands (Coche, Cubagua, Isla de Aves, Islas de Aves, La Blanquilla, La Orchila, La Tortuga, Los Hermanos, Los Monjes, Los Roques, Los Testigos)

ZA Albania
1 Durres, Elbasan, Librazhd, Lushnje, Tirana
2 Berat, Fier, Gramsh, Korce, Pogradec, Skrapar
3 Gjirokaster, Kolonje, Permet, Sarande, Tepelene, Vlore
4 Dibre, Kruje, Lezhe, Mat, Mirdite
5 Kukes, Puke, Shkoder, Tropoje

ZF Cayman Islands
1 Grand Cayman
2 Guest Licenses
8 Little Cayman Island
9 Cayman Brac Island

ZP Paraguay
1 Boqueron, Chaco, Nueva Asuncion
2 Alto Paraguay, Presidente Hayes
3 Amambay, Concepcion
4 Canindeyu, San Pedro
5 Asuncion
6 Central, Cordillera, Paraguari
7 Caaguazu, Caazapa, Guaira
8 Misiones, Neembucu
9 Alto Parana, Itapua
Ø Sonderrufzeichen

ZR, ZS, ZU Republic of South Africa (ZR VHF Licenses, ZU Novice Class)
1 Cape Province (Western Sector)
2 Cape Province (Eastern Sector)
3 Cape Province (North of 30° Latitude)
4 Orange Free State
5 Natal
6 Transvaal
7 Marion Island
8 Prince Edward Island
9 Walvis Bay
Ø Penguin Island

ZV, ZW, ZX, ZY, ZZ See PP

5N Nigeria
1 Ogun, Oyo
2 Kwara, Niger
3 Bendel, Ondo
4 Anambra, Rivers
5 Akwa Ibom, Cross River, Imo
6 Benue, Plateau
7 Bauchi, Gongola
8 Borno, Kano
9 Kaduna, Katsina, Sokoto
Ø Abuja, Lagos

6W Senegal
1 Dakar
2 Ziguinchor
3 Diourbel
4 Saint Louis
5 Tambacounda
6 Kaolack
7 Thies
8 Louga
9 Fatick
Ø Kolda

7J, 7K, 7L, 7M, 7N, 8J See JA

9H Malta
1 Malta
3 Guest Licenses, Special Calls
4 Gozo
5 VHF Licenses
8 Comino

9L Sierra Leone
1 Western Region
2 Northern Province
3 Southern Province
4 Eastern Province
7 Novice Class
8 VHF License

HF DIGITAL RADIO

If you are new to the world of high frequency digital communications, you have a great new aspect of the hobby waiting for you. Teleprinting via radio (radioteletype, or "RTTY") on the amateur bands was first authorized by the FCC in the early 1950s. Some stations still use the old mechanical machines with dripping oil and noisy gears, but the advent of the ubiquitous personal computer has completely revolutionized the mode. The development of inexpensive solid state modems (sometimes called TNCs, Terminal Units, or Interface Units) has put this aspect of the hobby within the reach of most amateurs. These interface devices enable communication between your radio and your keyboard and CRT display. More recently, the TNC function has been incorporated directly into the computer, thereby eliminating an extra piece of station hardware.

One of the unique aspects of digital radio is the convenience of printing out hard copy of your QSOs. This is great for your own personal scrapbook, for traffic handling, or other appropriate record. You can share your printout of a particularly interesting QSO with your pals at the local radio club or hamfest.

While competition for rare DX, and during contests, is as fierce on RTTY as on CW and SSB, there is a whole new dimension of friendliness that pervades digital radio. For years RTTY has been known as the "gentlemen's mode," and, to a great extent, it still is.

Even if you are not the world's greatest typist, that is no detriment to enjoying this fascinating aspect of our hobby.

RTTY

RTTY (radioteletype) is one of the more common communications protocols used in the HF bands. It is a half-duplex, non error-correcting mode that can be used by any number of stations on a frequency in a round-table fashion. Since there is no error-correction, it suffers from noisy environments, and a good signal-to-noise ratio is needed for reasonable copy. Note that transmit/receive switching is manual, so all parties in a roundtable need to agree on who transmits next. It is primarily used for single keyboard-to-keyboard contacts. RTTY uses Baudot character encoding (also known as ITA2), which is a 5-bit code. Note that 5 bits is only 32 possible combinations, which is not enough for a full alphanumeric set, much less mixed-case alphabetics. Baudot (and RTTY) gets around this limitation by defining two "shifts" which switch between a "letters case," and a "figures case." On older RTTY setups (ones which actually use a teletype, for instance), you have to worry about the letters/figures shift. For example, the RST signal report "599" is often sent both as "599" and "TOO" (which is the letter-case equivalent) to ensure copy if the receiving station has inadvertently missed the "figures-shift" character. However, most TNCs and multimode digital controllers now take care of those shift characters automatically, sending them as necessary for the data being transmitted. Lower case is not used on Baudot RTTY. ASCII can be used in RTTY as well, but it is very uncommon.

If you are migrating from CW or SSB to RTTY, you will find that contacts are made in very much the same manner with which you are accustomed. Conversational QSOs are established by calling CQ, answering a CQ, or a QRZ?. Selective area CQs (e.g., CQ Pacific) are common. As with any new mode, the best way to learn the prevailing operating practices is to listen before transmitting.

Most RTTY QSOs are carried on at 60 wpm (45.45 baud), although you may sometimes find a foreign station using 67 wpm (50 baud). This will be evident if you are getting less than perfect copy even with a 599 QRM-free signal. In that case the sender is probably using old equipment and cannot change. Adjust your baud rate to match his. Another problem often arises when an operator inadvertently uses Upper Sideband—by convention, all RTTY and AMTOR operation is done on Lower Sideband, regardless of frequency band. If you cannot get meaningful copy on a loud station, the sender is probably on the wrong sideband. Try calling on the same sideband that he is using, and ask him to switch to the correct one.

Very little RTTY DXing is done on 160 and 80 meters, although 40 and 80 meters can be quite active during RTTY contests. Most favored bands are 15 and 20 meters. In favorable parts of the sunspot cycle, 10 meters can be active. There is practically no RTTY activity on 12, 17, and 30 meters, without having a prior agreed-upon schedule.

AMTOR

During the 1970s, the Dutch government developed a system of digital communication called SITOR. It was designed to provide reliable RTTY communication under adverse conditions, while still maintaining an extremely low error-rate. The SITOR protocol was meant primarily for maritime use. It was so reliable a system that it was soon in use worldwide. In the early 1980s, Peter Martinez, G3PLX, made several minor changes to the SITOR protocol and called it AMTOR. The FCC authorized its use by U. S. amateurs beginning in January of 1983. AMTOR is different from any digital mode you may have used, in that it is the only synchronous type of RTTY authorized at the present time. "Synchronous" means that the two stations in an AMTOR ARQ contact are synchronized (linked) with each other. Most AMTOR activity is found on 20 meters. Look for it around 14.075. You will also find activity around 3.650, 7.050, and 21.075.

There are three modes in AMTOR. The first is ARQ, an acronym for Automatic Repeat Request, sometimes called Mode A. It makes the familiar "chirp chirp" sound you have often heard. The second mode is FEC, an acronym for Forward Error Correcting. It is sometimes called Mode B. The sound of an FEC transmission is similar to that of Baudot RTTY. The third mode is called Mode L, the Listen mode. It allows an operator to decode an ARQ signal even though he is not one of the two stations that are linked.

This description of the AMTOR ARQ mode refers to the "information sending station" and the "information receiving station." This is because when two stations are linked in Mode A, *both* stations are transmitting at intervals, thus it would be incorrect to refer to one as the "transmitting station" and the other as the "receiving station." In an ARQ link, the timing is set by the station that initiated the contact. It is called the "master" station, with the other station being the "slave." In AMTOR, the "ARQ Cycle" is 450 milliseconds long. It starts with the information-sending station transmitting a data-burst consisting of three characters. Since AMTOR uses a seven-bit code, and the data-transfer rate is fixed at 100 baud, this data-burst takes 210 milliseconds. Next there is an 85 millisecond period of silence, during which the receiving station checks the three characters for validity. If the data-burst passes the check, the receiving station prints it, and sends back a single character control code. This takes 70 milliseconds. The control code (an ACK) says, "OK, I got it, send the next burst." If the data-burst does not pass the check, the receiving station prints nothing and returns a control code (a NAK) that says, "Hey, I didn't get it. Send it again." The sending station will continue to repeat the data-burst until it gets an ACK. The control code is followed by another 85 milliseconds of silence, and the cycle begins again with either the next data-burst if the information sending station received an ACK, or a repeat of the last data-burst if it got a NAK.

The AMTOR ARQ mode has often been referred to as error-free. That is not quite true. Errors are possible, but the error rate is so extremely low that it is *virtually* error free. The method of error detection used is quite simple. Five of the bits in each character of the AMTOR code are information-bearing bits. The other two are used for error detection. The five information-bearing bits in each character are identical to the five information-bearing bits for that character in the Baudot code. Each of the two error detection bits can be either a mark or a space. The code is arranged so that every AMTOR character contains four marks and three spaces. A three character data-burst then, contains a total of twelve marks and nine spaces. All the information receiving station must do, therefore, is count the total number of marks and spaces in the data-burst it received to detect whether or not there has been an error. While data is not being transferred, the information-sending station transmits idle signals to maintain the link.

The second AMTOR mode is FEC. This mode is not synchronous, and the stations involved are not linked, but they do operate in phase with each other. In order for them to stay in phase, each FEC transmission is started with several sets of "phasing pairs."

These are repeated at regular intervals during the course of the transmission, so that the two stations can stay in phase. While no data is being transferred, idle signals are transmitted to keep the two stations in phase. In Mode B, each character is transmitted twice, 350 milliseconds apart. The receiving station prints a character the first time it is received if the mark/space count is correct. If it were received correctly the first time it was sent, it will be printed and ignored the second time it is received. If it were incorrect the first time it was received, it will be ignored, and will be printed the second time it is sent if it is received correctly. This method of error detection is much less effective than that used in ARQ, and the error-rate is considerably higher than it is in that mode. Although higher than in ARQ, the error-rate is still far lower than it is in other forms of RTTY.

The third AMTOR mode is called Mode L, or the "Listen" mode. It allows an operator to print ARQ data-bursts even though he is not linked to the information sending station. There is no error detection at all in the Listen mode, and if the station being monitored is asked for repeats (RQs), they will be printed.

To make a contact on AMTOR, you call CQ very much the same as on RTTY or CW, except that you must use the FEC (Forward Error Correction) mode, sometimes called Mode B. An FEC transmission sounds very much like fast RTTY. Most newcomers get frustrated when starting because they do not seem to be able to get answers to their CQs. The trick is to allow three to six seconds of idles at the beginning of your transmission. Without sufficient idles, listening stations will not be able to "sync" with you. When you call CQ, you include your "Selcal" in addition to your regular callsign. Selcal is an acronym for Selective Call. The convention is to derive your selcal from the first and the three trailing letters of your callsign. In the case of a one-by-two callsign such as W1AW, the first letter is repeated, followed by the two trailing letters, so its selcal would be WWAW. If the callsign is a two-by-one, the first letter is repeated twice, followed by the trailing letter. The selcal of WZ1R, for example, would be WWZR. A two-by-two callsign such as UW9AR, results in a selcal of UWAR. For a two- by-three callsign like WN4KKN, the selcal would be WKKN. While it is not necessary to follow this convention, since any four letters can be a selcal it is a good idea to do so. If you do, then any operator who knows your callsign can deduce your selcal.

Following your CQ, return to AMTOR Standby and wait for a reply. If you receive a response to your CQ, it could be in FEC, although it is much more likely that it will be in ARQ. If the response is in ARQ, your station will begin the ARQ cycle, and you will see that idle signals are being received. At this point, the link is established and your station is ready to receive text. Now the other operator need only open his transmit buffer, type the text, and it will be sent to you. If text stops appearing on your screen, just stand by. Your station is probably requesting repeats because it received a data-burst incorrectly. You will soon receive the block correctly, and traffic will begin to flow again. When the other station is ready to receive information from you, the operator will turn the link over to you, and it will be your turn to send text to him. He will do this by sending you a turnover sequence. That is the two characters "Plus-Question mark" (+?). You will know when the turnover has been made by the change in rhythm of your station's transmissions. Before the turnover, your station was sending single character data-bursts 70 milliseconds in length. When the turnover occurs, it will begin transmitting three character data- bursts 210 milliseconds in length. When the turnover has been made, simply open your transmit buffer and begin typing text for transmission. When you are transmitting text in ARQ, you will see it pop onto your screen in three character blocks, as the blocks are acknowledged by the receiving station. If this text stops appearing and nothing seems to be happening, it just means that the receiving station is requesting repeats because it received the last data-burst your station sent incorrectly. Stand by. The incorrect block will soon be acknowledged, and traffic will flow again. When you are ready to receive text again, reverse the link by sending the turnover sequence (+?).

The second way to initiate a contact is to answer another station's CQ. When a station calls CQ in FEC, its selcal should be included. If it is not, you can deduce what it is. To answer the CQ, just start an ARQ transmission. When you do this, your program will ask for the selcal of the station you wish to call. When you enter it, the ARQ cycle will start, with your station transmitting the other station's selcal. You will soon hear the other station responding with control codes, and you will see an indication that your station is sending idle signals. Now the link is established. Just open your transmit buffer and type in text for transmission. When you are ready for the other station's reply, send the turnover (+?) and reverse the link.

The third way to initiate a contact is to call a specific station in ARQ. Usually, this will happen when you have been watching an ARQ contact in the Listen mode, and you want to call one of the stations when they finish. In this case, since you have been "eavesdropping," you already know the selcal of the station you want to call. You also know it is on frequency, since the contact has just been terminated. Call the station by starting an ARQ transmission just as though you were replying to a CQ call.

There are two important control codes used in AMTOR. The first is "Control-C." It is used to force a changeover. If the other station in an ARQ link is the information-sending station, and you want to reverse the link without waiting for it to send the changeover sequence, you can do so by sending it a Control-C. The second code is "Control-D." It is used to break an ARQ link. An ARQ contact should *always* be ended with a Control D.

The T/R switching time of your rig should be on the order of 25 milliseconds for best ARQ operation. All newer rigs and most older ones easily meet this standard. Some rigs designed before AMTOR came into use, however, may require simple modifications. Since the ARQ cycle requires your rig to return to full receive sensitivity quickly, always set your AGC for fast release, or turn it off entirely.

(This section was written from material supplied by W2JGR, KD6GGD, and a file on the ARRL BBS written by N9ANL.)

OPERATING ON THE VHF FREQUENCIES AND ABOVE

Some of the most interesting and exciting Ham Radio operating takes place on the VHF, UHF and higher frequency bands. The sheer volume of spectrum, accounting for greater than 99% of the U.S. allocations, allows for the peaceful coexistence of a nearly endless variety of operating modes and styles. The 16 bands above 30 MHz span frequencies between 50 and 250,000 MHz and total over 20,000 MHz of Amateur band space. This large range of frequencies, and the desire to make the best use of them, has drawn many Amateurs into exploring and enjoying the bands above 10 meters.

When most Hams think of the frequencies of VHF and above they might consider FM repeater or packet operations. Others may think of satellites, ATV or SSB/CW work. It all depends on what you have discovered that interests you. The more common applications of the VHF and UHF spectrum, such as FM repeater, packet, satellite, and ATV operations, are aptly described elsewhere in this Almanac. The principal subject of this section is to describe so called weak signal operation on the bands above 50 MHz.

Weak signal work is the art of contacting distant stations by making the best use of equipment, antennas, band conditions, and operating skills. Although there a number of enhanced propagation modes that allow for contacts with stations several hundred, if not thousands, miles distant, the normal mode of propagation on the VHF and above bands is ground wave. For stations that are well equipped and have well placed directive antennas, reliable contacts can be routine with similarly equipped stations 300-400 miles away. Some of the key elements to successful and enjoyable weak signal work is to know where the activity is on the band and in what direction to point your antenna.

Calling Frequencies

The best place to start looking for VHF or UHF QSOs is on the calling frequencies. The following Table indicates the calling frequencies for the lower seven VHF/UHF bands allocated in North America.

Band (MHz)	Calling Frequency
50	50.110 for DX
	50.125 for Domestic QSOs
144	144.200
222	222.100
432	432.100
902	903.100
1296	1296.100
2304	2304.100

It is common practice to CQ on the calling frequency if it is not already in use. Amateurs active on the VHF and UHF bands often leave a receiver or two on the calling frequencies when they are in the shack so that they can keep track of band conditions and catch other VHFers without having to constantly tune the band.

Antennas

One of the advantages of VHF/UHF and Microwave operation is that an antenna comparable in size to, say, an average 10/15/20 meter triband Yagi has considerably more gain and directivity at VHF/UHF than the tribander does at HF. This is attributed to the inverse relationship between frequency and wavelength: the higher in frequency you go, the better the antenna performance at a given size.

For some very practical reasons, FM operation, which is primarily mobile, uses vertically polarized antennas. The use of vertically polarized antennas for FM mobile work has also been adopted for base station FM voice and packet operations. SSB and CW stations generally operate with horizontally polarized antennas, even when mobile. There is no clear advantage to one or the other in terms of performance for weak signal work. The important thing is that both stations use the same polarization. The most common antenna type is the long Yagi on the bands 50-432 MHz and the loop Yagi on 903 and 1296. Reflector antennas such as the common "dish" antenna are generally employed on the bands above 1296 Mhz.

Rigs for VHF and Above

The most popular and straightforward radios for 50-1296 MHz are the multimode (usually FM/SSB/CW) rigs. They come in basically three flavors: single-band mobile rigs, single-band base rigs, and multi-band base rigs. Most of these radios are quite similar to HF rigs in their features and operation, but generally transmit lower power levels in the 25 watt range. To boost output power levels, most amateurs couple their 25 watt radios to solid state "brick" amplifiers that are powered from 13.8 volts and amplify to typically about 150 watts. There are several commercial sources of these amplifiers, providing various output power levels and amplifier gains.

The easiest avenue to SSB/CW operation on 903, 1296, 2304 and 3456 is the "no-tune" transverter connected to a 144 MHz radio. These transverters take advantage of microwave monolithic integrated circuit technology in printed circuit boards employing etched tuned circuits. This design approach allows transverters to be constructed and tuned up with a minimum of adjustment as compared with earlier designs. Amateurs are getting on these higher bands like never before using these transverters, which are available in kit or fully constructed form.

Equipment for operation on 5760 and above is generally homebrew, but often employs surplus or used commercial pieces to keep costs down. The 10 GHz band is the most popular microwave band largely due to the availability of wide-band Gunn diode-based systems. There is even a commercially available 10 GHz FM transceiver with a built-in horn antenna for the amateur.

Grid Squares

While large antenna gain can help result in the ability to work over long distances, with it comes a commensurate increase in antenna directivity. Of course, you need to know where to point such directive antennas if they are to be useful. To make it easier to quickly know in what direction to turn your antenna, the earth has been mapped into 32,400 rectangles, called grid squares. Each square encompasses 1 degree of latitude and 2 degrees of longitude and has its own unique four-character designator. Almost all QSOs first begin with an exchange of grid squares, allowing both ends to quickly align their antennas.

Propagation

What follows describes a few common propagation modes capable of extending your range beyond what can be expected under average conditions.

E-Skip

This propagation mode, which is also called Sporadic-E, is common on the 6-meter band during the period of late May through July. E-skip usually produces contacts with stations that are 1100-1400 miles distant. During a Sporadic-E opening, radio waves propagate by refracting off of ionized regions in the E-layer, which is about 50 miles above the earth.

Tropo

Unlike E-skip, tropo openings have their greatest effect on the frequencies above 144 MHz. While there is a variety of types of tropo, they are all generally characterized by the refraction of radio waves at the temperature boundaries of lower atmospheres. Tropo openings can be local, providing enhancement within 100-200 miles, or long distance, allowing contacts with stations more than 1,000 miles distant. Unlike most of the propagation modes at HF, tropo is often developed and affected by the earth's weather patterns.

Aurora

The same aurora borealis that is such a treat to the eye can provide some exciting DX to the wary VHF operator on the bands 50-432. When charged particles thrown off by the sun during a solar storm interact with the earth's upper atmosphere over the north or south poles, there is the potential for the creation of large ionized polar regions. These regions can support extended VHF propagation for many hundreds of miles. If an aurora is suspected (if the WWV solar K index is above 4, for example), North American Hams should turn their antennas north and listen for Au. Unique to auroral propagation is the characteristic "buzz" or raspy sound to the signals. The signal distortion doesn't impact the effectiveness of CW, but it can make SSB contacts difficult.

Meteor-Scatter

Meteors strike and vaporize in the earth's upper atmosphere everyday. Meteors leave an ionized trail about 50-75 miles above the earth, supporting communications out to about 1400 miles. These ionized trails are such that signals on 10 and 6 meters are refracted particularly well and, to a lesser extent, signals on 2 meters and above. QSOs via meteor-scatter can be particularly challenging, as the ionized trail from a meteor may last anywhere from milliseconds to a minute or more. Stations often refer to meteor trail-induced receptions of distant stations as meteor bursts or pings if they are of very short duration. While skilled, persistent operators can work meteor-scatter almost any morning on 6 meters, the best chance to work meteor-scatter is during a meteor shower. The following table lists the meteor showers that occur every year during which amateurs can look for extended propagation.

Shower	Date(s)
Quadrantids	Jan 3-5
Lyrids	Apr 19-23
Eta Aquarids	May 1-6
Arietids	June 2-14
Delta Aquarids	July 26-31
Perseids	July 27-August 14
Orionids	Oct 18-23
Taurids	Oct 26-Nov 16
Leonids	Nov 14-18
Geminids	Dec 10-14
Ursids	Dec 22

Typically, the two most productive meteor showers for the amateur are the yearly Perseids and the Geminids.

In addition to the propagation modes described above, there are several others, such as double-hop E-skip, F-layer, and transequatorial, that can greatly extend your VHF horizon. Part of the fun of operating VHF and above is working distant stations by rare and exotic propagation.

Hilltopping and Contesting

One popular way to dramatically improve your QSO range on VHF and above is to operate from a hilltop, mountaintop, or any other elevated spot that provides a clear shot in the direction in which you want to operate. The improvement in range becomes more significant as your frequency of operation increases. Microwave contacts that are impossible when operating from a valley become easy if you move to a hilltop that provides a line-of-sight or nearly line-of-sight path.

Many stations enjoy hilltopping during VHF/UHF contests. Hilltopping contest stations can pull in many hundreds of QSOs without an elaborate setup. Small antennas, often short Yagis, can be very effective and easily mounted on a short mast that can be hand-rotated. Radios are usually multi-mode solid-state rigs plus solid-state "brick" amplifiers in the 50-150 watt class. Dozens of stations travel to hilltops in exotic grid squares during the contests to pass out rare multipliers and to feel the rush of being on the other end of a pile-up.

VHF/UHF Contests that Occur Every Year

ARRL VHF Sweepstakes	January
ARRL June VHF QSO Party	June
CQ VHF WPX Contest	July
ARRL UHF Contest	August
ARRL September VHF QSO Party	September
ARRL EME Contest	Oct-Nov

Courtesy of Ed Parsons, K1TR

VHF/UHF/MICROWAVE/LIGHTWAVE DX RECORDS

History

Amateur radio operators were quick to exploit the HF bands but before WW II the frequencies above 30 MHz were treated more as a curiosity or experimental area rather than a useful frequency spectrum. Furthermore, there weren't many high power tubes available, especially above 150 MHz.

After WW II when VHF/UHF equipment did become available, it was mostly obsolete RADAR gear that had poor frequency stability and low output power. Hence it was only usable on FM and later on AM. In the 1950's crystal controlled receivers and transmitters finally reached the 2-meter band and narrower band operation such as CW and later SSB became available.

In North America in the early years following WW II the primary DX was conducted on 6 and 2 meters in the quest for the WAS award. 6-meters of course was not too difficult since sporadic E and, at sunspot peaks, F2 propagation was available. However, 2-meter DXers had to primarily rely on tropospheric and meteors scatter propagation with no chance of completing a WAS award.

In the 1960's the Europeans invented the so called "Locator" system to pinpoint ones latitude and longitude. Later this evolved into a competition to see how many different locators you could contact. However, due to the way locators were originally designated, this system was not usable outside Europe.

Meanwhile, new propagation modes, better equipment, especially with the arrival of the transistor and FET improved operating techniques, higher gain antenna systems, and EME communications opened up new horizons but WAS and WAC were still the big awards here in North America. Some DX records were made but these were often overshadowed by "special" regions of the world that exhibited unusual propagation such as the tropo paths from California to Hawaii or over the Mediterranean Sea and the Great Australian Bight.

In 1983 the ARRL introduced the VUCC (VHF/UHF Century Club) award using the "Maidenhead" world-wide grid locator system. This is now well entrenched and has improved activity as well as DX chasing., However, there was still no real incentive to "improve the state of the art" in equipment and DXing since many of the long DX records were not easily exceeded in North America. Figure 1 shows the DX table as it appeared in 1984. Note that the only North American record were on 2 meters and the 135-cm band, the later not available outside of region 2!

Hence, in 1985 I introduced a new system whereby DX records in North America were treated as a separate entity. Furthermore, a separate record was established for each type of radio propagation on each VHF band above 6 meters. The 6-meter band was not listed since it frequently has mixed modes and even "long path" DX where the distances are greater than half-way around the world. Finally, in February 1989 I added the OL (over-land) and OW (over-water) designations to further enhance the challenges. To qualify for an OW DX record, the path must be at least 75% over water and must exceed the equivalent OL path distance.

Why are VHF and above DX records important?

1. They provide a challenge as described by the old saw: "because it's there."
2. They improve the state of the art (SOA) in radio propagation.
3. They set the pace for the design of SOA antennas, receivers, & transmitters.
4. They help determine the best transmission mode (CW, SSB, FM, etc.).
5. They require improved operating techniques to make new DX records.

What are some of the improvements brought forth primarily because DX records were being pursued?

1. New propagation modes such as TE, EME, FAI, Aurora, etc.
2. High stability narrowband receivers and transmitters have been developed that permit CW and SSB operation as high as 48 GHz!
3. New almost noiseless receivers have been developed that operate beyond the microwave region (above 10 GHz).
4. High gain low side lobe antenna systems are now common place.
5. High power vacuum tube and solid state transmitters are now available.
6. Improved operating techniques using the most optimum communications mode now allow almost routine contacts using meteor scatter and EME.
7. You tell me!

Current DX record tables (See following information) DX records serve a very useful purpose

1. They are sort of a "yard stick" that can be used to measure our accomplishments against those of our peers.
2. They give us a good idea of what can be accomplished on each of the bands above 50 MHz as well as the propagation modes available.
3. They tell us which Amateurs are in the forefront of technology thus providing a person or persons that can be contacted to help us along without having to "reinvent the wheel."

References

1. Joe Reisert, W1JR, "The VHF/UHF primer: an introduction to propagation," *Ham Radio Magazine*, July 1984, pg. 14.
2. Joe Reisert, W1JR, "Propagation update," *Ham Radio Magazine*, July 1985, pg. 86.
3. Joe Reisert, W1JR, "Propagation update—part 3," *Ham Radio Magazine*, July 1988, pg. 38.
4. Joe Reisert, W1JR, "DX records on 50 MHz and above," *Ham Radio Magazine*, Jan. 1989, pg. 48.
5. Joe Reisert, W1JR, "DX records on 50 MHz and above: part 2," *Ham Radio Magazine*, Feb. 1989, pg. 42.

Courtesy of Joe Reisert, W1JR (evhfc91)
16 May 1991

WORLD-WIDE VHF/UHF RECORD HOLDERS

Note: The information and format used in this table is copyrighted in 1989 and registered at the U. S. Patent Office by Joseph H. Reisert, W1JR, and may not be reprinted or used in any form without the written permission of the author.

Joseph H. Reisert, W1JR (wwvhfuhf),
Revised 93-09-23

World Wide Claimed VHF/UHF/SHF Terrestrial DX Records (notes 1 & 2)

Frequency	Record Holders	Date	Mode	Miles (km)
50 MHz	Note 3			
70 MHz	GW4ASR/P(IO82JG)-5B4CY (KM64MR)	1981-06-07	Es	2153 (3465)
144 MHz	I4EAT (JN54VG)-ZS3B (JG73OI)	1979-03-30	TE	4884 (7860)
220 MHz	KP4EOR (FK68XM)-LU7DJZ (GFØ5RJ)	1983-03-09	TE	3670 (5906)
432 MHz	KH6HME (BK29GO)-XE2GXQ/P (DL29CX)	1989-07-15	Duct	2575 (4143)
902 MHz	KH6HME (BK29GO)-N6CA/6 (DMØ3TR)	1993-08-23	Duct	2469 (3973)
1296 MHz	KH6HME (BK29GO)-XE2GXQ/P (DL29CX)	1989-07-15	Duct	2575 (4143)
2304 MHz	VK5QR (PF95HD)-VK6WG/P (OF85WA)	1978-02-17	Duct	1170 (1883)
3456 MHz	KH6HME (BK29GO)-N6CA/6 (DMØ3TR)	1991-07-28	Duct	2469 (3973)
5760 MHz	KH6HME (BK29GO)-N6CA/6 (DMØ3TR)	1991-07-29	Duct	2469 (3973)
10.3 GHz	IØSNY/EA9 (IM75IV)-IØYLI/IE9(JM68NR)	1983-07-08	Duct	1032 (1660)
24 GHz	IØSNY/IC8 (JN6ØWR)-I8YZO/8 (JM78WE)	1984-08-11	LOS	206 (331)
47 GHz	HB9MIN (JN47GF)-HB9MIO (JN37MD)	1992-09-15	LOS	103 (166)
76 GHz	OE9PMJ/9 (JN48—)-OE9FKI/9 (JN48—)	1989-09-18	LOS	1.3 (2.1)
145 GHz	WA1MBA (FN32RI)-WB2BYW (FN32RJ)	1993-05-02	LOS	2.4 (3.75)
474 THz	K6MEP/6 (DMØ4MS)-WA6EJO/6 (DMØ5XA)	1991-06-09	LOS	57 (92)
678 THz	KY7B/7 (DM42MS)-WA7LYI/7 (DM34TF)	1991-06-08	LOS	154 (248)

Notes:

1. The information within the brackets ( ) after the call sign is the grid square locator.
2. Distances have been calculated assuming a spherical earth model. The actual latitude and longitude are used rather than grid square centers which are less accurate.
3. 6 meters has been left blank on this listing because long-path QSO's (those exceeding approximately 12430 miles or 20000 km) have been reported during solar cycles 19, 21, and 22.

Reprinted with permission.

NORTH AMERICAN VHF/UHF RECORD HOLDERS

Note: The information and format used in this table is copyrighted in 1989 and registered at U.S. Patent Office by Joseph H. Reisert, W1JR, and may not be reprinted or used in any form without the written permission of the author.

Joseph. H. Reisert, W1JR (navhfuhf)
Revised 93-09-11

N. American VHF and Above Claimed DX Records (notes 1, 2 & 3)

Frequency	Record Holders	Date	Mode	DX Miles (km)
50 MHz	(Note 4)			
EME	WA4NJP (EM84DG)-ZL2BGJ (RF7ØDX)	1988-09-08	cw	8258 (13288)
144 MHz				
Aurora	KA1ZE (FN31TU)-WAØTKJ/WBØDRL (EM18CT)	1986-02-08	cw	1347 (2167)
EME	VE1UT (FN63XV)-VK5MC (QFØ2EJ)	1984-04-07	cw	10,985 (17676)
FAI	W5HUQ/4 (EM9ØGC)-W5UN (DM82WA)	1983-07-25	cw	1228 (1976)
MS	K5UR (EM35WA)-KP4EKG (FK68VG)	1985-12-13	ssb	1960 (3153)
Spor. E.	WA4CQG (EM72FO)-W7YOZ (CN87VR)	1988-06-06	ssb	2172 (3495)
TE	KP4EOR (FK78AJ)-LU5DJZ (GF11LU)	1978-02-12	ssb	3933 (6328)
Tropo OL	K1RJH (FN31XH)-K5WXZ (EM12QW)	1968-10-08	cw	1468 (2362)
Tropo OW	KH6HME (BK29GO)-XE2GXQ (DL28UQ)	1989-07-13	ssb	2657 (4276)
220 MHz				
Aurora	WC2K (FM29PT)-WB5LUA (EM13QC)	1989-03-13	cw	1298 (2089)
EME	K1WHS (FM43MK)-KH6BFZ (BL11CJ)	1983-11-17	cw	5058 (8139)
MS	W1JR (FN42HN)-KØALL (EN16OU)	1988-08-13	ssb	1274 (2057)
Spor. E	K5UGM (EM12MS)-W5HUQ/4 (EM9ØGC)	1987-06-14	cw/ssb	932 (1499)
TE	KP4EOR (FK78AJ)-LU7DJZ (GFØ5RJ)	1983-03-09	cw/ssb	3670 (5906)
Tropo OL	K5SW (EM25HR)-W2SZ/1 (FN32KP)	1992-09-13	cw	1275 (2050)

Tropo OW	KH6HME (BK29GO)-XE2GXQ (DL29CX)	1989-07-15	NBFM	2575 (4143)
432 MHz				
Aurora	W3IP (FM19PD)-WB5LUA (EM13QC)	1986-02-08	cw	1182 (1901)
EME	K2UYH (FN2ØQG)-VK6ZT (OF78VB)	1983-01-29	cw	11,567 (18612)
MS	KD5RO (FN13FB)-WB5LUA (EM13QC)	1988-12-13	cw	1239 (1994)
Tropo OL	KM1H (FN42HR)-WA4MJE (EL94HQ)	1992-12-16	ssb	1370 (2204)
Tropo OW	KH6HME (BK29GO)-XE2GXQ (DL29CX)	1989-07-15	ssb	2575 (4143)
902 MHz				
Aurora	K3HZO (FM18QP)-WA3NZL (FM19JG)	91-11-08	cw	54 (87)
EME	AF1T (FN43ED)-K5JL (EM15DQ)	1990-05-27	cw	1476 (2376)
Tropo OL	W4WSR (EL96WW)-WB5LUA (EM13QC)	1989-03-14	cw	1072 (1726)
Tropo OW	KH6HME (BK29GO)-N6CA/6 (DMØ3TR)	1993-08-23	cw	2469 (3973)
1296 MHz				
EME	K2UYH (FN2ØQG)-VK5MC (QFØ2EJ)	1981-12-06	cw	10,562 (16995)
Tropo OL	WB3CZG (FN21AX)-KD5RO (EM13PA)	1986-11-29	cw	1287 (2070)
Tropo OW	KH6HME (BK29GO)-XE2GXQ (DL29CX)	1989-07-15	ssb	2575 (4143)
2304 MHz				
EME	W3IWI/8 (FMØ8CK)-ZL2AQE (RE78JS)	1987-10-18	cw	8658 (13931)
Tropo OL	KD5RO (EM13PA)-W8YIO (EN82BE)	1986-11-29	cw	940 (1513)
3456 MHz				
EME	W7CNK/5 (EM15FI)-KØKE/0 (DM79NØ)	1987-04-12	cw	498 (802)
Tropo OL	WB5LUA (EM13QC)-W9ZIH (EM51MU)	1992-05-01	cw	736 (1184)
Tropo OW	KH6HME (BK29GO)-N6CA/6 (DMØ3TR)	1991-07-28	cw	2469 (3973)
5760 MHz				
EME	WA5TNY (EM12KV)-W7CNK/5 (EM15FI)	1987-04-24	cw	174 (279)
Tropo OL	N5JJZ/5 (EM26CB)-WA5ICW/5 (DM86LR)	1988-07-10	ssb	404 (650)
Tropo OW	KH6HME (BK29GO)-N6CA/6 (DMØ3TR)	1991-07-29	cw	2469 (3973)
10.368 GHz				
EME	SM4DHN (JP6ØUB)-WA7CJO (DM33XL)	1990-12-02	cw/ssb	5241 (8432)
Tropo OL	WB7ABP/P (CN81QB)-WBØHLC/6 (DMØ4MS)	1988-08-06	cw/ssb	479 (770)
Tropo OW	NN6W/6 (CM94XM)-XE2GFH (DL27VL)	1988-09-11	mcw	595 (958)
24.192 GHz				
LOS	KK6TG/6 (CM98MR)-WB7ABP/6 (CN8ØON)	1992-09-12	cw	159 (256)
	WA3RMX/7 (CN93IQ)-WB7UNU/7 (CN95DH)	1986-08-23	ssb	116 (186)
47.040 GHz				
LOS	WA3RMX/7 (CN82VW)-K7AUO/7 (CN82PB)	1988-08-06	cw/ssb	65.3 (105)
75-120 GHz	None reported			
145 GHz	WA1MBA/1 (FN32RI)-WB2BYW (FN32RJ)	1993-05-02	cw	2.4 (3.75)
300 GHz and above (note 5)				
474 THz				
LOS	K6MEP/6 (DMØ4MS)-WA6EJO/6 (DMØ5XA)	1991-06-09	Laser	57 (92)
678 THz				
LOS	KY7B/7 (DM42OK)-WA7LYI/7 (DM34TF)	1991-06-08	Laser	154 (248)

Notes:

1. The records are listed alphabetically by mode. Tropo OL is over land. Tropo OW is over water where at least 75% of the path is over water. Tropo OW records are only listed when they exceed the tropo OL DX record.
2. The information within the brackets ( ) following the call sign is the grid square locator.
3. Distances have been calculated assuming a spherical earth model using the actual latitude and longitude rather than grid square centers which is less accurate.
4. 6-meters records, excepting EME, were left off since the primary propagation mode is often hard to distinguish. Also long-path QSO's have been reported during solar cycles 19, 21, and 22 which exceed approximately 12430 miles (20000 km).
5. There have been very few reports of contacts in the wide open frequency allocation above 300 GHz. Therefore, at least for the time being, we will list those records that show considerable distance at widely different frequencies.

Reprinted with permission.

WORLD-WIDE EARTH-MOON-EARTH RECORDS

Note: The information and format used in this table is copyrighted in 1989 and registered at U.S. Patent Office by Joseph H. Reisert, W1JR, and may not be reprinted or used in any form without the written permission of the author.

Joseph H. Reisert, W1JR (wwemerec)
Revised 93-09-08

World Wide Claimed VHF/UHF/SHF EME DX Records (notes 1 & 2)

Frequency	Record holders	Date	Mode	Miles (km)
50 MHz	WA4NJP (EM84DG)-ZL2BGJ (RF7ØDX)	1988-09-08	cw	8258 (13288)
144 MHz	K6MYC/KH6 (BK29AO)-ZS6ALE (KG43RC)	1983-02-18	cw	12091 (19455)
220 MHz	K1WHS (FN43MK)-KH6BFZ (BL11CJ)	1983-11-17	cw	5058 (8139)
432 MHz	G3SEK (IO91IP)-ZL3AAD (RE66GR)	1989-03-12	cw	11724 (18864)
902 MHz	AF1T (FN43ED)-K5JL (EM15DQ)	1990-05-27	cw	1476 (2376)
1296 MHz	PAØSSB (JO11WI)-ZL3AAD (RE66GR)	1983-06-13	cw	11595 (18657)
2304 MHz	W3IWI/8 (FMØ8CK)- ZL2AQE (RE78JS)	1987-10-18	cw	8658 (13931)
3456 MHz	W7CNK/5 (EM15FI)-KØKE (DM79NO)	1987-04-06	cw	498 (802)
5760 MHz	WA5TNY (EM12KV)-W7CNK/5 (EM15FI)	1987-04-24	cw	174 (279)
10,368 MHz	SM4DHN (JP6ØUB)-WA7CJO (DM33XL)	1990-12-02	cw/ssb	5241 (8432)
24,000 MHz and above:	None reported			

Notes:

1. The information within the brackets ( ) following the call signs is the grid square locator.
2. The distances shown have been calculated assuming a spherical earth model. The actual latitudes and longitude are use rather than grid square centers which are less accurate.

Reprinted with permission.

CONTESTS

Contest Operating—A Tutorial

Ham radio is a competitive hobby. Active amateurs often find themselves engaged in competition by working a rare country, satisfying the requirements for a new award, or setting a long distance record on a UHF band. However, even when considering these endeavors in our hobby, there is nothing that is more competitive than the sport of contesting.

Contesting's beginnings took place over 60 years ago. The concept was originally developed as an attempt to improve the operating ability of amateurs around the world and advance the state of the art. Those goals remain in effect in today's contests.

When considering contesting, the most fundamental question one can ask is: "What is a Contest?" The basic definition is simply a scheduled operating event designed to encourage amateurs to contact as many other stations as possible over a fixed period of time and frequency spectrum. These events range from domestic affairs to worldwide phenomena such as the CQ World Wide. With dozens of contests being held annually around the world, contests have become a fundamental part of amateur radio.

Contest operating ability and knowledge is an acquired skill. While many operators have "instinctive proficiency" (e.g., capability to copy fast CW, good hearing, ability to process information quickly, etc.), the fastest way to improve your skill set is to meet other contesters and dive right into the fray.

Contests can be intimidating to the first-timer. On CW, there are seemingly hundreds of stations sending at least 30 WPM. When listening to SSB, you find world class experts working each other at rates of 350 QSOs per hour. The new competitor says: "that's not an environment for me!" The key is to remember that each and every station you hear in a contest was once a newcomer! The champions of the 90s were the newcomers of the 70s.

Here are a few basic points to keep in mind while operating:

1) Always sign your entire callsign when calling another station.

2) Accuracy is more important than speed. However, try to say/send the minimum amount of information necessary to complete a valid QSO as defined by the rules. Inaccurate logging will be found by the contest sponsor, and disqualification can result!

3) Practice, practice, practice. Not every contest is a "free for all." Many competitions are low key and offer a more subdued environment to hone your operating skills.

4) Practice your operating skills outside of contests. There is no substitute for improved CW skills and good ears on SSB.

5) Never give up or feel dismayed. Success in contesting is always a relative term. Most competing stations will never win. Those having the most fun compete against their previous accomplishments or a variety of other personal goals.

Frequently-Asked Questions about Contest Operating

Are contests only for big stations?

NO! If contests were only for big stations, there wouldn't be contests; there just aren't enough big stations to go around. A good operator at a modest station can beat a mediocre operator at a big station. Skill counts more than size.

What kind of radio/options should I be using?

From a contesting perspective, there are some *basic* features you should demand when selecting the "right radio." These include:

* Solid state finals—Critical for fast band changing.

* Digital displays—Reduces eye strain while operating and critical when packet spotting or meeting schedules.

* Selectable filtering options—The ability to copy through heavy QRM is never more needed than during a contest.

* RIT/XIT—Many stations call you off frequency during QSO runs. The RIT/XIT functions solve this common problem.

* Dual VFOs—Absolutely mandatory for 80/40 meter SSB. Also, more DX contesters are using split operation on other bands.

* Selectable attenuation—This is a necessary function on 40 meter to eliminate intermodulation problems from overseas broadcast stations.

* Programmable memories—Useful to program pileup frequencies or packet radio spots.

* Speech compression—A clear differentiator for phone contest operating. Audio punch is absolutely critical, especiallly when running low power.

* Noise blanking capability—Helpful for copying weak stations during high noise periods.

Some of the more *advanced* features to consider include:

* Computer interface (RS-232)—Absolutely critical if you plan to interface your computer logging program or packet radio spotting system to the transceiver.

* Independent tuning dials for main/sub VFOs—Extremely practical feature for separately tuning each VFO to allow VFO-independent band scanning and multiplier chasing.

* Antenna tuner—Useful for odd high-SWR antenna scenarios or when the input SWR to your amplifier is too high on certain bands.

* Electronic Keyer—Although most stations have a separate keyer accessory, backup devices such as these are always useful.

* Front panel control access—Helps the ease of adjustment for commonly changed settings (e.g., VOX settings, keyer speed).

* Full break-in—Nice CW feature that enhances your operating style in pileups by allowing you to time your calls.

Many of these features define a quality transceiver for any use within amateur radio. However, their absence in the competitive world of contest operating can dramatically impact your score. Not unlike most consumer purchases, it is easy to get caught up in the feature/function war between manufacturers. Don't forget that there is nothing better than good old fashioned word of mouth, especially if you can get it from an experienced contest operator.

A second consideration in equipment has arisen in recent years—the computer. While operating from a big contest station, you can sometimes find yourself looking for the radio in the maze of 386s, 486s, TNCs, keyboards, displays, cables, and other "amateur" support equipment. The guidelines for computers in amateur radio should parallel the same requirements for any home system. In today's world, a 286 system is barely adequate, while a 386 (or 386SX) is the model of choice. Nowadays, a contest station without a computer is only slightly less inept than one without antennas!

The final area to contemplate is the myriad of accessories (mostly homebrew) that can help differentiate a contest station. Consider issues such as audio and antenna switching, remote access to station functions, etc.

What about antennas?

Antenna selection decisions are usually determined by several factors such as money, time, and/or real estate. The guidelines for choosing antennas should be no different for a contest station than any other amateur setup. After all, whether you are interested in contesting, DXing, or casual ragchewing, you want to have the best signal possible.

For years, contesters have led the field in antenna innovation. Although most amateurs have limited resources to play in the mega-station field, a simple setup with a 60-foot tower, tribander for 10/15/20, two-element short yagi for 40, and a few strategically placed dipoles can do amazing things. Another alternative is to focus on a single band and place all your efforts in that direction.

And, don't forget that remarkable accomplishments are possible with only wire antennas. A quick tour through the ARRL antenna handbook (and other publications) will not only educate you, but offer low cost alternatives for the newcomer.

How do I choose my operating category?

Choosing an operating category begins by reading the rules and understanding your options. Multioperator competition is an excellent entry point for the "novice" contester, by teaming up with an experienced contester who will allow you to "help out" at his station.

In recent years, the growth of packet radio (and resultant "Single-operator-assisted" categories) has led many to believe that operating with packet spotting assistance is probably the most fun for a new contester from a small station. You have the combined advantage of making lots of interesting QSOs while honing your natural skills. It also reduces your loneliness during slow-rate periods. Simply put, it is a lot of fun!

How can I maximize my score from a small station?

Most of the strategic skill in contest operating is fundamentally based on common sense. Unfortunately, not everyone has the opportunity to operate from a contest "superstation." The vast majority of competitors use tri-banders and dipoles.

For most people, contesting is a sport that allows us to operate and "see what we can do." The issue of maximizing your score begins with an honest assessment of your station's strengths and weaknesses. If you are using a dipole on 40 meters, it is going to be difficult to compete against the crowd of stations with large beams at the low end of the band. However, tuning up and down the band and calling stations can be very productive. Secondly, selection of operating times is key. If you have limited operating time, try to choose a schedule that matches the times when conditions are optimum for peak rates (e.g., 15 meters in the morning for Europe in DX contests).

Operating from smaller stations actually forces you to be a better operator. It requires that you be more clever in signing your callsign in pileups (brute force just doesn't work). A strategic callsign placement during a lull in a pile often pays off! More important, the small station can still be very effective during the peak times of activity. Use your VFO to tune, tune, and tune again. And when you feel there is opportunity to make QSOs faster by calling CQ, stay high in the band and avoid the "big guns."

Where can I get more information about contests?

CQ Magazine and the ARRL Contest Branch can help you with additional information. The *National Contest Journal* is an excellent magazine that is exclusively focused on contesting. It includes interesting articles and features, and can help identify specific contesters who would be willing to answer questions and provide direction to the new operator.

Also, depending on your geographic location, there are a number of active contest clubs around the world that are interested in gaining new members. The following, while not a complete list of these clubs, can help you get started.

Contest Club	***Geography***	***Contact(s)***
Colorado Contest Conspiracy	Denver	WØUN
Florida West Coast DX Ring	Florida	K4XS
Frankford Radio Club	Philadelphia	N2VW, K3WW
Kentucky Contest Group	KY/OH/IN	ND4Y
Left Coast Contest Club	WA/OR	WY7I
Mad River Radio Club	OH/MI	K8CC
North Coast Contest Club	Ohio/PA	K3LR
North Texas Contest Club	Dallas	KS1G
Northern California Contest Club	No. Calif.	N6IP
Potomac Valley Radio Club	MD/VA	K3NA, KE3Q
Society of Midwest Contesters	IL/IN/WI/MO	WB9TIY
Southeast DX Club	Atlanta	KI4XO
Southern California Contest Club	Los Angeles	WA6OTU
Texas DX Society	Houston	W5ASP
Yankee Clipper Contest Club	New England	K2WR, K1XM

(Courtesy of John Dorr, K1AR)

Contest	*Wkend./Mo.*	*Hours*	*Sponsor Address*
ARRL Straight Key Night	1/JAN	varies	ARRL, 225 Main St., Newington, CT 06111
ARRL RTTY Roundup	1/JAN	24/30	ARRL, 225 Main St., Newington, CT 06111
AGCW-DL QRP CW Winter Contest	1/JAN	15	DJ7ST, Dr.H.Weber, Schesierweg 13,W-3320, Salzgitter, Germany
Michigan QRP Club CW Contest	1/JAN	36	N8CQA,654 Georgia, Marysville, MI 48040
Hunting Lions in the air CW Contest	1/JAN	36	LIONS, P.O. Box 106, 64223 Flen, Sweden
NCJ N.A.QSO Party-CW	2/JAN	10/12	KZ2S, John Golomb, 107 Bailey Corner Road,Wall, NJ 07719
JA Int'l CW Contest (160,80,40M)	2/JAN	48	'59 Magazine Contest, P.O. Box 59, Kamata, Tokyo 144, Japan
Hunting Lions in the air SSB Contest	2/JAN	36	LIONS, P.O. Box 106, 64223 Flen, Sweden
NCJ N.A. QSO Party-SSB	3/JAN	10/12	KZ2S, John Golomb, 107 Bailey Corner Road, Wall, NJ 07719
HA DX CW Contest	3/JAN	24	MRASZ, P.O.Box 11, H-1400 Budapest, Hungary
CQ WW DX 160m CW Contest	4/JAN	42	CQ 160 CW Contest, 76 N. Broadway, Hicksville, NY 11801
ARRL VHF Sweepstakes	4/JAN	33	ARRL, 225 Main St., Newington, CT 06111
REF CW Contest	4/JAN	36	R.E.F., P.O.Box 2129, F-37021 Tours Cedex, France
U.B.A. SSB Contest	4/JAN	24	UBA-HF, ON6JG Oude Gengarmeriestraat 62, B-2220 Heist Op Den Berg, Belgium
ARRL Novice Round-Up	4/JAN->1/FEB	1 week	ARRL, 225 Main St., Newington, CT 06111
NCJ N.A. Sprint-CW	1/FEB	4	N6TR, Larry "Tree" Tyree, 15125 SE Bartell Rd., Boring, OR 97009
YL-ISSB CW QSO Party	1/FEB	24	K0ETA, RR 4 Box 213-6, Stockton, MO 65785
Maine State QSO Party	1/FEB	48	PAWA, P.O. Box 1605, Portland, ME 04104
QCWA QSO Party CW	1/FEB	25	QCWA,W1EES, 75 Chestnut Circle, West Suffield, CT 06093
Classic Radio Exchange	1/FEB	48	W8KGI, P.O.Box 581, Sandia Park, NM 87047
NCJ's N.A. Sprint-SSB	2/FEB	4	K7GM, Ric Niswander, P.O.Box 3778, Greenville, NC 27836-1778
Utah 160m Challenge	2/FEB	48	WE7H, 68 South 300 West, Brigham City, UT 84302
EA RTTY Contest	2/FEB	24	EA1MV, EA RTTY, P.O.Box 240, 09400-Aranda, DeDuero, Burgos, Spain
Dutch "PACC" Contest	2/FEB	24	PACC, PA0INA, P.O. Box 499, 4600 AL Bergen op Zoom, The Netherlands
YLRL YL-OM SSB Contest	2/FEB	24	WO6X, 473 Palo Verde Dr., Sunnyvale, CA 94086

New Hampshire QSO Party	2/FEB	18	GEARS, P.O.Box 1076, Claremont, NH 03743-1076
ARRL DX CW Contest	3/FEB	48	ARRL, 225 Main St., Newington, CT 06111
YLRL YL-OM CW Contest	4/FEB	24	WO6X, 473 Palo Verde Dr., Sunnyvale, CA 94086
CQ WW DX 160m SSB Contest	4/FEB	42	CQ 160 PH Contest, 76 N. Broadway, Hicksville, NY 11801
REF SSB Contest	4/FEB	36	R.E.F., P.O.Box 2129, F-37021 Tours Cedex, France
RSGB 7 MHz CW Contest	4/FEB	18	G3UFY, HF Contests, 77 Bensham Manor Rd, Thornton Heath, Surrey CR7 7AF, UK
U.B.A. CW Contest	4/FEB	24	UBA-HF, ON6JG, Oude Gengarmeriestraat 62,B-2220 Heist Op Den Berg, Belguim
ARRL DX SSB Contest	1/MAR	48	ARRL, 225 Main St., Newington, CT 06111
YL-ISSB SSB QSO Party	2/MAR	48	K0ETA, RR 4 Box 213-6, Stockton, MO 65785
QCWA QSO Party-SSB	2/MAR	25	QCWA, W1EES, 75 Chestnut Circle, West Suffield, CT 06093
Wisconsin State QSO Party	2/MAR	7	WARAC, P.O. Box 1072, Milwaukee, WI 53201
Bermuda Contest	3/MAR	48	RSB, P.O.Box HM275, Hamilton HM AX, Bermuda
Virginia State QSO Party	3/MAR	32	W3FTG, 3627 Great Laurel Ln., Fairfax, VA 22033-1212
BARTG Spring RTTY Contest	3/MAR	30	G4SKA, 32 Wellbrook St., Tiverton, Devon, EX16 5JW, UK
CQ WW WPX SSB Contest	4/MAR	48	CQ WPX SSB Contest, 76 N. Broadway, Hicksville, NY 11801
Poisson d'Avril Contest	1/APR	42	Doug Grant, K1DG, 144 Kendall Pond Rd., Windham, NH 03087
ARCI QRP CW Spring QSO Party	1/APR	24	K5VOL, ARCI Contest Mgr, 835 Surryse Rd., Lake Zurich, IL 60047
SP DX Contest	1/APR	36	PZK, P.O.Box 61, PL-64100 Leszno 1, Poland
ARRL VHF/UHF Spring Sprint-144MHz	1/APR	4	ARRL 225 Main St., Newington, CT 06111
JA Int'l CW Contest (20,15,10M)	2/APR	48	'59 Magazine Contest, P.O.Box 59, Kamata, Tokyo 144, Japan
Yuri Gagarin Cup - CW	2/APR	24	KCRC, P.O. Box 88, Moscow, Russia
Holyland DX Contest SSB,CW	2/APR	24	Israel ARC Box 17600, Tel Aviv, 61176 Israel
ARRL VHF/UHF Spring Sprint - 222 MHz	2/APR	4	ARRL, 225 Main St., Newington, CT 06111
SARTG AMTOR Contest	3/APR	24	SM4CMG, Skulsta 1258, S-710 41 Fellingsbro, Sweden.
QST QSO Award Party	3/APR	24	VE3IAE, 19 Honeysuckle Crese, London, Ontario N5Y 4P3, Canada
Connecticut QSO Party	3/APR	28	CARA, P.O. Box 3441, Danbury, CT 06813-3441

Spring NWQRP Sprint-CW	3/APR	4	WU7F, 6822 131 Ave. SE, Bellevue, WA 98006
ARRL VHF/UHF Spring Sprint-432 MHz	3/APR	4	ARRL, 225 Main St., Newington, CT 06111
MARAC SSB County Hunters Contest	3/APR	48	WA5DTK, 1504 McCann Rd., Longview, TX 75601-3853
Swiss HELVETIA Contest SSB,CW	4/APR	24	HB9AGA, Gantrischweg 1, CH-3114 Oberwichtrach, Switzerland
Georgia QSO Party	4/APR	28	Dixie DXers-N4UZ, 755 Waddell Rd., Bremen, GA 30110
ARI Int'l DX Contest SSB, CW, RTTY	1/MAY	24	I2UIY, ARI Contest Mgr, P.O. Box 14, 27043 Broni (PV), Italy
MARAC CW County Hunters Contest	1/MAY	48	WA5DTK, 1504 McCann Rd., Longview, TX 75601-3853
ARRL UHF Spring Sprint-902/1296/2304 MHz	1/MAY	4	ARRL, 225 Main St., Newington, CT 06111
Texas State QSO Party	1/MAY	48	TDXS, P.O. Box 540291, Houston, TX 77254-0291
Oregon State QSO Party	1/MAY	48	W7ZM, 19821 Ponderosa St., Bend, OR 97702
10-X Int'l Spring CW QSO Party	1/MAY	48	N8FU, 4441 Andreas Ave., Cincinnati, OH 45211
CQ-M Contest SSB,CW	2/MAY	24	KCRC, P.O.Box 88, Moscow, Russia
ARI A.VOLTA RTTY Contest	2/MAY	24	P.O. Box 55, 22063 Cantu', Italy
Massachusetts QSO Party	2/MAY	30	Boston ARC, P.O. Box 15585, Kenmore Station, MA 02215
Nevada State QSO Party	2/MAY	48	NW7O, 4120 Oakhill Ave., Las Vegas, NV 89121
Danish SSTV Contest	2/MAY	48	Carl Emkjer, Soborghus Park 8, DK-2860 Soborg, Denmark
Michigan State QSO Party	3/MAY	24	K8ED, 27600 Franklin Rd., Apt 816, Southfield, MI 48034
ARRL Spring Sprint-50 MHz	3/MAY	4	ARRL, 225 Main St., Newington, CT 06111
ARAL DX Contest	4/MAY	14	ARAL, P.O. Box 296, Leira Codex 2403, Portugal
CQ WW WPX CW Contest	4/MAY	48	CQ WPX CW Contest, 76 N. Broadway, Hicksville, NY 11801
RSGB National Field Day	1/JUN	24	G3UFY, HF Contests, 77 Bensham Manor Rd, Thornton Heath, Surrey, CR7 7AF, UK
PORTUGAL Day Contest	1/JUN	24	
ARRL June VHF Contest	2/JUN	33	ARRL, 225 Main St., Newington, CT 06111
ANARTS WW RTTY Contest	2/JUN	48	ANARTS, P.O. Box 860, Crow's Nest, NSW 2065, Australia
ALL ASIAN CW Contest	3/JUN	48	J.A.R.L., P.O. Box 377, Tokyo Central, Japan
SMIRK 50 MHz QSO Party	3/JUN	48	W5OZI, P.O. Box 393, Junction, TX 78649
ARRL Field Day	4/JUN	27	ARRL, 225 Main St., Newington, CT 06111

R.A.C. CANADA Day Contest	1/JUL	24	R.A.C., P.O. Box 356, Kingston, Ontario, K7L 4W2, Canada.
Venezuela Independence Day SSB Contest	1/JUL	48	RCV, P.O. Box 2285, Caracas 1010-A,Venezuela
IARU HF Championship SSB-CW	2/JUL	24	IARU HQ, Box 310905, Newington, CT 06131-0905
CQ WW WPX VHF Contest	2/JUL	27	N6CL, Joe Lynch, P.O. Box 73, Oklahoma City, OK 73101
ARCI QRP Summer Homebrew Sprint-CW	2/JUL	4	K5VOL, ARCI Contest Mgr, 835 Surryse Rd., Lake Zurich, IL 60047
Colombian Independence Day Contest	3/JUL	24	LCRA, P.O. Box 584, Bogota, Columbia
SEANET CW Contest	3/JUL	48	SEANET, Maxwell Rd., P.O. Box 2728, Singapore 9047, Singapore
AGCW-DL QRP CW Summer Contest	3/JUL	24	DJ7ST, Dr.H.Weber, Schesierweg 13, W-3320, Salzgitter, Germany
Venezuela Independence Day CW Contest	4/JUL	48	RCV, P.O. Box 2285, Caracas 1010-A,Venezuela
RSGB IOTA HF Contest	4/JUL	24	G3UFY, HF Contests, 77 Bensham Manor Rd, Thornton Heath, Surrey CR7 7AF, UK
NCJ N.A. QSO Party-CW	1/AUG	10/12	KZ2S, John Golomb, 107 Bailey Corner Road, Wall, NJ 07719
QRP ARCI Summer SSB QSO Party	1/AUG	4	K5VOL, ARCI Contest Mgr, 835 Surryse Rd., Lake Zurich, IL 60047
10-X Summer Phone QSO Party	1/AUG	48	K0PVI, P.O. Box 112, Watkins, CO 80137
ARRL UHF Contest	1/AUG	24	ARRL, 225 Main St., Newington, Ct., 06111
YO DX HF Contest	1/AUG	20	RARF, P.O. Box 05-50, R-76100 Bucharest, Romania
WAE CW Contest	2/AUG	36	WAEDC, P.O.Box 1126, D-74370, Serhiem, Germany
Maryland-D.C. QSO Party	2/AUG	19	Antietam Radio Assn., P.O. Box52, Hagerstown, MD 21741
SARTG WW RTTY Contest	3/AUG	10/12	SM4CMG Skulsta 1258, S-710 41 Fellingsbro, Sweden
SEANET SSB Contest	3/AUG	48	SEANET, Maxwell Rd., P.O. Box 2728, Singapore 9047, Singapore
New Jersey State QSO Party	3/AUG	17	EARA, P.O. Box 528, Englewood, NJ 07631-0528
ARRL 10Ghz Cumulative Contest-Part 1	3/AUG	24	ARRL, 225 Main St., Newington, CT 06111
Empire State (N.Y.) QSO Party	4/AUG	30	K2VV, P.O. Box 460, Hagaman, NY 12086
NCJ N.A. Sprint-CW	1/SEPT	4	K7GM, Ric Niswander, P.O. Box 3778, Greenville, NC 27836-1778
R.A.C. VHF/UHF Sprint-902/1296/2304 MHz	1/SEPT	4	R.A.C., P.O. Box 356, Kingston, Ontario, K7L 4W2, Canada
LZ-DX-Contest	1/SEPT	48	BFRA, P.O. Box 830, Sofia 1000, Bulgaria

All-Asian SSB Contest	1/SEPT	48	J.A.R.L., P.O. Box 377, Tokyo Central, Japan
WAE DARC SSB Contest	2/SEPT	36	WAEDC, P.O. Box 1126, D-74370, Serhiem, Germany
ARRL VHF QSO Party	2/SEPT	33	ARRL 225 Main St., Newington, CT 06111
NCJ's N.A. Sprint-SSB	2/SEPT	4	N6TR, Larry "Tree" Tyree, 15125 SE Bartell Rd., Boring, OR 97009
R.A.C. VHF/UHF Sprint-432 MHz	2/SEPT	4	R.A.C., P.O. Box 356, Kingston, Ontario, K7L 4W2, Canada
Montana State QSO Party	2/SEPT	48	MT HF SOCIETY, 1009 Madison Ave., Helena, MT 59601
ARRL 10 Ghz Cumulative Contest-Part 2	3/SEPT	24	ARRL, 225 Main St., Newington, CT 06111
R.A.C. VHF/UHF Sprint-220MHz	3/SEPT	4	R.A.C., P.O.Box 356, Kingston, Ontario, K7L 4W2, Canada
Scandinavian CW Contest	3/SEPT	27	LA4YW, NRRL HF Contest Mgr, P.O. Box142, N-7078 Saupstad, Norway
CQ WW RTTY Contest	4/SEPT	48	KT1N, Roy Gould, CQ RTTY Contest Mgr, P.O. Box DX, Stow, MA 01701
R.A.C. VHF/UHF Sprint-144MHz	4/SEPT	4	R.A.C., P.O. Box 356, Kingston, Ontario, K7L 4W2, Canada
Scandinavian SSB Contest	4/SEPT	27	LA4YW, NRRL HF Contest Mgr, P.O. Box142, N-7078 Saupstad, Norway
Washington State Salmon Run	4/SEPT	31	WWDXClub, W7FR, P.O. Box 224, Mercer Island, WA 98040
Classic Radio Exchange	4/SEPT	48	W8KGI, P.O.Box 581, Sandia Park, NM 87047
VK/ZL SSB DX Contest	1/OCT	24	NZART, ZL1AAS, 46 Sandpit Rd., Howick, 1705, New Zealand
California QSO Party (CQP)	1/OCT	30	NCCC, K6PU, P.O. Box 853, Pine Grove, CA 95665
F9AA Cup Contest	1/OCT	24	Coupe Fernand Raoult, 11 Rue de Bordeaux, 94700 Maisons Alfort, France
R.A.C. VHF/UHF Sprint-50MHz	1/OCT	48	R.A.C., P.O.Box 356, Kingston, Ontario, K7L 4W2, Canada
VK/ZL CW DX Contest	2/OCT	24	NZART, ZL1AAS, 146 Sandpit Rd., Howick, 1705, New Zealand
RSGB 21/28 MHz SSB Contest	2/OCT	14	G3UFY, HF Contests, 77 Bensham Manor Rd, Thornton Heath, Surrey CR7 7AF, UK
Illinois State QSO Party	2/OCT	8	RAMS, WB9GOJ, 9134 Ewing Ave., Evanston, IL 60203
RSGB 21 MHz CW Contest	3/OCT	14	G3UFY, HF Contests, 77 Bensham Manor Rd, Thornton Heath, Surrey CR7 7AF, UK
ARCI QRP CW Contest	3/OCT	36	K5VOL, ARCI Contest Mgr, 835 Surryse Rd., Lake Zurich, IL 60047
W.A.G. Worked All Germany	3/OCT	24	DL1DTL, P.O.Box 427, 0-8072 Dresden, Germany

All-Asian SSB Contest	4/OCT	48	J.A.R.L., P.O. Box 377, Tokyo Central, Japan
CQ WW DX PHONE Contest	5/OCT	48	CQ WW PH Contest, 76 N. Broadway, Hicksville, NY 11801
ARRL Sweepstakes CW	1/NOV	24/30	ARRL, 225 Main St., Newington, CT 06111
JA Int'l DX SSB Contest	1/NOV	48	'59 Magazine Contest, P.O. Box 59, Kamata, Tokyo 144, Japan
OK DX Contest	2/NOV	24	CRK, P.O. Box 69, 11327 Praha 1, Czech Republic
WAE DARC RTTY Contest	2/NOV	36	WAEDC, P.O.Box 1126,D-74370, Serhiem, Germany
ARRL E-M-E Contest	2/NOV	48	ARRL, 225 Main St., Newington, CT 06111
ARRL Sweepstakes SSB	3/NOV	24/30	ARRL, 225 Main St., Newington, CT 06111
CQ WW DX CW Contest	4/NOV	48	CQ WW CW Contest, 76 N. Broadway, Hicksville, NY 11801
ARRL 160m DX Contest	1/DEC	42	ARRL 225 Main St., Newington, CT 06111
ARRL 10m DX Contest	2/DEC	36/48	ARRL 225 Main St., Newington, CT 06111

HIGHEST REPORTED RATES IN CONTEST OPERATIONS (QSO'S PER HOUR)

DX Contests, DXpeditions—DX Side

CW

234	WN4KKN at HC8N	CQWW CW	1992	15M 21Z Saturday
231	KC1F at NP4A	CQWW M/S	1982	
230	WB9JKI at V31A	CQ WW	1987	
223	LU8DQ at ZP5Y	1990	CQWW	10M 18Z D1
215	W2GD at P4ØGD	1987	CQWW	
212	WN4KKN at HC8N	1992	CQWW	10M 19Z D1
212	WN4KKN at TI1C	1993	ARRL DX	First hour 20M
211	W6QHS at P49V	ARRL CW DX	1993	15M
209	WN4KKN at TI1C	1993	ARRL DX	20Z 15M
208	WN4KKN at ZPØY	CQWW 1	1990 and 1991,	both 10M D1 18Z
207	WN4KKN at TI1C	1993	ARRL DX	03Z 40M
206	WN4KKN at TI1C	1993	ARRL DX	15Z 10M
204	WN4KKN at TI1C	1993	ARRL DX	21Z 15M
201	WN4KKN at HC8N	1992	CQWW	10M 18Z D1
200	K7SS at K7SS/KH6	ARRL DX		
200	K6NA at KP6BD	1977	Kingman Reef DXpedition.	
198	K8MR at VP2E	1982	ARRL DX	
193	K1MM at 1S1DX	April 1979		15M 13Z
180	K1MM at 1S1DX	April 1979		10M 04Z

Phone

457	KRØY at P40L	1993	CQWW	First Hour 20M
385	K5ZD at NP4A	1980	CQWW	
371	K1AR at TI1J	1989	CQWW	
370	K1DG at KP2A	1988	CQWW	
365	K3NA at PJ9JR	1979	CQWW	
350	K5RX at VP2EC	1987	CQWW	
341	KØGU at VP2KBU	1984	ARRL DX	10M Day 1
337	WB2CHO at VP2ML	ARRL DX		
337	K1MM at LU2MM	1983	ARRL DX	15M 00Z
334	KP2A	CQWW	1992	20M 01Z Day 1
334	K5TSQ at 6D2X	1993	ARRL DX	First hour 15M
325	K1MM at LU2MM	1983	ARRL DX	15M 01Z
321	FS/KC1F	1989	CQWW	15M 1st hour

320	V31DX	1992	CQWW	10M
317	WB5VZL at HR6A	1987	ARRL DX	
315	AA5B at ZF2HM	1984	ARRL DX	15/20M
310	KP2A	CQWW	1992	20M 00Z Day 1
310	AA5B at ZF2HM	ARRL DX		
289	WB5VZL at 6D2X	1993	ARRL DX	First hour 10M

DX Contests—U.S. Side

SSB

221	KC1F at K1EA	CQWW	1988	10M 12Z D1
220	K1AR at K1EA	CQWW	1992	10M 12Z D1
200	AA6TT	CQWW	1992	15M 00Z D1 M/M
177	N2RM	CQWW	1992	15M 12Z D1 M/M
175	K1DG	CQWW	1992	15M/10M 17Z D1
174	K3LR at K3TUP	CQWW	1988	15M/10M 12Z D1
173	K1AR at K1EA	CQWW	1992	10M/15M 13Z D1
172	K1AR at K1EA	CQWW	1992	20M 19Z D1
172	K1DG ARRL	DX	1993	
166	N6BV/1 ARRL	DX	1993	10M 14Z
161	KI3V at NZ7E	ARRL DX	1992	
160	K1KI	ARRL DX	1986	20M 13Z D1

CW

160	K1EA using KC1XX at K1EA	1993	WAE 15M	
152	K1DG (K1DG, WZ1R oprs.)	CQWW	1992	15M/10M 12Z D1
142	K1TO at K1KI	CQWW	1992	15/10M 12Z D1
128	K1KI	CQM	1985	20M
125	K1KI	ARRL DX	1987	20M 11Z D1

ARRL 10M Contest

244	AA5B	1990		
235	AA5B	1988		
181	K1KI	1980	SSB	16Z
152	K1KI	1992	CW	13Z

ARRL SS

Phone

186	KI3V 1992 First hour 10M
175	WB5VZL at N5AU 1986 First hour, 20/15M
174	N2IC at KP2A 1988, First hour, 10M
173	K5ZD at N5AU 1980 First hour
170	AA5B (twice)
153	N6BV at N6RO 1987 First hour
140	K1KI 1985 40M 01Z

CW

105	N6TR 1981 First hour
100	KI3V 1992 First hour 15M
100	K5ZD at N5AU First hour (several times 1980-84)
93	K1KI 1990 20M 12Z

Courtesy of National Contest Journal Mar/Apr 1988, K1AR column in CQ Magazine, CQ-CONTEST@TGV.COM, and various reporters.

OPERATING ON THE AMATEUR HF BANDS

Amateur Radio as an avocation for experimenters and communicators began at the start of this century with the use of frequencies below the present High Frequency bands (1.8 to 30 MHz) and now includes allocations reaching to 250 GHz. Until the 1970s, the HF bands were the medium used for all international and coast-to-coast radio communications by hams as well as commercial services. These frequencies still carry a great deal of commercial worldwide traffic, as well as including all phases of ham interests from across town to cross-country ragchewing, DXing, contesting, public service work and experimentation. In the past, most hams were first exposed to HF; quite often they later began to utilize the VHF bands also for satellites, local repeaters, and easy antenna experimentation.

More recently, many hams have reversed this trend; they are first exposed to 2 meter repeater operation and then become curious about the worldwide capabilities of the HF bands. This section will provide an introduction to each of the Amateur bands from 10 to 160 meters.

10 Meters

One band that older and newer hams have in common is the 10 meter. It has long been appreciated by newcomers for the ease of worldwide communications with low power and small gain-type antennas. There is plenty of spectrum to accommodate modes from CW and SSB to FM, AM and satellites; and the band is available to all U.S. amateur license classes except the codeless Technician.

Those who have been active through a few sunspot cycles remember how easy it was to work DX on this band when the MUF (Maximum Usable Frequency) was high and how dead the receiver can sound six years later. This phenomenon spurred the creation of a group, the 10-X International Net, whose purpose is to promote activity. Because 10 meters shows some of the propagation characteristics of the higher (VHF) bands, it is well known that listening is not proof that the band is closed. Short but excellent openings are always possible, waiting to be discovered by those who call CQ.

The most popular station setup for 10 meters is probably a barefoot (100 watt) transceiver and a small tribander (three-element 10,15 and 20 meter) or monoband 10 meter beam at rooftop level. Linear amplifiers and higher antennas are not really needed, but do put the antenna as high as you can. Small TV rotators will easily handle these antennas. Because of the large amount of spectrum available, it is important to tune slowly but completely. You may find an easily workable but weak station in a state you need 300 miles away or a new friend on an island in the South Pacific. You will be weak at his location also but, because of the lack of static and the avoidance of big pileups, a good contact can result.

15 Meters

As we tune lower in frequency (the WARC bands of 17, 12 and 30 meters are covered later), band conditions become more predictable and more congested. Fifteen meter long-haul DX is more common during low sunspot times than on 10 meters, and contacts across the U.S. are possible almost every day. There are more nets found on 15 than on 10 meters, including weather emergency, Red Cross, U.S. State Department hams overseas and DX nets.

There is no Novice/Technician SSB allocation and *all* license classes are limited to 200 watts in the Novice subband, unlike 10 meters. This doesn't mean that DXCC is impossible for Novice/Technicians because of the CW limitation. In 1957, KN4RID (now WØZV) became the first Novice to gain the DXCC award. He was limited by the regulations at that time to 75 watts, crystal control and a one-year maximum license term. Novice Worked All Zones has also been earned on this band.

More hams will be using higher power here because of the increased competition for less band space. The three-element tribander is still the most popular antenna, but it won't take long chasing DX or contest points to wish for a little more gain and height. As with 10 meters it is important to begin checking this band to the north and east from the time of your sunrise for the first DX openings. A good guide is to "follow the path of the sun" with your directional antenna; as your daylight begins to fade signals from the west and north will peak.

20 Meters

If any HF band could be labeled "workhorse" or the "band for all seasons" this is the one. Whether it is talking from Michigan to your brother in Florida every day, or reaching the DXCC Honor Roll using one band only, this is the place. There are good days and bad ones, and sunspots do take their effect, but for overall predictability no band is better than 20. Once again these bonuses attract more occupants, more power and bigger antennas. There are more DX nets, hurricane nets, maritime mobile nets and old friend nets on 20 meter SSB than elsewhere. Add the popular Slow Scan TV area around 14.230 MHz, HF packet links around 14.105 MHz, and the popularity of all of the digital modes below 14.1 MHz to good propagation characteristics and the possible congestion is obvious.

While plenty of contacts of all types can be made with 100 watts and a low tribander, you may find your frustration level raised often. The average three-band antenna is a compromise on 20; gain and front to back (F/B) both suffer in exchange for the small size. A six-element triband beam is one answer; a three-element or more 20 meter beam at 50 to 60 feet will definitely prove worthwhile. Front to back ratio takes on more importance on 20 meters and the lower bands because short skip propagation is common. This is most apparent on 20 during mid-day, when stations 300 to 500 miles away will sound like they are down the street. It becomes difficult to find a clear frequency to talk to your brother on unless you can lessen interference in unwanted directions. Another advantage of improved gain and F/B ratio is the ability to more easily work stations via the long path. While long path contacts happen on 15 and 10 meters, especially from the west coast, they are more common on 20 meters. It is often easier to contact Asia and the Indian Ocean area from the U.S. in the morning by beaming the opposite direction from your beam heading chart; in the afternoon the same is true for the Pacific and Australia.

40 Meters

Here is the band that is most obviously shared with other services. It won't take very long to discover 500 KW international broadcasters. They make forty especially challenging for Novice and SSB operations, but they also indicate the distance that can be covered at this portion of the spectrum. During the day, 40 meters is a dependable band for contacts up to 1500 miles. That holds true at night, but it is also possible to contact any point on earth, and you don't need 500 KW to do it. Some hams have all the countries on the DXCC list on 40 meters, and it is a very important band for all types of contesting, domestic as well as DX. During the day there are regional nets on CW, SSB and digital modes. At night there are SSB nets to help overcome the obstacles of working DX stations with split frequencies and broadcast interference to contend with. Because almost all amateur stations outside ITU Region 2 are limited to 7.000 to 7.100 MHz, and the U.S. SSB allocation starts at 7.150 MHz, the majority of U.S. to DX contacts on SSB require the use of split frequency operation. CW and digital modes follow the practices of the higher bands, but they do tend to be compressed lower in frequency because of the presence of non-U.S. SSB hams.

There is no question that one of the shortened two-element beams is a big help in dealing with the competition of all kinds on 40. Other antennas do very well; dipoles and open-wire fed wires can be very useful, especially if some tall trees are handy. Single or multiple verticals also work well for some; make sure you understand their use on the lower bands before expecting good DX results. An amplifier is helpful at night, as it is on 80 and 160 meters, but is not necessary. Note that the majority of articles on building low power portable rigs focus on 40 meters. Look around 7.040 MHz for QRP operators.

80 Meters

The things that most hams think of when the 80 and 160 meter bands are discussed are the very large antennas that are needed and the annoying natural and man-made noise levels. Keep in mind that the first hams were restricted to 200 meters and down, and that these bands were very popular years before our sophisticated equipment and computer-aided antenna designs were available. Prior to the immense growth of two-meter repeater systems in the 1970s, most local ragchewing, traffic handling, and emergency communications took place on 80 (and 75 meters, as the phone portion is called). There are many ways to cope with the obstacles that appear to preclude enjoying "the low bands."

For regional communications, narrow bandwidth antennas like short loaded dipoles, verticals and other designs combined with an antenna tuner perform well. Even very low fully sized dipoles or inverted vee's bent to fit into the available space will put out very good signals for a few hundred miles, as well as providing less capture area for noise. For consistently greater distance coverage, as well as better bandwidth, it helps to have a full size dipole up higher; 50 feet or better can often be achieved by making use of trees, ropes and ingenuity. Those who hope to reach the 300 country mark on 80 usually use some variety of phased array: slopers, high wires, or verticals. Separate lower noise receiving antennas are also popular.

Eighty meters is usually the hardest band for those chasing the very popular Five Band Worked All Zones Award. Over 360 have completed all 40 zones on all five major HF bands; chasing the last few zones on 80 meters is an experience they all share. In common "the last one" was a zone with very low human population, few if any hams and on the other side of the world. Contacting that zone requires knowledge of propagation, operating times or plans of DXpeditions, good conditions at both ends of the contact, persistence on the part of both operators, very good ears and often lack of sleep. Once you have trained on this band, move down one to 160.

160 Meters

There seems to be two kinds of hams who operate on 160. Many find it a good band for nightly ragchews with much less congestion than 75 meters. Antenna experimentation and comparisons are a popular topic. The other operators are the DXers. During the day tuning across the band will usually reveal no signals at all; you may discover a strange noise every 15 kHz. That's a harmonic from a local TV set. In the summer you can hear the static from every thunderstorm within hundreds of miles. At night the band will seem to come alive, especially in the fall through spring seasons. You may hear many strong signals, mostly on CW, but not the station they are calling and working. If you tune above 1850 kHz you will find loud SSB stations ragchewing. To join in on local contacts the same compromise type antennas used on 80 will work. Not many suburbanites have room for anything else; even a dipole is 270 feet long on this band.

Working DX on 160 meters involves some discovery. You need to find those signals that you missed when you first tuned by; they are weak compared to most of the DX you are used to hearing on the higher bands. You also need to learn how to use your receiver to improve the signal-to-noise ratio and pull those weak signals out of the higher background noise level. Do some reading on Beverage or steering-wave longwire antenna types and on loop receiving antennas. Often, switching to a 40-meter or other antenna to listen will help in copying a weak signal. Towers used to support HF beams are often used successfully on 160 by shunt feeding them or as supports for inverted-L type antennas. The author has confirmed over 220 countries with a full-sized inverted vee, supported at the 70-foot level on a tower. Keep in mind that contrary to first impression, 160 conditions can be quite different from those on 80 meters. The noise, QSB and propagation may be the exact opposite of those found on the same night on 80 meters.

The "WARC" Bands—12, 17, and 30 Meters

The World Administrative Radio Conference held in 1979 included a major Amateur radio presence by the IARU. The Amateur bands were reconfirmed at an international level, and new allocations were added for the Amateur satellite service as well as three new HF bands. Access in the U.S. to those HF bands was fully gained in 1989.

As you would expect, the bands of 12, 17 and 30 meters share many of the characteristics of those bands that are their close neighbors, such as propagation and antenna size. Where they differ greatly is in their relatively small frequency allocations and lack of congestion. Each band at times has propagation advantages; 12 is often open when 10 is not. Seventeen meters can be the best long-haul DX and ragchew band when 15 is not really open and 20 is too crowded. Thirty meters, with a 200-watt power limit and a shared band outside of the U.S., still provides almost around the clock DX possibilities and supports a large amount of digital activity including HF packet links. Many hams are using unusual antennas on the WARC bands; 80-meter antennas on 30 meters, 40-meter antennas on 17 and 12 meters are common. There are many three-band antennas available, from simple wires to three-band yagis. A newly popular solution is the log periodic array, for coverage of 20, 17, 15, 12 and 10 meters, and sometimes 30 meters as well.

(Courtesy of Jim Dionne, K1MEM)

PHONETIC ALPHABET/PHRASES

	English	German	French	Italian	Spanish	Portuguese	Russian (Phonetic)	Russian (Phonetic)
A	Alpha	Anton	Alfa	Alfa	Alfa	Antena	Anatoli	Anna
B	Bravo	Berta	Bravo	Bravo	Brasil	Bateria Baris	Borja	
C	Charlie	Caser	Charlie	Canada	Canada	Condensador	Tsentralnii	Tsentr
D	Delta	Dora	Delta	Delta	Delta	Detector	Dimitri Dima	
E	Echo	Emil	Echo	Europa	Espana	Estatico	Jelena	Jelena
F	Foxtrot	Friedrich	Foxtrot	Firenze	Francia	Filamento	Fjodor	Fedja
G	Golf	Gustav	Golf	Guatemala	Guatemala	Grade	Grigorii	Galja
H	Hotel	Heinrich	Hotel	Hotel	Hotel	Hotel	Hariton	Hariton
I	India	Ida	India	Italia	Italia	Intensidade	Ivan	Ivan
J	Juliet	Julius	Juliett	Juventus	Japon	Juliete	Ivan krakii	Ivan krakii
K	Kilo	Konrad	Kilo	Kilometro	Kilo	Kilo	Kanstantin	Kilavat
L	Lima	Ludwig	Lima	Lima	Lima	Lampada	Leanit	Leanit
M	Mike	Martha	Mike	Messico	Mejico	Manipulador	Mihail	Misa
N	November	Nordpol	November	Novembre	Noviembre	Negativo	Nikalai	Nina
O	Oscar	Otto	Oscar	Otranto	Oscar	Onda	Olga	Olja
P	Papa	Paula	Papa	Palermo	Papa	Placa	Pavel	Pavel
Q	Quebec	Quelle	Quebec	Quebec	Quito	Quadro	Ssuka	Ssuka
R	Romeo	Richard	Romeo	Romeo	Radio	Radio	Raman	Roma
S	Sierra	Siegfried	Sierra	Santiago	Santiago	Sintonia	Sergei	Sergei
T	Tango	Theodur	Tango	Tango	Tango	Terra	Tamara	Tanja
U	Uniform	Ulrich	Uniform	Universita	Universidad	Unidade	Uljana	Uljana
V	Victor	Viktor	Victor	Venezia	Victor	Valvula	Zenja	Zenja
W	Whisky	Wilhelm	Whisky	Whisky	Whisky	Watt	Vasilii	Viktar
X	X-ray	Xanthippe	X-ray	Xilofono	Xilofono	Xilofono	Mjahkii znak	Znak
Y	Yankee	Ypsilon	Yankee	Yokohama	Yucatan	Yucatan	Igrek	Igrek
Z	Zulu	Zeppelin	Zulu	Zelanda	Zulu	Zulu	Zinaida	Zoja

From The Radio Amateur's Conversation Guide, *by Jukka Heikinheimo, OH1BR and Miika Heikinheimo, OH2BAD. Reprinted with permission.*

NUMBERS—CARDINALS AND ORDINALS

	English		German		French		Italian		Spanish		Portuguese		Russian (Phonetic)		Japanese
	card.	ord.	card.	ord.	card.	ord.	card.	ord.	card.	ord.	card.	ord.	card.	ord.	card.
0	zero		null		zero		zero		cero		zero		nol		zero, maru
1	one	first	eins	erste	un	premier	uno	primo	uno	primero	um	primeiro	adin	pjervyi	ichi
2	two	second	zwei	zweite	deux	deuxieme	due	secondo	dos	segundo	dois	segundo	dva, dvie	ftaroi	ni
3	three	third	drei	dritte	trois	troisieme	tre	terzo	tres	tercero	tres	terceiro	tri	tretii	san
4	four	fourth	vier	vierte	quatre	quartrieme	quattro	quarto	cuarto	cuarto	quatro	quarto	cetire	cetvjortyi	shi, yon
5	five	fifth	funf	funfte	cinq	cinquieme	cinque	quinto	cinco	quinto	cinco	quinto	pjat	pjatyi	go
6	six	sixth	sechs	sechste	six	sixieme	sei	sesto	seis	sexto	seis	sexto	sest	sestoi	roku
7	seven	seventh	sieben	siebte	sept	septieme	sette	settimo	siete	septimo	sete	setimo	siem	sedmoi	shichi, nana
8	eight	eighth	acht	achte	huit	huitieme	otto	ottavo	ocho	octavo	oito	oitavo	vosiem	vasmoi	hachi
9	nine	ninth	neun	neunte	neuf	neuvieme	nove	nono	nueve	noveno	nove	nono	djevit	divjatyi	kyu
10	ten	tenth	zwehn	zehnte	dix	dixieme	dieci	decimo	diez	decimo	dez	decimo	djesit	disjatyi	ju
11	eleven		elf		onze		undici		once		onze		adinnatsat		juichi
12	twelve		zwolf		douze		dodici		doce		doze		dvenatsat		juni
13	thirteen		dreizehn		treize		tredici		trece		treze		trinatsat		jusan
14	fourteen		veirzehn		quatorze		quattordici		catorce		quatorze		cetirnatsat		jushi, juyon
15	fifteen		funfzehn		quinze		quindici		quince		quinze		pitnatsat		jugo
16	sixteen		sechzehn		seize		sedici		diez y seis		dezesseis		sestnatsat		juroku
17	seventeen		siebzehn		dix-sept		diciassette		diez y siete		dezessete		semnatsat		jushichi
18	eighteen		achtzehn		dix-huit		diciotto		diez y ocho		dezoito		vosemnatsat		juhachi
19	nineteen		neunzehn		dix-neuf		diciannove		diez y nueve		dezenove		djevitnatsat		jukyu, juku
20	twenty		zwanzig		vingt		venti		veinte		vinte		dvatsat		niju
21	twenty-one		einundzwanzig		vingt et un		ventuno		veintiuno		vinte e um		dvatsat adin		nijuichi
22	twenty-two		zweiundzwanzig		vingt deux		ventidue		veintidos		vinte e dois		dvatsat dva		nijuni
23	twenty-three		dreiundzwanzig		vingt trois		ventitre		veintitres		vinte e tres		dvatsat tri		nijusan
30	thirty		dreissig		trente		trenta		treinta		trinta		tritsat		sanju
40	forty		vierzig		quarante		quaranta		cuarenta		quarenta		sorak		yonju, shiju
50	fifty		funfzig		cinquante		cinquanta		cincuenta		cinquenta		pidisjat		goju
60	sixty		sechzig		soixante		sessanta		sesenta		sessenta		sestdesjat		rokuju
70	seventy		siebzig		soixante dix		settanta		setanta		setenta		siemdesjat		nanaju,hichiju
80	eighty		achzig		quatre-vingt		ottanta		ochenta		oitenta		vosemdesjat		hachiju
90	ninety		neunzig		quatre vingt dix		novanta		noventa		noventa		divjanosta		kyuju
100	one hundred		hundert		cent		cento		cien		cem		sto		hyaku
1000	one thousand		tausend		mille		mille		mil		mil		tisaca		sen

From The Radio Amateur's Conversation Guide, by Jukka Heikinheimo, OH1BR and Miika Heikinheimo, OH2BAD. Courtesy of Jukka Heikinheimo, OH1BR

OFTEN USED RADIO PHRASES

Phrases will be presented in the following sequence: English, German, French, Italian, Spanish, Portuguese, Russian (Phonetic), and Japanese.

Please give me another [a long] call.
Bitte geben Sie mir noch einmal einen [langen] Anruf.
S'il vous plait, donnez a nouveau [longuement] votre indicatif.
Per favore ripeti la chiamata [a lungo].
Por favor deme [una] otra llamada [larga].
Por favor, de-me uma outra [longa] chamada.
Pazalsta, pazavitje minja jisso ras. Pazalsta, daitje mnie dlinnyi vyizaf.
Moichido call kudasai. [long call de onegai shimasu.]

Please repeat your call-sign slowly several times.
Bitte wiederholen SieIhr Rufzeichen langsam mehrere Male.
S'il vous plait, repetez lentement votre indicatif plusieurs fois.
Per favore ripeti lentamente il tuo nominativo parecchie volte.
Por favor repita despacio varias veces su indicativo.
Por favor repita seu indicativo vagarosamente varias vezes.
Pazalsta, paftaritje mjedlenna vas pazyivnoi njeskalka ras.
Yukkurito nankaika call-sign o kurikaeshitekudasai.

What is your call-sign?
Was ist Ihr Rufzeichen?
Quel est votre indicatif?
Qual' e il tuo nominativo?
Cual es su indicativo?
Qual e seu indicativo?
Kakoi vas pazyivnoi?
Call-sign wa nandesuka?

I cannot copy you at the moment.
Ich kann Sie im Augenblick nicht lesen.
Je ne peux pas vous copier en ce moment.
Al momento non riesco piu' a copiarti.
No le peudo copiar por lel momento.
Eu nao posso lhe copiar no momento.
Ja vas sicas ni razbiraju.
Genzai anatao copy-dekimasen.

Thank you very much for your call.
Ich danke Ihnen vielmals fur Ihern Anruf.
Merci beaucoup pour votre appel.
Grazie molte per la tua chiamata.
Muchas gracias por su llamada.
Muito obrigado pela sua chamada.
Ocen blagadaren vam zavas vyizaf.
Oyobidashi domo arigato gozaimasu.

Good morning	Good afternoon	Good evening	Good night
Guten Morgen	Guten Tag	Guten Abend	Gute Nacht
Bonjour	Bon apres-midi	Bonsoir	Bonne nuit
Buon giorno	Buon pomeriggio	Buona sera	Buona notte
Buenos dias	Buenas tardes	Buenos tardes	Buenas noches
Bom dia	Boa tarde	Boa noite	Boa noite
Dobraje utra	Dobryi djen	Dobryi vjecer	Dobrai noci
Ohayogozaimasu	Konnichiwa	Konbanwa	Sayonara

It is very nice to meet you for the first time.
Es ist sehr nett Sie das erste Mal zu treffen.
C'est tres agreable de vous rencontrer pour la premiere fois.
Molto lieto di incontrarti per la prima volta.
Encantado de conocerle por primera vez.
E muito agradavel encontrar voce pela primeira vez.
Ocen prijatna fstretit vas fpervyie.
Hajimete omenikakarete totemo ureshikuomoimasu.

Your report is five and nine.
Der rapport fur Sie ist funf and neun.
Votre report est cinq neuf.
Il tuo rapporto e cinque nove.
Su reporte es cinco nueve.
Sua reportagem e cinco e nove.
Vas silisu pjat djevit.
Anatano report wa go kyu [gojukyu] desu.

What is my report?
Was ist mein Rapport?
Quel est mon report?
Qual' e il mio rapporto?
Cual es mi reporte?
Qual e a minha reportagem?
Kak vyi minja prinimajetje?
Watashino report wa nandesuka?

My name is Laurie.
Mein Name ist Bernd.
Mon nom est Bernard.
Il mio nome e Toni.
Mi nombre es Jorge.
Meu nome e Gerson.
Majo imja pabukvam.
Watashino namae wa Nao desu.

What is your name?
Wie ist Ihr Name?
Quel est votre nom?
Qual' e il tuo nome?
Cual es su nombre?
Qual e o seu nome?
Vase imja ? [Kak vazzavut ?]
Anatano namae wa nandesuka?

My antenna is ten meters high.
Meine Antenne ist in einer Hohe von zehn Metern.
Mon antenne est a dix metres de hauteur.
La mia antenna si trova a dieci metri di altezza.
Mi antena esta a una altura de diez metros.
Minha antena esta numa altura de dez metros.
Maja antjenna navisatje disjati mjetraf.
Watashi no antenna wa takasa ju meter desu.

I have recently put up a new antenna.
Neulich habe ich eine Antenne aufgestellt.
J'ai recemment monte une nouvelle antenne.
Ho montato recentemente un antenna nuova.
Recientemente he colocado una nova antena.
Eu levantei recentemente uma novwa antena
Nidavna ja ustanavil novuju antjennu.
Saikin atara shii antenna o age mashita.

I'd like to compare two antennas. Could you give me a comparative report?

Ich wurde gerne zwei Antennen miteeinander vergleichen. Konnten Sie mir einen Vergliech-Rapport geben?

Je voudrais comparar deux antennes. Pourriez vous me donner un report comparatif?

Desidererei paragonare due antenne. Puoi darmi un rapporto comparativo?

Querria comparar dos antenas. Podria darme un reporte comparativo?

Eu gostaria de comparar duas antenas. Voce poderia me dar uma reportagem comparativa?

Ja hatjel byi sravnit dvje antjennyi. Nje dadite li vyi sravnitelnuju atsenku?

Nihon no antenna o kurabe tai to omoimasu. Hikakushita report o itadakemasuka?

The weather here is 1. very fine 2. clear 3. cloudy 4. rainy 5. windy 6. foggy 7. warm 8. cold. It is snowing.

Das Wetter hier ist 1. sehr 2. klar 3. bewolkt 4. regnerisch 5. windig 6. neblig 7. warm 8. kalt. Es schneit gerade.

Ici le temps est 1. tres beau 2. beau 3. nuageux 4. pluvieux 5. venteux 6. brumeux 7. chaud 8. froid. Il neige.

Il tempo qui e 1. molto bello 2. sereno 3. nuvuloso 4. piovoso 5. ventoso 6. nebbioso 7. caldo 8. freddo. Sta nevicando.

El tempo aqui es 1. muy bueno 2. despejado 3. nublado 4. illuvioso 5. ventoso 6. nebuloso 7. caluroso 8. frio. Esta nevando.

O tempo aqui esta 1. muito bom 2. claro 3. nublado 4. chuvoso 5. tempestuoso 6. nevoado 7. calorento 8. frio. Esta nevando.

Pagoda zdjes 1. prikrasnaja 2. jasnaja 3. Zdjes oblacna 4. Idjot dozd 5. Zdjes silnyi vjeter 6. Unas tuman 7. zaraja 8. halodnaja. Idjot snjek.

Kochirano tenkiwa 1. kaiseidesu 2. haredesu 3. kumoridesu 4. amedesu 5. kazega fuiteimasu 6. kiriga deteimasu 7. atatakadesu 8. samuidesu. Yukiga futteimasu.

The temperature here is minus 10 [plus 25] degrees centigrade.
Die Temperatur hier betragt minus 10 [plus 25] Grad celsius.
Ici la temperature qui est de moins 10 [plus 25] degres centigrades.
La temperatura qui e meno 10 [plus 25] gradi centigradi.
La temperaturr es de 10 grados cent.

Foreign Ham Radio Phrases from The Radio Amateur's Conversation Guide,
by Jukka Heikinheimo, OH1BR and Miike Heikinheimo, OH2BAD. Courtesy of Jukka Heikinheimo, OH1BR.

REPEATER OPERATING PRACTICES

The following suggestions will assist you in operating a repeater like you've been doing it for years.

1) Monitor the repeater to become familiar with any peculiarities in its operation.

2) To initiate a contact simply indicate that you are on frequency. Various geographical areas have different practices on making yourself known, but, generally, "This is NUØX monitoring" will suffice. Please don't "ker-chunk" the repeater "just to see if it's working."

3) Identify legally; you must identify at the end of a transmission or series of transmissions and at least once each 10 minutes during the communication.

4) Pause between transmissions. This allows other hams to use the repeater (someone may have an emergency). On most repeaters a pause is necessary to reset the timer.

5) Keep transmissions short and thoughtful. Your "monologue" may prevent someone with an emergency from using the repeater. If you talk long enough, you may actually time out the repeater. Your transmissions are being heard by many listeners including non-hams with "public service band" monitors and scanners; don't give a bad impression of our service.

6) Use simplex whenever possible. If you can complete your QSO on a direct frequency, there is no need to tie up the repeater and prevent others from using it.

7) Use the minimum amount of power necessary to maintain communications. This FCC regulation {(97.313(a)} minimizes the possibility of accessing distant repeaters on the same frequency.

8) Don't break into a contact unless you have something to add. Interrupting is no more polite on the air than it is in person.

9) Repeaters are intended primarily to facilitate mobile operation. During the commuter rush hours, base stations should relinquish the repeater to mobile stations; some repeater groups have rules that specifically address this practice.

10) Many repeaters are equipped with autopatch facilities which, when properly accessed, connect the repeater to the telephone system to provide a public service. The FCC forbids using the autopatch for anything that could be construed as business communications. Nor shall an autopatch be used to avoid a toll call. Do not use an autopatch where regular telephone service is available. Autopatch privileges that are abused may be rescinded.

15) All repeaters are assembled and maintained at considerable expense and inconvenience. Usually an individual or group is responsible, and those who are regular users of a repeater should support the efforts of keeping the repeater on the air.

With an increase in the number of reports of repeater-to-repeater interference, the FCC is placing more emphasis on repeaters being coordinated. Repeater coordination is an example of voluntary self-regulation within the Amateur service. Non-coordinated repeater operation may imply non-conformance with locally recognized band plans (e.g., an unusual frequency split) or simply that the repeater trustee has not yet applied for, or received "official" recognition from the Frequency Coordinator.

(Courtesy of the ARRL)

ARRL AND ITU REGION 1 VHF-UHF BAND PLANS

Although the FCC rules set aside portions of some bands for specific modes, there's still a need to further organize our space among user groups by "gentlemen agreements." These agreements, or band plans, usually emerge by consensus of the band occupants, and are sanctioned by a national body like ARRL.

VHF-UHF Band Plans

When considering frequencies for use in conjunction with a repeater, be sure that both the input and output fall within subbands authorized for repeater use, and do not extend past the subband edges. FCC regulation 97.205(b) defines frequencies which are currently available for repeater use.

For example, a two-meter repeater on exactly 145.50 MHz would be "out-of-band," as the deviation will put the signal outside of the authorized band segment.

Packet-radio operations under automatic control should be guided by Section, 97.109(d) of the FCC rules.

Regional Frequency Coordination

The ARRL supports regional frequency coordination efforts by amateur groups. Band plans published in the ARRL Repeater Directory are recommendations based on a consensus as to good amateur operating practice on a nationwide basis. In some cases, however, local conditions may dictate a variation from the national band plan. In these cases, the written determination of the regional frequency coordinatin body shall prevail and be considered good amateur operating practice in that region.

29.400–29.700 MHz
28.000–28.070 CW
28.070-–28.150 RTTY
28.150–28.190 CW
28.190–28.200 New beacon subband (*)
28.200–28.300 Old beacon subband (*)
28.300–29.340 Phone
29.304–29.510 Satellites
29.510–29.590 Repeater inputs
29.600 FM simplex calling
29.610–29.740 Repeater,outputs

(*) User Note: The FCC states in 97.203(d) that automatically controlled beacons may only operate on 28.20–28.30 MHz.

50 -54 MHz

50.0–50.1 CW beacons
54.064–50.080 Beacon subband
50.1-50.3 SSB, CW
50.10-50.125 DX window
50.125 SSB calling
50.3-50.6 all modes
50.6-50.8 non-voice communications
50.62 digital (packet) calling
54.8-51.0 radio remote control (24-kHz channels)

Note: Activities above 51.14 MHz are set on 20-kHz-spaced "even channels"

51.4-51.1 Pacific DX window
51.12-51.48 repeater inputs (19 channels)

51.12-51.58 digital repeater inputs
51.5-51.6 simplex (6 channels)
51.62-51.98 repeater outputs (19 channels)
51.62-51.68 digital repeater outputs
52.0-52.48 repeater inputs (except as noted; 23 channels)
52.02, 52.04 FM simplex
52.2 TEST PAIR (input)
52.5-52.98 repeater output (except as noted; 23 channels)
52.525 primary FM simplex
52.54 secondary FM simplex
52.7 TEST PAIR (output)
53.0-53.48 repeater inputs (except as noted; 19 channels)
53.0 remote base FM simplex
53.02 simplex
53.1, 53.2 radio remote control
53.3, 53.4
53.5-53.98 repeater outputs (except as noted; 19 channels)
53.5, 53.6 radio remote control
53.7, 53.8
53.52-53.9 simplex

144–148 MHz

144.00-144.05 EME (CW)
144.05-144.10 General CW and weak signals
144.10-144.20 EME and weak-signal SSB
144.200 National calling frequency
144.20-144.275 General SSB operation
144.275-144.300 Propagation beacons
144.30-144.50 New OSCAR subband
144.50-144.60 Linear translator inputs
144.60-144.90 FM repeater inputs
144.90-145.10 Weak signal and fm simplex
(145.01,03,05,07,09 are widely used for packet radio)
145.10-145.20 Linear translator outputs
145.20-145.50 FM repeater outputs
145.50-145.80 Miscellaneous and experimental modes
145.80-146.00 OSCAR subband
146.01-147.37 Repeater inputs
146.40-146.58 Simplex
146.61-147.39 Repeater outputs
147.42-147.57 Simplex
147.60-147.99 Repeater inputs

Notes: The frequency 146.40 MHz is used in some areas as a repeater input.

1) Automatic/unattended operations should be conducted on 145.01, 145.03, 145.05, 145.07 and 145.09 MHz.

a) 145.01 should be reserved for inter-LAN use.

b) Use of the remaining frequencies should be determined by local user groups.

2) Additional frequencies within the two-meter band may be designated for packet radio use by local coordinators.

Simplex frequencies:

(*)146.415 (*)146.475 146.535 146.595 147.465 547.525
(*)546.430 (*)146.490 146.550 147.420 147.480 147.540 (*)146.445
(*)146.505 146.565 147.435 147.495 147.555 (*)146.460
(#)146.520 146.580 147.450 147.510 147.570 147.585

(*) May also be a repeater (input/output). See repeater pairs listing

(#) National Simplex Frequency

Several states have chosen to realign the 146-148 MHz band, using 20 kHz spacing between channels. This choice was made to gain additional repeater pairs.

The transition from 30 to 20 kHz spaking is taking place on a case-by-case basis as the need for additional pairs occurs.

Typically the repeater on an odd numbered pair, will shift to 14 kHz, up or down, creating a new set on an even numbered channel. For example, the pair of 146.13/73 would change to 146.12/72 or 146.14/74 while the pairs of 146.10/70 and 146.16/76 would be left unchanged.

222–225 MHz

222.04-222.15 Weak signal modes
222.00-222.425 UME
222.05-222.064 Propagation beacons
222.1 SSB & CW Calling
222.50-222.150 Weak signal CW & SSB
222.15-222.25 Local coordinator's option:
weak signal, ACSB, repeater inputs and control
222.25-223.38 FM repeater inputs only
223.40-223.52 FM simplex
223.54 Simplex calling
223.52-223.223.64 Digital packet
223.64-223.70 Links control
223.71-223.85 Local coordinator's option;
FM simplex packet repeater outputs
223.85-224.98 Repeater outputs only

Simplex frequencies:

223.42 223.52 223.62 223.72 223.82 223.44 223.54
223.64 223.74 223.84 223.46 223.56 223.66 223.76
223.48 223.58 223.68 223.78 (*)223.50 223.60 223.70
223.80

(*) National Simplex Frequency

420–450 MHz

420.00-426.00 ATV repeater or simplex with 421.25 MHz video carrier, control links and experimental
426.00-432.00 ATV simplex with 427.25 MHz video carrier frequency
432.00-432.07 EME (Earth-Moon-Earth)
432.07-432.10 Weak signal CW
432.10 Calling frequency
432.10-432.30 Mixed-mode and weak-signal work
432.30-432.40 Propagation beacons
432.40-433.00 Mixed-mode and weak signal work
433.00-435.00 Auxiliary/repeater links
435.00-438.00 Satellite only (internationally)
438.00-444.00 ATV repeater input with 439.250-MHz video carrier frequency and repeater links
442.00-445.00 Repeater inputs and outputs (local option)
445.00-447.00 Shared by auxiliary and control links, repeaters and simplex (local option)
446.00 National simplex frequency
447.00-450.00 Repeater inputs and outputs (local option)

902–928 MHz

902.0-903.0 Weak signal (902.1 calling frequency)
902.1 Calling frequency
903.0-906.0 Digital (903.1 alternate calling frequency)
906.0-909.0 FM repeater outputs
909.0-915.0 Amateur TV
915.0-918.0 Digital
918.0-921.0 FM repeater inputs
921.0-927.0 Amateur TV
927.0-928.0 FM simplex and links

Notes: Adopted by the ARRL Board of Directors in July, 1989. The following packet radio frequency recommendations were adopted by the ARRL Board of Directors in January, 1988 as interim guidance. Two 3-MHz-bandwidth channels are recommended for 1.5 Mbit/s links. They are 903-906 MHz and 914-917 MHz with 10.7 MHz spacing.

1) Extracts of FCC Rules & Regulations, 97.303(g)(1). No amateur station shall transmit from within the states of Colorado and Wyoming, bounded on the south by latitude 39 degrees North, on the north by latitude 42 degrees North, on the east by longitude 105 degrees West, and on the west by longitude 108 degrees West. This band is allocated on a secondary basis to the Amateur Service subject to not causing harmful interference to, and not receiving protection from any interference due to the operation of industrial, scientific and medical devices, automatic vehicle monitoring systems or government stations authorized in this band.

2) Coordinated frequency assignments are required.

3) ATV assignments should be made according to modulation type, e.g., VSB-ATV, SSB-ATV or combinations. Coordination of multiple users of a single channel in a local area can be achieved through isolation by means of cross-polarization and directional antennas.

4) Coordinated assignments at 100 kHz until allocations are filled, then assign 50 kHz until allocations are filled, before assigning 25 kHz channels.

5) Simplex services only; permanent users shall not be coordinated in this segment. High altitude repeaters or other unattended fixed operations are not permitted.

6) Voice and non-voice operation.

7) Spread-spectrum requires FCC authorization.

8) Consult FCC (97.307) for allowable data rates and bandwidths.

1240 - 1300 MHz

1244-1246 ATV #1

1246-1248 Narrow-bandwidth FM point-to-point links end digitel, duplex with 5258-1264.

1248-1252 Digital,Communications

1252-1258 ATV #2

1258-1260 Narrow-bandwidth FM point-to-point links and digital duplexed with 1246-1252

1264-1270 Satellite uplinks experimental simplex ATV

1270-1276 Repeater inputs, FM and linear, paired with 1282-1288. (239 pairs every 25 kHz, e.g., 1270.025, 450, etc.)

1271/1283 Non-coordinated test pair

1276-1282 ATV #3

1282-1288 Repeater outputs paired with 1270-1276

1288-1294 Wide Band experimental, simplex ATV

1294-1295 Narrow band FM simplex, 25-kHz channels

1294.50 National FM Simplex calling

1295-1297 Narrow band weak signal (no FM)

1295-1295.80 ATV, FAX, ACSSB experimental

1295-1296 Reserved for EME, CW expansion

1296-1296.05 EME exclusive

1296.07-1296.08 CW beacons

1296.1 CW/SSB calling frequency

1296.40-1296.60 Crossband linear translator output

1296.80-1297.00 Experimental beacons (exclusive)

1297-1300 Digital communication

2300 - 2310 and 2390 - 2450 MHz

2300-2302 High-rate data

2303-2303.5 Packet radio

2303.5-2303.8 RTTY packet

2303.8-2303.9 Packet, RTTY, CW, EME

2303.9-2304.1 CW, EME

2304.1 Calling frequency

2304.1-2304.2 CW, EME, SSB

2304.2-2304.3 SSB, SSTV, FAX, Packet, AM, AMTOR

2304.3-2304.32 Propagation beacon network

2304.32-2304.4 General propagation beacons

2304.4-2304.5 SSB, SSTV, ACSSB, FAX, Packet, AM, AMTOR experimental

2304.5-2304.7 Crossband linear translator input

2304.7-2304.9 Crossband linear translator output

2304.9-2305 Experimental beacons

2305-2305.2 FM simplex (25-kHz spacing)

2305.2 FM simplex calling frequency

2305.2-2306 FM simplex (25-kHz spacing)

2306-2309 FM repeaters (25-kHz) input

2309-2310 Control and auxiliary links

2390-2396 Fast-scan TV

2396-2399 High-rate data

2399-2399.5 Packet

2399.5-2400 Control and auxiliary links

2400-2403 Satellite

2403-2408 Satellite high-rate data

2408-2410 Satellite

2410-2413 FM repeaters (25-kHz spacing) output

2413-2418 High-rate data

2418-2430 Fast-scan TV

2430-2433 Satellite

2433-2438 Satellite high-rate data

2438-2450 Wideband FM, FSTV, FMTV, SS experimental

3300 - 3500 MHz

The following beacon subband was adopted by the ARRL Board of Directors in July, 1988.

3456.3-3456.4 Propagation beacons

5650 - 5925 MHz

The following beacon subband was adopted by the ARRL Board of Directors in July, 1988.

5760.3–5760.4 Propagation beacons

10.000 - 10.500 GHz

The following subband recommendation was adopted by the ARRL Board of Directors in January, 1987

10.368 GHz Narrow-band calling frequency

The following beacon subband was adopted by the ARRL Board of Directors in July, 1988.

10368.3-10368.4 Propagation beacons

ITU Region 1 (Europe and Africa) 144-146 MHz Band Plan

144-144.01 EME

144.05 CW calling, once contact has been established, move off frequency

144.10 CW random meteor scatter

144.15 Upper limit CW exclusive

144.20 SSB random meteor scatter

144.30 SSB calling, once contact has been established, move off frequency

144.40 SSB meteor scatter reference frequency

144.50 SSTV calling, upper limit CW/SSB exclusive

144.60 RTTY calling

144.675 Data transmission calling frequency

144.70 FMX calling

144.845-144.990 Beacon exclusive

145-145.175 Repeater inputs RØ/ to R7

145.2-145.575 Channelized FM simplex

145.5 FM calling frequency, once contact has been established, move off frequency

145.6-145.775 Repeater outputs RØ/ to R7

145.8-146 Space communications, CW/SSB uplink only

Repeater channels (input/output)

RØ/ 145.000/145.600

R1 145.025/145.625

R2 145.050/145.650

R3 145.075/146.675

R4 145.100/145.700

R5 145.125/145.725

R6 145.150/146.750

R7 145.175/145.775

Packet frequencies most widely used are:

144.650 144.675 432.675

Simplex Channels

S10 145.25

S11 145.275

S12 145.30

S13 145.325

S14 145.35

S15 145.375

S16 145.40

S17 145.45

S18 145.45

S19 145.475

S20 145.50–Most common simplex calling frequency, once contact has been established, move off frequency
S21 145.525
S22 145.55
S23 145.575

UK repeaters require a 1750-Hz (+/- 25-Hz) tone burst of about 200-ms duration to open the repeater. It is best to transmit this tone at the start of each transmission. Belgian repeaters require a 3-second tone burst. Swiss repeaters require an 1800-Hz tone burst.

Note: Several French repeaters are on nonstandard frequency pairs. Those pairs are:
144.725/146.325 144.825/145.425
144.750/145.350 44.850/145.450
144.800/145.400 144.875/145.475

(Courtesy of the ARRL)

CTCSS TONE FREQUENCIES

Frequency (Hz)	"P/L" Designator
67.0	XZ
69.3	WZ
71.9	XA
74.4	WA
77.0	XB
79.7	WB
82.5	YZ
85.4	YA
88.5	YB
91.5	ZZ
94.8	ZA
97.4	ZB
100.0	1Z
103.5	1A
107.2	1B
110.9	2Z
114.8	2A
118.8	2B
123.0	3Z
127.3	3A
131.8	3B
136.5	4Z
141.3	4A
146.2	4B
151.4	5Z
156.7	5A
162.2	5B
167.9	6Z
173.8	6A
179.9	6B
186.2	7Z
192.8	7A
203.5	M1
206.5	8Z
210.7	M2
218.1	M3
225.7	M4
229.1	9Z
233.6	M5
241.8	M6
250.3	M7
254.1	ØZ

VHF REPEATER FREQUENCY COORDINATORS

Frequency coordinators are volunteers normally appointed by a coordinating body. The ARRL Repeater Directory reports only the fact of coordination or non-coordination as instructed by the coordinating body. The ARRL is not a frequency coordinator, nor does the ARRL "certify" coordinators. Publication in the Repeater Directory does not constitute nor imply endorsement or recognition of the authority of such coordinators, as coordinators derive their authority from the voluntary participation of the entire amateur community in the areas they serve.

In some cases the person or group listed only compiles the information for listings in the RD. In other cases the listed individual or group offers guidance but not coordination.

Frequency coordinators keep extensive records of repeater input, output and control frequencies, including those not published in directories (at the owner's request). The coordinator will recommend frequencies for a proposed repeater in order to minimize interference with other repeaters and simplex operations. Therefore, anyone considering the installation of a repeater should check with the local frequency coordinator prior to such installation.

The following is a listing of groups or individuals for the United States and Canada who are active in frequency coordination and are acknowledged, by virtue of the recognition accorded them by the entire amateur community, as the sole frequency coordinators in their respective jurisdictions. Listings appear in order of largest parent organizations (MACC, SERA), followed by states, listed in alphabetical order, followed by packet radio coordinating groups and individuals.

The following states are members of the Mid-America Coordination Council, Inc. (MACC):

ARKANSAS - MACC
Fred Short, KI5KH, 7201 Walnut Rd., North Little Rock, AR 72116

COLORADO - MACC
Whitman E. Brown, WBØCJX, 14418 W. Ellsworth Place, Golden, CO 80401-5324

ILLINOIS - MACC
Jay Finn, WD9ENR, PO Box 615, Ramsey, IL 62080

INDIANA - MACC
52 MHz, Dave Crockett, WA9ZCE , PO Box 68104, Indianapolis, IN 46268
29 and 144 MHz, Walter A. Breining, N9WB, RR 1, Spiceland, IN 47385
222 MHz, Martin Hensley, KA9PCT, 1506 S. Parker Dr., Evensville, IN 47714
440 MHz, Jeff Tucker, KB9KIX, 1959 S. Brown Av., Terra Haute, IN 47803
902 & Above/Packet, Ron Pogue,,KD9QB, 210 Westminister Dr.., Noblesville, IN 46460

IOWA - MACC
Denny Crabb, WBØGGI, 1306 4th Av. N., Denison, IA 51442
Al Groff, KØVM, 5446 Council St., NE, Cedar Rapids, IA 52402

KANSAS - MACC
Wayne Fowler Jr., KAØE, 4708 Bluejacket, Shawnee, KS 67871
Western KS: Rod Hogg, KØEQH, 1206 Santa Fe, Scott City, KS 67871
Kansas City: Jasper Simpson, WØZGK, 1812 N 40th St., Kansas City, KS 66102
Eastern KS: Jess Sherwood, NXØY, 9541 Granada, Overland Park, KS 66207

MINNESOTA - MACC
Paul Emeott, KØLAV, 3960 Schuneman Rd., White Bear Lake, MN 55110

MISSOURI - MACC
Wayland N. "Mac" McKenzie, K4CHS, 8000 S. Barry Rd., Columbia, MO 65201
Western MO: Wayne Fowler Jr., KAØE, 4708 Bluejacket, Shawnee, KS 66203
Kansas City: Jasper Simpson, WØZGK, 1812 N 40th St., Kansas City, KS 66102
St. Louis: Jeff Young, KB3HF, 6 Long Branch Ct., St. Peters, MO 63376

MONTANA - MACC
Kenneth G. Kopp, KØPP, Box 848, Anaconda, MT 59711-0848, 406-797-3340

NEBRASKA - MACC
John Gebuhr, WBØCMC, 2340 N 64th St., Omaha, NE 68104
NORTH DAKOTA - MACC
Stanley E. Kittelson, WDØDAJ, 261 10th St. E., Dickinson, ND 58601
OHIO - MACC
Ken Bird, WB8SMK, 244 N Parkway Rd., Delaware, OH 43015
OKLAHOMA - MACC
Glen Turner, NF7T, RR 1, Box 53, Purcell, OK 73080
SOUTH DAKOTA - MACC
Richard Neish, WØSIR, PO Box 100, Chester, SD 57016
UPPER PENINSULA MICHIGAN - MACC
UPARRA Coordinations, PO Box 951, Escanaba, MI 49829
David Reinhart, KV9P, PO Box 218, Alpha, MI 49902
WESTERN WASHINGTON - MACC
Frequency Coordination, Suite 254, 14241 Woodinville-Duval Rd., Woodinville, WA 98072
WISCONSIN - MACC
Nels Harvey, WA9JOB, PO Box 23166, Milwaukee, WI 53233
WYOMING - MACC
Don Breazile, N7MYR, 4406 Greenhill Ct., Cheyenne, WY 82001

The following states are members of the South Eastern Repeater Association (SERA):
GEORGIA - SERA
Director: Stu Sims, N4MXC, 112 Carol Dr., Cochran, GA 31014
Vice-Director: Mike Flammia, N4PLM, 5303 Driskell Dr., Winston, GA 30187
Asst. Director: Bert Coker, N4BZJ, 2102 Milican Ln., Dalton, GA 30721
KENTUCKY - SERA
Director: Terry Estes, WB4ASZ, 27 Mahan Ct., Winchester, KY 40391-1658
Vice-Director: Jeffrey Martin, N5KOL, 308 Marylan Av., Bowling Green, KY 42101
MISSISSIPPI - SERA
Director South: Steve Grantham, N5DWU, PO Box 127, Ellisville, MS 39437
Vice-Director North: Jim Akers, W5VZF, 21 Whispering Pines, Starkville, MS 39759
NORTH CAROLINA - SERA
Director: Danny Hampton, KM4OX, PO Box 19122, Raleigh, NC 27609-9797
Vice Director: Norman Harrill, N4NH, #7 Skylyn Ct., Asheville, NC 28806
Asst. Director: Pamela Glaub, KC4SWM, PO Box 19122, Raleigh, NC 27609-9122
SOUTH CAROLINA - SERA
Director: Bill Jones, N4MNH, 1609 Bur-Clare Rd., Charleston, SC 29412-8148
Vice Director: Gary Foster, WD8OXE, 670 Foster Rd., Inman, SC 29349
TENNESSEE - SERA
Director: Johnny Wofford,,WA4ETE, 2966 Cordell, Memphis, TN 38118
Vice-Director: Tim Berry, WB4GBI, 214 Echodale Ln., Knoxville, TN 37920-5042
Freq. Coord (W-TN): Dave Meier, N4MW, 3205 Covington Pike, Memphis, TN 38128
Asst. Director: Brad Adams, N4PYI, 520 Columbus Dr., Hermitage, TN 37076
VIRGINIA - SERA
Director: Wally Burkett, WA4KXV, 242 Raintree Rd., Virginia Beach, VA 23452
Vice-Director: Don Williams, WA4K, 412 Ridgeway Dr., Bluefield, VA 24605-1630
WEST VIRGINIA - SERA
Director: R.T. (Dick) Fowler, N8FMD, Route 3, Box 52, Clarksburg, WV 28301
Vice-Director South: H. Alex Hedrick, Jr., N8FWL, PO Box 417, Beckley, WV 25802
Asst. Director: G. David Ramezan, KA8ZXP, PO Box 20, Normantown, WV 25267

Other coordination organizations listed alphabetically by state.
ALABAMA
Alabama Repeater Council, Inc., Steve Flory, WA4OUE (FC), PO Box 1305, Decatur, AL 35602
Jack Flory, W4RXH (SEC), 1903 Woodmeade St., Decatur, AL 35601
ALASKA
Mel Bowns, KL7GG, HC 83, Box 1599, Eagle River, AK 99577
ALASKA - NORTH & WESTERN INTERIOR
Jerry Curry, KL7EDK, 940 Vide Way, Fairbanks, AK 99712
ALASKA - SOUTHEAST
Edward Shilling, W6SJJ, PO Box 1087, Petersburg, AK 99833
ALBERTA
Ken Oelke, VE6AFO, 7136 Temple Dr. NE, Calgary, AB T1Y 4E7, CANADA
James Sketchly, VE6APO, Box 1063-A, RR 1, Sylvan Lake, AB T0M 1Z0, CANADA
ARIZONA
Arizona Council of Amateur, Radio Clubs, Ralph Turk, W7HSG, Chairman, 5232 W. Calle Paint, Tucson, AZ 85741
BRITISH COLUMBIA
Ken Oelke, VE3AFO, 7136 Temple Drive NE, Calgary, AB T1Y 4E7, CANADA
CALIFORNIA - NORTH
Northern Amateur Relay Council of California, Inc. (NARCC), Bob Wilkins, N6FRI, PO Box 60531, Sunnyvale, CA 94088
CALIFORNIA - SOUTH
Southern California Repeater and Remote Base Association (SCRRBA), PO Box 5967, Pasadena, CA 91117
220 Spectrum Management Assn., 220 SMA, PO Box 6080, Anaheim, CA 92816-6080
Two Meter Area Spectrum Management Association, TASMA, PO Box 6080, Anaheim, CA 92816-6080
CONNECTICUT: See New York City - Long Island
DELAWARE: See Maryland
DISTRICT OF COLUMBIA: See Maryland
FLORIDA
Florida Repeater Council, Inc. FRC - Secretary, Charles Burkey, K4EVA, 810 E. Wisconsin Av., DeLand, FL 32724
FRC - President - DBM, Walter Maxwell, W2DU, 243 N. Cranor Av., DeLand, FL 32720
HAWAII
Hawaii State Repeater Advisory Council, Pat Corrigan, KH6DD, PO Box 67, Honolulu, HI 96810
IDAHO
(south and east) Ronnie E. Moss, K7ENE, 5330 S 2000 W., Rexburg, ID 83440
(north and west) Larry E. Smith, W7ZRQ, 8106 Bobran St., Boise, ID 83709
(panhandle and eastern Washington) Doug Rider, KC7JC, E. 11516 Mission Ave., Spokane, WA 99206
LOUISIANA
Louisiana Council of Amateur Radio Clubs, Tom Palko, WB5ASD, PO Box 8762, Alexandria, LA 71306-1762
Dave Breeding, KF5JC, 17330 Sanders Rd., Franklinton, LA 70438
MAINE: See Massachusetts
MANITOBA
Thomas Blair, VE4TOM, 121 Miramar Rd., Winnipeg, MB R3R 1E4, CANADA
MARYLAND
The Middle Atlantic FM and Repeater Council, R. Gary Hendrickson, W3DTN, 1419 Larch Rd., Severn, MD 21144
MASSACHUSETTS
New England Spectrum Management Council (52 MHz), Alan D. Tasker, WA1NYR, 64 Dyer St., N Billerica, MA 01862
(222 MHz) Chandler S. Eaton, Jr., W1IFL, 126 Haynes Rd., Sudbury, MA 01776
(29 MHz) Roger Perkins, W1OJ, Old Bay Rd., Bolton, MA 01740
(440 MHz) Ken Chilton, KA1TIH, 53 Alan Rd., Marlboro, MA 01752
(902 and above) Lewis D. Collins, W1GXT, 10 Marshall Terrace, Wayland, MA 01778

(144): Bob Skinner, WA1YEG, Governor Dinsmore Rd., Windham, NH 03087

MICHIGAN

Michigan Area Repeater Council (MARC), 34201 66th St., Bangor, MI 49013

Don Bridgewater, K5IMR, (Pres.), 2291 Packard Hwy., Charlotte, MI 48813

(Lower, 29 -,52 - 144 MHz) Larry French, NW8J, 12215 Meyers Lake Av., NE, Cedar Springs, MI 49319

(Lower 440 - 222 MHz) Vince Vielhaber, KA8CSH, 790 Glaspie Rd., Oxford, MI 48371

NEVADA

(northern) CARCON - FC, Jay Ranney, K7WYC, 430 McClure Cir., Starks, NV 89431-1242

Secretary/Correspondence, PO Box 7523, Reno, NV 89510-7523

(southern) R. Scott Fowler, WA7GIV, 2208 Jansen Ave., Las Vegas, NV 89101

NEW HAMPSHIRE: See Massachusetts

NEW JERSEY (northern) See New York (NYC-LI); (southern) See Pennsylvania (eastern)

NEW MEXICO

New Mexico Frequency Coordinating Committee, Matt Maio, N5FDO, 4676 Platinum, Rio Rancho, NM 87124

NEW YORK (New York City - Long Island, northern New Jersey and Connecticut)

Tri-State Amateur Repeater Council (TSARC), TSARC, PO Box 1356, West Babylon, NY,11704-1356

TSARC,- Secretary, Harold Bacon, KA1ILH, PO Box 284 , Southington, CT 06489

(upstate - except [Clinton and N. Essex Counties—see Vermont], [Franklin and St. Lawrence Counties—see St. Lawrence, Seaway Valley), Upper New York Repeater Council (UNYREPCO)

Phil Bradway, KB2HQ, 1119 Hedgewood Ln., Schenectady, NY 12309

(western New York [west of Rochester] and southern Ontario): Western New York - Southern Ontario Repeater Council (WNYSORC)

Frequency Coordinator, PO Box 79519 - Gagemount Postal Outlet, Hamilton, ON L8T 5A2, CANADA

(eastern Ontario - St. Lawrence Seaway Vly.): St. Lawrence Valley Repeater Council (SLVRC) Graham Ide, VE3BYT, 43 Quinpool Crescent, Nepean, ON K2H 6H9, CANADA

ONTARIO

(western New York and southern Ontario), Western New York - Southern Ontario Repeater Council (WNYSORC)

Frequency Coordinator, PO Box 79519 - Gagemount Postal Outlet, Hamilton, ON L8T 5A2, CANADA

(eastern Ontario - St. Lawrence Seaway Valley): St. Lawrence Valley Repeater Association (SLVRA)

Graham Ide, VE3BYT, 43 Quinpool Crescent, Nepean, ON K2H 6H9, CANADA

OREGON (also Vancouver, WA)

Oregon Region Relay Council, Inc.

Frequency Coordinator, PO Box 25451, Portland, OR 97225-0451

PENNSYLVANIA (eastern Pennsylvania and southern New Jersey)

The Philadelphia Area Repeater Council (TPARC)

Jerry Smedley, WB3BLG, PO Box 36, Croydon, PA 19021, 215-788-0759

(western): Western Pennsylvania Repeater Council (WPRC)

Frequency Coordinations, PO Box 81020, Pittsburgh, PA 15217

Membership Information, c/o Bruce Taylor, WB3AYA, PO Box 81020, Pittsburgh, PA 15217

Frequency Coordinator, Edward C. DeHart, WA3YOA, 2714 Sapling Dr., Allison Park, PA 15101

PUERTO RICO

PR/VI VFC, PO Box 191917, San Juan, PR 00919-1917

QUEBEC

RAQI, Frequency Coordinator, C.P. 1000 Succ. M., Montreal, PQ H1V 3R2 CANADA

(Ottawa Valley - St. Lawrence Seaway Valley): St. Lawrence Valley Repeater Association (SLVRA)

Graham Ide, VE3BYT, 43 Quinpool Crescent, Nepean, ON K2H 6H9, CANADA

RHODE ISLAND: See Massachusetts

SASKATCHEWAN

Ken Nyeste, VE5NR, 123 Holland Rd., Saskatoon, SK S7H 4Z5, CANADA

TEXAS

Texas VHF-FM Society, Inc., Merle Taylor, WB5EPI, 910 Kingston Dr., Mansfield, TX 76063-2650

UTAH

Utah VHF Society, John Lloyd, K7JL, 11560 S. Sandy Creek Dr. Sandy, UT 84094

VERMONT (also Clinton and N. Essex Counties of New York)

Vermont Independent Repeater

Coordinating Committee VIRCC, PO Box 99, Essex, VT 05451

VIRGINIA - NORTHERN: See Maryland

WASHINGTON - EASTERN (also Idaho panhandle)

Doug Rider, KC7JC, E. 11516 Mission Ave., Spokane, WA 99206

WEST VIRGINIA - EASTERN PANHANDLE: See Maryland

CANADA (areas not included above): In areas of Canada, where no frequency coordination exists, please notify the following of any new repeaters or changes for inclusion in the ARRL Repeater Directory. The address is:

Ken Oelke, VE6AFO, 7136 Temple Drive NE, Calgary, AB T1Y 4E7

Packet - Coordination

CALIFORNIA

Frequency Coordinator, PO Box 4425, Carson, CA 90749

CALIFORNIA - SOUTH

Karl Pagel, N6BVU, PO Box 6080, Anaheim, CA 92816-6080

INDIANA

Indiana Digital Experimenters Association (IDEA), John Gooldy, WJ9U, 1712 Mulberry Cir., Noblesville, IN 46060

FLORIDA

Florida Amateur Digital Communications Association (FADCA), John P. Paxton, KB4RLL, 6333 NE 120th St., Okeechobee, FL 34972

KANSAS

Kansas Digital Coordination Committee (KDCC), Karl Medcalf, WK5M, RR 2 Box 239, Lawrence, KS 6604

MARYLAND

Packet Liaison Committee (PLC), John G. Hengen, K3HOI, 9128 Windemere Way, Savage, MD 20763

Digital Mid-Atlantic Radio Council (DMARC), Thomas Dove, K3ORC, 22-H Queen Victoria Way, Chester, MD 21619

MICHIGAN

(MIPAC), Jay Nugent, WB8TKL, 3081 Braeburn Cir., Ann Arbor, MI 48104

ILLINOIS

Northern Illinois Packet Radio Frequency Council (NIPRFC), Mark Thompson, WB9QZB, PO Box 357, Mount Prospect, IL 60056

(NIPRFC), Carl Bergstedt, K9VXW, 308 W. Osage Ln., Naperville, IL 60540-7821

(NIPRFC), William R. Davidson, KA9SWW, 3122 N. Drake Av., Chicago, IL 60618

TEXAS

Texas Packet Radio Society (TPRS), Harry Ridenour, NØCCW, 14218 Ridgedale, San Antonio, TX 78233

WISCONSIN

Wisconsin Amateur Packet Radio (WAPR), Joel Eschmann, K9MLD, 6964 Meadowdale Dr., Hartford, WI 53027

(Courtesy of the ARRL)

MOST COMMON REPEATER OUTPUT FREQUENCIES IN NORTH AMERICA

50-54 MHz

Rank	Freq.	Count
1	53.010	30
2	53.050	17
3	53.030	16
4	53.070	13
5	53.130	12
6	53.250	12 (tie)
7	53.110	11
8	53.170	11 (tie)
9	53.210	11 (tie)
10	53.090	10
	53.150	10 (tie)

144-148 MHz

Rank	Freq.	Count
1	146.940	156
2	146.760	146
3	146.880	134
4	146.820	131
5	147.000	125
6	146.640	115
7	146.700	114
8	147.300	105
9	147.360	103
10	146.790	102

222-225 MHz

Rank	Freq.	Count
1	224.940	54
2	223.940	48
3	224.760	41
4	224.860	40
5	224.100	38
6	224.820	38
7	224.200	36
8	224.600	35
9	224.700	35
10	224.740	35
	224.960	35 (tie)
	224.980	35 (tie)

420-450 MHz

Rank	Freq.	Count
1	444.500	77
2	444.900	70
3	444.950	69
4	444.100	68
5	444.000	66
6	444.800	65
7	444.200	64
8	444.850	60
9	444.700	58
10	444.400	55

STATES WITH THE MOST REPEATERS BY BAND

50-54 MHz

Rank	State	No. Repeaters
1	California	62
2	New York	35
3	Pennsylvania	29
4	New Jersey	19
5	Massachusetts	17
6	Virginia	15
7	Ohio	14
8	North Carolina	14
9	Michigan	13
10	Florida	12
	Tennessee	12
	Texas	12
	Washington	12

144-148 MHz

Rank	State	No. Repeaters
1	California	529
2	Texas	456
3	Florida	271
4	Ohio	267
5	New York	241
6	Pennsylvania	241
7	Tennessee	184
8	Illinois	171
9	Michigan	168
10	Georgia	165

222-225 MHz

Rank	State	No. Repeaters
1	California	328
2	Texas	101
3	Pennsylvania	95
4	Ohio	86
5	New York	77
6	Illinois	73
7	Florida	57
8	New Jersey	55
9	Michigan	54
10	Massachusetts	48

420-450 MHz

Rank	State	No. Repeaters
1	California	898
2	Texas	418
3	New York	308
4	Florida	214
5	Ohio	212
6	Washington	190
7	Illinois	173
8	Arizona	171
9	New Jersey	162
10	Michigan	157

K5XI's 20-Meter array in South Central Texas. As far as we've been able to determine, it is the highest tower constructed exclusively for a private ham radio station. See *Antennas* section for details.

Joe Reisert, W1JR- Holder of 12-Band Worked-All-Continents, 12-Band Worked-All-States, and 10-Band DXCC (30M awards are unofficial). See *Awards* section for details.

Jim Tucker, WM5G, proudly stands in front of his Garland, Texas super-station.

Work moonbounce Texas-style with this 2M EME array at the Merit, Texas location of Gerald Williamson, K5GW.

Imagine looking out your skylight and seeing the VHF arrays of Steve Powlishen, K1FO in Madison, Connecticut.

Only the sunshine highlights the awesome antennas belonging to Greg McIntire, AA5C of Princeton, Texas.

Don't most hams wish they had one of these in their back yard? The 40 foot dish EME antenna at Allen Katz, K2UYH in Robbinsville, New Jersey.

There's nothing like the Rocky Mountains to inspire you to climb your tower like the Nederland, Colorado QTH of Ron Stockton, NØRR.

Roger Cardinal Mahony, W6QYI—Roman Catholic Archbishop of Los Angeles.

Joe Rudi, NK7U, played major league baseball for 16 years and is a three-time winner of the Gold Glove Award. His station in Oregon includes eight towers up to 200 feet tall and over 50 antennas.

Larry Junstrom, KN4UB (rear, center wearing black hat), bass guitarist for the Southern rock band ".38 Special, " also previously played with the rock group "Lynyrd Skynyrd."

Roy Neal, K6DUE—retired television journalist, NBC.

VHF DIGITAL AMATEUR RADIO

The following tutorial section is derived from the Digital Radio Frequently Asked Questions (FAQ) list, Version 1.18.1 (last modified 9/22/93). It is reprinted here with the permission of author Steve Watt, KD6GGD. Please send corrections and additions to:

digital-faq@wattres.sj.ca.us via Internet, or via Packet Radio to:

KD6GGD @ NØARY.#NOCAL.CA.USA.NA

The Digital Radio FAQ list is posted on a monthly basis to rec.radio.amateur.digital.misc, rec.radio.info, rec.answers, and news.answers. The current version of this document is available via anonymous FTP atftp.cs.buffalo.edu.

Many FAQs, including this one, are available on the archive sitertfm.mit.edu in the directory pub/usenet/news.answers. The name under which a FAQ is archived appears in the Archive-Name: line at the top of the article. This FAQ is archived as radio/amateur/digital-faq.

There is also a mail server on rtfm.mit.edu, which can be addressed as mail-server@rtfm.mit.edu. For details on how to operate this server, send a message to that address with the word "help" in the BODY of the message.

Basic Packet Radio Information

What is packet radio?

Packet radio is one method of digital communications via amateur radio. Packet radio takes any digital data stream and sends that via radio to another amateur radio station. Packet radio is so named because it sends the data in small bursts, or packets.

What can I do on packet radio?

Keyboard-to-Keyboard contacts: Like other digital communications modes, packet radio can be used to talk to other amateurs. For those who cannot use HF frequencies, two amateurs can talk to each other from long distances using the packet radio network.

Packet BBS operations: Many cities have one or more packet Bulletin Board System (BBS) available on the local packet network. Amateurs can check into the BBSs and read messages from other packet users on almost any topic. BBSs are networked together over the packet network to allow messages to reach a broader audience than just your local BBS users. Private messages may also be sent to other packet operators, either locally or by those who use other BBSs. BBSs have the latest ARRL, AMSAT, and propagation bulletins. Many BBSs have a file section containing various text files full of information on amateur radio in general.

DX Packet Cluster:

A recent development is use of packet radio for DX spotting. HF operators connect to the local DX PacketCluster (tm) for the latest reports on DX. Often a user will "spot" some hot DX and distribute the DX report real time. A list of PacketCluster nodes can be found elsewhere in this Almanac.

File Transfer:

With special software, amateurs can pass any binary files to other amateurs. Currently, this is done with TCP/IP communications, YAPP, and other specialized protocols.

Satellite Communications:

Many of the amateur radio satellites contain microcomputer systems that can provide special information to amateurs. Some satellites contain CCD cameras on board and you can download images of the earth and the stars. Others provide store and forward packet mailboxes to allow rapid message transfers over long distances. Some satellites use AX.25, some use special packet protocols developed for satellite communications. A few transmit AX.25 packets over FM transmitters, but most use SSB transmissions.

Why packet over other digital modes?

Packet has three great advantages over most of the other digital modes: transparency, error correction, and automatic control.

The operation of a packet station is transparent to the end user; connect to the other station, type in your message, and it is sent automatically. The Terminal Node Controller (TNC) automatically divides the message into packets, keys the transmitter and sends the packets. While receiving packets, the TNC automatically decodes, checks for errors, and displays the received messages. In addition, any packet TNC can be used as a packet relay station, sometimes called a digipeater. This allows for greater range by stringing several packet stations together.

Packet radio provides error-free communications because of built-in error detection schemes. If a packet is received, it is checked for errors and will be displayed only if it is correct.

With VHF/UHF packet, many countries allow packet operators to operate in automatic control mode. This means that you can leave your packet station on constantly. Other users can connect to you at any time they wish to see if you are home. Some TNCs even have Personal BBSs (sometimes called mailboxes) so other amateurs can leave you messages if you are not at home.

The most important advantage of packet over other modes is the ability for many users to be able to use the same frequency channel simultaneously. No other digital mode yet gives this ability.

What elements make up a packet station?

TNC (Terminal Node Controller): A TNC contains a modem, a CPU, and the associated circuitry required to convert between RS-232 and the packet radio protocol in use. It assembles a packet from some of the data on the serial line, computing an error check (CRC) for the packet, modulates it into audio frequencies, and puts out appropriate signals to transmit that packet over the connected radio. It also reverses the process, translating the audio that the connected radio receives into a byte stream on the RS-232 port.

Most TNCs currently use 1200 BPS (bits per second) for local VHF and UHF packet, and 300 BPS for longer distance, lower bandwidth HF communication. Higher speeds are available for use in the VHF, UHF, and especially microwave region, but they often require unusual hardware and drivers.

Computer or Terminal: This is the user interface. A computer running a terminal emulator program, a packet-specific program, or just a dumb terminal can be used. For computers, almost any phone modem communications program can be adapted for packet use, but there are also customized packet radio programs available.

A radio: For 1200 BPS UHF/VHF packet, commonly available narrow band FM voice radios are used. For HF packet, 300 BPS data is used over single-sideband modulation. For high speed packet (anything greater than 1200 BPS), special radios or modified FM radios must be used.

What do you mean we can all use the same channel?

Packet radio uses a protocol called AX.25. AX.25 specifies channel access (ability to transmit on the channel) to be handled by CSMA (Carrier Sense Multiple Access). If you need to transmit, your TNC monitors the channel to see if someone else is transmitting. If no one else is transmitting, then the TNC keys up the radio, and sends its packet. All the other stations hear the packet and do not transmit until you are done. Unfortunately, two stations could accidentally transmit at the same time. This is called a collision. If a collision occurs, neither TNC will receive a reply back from the last packet it sent. Each TNC will wait a random amount of time and then retransmit the packet.

In actuality, a more complex scheme is used to determine when the TNC transmits. See the "AX.25 Protocol Specification" for more information.

What is AX.25?

AX.25 (Amateur X.25) is the communications protocol used for packet radio. A protocol is a standard for how two computer systems are to communicate with each other, somewhat analogous to using business format when writing a business letter. AX.25 was developed in the 1970s and based on the wired network protocol X.25. Because of the difference in the transport medium (radios vs.

wires) and because of different addressing schemes, X.25 was modified to suit amateur radio's needs. AX.25 includes a digipeater field to allow other stations to automatically repeat packets to extend the range of transmitters. One advantage of AX.25 is that every packet sent contains the sender's and recipient's amateur radio callsigns, thus providing station identification with every transmission.

Commonly used terms in Amateur Packet Radio

44 net—The class A network designator for TCP/IP amateur packet radio. All numerical TCP/IP addresses are in the format 44.xxx.xxx.xxx.

AFSK—Audio Frequency Shift Keying. A method of representing digital information by using different audio frequencies modulated on a carrier.

AMPR—Amateur Packet Radio.

ampr.org—The high level domain recognized on Internet for amateur packet radio TCP/IP.

AMTOR—Amateur Teleprinting Over Radio. This protocol allows error-free point-to-point or multicast, single user per channel communications. Usually used on HF, but not VHF or above.

ARQ—Automatic Resend Request. This is the point-to-point error correcting mode for AMTOR. It works by sending bursts of three characters, and then the other station sends an OK/NotOK code for those 3 characters.

AX.25—Amateur X.25 protocol. The basis of most packet systems.

CRC—Cyclic Redundancy Check. The error detection scheme included in each packet. Verifies that the packet was received error-free.

CSMA—Carrier Sense Multiple Access. A system allowing many stations to use the same radio frequency simultaneously for packet communications.

digi—Short name for a digipeater

digipeater—A packet radio station used for repeating packets.

FEC—Forward Error Correction. This is the multicast method of (almost) error-corrected communications on AMTOR. It works by sending each character twice.

FM—Frequency Modulation. The radio modulation scheme used for VHF and UHF packet communications.

FSK—Frequency Shift Keying. A method of representing digital information by shifting the radio carrier frequency different amounts to represent ones and zeros.

HDLC—(High-Level Data Link Control Procedures) A standard for high level link control. (ISO 3309)

KA9Q NOS—(KA9Q Network Operating System). A TCP/IP program originally developed by Phil Karn, KA9Q. Currently there are many different versions available.

KA-Node—A simple networking scheme developed by TNC maker Kantronics.

KISS—Keep It Simple Stupid. A simple interface developed for communications between TNCs and computers. This allows for most of the packet processing to be handled by the computer. Commonly used with packet TCP/IP software.

LAN—Local Area Network. A packet network developed for communications throughout a city or region. Often, the LAN uses separate frequencies from inter-city packet links.

modem—MODulator/DEModulator. Converts the analog signals into a binary data stream (a series of ones and zeros) for the TNC or a microcomputer. First step in decoding packets. It also converts binary data to analog, which is the last step in encoding packets.

NET/ROM—A scheme for packet radio networking.

NODE—A network node. Often a network node running NET/ROM.

PPP—Point to Point Protocol. PPP is another protocol used for moving IP frames over a serial line. It supports host authentication, and non-transparent serial lines. It also has a standard way of negotiating header (and potentially data) compression over the line. See also SLIP.

protocol—A standard used for intercommunications between different computer systems.

RS-232 (RS-323C)—A (more or less) standard for interconnection of serial peripherals to small computer systems. In packet radio, RS-232 is the most common interface between TNCs and the Computer/Terminal.

RTTY—Radio TeleTYpe. This protocol allows point-to-point or multicast, single user per channel communications, without error correction.

SLIP—Serial Line Internet Protocol. A trivial protocol for putting IP frames over a serial line to do (potentially) cheap TCP/IP networking. Approximately the same as KISS, except over wireline networks. See also PPP.

SSB - Single Side Band. The radio modulation scheme used for HF packet and satellite packet communications.

TAPR —Tucson Amateur Packet Radio. Was the first group to create a packet radio TNC using AX.25. Soon a TAPR TNC became cloned by many others. TAPR continues development of packet radio equipment.

TCP/IP—Transmission Control Protocol/Internet Protocol. A set of utility programs used over AX.25.

TNC—Terminal Node Controller.

Do's and Don'ts : Rules and Regulations

NOTE: These regulations apply only to amateurs regulated by the FCC (United States), but often are similar to regulations in other countries. Please bring any notable exceptions to the attention of KD6GGD.

Although there are no specific rules that apply to amateur packet radio, the general amateur radio rules force some restrictions on packet usage.

Can I set up a TNC at home and one at work so I can check my Electronic mail via packet?

This cannot be done without special restrictions. Amateur radio rules prohibit any business. Since you could have mail from your boss (or maybe even someone selling you something over Internet), that would constitute business activity and is specifically prohibited.

Profanity can also be a complication. Since you have no control over the language used in E-mail, proper filtering is required. Since no filter scheme can catch every offense, it is best to say every message must be hand filtered.

I would like to set up a packet radio gateway between a land line computer network and the packet network. Is this possible?

Yes, and there are several such gateways in use, but they must be managed with caution. Electronic mail may be passed FROM the packet network INTO the land line network without intervention. However, mail passed TO packet radio is considered third party traffic (the sender is not an amateur) and these messages must be hand filtered to ensure that rules of message content are followed.

It's my license if I use packet radio illegally anyway, so what does anyone else care!?

Packet radio is one of the few NETWORKED systems in amateur radio. Many people have helped develop the network and there are many amateurs who own parts of the packet radio network. Sending packet BBS mail, digipeating, and sharing the channel involves the licenses of MANY people. Because of FCC rules stating that anything to come out of a transmitter (either in automatic mode or via your direct control) is the licensee's responsibility, one illegal message sent over the packet radio network could literally jeopardize the licenses of thousands of other amateurs. When in doubt, it is best to check with other amateurs about sending the message before it is sent.

I have some ideas on how to use packet radio in a new way, but I don't know if it is legal. Who could tell me if I can do it legally?

The best source for legal assistance is your national amateur radio association. In the United States, that is the American Radio Relay League (ARRL). Another good place for such conversations is over Usenet/packet mailing lists, or the amateur radio BBS network.

Computing Network Resources for Amateur Packet radio

This section summarizes the resources available on Internet for amateur packet radio operators.

Newsgroups/mailing lists related to Packet Radio

This is a list of all groups that regularly discuss amateur packet radio. For newsgroups, join the group through use of your news reader. For mailing lists, add a '-request' to the end of the list name to request subscriptions. For listserv groups, send mail to 'listserv' at the node which contains the list. The first line of the mail should be 'SUBSCRIBE groupname yourname'. Send the command 'help' for more information.

rec.radio.amateur.packet (Newsgroup): General discussions involving Packet Radio. This group was deleted on 21 September 93!

rec.radio.amateur.digital.misc (Newsgroup): General discussions about all aspects of digital transmissions over Amateur Radio. This group is a replacement for rec.radio.amateur.packet.

rec.radio.amateur.equipment (Newsgroup): May contain discussions about equipment related to digital amateur radio, specifically HF rigs that are good for HF digital modes, and the like.

packet-radio@ucsd.edu (Listserv group): General discussions involving packet radio and packet-related issues.

ham-digital@ucsd.edu (Listserv group): A digest redistribution of the rec.radio.amateur.digital.misc Usenet discussion.

hs-modem@wb3ffv.ampr.org (Mailing list): Discussion of high speed modems and radios available and future plans. Also includes discussion of networking using high speed modems. This list is not very active.

tcp-group@ucsd.edu (Mailing list): Group discussion of technical developments of TCP/IP over packet radio and use of the NOS TCP/IP programs.

gateways@uhm.ampr.org (Mailing list): Discussion of current gateways and future plans for gateways. May deal with sensitive Internet working issues.

listserv@knuth.mtsu.edu : Has several interesting mailing lists available:

GRAPES-L—Discussions with GRAPES (Georgia Radio Amateur Packet Enthusiasts Society) on 56kb WANs and the WA4DSY 56kb RF modem that they distribute.

TENNET-L—Tennessee's efforts at a coordinated high-speed RF packet network

GRACILIS-L—Discussions on Gracilis tcp/ip packet equipment. Includes some of the people from Gracilis.

KA9Q-UNIX—Discussions on porting and using various versions of KA9Q Unix/Xenix NET/NOS under any of a variety of Unix/Xenix variants.

TNV-HAMS—General discussions among e-mail connected amateur radio operators in and surrounding Tennessee

Send a message with a body of "HELP" to get help from the list server. Also, Internet users may now INTERACTIVELY work with the ListServ there by:

telnet knuth.mtsu.edu 372

or

telnet 161.45.1.1 372

For all lists at ucsd.edu, archives may be found via anonymous FTP at ucsd.edu. Some listserv groups also have archives. Send the command 'help' to the group's listserv for more information. Digest mailings for the ucsd.edu discussions are also available. Send mail to listserv@ucsd.edu with the first line being 'longindex' for more information.

Terry Stader (KA8SCP) <tstader@aol.com> maintains a list of Mac packet-related software, and posts it periodically (somewhat less often than monthly) to rec.radio.amateur.digital.misc.

Carl Trommel <carl@codewks.nacjack.gen.nz> posts the weekly news bulletin of the ZL Data Group to rec.radio.amateur.digital.misc. This bulletin covers the current happenings in New Zeland's packet network.

There appears to be a mailing list about NOS on hydra.carleton.ca. Send a message to nos-bbs-request@hydra.carleton.ca. The list name is nos-bbs@hydra.carleton.ca.

Anonymous FTP sites and electronic mail servers available for getting packet radio information and programs

This is a sampling of FTP sites that carry amateur packet radio related files. Consult the Archie archive server for information on locating particular files. For more information on using archie, send mail to archie@cs.mcgill.edu with the line 'help.'

ucsd.edu

Primary distribution site of KA9Q's derived TCP/IP packages. Also, general packet radio information in the /hamradio/packet subdirectory.

wsmr-simtel20.army.mil

Very large collection of amateur radio software. Note that there are persistent rumors about Simtel20 going away for budgetary reasons.

wuarchive.wustl.edu

Mirror site of Simtel20 archives. Unix directory structure, which is easier to use then the simtel 20 archive.

tomcat.gsfc.nasa.gov

Packet software including Baycomm, ROSE, G8BPQ, NOS, etc.

akutaktak.andrew.cmu.edu

SoftKiss for the Mac, in /aw0g. Requires NET/Mac. SoftKiss is an init/cdev/driver that allows a MAC to do packet using a Poor Man's Packet modem.

sumex-aim.stanford.edu

NET/Mac is the port of KA9Q's NET program. It doesn't have nifty features like scrolling or saving the windows, but the individual sessions can be recorded into a file.

Internet / Packet Radio BBS Gateways

There are currently two comprehensive gateways between the Internet and the packet radio BBS system. One is run by Jim Durham, W2XO, in Pennsylvania and the other, which allows access to PBBS bulletins, as well as mail, is run by Bob Arasmith, NØARY, in California.

The W2XO Gateway

To mail from Internet to Packet:

1. Mail to: "bbs@w2xo.pgh.pa.us"
2. Make the first line of the text a Packet BBS "send" command, i.e: SP TOCALL @ BBSCALL.ROUTING-HINTS < FROMCALL
3. The "subject" line of the Internet mail becomes the "title" line of the Packet BBS mail.

NOTE: Because of FCC regulations, Jim must hand filter each message sent FROM Internet TO the Amateur Packet Radio BBS system. Messages should be of minimal length and appropriate content. Refer to "Do's and Don'ts: Rules and Regulations" regarding appropriate usage of packet radio for more information. Always include the routing hints with the BBS callsign.

To mail from Packet to Internet:

1. The amateur radio operator must have his callsign registered in the gateway alias list. If you want to mail from packet to a specific amateur on Internet, send mail to: 'durham@w2xo.pgh.pa.us' (Internet) or 'W2XO @ W2XO.#WPA.PA.USA.NOAM' (Packet BBS mail) with his/her amateur callsign and their Internet address.

2. Once the above is accomplished, packet BBS mail should be sent to 'CALL @ W2XO.#WPA.PA.USA.NOAM'. The mail will automatically be forwarded to the Internet address of the amateur with the 'CALL' callsign.

Jim Durham's Internet address is 'durham@w2xo.pgh.pa.us'.

The NØARY Internet mail <-> full packet BBS gateway

Bob Arasmith, NØARY, runs a gateway between the Internet mail system and the PBBS system. His gateway allows you to read, post, and respond to other postings on the PBBS system via e-mail. For more information, send mail to gateway_info@arasmith.com.

The N6QMY Internet mail <-> full packet BBS gateway

Patrick Mulrooney, N6QMY, also runs a gateway between the Internet mail system and the PBBS system. His gateway allows you to read, post, and respond to other postings on the PBBS system via e-mail. For more information, send mail to gateway-info@lbc.com.

Users are required to register with the gateway to allow automatic forwarding of mail from the Internet to Packet. No registration is needed to send mail from Packet to the Internet. To register, send the following information to gateway-request@lbc.com:

CALL:
FIRST NAME:
LAST NAME:
CITY & ST:
COUNTRY
ZIP:
HOME BBS:

LAN Gateways (Packet wormholes via Internet)

Currently a group of amateurs is experimenting with connecting packet LANs together via Internet IP inside IP Encapsulation. Some of the gateways only accept TCP/IP packets, others AX.25 packets. These gateways use the Internet as a transport medium, thus it is impossible to access the packet radio network from Internet. For more information, join the Gateways mailing list by sending mail to "gateways-request@uhm.ampr.org".

Networking and special packet protocols

This is a sample of some of the more popular networking schemes available today. By far, there are more customized networking schemes used than listed. Consult your local packet network guru for specific network information.

Are there any other protocols in use other than AX.25?

AX.25 is considered the defacto standard protocol for amateur radio use and is even recognized by many countries as a legal operation mode. However, there are other standards. TCP/IP is used in some areas for amateur radio. Also, some networking protocols use other packet formats than AX.25.

Often, special packet radio protocols are encapsulated within AX.25 packet frames. This is done to insure compliance with regulations requiring packet radio transmissions to be in the form of AX.25. However, details of AX.25 encapsulation rules vary from country to country.

What is TCP/IP?

TCP/IP stands for Transmission Control Protocol/Internet Protocol. This is commonly used over the Internet wired computer network. The TCP/IP suite contains different transmission facilities such as FTP (File Transfer Protocol), SMTP (Simple Mail Transport Protocol), Telnet (Remote terminal protocol), and NNTP (Net News Transfer Protocol)

TCP/IP doesn't use all of the AX.25 protocol. Instead, it uses special AX.25 packets called Unnumbered Information (UI) packets and then puts its own special protocol (called IP) on top of AX.25. This is used to increase efficiency of its transmissions, since IP does not require packets to be "reliable," that is to say, guaranteed delivered error-free. TCP handles the retransmission of lost and garbled packets in its own way, at a higher level. Therefore the extra information in an AX.25 "VC" (virtual circuit) frame is not useful, and thus consuming needed bandwidth.

The KA9Q NOS program (also called NET) is the most commonly used version of TCP/IP in packet radio. NOS originally was written for the PC compatible. However, NOS has been ported to many different computers such as the Amiga, Macintosh, Unix, and others. Smaller computers like the Commodore 64 and the Timex-Sinclar do not currently have version of NOS available.

Networking Schemes

During the early days of amateur packet radio, it became apparent that a packet network was needed. To this end, the following packet network schemes where created.

Digipeaters

The first networking scheme with packet radio was Digipeaters. Digipeaters would simply look at a packet, and if its call was in the digipeater field, would resend the packet. Digipeaters allow the extension of range of a transmitter by retransmitting any packets addressed to the digipeater.

This scheme worked well with only a few people on the radio channel. However, as packet became more popular, digipeaters soon were clogging up the airwaves with traffic being repeated over long distances. Also, if a packet got lost by one of the digipeaters, the originator station would have to retransmit the packet again, forcing every digipeater to transmit again and causing more congestion.

KA-Nodes

Kantronics improved on the digipeater slightly and created KA-Nodes. As with digipeaters, KA-Nodes simply repeat AX.25 frames. However, a KA-Node acknowledges every transmission each link instead of over the entire route. Therefore, instead of an end-to-end acknowledgment, KA-Nodes allow for more reliable connections with fewer timeouts, because acknowledgments are only carried on one link. KA-Nodes, therefore, are more reliable than digipeaters, but are not a true network. It is similar to having to wire your own telephone network to make a phone call.

NET/ROM

NET/ROM was one of the first networking schemes to try to address the problems with digipeaters. A user connects to a NET/ROM station as if connecting to any other packet station. From there, he can issue commands to instruct the station to connect to another user locally or connect to another NET/ROM station. This connect, then connect again, means that to a user's TNC, you are connected to a local station only and its transmissions do not have to be digipeated over the entire network and risk losing packets. This local connection proved to be more reliable.

NET/ROM is a commercial firmware (software put on a chip) program that is used as a replacement ROM in TAPR type TNCs. Other programs are available to emulate NET/ROM. Among them are TheNet, G8BPQ node switch, MSYS, and some versions of NET.

NET/ROM nodes, at regular intervals, transmit to other nodes their current list of known nodes. This is good because as new nodes come on-line, they are automatically integrated in the network. However, if band conditions such as ducting occur, ordinarily unreachable nodes can be entered into node lists. This causes the NET/ROM routing software to choose routes to distant nodes that are impossible. This problem requires users to develop a route to a distant node manually defining each hop instead of using the automatic routing feature.

ROSE

ROSE is another networking protocol derived from X.25. Each ROSE node has a static list of the nodes it can reach. For a user to use a ROSE switch, he issues a connect with the destination station and in the digipeater field places the call of the local rose switch and the distant rose switch the destination station can hear. Other than that, the network is completely transparent to the user.

ROSE's use of static routing tables ensures that ROSE nodes don't attempt to route packets through links that aren't reliably reachable, as NET/ROM nodes often do. However, ROSE suffers from the inability to automatically update its routing tables as new nodes come online. The operators must manually update the routing tables, which is why ROSE networks require more maintenance.

BBS message transfer

Many of the BBS programs used in packet radio allow for mail and bulletins to be transferred over the packet radio network. The BBSs use a special forwarding protocol developed originally by Hank Oredsen, WØRLI.

Besides full service BBSs, many TNC makers have developed Personal BBS software to allow full service BBSs to forward mail directly to the amateur's TNC. This allows operators to receive packet mail at night and avoid tying up the network during busy hours.

CW OPERATING

The first radio operators, amateur and professional, used telegraphy for message transmission. Proficiency in the "International Morse Code" has long been a requirement for amateur licensing. CW has fallen somewhat in popularity and was determined to be an impediment to the growth of amateur radio, and several countries (including the United States) have developed classes of license that do not require Morse code proficiency.

Organizations Devoted to CW Operation

Several amateur radio organizations are dedicated to CW operation. The best-known is the prestigious "First-class CW Operators Club," more commonly known as the FOC. Membership in this organization is by invitation only, with a formal process of nomination and sponsorship. Selection is done on the basis of CW proficiency, activity, and operating skill. Maximum membership at any one time is limited, and there have been approximately 1,600 members in the club's history. FOC members can usually be found operating on or near the unofficial club frequencies, 25 kHz above the bottom of each CW band.

A somewhat less formal organization is called the "Chicken Fat Operators," or CFO. It is "dedicated to competent Morse code operations in the Amateur Service." Founded in 1979 by W9WBL and W9TO (designer of the "TO" keyer manufactured by Hallicrafters for many years), this group can be found between 7030 and 7035 most evenings. The informal membership qualification is comfortable copy by ear at 45 WPM. No formal submission or proof is required. There have been approximately 950 members of the CFO club in approximately 30 countries, and a newsletter called "Key Clucks" is published. Members occasionally end their QSOs with a distinctive signature which sounds like a chicken's cluck. WB9LTN is currently in charge of the CFO's affairs.

Perhaps the most elite club of CW operators was the "Five Stars" club, founded by Bill Eitel, W6UF, in the 1970s. This group was as informal as the CFO group, but required CW proficiency at 80 words per minute! Paper-copy was not required to qualify for membership—merely the ability to copy by ear and correctly answer questions sent by a carefully-calibrated keyboard. Eitel stopped issuing membership certificates after qualifying 10 members, not for lack of applicants, but from lack of time. The club has not been formally active since W6UF's death in 1989, but some of the members remain active, still casually conversing on the bands at 70-80 WPM. One member still active on the bands is Florence, W7QYA, who began her high-speed CW career as an operator for the Federal Aviation Administration, on radiotelegraph circuits in Alaska.

Q SIGNALS

Given below are a number of Q signals whose meanings most often need to be expressed with brevity and clarity in amateur work. (Q abbreviations take the form of questions only when each is sent followed by a question mark.)

QRG	Will you tell me my exact frequency (or that of ____)? Your exact frequency (or that of ____) is ____ kHz.
QRH	Does my frequency vary? Your frequency varies.
QRI	How is the tone of my transmission? The tone of your transmission is ____ (1. Good; 2. Variable; 3. Bad).
QRJ	Are you receiving me badly? I cannot receive you. Your signals are too weak.
QRK	What is the intelligibility of my signals (or those of ____)? the intelligibility of your signals (or those of ____) is ____ (1. Bad; 2. Poor; 3. Fair; 4. Good; 5. Excellent).
QRL	Are you busy? I am busy (or I am busy with ____). Please do not interfere.
QRM	Is my transmission being interfered with? Your transmission is being interfered with ____ (1. Nil; 2. Slightly; 3. Moderately; 4. Severely; 5. Extremely.)
QRN	Are you troubled by static? I am trouble by static ____ (1–5 as under QRM).
QRO	Shall I increase power? Increase power.
QRP	Shall I decrease power? Decrease power.
QRQ	Shall I send faster? Send faster (____ WPM).
QRS	Shall I send more slowly? Send more slowly (____ WPM).
QRT	Shall I stop sending? Stop sending.
QRU	Have you anything for me? I have nothing for you.
QRV	Are you ready? I am ready.
QRW	Shall I inform ____ that you are calling on ____ kHz? Please inform ____ that I am calling on ____ kHz.
QRX	When will you call me again? I will call you again at ____ hours (on ____ kHz).
QRY	What is my turn? Your turn is numbered ____.
QRZ	Who is calling me? You are being called by ____ (on ____ kHz).
QSA	What is the strength of my signals (or those of ____)? The strength of your signals (or those of ____) is ____ (1. Scarcely perceptible; 2. Weak; 3. Fairly good; 4. Good; 5. Very good).
QSB	Are my signals fading? Your signals are fading.
QSD	Is my keying defective? Your keying is defective.
QSG	Shall I send ____ messages at a time? Send ____ messages at a time.
QSK	Can you hear me between your signals and if so can I break in on your transmission? I can hear you between my signals; break in on my transmission.
QSL	Can you acknowledge receipt? I am acknowledging receipt.
QSM	Shall I repeat the last message which I sent you, or some previous message? Repeat the last message which you sent me (or message[s] number[s] ____).
QSN	Did you hear me (or ____) on ____ kHz? I did hear you (or ____) on ____ kHz.
QSO	Can you communicate with ____ direct or by relay? I can communicate with ____ direct (or by relay through ____).
QSP	Will you relay to ____? I will relay to ____.
QST	General call preceding a message addressed to all amateurs and ARRL members. This is in effect "CQ ARRL."
QSU	Shall I send or reply on this frequency (or on ____ kHz)? Send a series of Vs on this frequency (or ____ kHz).
QSW	Will you send on this frequency (or on ____ kHz)? I am going to send on this frequency (or on ____ kHz).
QSX	Will you listen to ____ on ____ kHz? I am listening to ____ on ____ kHz.
QSY	Shall I change to transmission on another frequency? Change to transmission on another frequency (or on ____ kHz).
QSZ	Shall I send each word or group more than once? Send each word or group twice (or ____ times).
QTA	Shall I cancel message number ____? Cancel message number ____.
QTB	Do you agree with my counting of words? I do not agree with your counting of words. I will repeat the first letter or digit of each word or group.
QTC	How many messages have you to send? I have ____ messages for you (or for ____).
QTH	What is your location? My location is ____.
QTR	What is the correct time? The time is ____.

THE FASTEST CW OPERATOR IN HISTORY

McElroy, Theodore R. (1901–1963)

Ted McElroy is well-known among hams as a maker of telegraph keys in the 1930s and as the "World's Champion Radio Telegrapher" who set the official record of 75.2 words per minute in 1939 at a hamfest in Asheville, NC. But behind those bare facts was one of the most colorful telegraphers the world has known.

"Teddy" McElroy, as he was called by his friends, was born in Somerville, MA, on September 15, 1901. He attended the local public schools and, by age 14, was working part-time as a messenger for the Western Union. While in the seventh grade, Teddy took a typing course, at which he excelled. After attending Somerville High School for a few months, he left at age 15 to become a full-time telegraph operator.

McElroy worked at various Western Union offices around Boston and southern New Hampshire, and quickly became one of the company's best telegraphers. After World War II, he took a job with RCA at its transatlantic station on Cape Cod. Because it was a radio station, he had to learn the Continental (International Morse) code. He did so easily. This experience would have far-reaching consequences for McElroy.

RCA moved its operation to New York. Unhappy in that city, McElroy became involved in union organizing on behalf of telegraphers. He soon found himself on the street, and returned to Boston and the Western Union.

In the spring of 1922, impressed with his speed and knowing of his experience with Continental code, McElroy's boss entered him in a code receiving competition at the Boston Radio Exposition. There, in his first official contest, McElroy beat the competition and set a new world's record of 51.5 words per minute. The same year, at contests in New York and Chicago, he successfully defended his title and increased the world's record to 56.5 words per minute.

Ted married Margaret Frances Coleman of South Boston in 1925. Their only child, John Charles, was born the following year. Now a husband and father, Ted left the field of telegraphy and took jobs as a sales representative for various companies. He had not heard the code for several years when the next important code contest was announced.

The World-Wide ARRL Convention was held during the Chicago World's Fair in August, 1933. The Western Union sponsored McElroy as their entry against the best telegraphers in the world. Even without recent professional experience, McElroy put up a good fight. But it wasn't quite good enough. Both Joseph W. Chaplin, representing Press Wireless, and McElroy achieved a speed of 54.1 words per minute—but Chaplin made only five errors, while McElroy made eight. Ted's 1922 record meant he was still the world's fastest telegrapher, but he was no longer its champion.

In 1934, "T.R. McElroy" started manufacturing telegraph keys at his home in Boston. Over the next seven years, he would come up with more than a dozen different variations or models of his semi-automatic "Mac-Key" and straight keys. Perhaps his two most famous and collectible keys are the Super Stream-speed bug, with its all-chrome teardrop shaped base, and the chrome-plated teardrop "Streamkey" straight key.

In 1935, Ted attended a meeting of the Cape Cod Radio Club to demonstrate his code receiving abilities. The awed members gave him a certificate attesting to his amazing run of 77 words per minute. Showing that this was no fluke, McElroy participated in the contest held six months later in Brockton, MA. This time, Joe Chaplin was the loser and McElroy set a new record of 69 words per minute.

The next official contest was held in Asheville, NC. It was there that McElroy again beat all challengers to his title with a new record of 75.2 words per minute. It was the last official competition ever held; McElroy's record still stands today. (The world record for sending with a straight key is 35 wpm, set on November 9, 1942 by Harry A. Turner of the U.S. Army Signal Corps at Camp Crowder MO.)

McElroy was licensed as W1JYN in 1936, but it is not known if he was active on the amateur bands. During WWII, McElroy manufactured code training equipment for the military. As an promotional device, he designed his famous "Chart of Codes and Signals," which he introduced at the 1943 annual meeting of the Veteran Wireless Operators of America. Thousands of the colorful charts were given to anyone who asked. Few of those charts survive today.

McElroy made millions of dollars from his military contracts during the war and, after the war, lost it as quickly. He sold his company in 1955 and became a sales representative for an electronics company in New York. Ted McElroy died at his home in Littleton, MA, on November 12, 1963.

(Contributed by Tom French, W1IMQ. Tom is the author of McElroy: World's Champion Radio Telegrapher, *an illustrated biography available for $19.95 plus $2.00 s/h from Artifax Books, Box 88, Maynard MA 01754.)*

CW ABBREVIATIONS

AA	All After
AB	All before
ABT	About
ADR	Address
AF	Africa
AGN	Again
AM	Amplitude Modulation
AMP	Unit of Current, Power Amplifier
ANI	Any
ANT	Antenna
AS	Asia
AU	Aurora
AWDH	(See you later) GERMAN
AWS	Auf Weidersehen (Good-bye) GERMAN
BCI	Broadcast Interference
BCL	Broadcast Listener
BCNU	Be seeing you
BCP	Beaucoup (Much) FRENCH
BD	Bad
BEV	Beverage Receive Antenna
BJR	Bonjour (Hello, Good Morning) FRENCH
BK	Break, Back
BLV	Believe
BN	All between, Been,
BSR	Bonsoir (Good evening) FRENCH
BTR	Better
BUG	Semi-Automatic key
BURO	QSL Bureau
B4	Before
C	yes, centigrade, Celsius
CFM, CFMD	Confirm, Confirmed
CK	Check
CL	Closing my station
CLD, CLG	Called, calling
CNT	Cannot
CONDX	Condition
CONGRATS	Congratulations
CQ	General Call
CUAGN	See you again
CUD	Could
CUL	See you later
CUM	Come
CW	Continuous Wave
DE	From
DF	Direction Finding
DLD, DLVD	Delivered
DR	Dear
DS	Danke schon (Thanks) GERMAN
DSW	Do svidaniya (Good-bye) RUSSIAN
DUPE	QSO B4, Duplicate
DX	Long distance
ENUF	Enough
ES	And
EU	Europe
EX	Excellent, Formerly
FB	Fine Business
FER	For
FONE	Phone-Voice transmission
FM	Frequency Modulation
FOT	Frequency of optimum traffic
FREQ	Frequency
FT	Feet
GA	Go ahead-or-Good afternoon
GB	Good-bye
GD	Good day
GE	Good evening
GG	Going
GL	Good Luck
GLD	Glad

GM	Good morning
GN	Good night
GND,,GRND	Ground
GP	Ground plane vertical antenna
GUD	Good
HEJ	Hey (Cheerio) SWEDISH
HI	C.W. Laughter
HLV	Hasta La vista (See you later) SPANISH
HNY	Happy New Year
HPE	Hope
HR	Here, Hear
HRD	Heard
HV	Have
HVY	Heavy
HW	How
INFO	Information
KW	Kilowatt
LID	Poor operator
LIL	Little
LOC	Location
LP	Long path
LSB	Lower side band
LSN	Listen
LTR	Letter
LUF	Least usable frequency
M, MTRS	Meters
MA, MILS	Milliamperes
MCI	Merci (Thank you) FRENCH
MIN	Minute
MM	Multi-Operator Multi-Transmitter
MNI	Many
MOD	Modulation
MS	Meteor Scatter, Multi-operator Single-transmitter
MSG	Message
MUF	Maximum usable frequency
N	No
NA	North America
NCS	Net Control Station
NIL	No, Nothing
NR	Near, Number
NW	Now, Northwest
OB	Old Boy
OC	Old Chap
OM	Old Man
OP, OPR, OPS	Operator(s)
OT	Old timer
PA	Power/Final Amplifier
PAC	Pacific
PHONE	Telephone, Voice transmission
PKT	Packet
PSE	Please
PWR	Power
R	Received
RCD	Received
RCVR, RX	Receiver
RFI	Radio Frequency Interference
RIG	Radio, Station equipment
RPT	Repeat
RPRT	Report, Repeater
RS	Radiosputnik
RST	Readability, Strength, Tone
RTTY	RadioTeletype
SA	Say again, South America
SAE	Self-Addressed-Envelope
SAT	Saturday
SASE	Self-Addressed-Stamped-Envelope
SSB	Single Side Band, Voice
SED	Said
SHACK	Radio equiptment location
SID	Sudden Ionospheric Disturbance
SIG, SIGS	Signal(s)
SKED	Schedule
SN	Soon, Serial Number
SO	Single-Operator
SP	Short path
SRI	Sorry
STN	Station
SUM	Some
SUN	Sunday
SVP	S'il vous plait (Please) FRENCH
SWL	Short Wave Listener
TCVR, TRX	Transceiver
TEMP	Temperature
TEST	Contest
TFC	Traffic
TKS, TNX	Thanks
TMW, TMRW	Tomorrow
TU	Thank you
TVI	Television Interference
TX	Transmitter
TXT	Text
U	You
UR	You are, Your
USB	Upper side band
UTC	Coordinated Universal Time (G.M.T.)
VERT	Vertical Antenna
VFO	Variable Frequency Oscillator
VG	Very Good
VIA	QSL to (i.e. QSL VIA)
VY	Very
WID	With, Wide
WKD	Worked
WKG	Working
WL	Will
WPM	Words per minute
WUD	Would
WX	Weather
XMAS	Christmas
XMTR	Transmitter
XTAL	Crystal
XYL	Wife
YDAY	Yesterday
YL	Young Lady
55	Best Success—EASTERN EUROPE
73	Best Wishes
88	Love and Kisses

THE RST SYSTEM

Readability

1—Unreadable.
2—Barely readable, occasional words distinguishable.
3—Readable with considerable difficulty.
4—Readable with practically no difficulty.
5—Perfectly readable.

Signal Strength

1—Faint signals barely perceptible.
2—Very weak signals.
3—Weak signals.
4—Fair signals.
5—Fairly good signals.
6—Good signals.
7—Moderately good signals.
8—Strong signals.
9—Extremely strong signals.

Tone

1—Sixty-cycle AC or less, very rough and broad.
2—Very rough AC, very and broad.
3—Rough AC tone, rectified but not filtered.
4—Rough note, some trace of filtering.
5—Filtered rectified AC but strongly ripple-modulated.
6—Filtered tone, definite trace of ripple modulation.
7—Near pure tone, trace of ripple modulation.
8—Near perfect tone, slight trace of modulation.
9—Perfect tone, no trace of ripple or modulation of any kind.

The "tone" report refers only to the purity of the signal, and has no connection with its stability or freedom from clicks or chirps. If the signal has the characteristic steadiness of crystal control, add X to the report (e.g., RST 469X). If it has a chirp or "tail" (either on "make" or "break") add C (e.g., 469C). If it has clicks or noticeable other keying transients, add K (e.g., 469K). Of course, a signal could have both chirps and clicks, in which case both C and K could be used (e.g., RST 469CK).

W1AW schedule

Pacific	Mtn	Cent	East	Sun	Mon	Tue	Wed	Thu	Fri	Sat
6 am	7 am	8 am	9 am			Fast Code	Slow Code	Fast Code	Slow Code	
7 am	8 am	9 am	10 am			Code Bulletin				
8 am	9 am	10 am	11 am			Teleprinter Bulletin				
9 am	10 am	11 am	noon							
10 am	11 am	noon	1 pm		Visiting Operator Time					
11 am	noon	1 pm	2 pm							
noon	1 pm	2 pm	3 pm							
1 pm	2 pm	3 pm	4 pm	Slow Code	Fast Code	Slow Code	Fast Code	Slow Code	Fast Code	Slow Code
2 pm	3 pm	4 pm	5 pm	Code Bulletin						
3 pm	4 pm	5 pm	6 pm	Teleprinter Bulletin						
4 pm	5 pm	6 pm	7 pm	Fast Code	Slow Code	Fast Code	Slow Code	Fast Code	Slow Code	Fast Code
5 pm	6 pm	7 pm	8 pm	Code Bulletin						
6 pm	7 pm	8 pm	9 pm	Teleprinter Bulletin						
6^{45} pm	7^{45} pm	8^{45} pm	9^{45} pm	Voice Bulletin						
7 pm	8 pm	9 pm	10 pm	Slow Code	Fast Code	Slow Code	Fast Code	Slow Code	Fast Code	Slow Code
8 pm	9 pm	10 pm	11 pm	Code Bulletin						
9 pm	10 pm	11 pm	Mdnte	Teleprinter Bulletin						
9^{45} pm	10^{45} pm	11^{45} pm	12^{45} am	Voice Bulletin						

Morse Code transmissions:

requencies are 1.818, 3.5815, 7.0475, 14.0475, 18.0975, 21.0675, 28.0675 and 147.555 MHz.

low Code = practice sent at 5, 7-1/2, 10, 13 and 15 WPM.

ast Code = practice sent at 35, 30, 25, 20, 15, 13 and 10 WPM.

ode practice text is from the pages of *QST*. The source is given at the beginning of each practice session and alternate speeds within each session. For xample, "Text is from July 1992 *QST*, pages 9 and 81" indicates that the plain text is from the article on page 9 and mixed number/letter groups are rom page 81.

ode bulletins are sent at 18 WPM.

Teleprinter transmissions:

requencies are 3.625, 7.095, 14.095, 18.1025, 21.095, 28.095 and 147.555 MHz.

ulletins are send at 45.45-baud Baudot and 100 baud AMTOR, FEC Mode B. 110-baud ASCII will be sent only as time allows.

n Tuesdays and Saturdays at 6:30 P.M. Eastern time, Keplerian Elements for many amateur satellites are sent on the regular teleprinter frequencies.

Voice transmissions:

requencies are 1.855, 3.99, 7.29, 14.29, 18.16, 21.39, 28.59 and 147.555 MHz.

Miscellanea:

n Fridays, UTC, a DX bulletin replaces or is added to the regular bulletins.

V1AW is open to visitors during normal operating hours: from 1:00 P.M. until 1 A.M. on Mondays, 9 A.M. until 1 A.M. Tuesday through Friday, from P.M. to 1 A.M. on Saturday, and from 3:30 P.M. to 1 A.M. on Sundays. FCC licensed amateurs may operate the station from 1 - 4 P.M. Monday hrough Saturday. Be sure to bring your current FCC amateur license or a photocopy.

n a communications emergency, monitor W1AW for special bulletins as follows: voice on the hour, teleprinter at 15 minutes past the hour, and CW on he half hour.

leadquarters and W1AW are closed on New Year's Day, President's Day, Good Friday, Memorial Day, Independence Day, Labor Day, Thanksgiving nd the following Friday, and Christmas Day. On the first Thursday of September, Headquarters and W1AW will be closed during the afternoon.

ZONE LIST (ITU)

Prefix	Zone	Formerly
1A	28	
1S	50	
3A	27	
3B6-9	53	
3C	47	
3CØ	52	
3D2-All	56	
3DAØ	57	
3V	37	
3W	46	
3Y/B	67	
3Y/P	72	
4J1	29	
4K2	75	was UA1O
4S	41	
4U1ITU	28	
4U1VIC	28	
4U1UN	08	
4X	39	
5A	38	
5B	39	
5H	53	
5N	46	
5R	53	
5T	46	
5U	46	
5V	46	
5W	62	
5X	48	
5Z	48	
6W	46	
6Y	11	
7O	39	
7P	57	
7Q	53	
7X	37	
8P	11	
8Q	41	
8R	12	
9A	28	was YU2
9G	46	
9H	28	
9J	53	
9K	39	
9L	46	
9M2,4	54	
9M6,8	54	
9N	42	
9Q	52	
9U	52	
9V	54	
9X	52	
9Y	11	
A2	57	
A3	62	
A4	39	
A5	41	
A6	39	
A7	39	
A9	39	
AP	41	
BV	44	
BY	33,42,43,44	
C2	65	
C3	27	
C5	46	
C6	11	
C9	53	
CE	14,16	
CEØA	63	
CEØX,Z	14	
CO	11	
CN	37	
CP	12,14	
CT	37	
CT3	36	
CU	36	was CT2
CX	14	
CY9,Ø	09	
D2	52	
D4	46	
D6	53	
DA-DL	28	
DU	50	
EA	37	
EA6	37	
EA8	36	
EA9	37	
EI	27	
EL	46	
EP	40	
ES	29	
ET	48	
F	27	
FG	11	
FJ,FS	11	
FH	53	
FK	56	
FM	11	
FO/C	10	
FO	63	
FP	09	
FR	53	
FT8W	68	
FT8X	68	
FT8Z	68	
FW	62	
FY	12	
G	27	
H4	51	
HA	28	
HB	28	
HC	12	
HH	11	
HI	11	
HK	12	
HKØ/M	12	
HKØ/A	11	
HL	44	
HP	11	
HR	11	
HS	49	
HV	28	
HZ	39	
I	28	
J2	48	
J3	11	
J5	26	
J6	11	
J7	11	
J8	11	
JA	45	
JD/M	90	
JD/O	45	
JT	32,33	
JW	18	
JX	18	
JY	39	
K	06,07,08	
KC6	64	
KG4	11	
KHØ	64	
KH1	61,62	
KH2	64	

KH3	61	
KH4	61	
KH5	61	
KH6	61	
KH7	61	
KH8	62	
KH9	65	
KL7	01,02	
KP1-5	11	
LA	18	
LU	14,16	
LX	27	
LY	29	
LZ	28	
OA	12	
OD	39	
OE	28	
OH	18	
OHØ	18	
OJØ	18	
OK	28	
OM	28	
ON	27	
OX	05,75	
OY	18	
OZ	18	
P29	51	
P4	11	
P5	44	
PA	27	
PJ	11	
PY	12,13,15	
PYØ/F	13	
PYØ/P	13	
PYØ/T	15	
PZ	12	
S0	37	
S2	41	
S5	28	was YU3
S7	53	
S9	47	
SM	18	
SP	28	
ST	47,48	
SU	38	
SV,J4	28	
T2	28	
T3Ø	65	
T31	62	
T32	61,63	
T33	65	
T5	48	
T7	28	
T9	28	was YU4,4N4
TA	39	
TF	17	
TG	11	
TI	11	
TJ	47	
TK	28	
TL	47	
TN	52	
TR	52	
TT	47	
TU	46	
TZ	46	
R,UA-UI	19,20,29,30	
R2	29	was UA2
R9,Ø	20-26,30,35,75	was UA9,Ø
UR-UZ	29	was UB
EU-EW	29	was UC
4J,4K	29	was UD

4L	29	was UF
EK	29	was UG
EZ	30	was UH
UK	30	was UI
EY	30	wasUJ
UN-UQ	30	was UL
EX	30	was UM
U1	29	was UN1
ER	29	was UO
V2	11	
V3	11	
V4	11	
V5	57	
V6	65	
V7	65	
V8	54	
VE	02,03,04,09,75	
VK	55,58,59	
VK9/L	60	
VK9/W	55	
VK9/X	54	
VK9/C,K	54	
VK9/M	56	
VK9/N	60	
VKØ/H	68	
VKØ/M	60	
VP2	11	
VP5	11	
VP8/F	16	
VP8	73	
VP9	11	
VQ9	41	
VR6	63	
VS6,VR2	44	
VU	41	
VU/L	41	
VU/A	49	
XE	10	
XF4	10	
XT	46	
XU	49	
XW	49	
XX	44	
XZ	49	
YA	40	
YB	51,54	
YI	39	
YJ	56	
YK	39	
YL	29	
YN	11	
YO	28	
YS	11	
YU	28	
YV	12	
YVØ	11	
Z2	53	
Z3	28	was YU5,4N5
ZA	28	
ZB	37	
ZC	39	
ZD7	66	
ZD8	66	
ZD9	66	
ZF	11	
ZK1-3	62	
ZL	60	
ZP	14	
ZS	57	
ZS8	57	
ZS9	57	was ZS1
ZSØ	57	

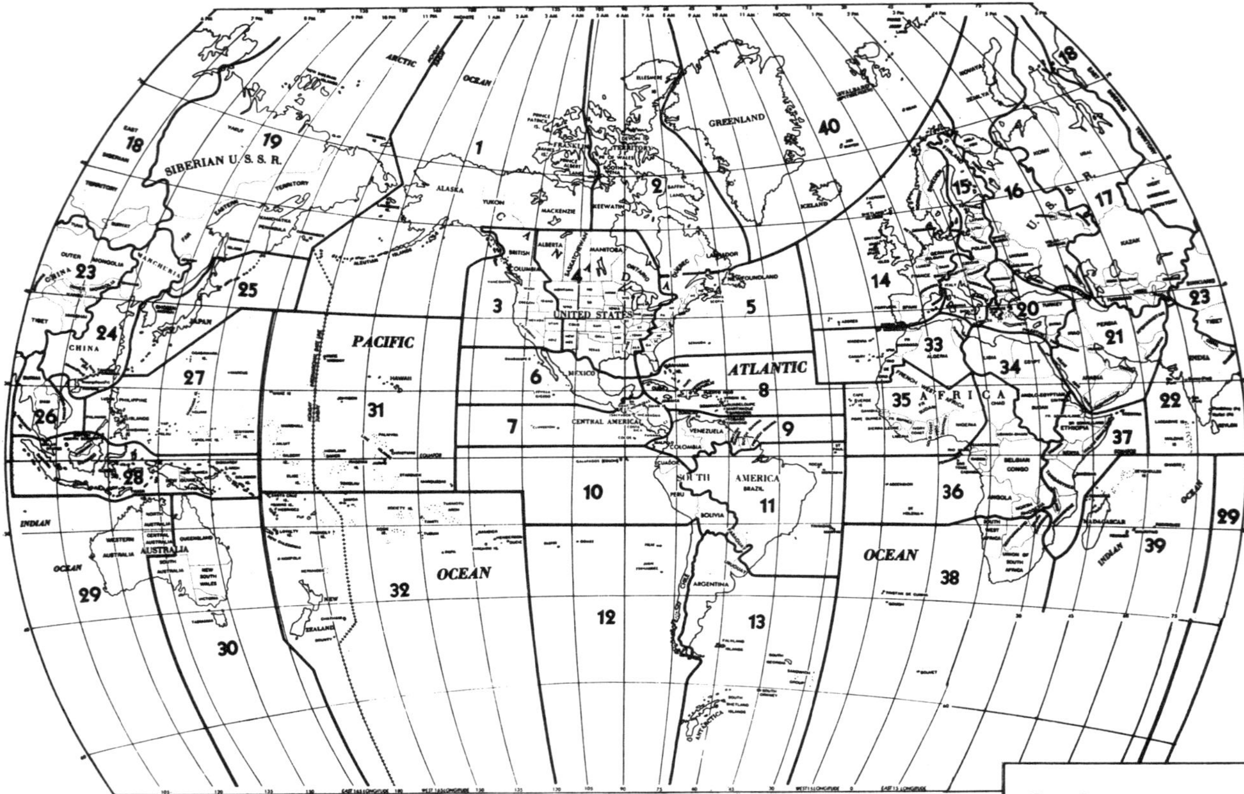

CQ DX ZONES OF THE WORLD

NOTE: This map is a reproduction of the official 1947 CQ WAZ Map, and is intended to be used for general reference only. Over the years numerous adjustments have been made to Zone boundaries for various reasons. Always consult the latest CQ WAZ Rules for the most up-to-date Zone delineations.

LATITUDE AND LONGITUDE FOR SELECTED LOCATIONS

NOTE: South Latitudes and East Longitudes are shown as negative values)

PFX	City/State/Country	LAT	LONG
A4	MUSCAT, OMAN	23.23	-58.30
AP	KARACHI, PAKISTAN	24.59	-68.56
BV	TAIPEI, TAIWAN	25.02	-121.38
BY	CHUNKING, CHINA	29.38	-107.30
BY	BEIJING, CHINA	39.55	-116.23
C2	REP.OF NAURU	-0.30	-167.00
C3	ANDORRA	42.30	-2.00
C6	NASSAU, BAHAMAS	22.05	77.20
C9	MAPUTO, MOZAMBIQUE	-26.50	-32.30
CE	SANTIAGO, CHILE	-33.26	70.40
CEØA	EASTER ISLAND	-26.50	109.00
CN	CASABLANCA, MOROCCO	33.32	7.41
CP	LAPAZ, BOLIVIA	-16.31	68.03
CT	LISBON, PORTUGAL	38.42	9.05
CU	SAO MIGUEL IS., AZORES	37.59	26.38
CX	MONTEVIDEO, URUGUAY	-34.50	56.10
D6	COMOROS	-12.30	-42.45
DJ	BONN, GERMANY	50.44	-7.06
DU	MANILA, PHILIPPINES	14.37	-121.00
EA6	BALEARIC ISLANDS	39.25	-1.28
EA8	CANARY ISLANDS	29.15	16.30
EI	DUBLIN, REP. IRELAND	53.20	6.15
ET	ADDIS ABABA, ETHIOPIA	9.00	-38.44
FT_X	KERGUELEN	-49.50	-69.30
FG	GUADELOUPE	16.40	61.10
FK	NOUMEA, NEW CALEDONIA	-22.18	-166.48
FO	CLIPPERTON ISL.	11.00	110.00
FO	PAPEETE, POLYNESIA	-17.30	149.30
FP	ST. PIERRE & MIQUELON	46.47	56.11
FR	REUNION	-21.06	-55.36
FY	CAYENNE, FR. GUIANA	4.56	52.18
G	LONDON, ENGLAND	51.30	0.07
HA	BUDAPEST, HUNGARY	47.30	-19.05
HC	QUITO, ECUADOR	-0.17	78.32
HC8	GALAPAGOS ISLS.	-0.17	92.00
HP	PANAMA CITY, PANAMA	8.35	81.08
HS	BANGKOK, THAILAND	13.50	-100.29
I	ROME, ITALY	41.52	-12.37
JA	TOKYO, JAPAN	35.41	-139.44
JD	MINAMI TORI-SHIMA	24.00	-155.00
JT	ULAN BATOR, MONGOLIA	47.56	-107.00
JW	SVALBARD	77.00	-20.00
KC4	McMURDO, ANTARCTICA	-78.00	-167.00
KC6	W. CAROLINE ISL.	9.00	-138.20
KH6	HILO, HAWAII	19.44	155.01
KL7	FAIRBANKS, ALASKA	64.50	147.48
KL7	JUNEAU, ALASKA	58.25	134.30
KP2	VIRGIN ISLANDS	18.15	64.00
LA	OSLO, NORWAY	59.56	-10.41
LZ	SOFIA, BULGARIA	42.43	-23.20
OH	HELSINKI, FINLAND	60.10	-24.53
OX	GODTHAAB, GREENLAND	64.10	51.32
P2	MADANG P.N.G.	-5.15	-145.45
PY	RIO DE JANEIRO, BRAZIL	-22.50	43.20
PY	NATAL, BRAZIL	-6.00	35.13
SU	CAIRO, EGYPT	30.00	-31.17
T3	CENTRAL KIRIBATI	-4.00	171.00
T5	MOGADISHU, SOMALIA	2.08	-45.22
TA	ANKARA, TURKEY	39.55	-32.50
TF	REYKJAVIK, ICELAND	64.09	21.39
TJ	YAOUNDE, CAMEROON	3.52	-11.31
TT	FT.LAMY, CHAD	12.07	-15.03
UA3	MOSCOW, EUR. RUSSIA	55.45	-37.37
4K2	FRANZ JOSEF LAND	81.32	-40.00
UA9	NOVOSIBIRSK, RUSSIA	55.09	-82.58
UA9	PERM, ASIATIC RUSSIA	58.00	-56.15
UAØ	KHABAROVSK, AS. RUSSIA	48.35	-135.12
UAØ	YAKUTSK, AS. RUSSIA	62.13	-129.49
UAØ	MAGADAN, AS. RUSSIA	59.28	-143.32
UAØ	USTOLENEK, AS. RUSSIA	72.52	-120.15
UD6	BAKU, AZERBAIJAN	40.28	-49.45
UH8	ASHKHABAD, TURKOMAN	39.45	-58.13
UN7	ALMA-ATA KAZAKH	43.19	-77.08
V3	BELIZE, BELIZE	17.31	88.10
V85	BRUNEI	5.00	-114.59
VE1	Halifax, N.S.	44.39	63.36
VE2	Quebec City, Que.	46.49	71.13
VE3	Ottawa, Ont.	46.05	77.20
VE4	Winnipeg, Mb.	49.53	97.09
VE5	Regina, Sk.	50.25	104.39
VE6	Edmondton, Al.	53.33	113.28
VE7	Prince Rupert, B.C.	54.19	130.19
VE8	Yellowknife, NWT	62.29	114.38
VO2	Goose Bay, Labrador	53.19	60.33
VY1	Whitehorse, Yukon	60.39	135.01
VK1	CANBERRA, AUSTRALIA	-35.21	-149.10
VK4	BRISBANE, AUSTRALIA	-27.30	-153.10
VK6	PERTH, AUSTRALIA	-31.50	-116.10
VK8	DARWIN, AUSTRALIA	-12.25	-131.00
VK9	COCOS (KEELING) IS.	-11.50	-90.50
VK9	NORFOLK ISLAND	-27.10	-166.50
VKØ	MACQUARIE ISLAND	-54.36	-158.45
VP8	FALKLAND ISLANDS	-50.45	61.00
VP8	SO. SANDWICH IS.	-58.00	27.00
VP8	SO. SHETLAND IS.	-62.00	58.50
VP9	BERMUDA	32.20	64.45
VQ9	DIEGO GARCIA CHAGOS	-7.30	-72.40
VR6	PITCAIRN IS.	-24.30	133.00
VU7	ANDAMAN IS.	11.38	-92.17
VU7	LACCADIVE IS.	11.00	-73.02
WØ	Denver, CO	39.44	104.59
WØ	DesMoines, IA	41.35	93.37
WØ	Topeka, KS	39.02	95.41
WØ	Minneapolis, MN	44.58	93.15
WØ	Jefferson City, MO	38.34	92.10
WØ	Lincoln, NE	40.49	96.43
WØ	Bismark, ND	46.48	100.46
WØ	Pierre, SD	44.22	100.20

W1	Augusta, ME	44.19	69.42
W1	Boston, MA	42.15	71.07
W1	Concord, NH	43.10	71.30
W1	Hartford, CT	41.45	72.40
W1	Montpelier, VT	44.20	72.35
W1	Providence, RI	41.50	71.23
W2	Albany, NY	42.40	73.50
W2	Trenton, NJ	40.13	74.46
W3	Dover, DE	39.10	76.30
W3	Harrisburg, PA	40.15	76.50
W3	Washington, D.C.	38.50	77.00
W4	Atlanta, GA	33.45	84.23
W4	Columbia, SC	34.00	81.00
W4	Frankfort, KY	38.10	84.55
W4	Montgomery, AL	32.23	86.17
W4	Nashville, TN	36.10	86.48
W4	Raleigh, NC	35.45	78.39
W4	Richmond, VA	37.35	77.30
W4	Tallahassee, FL	30.25	84.17
W5	Austin, TX	30.15	97.42
W5	Baton Rouge, LA	30.28	91.10
W5	Jackson, MS	32.17	90.10
W5	Little Rock, AR	34.42	92.16
W5	Oklahoma City, OK	35.27	97.32
W5	SantaFe, NM	35.10	106.00
W6	Los Angeles, CA	34.00	118.15
W6	San Francisco, CA	37.45	122.26
W7	Boise, ID	43.38	116.12
W7	Carson City, NV	39.10	119.45
W7	Cheyenne, WY	41.10	104.49
W7	Olympia, WA	47.02	122.52
W7	Phoenix, AZ	3.30	112.00
W7	Salem, OR	44.55	123.03
W7	Salt Lake City, UT	40.45	111.52
W8	Charleston, WV	38.20	81.35
W8	Columbus, OH	40.00	83.00
W8	Lansing, MI	42.45	84.35
W9	Indianapolis, IN	39.45	86.08
W9	Madison, WI	43.05	89.23
W9	Springfield, IL	39.45	89.37
XE1	MEXICO CITY, MEXICO	19.28	99.09
XW	VIENTIANE, LAOS	18.07	-102.33
YA	KABUL, AFGHANISTAN	34.39	-69.14
YB	JAKARTA, INDONESIA	-6.17	-106.45
ZD8	ASCENSION IS.	-8.00	13.00
ZD9	TRISTAN DA CUNHA	-35.30	12.15
ZF	CAYMAN IS.	19.30	80.30
ZL1	AUCKLAND, NEW ZEALAND	-36.53	-174.45
ZL4	DUNEDIN, NEW ZEALAND	-45.48	-170.32
ZP	ASUNCION, PARAGUAY	-25.25	57.30
ZS1	CAPETOWN, SO. AFRICA	-33.48	-18.28
ZS8	Pr. EDWARD & MARION	-46.36	-37.57
1S	SPRATLY IS.	8.38	-111.54
3V	TUNIS, TUNISIA	36.59	-10.06
3Y	BOUVET IS.	-54.26	-3.24
3Y	PETER 1ST IS.	-68.00	91.00
4U	UNITED NATIONS HQ	40.40	73.58
4X	ISRAEL	32.40	-34.00
5R	TANANARIVE, MALAGASY	-18.51	-47.40
5W	WESTERN SAMOA	-14.30	172.00
5Z	NAIROBI, KENYA	-1.17	-36.49
6W	DAKAR, SENEGAL	14.40	17.26
7O	ADEN, YEMEN P. DEM.	12.48	-45.00
7P	LESOTHO	-29.45	-28.07
8Q	MALDIVE IS.	4.30	-71.30
9G	ACCRA, GHANA	5.33	0.13
9J	LUSAKA, ZAMBIA	-15.25	-28.17
9K	KUWAIT	29.00	-48.45
9N	KATMANDU, NEPAL	27.49	-85.21
9Q	KINSHASA, ZAIRE	-4.18	-15.18
9V	SINGAPORE	1.22	-103.45
9X	RWANDA	-2.10	-29.37
9Y	TRINIDAD	10.00	61.00

HOW TO DETERMINE YOUR GRID SQUARE WITHOUT A MAP.

You will need your longitude and latitude rounded up to the nearest minute. Save the number obtained from each step, for it will be used in the next.

First use your longitude:

1. Convert the minutes portion of the longitude from minutes to decimal by dividing by 60.

2. For North America and locations of West longitude, subtract your longitude from 180 degrees. For location of East longitude, add 180 degrees.

3. Next divide this value by 20. The whole number result will be used to determine the first digit of your Grid, as follows:

0=A, 1=B, 2=C thru to 18=R .

4. For the the third digit, multiply this last number by 10. The digit immediately before the decimal point is the third digit of your Grid.

5. Use only the decimal portion of this last number and multiply by 24. The digit immediately before the decimal point is used to determine the fifth digit of your Grid.

0=A, B=1, C=2, thru to X=24.

Now use your Latitude:

1. If your Latitude is North, add 90. If your latitude is South, subtract your latitude from 90.

2. Divide this number by 10. The whole number result will be used to determine the second digit of your Grid, as follows:

0=A, B=1, C=2 thru to 18=R.

3. Now, multiply this number by 10. The digit immediately before the decimal point is the fouth digit of your Grid.

4. Use only the decimal portion of this last number and multiply by 24. The digit immediately before the decimal point is used to determine the sixth digit of your Gird, as follows:

0=A, 1=B, 2=C thru to 18=R.

This completes your Six digit Grid Location.

Expressed in another form:

Longitude = (20A + 2C + E/12) Degrees East.

Latitude = (10B + 1D + F/24) Degrees North

Grid Locator of "ABCDEF," where C and D are numbers and A, B, E and F are represented as letters.

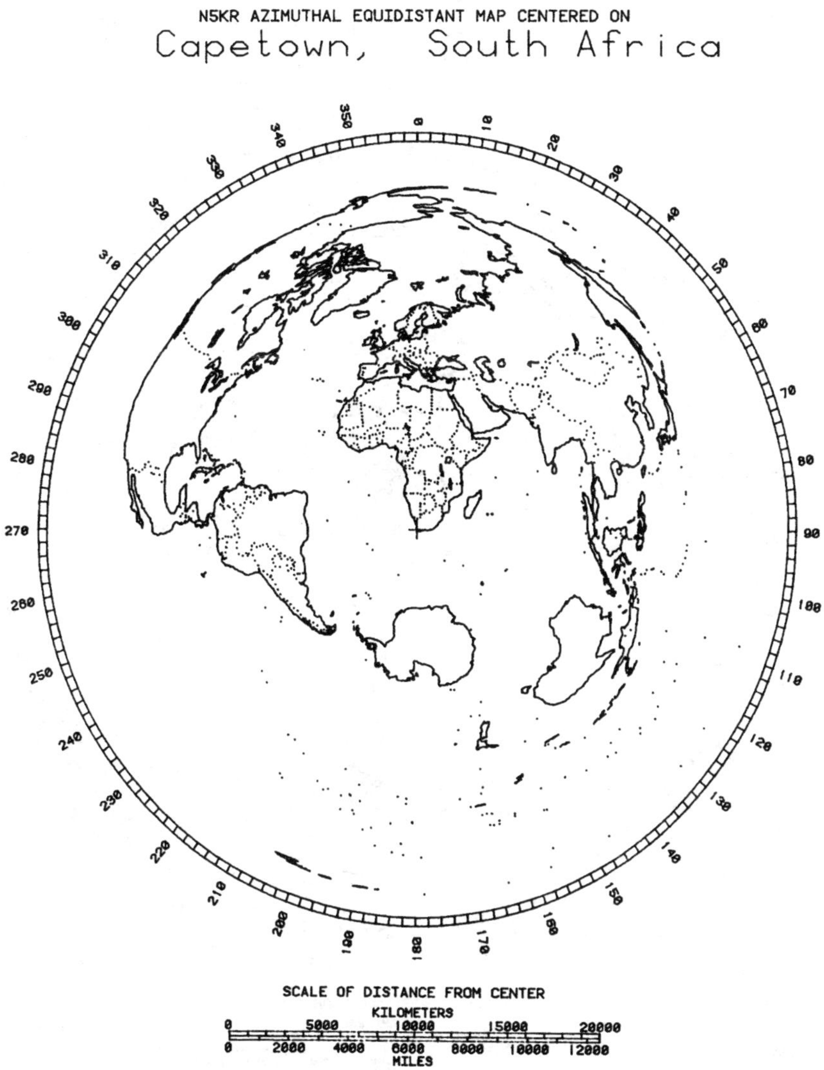
N5KR AZIMUTHAL EQUIDISTANT MAP CENTERED ON
Capetown, South Africa
SCALE OF DISTANCE FROM CENTER
KILOMETERS
0 5000 10000 15000 20000
0 2000 4000 6000 8000 10000 12000
MILES

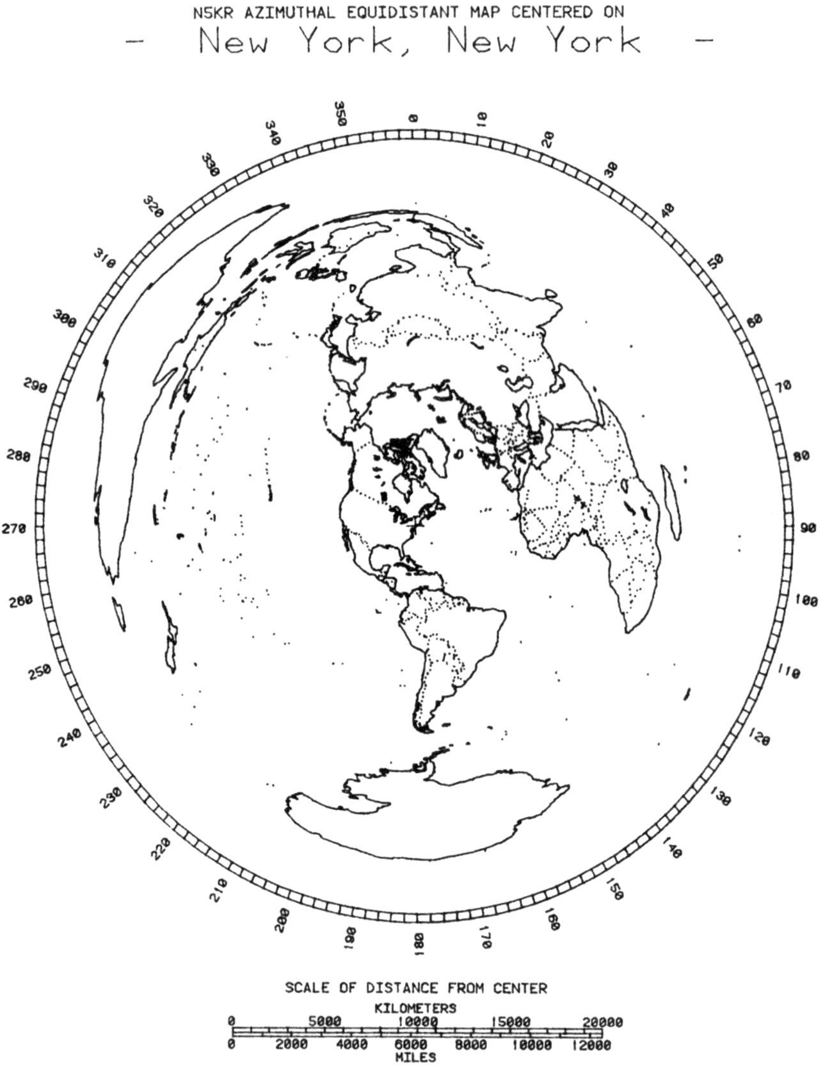
N5KR AZIMUTHAL EQUIDISTANT MAP CENTERED ON
- New York, New York -
SCALE OF DISTANCE FROM CENTER
KILOMETERS
0 5000 10000 15000 20000
0 2000 4000 6000 8000 10000 12000
MILES

N5KR AZIMUTHAL EQUIDISTANT MAP CENTERED ON

— Miami, Florida —

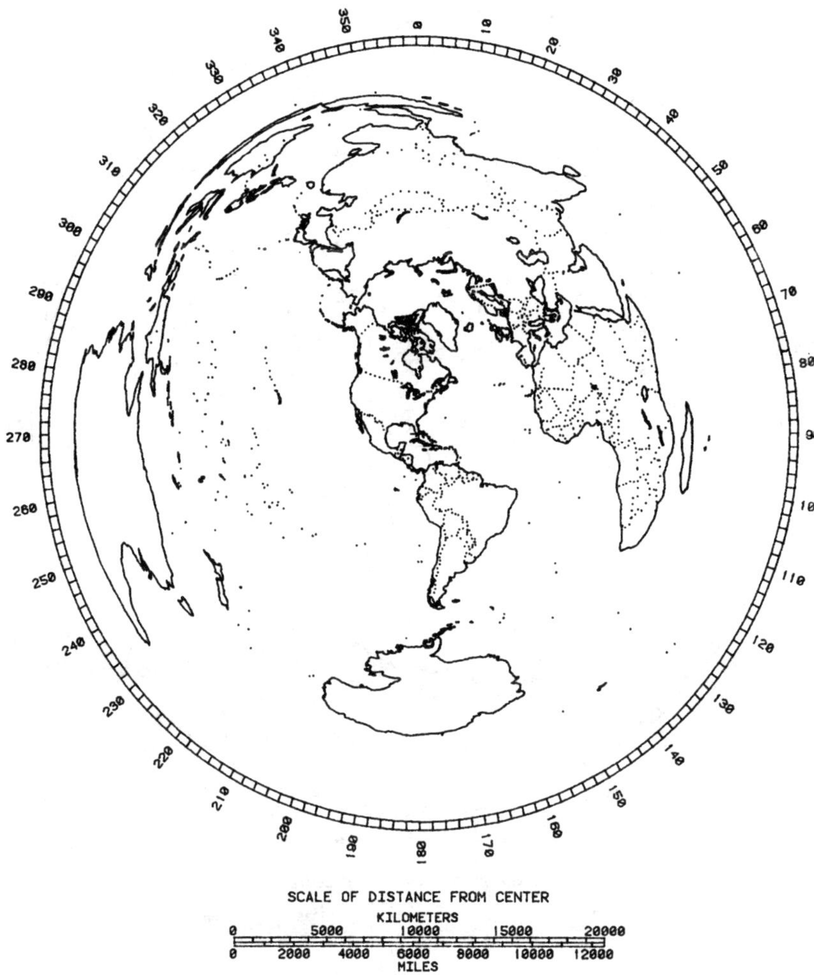

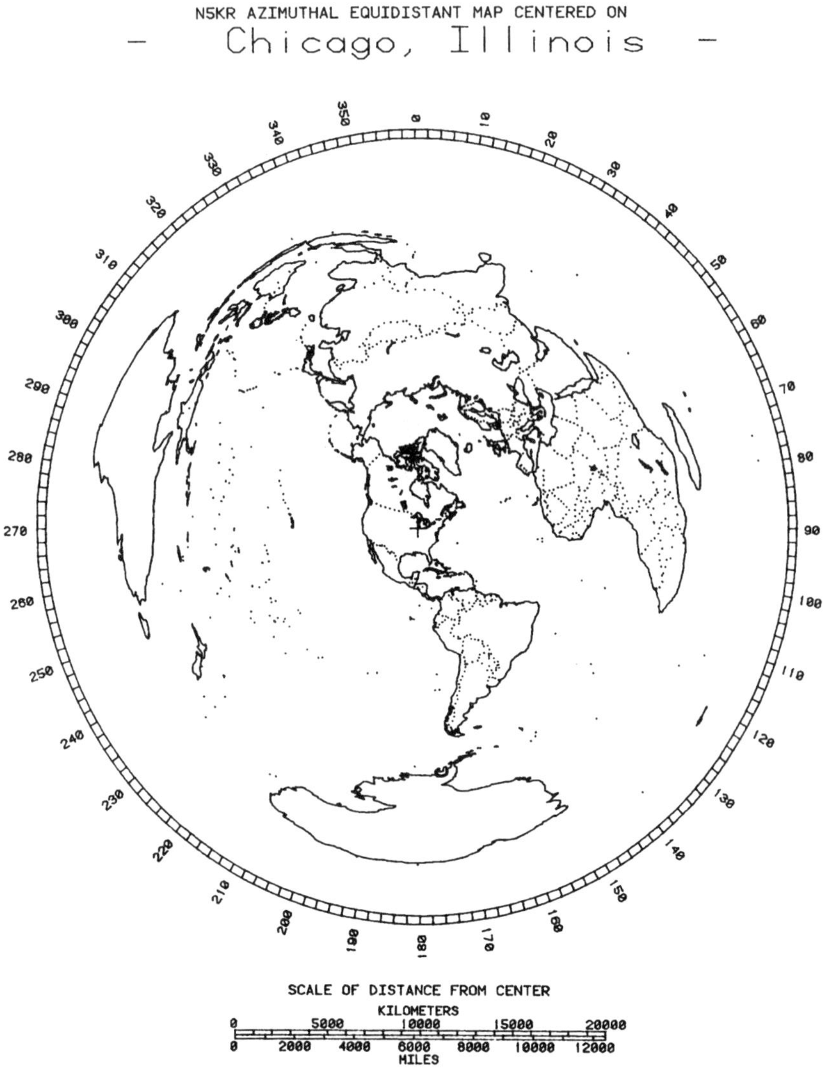
N5KR AZIMUTHAL EQUIDISTANT MAP CENTERED ON
- Chicago, Illinois -
0
10
20
30
40
50
60
70
80
90
100
110
120
130
140
150
160
170
180
190
200
210
220
230
240
250
260
270
280
290
300
310
320
330
340
350
SCALE OF DISTANCE FROM CENTER
KILOMETERS
0 5000 10000 15000 20000
0 2000 4000 6000 8000 10000 12000
MILES

N5KR AZIMUTHAL EQUIDISTANT MAP CENTERED ON

— Dallas, Texas —

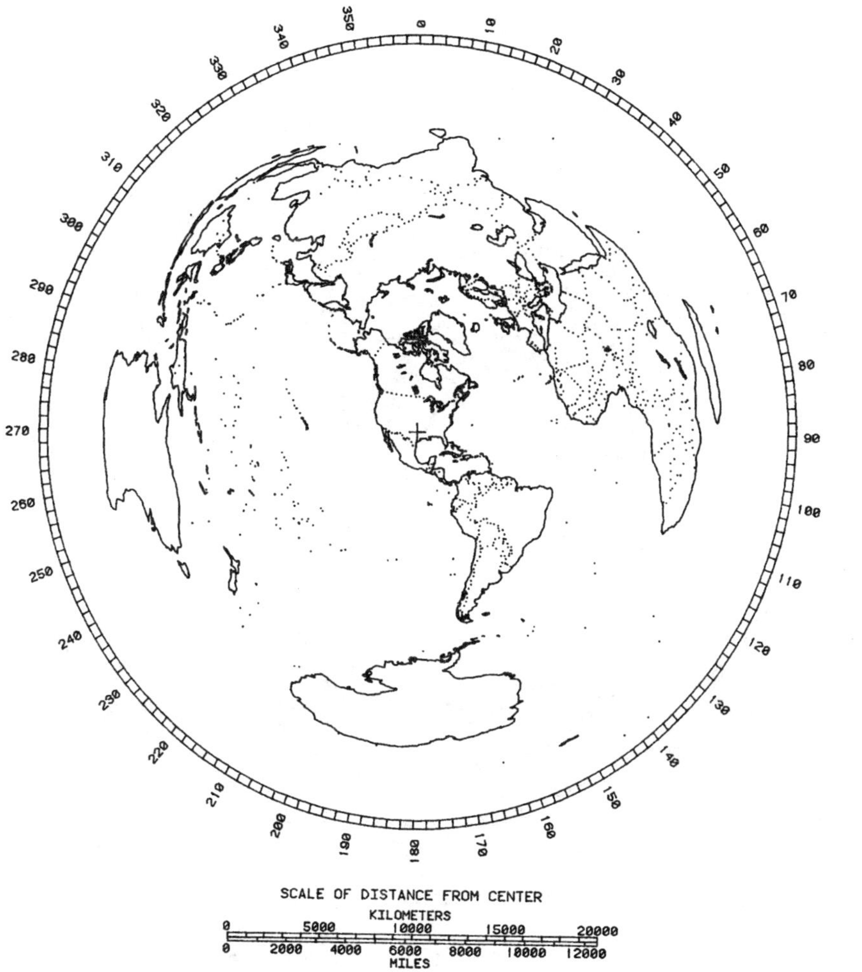

N5KR AZIMUTHAL EQUIDISTANT MAP CENTERED ON
- Seattle, Washington -
0
10
20
30
40
50
60
70
80
90
100
110
120
130
140
150
160
170
180
190
200
210
220
230
240
250
260
270
280
290
300
310
320
330
340
350
SCALE OF DISTANCE FROM CENTER
KILOMETERS
0 5000 10000 15000 20000
0 2000 4000 6000 8000 10000 12000
MILES

N5KR AZIMUTHAL EQUIDISTANT MAP CENTERED ON

– San Francisco, CA –

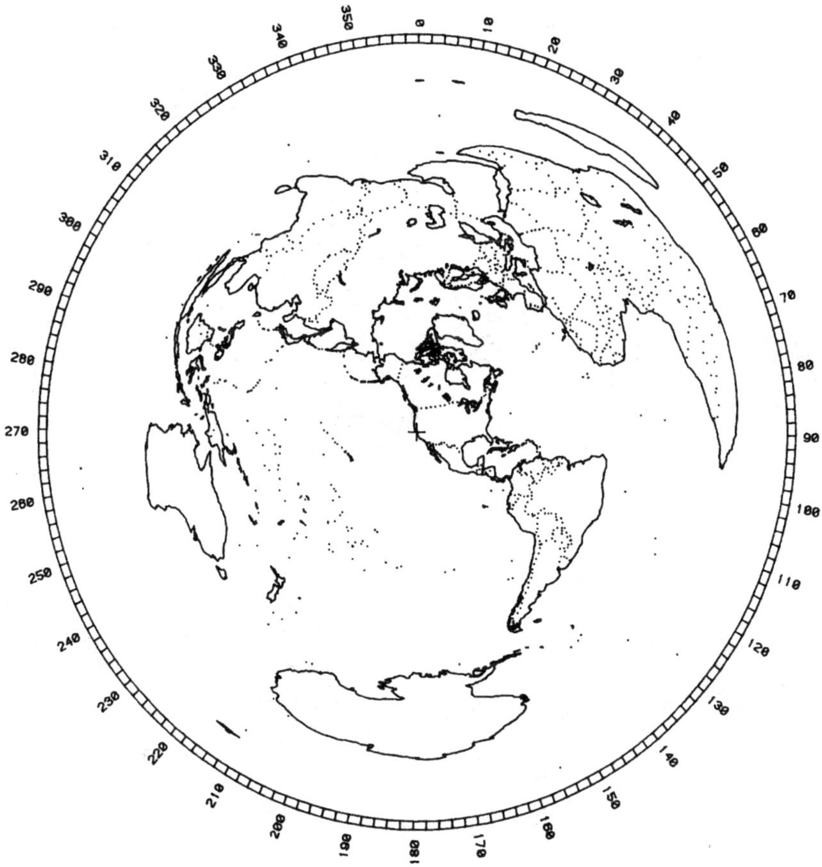

SCALE OF DISTANCE FROM CENTER

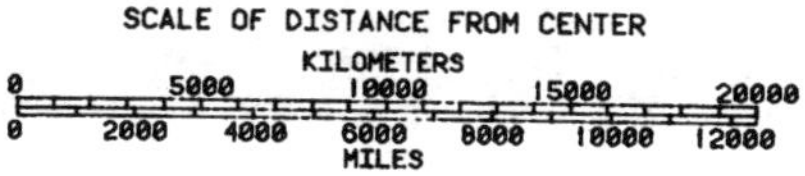

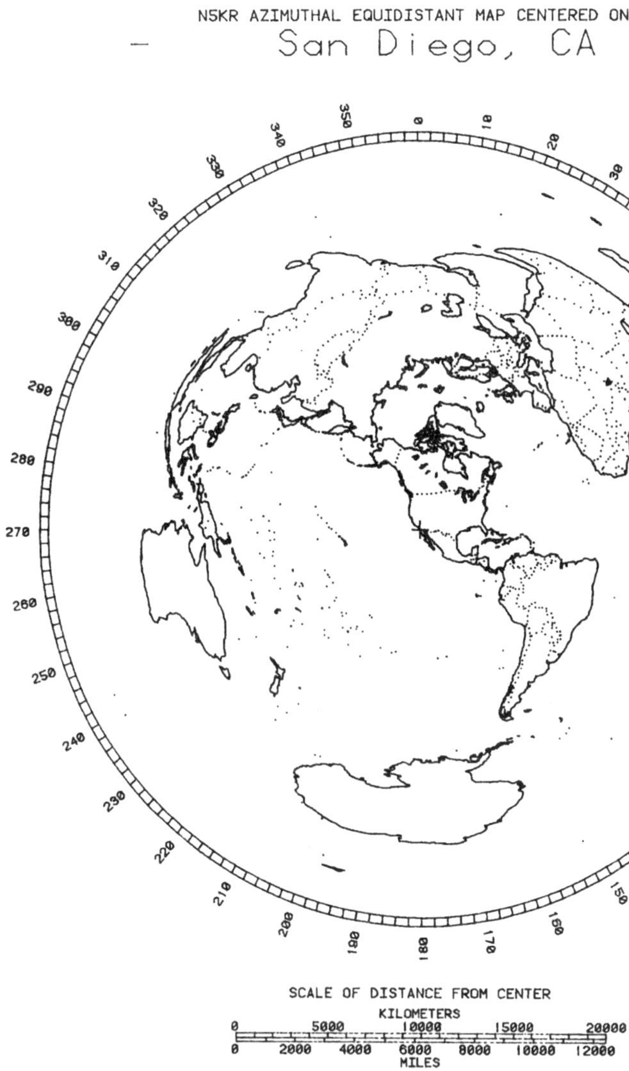
N5KR AZIMUTHAL EQUIDISTANT MAP CENTERED ON
San Diego, CA
0
10
20
30
40
50
60
70
80
90
100
110
120
130
140
150
160
170
180
190
200
210
220
230
240
250
260
270
280
290
300
310
320
330
340
350
SCALE OF DISTANCE FROM CENTER
KILOMETERS
0 5000 10000 15000 20000
0 2000 4000 6000 8000 10000 12000
MILES

N5KR AZIMUTHAL EQUIDISTANT MAP CENTERED ON

— Denver, Colorado —

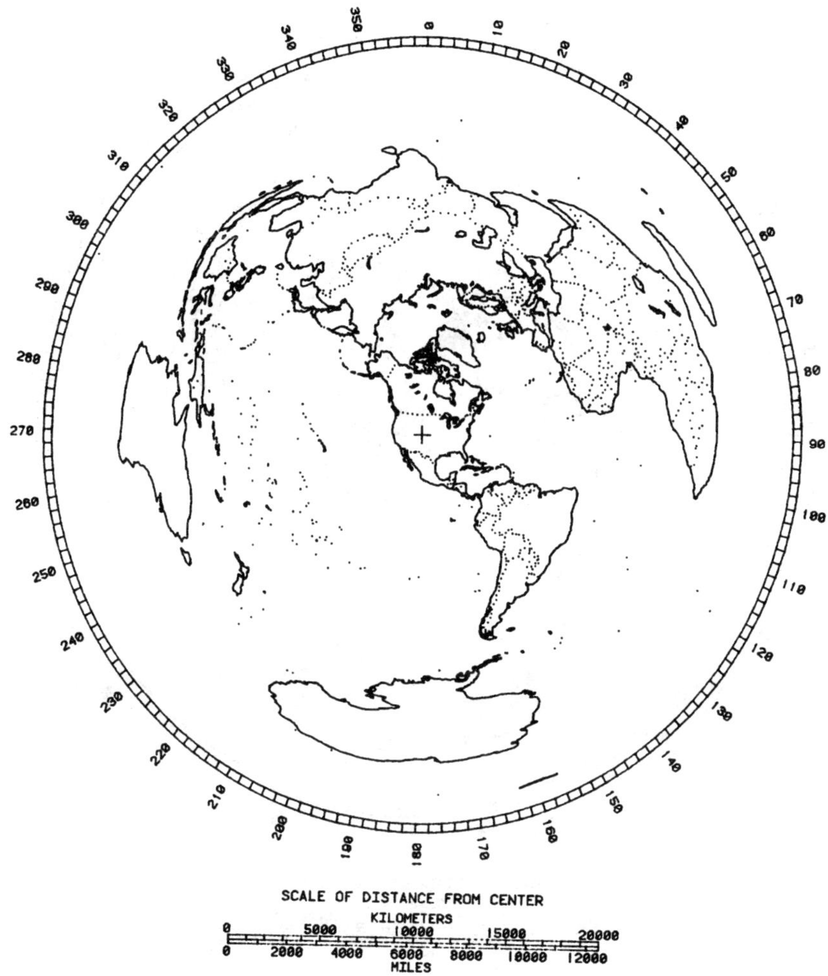

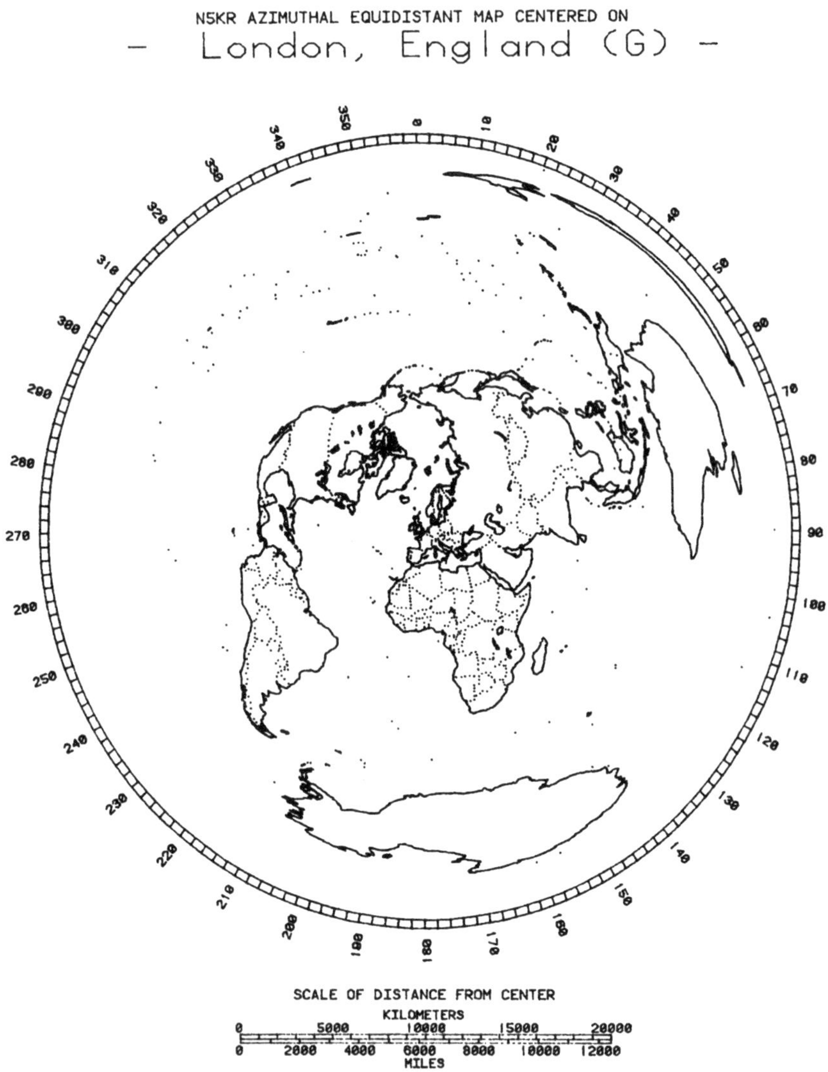
N5KR AZIMUTHAL EQUIDISTANT MAP CENTERED ON
- London, England (G) -
0
10
20
30
40
50
60
70
80
90
100
110
120
130
140
150
160
170
180
190
200
210
220
230
240
250
260
270
280
290
300
310
320
330
340
350
SCALE OF DISTANCE FROM CENTER
KILOMETERS
0 5000 10000 15000 20000
0 2000 4000 6000 8000 10000 12000
MILES

N5KR AZIMUTHAL EQUIDISTANT MAP CENTERED ON

– Rome, Italy (I0) –

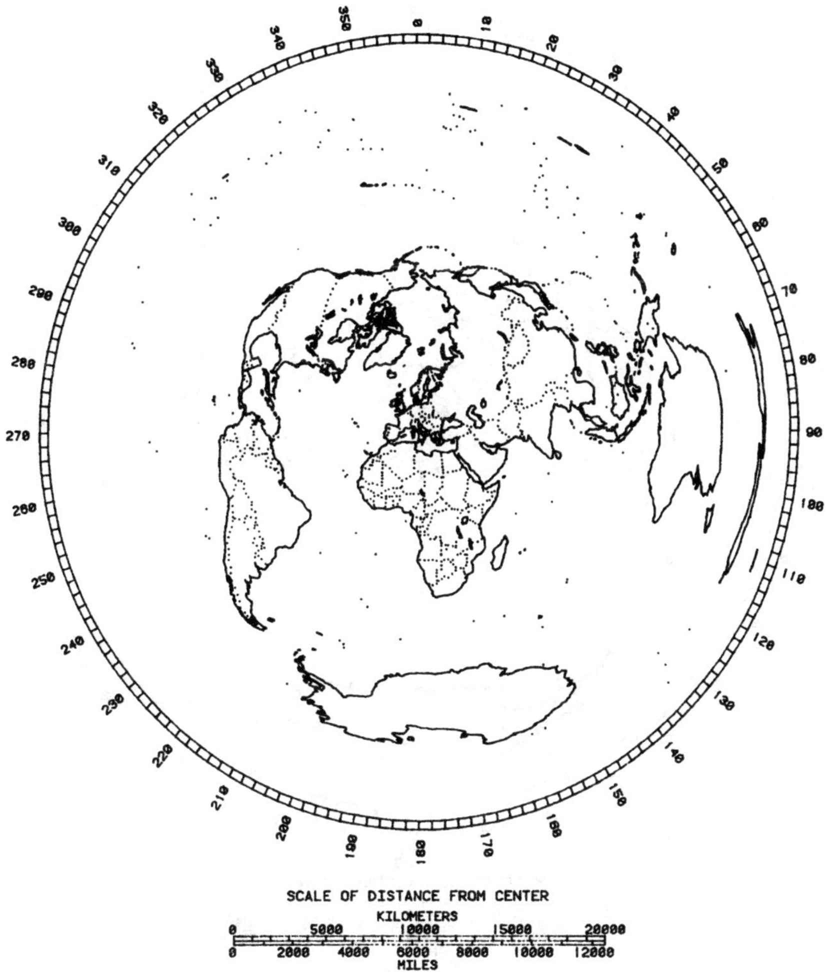

N5KR AZIMUTHAL EQUIDISTANT MAP CENTERED ON

- Moscow, Russia (UA3) -

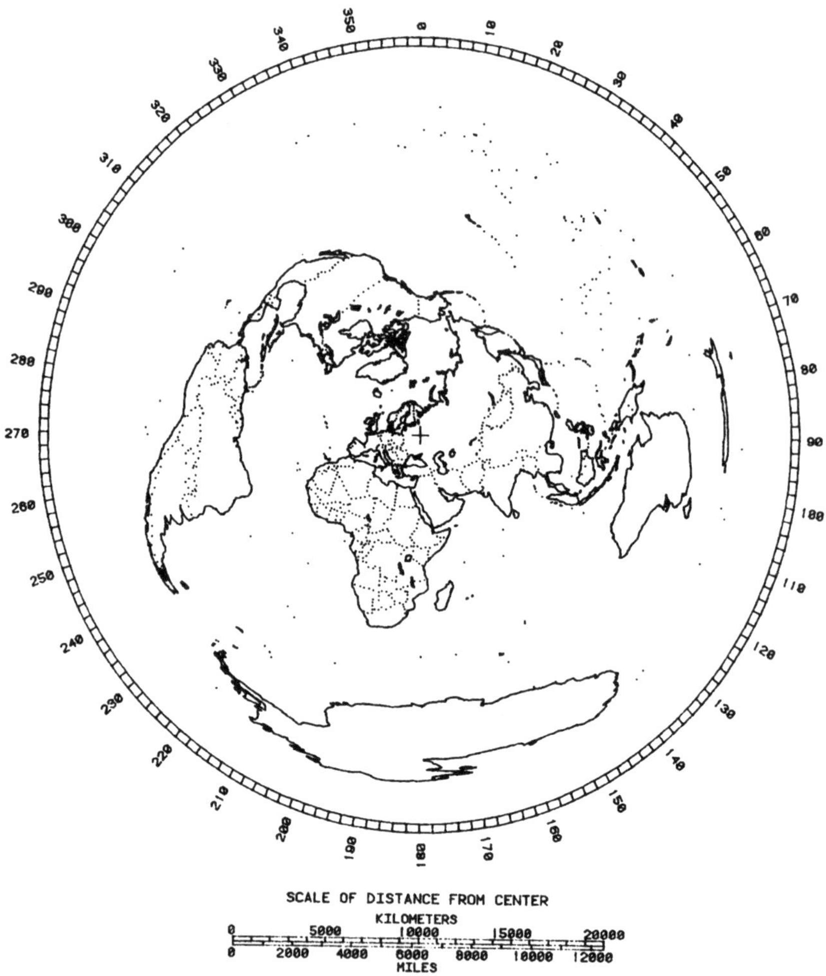

N5KR AZIMUTHAL EQUIDISTANT MAP CENTERED ON

- Tokyo, Japan (JA1) -

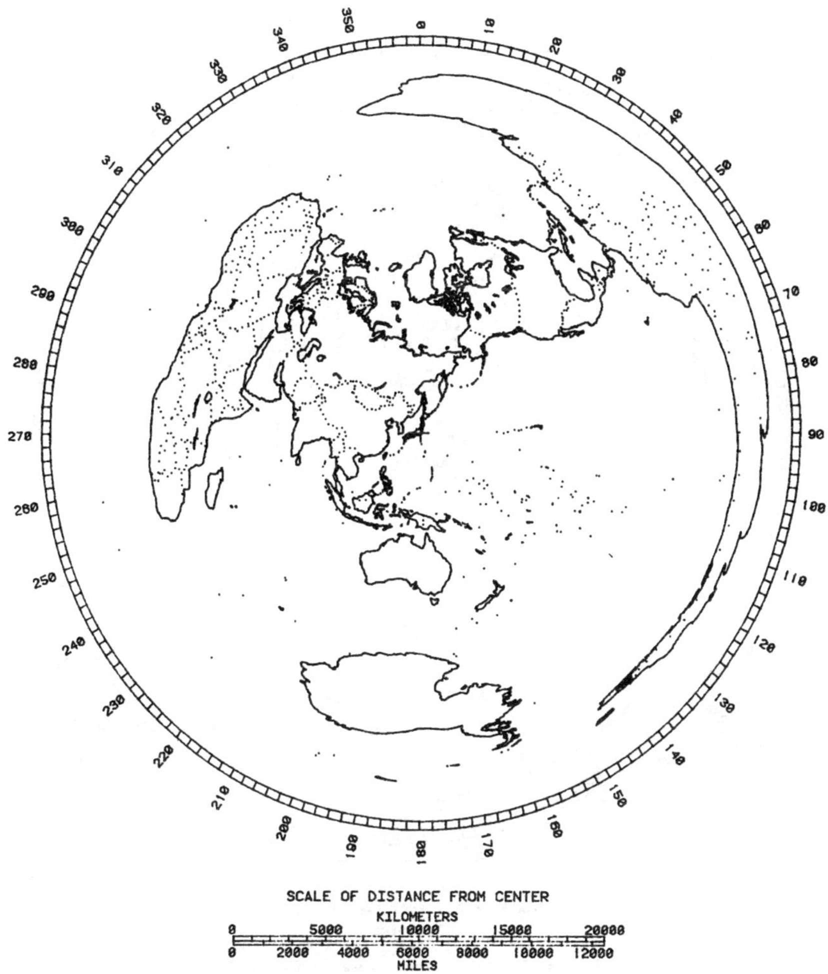

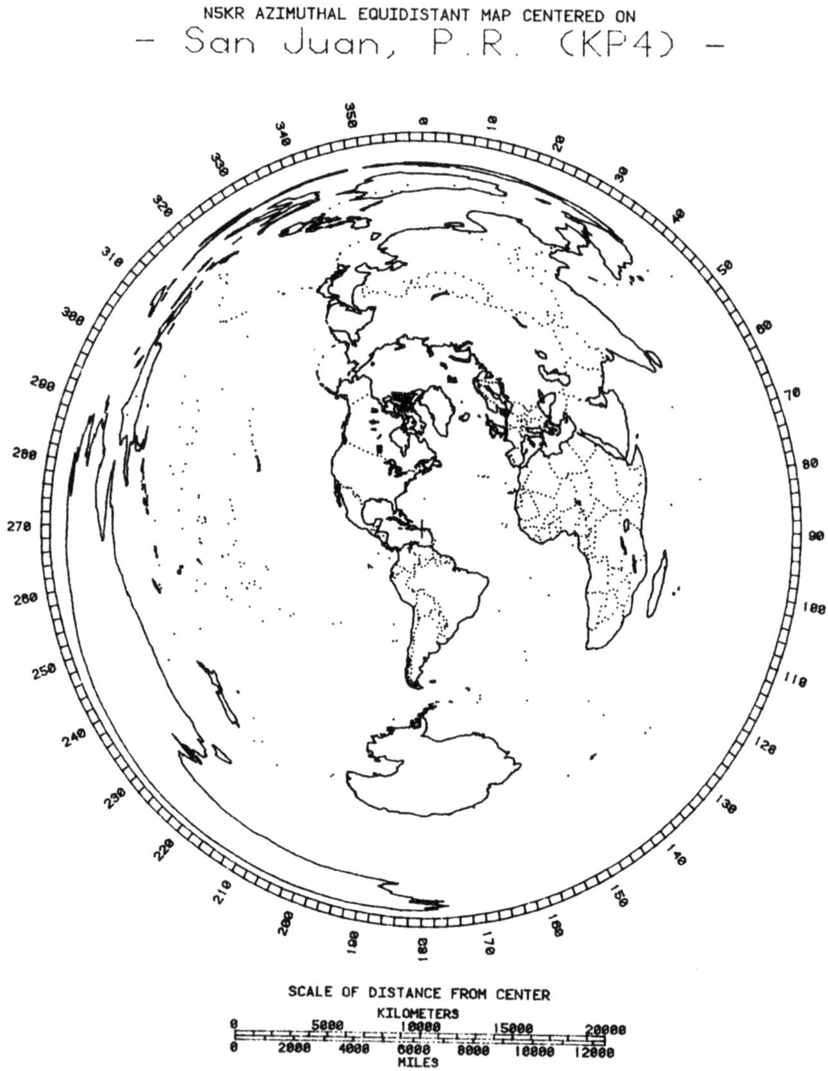
N5KR AZIMUTHAL EQUIDISTANT MAP CENTERED ON
- San Juan, P.R. (KP4) -
SCALE OF DISTANCE FROM CENTER
KILOMETERS
0 5000 10000 15000 20000
0 2000 4000 6000 8000 10000 12000
MILES

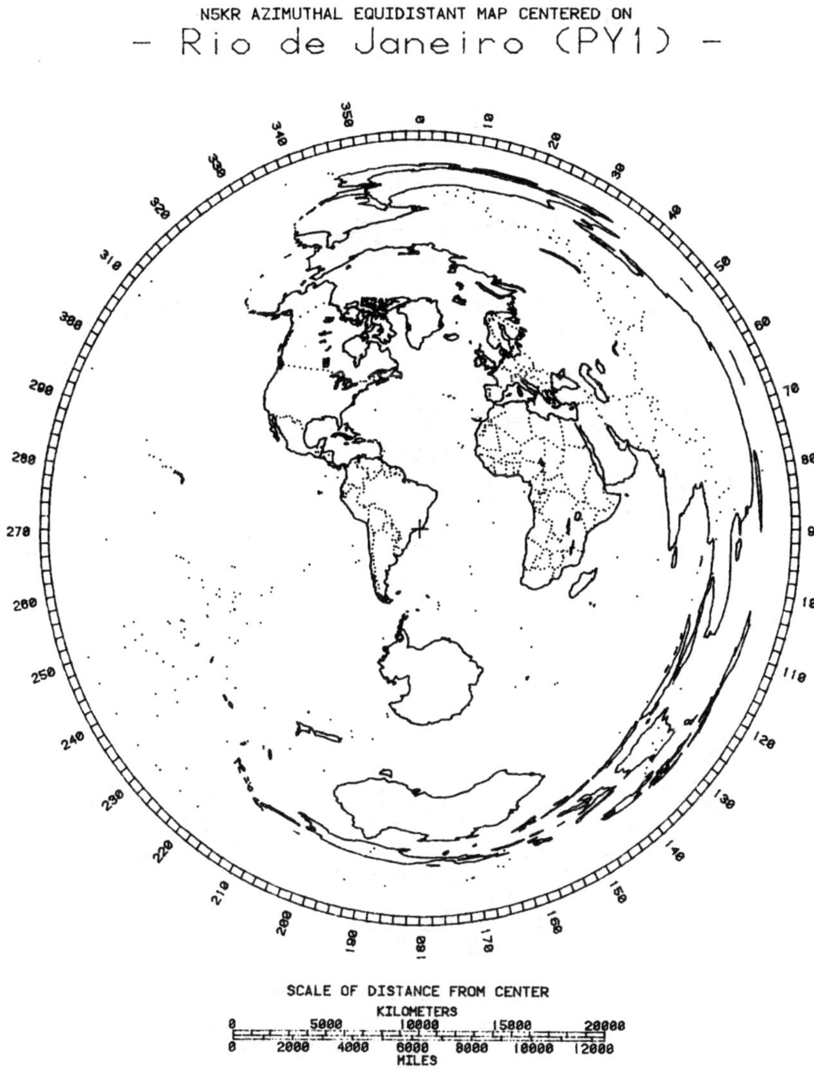
N5KR AZIMUTHAL EQUIDISTANT MAP CENTERED ON
- Rio de Janeiro (PY1) -
0
10
20
30
40
50
60
70
80
90
100
110
120
130
140
150
160
170
180
190
200
210
220
230
240
250
260
270
280
290
300
310
320
330
340
350
SCALE OF DISTANCE FROM CENTER
KILOMETERS
0 5000 10000 15000 20000
0 2000 4000 6000 8000 10000 12000
MILES

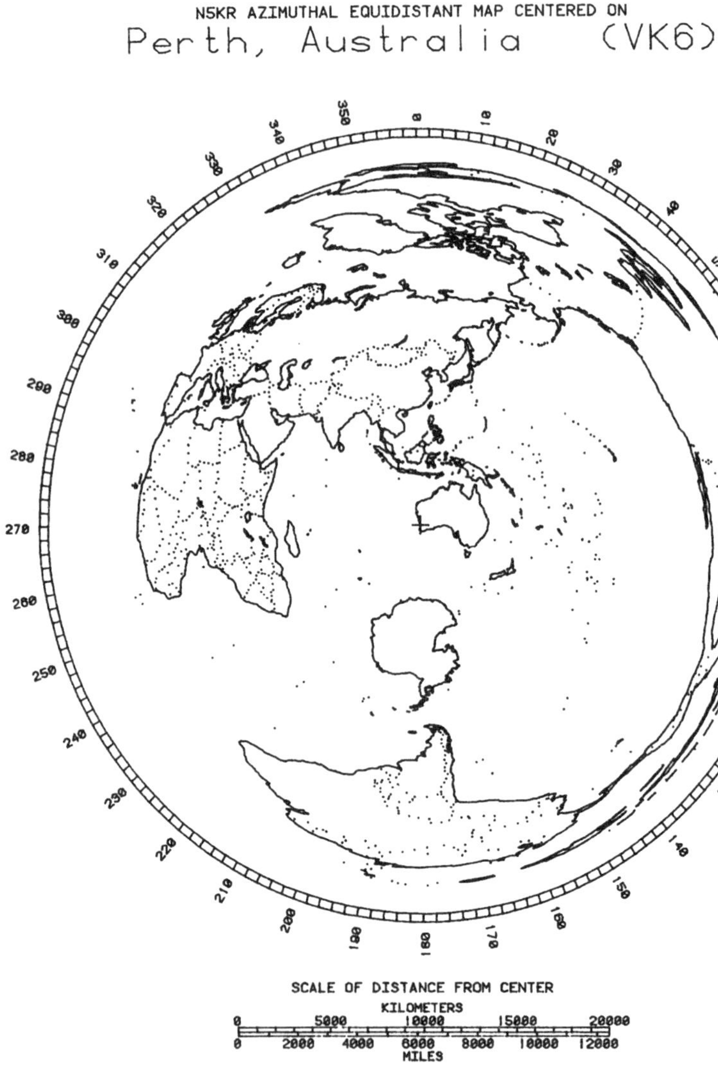
N5KR AZIMUTHAL EQUIDISTANT MAP CENTERED ON
Perth, Australia (VK6)
SCALE OF DISTANCE FROM CENTER
KILOMETERS
0 5000 10000 15000 20000
0 2000 4000 6000 8000 10000 12000
MILES

N5KR AZIMUTHAL EQUIDISTANT MAP CENTERED ON

Melbourne, Australia VK3

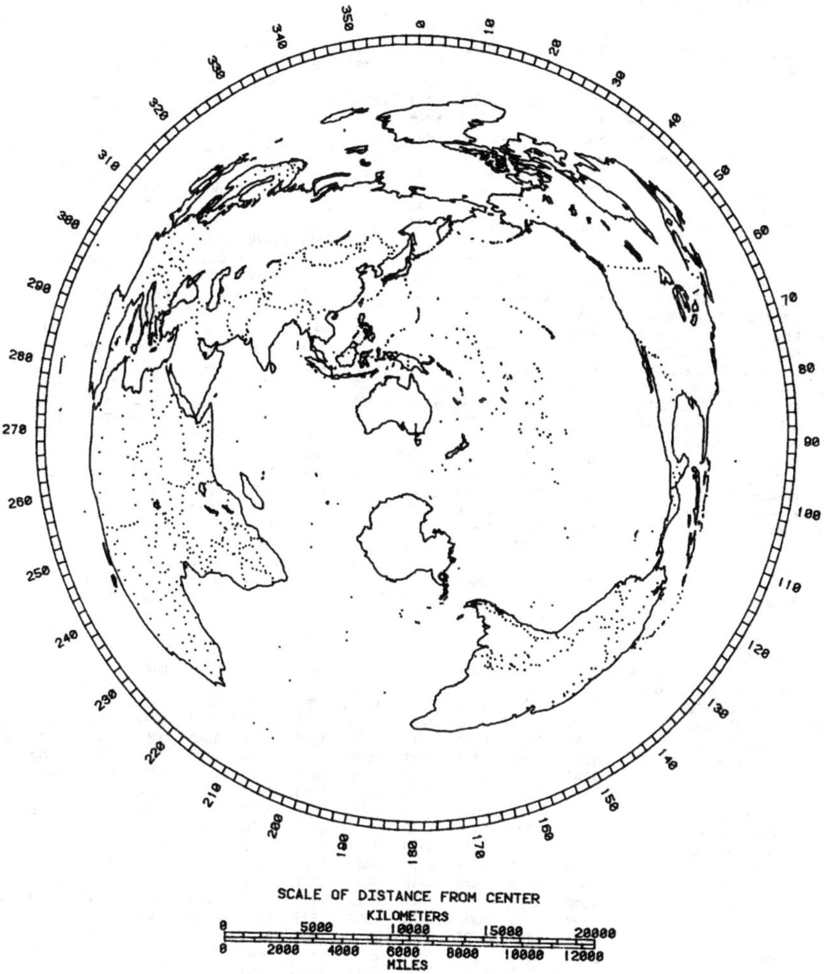

		A4	BY	CE	CT	CU	CX	DU	FO	FY	G	HA	HC
A4	MUSCAT OMAN	0	3522	9294	4044	4985	8475	4095	10594	7380	3627	2727	9137
BY	PEKING CHINA	3522	0	11834	6000	6562	11889	1768	7211	9249	5053	4554	9534
CE	SANTIAGO CHILE	9294	11834	0	6350	5682	832	10937	4908	2907	7246	7857	2344
CT	LISBON PORTUGAL	4043	6000	6350	0	950	5900	7537	9622	3566	983	1533	5128
CU	SAO MIGUEL IS AZORES	4984	6562	5682	950	0	5370	8234	8707	2794	1585	2371	4218
CX	MONTEVIDEO URUGUAY	8475	11889	832	5900	5370	0	11020	5695	2756	6855	7335	2786
DU	MANILA PHILIPPINES	4095	1768	10937	7537	8234	11020	0	6502	11002	6665	6012	10767
FO	PAPEETE POLYNESIA	10594	7211	4908	9622	8707	5695	6502	0	6767	9535	10251	4935
FY	CAYENNE FR. GUIANA	7380	9249	2907	3566	2794	2756	11002	6767	0	4378	5098	1844
G	LONDON ENGLAND	3627	5053	7246	983	1585	6855	6665	9535	4378	0	901	5732
HA	BUDAPEST HUNGARY	2726	4554	7857	1533	2371	7335	6012	10251	5098	901	0	6582
HC	QUITO ECUADOR	9136	9534	2344	5128	4218	2786	10767	4935	1844	5732	6582	0
HS	BANKOK THAILAND	2814	2042	10964	6626	7479	10374	1373	7814	10156	5913	5114	11489
I	ROME ITALY	2913	5040	7398	1160	2077	6849	6446	10431	4706	895	501	6285
JA	TOYKO JAPAN	4819	1302	10699	6920	7267	11530	1859	5914	9517	5936	5617	8964
JT	ULAN BATOR MONGOLIA	3134	722	11418	5278	5847	11176	2435	7737	8568	4331	3844	9120
KH6	HILO HAWAII	8691	5278	6644	7830	7225	7467	5494	2600	6919	7280	7771	5343
KL7	FAIRBANKS ALASKA	6176	3921	7926	4940	4656	8408	5337	5684	6066	4212	4639	5633
KL7	JUNEAU ALASKA	6741	4527	7315	5034	4602	7834	5869	5296	5641	4427	4972	5048
KP2	VIRGIN ISLANDS	7602	8411	3594	3559	2625	3700	10133	6285	1211	4117	4974	1615
LA	OSLO NORWAY	3402	4361	7901	1699	2219	7554	6016	9330	5003	715	922	6203
LZ	SOFIA BULGARIA	2406	4563	7912	1707	2610	7325	5911	10632	5255	1250	390	6826
P2	MADANG P.N.G.	6183	3633	8851	9632	10117	9314	2179	4464	11185	8684	8145	9350
PY	RIO DJANEIRO BRAZIL	7531	10754	1812	4790	4335	1134	11255	6704	2010	5758	6203	2830
T5	MOGADISHU SOMALIA	1710	5119	7782	4247	5146	6950	5217	10978	6727	4299	3503	8552
TF	REYKJAVIK ICELAND	4474	4888	7242	1830	1818	7087	6643	8395	4362	1167	1901	5280
TJ	YAOUNDE CAMEROON	3407	6822	5911	2730	3362	5121	7440	10816	4391	3356	3046	6217
UA3	MOSCOW EUR. RUSSIA	2473	3596	8772	2423	3138	8296	5127	9762	5928	1552	972	7221
UA9	NOVOSIBIRSK RUSSIA	2524	1852	10464	4155	4782	10040	3453	8667	7560	3228	2705	8497
UA9	PERM ASIATIC RUSSIA	2392	2879	9467	3130	3796	9014	4443	9344	6590	2221	1686	7744
UA0	YAKUTSK AS RUSSIA	4195	1638	10247	5095	5386	10519	3314	6996	7790	4114	3953	7905
UA0	OKHOTSK AS RUSSIA	4661	1789	10053	5471	5676	10508	3301	6498	7898	4502	4407	7761
UA0	UST OLENEK AS RUSSIA	4108	2278	9677	4359	4613	9798	4021	7378	7046	3388	3330	7351
UL7	ALMA-ATA KAZAKH	1736	2020	10569	4294	5067	9891	3252	9202	7847	3482	2762	9098
V3	BELIZE BELIZE	8817	8159	3701	4887	3940	4178	9450	4798	2572	5190	6091	1391
V85	BRUNEI	3959	2411	10431	7759	8573	10291	779	6700	11314	6989	6233	11440
VE1	Halifax N.S.	6482	6589	5408	2788	1953	5507	8325	6845	2826	2872	3769	3234
VE2	Quebec City Que.	6657	6421	5539	3115	2319	5713	8119	6543	3103	3098	3979	3281
VE3	Ottawa Ont.	6892	6430	5505	3409	2613	5739	8084	6255	3211	3365	4238	3201
VE4	Winnipeg Mb.	7153	5902	5976	4164	3466	6361	7408	5625	4046	3912	4708	3633
VE5	Regina Sk.	7229	5715	6148	4439	3773	6583	7158	5410	4349	4126	4887	3822
VE6	Edmondton Al.	7093	5327	6527	4638	4046	6993	6734	5343	4779	4219	4918	4218
VE7	Prince Rupert B.C.	7037	4824	7015	5124	4624	7556	6118	5081	5455	4580	5174	4769
VE8	Yellowknife NWT	6486	4816	7054	4332	3869	7452	6327	5832	5049	3791	4419	4718
VO2	Goose Bay Labrador	6007	5988	6019	2598	1921	6090	7737	7121	3372	2471	3341	3841
VY1	Whitehorse Yukon	6574	4410	7435	4926	4526	7932	5791	5451	5675	4294	4822	5151
VK1	CANBERRA AUSTRALIA	7165	5598	7026	11208	12131	7314	3910	3941	9921	10548	9761	8499
VK4	BRISBANE AUSTRALIA	7210	5219	7335	11145	11703	7717	3617	3710	10141	10267	9612	8506
VK6	PERTH AUSTRALIA	5385	4952	7899	9349	10292	7798	3222	5846	10425	8996	8102	10011
VP8	SO. SHETLAND IS.	8499	10887	2044	7475	7128	1878	9155	5172	4632	8459	8674	4387
VP9	BERMUDA	7062	7439	4556	3111	2171	4670	9164	6540	2055	3446	4342	2424
VQ9	DIEGO GARCIA CHAGOS	2336	4296	8718	6096	7036	7997	3644	9092	8647	5894	5002	10372
W0	Denver CO	7941	6343	5505	4850	4070	6013	7653	4868	4052	4682	5496	3226
W0	DesMoines IA	7600	6495	5379	4275	3471	5783	7964	5401	3584	4183	5031	3039
W0	Topeka KS.	7806	6613	5252	4456	3636	5688	8033	5208	3585	4385	5236	2923
W0	Minneapolis MN	7384	6286	5594	4152	3382	5976	7788	5555	3701	4008	4844	3250
W0	Jefferson City MO	7747	6717	5157	4308	3472	5564	8177	5342	3406	4275	5139	2817
W0	Lincoln NE	7718	6479	5387	4441	3641	5821	7904	5241	3693	4334	5175	3057
W0	Bismark ND	7411	6019	5846	4410	3687	6277	7461	5360	4073	4179	4977	3517
W0	Pierre SD	7562	6178	5684	4477	3725	6127	7599	5261	3973	4285	5098	3360
W1	Augusta ME	6724	6600	5367	3086	2254	5529	8304	6552	2916	3134	4025	3126
W1	Boston MA	6874	6735	5225	3194	2340	5404	8426	6436	2823	3275	4169	2972
W1	Concord NH	6844	6671	5288	3194	2351	5470	8361	6440	2888	3253	4145	3030
W1	Hartford CT	6955	6761	5192	3280	2423	5389	8439	6349	2834	3359	4252	2924
W1	Montpelier VT	6825	6584	5369	3223	2396	5561	8269	6419	2984	3249	4136	3101
W1	Providence RI	6904	6763	5196	3216	2358	5379	8451	6413	2805	3304	4198	2941
W2	Albany NY	6947	6684	5263	3315	2472	5470	8356	6320	2924	3365	4254	2985
W2	Trenton NJ	7107	6851	5090	3419	2551	5314	8509	6207	2806	3511	4405	2805
W3	Dover DE	7223	6908	5025	3531	2658	5270	8547	6093	2805	3629	4522	2725
W3	Harrisburg PA	7179	6830	5102	3520	2657	5347	8470	6109	2875	3594	4484	2800
W3	Washington D.C.	7258	6925	5005	3565	2690	5256	8559	6060	2804	3664	4557	2701
W4	Atlanta GA	7789	7172	4722	4087	3192	5074	8694	5535	2861	4203	5095	2379
W4	Columbia SC	7656	7205	4703	3907	3006	5015	8772	5714	2721	4053	4949	2372
W4	Frankfort KY	7561	6871	5026	3973	3112	5364	8416	5658	3073	4013	4895	2684
W4	Montgomery AL	7931	7230	4655	4229	3331	5034	8716	5393	2896	4348	5239	2310
W4	Nashville TN	7734	6972	4916	4129	3257	5282	8480	5499	3070	4183	5067	2571

HS	I	JA	JT	KH6	KL7	KL7	KP2	LA	LZ	P2	PY	T5	TF	TJ	UA3	UA9
2814	2914	4819	3134	8692	6177	6742	7603	3402	2407	6183	7531	1710	4474	3407	2474	2525
2042	5040	1302	722	5278	3921	4527	8411	4361	4563	3633	10754	5119	4888	6822	3596	1852
10964	7398	10699	11418	6644	7926	7315	3594	7901	7912	8851	1812	7782	7242	5911	8772	10464
6626	1160	6920	5278	7830	4940	5034	3559	1699	1707	9632	4790	4247	1830	2730	2423	4155
7479	2077	7267	5847	7225	4656	4602	2625	2219	2610	10117	4335	5146	1818	3362	3138	4782
10374	6849	11530	11176	7467	8408	7834	3700	7554	7325	9314	1134	6950	7087	5121	8296	10040
1373	6446	1859	2435	5494	5337	5869	10133	6016	5911	2179	11255	5217	6643	7440	5127	3453
7814	10431	5914	7737	2600	5684	5296	6285	9330	10632	4464	6704	10978	8395	10816	9762	8667
10156	4706	9517	8568	6919	6066	5641	1211	5003	5255	11185	2010	6727	4362	4391	5928	7560
5913	895	5936	4331	7280	4212	4427	4117	715	1250	8684	5758	4299	1167	3356	1552	3228
5114	501	5617	3844	7771	4639	4972	4974	922	390	8145	6203	3503	1901	3046	972	2705
11489	6285	8964	9120	5343	5633	5048	1615	6203	6826	9350	2830	8552	5280	6217	7221	8497
0	5471	2857	2383	6801	5962	6569	9973	5382	4921	3369	9980	3844	6253	6081	4381	3003
5471	0	6117	4334	8101	4984	5261	4703	1249	549	8603	5715	3410	2047	2625	1471	3196
2857	6117	0	1865	4064	3507	4015	8393	5220	5697	2852	11521	6372	5460	8114	4645	2959
2383	4334	1865	0	5565	3682	4309	7824	3641	3872	4356	10047	4817	4207	6268	2880	1138
6801	8101	4064	5565	0	3131	2853	5857	6868	8115	4373	8069	10381	6126	10559	7163	6245
5962	4984	3507	3682	3131	0	628	4895	3741	4987	5871	8056	7756	3118	7569	4097	3722
6569	5261	4015	4309	2853	628	0	4441	4052	5341	6152	7586	8258	3276	7747	4544	4326
9973	4703	8393	7824	5857	4895	4441	0	4599	5234	10230	3161	7431	3727	5180	5612	7001
5382	1249	5220	3641	6868	3741	4052	4599	0	1302	7982	6467	4394	1073	3871	1022	2562
4921	549	5697	3872	8115	4987	5341	5234	1302	0	8079	6192	3113	2290	2778	1102	2743
3369	8603	2852	4356	4373	5871	6152	10230	7982	8079	0	10394	6941	8312	9277	7213	5477
9980	5715	11521	10047	8069	8056	7586	3161	6467	6192	10394	0	6185	6117	4124	7167	8909
3844	3410	6372	4817	10381	7756	8258	7431	4394	3113	6941	6185	0	5402	2336	3727	4219
6253	2047	5460	4207	6126	3118	3276	3727	1073	2290	8312	6117	5402	0	4478	2045	3278
6081	2625	8114	6268	10559	7569	7747	5180	3871	2778	9277	4124	2336	4478	0	3862	5268
4381	1471	4645	2880	7163	4097	4544	5612	1022	1102	7213	7167	3727	2045	3862	0	1744
3003	3196	2959	1138	6245	3722	4326	7001	2562	2743	5477	8909	4219	3278	5268	1744	0
3807	2182	3940	2163	6769	3854	4379	6166	1595	1765	6502	7885	3902	2467	4443	717	1027
3637	4447	1881	1322	4538	2362	2988	6821	3404	4129	4733	9689	5905	3580	6853	3027	1708
3831	4895	1650	1662	4053	2133	2738	6842	3803	4601	4469	9876	6372	3858	7342	3499	2198
4152	3808	2655	1769	4807	2113	2726	6133	2690	3557	5507	8916	5768	2805	6332	2471	1611
2460	3195	3298	1467	6964	4578	5184	7515	2922	2667	5411	8788	3447	3819	4816	1933	857
10184	5944	7602	7813	4348	4245	3656	1587	5469	6421	8694	4113	8987	4426	6767	6471	7383
1159	6612	2638	3001	6097	6112	6648	10820	6403	6063	2236	10526	4799	7161	7114	5438	3890
8268	3691	6692	6010	5333	3327	3033	1822	3119	4121	9181	4831	7029	2093	5296	4128	5265
8209	3950	6417	5885	4943	2991	2662	2013	3259	4346	8815	5113	7331	2196	5675	4240	5229
8288	4227	6330	5931	4661	2855	2476	2066	3489	4610	8614	5212	7618	2419	5966	4451	5344
7900	4807	5577	5523	3762	2072	1594	2847	3848	5097	7680	6001	8205	2807	6826	4685	5175
7738	5021	5313	5382	3452	1827	1303	3143	4002	5277	7350	6282	8390	2991	7125	4785	5126
7362	5106	4885	5032	3201	1415	872	3575	4008	5306	6947	6714	8394	3058	7359	4704	4864
6865	5435	4260	4621	2718	942	315	4246	4252	5550	6265	7365	8522	3417	7853	4798	4638
6829	4656	4516	4468	3514	1016	734	3881	3498	4801	6841	7041	7845	2625	7059	4128	4250
7657	3341	6164	5399	5308	2930	2744	2427	2608	3713	8792	5357	6744	1548	5264	3592	4656
6452	5119	3946	4171	2987	491	167	4484	3904	5188	6163	7640	8092	3150	7627	4381	4165
4651	10065	4941	6310	5271	7697	7801	10084	9926	9528	2089	8328	7074	10401	8962	8996	7364
4534	10004	4448	5940	4755	7106	7217	9988	9581	9454	1611	8783	7369	9886	9422	8744	7039
3318	8285	4904	5535	6855	8355	8742	11489	8613	7792	2649	8417	5174	9563	7212	7590	6318
8943	8176	10446	11304	7620	9859	9231	5548	9174	8516	7608	2797	6790	8913	5814	9616	10986
9094	4167	7471	6862	5510	4015	3625	973	3817	4656	9714	4062	7296	2857	5270	4840	6092
2408	5084	5264	4360	9130	8011	8637	9425	5736	4645	5012	7625	1994	6809	4284	4803	4365
8383	5572	5793	6065	3251	2421	1822	2849	4644	5884	7465	5864	8981	3597	7415	5479	5860
8497	5061	6117	6120	3857	2631	2103	2372	4224	5412	8017	5486	8466	3155	6809	5127	5745
8631	5260	6177	6264	3739	2719	2164	2375	4431	5616	7961	5446	8662	3362	6956	5333	5924
8278	4893	5952	5897	3892	2451	1951	2494	4021	5227	7961	5636	8304	2957	6738	4910	5512
8719	5142	6326	6341	3927	2847	2310	2195	4356	5515	8152	5286	8532	3284	6778	5280	5951
8497	5215	6050	6131	3693	2586	2035	2482	4357	5558	7877	5569	8623	3292	6978	5244	5802
8039	5073	5612	5677	3555	2132	1598	2864	4117	5366	7579	5989	8474	3077	7049	4947	5385
8202	5177	5746	5843	3542	2280	1730	2762	4248	5485	7639	5867	8584	3199	7084	5094	5554
8366	3969	6605	6055	5046	3174	2832	1829	3338	4384	8983	4926	7323	2288	5593	4333	5376
8518	4101	6705	6200	5004	3250	2881	1708	3492	4525	9019	4830	7438	2445	5657	4490	5532
8460	4086	6640	6137	4973	3187	2823	1774	3457	4504	8965	4895	7435	2405	5679	4450	5476
8565	4187	6702	6235	4932	3233	2849	1700	3570	4609	8976	4837	7525	2519	5736	4564	5585
8388	4092	6544	6057	4906	3090	2728	1867	3431	4499	8872	4992	7456	2372	5735	4417	5411
8549	4128	6726	6229	4996	3266	2892	1684	3524	4553	9026	4811	7461	2477	5670	4521	5563
8504	4201	6614	6166	4862	3143	2758	1786	3554	4615	8887	4926	7555	2497	5796	4542	5532
8683	4336	6748	6341	4843	3260	2850	1645	3721	4761	8946	4799	7666	2669	5845	4714	5713
8763	4453	6768	6410	4763	3270	2839	1626	3835	4878	8906	4786	7779	2780	5939	4825	5804
8689	4425	6693	6334	4734	3198	2772	1699	3786	4844	8852	4859	7765	2727	5954	4772	5734
8788	4488	6775	6432	4740	3274	2838	1620	3869	4914	8894	4782	7812	2814	5966	4859	5831
9126	5027	6852	6744	4380	3356	2841	1650	4393	5453	8669	4747	8333	3330	6402	5371	6243
9123	4865	6946	6749	4570	3440	2947	1509	4270	5301	8843	4639	8150	3214	6208	5259	6199
8820	4859	6586	6438	4321	3081	2587	1863	4159	5262	8531	4999	8216	3088	6396	5120	5945
9205	5172	6865	6822	4282	3383	2850	1692	4533	5598	8595	4749	8474	3467	6523	5507	6350
8943	5027	6637	6559	4227	3143	2625	1858	4331	5433	8483	4963	8375	3261	6517	5291	6094

		A4	BY	CE	CT	CU	CX	DU	FO	FY	G	HA	HC
W4	Raleigh NC	7477	7116	4804	3735	2839	5083	8720	5887	2707	3873	4769	2487
W4	Richmond VA	7340	7005	4922	3624	2740	5182	8629	5999	2756	3741	4636	2614
W4	Tallahassee FL	7969	7395	4496	4195	3281	4861	8894	5430	2722	4363	5260	2152
W5	Austin TX	8402	7113	4737	4878	3999	5242	8401	4750	3427	4911	5783	2455
W5	Baton Rouge LA	8201	37258	94609	4544	3647	5049	8652	5078	3077	4641	5528	2278
W5	Jackson MS	8063	7162	4710	4428	3539	5130	8590	5195	3085	4509	5394	2372
W5	Little Rock AR	7982	6962	4907	4446	3579	5335	8384	5186	3273	4471	5345	2572
W5	Oklahoma City OK	8073	6795	5062	4672	3828	5535	8150	4976	3561	4635	5493	2753
W5	Santa Fe NM	8259	6585	5257	5077	4263	5801	7816	4605	3996	4960	5789	3019
W6	Los Angeles CA	8459	6250	5583	5669	4901	6216	7291	4096	4651	5440	6211	3492
W6	San Francisco CA	8205	5902	5932	5665	4951	6563	6961	4191	4923	5352	6082	3830
W7	Boise ID	7788	5796	6043	5152	4460	6599	7031	4707	4686	4833	5572	3816
W7	Carson City NV	8107	5921	5913	5492	4776	6520	7039	4348	4796	5191	5931	3765
W7	Cheyenne WY	7844	6262	5588	4787	4019	6085	7593	4944	4082	4602	5410	3299
W7	Olympia WA	7564	5408	6429	5242	4620	6996	6633	4745	5054	4828	5510	4215
W7	Pheonix AZ	8450	6493	5342	5418	4617	5939	7612	4288	4293	5261	6068	3185
W7	Salem OR	7710	5511	6325	5348	4705	6909	6696	4611	5036	4954	5646	4135
W7	Salt Lake City UT	7956	6087	5753	5101	4361	6301	7327	4679	4418	4857	5634	3518
W8	Charleston WV	7443	6907	5003	3805	2937	5306	8491	5822	2947	3872	4760	2672
W8	Columbus OH	7398	6776	5130	3826	2976	5441	8354	5810	3082	3852	4733	2795
W8	Lansing MI	7292	6572	5332	3824	3006	5648	8147	5832	3272	3788	4657	2994
W9	Indianapolis IN	7508	6747	5148	3984	3140	5491	8288	5657	3194	3986	4861	2804
W9	Madison WI	7404	6476	5412	4036	3234	5771	8004	5637	3470	3955	4810	3068
W9	Springfield IL	7607	6688	5196	4148	3315	5572	8189	5501	3340	4120	4987	2851
XE1	MEXICO CITY MEXICO	9108	7733	4105	5387	4463	4689	8825	4244	3303	5543	6434	1950
YA	KABUL AFGANISTAN	1010	2585	10146	4208	5075	9370	3486	9789	7754	3540	2704	9273
ZD8	ASCENSION IS.	5282	8618	4056	3234	3293	3296	9285	8958	2849	4178	4303	4538
ZF	CAYMAN IS.	8378	8183	3711	4397	3448	4076	9656	5309	2146	4759	5657	1372
ZL1	AUCKLAND NEWZEALAND	8579	6464	6004	12183	11255	6495	4982	2564	8732	11387	10991	7120
ZP	ASUNCION PARAGUAY	8440	11365	964	5418	4811	655	11675	5802	2123	6343	6908	2230
ZS1	CAPE TOWN SO.AFRICA	4743	8036	4937	5306	5737	4149	7480	8793	5315	5996	5613	6603
4X	ISRAEL	1619	4447	8172	2429	3375	7461	5502	11362	5815	2147	1287	7523
5R	TANANARIVE MALAGASY	3006	5991	6996	5404	6201	6218	5493	9669	6973	5645	4911	8551
5W	WESTERN SAMOA	9089	5922	6296	10459	9765	7023	4996	1527	8282	9833	10061	6440
6W	DAKAR SENEGAL	4940	7633	4825	1735	1705	4256	8943	9228	2461	2718	3079	4294
9N	KATMANDU NEPAL	1695	1952	10953	5261	6110	10121	2457	8908	8814	4548	3744	10247
9Q	KINSHASA ZAIRE	3479	6990	5817	3351	3963	4996	7336	10587	4705	3958	3583	6475
9Y	TRINIDAD IS.	7739	8977	3064	3753	2873	3111	10722	6302	690	4436	5244	1397

		UA9	UA0	UA0	UA0	UL7	V3	V85	VE1	VE2	VE3	VE4	VE5
A4	MUSCAT OMAN	2392	4196	4662	4109	1737	8818	3959	6483	6657	6892	7153	7229
BY	PEKING CHINA	2879	1638	1789	2278	2020	8159	2411	6589	6421	6430	5902	5715
CE	SANTIAGO CHILE	9467	10247	10053	9677	10569	3701	10431	5408	5539	5505	5976	6148
CT	LISBON PORTUGAL	3130	5095	5471	4359	4294	4887	7759	2788	3115	3409	4164	4439
CU	SAO MIGUEL IS AZORES	3796	5386	5676	4613	5067	3940	8573	1953	2319	2613	3466	3773
CX	MONTEVIDEO URUGUAY	9014	10519	10508	9798	9891	4178	10291	5507	5713	5739	6361	6583
DU	MANILA PHILIPPINES	4443	3314	3301	4021	3252	9450	779	8325	8119	8084	7408	7158
FO	PAPEETE POLYNESIA	9344	6996	6498	7378	9202	4798	6700	6845	6543	6255	5625	5410
FY	CAYENNE FR. GUIANA	6590	7790	7898	7046	7847	2572	11314	2826	3103	3211	4046	4349
G	LONDON ENGLAND	2221	4114	4502	3388	3482	5190	6989	2872	3098	3365	3912	4126
HA	BUDAPEST HUNGARY	1686	3953	4407	3330	2762	6091	6233	3769	3979	4238	4708	4887
HC	QUITO ECUADOR	7744	7905	7761	7351	9098	1391	11440	3234	3281	3201	3633	3822
HS	BANKOK THAILAND	3807	3637	3831	4152	2460	10184	1159	8268	8209	8288	7900	7738
I	ROME ITALY	2182	4447	4895	3808	3195	5944	6612	3691	3950	4227	4807	5021
JA	TOYKO JAPAN	3940	1881	1650	2655	3298	7602	2638	6692	6417	6330	5577	5313
JT	ULAN BATOR MONGOLIA	2163	1322	1662	1769	1467	7813	3001	6010	5885	5931	5523	5382
KH6	HILO HAWAII	6769	4538	4053	4807	6964	4348	6097	5333	4943	4661	3762	3452
KL7	FAIRBANKS ALASKA	3854	2362	2133	2113	4578	4245	6112	3327	2991	2855	2072	1827
KL7	JUNEAU ALASKA	4379	2988	2738	2726	5184	3656	6648	3033	2662	2476	1594	1303
KP2	VIRGIN ISLANDS	6166	6821	6842	6133	7515	1587	10820	1822	2013	2066	2847	3143
LA	OSLO NORWAY	1595	3404	3803	2690	2922	5469	6403	3119	3259	3489	3848	4002
LZ	SOFIA BULGARIA	1765	4129	4601	3557	2667	6421	6063	4121	4346	4610	5097	5277
P2	MADANG P.N.G.	6502	4733	4469	5507	5411	8694	2236	9181	8815	8614	7680	7350
PY	RIO DJANEIRO BRAZIL	7885	9689	9876	8916	8788	4113	10526	4831	5113	5212	6001	6282
T5	MOGADISHU SOMALIA	3902	5905	6372	5768	3447	8987	4799	7029	7331	7618	8205	8390
TF	REYKJAVIK ICELAND	2467	3580	3858	2805	3819	4426	7161	2093	2196	2419	2807	2991
TJ	YAOUNDE CAMEROON	4443	6853	7342	6332	4816	6767	7114	5296	5675	5966	6826	7125
UA3	MOSCOW EUR. RUSSIA	717	3027	3499	2471	1933	6471	5438	4128	4240	4451	4685	4785
UA9	NOVOSIBIRSK RUSSIA	1027	1708	2198	1611	857	7383	3890	5265	5229	5344	5175	5126
UA9	PERM ASIATIC RUSSIA	0	2409	2899	1967	1353	6832	4807	4549	4595	4767	4828	4864
UA0	YAKUTSK AS RUSSIA	2409	0	497	775	2461	6547	4022	5012	4811	4801	4271	4101
UA0	OKHOTSK AS RUSSIA	2899	497	0	1114	2925	6376	4051	5076	4832	4783	4150	3941
UA0	UST OLENEK AS RUSSIA	1967	775	1114	0	2465	6054	4690	4312	4146	4172	3766	3651
UL7	ALMA-ATA KAZAKH	1353	2461	2925	2465	0	8125	3506	5891	5911	6060	5984	5955
V3	BELIZE BELIZE	6832	6547	6376	6054	8125	0	10213	2351	2241	2067	2290	2447
V85	BRUNEI	4807	4022	4051	4690	3506	10213	0	8998	8830	8820	8180	7936

HS	I	JA	JT	KH6	KL7	KL7	KP2	LA	LZ	P2	PY	T5	TF	TJ	UA3	UA9
9003	4686	6913	6639	4683	3406	2938	1503	4094	5121	8914	4657	7980	3042	6066	5087	6057
8875	4560	6836	6517	4726	3332	2884	1564	3955	4990	8912	4725	7871	2901	5997	4946	5921
9356	5170	7044	6973	4417	3559	3029	1523	4582	5611	8749	4569	8428	3525	6422	5570	6471
9152	5766	6545	6816	3622	3192	2595	2266	5010	6156	7974	5140	9124	3937	7211	5933	6531
9273	5475	6793	6899	4010	3360	2792	1897	4798	5891	8353	4856	8789	3728	6827	5756	6506
9167	5347	6733	6788	4057	3278	2722	1890	4660	5759	8380	4901	8675	3590	6748	5618	6377
8974	5325	6527	6599	3926	3073	2516	2071	4584	5717	8220	5104	8689	3510	6836	5522	6217
8826	5505	6291	6475	3628	2880	2299	2364	4695	5871	7918	5361	8897	3625	7115	5600	6172
8626	5846	5964	6340	3151	2672	2057	2814	4948	6174	7450	5729	9256	3894	7577	5795	6169
8258	6335	5473	6118	2452	2459	1834	3491	5324	6601	6759	6287	9715	4315	8245	6069	6145
7910	6245	5134	5778	2313	2134	1515	3742	5177	6471	6534	6610	9565	4203	8313	5865	5840
7835	5727	5175	5583	2775	1901	1276	3479	4673	5962	6865	6496	9067	3688	7821	5397	5515
7945	6085	5200	5766	2485	2098	1471	3607	5030	6321	6682	6520	9423	4047	8138	5740	5779
8301	5493	5733	5976	3278	2341	1749	2875	4554	5798	7459	5914	8900	3510	7372	5383	5762
7445	5712	4776	5219	2609	1540	912	3843	4594	5896	6544	6889	8958	3664	7955	5241	5214
8522	6151	5779	6310	2797	2628	2001	3131	5205	6456	7118	5956	9559	4167	7937	6010	6242
7543	5841	4843	5338	2519	1667	1040	3828	4732	6033	6527	6840	9102	3793	8052	5386	5353
8128	5752	5472	5859	2915	2182	1562	3217	4753	6024	7097	6205	9137	3735	7720	5528	5749
8823	4709	6677	6448	4499	3169	2698	1743	4044	5122	8691	4896	8051	2979	6215	5019	5909
8704	4700	6539	6325	4413	3031	2561	1879	3996	5100	8573	5033	8065	2926	6280	4959	5806
8507	4652	6335	6127	4320	2828	2368	2075	3892	5031	8418	5233	8041	2819	6340	4837	5628
8703	4842	6458	6320	4248	2953	2461	1985	4107	5232	8428	5125	8217	3034	6446	5057	5843
8448	4829	6174	6065	4077	2669	2179	2264	4017	5189	8186	5409	8232	2945	6576	4936	5630
8670	4985	6347	6288	4064	2851	2337	2128	4212	5361	8255	5249	8372	3138	6629	5144	5860
9769	6364	7016	7501	3616	3831	3212	2294	5705	6793	7966	4762	9597	4634	7458	6654	7274
2418	3053	3887	2135	7682	5274	5868	7657	3106	2503	5662	8335	2719	4114	4248	2085	1560
7912	3804	9856	7994	9763	7940	7801	3918	4866	4179	10701	2253	4078	5001	1876	5260	6901
10125	5479	7797	7748	4801	4336	3788	1080	5094	5972	9169	3850	8467	4082	6255	6110	7182
5947	11415	5489	7182	4376	7307	7188	8671	10687	10867	2849	7618	8421	10425	9912	10059	8315
10791	6441	11184	10659	7238	7800	7245	3045	7022	6950	9798	911	7078	6478	5033	7841	9569
6296	5237	9143	7836	11376	10208	10328	6493	6486	5291	8062	3774	3034	7105	2639	6284	7221
4344	1330	5700	3835	8761	5695	6115	5985	2161	904	7670	6367	2232	3186	2462	1603	2806
4241	4751	7075	5882	10949	9173	9704	7984	5820	4523	6622	5774	1456	6789	2914	5183	5512
6289	10517	4682	6547	2629	5622	5452	7681	9287	10277	2938	8107	9741	8720	11654	9175	7624
7752	2594	8644	6924	8694	6361	6278	3085	3432	3089	11113	3123	4360	3422	2104	4044	5785
1370	4110	3198	1809	7230	5430	6057	8644	4046	3561	4618	9226	3176	4978	5103	3031	1891
5962	3192	8292	6512	11178	8165	8364	5608	4441	3284	8947	4106	2120	5091	621	4335	5597
10349	4913	8996	8360	6238	5495	5029	603	4986	5460	10568	2563	7298	4195	4979	5973	7471

VE6	VE7	VE8	VO2	VY1	VK1	VK4	VK6	VP8		VQ9	W0	W0	W0	W0	W0	W0
7094	7037	6487	6008	6575	7165	7210	5385	8498	7062	2336	7941	7600	7806	7384	7748	7718
5327	4824	4816	5988	4410	5598	5219	4952	10887	7439	4296	6343	6495	6613	6286	6717	6479
6527	7015	7054	6019	7435	7026	7335	7899	2044	4556	8718	5505	5379	5252	5594	5157	5387
4638	5124	4332	2598	4926	11208	11145	9349	7475	3111	6096	4850	4275	4456	4152	4308	4441
4046	4624	3869	1921	4526	12131	11703	10292	7128	2171	7036	4070	3471	3636	3382	3472	3641
6993	7556	7452	6090	7932	7314	7717	7798	1878	4670	7997	6013	5783	5688	5976	5564	5821
6734	6118	6327	7737	5791	3910	3617	3222	9155	9164	3644	7653	7964	8033	7788	8177	7904
5343	5081	5832	7121	5451	3941	3710	5846	5172	6540	9092	4868	5401	5208	5555	5342	5241
4779	5455	5049	3372	5675	9921	10141	10425	4632	2055	8647	4052	3584	3585	3701	3406	3693
4219	4580	3791	2471	4294	10548	10267	8996	8459	3446	5894	4682	4183	4385	4008	4275	4334
4918	5174	4419	3341	4822	9761	9612	8102	8674	4342	5002	5496	5031	5236	4844	5139	5175
4218	4769	4718	3841	5151	8499	8506	10011	4387	2424	10372	3226	3039	2923	3250	2817	3057
7362	6865	6829	7657	6452	4651	4534	3318	8943	9094	2408	8383	8497	8631	8278	8719	8497
5106	5435	4656	3341	5119	10065	10004	8285	8176	4167	5084	5572	5061	5260	4893	5142	5215
4885	4260	4516	6164	3946	4941	4448	4904	10446	7471	5264	5793	6117	6177	5952	6326	6050
5032	4621	4468	5399	4171	6310	5940	5535	11304	6862	4360	6065	6120	6264	5897	6341	6131
3201	2718	3514	5308	2987	5271	4755	6855	7620	5510	9130	3251	3857	3739	3892	3927	3693
1415	942	1016	2930	491	7697	7106	8355	9859	4015	8011	2421	2631	2719	2451	2847	2586
872	315	734	2744	167	7801	7217	8742	9231	3625	8637	1822	2103	2164	1951	2310	2035
3575	4246	3881	2427	4484	10084	9988	11489	5548	973	9425	2849	2372	2375	2494	2195	2482
4008	4252	3498	2608	3904	9926	9581	8613	9174	3817	5736	4644	4224	4431	4021	4356	4357
5306	5550	4801	3713	5188	9528	9454	7792	8516	4656	4645	5884	5412	5616	5227	5515	5558
6947	6265	6841	8792	6163	2089	1611	2649	7608	9714	5012	7465	8017	7961	7961	8152	7877
6714	7365	7041	5357	7640	8328	8783	8417	2797	4062	7625	5864	5486	5446	5636	5286	5569
8394	8522	7845	6744	8092	7074	7369	5174	6790	7296	1994	8981	8466	8662	8304	8532	8623
3058	3417	2625	1548	3150	10401	9886	9563	8913	2857	6809	3597	3155	3362	2957	3284	3292
7359	7853	7059	5264	7627	8962	9422	7212	5814	5270	4284	7415	6809	6956	6738	6778	6978
4704	4798	4128	3592	4738	8996	8744	7590	9616	4840	4803	5479	5127	5333	4910	5280	5244
4864	4638	4250	4656	4165	7364	7039	6318	10986	6092	4365	5860	5745	5924	5512	5951	5802
4704	4664	4095	3969	4212	8342	8051	7097	10254	5324	4614	5593	5336	5534	5106	5515	5429
3731	3299	3192	4431	2852	6821	6327	6536	12158	5849	5676	4762	4867	4995	4654	5089	4860
3543	3037	3058	4527	2621	6553	6028	6494	11667	5887	6005	4554	4734	4840	4535	4954	4705
3335	3040	2742	3716	2568	7596	7098	7230	11676	5161	5927	4362	4362	4514	4136	4581	4383
5710	5496	5094	5301	5023	7065	6852	5743	10231	6677	3519	6692	6538	6724	6304	6735	6606
2833	3378	3355	2881	3761	8729	8493	10616	5724	1780	10963	1834	1692	1553	1917	1473	1687
7512	6898	7095	8393	6569	3559	3391	2543	8477	9849	3040	8430	8741	8812	8562	8955	8683

		UA9	UA0	UA0	UA0	UL7	V3	V85	VE1	VE2	VE3	VE4	VE5
VE1	Halifax N.S.	4549	5012	5076	4312	5891	2351	8998	0	395	672	1598	1928
VE2	Quebec City Que.	4595	4811	4832	4146	5911	2241	8830	395	0	295	1202	1533
VE3	Ottawa Ont.	4767	4801	4783	4172	6060	2067	8820	672	295	0	949	1283
VE4	Winnipeg Mb.	4828	4271	4150	3766	5984	2290	8180	1598	1202	949	0	333
VE5	Regina Sk.	4864	4101	3941	3651	5955	2447	7936	1928	1533	1283	333	0
VE6	Edmondton Al.	4704	3731	3543	3335	5710	2833	7512	2284	1894	1669	740	432
VE7	Prince Rupert B.C.	4664	3299	3037	3040	5496	3378	6898	2948	2563	2349	1425	1108
VE8	Yellowknife NWT	4095	3192	3058	2742	5094	3355	7095	2340	1988	1839	1091	913
VO2	Goose Bay Labrador	3969	4431	4527	3716	5301	2881	8393	613	650	896	1569	1860
VY1	Whitehorse Yukon	4212	2852	2621	2568	5023	3761	6569	3017	2656	2486	1638	1367
VK1	CANBERRA AUSTRALIA	8342	6821	6553	7596	7065	8729	3559	10594	10211	9923	9031	8713
VK4	BRISBANE AUSTRALIA	8051	6327	6028	7098	6852	8493	3391	10087	9694	9416	8496	8172
VK6	PERTH AUSTRALIA	7097	6536	6494	7230	5743	10616	2543	11542	11321	11209	10315	9990
VP8	SO. SHETLAND IS.	10254	12158	11667	11676	10231	5724	8477	7368	7545	7534	8011	8163
VP9	BERMUDA	5324	5849	5887	5161	6677	1780	9849	852	1056	1160	2050	2374
VQ9	DIEGO GARCIA CHAGOS	4614	5676	6005	5927	3519	10963	3040	8765	8977	9223	9442	9460
W0	Denver CO	5593	4762	4554	4362	6692	1834	8430	2120	1751	1456	797	737
W0	DesMoines IA	5336	4867	4734	4362	6538	1692	8741	1518	1161	866	597	805
W0	Topeka KS.	5534	4995	4840	4514	6724	1553	8812	1683	1341	1049	752	898
W0	Minneapolis MN	5106	4654	4535	4136	6304	1917	8562	1444	1063	772	385	648
W0	Jefferson City MO	5515	5089	4954	4581	6735	1473	8955	1524	1200	915	819	1020
W0	Lincoln NE	5429	4860	4705	4383	6606	1687	8683	1688	1329	1034	626	764
W0	Bismark ND	5073	4401	4246	3936	6204	2145	8239	1780	1388	1111	269	305
W0	Pierre SD	5233	4564	4402	4105	6372	1983	8378	1793	1408	1120	409	463
W1	Augusta ME	4715	4993	5018	4323	6042	2137	9010	301	187	390	1337	1671
W1	Boston MA	4874	5122	5133	4461	6200	1981	9142	411	314	405	1345	1678
W1	Concord NH	4826	5056	5067	4397	6150	2021	9077	406	252	350	1295	1629
W1	Hartford CT	4940	5141	5142	4490	6262	1907	9164	497	356	378	1297	1629
W1	Montpelier VT	4778	4967	4974	4312	6095	2060	8989	442	183	260	1210	1543
W1	Providence RI	4906	5148	5157	4489	6232	1949	9169	436	343	416	1349	1681
W2	Albany NY	4903	5062	5057	4416	6219	1934	9084	526	308	287	1209	1541
W2	Trenton NJ	5083	5225	5208	4587	6400	1759	9245	645	488	425	1272	1598
W3	Dover DE	5187	5276	5245	4651	6500	1650	9291	762	591	479	1250	1569
W3	Harrisburg PA	5125	5199	5169	4575	6434	1709	9214	738	532	403	1187	1509
W3	Washington D.C.	5218	5293	5258	4672	6530	1617	9305	797	623	500	1246	1562
W4	Atlanta GA	5695	5534	5436	4974	6980	1145	9468	1336	1134	928	1288	1539
W4	Columbia SC	5611	5567	5492	4980	6914	1221	9539	1180	1021	855	1368	1643
W4	Frankfort KY	5419	5233	5144	4668	6691	1439	9186	1186	915	669	1009	1283
W4	Montgomery AL	5821	5595	5480	5053	7097	1033	9493	1481	1274	1058	1330	1557
W4	Nashville TN	5584	5336	5229	4791	6848	1290	9255	1346	1087	842	1079	1324
W4	Raleigh NC	5449	5480	5426	4874	6760	1387	9478	1000	854	716	1345	1641
W4	Richmond VA	5308	5371	5330	4755	6620	1528	9380	870	713	586	1289	1599
W4	Tallahassee FL	5910	5758	5651	5203	7203	923	9671	1491	1329	1144	1501	1735
W5	Austin TX	6150	5523	5325	5088	7338	1064	9173	2095	1816	1545	1355	1437
W5	Baton Rouge LA	6035	5637	5483	5141	7280	913	9431	1785	1550	1309	1376	1543
W5	Jackson MS	5898	5536	5394	5027	7147	1027	9370	1659	1415	1171	1267	1453
W5	Little Rock AR	5772	5339	5191	4842	7000	1213	9163	1659	1374	1107	1076	1250
W5	Oklahoma City OK	5799	5190	5011	4737	6979	1365	8929	1886	1566	1280	996	1092
W5	Santa Fe NM	5913	5028	4796	4655	7006	1638	8587	2310	1962	1668	1109	1055
W6	Los Angeles CA	6067	4798	4493	4556	7002	2177	8040	2952	2582	2288	1531	1324
W6	San Francisco CA	5816	4459	4147	4241	6698	2496	7716	3026	2640	2353	1500	1235
W7	Boise ID	5397	4263	4010	3950	6368	2432	7806	2560	2168	1890	995	715
W7	Carson City NV	5715	4444	4152	4191	6636	2411	7802	2852	2466	2180	1327	1068
W7	Cheyenne WY	5494	4675	4474	4268	6594	1908	8371	2075	1700	1407	706	638
W7	Olympia WA	5175	3897	3626	3626	6071	2831	7409	2785	2390	2131	1187	859
W7	Pheonix AZ	6073	4989	4716	4684	7093	1842	8370	2663	2308	2013	1360	1225
W7	Salem OR	5322	4016	3734	3761	6211	2759	7468	2845	2450	2183	1251	932
W7	Salt Lake City UT	5575	4543	4300	4203	6596	2134	8101	2427	2045	1755	949	751
W8	Charleston WV	5344	5269	5202	4680	6635	1491	9253	1024	786	577	1105	1401
W8	Columbus OH	5264	5138	5067	4556	6543	1583	9117	1038	754	507	968	1267
W8	Lansing MI	5115	4933	4860	4357	6378	1755	8910	1052	711	424	773	1084
W9	Indianapolis IN	5337	5109	5017	4550	6598	1540	9058	1196	892	622	881	1159
W9	Madison WI	5174	4840	4738	4297	6404	1766	8775	1282	922	626	596	879
W9	Springfield IL	5396	5054	4939	4522	6632	1538	8964	1365	1041	757	789	1034
XE1	MEXICO CITY MEXICO	6896	6189	5948	5802	8087	731	9559	2675	2458	2216	2103	2157
YA	KABUL AFGANISTAN	1719	3193	3654	3169	732	8532	3561	6206	6290	6477	6532	6542
ZD8	ASCENSION IS.	5944	8243	8668	7556	6598	5417	8855	4801	5191	5428	6377	6711
ZF	CAYMAN IS.	6533	6546	6438	5979	7864	519	10435	1988	1957	1843	2288	2509
ZL1	AUCKLAND NEWZEALAND	9343	7282	6886	8000	8234	7314	4803	9395	9068	8774	8023	7752
ZP	ASUNCION PARAGUAY	8549	9864	9868	9150	9604	3609	10932	4852	5059	5089	5737	5972
ZS1	CAPE TOWN SO.AFRICA	6704	8925	9403	8669	6479	7815	6779	7457	7851	8099	9048	9381
4X	ISRAEL	2035	4421	4917	3995	2429	7274	5503	5008	5245	5512	5993	6161
5R	TANANARIVE MALAGASY	5328	7113	7533	7112	4680	9535	4860	8154	8509	8804	9541	9771
5W	WESTERN SAMOA	8536	6148	5676	6734	7940	6119	5173	7812	7446	7152	6326	6036
6W	DAKAR SENEGAL	4762	6830	7199	6090	5747	4669	8899	3391	3786	4055	4988	5316
9N	KATMANDU NEPAL	2511	3107	3472	3364	1163	9268	2501	7055	7071	7211	7061	6992
9Q	KINSHASA ZAIRE	4860	7250	7747	6799	5045	7188	6903	5881	6265	6553	7430	7734
9Y	TRINIDAD IS.	6576	7408	7442	6706	7904	1891	11355	2397	2611	2670	3439	3727

VE6	VE7	VE8	VO2	VY1	VK1	VK4	VK6	VP8		VQ9	W0	W0	W0	W0	W0	W0
2284	2948	2340	613	3017	10594	10087	11542	7368	852	8765	2120	1518	1683	1444	1524	1688
1894	2563	1988	650	2656	10211	9694	11321	7545	1056	8977	1751	1161	1341	1063	1200	1329
1669	2349	1839	896	2486	9923	9416	11209	7534	1160	9223	1456	866	1049	772	915	1034
740	1425	1091	1569	1638	9031	8496	10315	8011	2050	9442	797	597	752	385	819	626
432	1108	913	1860	1367	8713	8172	9990	8163	2374	9460	737	805	898	648	1020	764
0	685	617	2125	943	8412	7852	9575	8517	2789	9229	1033	1232	1305	1080	1442	1173
685	0	796	2725	472	7805	7231	8890	8917	3475	8953	1545	1882	1921	1753	2079	1796
617	796	0	2014	683	8535	7951	9369	9076	3000	8613	1621	1679	1802	1476	1901	1668
2125	2725	2014	0	2695	10530	9956	10935	7961	1463	8331	2263	1721	1919	1568	1804	1879
943	472	683	2695	0	7864	7277	8725	9373	3643	8486	1932	2173	2248	2007	2385	2116
8412	7805	8535	10530	7864	0	590	1904	5531	10481	5155	8475	9081	8928	9150	9100	8912
7852	7231	7951	9956	7277	590	0	2229	6002	10146	5395	7995	8603	8467	8648	8648	8436
9575	8890	9369	10935	8725	1904	2229	0	5942	12363	3256	10081	10658	10578	10610	10770	10509
8517	8917	9076	7961	9373	5531	6002	5942	0	6521	6974	7484	7413	7276	7632	7192	7410
2789	3475	3000	1463	3643	10481	10146	12363	6521	0	9207	2283	1705	1785	1753	1593	1854
9229	8953	8613	8331	8486	5155	5395	3256	6974	9207	0	10197	9928	10133	9706	10083	10036
1033	1545	1621	2263	1932	8475	7995	10081	7484	2283	10197	0	608	498	697	690	441
1232	1882	1679	1721	2173	9081	8603	10658	7413	1705	9928	608	0	207	234	222	169
1305	1921	1802	1919	2248	8928	8467	10578	7276	1785	10133	498	207	0	427	192	134
1080	1753	1476	1568	2007	9150	8648	10610	7632	1753	9706	697	234	427	0	445	335
1442	2079	1901	1804	2385	9100	8648	10770	7192	1593	10083	690	222	192	445	0	287
1173	1796	1668	1879	2116	8912	8436	10509	7410	1854	10036	441	169	134	335	287	0
727	1383	1210	1812	1669	8826	8306	10228	7866	2135	9686	532	504	594	382	716	459
867	1497	1375	1882	1810	8803	8298	10286	7701	2077	9847	398	389	438	350	581	306
2048	2723	2167	746	2831	10298	9802	11509	7366	869	9028	1822	1218	1382	1153	1223	1388
2072	2754	2237	905	2889	10230	9756	11604	7231	768	9170	1761	1153	1301	1118	1132	1321
2019	2700	2174	860	2829	10210	9728	11540	7296	832	9147	1737	1129	1285	1082	1121	1298
2030	2714	2218	974	2863	10149	9681	11587	7206	782	9254	1686	1077	1221	1054	1049	1245
1929	2608	2078	824	2733	10156	9662	11443	7382	929	9138	1680	1076	1241	1013	1085	1245
2079	2761	2252	937	2902	10215	9746	11621	7204	750	9198	1751	1142	1287	1114	1115	1310
1940	2624	2127	949	2772	10092	9614	11496	7282	873	9256	1621	1013	1165	976	1000	1181
2012	2697	2243	1122	2873	10031	9580	11588	7114	777	9406	1591	986	1112	992	933	1149
1990	2674	2255	1232	2870	9930	9490	11555	7056	808	9523	1512	913	1025	944	841	1072
1927	2612	2182	1179	2801	9923	9471	11499	7133	865	9487	1483	878	1003	893	824	1041
1986	2669	2260	1266	2871	9900	9463	11543	7037	820	9558	1490	894	1001	933	816	1051
1969	2619	2378	1784	2906	9418	9025	11229	6766	1138	10097	1208	738	725	905	545	833
2076	2740	2445	1666	3003	9608	9219	11422	6745	945	9945	1377	862	884	997	695	979
1716	2383	2091	1558	2642	9472	9034	11161	7070	1202	9889	1080	517	583	636	393	654
1981	2615	2421	1924	2924	9284	8900	11116	6697	1253	10242	1157	752	698	945	539	819
1753	2404	2170	1730	2691	9336	8914	11082	6958	1282	10062	1018	523	524	694	337	623
2072	2748	2399	1495	2983	9769	9364	11536	6841	828	9766	1458	899	959	994	767	1036
2026	2707	2320	1354	2921	9858	9434	11557	6956	806	9635	1483	899	988	960	798	1049
2160	2795	2592	1977	3102	9347	8988	11217	6539	1157	10253	1330	929	877	1116	718	999
1791	2314	2350	2442	2704	8604	8211	10429	6731	1941	10737	772	814	616	1043	654	731
1944	2534	2445	2196	2884	8968	8590	10814	6637	1557	10528	1007	779	644	1007	562	779
1864	2473	2346	2060	2807	9069	8677	10890	6744	1479	10392	972	669	559	890	447	691
1659	2268	2148	2004	2601	9013	8594	10780	6936	1587	10319	779	480	353	710	266	486
1467	2034	2006	2165	2398	8751	8315	10484	7070	1882	10400	503	473	267	693	365	372
1320	1762	1922	2516	2180	8303	7851	10007	7209	2359	10515	320	802	627	952	798	637
1369	1519	1972	3073	1989	7645	7172	9307	7409	3058	10470	831	1436	1295	1522	1480	1267
1171	1202	1739	3070	1675	7570	7068	9133	7744	3230	10135	948	1546	1445	1581	1636	1385
696	972	1302	2563	1412	8046	7526	9505	7961	2857	9876	637	1152	1106	1133	1293	1012
1036	1156	1624	2897	1624	7744	7240	9293	7766	3070	10109	787	1379	1285	1408	1478	1220
944	1478	1526	2195	1854	8519	8029	10087	7573	2276	10098	99	580	503	638	693	422
610	598	1113	2699	1061	7857	7313	9193	8319	3170	9548	1025	1483	1469	1418	1648	1361
1386	1689	2004	2840	2142	7945	7490	9651	7231	2715	10607	579	1147	983	1271	1158	978
735	724	1258	2789	1194	7782	7246	9173	8196	3190	9678	986	1489	1454	1448	1639	1356
886	1263	1504	2503	1691	8167	7669	9719	7687	2644	10114	369	948	864	983	1055	791
1832	2508	2165	1436	2744	9651	9215	11331	7045	1032	9761	1255	674	760	755	571	822
1697	2375	2028	1395	2606	9599	9145	11220	7173	1143	9726	1161	564	678	623	499	722
1509	2192	1822	1317	2409	9550	9070	11067	7376	1297	9628	1076	468	633	457	490	638
1591	2261	1963	1519	2516	9433	8979	11069	7191	1294	9843	998	411	511	510	333	561
1310	1985	1681	1488	2231	9314	8829	10835	7455	1528	9740	838	239	430	231	344	407
1465	2122	1880	1649	2401	9254	8795	10890	7236	1473	9944	814	244	327	404	159	380
2473	2910	3060	3105	3340	8180	7875	10082	6048	2300	11435	1441	1561	1366	1792	1383	1481
6335	6176	5717	5652	5704	7057	6951	5508	9499	6924	2918	7278	7053	7249	6822	7234	7141
7086	7747	7073	5059	7754	9216	9807	8095	4372	4395	5847	6670	6100	6172	6133	5980	6248
2927	3537	3380	2564	3870	9230	9010	11089	5755	1316	10448	2014	1707	1623	1903	1489	1754
7561	7088	7883	9588	7301	1426	1413	3305	4986	9086	6561	7334	7908	7726	8032	7875	7741
6390	6980	6825	5437	7333	7885	8244	8453	2526	4014	8384	5436	5168	5085	5354	4952	5217
9735	10358	9602	7634	10230	6689	7260	5422	3769	7068	3888	9324	8772	8830	8811	8639	8915
6164	6350	5632	4616	5955	8779	8824	6957	8256	5496	3759	6783	6317	6521	6131	6419	6462
9828	9976	9298	7997	9538	6082	6511	4300	5571	8183	1850	10254	9669	9837	9556	9670	9838
5822	5342	6137	7894	5571	2799	2407	4635	6056	7740	7747	5695	6294	6133	6384	6302	6124
5645	6268	5544	3543	6213	10774	11354	9282	5741	3204	6350	5443	4837	4956	4813	4769	5001
6698	6373	6096	6465	5908	6021	5893	4588	9551	7834	2580	7717	7636	7812	7402	7842	7687
7977	8474	7679	5874	8242	8377	8865	6689	5430	5795	3942	7992	7383	7521	7325	7339	7551
4159	4824	4482	2990	5078	9848	9901	10909	4972	1560	9262	3383	2942	2927	3079	2754	3041

		W0	W0	W1	W1	W1	W1	W1	W1	W2	W2	W3	W3
A4	MUSCAT OMAN	7412	7562	6725	6874	6845	6955	6825	6905	6947	7108	7224	7179
BY	PEKING CHINA	6019	6178	6600	6735	6671	6761	6584	6763	6684	6851	6908	6830
CE	SANTIAGO CHILE	5846	5684	5367	5225	5288	5192	5369	5196	5263	5090	5025	5102
CT	LISBON PORTUGAL	4410	4477	3086	3194	3194	3280	3223	3216	3315	3419	3531	3520
CU	SAO MIGUEL IS AZORES	3687	3725	2254	2340	2351	2423	2396	2358	2472	2551	2658	2657
CX	MONTEVIDEO URUGUAY	6277	6127	5529	5404	5470	5389	5561	5379	5470	5314	5270	5347
DU	MANILA PHILIPPINES	7461	7599	8304	8426	8361	8439	8269	8451	8356	8509	8547	8470
FO	PAPEETE POLYNESIA	5360	5261	6552	6436	6440	6349	6419	6413	6320	6207	6093	6109
FY	CAYENNE FR. GUIANA	4073	3973	2916	2823	2888	2834	2984	2805	2924	2806	2805	2875
G	LONDON ENGLAND	4179	4285	3134	3275	3253	3359	3249	3304	3365	3511	3629	3594
HA	BUDAPEST HUNGARY	4977	5098	4025	4169	4145	4252	4136	4198	4254	4405	4522	4484
HC	QUITO ECUADOR	3517	3360	3126	2972	3030	2924	3101	2941	2985	2805	2725	2800
HS	BANKOK THAILAND	8039	8202	8366	8518	8460	8565	8388	8549	8504	8683	8763	8689
I	ROME ITALY	5073	5177	3969	4101	4086	4187	4092	4128	4201	4336	4453	4425
JA	TOYKO JAPAN	5612	5746	6605	6705	6640	6702	6544	6726	6614	6748	6768	6693
JT	ULAN BATOR MONGOLIA	5677	5843	6055	6200	6137	6235	6057	6229	6166	6341	6410	6334
KH6	HILO HAWAII	3555	3542	5046	5004	4973	4932	4906	4996	4862	4843	4763	4734
KL7	FAIRBANKS ALASKA	2132	2280	3174	3250	3187	3233	3090	3266	3143	3260	3270	3198
KL7	JUNEAU ALASKA	1598	1730	2832	2881	2823	2849	2728	2892	2758	2850	2839	2772
KP2	VIRGIN ISLANDS	2864	2762	1829	1708	1774	1700	1867	1684	1786	1645	1626	1699
LA	OSLO NORWAY	4117	4248	3338	3492	3457	3570	3431	3524	3554	3721	3835	3786
LZ	SOFIA BULGARIA	5366	5485	4384	4525	4504	4609	4499	4553	4615	4761	4878	4844
P2	MADANG P.N.G.	7579	7639	8983	9019	8965	8976	8872	9026	8887	8946	8906	8852
PY	RIO DJANEIRO BRAZIL	5989	5867	4926	4830	4895	4837	4992	4811	4926	4799	4786	4859
T5	MOGADISHU SOMALIA	8474	8584	7323	7438	7435	7525	7456	7461	7555	7666	7779	7765
TF	REYKJAVIK ICELAND	3077	3199	2288	2445	2405	2519	2372	2477	2497	2669	2780	2727
TJ	YAOUNDE CAMEROON	7049	7084	5593	5657	5679	5736	5735	5670	5796	5845	5939	5954
UA3	MOSCOW EUR. RUSSIA	4947	5094	4333	4490	4450	4564	4417	4521	4542	4714	4825	4772
UA9	NOVOSIBIRSK RUSSIA	5385	5554	5376	5532	5476	5585	5411	5563	5532	5713	5804	5734
UA9	PERM ASIATIC RUSSIA	5073	5233	4715	4874	4826	4940	4778	4906	4903	5083	5187	5125
UA0	YAKUTSK AS RUSSIA	4401	4564	4993	5122	5056	5141	4967	5148	5062	5225	5276	5199
UA0	OKHOTSK AS RUSSIA	4246	4402	5018	5133	5067	5142	4974	5157	5057	5208	5245	5169
UA0	UST OLENEK AS RUSSIA	3936	4105	4323	4461	4397	4490	4312	4489	4416	4587	4651	4575
UL7	ALMA-ATA KAZAKH	6204	6372	6042	6200	6150	6262	6095	6232	6219	6400	6500	6434
V3	BELIZE BELIZE	2145	1983	2137	1981	2021	1907	2060	1949	1934	1759	1650	1709
V85	BRUNEI	8239	8378	9010	9142	9077	9164	8989	9169	9084	9245	9291	9214
VE1	Halifax N.S.	1780	1793	301	411	406	497	442	436	526	645	762	738
VE2	Quebec City Que.	1388	1408	187	314	252	356	183	343	308	488	591	532
VE3	Ottawa Ont.	1111	1120	390	405	350	378	260	416	287	425	479	403
VE4	Winnipeg Mb.	269	409	1337	1345	1295	1297	1210	1349	1209	1272	1250	1187
VE5	Regina Sk.	305	463	1671	1678	1629	1629	1543	1681	1541	1598	1569	1509
VE6	Edmondton Al.	727	867	2048	2072	2019	2030	1929	2079	1940	2012	1990	1927
VE7	Prince Rupert B.C.	1383	1497	2723	2754	2700	2714	2608	2761	2624	2697	2674	2612
VE8	Yellowknife NWT	1210	1375	2167	2237	2174	2218	2078	2252	2127	2243	2255	2182
VO2	Goose Bay Labrador	1812	1882	746	905	860	974	824	937	949	1122	1232	1179
VY1	Whitehorse Yukon	1669	1810	2831	2889	2829	2863	2733	2902	2772	2873	2870	2801
VK1	CANBERRA AUSTRALIA	8826	8803	10298	10230	10210	10149	10156	10215	10092	10031	9930	9923
VK4	BRISBANE AUSTRALIA	8306	8298	9802	9756	9728	9681	9662	9746	9614	9580	9490	9471
VK6	PERTH AUSTRALIA	10228	10286	11509	11604	11540	11587	11443	11621	11496	11588	11555	11499
VP8	SO. SHETLAND IS.	7866	7701	7366	7231	7296	7206	7382	7204	7282	7114	7056	7133
VP9	BERMUDA	2135	2077	869	768	832	782	929	750	873	777	808	865
VQ9	DIEGO GARCIA CHAGOS	9686	9847	9028	9170	9147	9254	9138	9198	9256	9406	9523	9487
W0	Denver CO	532	398	1822	1761	1737	1686	1680	1751	1621	1591	1512	1483
W0	DesMoines IA	504	389	1218	1153	1129	1077	1076	1142	1013	986	913	878
W0	Topeka KS.	594	438	1382	1301	1285	1221	1241	1287	1165	1112	1025	1003
W0	Minneapolis MN	382	350	1153	1118	1082	1054	1013	1114	976	992	944	893
W0	Jefferson City MO	716	581	1223	1132	1121	1049	1085	1115	1000	933	841	824
W0	Lincoln NE	459	306	1388	1321	1298	1245	1245	1310	1181	1149	1072	1041
W0	Bismark ND	0	169	1501	1483	1442	1423	1365	1481	1342	1371	1327	1274
W0	Pierre SD	169	0	1503	1467	1432	1400	1363	1462	1324	1331	1273	1228
W1	Augusta ME	1501	1503	0	158	119	231	142	191	233	383	498	459
W1	Boston MA	1483	1467	158	0	65	86	161	32	142	236	353	327
W1	Concord NH	1442	1432	119	65	0	113	97	92	121	264	379	340
W1	Hartford CT	1423	1400	231	86	113	0	178	66	91	152	269	240
W1	Montpelier VT	1365	1363	142	161	97	178	0	182	125	305	409	355
W1	Providence RI	1481	1462	191	32	92	66	182	0	140	208	325	303
W2	Albany NY	1342	1324	233	142	121	91	125	140	0	181	284	232
W2	Trenton NJ	1371	1331	383	236	264	152	305	208	181	0	117	109
W3	Dover DE	1327	1273	498	353	379	269	409	325	284	117	0	77
W3	Harrisburg PA	1274	1228	459	327	340	240	355	303	232	109	77	0
W3	Washington D.C.	1316	1258	533	388	413	304	442	360	317	152	35	98
W4	Atlanta GA	1242	1122	1069	928	950	843	964	900	843	692	574	611
W4	Columbia SC	1357	1252	932	781	812	701	842	751	717	549	434	488
W4	Frankfort KY	1000	905	894	779	781	693	767	758	661	560	458	455
W4	Montgomery AL	1254	1120	1213	1073	1094	988	1106	1045	986	837	719	755
W4	Nashville TN	1027	908	1059	936	943	850	935	913	826	709	599	609
W4	Raleigh NC	1370	1285	756	603	637	524	673	573	547	373	263	326

W3	W4	W4	W4	W4	W4	W4	W4	W4	W5	W5	W5	W5	W5	W5	W6	W6
]7259	7790	7656	7562	7931	7734	7478	7341	7969	8402	8201	8063	7983	8073	8260	8460	8206
6925	7172	7205	6871	7230	6972	7116	7005	7395	7113	7258	7162	6962	6795	6585	6250	5902
5005	4722	4703	5026	4655	4916	4804	4922	4496	4737	4609	4710	4907	5062	5257	5583	5932
3565	4087	3907	3973	4229	4129	3735	3624	4195	4878	4544	4428	4446	4672	5077	5669	5665
2690	3192	3006	3112	3331	3257	2839	2740	3281	3999	3647	3539	3579	3828	4263	4901	4951
5256	5074	5015	5364	5034	5282	5083	5182	4861	5242	5049	5130	5335	5535	5801	6216	6563
8559	8694	8772	8416	8716	8480	8720	8629	8894	8401	8652	8590	8384	8150	7816	7291	6961
6060	5535	5714	5658	5393	5499	5887	5999	5430	4750	5078	5195	5186	4976	4605	4096	4191
2804	2861	2721	3073	2896	3070	2707	2756	2722	3427	3077	3085	3273	3561	3996	4651	4923
3664	4203	4053	4013	4348	4183	3873	3741	4363	4911	4641	4509	4471	4635	4960	5440	5352
4557	5095	4949	4895	5239	5067	4769	4636	5260	5783	5528	5394	5345	5493	5789	6211	6082
2701	2379	2372	2684	2310	2571	2487	2614	2152	2455	2278	2372	2572	2753	3019	3492	3830
8788	9126	9123	8820	9205	8943	9003	8875	9356	9152	9273	9167	8974	8826	8626	8258	7910
4488	5027	4865	4859	5172	5027	4686	4560	5170	5766	5475	5347	5325	5505	5846	6335	6245
6775	6852	6946	6586	6865	6637	6913	6836	7044	6545	6793	6733	6527	6291	5964	5473	5134
6432	6744	6749	6438	6822	6559	6639	6517	6973	6816	6899	6788	6599	6475	6340	6118	5778
4740	4380	4570	4321	4282	4227	4683	4726	4417	3622	4010	4057	3926	3628	3151	2452	2313
3274	3356	3440	3081	3383	3143	3406	3332	3559	3192	3360	3278	3073	2880	2672	2459	2134
2838	2841	2947	2587	2850	2625	2938	2884	3029	2595	2792	2722	2516	2299	2057	1834	1515
1620	1650	1509	1863	1692	1858	1503	1564	1523	2266	1897	1890	2071	2364	2814	3491	3742
3869	4393	4270	4159	4533	4331	4094	3955	4582	5010	4798	4660	4584	4695	4948	5324	5177
4914	5453	5301	5262	5598	5433	5121	4990	5611	6156	5891	5759	5717	5871	6174	6601	6471
8894	8669	8843	8531	8595	8483	8914	8912	8749	7974	8353	8380	8220	7918	7450	6759	6534
4782	4747	4639	4999	4749	4963	4657	4725	4569	5140	4856	4901	5104	5361	5729	6287	6610
7812	8333	8150	8216	8474	8375	7980	7871	8428	9124	8789	8675	8689	8897	9256	9715	9565
2814	3330	3214	3088	3467	3261	3042	2901	3525	3937	3728	3590	3510	3625	3894	4315	4203
5966	6402	6208	6396	6523	6517	6066	5997	6422	7211	6827	6748	6836	7115	7577	8245	8313
4859	5371	5259	5120	5507	5291	5087	4946	5570	5933	5756	5618	5522	5600	5795	6069	5865
5831	6243	6199	5945	6350	6094	6057	5921	6471	6531	6506	6377	6217	6172	6169	6145	5840
5218	5695	5611	5419	5821	5584	5449	5308	5910	6150	6035	5898	5772	5799	5913	6067	5816
5293	5534	5567	5233	5595	5336	5480	5371	5758	5523	5637	5536	5339	5190	5028	4798	4459
5258	5436	5492	5144	5480	5229	5426	5330	5651	5325	5483	5394	5191	5011	4796	4493	4147
4672	4974	4980	4668	5053	4791	4874	4755	5203	5088	5141	5027	4842	4737	4655	4556	4241
6530	6980	6914	6691	7097	6848	6760	6620	7203	7338	7280	7147	7000	6979	7006	7002	6698
1617	1145	1221	1439	1033	1290	1387	1528	923	1064	913	1027	1213	1365	1638	2177	2496
9305	9468	9539	9186	9493	9255	9478	9380	9671	9173	9431	9370	9163	8929	8587	8040	7716
797	1336	1180	1186	1481	1346	1000	870	1491	2095	1785	1659	1659	1886	2310	2952	3026
623	1134	1021	915	1274	1087	854	713	1329	1816	1550	1415	1374	1566	1962	2582	2640
500	928	855	669	1058	842	716	586	1144	1545	1309	1171	1107	1280	1668	2288	2353
1246	1288	1368	1009	1330	1079	1345	1289	1501	1355	1376	1267	1076	996	1109	1531	1500
1562	1539	1643	1283	1557	1324	1641	1599	1735	1437	1543	1453	1250	1092	1055	1324	1235
1986	1969	2076	1716	1981	1753	2072	2026	2160	1791	1944	1864	1659	1467	1320	1369	1171
2669	2619	2740	2383	2615	2404	2748	2707	2795	2314	2534	2473	2268	2034	1762	1519	1202
2260	2378	2445	2091	2421	2170	2399	2320	2592	2350	2445	2346	2148	2006	1922	1972	1739
1266	1784	1666	1558	1924	1730	1495	1354	1977	2442	2196	2060	2004	2165	2516	3073	3070
2871	2906	3003	2642	2924	2691	2983	2921	3102	2704	2884	2807	2601	2398	2180	1989	1675
9900	9418	9608	9472	9284	9336	9769	9858	9347	8604	8968	9069	9013	8751	8303	7645	7570
9463	9025	9219	9034	8900	8914	9364	9434	8988	8211	8590	8677	8594	8315	7851	7172	7068
11543	11229	11422	11161	11116	11082	11536	11557	11217	10429	10814	10890	10780	10484	10007	9307	9133
7037	6766	6745	7070	6697	6958	6841	6956	6539	6731	6637	6744	6936	7070	7209	7409	7744
820	1138	945	1202	1253	1282	828	806	1157	1941	1557	1479	1587	1882	2359	3058	3230
9558	10097	9945	9889	10242	10062	9766	9635	10253	10737	10528	10392	10319	10400	10515	10470	10135
1490	1208	1377	1080	1157	1018	1458	1483	1330	772	1007	972	779	503	320	831	948
894	738	862	517	752	523	899	899	929	814	779	669	480	473	802	1436	1546
1001	725	884	583	698	524	959	988	877	616	644	559	353	267	627	1295	1445
933	905	997	636	945	694	994	960	1116	1043	1007	890	710	693	952	1522	1581
816	545	695	393	539	337	767	798	718	654	562	447	266	365	798	1480	1636
1051	833	979	654	819	623	1036	1049	999	731	779	691	486	372	637	1267	1385
1316	1242	1357	1000	1254	1027	1370	1342	1432	1154	1239	1147	944	801	848	1269	1265
1258	1122	1252	905	1120	908	1285	1273	1300	984	1081	997	792	632	702	1191	1232
533	1069	932	894	1213	1059	756	616	1245	1805	1508	1378	1366	1586	2009	2653	2735
388	928	781	779	1073	936	603	467	1094	1686	1374	1248	1251	1489	1927	2588	2690
413	950	812	781	1094	943	637	497	1126	1691	1390	1261	1253	1481	1912	2566	2660
304	843	701	693	988	850	524	385	1014	1599	1288	1161	1165	1404	1846	2511	2619
442	964	842	767	1106	935	673	531	1153	1676	1392	1259	1236	1449	1868	2511	2594
360	900	751	758	1045	913	573	437	1064	1663	1348	1222	1230	1470	1912	2576	2682
317	843	717	661	986	826	547	405	1028	1572	1276	1146	1134	1360	1792	2449	2548
152	692	549	560	837	709	373	233	862	1458	1139	1015	1029	1280	1732	2408	2533
35	574	434	458	719	599	263	121	747	1346	1023	899	921	1180	1639	2321	2458
98	611	488	455	755	609	326	187	797	1359	1050	922	926	1172	1623	2299	2425
0	539	400	429	684	567	231	90	712	1313	988	865	889	1151	1612	2296	2437
539	0	194	305	144	215	353	467	230	815	456	349	454	755	1232	1932	2135
400	194	0	360	324	359	179	315	313	1008	641	542	643	942	1419	2120	2313
429	305	360	0	406	172	383	405	536	910	639	502	472	721	1183	1872	2028
684	144	324	406	0	262	494	612	179	689	316	226	379	678	1145	1843	2063
567	215	359	172	262	0	456	522	422	749	466	329	323	602	1077	1775	1956
231	353	179	383	494	456	0	141	491	1164	809	700	770	1058	1533	2230	2403

		W0	W0	W1	W1	W1	W1	W1	W1	W2	W2	W3	W3
W4	Richmond VA	1342	1273	616	467	497	385	531	437	405	233	121	187
W4	Tallahassee FL	1432	1300	1245	1094	1126	1014	1153	1064	1028	862	747	797
W5	Austin TX	1154	984	1805	1686	1691	1599	1676	1663	1572	1458	1346	1359
W5	Baton Rouge LA	1239	1081	1508	1374	1390	1288	1392	1348	1276	1139	1023	1050
W5	Jackson MS	1147	997	1378	1248	1261	1161	1259	1222	1146	1015	899	922
W5	Little Rock AR	944	792	1366	1251	1253	1165	1236	1230	1134	1029	921	926
W5	Oklahoma City OK	801	632	1586	1489	1481	1404	1449	1470	1360	1280	1180	1172
W5	Santa Fe NM	848	702	2009	1927	1912	1846	1868	1912	1792	1732	1639	1623
W6	Los Angeles CA	1269	1191	2653	2588	2566	2511	2511	2576	2449	2408	2321	2299
W6	San Francisco CA	1265	1232	2735	2690	2660	2619	2594	2682	2548	2533	2458	2425
W7	Boise ID	780	788	2279	2252	2215	2187	2141	2248	2110	2119	2059	2016
W7	Carson City NV	1090	1059	2562	2519	2488	2449	2421	2512	2377	2365	2292	2258
W7	Cheyenne WY	438	316	1779	1727	1699	1654	1637	1718	1585	1566	1493	1459
W7	Olympia WA	1038	1098	2521	2516	2472	2460	2390	2517	2376	2410	2363	2312
W7	Pheonix AZ	1090	975	2362	2285	2268	2204	2220	2270	2148	2092	1999	1983
W7	Salem OR	1076	1113	2573	2559	2517	2499	2439	2557	2418	2440	2386	2339
W7	Salt Lake City UT	692	636	2135	2089	2058	2018	1994	2081	1947	1933	1861	1827
W8	Charleston WV	1132	1054	740	613	623	526	623	590	508	386	279	286
W8	Columbus OH	1003	934	741	636	632	552	610	618	511	435	350	326
W8	Lansing MI	838	794	751	685	660	612	609	676	544	536	488	436
W9	Indianapolis IN	879	793	897	800	791	717	762	783	670	601	514	492
W9	Madison WI	611	553	983	927	899	855	841	919	785	778	721	675
W9	Springfield IL	740	633	1065	977	963	895	926	961	843	785	699	676
XE1	MEXICO CITY MEXICO	1889	1720	2408	2268	2289	2183	2297	2240	2179	2032	1915	1949
YA	KABUL AFGANISTAN	6769	6933	6398	6556	6513	6627	6471	6588	6597	6773	6881	6823
ZD8	ASCENSION IS.	6510	6468	5042	5034	5081	5088	5167	5033	5173	5140	5194	5241
ZF	CAYMAN IS.	2204	2060	1822	1663	1715	1603	1773	1631	1651	1469	1378	1448
ZL1	AUCKLAND NEWZEALAND	7776	7708	9097	8990	8989	8903	8960	8968	8868	8765	8653	8664
ZP	ASUNCION PARAGUAY	5668	5523	4874	4751	4816	4736	4908	4726	4819	4664	4623	4700
ZS1	CAPE TOWN SO.AFRICA	9189	9145	7710	7710	7756	7766	7839	7709	7850	7819	7871	7919
4X	ISRAEL	6262	6385	5278	5415	5396	5500	5395	5443	5509	5651	5768	5737
5R	TANANARIVE MALAGASY	9799	9879	8455	8538	8552	8620	8597	8554	8672	8739	8839	8847
5W	WESTERN SAMOA	6092	6044	7512	7434	7418	7352	7370	7418	7299	7232	7131	7125
6W	DAKAR SENEGAL	5167	5163	3666	3696	3730	3765	3803	3702	3838	3851	3931	3960
9N	KATMANDU NEPAL	7262	7431	7204	7363	7312	7424	7255	7395	7379	7560	7658	7591
9Q	KINSHASA ZAIRE	7647	7673	6174	6230	6255	6306	6316	6241	6371	6408	6497	6517
9Y	TRINIDAD IS.	3441	3330	2425	2309	2374	2303	2468	2286	2389	2249	2228	2302

		W7	W7	W7	W7	W7	W7	W7	W8	W8	W8	W9	W9
A4	MUSCAT OMAN	7788	8108	7844	7565	7565	7711	7956	7444	7399	7293	7509	7405
BY	PEKING CHINA	5796	5921	6262	5408	5408	5511	6087	6907	6776	6572	6747	6476
CE	SANTIAGO CHILE	6043	5913	5588	6429	6429	6325	5753	5003	5130	5332	5148	5412
CT	LISBON PORTUGAL	5152	5492	4787	5242	5242	5348	5101	3805	3826	3824	3984	4036
CU	SAO MIGUEL IS AZORES	4460	4776	4019	4620	4620	4705	4361	2937	2976	3006	3140	3234
CX	MONTEVIDEO URUGUAY	6599	6520	6085	6996	6996	6909	6301	5306	5441	5648	5491	5771
DU	MANILA PHILIPPINES	7031	7039	7593	6633	6633	6696	7327	8491	8354	8147	8288	8004
FO	PAPEETE POLYNESIA	4707	4348	4944	4745	4745	4611	4679	5822	5810	5832	5657	5637
FY	CAYENNE FR. GUIANA	4686	4796	4082	5054	5054	5036	4418	2947	3082	3272	3194	3470
G	LONDON ENGLAND	4833	5191	4602	4828	4828	4954	4857	3872	3852	3788	3986	3955
HA	BUDAPEST HUNGARY	5572	5931	5410	5510	5510	5646	5634	4760	4733	4657	4861	4810
HC	QUITO ECUADOR	3816	3765	3299	4215	4215	4135	3518	2672	2795	2994	2804	3068
HS	BANKOK THAILAND	7835	7945	8301	7445	7445	7543	8128	8823	8704	8507	8703	8448
I	ROME ITALY	5727	6085	5493	5712	5712	5841	5752	4709	4700	4652	4842	4829
JA	TOYKO JAPAN	5175	5200	5733	4776	4776	4843	5472	6677	6539	6335	6458	6174
JT	ULAN BATOR MONGOLIA	5583	5766	5976	5219	5219	5338	5859	6448	6325	6127	6320	6065
KH6	HILO HAWAII	2775	2485	3278	2609	2609	2519	2915	4499	4413	4320	4248	4077
KL7	FAIRBANKS ALASKA	1901	2098	2341	1540	1540	1667	2182	3169	3031	2828	2953	2669
KL7	JUNEAU ALASKA	1276	1471	1749	912	912	1040	1562	2698	2561	2368	2461	2179
KP2	VIRGIN ISLANDS	3479	3607	2875	3843	3843	3828	3217	1743	1879	2075	1985	2264
LA	OSLO NORWAY	4673	5030	4554	4594	4594	4732	4753	4044	3996	3892	4107	4017
LZ	SOFIA BULGARIA	5962	6321	5798	5896	5896	6033	6024	5122	5100	5031	5232	5189
P2	MADANG P.N.G.	6865	6682	7459	6544	6544	6527	7097	8691	8573	8418	8428	8186
PY	RIO DJANEIRO BRAZIL	6496	6520	5914	6889	6889	6840	6205	4896	5033	5233	5125	5409
T5	MOGADISHU SOMALIA	9067	9423	8900	8958	8958	9102	9137	8051	8065	8041	8217	8232
TF	REYKJAVIK ICELAND	3688	4047	3510	3664	3664	3793	3735	2979	2926	2819	3034	2945
TJ	YAOUNDE CAMEROON	7821	8138	7372	7955	7955	8052	7720	6215	6280	6340	6446	6576
UA3	MOSCOW EUR. RUSSIA	5397	5740	5383	5241	5241	5386	5528	5019	4959	4837	5057	4936
UA9	NOVOSIBIRSK RUSSIA	5515	5779	5762	5214	5214	5353	5749	5909	5806	5628	5843	5630
UA9	PERM ASIATIC RUSSIA	5397	5715	5494	5175	5175	5322	5575	5344	5264	5115	5337	5174
UA0	YAKUTSK AS RUSSIA	4263	4444	4675	3897	3897	4016	4543	5269	5138	4933	5109	4840
UA0	OKHOTSK AS RUSSIA	4010	4152	4474	3626	3626	3734	4300	5202	5067	4860	5017	4738
UA0	UST OLENEK AS RUSSIA	3950	4191	4268	3626	3626	3761	4203	4680	4556	4357	4550	4297
UL7	ALMA-ATA KAZAKH	6368	6636	6594	6071	6071	6211	6596	6635	6543	6378	6598	6404
V3	BELIZE BELIZE	2432	2411	1908	2831	2831	2759	2134	1491	1583	1755	1540	1766
V85	BRUNEI	7806	7802	8371	7409	7409	7468	8101	9253	9117	8910	9058	8775
VE1	Halifax N.S.	2560	2852	2075	2785	2785	2845	2427	1024	1038	1052	1196	1282

W3	W4	W4	W4	W4	W4	W4	W4	W4	W5	W5	W5	W5	W5	W5	W6	W6
90	467	315	405	612	522	141	0	628	1259	921	803	845	1118	1587	2277	2431
712	230	313	536	179	422	491	628	0	799	409	369	550	841	1299	1990	2223
1313	815	1008	910	689	749	1164	1259	799	0	389	466	441	359	589	1226	1501
1988	456	641	639	316	466	809	921	409	389	0	138	299	504	919	1596	1847
865	349	542	502	226	329	700	803	369	466	138	0	206	475	929	1623	1853
889	454	643	472	379	323	770	845	550	441	299	206	0	302	777	1478	1686
1151	755	942	721	678	602	1058	1118	841	359	504	475	302	0	477	1177	1385
1612	1232	1419	1183	1145	1077	1533	1587	1299	589	919	929	777	477	0	700	928
2296	1932	2120	1872	1843	1775	2230	2277	1990	1226	1596	1623	1478	1177	700	0	348
2437	2135	2313	2028	2063	1956	2403	2431	2223	1501	1847	1853	1686	1385	928	348	0
2042	1831	1989	1665	1790	1630	2048	2051	1965	1370	1642	1609	1415	1139	797	673	520
2272	1986	2161	1867	1920	1802	2245	2268	2085	1389	1719	1716	1541	1243	804	365	174
1473	1227	1387	1075	1186	1028	1456	1472	1363	851	1060	1014	814	557	419	884	966
2350	2193	2340	2001	2163	1985	2382	2370	2341	1769	2032	1993	1794	1528	1195	931	641
1972	1583	1773	1544	1488	1435	1891	1947	1632	867	1236	1266	1129	833	360	360	654
2371	2179	2335	2005	2140	1976	2388	2385	2315	1705	1989	1959	1765	1487	1121	795	495
1841	1578	1746	1441	1524	1386	1822	1840	1695	1073	1356	1333	1145	858	500	582	601
249	352	300	180	488	323	240	228	567	1073	769	638	642	901	1364	2052	2203
329	438	428	163	556	335	377	339	665	1066	802	665	625	852	1297	1973	2107
479	621	634	317	721	470	577	516	852	1126	922	784	692	855	1259	1905	2006
491	425	487	127	508	250	492	488	653	924	701	562	484	689	1131	1807	1946
708	698	772	412	757	496	762	730	918	997	876	746	598	682	1041	1669	1763
676	505	619	275	542	291	658	669	711	799	647	517	378	525	950	1623	1762
1879	1340	1498	1547	1195	1374	1677	1804	1197	750	908	1045	1133	1108	1161	1542	1883
6914	7405	7311	7134	7534	7300	7144	7003	7616	7866	7754	7616	7492	7512	7597	7663	7373
5210	5475	5296	5594	5553	5654	5213	5201	5402	6178	5799	5770	5926	6228	6699	7393	7609
1350	1012	1001	1315	958	1212	1127	1261	789	1305	1007	1065	1271	1512	1891	2515	2805
8619	8099	8279	8210	7957	8055	8451	8561	7994	7306	7642	7757	7738	7511	7105	6516	6524
4610	4448	4381	4734	4416	4659	4442	4538	4241	4672	4453	4526	4732	4947	5245	5714	6055
7886	8116	7947	8261	8178	8306	7878	7874	8014	8743	8388	8383	8557	8855	9307	9965	10235
5804	6343	6186	6160	6488	6330	6007	5878	6494	7058	6786	6655	6618	6776	7076	7485	7335
8868	9316	9122	9297	9436	9426	8979	8904	9331	10125	9738	9662	9748	10019	10464	11069	10992
7102	6632	6825	6673	6502	6539	6978	7062	6584	5816	6190	6283	6216	5952	5506	4864	4828
3955	4342	4149	4377	4453	4479	4023	3971	4340	5137	4748	4680	4789	5081	5556	6249	6383
7687	8124	8067	7829	8235	7981	7917	7778	8350	8413	8397	8268	8108	8055	8017	7889	7557
6523	6933	6739	6950	7047	7062	6608	6547	6933	7731	7342	7273	7377	7664	8134	8816	8906
2222	2209	2084	2443	2231	2422	2094	2162	2054	2739	2396	2411	2604	2886	3312	3962	4239

W9	XE1	YA	ZD8	ZF	ZL1	ZP	ZS1	4X	5R	5W	6W	9N	9Q	9Y
7608	9108	1011	5282	8379	8578	8440	4743	1619	3005	9089	4940	1696	3479	7739
6688	7733	2585	8618	8183	6464	11365	8036	4447	5991	5922	7633	1952	6990	8977
5196	4105	10146	4056	3711	6004	964	4937	8172	6996	6296	4825	10953	5817	3064
4148	5387	4208	3234	4397	12183	5418	5306	2429	5404	10459	1735	5261	3351	3753
3315	4463	5075	3293	3448	11255	4811	5737	3375	6201	9765	1705	6110	3963	2873
5572	4689	9370	3296	4076	6495	655	4149	7461	6218	7023	4256	10121	4996	3111
8189	8825	3486	9285	9656	4982	11675	7480	5502	5493	4996	8943	2457	7336	10722
5501	4244	9789	8958	5309	2564	5802	8793	11362	9669	1527	9228	8908	10587	6302
3340	3303	7754	2849	2146	8732	2123	5315	5815	6973	8282	2461	8814	4705	690
4120	5543	3540	4178	4759	11387	6343	5996	2147	5645	9833	2718	4548	3958	4436
4987	6434	2704	4303	5657	10991	6908	5613	1287	4911	10061	3079	3744	3583	5244
2851	1950	9273	4538	1372	7120	2230	6603	7523	8551	6440	4294	10247	6475	1397
8670	9769	2418	7912	10125	5947	10791	6296	4344	4241	6289	7752	1370	5962	10349
4985	6364	3053	3804	5479	11415	6441	5237	1330	4751	10517	2594	4110	3192	4913
6347	7016	3887	9856	7797	5489	11184	9143	5700	7075	4682	8644	3198	8292	8996
6288	7501	2135	7994	7748	7182	10659	7836	3835	5882	6547	6924	1809	6512	8360
4064	3616	7682	9763	4801	4376	7238	11376	8761	10949	2629	8694	7230	11178	6238
2851	3831	5274	7940	4336	7307	7800	10208	5695	9173	5622	6361	5430	8165	5495
2337	3212	5868	7801	3788	7188	7245	10328	6115	9704	5452	6278	6057	8364	5029
2128	2294	7657	3918	1080	8671	3045	6493	5985	7984	7681	3085	8644	5608	603
4212	5705	3106	4866	5094	10687	7022	6486	2161	5820	9287	3432	4046	4441	4986
5361	6793	2503	4179	5972	10867	6950	5291	904	4523	10277	3089	3561	3284	5460
8255	7966	5662	10701	9169	2849	9798	8062	7670	6622	2938	11113	4618	8947	10568
5249	4762	8335	2253	3850	7618	911	3774	6367	5774	8107	3123	9226	4106	2563
8372	9597	2719	4078	8467	8421	7078	3034	2232	1456	9741	4360	3176	2120	7298
3138	4634	4114	5001	4082	10425	6478	7105	3186	6789	8720	3422	4978	5091	4195
6629	7458	4248	1876	6255	9912	5033	2639	2462	2914	11654	2104	5103	621	4979
5144	6654	2085	5260	6110	10059	7841	6284	1603	5183	9175	4044	3031	4335	5973
5860	7274	1560	6901	7182	8315	9569	7221	2806	5512	7624	5785	1891	5597	7471
5396	6896	1719	5944	6533	9343	8549	6704	2035	5328	8536	4762	2511	4860	6576
5054	6189	3193	8243	6546	7282	9864	8925	4421	7113	6148	6830	3107	7250	7408
4939	5948	3654	8668	6438	6886	9868	9403	4917	7533	5676	7199	3472	7747	7442
4522	5802	3169	7556	5979	8000	9150	8669	3995	7112	6734	6090	3364	6799	6706
6632	8087	732	6598	7864	8234	9604	6479	2429	4680	7940	5747	1163	5045	7904
1538	731	8532	5417	519	7314	3609	7815	7274	9535	6119	4669	9268	7188	1891
8964	9559	3561	8855	10435	4803	10932	6779	5503	4860	5173	8899	2501	6903	11355
1365	2675	6206	4801	1988	9395	4852	7457	5008	8154	7812	3391	7055	5881	2397

		W7	W7	W7	W7	W7	W7	W7	W8	W8	W8	W9	W9
VE2	Quebec City Que.	2168	2466	1700	2390	2390	2450	2045	786	754	711	892	922
VE3	Ottawa Ont.	1890	2180	1407	2131	2131	2183	1755	577	507	424	622	626
VE4	Winnipeg Mb.	995	1327	706	1187	1187	1251	949	1105	968	773	881	596
VE5	Regina Sk.	715	1068	638	859	859	932	751	1401	1267	1084	1159	879
VE6	Edmondton Al.	696	1036	944	610	610	735	886	1832	1697	1509	1591	1310
VE7	Prince Rupert B.C.	972	1156	1478	598	598	724	1263	2508	2375	2192	2261	1985
VE8	Yellowknife NWT	1302	1624	1526	1113	1113	1258	1504	2165	2028	1822	1963	1681
VO2	Goose Bay Labrador	2563	2897	2195	2699	2699	2789	2503	1436	1395	1317	1519	1488
VY1	Whitehorse Yukon	1412	1624	1854	1061	1061	1194	1691	2744	2606	2409	2516	2231
VK1	CANBERRA AUSTRALIA	8046	7744	8519	7857	7857	7782	8167	9651	9599	9550	9433	9314
VK4	BRISBANE AUSTRALIA	7526	7240	8029	7313	7313	7246	7669	9215	9145	9070	8979	8829
VK6	PERTH AUSTRALIA	9505	9293	10087	9193	9193	9173	9719	11331	11220	11067	11069	10835
VP8	SO. SHETLAND IS.	7961	7766	7573	8319	8319	8196	7687	7045	7173	7376	7191	7455
VP9	BERMUDA	2857	3070	2276	3170	3170	3190	2644	1032	1143	1297	1294	1528
VQ9	DIEGO GARCIA CHAGOS	9876	10109	10098	9548	9548	9678	10114	9761	9726	9628	9843	9740
W0	Denver CO	637	787	99	1025	1025	986	369	1255	1161	1076	998	838
W0	DesMoines IA	1152	1379	580	1483	1483	1489	948	674	564	468	411	239
W0	Topeka KS.	1106	1285	503	1469	1469	1454	864	760	678	633	511	430
W0	Minneapolis MN	1133	1408	638	1418	1418	1448	983	755	623	457	510	231
W0	Jefferson City MO	1293	1478	693	1648	1648	1639	1055	571	499	490	333	344
W0	Lincoln NE	1012	1220	422	1361	1361	1356	791	822	722	638	561	407
W0	Bismark ND	780	1090	438	1038	1038	1076	692	1132	1003	838	879	611
W0	Pierre SD	788	1059	316	1098	1098	1113	636	1054	934	794	793	553
W1	Augusta ME	2279	2562	1779	2521	2521	2573	2135	740	741	751	897	983
W1	Boston MA	2252	2519	1727	2516	2516	2559	2089	613	636	685	800	927
W1	Concord NH	2215	2488	1699	2472	2472	2517	2058	623	632	660	791	899
W1	Hartford CT	2187	2449	1654	2460	2460	2499	2018	526	552	612	717	855
W1	Montpelier VT	2141	2421	1637	2390	2390	2439	1994	623	610	609	762	841
W1	Providence RI	2248	2512	1718	2517	2517	2557	2081	590	618	676	783	919
W2	Albany NY	2110	2377	1585	2376	2376	2418	1947	508	511	544	670	785
W2	Trenton NJ	2119	2365	1566	2410	2410	2440	1933	386	435	536	601	778
W3	Dover DE	2059	2292	1493	2363	2363	2386	1861	279	350	488	514	721
W3	Harrisburg PA	2016	2258	1459	2312	2312	2339	1827	286	326	436	492	675
W3	Washington D.C.	2042	2272	1473	2350	2350	2371	1841	249	329	479	491	708
W4	Atlanta GA	1831	1986	1227	2193	2193	2179	1578	352	438	621	425	698
W4	Columbia SC	1989	2161	1387	2340	2340	2335	1746	300	428	634	487	772
W4	Frankfort KY	1665	1867	1075	2001	2001	2005	1441	180	163	317	127	412
W4	Montgomery AL	1790	1920	1186	2163	2163	2140	1524	488	556	721	508	757
W4	Nashville TN	1630	1802	1028	1985	1985	1976	1386	323	335	470	250	496
W4	Raleigh NC	2048	2245	1456	2382	2382	2388	1822	240	377	577	492	762
W4	Richmond VA	2051	2268	1472	2370	2370	2385	1840	228	339	516	488	730
W4	Tallahassee FL	1965	2085	1363	2341	2341	2315	1695	567	665	852	653	918
W5	Austin TX	1370	1389	851	1769	1769	1705	1073	1073	1066	1126	924	997
W5	Baton Rouge LA	1642	1719	1060	2032	2032	1989	1356	769	802	922	701	876
W5	Jackson MS	1609	1716	1014	1993	1993	1959	1333	638	665	784	562	746
W5	Little Rock AR	1415	1541	814	1794	1794	1765	1145	642	625	692	484	598
W5	Oklahoma City OK	1139	1243	557	1528	1528	1487	858	901	852	855	689	682
W5	Santa Fe NM	797	804	419	1195	1195	1121	500	1364	1297	1259	1131	1041
W6	Los Angeles CA	673	365	884	931	931	795	582	2052	1973	1905	1807	1669
W6	San Francisco CA	520	174	966	641	641	495	601	2203	2107	2006	1946	1763
W7	Boise ID	0	359	604	399	399	349	297	1827	1714	1583	1564	1341
W7	Carson City NV	359	0	799	565	565	431	431	2040	1942	1836	1782	1593
W7	Cheyenne WY	604	799	0	979	979	953	368	1244	1143	1041	984	800
W7	Olympia WA	399	565	979	0	0	146	697	2152	2030	1876	1891	1642
W7	Pheonix AZ	734	581	659	1093	1093	982	500	1725	1657	1611	1490	1386
W7	Salem OR	349	431	953	146	146	0	634	2163	2046	1903	1900	1665
W7	Salt Lake City UT	297	431	368	697	697	634	0	1612	1511	1405	1352	1162
W8	Charleston WV	1827	2040	1244	2152	2152	2163	1612	0	138	343	262	523
W8	Columbus OH	1714	1942	1143	2030	2030	2046	1511	138	0	206	166	392
W8	Lansing MI	1583	1836	1041	1876	1876	1903	1405	343	206	0	222	243
W9	Indianapolis IN	1564	1782	984	1891	1891	1900	1352	262	166	222	0	284
W9	Madison WI	1341	1593	800	1642	1642	1665	1162	523	392	243	284	0
W9	Springfield IL	1390	1599	803	1727	1727	1730	1171	441	350	332	184	229
XE1	MEXICO CITY MEXICO	1938	1831	1534	2324	2324	2226	1650	1674	1710	1817	1599	1726
YA	KABUL AFGANISTAN	7012	7299	7179	6738	6738	6880	7221	7053	6978	6833	7055	6893
ZD8	ASCENSION IS.	7252	7457	6670	7548	7548	7580	7036	5427	5537	5676	5690	5915
ZF	CAYMAN IS.	2646	2694	2067	3039	3039	2991	2356	1301	1423	1622	1437	1707
ZL1	AUCKLAND NEWZEALAND	7038	6696	7398	6955	6955	6847	7085	8379	8357	8358	8199	8147
ZP	ASUNCION PARAGUAY	6041	5995	5503	6440	6440	6364	5743	4668	4804	5011	4861	5143
ZS1	CAPE TOWN SO.AFRICA	9925	10098	9333	10226	10226	10258	9693	8098	8212	8355	8361	8593
4X	ISRAEL	6835	7191	6696	6740	6740	6881	6911	6017	5999	5934	6133	6093
5R	TANANARIVE MALAGASY	10477	10836	10191	10409	10409	10550	10490	9117	9171	9206	9337	9430
5W	WESTERN SAMOA	5331	5002	5746	5220	5220	5117	5410	6852	6801	6761	6635	6531
6W	DAKAR SENEGAL	5945	6214	5417	6175	6175	6236	5783	4197	4281	4377	4446	4621
9N	KATMANDU NEPAL	7309	7529	7621	6969	6969	7097	7567	7783	7686	7513	7730	7521
9Q	KINSHASA ZAIRE	8423	8732	7954	8570	8570	8664	8308	6770	6843	6915	7009	7155
9Y	TRINIDAD IS.	4019	4115	3418	4395	4395	4369	3745	2333	2471	2670	2568	2850

W9	XE1	YA	ZD8	ZF	ZL1	ZP	ZS1	4X	5R	5W	6W	9N	9Q	9Y
1041	2458	6290	5191	1957	9068	5059	7851	5245	8509	7446	3786	7071	6265	2611
757	2216	6477	5428	1843	8774	5089	8099	5512	8804	7152	4055	7211	6553	2670
789	2103	6532	6377	2288	8023	5737	9048	5993	9541	6326	4988	7061	7430	3439
1034	2157	6542	6711	2509	7752	5972	9381	6161	9771	6036	5316	6992	7734	3727
1465	2473	6335	7086	2927	7561	6390	9735	6164	9828	5822	5645	6698	7977	4159
2122	2910	6176	7747	3537	7088	6980	10358	6350	9976	5342	6268	6373	8474	4824
1880	3060	5717	7073	3380	7883	6825	9602	5632	9298	6137	5544	6096	7679	4482
1649	3105	5652	5059	2564	9588	5437	7634	4616	7997	7894	3543	6465	5874	2990
2401	3340	5704	7754	3870	7301	7333	10230	5955	9538	5571	6213	5908	8242	5078
9254	8180	7057	9216	9230	1426	7885	6689	8779	6082	2799	10774	6021	8377	9848
8795	7875	6951	9807	9010	1413	8244	7260	8824	6511	2407	11354	5893	8865	9901
10890	10082	5508	8095	11089	3305	8453	5422	6957	4300	4635	9282	4588	6689	10909
7236	6048	9499	4372	5755	4986	2526	3769	8256	5571	6056	5741	9551	5430	4972
1473	2300	6924	4395	1316	9086	4014	7068	5496	8183	7740	3204	7834	5795	1560
9944	11435	2918	5847	10448	6561	8384	3888	3759	1850	7747	6350	2580	3942	9262
814	1441	7278	6670	2014	7334	5436	9324	6783	10254	5695	5443	7717	7992	3383
244	1561	7053	6100	1707	7908	5168	8772	6317	9669	6294	4837	7636	7383	2942
327	1366	7249	6172	1623	7726	5085	8830	6521	9837	6133	4956	7812	7521	2927
404	1792	6822	6133	1903	8032	5354	8811	6131	9556	6384	4813	7402	7325	3079
159	1383	7234	5980	1489	7875	4952	8639	6419	9670	6302	4769	7842	7339	2754
380	1481	7141	6248	1754	7741	5217	8915	6462	9838	6124	5001	7687	7551	3041
740	1889	6769	6510	2204	7776	5668	9189	6262	9799	6092	5167	7262	7647	3441
633	1720	6933	6468	2060	7708	5523	9145	6385	9879	6044	5163	7431	7673	3330
1065	2408	6398	5042	1822	9097	4874	7710	5278	8455	7512	3666	7204	6174	2425
977	2268	6556	5034	1663	8990	4751	7710	5415	8538	7434	3696	7363	6230	2309
963	2289	6513	5081	1715	8989	4816	7756	5396	8552	7418	3730	7312	6255	2374
895	2183	6627	5088	1603	8903	4736	7766	5500	8620	7352	3765	7424	6306	2303
926	2297	6471	5167	1773	8960	4908	7839	5395	8597	7370	3803	7255	6316	2468
961	2240	6588	5033	1631	8968	4726	7709	5443	8554	7418	3702	7395	6241	2286
843	2179	6597	5173	1651	8868	4819	7850	5509	8672	7299	3838	7379	6371	2389
785	2032	6773	5140	1469	8765	4664	7819	5651	8739	7232	3851	7560	6408	2249
699	1915	6881	5194	1378	8653	4623	7871	5768	8839	7131	3931	7658	6497	2228
676	1949	6823	5241	1448	8664	4700	7919	5737	8847	7125	3960	7591	6517	2302
676	1879	6914	5210	1350	8619	4610	7886	5804	8868	7102	3955	7687	6523	2222
505	1340	7405	5475	1012	8099	4448	8116	6343	9316	6632	4342	8124	6933	2209
619	1498	7311	5296	1001	8279	4381	7947	6186	9122	6825	4149	8067	6739	2084
275	1547	7134	5594	1315	8210	4734	8261	6160	9297	6673	4377	7829	6950	2443
542	1195	7534	5553	958	7957	4416	8178	6488	9436	6502	4453	8235	7047	2231
291	1374	7300	5654	1212	8055	4659	8306	6330	9426	6539	4479	7981	7062	2422
658	1677	7144	5213	1127	8451	4442	7878	6007	8979	6978	4023	7917	6608	2094
669	1804	7003	5201	1261	8561	4538	7874	5878	8904	7062	3971	7778	6547	2162
711	1197	7616	5402	789	7994	4241	8014	6494	9331	6584	4340	8350	6933	2054
799	750	7866	6178	1305	7306	4672	8743	7058	10125	5816	5137	8413	7731	2739
647	908	7754	5799	1007	7642	4453	8388	6786	9738	6190	4748	8397	7342	2396
517	1045	7616	5770	1065	7757	4526	8383	6655	9662	6283	4680	8268	7273	2411
378	1133	7492	5926	1271	7738	4732	8557	6618	9748	6216	4789	8108	7377	2604
525	1108	7512	6228	1512	7511	4947	8855	6776	10019	5952	5081	8055	7664	2886
950	1161	7597	6699	1891	7105	5245	9307	7076	10464	5506	5556	8017	8134	3312
1623	1542	7663	7393	2515	6516	5714	9965	7485	11069	4864	6249	7889	8816	3962
1762	1883	7373	7609	2805	6524	6055	10235	7335	10992	4828	6383	7557	8906	4239
1390	1938	7012	7252	2646	7038	6041	9925	6835	10477	5331	5945	7309	8423	4019
1599	1831	7299	7457	2694	6696	5995	10098	7191	10836	5002	6214	7529	8732	4115
803	1534	7179	6670	2067	7398	5503	9333	6696	10191	5746	5417	7621	7954	3418
1727	2324	6738	7548	3039	6955	6440	10226	6740	10409	5220	6175	6969	8570	4395
1309	1250	7721	7034	2160	6765	5414	9608	7353	10817	5150	5915	8044	8495	3605
1730	2226	6880	7580	2991	6847	6364	10258	6881	10550	5117	6236	7097	8664	4369
1171	1650	7221	7036	2356	7085	5743	9693	6911	10490	5410	5783	7567	8308	3745
441	1674	7053	5427	1301	8379	4668	8098	6017	9117	6852	4197	7783	6770	2333
350	1710	6978	5537	1423	8357	4804	8212	5999	9171	6801	4281	7686	6843	2471
332	1817	6833	5676	1622	8358	5011	8355	5934	9206	6761	4377	7513	6915	2670
184	1599	7055	5690	1437	8199	4861	8361	6133	9337	6635	4446	7730	7009	2568
229	1726	6893	5915	1707	8147	5143	8593	6093	9430	6531	4621	7521	7155	2850
0	1511	7115	5867	1499	8034	4951	8536	6265	9515	6457	4631	7751	7193	2701
1511	0	8614	6149	1213	6803	4172	8510	7683	10265	5474	5353	9149	7902	2623
7115	8614	0	6090	8193	8364	9216	5753	2019	3955	8403	5456	1060	4409	7947
5867	6149	6090	0	4963	9288	3159	2678	4172	4123	10310	1593	6978	1958	3525
1499	1213	8193	4963	0	7808	3463	7450	6805	9059	6639	4153	9026	6689	1455
8034	6803	8364	9288	7808	0	6948	7314	10198	7264	1746	10720	7305	9291	8505
4951	4172	9216	3159	3463	6948	0	4495	7219	6549	7234	3861	10136	5014	2456
8536	8510	5753	2678	7450	7314	4495	0	4698	2069	9022	4094	6099	2046	6003
6265	7683	2019	4172	6805	10198	7219	4698	0	3668	10369	3443	3051	2830	6128
9515	10265	3955	4123	9059	7264	6549	2069	3668	0	8881	4992	4088	2401	7646
6457	5474	8403	10310	6639	1746	7234	9022	10369	8881	0	10729	7436	11036	7777
4631	5353	5456	1593	4153	10720	3861	4094	3443	4992	10729	0	6495	2594	2951
7751	9149	1060	6978	9026	7305	10136	6099	3051	4088	7436	6495	0	5148	8982
7193	7902	4409	1958	6689	9291	5014	2046	2830	2401	11036	2594	5148	0	5337
2701	2623	7947	3525	1455	8505	2456	6003	6128	7646	7777	2951	8982	5337	0

1988

January

S	M	T	W	T	F	S
					1	2
3	4	5	6	7	8	9
10	11	12	13	14	15	16
17	18	19	20	21	22	23
24	25	26	27	28	29	30
31						

February

S	M	T	W	T	F	S
	1	2	3	4	5	6
7	8	9	10	11	12	13
14	15	16	17	18	19	20
21	22	23	24	25	26	27
28	29					

March

S	M	T	W	T	F	S
		1	2	3	4	5
6	7	8	9	10	11	12
13	14	15	16	17	18	19
20	21	22	23	24	25	26
27	28	29	30	31		

April

S	M	T	W	T	F	S
					1	2
3	4	5	6	7	8	9
10	11	12	13	14	15	16
17	18	19	20	21	22	23
24	25	26	27	28	29	30

May

S	M	T	W	T	F	S
1	2	3	4	5	6	7
8	9	10	11	12	13	14
15	16	17	18	19	20	21
22	23	24	25	26	27	28
29	30	31				

June

S	M	T	W	T	F	S
			1	2	3	4
5	6	7	8	9	10	11
12	13	14	15	16	17	18
19	20	21	22	23	24	25
26	27	28	29	30		

July

S	M	T	W	T	F	S
					1	2
3	4	5	6	7	8	9
10	11	12	13	14	15	16
17	18	19	20	21	22	23
24	25	26	27	28	29	30
31						

August

S	M	T	W	T	F	S
	1	2	3	4	5	6
7	8	9	10	11	12	13
14	15	16	17	18	19	20
21	22	23	24	25	26	27
28	29	30	31			

September

S	M	T	W	T	F	S
				1	2	3
4	5	6	7	8	9	10
11	12	13	14	15	16	17
18	19	20	21	22	23	24
25	26	27	28	29	30	

October

S	M	T	W	T	F	S
						1
2	3	4	5	6	7	8
9	10	11	12	13	14	15
16	17	18	19	20	21	22
23	24	25	26	27	28	29
30	31					

November

S	M	T	W	T	F	S
		1	2	3	4	5
6	7	8	9	10	11	12
13	14	15	16	17	18	19
20	21	22	23	24	25	26
27	28	29	30			

December

S	M	T	W	T	F	S
				1	2	3
4	5	6	7	8	9	10
11	12	13	14	15	16	17
18	19	20	21	22	23	24
25	26	27	28	29	30	31

1989

January

S	M	T	W	T	F	S
1	2	3	4	5	6	7
8	9	10	11	12	13	14
15	16	17	18	19	20	21
22	23	24	25	26	27	28
29	30	31				

February

S	M	T	W	T	F	S
			1	2	3	4
5	6	7	8	9	10	11
12	13	14	15	16	17	18
19	20	21	22	23	24	25
26	27	28				

March

S	M	T	W	T	F	S
			1	2	3	4
5	6	7	8	9	10	11
12	13	14	15	16	17	18
19	20	21	22	23	24	25
26	27	28	29	30	31	

April

S	M	T	W	T	F	S
						1
2	3	4	5	6	7	8
9	10	11	12	13	14	15
16	17	18	19	20	21	22
23	24	25	26	27	28	29
30						

May

S	M	T	W	T	F	S
	1	2	3	4	5	6
7	8	9	10	11	12	13
14	15	16	17	18	19	20
21	22	23	24	25	26	27
28	29	30	31			

June

S	M	T	W	T	F	S
				1	2	3
4	5	6	7	8	9	10
11	12	13	14	15	16	17
18	19	20	21	22	23	24
25	26	27	28	29	30	

July

S	M	T	W	T	F	S
						1
2	3	4	5	6	7	8
9	10	11	12	13	14	15
16	17	18	19	20	21	22
23	24	25	26	27	28	29
30	31					

August

S	M	T	W	T	F	S
		1	2	3	4	5
6	7	8	9	10	11	12
13	14	15	16	17	18	19
20	21	22	23	24	25	26
27	28	29	30	31		

September

S	M	T	W	T	F	S
					1	2
3	4	5	6	7	8	9
10	11	12	13	14	15	16
17	18	19	20	21	22	23
24	25	26	27	28	29	30

October

S	M	T	W	T	F	S
1	2	3	4	5	6	7
8	9	10	11	12	13	14
15	16	17	18	19	20	21
22	23	24	25	26	27	28
29	30	31				

November

S	M	T	W	T	F	S
			1	2	3	4
5	6	7	8	9	10	11
12	13	14	15	16	17	18
19	20	21	22	23	24	25
26	27	28	29	30		

December

S	M	T	W	T	F	S
					1	2
3	4	5	6	7	8	9
10	11	12	13	14	15	16
17	18	19	20	21	22	23
24	25	26	27	28	29	30
31						

1990

January

S	M	T	W	T	F	S
	1	2	3	4	5	6
7	8	9	10	11	12	13
14	15	16	17	18	19	20
21	22	23	24	25	26	27
28	29	30	31			

February

S	M	T	W	T	F	S
				1	2	3
4	5	6	7	8	9	10
11	12	13	14	15	16	17
18	19	20	21	22	23	24
25	26	27	28			

March

S	M	T	W	T	F	S
				1	2	3
4	5	6	7	8	9	10
11	12	13	14	15	16	17
18	19	20	21	22	23	24
25	26	27	28	29	30	31

April

S	M	T	W	T	F	S
1	2	3	4	5	6	7
8	9	10	11	12	13	14
15	16	17	18	19	20	21
22	23	24	25	26	27	28
29	30					

May

S	M	T	W	T	F	S
		1	2	3	4	5
6	7	8	9	10	11	12
13	14	15	16	17	18	19
20	21	22	23	24	25	26
27	28	29	30	31		

June

S	M	T	W	T	F	S
					1	2
3	4	5	6	7	8	9
10	11	12	13	14	15	16
17	18	19	20	21	22	23
24	25	26	27	28	29	30

July

S	M	T	W	T	F	S
1	2	3	4	5	6	7
8	9	10	11	12	13	14
15	16	17	18	19	20	21
22	23	24	25	26	27	28
29	30	31				

August

S	M	T	W	T	F	S
			1	2	3	4
5	6	7	8	9	10	11
12	13	14	15	16	17	18
19	20	21	22	23	24	25
26	27	28	29	30	31	

September

S	M	T	W	T	F	S
						1
2	3	4	5	6	7	8
9	10	11	12	13	14	15
16	17	18	19	20	21	22
23	24	25	26	27	28	29
30						

October

S	M	T	W	T	F	S
	1	2	3	4	5	6
7	8	9	10	11	12	13
14	15	16	17	18	19	20
21	22	23	24	25	26	27
28	29	30	31			

November

S	M	T	W	T	F	S
				1	2	3
4	5	6	7	8	9	10
11	12	13	14	15	16	17
18	19	20	21	22	23	24
25	26	27	28	29	30	

December

S	M	T	W	T	F	S
						1
2	3	4	5	6	7	8
9	10	11	12	13	14	15
16	17	18	19	20	21	22
23	24	25	26	27	28	29
30	31					

1991

January

S	M	T	W	T	F	S
		1	2	3	4	5
6	7	8	9	10	11	12
13	14	15	16	17	18	19
20	21	22	23	24	25	26
27	28	29	30	31		

February

S	M	T	W	T	F	S
					1	2
3	4	5	6	7	8	9
10	11	12	13	14	15	16
17	18	19	20	21	22	23
24	25	26	27	28		

March

S	M	T	W	T	F	S
					1	2
3	4	5	6	7	8	9
10	11	12	13	14	15	16
17	18	19	20	21	22	23
24	25	26	27	28	29	30
31						

April

S	M	T	W	T	F	S
	1	2	3	4	5	6
7	8	9	10	11	12	13
14	15	16	17	18	19	20
21	22	23	24	25	26	27
28	29	30				

May

S	M	T	W	T	F	S
			1	2	3	4
5	6	7	8	9	10	11
12	13	14	15	16	17	18
19	20	21	22	23	24	25
26	27	28	29	30	31	

June

S	M	T	W	T	F	S
						1
2	3	4	5	6	7	8
9	10	11	12	13	14	15
16	17	18	19	20	21	22
23	24	25	26	27	28	29
30						

July

S	M	T	W	T	F	S
	1	2	3	4	5	6
7	8	9	10	11	12	13
14	15	16	17	18	19	20
21	22	23	24	25	26	27
28	29	30	31			

August

S	M	T	W	T	F	S
				1	2	3
4	5	6	7	8	9	10
11	12	13	14	15	16	17
18	19	20	21	22	23	24
25	26	27	28	29	30	31

September

S	M	T	W	T	F	S
1	2	3	4	5	6	7
8	9	10	11	12	13	14
15	16	17	18	19	20	21
22	23	24	25	26	27	28
29	30					

October

S	M	T	W	T	F	S
		1	2	3	4	5
6	7	8	9	10	11	12
13	14	15	16	17	18	19
20	21	22	23	24	25	26
27	28	29	30	31		

November

S	M	T	W	T	F	S
					1	2
3	4	5	6	7	8	9
10	11	12	13	14	15	16
17	18	19	20	21	22	23
24	25	26	27	28	29	30

December

S	M	T	W	T	F	S
1	2	3	4	5	6	7
8	9	10	11	12	13	14
15	16	17	18	19	20	21
22	23	24	25	26	27	28
29	30	31				

1992

January

S	M	T	W	T	F	S
			1	2	3	4
5	6	7	8	9	10	11
12	13	14	15	16	17	18
19	20	21	22	23	24	25
26	27	28	29	30	31	

February

S	M	T	W	T	F	S
						1
2	3	4	5	6	7	8
9	10	11	12	13	14	15
16	17	18	19	20	21	22
23	24	25	26	27	28	29

March

S	M	T	W	T	F	S
1	2	3	4	5	6	7
8	9	10	11	12	13	14
15	16	17	18	19	20	21
22	23	24	25	26	27	28
29	30	31				

April

S	M	T	W	T	F	S
			1	2	3	4
5	6	7	8	9	10	11
12	13	14	15	16	17	18
19	20	21	22	23	24	25
26	27	28	29	30		

May

S	M	T	W	T	F	S
					1	2
3	4	5	6	7	8	9
10	11	12	13	14	15	16
17	18	19	20	21	22	23
24	25	26	27	28	29	30
31						

June

S	M	T	W	T	F	S
	1	2	3	4	5	6
7	8	9	10	11	12	13
14	15	16	17	18	19	20
21	22	23	24	25	26	27
28	29	30				

July

S	M	T	W	T	F	S
			1	2	3	4
5	6	7	8	9	10	11
12	13	14	15	16	17	18
19	20	21	22	23	24	25
26	27	28	29	30	31	

August

S	M	T	W	T	F	S
						1
2	3	4	5	6	7	8
9	10	11	12	13	14	15
16	17	18	19	20	21	22
23	24	25	26	27	28	29
30	31					

September

S	M	T	W	T	F	S
		1	2	3	4	5
6	7	8	9	10	11	12
13	14	15	16	17	18	19
20	21	22	23	24	25	26
27	28	29	30			

October

S	M	T	W	T	F	S
				1	2	3
4	5	6	7	8	9	10
11	12	13	14	15	16	17
18	19	20	21	22	23	24
25	26	27	28	29	30	31

November

S	M	T	W	T	F	S
1	2	3	4	5	6	7
8	9	10	11	12	13	14
15	16	17	18	19	20	21
22	23	24	25	26	27	28
29	30					

December

S	M	T	W	T	F	S
		1	2	3	4	5
6	7	8	9	10	11	12
13	14	15	16	17	18	19
20	21	22	23	24	25	26
27	28	29	30	31		

1993

January

S	M	T	W	T	F	S
					1	2
3	4	5	6	7	8	9
10	11	12	13	14	15	16
17	18	19	20	21	22	23
24	25	26	27	28	29	30
31						

February

S	M	T	W	T	F	S
	1	2	3	4	5	6
7	8	9	10	11	12	13
14	15	16	17	18	19	20
21	22	23	24	25	26	27
28						

March

S	M	T	W	T	F	S
	1	2	3	4	5	6
7	8	9	10	11	12	13
14	15	16	17	18	19	20
21	22	23	24	25	26	27
28	29	30	31			

April

S	M	T	W	T	F	S
				1	2	3
4	5	6	7	8	9	10
11	12	13	14	15	16	17
18	19	20	21	22	23	24
25	26	27	28	29	30	

May

S	M	T	W	T	F	S
						1
2	3	4	5	6	7	8
9	10	11	12	13	14	15
16	17	18	19	20	21	22
23	24	25	26	27	28	29
30	31					

June

S	M	T	W	T	F	S
		1	2	3	4	5
6	7	8	9	10	11	12
13	14	15	16	17	18	19
20	21	22	23	24	25	26
27	28	29	30			

July

S	M	T	W	T	F	S
				1	2	3
4	5	6	7	8	9	10
11	12	13	14	15	16	17
18	19	20	21	22	23	24
25	26	27	28	29	30	31

August

S	M	T	W	T	F	S
1	2	3	4	5	6	7
8	9	10	11	12	13	14
15	16	17	18	19	20	21
22	23	24	25	26	27	28
29	30	31				

September

S	M	T	W	T	F	S
			1	2	3	4
5	6	7	8	9	10	11
12	13	14	15	16	17	18
19	20	21	22	23	24	25
26	27	28	29	30		

October

S	M	T	W	T	F	S
					1	2
3	4	5	6	7	8	9
10	11	12	13	14	15	16
17	18	19	20	21	22	23
24	25	26	27	28	29	30
31						

November

S	M	T	W	T	F	S
	1	2	3	4	5	6
7	8	9	10	11	12	13
14	15	16	17	18	19	20
21	22	23	24	25	26	27
28	29	30				

December

S	M	T	W	T	F	S
			1	2	3	4
5	6	7	8	9	10	11
12	13	14	15	16	17	18
19	20	21	22	23	24	25
26	27	28	29	30	31	

1994

January
S	M	T	W	T	F	S
						1
2	3	4	5	6	7	8
9	10	11	12	13	14	15
16	17	18	19	20	21	22
23	24	25	26	27	28	29
30	31					

February
S	M	T	W	T	F	S
		1	2	3	4	5
6	7	8	9	10	11	12
13	14	15	16	17	18	19
20	21	22	23	24	25	26
27	28					

March
S	M	T	W	T	F	S
		1	2	3	4	5
6	7	8	9	10	11	12
13	14	15	16	17	18	19
20	21	22	23	24	25	26
27	28	29	30	31		

April
S	M	T	W	T	F	S
					1	2
3	4	5	6	7	8	9
10	11	12	13	14	15	16
17	18	19	20	21	22	23
24	25	26	27	28	29	30

May
S	M	T	W	T	F	S
1	2	3	4	5	6	7
8	9	10	11	12	13	14
15	16	17	18	19	20	21
22	23	24	25	26	27	28
29	30	31				

June
S	M	T	W	T	F	S
			1	2	3	4
5	6	7	8	9	10	11
12	13	14	15	16	17	18
19	20	21	22	23	24	25
26	27	28	29	30		

July
S	M	T	W	T	F	S
					1	2
3	4	5	6	7	8	9
10	11	12	13	14	15	16
17	18	19	20	21	22	23
24	25	26	27	28	29	30
31						

August
S	M	T	W	T	F	S
	1	2	3	4	5	6
7	8	9	10	11	12	13
14	15	16	17	18	19	20
21	22	23	24	25	26	27
28	29	30	31			

September
S	M	T	W	T	F	S
				1	2	3
4	5	6	7	8	9	10
11	12	13	14	15	16	17
18	19	20	21	22	23	24
25	26	27	28	29	30	

October
S	M	T	W	T	F	S
						1
2	3	4	5	6	7	8
9	10	11	12	13	14	15
16	17	18	19	20	21	22
23	24	25	26	27	28	29
30	31					

November
S	M	T	W	T	F	S
		1	2	3	4	5
6	7	8	9	10	11	12
13	14	15	16	17	18	19
20	21	22	23	24	25	26
27	28	29	30			

December
S	M	T	W	T	F	S
				1	2	3
4	5	6	7	8	9	10
11	12	13	14	15	16	17
18	19	20	21	22	23	24
25	26	27	28	29	30	31

1995

January
S	M	T	W	T	F	S
1	2	3	4	5	6	7
8	9	10	11	12	13	14
15	16	17	18	19	20	21
22	23	24	25	26	27	28
29	30	31				

February
S	M	T	W	T	F	S
			1	2	3	4
5	6	7	8	9	10	11
12	13	14	15	16	17	18
19	20	21	22	23	24	25
26	27	28				

March
S	M	T	W	T	F	S
			1	2	3	4
5	6	7	8	9	10	11
12	13	14	15	16	17	18
19	20	21	22	23	24	25
26	27	28	29	30	31	

April
S	M	T	W	T	F	S
						1
2	3	4	5	6	7	8
9	10	11	12	13	14	15
16	17	18	19	20	21	22
23	24	25	26	27	28	29
30						

May
S	M	T	W	T	F	S
	1	2	3	4	5	6
7	8	9	10	11	12	13
14	15	16	17	18	19	20
21	22	23	24	25	26	27
28	29	30	31			

June
S	M	T	W	T	F	S
				1	2	3
4	5	6	7	8	9	10
11	12	13	14	15	16	17
18	19	20	21	22	23	24
25	26	27	28	29	30	

July
S	M	T	W	T	F	S
						1
2	3	4	5	6	7	8
9	10	11	12	13	14	15
16	17	18	19	20	21	22
23	24	25	26	27	28	29
30	31					

August
S	M	T	W	T	F	S
		1	2	3	4	5
6	7	8	9	10	11	12
13	14	15	16	17	18	19
20	21	22	23	24	25	26
27	28	29	30	31		

September
S	M	T	W	T	F	S
					1	2
3	4	5	6	7	8	9
10	11	12	13	14	15	16
17	18	19	20	21	22	23
24	25	26	27	28	29	30

October
S	M	T	W	T	F	S
1	2	3	4	5	6	7
8	9	10	11	12	13	14
15	16	17	18	19	20	21
22	23	24	25	26	27	28
29	30	31				

November
S	M	T	W	T	F	S
			1	2	3	4
5	6	7	8	9	10	11
12	13	14	15	16	17	18
19	20	21	22	23	24	25
26	27	28	29	30		

December
S	M	T	W	T	F	S
					1	2
3	4	5	6	7	8	9
10	11	12	13	14	15	16
17	18	19	20	21	22	23
24	25	26	27	28	29	30
31						

1996

January
S	M	T	W	T	F	S
	1	2	3	4	5	6
7	8	9	10	11	12	13
14	15	16	17	18	19	20
21	22	23	24	25	26	27
28	29	30	31			

February
S	M	T	W	T	F	S
				1	2	3
4	5	6	7	8	9	10
11	12	13	14	15	16	17
18	19	20	21	22	23	24
25	26	27	28	29		

March
S	M	T	W	T	F	S
					1	2
3	4	5	6	7	8	9
10	11	12	13	14	15	16
17	18	19	20	21	22	23
24	25	26	27	28	29	30
31						

April
S	M	T	W	T	F	S
	1	2	3	4	5	6
7	8	9	10	11	12	13
14	15	16	17	18	19	20
21	22	23	24	25	26	27
28	29	30				

May
S	M	T	W	T	F	S
			1	2	3	4
5	6	7	8	9	10	11
12	13	14	15	16	17	18
19	20	21	22	23	24	25
26	27	28	29	30	31	

June
S	M	T	W	T	F	S
						1
2	3	4	5	6	7	8
9	10	11	12	13	14	15
16	17	18	19	20	21	22
23	24	25	26	27	28	29
30						

July
S	M	T	W	T	F	S
	1	2	3	4	5	6
7	8	9	10	11	12	13
14	15	16	17	18	19	20
21	22	23	24	25	26	27
28	29	30	31			

August
S	M	T	W	T	F	S
				1	2	3
4	5	6	7	8	9	10
11	12	13	14	15	16	17
18	19	20	21	22	23	24
25	26	27	28	29	30	31

September
S	M	T	W	T	F	S
1	2	3	4	5	6	7
8	9	10	11	12	13	14
15	16	17	18	19	20	21
22	23	24	25	26	27	28
29	30					

October
S	M	T	W	T	F	S
		1	2	3	4	5
6	7	8	9	10	11	12
13	14	15	16	17	18	19
20	21	22	23	24	25	26
27	28	29	30	31		

November
S	M	T	W	T	F	S
					1	2
3	4	5	6	7	8	9
10	11	12	13	14	15	16
17	18	19	20	21	22	23
24	25	26	27	28	29	30

December
S	M	T	W	T	F	S
1	2	3	4	5	6	7
8	9	10	11	12	13	14
15	16	17	18	19	20	21
22	23	24	25	26	27	28
29	30	31				

1997

January
S	M	T	W	T	F	S
			1	2	3	4
5	6	7	8	9	10	11
12	13	14	15	16	17	18
19	20	21	22	23	24	25
26	27	28	29	30	31	

February
S	M	T	W	T	F	S
						1
2	3	4	5	6	7	8
9	10	11	12	13	14	15
16	17	18	19	20	21	22
23	24	25	26	27	28	

March
S	M	T	W	T	F	S
						1
2	3	4	5	6	7	8
9	10	11	12	13	14	15
16	17	18	19	20	21	22
23	24	25	26	27	28	29
30	31					

April
S	M	T	W	T	F	S
		1	2	3	4	5
6	7	8	9	10	11	12
13	14	15	16	17	18	19
20	21	22	23	24	25	26
27	28	29	30			

May
S	M	T	W	T	F	S
				1	2	3
4	5	6	7	8	9	10
11	12	13	14	15	16	17
18	19	20	21	22	23	24
25	26	27	28	29	30	31

June
S	M	T	W	T	F	S
1	2	3	4	5	6	7
8	9	10	11	12	13	14
15	16	17	18	19	20	21
22	23	24	25	26	27	28
29	30					

July
S	M	T	W	T	F	S
		1	2	3	4	5
6	7	8	9	10	11	12
13	14	15	16	17	18	19
20	21	22	23	24	25	26
27	28	29	30	31		

August
S	M	T	W	T	F	S
					1	2
3	4	5	6	7	8	9
10	11	12	13	14	15	16
17	18	19	20	21	22	23
24	25	26	27	28	29	30
31						

September
S	M	T	W	T	F	S
	1	2	3	4	5	6
7	8	9	10	11	12	13
14	15	16	17	18	19	20
21	22	23	24	25	26	27
28	29	30				

October
S	M	T	W	T	F	S
			1	2	3	4
5	6	7	8	9	10	11
12	13	14	15	16	17	18
19	20	21	22	23	24	25
26	27	28	29	30	31	

November
S	M	T	W	T	F	S
						1
2	3	4	5	6	7	8
9	10	11	12	13	14	15
16	17	18	19	20	21	22
23	24	25	26	27	28	29
30						

December
S	M	T	W	T	F	S
	1	2	3	4	5	6
7	8	9	10	11	12	13
14	15	16	17	18	19	20
21	22	23	24	25	26	27
28	29	30	31			

1998

January
S	M	T	W	T	F	S
				1	2	3
4	5	6	7	8	9	10
11	12	13	14	15	16	17
18	19	20	21	22	23	24
25	26	27	28	29	30	31

February
S	M	T	W	T	F	S
1	2	3	4	5	6	7
8	9	10	11	12	13	14
15	16	17	18	19	20	21
22	23	24	25	26	27	28

March
S	M	T	W	T	F	S
1	2	3	4	5	6	7
8	9	10	11	12	13	14
15	16	17	18	19	20	21
22	23	24	25	26	27	28
29	30	31				

April
S	M	T	W	T	F	S
			1	2	3	4
5	6	7	8	9	10	11
12	13	14	15	16	17	18
19	20	21	22	23	24	25
26	27	28	29	30		

May
S	M	T	W	T	F	S
					1	2
3	4	5	6	7	8	9
10	11	12	13	14	15	16
17	18	19	20	21	22	23
24	25	26	27	28	29	30
31						

June
S	M	T	W	T	F	S
	1	2	3	4	5	6
7	8	9	10	11	12	13
14	15	16	17	18	19	20
21	22	23	24	25	26	27
28	29	30				

July
S	M	T	W	T	F	S
			1	2	3	4
5	6	7	8	9	10	11
12	13	14	15	16	17	18
19	20	21	22	23	24	25
26	27	28	29	30	31	

August
S	M	T	W	T	F	S
						1
2	3	4	5	6	7	8
9	10	11	12	13	14	15
16	17	18	19	20	21	22
23	24	25	26	27	28	29
30	31					

September
S	M	T	W	T	F	S
		1	2	3	4	5
6	7	8	9	10	11	12
13	14	15	16	17	18	19
20	21	22	23	24	25	26
27	28	29	30			

October
S	M	T	W	T	F	S
				1	2	3
4	5	6	7	8	9	10
11	12	13	14	15	16	17
18	19	20	21	22	23	24
25	26	27	28	29	30	31

November
S	M	T	W	T	F	S
1	2	3	4	5	6	7
8	9	10	11	12	13	14
15	16	17	18	19	20	21
22	23	24	25	26	27	28
29	30					

December
S	M	T	W	T	F	S
		1	2	3	4	5
6	7	8	9	10	11	12
13	14	15	16	17	18	19
20	21	22	23	24	25	26
27	28	29	30	31		

1999

January
S	M	T	W	T	F	S
					1	2
3	4	5	6	7	8	9
10	11	12	13	14	15	16
17	18	19	20	21	22	23
24	25	26	27	28	29	30
31						

February
S	M	T	W	T	F	S
	1	2	3	4	5	6
7	8	9	10	11	12	13
14	15	16	17	18	19	20
21	22	23	24	25	26	27
28						

March
S	M	T	W	T	F	S
	1	2	3	4	5	6
7	8	9	10	11	12	13
14	15	16	17	18	19	20
21	22	23	24	25	26	27
28	29	30	31			

April
S	M	T	W	T	F	S
				1	2	3
4	5	6	7	8	9	10
11	12	13	14	15	16	17
18	19	20	21	22	23	24
25	26	27	28	29	30	

May
S	M	T	W	T	F	S
						1
2	3	4	5	6	7	8
9	10	11	12	13	14	15
16	17	18	19	20	21	22
23	24	25	26	27	28	29
30	31					

June
S	M	T	W	T	F	S
		1	2	3	4	5
6	7	8	9	10	11	12
13	14	15	16	17	18	19
20	21	22	23	24	25	26
27	28	29	30			

July
S	M	T	W	T	F	S
				1	2	3
4	5	6	7	8	9	10
11	12	13	14	15	16	17
18	19	20	21	22	23	24
25	26	27	28	29	30	31

August
S	M	T	W	T	F	S
1	2	3	4	5	6	7
8	9	10	11	12	13	14
15	16	17	18	19	20	21
22	23	24	25	26	27	28
29	30	31				

September
S	M	T	W	T	F	S
			1	2	3	4
5	6	7	8	9	10	11
12	13	14	15	16	17	18
19	20	21	22	23	24	25
26	27	28	29	30		

October
S	M	T	W	T	F	S
					1	2
3	4	5	6	7	8	9
10	11	12	13	14	15	16
17	18	19	20	21	22	23
24	25	26	27	28	29	30
31						

November
S	M	T	W	T	F	S
	1	2	3	4	5	6
7	8	9	10	11	12	13
14	15	16	17	18	19	20
21	22	23	24	25	26	27
28	29	30				

December
S	M	T	W	T	F	S
			1	2	3	4
5	6	7	8	9	10	11
12	13	14	15	16	17	18
19	20	21	22	23	24	25
26	27	28	29	30	31	

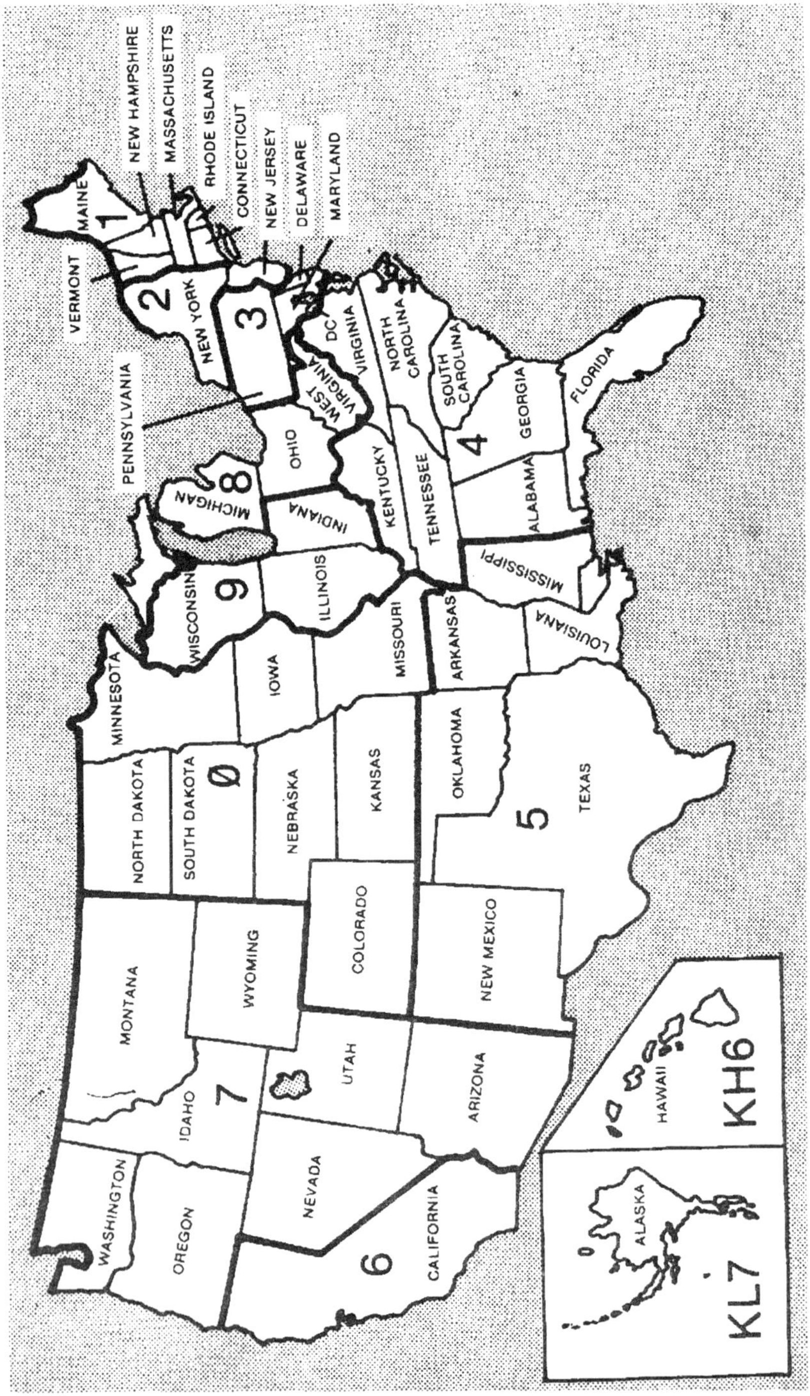

VERMONT
MAINE
1
NEW HAMPSHIRE
MASSACHUSETTS
RHODE ISLAND
CONNECTICUT
NEW JERSEY
DELAWARE
MARYLAND
2
NEW YORK
3
PENNSYLVANIA
DC
VIRGINIA
WEST VIRGINIA
NORTH CAROLINA
SOUTH CAROLINA
4
GEORGIA
FLORIDA
ALABAMA
MISSISSIPPI
TENNESSEE
KENTUCKY
OHIO
8
MICHIGAN
INDIANA
ILLINOIS
9
WISCONSIN
MINNESOTA
IOWA
MISSOURI
ARKANSAS
LOUISIANA
5
TEXAS
OKLAHOMA
KANSAS
NEBRASKA
Ø
SOUTH DAKOTA
NORTH DAKOTA
MONTANA
WYOMING
COLORADO
NEW MEXICO
ARIZONA
UTAH
7
IDAHO
NEVADA
WASHINGTON
OREGON
6
CALIFORNIA
HAWAII
KH6
ALASKA
KL7

PROPAGATION FORECASTS FOR 1994

The following pages are W3ASK's propagation predictions for Northern Hemisphere locations for 1994. While this data can be used for general guidelines, day-to-day propagation will vary considerably. To get a better idea of the propagation expected for any particular day, consult the monthly Propagation column in CQ and monitor WWV for unusual short-term events.

HOW TO USE THE DX PROPAGATION CHARTS

1. Use chart appropriate to your transmitter location. The Eastern USA Chart can be used in the 1, 2, 3, 4, 8, KP4, KG4, and KV4 areas in the USA and adjacent call areas in Canada; the Central USA Chart in the 5, 9, and 0 areas; the Western USA Chart in the 6 and 7 areas; and with somewhat less accuracy in the KH6 and KL7 areas.

2. The predicted times of openings are found under the appropriate meter band column (10 through 80 meters) for a particular DX region, as shown in the left-hand column of the charts. An * indicates the best time to listen for 160 meter openings.

3. The propagation index is the number that appears in ( ) after the time of each predicted opening. The index indicates the number of days during the month on which the opening is expected to take place as follows:

(4) Opening should occur on more than 22 days
(3) Opening should occur between 14 and 22 days
(2) Opening should occur between 7 and 13 days
(1) Opening should occur on less than 7 days

Refer to the "Last Minute Forecast" at the beginning of this column for the actual dates on which an opening with a specific *propagation index* is likely to occur, and the signal quality that can be expected.

4. Times shown in the charts are in the 24-hour system, where 00 is midnight; 12 is noon; 01 is 1 A.M.; 13 is 1 P.M., etc. Appropriate *daylight* time is used, not GMT. To convert to GMT, add to the times shown in the appropriate chart 7 hours in PDT Zone, 6 hours in MDT Zone, 5 hours in CDT Zone, and 4 hours in EDT Zone. For example, 14 hours in Washington, D.C. is 18 GMT. When it is 20 hours in Los Angeles, it is 03 GMT, etc.

5. The charts are based upon a transmitted power of 250 watts CW, or 1 kw, PEP on sideband, into a dipole antenna a quarter-wavelength above ground on 160 and 80 meters, and a half-wavelength above ground on 40 and 20 meters, and a wavelength above ground on 15 and 10 meters. For each 10 dB gain above these reference levels, the *propagation index* will increase by one level; for each 10 dB loss, it will lower by one level.

6. Propagation data contained in the charts has been prepared from basic data published by the Institute for Telecommunication Sciences of the U.S. Dept of Commerce, Boulder, Colorado 80302.

Spring 1994
Time Zone: EST (24-Hour Time)
EASTERN USA To:

Reception Area	*10 Meters*	*15 Meters*	*20 Meters*	*40/80 Meters*
Western & Central Europe & North Africa	09-11 (1) 11-13 (2) 13-14 (1)	07-08 (1) 08-09 (3) 09-12 (4) 12-13 (3) 13-15 (2) 15-16 (1)	04-07 (1) 07-09 (4) 09-12 (3) 12-15 (4) 15-17 (3) 17-19 (2) 19-21 (1)	17-19 (1) 19-20 (2) 20-01 (3) 01-02 (2) 02-03 (1) 19-21 (1)* 21-22 (2)* 22-23 (3)* 23-00 (2)* 00-01 (1)*
Northern Europe & European USSR	08-12 (1)	07-08 (1) 08-11 (2) 11-14 (1)	05-07 (1) 07-09 (3) 09-11 (2) 11-13 (3) 13-14 (2) 14-18 (1)	18-20 (1) 20-22 (2) 22-02 (1) 20-00 (1)*
Eastern Mediter-ranean	09-13 (1)	08-09 (1) 09-11 (3) 11-13 (2) 13-15 (1)	07-09 (2) 09-12 (1) 12-14 (2) 14-16 (1) 16-18 (3) 18-22 (2) 22-23 (1) 04-07 (1)	19-20 (1) 20-22 (2) 22-23 (1) 20-22 (1)*
East Africa	10-13 (1) 13-15 (2) 15-16 (1)	07-08 (1) 08-13 (2) 13-16 (3) 16-17 (2) 17-18 (1)	06-07 (1) 07-09 (2) 09-13 (1) 13-18 (2) 18-21 (3) 21-23 (2) 23-01 (1)	19-00 (1) 21-23 (1)*
West & Central Africa	11-14 (1) 14-16 (2) 16-17 (1)	07-08 (1) 08-09 (2) 09-11 (3) 11-14 (4) 14-16 (3) 16-17 (2) 17-19 (1)	07-09 (2) 09-12 (1) 12-13 (2) 13-15 (3) 15-18 (4) 18-19 (3) 19-22 (2) 22-07 (1)	18-20 (1) 20-22 (2) 22-01 (1) 21-23 (1)*
South Africa	10-11 (1) 11-12 (2) 12-14 (1)	07-09 (1) 09-13 (2) 13-15 (3) 15-17 (2) 17-18 (1)	05-14 (1) 14-16 (2) 16-18 (3) 18-20 (2) 20-23 (1) 23-01 (2) 01-03 (1)	21-23 (1) 23-00 (2) 00-01 (1) 23-01 (1)*
Central & South Asia	*Nil*	07-09 (1) 18-20 (1)	07-10 (1) 19-22 (1)	05-07 (1) 19-21 (1)
Southeast Asia	*Nil*	07-09 (1) 18-20 (1)	06-07 (1) 07-09 (2) 09-10 (1) 19-21 (1)	06-08 (1) 17-20 (1)
Far East	17-19 (1)	07-09 (1) 16-17 (1) 17-19 (2) 19-21 (1)	06-07 (1) 07-09 (2) 09-11 (1) 17-20 (1) 20-22 (2) 22-00 (1)	05-08 (1) 06-07 (1)*
Guam & Pacific Islands	13-15 (1) 15-17 (2) 17-18 (1)	12-15 (1) 15-17 (2) 17-19 (3) 19-20 (2) 20-21 (1)	01-07 (1) 07-10 (2) 10-19 (1) 19-01 (2)	00-02 (1) 02-06 (3) 06-07 (2) 07-08 (1) 02-03 (1)* 03-05 (2)* 05-06 (1)*
Australia & New Zealand	16-18 (1)	08-12 (1) 15-17 (1) 17-20 (2) 20-22 (1)	00-03 (2) 03-07 (1) 07-09 (3) 09-10 (2) 10-13 (1) 13-15 (2) 15-19 (1) 19-22 (2) 22-00 (3)	03-05 (1) 05-07 (2) 07-09 (1) 04-05 (1)* 05-06 (2)* 06-07 (1)*
Northern & Central South America	08-10 (1) 10-12 (2) 12-15 (3) 15-16 (2) 16-18 (1)	07-08 (1) 08-11 (3) 11-14 (2) 14-15 (3) 15-17 (4) 17-19 (3) 19-20 (2)	00-03 (2) 03-06 (1) 06-07 (2) 07-09 (4) 09-11 (3) 11-15 (2) 15-17 (3)	18-19 (1) 19-20 (2) 20-03 (3) 03-05 (2) 05-07 (1) 19-21 (1)* 21-02 (2)*

		20-21 (1)	17-22 (4) 22-00 (3)	02-06 (1)*
Southern Brazil, Argentina, Chile & Uruguay	09-11 (1) 11-13 (2) 13-15 (3) 15-16 (2) 16-18 (1)	07-08 (1) 08-10 (3) 10-15 (2) 15-17 (4) 17-18 (3) 18-19 (2) 19-20 (1)	04-06 (1) 06-08 (2) 08-15 (1) 15-16 (2) 16-17 (3) 17-19 (4) 19-01 (3) 01-04 (2)	19-21 (1) 21-03 (2) 03-07 (1) 21-06 (1)*
McMurdo Sound, Antarctica	11-13 (1) 13-16 (2) 16-18 (1)	08-10 (1) 15-17 (1) 17-19 (2) 19-21 (1)	04-07 (1) 07-09 (2) 09-12 (1) 15-18 (1) 18-21 (2) 21-00 (3) 00-04 (2)	23-05 (1)

Time Zones: CST & MST (24-Hour Time)
CENTRAL USA To:

Reception Area	*10 Meters*	*15 Meters*	*20 Meters*	*40/80 Meters*
Western & Central Europe & North Africa	09-12 (1)	07-08 (1) 08-09 (2) 09-12 (3) 12-14 (2) 14-15 (1)	05-07 (1) 07-09 (3) 09-11 (2) 11-14 (3) 14-17 (2) 17-20 (1)	17-19 (1) 19-22 (2) 22-02 (1) 20-21 (1)* 21-22 (2)* 22-00 (1)*
Northern Europe & European USSR	08-11 (1)	07-09 (1) 09-11 (2) 11-13 (1)	06-07 (1) 07-09 (2) 09-11 (1) 11-13 (2) 13-17 (1)	19-01 (1) 20-23 (1)*
Eastern Mediter-ranean	09-12 (1)	07-09 (1) 09-12 (2) 12-14 (1)	23-02 (1) 07-12 (1) 12-17 (2) 17-22 (1)	19-23 (1) 20-22 (1)*
East Africa	10-15 (1)	07-10 (1) 10-15 (2) 15-17 (1)	06-12 (1) 12-17 (2) 17-20 (3) 20-21 (2) 21-23 (1)	19-21 (1) 20-22 (1)*
West & Central Africa	11-13 (1) 13-15 (2) 15-16 (1)	07-08 (1) 08-10 (2) 10-12 (3) 12-14 (4) 14-15 (3) 15-16 (2) 16-18 (1)	07-12 (1) 12-13 (2) 13-15 (3) 15-17 (4) 17-20 (2) 20-00 (1)	18-19 (1) 19-21 (2) 21-00 (1) 20-22 (1)*
South Africa	10-13 (1)	07-09 (1) 09-13 (2) 13-14 (3) 14-16 (2) 16-17 (1)	05-14 (1) 14-16 (2) 16-18 (3) 18-19 (2) 19-21 (1) 00-02 (1)	23-00 (1) 23-00 (1)*
Central & South Asia	17-19 (1)	07-10 (1) 18-20 (1)	06-07 (1) 07-09 (2) 09-11 (1) 19-22 (1)	06-08 (1) 19-21 (1)
Southeast Asia	09-11 (1) 16-19 (1)	08-11 (1) 16-17 (1) 17-19 (2) 19-20 (1)	06-07 (1) 07-09 (2) 09-12 (1) 17-18 (1) 18-10 (2) 20-22 (1)	06-08 (1) 17-19 (1)
Far East	15-18 (1)	07-09 (1) 14-16 (1) 16-19 (2) 19-21 (1)	07-09 (2) 09-11 (1) 17-20 (1) 20-00 (2) 00-07 (1)	02-05 (1) 05-07 (2) 07-09 (1) 05-07 (1)*
Guam & Pacific Islands	12-15 (1) 15-17 (2) 17-19 (1)	10-13 (1) 13-16 (2) 16-19 (3) 19-20 (2) 20-21 (1)	06-07 (2) 07-09 (3) 09-11 (2) 11-18 (1) 18-20 (2) 20-22 (3) 22-00 (2) 00-06 (1)	22-01 (1) 01-06 (3) 06-07 (2) 07-09 (1) 00-03 (1)* 03-06 (2)* 06-07 (1)*
Australia & New Zealand	15-17 (1)	09-12 (1) 12-17 (2) 17-19 (3) 19-20 (2) 20-22 (1)	07-09 (2) 09-17 (1) 17-20 (2) 20-00 (3) 00-03 (2) 03-07 (1)	02-04 (1) 04-07 (2) 07-09 (1) 04-05 (1)* 05-07 (2)* 07-08 (1)*
Northern & Central South America	09-11 (1) 11-13 (2) 13-14 (3) 14-15 (2) 15-17 (1)	06-07 (1) 07-08 (2) 08-14 (3) 14-16 (4) 16-18 (3) 18-19 (2) 19-20 (1)	06-07 (2) 07-11 (3) 11-14 (2) 14-16 (3) 16-20 (4) 20-22 (3) 22-02 (2) 02-06 (1)	18-19 (1) 19-20 (2) 20-02 (3) 02-04 (2) 04-06 (1) 20-21 (1)* 21-02 (2)* 02-06 (1)*
Southern Brazil, Argentina, Chile & Uruguay	08-11 (1) 11-13 (2) 13-15 (3) 15-16 (2) 16-18 (1)	07-08 (1) 08-13 (2) 13-15 (3) 15-17 (4) 17-18 (3) 18-19 (2) 19-20 (1)	06-08 (2) 08-15 (1) 15-16 (2) 16-18 (4) 18-22 (3) 22-04 (2) 04-06 (1)	19-22 (1) 21-03 (2) 03-06 (1) 21-05 (1)*
McMurdo Sound, Antarctica	11-13 (1) 13-15 (2) 15-18 (1)	13-16 (1) 16-18 (2) 18-20 (1)	07-09 (2) 09-12 (1) 15-18 (1) 18-20 (2) 20-23 (3) 23-03 (2) 03-07 (1)	00-06 (1)

Time Zone: PST (24-Hour Time)
WESTERN USA To:

Reception Area	*10 Meters*	*15 Meters*	*20 Meters*	*40/80 Meters*
Western & Central Europe & North Africa	09-11 (1)	08-10 (1) 10-12 (2) 12-15 (1)	23-01 (1) 06-08 (1) 08-12 (2) 12-14 (3) 14-16 (2) 16-20 (1)	18-00 (1) 20-22 (1)*
Northern Europe & European USSR	*Nil*	08-12 (1)	23-01 (1) 06-07 (1) 07-09 (2) 09-13 (1)	19-23 (1) 20-22 (1)*
Eastern Mediter-ranean & East Africa	*Nil*	07-11 (1)	06-09 (1) 09-11 (2) 11-15 (1) 18-21 (1)	18-21 (1)
West & Central Africa	11-16 (1)	06-08 (1) 08-15 (2) 15-17 (3) 17-18 (2) 18-19 (1)	05-10 (1) 10-15 (2) 15-18 (3) 18-20 (2) 20-22 (1)	18-22 (1) 19-21 (1)*
South Africa	10-13 (1)	08-10 (1) 10-14 (2) 14-16 (1)	05-14 (1) 14-16 (2) 16-18 (3) 18-20 (1) 00-02 (1)	19-22 (1) 20-21 (1)*

Central Asia	17-19 (1)	07-09 (1) 16-17 (1) 17-19 (2) 19-21 (1)	06-07 (1) 07-09 (2) 09-11 (1) 17-19 (1) 19-20 (2) 20-22 (1)	05-08 (1)
Southeast Asia	16-19 (1) 09-11 (1)	08-09 (1) 09-10 (2) 10-14 (1) 14-17 (2) 17-18 (3) 18-19 (2) 19-21 (1)	07-08 (1) 08-10 (3) 10-11 (2) 11-21 (1) 21-00 (2) 00-02 (1)	00-02 (1) 02-06 (2) 06-08 (1) 02-06 (1)*
Far East	14-15 (1) 15-16 (2) 16-18 (1)	12-14 (1) 14-18 (2) 18-20 (3) 20-22 (1)	08-10 (2) 10-20 (1) 20-22 (2) 22-00 (3) 00-04 (2) 04-08 (1)	00-02 (1) 02-06 (2) 06-08 (1) 02-08 (1)*
Guam & Pacific Islands	12-15 (1) 15-17 (2) 17-19 (1)	08-12 (1) 12-16 (2) 16-17 (3) 17-18 (4) 18-20 (3) 20-21 (1)	09-10 (2) 10-12 (4) 12-16 (3) 16-19 (4) 19-20 (3) 20-00 (2) 00-09 (1)	19-20 (1) 20-22 (2) 22-06 (4) 06-08 (2) 08-09 (1) 21-23 (1)* 23-06 (2)* 06-07 (1)*
Australia & New Zealand	11-15 (1) 15-17 (2) 17-18 (1)	10-12 (1) 12-17 (2) 17-19 (3) 19-20 (2) 20-21 (1)	07-08 (1) 08-10 (3) 10-12 (2) 12-17 (1) 17-18 (2) 18-20 (3) 20-22 (4) 22-00 (3) 00-02 (2) 02-04 (1)	00-03 (1) 03-05 (3) 05-07 (2) 07-08 (1) 02-03 (1) 03-05 (2) 05-07 (1)
Northern & Central South America	10-12 (1) 12-14 (2) 14-16 (1)	06-07 (1) 07-08 (2) 08-14 (3) 14-16 (4) 16-17 (3) 17-18 (2) 18-19 (1)	06-07 (2) 07-09 (3) 09-10 (2) 10-14 (1) 14-16 (2) 16-18 (4) 18-22 (3) 22-00 (2) 00-06 (1)	18-20 (1) 20-00 (3) 00-03 (2) 03-05 (1) 20-21 (1)* 21-01 (2)* 01-04 (1)*
Southern Brazil, Argentina, Chile & Uruguay	08-12 (1) 12-13 (2) 13-15 (3) 15-16 (2) 16-18 (1)	00-02 (1) 07-11 (1) 11-13 (2) 13-15 (3) 15-16 (4) 16-17 (3) 17-18 (2) 18-19 (1)	20-05 (2) 05-15 (1) 15-16 (2) 16-18 (4) 18-20 (3)	18-19 (1) 19-23 (2) 23-03 (1) 20-02 (1)*
McMurdo Sound, Antarctica	11-13 (1) 13-15 (2) 15-17 (1)	12-15 (1) 15-18 (2) 18-20 (1)	05-06 (1) 06-08 (2) 08-11 (1) 16-19 (1) 19-20 (2) 20-23 (3) 23-02 (2) 02-05 (1)	00-06 (1)

CQ Short-Skip Propagation Chart Spring 1994

Band Openings Given In Local Standard Time At Path Mid-Point Using 24-Hour Time System

Band (Meters)	*Distance From Transmitter (Miles)*			
	50–250	*250–750*	*750–1300*	*1300–2300*
10	*Nil*	*NIL*	08-09 (0-1) 09-12 (0-2) 12-14 (0-3) 14-16 (0-2) 16-18 (0-1)	08-09 (1-0) 09-12 (2-1) 12-14 (3-2) 14-16 (2-3) 16-17 (1-2) 17-18 (1) 18-20 (0-1)
15	*Nil*	08-09 (1) 09-15 (0-2) 15-17 (0-1)	07-08 (0-1) 08-09 (1) 09-10 (2) 10-15 (2-4) 15-17 (1-3) 17-18 (0-2) 18-20 (0-1)	07-08 (1-0) 08-09 (1) 09-10 (2-3) 10-15 (4) 15-17 (3) 17-18 (2-3) 18-20 (1-2) 20-21 (0-1)
20	11-13 (0-1) 13-15 (0-2) 15-16 (0-1)	07-10 (0-1) 10-11 (0-2) 11-13 (1-3) 13-15 (2-4) 15-16 (1-3) 16-18 (0-3) 18-20 (0-2) 20-07 (0-1)	06-08 (1-2) 08-10 (1-3) 10-13 (3-4) 13-15 (4) 15-18 (3-4) 18-20 (2-3) 20-22 (1-2) 22-06 (1)	06-07 (2-1) 07-08 (2) 08-10 (3) 10-15 (4-3) 15-18 (4) 18-20 (3-4) 20-22 (2-3) 22-02 (1-2) 02-06 (1)
40	06-07 (1-2) 07-09 (2-3) 09-18 (3-4) 18-19 (2-3) 19-21 (1-2) 21-00 (0-1)	06-07 (2-3) 07-09 (3-4) 09-11 (4-3) 11-13 (4-2) 13-15 (4-3) 15-18 (4) 18-19 (3-4) 19-20 (2-4) 20-21 (2-3) 21-00 (1-2) 00-06 (0-1)	06-07 (3-2) 07-08 (4-2) 08-09 (4-1) 09-11 (3-1) 11-13 (2-1) 13-15 (3-1) 15-17 (4-2) 17-19 (4-3) 19-20 (4) 20-21 (3-4) 21-00 (2-3) 00-02 (1-3) 02-06 (1-2)	06-08 (2-1) 08-15 (1-0) 15-16 (2-0) 16-17 (2-1) 17-19 (3-2) 19-21 (4-3) 21-22 (4) 22-00 (3-4) 00-02 (3) 02-05 (2-3) 05-06 (2)
80	07-08 (2-3) 08-11 (3-4) 11-18 (4-3) 18-20 (3-4) 20-22 (2-3) 22-02 (1-2) 02-05 (1) 05-07 (1-2)	07-08 (3-2) 08-11 (4-1) 11-16 (3-0) 16-18 (3-2) 18-20 (4-3) 20-22 (3-4) 22-02 (2-4) 02-05 (1-2) 05-07 (2)	07-08 (2-1) 08-11 (1-0) 11-16 (0) 16-18 (2-1) 18-20 (3-2) 20-02 (4) 02-05 (2-3) 05-07 (2)	07-08 (1-0) 08-16 (0) 16-18 (1-0) 18-20 (2-1) 20-22 (4-2) 22-02 (4-3) 02-05 (3-2) 05-07 (2-1)
160	05-07 (4-2) 07-09 (3-1) 09-17 (2-0) 17-19 (3-1) 19-20 (4-2) 20-05 (4)	05-06 (2-1) 06-07 (2-0) 07-09 (1-0) 09-17 (0) 17-19 (1-0) 19-20 (2) 20-22 (4-3) 22-03 (4) 03-05 (4-3)	05-06 (1) 06-19 (0) 19-20 (2-1) 20-22 (3-2) 22-03 (4-2) 03-05 (3-2)	05-06 (1-) 06-19 (0) 19-20 (1-0) 20-22 (2-1) 22-03 (2) 03-05 (2-1)

*Predicted 80 meter openings. Openings on 160 meters are also likely to occur during those times where 80 meter openings are shown with a forecast rating of (2), or higher.

HOW TO USE THE SHORT-SKIP CHARTS

1. In the Short-Skip Chart, the predicted times of openings can be found under the appropriate distance column of a particular meter band (10 through 160 meters) as shown in the left-hand column of the chart. For the Alaska and Hawaii Charts the predicted times of openings are found under the appropriate meter band column (15 through 80 meters) for a particular geographical region of the continental USA as shown in the left-hand column of the charts. An * indicates the best time to listen for 80 meter openings.

2. The propagation index is the number that appears in () after the time of each predicted opening. On the Short-Skip Chart, where two numerals are shown within a single set of parentheses, the first applies to the shorter distance for which the forecast is made, and the second to the greater distance. The index indicates the number of days during the month on which the opening is expected to take place, as follows:

(4) Opening should occur on more than 22 days
(3) Opening should occur between 14 and 22 days
(2) Opening should occur between 7 and 13 days
(1) Opening should occur on less than 7 days

Refer to the "Last Minute Forecast" at the beginning of this column for the actual dates on which an opening with a specific propagation index is likely to occur, and the signal quality that can be expected.

3. Times shown in the charts are in the 24-hour system, where 00 is midnight; 12 is noon; 01 is 1 AM; 13 is 1 PM, etc. On the Short-Skip Chart appropriate daylight time is used at the path midpoint. For example on a circuit between Maine and Florida, the time shown would be EDT, on a circuit between New York and Texas, the time at the midpoint would be CDT, etc. Times shown in the Hawaii Chart are in HST. To convert to standard time in other USA time zones add 2 hours in the PDT zone; 3 hours in the MDT zone; 4 hours in the CDT zone; and 5 hours in the EDT zone. Add 10 hours to convert from HST to GMT. For example, when it is 12 noon in Honolulu, it is 14 or 2 PM in Los Angeles; 17 or 5 PM in Washington, D.C.; and 22 GMT. Time shown in the Alaska Chart is given in GMT. To convert to daylight time in other areas of the USA subtract 8 hours in the PDT zone; 7 hours in the MDT zone; 6 hours in the CDT zone; and 5 hours in the EDT zone. For example, at 20 GMT it is 15 or 3 PM in New York City.

4. The Short-Skip Chart is based upon a transmitted power of 75 watts CW or 300 watts PEP on sideband; the Alaska and Hawaii Charts are based upon a transmitter power of 250 watts CW or 1 kw PEP on sideband. A dipole antenna a quarter-wavelength above ground is assumed for 160 and 80 meters, a half-wave above ground on 40 and 20 meters, and a wavelength above ground on 15 and 10 meters. For each 10 dB gain above these reference levels, the propagation index will increase by one level; for each 10 dB loss, it will lower by one level.

5. Propagation data contained in the charts has been prepared from basic data published by the Institute for Telecommunication Sciences of the U.S. Dept. of Commerce, Boulder, Colorado 80302.

ALASKA
Spring 1994
Openings Given in GMT

To:	10 Meters	15 Meters	20 Meters	40/80 Meters
Eastern USA	21-23 (1)	20-21 (1) 21-23 (2) 23-01 (1)	20-23 (1) 23-02 (2) 02-05 (1)	06-13 (1) 07-12 (1)*
Central USA	21-00 (1)	20-22 (1) 22-00 (2) 00-02 (1)	20-00 (1) 00-02 (2) 02-04 (3) 04-05 (2) 05-06 (1)	07-09 (1) 09-12 (2) 12-14 (1) 08-12 (1)*
Western USA	21-01 (1)	20-22 (1) 22-00 (2) 00-02 (3) 02-03 (2) 03-04 (1)	18-21 (1) 21-00 (2) 00-03 (3) 03-05 (2) 05-07 (1)	06-08 (1) 08-09 (2) 09-12 (3) 12-13 (2) 13-15 (1) 09-10 (1)* 10-12 (2)* 12-13 (1)*

See explanation in "How To Use Short-Skip Charts" in box at the beginning of this column.

* Indicates best time for 80 Meter openings. Openings on 160 Meters are also likely to occur during those times when 80 Meter openings are shown with a propagation index of (2), or higher.

Note: The Alaska and Hawaii Propagation Charts are intended for distances *greater* than 1300 miles. For shorter distances, use the preceding Short-Skip Propagation Chart.

HAWAII
Spring 1994
Openings Given in Hawaiian Standard Time

To:	10 Meters	15 Meters	20 Meters	40/80 Meters
Eastern USA	10-12 (1) 12-14 (2) 14-15 (1)	08-11 (1) 11-13 (2) 13-15 (3) 15-16 (2) 16-17 (1)	07-13 (1) 13-15 (2) 15-19 (3) 19-21 (2) 21-05 (1) 05-07 (2)	18-20 (1) 20-22 (2) 22-00 (3) 00-02 (2) 02-03 (1) 20-22 (1)* 22-01 (2)* 01-02 (1)*
Central USA	10-11 (1) 11-14 (2) 14-16 (1)	06-08 (1) 08-13 (2) 13-16 (3) 16-17 (2) 17-18 (1)	08-13 (1) 13-15 (2) 15-17 (3) 17-19 (4) 19-21 (3) 21-23 (2) 23-05 (1) 05-08 (2)	18-19 (1) 19-22 (2) 22-01 (3) 01-04 (2) 04-05 (1) 19-21 (1)* 21-02 (2)* 02-04 (1)*
Western USA	09-11 (1) 11-12 (2) 12-14 (3) 14-15 (2) 15-16 (1)	07-08 (1) 08-09 (2) 09-11 (3) 11-15 (4) 15-17 (3) 17-18 (2) 18-20 (1)	15-18 (4) 18-20 (3) 20-00 (2) 00-04 (1) 04-06 (2) 06-09 (4) 09-11 (3) 11-13 (2) 13-15 (3)	17-19 (1) 19-20 (2) 20-21 (3) 21-23 (4) 23-05 (3) 05-06 (2) 06-07 (1) 19-20 (1)* 20-22 (2)* 22-04 (3)* 04-05 (2)* 05-06 (1)*

Summer 1994
Time Zone: EDT (24-Hour Time)
EASTERN USA To:

	10 Meters	15 Meters	20 Meters	40/80 Meters
Western & Central Europe & North Africa	*Nil*	11-16 (1) 16-18 (2) 18-19 (1)	06-09 (2) 09-13 (1) 13-15 (2) 15-17 (3) 17-22 (4) 22-00 (3) 00-03 (2) 03-06 (1)	20-22 (1) 22-23 (2) 23-01 (3) 01-02 (2) 02-03 (1) 22-00 (1)* 00-01 (2)* 01-02 (1)*
Northern Europe & European USSR	*Nl*	14-18 (1)	09-15 (1) 15-18 (2) 18-19 (3) 19-21 (4) 21-23 (3) 23-02 (2) 02-07 (1) 07-09 (2)	21-22 (1) 22-00 (2) 00-02 (1) 21-00 (1)*
Eastern Mediterranean & Middle East	*Nil*	11-16 (1) 16-18 (2) 18-19 (1)	12-14 (1) 14-17 (2) 17-19 (3) 19-23 (4) 23-01 (3) 01-03 (2) 03-06 (1) 06-08 (2) 08-09 (1)	20-22 (1) 22-00 (2) 00-01 (1) 22-00 (1)*
Western Africa	16-18 (1)	10-12 (1) 12-14 (2) 14-15 (3) 15-17 (4) 17-19 (3) 19-20 (2) 20-22 (1)	03-07 (1) 07-09 (2) 09-15 (1) 15-16 (2) 16-17 (3) 17-23 (4) 23-01 (3) 01-03 (2)	20-22 (1) 22-00 (2) 00-02 (1) 22-00 (1)*
Eastern & Central Africa	16-17 (1)	11-14 (1) 14-15 (2) 15-16 (3) 16-17 (4) 17-18 (3) 18-19 (2) 19-20 (1)	14-16 (1) 16-17 (2) 17-18 (3) 18-21 (4) 21-23 (3) 23-02 (2) 02-06 (1)	21-00 (1)
Southern Africa	10-13 (1)	09-11 (1) 11-12 (2) 12-13 (3) 13-14 (2) 14-15 (1)	00-01 (1) 01-05 (2) 05-07 (1) 15-16 (1) 16-18 (2) 18-19 (1)	21-22 (1) 22-00 (2) 00-02 (1) 23-01 (1)*
Central & South Asia	*Nil*	10-12 (1) 19-22 (1)	17-20 (1) 20-23 (2) 23-03 (1) 06-09 (1)	19-21 (1)
Southeast Asia	*Nil*	10-12 (1) 19-21 (1)	19-21 (2) 21-23 (1) 23-01 (2) 01-02 (1) 06-07 (1) 07-09 (2) 09-11 (1)	*Nil*
Far East	*Nil*	10-12 (1) 17-18 (1) 18-20 (2) 20-21 (1)	06-07 (1) 07-09 (3) 09-10 (2) 10-12 (1) 19-20 (1) 20-23 (2) 23-00 (1)	*Nil*
South Pacific & New Zealand	18-21 (1)	15-17 (1) 17-19 (2) 19-21 (3) 21-22 (2) 22-23 (1)	18-21 (1) 21-23 (2) 23-01 (3) 01-03 (4) 03-04 (3) 04-07 (2) 07-09 (3) 09-10 (2) 10-12 (1)	01-03 (1) 03-06 (2) 06-08 (1) 04-06 (1)*
Australasia	18-20 (1)	10-12 (1) 18-19 (1) 19-20 (2) 20-21 (3) 21-22 (2) 22-23 (1)	23-01 (1) 01-02 (2) 02-04 (3) 04-05 (2) 05-07 (1) 07-09 (2) 09-10 (1) 16-18 (1)	03-04 (1) 04-06 (2) 06-07 (1) 04-06 (1)*
Caribbean, Central America & Northern Countries of South America	09-13 (1) 13-15 (2) 15-17 (3) 17-18 (2) 18-19 (1)	08-09 (1) 09-11 (1) 11-20 (4) 20-21 (3) 21-22 (2) 22-23 (1)	07-10 (4) 10-16 (3) 16-00 (4) 00-03 (3) 03-06 (2) 06-07 (3)	19-21 (1) 21-23 (2) 23-03 (3) 03-05 (2) 05-06 (1) 22-23 (1)* 23-04 (2)* 04-05 (1)*
Peru, Bolivia, Paraguay, Brazil, Chile, Argentina, & Uruguay	12-14 (1) 14-16 (2) 16-18 (3) 18-19 (1)	08-09 (1) 09-11 (2) 11-15 (1) 15-16 (2) 16-17 (3) 17-20 (4) 20-22 (3) 22-23 (2)	11-16 (1) 16-17 (2) 17-18 (3) 18-02 (4) 02-04 (3) 04-07 (2) 07-09 (3) 09-11 (2)	20-21 (1) 21-22 (2) 22-02 (3) 02-04 (2) 04-05 (1) 22-03 (1)*
McMurdo Sound, Antarctica	*Nil*	16-20 (1)	17-19 (1) 19-23 (2) 23-01 (3) 01-03 (2) 03-05 (1) 07-09 (1)	02-05 (1)

Time Zones: CDT & MDT
(24 Hour Time)
CENTRAL USA To:

	10 Meters	15 Meters	20 Meters	40/80 Meters
Western & Southern Europe & North Africa	*Nil*	15-18 (1)	05-06 (1) 06-08 (2) 08-15 (1) 15-17 (2) 17-18 (3) 18-20 (4) 20-22 (3) 22-00 (2) 00-02 (1)	20-23 (1) 23-01 (2) 01-02 (1) 22-00 (1)*
Northern & Central Europe & European USSR	*Nil*	13-17 (1)	05-06 (1) 06-09 (2) 09-15 15-18 (2) 18-21 (3) 21-00 (2) 00-01	20-00 (1)
Eastern Mediterranean & Middle East	*Nil*	15-18 (1)	13-16 (1) 16-18 (2) 18-22 (3) 22-00 (2) 00-01 (1) 07-09 (1)	21-23 (1)

	10 Meters	15 Meters	20 Meters	40/80 Meters
Western Africa	16-18 (1)	10-13 (1) 13-15 (2) 15-17 (3) 17-18 (2) 18-20 (1)	14-15 (1) 15-16 (2) 16-18 (3) 18-21 (4) 21-23 (3) 23-01 (2) 01-03 (1)	20-00 (1) 22-00 (1)*
Eastern & Central Africa	16-18 (1)	13-15 (1) 15-16 (2) 16-17 (3) 17-18 (2) 18-19 (1)	15-17 (1) 17-18 (2) 18-21 (3) 21-23 (2) 23-01 (1)	20-23 (1)
Southern Africa	10-12 (1)	09-10 (1) 10-12 (2) 12-13 (1)	22-00 (1) 00-03 (2) 03-07 (1) 13-15 (1) 15-17 (2) 17-19 (1)	21-22 (1) 22-00 (2) 00-01 (1) 22-00 (1)*
Central & South Asia	*Nil*	10-12 (1) 18-21 (1)	17-19 (1) 19-22 (2) 22-03 (1) 05-07 (1) 07-09 (2) 09-10 (1)	*Nil*
Southeast Asia	*Nil*	10-12 (1) 19-22 (1)	04-07 (1) 07-09 (2) 09-10 (1) 22-23 (1) 23-01 (2) 01-02 (1)	03-05 (1)
Far East	*Nil*	10-15 (1) 18-20 (1) 20-22 (2) 22-23 (1)	05-07 (2) 07-09 (3) 09-10 (2) 10-12 (1) 20-22 (1) 22-00 (2) 00-02 (3) 02-03 (2) 03-05 (1)	04-05 (1) 05-06 (2) 06-07 (1) 04-06 (1)*
South Pacific & New Zealand	18-20 (1)	13-16 (1) 16-18 (2) 18-20 (3) 20-21 (4) 21-22 (3) 22-23 (2) 23-00 (1)	17-19 (1) 19-23 (2) 23-01 (4) 01-05 (3) 05-07 (2) 07-09 (4) 09-11 (2) 11-13 (1)	23-01 (1) 01-03 (2) 03-05 (3) 05-07 (2) 07-08 (1) 01-04 (1)* 04-06 (2)* 06-07 (1)*
Australasia	17-20 (1)	14-15 (1) 15-17 (2) 17-19 (1) 19-20 (2) 20-21 (3) 21-22 (2) 22-23 (1)	22-00 (1) 00-01 (2) 01-05 (3) 05-07 (2) 07-09 (4) 09-11 (2) 11-12 (1)	01-03 (1) 03-07 (2) 07-08 (1) 03-06 (1)*
Caribbean, Central America & Northern Countries of South America	10-13 (1) 13-15 (2) 15-17 (3) 17-18 (2) 18-19 (1)	07-09 (1) 09-10 (2) 10-11 (3) 11-19 (4) 19-20 (3) 20-21 (2) 21-22 (1)	02-05 (2) 05-07 (3) 07-10 (4) 10-11 (3) 11-13 (2) 13-16 (3) 16-22 (4) 22-02 (3)	19-20 (1) 20-23 (4) 23-00 (3) 00-03 (2) 03-05 (3) 05-06 (1) 20-21 (1)* 21-23 (2)* 23-05 (1)*
Peru, Bolivia, Paraguay, Brazil, Chile, Argentina & Uruguay	12-14 (1) 14-15 (2) 15-17 (3) 17-18 (2) 18-19 (1)	07-08 (1) 08-10 (2) 10-14 (1) 14-16 (2) 16-19 (4) 19-20 (3) 20-22 (2) 22-23 (1)	14-16 (1) 16-17 (2) 17-18 (3) 18-23 (4) 23-02 (3) 02-05 (1) 05-07 (2) 07-10 (1)	20-21 (1) 21-22 (2) 22-02 (3) 02-03 (2) 03-05 (1) 20-03 (1)*
McMurdo Sound, Antarctica	*Nil*	15-16 (1) 16-19 (2) 19-21 (1)	17-19 (1) 19-23 (2) 23-01 (3) 01-03 (2) 03-05 (1) 07-09 (1)	03-06 (1)

Time Zone: PDT (24-Hour Time) WESTERN USA To:

	10 Meters	*15 Meters*	*20 Meters*	*40/80 Meters*
Western & Southern Europe & North Africa	*Nil*	09-11 (1) 15-17 (1)	05-06 (1) 06-08 (2) 08-15 (1) 15-21 (3) 21-23 (2) 23-03 (1)	20-23 (1)
Central & Northern Europe & European USSR	*Nil*	14-16 (1)	00-06 (1) 06-08 (2) 08-10 (1) 13-16 (1) 16-20 (2) 20-22 (3) 22-00 (2)	20-22 (1)
Eastern Mediterranean & Middle East	*Nil*	13-15 (1)	14-16 (1) 16-20 (2) 20-22 (3) 22-23 (2) 23-00 (1) 06-08 (1)	20-21 (1)
Western & Central Africa	14-16 (1)	07-09 (1) 11-13 (1) 13-17 (2) 17-18 (1)	14-16 (1) 16-18 (2) 18-20 (3) 20-21 (4) 21-23 (3) 23-03 (2) 03-04 (1) 07-09	20-22 (1)
Eastern Africa	*Nil*	13-16 (1)	16-19 (1) 19-22 (2) 22-00 (1)	*Nil*
Southern Africa	09-11 (1)	09-10 (1) 10-12 (2) 12-13 (1)	15-17 (1) 22-23 (1) 23-01 (2) 01-03 (1) 06-08 (1)	20-23 (1)
Central & South Asia	*Nil*	10-12 (1) 19-21 (1)	05-07 (1) 07-09 (2) 09-11 (1) 16-19 (1) 21-23 (1) 23-01 (2) 01-02 (1)	05-07 (1) 19-20 (1)
Southeast Asia	*Nil*	10-12 (1) 19-21 (1)	23-01 (1) 01-03 (2) 03-06 (3) 06-07 (2) 07-10 (1) 16-19 (1)	02-06 (1)
Far East	*Nil*	13-15 (1) 15-17 (2) 17-18 (3) 18-19 (2) 19-20 (1)	19-21 (1) 21-23 (2) 23-02 (3) 02-04 (4) 04-07 (2) 07-09 (3) 09-11 (2) 11-13 (1)	01-02 (1) 02-03 (2) 03-05 (3) 05-06 (2) 06-07 (1) 03-05 (1)*
South Pacific & New Zealand	13-15 (1) 15-18 (2) 18-20 (1)	10-12 (1) 12-15 (2) 15-18 (3) 18-20 (4) 20-21 (3) 21-22 (2) 22-23 (1)	17-19 (1) 19-21 (2) 21-02 (4) 02-06 (2) 06-08 (4) 08-10 (3) 10-11 (2) 11-12 (1)	22-23 (1) 23-01 (2) 01-06 (3) 06-07 (2) 07-08 (1) 23-02 (1)* 02-05 (2)* 05-06 (1)*

Australasia	15-17 (1) 17-20 (2) 20-21 (1)	13-15 (1) 15-18 (2) 18-19 (3) 19-21 (4) 21-22 (3) 22-23 (2) 23-00 (1)	20-22 (1) 22-23 (2) 23-00 (3) 00-03 (4) 03-05 (3) 05-06 (2) 06-08 (3) 08-09 (2) 09-13 (1) 13-15 (2) 15-17 (1)	22-00 (1) 00-01 (2) 01-05 (3) 05-06 (2) 06-08 (1) 01-04 (1)*
Caribbean, Central America & Northern Countries of South America	09-11 (1) 11-13 (2) 13-15 (1) 15-17 (2) 17-18 (1)	09-11 (1) 11-14 (2) 14-16 (3) 16-19 (4) 19-20 (2) 20-21 (1)	18-01 (4) 01-03 (3) 03-05 (2) 05-08 (3) 08-11 (2) 11-14 (1) 14-16 (2) 16-18 (3)	19-21 (1) 21-23 (3) 23-04 (2) 04-05 (1) 20-04 (1)*
Peru, Bolivia, Paraguay, Brazil, Chile, Argentina & Uruguay	13-15 (1) 15-16 (2) 16-18 (3) 18-19 (2) 19-20 (1)	08-11 (1) 11-16 (2) 16-17 (3) 17-19 (4) 19-20 (2) 20-21 (1)	14-16 (1) 16-18 (2) 18-19 (3) 19-23 (4) 23-01 (3) 01-02 (2) 02-05 (1) 05-07 (2) 07-10 (1)	20-21 (1) 21-00 (2) 00-02 (1) 02-03 (3) 03-04 (2) 04-05 (1) 02-04 (1)*
McMurdo Sound, Antarctica	*Nil*	17-21 (1)	16-18 (1) 18-19 (2) 19-24 (3) 24-03 (2) 03-07 (1)	00-06 (1)

* Indicates best time for eighty meter openings. Openings on 160 meters are also likely to occur during those times when 80 meter openings are shown with a propagation index of (2), or higher.

CQ Short-Skip Popagation Chart Summer 1994 Local Daylight Savings Time At Path Mid-Point

Band (Meters) *Distance Between Stations (Miles)*

	50-250	*250-750*	*750-1300*	*1300-2300*
10	*Nil*	10-21 (0-1)	08-10 (1) 10-13 (1-2) 13-15 (1-3) 15-16 (1-2) 16-21 (0-1)	08-10 (1) 10-13 (2) 13-15 (3) 15-16 (2-3) 16-17 (1-2) 17-19 (1) 19-21 (1-0)
15	*Nil*	08-10 (0-1) 10-15 (0-2) 15-21 (0-1)	08-09 (1) 09-10 (1-2) 10-15 (2-4) 15-17 (1-4) 17-18 (1-3) 18-20 (1-2) 20-21 (1) 21-08 (0-1)	08-09(1) 09-10 (2-3) 10-11 (4-3) 11-17 (4) 17-18 (3) 18-19 (2-3) 19-20 (2) 20-21 (1) 21-08 (1-0)
20	12-14 (0-1) 14-16 (0-2) 16-22 (0-1)	08-09 (0-1) 09-10 (0-2) 10-11 (0-3) 11-12 (0-4) 12-14 (1-4) 14-16 (2-4) 16-18 (1-4) 18-19 (1-3) 19-22 (1-2) 22-08 (0-1)	06-08 (1-2) 08-09 (1-3) 09-10 (2-4) 10-11 (3-4) 11-18 (4) 18-19 (3-4) 19-22 (2-3) 22-00 (1-2) 00-06 (1)	06-08 (2) 08-09 (3) 09-14 (4-2) 14-16 (4-3) 16-19 (4) 19-21 (3-4) 21-22 (3) 22-23 (2-3) 23-00 (2) 00-06 (1)
40	08-10 (1-3) 10-12 (2-4) 12-18 (3-4) 18-19 (2-3) 19-21 (1-2) 21-06 (0-1) 06-08 (0-2)	08-10 (3-4) 10-12 (4-3) 12-16 (4-2) 16-18 (4-3) 18-19 (3-4) 19-21 (2-4) 21-23 (1-4) 23-03 (1-3) 03-06 (1-2) 06-08 (2-3)	08-10 (4-2) 10-12 (3-1) 12-16 (2-1) 16-18 (3-2) 18-19 (4-2) 19-20 (4-3) 20-23 (4) 23-03 (3-4) 03-06 (2-3) 06-08 (3-4)	08-10 (2-1) 10-16 (1-0) 16-18 (2-1) 18-19 (2) 19-20 (3) 20-21 (4-3) 21-03 (4) 03-05 (3-4) 05-06 (3) 06-08 (4-3)
80	07-09 (3-4) 09-12 (4) 12-19 (4-3) 19-23 (4) 23-05 (3-4) 05-07 (2-3)	07-09 (4-2) 09-12 (4-1) 12-17 (3-1) 17-19 (3-2) 19-21 (4-3) 21-05 (4) 05-06 (3-4) 06-07 (3)	07-09 (2-1) 09-17 (1-0) 17-19 (2-1) 19-21 (3-2) 21-22 (4-3) 22-04 (4) 04-06 (4-3) 06-07 (3-2)	07-09 (1) 09-17 (0) 17-19 (1) 19-21 (2) 21-22 (3-2) 22-04 (4-3) 04-06 (3-2) 06-07 (2-1)
160	17-19 (1-0) 19-21 (2-1) 21-06 (4) 06-08 (3-2) 08-10 (2-1) 10-12 (1-0)	18-20 (1-0) 20-21 (1) 21-03 (4-3) 03-06 (3-2) 06-08 (2-1) 08-10 (1-0)	20-21 (1-0) 21-23 (3-1) 23-03 (3) 03-06 (2-1) 06-08 (1)	21-23 (1-0) 23-03 (3-2) 03-06 (1) 06-08 (1-0)

HAWAII Summer 1994 Openings Given in Hawaiian Standard Time

	10 Meters	*15 Meters*	*20 Meters*	*40/80 Meters*
Eastern States	08-10 (1) 10-13 (2) 13-14 (1)	07-11 (1) 11-12 (2) 12-14 (3) 14-15 (2) 15-16 (1)	11-13 (1) 13-14 (2) 14-18 (3) 18-20 (2) 20-04 (1) 04-07 (2) 07-08 (1)	18-20 (1) 20-22 (2) 22-00 (3) 00-02 (2) 02-03 (1) 10-21 (1)* 21-00 (2)* 00-01 (1)*
Central States	08-10 (1) 10-14 (2) 14-16 (1)	07-10 (1) 10-12 (2) 12-16 (3) 16-17 (2) 17-18 (1)	09-13 (1) 13-14 (2) 14-15 (3) 15-18 (4) 18-19 (3) 19-21 (2) 21-04 (1) 04-09 (2)	18-20 (1) 20-22 (2) 22-02 (3) 02-04 (2) 04-05 (1) 19-21 (1)* 21-00 (2)* 00-02 (1)*
Western States	08-09 (1) 09-10 (2) 10-15 (3) 15-16 (2) 16-17 (1)	07-09 (1) 09-10 (2) 10-13 (3) 13-15 (4) 15-16 (3) 16-17 (2) 17-19 (1)	10-12 (2) 12-14 (3) 14-18 (4) 18-20 (3) 20-00 (2) 00-05 (1) 05-06 (2) 06-10 (3)	18-19 (1) 19-20 (2) 20-02 (4) 02-04 (3) 04-05 (2) 05-06 (1) 19-20 (1)* 20-22 (2)* 22-02 (3)* 02-04 (2)* 04-05 (1)*

See explanation in "How To Use Short-Skip Charts" in box at the beginning of this column.

Note: The Alaska and Hawaii Propagation Charts are intended for distances *greater* than 1300 miles. For shorter distances, use the preceding Short-Skip Propagation Chart.

* Indicates best time to listen for 80 Meter openings. Openings on 160 Meters are also likely to occur during those times when 80 Meter openings are shown with a forecast rating of (2), or higher.

ALASKA
Summer 1994
Openings Given in GMT

	10 Meters	15 Meters	20 Meters	40/80 Meters
Eastern States	19-22 (1)	17-19 (1) 19-23 (2) 23-00 (1)	12-15 (1) 18-21 (1) 21-23 (2) 23-01 (3) 01-02 (2) 02-04 (1)	08-12 (1)
Central States	20-00 (1)	17-19 (1) 19-21 (2) 21-23 (3) 23-01 (2) 01-02 (1)	13-22 (1) 22-00 (2) 00-03 (3) 03-04 (2) 04-06 (1)	08-11 (1) 11-13 (2) 13-14 (1) 11-13 (1)*
Western States	20-22 (1) 22-01 (2) 01-02 (1)	18-21 (1) 21-22 (2) 22-00 (4) 00-01 (3) 01-02 (2) 02-03 (1)	16-18 (1) 18-20 (3) 20-00 (2) 00-02 (3) 02-03 (4) 03-04 (3) 04-05 (2) 05-07 (1,	08-11 (1) 11-14 (2) 14-16 (1) 11-14 (1)*

Fall 1994
Time Zone: EDT (24-Hour Time)
EASTERN USA To:

	10 Meters	15 Meters	20 Meters	40/80 Meters
Western & Central Europe & North Africa	09-11 (1) 11-12 (2) 12-14 (1)	08-09 (1) 09-11 (2) 11-14 (4) 14-15 (3) 15-16 (2) 16-17 (1)	03-04 (1) 04-06 (2) 06-10 (3) 10-12 (2) 12-15 (3) 15-17 (4) 17-19 (3) 19-20 (2) 20-21 (1)	18-19 (1) 19-21 (2) 21-23 (3) 23-02 (4) 02-03 (3) 03-04 (2) 04-05 (1) 20-22 (1)* 22-01 (2)* 01-04 (1)*
Northern Europe & European USSR	09-12 (1)	08-09 (1) 09-10 (2) 10-12 (3) 12-13 (2) 13-15 (1)	03-06 (1) 06-08 (2) 08-11 (3) 11-13 (2) 13-17 (3) 17-18 (2) 18-20 (1)	18-20 (1) 20-04 (2) 04-06 (1) 21-04 (1)*
Eastern Mediter ranean & Middle East	10-13 (1)	08-09 (1) 09-12 (2) 12-14 (3) 14-16 (2) 16-17 (1)	07-09 (2) 09-15 (1) 15-17 (2) 17-20 (3) 20-21 (2) 21-23 (1) 23-01 (2) 01-07 (1)	19-21 (1) 21-00 (2) 00-01 (1) 22-23 (1)*
Western Africa	11-13 (1) 13-14 (2) 14-16 (3) 16-17 (2) 17-18 (1)	07-09 (1) 09-13 (2) 13-15 (3) 15-17 (4) 17-18 (3) 18-19 (2) 19-20 (1)	05-08 (2) 08-15 (1) 15-17 (2) 17-18 (3) 18-21 (4) 21-23 (3) 23-03 (2) 03-05 (1)	20-23 (1) 23-02 (2) 02-04 (1) 00-03 (1)*
Eastern & Central Africa	13-15 (1) 15-17 (2) 17-18 (1)	08-09 (1) 09-13 (2) 13-15 (3) 15-17 (4) 17-18 (3) 18-19 (2) 19-20 (1)	12-14 (1) 14-17 (2) 17-21 (3) 21-01 (2) 01-02 (1)	20-02 (1) 00-01 (1)*
Southern Africa	09-11 (1) 11-13 (2) 13-14 (1)	08-11 (1) 11-12 (2) 12-13 (3) 13-15 (4) 15-16 (3) 16-17 (2) 17-18 (1)	14-16 (1) 16-19 (2) 19-23 (3) 23-01 (2) 01-02 (1) 06-08 (1)	19-22 (1) 22-00 (2) 00-02 (1) 23-01 (1)*
Central & South Asia	09-11 (1) 19-21 (1)	09-10 (1) 10-12 (2) 12-13 (1) 20-22 (1)	07-08 (1) 08-10 (2) 10-12 (1) 17-19 (1) 19-22 (2) 22-00 (1)	05-07 (1) 20-23 (1)
Southeast Asia	11-13 (1) 18-20 (1)	09-11 (1) 14-16 (1) 18-19 (1) 19-20 (2) 20-21 (1)	06-07 (1) 07-10 (2) 10-12 (1) 15-18 (1) 20-21 (1) 21-23 (2) 23-01 (1)	06-08 (1)
Far East	18-20 (1)	10-12 (1) 16-18 (1) 18-20 (2) 20-21 (1)	07-08 (1) 08-10 (2) 10-12 (1) 17-20 (1) 20-22 (2) 22-00 (1)	05-08 (1) 18-19 (1) 06-07 (1)*
South Pacific & New Zealand	09-15 (1) 15-17 (2) 17-19 (3) 19-20 (2) 20-21 (1)	09-14 (1) 14-18 (2) 18-20 (3) 20-21 (2) 21-22 (1)	08-10 (3) 10-12 (2) 12-20 (1) 20-23 (2) 23-03 (3) 03-07 (1)	01-02 (1) 02-03 (2) 03-06 (3) 06-08 (2) 08-09 (1) 03-05 (1)* 05-07 (2)* 07-08 (1)*
Austral asia	10-12 (1) 16-17 (1) 17-19 (2) 19-20 (1)	09-11 (1) 14-17 (1) 17-18 (2) 18-20 (3) 20-21 (2) 21-22 (1)	07-09 (2) 09-11 (3) 11-13 (2) 13-16 (1) 16-18 (2) 18-21 (1) 21-23 (2) 23-01 (3) 01-03 (2) 03-07 (1)	02-04 (1) 04-06 (2) 06-07 (3) 07-08 (2) 08-09 (1) 04-05 (1)* 05-06 (2)* 06-07 (1)*
Caribbean, Central America & Northern Countries of South America	10-11 (1) 11-14 (2) 14-17 (4) 17-18 (2) 18-19 (1)	08-09 (1) 09-10 (2) 10-13 (3) 13-18 (4) 18-19 (3) 19-20 (2) 20-21 (1)	04-06 (1) 06-07 (2) 07-08 (3) 08-10 (4) 10-15 (2) 15-17 (3) 17-22 (4) 22-03 (3) 03-04 (2)	19-20 (1) 20-21 (2) 21-04 (4) 04-06 (3) 06-07 (2) 07-08 (1) 21-23 (1)* 23-04 (2)* 04-06 (1)*
Peru, Bolivia, Paraguay, Brazil, Chile, Argentina, & Uruguay	09-10 (1) 10-12 (2) 12-14 (1) 14-15 (2) 15-17 (4) 17-18 (3) 18-19 (1)	08-09 (1) 09-11 (2) 11-14 (1) 14-16 (2) 16-17 (3) 17-19 (4) 19-20 (3) 20-21 (2) 21-22 (1)	11-16 (1) 16-17 (2) 17-20 (3) 20-01 (4) 01-03 (3) 03-04 (2) 04-07 (1) 07-08 (2) 08-10 (3) 10-11 (2)	21-00 (1) 00-05 (2) 05-07 (1) 01-06 (1)*
McMurdo Sound, Antarctica	16-18 (1)	12-15 (1) 15-18 (2) 18-19 (3) 19-20 (2) 20-21 (1)	16-18 (1) 18-21 (2) 21-23 (3) 23-01 (2) 01-03 (1) 07-09 (1)	23-01 (1) 01-05 (2) 04-06 (1) 04-06 (1)*

Time Zones: CDT & MDT (24-Hour Time) CETRAL USA To:

	10 Meters	15 Meters	20 Meters	40/80 Meters
Western & Central Europe & North Africa	09-12 (1)	08-10 (1) 10-11 (2) 11-13 (3) 13-14 (2) 14-16 (1)	06-07 (1) 07-10 (2) 10-13 (1) 13-14 (2) 14-16 (4) 16-17 (3) 17-20 (2) 20-23 (1)	18-20 (1) 20-23 (2) 23-01 (3) 01-02 (2) 02-03 (1) 21-23 (1)* 23-01 (2)* 01-02 (1)*
Northern Europe & European USSR	09-11 (1)	08-10 (1) 10-12 (2) 12-14 (1)	06-07 (1) 07-10 (2) 10-12 (1) 12-13 (2) 13-15 (3) 15-16 (2) 16-18 (1) 22-01 (1)	20-23 (1) 23-01 (2) 01-02 (1) 22-01 (1)*
Eastern Mediter-ranean & Middle East	10-12 (1)	08-10 (1) 10-13 (2) 13-14 (1)	06-07 (1) 07-09 (2) 09-15 (1) 15-18 (2) 18-21 (1) 21-23 (2) 23-00 (1)	20-23 (1) 21-23 (1)*
Western Africa	11-13 (1) 13-15 (2) 15-17 (1)	07-10 (1) 10-13 (2) 13-15 (3) 15-17 (4) 17-18 (2) 18-19 (1)	05-06 (1) 06-08 (2) 08-15 (3) 15-17 (2) 17-18 (3) 18-19 (4) 19-22 (3) 22-00 (2) 00-01 (1)	20-23 (1) 23-01 (2) 01-02 (1) 23-01 (1)*
Eastern & Central Africa	12-15 (1)	09-11 (1) 11-15 (2) 15-16 (3) 16-17 (2) 17-18 (1)	13-15 (1) 15-17 (2) 17-19 (3) 19-21 (2) 21-22 (1)	21-00 (1)
Southern Africa	10-11 (1) 11-13 (2) 13-14 (1)	07-09 (1) 09-12 (2) 12-13 (3) 13-14 (4) 14-15 (3) 15-16 (2) 16-17 (1)	06-08 (2) 08-14 (1) 14-16 (2) 16-19 (3) 19-21 (2) 21-23 (1) 23-01 (2) 01-02 (1)	20-21 (1) 21-23 (2) 23-01 (1) 21-23 (1)*
Central South Asia	09-11 (1) 18-20 (1)	09-11 (1) 18-19 (1) 19-21 (2) 21-22 (1)	07-08 (1) 08-10 (2) 10-12 (1) 17-19 (1) 19-21 (2) 21-23 (1)	06-08 (1) 19-21 (1)
Southeast Asia	10-12 (1) 18-20 (1)	09-11 (1) 14-17 (1) 17-19 (2) 19-21 (1)	06-08 (1) 08-10 (2) 10-13 (1) 16-21 (1) 21-00 (2) 00-02 (1)	05-09 (1)
Far East	17-18 (1) 18-19 (2) 19-20 (1)	10-16 (1) 16-18 (2) 18-20 (3) 20-21 (2) 21-22 (1)	07-08 (1) 08-10 (3) 10-12 (2) 17-21 (1) 21-00 (2) 00-02 (1)	03-05 (1) 05-08 (2) 08-09 (1) 06-08 (1)*
South Pacific & New Zealand	13-15 (1) 15-17 (2) 17-19 (3) 19-20 (2) 20-21 (1)	09-13 (1) 13-17 (2) 17-19 (4) 19-20 (3) 20-21 (2) 21-23 (1)	07-08 (2) 08-11 (3) 11-13 (2) 13-18 (1) 18-20 (2) 20-22 (3) 22-00 (4) 00-01 (3) 00-03 (2) 03-07 (1)	00-01 (1) 01-06 (3) 06-08 (4) 08-09 (2) 09-10 (1) 02-04 (1)* 04-07 (2)* 07-08 (1)*
Austral asia	14-16 (1) 16-18 (2) 18-19 (3) 19-20 (2) 20-21 (1)	09-11 (1) 13-17 (1) 17-19 (2) 19-20 (3) 20-21 (2) 21-22 (1)	16-18 (2) 18-21 (1) 21-23 (2) 23-03 (3) 03-04 (2) 04-07 (1) 07-09 (2) 09-11 (3) 11-13 (2) 13-16 (1)	02-03 (1) 03-05 (2) 05-07 (3) 07-08 (2) 08-09 (1) 05-06 (1)* 06-07 (2)* 07-08 (1)*
Caribbean, Central America & Northern Countries of South America	09-10 (1) 10-11 (2) 11-13 (3) 13-16 (4) 16-18 (2) 18-19 (1)	07-08 (1) 08-10 (2) 10-13 (3) 13-17 (4) 17-18 (3) 18-20 (2) 20-21 (1)	07-10 (4) 10-12 (3) 12-15 (2) 15-17 (3) 17-22 (4) 22-01 (3) 01-03 (2) 03-05 (1) 05-07 (2)	19-20 (1) 20-21 (2) 21-01 (3) 01-05 (4) 05-06 (3) 06-07 (2) 07-08 (1) 20-23 (1)* 23-05 (2)* 05-06 (1)*
Peru, Bolivia, Paraguay, Brazil, Chile, Argentina & Uruguay	09-10 (1) 10-13 (2) 13-15 (3) 15-17 (4) 17-18 (2) 18-19 (1)	07-08 (1) 08-11 (3) 11-15 (2) 15-16 (3) 16-19 (4) 19-20 (3) 20-21 (2) 21-22 (1)	04-08 (1) 08-10 (2) 10-16 (1) 16-18 (2) 18-20 (3) 20-23 (4) 23-02 (3) 02-04 (2)	21-00 (1) 00-04 (2) 04-06 (1) 01-05 (1)*
McMurdo Sound, Antarctica	15-18 (1)	11-16 (1) 16-18 (2) 18-19 (3) 19-20 (2) 20-21 (1)	08-09 (1) 17-19 (1) 19-20 (2) 20-23 (3) 23-00 (2) 00-03 (2)	00-03 (1) 03-05 (2) 05-07 (1) 04-06 (1)*

Time Zone: PDT (24-Hour Time) WESTERN USA To:

	10 Meters	15 Meters	20 Meters	40/80 Meters
Western Europe & North Africa	09-11 (1)	08-09 (1) 09-12 (2) 12-14 (1)	06-07 (1) 07-10 (2) 10-13 (1) 13-14 (2) 14-16 (3) 16-17 (2) 17-19 (1)	20-21 (1) 21-23 (2) 23-00 (1) 21-23 (1)*
Central & Northern Europe & European USSR	Nil	08-09 (1) 09-11 (2) 11-13 (1)	06-07 (1) 07-09 (2) 09-12 (1) 12-14 (2) 14-16 (2) 21-23 (1)	20-00 (1) 20-22 (1)*
Eastern Mediter ranean & Middle East	*Nil*	08-09 (1) 09-11 (2) 11-12 (1) 20-22 (1)	06-07 (1) 07-10 (2) 10-13 (1) 13-15 (2) 15-16 (1) 19-20 (1) 20-22 (2) 22-23 (1)	20-23 (1)

Western & Central Africa	11-12 (1) 12-14 (2) 14-15 (1)	08-10 (1) 10-13 (2) 13-16 (3) 16-17 (2) 17-18 (1)	06-07 (1) 07-09 (2) 09-14 (1) 14-15 (2) 15-16 (3) 16-18 (4) 18-20 (3) 20-22 (2) 22-00 (1)	21-00 (1)
Eastern Africa	11-14 (1)	10-13 (1) 13-16 (2) 16-17 (1)	07-09 (1) 12-15 (1) 15-19 (2) 19-21 (1)	20-22 (1)
Southern Africa	10-13 (1)	07-09 (1) 09-11 (2) 11-13 (3) 13-15 (2) 15-16 (1)	05-07 (1) 07-09 (2) 09-10 (1) 12-14 (1) 14-16 (2) 16-18 (3) 18-19 (2) 19-22 (1) 22-00 (2) 00-01 (1)	19-22 (1)
Central & South Asia	17-19 (1)	08-11 (1) 16-17 (1) 17-19 (2) 19-21 (1)	07-08 (1) 08-11 (2) 11-13 (1) 17-19 (1) 19-21 (2) 21-23 (1)	06-08 (1) 19-21 (1)
Southeast Asia	16-19 (1)	10-11 (1) 11-13 (2) 13-16 (1) 16-18 (2) 18-21 (1)	05-07 (1) 07-09 (3) 09-11 (2) 11-12 (1) 21-23 (1) 23-01 (2) 01-02 (1)	01-03 (1) 03-06 (2) 06-08 (1) 03-06 (1)*
Far East	16-17 (1) 17-18 (2) 18-19 (1)	14-15 (1) 15-17 (2) 17-19 (3) 19-20 (2) 20-21 (1)	07-08 (1) 08-09 (2) 09-10 (4) 10-13 (3) 13-15 (2) 15-20 (1) 20-22 (2) 22-00 (3) 00-01 (2) 01-03 (1)	01-03 (1) 03-07 (2) 07-08 (3) 08-09 (1) 03-05 (1)* 05-07 (2)* 07-08 (1)*
South Pacific & New Zealand	11-13 (1) 13-15 (2) 15-17 (3) 17-19 (2) 19-20 (1)	09-11 (1) 11-13 (3) 13-17 (2) 17-19 (3) 19-21 (4) 21-22 (3) 22-23 (2) 23-01 (1)	13-19 (1) 19-21 (2) 21-23 (3) 23-01 (4) 01-03 (3) 03-05 (2) 05-06 (1) 06-07 (2) 07-09 (3) 09-13 (2)	21-22 (1) 22-23 (2) 23-00 (3) 00-05 (4) 05-07 (3) 07-08 (2) 08-09 (1) 23-02 (1)* 02-06 (2)* 06-07 (1)*
Austral asia	14-15 (1) 15-17 (2) 17-19 (3) 19-20 (2) 20-21 (1)	08-10 (1) 13-17 (1) 17-19 (2) 19-21 (3) 21-22 (2) 22-23 (1)	19-21 (1) 21-23 (2) 23-01 (4) 01-03 (3) 03-04 (2) 04-07 (1) 07-08 (2) 08-10 (3) 10-12 (2) 12-13 (1)	01-02 (1) 02-03 (2) 03-06 (3) 06-08 (2) 08-09 (1) 02-04 (1)* 04-06 (2)* 06-07 (1)*
Caribbean, Central America & Northern Countries Of South America	09-10 (1) 10-11 (2) 11-13 (3) 13-15 (4) 15-16 (3) 16-17 (2) 17-18 (1)	07-08 (1) 08-10 (3) 10-12 (2) 12-15 (3) 15-17 (4) 17-18 (3) 18-19 (2) 19-20 (1)	06-08 (4) 08-10 (3) 10-15 (2) 15-17 (3) 17-23 (4) 23-01 (3) 01-03 (2) 03-05 (1) 05-06 (2)	19-21 (1) 21-02 (3) 02-04 (2) 04-07 (1) 20-22 (1)* 22-03 (2)* 03-05 (1)*
Peru, Bolivia, Paraguay, Brazil, Chile, Argentina, & Uruguay	09-10 (1) 10-12 (2) 12-14 (3) 14-16 (4) 16-17 (3) 17-18 (2)	07-08 (1) 08-09 (2) 09-13 (1) 13-15 (2) 15-16 (3) 16-19 (4) 19-20 (2) 20-21 (1)	06-15 (1) 15-17 (2) 17-19 (3) 19-23 (4) 23-01 (3) 01-06 (2)	21-23 (1) 23-02 (2) 02-04 (1) 00-03 (1)*
McMurdo Sound, Antarctica	14-18 (1)	11-15 (1) 15-17 (2) 17-19 (3) 19-20 (2) 20-21 (1)	08-10 (1) 17-19 (1) 19-20 (2) 20-23 (3) 23-01 (2) 01-03 (1)	01-03 (1) 03-05 (2) 05-07 (1) 03-06 (1)*

CQ Short-Skip Propagation Chart
Fall 1994
Local Daylight Savings Time At Path Mid-Point (24-Hour Time)

Band (Meters)	*Distance Between Stations (Miles)* 50-250	250-750	750-1300	1300-2300
10	*Nil*	10-21 (0-1)	08-10 (1) 10-13 (1-2) 13-15 (1-3) 15-16 (1-2) 16-21 (0-1)	08-10 (1) 10-13 (2) 13-15 (3) 15-16 (2-3) 16-17 (1-2) 17-19 (1) 19-21 (1-0)
15	*Nil*	08-10 (0-1) 10-15 (0-2) 15-21 (0-1)	08-09 (1) 09-10 (1-2) 10-15 (2-4) 15-17 (1-4) 17-18 (1-3) 18-20 (1-2) 20-21 (1) 21-08 (0-1)	08-09(1) 09-10 (2-3) 10-11 (4-3) 11-17 (4) 17-18 (3) 18-19 (2-3) 19-20 (2) 20-21 (1) 21-08 (1-0)
20	12-14 (0-1) 14-16 (0-2) 16-22 (0-1)	08-09 (0-1) 09-10 (0-2) 10-11 (0-3) 11-12 (0-4) 12-14 (1-4) 14-16 (2-4) 16-18 (1-4) 18-19 (1-3) 19-22 (1-2) 22-08 (0-1)	06-08 (1-2) 08-09 (1-3) 09-10 (2-4) 10-11 (3-4) 11-18 (4) 18-19 (3-4) 19-22 (2-3) 22-00 (1-2) 00-06 (1)	06-08 (2) 08-09 (3) 09-14 (4-2) 14-16 (4-3) 16-19 (4) 19-21 (3-4) 21-22 (3) 22-23 (2-3) 23-00 (2) 00-06 (1)
40	08-10 (1-3) 10-12 (2-4) 12-18 (3-4) 18-19 (2-3) 19-21 (1-2) 21-06 (0-1) 06-08 (0-2)	08-10 (3-4) 10-12 (4-3) 12-16 (4-2) 16-18 (4-3) 18-19 (3-4) 19-21 (2-4) 21-23 (1-4) 23-03 (1-3) 03-06 (1-2) 06-08 (2-3)	08-10 (4-2) 10-12 (3-1) 12-16 (2-1) 16-18 (3-2) 18-19 (4-2) 19-20 (4-3) 20-23 (4) 23-03 (3-4) 03-06 (2-3) 06-08 (3-4)	08-10 (2-1) 10-16 (1-0) 16-18 (2-1) 18-19 (2) 19-20 (3) 20-21 (4-3) 21-03 (4) 03-05 (3-4) 05-06 (3) 06-08 (4-3)

80	07-09 (3-4) 09-12 (4) 12-19 (4-3) 19-23 (4) 23-05 (3-4) 05-07 (2-3)	07-09 (4-2) 09-12 (4-1) 12-17 (3-1) 17-19 (3-2) 19-21 (4-3) 21-05 (4) 05-06 (3-4) 06-07 (3)	07-09 (2-1) 09-17 (1-0) 17-19 (2-1) 19-21 (3-2) 21-22 (4-3) 22-04 (4) 04-06 (4-3) 06-07 (3-2)	07-09 (1) 09-17 (0) 17-19 (1) 19-21 (2) 21-22 (3-2) 22-04 (4-3) 04-06 (3-2) 06-07 (2-1)
160	17-19 (1-0) 19-21 (2-1) 21-06 (4) 06-08 (3-2) 08-10 (2-1) 10-12 (1-0)	18-20 (1-0) 20-21 (1) 21-03 (4-3) 03-06 (3-2) 06-08 (2-1) 08-10 (1-0)	20-21 (1-0) 21-23 (3-1) 23-03 (3) 03-06 (2-1) 06-08 (1)	21-23 (1-0) 23-03 (3-2) 03-06 (1) 06-08 (1-0)

ALASKA
Fall 1994
Openings Given GMT

	10 Meters	15 Meters	20 Meters	40/80 Meters
Eastern States	19-22 (1)	17-19 (1) 19-23 (2) 23-00 (1)	12-15 (1) 18-21 (1) 21-23 (2) 23-01 (3) 01-02 (2) 02-04 (1)	08-12 (1)
Central States	20-00 (1)	17-19 (1) 19-21 (2) 21-23 (3) 23-01 (2) 01-02 (1)	13-22 (1) 22-00 (2) 00-03 (3) 03-04 (2) 04-06 (1)	08-11 (1) 11-13 (2) 13-14 (1) 11-13 (1)*
Western States	20-22 (1) 22-01 (2) 01-02 (1)	18-21 (1) 21-22 (2) 22-00 (4) 00-01 (3) 01-02 (2) 02-03 (1)	16-18 (1) 18-20 (3) 20-00 (2) 00-02 (3) 02-03 (4) 03-04 (3) 04-05 (2) 05-07 (1,	08-11 (1) 11-14 (2) 14-16 (1) 11-14 (1)*

HAWAII
Fall 1994
Openings Given in Hawaiian Standard Time

	10 Meters	15 Meters	20 Meters	40/80 Meters
Eastern States	08-10 (1) 10-13 (2) 13-14 (1)	07-11 (1) 11-12 (2) 12-14 (3) 14-15 (2) 15-16 (1)	11-13 (1) 13-14 (2) 14-18 (3) 18-20 (2) 20-04 (1) 04-07 (2) 07-08 (1)	18-20 (1) 20-22 (2) 22-00 (3) 00-02 (2) 02-03 (1) 10-21 (1)* 21-00 (2)* 00-01 (1)*
Central States	08-10 (1) 10-14 (2) 14-16 (1)	07-10 (1) 10-12 (2) 12-16 (3) 16-17 (2) 17-18 (1)	09-13 (1) 13-14 (2) 14-15 (3) 15-18 (4) 18-19 (3) 19-21 (2) 21-04 (1) 04-09 (2)	18-20 (1) 20-22 (2) 22-02 (3) 02-04 (2) 04-05 (1) 19-21 (1)* 21-00 (2)* 00-02 (1)*

Western States	08-09 (1) 09-10 (2) 10-15 (3) 15-16 (2) 16-17 (1)	07-09 (1) 09-10 (2) 10-13 (3) 13-15 (4) 15-16 (3) 16-17 (2) 17-19 (1)	10-12 (2) 12-14 (3) 14-18 (4) 18-20 (3) 20-00 (2) 00-05 (1) 05-06 (2) 06-10 (3)	18-19 (1) 19-20 (2) 20-02 (4) 02-04 (3) 04-05 (2) 05-06 (1) 19-20 (1)* 20-22 (2)* 22-02 (3)* 02-04 (2)* 04-05 (1)*

\# See explanation in "How To Use Short-Skip Charts" in box at the beginning of this column.

Note: The Alaska and Hawaii Propagation Charts are intended for distances *greater* than 1300 miles. For shorter distances, use the preceding Short-Skip Propagation Chart.

* Indicates best time to listen for 80 Meter openings. Openings on 160 Meters are also likely to occur during those times when 80 Meter openings are shown with a forecast rating of (2), or higher.

Winter 1994
Time Zone: EST (24-Hour Time)
EASTERN USA To:

Reception Area	*10 Meters*	*15 Meters*	*20 Meters*	*40/80* Meters*
Western & Central Europe & North Africa	09-11 (1)	07-08 (1) 08-09 (2) 09-11 (3) 11-13 (2) 13-14 (1)	06-07 (1) 07-09 (4) 09-11 (3) 11-13 (4) 13-14 (3) 14-15 (2) 15-17 (1)	15-16 (1) 16-17 (2) 17-19 (3) 19-00 (4) 00-02 (2) 02-03 (3) 03-05 (1) 17-19 (1)* 19-20 (2)* 20-02 (3)* 02-03 (2)* 03-04 (1)*
Northern Europe & European USSR	08-10 (1)	07-08 (1) 08-10 (2) 10-12 (1)	06-07 (1) 07-09 (3) 09-12 (2) 12-14 (1)	16-19 (1) 19-23 (2) 23-03 (1) 19-02 (1)*
Eastern Mediterranean & Middle East	08-10 (1)	08-09 (1) 09-10 (3) 10-11 (2) 11-12 (1)	06-09 (1) 09-10 (2) 10-13 (3) 13-15 (2) 15-17 (1)	18-20 (1) 20-22 (2) 22-00 (1) 20-23 (1)*
West Africa	09-11 (1) 11-13 (2) 13-15 (1)	07-08 (1) 08-09 (2) 09-12 (3) 12-14 (4) 14-15 (3) 15-16 (2) 16-17 (1)	06-07 (1) 07-09 (2) 09-13 (1) 13-15 (2) 15-17 (4) 17-18 (3) 18-19 (2) 19-20 (1)	18-22 (1) 22-00 (2) 00-03 (1) 03-04 (2) 00-02 (1)*
East & Central Africa	10-13 (1)	08-10 (1) 10-12 (2) 12-13 (3) 13-15 (2) 15-16 (1)	07-13 (1) 13-15 (2) 15-17 (3) 17-18 (2) 18-19 (1)	18-00 (1)

Southern Africa	09-10 (1) 10-12 (2) 12-13 (1)	07-09 (1) 09-12 (2) 12-14 (3) 14-15 (1)	07-09 (1) 12-14 (1) 14-15 (2) 15-17 (3) 17-18 (2) 18-20 (1)	18-19 (1) 19-21 (2) 21-00 (1) 19-22 (1)*
Central & South Asia	Nil	08-10 (1) 17-19 (1)	06-07 (1) 07-09 (2) 09-11 (1) 18-21 (1)	06-08 (1) 20-22 (1)
Southeast Asia	Nil	08-11 (1) 17-19 (1)	06-07 (1) 07-09 (2) 09-12 (1) 19-21 (1)	06-08 (1) 20-22 (1)
Far East	Nil	16-17 (1) 17-19 (2) 19-20 (1)	06-07 (1) 07-09 (2) 09-11 (1) 16-18 (1) 18-20 (2) 20-21 (1)	05-08 (1) 05-07 (1)*
South Pacific & New Zealand	13-17 (1)	11-14 (1) 14-15 (2) 15-17 (3) 17-18 (2) 18-20 (1)	03-07 (1) 07-09 (2) 09-11 (1) 16-18 (1) 18-20 (2) 20-22 (1)	01-02 (1) 02-04 (2) 04-07 (3) 07-08 (2) 08-09 (1) 04-05 (1)* 05-07 (2)* 07-08 (1)*
Australasia	16-18 (1)	09-12 (1) 15-16 (1) 16-18 (2) 18-20 (1)	06-07 (1) 07-10 (2) 10-14 (1) 14-16 (2) 16-18 (1) 18-20 (2) 20-22 (1)	03-05 (1) 05-07 (2) 07-09 (1) 05-08 (1)*
Caribbean, Central America & Northern Countries of South America	09-10 (1) 10-12 (2) 12-14 (1) 14-16 (2) 16-17 (1)	07-08 (1) 08-11 (3) 11-13 (2) 13-15 (4) 15-16 (3) 16-17 (2) 17-18 (1)	06-07 (2) 07-09 (4) 09-11 (3) 11-15 (2) 15-17 (3) 17-18 (4) 18-19 (3) 19-20 (2) 20-22 (1) 22-00 (2) 00-06 (1)	17-18 (1) 18-19 (2) 19-21 (3) 21-04 (4) 04-05 (3) 05-06 (2) 06-07 (1) 19-20 (1)* 20-22 (2)* 22-02 (3)* 02-04 (2)* 04-06 (1)*
Peru, Bolivia, Paraguay, Brazil, Chile, Argentina & Uruguay	09-12 (1) 12-15 (2) 15-16 (1)	07-08 (1) 08-10 (2) 10-12 (1) 12-14 (2) 14-16 (4) 16-17 (3) 17-18 (1)	13-14 (1) 14-15 (2) 15-17 (3) 17-18 (4) 18-19 (3) 19-20 (2) 20-22 (1) 22-00 (2) 00-03 (1) 05-06 (1) 06-08 (2) 08-09 (1)	19-21 (1) 21-02 (2) 02-05 (1) 21-03 (1)*
McMurdo Sound, Antarctica	Nil	07-10 (1) 16-18 (1)	07-09 (1) 17-18 (1) 18-22 (2) 22-00 (1) 00-02 (2) 02-03 (1)	00-05 (1)

**Predicted times of 80 meter openings. Openings on 160 meters are also likely to occur during those times when 80 meter openings are shown with a forecast rating of (2) or better.*

Winter 1994-1995
Time Zones: CST & MST (24-Hour Time)
CENTRAL USA To:

Reception Area	*10 Meters*	*15 Meters*	*20 Meters*	*40/80* Meters*
Western & Southern Europe & North Africa	09-11 (1)	07-08 (1) 08-09 (2) 09-11 (3) 11-12 (2) 12-13 (1)	06-08 (1) 08-09 (2) 09-12 (3) 12-13 (2) 13-15 (1) 22-00 (1)	16-18 (1) 18-20 (2) 20-00 (1) 00-02 (2) 02-03 (1) 17-20 (1)* 20-01 (2)* 01-02 (1)*
Northern & Central Europe & European U S S R	Nil	07-08 (1) 08-10 (2) 10-12 (1)	07-08 (1) 08-11 (2) 11-13 (1) 23-01 (1)	17-19 (1) 19-22 (2) 22-01 (1) 19-00 (1)*
Eastern Mediterranean & Middle East	Nil	08-11 (1)	06-09 (1) 09-12 (2) 12-14 (1) 22-00 (1)	18-20 (1) 20-22 (2) 22-23 (1) 20-22 (1)*
West & Central Africa	08-10 (1) 10-12 (2) 12-13 (1)	07-09 (1) 09-11 (2) 11-13 (3) 13-14 (2) 14-15 (1)	06-11 (1) 11-13 (2) 13-16 (3) 16-17 (2) 17-19 (1) 22-02 (1)	18-21 (1) 21-23 (2) 23-01 (1) 19-22 (1)*
East Africa	10-12 (1)	07-11 (1) 11-13 (2) 13-14 (1)	06-12 (1) 12-14 (2) 14-16 (3) 16-17 (2) 17-19 (1)	19-23 (1)
Southern Africa	08-09 (1) 09-12 (2) 12-13 (1)	07-09 (1) 09-11 (2) 11-13 (3) 13-15 (2) 15-16 (1)	07-13 (1) 13-15 (2) 15-17 (3) 17-18 (2) 18-20 (1) 23-01 (1)	18-19 (1) 19-21 (2) 21-23 (1)
Central & South Asia	Nil	08-10 (1) 19-21 (1)	06-07 (1) 07-09 (2) 09-11 (1) 19-22 (1)	06-08 (1) 19-21 (1)
Southeast Asia	Nil	08-11 (1) 17-20 (1)	07-08 (1) 08-10 (2) 10-12 (1) 16-17 (1) 17-19 (2) 19-20 (1)	04-07 (1)
Far East	Nil	07-09 (1) 16-17 (1) 17-19 (2) 19-20 (1)	06-07 (1) 07-09 (2) 09-11 (1) 15-17 (1) 17-19 (2) 19-21 (1)	02-04 (1) 04-06 (2) 06-07 (1) 04-07 (1)*
South Pacific & New Zealand	12-14 (1) 14-16 (2) 16-18 (1)	10-12 (1) 12-14 (2) 14-17 (3) 17-19 (2) 19-20 (1)	06-07 (1) 07-09 (3) 09-12 (2) 12-15 (1) 15-17 (2) 17-20 (3) 20-21 (2) 21-22 (1) 02-04 (1)	23-01 (1) 01-02 (2) 02-06 (3) 06-07 (2) 07-08 (1) 03-07 (1)*

Australasia	14-15 (1) 15-17 (2) 17-18 (1)	09-11 (1) 13-15 (1) 15-17 (3) 17-19 (2) 19-20 (1)	06-07 (1) 07-08 (2) 08-10 (3) 10-12 (2) 12-18 (1) 18-21 (2) 21-22 (1)	02-04 (1) 04-07 (2) 07-09 (1) 03-06 (1)*
Caribbean, Central America & Northern Countries of South America	08-10 (1) 10-14 (2) 14-16 (1)	07-08 (1) 08-09 (2) 09-13 (3) 13-16 (4) 16-17 (2) 17-19 (1)	06-07 (2) 07-11 (3) 11-14 (2) 14-16 (3) 16-18 (4) 18-19 (3) 19-20 (2) 20-22 (1) 22-00 (2) 00-06 (1)	18-20 (1) 20-22 (2) 22-03 (3) 03-05 (2) 05-07 (1) 19-21 (1)* 21-01 (2) 01-04 (1)*
Peru, Bolivia, Paraguay, Brazil, Chile, Argentina & Uruguay	08-11 (1) 11-15 (2) 15-17 (1)	07-08 (1) 08-13 (2) 13-15 (4) 15-16 (3) 16-17 (2) 17-19 (1)	05-06 (1) 06-08 (2) 08-10 (1) 12-14 (1) 14-15 (2) 15-17 (3) 17-19 (4) 19-20 (2) 20-22 (1) 22-00 (2) 00-03 (1)	19-21 (1) 21-02 (2) 02-05 (1) 21-04 (1)*
McMurdo Sound, Antarctica	Nil	07-09 (1) 16-18 (1)	06-07 (1) 07-09 (2) 09-11 (1) 17-18 (1) 18-22 (2) 22-00 (1) 00-02 (2) 02-03 (1)	22-05 (1)

Winter 1994-1995
Time Zone: PST (24-Hour Time)
WESTERN USA To:

Reception Area	*10 Meters*	*15 Meters*	*20 Meters*	*40/80* Meters*
Western & Southern Europe & North Africa	07-09 (1)	07-08 (1) 08-10 (2) 10-11 (1)	05-07 (1) 07-10 (2) 10-12 (1) 23-01 (1)	18-20 (1) 20-23 (2) 23-01 (1) 19-23 (1)*
Central & Northern Europe & European USSR	Nil	07-09 (1)	06-07 (1) 07-10 (2) 10-13 (1) 23-01 (1)	17-00 (1) 19-23 (1)*
Eastern Mediter-ranean & Middle East	Nil	07-09 (1)	06-07 (1) 07-09 (2) 09-11 (1) 21-23 (1)	18-21 (1)
West & Central Africa	09-12 (1)	07-09 (1) 09-10 (2) 10-12 (3) 12-13 (2) 13-14 (1)	06-10 (1) 10-13 (2) 13-16 (3) 16-18 (2) 18-19 (1)	18-22 (1)
East Africa	Nil	08-11 (1)	08-10 (1) 13-16 (1) 21-23 (1)	18-20 (1)
Southern Africa	08-11 (1)	06-08 (1) 08-10 (2) 10-12 (3) 12-13 (2) 13-14 (1)	07-11 (1) 11-13 (2) 13-16 (3) 16-18 (2) 18-19 (1) 00-02 (1)	18-20 (1)
Central & South Asia	Nil	09-11 (1) 17-19 (1)	08-10 (1) 17-19 (1) 19-20 (2) 20-21 (1)	05-07 (1) 18-20 (1)
Southeast Asia	15-18 (1)	09-11 (1) 15-16 (1) 16-18 (2) 18-19 (1)	07-09 (1) 09-11 (2) 11-16 (1) 16-19 (2) 19-20 (1)	03-08 (1)
Far East	15-17 (1)	14-15 (1) 15-16 (2) 16-17 (3) 17-18 (2) 18-19 (1)	08-10 (1) 13-14 (1) 14-15 (2) 15-18 (3) 18-19 (2) 19-21 (1)	00-01 (1) 01-03 (2) 03-06 (3) 06-08 (2) 08-10 (1) 02-08 (1)*
South Pacific & New Zealand	12-14 (1) 14-16 (2) 16-17 (1)	09-12 (1) 12-14 (2) 14-16 (4) 16-17 (3) 17-18 (2) 18-20 (1)	07-08 (1) 08-10 (2) 10-15 (1) 15-16 (2) 16-18 (4) 18-19 (3) 19-20 (2) 20-22 (1) 03-05 (1)	22-00 (1) 00-03 (2) 03-06 (3) 06-07 (2) 07-08 (1) 00-03 (1)* 03-06 (2)* 06-07 (1)*
Australasia	13-15 (1) 15-17 (2) 17-18 (1)	08-12 (1) 12-15 (2) 15-17 (3) 17-18 (2) 18-19 (1)	07-08 (1) 08-10 (3) 10-12 (2) 12-17 (1) 17-18 (2) 18-20 (3) 20-21 (2) 21-22 (1)	01-03 (1) 03-06 (2) 06-08 (1) 01-03 (1)* 03-06 (2)* 06-07 (1)*
Caribbean, Central America & Northern Countries of South America	09-11 (1) 11-14 (2) 14-16 (1)	06-07 (1) 07-08 (2) 08-12 (3) 12-14 (4) 14-15 (3) 15-16 (2) 16-17 (1)	06-07 (2) 07-09 (3) 09-13 (2) 13-15 (3) 15-17 (4) 17-18 (3) 18-20 (2) 20-22 (1) 22-00 (2) 00-06 (1)	18-20 (1) 20-22 (2) 22-02 (3) 02-04 (2) 04-05 (1) 19-21 (1)* 21-01 (2)* 01-04 (1)*
Peru, Bolivia, Paraguay, Brazil, Chile, Argentina & Uruguay	10-12 (1) 12-14 (2) 14-15 (1)	07-10 (1) 10-12 (2) 12-13 (3) 13-15 (4) 15-16 (2) 16-18 (1)	08-14 (1) 14-15 (2) 15-16 (3) 16-18 (4) 18-19 (3) 19-20 (2) 20-23 (1) 23-01 (2) 01-06 (1) 06-08 (2)	20-22 (1) 22-01 (2) 01-04 (1) 22-02 (1)*
McMurdo Sound, Antarctica	Nil	07-09 (1) 12-15 (1) 15-17 (2) 17-18 (1)	16-18 (1) 18-19 (2) 19-22 (3) 22-01 (2) 01-03 (1) 07-09 (1)	23-05 (1)

CQ Short-Skip Propagation Chart
Winter 1994-1995
Local standard Time
At Path Mid-Point (24-Hour Time)

Band (Meters)	Distance between stations (Miles) 50-250	250-750	750-1300	1300-2300
10	*Nil*	*Nil*	08-11 (0-1) 11-17 (0-2) 15-17 (0-1)	08-09 (1) 09-11 (1-2) 11-15 (2) 15-17 (1) 17-19 (0-1)
15	*Nil*	09-11 (0-1) 11-15 (0-2) 15-18 (0-1)	07-08 (0-1) 08-09 (0-2) 09-11 (1-3) 11-15 (2-4) 15-16 (1-3) 16-18 (1-2) 18-19 (0-1)	07-08 (1) 08-09 (2) 09-11 (3) 11-15 (4) 15-16 (3) 16-18 (2-3) 18-19 (1-2) 19-21 (0-1)
20	10-12 (0-1) 12-14 (0-2) 14-16 (0-1)	06-07 (0-1) 07-10 (0-2) 10-12 (1-3) 12-14 (2-4) 14-16 (1-4) 16-17 (0-3) 17-19 (0-2) 19-22 (0-1)	06-07 (1) 07-09 (2-3) 09-10 (2-4) 10-12 (3-4) 12-16 (4) 16-17 (3-4) 17-19 (2-3) 19-22 (1-2) 22-00 (0-1)	06-07 (1-2) 07-09 (3) 09-15 (4-3) 15-17 (4) 17-19 (3-4) 19-21 (2-3) 21-22 (2) 22-23 (1-2) 23-00 (1) 00-06 (0-1)
40	07-08 (0-2) 08-09 (1-3) 09-17 (3-4) 17-19 (2-3) 19-21 (1) 21-00 (0-1)	06-07 (0-2) 07-08 (2-3) 08-09 (3) 09-15 (4-3) 15-17 (4) 17-19 (3-4) 19-21 (1-3) 21-00 (1-2) 00-03 (0-2) 03-06 (0-1)	06-07 (2-3) 07-08 (3) 08-09 (3-2) 09-15 (3-1) 15-17 (4-2) 17-19 (4) 19-21 (3-4) 21-03 (2-4) 03-06 (1-3)	06-08 (3-2) 08-09 (2-1) 09-15 (1-0) 15-17 (2-0) 17-19 (4-3) 19-03 (4) 03-06 (3)
80	08-21 (4) 21-01 (3-4) 01-04 (2-3) 04-07 (1-2) 07-08 (3)	08-09 (4-2) 09-16 (4-1) 16-18 (4-3) 18-01 (4) 01-04 (3-4) 04-07 (2-3) 07-08 (3)	08-09 (2-1) 09-16 (1-0) 16-18 (3-1) 18-20 (4-3) 20-04 (4) 04-06 (3-4) 06-07 (3) 07-08 (3-1)	08-09 (1-0) 09-16 (0) 16-18 (1-0) 18-20 (3-2) 20-04 (4) 04-06 (4-2) 06-07 (3-1) 07-08 (1)
160	07-09 (3-2) 09-11 (2-0) 11-17 (1-0) 17-19 (3-2) 19-07 (4)	07-09 (2-1) 09-17 (0) 17-19 (2-1) 19-04 (4) 04-07 (4-2)	07-09 (1-0) 09-17 (0) 17-19 (1-0) 19-21 (4-2) 21-04 (4) 04-06 (2) 06-07 (2-1)	07-19 (0) 19-21 (2-1) 21-04 (4-2) 04-06 (2-1) 06-07 (1-0)

HAWAII
Winter 1994-1995
Openings Given in
Hawaiian Standard Time

To:	*10 Meters*	*15 Meters*	*20 Meters*	*40/80* Meters*
Eastern USA	08-10 (1) 10-12 (2) 12-14 (1)	07-08 (1) 08-12 (2) 12-14 (3) 14-15 (2) 15-17 (1)	06-08 (2) 08-13 (1) 13-14 (2) 14-17 (3) 17-20 (2) 20-00 (1)	16-18 (1) 18-02 (3) 02-04 (1) 18-20 (1)* 20-01 (2) 01-03 (1)*
Central USA	08-10 (1) 10-14 (2) 14-16 (1)	06-07 (1) 07-09 (3) 09-11 (2) 11-13 (3) 13-15 (4) 15-16 (3) 16-17 (2) 17-18 (1)	06-07 (2) 07-08 (3) 08-13 (2) 13-14 (3) 14-16 (4) 16-18 (3) 18-20 (2) 20-00 (1)	17-19 (1) 19-20 (2) 20-02 (3) 02-03 (2) 03-04 (1) 19-21 (1)* 21-02 (2)* 02-04 (1)*
Western USA	08-10 (1) 10-14 (2) 14-17 (1)	06-07 (1) 07-08 (2) 08-12 (3) 12-14 (4) 14-16 (3) 16-17 (2) 17-19 (1)	06-07 (2) 07-09 (4) 09-14 (3) 14-16 (4) 16-18 (3) 18-22 (2) 22-02 (1)	17-18 (1) 18-20 (2) 20-01 (4) 01-04 (3) 04-06 (2) 06-07 (1) 18-19 (1)* 19-21 (2)* 21-04 (3)* 04-05 (2)* 05-06 (1)*

ALASKA
Openings Given In GMT

To:	*10 Meters*	*15 Meters*	*20 Meters*	*40/80* Meters*
Eastern USA	19-22 (1)	16-18 (1) 18-21 (2) 21-23 (3) 23-00 (2) 00-01 (1)	18-21 (1) 21-23 (2) 23-01 (3) 01-02 (2) 02-04 (1)	06-12 (1) 07-11 (1)*
Central USA	19-23 (1)	17-18 (1) 18-21 (2) 21-00 (3) 00-01 (2) 00-01 (2) 01-02 (1)	17-20 (1) 20-23 (2) 23-02 (3) 02-03 (2) 03-05 (1)	06-14 (1) 07-12 (1)*
Western USA	19-21 (1) 21-23 (2) 23-00 (1)	17-20 (1) 20-21 (2) 21-22 (3) 22-00 (4) 00-01 (3) 01-02 (2) 02-03 (1)	14-17 (1) 17-20 (2) 20-22 (3) 22-00 (4) 00-02 (3) 02-04 (2) 04-06 (1)	02-03 (1) 03-05 (2) 05-14 (3) 14-15 (2) 15-16 (1)

SUNRISE/SUNSET FORMULAS

Each day is said to began with the sunrise and end at sunset. For Amateur Radio DXers, these times can be the most exciting! Most other folks, though, they see these times on calendars or during the evening weather forecast, but otherwise take for granted that the sun will rise today and set tonight and return tomorrow.

There presently exist many methods of calculating sunrise and sunset times. With maps and slides, globes and lights, or maps that move and computer programs from crude to multi-colored, one can easily estimate a sunrise or sunset, but each has an inherent inaccuracy. Some are larger than others. Corrections may be needed for leap year, leap second, non-circular Earth orbit, and the varying speed of Earth's travel and rotation. For higher accuracy, and to determine the times for other locations, a computer program is the answer. Each program author uses a variation on a standard formula to increase accuracy, or correction factors must be added.

The declination of the sun, caused by the Earth's axis angle relative to the sun, is one of the important variables. The Earth axis is tilted 23.5 degrees relative to its solar orbit. As the Earth rotates around the sun, the North and South Poles can be the exact distance from the sun. This occurs on March 21st and September 21st, when the sun's declination is zero degrees. This marks the time on the Earth when the length of day (12 hours) equals the length of night (12 hours), giving us the term "Equinox": "Equi-" meaning equal and "-nox" meaning night.

When the Earth's North Pole is farther away from the sun than the South Pole, the declination of the sun is negative (up to -23.5 degrees on December 21st). When the South Pole is farther from the sun than the North pole, the declination is positive (up to +23.5 degrees on June 21st).

To calculate the sun's declination, you will need to know the date on the Julian calendar and have a trigonometric table or a calculator that will process trigonometric functions. Since the Julian calendar is the standard calendar we use, simple count the number of days since January 1 to your target day.

$$A = -23.5 \times \text{SIN} (360 \times (d - 80/365))$$

Where A = Sun declination; d = Day of the Year

Next, this sun declination angle can be used to directly calculate the sunrise or sunset time of the target location on this target day. You'll also need to know the Latitude and Longitude of the target location.

$$\text{Sunrise} = (LONG/15) + \cos^{\underline{\ 1\ }} \frac{(\tan[A] \times \tan[LAT])}{15}$$

Where A = Sun declination; LONG = Longitude in Degrees; LAT = Latitude in Degrees
Values for LAT and LONG must be positive for targets North and West.

$$\text{Sunset} = (LONG/15) - \cos^{\underline{\ 1\ }} \frac{(\tan[A] \times \tan[LAT])}{15}$$

Where A = Sun declination; LONG = Target Longitude; LAT = Target Latitude

The answer will be a decimal representation of the time the terminator crosses the target location relative to the Zero meridian. (0, 0 - UTC). To convert the decimal portion of the calculated time, multiply by 60. (i. e., sunrise time was calculated as 10.88. Multiply .88 x 60 = 52.8 minutes. Therefore, the calculated sunrise would be 10:52.48 Z (UTC)).

Due to the previously mentioned variables, corrections are required to each sunrise and sunset formula result. Add or subtract the following number of minutes from your times for your day.

Jan01	+3	Apr01	+4	Jul01	+4	Oct01	-10
Jan16	+9	Apr16	0	Jul15	+6	Oct16	-14
Feb01	+14	May01	-3	Aug01	+6	Nov01	-16
Feb15	+14	May16	-4	Aug16	+4	Nov16	-15
Mar01	+13	Jun01	-2	Sep01	0	Dec01	-11
Mar15	+9	Jun16	0	Sep16	-5	Dec16	-5

The terminator is a line, perpendicular to the light rays from the sun, marking the transition on the Earth's surface between the nighttime portion and the daylight portion. This would mark the beginning of the twilight zone or Gray-Line area.

The sunrise and sunset periods are the most exciting times of radio propagation.

Other sunrise/sunset and Gray-Line reading includes *Low-Band DXing*, by John Devoldere, ON4UN, available through the ARRL and amateur bookstores; *Long-Path Propagation*, by Bob Brown, NM7M, available directly from the author; *An Introduction to Gray-Line DXing*, by Tom Russell, N4KG, published in *QST*, November 1992; *The ARRL Antenna Book*, edited by Gerald Hall, K1TD, published by the ARRL; *Ionospheric Radio*, by Kenneth Davies, published by Peter Peregrinus, Ltd. and available through the I.E.E.E.

SUNRISE/SUNSET CALCULATION SOFTWARE

```
9 CLS
10 CLEAR , 64000, 4096
15 REM ORIGINAL PROGRAM BY Van Heddegem ON4HW
17 D = 59
20 PI = 3.1415927#
30 SW = -.97599592#
40 CW = .21778881#
50 SE = .39777961#
60 CE = .9174811
61 K1 = -.014834754#
62 n$ = "b:\latlong"
63 OPEN n$ FOR INPUT ACCESS READ AS #1 LEN = 43
64 na$ = "a:\srssw_of.e28"
65 OPEN na$ FOR OUTPUT AS #2
67 IF EOF(1) THEN CLOSE : GOTO 500
69 FOR L = 1 TO 181
70 INPUT #1, L$
72 pf$ = LEFT$(L$, 4)
73 ct$ = MID$(L$, 6, 19)
74 at$ = MID$(L$, 30, 6)
75 on$ = RIGHT$(L$, 7)
79 REM PRINT #2, pf$;
80 REM PRINT #2, ct$;
88 RSET at$ = at$
89 LA = VAL(at$)
90 RSET on$ = on$
91 LO = VAL(on$)
120 LO = LO * PI / 180
130 LA = LA * PI / 180
160 M = (2 * PI * D + LO) / 365.24219# - .052708
170 L = M - 1.351248
180 C1 = 1 - .03343 * COS(M)
190 C2 = .99944 * SIN(M) / C1
200 C3 = (COS(M) - .03343) / C1
210 C4 = SW * C3 + CW * C2
220 C5 = CW * C3 - SW * C2
230 C6 = SE * C4: REM SINE OF SUN DECLINATION
240 B1 = K1 - C6 * SIN(LA)
250 B2 = (COS(LA)) ^ 2 * (1 - C6 ^ 2) - B1 ^ 2
260 IF B2 <= 0 THEN R$ = "NO.SR": S$ = "NO.SS": GOTO 345
270 B3 = ATN(B1 / SQR(B2)) - PI / 2
280 B4 = ATN((COS(L) * CE * C4 - SIN(L) * C5) / (SIN(L) * CE
 * C4 + COS(L) * C5))
290 GOSUB 370
300 R$ = STR$(B6)
310 B3 = -B3
320 GOSUB 370
330 S$ = STR$(B6)
345 WRITE #2, R$, S$
350 NEXT L: REM GOTO 440
370 B5 = B4 + B3 + LO + PI
380 IF B5 < 0 THEN B5 = B5 + 2 * PI
390 B5 = INT(B5 * 720 / PI + .5): REM MINUTES PAST 0000
 UTC
400 IF B5 > 1439 THEN B5 = B5 - 1440
410 B6 = .4 * INT(B5 / 60) + B5 / 100: REM TIME IN HH.MM
420 RETURN
440 REM IF D < 344 THEN LET D = D + 14: GOTO 160
450 REM IF D > 356 THEN GOTO 9
460 REM RETURN
500 END
```

Prefix City Country	Jan14 Sunrise	Jan 14 Sunset	Jan 28 Sunrise	Jan 28 Sunset	Feb 14 Sunrise	Feb 14 Sunset	Feb 28 Sunrise	Feb 28 Sunset	Mar 14 Sunrise	Mar 14 Sunset	Mar 28 Sunrise	Mar 28 Sunset
A4 MUSCAT OMAN	02:50	13:39	02:48	13:49	02:40	14:00	02:30	14:08	02:17	14:14	02:03	14:20
AP KARACHI PAKISTAN	02:11	12:55	02:09	13:05	02:00	13:17	01:49	13:25	01:36	13:32	01:21	13:38
BV TAIPEI TAIWAN	22:40	09:24	22:38	09:34	22:30	09:46	22:18	09:54	22:05	10:01	21:51	10:07
BY CHUNKING CHINA	23:46	10:11	23:42	10:23	23:31	10:37	23:18	10:47	23:03	10:57	22:46	11:05
BY BEIJING CHINA	23:35	09:11	23:27	09:27	23:10	09:47	22:51	10:03	22:30	10:18	22:07	10:33
C2 REP. OF NAURU	18:56	07:05	19:00	07:09	19:02	07:10	19:01	07:09	18:58	07:05	18:54	07:01
C3 ANDORRA	07:20	16:42	07:11	16:59	06:52	17:21	06:31	17:39	06:08	17:56	05:43	18:12
C6 NASSAU BAHAMAS	11:51	22:45	11:49	22:55	11:42	23:05	11:32	23:12	11:20	23:18	11:07	23:23
C9 MAPUTO MOZAMBIQUE	03:09	16:49	03:20	16:46	03:33	16:36	03:42	16:24	03:50	16:09	03:57	15:54
CE SANTIAGO CHILE	09:47	23:56	10:00	23:51	10:17	23:37	10:29	23:21	10:41	23:04	10:51	22:45
CEØ EASTER ISLAND	12:35	02:15	12:46	02:12	12:59	02:02	13:08	01:49	13:16	01:35	13:23	01:20
CN CASABLANCA MOROCCO	07:35	17:44	07:03	17:57	07:17	18:13	07:02	18:25	06:44	18:37	06:25	18:47
CP LA PAZ BOLIVIA	10:10	23:12	10:19	23:11	10:27	23:06	10:31	22:58	10:35	22:49	10:37	22:38
CT LISBON PORTUGAL	07:54	17:37	07:46	17:52	07:30	18:11	07:12	18:27	06:51	18:41	06:29	18:55
CU SAO MIGUEL IS.AZORES	09:02	18:49	08:55	19:04	08:39	19:23	08:21	19:38	08:01	19:51	07:39	20:05
CX MONTEVIDEO URUGUAY	08:45	23:02	08:59	22:56	09:17	22:41	09:30	22:25	09:42	22:06	09:53	21:47
D6 COMOROS	02:54	15:41	03:01	15:42	03:08	15:39	03:11	15:33	03:12	15:25	03:13	15:16
DJ BONN GERMANY	07:29	15:52	07:15	16:14	06:48	16:44	06:20	17:09	05:50	17:32	05:19	17:55
DU MANILA PHILIPPINES	22:24	09:45	22:25	09:52	22:21	10:00	22:14	10:04	22:05	10:06	21:55	10:08
EA6 BALEARIC ISLANDS	07:13	16:52	07:06	17:08	06:49	17:28	06:30	17:44	06:09	17:59	05:47	18:13
EA8 CANARY ISLANDS	08:01	18:28	07:58	18:40	07:47	18:54	07:34	19:04	07:18	19:13	07:02	19:21
EI DUBLIN REP IRELAND	08:34	16:33	08:18	16:58	07:47	17:31	07:17	17:58	06:44	18:25	06:11	18:50
ET ADDIS-ABABA ETHIOPIA	03:44	15:23	03:46	15:29	03:44	15:34	03:40	15:36	03:33	15:36	03:25	15:36
FT_8 KERGUELEN	23:33	15:28	23:55	15:14	00:25	14:48	00:49	14:21	01:12	13:51	01:34	13:21
FG GUADELOUPE	10:37	21:50	10:37	21:59	10:31	22:06	10:24	22:11	10:14	22:14	10:03	22:17
FK NOUMEA NEW CALEDON	18:20	07:43	18:30	07:41	18:41	07:33	18:48	07:23	18:54	07:11	18:59	06:58
FO CLIPPERTON ISL	13:43	01:15	13:44	01:22	13:41	01:27	13:36	01:30	13:28	01:31	13:20	01:31
FO PAPEETE POLYNESIA	15:33	04:38	15:42	04:37	15:50	01:27	13:36	01:30	15:59	04:13	16:02	04:02
FP ST PIERRE & MIQUELON	11:26	20:21	11:15	20:40	10:52	21:06	10:28	21:27	10:01	21:47	09:34	22:07
FR REUNION	01:47	15:05	01:57	15:04	02:07	14:57	02:14	14:47	02:19	14:35	02:23	14:23
FY CAYENNE FR.GUIANA	09:42	21:34	09:45	21:39	09:45	21:42	09:41	21:43	09:36	21:41	09:30	21:39
G LONDON ENGLAND	08:01	16:17	07:46	16:40	07:18	17:11	06:50	17:36	06:19	18:01	05:47	18:25
HA BUDAPEST HUNGARY	06:28	15:17	06:16	15:37	05:53	16:03	05:28	16:25	05:01	16:46	04:33	17:06
HC QUITO ECUADOR	11:19	23:27	11:23	23:31	11:25	23:32	11:23	23:30	11:20	23:27	11:16	23:23
HC8 GALAPAGOS ISLS	12:13	00:21	12:17	00:25	12:18	00:26	12:17	00:24	12:14	00:21	12:10	00:17
HP PANAMA CITY PANAMA	11:43	23:23	11:45	23:29	11:43	23:34	11:39	23:36	11:32	23:36	11:25	23:35
HS BANGKOK THAILAND	23:45	11:08	23:46	11:16	23:42	11:22	23:36	11:26	23:27	11:28	23:18	11:30
I ROME ITALY	06:36	16:01	06:27	16:18	06:08	16:39	05:48	16:57	05:25	17:13	05:01	17:29
JA TOYKO JAPAN	21:51	07:48	21:45	08:03	21:31	08:20	21:14	08:34	20:55	08:46	20:35	08:58
JD MINAMI TORI-SHIMA	20:25	07:12	20:23	07:22	20:15	07:34	20:04	07:41	19:51	07:48	19:37	07:54
JT ULAN-BATOR MONGOLIA	00:38	09:23	00:26	09:43	00:02	10:10	23:37	10:32	23:10	10:53	22:41	11:14
JW SVALBARD	NO:SR	NO:SS	NO:SR	NO:SS	09:50	11:59	07:11	14:34	05:25	16:14	03:45	17:46
KC4 McMurdo Antarctica	NO:SR	NO:SS	NO:SR	NO:SS	NO:SR	NO:SS	15:42	10:28	17:46	08:18	19:27	06:28
KC6 W CAROLINE ISL	21:06	08:45	21:08	08:51	21:06	08:56	21:01	08:58	20:55	08:58	20:47	08:57

Prefix City Country	Apr 14 Sunrise	Apr 14 Sunset	Apr 28 Sunrise	Apr 28 Sunset	May 14 Sunrise	May 14 Sunset	May 28 Sunrise	May 28 Sunset	Jun 14 Sunrise	Jun 14 Sunset	Jun 28 Sunrise	Jun 28 Sunset
A4 MUSCAT OMAN	01:47	14:26	01:35	14:32	01:25	14:39	01:20	14:46	01:19	14:53	01:22	14:56
AP KARACHI PAKISTAN	01:04	13:46	00:52	13:52	00:41	14:00	00:35	14:07	00:34	14:14	00:37	14:18
BV TAIPEI TAIWAN	21:33	10:15	21:21	10:21	21:10	10:29	21:05	10:36	21:03	10:44	21:06	10:47
BY CHUNKING CHINA	22:26	11:15	22:12	11:24	21:59	11:34	21:52	11:42	21:49	11:51	21:52	11:54
BY BEIJING CHINA	21:40	10:50	21:20	11:04	21:02	11:20	20:51	11:32	20:45	11:44	20:48	11:47
C2 REP. OF NAURU	18:50	06:56	18:47	06:53	18:45	06:51	18:46	06:52	18:49	06:55	18:52	06:58
C3 ANDORRA	05:14	18:31	04:53	18:47	04:32	19:04	04:20	19:18	04:14	19:30	04:16	19:34
C6 NASSAU BAHAMAS	10:51	23:29	10:40	23:34	10:31	23:41	10:26	23:47	10:25	23:53	10:28	23:57
C9 MAPUTO MOZAMBIQUE	04:05	15:36	04:12	15:23	04:21	15:12	04:28	15:06	04:36	15:04	04:39	15:07
CE SANTIAGO CHILE	11:03	22:23	11:14	22:07	11:25	21:52	11:35	21:44	11:44	21:41	11:47	21:44
CEØ EASTER ISLAND	13:31	01:02	13:39	00:49	13:47	00:37	13:55	00:32	14:02	00:30	14:05	00:33
CN CASABLANCA MOROCCO	06:03	19:00	05:46	19:10	05:32	19:22	05:23	19:32	05:20	19:41	05:23	19:45
CP LA PAZ BOLIVIA	10:40	22:25	10:43	22:17	10:47	22:10	10:52	22:07	10:58	22:07	11:01	22:10
CT LISBON PORTUGAL	06:03	19:11	05:44	19:24	05:26	19:39	05:16	19:51	05:11	20:02	05:13	20:05
CU SAO MIGUEL IS.AZORES	07:14	20:20	06:55	20:33	06:38	20:48	06:28	20:59	06:23	21:10	06:26	21:13
CX MONTEVIDEO URUGUAY	10:07	21:24	10:18	21:07	10:30	20:52	10:40	20:43	10:49	20:40	10:53	20:43
D6 COMOROS	03:14	15:05	03:16	14:58	03:19	14:52	03:22	14:50	03:27	14:51	03:30	14:54
DJ BONN GERMANY	04:42	18:23	04:13	18:45	03:46	19:10	03:28	19:29	03:18	19:45	03:20	19:49
DU MANILA PHILIPPINES	21:44	10:10	21:35	10:12	21:29	10:16	21:26	10:20	21:26	10:25	21:29	10:29
EA6 BALEARIC ISLANDS	05:20	18:29	05:00	18:43	04:42	18:59	04:31	19:11	04:26	19:22	04:29	19:25
EA8 CANARY ISLANDS	06:42	19:31	06:28	19:39	06:15	19:49	06:08	19:58	06:06	20:06	06:09	20:09
EI DUBLIN REP IRELAND	05:30	19:21	04:59	19:46	04:28	20:14	04:08	20:36	03:57	20:53	03:59	20:57
ET ADDIS-ABABA ETHIOPIA	03:16	15:35	03:10	15:35	03:06	15:37	03:04	15:40	03:06	15:44	03:09	15:47
FT_8 KERGUELEN	02:00	12:45	02:22	12:18	02:45	11:52	03:03	11:36	03:17	11:26	03:21	11:29
FG GUADELOUPE	09:51	22:20	09:42	22:23	09:34	22:28	09:31	22:32	09:31	22:38	09:34	22:41
FK NOUMEA NEW CALEDON	19:05	06:43	19:10	06:31	19:16	06:22	19:23	06:17	19:29	06:16	19:32	06:19
FO CLIPPERTON ISL	13:10	01:31	13:03	01:32	12:58	01:35	12:56	01:38	12:57	01:43	13:00	01:46
FO PAPEETE POLYNESIA	16:05	03:49	16:09	03:40	16:13	03:33	16:18	03:29	16:24	03:30	16:27	03:32
FP ST PIERRE & MIQUELON	09:01	22:30	08:36	22:49	08:12	23:10	07:58	23:26	07:50	23:39	07:52	23:43
FR REUNION	02:29	14:08	02:33	13:57	02:39	13:48	02:45	13:44	02:52	13:43	02:55	13:46
FY CAYENNE FR.GUIANA	09:23	21:36	09:18	21:35	09:15	21:36	09:15	21:38	09:17	21:41	09:20	21:44
G LONDON ENGLAND	05:09	18:53	04:40	19:16	04:12	19:42	03:53	20:02	03:43	20:18	03:45	20:22
HA BUDAPEST HUNGARY	03:59	17:29	03:34	17:49	03:09	18:11	02:54	18:27	02:46	18:41	02:48	18:45
HC QUITO ECUADOR	11:11	23:18	11:09	23:15	11:07	23:14	11:08	23:14	11:11	23:17	11:14	23:20
HC8 GALAPAGOS ISLS	12:05	00:12	12:02	00:09	12:01	00:08	12:02	00:08	12:05	00:11	12:08	00:14
HP PANAMA CITY PANAMA	11:16	23:34	11:10	23:34	11:06	23:36	11:04	23:39	11:06	23:43	11:09	23:46
HS BANGKOK THAILAND	23:06	11:31	22:58	11:33	22:52	11:37	22:49	11:41	22:50	11:46	22:53	11:49
I ROME ITALY	04:33	17:48	04:11	18:03	03:51	18:20	03:40	18:34	03:34	18:45	03:36	18:49
JA TOYKO JAPAN	20:12	09:12	19:54	09:24	19:38	09:37	19:29	09:48	19:24	09:57	19:27	10:01
JD MINAMI TORI-SHIMA	19:21	08:00	19:09	08:07	18:59	08:14	18:53	08:21	18:52	08:28	18:54	08:31
JT ULAN-BATOR MONGOLIA	22:07	11:38	21:41	11:58	21:16	12:20	21:01	12:37	20:52	12:52	20:54	12:55
JW SVALBARD	01:24	19:57	NO:SR	NO:SS	NO:SR	NO:SS	NO:SR	NO:SS	NO:SR	NO:SS	NO:SR	NO:SS
KC4 McMurdo Antarctica	21:39	04:06	NO:SR	NO:SS	NO:SR	NO:SS	NO:SR	NO:SS	NO:SR	NO:SS	NO:SR	NO:SS
KC6 W CAROLINE ISL	20:38	08:57	20:32	08:57	20:27	08:59	20:26	09:02	20:27	09:06	20:30	09:09

Prefix City Country	July 14 Sunrise	July 14 Sunset	July 28 Sunrise	July 28 Sunset	Aug 14 Sunrise	Aug 14 Sunset	Aug 28 Sunrise	Aug 28 Sunset	Sep 14 Sunrise	Sep 14 Sunset	Sept 28 Sunrise	Sept 28 Sunset
A4 MUSCAT OMAN	01:28	14:55	01:34	14:51	01:41	14:41	01:46	14:29	01:52	14:12	01:56	13:58
AP KARACHI PAKISTAN	00:43	14:17	00:49	14:12	00:57	14:01	01:03	13:49	01:09	13:31	01:15	13:16
BV TAIPEI TAIWAN	21:12	10:46	21:18	10:42	21:26	10:31	21:32	10:18	21:38	10:01	21:44	09:46
BY CHUNKING CHINA	21:59	11:53	22:06	11:47	22:16	11:33	22:24	11:19	22:33	10:59	22:41	10:42
BY BEIJING CHINA	20:57	11:43	21:08	11:34	21:24	11:15	21:37	10:55	21:53	10:28	22:06	10:05
C2 REP. OF NAURU	18:55	07:01	18:56	07:01	18:54	07:00	18:51	06:57	18:45	06:51	18:40	06:47
C3 ANDORRA	04:27	19:29	04:39	19:18	04:56	18:57	05:11	18:36	05:29	18:06	05:44	17:42
C6 NASSAU BAHAMAS	10:34	23:56	10:39	23:52	10:46	23:42	10:51	23:31	10:56	23:15	10:59	23:01
C9 MAPUTO MOZAMBIQUE	04:38	15:13	04:33	15:20	04:21	15:28	04:08	15:35	03:50	15:42	03:34	15:48
CE SANTIAGO CHILE	11:45	21:52	11:38	22:00	11:23	22:12	11:07	22:22	10:44	22:33	10:25	22:42
CEØ EASTER ISLAND	14:04	00:40	13:59	00:46	13:47	00:55	13:34	01:01	13:15	01:08	13:00	01:14
CN CASABLANCA MOROCCO	05:31	19:42	05:39	19:35	05:51	19:20	06:01	19:03	06:13	18:41	06:22	18:21
CP LA PAZ BOLIVIA	11:01	22:15	10:59	22:19	10:51	22:23	10:42	22:25	10:29	22:27	10:18	22:29
CT LISBON PORTUGAL	05:23	20:01	05:33	19:52	05:48	19:34	06:01	19:15	06:16	18:49	06:28	18:26
CU SAO MIGUEL IS.AZORES	06:35	21:10	06:45	21:01	07:20	00:43	07:12	20:24	07:26	19:59	07:38	19:37
CX MONTEVIDEO URUGUAY	10:50	20:51	10:43	21:00	10:27	21:12	10:10	21:22	09:47	21:34	09:27	21:45
D6 COMOROS	03:31	14:58	03:29	15:01	03:24	15:04	03:16	15:05	03:05	15:05	02:55	15:05
DJ BONN GERMANY	03:34	19:41	03:51	19:25	04:16	18:57	04:37	18:29	05:04	17:52	05:25	17:20
DU MANILA PHILIPPINES	21:34	10:29	21:38	10:27	21:41	10:20	21:43	10:12	21:44	10:00	21:45	09:49
EA6 BALEARIC ISLANDS	04:38	19:21	04:49	19:12	05:05	18:53	05:18	18:34	05:33	18:07	05:46	17:44
EA8 CANARY ISLANDS	06:16	20:08	06:23	20:02	06:33	19:49	06:41	19:34	06:50	19:14	06:57	18:57
EI DUBLIN REP IRELAND	04:14	20:47	04:33	20:30	05:01	19:58	05:25	19:28	05:55	18:47	06:19	18:13
ET ADDIS-ABABA ETHIOPIA	03:13	15:49	03:15	15:48	03:17	15:43	03:17	15:37	03:15	15:27	03:14	15:19
FT_8 KERGUELEN	03:14	11:41	03:00	11:57	02:34	12:20	02:07	12:40	01:31	13:05	01:00	13:26
FG GUADELOUPE	09:39	22:42	09:43	22:39	09:48	22:31	09:50	22:22	09:53	22:09	09:54	21:57
FK NOUMEA NEW CALEDON	19:32	06:25	19:28	06:30	19:19	06:37	19:08	06:41	18:52	06:46	18:38	06:50
FO CLIPPERTON ISL	13:04	01:47	13:07	01:46	13:10	01:40	13:10	01:33	13:10	01:22	13:09	01:13
FO PAPEETE POLYNESIA	16:27	03:38	16:24	03:42	16:17	03:46	16:07	03:49	15:54	03:52	15:42	03:53
FP ST PIERRE & MIQUELON	08:04	23:37	08:19	23:24	08:40	22:59	08:58	22:35	09:20	22:01	09:38	21:33
FR REUNION	02:55	13:52	02:51	13:57	02:42	14:03	02:31	14:07	02:16	14:11	02:03	14:15
FY CAYENNE FR.GUIANA	09:23	21:46	09:25	21:46	09:25	21:43	09:24	21:38	09:20	21:30	09:17	21:23
G LONDON ENGLAND	03:59	20:13	04:17	19:57	04:43	19:28	05:05	18:59	05:32	18:21	05:54	17:49
HA BUDAPEST HUNGARY	03:00	18:39	03:15	18:25	03:37	18:00	03:55	17:35	04:18	17:01	04:37	16:33
HC QUITO ECUADOR	11:17	23:23	11:17	23:24	11:16	23:22	11:12	23:19	11:07	23:13	11:02	23:09
HC8 GALAPAGOS ISLS	12:11	00:17	12:11	00:18	12:10	00:16	12:06	00:13	12:01	00:07	11:56	00:02
HP PANAMA CITY PANAMA	11:13	23:48	11:15	23:47	11:17	23:42	11:16	23:36	11:15	23:26	11:13	23:18
HS BANGKOK THAILAND	22:57	11:50	23:01	11:48	23:04	11:41	23:06	11:33	23:07	11:21	23:07	11:11
I ROME ITALY	03:46	18:44	03:58	18:34	04:15	18:13	04:30	17:52	04:47	17:24	05:02	16:59
JA TOYKO JAPAN	19:35	09:58	19:45	09:50	19:58	09:34	20:09	09:17	20:22	08:53	20:32	08:32
JD MINAMI TORI-SHIMA	19:01	08:31	19:07	08:26	19:14	08:16	19:19	08:04	19:25	07:47	19:30	07:32
JT ULAN-BATOR MONGOLIA	21:07	12:49	21:21	12:35	21:44	12:10	22:03	11:45	22:26	11:10	22:45	10:41
JW SVALBARD	NO:SR	NO:SS	NO:SR	NO:SS	NO:SR	NO:SS	00:55	20:28	03:13	17:59	04:44	16:18
KC4 McMurdo Antarctica	NO:SR	NO:SS	NO:SR	NO:SS	NO:SR	NO:SS	22:17	03:30	19:47	05:49	17:59	07:27
KC6 W CAROLINE ISL	20:34	09:11	20:37	09:09	20:38	09:05	20:38	08:58	20:37	08:49	20:35	08:40

Prefix City Country	Oct 14 Sunrise	Oct 14 Sunset	Oct 28 Sunrise	Oct 28 Sunset	Nov 14 Sunrise	Nov 14 Sunset	Nov 28 Sunrise	Nov 28 Sunset	Dec 14 Sunrise	Dec 14 Sunset	Dec 28 Sunrise	Dec 28 Sunset
A4 MUSCAT OMAN	02:02	13:43	02:09	13:31	02:19	13:22	02:28	13:19	02:39	13:22	02:46	13:28
AP KARACHI PAKISTAN	01:21	13:00	01:29	12:48	01:39	12:38	01:49	12:34	02:00	12:37	02:07	12:43
BV TAIPEI TAIWAN	21:50	09:29	21:58	09:17	22:08	09:07	22:18	09:04	22:29	09:06	22:37	09:12
BY CHUNKING CHINA	22:50	10:23	22:59	10:09	23:12	09:56	23:24	09:51	23:36	09:52	23:43	09:58
BY BEIJING CHINA	22:22	09:39	22:37	09:20	22:57	09:01	23:12	08:52	23:27	08:50	23:35	08:56
C2 REP. OF NAURU	18:35	06:42	18:32	06:40	18:32	06:40	18:35	06:44	18:41	06:50	18:48	06:57
C3 ANDORRA	06:02	17:14	06:19	16:53	06:40	16:32	06:57	16:22	07:13	16:19	07:21	16:25
C6 NASSAU BAHAMAS	11:05	22:46	11:11	22:36	11:20	22:27	11:29	22:25	11:40	22:28	11:47	22:34
C9 MAPUTO MOZAMBIQUE	03:17	15:56	03:04	16:04	02:53	16:16	02:48	16:27	02:50	16:38	02:56	16:46
CE SANTIAGO CHILE	10:04	22:54	09:48	23:05	09:33	23:21	09:27	23:34	09:27	23:47	09:33	23:55
CEØ EASTER ISLAND	12:42	01:22	12:29	01:30	12:18	01:42	12:14	01:53	12:16	02:05	12:23	02:12
CN CASABLANCA MOROCCO	06:34	18:00	06:45	17:44	07:00	17:30	07:13	17:23	07:26	17:24	07:34	17:30
CP LA PAZ BOLIVIA	10:05	22:31	09:57	22:35	09:51	22:42	09:50	22:50	09:53	23:00	10:00	23:07
CT LISBON PORTUGAL	06:43	18:02	06:58	17:43	07:16	17:25	07:31	17:17	07:46	17:15	07:53	17:22
CU SAO MIGUEL IS.AZORES	07:53	19:13	08:07	18:54	08:25	18:37	08:40	18:29	08:54	18:28	09:01	18:34
CX MONTEVIDEO URUGUAY	09:05	21:57	08:48	22:09	08:32	22:26	08:25	22:39	08:25	22:53	08:31	23:00
D6 COMOROS	02:45	15:06	02:38	15:08	02:33	15:13	02:33	15:20	02:38	15:29	02:44	15:36
DJ BONN GERMANY	05:51	16:45	06:14	16:17	06:43	15:49	07:06	15:33	07:25	15:26	07:33	15:32
DU MANILA PHILIPPINES	21:47	09:38	21:50	09:30	21:56	09:25	22:03	09:24	22:12	09:28	22:19	09:35
EA6 BALEARIC ISLANDS	06:02	17:19	06:17	17:00	06:36	16:41	06:51	16:33	07:06	16:31	07:13	16:37
EA8 CANARY ISLANDS	07:06	18:39	07:15	18:25	07:28	18:13	07:39	18:08	07:51	18:09	07:59	18:16
EI DUBLIN REP IRELAND	06:48	17:35	07:14	17:04	07:46	16:33	08:11	16:15	08:32	16:06	08:40	16:12
ET ADDIS-ABABA ETHIOPIA	03:13	15:10	03:14	15:04	03:18	15:01	03:23	15:02	03:31	15:07	03:38	15:14
FT_8 KERGUELEN	00:26	13:51	23:58	14:14	23:30	14:42	23:14	15:05	23:08	15:24	23:13	15:33
FG GUADELOUPE	09:57	21:45	10:01	21:37	10:08	21:30	10:15	21:30	10:24	21:33	10:32	21:40
FK NOUMEA NEW CALEDON	18:23	06:56	18:12	07:02	18:03	07:11	18:00	07:21	18:02	07:31	18:09	07:38
FO CLIPPERTON ISL	13:09	01:04	13:11	00:57	13:15	00:53	13:21	00:54	13:30	00:59	13:37	01:06
FO PAPEETE POLYNESIA	15:29	03:57	15:20	04:01	15:14	04:09	15:13	04:16	15:16	04:26	15:23	04:33
FP ST PIERRE & MIQUELON	10:00	21:02	10:20	20:38	10:45	20:14	11:04	20:01	11:21	19:57	11:29	20:03
FR REUNION	01:48	14:20	01:38	14:25	01:29	14:34	01:27	14:43	01:30	14:54	01:36	15:01
FY CAYENNE FR.GUIANA	09:15	21:16	09:14	21:12	09:16	21:11	09:21	21:13	09:28	21:19	09:35	21:26
G LONDON ENGLAND	06:21	17:13	06:45	16:44	07:15	16:15	07:38	15:58	07:58	15:52	08:06	15:57
HA BUDAPEST HUNGARY	04:59	16:01	05:20	15:36	05:45	15:11	06:05	14:57	06:23	14:53	06:31	14:59
HC QUITO ECUADOR	10:57	23:04	10:54	23:02	10:55	23:02	10:58	23:06	11:04	23:13	11:11	23:19
HC8 GALAPAGOS ISLS	11:51	23:58	11:48	23:56	11:48	23:56	11:52	00:00	11:58	00:06	12:05	00:13
HP PANAMA CITY PANAMA	11:12	23:09	11:13	23:04	11:17	23:01	11:22	23:03	11:30	23:08	11:37	23:15
HS BANGKOK THAILAND	23:09	11:00	23:11	10:53	23:17	10:48	23:24	10:48	23:32	10:52	23:40	10:58
I ROME ITALY	05:19	16:32	05:36	16:11	05:56	15:51	06:13	15:41	06:28	15:39	06:36	15:45
JA TOYKO JAPAN	20:45	08:10	20:58	07:52	21:14	07:36	21:28	07:29	21:42	07:28	21:49	07:35
JD MINAMI TORI-SHIMA	19:36	07:16	19:43	07:05	19:53	06:55	20:03	06:52	20:14	06:54	20:21	07:01
JT ULAN-BATOR MONGOLIA	23:08	10:09	23:28	09:43	23:54	09:18	00:15	09:04	00:33	08:59	00:41	09:05
JW SVALBARD	06:33	14:20	08:49	11:59	NO:SR	NO:SS	NO:SR	NO:SS	NO:SR	NO:SS	NO:SR	NO:SS
KC4 McMurdo Antarctica	15:40	09:36	NO:SR	NO:SS	NO:SR	NO:SS	NO:SR	NO:SS	NO:SR	NO:SS	NO:SR	NO:SS
KC6 W CAROLINE ISL	20:34	08:32	20:35	08:26	20:39	08:23	20:44	08:24	20:52	08:29	20:59	08:36

Prefix City Country	Jan 14 Sunrise	Jan 14 Sunset	Jan 28 Sunrise	Jan 28 Sunset	Feb 14 Sunrise	Feb 14 Sunset	Feb 28 Sunrise	Feb 28 Sunset	Mar 14 Sunrise	Mar 14 Sunset	Mar 28 Sunrise	Mar 28 Sunset
KH6 HILO HAWAII	16:57	04:01	16:56	04:09	16:50	04:19	16:41	04:25	16:30	04:29	16:18	04:33
KL7 FAIRBANKS ALASKA	19:31	00:29	18:52	01:16	17:56	02:15	17:07	03:01	16:16	03:45	15:25	04:28
KL7 JUNEAU ALASKA	17:35	00:38	17:12	01:09	16:34	01:50	15:58	02:24	15:19	02:56	14:39	03:28
KP2 VIRGIN ISLANDS	10:51	21:59	10:50	22:07	10:44	22:16	10:36	22:21	10:26	22:25	10:14	22:29
LA OSLO NORWAY	08:07	14:45	07:42	15:18	07:01	16:02	06:22	16:39	05:40	17:13	04:58	17:48
LZ SOFIA BULGARIA	05:55	15:15	05:46	15:33	05:27	15:55	05:06	16:13	04:42	16:30	04:18	16:46
OH HELSINKI FINLAND	07:12	13:46	06:47	14:20	06:05	15:05	05:25	15:41	04:44	16:16	04:01	16:51
OX GODTHAAB GREENLAND	12:58	18:12	12:21	18:56	11:28	19:53	10:40	20:37	09:51	21:20	09:02	22:02
P2 MADANG P.N.G.	20:14	08:38	20:19	08:40	20:23	08:40	20:23	08:36	20:22	08:31	20:20	08:25
PY RIO DE JANEIRO BR.	08:20	21:44	08:30	21:42	08:41	21:34	08:48	21:24	08:54	21:11	08:59	20:58
PY NATAL BRAZIL	08:16	20:43	08:22	20:45	08:26	20:44	08:27	20:41	08:26	20:35	08:24	20:29
SU CAIRO EGYPT	04:52	15:15	04:48	15:27	04:37	15:42	04:23	15:52	04:07	16:02	03:50	16:10
T3 CENTRAL KIRIBATI	17:23	05:43	17:28	05:46	17:31	05:45	17:31	05:42	17:29	05:38	17:27	05:32
T5 MOGADISHU SOMALIA	03:07	15:08	03:11	15:12	03:11	15:14	03:09	15:14	03:05	15:11	03:00	15:08
TA ANKARA TURKEY	05:09	14:46	05:01	15:01	04:44	15:22	04:25	15:38	04:04	15:53	03:41	16:07
TF REYKJAVIK ICELAND	10:58	16:12	10:22	16:57	09:29	17:53	08:41	18:38	07:52	19:20	07:02	20:02
TJ YAOUNDE CAMEROON	05:25	17:20	05:28	17:25	05:28	17:28	05:26	17:28	05:21	17:26	05:15	17:24
TT FT.LAMY CHAD	05:24	16:53	05:25	17:00	05:22	17:06	05:16	17:09	05:08	17:10	05:00	17:11
UA3 MOSCOW EUR.RUSSIA	05:52	13:25	05:33	13:52	04:59	14:29	04:26	14:59	03:50	15:28	03:14	15:56
4K2 FRANZ JOSEF LAND	NO:SR	NO:SS	NO:SR	NO:SS	NO:SR	NO:SS	07:42	11:24	04:26	14:33	01:51	17:00
UA9 NOVOSIBIRSK RUSSIA	02:47	10:27	02:29	10:53	01:56	11:29	01:24	11:58	00:49	12:27	00:13	12:54
UA9 PERM AS.RUSSIA	04:51	11:56	04:29	12:26	03:52	13:07	03:16	13:40	02:37	14:12	01:58	14:43
UAØ KHABAROVSK AS.RUSSIA	22:48	07:28	22:35	07:48	22:11	08:16	21:46	08:38	21:18	09:00	20:48	09:21
UA Ø YAKUTSK AS.RUSSIA	00:32	06:27	00:02	07:05	23:15	07:55	22:32	08:36	21:46	09:15	21:00	09:52
UAØ OKHOTSK AS.RUSSIA	23:13	05:56	22:49	06:28	22:08	07:12	21:30	07:47	20:50	08:21	20:08	08:55
UAØ UST-OLENEK AS.RUSSIA	NO:SR	NO:SS	NO:SR	NO:SS	01:19	07:08	23:54	08:30	22:37	09:41	21:20	10:49
UD6 BAKU AZERBAIJAN	04:03	13:36	03:55	13:52	03:37	14:13	03:18	14:30	02:56	14:45	02:33	15:00
UH8 ASHKHABAD TURKOMAN	03:27	13:04	03:20	13:20	03:02	13:40	02:44	13:56	02:22	14:11	02:00	14:26
UN7 ALMA-ATA KAZAKH	02:22	11:38	02:13	11:56	01:53	12:19	01:32	12:37	01:08	12:54	00:43	13:11
V3 BELIZE BELIZE	12:26	23:37	12:26	23:45	12:20	23:54	12:12	23:59	12:02	00:02	11:51	00:05
V85 BRUNEI	22:33	10:24	22:36	10:30	22:36	10:33	22:32	10:33	22:27	10:32	22:21	10:30
VE1 Halifax N.S.	11:49	20:57	11:39	21:16	11:18	21:40	10:55	21:59	10:30	22:17	10:04	22:35
VE2 Quebec City Que.	12:27	21:21	12:15	21:40	11:52	22:06	11:28	22:27	11:01	22:47	10:34	23:07
VE3 Ottawa Ont.	12:49	21:48	12:37	22:07	12:15	22:32	11:52	22:52	11:26	23:12	10:59	23:31
VE4 Winnipeg Mb.	14:22	22:53	14:08	23:15	13:42	23:44	13:15	00:07	12:46	00:30	12:16	00:52
VE5 Regina Sk.	14:54	23:21	14:40	23:43	14:13	00:12	13:46	00:37	13:16	01:00	12:45	01:23
VE6 Edmondton Al.	15:44	23:42	15:27	00:07	14:56	00:40	14:26	01:07	13:53	01:34	13:19	02:00
VE7 Prince Rupert B.C.	16:55	00:45	16:37	01:11	16:05	01:45	15:34	02:14	15:00	02:41	14:25	03:08
VE8 Yellowknife NWT	16:51	22:44	16:20	23:23	15:32	00:14	14:48	00:55	14:02	01:34	13:15	02:12
VO2 Goose Bay Labrador	12:11	20:11	11:54	20:36	11:24	21:09	10:54	21:36	10:21	22:02	09:47	22:28
VY1 Whitehorse Yukon	17:56	00:23	17:29	00:58	16:46	01:44	16:05	02:21	15:23	02:57	14:39	03:33
VK1 CANBERRA AUSTRALIA	19:02	09:22	19:16	09:16	19:34	09:01	19:48	08:45	20:00	08:26	20:12	08:06
VK4 BRISBANE AUSTRALIA	19:04	08:48	19:16	08:44	19:29	08:34	19:39	08:22	19:47	08:07	19:54	07:52
VK6 PERTH AUSTRALIA	21:23	11:25	21:36	11:20	21:51	11:08	22:03	10:53	22:13	10:37	22:23	10:19
VK8 DARWIN AUSTRALIA	21:01	09:48	21:08	09:49	21:15	09:46	21:18	09:40	21:19	09:32	21:20	09:23
VK9 COCOS (KEELING) IS	23:43	12:28	23:50	12:29	23:56	12:26	23:59	12:20	00:00	12:12	00:01	12:04

Prefix City Country	Apr 14 Sunrise	Apr 14 Sunset	Apr 28 Sunrise	Apr 28 Sunset	May 14 Sunrise	May 14 Sunset	May 28 Sunrise	May 28 Sunset	Jun 14 Sunrise	Jun 14 Sunset	Jun 28 Sunrise	Jun 28 Sunset
KH6 HILO HAWAII	16:04	04:38	15:53	04:42	15:45	04:48	15:41	04:53	15:41	05:00	15:44	05:03
KL7 FAIRBANKS ALASKA	14:22	05:21	13:31	06:07	12:34	07:01	11:46	07:50	11:03	08:40	11:04	08:45
KL7 JUNEAU ALASKA	13:51	04:06	13:13	04:38	12:35	05:13	12:09	05:41	11:52	06:04	11:55	06:08
KP2 VIRGIN ISLANDS	10:01	22:32	09:51	22:36	09:43	22:41	09:40	22:47	09:40	22:52	09:42	22:56
LA OSLO NORWAY	04:07	18:29	03:26	19:03	02:45	19:43	02:15	20:14	01:55	20:40	01:56	20:44
LZ SOFIA BULGARIA	03:49	17:06	03:27	17:22	03:06	17:40	02:54	17:53	02:48	18:05	02:50	18:09
OH HELSINKI FINLAND	03:09	17:33	02:29	18:08	01:46	18:47	01:16	19:19	00:55	19:45	00:57	19:50
OX GODTHAAB GREENLAND	08:01	22:52	07:11	23:36	06:17	00:28	05:33	01:13	04:57	01:56	04:57	02:01
P2 MADANG P.N.G.	20:18	08:18	20:16	08:13	20:17	08:10	20:19	08:10	20:22	08:12	20:25	08:14
PY RIO DE JANEIRO BR.	09:05	20:42	09:11	20:31	09:18	20:21	09:24	20:16	09:31	20:16	09:34	20:18
PY NATAL BRAZIL	08:22	20:21	08:21	20:16	08:22	20:13	08:24	20:12	08:27	20:14	08:30	20:17
SU CAIRO EGYPT	03:30	16:21	03:16	16:29	03:03	16:40	02:56	16:48	02:53	16:57	02:56	17:00
T3 CENTRAL KIRIBATI	17:24	05:25	17:22	05:21	17:22	05:19	17:24	05:19	17:27	05:21	17:30	05:24
T5 MOGADISHU SOMALIA	02:54	15:04	02:51	15:02	02:48	15:01	02:49	15:03	02:51	15:06	02:54	15:09
TA ANKARA TURKEY	03:14	16:24	02:54	16:39	02:36	16:54	02:25	17:07	02:19	17:18	02:22	17:21
TF REYKJAVIK ICELAND	06:02	20:53	05:12	21:36	04:18	22:28	03:34	23:13	02:57	23:56	02:58	00:01
TJ YAOUNDE CAMEROON	05:09	17:20	05:04	17:19	05:02	17:19	05:01	17:21	05:04	17:24	05:07	17:27
TT FT.LAMY CHAD	04:49	17:12	04:42	17:13	04:36	17:16	04:34	17:20	04:35	17:25	04:38	17:28
UA3 MOSCOW EUR.RUSSIA	02:30	16:30	01:56	16:59	01:22	17:30	00:59	17:54	00:45	18:14	00:47	18:18
4K2 FRANZ JOSEF LAND	NO:SR	NO:SS	NO:SR	NO:SS	NO:SR	NO:SS	NO:SR	NO:SS	NO:SR	NO:SS	NO:SR	NO:SS
UA9 NOVOSIBIRSK RUSSIA	23:30	13:27	22:57	13:55	22:24	14:25	22:02	14:49	21:48	15:08	21:50	15:13
UA9 PERM AS.RUSSIA	01:10	15:21	00:33	15:53	23:55	16:28	23:29	16:55	23:12	17:18	23:14	17:22
UAØ KHABAROVSK AS.RUSSIA	20:14	09:46	19:47	10:07	19:22	10:29	19:05	10:47	18:56	11:02	18:59	11:06
UAØ YAKUTSK AS.RUSSIA	20:04	10:39	19:19	11:18	18:31	12:03	17:56	12:40	17:29	13:12	17:29	13:18
UAØ OKHOTSK AS.RUSSIA	19:18	09:35	18:38	10:09	17:57	10:47	17:28	11:17	17:09	11:43	17:10	11:48
UAØ UST-OLENEK AS.RUSSIA	19:43	12:16	18:06	13:47	NO:SR	NO:SS	NO:SR	NO:SS	NO:SR	NO:SS	NO:SR	NO:SS
UD6 BAKU AZERBAIJAN	02:06	15:17	01:46	15:32	01:27	15:48	01:15	16:01	01:10	16:12	01:12	16:15
UH8 ASHKHABAD TURKOMAN	01:33	14:43	01:13	14:57	00:55	15:12	00:44	15:25	00:38	15:36	00:41	15:39
UN7 ALMA-ATA KAZAKH	00:13	13:31	23:51	13:48	23:30	14:06	23:17	14:20	23:10	14:32	23:13	14:36
V3 BELIZE BELIZE	11:38	00:08	11:29	00:12	11:21	00:17	11:18	00:22	11:18	00:28	11:20	00:31
V85 BRUNEI	22:14	10:27	22:09	10:26	22:06	10:27	22:06	10:29	22:08	10:32	22:11	10:35
VE1 Halifax N.S.	09:33	22:56	09:10	23:14	08:48	23:33	08:35	23:48	08:28	00:00	08:31	00:04
VE2 Quebec City Que.	10:01	23:30	09:36	23:49	09:12	00:10	08:58	00:26	08:50	00:40	08:52	00:43
VE3 Ottawa Ont.	10:26	23:53	10:02	00:12	09:39	00:32	09:25	00:48	09:17	01:01	09:20	01:05
VE4 Winnipeg Mb.	11:40	01:19	11:12	01:40	10:45	02:04	10:29	02:23	10:19	02:38	10:22	02:41
VE5 Regina Sk.	12:09	01:50	11:41	02:12	11:13	02:36	10:56	02:55	10:47	03:11	10:49	03:14
VE6 Edmondton Al.	12:38	02:31	12:07	02:56	11:36	03:25	11:16	03:46	11:04	04:04	11:06	04:07
VE7 Prince Rupert B.C.	13:44	03:40	13:11	04:06	12:40	04:35	12:19	04:58	12:06	05:16	12:09	05:20
VE8 Yellowknife NWT	12:19	02:59	11:34	03:39	10:45	04:25	10:09	05:03	09:42	05:35	09:43	05:40
VO2 Goose Bay Labrador	09:07	22:58	08:36	23:24	08:05	23:52	07:46	00:13	07:34	00:30	07:36	00:34
VY1 Whitehorse Yukon	13:47	04:15	13:05	04:51	12:22	05:32	11:51	06:05	11:30	06:32	11:32	06:36
VK1 CANBERRA AUSTRALIA	20:25	07:43	20:37	07:26	20:49	07:10	21:00	07:01	21:09	06:57	21:13	07:00
VK4 BRISBANE AUSTRALIA	20:03	07:33	20:10	07:20	20:19	07:08	20:27	07:02	20:34	07:00	20:38	07:03
VK6 PERTH AUSTRALIA	22:34	09:58	22:44	09:42	22:55	09:29	23:04	09:21	23:12	09:18	23:16	09:21
VK8 DARWIN AUSTRALIA	21:21	09:12	21:22	09:05	21:25	08:59	21:29	08:57	21:34	08:58	21:37	09:01
VK9 COCOS (KEELING) IS	00:01	11:53	00:03	11:46	00:05	11:41	00:09	11:39	00:13	11:40	00:17	11:43

Prefix City Country	July 14 Sunrise	July 14 Sunset	July 28 Sunrise	July 28 Sunset	Aug 14 Sunrise	Aug 14 Sunset	Aug 28 Sunrise	Aug 28 Sunset	Sep 14 Sunrise	Sep 14 Sunset	Sept 28 Sunrise	Sept 28 Sunset
KH6 HILO HAWAII	15:49	05:03	15:54	04:59	16:00	04:50	16:03	04:40	16:07	04:25	16:10	04:12
KL7 FAIRBANKS ALASKA	11:49	08:05	12:35	07:21	13:32	06:20	14:17	05:29	15:08	04:26	15:49	03:35
KL7 JUNEAU ALASKA	12:15	05:53	12:40	05:29	13:16	04:49	13:47	04:12	14:24	03:24	14:54	02:44
KP2 VIRGIN ISLANDS	09:48	22:56	09:52	22:53	09:57	22:44	10:01	22:34	10:03	22:20	10:06	22:08
LA OSLO NORWAY	02:19	20:27	02:47	20:01	03:27	19:18	04:00	18:37	04:40	17:46	05:13	17:04
LZ SOFIA BULGARIA	03:01	18:04	03:13	17:53	03:31	17:32	03:46	17:11	04:04	16:41	04:19	16:16
OH HELSINKI FINLAND	01:20	19:33	01:48	19:06	02:29	18:22	03:03	17:42	03:43	16:50	04:16	16:07
OX GODTHAAB GREENLAND	05:35	01:29	06:17	00:48	07:11	23:51	07:54	23:02	08:43	22:01	09:23	21:11
P2 MADANG P.N.G.	20:27	08:18	20:27	08:20	20:24	08:20	20:19	08:18	20:11	08:15	20:04	08:12
PY RIO DE JANEIRO BR.	09:34	20:24	09:29	20:30	09:19	20:37	09:08	20:41	08:52	20:47	08:38	20:51
PY NATAL BRAZIL	08:32	20:21	08:32	20:23	08:28	20:23	08:23	20:22	08:15	20:19	08:08	20:16
SU CAIRO EGYPT	03:03	16:58	03:11	16:52	03:21	16:39	03:29	16:24	03:38	16:04	03:46	15:46
T3 CENTRAL KIRIBATI	17:32	05:27	17:32	05:28	17:29	05:28	17:25	05:26	17:17	05:22	17:11	05:19
T5 MOGADISHU SOMALIA	02:57	15:11	02:58	15:12	02:58	15:09	02:55	15:05	02:51	14:59	02:46	14:53
TA ANKARA TURKEY	02:31	17:17	02:42	17:08	02:58	16:49	03:11	16:29	03:27	16:02	03:41	15:39
TF REYKJAVIK ICELAND	03:36	23:29	04:17	22:49	05:11	21:52	05:54	21:02	06:43	20:02	07:24	19:12
TJ YAOUNDE CAMEROON	05:10	17:30	05:11	17:29	05:11	17:26	05:09	17:22	05:05	17:14	05:02	17:08
TT FT.LAMY CHAD	04:42	17:29	04:45	17:27	04:48	17:21	04:49	17:14	04:49	17:03	04:49	16:53
UA3 MOSCOW EUR.RUSSIA	01:04	18:07	01:25	17:47	01:57	17:12	02:24	16:38	02:57	15:54	03:24	15:17
4K2 FRANZ JOSEF LAND	NO:SR	NO:SS	NO:SR	NO:SS	NO:SR	NO:SS	NO:SR	NO:SS	01:03	17:29	03:31	14:51
UA9 NOVOSIBIRSK RUSSIA	22:06	15:02	22:27	14:42	22:58	14:08	23:24	13:36	23:56	12:52	00:22	12:16
UA9 PERM AS.RUSSIA	23:33	17:09	23:57	16:46	00:33	16:07	01:03	15:30	01:40	14:42	02:10	14:02
UAØ KHABAROVSK AS.RUSSIA	19:11	10:59	19:26	10:45	19:49	10:19	20:08	09:53	20:32	09:18	20:52	08:49
UAØ YAKUTSK AS.RUSSIA	17:57	12:56	18:30	12:24	19:17	11:34	19:55	10:50	20:40	09:54	21:16	09:08
UAØ OKHOTSK AS.RUSSIA	17:31	11:32	17:58	11:07	18:37	10:25	19:09	09:46	19:48	08:56	20:20	08:14
UAØ UST-OLENEK AS.RUSSIA	NO:SR	NO:SS	NO:SR	NO:SS	17:44	14:24	19:24	12:38	20:52	10:58	21:58	09:42
UD6 BAKU AZERBAIJAN	01:22	16:11	01:33	16:02	01:49	15:42	02:03	15:22	02:19	14:55	02:33	14:31
UH8 ASHKHABAD TURKOMAN	00:50	15:35	01:01	15:26	01:17	15:07	01:30	14:47	01:46	14:20	01:59	13:57
UN7 ALMA-ATA KAZAKH	23:23	14:31	23:36	14:20	23:54	13:59	00:09	13:37	00:28	13:07	00:44	12:41
V3 BELIZE BELIZE	11:26	00:31	11:30	00:28	11:35	00:20	11:38	00:10	11:40	23:57	11:42	23:45
V85 BRUNEI	22:14	10:37	22:16	10:37	22:16	10:34	22:15	10:29	22:11	10:21	22:08	10:14
VE1 Halifax N.S.	08:42	23:58	08:55	23:47	09:14	23:24	09:31	23:01	09:51	22:30	10:07	22:03
VE2 Quebec City Que.	09:04	00:37	09:19	00:24	09:40	23:59	09:58	23:35	10:20	23:02	10:38	22:33
VE3 Ottawa Ont.	09:32	00:59	09:46	00:46	10:06	00:22	10:24	23:58	10:45	23:26	11:03	22:58
VE4 Winnipeg Mb.	10:35	02:33	10:52	02:19	11:16	01:51	11:36	01:24	12:02	00:47	12:23	00:16
VE5 Regina Sk.	11:03	03:06	11:20	02:51	11:44	02:22	12:05	01:55	12:31	01:18	12:53	00:46
VE6 Edmondton Al.	11:22	03:57	11:41	03:39	12:10	03:07	12:34	02:36	13:04	01:55	13:29	01:21
VE7 Prince Rupert B.C.	12:25	05:09	12:45	04:50	13:15	04:17	13:40	03:45	14:11	03:03	14:36	02:28
VE8 Yellowknife NWT	10:13	05:16	10:47	04:43	11:35	03:52	12:13	03:07	12:59	02:10	13:36	01:23
VO2 Goose Bay Labrador	07:51	00:24	08:11	00:07	08:39	23:35	09:03	23:04	09:32	22:24	09:57	21:50
VY1 Whitehorse Yukon	11:56	06:17	12:25	05:49	13:07	05:03	13:42	04:22	14:23	03:29	14:57	02:46
VK1 CANBERRA AUSTRALIA	21:10	07:08	21:03	07:17	20:47	07:29	20:30	07:40	20:06	07:52	19:46	08:03
VK4 BRISBANE AUSTRALIA	20:37	07:09	20:32	07:16	20:20	07:25	20:07	07:31	19:48	07:39	19:32	07:45
VK6 PERTH AUSTRALIA	23:14	09:28	23:08	09:36	22:54	09:47	22:38	09:56	22:17	10:06	21:59	10:14
VK8 DARWIN AUSTRALIA	21:38	09:05	21:36	09:08	21:31	09:11	21:23	09:12	21:12	09:12	21:02	09:12
VK9 COCOS (KEELING) IS	00:18	11:47	00:16	11:50	00:11	11:53	00:03	11:53	23:52	11:53	23:43	11:53

Prefix City Country	Oct 14 Sunrise	Oct 14 Sunset	Oct 28 Sunrise	Oct 28 Sunset	Nov 14 Sunrise	Nov 14 Sunset	Nov 28 Sunrise	Nov 28 Sunset	Dec 14 Sunrise	Dec 14 Sunset	Dec 28 Sunrise	Dec 28 Sunset
KH6 HILO HAWAII	16:14	03:58	16:19	03:49	16:28	03:41	16:36	03:40	16:46	03:43	16:53	03:50
KL7 FAIRBANKS ALASKA	16:38	02:37	17:23	01:47	18:20	00:51	19:07	00:11	19:49	23:42	19:58	23:46
KL7 JUNEAU ALASKA	15:30	01:59	16:02	01:22	16:42	00:43	17:12	00:19	17:38	00:07	17:46	00:12
KP2 VIRGIN ISLANDS	10:09	21:55	10:14	21:46	10:21	21:39	10:29	21:38	10:39	21:42	10:46	21:48
LA OSLO NORWAY	05:51	16:16	06:26	15:36	07:09	14:54	07:43	14:27	08:11	14:12	08:20	14:17
LZ SOFIA BULGARIA	04:37	15:49	04:54	15:27	05:16	15:06	05:33	14:56	05:48	14:53	05:56	14:59
OH HELSINKI FINLAND	04:55	15:19	05:30	14:39	06:14	13:56	06:48	13:28	07:16	13:13	07:25	13:17
OX GODTHAAB GREENLAND	10:10	20:14	10:53	19:27	11:48	18:33	12:33	17:55	13:12	17:29	13:21	17:33
P2 MADANG P.N.G.	19:57	08:10	19:53	08:09	19:51	08:12	19:53	08:16	19:58	08:24	20:05	08:31
PY RIO DE JANEIRO BR.	08:22	20:56	08:11	21:03	08:02	21:13	07:59	21:22	08:02	21:33	08:08	21:40
PY NATAL BRAZIL	08:00	20:14	07:56	20:14	07:54	20:17	07:56	20:21	08:01	20:29	08:08	20:36
SU CAIRO EGYPT	03:55	15:27	04:05	15:13	04:18	15:00	04:30	14:55	04:42	14:56	04:49	15:03
T3 CENTRAL KIRIBATI	17:05	05:16	17:01	05:15	17:00	05:17	17:02	05:22	17:08	05:29	17:15	05:36
T5 MOGADISHU SOMALIA	02:43	14:47	02:41	14:44	02:42	14:44	02:46	14:47	02:53	14:53	03:00	15:00
TA ANKARA TURKEY	03:57	15:13	04:12	14:54	04:31	14:35	04:47	14:26	05:01	14:24	05:09	14:30
TF REYKJAVIK ICELAND	08:11	18:15	08:54	17:27	09:48	16:33	10:33	15:56	11:12	15:30	11:22	15:34
TJ YAOUNDE CAMEROON	04:59	17:02	04:58	16:58	05:00	16:57	05:04	16:59	05:11	17:05	05:18	17:12
TT FT.LAMY CHAD	04:49	16:43	04:51	16:36	04:56	16:32	05:03	16:32	05:11	16:37	05:18	16:43
UA3 MOSCOW EUR.RUSSIA	03:56	14:36	04:25	14:02	05:00	13:27	05:28	13:07	05:51	12:56	05:59	13:02
4K2 FRANZ JOSEF LAND	06:43	11:29	NO:SR	NO:SS	NO:SR	NO:SS	NO:SR	NO:SS	NO:SR	NO:SS	NO:SR	NO:SS
UA9 NOVOSIBIRSK RUSSIA	00:53	11:36	01:21	11:03	01:56	10:29	02:23	10:09	02:46	09:59	02:54	10:04
UA9 PERM AS.RUSSIA	02:45	13:18	03:17	12:41	03:56	12:02	04:27	11:39	04:52	11:26	05:01	11:31
UAØ KHABAROVSK AS.RUSSIA	21:15	08:16	21:37	07:50	22:03	07:23	22:24	07:09	22:43	07:04	22:51	07:09
UAØ YAKUTSK AS.RUSSIA	21:59	08:16	22:38	07:32	23:26	06:44	00:05	06:12	00:38	05:51	00:48	05:55
UAØ OKHOTSK AS.RUSSIA	20:58	07:27	21:32	06:48	22:14	06:06	22:47	05:40	23:15	05:25	23:24	05:29
UAØ UST-OLENEK AS.RUSSIA	23:16	08:15	00:34	06:52	03:17	04:09	NO:SR	NO:SS	NO:SR	NO:SS	NO:SR	NO:SS
UD6 BAKU AZERBAIJAN	02:49	14:05	03:05	13:45	03:25	13:26	03:40	13:17	03:55	13:15	04:03	13:21
UH8 ASHKHABAD TURKOMAN	02:15	13:32	02:30	13:12	02:49	12:54	03:05	12:45	03:19	12:43	03:27	12:49
UN7 ALMA-ATA KAZAKH	01:02	12:13	01:20	11:51	01:42	11:30	01:59	11:19	02:15	11:16	02:23	11:22
V3 BELIZE BELIZE	11:45	23:32	11:49	23:24	11:57	23:17	12:05	23:16	12:14	23:20	12:21	23:26
V85 BRUNEI	22:06	10:07	22:05	10:03	22:07	10:01	22:12	10:04	22:19	10:09	22:26	10:16
VE1 Halifax N.S.	10:27	21:34	10:45	21:11	11:08	20:49	11:27	20:38	11:43	20:34	11:51	20:40
VE2 Quebec City Que.	11:00	22:02	11:20	21:38	11:45	21:14	12:04	21:01	12:22	20:57	12:29	21:03
VE3 Ottawa Ont.	11:24	22:28	11:43	22:03	12:07	21:40	12:26	21:28	12:43	21:24	12:51	21:30
VE4 Winnipeg Mb.	12:47	23:42	13:10	23:15	13:38	22:48	14:00	22:33	14:18	22:27	14:26	22:33
VE5 Regina Sk.	13:18	00:12	13:41	23:44	14:10	23:16	14:32	23:01	14:51	22:55	14:59	23:01
VE6 Edmondton Al.	13:58	00:43	14:24	00:12	14:56	23:40	15:21	23:22	15:42	23:14	15:50	23:20
VE7 Prince Rupert B.C.	15:06	01:49	15:33	01:17	16:07	00:44	16:32	00:26	16:54	00:17	17:02	00:23
VE8 Yellowknife NWT	14:19	00:31	14:58	23:46	15:48	22:58	16:27	22:25	17:00	22:05	17:09	22:10
VO2 Goose Bay Labrador	10:25	21:12	10:51	20:41	11:23	20:10	11:48	19:52	12:09	19:44	12:17	19:49
VY1 Whitehorse Yukon	15:37	01:57	16:13	01:16	16:58	00:32	17:33	00:04	18:02	23:48	18:10	23:53
VK1 CANBERRA AUSTRALIA	19:24	08:16	19:06	08:28	18:50	08:45	18:43	08:59	18:42	09:13	18:48	09:20
VK4 BRISBANE AUSTRALIA	19:14	07:54	19:01	08:02	18:49	08:14	18:44	08:25	18:46	08:37	18:52	08:44
VK6 PERTH AUSTRALIA	21:39	10:25	21:23	10:36	21:09	10:50	21:03	11:03	21:03	11:15	21:10	11:23
VK8 DARWIN AUSTRALIA	20:52	09:13	20:45	09:15	20:40	09:20	20:40	09:27	20:45	09:35	20:51	09:42
VK9 COCOS (KEELING) IS	23:33	11:53	23:26	11:55	23:22	12:00	23:22	12:06	23:26	12:15	23:33	12:22

Prefix City Country	Jan14 Sunrise	Jan 14 Sunset	Jan 28 Sunrise	Jan 28 Sunset	Feb 14 Sunrise	Feb 14 Sunset	Feb 28 Sunrise	Feb 28 Sunset	Mar 14 Sunrise	Mar 14 Sunset	Mar 28 Sunrise	Mar 28 Sunset
VK9 NORFOLK ISLAND	18:10	07:52	18:22	07:49	18:35	07:39	18:44	07:27	18:52	07:13	18:59	06:57
VKØ MACQUARIE ISLAND	17:11	09:56	17:38	09:38	18:14	09:05	18:43	08:32	19:11	07:58	19:38	07:23
VP8 FALKLAND ISLANDS	08:11	00:14	08:34	23:55	09:05	23:31	09:30	23:03	09:54	22:33	10:17	22:02
VP8 SO.SANDWICH IS	05:12	22:42	05:44	22:18	06:26	21:38	07:00	21:01	07:33	20:22	08:04	19:43
VP8 SO.SHETLAND IS	06:40	01:25	07:22	00:52	08:14	00:02	08:56	23:18	09:35	22:32	10:12	21:46
VP9 BERMUDA	11:21	21:35	11:16	21:48	11:03	22:03	10:49	22:15	10:32	22:25	10:14	22:35
VQ9 DIEGO GARCIA	01:02	13:34	01:08	13:36	01:13	13:34	01:14	13:30	01:14	13:24	01:13	13:17
VR6 PITCAIRN IS	14:16	03:46	14:26	03:44	14:38	03:35	14:46	03:24	14:53	03:10	14:59	02:56
VU7 ANDAMAN IS	00:14	11:45	00:16	11:51	00:13	11:57	00:07	12:00	00:00	12:02	23:51	12:02
VU7 LACCADIVE IS	01:30	13:03	01:32	13:09	01:29	12:15	01:24	13:18	01:16	13:19	01:08	13:19
WØ Denver CO	14:20	23:58	14:12	00:14	13:55	00:34	13:36	00:50	13:14	01:05	12:52	01:19
WØ Des Moines IA	13:40	23:07	13:31	23:24	13:12	23:45	12:52	00:02	12:29	00:19	12:06	00:34
WØ Topeka KS	13:41	23:22	13:33	23:38	13:16	23:58	12:58	00:13	12:37	00:27	12:15	00:41
WØ Minneapolis MN	13:48	22:55	13:38	23:14	13:17	23:38	12:54	23:57	12:29	00:16	12:03	00:34
WØ Jefferson City MO	13:25	23:09	13:18	23:25	13:02	23:44	12:43	23:59	12:23	00:14	12:01	00:27
WØ Lincoln NE	13:50	23:22	13:41	23:38	13:23	23:59	13:04	00:15	12:42	00:31	12:18	00:46
WØ Bismark ND	14:25	23:19	14:13	23:39	13:50	00:04	13:26	00:25	12:59	00:46	12:32	01:05
WØ Pierre SD	14:15	23:25	14:05	23:44	13:44	00:07	13:22	00:26	12:57	00:45	12:31	01:02
W1 Augusta ME	12:12	21:23	12:02	21:41	11:41	22:05	11:19	22:24	10:55	22:42	10:29	22:59
W1 Boston MA	12:12	21:35	12:03	21:52	11:34	22:14	11:23	22:32	11:00	22:48	10:35	23:04
W1 Concord NH	12:16	21:34	12:06	21:51	11:46	22:14	11:25	22:32	11:01	22:50	10:37	23:06
W1 Hartford CT	12:16	21:43	12:07	21:59	11:49	22:21	11:28	22:38	11:06	22:55	10:42	23:10
W1 Montpelier VT	12:24	21:34	12:14	21:53	11:53	22:16	11:31	22:35	11:06	22:54	10:40	23:11
W1 Providence RI	12:11	21:37	12:03	21:54	11:44	22:16	11:23	22:33	11:01	22:49	10:37	23:05
W2 Albany NY	12:24	21:44	12:15	22:02	11:55	22:24	11:34	22:42	11:11	22:59	10:46	23:15
W2 Trenton NJ	12:20	21:55	12:12	22:11	11:55	22:32	11:35	22:48	11:14	23:03	10:51	23:18
W3 Dover DE	12:24	22:05	12:17	22:21	12:00	22:41	11:41	22:56	11:20	23:11	10:58	23:25
W3 Harrisburg PA	12:29	22:04	12:21	22:20	12:03	22:40	11:44	22:56	11:22	23:12	10:59	23:26
W3 Washington D.C.	12:26	22:08	12:18	22:24	12:01	22:43	11:43	22:58	11:22	23:13	11:23	00:26
W4 Atlanta GA	12:43	22:50	12:37	23:03	12:24	23:20	12:08	23:32	11:50	23:44	11:32	23:54
W4 Columbia SC	12:30	22:36	12:24	22:49	12:11	23:06	11:55	23:18	11:37	23:30	11:18	23:41
W4 Frankfort KY	12:55	22:41	12:48	22:57	12:32	23:16	12:14	23:31	11:54	23:45	11:32	23:58
W4 Montgomery AL	12:47	23:01	12:42	23:14	12:30	23:29	12:15	23:41	11:58	23:52	11:40	00:01
W4 Nashville TN	12:58	22:54	12:52	23:08	12:37	23:26	12:20	23:40	12:01	23:53	11:40	00:05
W4 Raleigh NC	12:24	22:22	12:18	22:37	12:04	22:54	11:47	23:08	11:28	23:20	11:08	23:32
W4 Richmond VA	12:24	22:13	12:17	22:28	12:02	22:47	11:44	23:02	11:24	23:15	11:03	23:28
W4 Tallahassee FL	12:35	22:57	12:31	23:09	12:19	23:24	12:05	23:34	11:49	23:44	11:32	23:53
W5 Austin TX	13:28	23:51	13:24	00:03	13:13	00:18	12:59	00:28	12:43	00:38	12:26	00:46
W5 Baton Rouge LA	13:02	23:24	12:58	23:37	12:47	23:51	12:33	00:02	12:17	00:11	12:00	00:20
W5 Jackson MS	13:02	23:16	12:58	23:29	12:45	23:45	12:30	23:56	12:13	00:07	11:55	00:17
W5 Little Rock AR	13:16	23:19	13:11	23:33	12:57	23:50	12:41	00:03	12:22	00:15	12:03	00:26
W5 Oklahoma City OK	13:39	23:39	13:33	23:53	13:19	00:10	13:02	00:23	12:43	00:36	12:24	00:47
W5 Santa Fe NM	14:12	00:13	14:06	00:27	13:52	00:44	13:36	00:58	13:17	01:10	12:57	01:21
W6 Los Angeles CA	14:59	01:05	14:53	01:19	14:39	01:35	14:24	01:48	14:06	01:59	13:47	02:10
W6 San Francisco CA	15:24	01:13	15:17	01:28	15:01	01:47	14:44	02:01	14:23	02:15	14:02	02:28
W7 Boise ID	15:16	00:31	15:06	00:49	14:46	01:12	14:24	01:31	14:00	01:48	13:35	02:05

Prefix City Country	Apr 14 Sunrise	Apr 14 Sunset	Apr 28 Sunrise	Apr 28 Sunset	May 14 Sunrise	May 14 Sunset	May 28 Sunrise	May 28 Sunset	Jun 14 Sunrise	Jun 14 Sunset	Jun 28 Sunrise	Jun 28 Sunset
VK9 NORFOLK ISLAND	19:08	06:39	19:15	06:26	19:24	06:14	19:32	06:08	19:39	06:06	19:42	06:09
VKØ MACQUARIE ISLAND	20:11	06:41	20:37	06:09	21:05	05:37	21:27	05:17	21:45	05:05	21:49	05:06
VP8 FALKLAND ISLANDS	10:44	21:25	11:06	20:57	11:30	20:30	11:49	20:13	12:04	20:04	12:07	20:06
VP8 SO.SANDWICH IS	08:41	18:56	09:12	18:20	09:45	17:43	10:11	17:19	10:32	17:04	10:36	17:06
VP8 SO.SHETLAND IS	10:57	20:52	11:34	20:09	12:16	19:25	12:49	18:53	13:16	18:32	13:21	18:33
VP9 BERMUDA	09:52	22:47	09:36	22:57	09:22	23:08	09:14	23:18	09:11	23:27	09:14	23:30
VQ9 DIEGO GARCIA	01:11	13:09	01:11	13:03	01:12	12:59	01:14	12:58	01:18	13:00	01:22	13:03
VR6 PITCAIRN IS	15:06	02:39	15:12	02:27	15:19	02:17	15:26	02:12	15:33	02:11	15:36	02:14
VU7 ANDAMAN IS	23:41	12:02	23:33	12:04	23:28	12:07	23:26	12:10	23:27	12:15	23:30	12:18
VU7 LACCADIVE IS	00:58	13:19	00:51	13:20	00:46	13:23	00:44	13:26	00:45	13:31	00:48	13:34
WØ Denver CO	12:25	01:36	12:05	01:50	11:47	02:06	11:36	02:18	11:31	02:29	11:34	02:32
WØ DesMoines IA	11:37	00:53	11:16	01:08	10:57	01:25	10:45	01:38	10:40	01:49	10:42	01:53
WØ Topeka KS	11:49	00:58	11:29	01:11	11:11	01:27	11:01	01:39	10:56	01:49	10:59	01:53
WØ Minneapolis MN	11:32	00:56	11:08	01:13	10:46	01:33	10:33	01:48	10:26	02:00	10:28	02:04
WØ Jefferson City MO	11:35	00:43	11:16	00:56	10:58	01:11	10:48	01:23	10:44	01:34	10:46	01:37
WØ Lincoln NE	11:51	01:04	11:30	01:19	11:11	01:35	11:00	01:48	10:55	01:59	10:57	02:03
WØ Bismark ND	11:59	01:28	11:34	01:47	11:10	02:08	10:56	02:24	10:48	02:38	10:51	02:41
WØ Pierre SD	12:01	01:23	11:38	01:40	11:16	01:59	11:03	02:14	10:56	02:26	10:59	02:30
W1 Augusta ME	09:58	23:20	09:35	23:37	09:14	23:56	09:01	00:11	08:54	00:24	08:57	00:27
W1 Boston MA	10:07	23:23	09:45	23:39	09:25	23:56	09:13	00:10	09:07	00:22	09:10	00:25
W1 Concord NH	10:07	23:26	09:45	23:42	09:24	00:00	09:12	00:14	09:06	00:26	09:08	00:30
W1 Hartford CT	10:13	23:29	09:52	23:44	09:33	00:01	09:21	00:15	09:15	00:26	09:18	00:30
W1 Montpelier VT	10:10	23:32	09:47	23:49	09:25	00:08	09:12	00:23	09:05	00:35	09:08	00:39
W1 Providence RI	10:08	23:24	09:47	23:39	09:27	23:56	09:16	00:10	09:10	00:21	09:12	00:25
W2 Albany NY	10:17	23:35	09:55	23:51	09:35	00:09	09:22	00:22	09:16	00:34	09:19	00:38
W2 Trenton NJ	10:24	23:35	10:04	23:50	09:45	00:06	09:34	00:18	09:29	00:29	09:31	00:33
W3 Dover DE	10:32	23:41	10:12	23:55	09:54	00:10	09:44	00:22	09:39	00:33	09:42	00:36
W3 Harrisburg PA	10:32	23:44	10:12	23:58	09:53	00:14	09:42	00:27	09:37	00:38	09:39	00:41
W3 Washington D.C.	10:34	23:43	10:15	23:56	09:57	00:11	09:47	00:23	09:42	00:34	09:45	00:37
W4 Atlanta GA	11:09	00:07	10:53	00:18	10:38	00:30	10:30	00:40	10:26	00:49	10:29	00:52
W4 Columbia SC	10:55	23:54	10:39	00:04	10:24	00:17	10:15	00:27	10:12	00:36	10:15	00:39
W4 Frankfort KY	11:07	00:14	10:48	00:27	10:30	00:41	10:20	00:53	10:16	01:03	10:18	01:07
W4 Montgomery AL	11:18	00:13	11:02	00:23	10:48	00:35	10:40	00:44	10:37	00:53	10:40	00:56
W4 Nashville TN	11:16	00:19	10:59	00:31	10:42	00:45	10:33	00:55	10:29	01:05	10:32	01:08
W4 Raleigh NC	10:44	23:46	10:27	23:58	10:11	00:11	10:02	00:22	09:58	00:31	10:00	00:35
W4 Richmond VA	10:38	23:43	10:19	23:56	10:02	00:11	09:52	00:22	09:48	00:32	09:51	00:35
W4 Tallahassee FL	11:12	00:03	10:57	00:12	10:44	00:23	10:37	00:32	10:34	00:40	10:37	00:43
W5 Austin TX	12:06	00:57	11:51	01:06	11:38	01:16	11:31	01:25	11:28	01:33	11:31	01:36
W5 Baton Rouge LA	11:39	00:31	11:25	00:40	11:11	00:50	11:04	00:59	11:02	01:08	11:04	01:11
W5 Jackson MS	11:34	00:29	11:18	00:39	11:04	00:50	10:56	00:59	10:53	01:08	10:56	01:11
W5 Little Rock AR	11:40	00:39	11:23	00:51	11:07	01:03	10:59	01:14	10:55	01:23	10:58	01:26
W5 Oklahoma City OK	12:00	01:01	11:43	01:13	11:27	01:26	11:18	01:37	11:14	01:46	11:17	01:49
W5 Santa Fe NM	12:34	01:35	12:17	01:46	12:01	01:59	11:53	02:10	11:49	02:19	11:52	02:22
W6 Los Angeles CA	13:24	02:23	13:08	02:33	12:53	02:46	12:44	02:56	12:41	03:05	12:44	03:08
W6 San Francisco CA	13:37	02:43	13:18	02:56	13:01	03:11	12:51	03:22	12:47	03:32	12:50	03:36
W7 Boise ID	13:05	02:26	12:43	02:42	12:22	03:01	12:09	03:15	12:03	03:27	12:05	03:30

Prefix City Country	July 14 Sunrise	July 14 Sunset	July 28 Sunrise	July 28 Sunset	Aug 14 Sunrise	Aug 14 Sunset	Aug 28 Sunrise	Aug 28 Sunset	Sep 14 Sunrise	Sep 14 Sunset	Sept 28 Sunrise	Sept 28 Sunset
VK9 NORFOLK ISLAND	19:42	06:15	19:36	06:22	19:25	06:30	19:12	06:37	18:53	06:44	18:37	06:51
VK0 MACQUARIE ISLAND	21:40	05:21	21:22	05:40	20:51	06:09	20:19	06:34	19:37	07:05	19:02	07:30
VP8 FALKLAND ISLANDS	12:00	20:20	11:45	20:36	11:17	21:00	10:50	21:21	10:13	21:47	09:41	22:09
VP8 SO.SANDWICH IS	10:23	17:24	10:02	17:47	09:24	18:21	08:48	18:51	08:02	19:26	07:22	19:56
VP8 SO.SHETLAND IS	13:02	18:57	12:34	19:27	11:48	20:10	11:05	20:46	10:11	21:29	09:25	22:05
VP9 BERMUDA	09:22	23:28	09:30	23:21	09:42	23:06	09:51	22:50	10:01	22:28	10:10	22:10
VQ9 DIEGO GARCIA	01:23	13:07	01:23	13:09	01:19	13:10	01:13	13:09	01:04	13:07	00:56	13:05
VR6 PITCAIRN IS	15:35	02:20	15:31	02:26	15:20	02:33	15:08	02:39	14:51	02:45	14:36	02:50
VU7 ANDAMAN IS	23:34	12:19	23:37	12:18	23:40	12:12	23:41	12:04	23:40	11:54	23:40	11:44
VU7 LACCADIVE IS	00:52	13:35	00:55	13:34	00:57	13:28	00:58	13:21	00:57	13:10	00:57	13:01
WØ Denver CO	11:43	02:28	11:54	02:18	12:10	01:59	12:23	01:39	12:39	01:12	12:52	00:49
WØ DesMoines IA	10:52	01:48	11:04	01:38	11:21	01:17	11:35	00:56	11:53	00:28	12:07	00:04
WØ Topeka KS	11:08	01:49	11:19	01:39	11:34	01:21	11:47	01:01	12:02	00:35	12:15	00:12
WØ Minneapolis MN	10:39	01:58	10:53	01:46	11:12	01:23	11:29	01:00	11:49	00:28	12:06	00:02
WØ Jefferson City MO	10:56	01:33	11:06	01:24	11:21	01:06	11:33	00:47	11:48	00:21	12:01	23:58
WØ Lincoln NE	11:07	01:58	11:19	01:48	11:35	01:28	11:49	01:08	12:05	00:40	12:19	00:16
WØ Bismark ND	11:03	02:35	11:17	02:22	11:38	01:57	11:56	01:33	12.18	01:00	12:37	00:31
WØ Pierre SD	11:10	02:24	11:23	02:12	11:42	01:50	11:58	01:27	12:18	00:56	12:34	00:30
W1 Augusta ME	09:08	00:22	09:21	00:10	09:40	23:48	09:56	23:25	10:15	22:54	10:32	22:28
W1 Boston MA	09:20	00:20	09:32	00:10	09:50	23:49	10:04	23:27	10:22	22:58	10:37	22:34
W1 Concord NH	09:19	00:25	09:31	00:14	09:49	23:52	10:05	23:30	10:23	23:00	10:39	22:35
W1 Hartford CT	09:28	00:25	09:40	00:14	09:57	23:54	10:11	23:33	10:29	23:04	10:43	22:40
W1 Montpelier VT	09:19	00:33	09:32	00:21	09:51	23:59	10:07	23:36	10:27	23:05	10:43	22:39
W1 Providence RI	09:23	00:20	09:34	00:10	09:52	23:49	10:06	23:28	10:24	22:59	10:38	22:35
W2 Albany NY	09:29	00:33	09:42	00:22	09:59	00:01	10:15	23:39	10:33	23:10	10:48	22:45
W2 Trenton NJ	09:41	00:29	09:52	00:19	10:08	23:59	10:22	23:39	10:38	23:12	10:51	22:49
W3 Dover DE	09:51	00:32	10:02	00:23	10:17	00:04	10:30	23:45	10:45	23:18	10:58	22:56
W3 Harrisburg PA	09:49	00:37	10:00	00:27	10:16	00:08	10:30	23:48	10:46	23:20	11:00	22:57
W3 Washington D.C.	09:54	00:33	10:05	00:24	10:20	00:06	10:32	23:46	10:48	23:20	11:00	22:58
W4 Atlanta GA	10:37	00:50	10:46	00:42	10:58	00:27	11:08	00:10	11:19	23:47	11:29	23:28
W4 Columbia SC	10:23	00:37	10:32	00:29	10:44	00:14	10:54	23:57	11:06	23:34	11:16	23:14
W4 Frankfort KY	10:28	01:03	10:38	00:54	10:53	00:36	11:05	00:17	11:20	23:51	11:32	23:29
W4 Montgomery AL	10:48	00:54	10:56	00:47	11:08	00:32	11:17	00:16	11:28	23:54	11:36	23:36
W4 Nashville TN	10:41	01:05	10:50	00:57	11:04	00:40	11:15	00:22	11:28	23:58	11:39	23:37
W4 Raleigh NC	10:09	00:32	10:19	00:24	10:32	00:07	10:43	23:49	10:56	23:25	11:06	23:05
W4 Richmond VA	10:00	00:32	10:10	00:23	10:24	00:06	10:36	23:47	10:50	23:22	11:02	23:00
W4 Tallahassee FL	10:44	00:41	10:52	00:35	11:03	00:21	11:11	00:06	11:20	23:46	11:28	23:28
W5 Austin TX	11:39	01:35	11:46	01:28	11:57	01:15	12:05	01:00	12:14	00:39	12:22	00:22
W5 Baton Rouge LA	11:12	01:09	11:20	01:02	11:30	00:49	11:38	00:34	11:48	00:13	11:56	23:55
W5 Jackson MS	11:04	01:09	11:12	01:02	11:23	00:47	11:32	00:32	11:43	00:10	11:52	23:51
W5 Little Rock AR	11:06	01:23	11:15	01:16	11:28	01:00	11:38	00:43	11:51	00:19	12:01	23:59
W5 Oklahoma City OK	11:25	01:46	11:35	01:38	11:48	01:22	11:59	01:05	12:11	00:41	12:22	00:20
W5 Santa Fe NM	12:00	02:19	12:09	02:12	12:22	01:55	12:33	01:38	12:45	01:14	12:56	00:54
W6 Los Angeles CA	12:52	03:06	13:01	02:58	13:13	02:42	13:23	02:26	13:50	02:20	13:45	01:43
W6 San Francisco CA	12:59	03:32	13:09	03:23	13:24	03:05	13:36	02:47	13:35	02:03	14:02	01:59
W7 Boise ID	12:16	03:25	12:29	03:14	12:47	02:52	13:03	02:30	13:22	01:59	13:38	01:34

Prefix City Country	Oct 14 Sunrise	Oct 14 Sunset	Oct 28 Sunrise	Oct 28 Sunset	Nov 14 Sunrise	Nov 14 Sunset	Nov 28 Sunrise	Nov 28 Sunset	Dec 14 Sunrise	Dec 14 Sunset	Dec 28 Sunrise	Dec 28 Sunset
VK9 NORFOLK ISLAND	18:19	06:59	18:06	07:07	17:55	07:19	17:50	07:30	17:52	07:42	17:58	07:49
VKØ MACQUARIE ISLAND	18:22	08:01	17:49	08:29	17:14	09:04	16:54	09:31	16:43	09:55	16:48	10:04
VP8 FALKLAND ISLANDS	09:06	22:35	08:37	22:59	08:08	23:28	07:52	23:51	07:45	00:11	07:51	00:19
VP8 SO.SANDWICH IS	06:37	20:32	05:59	21:04	05:19	21:46	04:54	22:18	04:40	22:45	04:45	22:53
VP8 SO.SHETLAND IS	08:33	22:48	07:48	23:28	06:58	00:19	06:23	01:00	06:00	01:36	06:04	01:46
VP9 BERMUDA	10:21	21:49	10:32	21:34	10:47	21:20	10:59	21:14	11:12	21:15	11:19	21:21
VQ9 DIEGO GARCIA	00:48	13:03	00:43	13:04	00:40	13:07	00:42	13:12	00:47	13:20	00:54	13:27
VR6 PITCAIRN IS	14:20	02:57	14:08	03:04	13:58	03:15	13:55	03:25	13:57	03:35	14:04	03:43
VU7 ANDAMAN IS	23:40	11:34	23:42	11:28	23:47	11:24	23:53	11:24	00:01	11:29	00:08	11:35
VU7 LACCADIVE IS	00:57	12:52	00:58	12:45	01:03	12:41	01:09	12:42	01:17	12:47	01:24	12:53
WØ Denver CO	13:08	00:24	13:23	00:05	13:42	23:46	13:58	23:37	14:12	23:36	14:20	23:42
WØ Des Moines IA	12:24	23:37	12:40	23:16	13:01	22:57	13:17	22:47	13:33	22:45	13:40	22:51
WØ Topeka KS	12:30	23:48	12:45	23:28	13:04	23:11	13:19	23:02	13:33	23:01	13:41	23:07
WØ Minneapolis MN	12:26	23:32	12:45	23:09	13:08	22:47	13:26	22:35	13:43	22:32	13:50	22:38
WØ Jefferson City MO	12:16	23:34	12:30	23:15	12:48	22:58	13:03	22:49	13:18	22:48	13:25	22:54
WØ Lincoln NE	12:36	23:50	12:52	23:30	13:12	23:11	13:28	23:01	13:43	23:00	13:50	23:06
WØ Bismark ND	12:58	00:00	13:18	23:36	13:43	23:12	14:02	22:59	14:20	22:55	14:27	23:01
WØ Pierre SD	12:54	00:01	13:12	23:38	13:35	23:17	13:53	23:05	14:09	23:02	14:17	23:08
W1 Augusta ME	10:51	21:59	11:09	21:36	11:32	21:14	11:50	21:03	12:06	21:00	12:14	21:06
W1 Boston MA	10:55	22:07	11:11	21:45	11:33	21:25	11:49	21:15	12:05	21:13	12:12	21:19
W1 Concord NH	10:57	22:07	11:14	21:45	11:36	21:24	11:54	21:14	12:09	21:11	12:17	21:17
W1 Hartford CT	11:01	22:13	11:17	21:52	11:38	21:32	11:54	21:23	12:09	21:20	12:17	21:27
W1 Montpelier VT	11:03	22:10	11:21	21:48	11:44	21:26	12:01	21:15	12:18	21:11	12:25	21:18
W1 Providence RI	10:56	22:08	11:12	21:47	11:33	21:27	11:49	21:17	12:04	21:15	12:12	21:21
W2 Albany NY	11:06	22:17	11:23	21:55	11:45	21:35	12:02	21:24	12:17	21:22	12:25	21:28
W2 Trenton NJ	11:08	22:23	11:23	22:03	11:42	21:44	11:58	21:35	12:13	21:34	12:20	21:40
W3 Dover DE	11:14	22:31	11:28	22:12	11:47	21:54	12:02	21:45	12:17	21:44	12:24	21:50
W3 Harrisburg PA	11:16	22:31	11:31	22:11	11:51	21:53	12:07	21:43	12:21	21:42	12:29	21:48
W3 Washington D.C.	11:15	22:33	11:30	22:14	11:48	21:56	12:03	21:48	12:18	21:47	12:25	21:53
W4 Atlanta GA	11:41	23:07	11:52	22:51	12:08	22:36	12:21	22:30	12:34	22:30	12:41	22:36
W4 Columbia SC	11:28	22:53	11:39	22:37	11:55	22:22	12:08	22:16	12:21	22:16	12:28	22:22
W4 Frankfort KY	11:46	23:05	12:00	22:47	12:19	22:29	12:33	22:21	12:48	22:20	12:55	22:27
W4 Montgomery AL	11:47	23:15	11:58	23:00	12:13	22:46	12:25	22:40	12:38	22:41	12:45	22:47
W4 Nashville TN	11:52	23:14	12:05	22:57	12:22	22:41	12:36	22:34	12:50	22:33	12:57	22:40
W4 Raleigh NC	11:19	22:42	11:32	22:25	11:49	22:09	12:02	22:02	12:16	22:02	12:23	22:08
W4 Richmond VA	11:16	22:36	11:30	22:18	11:48	22:01	12:02	21:53	12:16	21:52	12:24	21:59
W4 Tallahassee FL	11:38	23:09	11:48	22:54	12:01	22:42	12:13	22:37	12:25	22:38	12:32	22:44
W5 Austin TX	12:32	00:02	12:41	23:48	12:55	23:36	13:06	23:31	13:18	23:32	13:26	23:38
W5 Baton Rouge LA	12:06	23:36	12:15	23:22	12:29	23:09	12:41	23:04	12:53	23:05	13:00	23:12
W5 Jackson MS	12:03	23:31	12:14	23:15	12:28	23:02	12:41	22:56	12:53	22:57	13:00	23:03
W5 Little Rock AR	12:13	23:37	12:25	23:21	12:41	23:06	12:54	22:59	13:08	22:59	13:15	23:05
W5 Oklahoma City OK	12:35	23:58	12:47	23:41	13:04	23:25	13:17	23:18	13:31	23:18	13:38	23:25
W5 Santa Fe NM	13:08	00:32	13:21	00:15	13:37	00:00	13:50	23:53	14:04	23:53	14:11	23:59
W6 Los Angeles CA	13:57	01:22	14:08	01:06	14:24	00:51	14:37	00:45	14:50	00:45	14:57	00:51
W6 San Francisco CA	14:16	01:36	14:30	01:17	14:48	01:00	15:03	00:52	15:17	00:52	15:24	00:58
W7 Boise ID	13:57	01:05	14:14	00:43	14:36	00:22	14:54	00:11	15:10	00:08	15:17	00:15

Prefix City Country	Jan14 Sunrise	Jan 14 Sunset	Jan 28 Sunrise	Jan 28 Sunset	Feb 14 Sunrise	Feb 14 Sunset	Feb 28 Sunrise	Feb 28 Sunset	Mar 14 Sunrise	Mar 14 Sunset	Mar 28 Sunrise	Mar 28 Sunset
W7 Carson City NV	15:17	00:58	15:10	01:14	14:53	01:34	14:34	01:49	14:13	02:04	13:51	02:18
W7 Cheyenne WY	14:23	23:53	14:15	00:10	13:56	00:31	13:36	00:48	13:14	01:03	12:51	01:19
W7 Olympia WA	15:54	00:47	15:42	01:06	15:19	01:33	14:55	01:54	14:28	02:14	14:00	02:34
W7 Pheonix AZ	14:32	00:41	14:27	00:54	14:14	01:11	13:58	01:23	13:41	01:34	13:22	01:45
W7 Salem OR	15:47	00:55	15:37	01:13	15:16	01:37	14:53	01:57	14:28	02:15	14:02	02:33
W7 Salt Lake City UT	14:50	00:22	14:42	00:39	14:24	01:00	14:04	01:16	13:42	01:32	13:19	01:47
W8 Charleston WV	12:43	22:28	12:35	22:43	12:19	23:02	12:01	23:17	11:40	23:31	11:19	23:45
W8 Columbus OH	12:53	22:29	12:45	22:45	12:27	23:05	12:08	23:17	11:47	23:36	11:24	23:51
W8 Lansing MI	13:07	22:27	12:58	22:45	12:38	23:07	12:17	23:25	11:54	23:42	11:29	23:58
W9 Indianapolis IN	13:04	22:42	12:57	22:58	12:39	23:18	12:20	23:34	11:59	23:49	11:36	00:03
W9 Madison WI	13:27	22:46	13:18	23:03	12:58	23:26	12:37	23:44	12:13	00:01	11:48	00:18
W9 Springfield IL	13:18	22:56	13:11	23:12	12:53	23:32	12:34	23:48	12:13	00:03	11:50	00:17
XE1 MEXICO CITY MEXICO	13:13	00:17	13:13	00:26	13:06	00:35	12:57	00:41	12:46	00:46	12:35	00:49
XW VIENTIANE LOAS	23:44	10:53	23:44	11:01	23:38	11:10	23:30	11:15	23:20	11:19	23:08	11:22
YA KABUL AFGANISTAN	02:30	12:33	02:25	12:47	02:11	13:04	01:55	13:17	01:37	13:29	01:17	13:40
YB JAKARTA INDONESIA	22:48	11:15	22:54	11:18	22:58	11:17	22:59	11:13	22:58	11:07	22:56	11:01
ZD8 ASCENSION IS.	06:44	19:17	06:50	19:19	06:55	19:17	06:57	19:13	06:56	19:07	06:55	18:59
ZD9 TRISTAN DA CUNHA	05:48	20:08	06:02	20:01	06:20	19:47	06:34	19:30	06:46	19:11	06:58	18:51
ZF CAYMAN IS.	11:59	23:03	11:58	23:12	11:52	23:21	11:43	23:27	11:32	23:31	11:20	23:35
ZL1 AUCKLAND NZ	17:16	07:43	17:31	07:37	17:49	07:21	18:04	07:04	18:17	06:44	18:30	06:24
ZL4 DUNEDIN NZ	17:05	08:28	17:24	08:17	17:50	07:54	18:10	07:31	18:30	07:05	18:49	06:38
ZP ASUNCION PARAGUAY	09:12	22:46	09:22	22:43	09:35	22:34	09:34	22:22	09:50	22:09	09:57	21:54
ZS1 CAPETOWN S.AFRICA	03:49	18:00	04:03	17:55	04:20	17:41	04:32	17:26	04:44	17:08	04:54	16:49
ZS8 Pr.EDWARD & MARION	01:53	17:21	02:13	17:09	02:39	16:46	03:00	16:22	03:20	15:55	03:40	15:28
1S SPRATLY IS.	22:51	10:31	22:53	10:37	22:51	10:42	22:47	10:44	22:40	10:44	22:33	10:43
3V TUNIS TUNISIA	06:32	16:24	06:26	16:39	06:11	16:57	05:53	17:11	05:34	17:25	05:13	17:37
3Y BOUVET IS.	03:34	20:16	04:01	19:57	04:37	19:25	05:06	18:52	05:34	18:18	06:01	17:43
3Y PETER 1ST IS.	NO:SR	NO:SS	08:18	04:16	09:44	02:53	10:43	01:51	11:36	00:51	12:27	23:52
4U UNITED NATIONS HQ	12:18	21:51	12:10	22:07	11:52	22:28	11:33	22:45	11:11	23:00	10:47	23:15
4X ISRAEL	04:47	14:59	04:42	15:12	04:29	15:27	04:14	15:39	03:57	15:50	03:39	16:00
5R TANANARIVE MALAGASY	02:23	15:33	02:32	15:32	02:41	15:26	02:47	15:17	02:51	15:07	02:55	14:55
5W WESTERN SAMOA	17:10	06:04	17:18	06:04	17:25	06:00	17:29	05:53	17:31	05:44	17:33	05:34
5Z NAIROBI KENYA	03:36	15:47	03:40	15:51	03:42	15:52	03:41	15:50	03:39	15:46	03:35	15:41
6W DAKAR SENEGAL	07:38	18:59	07:39	19:06	07:35	19:13	07:28	19:17	07:19	19:20	07:09	19:21
7O ADEN YEMAN P.DEM.	03:25	14:52	03:26	14:59	03:23	15:05	03:17	15:09	03:09	15:10	03:00	15:11
7P LESOTHO	03:20	17:13	03:32	17:09	03:47	16:57	03:57	16:44	04:06	16:28	04:15	16:11
8Q MALDIVE IS	01:26	13:19	01:29	13:24	01:29	13:27	01:26	13:28	01:21	13:26	01:15	13:24
9G ACCRA GHANA	06:15	18:04	06:17	18:10	06:17	18:13	06:13	18:14	06:08	18:13	06:02	18:11
9J LUSAKA ZAMBIA	03:47	16:44	03:55	16:44	04:02	16:40	04:07	16:33	04:10	16:23	04:12	16:13
9K KUWAIT	03:40	14:08	03:36	14:19	03:26	14:33	03:13	14:43	02:57	14:52	02:41	15:00
9N KATMANDU NEPAL	01:11	11:43	01:08	11:55	00:58	12:08	00:45	12:17	00:31	12:26	00:15	12:33
9Q KINSHASA ZAIRE	04:57	17:18	05:02	17:21	05:05	17:21	05:06	17:18	05:04	17:13	05:02	17:07
9V SINGAPORE	23:12	11:15	23:16	11:19	23:17	11:21	23:15	11:20	23:12	11:18	23:07	11:14
9X RWANDA	04:03	16:17	04:08	16:21	04:10	16:21	04:10	16:19	04:07	16:15	04:04	16:10
9Y TRINIDAD IS.	10:25	22:01	10:27	22:07	10:24	22:12	10:19	22:14	10:12	22:15	10:04	22:15

Prefix City Country	Apr 14 Sunrise	Apr 14 Sunset	Apr 28 Sunrise	Apr 28 Sunset	May 14 Sunrise	May 14 Sunset	May 28 Sunrise	May 28 Sunset	Jun 14 Sunrise	Jun 14 Sunset	Jun 28 Sunrise	Jun 28 Sunset
W7 Carson City NV	13:25	02:34	13:05	02:48	12:47	03:03	12:37	03:15	12:32	03:26	12:35	03:29
W7 Cheyenne WY	12:23	01:37	12:02	01:52	11:43	02:08	11:31	02:21	11:26	02:33	11:28	02:36
W7 Olympia WA	13:27	02:57	13:02	03:16	12:38	03:38	12:23	03:54	12:16	04:07	12:18	04:11
W7 Pheonix AZ	13:00	01:57	12:43	02:08	12:29	02:20	12:21	02:30	12:17	02:39	12:20	02:42
W7 Salem OR	13:31	02:55	13:07	03:12	12:45	03:32	12:32	03:47	12:25	03:59	12:28	04:03
W7 Salt Lake City UT	12:51	02:05	12:31	02:19	12:12	02:36	12:01	02:48	11:55	03:00	11:58	03:03
W8 Charleston WV	10:53	00:01	10:34	00:14	10:17	00:29	10:07	00:40	10:02	00:51	10:05	00:54
W8 Columbus OH	10:57	00:08	10:37	00:22	10:18	00:38	10:07	00:51	10:02	01:02	10:05	01:05
W8 Lansing MI	11:00	00:18	10:38	00:34	10:18	00:52	10:05	01:05	09:59	01:17	10:02	01:21
W9 Indianapolis IN	11:10	00:20	10:50	00:34	10:32	00:50	10:21	01:03	10:16	01:13	10:18	01:17
W9 Madison WI	11:19	00:37	10:57	00:54	10:36	01:12	10:24	01:26	10:17	01:38	10:20	01:41
W9 Springfield IL	11:24	00:34	11:04	00:48	10:45	01:04	10:35	01:16	10:30	01:27	10:32	01:31
XE1 MEXICO CITY MEXICO	12:20	00:54	12:10	00:58	12:02	01:04	11:58	01:09	11:58	01:15	12:01	01:19
XW VIENTIANE LOAS	22:55	11:26	22:45	11:30	22:37	11:35	22:34	11:40	22:34	11:46	22:36	11:49
YA KABUL AFGANISTAN	00:54	13:53	00:37	14:04	00:22	14:17	00:13	14:27	00:09	14:37	00:12	14:40
YB JAKARTA INDONESIA	22:54	10:53	22:53	10:48	22:54	10:45	22:56	10:44	23:00	10:46	23:03	10:49
ZD8 ASCENSION IS.	06:54	18:51	06:54	18:45	06:55	18:41	06:58	18:40	07:02	18:42	07:05	18:45
ZD9 TRISTAN DA CUNHA	07:11	18:28	07:23	18:10	07:36	17:55	07:46	17:46	07:55	17:42	07:59	17:45
ZF CAYMAN IS.	11:06	23:39	10:56	23:44	10:47	23:49	10:43	23:55	10:43	00:01	10:46	00:04
ZL1 AUCKLAND NZ	18:44	05:59	18:56	05:41	19:10	05:25	19:21	05:15	19:31	05:11	19:35	05:13
ZL4 DUNEDIN NZ	19:11	06:07	19:29	05:43	19:48	05:20	20:03	05:06	20:16	04:59	20:20	05:01
ZP ASUNCION PARAGUAY	10:04	21:37	10:11	21:25	10:19	21:14	10:26	21:08	10:33	21:07	10:36	21:10
ZS1 CAPETOWN S.AFRICA	05:07	16:26	05:18	16:10	05:29	15:55	05:39	15:47	05:48	15:44	05:52	15:47
ZS8 Pr.EDWARD & MARION	04:02	14:55	04:21	14:31	04:41	14:08	04:57	13:54	05:10	13:46	05:14	13:49
1S SPRATLY IS.	22:24	10:42	22:18	10:42	22:14	10:44	22:12	10:47	22:14	10:51	22:17	10:54
3V TUNIS TUNISIA	04:48	17:52	04:30	18:05	04:13	18:19	04:04	18:30	03:59	18:40	04:02	18:43
3Y BOUVET IS.	06:32	17:02	06:58	16:30	07:27	15:59	07:48	15:39	08:06	15:27	08:10	15:29
3Y PETER 1ST IS.	13:29	22:40	14:21	21:42	15:27	20:34	16:32	19:31	NO:SR	NO:SS	NO:SR	NO:SS
4U UNITED NATIONS HQ	10:20	23:33	10:00	23:47	09:41	00:04	09:29	00:16	09:24	00:28	09:27	00:31
4X ISRAEL	03:17	16:12	03:01	16:22	02:47	16:34	02:39	16:43	02:36	16:52	02:38	16:56
5R TANANARIVE MALAGASY	02:59	14:41	03:03	14:32	03:08	14:23	03:13	14:20	03:19	14:20	03:22	14:22
5W WESTERN SAMOA	17:35	05:22	17:37	05:14	17:40	05:08	17:45	05:06	17:50	05:06	17:53	05:09
5Z NAIROBI KENYA	03:31	15:36	03:28	15:33	03:27	15:31	03:28	15:31	03:31	15:34	03:34	15:37
6W DAKAR SENEGAL	06:57	19:23	06:49	19:26	06:42	19:30	06:40	19:34	06:40	19:39	06:43	19:42
7O ADEN YEMAN P.DEM.	02:49	15:12	02:41	15:14	02:35	15:17	02:33	15:21	02:34	15:26	02:37	15:29
7P LESOTHO	04:25	15:51	04:34	15:37	04:43	15:24	04:52	15:17	05:00	15:15	05:03	15:18
8Q MALDIVE IS	01:08	13:21	01:04	13:20	01:01	13:20	01:00	13:22	01:02	13:25	01:05	13:28
9G ACCRA GHANA	05:54	18:08	05:49	18:08	05:46	18:08	05:46	18:10	05:48	18:14	05:50	18:17
9J LUSAKA ZAMBIA	04:14	16:01	04:16	15:53	04:20	15:46	04:25	15:43	04:30	15:44	04:33	15:46
9K KUWAIT	02:21	15:10	02:07	15:18	01:55	15:28	01:48	15:36	01:46	15:44	01:48	15:48
9N KATMANDU NEPAL	23:56	12:42	23:43	12:50	23:31	12:59	23:24	13:07	23:22	13:15	23:25	13:18
9Q KINSHASA ZAIRE	04:59	17:00	04:57	16:56	04:57	16:53	04:59	16:53	05:02	16:55	05:05	16:58
9V SINGAPORE	23:01	11:10	22:58	11:08	22:56	11:07	22:56	11:08	22:59	11:11	23:02	11:14
9X RWANDA	04:00	16:04	03:58	16:01	03:57	15:59	03:58	15:59	04:02	16:01	04:05	16:04
9Y TRINIDAD IS.	09:55	22:15	09:48	22:15	09:43	22:17	09:42	22:21	09:43	22:25	09:46	22:28

Prefix City Country	July 14 Sunrise	July 14 Sunset	July 28 Sunrise	July 28 Sunset	Aug 14 Sunrise	Aug 14 Sunset	Aug 28 Sunrise	Aug 28 Sunset	Sep 14 Sunrise	Sep 14 Sunset	Sept 28 Sunrise	Sept 28 Sunset
W7 Carson City NV	12:44	03:25	12:55	03:16	13:10	02:57	13:23	02:38	13:39	02:11	13:51	01:49
W7 Cheyenne WY	11:38	02:32	11:50	02:21	12:07	02:01	12:21	01:41	12:38	01:12	12:52	00:49
W7 Olympia WA	12:30	04:04	12:45	03:51	13:06	03:26	13:24	03:01	13:47	02:28	14:05	02:00
W7 Pheonix AZ	12:28	02:39	12:37	02:32	12:49	02:17	12:59	02:00	13:10	01:38	13:20	01:18
W7 Salem OR	12:39	03:57	12:52	03:45	13:12	03:22	13:28	02:59	13:49	02:27	14:05	02:01
W7 Salt Lake City UT	12:08	02:59	12:19	02:48	12:36	02:29	12:50	02:08	13:06	01:40	13:20	01:17
W8 Charleston WV	10:14	00:50	10:24	00:41	10:39	00:23	10:51	00:04	11:06	23:38	11:18	23:16
W8 Columbus OH	10:15	01:01	10:26	00:51	10:42	00:32	10:55	00:12	11:11	23:45	11:24	23:22
W8 Lansing MI	10:12	01:16	10:25	01:05	10:42	00:44	10:58	00:22	11:16	23:53	11:31	23:27
W9 Indianapolis IN	10:28	01:13	10:39	01:03	10:55	00:44	11:08	00:24	11:24	23:57	11:37	23:34
W9 Madison WI	10:31	01:36	10:43	01:25	11:01	01:04	11:16	00:42	11:35	00:12	11:50	23:47
W9 Springfield IL	10:42	01:27	10:53	01:17	11:09	00:58	11:22	00:38	11:38	00:11	11:51	23:48
XE1 MEXICO CITY MEXICO	12:06	01:19	12:11	01:15	12:17	01:06	12:20	00:56	12:24	00:41	12:26	00:29
XW VIENTIANE LOAS	22:42	11:49	22:46	11:46	22:51	11:38	22:54	11:28	22:57	11:15	22:59	11:03
YA KABUL AFGANISTAN	00:20	14:37	00:29	14:30	00:42	14:14	00:52	13:57	01:04	13:34	01:14	13:14
YB JAKARTA INDONESIA	23:05	10:52	23:05	10:54	23:01	10:55	22:56	10:54	22:47	10:51	22:40	10:48
ZD8 ASCENSION IS.	07:07	18:49	07:06	18:51	07:02	18:52	06:56	18:51	06:47	18:49	06:39	18:47
ZD9 TRISTAN DA CUNHA	07:56	17:53	07:48	18:02	07:32	18:15	07:15	18:26	06:52	18:38	06:31	18:49
ZF CAYMAN IS.	10:51	00:04	10:56	00:01	11:02	23:52	11:06	23:41	11:09	23:27	11:12	23:14
ZL1 AUCKLAND NZ	19:32	05:22	19:24	05:31	19:07	05:45	18:49	05:56	18:25	06:09	18:04	06:21
ZL4 DUNEDIN NZ	20:15	05:12	20:03	05:25	19:41	05:45	19:17	06:02	18:45	06:23	18:18	06:40
ZP ASUNCION PARAGUAY	10:35	21:16	10:30	21:22	10:19	21:30	10:07	21:36	09:49	21:43	09:34	21:48
ZS1 CAPETOWN S.AFRICA	05:49	15:55	05:42	16:03	05:27	16:15	05:11	16:25	04:48	16:36	04:29	16:46
ZS8 Pr.EDWARD & MARION	05:08	14:00	04:56	14:14	04:32	14:34	04:08	14:51	03:35	15:13	03:08	15:31
1S SPRATLY IS.	22:20	10:56	22:23	10:55	22:25	10:50	22:24	10:44	22:23	10:34	22:21	10:26
3V TUNIS TUNISIA	04:11	18:40	04:21	18:32	04:34	18:14	04:46	17:56	05:00	17:31	05:11	17:10
3Y BOUVET IS.	08:00	15:44	07:42	16:03	07:11	16:32	06:39	16:57	05:58	17:27	05:22	17:52
3Y PETER 1ST IS.	16:51	19:28	15:50	20:31	14:37	21:40	13:38	22:33	12:27	23:32	11:29	00:21
4U UNITED NATIONS HQ	09:37	00:27	09:48	00:17	10:04	23:57	10:18	23:37	10:34	23:09	10:48	22:45
4X ISRAEL	02:46	16:53	02:54	16:47	03:06	16:32	03:15	16:16	03:26	15:54	03:35	15:35
5R TANANARIVE MALAGASY	03:22	14:28	03:19	14:32	03:11	14:37	03:01	14:41	02:47	14:44	02:35	14:46
5W WESTERN SAMOA	17:54	05:14	17:51	05:18	17:44	05:21	17:36	05:23	17:24	05:24	17:13	05:24
5Z NAIROBI KENYA	03:37	15:40	03:37	15:41	03:35	15:40	03:32	15:37	03:26	15:32	03:20	15:27
6W DAKAR SENEGAL	06:48	19:43	06:52	19:41	06:55	19:34	06:57	19:25	06:58	19:13	06:59	19:03
7O ADEN YEMAN P.DEM.	02:41	15:30	02:45	15:28	02:48	15:22	02:49	15:14	02:49	15:03	02:49	14:53
7P LESOTHO	05:02	15:25	04:56	15:32	04:43	15:42	04:28	15:50	04:08	15:59	03:51	16:06
8Q MALDIVE IS	01:09	13:31	01:11	13:30	01:11	13:27	01:09	13:22	01:05	13:15	01:02	13:08
9G ACCRA GHANA	05:54	18:19	05:56	18:19	05:56	18:15	05:55	18:10	05:52	18:02	05:49	17:55
9J LUSAKA ZAMBIA	04:34	15:51	04:32	15:55	04:25	15:59	04:16	16:01	04:04	16:02	03:53	16:03
9K KUWAIT	01:55	15:46	02:03	15:40	02:12	15:27	02:20	15:13	02:29	14:53	02:36	14:36
9N KATMANDU NEPAL	23:31	13:17	23:38	13:12	23:48	12:59	23:55	12:46	00:03	12:27	00:09	12:10
9Q KINSHASA ZAIRE	05:08	17:01	05:08	17:03	05:05	17:03	05:00	17:01	04:52	16:57	04:46	16:54
9V SINGAPORE	23:05	11:17	23:06	11:17	23:05	11:15	23:02	11:11	22:57	11:05	22:53	10:59
9X RWANDA	04:07	16:07	04:07	16:09	04:05	16:08	04:01	16:05	03:55	16:00	03:49	15:56
9Y TRINIDAD IS.	09:50	22:30	09:53	22:28	09:55	22:23	09:55	22:16	09:54	22:06	09:53	21:57

Prefix City Country	Oct 14 Sunrise	Oct 14 Sunset	Oct 28 Sunrise	Oct 28 Sunset	Nov 14 Sunrise	Nov 14 Sunset	Nov 28 Sunrise	Nov 28 Sunset	Dec 14 Sunrise	Dec 14 Sunset	Dec 28 Sunrise	Dec 28 Sunset
W7 Carson City NV	14:07	01:24	14:21	01:04	14:40	00:47	14:55	00:38	15:10	00:37	15:17	00:43
W7 Cheyenne WY	13:09	00:22	13:25	00:02	13:45	23:42	14:01	23:33	14:16	23:31	14:24	23:37
W7 Olympia WA	14:27	01:28	14:47	01:04	15:12	00:39	15:32	00:27	15:49	00:22	15:57	00:29
W7 Pheonix AZ	13:31	00:57	13:43	00:41	13:58	00:27	14:11	00:21	14:24	00:21	14:31	00:28
W7 Salem OR	14:25	01:31	14:44	01:08	15:07	00:46	15:25	00:35	15:42	00:31	15:49	00:37
W7 Salt Lake City UT	13:37	00:51	13:52	00:30	14:12	00:11	14:28	00:02	14:43	00:00	14:51	00:07
W8 Charleston WV	11:33	22:52	11:47	22:33	12:06	22:16	12:20	22:08	12:35	22:06	12:42	22:13
W8 Columbus OH	11:40	22:56	11:56	22:36	12:15	22:18	12:31	22:09	12:45	22:07	12:53	22:14
W8 Lansing MI	11:49	23:00	12:06	22:38	12:28	22:18	12:45	22:07	13:00	22:05	13:08	22:11
W9 Indianapolis IN	11:53	23:09	12:08	22:49	12:27	22:31	12:42	22:22	12:57	22:21	13:05	22:27
W9 Madison WI	12:09	23:19	12:26	22:57	12:48	22:36	13:05	22:26	13:21	22:23	13:28	22:29
W9 Springfield IL	12:07	23:23	12:22	23:03	12:41	22:45	12:56	22:36	13:11	22:34	13:19	22:41
XE1 MEXICO CITY MEXICO	12:30	00:15	12:35	00:06	12:44	23:58	12:52	23:57	13:02	00:00	13:09	00:07
XW VIENTIANE LOAS	23:03	10:50	23:07	10:41	23:15	10:34	23:22	10:32	23:32	10:36	23:39	10:42
YA KABUL AFGANISTAN	01:27	12:52	01:39	12:35	01:55	12:20	02:08	12:13	02:21	12:13	02:29	12:19
YB JAKARTA INDONESIA	22:33	10:46	22:28	10:46	22:26	10:49	22:27	10:54	22:33	11:02	22:39	11:09
ZD8 ASCENSION IS.	06:30	18:46	06:25	18:47	06:22	18:50	06:23	18:56	06:29	19:04	06:35	19:11
ZD9 TRISTAN DA CUNHA	06:09	19:02	05:51	19:15	05:35	19:31	05:28	19:45	05:27	19:59	05:34	20:06
ZF CAYMAN IS.	11:16	23:01	11:21	22:51	11:29	22:44	11:37	22:42	11:47	22:45	11:54	22:52
ZL1 AUCKLAND NZ	17:40	06:35	17:22	06:48	17:05	07:06	16:57	07:20	16:55	07:35	17:01	07:42
ZL4 DUNEDIN NZ	17:48	07:01	17:23	07:20	16:59	07:45	16:46	08:04	16:42	08:22	16:47	08:30
ZP ASUNCION PARAGUAY	09:17	21:55	09:05	22:03	08:55	22:14	08:51	22:24	08:53	22:35	09:00	22:43
ZS1 CAPETOWN S.AFRICA	04:07	16:58	03:51	17:09	03:36	17:25	03:29	17:38	03:29	17:51	03:35	17:59
ZS8 Pr.EDWARD & MARION	02:36	15:53	02:11	16:13	01:47	16:38	01:34	16:58	01:29	17:16	01:35	17:24
1S SPRATLY IS.	22:20	10:18	22:21	10:12	22:24	10:09	22:30	10:10	22:38	10:15	22:45	10:22
3V TUNIS TUNISIA	05:25	16:47	05:38	16:29	05:56	16:12	06:10	16:04	06:24	16:04	06:32	16:10
3Y BOUVET IS.	04:43	18:23	04:10	18:51	03:36	19:26	03:16	19:52	03:06	20:15	03:11	20:24
3Y PETER 1ST IS.	10:20	01:20	09:18	02:17	07:56	03:40	NO:SR	NO:SS	NO:SR	NO:SS	NO:SR	NO:SS
4U UNITED NATIONS HQ	11:05	22:19	11:20	21:59	11:40	21:40	11:56	21:31	12:11	21:29	12:19	21:35
4X ISRAEL	03:46	15:14	03:57	14:59	04:12	14:45	04:24	14:39	04:37	14:39	04:45	14:45
5R TANANARIVE MALAGASY	02:21	14:50	02:12	14:55	02:04	15:03	02:03	15:11	02:06	15:21	02:13	15:28
5W WESTERN SAMOA	17:02	05:26	16:55	05:29	16:49	05:35	16:49	05:43	16:53	05:52	17:00	05:59
5Z NAIROBI KENYA	03:15	15:23	03:12	15:21	03:12	15:22	03:15	15:26	03:21	15:33	03:28	15:40
6W DAKAR SENEGAL	07:01	18:51	07:04	18:44	07:10	18:38	07:17	18:38	07:26	18:42	07:33	18:49
7O ADEN YEMAN P.DEM.	02:50	14:43	02:52	14:36	02:57	14:31	03:04	14:31	03:13	14:36	03:20	14:42
7P LESOTHO	03:32	16:16	03:18	16:25	03:05	16:39	03:00	16:50	03:01	17:03	03:07	17:10
8Q MALDIVE IS	00:59	13:01	00:59	12:57	01:01	12:56	01:05	12:58	01:12	13:04	01:19	13:11
9G ACCRA GHANA	05:47	17:48	05:46	17:43	05:49	17:42	05:53	17:44	06:01	17:49	06:08	17:56
9J LUSAKA ZAMBIA	03:41	16:05	03:33	16:09	03:27	16:15	03:26	16:23	03:30	16:32	03:37	16:39
9K KUWAIT	02:45	14:18	02:54	14:04	03:07	13:52	03:18	13:47	03:30	13:49	03:37	13:55
9N KATMANDU NEPAL	00:17	11:52	00:26	11:39	00:38	11:28	00:49	11:23	01:00	11:25	01:08	11:31
9Q KINSHASA ZAIRE	04:39	16:51	04:35	16:50	04:34	16:52	04:36	16:57	04:42	17:04	04:49	17:11
9V SINGAPORE	22:49	10:54	22:47	10:51	22:47	10:51	22:51	10:54	22:58	11:00	23:05	11:07
9X RWANDA	03:43	15:52	03:40	15:51	03:39	15:52	03:42	15:56	03:48	16:03	03:55	16:10
9Y TRINIDAD IS.	09:52	21:48	09:54	21:42	09:58	21:39	10:04	21:40	10:12	21:45	10:19	21:51

HOW THE NCDXF/IARU 14.1 MHZ BEACON NETWORK BEGAN

Shortly after the formation of the Northern California DX Foundation (NCDXF) in October 1972, the newly formed Board of Directors decided that the organization should expand its horizons to include something of a scientific nature in which all amateurs—DXers and non-DXers alike—could participate. NCDXF support for DXpeditions and overseas operations would be a priority because DXers of the world would be the major contributors to the Foundation. But we hoped to do more than just send radios and DXpeditions and print QSL cards.

We consulted our Scientific Advisor, Dr. O.G. "Mike" Villard, Jr., W6QYT, Professor of Electrical Engineering at Stanford University and Senior Research Scientist at Stanford Research Institute (now SRI International). Mike had an idea. He was concerned about the disappearance of fishing and other boats in Alaskan waters every year. He believed that if the circulation of the Arctic currents were better understood, searching rescue ships would have a clearer idea where to look, thus increasing the chance for finding small lost boats. To help solve this problem, Mike suggested the possibility that a floating beacon be dropped into these Alaskan currents. This could be tracked by amateurs around the world to monitor the drifting course of the beacons.

Mike had a friend with just such a drifting beacon which would transmit on 20 meters with 1 watt or 25 watts, and it was being tested in Washington, D.C. Mike arranged for his friend to turn on the beacon one Saturday morning, and we organized a listening group on 20 meters via the Northern California DX Club 2-meter network. The beacon was easily readable with 25 watts, and pretty good with just one watt. So even the 1-watt QRP transmission could be monitored and useful to amateurs some distance away.

There was One Big Problem with the drifting beacons: their cost of $25,000 each was about 25 times greater than NCDXF had in the treasury. In addition, the beacons were non-recoverable. The idea of a beacon remained appealing, however, and with further thought, the development of a series of relatively low-cost stationary beacons world-wide appeared possible. It would be much cheaper and would still work!

We set up a series of brown bag lunch meetings at SRI to explore possibilities. To do the heavy thinking, we recruited some of the fellows who had worked on Oscar I–IV: Chuck Towns, K6LFH, who was president of Project Oscar at the time; Lance Ginner; and Board Member Jim Maxwell, W6CF, who was always full of imagination and creative thoughts.

After a month or so of meetings, we agreed it would be possible to develop a world-wide beacon network. It would feature all beacons transmitting the same message, each about one minute in length, all on the same frequency, one after the other, and going around the world. At Mike's suggestion, we also planned to step down the power output of the beacons in 10 dB steps, beginning at 100 watts. The beacon would come on the air with 100 watts, sign the beacon callsign, then step down to each of four power levels, 100, 10, 1, 0.1 watt, and finally back to 100 watts for the sign-off call. Each power level would last about 10 seconds before automatically switching to the next level.

All this planning and daydreaming was just fine, but who was going to design and build this thing? We turned to Chuck Towns and he looked deep into the engineering talent of Project Oscar and came up with an enthusiastic, knowledgeable designer and builder, Jim Ouimet, K6OPO.

One seemingly small matter had to be addressed now, but it was potentially the biggest hurdle. We would need an FCC license! So we wrote a letter to Mr. A. Prose Walker, W4BW, then Chief of the Amateur Branch of the FCC. We received a prompt answer from him saying, essentially, he thought this was a good idea. The plan showed the creative ingenuity that amateurs had used in creating Oscar-1. It was a program that would be for the benefit and interest of all amateurs world-wide, and thus of interest to the WARC-79 planners (he expressed this sentiment personally later). He invited us to join as a member of the WARC-79 group which was beginning to develop the amateur agenda for that important international conference. The NCDXF/IARU World-Wide Beacon Network owes its existence to the early encouragement of Mr. A. Prose Walker.

Attending WARC-79 meetings in Washington offered the all-important opportunity to discuss with the FCC Amateur Branch engineers what requirements we would have to meet before submitting the proper application for an unmanned, automatic beacon on 14 MHz. One requirement was that we submit a contour map showing the beacon location, as well as the location of all amateur station operators in the San Francisco Bay Area who would be monitoring the beacon 24 hours a day. This was a precaution in case the beacon drifted off frequency, the keying mechanism failed, or anything else went wrong (the map requirement was the same as for early 2-meter repeaters). A lot of Northern California DX Club members did not realize they were now expected to have a receiver on 14.1 MHz day and night, and listen to it...continuously!

Meanwhile, back in Palo Alto, CA, Jim Ouimet was busy designing and building the beacon. He became so busy at work that he had to turn beacon construction over to a colleague. But the work proceeded and, on bench tests, did exactly what it was supposed to do.

The license arrived and we were assigned the call WB6ZNL, not exactly a nice, crisp, short beacon-type call, but it was a license and we were elated and grateful!

In 1979, the beacon was put in operation from a trailer on a low hill overlooking the Stanford University campus. It worked remarkably well, transmitting a one-minute message every 10 minutes for about two years. We received reports from all over the world telling of its reception. So the beacon was doing what it was supposed to do.

Now all we needed was to build eight or nine beacons and distribute them around the world. But there was another problem. Our beacon transmitter was very complicated to build and, we had to admit it, a real boat anchor. Also, Jim Ouimet was being sent world-wide by his company for extended periods. We definitely had a problem in manufacturing those other beacons.

About this time, Dave Lesson, W6QHS, came on the Board of Directors of NCDXF. We described the problem to Dave and he went to work in his lab. He came up with a solution: use a Kenwood TS-120 as the beacon transmitter and build a black box to control the entire system. Dave built the control unit and hooked it up to the TS-120 and, Voila!, we had a beacon transmitter that an amateur with an average build and strength could lift.

We now needed eight more beacons. Who was going to build them? Fortunately, the late Cam Pierce, K6RU, another NCDXF Board Member, took on the project with great enthusiasm. He had the control circuit boards designed and built, cabinets designed and made, cables fabricated, and the units tested. He turned on a real engineering production line.

The new beacons worked beautifully. We put up two quad loops at right angles, complete with a phasing box, designed by Mike Stahl, K6MYC, then at KLM Electronics. At about the same time, we received the call W6WX/B for the beacon. NCDXF had acquired the call after the untimely death of a well-known local DXer, Dave Baker, W6WX. That beacon was on the air almost continuously until 1990—when it was stolen from the trailer!

As Cam Pierce was building beacons, we began to contact potential beacon station operators spaced around the world. At the United Nations, we talked to Dr. Max de Hensler, HB9RS, "Mr. U.N. Amateur Radio." Max immediately said yes, he would like to operate a beacon there. Martti Laine, OH2BH, arranged for a beacon at the University of Helsinki and also in Madeira. Local DX Club friend Bruno Bienenfeld, AA6AD, introduced us to an astronomy professor, Dr. Ahron Slonim, 4X4FQ, at his alma mater, Tel Aviv University. Kan Mizoguchi, JA1BK, introduced the beacon idea to the JARL. We also contacted old DX friend ZS6DN for a good location in the Southern Hemisphere. And at Honolulu City College, we spoke with Professor Bob Jones, KH6O. Later we received approval from Radio Club Argentina to put a beacon in Buenos Aires. Here were eight groups ready to operate a beacon and join W6WX/B at Stanford to complete the first World-Wide Beacon Network.

These new beacons were unique. Each would transmit the same one-minute message in sequence one after the other on 14.1 MHz. The message was the same as before: callsign at 100 watts, then four 9-second dashes at power levels descending from 100 watts to 10 watts, to 1 watt, to 0.1 watt—then back to 100 watts to sign-off. This same message has been transmitted on 14.1 MHz by beacons for almost 14 years.

Beacons were distributed to the operators as they were completed and tested. They have all been in almost continuous operation since being put on the air. We have had two thefts, one at W6WX/B, the other at JA2IGY. Lightning struck a tree which crashed into the antenna at ZS6DN/B. A hurricane flattened the vertical at KH6O/B. Once in a great while something did go wrong with the beacon or power supply, but was repaired locally. But the TS-120s, in general, have been remarkably free of problems. This is a very good record, considering that the beacons have been on the air for between 10 to 12 years each.

The International Amateur Radio Union (IARU) had been interested in beacons on a world-wide basis for many years. In 1984, at an IARU Advisory Council meeting, Alberto Shaio, HK3DEU, then Secretary of Region 2 of IARU, had an idea. He suggested that a frequency and time-sharing network, as used in the NCDXF system, would be the best way to present beacons on a world-wide basis. We talked it over and have been working together ever since.

About four years ago, it was decided that the network should be expanded and up-graded to a multiband network. Also, we had ideas about expanding the number of beacons and making the entire system multiband. But back to the old problem—who would do the work?

Quite fortuitously, at a meeting of the Northern California Contest Club, this writer met Bob Fabry, N6EK, retired Professor of Computer Science at the University of California, Berkeley. Somehow we drifted into a conversation about beacons and Bob said he would be interested in building rather than programming for a while. I suggested he talk to Dave Lesson, W6QHS, who designed the present generation of beacons, and who just happened to be sitting at the next table. They immediately started drawing pictures on the table and closely collaborated over many months until Bob had a prototype. Thus was born the new generation of beacons.

We wanted to shorten the time of each beacon's transmission so we could increase the number of beacons without stretching listening time beyond listener attention span. So, Bob recorded beacon messages at various speeds, from about 10 to 20 seconds; that is, beacon call, then four short, power-stepping dashes only. He played the tape for the Directors of NCDXF, and we voted unanimously that 12 seconds would be about right. The same tape was played for a meeting of the Executive Committee of IARU Region 2. They agreed that 12-15 seconds was good.

Using the technology available in the TS-140, Bob constructed a unit to control the functions of band-switching and power-stepping the beacon. He also used the new Trimble Global Positioning System (GPS) receiver as a time control unit to assure accurate functions. Everything's state-of-the-art in this new system!

As this new beacon was being crafted, we went to work with the IARU to secure additional locations for the beacons. One big consideration was to increase the number of locations in the Southern Hemisphere. To date, Radio Club Peruano, Radio Club Venezuelano, the New Zealand Amateur Radio Transmitters and the Radio Club of Sri Lanka have accepted invitations to join the network. An invitation has also been extended to Australia. We hope someday to add a beacon in Central Asia, bringing to 15 the total network of beacons.

Frequencies were chosen for the five new bands after a survey of several months by Bob Knowles, ZL1BAD, and his world-wide crew at the IARU Monitoring Service. Frequencies chosen were 14.100-18.110-21.150-24.930- 28.200 MHz. We are quite aware that 14.1 MHz is in the middle of packet station QRM. However, W6WX/B is limited to that frequency because of our FCC license. Actually 14.100 MHz has been designated on the IARU band-plan as a "guarded" beacon frequency for many years. We are hopeful that packeteers will give a little up or down and keep 14.100 clear for the Network.

That is where we are today. Within a year or so, we hope to have the new fast Beacon Network on five bands. The listener can listen for 14 beacons transmitting around the world in about three minutes. Or he may monitor a single beacon, switching through five bands in a little over a minute.

We are grateful to the 14 Universities, National Societies and individuals who have volunteered to operate the beacons in this expanded network. You will be reading more about these operators as beacons are distributed to them during 1994.

It will be interesting to monitor the increase in HF band activity as the sunspot cycle passes through minimum and begins its climb back to DX glory!

Northern California DX Foundation/International Amateur Radio Union
14.100 MHz World-Wide Beacon Network

Minute	Callsign	Location
:00	4U1UN/B	United Nations Headquarters, NY
:01	W6WX/B	Stanford University, Palo Alto, CA.
:02	KH6O/B	Honolulu City College, HI
:03	JA2IGY/B	Japan
:04	4X6TU/B	Tel Aviv, Israel
:05	OH2B	Helsinki, Finland
:06	CT3B	Madeira Island
:07	ZS6DN/B	Irene, South Africa
:08	LU4AA	Buenos Aires, Argentina

58 Second Message Format

100Watts	QST DE W6WX/B BEACON
100Watts	-(9Seconds)
10Watts	-(9Seconds)
1Watt	-(9Seconds)
0.1Watt	-(9Seconds)
100Watts	W6WX/BSK

Provided by John G. Troster, W6ISQ, NCDXF Beacon Coordinator, IARU International Beacon Coordinator

10 METER BEACON LIST

Freq.	Call	Operation	LOCATION	NOTES
28.175	VE3TEN	C	OTTAWA, ONT.	10W, GP
28.191	VE6YF		EDMONTON, ALTA.	10W
28.195	IY4MROBOT		BOLOGNA, ITALY	20W, 5/8GP
28.200	GB3SX	C	CROWBOROUGH, ENGLAND	8W, DIPOLE
28.201	LU8ED		ARGENTINA	5W

28.202	KE5GYI		ARLINGTON, TX	5W, VERTICAL
28.2025	ZS5VHF		NATAL, RSA	5W, GP
28.204	DLIGI	C	GERMANY	100W, VERTDIPOLE
28.205	KA3OEM		MEADVILLE, PA	27W, YAGI/WEST
28.206	KJ4X		PICKENS, SC	2W, VERTICAL
28.2075	W8FKL	C	VENICE, FL	10W, VERT
28.208	WA1IOB	C	MARLBORO, MA	75W, VERT
28.209	NX2O	C	STATEN ISLAND, NY	10W, GP
28.210	3B8MS	C	MAURITIUS	GP
28.210	K4KMZ	I	ELIZABETHTOWN, KY	20W, VERT
28.210	KC4DPC	C	WILMINGTON, NC	4W, DIPOLE
28.212	EA6RCM		PALMA DE MALLORCA	4W, 5ELYAGINNE
28.2125	ZD9GI	C	GOUGH ISLAND	GP
28.213	PT7BCN	C	CEARA, BRAZIL	
28.216	GB3RAL	C	SLOUGH, ENGLAND	20W, GP
28.2175	WB9VMY	C	CALUMET, OK	2W, DIPOLE
28.218	W8UR	C	MACKINAC ISLAND, MI	0.5W, VERT
28.2185	PT8AA		RIO BRANCO, BRAZIL	5W, GP
28.2195	LU4XS		CAPE HORN, ARGENTINA	
28.220	5B4CY	C	CYPRUS	26W, GP
28.221	PY2GOB		SAN PAULO, BRAZIL	15W, VERT
28.222	W9UXO	C	NR CHICAGO, IL	10W, GP
28.2225	HG2BHA	C	TAPOLCA, HUNGARY	10W, GP
28.225	N6TWX	I	GRASS VALLEY, CA	30W, 3ELYAGI
28.225	KW7Y		EVERETT, WA	4W, OMNI
28.225	PY2AMI	C	SAO PAULO, BRAZIL	5W, DIOPOLE
28.2275	EA6AU	C	MALLORCA, BALEARIC IS	10W, 5/8GP
28.230	ZL2MHF	C	MT.CLMIE, NEW ZEALAND	50W, VERTDIPOLE
28.232	W7JPI	C	SONOITA, AZ	5W, 3ELYAGINE
28.233	KD4EC	C	JUPITER, FL	7W, GP
28.235	VP9BA	C	HAMILTON, BERMUDA	10W, GP
28.237	NV6A	C	SAN DIEGO, CA	0.5W, VERT
28.2375	LA5TEN	C	OSLO, NORWAY	10W, 5/8GP
28.2405	5Z4ERR	C	KIAMBU, KENYA	
28.244	WA6APQ	C	LONG BEACH, CA	30W, Vert
28.245	A92C		BAHRAIN	DIPOLENW/SE
28.2455	ZS1CTB	C	CAPETOWN, RSA	20W, 1/4VERT
28.246	N8KHE	C	MACKINAW, MI	0.050W, VERT
28.2475	EA2HB	I	SPAIN	6W, GP
28.248	K1BZ	C	BELFAST, ME	5W, VERTDIPOLE
28.2495	EA3JA		BARCELONA, SPAIN	
28.250	W3SV	C	ELVERSON, PA	10W, VERT
28.250	KØHTF	C	DES MOINES, IA	2W, GP
28.250	Z21ANB	C	BULAWAYO, ZIMBABWE	8W, GP
28.250	WA4SLT	I	HASTINGS, FL	20W, Vert
28.2505	4N3ZHK	C	MT. KUM, YUGOSLAVIA	1W, VERT
28.252	WJ7X	C	SEATTLE, WA	5W, RINGO
28.2525	OH2TEN		FINLAND	
28.255	LUIUG	G	RALPICO, ARGENTINA	5W, GP
28.2575	DKØTEN	C	ARBEITSGEN, GERMANY	40W, GP
28.258	WB4JHS	I	KISSIMMEE, FL	5W, VERT
28.259	WB9FVR	C	PEMBROKE PINES, FL	1W, DIPOLE
28.260	VK5WI	C	ADELAIDE, AUSTRALIA	10W, GP
28.262	VK2RSY	C	SYDNEY, NSW, AUSTRALIA	25W, GP
28.263	N6PEQ	C?	TUSTIN, CA	2W, HORZDIPOLE
28.264	VK6RWA	C	PERTH, WA, AUSTRALIA	
28.265	VK4RIK		CAIRNS, AUSTRALIA	
28.265	SV3AQR/B	C	AMALIAS, GREECE	4W, GP
28.266	VK6RTW	C	ALBANY, WA, AUSTRALIA	
28.266	KB4UPI	C	BIRMINGTON, AL	20W, 1/4VERT
28.268	VK8VF		DARWIN, AUSTRALIA	
28.2685	W9KFO	I	EATON, IL	0.750W, VERT
28.270	ZS6PW	C	PRETORIA, RSA	10W, 3ELYAGI
28.270	VK4RTL	C	TOWNSVILLE, QLD, AUSTRALIA	
28.2705	KF4MS	C	ST PETERSBURG, FL	5W
28.2725	9L1FTN	I	FREETOWN, SIERRALEONE	10W, VERTDIPOLE
28.2745	ZS1LA		STILL BAY, RSA	20W, 3ELYAGINW
28.275	AL7GQ	C	DENVER, CO	1W, LOOP
28.2755	N6RDX	I	STOCKTON, CA	20W, 3ELYAGI
28.277	DFØAAB	C	KIEL, GERMANY	10W, GP
28.280	LU8EB		ARGENTINA	5W
28.282	VE1MUF	C	FREDRICKTON, NB, CANADA	0.5W, DIPOLE

28.282	VE2HOT	C	BEACONSFIELD, QUE, CANADA	5W, VERTDIPOLE
28.2825	OKØEG	C	HRADECKRALOVE, CZECH	10W, DIPOLE
28.284	VP8ADE	C	ADELAIDE IS, NR ANTARCTICA	8W, VBEAMTOENGLAND
28.285	N2JNT	C	TROY, NY	1W, GP
28.286	KE2DI	NR	ROCHESTER, NY	2W, VERTDIPOLE
28.286	KK4M	C	LAS VEGAS, NV	5W, VERT
28.287	W8OMV	NR	ASHVILLE, NC	5W, GP
28.287	H44SI	C	SOLOMON IS	15W
28.288	W2NZH	I	MOORESTOWN, NJ	3WGP
28.290	SK5TEN		SWEDEN	5W, «_
28.290	VS6TEN	C	HONG KONG	10W, VERT
28.292	ZD8HF		ASCENSION ISLAND	
28.2925	LU2FFV		SAN JORGE, ARGENTINA	5W, GP
28.284	KEØUL		GREELY, CO	5WOmnivert
28.295	WC8E	I	CINCINNATI, OHIO	10W, RINGO
28.295	W3VD	C	LAUREL, MD	1, 5W, VERTDIPOLE
28.297	WA4DJS	I	FT LAUDERDALE, FL	30W, GP
28.3025	PT7AAC		FORTALEZA, BRAZIL	5W, GP-CODEPRACTICE
28.993	DFØANN	C	NUREMBERG, GERMANY	0.30W, 1-ELDELTALOOP

C=Continuous; I=Intermittent

Compiled by K2OLG, April 21, 1993
Copy supplied compliments of The DX Bulletin, Box 50 Fulton CA
95439 USA

6 METER BEACON LIST

FREQ	CALLSIGN	LOCATION	GRID	POWER
48.238-262	TV VIDEO	WESTERN EUROPE	JN18	KW+
49.500	"FM AUDIO"	SOUTH AMERICA	FJ24	KW
49.545	"RADIO"	SOUTH AMERICA	FJ24	KW
49.575	"RADIO"	COLUMBIA	FJ24	KW
49.580	"RADIO"	PUERTO RICO	FK68	*
49.740	TV VIDEO	EASTERN EUROPE	KN04	KW+
49.750	TV VIDEO	EASTERN EUROPE	KO59	KW+
49.760	TV VIDEO	EASTERN EUROPE	KO00	KW+
50.000	GB3BUX	ENGLAND	IO93	15
50.003	7Q7SIX	MALAWI	KH75	*
50.004	PJ2SIX	CURACAO ISL.	FK52	22
50.005	ZS2SIX	REP.OF SO.AFRICA	KF25	25
50.008	DX1HB	PHILLIPINES	PK04	20
50.008	HIØVHF	DOMINICAN REPUBLIC	FK58	*
50.008	KØGUV	MINNESOTA	EN26	18
50.008	XE2HWB	BAJA MEXICO	DL44	10
50.010	JA2IGY	JAPAN	PM84	10
50.011	VP2A	ANGUILLA	FK88	50
50.012	OZ4VM	DENMARK	JO46	10
50.014	9M6SMC	SABAH-EAST MALAYSIA	OJ51	*
50.014	CU3URA	AZORES	HM68	5
50.014	S55ZRS	SLOVENIA	JN76	10
50.015	PJ4B	BONAIRE ISL.	FK52	10
50.015	SZ2DH	GREECE	KM27	5
50.017	JA6YBR	JAPAN	PM51	50
50.018	V51VHF	NAMIBIA	JG87	60
50.019	CX1CCC	URUGUAY	GF15	5
50.019	P29BPL	PAPUA-NEW GUINEA	QI30	*
50.020	GB3SIX	WALES	IO73	100
50.021	OZ7IGY	DENMARK	JO55	30
50.0215	FR5SIX	REUNION ISL.	LG78	2
50.023	LXØSIX	LUXEMBOURG	JN39	5
50.0245	ZP5AA	PARAGUAY	GG14	5
50.025	OH1SIX	FINLAND	KP11	50
50.025	YV4AB	VENEZUELA	FK50	15
50.026	9H1SIX	MALTA	JM75	7
50.027	JA7ZMA	JAPAN	QM07	50
50.027	ZS6PW	REP.OF SO.AFRICA	KG44	*

50.028	XE2UZL	BAJA MEXICO	DM10	25
50.030	CTØWW	PORTUGAL	IN61	40
50.030	WD4KPD	NORTH CAROLINA	FM15	*
50.0325	ZD8VHF	ASCENSION ISL.	II22	40
50.033	LU8YYO	ARGENTINA	FF50	10
50.033	UL7GCC	KAZAKHSTAN	MN83	*
50.033	VE6MTR	ALBERTA	DO33	*
50.035	ZB2VHF	GIBRALTAR	IM76	50
50.036	UL8GDD	KAZAKHSTAN	MN83	*
50.039	FY7THF	FRENCH GUYANA	GJ35	100
50.040	KP4BZ	PUERTO RICO	FK78	*
50.040	SV1SIX	GREECE	KM17	30
50.040	VO1ZA	NEWFOUNDLAND	GN37	1
50.042	GB3MCB	ENGLAND	IO70	14
50.042	YV5ZZ	VENEZUELA	FK60	*
50.043	ZL3MHF	NEW ZEALAND	RE66	20
50.045	JD1BFI	OGASAWARA ISL.	QL17	5
50.045	JR6YAG	JAPAN	PL36	20
50.045	OX3VHF	GREENLAND	GP60	20
50.046	VK8RAS	AUSTRALIA	PG66	15
50.0465	4N1SIX	YUGOSLAVIA	KN04	*
50.048	FX4SIX	FRANCE	JN06	10
50.048	JA7YYL	JAPAN	QM08	1
50.050	FO5DR	TAHITI ISL.	BH52	50
50.050	GB3NHQ	ENGLAND	IO91	15
50.050	VE7BEE	BRITISH COLUMBIA	DN09	10
50.050	ZS6DN	REP.OF SO.AFRICA	KG44	100
50.051	LA7SIX	NORWAY	JP99	20
50.052	P43AS	ARUBA	FK52	*
50.052	Z21SIX	ZIMBABWE	KH52	*
50.054	JA5FFJ	JAPAN	PM63	3
50.054	OZ6VHF	DENMARK	JO57	25
50.054	VK3SIX	AUSTRALIA	QF02	10
50.057	TF3SIX	ICELAND	HP94	15
50.057	VK7RSB	AUSTRALIA	QE37	100
50.057	VK8VF	AUSTRALIA	PH57	25
50.058	VK4RGG	AUSTRALIA	QG62	6
50.059	VE3UBL	ONTARIO	FN03	10
50.060	GB3RMK	SCOTLAND	IO77	40
50.060	K4TQR	ALABAMA	EM63	5
50.060	PY1AA	BRAZIL	GG87	2
50.060	PY2AA	BRAZIL	GG66	15
50.060	W5VAS	LOUISIANA	EM50	10
50.061	WBØRMO	NEBRASKA	EN10	100
50.062	KH6HME	HAWAII	BK29	20
50.062	WA8HTL	MICHIGAN	EN82	*
50.062	WA8R	KENTUCKY	EM79	1
50.062	WB2MAI	NEW JERSEY	FN30	*
50.0625	GB3NGI	NORTHERN IRELAND	IO65	25
50.063	KB6BKN	CALIFORNIA	CM88	3
50.063	W3VD	MARYLAND	FM19	10
50.064	GB3LER	SHETLAND ISLS.	IP90	45
50.064	KH3AF	JOHNSTON ISL.	AK56	15
50.064	VE5US	SASKATCHEWAN	DO61	*
50.064	WD7Z	ARIZONA	DM24	75
50.065	KAØCND/IJR	COLORADO	DM79	20
50.0655	GB3IOJ	JERSEY-CHANNEL ISL.	IN89	10
50.066	KB5KYB	MISSISSIPPI	EM50	4
50.066	VK6RPR	AUSTRALIA	OF78	10
50.066	WB4AEG	GEORGIA	EM74	*
50.067	KA5FYI	TEXAS	EM10	2
50.067	KD4LP	TENNESSEE	EM86	5
50.067	N5OQT	LOUISIANA	EM40	*
50.067	N7DB	OREGON	CN85	10
50.067	OH9SIX	FINLAND	KP36	50
50.067	WA1OJB	MAINE	FN54	30

50.067	WZ8D	OHIO	EM79	6
50.069	K6FV	CALIFORNIA	CM87	100
50.069	N4XND	VIRGINIA	FM17	*
50.069	W4RFR	TENNESSEE	EM66	2
50.069	W7US	ARIZONA	DM42	2
50.070	EA3VHF	SPAIN	JN01	1
50.070	KØHTF	IOWA	EN31	2
50.070	K4AUG	VIRGINIA	EM97	1
50.070	KB4UPI	ALABAMA	EM63	5
50.070	KK4M/7	NEVADA	DM36	5
50.070	KM4ME	ALABAMA	EM65	10
50.070	N4MW	TENNESSEE	EM55	4
50.070	W2CAP/1	MASSACHUSETTS	FN41	15
50.070	WA7ECY	OREGON	CN85	10
50.071	WØVD	MISSOURI	EM27	10
50.072	KS2T	NEW JERSEY	FM29	10
50.072	KW2T	NEW YORK	FN13	1
50.072	N5DUH	LOUISIANA	EM32	*
50.072	WB9STR	ILLINOIS	EN61	5
50.073	KH6HI	HAWAII	BL01	80
50.073	VE1MQ	NEW BRUNSWICK	FN65	5
50.073	WB4WTC	VIRGINIA	FM06	10
50.074	K5ZXE	OKLAHOMA	EM14	*
50.074	NN7K	OREGON	CN92	1
50.074	WB5DSH	OKLAHOMA	EM15	30
50.075	EA8SIX	CANARY ISL.	IL28	10
50.075	NL7XM/2	NEW YORK	FN30	1/10
50.075	PY2AMI	BRAZIL	GG67	5
50.075	VS6SIX	HONG KONG	OL72	10
50.075	WA4IOB	GEORGIA	EM73	2
50.075	WB4OSN	FLORIDA	EL96	3
50.076	K7IHZ	ARIZONA	DM43	10
50.076	KL7GLK/3	MARYLAND	FM18	1
50.076	LU1DMA	ARGENTINA	FF57	10
50.077	NØLL	KANSAS	EM09	21
50.077	WB2CUS/3	PENNSYLVANIA	FN10	1
50.0775	VK4BRG	AUSTRALIA	QG48	3
50.078	OD5SIX	LEBANON	KM75	10
50.078	PT7BCN	BRAZIL	HI06	5
50.078	W8UR	MICHIGAN	EN75	2
50.079	JX7DFA	JAN MAYEN ISL.	IQ51	10
50.079	TI2NA	COSTA RICA	EJ79	20
50.079	W6SKC/7	ARIZONA	DM41	5
50.080	"FM AUDIO"	MALI-WEST AFRICA	IK62	10 KW
50.080	SK6SIX	SWEDEN	JO57	1/10
50.080	WB4OOJ	FLORIDA	EL87	12
50.081	LU3EMK	ARGENTINA	GF05	*
50.082	HC8SIX	GALAPAGOS ISLS.	EI59	4
50.084	3D2FJ	FIJI ISLS.	RH82	20
50.084	WA4NTF	GEORGIA	EM81	*
50.086	VP2MO	MONTSERRAT ISL.	FK86	10
50.0865	LU1MA	ARGENTINA	FF57	8
50.088	VE2TWO	QUEBEC	FO13	15
50.092	HC2FG	ECUADOR	FI97	50
50.093	CN6VHF	MOROCCO	IM64	8
50.094	TU2VHF	IVORY COAST	IJ76	*
50.095	PY5XX	BRAZIL	GG54	50
50.098	LU2MFO	ARGENTINA	FF97	4
50.099	"FM AUDIO"	BORDEAUX,FRANCE	IN95	10KW
50.100	CTØSMB	PORTUGAL	IN61	*
50.100	XE3WMA	YUCATAN,MEXICO	EL51	*
50.120	FC1JUC	FRANCE	JN35	*
50.150	"FM AUDIO"	MONACO	JN33	10KW

Compiled by K1TOL and K1GPJ August 1993

** Information not available at press time.*

OTHER HF BEACONS

The International Telecommunication Union (ITU) has activated a new HF beacon transmittter in Sveio, Norway, as part of a worldwide HF field strength measurement campaign. The new beacon was provided by the Norwegian Telecommunications Regulatory Authority and Norwegian Telecom, and joins a similar beacon station on the air from Australia since 1990.

LN2A operates 24 hours a day, 1 kW on CW to a 5-band trap vertical antenna. VK4IPS in Brisbane, Australia also operates 24 hours a day, running 1 kW to an omni-directional spiral antenna.

The schedule of frequencies (in kHz) for both is as follows:

Time (min past hr)	VK4IPS	LN2A
00, 20, 40	5470	14405
04, 24, 44	7870	20945
08, 28, 48	10407	5470
12, 32, 52	14405	7870
16, 36, 56	20945	10407

A new beacon began operation May 13, 1993 from Cape Prince of Wales, Alaska (67N, 168W). Transmissions are narrowband CW and FSK. Its call sign is NAF and it runs 100 watts to a 3-band fan dipole on the following schedule (all frequencies in kHz):

Time (min past hr)	Frequency
00, 01	5604
20, 21	11004
40, 41	16804

The beacon will be monitored by government facilities in Fairbanks, Alaska; Seattle, Washington; State College, Pennsylvania; and San Diego, California. The project's sponsor is the Naval Security Group Command in Washington, D.C.

A government spokesman said the project is "purely scientific." The purpose of the project is described as to provide a "rigorous verification" of field strength models done by HF propagation prediction programs like IONCAP which are used, for example, to generate the predictions published each month in *QST*.

Reception reports are encouraged and will be acknowledged with a colorful QSL card. Send them to:

Bob Rose, K6GKU, Code 54, NRaD Division, NCCOSC, 271 Catalina Blvd., San Diego CA 92152; or...

Dr. Gus Lott, KR4K, Code GX, COMNAVSECGRU, 3801 Nebraska Ave NW, Washington DC 20393

Another beacon, from Rarotonga in the South Cook Islands, was scheduled to go on the air in the fall of 1993, on low VHF frequencies as well as the three NAF frequencies.

WWV/WWVH/WWVB INFORMATION

The following is excerpted from NIST Time and Frequency Services [Special Publication 432 (Revised 1990)]. A complete copy is available from NIST.

Abstract

NIST Time and Frequency Services [Special Publication 432 (Revised 1990)] is a revision of SP 432, last published in 1979. It describes services available, as of December 1990, from NIST radio stations WWV, WWVH, and WWVB; from GOES satellites; from Loran-C; by telephone (voice and modem); and from the NIST Frequency Measurement Service.

Key words: broadcast of standard frequencies; computer time setting; frequency calibrations; GOES satellite; high frequency; low frequency; satellite time code; shortwave; standard frequencies; time calibrations; time signals.

Introduction

Precise time and frequency information is needed by electric power companies, radio and television stations, telephone companies, air traffic control systems, participants in space exploration, computer networks, scientists monitoring data of all kinds, and navigators of ships and planes. These users need to compare their own timing equipment to a reliable, internationally recognized standard. The National Institute of Standards and Technology (NIST), formerly the National Bureau of Standards, provides this standard for most users in the United States.

NIST began broadcasting time and frequency information from radio station WWV in 1923. Since then, NIST has expanded its time and frequency services to meet the needs of a growing number of users. NIST time and frequency services are convenient, accurate, and easy to use. They contribute greatly to the nation's space and defense programs, to manufacturers, and to transportation and communications. In addition, NIST services are widely used by the general public.

Broadcast services include radio signals from NIST radio stations WWV, WWVH, and WWBV; the GOES satellites, and Loran-C. Services are also available using telephone voice and data lines. This is a guide to these services.

Shortwave Services—WWV and WWVH

NIST operates two high-frequency (shortwave) radio stations, WWV and WWVH. WWV is in Ft. Collins, CO, and WWVH is in Kauai, HI. Both stations broadcast continuous time and frequency signals on 2.5, 5, 10, and 15 MHz. WWV also broadcasts on 20 MHz. All frequencies provide the same information. Although radio reception conditions in the high-frequency band vary greatly with factors such as location, time of year, time of day, the particular frequency being used, atmospheric and ionospheric propagation conditions, and the type of receiving equipment used, at least one frequency should be usable at all times. As a general rule, frequencies above 10 MHz work best in the daytime, and the lower frequencies work best at night.

Summary of Radio Broadcast Services

Characteristics & Services:	WWV		WWVH		WWVB
Date Service Began	March 1923		November 1948		July 1956
Geographical Coordinates	40° 40' 49.0" N 105° 02' 27.0" W		21° 59' 26.0" N 159° 46' 00.0" W		40° 40' 28.3" N 105° 02' 39.5" W
Standard Carrier Frequencies	2.5 & 20 MHz	5, 10, & 15 MHz	2.5 MHz	5, 10, & 15 MHz	60 kHz
Power	2500 W	10,000 W	5000 W	10,000 W	13,000 W
Standard Audio Frequencies	440 (A above middle C), 500, & 600 Hz				—
Time Intervals	1 pulse/s; minute mark; hour mark				s; min.
Time Signals: Voice	Once per minute				—
Time Signals: Code	BCD code on 100-Hz subcarrier, 1 puls/s				BCD code
UT1 Corrections	UT1 corrections are broadcast with an accuracy of ±0.1 s				
Special Announcements	Omega Reports, Geoalerts, Marine Storm Warnings, Global Positioning System Status Reports				—

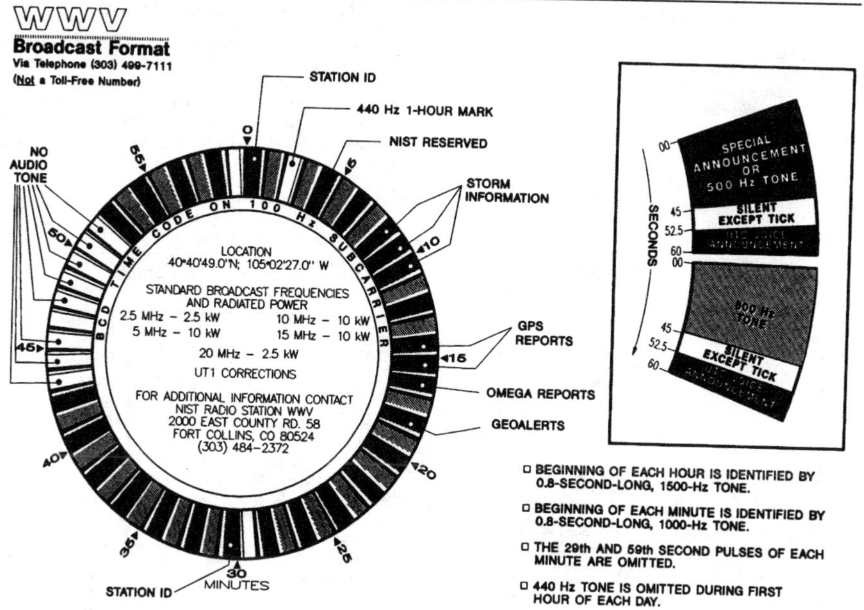

Figure 1

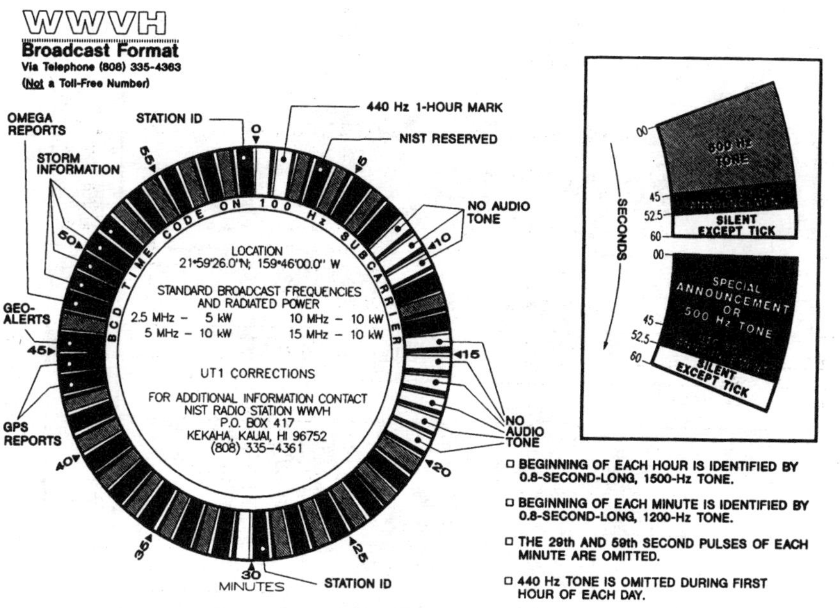

Figure 2

Services provided by WWV and WWVH include:

- Time announcements
- Standard time intervals
- Standard frequencies
- UT1 time corrections
- BCD time code
- Geophysical alerts
- Marine storm warnings
- OMEGA Navigation System status reports
- Global Positioning System (GPS) status reports

Figures 1 and 2 show the hourly broadcast schedules of these services along with station location, radiated power, and details of the modulation.

Accuracy and Stability

WWV and WWVH are referred to the primary NIST Frequency Standard and related NIST atomic time scales in Boulder, CO. The frequencies as transmitted are accurate to about 1 part in 100 billion (1×10^{-11}) for frequency and about 0.01 ms for timing. The day-to-day deviations are normally less than 1 part in 1, 000 billion (1×10^{-12}). However, the received accuracy is far less due to various propagation effects. The usable received accuracy is about 1 part in 10 million for frequency (1×10^{-7}) and about 1 ms for timing.

Radiated Power, Antennas, and Modulation

WWV and WWVH radiate 10, 000 W on 5, 10, and 15 MHz. The radiated power is lower on the other frequencies: WWV radiates 2500 W on 2.5 and 20 MHz while WWVH radiates 5000 W on 2.5 MHz and does not broadcast on 20 MHz.

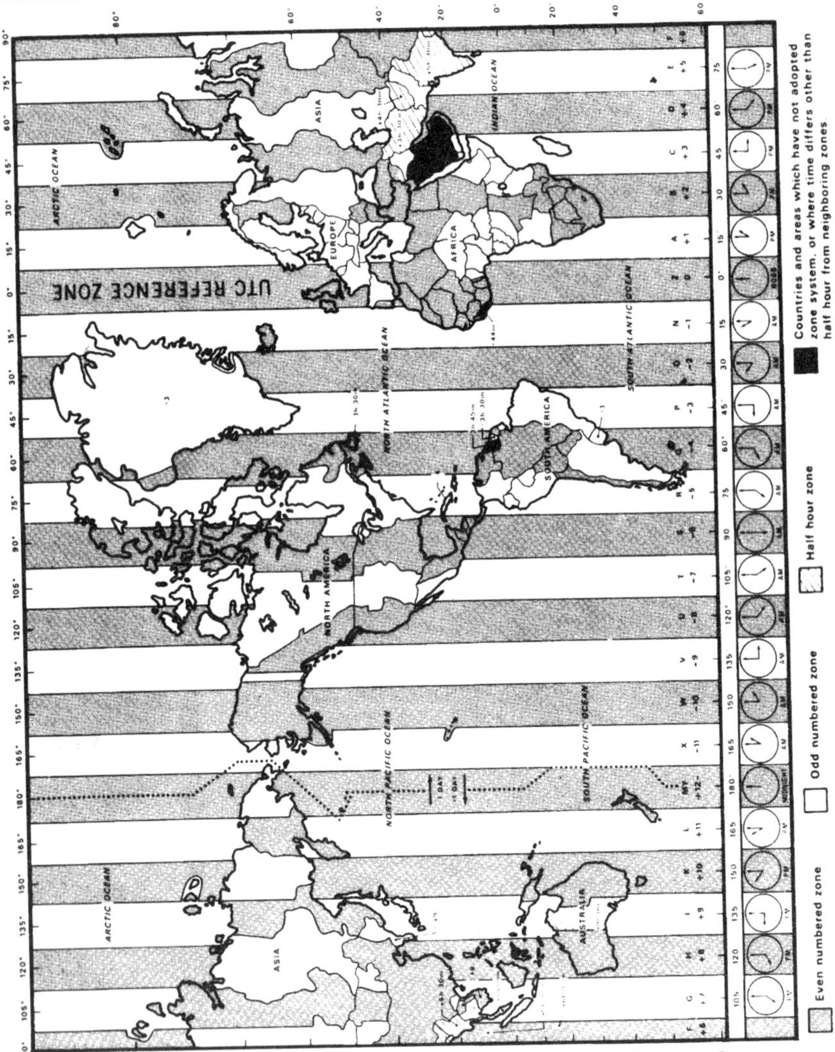

Figure 3

The WWV antennas are half-wave dipoles that radiate omnidirectional patterns. The 2.5-MHz antenna at WWVH is also of this type. The other antennas at WWVH are phased vertical half-wave dipole arrays. They radiate a cardioid pattern with the maximum gain pointed toward the west.

Both stations use double sideband amplitude modulation. The modulation level is 50 percent for the steady tones, 25 percent for the BCD time code, 100 percent for the seconds pulses and the minute and hour markers, and 75 percent for the voice announcements.

Time Announcements

Voice announcements are made from WWV and WWVH once every minute. Since both stations can be heard in some locations, a man's voice is used on WWV, and a woman's voice is used on WWVH to reduce confusion. The WWVH announcement occurs first, at about 15 s before the minute. The WWV announcement follows at about 7.5 s before the minute. Though the announcements occur at different times, the tone markers are transmitted at the exact same time from both stations. However, they may not be received at exactly the same instant due to differences in the propagation delays from the two station sites.

The announced time is "Coordinated Universal Time" (UTC). UTC was established by international agreement in 1972, and is governed by the International Bureau of Weights and Measures (BIPM) in Paris, France. Coordination with the international UTC time scale keeps NIST time signals in close agreement with signals from other time and frequency stations throughout the world.

UTC differs from your local time by a specific number of hours. The number of hours depends on the number of time zones between your location and the location of the zero meridian (which passes through Greenwich, England). When local time changes from Daylight Saving to Standard Time, or vice versa, UTC does not change. However, the difference between UTC and local time does change—by 1 hour. Use the chart of world time zones (figure 3) to find out how many hours to add to or subtract from UTC to obtain your local standard time. If DST is in effect at your location, subtract 1 hour less in the U.S. than shown on the chart. Thus, Eastern Daylight Time (EDT) is only 4 hours behind UTC, not 5 as shown on the chart for EST.

UTC is a 24-hour clock system. The hours are numbered beginning with 00 hours at midnight through 12 hours at noon to 23 hours and 59 minutes just before the next midnight.

The international agreement that established UTC in 1972 also specified that occasional adjustments of exactly 1 s will be made to UTC so that UTC should never differ from a particular astronomical time scale, UT1, by more than 0.9 s. This was done as a convenience for some time-broadcast users, such as boaters using celestial navigation, who need to know time that is based on the rotation of the Earth. These occasional 1-s adjustments are known as "leap seconds." When deemed necessary by the International Earth Rotation Service in Paris, France, the leap seconds are inserted into UTC, usually at the end of June or at the end of December, making that month 1 s longer than usual. Typically, a leap second has been inserted at intervals of 1 to 2 years.

Standard Time Intervals

The most frequent sounds heard on WWV and WWVH are the seconds pulses. These pulses are heard every second except on the 29th and 59th seconds of each minute. The first pulse of each hour is an 800-ms pulse of 1500 Hz. The first pulse of each minute is an 800-ms pulse of 1000 Hz at WWV and 1200 Hz at WWVH. The remaining seconds pulses are short audio bursts (5-ms pulses of 1000 Hz at WWV and 1200 Hz at WWVH) that sound like the ticking of a clock.

Each seconds pulse is preceded by 10 ms of silence and followed by 25 ms of silence. The silence makes it easier to pick out the pulse. The total 40-ms protected zone around each seconds pulse is shown in figure 4.

Standard Audio Frequencies

In alternate minutes during most of each hour, 500-Hz or 600-Hz audio tones are broadcast. A 440-Hz tone (the musical note A above middle C) is broadcast once each hour. In addition to being a musical standard, the 440-Hz tone provides an hourly marker for chart recorders and other automated devices. The 440-Hz tone is omitted, however, during the first hour of each UTC day. See figures 1 and 2 for further details.

Silent Periods

The silent periods are without tone modulation. However, the carrier frequency, seconds pulses, time announcements, and the 100-Hz BCD time code continue during the silent periods. In general, one station will not broadcast an audio tone while the other station is broadcasting a voice message.

On WWV, the silent period extends from 43 to 46 and from 47 to 52 minutes after the hour. WWVH has two silent periods; from 8 to 11 minutes after the hour, and from 14 to 20 minutes after the hour. Minutes 29 and 59 on WWV and minutes 00 and 30 on WWVH are also silent.

BCD Time Code

WWV and WWVH continuously broadcast a binary coded decimal (BCD) time code on a 100-Hz subcarrier. The time code presents UTC information in serial fashion at a rate of 1 pulse per second. The information carried by the time code includes the current minute, hour, and day of the year. The time code also contains the 100-Hz frequency from the subcarrier. The 100-Hz frequency may be used as a standard with the same accuracy as the audio frequencies.

At the time of publication of this revision of Special Publication 432 (late 1990), further changes to the content of the WWV and WWVH time codes are in the planning stage. The proposed changes will not affect currently encoded information, but will add information in the form of the last two digits of the current year, improved indicators for when Daylight Saving Time is in effect, and a warning for the insertion of a leap second at the end of the current month.

UT1 Time Corrections

The UTC time scale broadcast by WWV and WWVH meets the needs of most users. UTC runs at an almost perfectly constant rate, since its rate is based on cesium atomic frequency standards. Somewhat surprisingly, some users need time less stable than UTC but related to the rotation of the Earth. Applications such as celestial navigation, satellite observations of the Earth, and some types of surveying require time referenced to the rotational position of the Earth. These users rely on the UT1 time scale. UT1 is derived by astronomers who monitor the speed of the Earth's rotation.

You can obtain UT1 time by applying a correction to the UTC time signals broadcast from WWV and WWVH. UT1 time corrections are included in the WWV and WWVH broadcasts at two levels of accuracy. First, for those users only needing UT1 to within 1 s, occasional corrections of exactly 1 s are inserted into the UTC time scale. These corrections, called leap seconds, keep UTC within ±0.9 s of UT1. Leap seconds are coordinated under international agreement by the International Earth Rotation Service in

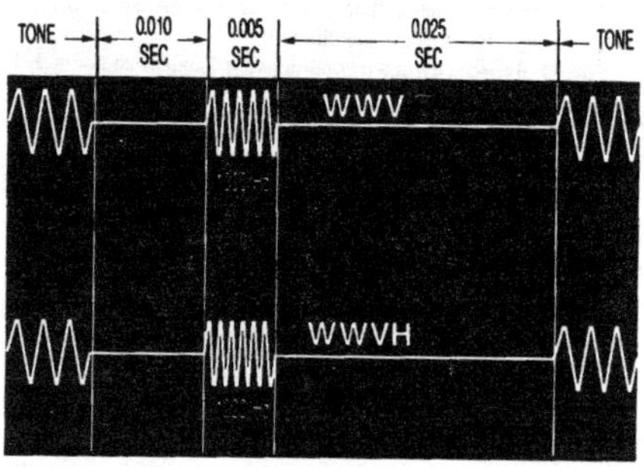

Figure 4

Paris, France. Leap seconds can be either positive or negative, but so far, only positive leap seconds have been needed. A positive leap second is normally added every 1 or 2 years, usually on June 30 or December 31.

The second level of correction is for the small number of users needing UT1 accurate to within 0.1 s. These corrections are encoded into the broadcasts by using doubled ticks during the first 16 s of each minute. The amount of correction (in tenths of 1 s) is determined by counting the number of successive doubled ticks heard each minute. The sign of the correction depends on whether the doubled ticks are in the first 8 s of the minute or in the second 8 s. If the doubled ticks are in the first 8 s (1–8) the sign is positive, and if they are in the second 8 s (9–16) the sign is negative. For example, if ticks 1, 2, and 3 are doubled, the correction is "plus" 0.3 s. This means that UT1 equals UTC + 0.3 s. If UTC is 8:45:17, then UT1 is 8:45:17.3. If ticks 9, 10, 11, and 12 are doubled, the correction is "minus" 0.4 s. If UTC is 8:45:17, then UT1 is 8:45:16.6. An absence of doubled ticks indicates that the current correction is 0.

Official Announcements

Announcement segments 45 s long are available by subscription to other Federal agencies (see figures 1 & 2). These segments are used for public service messages. The accuracy and content of these messages is the responsibility of the originating agency.

For information about the availability of these segments, contact the NIST Time and Frequency Division.

The segments currently in use (late 1990) are described below. Since these are subject to change from time to time, contact NIST for more current status information.

OMEGA Navigation System Status Reports—The OMEGA Navigation System status reports are voice announcements broadcast on WWV at 16 minutes after the hour, and on WWVH at 47 minutes after the hour. The OMEGA Navigation System consists of eight radio stations transmitting in the 10- to 14-kHz frequency band. These stations serve as international aids to navigation. The status reports are updated as necessary by the U.S. Coast Guard.

For more information about the OMEGA Navigation System or these announcements, contact: Commanding Officer, U.S. Coast Guard OMEGA Navigation System Center, 7323 Telegraph Road, Alexandria, VA 22310-3998; telephone (703) 866-3800.

Geophysical Alerts—Current geophysical alerts (Geo-alerts) are broadcast in voice from WWV at 18 minutes after the hour and from WWVH at 45 minutes after the hour. The messages are less than 45 s in length and are updated every 3 hours (typically at 0000, 0300, 0600, 0900, 1200, 1500, 1800, and 2100 UTC). Hourly updates are made when necessary.

Part A of the message gives the solar-terrestrial indices for the day: specifically the 1700 UTC solar flux from Ottowa, Canada, at 2800 MHz, the estimated A-index for Boulder, CO, and the current Boulder K-index.

Part B gives the solar-terrestrial conditions for the previous 24 hours.

Part C gives optional information on current conditions that may exist (that is, major flares, proton or polar cap absorption [PCA] events, or stratwarm conditions).

Part D gives the expected conditions for the next 24 hours. For example:

A) "Solar-terrestrial indices for 26 October follow: Solar flux 173 and estimated Boulder A-index 20; repeat: Solar flux one-seven-three and estimated Boulder A-index two-zero.The Boulder K-index at 1800 UTC on 26 October was four; Repeat: four."

B) "Solar-terrestrial conditions for the last 24 hours follow:
Solar activity was high.
Geomagnetic field was unsettled to active."

C) "A major flare occurred at 1648 UTC on 26 October. A satellite proton event and PCA are in progress."

D) "The forecast for the next 24 hours follows:
Solar activity will be moderate to high. The geomagnetic field will be active."

Definitions

1. Solar Activity is defined as transient perturbations of the solar atmosphere as measured by enhanced x-ray emission, typically associated with flares. Five standard terms are used to describe solar activity:

Very Low:	X-ray events less than C-class.
Low:	C-class x-ray events.
Moderate:	isolated (1 to 4) M-class x-ray events.
High	several (5 or more) M-class x-ray events, or isolated (1 to 4) M5 or greater x-ray events.
Very High	several M5 or greater x-ray events.

2. The geomagnetic field experiences natural variations classified quantitatively into six standard categories depending upon the amplitude of the disturbance. The Boulder K- and estimated A-indices determine the category according to the following table:

Condition	Range of A-index	Typical K-indices
Quiet	$0 \le A < 8$	usually no K-indices > 2
Unsettled	$8 \le A < 16$	usually no K-indices > 3
Active	$16 \le A < 30$	a few K-indices of 4
Minor storm	$30 \le A \le 50$	K-indices mostly 4 and 5
Major storm	$50 \le A < 100$	some K-indices 6 or greater
Severe storm	$100 \le A$	some K-indices 7 or greater.

3. Solar Flares are classified by their x-ray emission as:

Peak Flux Range (1–8 Angstroms)

Class	SI system (W m^{-2})	cgs system (erg cm^{-2} s^{-1})
A	Ø < 10-7	Ø<10-4
B	10-7 ≤ Ø < 10-6	10-4 ≤ Ø < 10-3
C	10-6 ≤ Ø < 10-5	10-3 ≤ Ø < 10-1
M	10-5 ≤ Ø < 10-4	10-2 ≤ Ø < 10-1
X	10-4 ≤ Ø	10-1 ≤ Ø

The letter designates the order of magnitude of the peak value. Following the letter the measured peak value is given. For descriptive purposes, a number from 1.0 to 9.9 is appended to the letter designation. The number acts as a multiplier. For example, a C3.2 event indicates an x-ray burst with peak flux of 3.2 x 10^{-6} Wm^{-2}.

Forecasts are usually issued only in terms of the broad C, M, and X categories. Since x-ray bursts are observed as a full-Sun value, bursts below the x-ray background level are not discernible. The background drops to class A level during solar minimum; only bursts that exceed B1.0 are classified as x-ray events. During solar maximum the background is often at the class M level, and therefore class A, B, and C x-ray bursts cannot be seen. Data are from the NOAA GOES satellites, monitored in real time at the NOAA Space Environment Services Center. Bursts greater than 1.2 x 10^{-3} Wm^{-2} may saturate the GOES detectors. If saturation occurs estimated peak flux values are reported.

4. The remainder of the report is as follows:

Major Solar Flare = flare which produces some geophysical effect, usually flares that have x-rays ≥ M5 class.

Proton Flare = protons by satellite detectors (or polar cap observed in time association with H-alpha flare.

Satellite Level Proton Event = proton enhancement detected by Earth-orbiting satellites with measured particle flux of at least 10 protons $cm^{-2}s^{-1}sr^{-1}$ at ≥ 10 MeV.

Polar Cap Absorption = proton-induced absorption ≥ 2 dB daytime, 0.5 dB night, as measured by a 20-MHz riometer located within the polar cap.

Stratwarm = reports of stratospheric warmings in the high latitude regions of the winter hemisphere of the Earth associated with gross distortions of the normal circulation associated with the winter season.

To hear these Geophysical Alert messages by telephone (at any minute of the hour, but without time information), dial (303) 497-3235.

Inquiries regarding these messages should be addressed to: Space Environment Services Center, NOAA R/E/SE2, 325 Broadway, Boulder, CO 80303-3328. Or call (303) 497-5127.

Marine Storm Warnings—Marine storm warnings are broadcast for the marine areas that the United States has warning responsibility for under international agreement. The storm warning information is provided by the National Weather Service. Storm warnings for the Atlantic and eastern North Pacific are broadcast by voice on WWV at 8, 9, and 10 minutes after the hour. Storm warnings for the western, eastern, southern, and north Pacific are broadcast by WWVH at 48, 49, 50, and 51 minutes after the hour. An additional segment (at 11 minutes after the hour on WWV and at 52 minutes after the hour on WWVH) is used occasionally if there are unusually widespread storm conditions. The brief voice messages warn mariners of storm threats present in their areas.

The storm warnings are based on the most recent forecasts. Updated forecasts are issued by the National Weather Service at 0500, 1100, 1700, and 2300 UTC for WWV; and at 0000, 0600, 1200, and 1800 UTC for WWVH.

A typical storm warning announcement text is as follows:

> North Atlantic weather West of 35 West at 1700 UTC; Hurricane Donna, intensifying, 24 North, 60 West, moving northwest, 20 knots, winds 75 knots; storm, 65 North, 35 West, moving east, 10 knots; winds 50 knots, seas 15 feet.

For more information about marine storm warnings, write to: The Director, National Weather Service, Silver Spring, MD 20910.

Global Positioning System (GPS) Status Announcements—Since March 1990 the U.S. Coast guard has sponsored two voice announcements per hour on WWV and WWVH, giving current status information about the GPS satellites and related operations. The 45-s announcements begin at 14 and 15 minutes after each hour on WWV and at 43 and 44 minutes after each hour on WWVH. For further information, contact the Commanding Officer, U.S. Coast Guard Center, 7323 Telegraph Road, Alexandria, VA 22310-3998.

WWV and WWVH Audio Signals by Telephone

The audio portions of the WWV and WWVH broadcasts can be heard by telephone. The accuracy of the telephone time signals is normally 20 ms or better in the continental United States. In rare instances when the telephone connection is made by satellite, there is an additional delay of 0.25 to 0.5 s.

To hear these broadcasts, dial (303) 499-7111 for WWV, and (808) 335-4363 for WWVH. Callers are disconnected after three minutes. These are not toll-free numbers; callers outside the local calling area are charged for the call at regular long-distance rates.

Low-Frequency Service—WWVB

Radio station WWVB is located on the WWV site near Ft. Collins, CO. WWVB continuously broadcasts time and frequency signals at 60 kHz, primarily for the continental United States. WWVB does not broadcast voice announcements, but provides standard time information, including the year; time intervals; Daylight Saving Time, leap second, and leap-year indicators; and UT1 corrections by means of a BCD time code. In addition, the 60-kHz carrier frequency provides an accurate frequency standard which is referenced to the NIST Frequency Standard.

Accuracy and Stability

The transmitted accuracy of WWVB is normally better than 1 part in 100 billion (1×10^{-11}). Day-to-day deviations are less than 5 parts in 1000 billion (5×10^{-12}). The BCD time code can be received and used with an accuracy of approximately 0.1 ms. Propagation effects are minor compared to those of WWV and WWVH. When proper receiving and averaging techniques are used, the received accuracy of WWVB should be nearly as good as the transmitted accuracy.

Station Identification

WWVB identifies itself by advancing its carrier phase 45° at 10 minutes after the hour and returning to normal phase at 15 minutes after the hour. WWVB is also identified by its unique time code.

Radiated Power, Antenna, and Coverage

The effective radiated power from WWVB is 13, 000 watts. The antenna is a 122-m, top-loaded vertical, installed over a radial ground screen. Some measured field intensity contours are shown in the coverage map in figure 5.

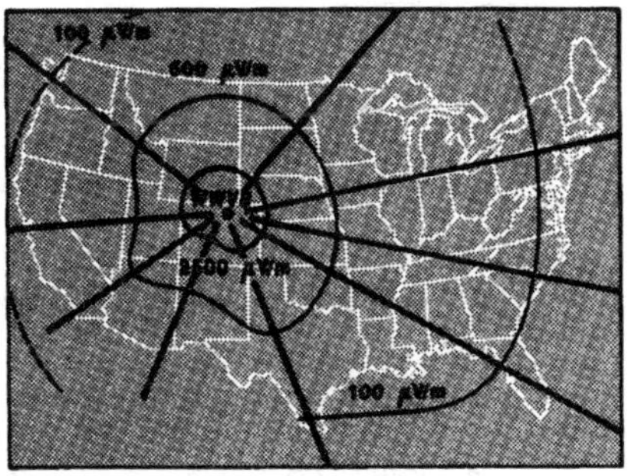

Figure 5

WWVB Time Code

The WWVB time code is synchronized with the 60-kHz carrier and is broadcast continuously at a rate of 1 pulse per second using pulse-width modulation. Each pulse is generated by reducing the carrier power 10 dB at the start of the second, so that the leading edge of every negative-going pulse is on time. Full power is restored either 0.2, 0.5, or 0.8 s later to convey either a binary "0, " "1, " or a position marker, respectively. Details of the time code are in appendix C.

The WWVB code contains information on the current year (since early 1990), day of year, hour, minute, second, status of Daylight Saving Time, leap year, and a leap-second warning (planned for mid-1991 implementation). Since the WWVB code is undergoing some revision, users are encouraged to contact the NIST Time and Frequency Division for the most current information.

How NIST Controls the Transmitted Frequencies

Figure 6 shows the relationship between the NIST broadcasts, the primary NIST Frequency Standard, and the NIST atomic time scale. The NIST Frequency Standard and atomic time scale systems are located in Boulder, CO. They include:

- The primary NIST Frequency Standard. This standard is a laboratory cesium beam device, built and maintained by NIST. It provides a frequency and time interval reference, based on the international definition of the second.
- A group of commercial cesium standards, hydrogen maser frequency standards, and possibly other devices. These are kept in controlled environments, and serve as the continuously operating "working" standards.
- Sophisticated time comparison equipment, computer systems, and computer software. This equipment generates a composite

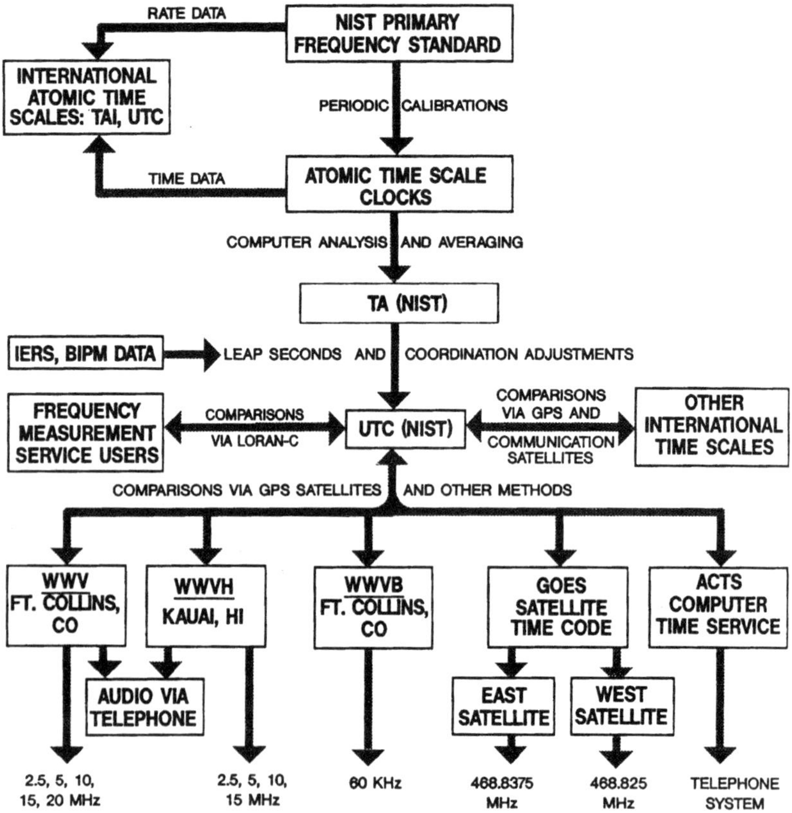

Figure 6

time scale that is better than any of the individual standards. The composite time scale, TA(NIST), is based on (approximately) annual calibrations of the working standards using the primary NIST Frequency Standard.

- Provisions for inserting small adjustments and leap seconds into the time scale. These adjustments let NIST generate UTC(NIST), an internationally coordinated UTC time scale. UTC(NIST) is distributed to users of the services described in this booklet, including WWH, WWVH, WWVB, the GOES satellites, the Frequency Measurement Service, and the telephone services.

The NIST radio station sites (Fort Collins, CO, and Kauai, HI) each have three commercial atomic standards that emulate UTC(NIST). Each standard can provide the frequency input to the station's time-code generators and transmitters.

The local standards at each station are compared to the UTC(NIST) time scale in Boulder, CO. These comparisons are made using GPS (Global Positioning System) satellites. GPS consists of orbiting navigation satellites that broadcast precise timing signals. These signals are received simultaneously at Boulder and at both radio station sites. The results obtained at the radio stations are then compared to the results obtained in Boulder. The timing differences (accurate to less than 100 ns), are then used to calibrate the local standards.

Other time and frequency resources are also used to check the local standards. These include portable clocks (physically carried to the radio station sites), Loran-C, and GOES satellite broadcasts.

GOES Satellite Time Services

In 1974, NIST began broadcasting a time code from the GOES (Geostationary Operational Environmental Satellite) satellites of the National Oceanic and Atmospheric Administration (NOAA). This cooperative arrangement between NIST and NOAA was formalized by a renewable agreement, the latest version of which extends until 1997. The primary purpose of the GOES satellites is to collect environmental data from thousands of sensing platforms located throughout the Western Hemisphere and to relay this information to a central processing facility from where it is made available to interested organizations, such as the World Meteorological Organization, radio and TV stations, and various government agencies. The time code is referenced to UTC(NIST) and is broadcast continuously to the entire Western Hemisphere from two satellites (GOES/East and GOES/West).

GOES time-code receivers are commercially available. Some of them provide timing signals accurate to within 100 μs over periods of hours, months, or years. Other versions are accurate to within 1–2 ms over the same time periods.

Inquiries about NIST Time and Frequency Services

If you have specific questions about the operations of NIST radio stations, contact:

Engineer-in-Charge, NIST Radio Stations WWV and WWVB, 2000 East County Road 58, Fort Collins, CO 80524; (303) 484-2372. Or...

Engineer-in-Charge, NIST Radio Station WWVH, P.O. Box 417, Kekaha, Kauai, HI 96752; (808) 335-4361.

If you have specific questions about the other time and frequency services, contact:

NIST Time and Frequency Services, 847.40, National Institute of Standards and Technology, 325 Broadway, Boulder, CO 80303-3328; (303) 497-3294.

Tours of NIST Facilities

Public guided tours of the NIST Laboratories in Boulder are held twice a week from Memorial Day to Labor Day, and once a week the rest of the year. They offer a chance to see the NIST Atomic Clock that provides the basis for the time and frequency services, as well as visiting other laboratories of NIST and the National Oceanic and Atmospheric Administration.

Contact the Tour Program Office, Division 360.06, NIST, 325 Broadway, Boulder, CO 80303-3328; telephone (303) 497-5507; for information about when tours are scheduled or to arrange special tours for groups of 15 to 30 people.

There are no public tours available to the radio stations.

A Brief History of NIST Time and Frequency Services

March	1923	First scheduled broadcasts of WWV, Washington, D.C.
April	1933	WWV gets first 20-kW transmitter, Beltsville, MD.
January	1943	WWV relocated to Greenbelt, MD.
November	1948	WWVH commenced broadcasts, Maui, HI.
January	1950	WWV added voice announcements.
July	1956	WWVB began 60-kHz broadcasts (as KK2XEI), Sunset, CO.
April	1960	WWVL began 20-kHz experimental broadcasts, Sunset, CO.
July	1963	WWVB began high power broadcasts, Ft. Collins, CO.
August	1963	WWVL began high power broadcasts, Ft. Collins, CO.
July	1964	WWVH added voice announcements.
December	1966	WWV relocated to Ft. Collins, CO.
July	1971	WWVH relocated to Kauai, HI.
June	1972	First leap second in history was added to UTC time scale.
July	1972	WWVL went off the air.
January	1974	Voice announcements changed from GMT to UTC (WWV/WWVH).
July	1974	GOES satellite time code initiated.
March	1975	Frequency calibration using network color TV became a nationwide service.
August	1975	Line-10 time comparisons using TV synchronization pulses became a nationwide service.
February	1977	20- and 25-MHz broadcasts from WWV and 20-MHz broadcasts from WWVH were discontinued.
December	1978	20-MHz broadcasts from WWV were rein stated.
February	1984	Frequency Measurement Service began.
March	1988	Automated Computer Time Service (ACTS) began on experimental basis.

The Sun, the Ionosphere, and the Radio Amateur

Most amateurs know that the sun plays an important role in radio propagation. Numerous books and papers have been written on the subject. The most popular is probably *The Shortwave Propagation Handbook,* by George Jacobs, W3ASK, and Theodore Cohen, N4XX. It provides detailed explanations of the science of propagation forecasting.

Sunspot Numbers

In 1748, the Swiss astronomer Johann Rudolph Wolf introduced a daily measurement of sunspot number. His method, which is still used today, counts the total number of spots visible on the face of the sun and the number of groups into which they cluster, because neither quantity alone satisfactorily measures sunspot activity.

An observer computes a daily sunspot number by multiplying the number of groups he sees by 10 and then adding this product to the total count of individual spots. Results, however, vary greatly since the measurement strongly depends on observer interpretation and experience and on the stability of the Earth's atmosphere above the observation site. Moreover, the use of Earth as a platform from which to record these numbers contributes to their variability, too, because the sun rotates and the evolving spot groups are distributed unevenly across solar longitudes. To compensate for these limitations, each daily international number is computed as a weighted average of measurements made from a network of cooperating observatories.

Two sets of monthly sunspot numbers are recorded: a "mean" number and a "smoothed" number (both are included here). The smoothed count best approximates the sunspot cycle, but due to the data required for the smoothing, a given month's smoothed number is not available until six months later. The monthly mean number is available immediately.

How do sunspot numbers in these tables compare with the largest values ever recorded? The highest daily count on record occurred December 24 and 25, 1957. On both of those days the sunspot number totaled 355. In contrast, during years near the minimum of the spot cycle, the count can fall to zero. Today, much more sophisticated measurements of solar activity are made routinely, but none has the link with the past that sunspot numbers have. In 1994, sunspot Cycle 22 is declining. Current predictions call for the minimum to occur between late 1996 and mid-1997.

Monthly Mean Sunspot Numbers

Year	Jan	Feb	Mar	Apr	May	Jun	Jul	Aug	Sep	Oct	Nov	Dec
1749	58.0	62.6	70.0	55.7	85.0	83.5	94.8	66.3	75.9	75.5	158.6	85.2
1750	73.3	75.9	89.2	88.3	90.0	100.0	85.4	103.0	91.2	65.7	63.3	75.4
1751	70.0	43.5	45.3	56.4	60.7	50.7	66.3	59.8	23.5	23.2	28.5	44.0
1752	35.0	50.0	71.0	59.3	59.7	39.6	78.4	29.3	27.1	46.6	37.6	40.0
1753	44.0	32.0	45.7	38.0	36.0	31.7	22.0	39.0	28.0	25.0	20.0	6.7
1754	0.0	3.0	1.7	13.7	20.7	26.7	18.8	12.3	8.2	24.1	13.2	4.2
1755	10.2	11.2	6.8	6.5	0.0	0.0	8.6	3.2	17.8	23.7	6.8	20.0
1756	12.5	7.1	5.4	9.4	12.5	12.9	3.6	6.4	11.8	14.3	17.0	9.4
1757	14.1	21.2	26.2	30.0	38.1	12.8	25.0	51.3	39.7	32.5	64.7	33.5
1758	37.6	52.0	49.0	72.3	46.4	45.0	44.0	38.7	62.5	37.7	43.0	43.0
1759	48.3	44.0	46.8	47.0	49.0	50.0	51.0	71.3	77.2	59.7	46.3	57.0
1760	67.3	59.5	74.7	58.3	72.0	48.3	66.0	75.6	61.3	50.6	59.7	61.0
1761	70.0	91.0	80.7	71.7	107.2	99.3	94.1	91.1	100.7	88.7	89.7	46.0
1762	43.8	72.8	45.7	60.2	39.9	77.1	33.8	67.7	68.5	69.3	77.8	77.2
1763	56.5	31.9	34.2	32.9	32.7	35.8	54.2	26.5	68.1	46.3	60.9	61.4
1764	59.7	59.7	40.2	34.4	44.3	30.0	30.0	30.0	28.2	28.0	26.0	25.7
1765	24.0	26.0	25.0	22.0	20.2	20.0	27.0	29.7	16.0	14.0	14.0	13.0
1766	12.0	11.0	36.6	6.0	26.8	3.0	3.3	4.0	4.3	5.0	5.7	19.2
1767	27.4	30.0	43.0	32.9	29.8	33.3	21.9	40.8	42.7	44.1	54.7	53.3
1768	53.5	66.1	46.3	42.7	77.7	77.4	52.6	66.8	74.8	77.8	90.6	111.8
1769	73.9	64.2	64.3	96.7	73.6	94.4	118.6	120.3	148.8	158.2	148.1	112.0
1770	104.0	142.5	80.1	51.0	70.1	83.3	109.8	126.3	104.4	103.6	132.2	102.3
1771	36.0	46.2	46.7	64.9	152.7	119.5	67.7	58.5	101.4	90.0	99.7	95.7
1772	100.9	90.8	31.1	92.2	38.0	57.0	77.3	56.2	50.5	78.6	61.3	64.0
1773	54.6	29.0	51.2	32.9	41.1	28.4	27.7	12.7	29.3	26.3	40.9	43.2
1774	46.8	65.4	55.7	43.8	51.3	28.5	17.5	6.6	7.9	14.0	17.7	12.2
1775	4.4	0.0	11.6	11.2	3.9	12.3	1.0	7.9	3.2	5.6	15.1	7.9
1776	21.7	11.6	6.3	21.8	11.2	19.0	1.0	24.2	16.0	30.0	35.0	40.0
1777	45.0	36.5	39.0	95.5	80.3	80.7	95.0	112.0	116.2	106.5	146.0	157.3
1778	177.3	109.3	134.0	145.0	238.9	171.6	153.0	140.0	171.7	156.3	150.3	105.0
1779	114.7	165.7	118.0	145.0	140.0	113.7	143.0	112.0	111.0	124.0	114.0	110.0
1780	70.0	98.0	98.0	95.0	107.2	88.0	86.0	86.0	93.7	77.0	60.0	58.7

Year	Jan	Feb	Mar	Apr	May	Jun	Jul	Aug	Sep	Oct	Nov	Dec
1781	98.7	74.7	53.0	68.3	104.7	97.7	73.5	66.0	51.0	27.3	67.0	35.2
1782	54.0	37.5	37.0	41.0	54.3	38.0	37.0	44.0	34.0	23.2	31.5	30.0
1783	28.0	38.7	26.7	28.3	23.0	25.2	32.2	20.0	18.0	8.0	15.0	10.5
1784	13.0	8.0	11.0	10.0	6.0	9.0	6.0	10.0	10.0	8.0	17.0	14.0
1785	6.5	8.0	9.0	15.7	20.7	26.3	36.3	20.0	32.0	47.2	40.2	27.3
1786	37.2	47.6	47.7	85.4	92.3	59.0	83.0	89.7	111.5	112.3	116.0	112.7
1787	134.7	106.0	87.4	127.2	134.8	99.2	128.0	137.2	157.3	157.0	141.5	174.0
1788	138.0	129.2	143.3	108.5	113.0	154.2	141.5	136.0	141.0	142.0	94.7	129.5
1789	114.0	125.3	120.0	123.3	123.5	120.0	117.0	103.0	112.0	89.7	134.0	135.5
1790	103.0	127.5	96.3	94.0	93.0	91.0	69.3	87.0	77.3	84.3	82.0	74.0
1791	72.7	62.0	74.0	77.2	73.7	64.2	71.0	43.0	66.5	61.7	67.0	66.0
1792	58.0	64.0	63.0	75.7	62.0	61.0	45.8	60.0	59.0	59.0	57.0	56.0
1793	56.0	55.0	55.5	53.0	52.3	51.0	50.0	29.3	24.0	47.0	44.0	45.7
1794	45.0	44.0	38.0	28.4	55.7	41.5	41.0	40.0	11.1	28.5	67.4	51.4
1795	21.4	39.9	12.6	18.6	31.0	17.1	12.9	25.7	13.5	19.5	25.0	18.0
1796	22.0	23.8	15.7	31.7	21.0	6.7	26.9	1.5	18.4	11.0	8.4	5.1
1797	14.4	4.2	4.0	4.0	7.3	11.1	4.3	6.0	5.7	6.9	5.8	3.0
1798	2.0	4.0	12.4	1.1	0.0	0.0	0.0	3.0	2.4	1.5	12.5	9.9
1799	1.6	12.6	21.7	8.4	8.2	10.6	2.1	0.0	0.0	4.6	2.7	8.6
1800	6.9	9.3	13.9	0.0	5.0	23.7	21.0	19.5	11.5	12.3	10.5	40.1
1801	27.0	29.0	30.0	31.0	32.0	31.2	35.0	38.7	33.5	32.6	39.8	48.2
1802	47.8	47.0	40.8	42.0	44.0	46.0	48.0	50.0	51.8	38.5	34.5	50.0
1803	50.0	50.8	29.5	25.0	44.3	36.0	48.3	34.1	45.3	54.3	51.0	48.0
1804	45.3	48.3	48.0	50.6	33.4	34.8	29.8	43.1	53.0	62.3	61.0	60.0
1805	61.0	44.1	51.4	37.5	39.0	40.5	37.6	42.7	44.4	29.4	41.0	38.3
1806	39.0	29.6	32.7	27.7	26.4	25.6	30.0	26.3	24.0	27.0	25.0	24.0
1807	12.0	12.2	9.6	23.8	10.0	12.0	12.7	12.0	5.7	8.0	2.6	0.0
1808	0.0	4.5	0.0	12.3	13.5	13.5	6.7	8.0	11.7	4.7	10.5	12.3
1809	7.2	9.2	0.9	2.5	2.0	7.7	0.3	0.2	0.4	0.0	0.0	0.0
1810	0.0	0.0	0.0	0.0	0.0	0.0	0.0	0.0	0.0	0.0	0.0	0.0
1811	0.0	0.0	0.0	0.0	0.0	0.0	6.6	0.0	2.4	6.1	0.8	1.1
1812	11.3	1.9	0.7	0.0	1.0	1.3	0.5	15.6	5.2	3.9	7.9	10.1
1813	0.0	10.3	1.9	16.6	5.5	11.2	18.3	8.4	15.3	27.8	16.7	14.3
1814	22.2	12.0	5.7	23.8	5.8	14.9	18.5	2.3	8.1	19.3	14.5	20.1
1815	19.2	32.2	26.2	31.6	9.8	55.9	35.5	47.2	31.5	33.5	37.2	65.0
1816	26.3	68.8	73.7	58.8	44.3	43.6	38.8	23.2	47.8	56.4	38.1	29.9
1817	36.4	57.9	96.2	26.4	21.2	40.0	50.0	45.0	36.7	25.6	28.9	28.4
1818	34.9	22.4	25.4	34.5	53.1	36.4	28.0	31.5	26.1	31.6	10.9	25.8
1819	32.8	20.7	3.7	20.2	19.6	35.0	31.4	26.1	14.9	27.5	25.1	30.6
1820	19.2	26.6	4.5	19.4	29.3	10.8	20.6	25.9	5.2	8.9	7.9	9.1
1821	21.5	4.2	5.7	9.2	1.7	1.8	2.5	4.8	4.4	18.8	4.4	0.2
1822	0.0	0.9	16.1	13.5	1.5	5.6	7.9	2.1	0.0	0.4	0.0	0.0
1823	0.0	0.0	0.6	0.0	0.0	0.0	0.5	0.0	0.0	0.0	0.0	20.4
1824	21.7	10.8	0.0	19.4	2.8	0.0	0.0	1.4	20.5	25.2	0.0	0.8
1825	5.0	15.5	22.4	3.8	15.5	15.4	30.9	25.7	15.7	15.6	11.7	22.0
1826	17.7	18.2	36.7	24.0	32.4	37.1	52.5	39.6	18.9	50.6	39.5	68.1
1827	34.6	47.4	57.8	46.0	56.3	56.7	42.3	53.7	49.6	56.1	48.2	46.1
1828	52.8	64.4	65.0	61.1	89.1	98.0	54.2	76.4	50.4	54.7	57.0	46.9
1829	43.0	49.4	72.3	95.0	67.4	73.9	90.8	77.6	52.8	57.2	67.6	56.5
1830	52.2	72.1	84.6	106.3	66.3	65.1	43.9	50.7	62.1	84.4	81.2	82.1
1831	47.5	50.1	93.4	54.5	38.1	33.4	45.2	55.0	37.9	46.3	43.5	28.9
1832	30.9	55.6	55.1	26.9	41.3	26.7	14.0	8.9	8.2	21.1	14.3	27.5
1833	11.3	14.9	11.8	2.8	12.9	1.0	7.0	5.7	11.6	7.5	5.9	9.9
1834	4.9	18.1	3.9	1.4	8.8	7.8	8.7	4.0	11.5	24.8	30.5	34.5

Year	Jan	Feb	Mar	Apr	May	Jun	Jul	Aug	Sep	Oct	Nov	Dec
1835	7.5	24.5	19.7	61.5	43.6	33.2	59.8	59.0	100.8	95.2	100.0	77.5
1836	88.6	107.6	98.2	142.9	111.4	124.7	116.7	107.8	95.1	137.4	120.9	206.2
1837	188.0	175.6	134.6	138.2	111.7	158.0	162.8	134.0	96.3	123.7	107.0	129.8
1838	144.9	84.8	140.8	126.6	137.6	94.5	108.2	78.8	73.6	90.8	77.4	79.8
1839	105.6	102.5	77.7	61.8	53.8	54.6	84.8	131.2	132.7	90.9	68.8	63.7
1840	81.2	87.7	67.8	65.9	69.2	48.5	60.7	57.8	74.0	55.0	54.3	53.7
1841	24.1	29.9	29.7	40.2	67.5	55.7	30.8	39.3	36.5	28.5	19.8	38.8
1842	20.4	22.1	21.7	26.9	24.9	20.5	12.6	26.6	18.4	38.1	40.5	17.6
1843	13.3	3.5	8.3	9.5	21.1	10.5	9.5	11.8	4.2	5.3	19.1	12.7
1844	9.4	14.7	13.6	20.8	11.6	3.7	21.2	23.9	7.0	21.5	10.7	21.6
1845	25.7	43.6	43.3	57.0	47.8	31.1	30.6	32.3	29.6	40.7	39.4	59.7
1846	38.7	51.0	63.9	69.3	59.9	65.1	46.5	54.8	107.1	55.9	60.4	65.5
1847	62.6	44.9	85.7	44.7	75.4	85.3	52.2	140.6	160.9	180.4	138.9	109.6
1848	159.1	111.8	108.6	107.1	102.2	129.0	139.2	132.6	100.3	132.4	114.6	159.5
1849	157.0	131.7	96.2	102.5	80.6	81.1	78.0	67.7	93.7	71.5	99.0	97.0
1850	78.0	89.4	82.6	44.1	61.6	70.0	39.1	61.6	86.2	71.0	54.8	61.0
1851	75.5	105.4	64.6	56.5	62.6	63.2	36.1	57.4	67.9	62.5	51.0	71.4
1852	68.4	66.4	61.2	65.4	54.9	46.9	42.1	39.7	37.5	67.3	54.3	45.4
1853	41.1	42.9	37.7	47.6	34.7	40.0	45.9	50.4	33.5	42.3	28.8	23.4
1854	15.4	20.0	20.7	26.5	24.0	21.1	18.7	15.8	22.4	12.6	28.2	21.6
1855	12.3	11.4	17.4	4.4	9.1	5.3	0.4	3.1	0.0	9.6	4.2	3.1
1856	0.5	4.9	0.4	6.5	0.0	5.2	4.6	5.9	4.4	4.5	7.7	7.2
1857	13.7	7.4	5.2	11.1	28.6	16.0	22.2	16.9	42.4	40.6	31.4	37.2
1858	39.0	34.9	57.5	38.3	41.4	44.5	56.7	55.3	80.1	91.2	51.9	66.9
1859	83.7	87.6	90.3	85.7	91.0	87.1	95.2	106.8	105.8	114.6	97.2	81.0
1860	82.4	88.3	98.9	71.4	107.1	108.6	116.7	100.3	92.2	90.1	97.9	95.6
1861	62.3	77.7	101.0	98.5	56.8	88.1	78.0	82.5	79.9	67.2	53.7	80.5
1862	63.1	64.5	43.6	53.7	64.4	84.0	73.4	62.5	66.6	41.9	50.6	40.9
1863	48.3	56.7	66.4	40.6	53.8	40.8	32.7	48.1	22.0	39.9	37.7	41.2
1864	57.7	47.1	66.3	35.8	40.6	57.8	54.7	54.8	28.5	33.9	57.6	28.6
1865	48.7	39.3	39.5	29.4	34.5	33.6	26.8	37.8	21.6	17.1	24.6	12.8
1866	31.6	38.4	24.6	17.6	12.9	16.5	9.3	12.7	7.3	14.1	9.0	1.5
1867	0.0	0.7	9.2	5.1	2.9	1.5	5.0	4.8	9.8	13.5	9.6	25.2
1868	15.6	15.7	26.5	36.6	26.7	31.1	29.0	34.4	47.2	61.6	59.1	67.6
1869	60.9	59.9	52.7	41.0	103.9	108.4	59.2	79.6	80.6	59.3	78.1	104.3
1870	77.3	114.9	157.6	160.0	176.0	135.6	132.4	153.8	136.0	146.4	147.5	130.0
1871	88.3	125.3	143.2	162.4	145.5	91.7	103.0	110.1	80.3	89.0	105.4	90.4
1872	79.5	120.1	88.4	102.1	107.6	109.9	105.5	92.9	114.6	102.6	112.0	83.9
1873	86.7	107.0	98.3	76.2	47.9	44.8	66.9	68.2	47.1	47.1	55.4	49.2
1874	60.8	64.2	46.4	32.0	44.6	38.2	67.8	61.3	28.0	34.3	28.9	29.3
1875	14.6	21.5	33.8	29.1	11.5	23.9	12.5	14.6	2.4	12.7	17.7	9.9
1876	14.3	15.0	30.6	2.3	5.1	1.6	15.2	8.8	9.9	14.3	9.9	8.2
1877	24.4	8.7	11.9	15.8	21.6	14.2	6.0	6.3	16.9	6.7	14.2	2.2
1878	3.3	6.6	7.8	0.1	5.9	6.4	0.1	0.0	5.3	1.1	4.1	0.5
1879	1.0	0.6	0.0	6.2	2.4	4.8	7.5	10.7	6.1	12.3	13.1	7.3
1880	24.0	27.2	19.3	19.5	23.5	34.1	21.9	48.1	66.0	43.0	30.7	29.6
1881	36.4	53.2	51.5	51.6	43.5	60.5	76.9	58.4	53.2	64.4	54.8	47.3
1882	45.0	69.5	66.8	95.8	64.1	45.2	45.4	40.4	57.7	59.2	84.4	41.8
1883	60.6	46.9	42.8	82.1	31.5	76.3	80.6	46.0	52.6	83.8	84.5	75.9
1884	91.5	86.9	87.5	76.1	66.5	51.2	53.1	55.8	61.9	47.8	36.6	47.2
1885	42.8	71.8	49.8	55.0	73.0	83.7	66.5	50.0	39.6	38.7	30.9	21.7
1886	29.9	25.9	57.3	43.7	30.7	27.1	30.3	16.9	21.4	8.6	0.3	13.0
1887	10.3	13.2	4.2	6.9	20.0	15.7	23.3	21.4	7.4	6.6	6.9	20.7

Year	Jan	Feb	Mar	Apr	May	Jun	Jul	Aug	Sep	Oct	Nov	Dec
1888	12.7	7.1	7.8	5.1	7.0	7.1	3.1	2.8	8.8	2.1	10.7	6.7
1889	0.8	8.5	6.7	4.3	2.4	6.4	9.4	20.6	6.5	2.1	0.2	6.7
1890	5.3	0.6	5.1	1.6	4.8	1.3	11.6	8.5	17.2	11.2	9.6	7.8
1891	13.5	22.2	10.4	20.5	41.1	48.3	58.8	33.0	53.8	51.5	41.9	32.5
1892	69.1	75.6	49.9	69.6	79.6	76.3	76.5	101.4	62.8	70.5	65.4	78.6
1893	75.0	73.0	65.7	88.1	84.7	89.9	88.6	129.2	77.9	80.0	75.1	93.8
1894	83.2	84.6	52.3	81.6	101.2	98.9	106.0	70.3	65.9	75.5	56.6	60.0
1895	63.3	67.2	61.0	76.9	67.5	71.5	47.8	68.9	57.7	67.9	47.2	70.7
1896	29.0	57.4	52.0	43.8	27.7	49.0	45.0	27.2	61.3	28.7	38.0	42.6
1897	40.6	29.4	29.1	31.0	20.0	11.3	27.6	21.8	48.1	14.3	8.4	33.3
1898	30.2	36.4	38.3	14.5	25.8	22.3	9.0	31.4	34.8	34.4	30.9	12.6
1899	19.5	9.2	18.1	14.2	7.7	20.5	13.5	2.9	8.4	13.0	7.8	10.5
1900	9.4	13.6	8.6	16.0	15.2	12.1	8.3	4.3	8.3	12.9	4.5	0.3
1901	0.2	2.4	4.5	0.0	10.2	5.8	0.7	1.0	0.6	3.7	3.8	0.0
1902	5.5	0.0	12.4	0.0	2.8	1.4	0.9	2.3	7.6	16.3	10.3	1.1
1903	8.3	17.0	13.5	26.1	14.6	16.3	27.9	28.8	11.1	38.9	44.5	45.6
1904	31.6	24.5	37.2	43.0	39.5	41.9	50.6	58.2	30.1	54.2	38.0	54.6
1905	54.8	85.8	56.5	39.3	48.0	49.0	73.0	58.8	55.0	78.7	107.2	55.5
1906	45.5	31.3	64.5	55.3	57.7	63.2	103.6	47.7	56.1	17.8	38.9	64.7
1907	76.4	108.2	60.7	52.6	42.9	40.4	49.7	54.3	85.0	65.4	61.5	47.3
1908	39.2	33.9	28.7	57.6	40.8	48.1	39.5	90.5	86.9	32.3	45.5	39.5
1909	56.7	46.6	66.3	32.3	36.0	22.6	35.8	23.1	38.8	58.4	55.8	54.2
1910	26.4	31.5	21.4	8.4	22.2	12.3	14.1	11.5	26.2	38.3	4.9	5.8
1911	3.4	9.0	7.8	16.5	9.0	2.2	3.5	4.0	4.0	2.6	4.2	2.2
1912	0.3	0.0	4.9	4.5	4.4	4.1	3.0	0.3	9.5	4.6	1.1	6.4
1913	2.3	2.9	0.5	0.9	0.0	0.0	1.7	0.2	1.2	3.1	0.7	3.8
1914	2.8	2.6	3.1	17.3	5.2	11.4	5.4	7.7	12.7	8.2	16.4	22.3
1915	23.0	42.3	38.8	41.3	33.0	68.8	71.6	69.6	49.5	53.5	42.5	34.5
1916	45.3	55.4	67.0	71.8	74.5	67.7	53.5	35.2	45.1	50.7	65.6	53.0
1917	74.7	71.9	94.8	74.7	114.1	114.9	119.8	154.5	129.4	72.2	96.4	129.3
1918	96.0	65.3	72.2	80.5	76.7	59.4	107.6	101.7	79.9	85.0	83.4	59.2
1919	48.1	79.5	66.5	51.8	88.1	111.2	64.7	69.0	54.7	52.8	42.0	34.9
1920	51.1	53.9	70.2	14.8	33.3	38.7	27.5	19.2	36.3	49.6	27.2	29.9
1921	31.5	28.3	26.7	32.4	22.2	33.7	41.9	22.8	17.8	18.2	17.8	20.3
1922	11.8	26.4	54.7	11.0	8.0	5.8	10.9	6.5	4.7	6.2	7.4	17.5
1923	4.5	1.5	3.3	6.1	3.2	9.1	3.5	0.5	13.2	11.6	10.0	2.8
1924	0.5	5.1	1.8	11.3	20.8	24.0	28.1	19.3	25.1	25.6	22.5	16.5
1925	5.5	23.2	18.0	31.7	42.8	47.5	38.5	37.9	60.2	69.2	58.6	98.6
1926	71.8	69.9	62.5	38.5	64.3	73.5	52.3	61.6	60.8	71.5	60.5	79.4
1927	81.6	93.0	69.6	93.5	79.1	59.1	54.9	53.8	68.4	63.1	67.2	45.2
1928	83.5	73.5	85.4	80.6	77.0	91.4	98.0	83.8	89.7	61.4	50.3	59.0
1929	68.9	62.8	50.2	52.8	58.2	71.9	70.2	65.8	34.4	54.0	81.1	108.0
1930	65.3	49.9	35.0	38.2	36.8	28.8	21.9	24.9	32.1	34.4	35.6	25.8
1931	14.6	43.1	30.0	31.2	24.6	15.3	17.4	13.0	19.0	10.0	18.7	17.8
1932	12.1	10.6	11.2	11.2	17.9	22.2	9.6	6.8	4.0	8.9	8.2	11.0
1933	12.3	22.2	10.1	2.9	3.2	5.2	2.8	0.2	5.1	3.0	0.6	0.3
1934	3.4	7.8	4.3	11.3	19.7	6.7	9.3	8.3	4.0	5.7	8.7	15.4
1935	18.6	20.5	23.1	12.2	27.3	45.7	33.9	30.1	42.1	53.2	64.2	61.5
1936	62.8	74.3	77.1	74.9	54.6	70.0	52.3	87.0	76.0	89.0	115.4	123.4
1937	132.5	128.5	83.9	109.3	116.7	130.3	145.1	137.7	100.7	124.9	74.4	88.8
1938	98.4	119.2	86.5	101.0	127.4	97.5	165.3	115.7	89.6	99.1	122.2	92.7
1939	80.3	77.4	64.6	109.1	118.3	101.0	97.6	105.8	112.6	88.1	68.1	42.1
1940	50.5	59.4	83.3	60.7	54.4	83.9	67.5	105.5	66.5	55.0	58.4	68.3
1941	45.6	44.5	46.4	32.8	29.5	59.8	66.9	60.0	65.9	46.3	38.4	33.7

Year	Jan	Feb	Mar	Apr	May	Jun	Jul	Aug	Sep	Oct	Nov	Dec
1942	35.6	52.8	54.2	60.7	25.0	11.4	17.7	20.2	17.2	19.2	30.7	22.5
1943	12.4	28.9	27.4	26.1	14.1	7.6	13.2	19.4	10.0	7.8	10.2	18.8
1944	3.7	0.5	11.0	0.3	2.5	5.0	5.0	16.7	14.3	16.9	10.8	28.4
1945	18.5	12.7	21.5	32.0	30.6	36.2	42.6	25.9	34.9	68.8	46.0	27.4
1946	47.6	86.2	76.6	75.7	84.9	73.5	116.2	107.2	94.4	102.3	123.8	121.7
1947	115.7	133.4	129.8	149.8	201.3	163.9	157.9	188.8	169.4	163.6	128.0	116.5
1948	108.5	86.1	94.8	189.7	174.0	167.8	142.2	157.9	143.3	136.3	95.8	138.0
1949	119.1	182.3	157.5	147.0	106.2	121.7	125.8	123.8	145.3	131.6	143.5	117.6
1950	101.6	94.8	109.7	113.4	106.2	83.6	91.0	85.2	51.3	61.4	54.8	54.1
1951	59.9	59.9	55.9	92.9	108.5	100.6	61.5	61.0	83.1	51.6	52.4	45.8
1952	40.7	22.7	22.0	29.1	23.4	36.4	39.3	54.9	28.2	23.8	22.1	34.3
1953	26.5	3.9	10.0	27.8	12.5	21.8	8.6	23.5	19.3	8.2	1.6	2.5
1954	0.2	0.5	10.9	1.8	0.8	0.2	4.8	8.4	1.5	7.0	9.2	7.6
1955	23.1	20.8	4.9	11.3	28.9	31.7	26.7	40.7	42.7	58.5	89.2	76.9
1956	73.6	124.0	118.4	110.7	136.6	116.6	129.1	169.6	173.2	155.3	201.3	192.1
1957	165.0	130.2	157.4	175.2	164.6	200.7	187.2	158.0	235.8	253.8	210.9	239.4
1958	202.5	164.9	190.7	196.0	175.3	171.5	191.4	200.2	201.2	181.5	152.3	187.6
1959	217.4	143.1	185.7	163.3	172.0	168.7	149.6	199.6	145.2	111.4	124.0	125.0
1960	146.3	106.0	102.2	122.0	119.6	110.2	121.7	134.1	127.2	82.8	89.6	85.6
1961	57.9	46.1	53.0	61.4	51.0	77.4	70.2	55.8	63.6	37.7	32.6	39.9
1962	38.7	50.3	45.6	46.4	43.7	42.0	21.8	21.8	51.3	39.5	26.9	23.2
1963	19.8	24.4	17.1	29.3	43.0	35.9	19.6	33.2	38.8	35.3	23.4	14.9
1964	15.3	17.7	16.5	8.6	9.5	9.1	3.1	9.3	4.7	6.1	7.4	15.1
1965	17.5	14.2	11.7	6.8	24.1	15.9	11.9	8.9	16.8	20.1	15.8	17.0
1966	28.2	24.4	25.3	48.7	45.3	47.7	56.7	51.2	50.2	57.2	57.2	70.4
1967	110.9	93.6	111.8	69.5	86.5	67.3	91.5	107.2	76.8	88.2	94.3	126.4
1968	121.8	111.9	92.2	81.2	127.2	110.3	96.1	109.3	117.2	107.7	86.0	109.8
1969	104.4	120.5	135.8	106.8	120.0	106.0	96.8	98.0	91.3	95.7	93.5	97.9
1970	111.5	127.8	102.9	109.5	127.5	106.8	112.5	93.0	99.5	86.6	95.2	83.5
1971	91.3	79.0	60.7	71.8	57.5	49.8	81.0	61.4	50.2	51.7	63.2	82.2
1972	61.5	88.4	80.1	63.2	80.5	88.0	76.5	76.8	64.0	61.3	41.6	45.3
1973	43.4	42.9	46.0	57.7	42.4	39.5	23.1	25.6	59.3	30.7	23.9	23.3
1974	27.6	26.0	21.3	40.3	39.5	36.0	55.8	33.6	40.2	47.1	25.0	20.5
1975	18.9	11.5	11.5	5.1	9.0	11.4	28.2	39.7	13.9	9.1	19.4	7.8
1976	8.1	4.3	21.9	18.8	12.4	12.2	1.9	16.4	13.5	20.6	5.2	15.3
1977	16.4	23.1	8.7	12.9	18.6	38.5	21.4	30.1	44.0	43.8	29.1	43.2
1978	51.9	93.6	76.5	99.7	82.7	95.1	70.4	58.1	138.2	125.1	97.9	122.7
1979	166.6	137.5	138.0	101.5	134.4	149.5	159.4	142.2	188.4	186.2	183.3	176.3
1980	159.6	155.0	126.2	164.1	179.9	157.3	136.3	135.4	155.0	164.7	147.9	174.4
1981	114.0	141.3	135.5	156.4	127.5	90.9	143.8	158.7	167.3	162.4	137.5	150.1
1982	111.2	163.6	153.8	122.0	82.2	110.4	106.1	107.6	118.8	94.7	98.1	127.0
1983	84.3	51.0	66.5	80.7	99.2	91.1	82.2	71.8	50.3	55.8	33.3	33.4
1984	57.0	85.4	83.5	69.7	76.4	46.1	37.4	25.5	15.7	12.0	22.8	18.7
1985	16.5	15.9	17.2	16.2	27.5	24.2	30.7	11.1	3.9	18.6	16.2	17.3
1986	2.5	23.2	15.1	18.5	13.7	1.1	18.1	7.4	3.8	35.4	15.2	6.8
1987	10.4	2.4	14.7	39.6	33.0	17.4	33.0	38.7	33.9	60.6	39.9	27.1
1988	59.0	40.0	76.2	88.0	60.1	101.8	113.8	111.6	120.1	125.1	125.1	179.2
1989	161.3	165.1	131.4	130.6	138.5	196.2	126.9	168.9	176.7	159.4	173.0	165.5
1990	177.3	130.5	140.3	140.3	132.2	105.4	149.4	200.3	125.2	145.5	131.4	129.7
1991	136.9	167.5	141.9	140.0	121.3	169.7	173.7	176.3	125.3	144.1	108.2	144.4
1992	150.0	161.1	106.7	99.8	73.8	65.2	85.7	64.5	63.9	88.7	91.8	82.6
1993	59.3	91.0	69.8	62.0								

No observations were available during February 1824. The value shown was interpolated from the January and March monthly means of that year.

Smoothed Monthly Mean Sunspot Numbers

Year	Jan	Feb	Mar	Apr	May	Jun	Jul	Aug	Sep	Oct	Nov	Dec
1749							81.6	82.8	84.1	86.3	87.8	88.7
1750	89.0	90.2	92.3	92.6	88.2	83.8	83.3	81.8	78.6	75.4	72.9	69.6
1751	66.8	64.2	59.5	54.9	51.7	49.0	46.2	45.0	46.4	47.5	47.6	47.1
1752	47.2	46.4	45.3	46.4	47.8	48.0	48.2	47.8	46.0	44.1	42.2	40.9
1753	38.2	36.2	36.7	35.8	34.2	32.1	28.8	25.8	22.8	19.9	18.3	17.4
1754	17.1	15.8	13.9	13.0	12.7	12.3	12.6	13.4	14.0	13.9	12.7	10.7
1755	9.2	8.4	8.4	8.8	8.5	8.9	9.7	9.6	9.4	9.4	10.1	11.1
1756	11.5	11.4	11.3	10.6	10.7	10.6	10.3	10.9	12.4	14.1	16.0	17.1
1757	18.0	20.7	23.8	25.7	28.4	31.4	33.4	35.7	37.9	40.6	42.7	44.4
1758	46.5	46.8	47.2	48.4	47.7	47.2	48.0	48.2	47.7	46.6	45.6	46.0
1759	46.5	48.1	50.1	51.5	52.7	53.4	54.8	56.2	58.0	59.6	61.1	62.0
1760	62.5	63.3	62.8	61.8	62.0	62.7	63.0	64.4	66.0	66.8	68.8	72.4
1761	75.7	77.5	79.8	83.0	85.9	86.5	84.8	82.9	80.7	78.8	75.5	71.7
1762	68.3	64.8	62.5	60.4	59.0	59.9	61.7	60.5	58.3	56.7	55.3	53.2
1763	52.4	51.5	49.8	48.8	47.1	45.8	45.3	46.5	48.0	48.3	48.8	49.1
1764	47.8	46.9	45.4	43.0	40.8	37.8	34.9	32.0	29.9	28.8	27.3	25.8
1765	25.3	25.2	24.6	23.6	22.5	21.4	20.4	19.3	19.1	19.0	18.6	18.1
1766	16.4	14.4	12.8	12.0	11.2	11.2	12.1	13.5	14.5	15.9	17.2	18.6
1767	20.6	22.9	26.0	29.3	32.9	36.4	38.9	41.5	43.1	43.7	46.1	49.9
1768	53.0	55.4	57.8	60.6	63.5	67.4	70.7	71.5	72.1	75.1	77.2	77.8
1769	81.2	86.2	91.5	97.9	103.7	106.1	107.3	111.9	115.8	114.5	112.5	111.9
1770	111.1	110.9	109.3	105.2	102.3	101.2	98.0	91.1	85.7	84.9	88.9	93.9
1771	93.6	89.1	86.1	85.4	83.5	81.9	84.3	88.9	90.1	90.5	86.9	79.5
1772	77.3	77.6	75.4	72.8	70.7	67.8	64.6	60.1	58.3	56.7	54.3	53.3
1773	50.0	46.1	43.5	40.4	37.4	35.6	34.5	35.6	37.3	38.0	38.9	39.3
1774	38.9	38.2	37.1	35.6	34.2	31.9	28.9	24.4	19.8	16.6	13.3	10.6
1775	9.3	8.6	8.5	7.9	7.5	7.2	7.7	8.9	9.2	9.4	10.2	10.7
1776	11.0	11.7	12.9	14.5	16.3	18.5	20.8	22.8	25.2	29.6	35.6	41.0
1777	47.5	55.1	62.9	70.3	78.1	87.6	98.0	106.6	113.6	119.6	128.2	138.6
1778	144.8	148.4	151.9	156.3	158.5	156.5	151.8	151.5	153.2	152.5	148.4	141.9
1779	139.0	137.5	133.8	129.9	127.0	125.7	124.1	119.4	115.7	112.8	109.4	106.9
1780	103.5	100.0	98.2	95.5	91.3	86.9	86.0	86.2	83.4	80.4	79.2	79.5
1781	79.4	78.0	75.4	71.5	69.8	69.1	66.2	62.8	60.6	58.8	55.6	51.0
1782	47.0	44.5	42.9	42.0	40.4	38.7	37.4	36.3	36.0	35.0	33.2	31.3
1783	30.6	29.4	27.7	26.4	25.1	23.6	22.2	20.3	18.3	16.9	15.5	14.1
1784	12.3	10.8	10.0	9.7	9.8	10.0	9.9	9.6	9.5	9.7	10.5	11.9
1785	13.9	15.5	16.9	19.4	22.0	23.5	25.4	28.3	31.6	36.1	42.0	46.3
1786	49.6	54.5	60.7	66.7	72.6	79.3	86.9	93.4	97.5	100.9	104.4	107.9
1787	111.4	115.3	119.2	123.0	125.9	129.5	132.2	133.3	136.6	138.0	136.4	137.8
1788	140.7	141.2	140.4	139.1	136.6	132.8	129.9	128.7	127.6	127.3	128.3	127.3
1789	124.9	122.5	119.9	116.5	116.0	117.9	117.7	117.3	116.4	114.2	111.7	109.2
1790	106.0	103.4	101.2	99.6	97.2	92.5	88.6	84.6	81.0	79.4	77.8	75.9
1791	74.9	73.1	70.8	69.4	67.9	66.9	66.0	65.4	65.1	64.5	64.0	63.4
1792	62.2	61.9	62.2	61.8	61.3	60.5	60.0	59.5	58.8	57.6	56.2	55.4
1793	55.1	54.0	51.3	49.3	48.3	47.3	46.4	45.5	44.3	42.6	41.7	41.4
1794	40.7	40.7	40.7	39.3	39.6	40.8	40.0	38.9	37.6	36.2	34.7	32.7
1795	30.5	28.7	28.2	28.0	25.8	22.7	21.3	20.6	20.1	20.8	20.9	20.1
1796	20.2	19.8	19.0	18.8	17.8	16.6	15.7	14.6	13.3	11.6	9.9	9.5
1797	8.8	8.0	7.7	7.0	6.7	6.5	5.9	5.4	5.7	5.9	5.5	4.7
1798	4.1	3.8	3.5	3.2	3.2	3.8	4.1	4.4	5.1	5.8	6.5	7.3
1799	7.8	7.8	7.5	7.6	7.3	6.8	7.0	7.1	6.6	5.9	5.4	5.9
1800	7.2	8.8	10.1	10.9	11.5	13.2	15.3	17.0	18.5	20.4	22.8	24.3

Year	Jan	Feb	Mar	Apr	May	Jun	Jul	Aug	Sep	Oct	Nov	Dec
1801	25.2	26.6	28.3	30.0	32.1	33.7	34.9	36.5	37.7	38.6	39.6	40.7
1802	41.8	42.8	44.1	45.1	45.1	45.0	45.1	45.4	45.1	43.9	43.2	42.8
1803	42.4	41.7	40.8	41.2	42.5	43.1	42.9	42.6	43.2	45.1	45.7	45.2
1804	44.3	44.0	44.6	45.3	46.1	47.0	48.1	48.6	48.6	48.2	47.9	48.3
1805	48.9	49.2	48.8	47.1	44.9	43.1	41.3	39.8	38.4	37.2	36.3	35.2
1806	34.2	33.2	31.7	30.7	30.0	28.7	27.0	25.1	23.0	22.3	21.5	20.2
1807	18.9	17.6	16.3	14.7	13.0	11.1	9.6	8.7	8.0	7.1	6.8	7.0
1808	6.8	6.4	6.5	6.6	6.8	7.6	8.4	8.9	9.2	8.8	7.9	7.2
1809	6.7	6.1	5.3	4.6	4.0	3.0	2.2	1.6	1.1	1.0	0.8	0.4
1810	0.1	0.0	0.0	0.0	0.0	0.0	0.0	0.0	0.0	0.0	0.0	0.0
1811	0.3	0.6	0.7	1.0	1.3	1.4	1.9	2.4	2.5	2.6	2.6	2.7
1812	2.5	2.9	3.7	3.7	3.9	4.6	4.5	4.4	4.8	5.5	6.4	7.0
1813	8.1	8.6	8.7	10.1	11.5	12.0	13.1	14.1	14.3	14.8	15.1	15.3
1814	15.4	15.2	14.6	14.0	13.5	13.7	13.8	14.5	16.2	17.4	17.9	19.8
1815	22.2	24.8	27.6	29.2	30.7	33.5	35.7	37.5	41.0	44.1	46.7	47.6
1816	47.3	43.4	46.1	47.7	48.7	47.3	46.2	46.2	46.7	46.3	44.0	42.8
1817	43.2	44.5	45.0	43.2	41.6	41.1	41.0	39.5	35.0	32.4	34.1	35.2
1818	34.2	32.7	31.7	31.5	31.0	30.2	30.0	29.8	28.8	27.3	25.3	23.9
1819	24.0	23.9	23.2	22.5	23.0	23.7	23.4	23.1	23.4	23.4	23.7	23.1
1820	21.7	21.2	20.8	19.6	18.1	16.5	15.8	14.9	14.1	13.7	12.1	10.6
1821	9.5	7.8	6.9	7.3	7.5	7.0	5.7	4.7	5.0	5.6	5.7	5.9
1822	6.3	6.4	6.1	5.1	4.2	4.0	4.0	4.0	3.3	2.1	1.4	1.2
1823	0.6	0.2	0.1	0.1	0.1	0.9	2.7	4.0	4.5	5.3	6.2	6.3
1824	6.3	6.3	7.2	9.1	10.2	9.4	7.9	7.4	8.5	8.8	8.6	9.8
1825	11.7	14.0	14.8	14.2	14.3	15.7	17.1	17.7	18.4	19.9	21.4	23.0
1826	24.9	26.3	27.1	28.7	31.3	34.4	37.0	38.9	41.0	42.8	44.7	46.5
1827	46.9	47.1	49.0	50.5	51.2	50.6	50.5	51.9	52.9	53.9	55.9	59.0
1828	61.2	62.6	63.6	63.5	63.8	64.2	63.8	62.8	62.4	64.1	64.7	62.8
1829	63.3	64.9	65.1	65.3	65.8	66.7	67.4	68.7	70.2	71.2	71.7	71.3
1830	68.9	65.8	65.1	66.6	68.3	69.9	70.8	69.7	69.1	67.3	63.9	61.4
1831	60.2	60.4	59.6	57.0	53.8	50.0	47.1	46.7	45.3	42.5	41.5	41.4
1832	39.8	36.6	33.4	31.1	28.9	27.6	26.7	24.2	20.7	17.9	15.7	13.5
1833	12.1	11.7	11.7	11.3	10.3	9.3	8.3	8.1	7.9	7.5	7.3	7.4
1834	7.8	7.8	7.7	8.4	10.2	12.2	13.4	13.7	14.7	17.8	21.8	24.3
1835	27.5	31.9	37.9	44.6	50.4	55.1	60.2	67.1	73.8	80.5	86.7	93.3
1836	99.5	103.9	105.7	107.2	109.9	116.1	125.6	132.6	136.9	138.2	138.0	139.4
1837	142.7	145.8	146.9	146.4	145.2	141.5	136.5	130.9	127.4	127.2	127.8	126.2
1838	121.3	116.7	113.5	111.2	108.6	105.2	101.6	100.8	98.9	93.6	87.4	82.2
1839	79.6	80.8	85.4	87.9	87.5	86.5	84.7	83.0	81.5	80.7	81.5	81.9
1840	80.7	76.6	71.1	66.9	64.6	63.6	60.8	56.0	52.5	50.5	49.4	49.7
1841	48.7	46.7	44.3	41.8	39.5	37.4	36.7	36.2	35.5	34.5	32.1	28.9
1842	26.6	25.4	24.1	23.8	25.1	25.1	23.9	22.8	21.5	20.2	19.3	18.7
1843	18.1	17.4	16.2	14.2	12.0	10.9	10.5	10.8	11.5	12.2	12.3	11.7
1844	11.9	12.9	13.5	14.3	14.6	14.6	15.7	17.6	20.0	22.7	25.7	28.4
1845	29.9	30.7	31.9	33.7	35.7	38.5	40.6	41.5	42.6	44.0	45.0	46.9
1846	49.0	50.6	54.8	58.6	60.1	61.3	62.5	63.2	63.9	63.8	63.4	64.9
1847	66.0	69.8	75.6	83.1	91.5	96.6	102.5	109.3	113.0	116.6	120.3	123.0
1848	128.3	131.6	128.7	124.2	121.1	122.2	124.2	124.9	125.3	124.6	123.5	120.8
1849	116.5	110.9	107.7	104.9	101.7	98.5	92.6	87.5	85.2	82.2	79.0	77.7
1850	75.6	74.0	73.7	73.4	71.5	68.1	66.4	67.0	66.9	66.7	67.2	67.0
1851	66.6	66.3	65.4	64.2	63.7	64.0	64.2	62.3	60.6	60.8	60.9	59.9
1852	59.5	59.0	57.0	55.9	56.2	55.3	53.1	50.9	48.9	47.2	45.6	44.5
1853	44.3	45.0	45.2	44.0	41.9	39.9	38.0	35.9	34.3	32.7	31.3	30.1
1854	28.2	25.6	23.7	22.0	20.8	20.7	20.4	20.0	19.5	18.4	16.9	15.6

Year	Jan	Feb	Mar	Apr	May	Jun	Jul	Aug	Sep	Oct	Nov	Dec
1855	14.2	12.9	11.4	10.4	9.2	7.5	6.2	5.4	4.5	3.8	3.6	3.2
1856	3.3	3.6	3.9	3.9	3.8	4.1	4.9	5.5	5.8	6.2	7.6	9.3
1857	10.5	11.7	13.7	16.8	19.3	21.5	23.8	26.0	29.4	32.7	34.3	36.0
1858	38.6	41.7	44.8	48.5	51.5	53.6	56.7	60.7	64.3	67.6	71.7	75.5
1859	78.9	82.6	85.9	87.9	90.8	93.2	93.7	93.7	94.0	93.8	93.9	95.4
1860	97.2	97.9	97.0	95.4	94.4	95.1	94.9	93.7	93.3	94.5	93.6	90.6
1861	88.1	85.8	84.5	83.1	80.3	77.8	77.2	76.7	73.7	69.5	67.9	68.1
1862	67.7	66.7	65.3	63.7	62.5	60.8	58.5	57.6	58.2	58.6	57.6	55.4
1863	51.9	49.6	47.1	45.2	44.5	44.0	44.4	44.4	44.0	43.8	43.0	43.2
1864	44.8	46.0	46.6	46.6	47.2	47.5	46.6	45.9	44.4	43.1	42.5	41.3
1865	39.1	37.2	36.2	35.2	33.2	31.1	29.8	29.0	28.4	27.2	25.9	24.2
1866	22.8	21.0	19.4	18.7	17.9	16.8	15.0	12.1	9.9	8.7	7.8	6.7
1867	5.9	5.4	5.2	5.3	5.3	6.3	7.9	9.2	10.5	12.6	14.9	17.1
1868	19.3	21.5	24.2	27.6	31.7	35.5	39.2	42.9	45.8	47.1	50.5	56.9
1869	61.4	64.6	68.0	69.4	70.1	72.4	74.6	77.6	84.3	93.8	101.7	105.8
1870	110.0	116.2	121.6	127.5	134.0	138.0	139.6	140.5	140.2	139.6	138.5	135.4
1871	132.3	129.3	125.1	120.4	116.3	112.9	110.8	110.3	107.8	103.0	98.9	98.0
1872	98.9	98.3	99.0	101.0	101.9	101.9	102.0	101.7	101.6	100.9	97.4	92.2
1873	87.8	85.2	81.4	76.2	71.5	67.7	65.2	62.4	58.4	54.4	52.4	52.0
1874	51.8	51.5	50.4	49.1	47.4	45.5	42.7	39.1	36.8	36.1	34.6	32.7
1875	29.8	25.5	22.5	20.5	19.2	17.9	17.1	16.8	16.3	15.1	13.7	12.5
1876	11.7	11.6	11.7	12.0	11.8	11.4	11.7	11.9	10.8	10.6	11.8	13.0
1877	13.1	12.6	12.7	12.7	12.6	12.5	11.4	10.4	10.1	9.3	8.0	7.1
1878	6.6	6.0	5.3	4.6	4.0	3.5	3.3	3.9	2.4	2.3	2.4	2.2
1879	2.5	3.2	3.7	4.2	5.0	5.7	6.9	9.0	10.9	12.3	13.7	15.8
1880	17.7	19.8	23.9	27.6	29.7	31.3	32.8	34.4	36.8	39.5	41.6	43.6
1881	47.0	49.7	49.6	49.9	51.8	53.5	54.6	55.6	57.0	59.5	62.2	62.4
1882	60.4	58.4	57.9	57.8	58.9	59.9	60.3	60.0	58.1	56.5	54.6	54.5
1883	57.3	59.0	59.0	59.8	60.9	62.3	65.0	67.9	71.4	73.0	74.2	74.6
1884	72.4	71.7	72.4	71.3	67.8	64.6	61.4	58.8	56.6	54.2	53.6	55.2
1885	57.1	57.4	56.2	54.9	54.4	53.2	51.6	49.2	47.6	47.4	45.2	41.1
1886	37.2	34.3	32.2	30.2	27.5	25.8	24.6	23.2	20.5	16.7	14.7	13.8
1887	13.1	13.0	12.6	11.9	12.1	12.7	13.2	13.0	12.9	13.0	12.4	11.5
1888	10.3	8.6	7.9	7.8	7.8	7.3	6.3	5.8	5.8	5.8	5.6	5.3
1889	5.6	6.6	7.2	7.1	6.7	6.3	6.5	6.3	5.9	5.7	5.7	5.6
1890	5.5	5.0	5.0	5.8	6.6	7.0	7.4	8.6	9.8	10.8	13.1	16.5
1891	20.5	23.5	26.0	29.2	32.2	34.6	37.9	42.5	46.3	50.0	53.7	56.5
1892	58.4	62.0	65.2	66.4	68.1	71.0	73.2	73.4	73.9	75.3	76.3	77.0
1893	78.0	79.7	81.5	82.5	83.3	84.3	85.3	86.1	86.0	85.2	85.6	86.7
1894	87.9	86.2	83.2	82.5	81.6	79.4	77.2	75.6	75.3	75.4	73.8	71.3
1895	67.7	65.2	64.8	64.2	63.5	63.5	62.5	60.7	59.9	58.2	55.1	52.5
1896	51.5	49.6	48.0	46.5	44.5	43.0	42.3	41.6	39.5	38.0	37.1	35.2
1897	32.9	32.0	31.2	30.1	28.3	26.6	25.8	25.7	26.3	26.0	25.6	26.3
1898	26.0	25.6	25.4	25.7	27.5	27.6	26.3	24.7	22.7	21.9	21.1	20.3
1899	20.4	19.4	17.1	15.1	13.2	12.2	11.7	11.5	11.2	10.9	11.3	11.3
1900	10.7	10.5	10.6	10.6	10.4	9.9	9.1	8.2	7.6	6.8	5.9	5.4
1901	4.8	4.4	3.9	3.2	2.8	2.8	3.0	3.1	3.3	3.6	3.3	2.8
1902	2.6	2.7	3.1	3.9	4.7	5.0	5.2	6.0	6.8	7.9	9.5	10.6
1903	12.3	14.6	15.8	16.9	19.3	22.5	25.4	26.6	27.9	29.6	31.4	33.5
1904	35.5	37.7	39.7	41.1	41.5	41.6	42.9	46.4	49.8	50.5	50.7	51.3
1905	52.5	53.5	54.6	56.6	60.5	63.4	63.1	60.4	58.5	59.5	60.6	61.6
1906	63.4	64.2	63.8	61.3	55.9	53.5	55.1	59.6	62.7	62.4	61.7	60.1
1907	56.9	55.0	56.4	59.6	62.6	62.8	60.5	55.9	51.4	50.3	50.4	50.6

Year	Jan	Feb	Mar	Apr	May	Jun	Jul	Aug	Sep	Oct	Nov	Dec
1908	50.5	51.6	53.2	51.9	49.9	48.9	49.3	50.5	52.6	53.1	51.9	50.6
1909	49.4	46.4	41.6	40.7	42.2	43.3	42.6	40.7	38.2	35.4	33.8	32.8
1910	31.5	30.1	29.1	27.7	24.7	20.6	17.6	15.7	14.2	14.0	13.8	12.8
1911	12.0	11.2	10.0	7.6	6.0	5.9	5.6	5.1	4.6	4.0	3.3	3.2
1912	3.2	3.0	3.1	3.4	3.4	3.4	3.7	3.9	3.8	3.5	3.2	2.8
1913	2.6	2.5	2.2	1.8	1.7	1.6	1.5	1.5	1.6	2.4	3.3	4.0
1914	4.6	5.1	5.8	6.5	7.4	8.8	10.4	12.9	16.1	18.6	20.7	24.3
1915	29.4	34.8	38.9	42.3	45.3	46.9	48.3	49.8	51.5	53.9	56.9	58.6
1916	57.8	55.6	54.0	53.7	54.6	56.3	58.3	60.2	62.1	63.3	65.1	68.7
1917	73.4	81.2	89.7	94.1	96.3	100.7	104.8	105.4	104.2	103.5	102.2	98.3
1918	95.5	92.8	88.5	87.0	87.0	83.5	78.6	77.2	77.5	76.1	75.4	78.0
1919	78.4	75.2	72.8	70.4	67.4	64.6	63.7	62.8	61.9	60.5	56.7	51.4
1920	46.8	43.2	40.3	39.4	38.7	37.9	36.8	34.9	32.1	31.0	31.3	30.6
1921	31.0	31.7	31.1	29.0	27.3	26.5	25.3	24.4	25.5	25.8	24.3	22.5
1922	20.1	18.1	16.9	15.8	14.9	14.4	13.9	12.6	9.4	7.1	6.7	6.6
1923	6.4	5.9	6.0	6.6	6.9	6.4	5.6	5.6	5.7	5.8	6.8	8.1
1924	9.8	11.6	12.9	14.0	15.1	16.1	16.9	17.9	19.3	20.9	22.6	24.5
1925	25.9	27.1	29.3	32.6	35.9	40.9	47.2	51.8	55.6	57.7	58.9	60.9
1926	62.6	64.1	65.1	65.2	65.4	64.7	64.3	65.7	66.9	69.5	72.4	72.4
1927	72.0	71.8	71.7	71.7	71.6	70.5	69.1	68.4	68.3	68.4	67.7	69.0
1928	72.1	75.1	77.3	78.1	77.3	77.2	77.1	76.1	74.2	71.6	69.2	67.7
1929	66.2	64.3	61.3	58.6	59.6	63.0	64.8	64.0	62.8	61.1	60.6	57.5
1930	53.6	49.8	48.0	47.1	44.2	39.0	33.5	31.2	30.7	30.2	29.4	28.3
1931	27.6	26.9	25.9	24.2	22.6	21.6	21.1	19.7	17.8	16.3	14.8	14.8
1932	14.8	14.2	13.3	12.6	12.2	11.4	11.2	11.7	12.0	11.7	10.7	9.4
1933	8.4	7.9	7.7	7.5	6.9	6.2	5.4	4.3	3.4	3.6	4.6	5.4
1934	5.7	6.3	6.6	6.7	7.2	8.1	9.4	10.6	11.9	12.7	13.0	15.0
1935	17.6	19.6	22.0	25.6	29.9	34.2	37.9	42.0	46.5	51.3	55.0	57.2
1936	59.0	62.2	65.9	68.8	72.5	77.2	82.6	87.8	90.3	92.1	96.1	101.2
1937	107.6	113.5	116.7	119.2	119.0	115.8	113.0	111.2	110.9	110.6	110.8	109.8
1938	109.3	109.2	107.9	106.3	107.1	109.4	108.8	106.3	103.6	103.0	103.0	102.8
1939	101.1	96.9	97.4	97.9	95.2	90.9	87.6	85.5	85.5	84.3	79.6	76.3
1940	74.2	73.0	71.1	67.8	66.0	66.7	67.6	66.8	64.6	61.9	59.7	57.6
1941	56.6	54.7	52.8	52.4	51.2	49.0	47.0	47.0	47.6	49.1	50.2	47.8
1942	43.7	41.1	36.5	33.3	31.8	31.0	29.6	27.7	25.6	23.0	21.1	20.5
1943	20.1	19.9	19.6	18.8	17.5	16.5	16.0	14.4	12.6	10.8	9.2	8.6
1944	8.2	7.7	7.8	8.4	8.8	9.2	10.2	11.3	12.3	14.0	16.5	19.0
1945	21.9	23.8	25.1	28.1	31.7	33.1	34.3	38.6	43.9	48.1	52.1	56.0
1946	60.6	67.0	72.9	76.8	81.4	88.6	95.3	100.2	104.3	109.6	117.6	126.2
1947	131.7	136.8	143.4	149.0	151.8	151.7	151.2	148.9	145.5	145.7	146.2	145.3
1948	144.8	142.8	140.5	138.2	135.8	135.3	136.6	141.1	147.7	148.5	143.9	139.2
1949	136.6	134.5	133.2	133.0	134.8	136.0	134.4	130.0	124.4	121.0	119.6	118.0
1950	115.0	111.9	106.4	99.5	92.9	86.6	82.2	79.0	75.3	72.2	71.4	72.2
1951	71.7	69.5	69.8	70.7	70.2	69.8	68.6	66.3	63.3	59.2	53.0	46.8
1952	43.2	42.0	39.5	36.0	33.6	31.9	30.8	29.4	28.2	27.6	27.1	26.0
1953	24.1	21.6	19.9	18.9	17.4	15.2	12.8	11.5	11.4	10.4	8.8	7.4
1954	6.4	5.6	4.2	3.4	3.7	4.2	5.4	7.2	7.8	7.9	9.5	12.0
1955	14.2	16.4	19.5	23.4	28.8	35.1	40.1	46.5	55.5	64.4	73.0	81.0
1956	88.8	98.5	109.3	118.7	127.4	136.9	145.5	149.6	151.5	155.8	159.6	164.3
1957	170.2	172.2	174.3	181.0	185.5	187.9	191.4	194.4	197.3	199.5	200.8	200.1
1958	199.0	200.9	201.3	196.8	191.4	186.8	185.2	184.9	183.8	182.2	180.7	180.5
1959	178.6	176.9	174.5	169.2	165.1	161.4	155.8	151.3	146.3	141.1	137.2	132.5
1960	128.9	125.0	121.6	119.6	117.0	113.9	108.4	101.9	97.2	92.6	87.2	82.9

Year	Jan	Feb	Mar	Apr	May	Jun	Jul	Aug	Sep	Oct	Nov	Dec
1961	80.2	74.8	68.9	64.3	60.1	55.8	53.1	52.5	52.3	51.4	50.5	48.7
1962	45.2	41.8	39.8	39.4	39.2	38.3	36.8	34.9	32.7	30.8	30.0	29.8
1963	29.4	29.8	29.7	29.0	28.7	28.2	27.7	27.2	26.9	26.0	23.8	21.3
1964	19.5	17.8	15.4	12.7	10.9	10.2	10.3	10.2	9.9	9.6	10.2	11.0
1965	11.7	12.0	12.5	13.6	14.6	15.0	15.5	16.4	17.4	19.7	22.3	24.5
1966	27.7	31.3	34.5	37.4	40.7	44.6	50.3	56.6	63.1	67.6	70.2	72.7
1967	75.0	78.8	82.2	84.6	87.4	91.3	94.1	95.3	95.3	95.0	97.1	100.6
1968	102.6	102.9	104.7	107.2	107.6	106.6	105.2	104.8	107.0	109.9	110.6	110.1
1969	110.0	109.6	108.0	106.4	106.2	106.1	105.8	106.4	105.4	104.1	104.6	104.9
1970	105.6	106.0	106.2	106.1	105.8	105.3	103.8	101.0	97.2	93.9	89.4	84.1
1971	80.4	77.8	74.4	70.9	68.1	66.7	65.4	64.6	65.8	66.2	66.8	69.4
1972	70.8	71.2	72.4	73.4	72.9	70.5	68.2	65.5	62.2	60.6	58.7	55.1
1973	50.9	46.5	44.2	42.7	40.7	39.1	37.5	36.1	34.4	32.6	31.8	31.5
1974	32.7	34.4	34.0	33.9	34.6	34.5	34.0	33.1	32.1	30.3	27.6	25.2
1975	23.0	22.1	21.3	18.6	16.8	16.0	15.0	14.2	14.4	15.4	16.1	16.2
1976	15.2	13.2	12.2	12.6	12.5	12.2	12.9	14.0	14.3	13.4	13.5	14.8
1977	16.7	18.1	20.0	22.2	24.2	26.3	29.0	33.4	39.1	45.6	51.9	56.9
1978	61.3	64.5	69.6	76.9	83.2	89.3	97.4	104.0	108.4	111.1	113.3	117.7
1979	123.7	130.9	136.5	141.1	147.2	153.0	155.0	155.4	155.7	157.8	162.3	164.5
1980	163.9	162.6	160.9	158.7	156.3	154.7	152.8	150.3	150.1	150.2	147.7	142.7
1981	140.3	141.5	143.0	143.4	142.9	141.5	140.3	141.1	142.8	142.2	138.9	137.8
1982	137.0	133.3	129.2	124.3	119.9	117.3	115.2	109.4	101.0	95.7	94.7	94.6
1983	92.8	90.3	85.9	81.5	77.1	70.5	65.5	65.8	67.9	68.2	66.8	64.0
1984	60.2	56.4	53.0	49.8	47.5	46.5	44.2	39.6	33.9	28.9	24.7	21.7
1985	20.5	19.6	18.6	18.3	18.3	18.0	17.4	17.1	17.3	17.3	16.8	15.3
1986	13.8	13.1	13.0	13.7	14.3	13.8	13.7	13.2	12.3	13.2	14.9	16.3
1987	17.6	19.6	22.1	24.4	26.5	28.4	31.2	34.8	39.0	43.6	46.7	51.3
1988	58.2	64.6	71.3	77.5	83.8	93.7	104.3	113.7	121.2	125.3	130.4	137.6
1989	142.0	145.0	149.7	153.5	156.9	158.4	158.5	157.7	156.6	157.4	157.5	153.5
1990	150.6	152.9	152.0	149.3	147.0	143.8	140.6	140.5	142.1	142.1	141.7	143.9
1991	147.6	147.6	146.6	146.5	145.5	145.2	146.3	146.6	144.9	141.7	138.1	131.7
1992	123.7	115.4	108.2	103.3	100.3	97.1	90.7	84.0	79.5	77.0		

Each smoothed number represents the average of two adjacent 12-month running means of monthly means. Consider, for example, the June 1980 value. We built this number by first computing two 12-month means: one that averaged monthly means from December 1979 through November 1980 and a second that averaged means from January 1980 through December 1980. The June 1980 smoothed number equals the arithmetic average of these two running means.

Source: Solar-Terrestrial Physics Division, National Geophysical Data Center, 325 Broadway, Mail Code E/GC2, Boulder, CO 80303-3328 USA

WORLDWIDE INDICES

Daily Solar and Geomagnetic Terrestrial Data, September 1992 through August 1993

The following 13 observatories, which lie between 46 and 63 degrees north and south geomagnetic latitude, now contribute to the planetary indices: Lerwick (UK), Eskdalemuir (UK), Hartland (UK), Ottawa (Canada), Fredericksburg (USA), Meannook (Canada), Sitka (USA), Eyrewell (New Zealand), Canberra (Australia), Lovo (Sweden), Rude Skov (Denmark), Wingst (Germany), and Witteveen (The Netherlands).

Three-Hour-Range K-Index

K indices isolate solar particle effects on the earth's magnetic field; over a three-hour period, they classify into disturbance levels the range of variation of the more unsettled horizontal field component. Each activity level relates almost logarithmically to its corresponding disturbance amplitude. Three-hour indices discriminate conservatively between true magnetic field perturbations and the quiet-day variations produced by ionospheric currents.

K indices range in 28 steps from 0 (quiet) to 9 (greatly disturbed) with fractional parts expressed in thirds of a unit. The indices reported in the table below have been rounded to resemble the reports announced on WWV at 18 minutes after each hour.

Equivalent Amplitude, or A-Index

The A-index ranges from 0 to 400 and represents a K-value converted to a linear scale in gammas (nanoTeslas). A scale that measures equivalent disturbance amplitude of a station at which K=9 has a lower limit of 400 gammas.

Daily Sunspot Number, "SN"

"SN" in the table is the daily sunspot number for that date, unsmoothed, from the Royal Observatory in Brussels.

SFI—Solar Flux Index

The SFI column represents the Ottawa 10.7-cm (2800 MHz) Solar Radio Flux ADJUSTED TO 1 AU. Solar flux is measured at 1700 UT daily and expressed in units of 10 to the -22 Watts/meter^2 /hertz. The numbers here are the "observed" and "adjusted" values. Since the Solar Flux Index is closely followed by radio amateurs, it is instructive to know how this number is derived.

The sun emits radio energy with a slowly varying intensity. This radio flux, which originates from atmospheric layers high in the sun's chromosphere and low in its corona, changes gradually from day-to-day, in response to the number of spot groups on the disk. Radio intensity levels consist of emission from three sources: from the undisturbed solar surface, from developing active regions, and from short-lived enhancements above the daily level. Solar flux density at 2800 MHz has been recorded routinely by radio telescope near Ottawa since February 14, 1947. Each day, levels are determined at local noon (1700 GMT) and then corrected to within a few percent for factors such as antenna gain, atmospheric absorption, bursts in progress, and background sky temperature.

Three sets of flux values are recorded: the observed, the adjusted, and the absolute. Of the three, the observed numbers are the least refined, since they contain fluctuations as large as 7% that arise from the changing sun-earth distance, but they are perhaps more relevant in determining the sun's effect on radio wave propagation. In contrast, adjusted fluxes have this variation removed; these numbers reflect the energy flux received by a detector located at the mean distance (1AU) between sun and earth. Finally, the absolute levels carry the error reduction one step further; here each adjusted value is multiplied by 0.90 to compensate for uncertainties in antenna gain and in waves reflected from the ground.

Notes on the SFI data:

* Data for November 30, 1992 is corrected for a burst in progress
** Data for December 18, 1992 is a value enhanced by burst
*** Data for December 21, 1992 is a 2300 UT reading—1700 UT reading corrupted by wet snow on antenna
NA Data not available at press time

		K-Index								A-index										
Month	day	03Z	06Z	09Z	12Z	15Z	18Z	21Z	24Z	03Z	06Z	09Z	12Z	15Z	18Z	21Z	24Z	SN	adjSFI	obsSFI
Sep-92	1	1	1	0	0	1	1	0	0	4	3	2	0	3	3	2	2	47	101.6	99.8
	2	1	2	2	4	5	5	4	4	5	6	6	27	39	48	27	27	49	106.3	104.5
	3	3	5	6	5	5	6	5	4	18	48	67	56	39	67	56	32	44	108.9	107
	4	4	4	5	4	4	3	3	6	32	22	48	32	22	15	15	80	46	106.4	104.7
	5	5	5	4	4	3	3	4	3	56	39	32	22	15	12	27	18	47	121.2	119.3
	6	3	4	3	2	2	3	4	3	18	22	15	6	9	15	32	18	52	141.3	139.2
	7	4	3	3	4	4	3	4	3	22	18	18	32	27	18	27	12	44	133.6	131.7
	8	4	4	5	2	3	3	3	2	22	22	39	9	15	15	15	9	38	130.8	128.9
	9	5	7	6	7	7	5	6	5	56	111	80	154	111	48	67	48	57	118.5	116.9
	10	6	6	6	6	5	7	7	6	67	94	94	67	56	132	111	80	54	118.4	116.9
	11	6	4	4	3	3	5	3	3	94	32	32	18	15	39	18	12	59	120.1	118.6
	12	2	2	1	0	1	1	1	2	9	7	4	2	3	3	5	6	63	118.7	117.3
	13	1	1	1	1	1	1	2	2	5	5	4	4	3	3	7	6	77	128.8	127.3
	14	1	2	2	2	1	2	2	3	5	9	7	6	5	7	9	12	77	123.1	121.7
	15	3	3	3	2	2	3	2	1	12	18	12	7	7	12	7	5	75	121.5	120.2
	16	2	2	3	2	3	3	4	3	6	9	15	7	12	12	22	12	76	127.9	126.6
	17	6	7	7	7	5	5	7	6	67	111	154	111	56	48	132	67	62	120.6	119.4
	18	4	5	4	5	4	3	4	4	32	48	27	39	32	15	32	22	54	118.5	117.5
	19	3	3	2	3	3	2	4	1	18	18	7	15	12	9	22	5	63	113.4	112.5
	20	2	2	2	2	2	1	3	3	6	7	9	9	9	4	12	12	62	107.1	106.3
	21	1	1	2	1	1	1	2	4	4	5	6	4	3	5	6	22	65	110.4	109.5
	22	4	5	2	2	2	1	3	3	32	48	7	6	6	5	15	15	66	112.3	111.6
	23	3	3	3	2	2	1	2	1	12	18	12	7	6	5	7	4	89	112.6	111.9
	24	0	0	0	1	0	1	1	2	2	2	2	3	2	3	5	9	90	112.6	112
	25	3	1	2	3	3	2	3	3	15	5	6	12	12	7	18	12	75	116.5	115.9

Month	day	K-Index 03Z	06Z	09Z	12Z	15Z	18Z	21Z	24Z	A-Index 03Z	06Z	09Z	12Z	15Z	18Z	21Z	24Z	SN	adjSFI	obsSFI
	26	3	2	1	1	1	3	2	0	18	9	5	3	4	18	6	2	84	117.3	116.7
	27	1	1	1	1	2	1	1	1	3	4	4	4	6	3	4	3	86	121.6	121.1
	28	0	1	2	2	3	3	5	5	2	5	6	6	12	18	39	39	62	116.6	116.2
	29	4	7	7	6	5	5	5	4	27	111	111	67	56	48	48	27	72	117.7	117.3
	30	5	4	4	3	4	6	5	4	39	27	27	15	27	67	48	27	81	116.2	115.9
Oct-92	1	4	5	4	3	3	3	4	2	27	56	32	18	18	18	32	7	85	118.2	117.9
	2	4	3	2	2	2	2	1	2	22	15	7	7	6	7	5	6	98	119.5	119.4
	3	1	1	2	2	1	1	2	1	3	5	6	7	5	4	9	5	84	120.2	120.1
	4	3	4	2	1	1	0	1	1	12	22	9	4	4	2	3	3	105	126.1	126.1
	5	1	2	1	0	1	2	2	1	4	7	5	2	4	7	6	5	122	130.1	130.2
	6	4	3	1	2	3	2	1	1	22	15	5	7	12	7	4	4	119	137.3	137.4
	7	2	3	2	2	2	2	2	1	6	15	9	9	7	6	9	4	103	135.8	136.1
	8	3	2	1	0	0	1	3	3	18	9	3	2	0	4	18	12	88	125.4	125.6
	9	3	2	2	5	4	5	4	3	12	9	9	56	27	56	27	15	91	121	121.3
	10	1	2	3	3	3	1	1	3	4	6	15	18	12	5	5	15	73	112.1	112.5
	11	3	2	1	3	5	5	5	4	12	7	5	18	48	39	39	22	57	110	110.5
	12	3	4	5	4	6	4	3	2	15	27	48	32	94	32	15	9	41	106.5	107
	13	3	3	2	1	3	4	6	4	18	15	9	5	15	27	67	27	36	108.2	108.7
	14	3	4	3	3	3	2	5	6	18	22	18	18	12	9	39	67	43	104.9	105.5
	15	5	5	4	5	4	4	4	4	48	48	32	39	32	22	32	27	40	97.8	98.4
	16	5	4	4	3	3	3	2	4	48	32	22	18	12	15	9	22	54	99.9	100.6
	17	3	3	3	3	4	3	4	2	15	12	12	18	22	18	22	9	55	105.8	106.6
	18	3	1	1	1	3	2	3	4	12	5	5	4	18	9	12	27	73	111.4	112.3
	19	4	3	2	3	3	4	3	3	27	12	7	15	18	22	15	12	92	123.4	124.5
	20	4	4	2	2	2	1	1	1	32	27	6	9	6	4	5	5	75	131.9	133.1
	21	1	2	2	1	1	2	2	3	4	6	6	4	5	6	6	12	98	139.2	140.6
	22	3	2	1	1	3	3	1	2	18	7	3	4	15	15	5	6	104	149.2	150.7
	23	2	2	1	1	1	1	1	1	6	6	5	5	5	3	5	5	95	140.3	141.8
	24	1	1	0	0	0	1	0	2	4	4	2	2	2	3	0	6	114	145.1	146.8
	25	3	2	1	2	2	1	2	2	15	6	5	7	6	4	6	6	113	159.4	161.2
	26	3	3	3	2	2	2	4	3	18	15	12	7	6	7	27	18	125	167.9	169.9
	27	5	4	3	5	5	5	3	3	48	27	18	39	39	48	18	12	130	168.9	171.1
	28	4	3	3	4	2	3	3	3	32	15	18	27	9	18	12	18	131	172.3	174.7
	29	4	4	4	4	3	4	5	4	32	22	32	22	18	27	39	22	111	161.6	163.8
	30	3	3	3	3	4	4	2	3	15	15	15	12	22	22	9	15	100	225.8	229.1
	31	2	2	3	3	3	2	2	1	9	7	15	12	15	9	6	5	82	147.3	149.6
Nov-92	1	2	1	2	1	2	3	2	6	7	4	6	5	6	15	9	80	109	144.8	147.1
	2	5	5	4	3	3	1	3	3	39	56	22	18	12	5	18	15	88	138.8	141
	3	4	4	4	4	2	1	2	3	22	22	32	27	7	4	9	12	68	132.9	135.1
	4	2	3	3	4	4	5	3	5	9	15	15	27	32	48	15	39	86	140.4	142.8
	5	4	2	3	3	3	2	2	2	32	9	15	18	18	9	9	7	95	133.6	136
	6	3	2	3	2	4	4	2	3	15	9	15	7	22	22	9	12	95	130.5	132.9
	7	3	2	3	3	2	3	2	3	15	7	15	12	7	15	7	18	96	132.4	134.9
	8	3	2	2	1	2	2	3	4	18	7	7	5	7	7	15	22	74	129.7	132.2
	9	3	4	6	6	5	4	3	4	12	27	94	80	48	32	15	32	76	129.9	132.4
	10	3	3	2	3	2	3	2	3	15	12	9	15	7	18	9	15	78	133.7	136.4
	11	4	4	4	4	3	3	3	2	22	27	22	22	18	18	12	9	84	132	134.8
	12	3	3	3	3	3	3	3	4	15	18	12	18	15	12	15	27	83	124.7	127.4
	13	3	2	2	4	4	3	3	3	15	9	9	27	32	15	15	12	59	122.2	124.9
	14	3	2	2	3	3	3	3	2	12	9	9	15	18	12	12	9	69	123.4	126.1
	15	3	2	2	2	4	4	3	5	15	9	6	6	27	32	18	39	74	124.1	126.9
	16	4	2	2	2	1	1	3	3	22	9	7	6	5	5	15	15	84	133.7	136.7
	17	2	3	2	1	2	1	2	2	9	18	7	5	6	5	7	7	100	148.9	152.3
	18	3	1	1	1	1	2	3	1	12	4	3	5	4	9	15	3	102	158.2	161.9
	19	1	2	2	3	3	1	1	1	3	7	7	12	15	5	4	3	108	157.1	160.9
	20	1	0	1	1	1	0	2	2	3	2	3	4	3	2	6	9	98	155	158.8
	21	4	3	2	0	0	0	1	1	22	18	6	2	2	2	3	4	85	NA	165.3
	22	1	2	3	4	4	3	4	4	3	7	12	22	27	18	22	27	95	162	166.2
	23	5	6	4	3	3	5	3	3	39	67	32	18	18	39	15	18	115	171.7	176.2
	24	2	1	3	3	3	3	3	3	6	5	12	12	15	12	18	12	116	169.4	173.8
	25	3	2	2	4	4	2	2	3	12	7	7	22	22	7	7	15	125	162.4	166.8
	26	3	4	2	2	2	1	2	2	15	22	6	9	7	5	7	6	116	158.2	162.5
	27	1	1	2	1	2	2	0	1	5	5	6	4	9	6	2	5	116	152.6	156.8
	28	1	2	1	2	1	1	2	2	5	7	5	7	4	5	6	9	103	144.7	148.7
	29	1	1	2	1	2	2	1	0	5	4	6	5	9	6	4	2	88	136	139.8
	30	0	0	1	2	3	4	5	3	2	2	5	9	15	22	39	12	74	135.9	139.8*
Dec-92	1	4	3	4	3	3	3	2	3	27	12	22	18	15	18	7	18	65	127.1	131.4
	2	3	3	1	2	2	2	2	2	18	15	5	7	7	6	7	6	56	126	130.3
	3	3	3	2	3	3	4	3	3	18	18	6	18	12	22	12	15	59	121.3	125.5

		K-index								A-index										
Month	day	03Z	06Z	09Z	12Z	15Z	18Z	21Z	24Z	03Z	06Z	09Z	12Z	15Z	18Z	21Z	24Z	SN	adjSFI	obsSFI
	4	3	4	3	2	3	3	3	3	15	27	12	7	15	12	12	18	59	115.9	119.8
	5	4	3	2	1	1	1	0	0	22	12	7	4	4	5	2	2	51	112.4	116.3
	6	1	0	0	1	2	3	2	1	4	0	2	3	6	15	6	3	48	115.9	119.8
	7	0	1	3	2	4	1	2	5	2	5	15	9	32	4	9	48	34	116.1	120.1
	8	5	3	4	4	4	4	4	5	39	18	22	22	22	22	27	39	58	124.8	129
	9	3	3	3	3	4	4	3	3	18	15	15	15	32	27	12	15	96	129.6	134
	10	2	2	3	3	2	5	4	3	9	9	12	18	7	39	22	18	95	137.5	142.2
	11	3	2	2	2	2	2	2	3	18	9	6	6	7	9	9	12	132	159	164.4
	12	2	2	1	1	3	2	3	2	9	6	3	4	15	7	12	9	109	163.1	168.6
	13	3	3	2	2	2	2	1	2	15	15	6	6	7	7	5	6	113	167.6	173.3
	14	3	2	1	1	1	3	3	3	18	9	3	4	5	12	18	15	106	161.8	167.2
	15	4	3	2	2	2	3	3	4	27	15	7	9	9	12	12	22	112	150.4	155.5
	16	2	3	2	2	2	1	0	1	6	15	7	6	6	4	2	5	109	145.8	150.7
	17	0	1	3	3	4	6	5	3	2	4	18	12	27	67	56	15	105	145.5	150.3
	18	2	1	1	2	1	2	3	3	9	5	4	7	5	9	18	12	98	144.9	149.8**
	19	2	1	1	2	3	2	4	4	6	3	5	6	12	7	27	22	104	142.2	147
	20	2	3	4	3	3	3	3	2	7	15	22	12	12	15	15	7	97	143.2	147.9
	21	1	2	2	3	2	4	4	3	4	7	9	15	9	27	27	18	84	140.8	145.4***
	22	2	1	2	2	2	2	2	1	9	5	7	7	9	9	9	4	91	137.6	142.1
	23	1	3	2	2	3	2	2	1	5	12	9	7	15	7	7	3	84	139.3	143.8
	24	1	2	2	2	2	2	3	1	4	9	7	9	7	9	18	4	82	132	136.3
	25	0	0	1	1	1	2	2	2	2	2	3	4	5	7	7	7	81	132	136.2
	26	1	1	1	1	1	1	1	1	5	3	5	5	4	4	5	5	95	127.2	131.3
	27	1	0	1	0	0	0	3	5	3	2	3	2	2	2	12	39	73	121.2	125
	28	3	2	3	2	5	5	6	6	15	7	15	7	48	56	67	94	80	123.4	127.2
	29	6	6	5	4	4	5	4	3	67	67	48	27	32	56	22	15	78	121.3	125.1
	30	3	3	2	3	3	2	1	1	12	12	9	15	15	7	5	5	69	121.9	125.7
	31	3	2	3	2	3	3	1	1	15	9	12	9	18	15	5	4	59	125.8	129.7
Jan-93	1	2	3	3	2	2	2	2	3	7	18	15	7	7	7	7	15	46	118.3	122.3
	2	3	3	3	5	4	4	4	4	18	18	18	39	27	27	27	22	41	117.4	121.4
	3	5	5	4	4	3	4	4	4	56	48	27	32	18	32	27	22	38	120.6	124.7
	4	5	3	4	4	5	4	4	4	56	18	22	32	39	22	27	32	52	117.1	121.1
	5	3	4	3	4	3	2	3	3	18	22	15	22	18	9	15	15	71	120.8	124.9
	6	3	4	3	3	3	3	3	3	18	22	15	12	15	15	18	15	84	125.8	130.1
	7	3	4	2	4	3	4	5	5	12	22	9	27	12	27	39	39	81	126.3	130.6
	8	3	3	2	2	2	4	4	4	18	12	7	7	9	22	22	22	89	128.6	132.9
	9	4	3	3	2	3	3	3	3	27	12	18	9	18	18	12	12	94	124.5	128.8
	10	3	4	6	4	4	3	1	1	18	27	80	27	27	15	4	4	100	127.7	132.1
	11	2	2	1	3	5	4	4	4	7	9	5	18	56	27	22	27	91	127.4	131.7
	12	4	3	3	2	2	3	2	1	27	18	12	7	7	15	9	5	94	135.6	140.2
	13	2	1	1	2	3	3	2	5	7	5	5	7	12	18	7	39	96	136.6	141.3
	14	4	5	3	3	4	3	3	4	22	39	12	18	22	18	18	27	69	128.8	133.1
	15	3	3	2	3	2	3	3	4	18	15	7	12	9	15	12	22	58	121.9	126
	16	3	4	2	1	2	3	2	3	12	22	7	4	7	12	9	15	59	129.1	133.4
	17	4	3	4	3	2	2	2	1	22	15	27	15	9	6	6	5	62	121.9	126
	18	2	3	1	2	2	3	3	4	7	12	5	7	7	12	12	27	66	117.7	121.6
	19	4	3	3	4	2	3	5	5	27	18	12	22	9	12	39	39	68	112.7	116.4
	20	4	2	3	3	4	3	1	1	22	6	18	15	22	18	4	3	52	106.5	110
	21	2	3	1	2	2	1	1	1	9	18	5	6	6	5	3	3	47	103.3	106.6
	22	1	2	1	1	1	1	3	3	3	6	5	4	4	5	12	15	34	101	104.2
	23	2	1	0	0	1	0	1	2	9	3	2	0	4	2	4	6	30	102.7	106
	24	1	2	2	3	2	2	3	1	4	9	9	18	7	9	18	5	45	101.6	104.8
	25	1	1	2	3	5	4	5	4	3	3	6	15	56	27	56	32	51	102.6	105.8
	26	5	4	4	3	3	3	3	2	48	22	22	18	18	18	18	9	37	103.3	106.5
	27	2	3	3	3	2	3	2	2	7	15	15	12	9	15	9	7	43	107.6	110.9
	28	1	3	2	2	2	1	1	1	5	18	7	7	6	4	4	3	37	108.6	112
	29	1	1	1	1	1	1	1	2	3	4	5	5	4	4	5	9	35	110.7	114
	30	3	4	2	2	2	2	2	3	18	22	9	7	9	7	9	18	36	109.6	113
	31	4	5	6	6	5	5	6	6	32	56	80	67	48	39	67	80	32	115.6	119
Feb-93	1	5	4	5	4	3	5	3	4	48	27	39	27	18	48	18	22	22	121.5	125.1
	2	4	5	3	3	3	4	4	2	32	39	15	12	12	22	27	7	34	124.7	128.3
	3	1	3	2	1	1	1	3	4	5	12	6	5	4	5	18	22	73	133	136.9
	4	3	2	1	1	1	2	2	2	15	7	4	4	5	9	7	7	85	143.2	147.4
	5	1	1	2	1	1	2	2	2	5	4	9	5	3	6	6	9	119	155.6	160.1
	6	1	2	1	1	1	1	2	1	3	9	5	4	4	3	9	5	121	178.8	183.8
	7	1	4	4	4	2	4	5	5	5	27	32	27	9	22	56	39	128	171.2	175.9
	8	5	5	4	4	3	5	5	5	56	56	32	27	18	56	39	39	134	183.4	188.4
	9	4	5	3	5	4	4	4	3	22	39	18	39	27	32	27	18	126	180.3	185.1
	10	2	2	3	2	3	3	5	2	9	7	15	9	18	18	48	9	114	175	179.6
	11	4	3	3	3	3	3	3	5	27	18	15	12	15	18	18	39	95	168.8	173.2

Month	day	K-Index								A-Index										
		03Z	06Z	09Z	12Z	15Z	18Z	21Z	24Z	03Z	06Z	09Z	12Z	15Z	18Z	21Z	24Z	SN	adjSFI	obsSFI
	12	4	3	2	3	2	2	1	3	22	15	9	12	7	6	5	15	97	144.9	148.6
	13	4	3	2	2	3	2	2	3	27	12	6	7	12	7	7	15	92	131.7	135
	14	2	3	1	2	1	1	2	1	7	15	4	6	5	3	7	4	82	137.9	141.4
	15	1	1	1	2	2	1	1	1	3	5	3	6	7	4	4	3	73	131.6	134.8
	16	1	2	2	2	2	1	1	1	3	6	9	9	7	4	3	3	88	130.5	133.7
	17	2	4	4	5	7	6	2	1	7	27	22	39	111	67	9	5	68	121.4	124.3
	18	1	1	2	3	4	3	3	4	4	4	6	15	22	15	18	22	80	123.2	126
	19	3	1	3	2	1	1	2	1	15	4	12	6	5	4	7	4	88	113.4	116
	20	3	4	5	4	4	3	3	5	15	27	39	32	22	12	15	48	97	120.6	123.3
	21	2	3	4	4	4	5	5	4	9	15	22	27	27	48	39	27	92	120.3	122.9
	22	3	4	6	4	4	4	3	4	18	22	80	32	27	22	18	22	100	130.3	133.1
	23	3	3	1	2	2	3	2	1	12	15	5	7	7	12	6	4	101	129.6	132.3
	24	2	3	2	2	2	1	0	1	7	12	6	7	7	4	2	5	90	132.7	135.4
	25	1	3	2	1	2	2	1	1	4	12	7	5	7	7	4	3	88	125.5	128
	26	1	1	2	1	2	2	1	1	3	5	6	4	6	7	4	5	86	123.8	126.2
	27	1	1	1	1	1	0	1	3	3	3	3	3	4	2	3	15	86	121.6	124
	28	4	4	4	4	4	3	2	1	22	22	22	22	32	18	7	5	88	121.4	123.6
Mar-93	1	2	2	3	4	5	4	3	3	7	7	15	22	39	22	15	18	76	129.6	132
	2	2	3	5	3	3	4	4	5	6	18	39	18	15	27	32	39	80	141	143.5
	3	4	4	4	4	4	5	6	4	32	32	27	22	27	39	67	32	84	148.6	151.1
	4	6	5	4	3	1	3	3	1	67	48	22	12	5	15	12	5	93	163.8	166.5
	5	3	2	2	2	1	1	1	2	18	7	9	6	4	3	3	7	105	162.5	165.2
	6	1	1	2	3	2	2	3	2	5	3	7	12	7	7	15	7	96	164	166.6
	7	4	5	4	2	2	2	4	4	22	48	32	6	6	7	32	27	93	150.9	153.2
	8	3	3	3	2	3	5	4	6	18	18	18	7	18	39	22	94	82	144.3	146.4
	9	7	7	6	6	5	4	3	5	111	111	94	67	39	32	18	39	85	140.6	142.6
	10	5	3	2	1	3	2	1	3	48	18	7	5	18	7	4	12	81	146.7	148.7
	11	3	1	3	5	6	7	6	6	12	5	15	39	67	111	80	67	86	148	149.9
	12	6	3	3	3	3	4	5	4	67	18	15	15	12	27	48	22	77	158.7	160.6
	13	5	5	4	3	3	5	5	3	39	48	22	12	18	48	48	15	67	139.9	141.5
	14	3	3	3	4	4	4	4	4	12	12	18	27	27	27	27	32	56	134.2	135.7
	15	4	4	6	5	5	5	4	5	32	22	67	56	56	39	32	56	60	129.7	131.1
	16	4	5	5	5	3	6	5	2	32	48	56	39	12	67	48	9	56	120.5	121.7
	17	4	3	2	5	3	3	4	5	27	18	9	39	18	12	22	39	60	122.4	123.6
	18	5	4	4	3	3	2	2	2	48	22	22	18	15	6	7	9	69	126.2	127.3
	19	2	1	2	3	2	4	3	2	6	5	7	12	9	27	15	6	72	133.4	134.5
	20	2	4	4	5	4	4	3	2	9	27	22	39	27	22	12	9	70	127	128
	21	3	4	4	5	5	4	3	3	15	32	22	48	56	27	18	18	78	129.7	130.6
	22	4	3	4	4	3	4	4	4	22	18	27	32	18	32	27	27	73	126.6	127.5
	23	3	2	2	2	3	2	2	4	12	6	7	7	15	6	7	32	63	120.1	120.8
	24	4	6	7	6	5	4	3	4	27	80	154	80	39	32	18	32	42	114.4	115
	25	3	3	3	3	3	4	3	2	18	15	18	18	12	22	15	6	40	116	116.5
	26	1	2	1	2	2	1	3	2	4	9	5	7	6	5	15	9	46	116.4	116.9
	27	3	2	2	1	3	3	2	4	15	7	9	5	15	18	7	22	51	122.4	122.9
	28	4	3	2	2	2	3	4	5	22	12	7	9	7	15	27	39	51	125.8	126.2
	29	4	5	4	2	1	1	1	3	32	48	32	6	3	4	3	15	54	128.3	128.7
	30	3	2	3	3	4	5	3	2	18	9	18	15	27	39	15	9	58	128.7	129
	31	4	2	2	1	2	2	2	3	27	7	6	3	7	9	7	12	61	124.9	125.1
Apr-93	1	2	3	2	1	1	2	3	3	7	12	7	4	5	9	12	12	67	123.5	123.6
	2	1	1	2	1	1	1	1	1	4	5	6	5	3	3	4	5	67	120.7	120.8
	3	2	1	0	0	1	1	1	2	6	4	2	2	3	3	5	6	75	117	117
	4	2	2	1	1	5	6	7	8	6	6	4	5	48	80	132	179	67	116.4	116.3
	5	6	7	7	6	6	6	6	3	94	154	132	67	94	67	67	18	75	118.9	118.8
	6	2	2	2	3	3	3	2	5	7	9	7	12	15	15	9	39	89	133.1	132.8
	7	2	3	2	2	2	3	2	4	7	15	9	7	6	15	9	27	79	130	129.7
	8	2	3	4	4	4	4	5	3	9	15	27	27	32	32	48	15	81	143.5	143.1
	9	4	3	3	2	2	5	4	6	22	15	15	6	7	56	32	67	87	136	135.5
	10	4	4	4	2	3	3	3	3	32	22	27	9	15	15	15	12	74	139.2	138.6
	11	2	3	2	2	3	1	2	3	6	12	6	7	12	5	6	12	55	119.4	118.8
	12	4	5	3	2	1	1	2	2	32	56	12	6	5	3	6	6	37	103.7	103.2
	13	2	5	5	6	4	4	4	2	7	48	39	67	32	27	27	7	19	97.7	97.2
	14	4	4	3	3	1	4	4	4	22	32	18	18	5	22	22	22	15	92.8	92.2
	15	4	5	4	3	2	2	5	5	32	39	32	18	6	6	39	56	15	88.8	88.2
	16	3	5	4	2	2	3	3	2	18	39	22	7	7	15	12	9	15	90.9	90.2
	17	2	2	2	3	2	3	4	2	6	7	7	12	6	18	22	6	36	96.5	95.7
	18	4	4	3	4	4	3	3	1	22	32	18	32	22	18	12	5	49	106.6	105.7
	19	3	2	1	3	2	3	2	2	12	6	5	12	9	15	7	7	51	111.9	110.9
	20	3	5	4	3	4	4	3	3	18	48	22	18	27	22	15	12	89	119.9	118.8
	21	4	4	5	4	3	6	4	4	32	27	39	22	18	67	32	27	98	120.5	119.3
	22	4	3	3	2	2	4	5	4	22	12	15	6	9	27	48	32	93	118.4	117.1

Month	day	K-Index 03Z	06Z	09Z	12Z	15Z	18Z	21Z	24Z	A-Index 03Z	06Z	09Z	12Z	15Z	18Z	21Z	24Z	SN	adjSFI	obsSFI
	23	2	2	1	2	1	3	4	3	9	9	5	9	4	12	27	18	96	122.9	121.5
	24	3	2	2	2	3	3	2	1	15	6	7	9	12	12	7	5	98	130.3	128.8
	25	2	3	3	2	2	1	2	3	9	12	18	9	6	5	9	12	88	126.2	124.6
	26	1	1	2	1	2	1	1	1	4	4	7	4	6	5	5	3	50	125	123.3
	27	1	1	1	1	1	1	1	2	3	3	4	3	5	5	3	6	62	119.6	118
	28	1	1	1	1	2	2	2	1	5	4	4	4	6	6	6	3	51	115.2	113.6
	29	1	1	1	2	3	3	4	4	3	4	4	6	15	15	22	27	41	108.1	106.5
	30	4	3	3	2	2	2	3	2	32	15	12	6	9	9	15	7	38	107.4	105.8
May-93	1	3	3	1	2	2	0	0	0	15	18	5	9	6	2	2	2	33	104.2	102.6
	2	0	1	1	1	1	1	3	2	2	4	5	5	5	5	12	7	30	104.7	103.1
	3	2	1	2	2	3	2	1	1	9	5	7	9	15	7	3	5	42	108.9	107.1
	4	1	1	2	0	1	2	1	1	3	5	6	2	5	9	3	4	69	112.4	110.6
	5	1	2	2	1	3	1	0	1	4	6	7	5	15	3	2	4	80	120	117.9
	6	2	2	2	2	2	3	3	2	9	7	7	7	9	12	15	7	71	122.2	120
	7	1	3	2	2	3	3	4	5	4	12	7	7	18	18	27	48	74	133	130.6
	8	6	4	5	5	5	4	5	5	67	22	48	39	39	22	39	48	81	131.2	128.7
	9	5	6	5	4	4	4	5	5	56	80	48	27	32	27	56	56	87	131.5	129
	10	5	6	6	6	5	3	3	4	56	94	67	67	48	15	12	27	120	136.8	134.1
	11	1	2	1	1	1	1	1	2	5	6	5	3	4	3	4	6	125	134.7	132
	12	2	3	3	3	3	3	4	4	7	15	12	15	12	15	27	27	111	129	126.4
	13	4	2	0	0	1	2	4	3	27	9	2	2	3	6	22	12	85	122.4	119.8
	14	2	3	2	4	5	2	2	2	7	12	7	22	39	9	7	7	59	114.6	112.1
	15	2	2	2	2	3	3	4	3	9	6	9	9	15	15	32	12	51	106.7	104.4
	16	3	4	2	2	2	2	2	3	12	32	7	6	9	6	6	15	37	101.1	98.8
	17	3	4	2	2	2	2	5	4	15	27	7	6	9	9	48	27	32	98.4	96.2
	18	1	1	1	1	2	2	2	4	3	4	4	5	7	6	7	22	29	93.5	91.3
	19	2	2	3	2	3	3	3	2	6	9	12	7	15	12	18	6	13	93.1	90.9
	20	1	2	3	2	2	2	1	0	5	9	18	6	7	6	5	2	33	93.4	91.1
	21	1	0	0	1	0	1	1	1	4	2	2	3	2	3	4	3	27	93.3	91
	22	1	1	1	1	1	1	1	0	3	5	3	5	4	5	5	2	20	94.1	91.8
	23	0	0	0	0	1	0	1	0	2	2	2	2	5	2	3	0	23	97.3	94.9
	24	1	1	1	1	0	0	0	0	3	3	5	4	2	2	2	2	33	100.9	98.4
	25	1	1	0	0	0	0	0	0	3	3	0	0	2	2	2	2	53	102.4	99.8
	26	0	1	1	1	1	1	1	2	2	3	3	3	3	4	4	9	66	110.4	107.5
	27	2	4	4	3	3	2	3	3	9	27	27	18	18	7	18	18	59	122.7	119.5
	28	3	4	3	4	3	4	4	4	18	32	12	22	15	32	32	22	74	129.2	125.8
	29	4	2	2	3	1	2	2	2	22	7	7	18	4	6	6	7	88	132.5	129
	30	1	2	1	1	1	1	1	0	3	7	4	3	5	4	4	2	97	144.1	140.1
	31	1	1	1	1	2	1	2	1	4	3	3	5	9	5	6	3	96	142.1	138.2
Jun-93	1	2	1	1	1	2	1	1	0	7	4	3	3	6	3	3	2	105	140.4	136.6
	2	1	1	1	2	3	1	2	1	4	4	5	7	12	4	6	4	102	143.4	139.4
	3	2	2	3	3	3	4	3	3	9	7	15	18	18	22	12	12	101	140.4	136.4
	4	4	5	6	6	5	4	6	6	27	56	67	80	39	27	67	67	82	133.7	129.9
	5	6	5	4	4	4	4	5	3	67	56	32	27	22	22	48	18	74	137.7	133.8
	6	3	3	4	3	3	3	4	3	18	18	27	12	12	15	27	18	83	131.3	127.5
	7	3	2	3	4	4	3	3	4	18	7	18	32	32	18	18	27	70	115.7	112.3
	8	4	3	3	2	3	2	4	2	22	15	12	7	15	9	22	6	55	115.2	111.8
	9	2	1	1	1	1	1	1	2	9	5	4	5	5	5	5	9	46	118.9	115.4
	10	0	1	2	2	1	3	5	7	0	5	6	6	4	12	56	132	47	116	112.6
	11	4	2	2	2	2	2	2	2	27	7	6	6	6	7	9	6	35	104.9	101.8
	12	2	2	3	4	2	2	2	3	6	9	12	27	9	9	7	18	18	96.2	93.3
	13	2	3	4	3	3	2	2	3	9	12	22	18	12	6	9	12	10	89.4	86.6
	14	1	2	2	3	2	2	2	2	4	9	6	18	6	7	6	7	8	86.4	83.7
	15	2	2	2	1	1	1	1	1	7	9	7	5	5	3	3	3	9	84.6	82
	16	1	1	1	1	1	0	0	0	3	4	5	4	3	2	2	2	10	85	82.3
	17	1	1	1	1	1	1	2	2	3	3	4	4	5	4	7	6	17	86.1	83.4
	18	1	0	0	0	1	2	1	1	3	2	0	2	3	7	3	3	13	87.4	84.7
	19	0	2	2	1	2	1	2	2	2	6	6	4	6	5	6	6	15	88.8	86
	20	1	1	2	2	2	1	1	0	3	5	9	6	6	3	5	2	21	94.1	91.2
	21	0	0	0	0	0	1	0	0	2	0	0	2	2	3	2	2	25	94	91
	22	1	1	1	1	1	1	2	3	4	4	4	4	3	4	7	12	27	99.8	96.6
	23	3	2	1	3	3	3	5	3	12	6	5	12	18	15	56	15	51	113.1	109.4
	24	3	4	5	3	4	4	3	3	18	32	39	18	32	32	15	18	50	125.4	121.4
	25	3	2	4	4	3	3	3	3	15	9	32	27	15	18	12	12	55	122.6	118.7
	26	3	2	2	1	2	2	1	2	12	9	6	4	6	7	5	9	62	126	122
	27	2	1	1	2	1	2	1	1	7	5	5	9	5	7	5	3	67	131.7	127.5
	28	1	1	1	2	1	1	1	1	4	5	5	6	4	3	3	3	69	127.8	123.7
	29	2	2	2	3	3	3	1	2	7	9	6	18	18	12	4	7	75	126.7	122.6
	30	3	2	2	1	1	3	3	3	12	9	9	4	5	18	12	15	70	120.3	116.4

Month	day	K-Index 03Z	06Z	09Z	12Z	15Z	18Z	21Z	24Z	A-index 03Z	06Z	09Z	12Z	15Z	18Z	21Z	24Z	SN	adjSFI	obsSFI
Jul-93	1	3	4	3	4	4	2	4	4	15	27	15	27	32	9	22	32	58	111.8	108.1
	2	4	3	2	4	4	3	5	6	22	12	9	27	27	18	39	80	57	113.6	109.9
	3	5	4	4	2	3	2	3	3	56	32	27	6	12	9	12	15	66	114.2	110.5
	4	3	3	2	2	1	2	1	2	15	12	6	9	5	7	4	6	80	110.1	106.5
	5	2	3	1	0	1	1	1	1	7	12	3	2	3	4	4	3	68	103.9	100.5
	6	0	1	1	3	1	1	1	2	2	3	3	12	4	3	5	6	58	98.4	95.2
	7	3	3	2	1	1	1	2	1	15	12	7	4	5	5	9	5	45	96.5	93.4
	8	2	3	3	3	3	4	3	2	9	15	18	15	18	22	12	7	40	96.4	93.3
	9	3	3	2	2	4	4	2	2	12	18	9	7	27	32	7	7	38	93.2	90.2
	10	2	2	2	3	3	2	3	3	9	9	7	12	15	7	18	15	31	89	86.1
	11	4	5	4	3	2	3	2	1	22	48	32	18	7	18	7	5	35	85.8	83
	12	2	2	2	2	2	3	1	2	9	6	9	7	7	12	5	7	35	88.7	85.8
	13	2	3	3	2	3	2	2	2	9	12	15	9	12	7	6	6	51	89.5	86.6
	14	1	1	1	0	1	1	1	1	3	3	3	2	3	3	3	3	63	95.7	92.6
	15	1	2	1	1	2	1	2	2	4	6	5	3	6	4	6	7	66	96.3	93.2
	16	1	1	0	0	1	2	1	1	3	3	2	2	3	6	4	5	63	100.3	97.1
	17	1	1	1	1	1	1	0	1	4	3	3	3	4	3	2	3	67	102.6	99.3
	18	1	1	1	2	2	1	1	1	4	3	5	6	7	4	4	5	80	103.7	100.4
	19	1	2	1	2	1	1	1	2	5	6	4	6	5	4	5	7	76	104.1	100.8
	20	1	2	3	4	2	3	4	4	5	6	12	32	7	15	32	22	69	105.6	102.2
	21	3	4	3	3	3	2	3	3	12	22	12	12	18	9	12	12	64	108.9	105.4
	22	3	2	3	3	2	2	2	3	12	9	12	12	9	6	7	12	54	111.2	107.7
	23	2	2	2	1	2	1	0	1	9	9	6	5	6	4	2	4	68	113.3	109.8
	24	1	0	1	1	1	2	1	1	4	2	3	5	4	7	5	3	66	109.8	106.4
	25	3	2	1	1	1	1	1	1	12	7	4	4	3	3	3	3	61	105.1	101.9
	26	1	1	0	1	1	2	0	1	4	5	2	4	3	6	2	3	55	106.8	103.6
	27	2	1	1	2	3	3	3	2	6	3	3	7	15	15	18	9	66	106.4	103.2
	28	2	2	2	1	1	1	1	2	9	7	6	5	4	5	5	7	59	104.6	101.5
	29	2	1	2	2	4	4	5	3	6	4	7	7	27	32	48	12	47	103.5	100.4
	30	3	2	1	1	1	1	1	1	15	9	5	4	5	4	5	4	45	100.8	97.9
	31	2	2	1	2	2	1	1	1	9	9	4	6	6	3	5	5	46	99.1	96.2
Aug-93	1	1	0	0	0	0	1	1	1	5	2	2	2	2	4	4	3	38	102.8	NA
	2	1	1	1	0	0	0	1	1	3	4	4	2	2	2	5	4	40	103.7	NA
	3	1	1	1	1	2	2	2	2	5	3	4	5	6	7	9	7	36	100.8	NA
	4	2	2	2	2	4	5	4	5	6	6	9	9	32	48	32	56	35	98.9	NA
	5	5	5	3	3	2	2	3	1	48	39	18	12	6	7	12	5	26	97	NA
	6	1	2	4	3	3	4	3	2	3	7	27	18	18	22	12	6	49	97.1	NA
	7	3	4	3	3	3	2	3	4	12	27	12	15	12	7	12	22	43	93.8	NA
	8	2	2	3	3	1	2	1	1	7	7	15	12	5	6	3	4	47	93.4	NA
	9	3	2	2	3	2	2	3	2	12	9	7	18	9	9	15	6	59	99.1	NA
	10	1	1	1	3	2	2	2	2	5	3	5	15	6	6	6	7	65	104.5	NA
	11	2	2	1	1	1	0	1	1	6	6	4	4	4	2	3	3	73	111.2	NA
	12	1	2	2	2	2	1	0	2	4	9	9	6	7	5	2	6	58	103.2	NA
	13	1	2	1	1	1	1	1	1	5	6	4	4	5	5	3	4	60	99.2	NA
	14	0	0	0	0	0	1	1	0	2	0	0	2	2	3	3	2	39	94.6	NA
	15	1	0	1	1	2	4	3	5	3	2	3	4	6	32	18	48	29	92.8	NA
	16	5	5	6	6	5	6	7	6	56	48	80	94	56	67	132	94	21	92.4	NA
	17	7	5	3	2	2	2	2	1	111	56	15	6	9	6	9	5	29	95.1	NA
	18	3	4	4	3	3	3	3	3	15	22	22	18	18	18	15	12	28	94.3	NA
	19	3	3	2	2	2	2	3	3	18	12	9	7	7	7	18	15	28	93.9	NA
	20	3	2	2	2	1	1	2	1	12	6	9	7	4	5	6	3	22	93.8	NA
	21	1	2	2	1	1	1	1	1	5	6	6	5	4	3	4	3	31	97	NA
	22	1	1	1	2	1	1	2	2	4	5	5	9	4	4	6	9	42	96.2	NA
	23	2	1	1	0	0	1	1	0	7	4	3	2	2	3	3	2	42	94.8	NA
	24	0	1	1	2	2	1	1	2	0	3	5	7	6	3	4	6	56	92.5	NA
	25	2	0	0	1	1	1	1	1	6	2	2	4	3	3	3	5	53	90.6	NA
	26	2	1	1	1	2	1	2	2	7	3	5	5	6	5	7	7	44	90.2	NA
	27	2	1	2	3	5	6	4	4	7	4	6	12	39	80	32	27	46	89.4	NA
	28	2	2	1	3	3	3	2	3	9	7	5	15	15	12	9	15	48	90.2	NA
	29	3	3	3	2	3	1	1	3	15	15	12	7	12	3	4	15	49	91.7	NA
	30	1	1	1	1	0	1	1	2	5	5	5	3	2	3	3	6	37	90.7	NA
	31	2	2	1	1	1	1	1	1	7	6	4	3	5	4	5	5	28	90.6	NA

The information shown above was provided by the National Geophysical Data Center. For more information, their address is: NATIONAL GEOPHYSICAL DATA CENTER, 325 Broadway, Mail Code E/GC2, Boulder, Colorado 80303-3328 USA

This listing gives valuable information on manufacturers and/or importers of amateur radio transmitting equipment and supplies.

Beyond being a handy source of phone numbers and addresses, it also gives you insight to a company's business longevity and size, the latter by number of employees. Moreover, you'll learn which companies sell their own products directly to end users, usually through mail order rather than only dealers for resale.

The listing that follows, presents retail operations that sell transmitting products made or imprted by companies listed here.

While every effort has been made to create accurate and useful listings, we recognize errors and omissions may occur. Should any be observed, please inform us so they may be corrected in the next edition.

A

Alinco Electronics, Inc.
438 Amapola Ave., Suite 130
Torrance, CA 90501
Phone: 405 748-3066
FAX: 405 748-3077
Established: 1985; *Employs* 11
Sells through dealers.
Major Lines: VHF & UHF mobile transceivers, HT's, linear amplifiers, roof top towers.

Ameritron
921 Louisville Rd.
Starkville, MS 39759
Phone: 800 647-1800, 601 323-8211
FAX: 601 323-6551
Sells through dealers.
Major Lines: HF amplifiers, antenna tuners, remote antenna switches, dummy loads, in-rush current protectors, QSK switch.

Azden Corporation
147 New Hyde Park Road
Franklin Square, NY 11010
Phone: 516 328-7501
Sells direct and through dealers
Major Lines: VHF/UHF mobile & handheld radios, communications headphones with/without boom mike.

C

Communications Concepts, Inc.
508 Millstone Drive
Beavercreek, OH 45434
Phone: 513 426-8600
FAX: 513 429-3811
Established: 1978
Sells direct and through dealers.
Major Lines: HF and 2-meter amplifiers, ATV parts & hard to find components, metal clad, chip and arco caps, low-pass filters, transistors (ferrite).

E

Ehrhorn Technological Operations, Inc. (ETO)
4975 N. 30th St.
Colorado Springs, CO 80919-4101
Phone: 719 599-ETO1
FAX: 719 260-0395
Established: 1970
Sells direct.
Major Line: RF power amplifiers.

F

Falcon Communications
PO Box 8979
Newport Beach, CA 92658
Phone: 714 760-0340
FAX: 714 645-8156
Established: 1984
Sells direct.
Major Lines: RF power amplifiers, antennas.

H

Hamtronics, Inc.
65 Moul Road
Hilton, NY 14468-9535
Phone: 716 392-9430
FAX: 716 392-9420
Established: 1961
Sells direct.
Major Lines: VHF/UHF FM exciters, receivers, repeaters, PA's, preamps, RCVG & XMTG converters, autopatches & other repeater accessories, computer data links.

I

ICOM America, Inc.
2380 116th Avenue NE
Bellevue, WA 98004
Phone: 206 454-8155
Brochure Hot Line: 206 450-6088
Tech: 206 454-7619
Established: 1979
Sells through dealers.
Major Lines: HF/VHF/UHF base and mobile/handheld transceivers, 1.2 GHz/144 MHz/220 MHz/440 MHz repeaters, accessories, amplifiers, power supplies, antenna tuners.
Branch: 18102 Sky Park South, #52B
Irvine, CA 92714
Phone: 714 852-8026
Branch: 3071 #S Road Unit 9,
Richmond BC, Canada
Phone: 604 273-7400

J

Japan Radio Company, Ltd. (JRC)
430 Park Avenue, 2nd Floor
New York, NY 10022
Phone: 212 355-1180
FAX: 212 319-5227
Established: 1915
Sells through dealers.
Major Lines: HF transceivers, general-coverage receivers, linear amplifiers.

K

Kendecom Inc.
23 Elm Park
Groveland, MA 01834
Phone: 508 372-3442
FAX: 508 373-7304
Established: 1979; *Employs* 7
Sells direct.
Major Lines: Repeaters, controllers, RF equipment.

Kenwood Communications Corporation
2201 E. Dominguez Street
PO Box 22745
Long Beach, CA 90801
Phone: 213 639-4200
Tech: 213 639-7140
BBS: 213 761-8284 (8N1, 300/1200/2400)
Established: 1975
Sells through dealers.
Major Lines: HF/VHF/UHF base, mobile, portable transceivers and receivers, amplifiers, power supplies, manual and automatic antenna tuners, external speakers for base and mobile use, SWR and RF power meters, HF mobile antenna, dual band (2m/70cm) mobile antenna, headphones, microphones, and accessories.

M

Maggiore Electronic Lab
600 Westtown Road
West Chester, PA 19382
Phone: 215 436-6051
FAX: 215 436-6268
Established: 1968; *Employs* 8
Sells direct and through dealers.
Major Lines: VHF & UHF repeaters, transmitters, receivers, power amps. C.O.R. indentifiers, microprocessor repeater controller and auto patch.

Midland International Corp.
1690 N. Topping Avenue
Kansas City, MO 64120
Phone: 800 669-4567 x1165
Tech: 800-669-4567 x 57
Established: 1961; *Employs* 200
Sells through dealers.
Major Lines: VHF transceivers, antennas.

Mirage/KLM
PO Box 1000
16890 Church St.
Morgan Hill, CA 95038
Phone: 408 779-7363
FAX: 408 779-8845
Established: 1979; *Employs* 40
Sells through dealers.
Major Lines: Amateur radio amplifiers and antennas.
Branch Office:
KLM Antennas, Inc.
14792 172nd Drive, SE, #1
Monroe, WA 98272
Phone: 206 794-2923
FAX: 206 794-0294

Myers Engineering International
PO Box 15908
Ft. Lauderdale, FL 33318-5908
Phone: 305 572-8217
FAX: 305 572- 8273

N

Naval Electronics, Inc.
5417 Jetview Circle
Tampa, FL 33634
Phone: 813 885-6091
FAX: 813 885-3789
Established: 1984; *Employs* 6
Sells direct and through dealers.
Major Lines: PV-35R linear amplifier, HTS-2 audio booster, voice operated squelch.

O

Orion Business International
360 W. Bedford Ave., Suite 111
Fresno, CA 93711
Phone: 209 432-4155
FAX: 209 261-0662
Established: 1985
Sells through dealers.
Major Lines: Rotators, HT antennas, roof towers, Tokyo Hi-Power, HF Handheld radio, VHF/UHF amplifiers, transverters, Orion Roof Towers, Orion Intermod Filters, Orion Toroid Filters.

P

P.C. Electronics
2522 Paxson Lane
Arcadia, CA 91007
Phone: 818 447-4565
FAX: 818 447-0489
Established: 1965; *Employs* 10
Sells direct and through dealers.
Major Lines: Fast scan amateur television equipment, transmitters, transceivers, down converters, antennas, linear amps, accessories.

PKT Electronics, Inc.
2668 Haverstraw Ave.
Dayton, OH 45414
Phone/FAX: 513 454-0242
Major Line: Manufactures "PC Packet Station".

Pauldon
210 Utica Street
Tonawanda, NY 14150
Phone: 716 692-5451
Major Line: VHF/UHF amplifiers.

Pro•Am (Div. of Valor Enterprises Inc.)
1711 N. Commerce Drive
Piqua, OH 45356
Phone: 513 778-0074
FAX: 513 778-0259
Established: 1974; *Employs* 180
Sells through dealers.
Major Lines: Two meter base/mobile, multi-band base/mobile, 450 portables, HF yagis, scanner mobile/base, two-meter portable, HF mobile antenna, cellular, commercial, marine antennas and accessories, RV antennas, UHF/VHF amplifiers.
Branch Office:
185 W. Hamilton Street
West Milton, OH 45383
Phone: 513 698-4194

ProComm
1372 Harmony Court
Thousand Oaks, CA 91362
Phone: 805 497-2397
Major Lines: Motorola transceivers, frequency counters, simplex repeaters, discone/HF antennas, preamps, ranger transceivers.

R

RF Concepts, Div. of Kantronics
PO Box 11039
Reno, NV 89510-1039
Phone: 702 324-3290
FAX: 702 324-3289
Service: 913 842-4476
Established: 1987
Sells through dealers.
Major Lines: VHF all mode RF amplifiers 144-148 MHz, UHF all mode RF amplifiers 432-450 MHz, dual-band amplifiers.

Rabun Labs, Inc.
4407 Vineland Road, Suite D-18
Orlando, FL 32811
Phone: 407 246-1355; 800 788-1824
Established: 1990; *Employs* 6
Sells through dealers.
Major Lines: HF transceivers, Two Meter base/mobile, Multi-Band Base/Mobile, repeaters, packet controllers, computers, scanners, six-meter base/ mobile, ILD/P Lightning Protection System.

Radio Shack
1500 One Tandy Center
Ft. Worth, TX 76102
Phone: 817 390-3011
Established: 1921; *Employs* 39,000
Over 7,000 stores in the U.S.
Major Lines: Computers, scanners, antennas, transceivers, coax, plugs, jacks, parts and supplies.

S

SGC, Inc.
The SGC Building
13737 S.E. 26th St.
Bellevue, WA 98005
PO Box 3526
Bellevue, WA 98009
Phone: 206 746-6310
FAX: 206 746-6384
Established: 1972; *Employs* 100
Sells direct and through dealers.
Major Lines: Manufactures HF SSB radios, antenna couplers, power supplies, and antennas.

S&S Engineering
14102 Brown Road
Smithsburg, MD 21783
Phone: 301 416-0661
Established: 1989
Sells direct.
Major Lines: HF Transceiver Kits, QRP, CW; Accessories (Speed Keyers, Frequency Counters).

Spectrum Communications Corp.
1055 W. Germantown Pike
Norristown, PA 19403
Phone: 215 631-1710
FAX: 215 631-5017
Established: 1974; *Employs* 30
Sells direct.
Major Lines: VHF/UHF repeaters and amplifiers, repeater control boards, RF link and repeater receivers/transmitters and accessories.

Standard Amateur Radio Products, Inc.
PO Box 48480
Niles, IL 60648
Phone: 312 763-0081
Established: 1990
Sells through dealers.
Major Lines: VHF/UHF base/mobile and handheld transceivers; transceiver accessories.

T

TE Systems
PO Box 25845
Los Angeles, CA 90025
Phone: 213 478-0591
FAX: 213 473-4038
Established: 1982; *Employs* 28
Sells direct and through dealers.
Major Lines: RF power amplifiers (VHF, UHF, Microwave) low noise preamplifiers.

Ten-Tec, Inc.
1185 Dolly Parton Parkway
Sevierville, TN 37862
Phone: 615 453-7172
Tech: 615 428-0364
FAX: 615 428-4483
Established: 1968; *Employs* 120
Sells direct.
Major Lines: HF transceivers, mobile and base. HF amplifiers to 1500 watts. Mobile and base antenna tuners. Mobile antennas. Metal and plastic equipment enclosures. Custom tools and dies.

U

Uniden Corporation of America
4700 Amon Carter Blvd.
Ft. Worth, TX 76155
Phone: 817 858-3300
Tech: 317 841-8618
Established: 1979; *Employs* 350
Sells through dealers and distributors.
Major Lines: Cordless telephones, TADs, cellular telephones, scanners, radar detectors, citizen band radios, satellite receivers, 2-way commercial radios, marine radios and pagers, GMRS.

Y

Yaesu
17210 Edwards Road
Cerritos, CA 90701
Phone: 310 404-2700
FAX: 310 404-1210
Established: 1956
Sells through dealers.
Major Lines: HF, VHF, UHF all-mode transceiver, VHF and UHF FM mobiles and handhelds, HF amplifiers, antenna tuners, portable HF transceiver, HF receivers, headphones, microphones, power/SWR meters, antenna rotors, power supplies, speakers, and other related accessories.

CANADA

Vectronics Corporation Inc.
31 Estate Drive
Scarborough, Ontario MIH 222
Phone: 416 289-4637
Established: 1981; *Employs* 10
Sells through dealers.
Major Lines: HF amplifiers, HF antenna tuners, power supplies, HP/LP filters, dummy loads amplifier components.

The following listing consists of retailers who sell other makers' brands of radio products either through a retail store(s) or by mail order, or both. (Manufacturers or importers who sell only their own brands to end users are listed in the previous section.,

Top lines they carry are noted, as well as information concerning equipment trade-ins and on-site repairs. Additionally, the year the company was established, the number of employees, and branch store information, if any, are also indicated. Furthermore, key employee names and call signs are shown, enabling you to personalize your buying contacts.

Note that toll-free "800" telephone numbers should only be used to place a purchase order, not to gather general information, for repairs, etc. This reduces the time that other callers have to wait (it might be you!) for someone to take their order.

A

A-B-C Communications
17550 15th Avenue NE
Seattle, WA 98108
Phone: 206 364-8300
Sells via showroom and mail order.
Top Lines: ICOM, books, and all major antenna lines.

A-TECH Electronics
2210 W. Magnolia Blvd.
Burbank, CA 91506
Phone: 818 845-9203
FAX: 818 846-2298
Established: 1987; *Employs* 5
Sells via showroom and mail order.
Key Employees: Bill, N6MQS; Ted, KD6HGA.
Top Lines: Alinco, Larsen, Comet, Mirage, Kenwood, Yaesu, ICOM, NCG, ArtSci.
Accepts trade-ins and provides repairs.

Ack Radio Supply Company
3101 4th Avenue
South Birmingham, AL 35233
Phone: 205 322-0588; 800-338-4218
FAX: 205-322-0580
Established: 1947; *Employs* 5
Sells via showroom and mail order.
Key Employees: Larry N4HYX; Mike, KC4OIT; Bill; Kirk, N4WYC.
Top Lines: ICOM, Ten-Tec, MFJ, ARRL, Vibroplex, Bencher, Hustler, DAIWA.
Accepts Trade-Ins.
Branch: 554 Deering Road
Atlanta, GA 30367
Phone: 404 351-6340
FAX: 404 351-1879
Key Employees: Tommy W4RRW; Jim WA4APG.

Amateur & Advanced Communications
3208 Concord Pike, Rt 202
Wilmington, DE 19803
Phone: 302 478-2757
Established: 1977; *Employs* 2
Sells via showroom and mail order.
Key Employees: Gisele, K3WAJ
Top Lines: ARRL, Alinco, Ameritron, Cushcraft, MFJ, Ten-Tec, Alpha Delta, Hustler, Butternut, Larsen, Rohn, ProAm, Bencher, Henry, Kantronics, Astron, Shortwave Equipment, Ham Classes.
Provides repairs.

Amateur Communications, Etc.
263 Mink
San Antonio, TX 78213-3949
Phone: 512 733-0334;
512 734-7793-7794
Established: 1969; *Employs* 2
Sells via showroom and mail order.
Key Employees: Frank, WD5GZU; Steven, KA5SWI .
Top Lines: Ten-Tec, Tempo, Alinco, MFJ, Valor, Azden, William Nye, Hustler, Ranger.
Accepts trade-ins and provides repairs.

Amateur Electronic Supply, Inc.
5710 Good Hope Road
Milwaukee, WI 53223
Phone: 800 558-0411, 414 358-0333
Established: 1957; *Employs* 39
Sells via showroom and mail order.
Key Employees: Paul, W9KHO.
Top Lines: Kenwood, Yaesu, ICOM, Cushcraft, Hy-Gain, AEA, Kantronics, Nye-Viking, MFJ, Ten-Tec, Hustler, Mirage/KLM, Standard, Alinco. Large used gear inventory.
Accepts trade-ins and provides repairs.

Amateur Electronic Supply, Inc.
28940 Euclid Avenue
Wickliffe, OH 44092
Phone: 800 321-3594; 216 585-7388
Employs 8
Sells via showroom and mail order.
Key Employees: Dave, WB8BAG.
Top Lines: Kenwood, Yaesu, ICOM, Cushcraft, Hy-Gain, AEA, Kantronics, Nye-Viking, MFJ, Ten-Tec, Hustler. Large used gear inventory.
Accepts trade-ins and provides repair.

Amateur Electronic Supply, Inc.
621 Commonwealth Avenue
Orlando, FL 32803
Phone: 800 327-1917; 407 894-3238
Employs 11
Sells via showroom and mail order.
Key employees: Grant, K41QW.
Top Lines: Kenwood, Yaesu, ICOM, Cushcraft, Hy-Gain, AEA, Kantronics, Nye-Viking, MFJ, Ten-Tec, Hustler. Large used gear inventory.
Accepts trades-in and provides repairs.

Amateur Electronic Supply, Inc.
1898 Drew Street
Clearwater, FL 34625
Phone: 813 461-4267
FAX: 813 443-7893
Employs 4
Sells via showroom and mail order.
Key Employee: Len, K4BDP.
Top Lines: Kenwood, Yaesu, ICOM, Cushcraft, Hy-Gain, AEA, Kantronics, Nye-Viking, MFJ, Mirage/KLM. Large used gear inventory.
Accepts trade-in and provides repairs.

Amateur Electronic Supply, Inc.
1072 N. Rancho Drive
Las Vegas, NV 89106
Phone: 800 634-6227; 702 647-311 4
FAX: 702 647-3412
Employs 6
Sells via showroom and mail order.
Key Employees: Squeak, AD7K.
Top Lines: Kenwood, Yaesu, ICOM, Cushcraft, Hy-Gain, AEA, Kantronics, Nye-Viking, Mirage/KLM, Standard, MFJ, Ten-Tec. Large used gear inventory.
Accepts trade-ins and provides repairs.

Amateur Radio Supply, Co.
5963 Corson Avenue S. Suite #140
Seattle, WA 98108-2707
Phone: 206 767-3222
FAX: 206 763-8176
Established: 1956; *Employs* 8
Sells via showroom and mail order.
Key Employees: Sharon, KA7GEL; Al, KW7U; Eric, N7DLV, Frank, N7OF.
Top Lines: Kenwood, ICOM, Rohn, AEA, Cushcraft, B & W, Bird Wattmeters, Kantronics, Yaesu, Newtronics, NYE-Viking, Alinco, Comet, Valor, Larsen.

Amateur Radio Team 0f Spokane
S.25 Girard
Spokane, WA 99212
Phone: 509 928-3073
Established: 1976; *Employs* 2
Sells via showroom and mail order.
Key Employees: Art, WB7AUK and Joann, KA7SUZ.
Top Lines: ICOM, Astron, International Wire, MFJ, ARRL, Van Gordon, Bencher, AEA.
Accepts trade-ins.

American Electronics
164 Southpark Blvd.
PO Box 301
Greenwood, IN 46142
Phone: 317 888-7265; 800 872-1373
FAX: 317 888-7368
Established: 1965; *Employs* 8
Sells via showroom and phone/mail order to wholesale dealers.
Key Employees: Win, K9EMV; Mike, N9LPJ; Jon, N9KZB; John, N9KZG.
Top Lines: Kenwood, Dick Smith, Cushcraft, DAIWA, Hustler, Telex/Hy-Gain, ARRL, Uniden, AEI, Nye-Viking, Antenna Specialists, Valor, Maxon, Radio Amateur Callbook, Sangean, B & W, Trippe, W5YI, Heights, Wintenna, Tekk, Relm.
Provides repairs and custom installations.

Associated Radio Comm.
PO Box 4327
8012 Conser
Overland Park, KS 66204
Phone: 913 381-5900
FAX: 913 648-3020.
Established: 1945
Sells via showroom and mail order.
Top Lines: Kenwood, ICOM, Yaesu, Comet, Alinco, Kantronics, R.F. Concepts, Cushcraft, Maxrad, Hustler, B&W, NYE-Viking, Panasonic, Sangean, Uniden-Bearcat, Drake, Collins, AEA, Daiwa, Vectronics, MFJ, W5YI, Valor.
Accepts trade-ins and provides repairs.

Austin Amateur Radio Supply
5325 North IH-35
Austin, TX 78723
Phone: 512 454-2994; 800 423-2604
Established: 1986
Sells via showroom and mail order.
Top Lines: Kenwood, ICOM, Yaesu, Alinco, AEA, MFJ, Astron, Cushcraft, Hustler, Butternut, Larsen, Telex/Hy-Gain.

B

B.C. Communications, Inc.
The 211 Bldg.-Depot Road
Huntington Station, NY 11746
Phone: 516 549-8833
FAX: 516 549-8820
Established: 1972; *Employs* 12
Sells via showroom and mail order.
Key Employees: William, W2WBY.
Top Lines: Yaesu, MFJ, Larsen, William Nye-Viking, DAIWA, Kantronics, Astatic, Hustler, Newtronics, Valor, Mobile Mark, Bearcat, Uniden, Maxon, Mirage, B&W, Callbook, ARRL, KLM, Ameco, Bencher, etc.
Accepts trade-ins and provides repairs.

Barry Electronics, Corp.
512 Broadway
New York, NY 10012
Phone: 212 925-7000
FAX: 212 925-7001
Established: 1950; *Employs* 11
Sells via showroom and mail order "world wide".
Key Employees: Kitty, WA2BAP; Arnie, WB2YXB; Deanna, KB2JYL, Don, Anil.
Top Lines: Motorola, ICOM, Kenwood, Yaesu, Alinco, Standard, Hy-Gain, AEA, MFJ, Astron, B&W, Sony, Grundig, Sangean, Larsen, Comet, Diamond, Maxon, Relm, Mirage, Cushcraft, Hustler, Bencher, Astatic, ARRL Books, Tapes, ANLI Antennas, Belden coaxial cable, connectors, rotor cable. Books on Ham radio, modifications, theory, antennas, etc. Ranger, Ameco, RF Concepts, Kantronics. Scanners, Ace, ICOM, Uniden & scanner books.
Provides full-service lab for Ham and commercial repairs. Technical Assistance Specialist in Ham, Business and Government radios, CB.

Base Station, Inc.
1839 East Street
Concord, CA 94520
Phone: 510 685-7388
Established: 1976; *Employs* 5
Sells via showroom and mail order.
Key Employees: Art, AB6HB; Charley, N5TBV.
Top Lines: Yaesu, Mirage, Cushcraft, Larsen, MFJ, AEA, Nye-Viking, B&W, Bearcat, Uniden, Butternut, Astron, Sony, Hustler, Bencher, Astatic, Ameco, Tab Books, Gordon West Books & Tapes, W5YI Books and Software, ANLI Antennas, Diamond Antennas, Callbooks, ARRL publications.
Accepts trade-ins and provides repairs.

Burghardt Amateur Center, Inc.
PO Box 73,182 N. Maple St.
Watertown, SD 57201-0073
Phone: 605 886-7314; 800 927-4261
FAX: 605 886-3444
Established: 1931; *Employs* 10
Sells via showroom and mail order.
Key Employees: Darrell, WDØGDF; Tim, WDØFKC; Stan, WØIT; Jim, WBØMJY and David, KAØJDN.
Top Lines: Kenwood, ICOM, Yaesu, AEA, Kantronics, Astron, Ten-Tec,B&W, Cushcraft, Telex, MFJ.
Accepts trade-ins and provides repairs.

Burk Electronics
35 N. Kensington
LaGrange, IL 60525
Phone: 708 482-9310
Established: 1983; *Employs* 5
Sells via mail order.
Key Employees: Wayne, NA9B; Ann, AA9FN; Jeff, N9MLU; Maria, N9QWQ; James, N9MSX.
Top Lines: AEA, Alinco, Antenex, Ameritron, Ameco, Antenna Specialist, Antler, ARRL Publications, Bencher, Butternut, Comet, Diamond, Hustler, Larsen, Lunar, Maxrad, Mobile Mark, MFJ, *Radio Amateur Callbook*, Radio Publications, Pyramid, Sams, Smiley Antenna, TAB Books, Valor, Wintenna, Yaesu.
Accepts trade-ins, provides repairs and technical assistance.

C

C-Comm
6115 15th Avenue NW
Seattle, WA 98107
Phone: 800 426-6528; 206 784-7337 *FAX:* 206 784-0541
Established: 1976; *Employs* 7
Sells via showroom and mail order.
Key Employees: Frank, K7DS; George, K7HBN; Aaron, AA7IS; Dan, N7PSH and Dale, W7GAB.
Top Lines: ICOM, Kenwood, Yaesu, AEA, Cushcraft, Butternut, Telex/Hy-Gain, Astron, Hustler.
Provides repairs.

Colorado Comm Center
525 E. 70th Ave Suite 1W
Denver, CO 80229
Phone: 800 227-7373; 303 288-7373
Established: 1984; *Employs* 3
Sells via showroom and mail order.
Key Employees: Joel, KJØI.
Top Lines: Kenwood, Yaesu, ICOM, Astron, Comet.
Accepts trade-ins.

Communications Data Corporation
1051 Main Street
St. Joseph, MI 49085
Phone: 616 982-0404; 800 382-2562 *FAX:* 616 982-0433
Established: 1981; *Employs* 6
Sells via showroom and mail order.
Key Employees: Duane, KX8D; Barb, N8JML.
Top Lines: Yaesu, ICOM, Alinco, VoCom, Vibroplex, Bencher, RF Concepts, Comet, Hustler, Ameritron, ARRL, Astron, MFJ, Various computer products.

Comm-Pute, Inc.
1057 East 2100 South
Salt Lake City, UT 84106
Phone: 801 467-8873; 800 942-8873
Established: 1988; *Employs* 5
Sells via showroom and mail-order.
Key Employees: Preben, K7KMZ; Tim, W7IQY.
Top Lines: Kenwood, Yaesu, ICOM, Cushcraft, Larsen, B&W, AEA, Kantronics, Hustler, Bencher, Diamond.

D

DANDYS
120 North Washington
Wellington, KS 67152
Phone: 316 326-6314
Established: 1985; *Employs* 5
Sells via showroom and mail order.
Key Employees: Norm, NIØS; Dana, NØFYQ.
Top Lines: AEA, ARRL, Ameritron, Astron, Butternut, Kantronics, MFJ, Radio Shack, Comet, Diamond.
Accepts trade-ins.

Delaware Amateur Supply
71 Meadow Road
New Castle, DE 19720
Phone: 302 328-7728, 800 441-7008
Established: 1975
Sells via showroom and mail order.
Key Employees: Paul, WA3QPX; Rob, WA3QLS; Gail, KA31TN.
Top Lines: Kenwood, ICOM, Yaesu, Alinco, ARRL, Hy-Gain, MFJ, Standard, Cushcraft, Butternut, AEA, Kantronics, Mirage, Ameritron, Astron, Larsen, RF Concept, Heil Sound, Hustler, Bencher, Larsen, B&W, Diamond, ANLI, Van Gorden.

Dentronics
6102 Deland Road
Flushing, Ml 48433
Phone: 313 659-1776; 800 722-5488 *FAX:* 313 659-1280
Established: 1978; *Employs* 2
Sells via showroom and mail order.
Key Employee: Dennis, WB8QWL.
Top Lines: Kantronics, AEA, MFJ, DRSI, R.F. Concepts, Pac-Comm, Diamond, Sierra Computers.
Accepts trade-ins.

Doc's Communications
702 Chickamauga Avenue
Rossville, GA 30741
Phone: 404 866-2302; 404 861-5610 *FAX:* 404 866-6113
Established: 1975; *Employs* 6
Sells via showroom and mail order.
Key Employees: Maxine, N4ECA; Doc, KC4EV; John, WD4AQO; Pat; Jim; Darrel.
TopLines: ICOM, Kenwood, Yaesu, Alinco, MFJ, Larsen, Astron, Ameritron.
Accepts trade-ins and provides repairs.

E

El Original Electronics
1257 East Levee
Brownsville, TX 78520
Phone: 512 546-9846; 512 542-8507
Established: 1979; *Employs* 4
Sells via showroom.
Key Employee: Emilio, XE2XES.
Top Lines: Alinco, Azden, Kenwood, ICOM, Tempo, Yaesu, Larsen, Comet, Maxrad.

Electro-Comm
961 E.65th Street
Tacoma, WA 98404-2237
Phone/FAX: 206 473-9225; 800 821-9150
Established: 1984; *Employs* 3
Sells via showroom and mail order.
Key Employees: Joe, KA7DEX; Dick, WB7CRR; Deanna.
Top Lines: Alinco, Larsen, Mirage/KLM, Astron, MFJ, Anli, Pouch.

Electronic Center, Inc.
2809 Ross Avenue
Dallas, TX 75201
Phone: 214 969-1936
Established: 1960; *Employs* 2
Sells via showroom, hamfest, and mail order.
Key Employees: Mike, WB5E; Marcia, KA5ROJ; George, N5AXR; Clif, KA5IPF; Matt, KE5BJ.
Top Lines: Kenwood, ICOM, Yaesu, Rohn, Hustler, AEA, ARRL, Larsen, MFJ, Mirage/KLM .
Accepts trade-ins and provides repairs.

Electronic Equipment Bank (EEB)
323 Mill Street NW
Vienna,VA 22180
Phone: 800 368-3270, 703 938-3350 *FAX:* 703 938-6911
Established: 1971; *Employs* 22
Sells via showroom and mail order.
Key Employees: Ted, AA4GM, Dick, K4EIH; Bob, K7RDH; Ken, KC4YMD.
Top Lines: ICOM, Kenwood, Yaesu, AOR, Novex, Sony, DAIWA, Astron, AEA, Bird, Cushcraft, Hy-Gain, MFJ, Ten-Tec, Rohn, Emoto, Create, Datong.
Accepts trade-ins and provides repairs.

Electronic Specialists
Cinema Square Shopping Center
3830 Oleander Drive
Wilmington, NC 28403
Phone: 800 688-0073; 919 791-8885
Established: 1988
Sells via showroom and mail order.
Key Employees: Shirley, N4LFV; Dwight, K4YNY; Stanley, KC4DPC; Cindy, KC4DUK; Mike, N3DJT and Dennis, KC4YOU.
Top Lines: ICOM, Kenwood, Yaesu, AEA, Alinco, Cushcraft, Diamond, Larsen, Hustler, MFJ, Kantronics, RF Concepts, ARRL, Bencher, Astron, B&W, and Sangean.
Accepts trade-ins and provides repairs.

Eli's Amateur Radio, Inc.
2513 SW Ninth Avenue
Ft. Lauderdale, FL 33315
Phone: 305 525-0103, 305 944-3383; 800 780-0103;
FAX: 305 944-3383
Established: 1980; *Employs* 5
Sells via showroom and mail order.
Key Employees: Eli, M4BK; Al, N4AXQ; Jose, WT4G.
Top Lines: ICOM, Yaesu, Kenwood, Cushcraft, Hustler, AEA, Kantronics, Bird, DAIWA, MFJ, Antenna Specialists, Larsen, Diamond
Accepts trade-ins and provides repairs.

Erickson Communications
5456 N. Milwaukee Avenue
Chicago, I L 60630
Phone: 800 621-5802; 312 631-5181
Established: 1969; *Employs* 7
Sells via showroom and mail order.
Key Employees: Vince, KA9ZDM; Verne, K9TMR.
Top Lines: Kenwood, Yaesu, ICOM, Cushcraft, Hy-Gain, AEA, Kantronics, Nye-Viking, MFJ, Ten-Tec, Hustler.
Accepts trade-ins.

F

F & M Electronics
153 W. Railroad Street N
Pelham, GA 31779-1201
Established: 1978; *Employs* 6
Sells via showroom and mail order.
Key Employees: Mae, KB4LMX; Frank, N4AZM.
Top Lines: ICOM, Ten-Tec, Bencher, Callbook, Ameco, MFJ, Antenna Specialists, Hustler, Lunar, B& W, Alinco, Uniden, Alliance, Ranger, Wilson, Sangean, Butternut.
Accepts trade-ins and provides repairs.

G

Gilfer Radio
52 Park Avenue
Park Ridge, NJ 07656
Phone: 201 391-7887
FAX: 201 391-7433
Established: 1953; Employs 4
Sells via showroom and mail order.
Key Employee: Lee, WK2T.
Top Lines: Kenwood, AEA, Kantronics, Astron, ACE, Ameco, ICOM, Japan Radio Co., R.L. Drake, Datong and Dressler. Publisher of Ferrell's "Confidential Frequency List."

H

H.R. Electronics
722-24 Evanston Avenue
Muskegon, MI 49442
Phone: 616 722-2246
FAX: 616 722-4993
Established: 1978; *Employs* 3
Sells via showroom and mail order.
Key Employees: Sue, N8MMH; Dan, N8PPQ, Chuck, N8GNG.
Top Lines: M^2, ICOM, Alinco, Cushcraft, DAIWA, Hustler, Mirage/KLM, Van Gorden, Butternut, Rohn, B&W, Astron, Larsen, Spi-ro, MFJ, A/S, Grundig, ARRL, Callbooks, Bencher, Vibroplex, AEA, KPC, Ameco, Yaesu, Kenwood, Diamond, Comet, & Pouch.
Accepts trade-ins and provides repairs.

"Ham" Buerger, Inc.
417 Davisville Road
Willow Grove, PA 19090
Phone: 215 659-5900; 800 HAM-6606
Established: 1956; *Employs* 6
Sells via showroom and mail order.
Key Employees: Bob, WA3ZID, Brian Dave.
Top Lines: ICOM, Cushcraft, Hustler, MFJ, ARRL, Bearcat, ECG, NTE, PRB, Van Gorden.
Accepts trade-ins and provides repairs.

Ham Contact, The
PO Box 3624
Long Beach, CA 90803
Phone: 800 933-HAM4; 310 433-5860
Established: 1987; *Employs:* 4
Key Employees: Joe, N6YYO; Denise, N6YYN; Lee.
Top Lines: Kenwood, ICOM, Yaesu, Alinco, Standard, Mirage-KLM, Larsen, Comet, Diamond, MFJ.
Accepts trade-ins and provides repairs.

Ham Radio Outlet
933 N. Euclid Street
Anaheim, CA 92801
Phone: 800 854-6046
Local: 714 533-7373
FAX: 714 533-9485
Established: 1971; *Employs* 15
Sells via showroom and mail order.
Top Lines: Kenwood, ICOM, Yaesu, Alinco, US Tower, RFC, Rohn, AEA, Cushcraft, Hy-Gain, Butternut, Bird, Kantronics, Larsen, Diamond, NCG, MFJ, Ameritron, Standard, Bencher, Mirage/KLM, Orion, Sony, Astron, Hustler, M^2, Outbacker.
Accepts trade-ins and provides repairs.

Ham Radio Outlet
6071 Buford Highway
Atlanta, GA 30340
Phone: 404 263-0700; 800 444-7927
FAX: 404 263-9548
Established: 1971; *Employs* 5
Sells via showroom and mail order.
Key Employee: Mark, KJ4VO.
Top Lines: Kenwood, ICOM, Yaesu, Alinco, US Tower, RFC, Rohn, AEA, Cushcraft, Hy-Gain, Butternut, Bird, Kantronics, Larsen, Diamond, NCG, MFJ, Ameritron, Standard, Bencher, Mirage/KLM, Orion, Sony, Astron, Hustler, M^2, Outbacker.
Accepts trade-ins.

Ham Radio Outlet
8400 E. Lliff Avenue, #9
Denver, CO 80231
Phone: 303 745-7373; 800 444-9476
FAX: 303 745-7394
Employs: 5
Sells via showroom and mail order. Exports.
Key Employee: Joe, KDØGA.
Top Lines: Kenwood, ICOM, Yaesu, Alinco, US Tower, RFC, Rohn, AEA, Cushcraft, Hy-Gain, Butternut, Bird, Kantronics, Larsen, Diamond, NCG, MFJ, Ameritron, Standard, Bencher, Mirage/KLM, Orion, Sony, Astron, Hustler, M^2, Outbacker.
Accepts trade-ins.

Ham Radio Outlet
2210 Livingston Street
Oakland, CA 94606
Phone: 415 534-5757, 800 854-6046 *FAX:* 415 534-0729
Established: 1971; *Employs* 4
Sells via showroom and mail order.
Key Employee: Rich, WA9WYB.
Top Lines: Kenwood, ICOM, Yaesu, Alinco, US Tower, RFC, Rohn, AEA, Cushcraft, Hy-Gain, Butternut, Bird, Kantronics, Larsen, Diamond, NCG, MFJ, Ameritron, Standard, Bencher, Mirage/KLM, Orion, Sony, Astron, Hustler, M^2, Outbacker.
Accepts trade-ins.

Ham Radio Outlet
11705 SW Pacific Highway
Suite Z
Portland, OR 97223
Phone: 503 598-0555; 800 854-6046
FAX: 503 684-0469
Established: 1991; *Employs* 5
Sells via showroom and mail order.
Key Employee: Earl, KE7OA.
Top Lines: Kenwood, ICOM, Yaesu, Alinco, US Tower, RFC, Rohn, AEA, Cushcraft, Hy-Gain, Butternut, Bird, Kantronics, Larsen, Diamond, NCG, MFJ, Ameritron, Standard, Bencher, Mirage/KLM, Orion, Sony, Astron, Hustler, M^2, Outbacker.
Accepts trade-ins.

Ham Radio Outlet
1702 W. Camelback Road, Suite 4
Phoenix, AZ 85015
Phone: 602 242-3515, 800 854-6046 *FAX:* 602 242-3481
Established: 1971; *Employs* 5
Sells via showroom and mail order.
Key Employee: Gary, WB7SLY.
Top Lines: Kenwood, ICOM, Yaesu, Alinco, US Tower, RFC, Rohn, AEA, Cushcraft, Hy-Gain, Butternut, Bird, Kantronics, Larsen, Diamond, NCG, MFJ, Ameritron, Standard, Bencher, Mirage/KLM, Orion, Sony, Astron, Hustler, M^2, Outbacker.
Accepts trade-ins.

Ham Radio Outlet
224 N. Broadway
Salem, NH 03079
Phone: 603 898-3750, 800 444-0047 *FAX:* 603 898-1041
Established: 1986; *Employs* 8
Sells via showroom and mail order.
Key Employee: Chuck, KM4NZ.
Top Lines: Kenwood, ICOM, Yaesu, Alinco, US Tower, RFC, Rohn, AEA, Cushcraft, Hy-Gain, Butternut, Bird, Kantronics, Larsen, Diamond, NCG, MFJ, Ameritron, Standard, Bencher, Mirage/KLM, Orion, Sony, Astron, Hustler, M^2, Outbacker.
Accepts trade-ins.

Ham Radio Outlet
5375 Kearny Villa Road
San Diego, CA 92123
Phone: 619 560-4900, 800 854-6046 *FAX:* 619 560-1705
Established: 1971; *Employs* 5
Sells via showroom and mail order.
Key Employee: Tom, KM6K.
Top Lines: Kenwood, ICOM, Yaesu, Alinco, US Tower, RFC, Rohn, AEA, Cushcraft, Hy-Gain, Butternut, Bird, Kantronics, Larsen, Diamond, NCG, MFJ, Ameritron, Standard, Bencher, Mirage/KLM, Orion, Sony, Astron, Hustler, M^2, Outbacker.
Accepts trade-ins.

Ham Radio Outlet
510 Lawrence Expwy #102
Sunnyvale, CA 94086
Phone: 408 736-9496, 800 854-6046
FAX: 408 736-9499
Established: 1971; *Employs* 8
Sells via showroom and mail order. Exports.
Key Employee: Tom, KB6LUC.
Top Lines: Kenwood, ICOM, Yaesu, Alinco, US Tower, RFC, Rohn, AEA, Cushcraft, Hy-Gain, Butternut, Bird, Kantronics, Larsen, Diamond, NCG, MFJ, Ameritron, Standard, Bencher, Mirage/KLM, Orion, Sony, Astron, Hustler, M^2, Outbacker.
Accepts trade-ins.

Ham Radio Outlet
6265 Sepulveda Blvd.
Van Nuys, CA 91411
Phone: 818 988-2212; 800 854-6046 *FAX:* 818 988-4326
Established: 1971; *Employs* 5
Sells via showroom and mail order.
Key Employee: Jon, KB6ZBI .
Top Lines: Kenwood, ICOM, Yaesu, Alinco, US Tower, RFC, Rohn, AEA, Cushcraft, Hy-Gain, Butternut, Bird, Kantronics, Larsen, Diamond, NCG, MFJ, Ameritron, Standard, Bencher, Mirage/KLM, Orion, Sony, Astron, Hustler. M^2, Outbacker.
Accepts trade-ins.

Ham Radio Outlet
14803 Build America Drive, Bldg B
Woodbridge, VA 22191
Phone: 800 444-4799, 703 643-1063 *FAX:* 703 494-3679
Established: 1977; *Employs* 9
Sells via showroom and mail order.
Key Employee: Curtis, WB4KZL.
Top Lines: Kenwood, ICOM, Yaesu, Alinco, US Tower, RFC, Rohn, AEA, Cushcraft, Hy-Gain, Butternut, Bird, Kantronics, Larsen, Diamond, NCG, MFJ, Ameritron, Standard, Bencher, Mirage/KLM, Orion, Sony, Astron, Hustler, M^2, Outbacker.
Accepts trade-ins and provides repairs.

Ham Radio Toy Store, Inc.
117 West Wesley Street
Wheaton, IL 60187
Phone: 708 668-9577
FAX: 703 690-9335
Established: 1989; *Employs* 5
Sells via showroom and mail order.
Key Employee: Roberto, WA9E; Wayne, NA9B.
Top Lines: ICOM, Yaesu, Ameritron, AEA, Ameco, Antenna Specialist, Antenex, Antler, ARRL Publications, Belden, Bencher, Butternut, Comet, Diamond, Gordon West, Hustler, Larsen, Lunar, Maxrad, MFJ, Mobile Mark, *Radio Amateur Callbook*, Radio Publications, Pyramid, Sams, Smiley Antenna, Valor, Wintenna, Alinco, Sangean, W5YI, Alpha Delta, Radio School.
Accepts trade-ins and provides repairs.

Ham Station, Inc.
220 N. Fulton Avenue
Evansville, IN 47710
Phone: 800 729-4373, 812 422-0231
Established: 1979
Sells via showroom and mail order.
Key Employees: Dan, N9APA; Rick, WB9SAN; Mark, N9JBP and Jeff, KA9YKA.
Top Lines: ICOM, Kenwood, Yaesu, Alinco, Standard, AEA, MFJ, RFC, Cushcraft, Kantronics.
Accepts trade-ins and provides repairs.

Ham Store, The
5707A Mobud
San Antonio, TX 78238
Phone: 800 344-3144
FAX: 512 647-8007
Established: 1988; *Employs* 9
Sells via showroom and mail order.
Key Employees: Craig, KB5BI; Gary, WD5DUL; and Ed, KS5V.
Top Lines: Kenwood, Yaesu, ICOM, Alinco, Cushcraft, Hustler, Mirage/KLM, Astron, AEA, DAIWA, Genesys Products.
Accepts trade-ins and provides repairs.
Si Habla Espanol.

Hamtronics/Trevose
4033 Brownsville Road
Trevose, PA 19053
Phone: 215 357-1400; 800 426-2820 *FAX:* 215 355-8958
Established: 1954; *Employs* 14
Sells via showroom and mail order.
Key Employees: Dave, N3TS; Mike, KA3WVZ; Sam, N3DFV; Dave Jr., KA3BKG; Gene, WA3STW, Eva, WA3USJ; Marrion, WA3VEP; Jim, KA3JSO.
Top Lines: Kenwood, Yaesu, ICOM, Alinco, AEA, MFJ, Cushcraft, Astron, Hustler, JRC, Ameritron, Larsen, Kantronics, Rohn, Bencher, Heil, B&W, RF Concepts, Daiwa, Diamond, Comet.
Accepts trade-ins and provides repairs.

Hardin Electronics
5635 E. Rosedale Street
Ft. Worth, TX 76112
Phone: 800 433-3203; 817 429-9761 *FAX:* 817 457-2429
Established: 1965; *Employs* 20
Sells via showroom and mail order.
Key Employees: Lee, N5RAT; Richard, K5ZIM; Rick, N5QKB.
Top Lines: Kenwood, Standard, ICOM, Yaesu, Alinco, Larsen, Comet, Diamond, Daiwa, ARRL.
Accepts trade-ins and provides repairs.

Hatry Electronics
500 Ledyard Street
Hartford, CT 06114
Phone: 203 296-1881
FAX: 203 296-7110
Established: 1928; *Employs* 20
Sells via showroom and mail order.
Key Employees: Lenny, WA1VPT; Spiro, KJ1R.
Top Lines: ICOM, MFJ, B&W, Alinco, Ameco, Sangean, Van Gorden, Cushcraft, Larsen, Hustler.
Accepts trade-ins.

Heaster, Inc., Harold
84 North Tymber Creek Road
Ormond Beach, FL 32174
Phone: 904 673-4066
Established: 1984; *Employs* 5
Sells via showroom and mail order.
Key Employees: Harold, KE8MR; Vern, K3FOA; Barb, KA8RRD; Lewis, KC4DSQ; Jeff, KA8RRE.
Top Lines: Kenwood, ICOM, Larsen.
Accepts trade-ins.

Henry Radio Inc.
2050 South Bundy Drive
Los Angeles, CA 90025
Phone: 800 877-7979, 310 820-1234
FAX: 310 826-7790
Established: 1941; *Employs* 51
Sells via showroom.
Key Employees: Ray, WW6X; Fred, N6SFD; Leo, KJ6HI; Nate, KI6IK; Andy, N6UPM; Ted, W6YEY; Paul, N6VLV.
Top Lines: Kenwood, ICOM, Yaesu, Henry Amps, Tempo, Astron, Bird, Hy-Gain, Cushcraft, MFJ, Alinco.
Accepts trade-ins and provides repairs.

Hialeah Communications
801 Hialeah Drive
Hialeah, FL 33010
Phone: 305 885-9929
FAX: 305 888-8768
Established: 1978; *Employs* 20
Sells via showroom and mail order.
Key Employees: Sara, Ruben, Jose, Miguel, Juvenal.
Top Lines: Motorola, ICOM, Kenwood, Yaesu, Bird, CES, Larsen, Cushcraft, Antenna Specialists, Hustler.
Provides repairs.

Honolulu Electronics
819 Keeaumoku Street
Honolulu, HI 96814
Phone: 808 949-5564, 808 949-5565 *FAX:* 808 949-1209
Established 1932; *Employs* 20
Sells via showroom and mail order.
Key Employees: Tom, KH6BM; Richard, AH610; Mark, KH6GBL; Mel.
Top Lines: Kenwood, ICOM, Yaesu, Tri-Ex Towers, Belden Cables, Eimac Tubes, Alexander Nicad Batteries, Astron Power Supplies, KLM Antennas, AEA, Hy-Gain, MFJ, Cushcraft, Larsen, Fluke Meters, Maxrad Antennas, Alinco.
Provides repairs.

Hooper Electronics
1702 Pass Road
Biloxi, MS 39531
Phone: 601 432-1100; 601 432-0584 *FAX:* 601 432-7651
Established: 1960; *Employs* 110
Sells via showroom and mail order.
Key Employees: Dave, WB5KDV; Bill, W5WWJ; Joyce, WB5LKC; Wayne, KB5JCI.
Top Lines: ICOM, Kenwood, AEA, MFJ, Cushcraft, Hustler, Astron, Bird, Larsen. Antenna Specialist.
Accepts trade-ins.
Branch: 1700 Terry Road
Jackson, MS 38204
Phone: 601 353-0922, 601 354-4531 *FAX:* 601 948-3807
Key Employee: Dave Anderson, WB5KDV

J

J.R.S. Distributors, Inc.
646 W. Market Street
York, PA 17404
Phone: 717 854-8624
FAX: 717 854-8624
Established: 1925; *Employs* 3
Sells via showroom and mail order.
Key Employees: Jim, K3JFL; Jean, K30AU.
Top Lines: Kenwood, ICOM, Yaesu, Alinco, AEA, Bencher, Cushcraft, Butternut, Larsen, Nye-Viking, MFJ, Astron, ARRL Publications.
Accepts trade-ins and provides repairs.

Jun's Electronics
5563 Sepulveda Blvd.
Culver City, CA 90230
Phone: 213 390-8003, 800 882-1343 *FAX:* 213 390-4393
Established: 1975; *Employs* 8
Sells via showroom and mail order.
Key Employees: PJ, WA61BY; Raul, KB6GMR; Lisia, N6YCR; Rudy, KC6LYY, Rick, N6KIB; Kyung.
Top Lines: ICOM, Kenwood, Yaesu, Alinco, Grundig, Mirage/KLM, RF Concepts, Astron, Ameritron, AEA.
Provides repairs.

K

K-Com
Box 82
Randolph, OH 44265
Phone: 216 325-2110
Top Lines: Telephone Interface Filters.

KJI Electronics
66 Skytop Road
Cedar Grove, NJ 07009
Phone: 201 239-4389
Established: 1975; *Employs* 4
Sells via showroom and mail order.
Key Employees: Gene, K2KJI; Maryann, K2RVH, Chris.
Top Lines: ICOM, Kenwood, Yaesu, Azden, Alinco, KLM/Mirage, RF Concepts, Bencher, AEA, Kantronics, Larsen, Astron, Diamond, MFJ.
Accepts trade-ins and provides repairs.

L

LaRue Electronics
1112 Grandview Street
Scranton, PA 18509
Phone: 717 343-2124
Established: 1976; *Employs* 3
Sells via showroom and mail order.
Key Employees: Gene, K3HAM; Les, W3LPZ.
Top Lines: ICOM, AEA, Amphenol, Astron, Beckman, Belden, Bencher, Bird, Cushcraft, Larsen, Vibroplex, Weller, Xcelite, 3M.
Provides repairs.

Lentini Communications
21 Garfield Street
Newington, CT 06111
Phone: 203 666-6227, 800 666-0908
FAX: 203 667-3561
Established: 1954; *Employs* 5
Sells via showroom and mail order.
Key Employees: Alex, N1EBU; Mike, WIVLA; Martin, N1FOC; Bill, N1JBS; Jim, NIJYH.
Top Lines: Kenwood, Yaesu, ICOM, Alinco, Standard, Drake, Sony, Comet, Bencher, DAIWA, Hustler, Larsen, Uniden, Astatic, RF Concepts, NCG, MFJ, Austin Custom Antennas, Kantronics, Diamond, Alpha-Delta, AEA, Cushcraft.
Accepts trade-ins and provides repairs.

Long's Electronics
2630 South Fifth Avenue
Irondale, AL 35210
Phone: 800 633-3410, 800 292-8668
Established: 1971
Sells via showroom and direct mail.
Key Employees: Jimmy, W4ZRZ; Roy, N4AZU; Chris, KD4GUX; Tracy, KD4GVB; Ricky, KA4LIA; Charles, KD4GUS; John, KD4GUU; Jamie, KD4GUV; Steve, KD4GUZ; Karen, KD4GVH; Blanche, KD4GUR; Lynn, WB4RZN; Paul, N4ZS; Jimmy, KA4BVT; Jo Ann, KD4GUT; Dave, K4TWJ.
Top Lines: Kenwood, ICOM, MFJ, Cushcraft, Hy-Gain, Ameritron, Uniden, Rohn Towers, Sony, Panasonic, Simpson, B&K, Maxon, Hakko.

M

Maryland Radio Center
8576 Laureldale Drive
Laurel, MD 20707
Phone: 301 725-1212,800 447-7489; *FAX:* 301 725-1198
Established: 1986; *Employs* 9
Sells via showroom.
Key Employees: Jerry, WA3WZF; Steve, KD3EH; Mike, WA8MCQ; Ike, WB3LRM; John, N3FNG.
Top Lines: Kenwood, ICOM.
Accepts trade-ins and provides repairs.

Memphis Amateur Electronics, Inc.
1465 Wells Station Road
Memphis, TN 38108
Phone: 800 238-6168; 901 683-9125
Established: 1966; *Employs* 8
Sells via showroom and mail order.
Key Employees: Bill, W4TNP; Marshall, KU40; Stan, W4RMW; Chic, WB4KXN.
Top Lines: Kenwood, ICOM, MFJ, Cushcraft, Hustler, Larsen, Van Gorden, Astron, Hy-Gain, Alinco, Daiwa, Valor, Yaesu.
Accepts trade-ins and provides repairs.

Miami Radio Center
5590 W. Flagler Street
Miami, FL 33134
Phone: 305 264-8406
Established: 1980; *Employs* 6
Sells via showroom.
Top Lines: ICOM, Kenwood, Yaesu, Motorola, Cobra, Astron, Hustler, Mirage.

Michigan Radio
23040 Shoenherr
Warren, MI 48089
Phone: 313 771-4711; 800 878-4266
Service: 313 771-4712
FAX: 313 771-6546
Established: 1980; *Employs* 8
Sells via showroom and mail order.
Key Employees: Jerry, W8MR; Vicky, XYL W8MR; Thomas, KA8LSU; Dave, AA8DH; Chris, N8FZT; Rose; John.
Top Lines: Kenwood, ICOM, Yaesu, Standard, Alinco, Drake, Sangean, Rohn, Cushcraft, KLM, Hustler, Butternut, Diamond, Comet, Larsen, AEA, Alpha Delta, Astron, Bencher, Daiwa, Diamond, Heil, MFJ, RF Concepts, Kantronics, Van Gorden, ARRL, W5YI, Callbook, and more.
Accepts trade-ins and provides repairs.

Mike's Electronics
1001 NW 52nd Street
Ft. Lauderdale, FL 33309
Phone: 305 491-7110; 800 427-3066
Established 1980; *Employs* 3
Sells via showroom and mail order.
Key Employees: Walt, KN4SL; Mike, WB4RFC.
Top Lines: ICOM, Yaesu, Spirit, JPS, ANLI, Ham Stick, JRC, Pouch, ARRL, Radio Amateur Callbooks, Valor, Alpha Delta, VGE, NCG, Maxcom, Bearcat, SONY, Rohn, Butternut, Astron, Daiwa, AOR, Nye Viking, Kenwood, Cushcraft, Bencher, Hustler, AEA, Kantronics, RF, MFJ, Ritron, Jabro, Uniden, Comet, RF Concepts, Belden, Periphex.
Accepts trade-ins.

N

N & G Electronics
1950 NW 94th Avenue
Miami, FL 33172
Phone: 305 592-9685
Top Lines: Heathkit, ICOM, Kenwood, Yaesu, Interconnect Spec., Astron, Hy-Gain, Cushcraft, AEA, C.E.S., Hustler, Motorola, and many more.
Provides repairs.

O

Oklahoma Comm Center
9500 Cedar Lake Avenue., Suite 100
Oklahoma City, OK 73114
Phone: 405 478-2866, 800 765-4267 *FAX:* 405 478-4202
Established: 1989; Employs 8
Sells via showroom and mail order.
Key Employees: Craig, AH9B; Mike, WN5J; N5DDB;
Tony, KG5SA.
Top Lines: Alinco, ICOM, Comet, Diamond, Cushcraft, Yaesu, Kantronics, AEA, Astron, Larsen, Ameritron, Hy-Gain, Alpha Delta, Genesys.

Omni Electronics
1007 San Dario
Laredo, TX 78040
Phone: 210 725-OMNI
Established: 1984; *Employs* 8
Sells via showroom and mail order.
Key Employee: Eduardo, XE2HHC.
Top Lines: ICOM, Kenwood, Yaesu, Antenna Specialists, Telemobile, Tempo, CES, CSI, Anteco, Astron, Arco-Solar, Azden, Centurion, Hustler, Neutec, RF, Motorola, Standard.
Provides repairs.

P

Portland Radio Supply
234 SE Grand Avenue
Portland, OR 97214-1115
Phone: 503 233-4904
Established: 1932; *Employs* 7
Sells via showroom and mail order.
Key Employees: Doug, WA7EJP; Ken, WR7D; Rich, KG7FS; Stan, WB70KN; Stephanie.
Top Lines: ICOM, Kenwood, Yaesu, Rohn, Astron, Larsen, Hustler, ARRL, RF Concepts, MFJ, Grundig, Mouser, NTE.
Large selection of used gear.
Accepts trade-ins and consignments.

Q

Quement Electronics
1000 S. Bascom Avenue
San Jose, CA 95128
Phone: 408 998-5900
FAX: 408 292-9920
Established: 1933
Sells via showroom and mail order.
Top Lines: ICOM, Yaesu, Larsen, Cushcraft, Telex/Hy-Gain, MFJ, Alpha Delta, B&W, Butternut, Rohn, Alinco.

R

R.F. Enterprises
HC 86 Box 580
Merrifield, MN 56465
Phone: 218 765-3254, 800 233-2482
FAX: 218 765-3308
Established: 1982; *Employs* 3
Sells via showroom and mail/telephone order.
Top Lines: Yaesu, Rohn, Cushcraft, Mirage/KLM, Butternut, Hustler, MFJ, Kantronics, ICOM, AEA, Telex/HyGain, Ameritron, Belden, Andrew, Amphenol, Astron, Heil, Diamond, Vectronics, and Alpha Delta.

R & L Electronics
1315 Maple Avenue
Hamilton, OH 45011
Phone: 800 221-7735, 513 868-6399
FAX: 513 868-6574
Established: 1980; *Employs* 13
Sells via showroom and mail order.
Key Employees: Larry, N8CHL; Rita, WD8POC; Troy, N8ASZ; Roger, N8EKG.
Top Lines: Yaesu, Kenwood, ICOM, MFJ, Ten-Tec, Rohn, AEA, DAIWA, Cushcraft, Hustler.
Accepts trade-ins.
Branch: 8524 E. Washington St.
Indianapolis, IN 46219
Phone: 800 524-4889; 317 897-7362 *FAX:* 317 898-3027.
Established : 1992; *Employs* 5

Radio Center USA
630 NW Englewood Road
Kansas City, MO 64118
Phone: 800 821-7323; 816 459-8832
Established: 1980; *Employs* 9
Sells via showroom and mail order.
Key Employees: Larry, WØYY; Bill,
Top Lines: Kenwood, Yaesu, ICOM, AEA, MFJ, Hy-Gain, Cushcraft, Butternut, Kantronics, RF Concepts.
Accepts trade-ins and provides repairs.

Radio Center USA
12 Glen Carran Circle
Sparks, NV 89431
Phone: 800 345-5686; 702 331-7373 *FAX:* 702 331-3762
Established: 1986; *Employs* 3
Sells via showroom and mail order.
*Key Employees:*Jim, W6FHZ; Jane.
Top Lines: Kenwood, ICOM, Yaesu, AEA, MFJ, Hy-Gain, Cushcraft, Butternut, Kantronics, RF Concepts, Alinco.
Accepts trade-ins.

Radio City Inc.
2663 County Road I
Mounds View, MN 55330
Phone: 612 786-4475; 800 426-2891
Established: 1982; *Employs* 10
Sells via showroom and mail order.
Key Employees: Dan, KBØXC; Maline; Jim, KBØGGI; John, NØISL; Louis, KAØIPN.
Top Lines: Yaesu, ICOM, Kenwood, Alinco, Cushcraft, Comet, Telex, ARRL, Kantronics.
Accepts trade-ins; provides repairs.

Radio Place, The
5675A Power Inn Road
Sacramento, CA 95824
Phone: 916 387-0730; 916 387-0731 *FAX:* 916 387-0744
Established: 1976; *Employs* 10
Sells via showroom and mail order.
Key Employees: Glenn, WR60; Paul, KA6MHT; Gary, KI6T; Rudy, KC6MUR; Dale, KF7MI; Craig, N6YUV.
Top Lines: Yaesu, Cushcraft, Larsen, ARRL, MFJ, Astron, Kantronics, Ameritron, Diamond, DAIWA, Alinco, Hustler, Comet, AEA and books.
Provides repairs.

Rivendell Electronics
8 Londonderry Road
Derry, NH 03038
Phone: 603 434-5371
Established 1982; *Employs* 6
Sells via showroom and mail order.
Key Employees: Joe, KC1D; Peter, KI1M; Nancy, N1CXC; Herb, AK1V; Marybeth, N1KCB; Rob, N1ORI.
Top Lines: ICOM, AEA, B&W, Cushcraft, Hustler, Alinco, Larsen, MFJ, Rohn, Bencher, Kantronics, RF Concepts.
Accepts trade-ins and provides repairs.

Ross Distributing, Co.
PO Box 234
78 S. State Street
Preston, ID 83263
Phone: 208 852-0830; 208 852-0832
FAX: 208 852-0833
Established: 1953; *Employs* 5
Sells via showroom and mail order.
Key Employees: Ross, WB7BYZ; Karen, KA7BLB; Kathy, Gae, John, Shannon, Niko.
Top Lines: Kenwood, ICOM, Yaesu, AEA, Larsen, Kantronics, Cushcraft, Telex, MFJ, Astron, Butternut, Diamond.
Accepts trade-ins and used gear.

S

Satellite City
2663 Country Road I
Minneapolis, MN 55112
Phone: 800 426-2891, 612 786-4475
Established: 1986; *Employs* 10
Sells via showroom and mail order.
Key Employees: Dan, KBØXC; Louis, KAØIPN; John, NØISL; Jim, KBØGGT; Jim, KBØJZF; Maline, Denise, Dorothy, KBØJPS.
Top Lines: Yaesu, ICOM, Kenwood, Comet, RSGB, ARRL, Lakewood, Alinco, MFJ, Cushcraft, AEA, Kantronics, Astron, Butternut, Smiley, Larsen, Vibroplex, Bencher, DAIWA, Sony, Panasonic, Sangean, Grundig, RF Concepts, Mirage/KLM, Spi-Ro, Hustler, Rohn, Books, Cable & Connectors.
Accepts trade-ins and provides repairs.

Soundnorth Electronics
1802 Highway 53
International Falls, MN 56679
Phone: 218 283-9290, 800 932-3337
Established: 1976; *Employs* 7
Sells via showroom and mail order.
Key Employees: Terry, WVØG: Gale, WVØO; Dan, WZØA; Jami, WYØD; Mike, KBØDXW.
Top Lines: Alinco, DAIWA, NCG, Valor, ANTECO, Maxrad, JRC, T.E. Systems Amps, MFJ and all used gear.
Accepts trade-ins and provides repairs.

T

Tel-Com, Inc.
Electronic Communications
675 Great Road, Rt.119
Littleton, MA 01460
Phone: 508 486-3400; 508 486-3040
Established: 1978; *Employs* 5
Sells via showroom and mail order.
Key Employees: Jim, Fred, Roy, Greg.
Top Lines: Kenwood, ICOM, Astron, Bencher, AEA, Diamond, Ameritron, Mirage/KLM, Hustler, MFJ, RF Concepts, DAIWA, Amphenol, Unadilla, Larsen, ARRL, Callbook, Cushcraft, Uniden, plus more.
Provides in-house repairs.

Texas Towers
1108 Summit Avenue Ste.4
Plano, TX 75074
Phone: 800 272-3467; 214 422-7306
FAX: 214 881-0776
Established: 1976; *Employs* 6
Sells via showroom and mail order.
Key Employees: Gerald, K5GW; Matt, N5VQT; Neil, AA6TR.
Top Lines: Kenwood, ICOM, Yaesu, US Towers, Rohn, Telex/Hy-Gain, Cushcraft, Mirage/ KLM, Butternut, Astron, AEA, Ameritron, MFJ, Nye-Viking, Kantronics, RF Concepts, Diamond, Comet, Daiwa, Alinco, ANLI, Aluminum tubing, Andrew, Hustler.

U

Universal Radio Inc.
6830 Americana Parkway
Reynoldsburg, OH 43068
Phone: 614 866-4267; 800 431-3939
FAX: 614 866-2339
Established: 1942; *Employs* 20
Sells via showroom and mail order.
Key Employees: Steve, NI8F; Fred, N8EKU; Kristen, KA8YCO; Tom, W8OMV; Sam, N8JYV; Dave, N8FVL; Scott, KB2ARL; Jim, KC8XZ.
Top Lines: Kenwood, ICOM, Yaesu, Japan Radio, AEA, Info-Tech, Kantronics, Sony, Telex/Hy-Gain, Alpha-Delta, Sangean, Alinco, Standard, Astron, MFJ, Ameritron, Cushcraft, Hustler, Lowe, Grundig, ARRL.
Accepts trade-ins and provides repairs.

V

VHF Communications
453 Buffalo Street
Jamestown, NY 14701
Phone: 716 664-6345
800 752-8813 (*orders only*).
FAX: 716 487-0310
Established: 1971
Sells via showroom and mail order.
Key Employees: Gary, W2UCZ; Loretta.
Top Lines: ICOM, Unadilla, Vibroplex, AEA, Van Gorden, Nye-Viking, Hamtronics, RF Concepts, Kantronics, Sinclabs, KAIWA, DRSI, Larsen.
Accepts trade-ins and provides repairs.

Valley Radio Center
1522 N. 77 Sunshine Strip
Harlingen, TX 78550
Phone: 210 423-6407
FAX: 210 423-1705
Established: 1959; *Employs* 8
Sells via showroom and mail order.
Key Employees: Bob, WD5KBZ; Rick, WD5ADC; Pat, KB5AFG; Bill, WD5KBZ.
Top Lines: Kenwood, ICOM, Yaesu, Alinco, Larsen, Antenna Specialists, Hustler, B&W, Mirage/KLM, RF Concepts, AEA, Kantronics, Astron, CES, Connect System, Comm Systems.
Accepts trade-ins and provides repairs.

W

Western Radio Electronics, Inc.
4797 Ruffner Street
San Diego, CA 92111
Phone: 619 268-4400; 800 777-4973
FAX: 619 379-7048
Established: 1932
Top Lines: Antenna Specialist, Amphenol RF, Belden, ICOM, Larsen, Multiplier.
Contact: Paul Marquez.

Williams Radio Sales
600 Lakedale Road
Colfax, NC 27235
Phone: 919 993-5881
Established: 1974; *Employs* 3
Sells via showroom, hamfests and mail order.
Key Employees: Wayne, K4MOB; Gerry, KB4SEL; Chris.
Top Lines: Alinco, Larsen, ARRL books, W5YI, Pac Comm, Pouch, Batteries, Chargers, Pyramid.
Accepts trade-ins.

Canada

Atlantic Ham Radio, Ltd.
368 Wilson Avenue
Downsview, ONT M3H 1S9
Phone: 416 636-3636
FAX: 416 631-0747
Established: 1979; *Employs* 12
Sells via showroom and mail order.
Key Employees: Lutz; Mike, VE3HQW; Harry, VE3LLR; Nick, VE3SEC; Mario, VE2MBZ; Howard, VE2HNL; Steve, VE3OOS; Alan, VE3XAG.
Top Lines: Kenwood, ICOM, Yaesu, Sony, JRC, AEA, Kantronics, Hy-Gain, Cushcraft, MFJ, Astron, Nye-Viking, Uniden, Butternut, DAIWA, Hustler, Larsen, Alinco, Mirage/KLM.
Accepts trade-ins and provides repairs.

Com-West Radio Systems, Ltd.
48 East 69th Avenue
Vancouver, BC V5X 4K6
Phone: 604 321-1833
FAX: 604 321-6560
Sells via showroom and mail order.
Catalog available $2.00.
Key Employees: Ron, VE7XR; Stan, VE7STN; Al, VE7DL; Fred, VE7GGE; Michael, VE7CIP.
Service: Brian, VE7BWM; Robert, VE7HBG; Doug, VE7HDL.
Top Lines: ICOM, Kenwood, Yaesu, Cushcraft, Mirage/KLM, Larsen, AEA, Butternut, Hustler, Unadilla, Kantronics, ARRL, Astron, B&W, MFJ, Telex/ HyGain, Alinco.
Provides repairs.

Garantennas
721 River Street
Thunder Bay, Ont., P7A 3S7
Phone: 807 768-8164
FAX: 807 768-9838
Established: 1993; *Employs* 2
Sells via mail order.
Key Employees: Barry, VE3BGA; Skip, VE3BBS.

MacFarlane Electronic, Ltd., H.C.
R.R. #2
Battersea, ONT KOH 1H0
Phone: 613 353-2800
FAX: 613 353-1294
Established: 1958; *Employs* 4
Sells via showroom and mail order.
Key Employee: Harold, VE3BPM .
Top Lines: ICOM, Telex/Hygain, Cushcraft, Larsen, Hustler, Butternut, Diamond, ARRL Publications, Vibroplex, Uniden, Ten-Tec, MFJ, Nye-Viking, Bencher, AEA, B&W, Ameritron, Trylon Towers.
Accepts trade-ins and provides repairs.

R & S Electronics Ltd.
157 Main Street
Dartmouth, Nova Scotia B2X 1S1
Phone: 902 434-5235
FAX: 902 434-5590
Established: 1976; *Employs* 4
Sells via showroom and mail order.
Key Employee: Dick, VE1AI.
Top Lines: Kenwood, ICOM, Ten-Tec, Telex/Hy-Gain, Panasonic, Yaesu, Cushcraft, Mirage/KLM, JRC, MFJ, Uniden, AEA.
Accepts trade-ins and provides repairs.

Radio Progressive Inc.
8104-A Trans Canada Highway
Ville St. Laurent, Quebec H4S 1M5
Phone: 514 336-2423; 800 363-0930
FAX: 514 336-5929
Key Employees: Jean-Claude, VE2DRL; Joe, VE2ALE; Bruno, VE2JFX; Julio.
Top Lines: ICOM, Kenwood, Yaesu and many others.

This directory gives valuable information on manufacturers and/or importers of amateur radio equipment and supplies.

Beyond being a handy source of phone numbers and addresses, it also gives you insight to a company's business longevity and size, the latter by number of employees. Moreover, you'll learn which companies sell their own products directly to end users, usually through mail order, rather than only to dealers for resale.

A

ANLI Corp.
15344 E. Valley Blvd. #C
City of Industry, CA 91746
Phone: 800 666-2654
Tech: 818 369-2654
Established: 1963; *Employs* 45
Sells through dealers.
Major Lines: Antennas, HF Mobile Antennas.

Advanced Electronic Applications Inc. (AEA)
2006 196th St. SW
PO Box C-2160
Lynnwood, WA 98036
Phone: 206 774-5554
FAX: 206 775-2340
Tech. Support: 206 775-7373
Literature: 800 432-8873
Established: 1977
Sells through dealers.
Major Lines: Packet controllers, multimode data controllers, HF/VHF/UHF antennas, high speed radio modems, remote telephone and radio controllers for HF/VHF/UHF radios, weather FAX modems, CW keyers, ATV equipment, and antenna performance analyzers.

Alpha Delta Communications, Inc.
1232 E. Broadway, Suite 210
Tempe, AZ 85282
Phone: 602 966-2200
Established: 1981
Sells direct and through dealers.
Major Lines: Lightning/EMP ceramic gas tube Transi-Trap surge protectors, lightning/emp-protected DELTA-4 precision coaxial switches, HF (160 through 10 meter) NO-TRAP spacelimited sloper and dipole DX SERIES wire antennas.

American Antenna Corp.
1500 Executive Drive
Elgin, IL 60123
Phone: 800 323-6768; 708 888-7200
FAX: 708 888-7094
Established: 1977; *Employs* 125
Sells direct and through dealers.
Major Lines: Manufacturers of HF & VHF mobile antennas and accessories.

Antenna Mart
PO Box 699
Loganville, GA, 30249
Phone: 404 466-4353
FAX: 404 466-3095
Established: 1984; *Employs* 3
Major Lines: Quad antennas and parts. Heavy duty gin poles. HD mast pipes RF switches—remote type, dist, QSL holders, Seth Thomas 24 hr. clocks, Rotator capacitor kits & more.

Antenna Sales & Accessories (ASA)
PO Box 3461
Myrtle Beach, SC 29578
Phone: 800 722-2681
Tech: 800 722-2681
Established: 1991; Employs 3
Sells direct and through dealers.
Major Lines: Specializes in antennas: HF mobile, UHF & VHF mobiles, Rubberducks, UHF-VHF Base Antennas, Cellular, Scanner, C.B., Business & Marine, accessories.

Antenna Specialists Co.
30500 Bruce Industrial Pkway.
Cleveland, OH 44139
Phone: 216 349-8400
FAX: 216 349-8407
Established: 1953; *Employs* 500
Sells through dealers.
Major Lines: Two-way mobile and base communications antennas for CB, VHF, UHF, 800 MHz, 900 MHz, cellular, marine, amateur, monitor.

Antenna Supermarket
PO Box 563
Palatine, IL 60078
Phone: 708 359-7092
FAX: 708 359-8161
Established: 1974
Sells: direct and through dealers.
Major Lines: SWL antennas, multi-band SWL antennas, lightning surge arrestors.

Antenna Systems, Inc.
13662 SW Whitmore
Hillsboro, OR 97123
Phone: 503 628-3568
Established: 1987; *Employs* 4
Sells direct and through dealers.
Major Lines: Antenna products, baluns, center insulators, multiband antennas, single-band dipoles.

Antennaco, Inc.
PO Box 218C
Milford, NH 03055
Phone: 603 673-4347
Established: 1992
Sells direct and through dealers
Major Lines: HF Yagis, Quads, VHF/ UHF Verticals, yagis, dipole, arrays, custom mounting hardware, power dividers, stacking frames and harness tower standoffs, antenna kits, satellite antennas circular polarized.

Antennas West
PO Box 50062
1500 North 150 West
Provo, UT 84605
Phone: 801 373-8425
FAX: 801 375-4664
Order Line: 800 926-7373
Established: 1987; *Employs* 10
Catalog: Radio Adventure $1
Sells direct and through dealers.
Major Lines: HF antennas, VHF/UHF Antennas, Masts & Towers, Solar Power, Publications.

Austin Custom Antenna
10 Main Street
Gonic, NH 03839
Phone: 603 335-6339
FAX: 603 335-1756
Established: 1973; *Employs* 12
Sells direct and through dealers.
Major Lines: VHF/UHF fixed and mobile antennas, microwave and multiband-design antennas, including collinears.

B

Barker and Williamson
10 Canal Street
Bristol, PA 19007
Phone: 215 788-5581
FAX: 215 788-9577
Established: 1932; *Employs* 25
Sells direct and through dealers.
Major Lines: HF antennas, HF amplifiers, HF antenna tuners, baluns, coax switches, filters, coils, dummyload wattmeters, plate chokes, filament chokes, antenna wire, insulators, center connectors.

Bilal Company
137 Manchester Drive
Florissant, CO 80816
Phone: 719 687-0650
Established: 1980
Sells direct and through dealers.
Major Line: Reduced-space HF Antennas.

Broadcast Technical Services
11 Walnut Street
Marshfield, MA 02050
Phone: 617 837-2880
Sells direct.
Major Line: Sidekick VHF/UHF antennas.

Butternut Electronics
PO Box 1234
Olmito, TX 78575
Phone: 210 350-5711
Established: 1976; *Employs* 22
Sells through dealers.
Major Line: HF Antennas.

C

Cellular Security Group
4 Gerring Road
Gloucester, MA 01930
Phone: 508 281-8892
Established: 1990; *Employs* 3
Sells direct.
Major Line: VHF/UHF antennas .

Centurion International, Inc.
PO Box 82846
Lincoln, NE 68501-2846
Phone: 402 467-4491
FAX: 800 848-3825
Major Lines: Replacement antennas and batteries for two-way portable radios, cordless telephones & specialized OEM applications.

Com-Rad Industries
PO Box 88
4230 East Lake Road
Wilson, NY 14172
Phone: 716 751-4945
FAX: 716 751-9879
Established: 1979; *Employs* 2
Sells direct and through dealers.
Major Lines: Un-tenna line of low profile VHF and UHF antennas for amateur and commercial use.

ComTek Antennas, Inc.
PO Box 470565
Charlotte, NC 28247
Phone: 704 542-4808
Established: 1988
Sells direct.
Major Lines: Vertical phase box, phasing lines, antennas and switches.

Create Design Co., LTD
Phone: 703 938-8105
FAX: 703 938-6911
Major Lines: Amateur and Commercial Antennas, HF, VHF, UHF, Rotators, Highpower Baluns, Towers and RF Generator for Plasma Processing, etc.
Amateur Radio Sales:
Electronic Distributors Corp.
325 Mill Street
Vienna, VA 22180
Phone: 703 938-8105
FAX: 703 938-6911
Henry Radio, Inc. 2050 S. Bundy Drive
Los Angeles, CA 90025
Phone: Toll Free: 800 877-7979
Local: 213 820-1234
FAX: 310 826-7790

Cubex Company
25 S. Backus Avenue
Pasadena, CA 91107
Phone: 818 449-5925, 818 798-8106
Established: 1956; *Employs* 3
Sells direct.
Major Lines: Exclusive manufacturer of cubical quad beam antennas and accessories.

Cushcraft, Inc.
PO Box 4680
48 Perimeter Road
Manchester, NH 03108
Phone: 603 627-7877
FAX: 603 627-1764
Established: 1950
Sells through dealers.
Major Lines: HF/VHF/UHF antennas and accessories.

D

DC Sales
1602 Chestnut Ridge
Kingwood, TX 77339
Phone: 713 358-0051
Established: 1985; *Employs* 3
Sells direct and through dealers.
Major Lines: Antenna brackets (mobile), antennas (mobile).

DX Engineering
618 Spaulding Avenue
Brownsville, OR 97327
Phone: 503 466-3138
FAX: 503 466-5453
Established: 1989 *Employs* 3
Sells direct.
Major Lines: High performance, 40 through 6 meter, monoband yagi antennas, stacking systems, HF vertical phasing array switches, remote coax switches and accessories, high performance 10-20M log periodic antennas.

Delta Loop Antennas, Inc.
PO Box 274
Weston, VT 05161
Phone: 802 824-8161
Established: 1987
Sells direct.
Major Line: HF antennas .

Down East Microwave
Box 2310, RR1
Troy, ME 04987
Phone: 207 948-3741
FAX: 207 948-5157
Major Lines: UHF and microwave antennas and accessories, linears, amplifiers, preamps, microwave transverters and accessories, RF and microwave components.

E

Electron Processing, Inc.
PO Box 68
Cedar, MI 49621
Phone: 616 228-7020
Established: 1984; *Employs* 10
Sells direct.
Major Lines: Receiver preamplifiers, antennas, assorted accessories for Hams and SWL's.

Eur-Am Electronics
PO Box 990
Meredith, NH 03253
Phone: 603 279-1393
Established: 1982
Sells direct.
Major Lines: Computer programs for packet, European made antennas (mobile and base), 6M discones, mounting hardware.

F

Forbes Group, The
PO Box 445
5420 Whitney Blvd.
Rocklin, CA 95677
Phone: 916 624-7069; 800 551-5156
Sells direct.
Major Lines: Ventenna™ concealed antennas.

Force 12
3350 Scott Blvd., Bldg. 6102
Santa Clara,CA 94054
Phone: 408 988-2766; 800 248-1985
FAX: 408 988-2767
Major Lines: Large variety of HF antennas.

G

GAP Antenna Products Inc.
6010 Bldg. B, N. Old Dixie Hwy.
Vero Beach, FL 32967
Phone: 407 778-3728
Established: 1989; *Employs* 6
Sells direct.
Major Line: HF vertical and beam antennas utilizing GAP technology.

Genesys Products Group
5730 Mobud
San Antonio, TX 78238
Phone: 210 521-6868
FAX: 210 647-8007
Established: 1992
Sells through dealers
Major Lines: Dual band antennas, mount, accessories, wattmeters, spkr/ mikes, eartalk microphone, throat microphone.

H

Ham-Pro Antennas
6199-B Warehouse Way
Sacramento, CA 95826
Phone: 916 381-4469
FAX: 916 381-4332
Established: 1979
Sells direct.
Major Lines: HF and VHF beam antennas for the amateur. Studio to transmitter link antennas TV/FM broadcasting.

Hustler Antenna
One Newtronics Place
Mineral Wells, TX 76067
Phone: 817 325-1386; 800 949-9490
FAX: 817 328-1409
Established: 1968; *Employs* 100
Sells through dealers.
Major Line: Amateur, land-mobile, CB antennas and scanner antennas.

I

IVIE Technologies
1366 W. Center Street
Orem, UT 84057
Phone: 801 224-1800
FAX: 801 224-7526
Major Line: Ground cooperative antennas that can be laid on the ground.

J

J•Com
793 Canning Pkwy.
Victor, NY 14564
Phone: 716 924-0422
FAX: 716 924-4555
Established: 1990
Sells direct and through dealers.
MajorLines: Magic Notch automatic notch audio filter; Ventriloquist audio memory; Ham-Base software and databases; Stealth Antennas; SofTNC and packet modems. Other hardware and software accessories for the radio amateur.

Jo Gunn Enterprises
Route 1, Box 32C
Ethelsville AL 35461
Phone: 205 658-2229
FAX: 205 658-2259
Established: 1976; *Employs* 5
Sells direct/through distributors/dealers.
Major Lines: Mobile and base CB antennas, 10M amateur antennas, coax and accessories.

K

Kilo-Tec
PO Box 10
Oak View, CA 93022
Phone: 805 646-9645
FAX: 805 646-9645
Established: 1982
Sells direct and through dealers.
Major Lines: Antennas HF/VHF, ATU components & tuners, coax and antenna accessories, HV variable capacitors, roller inductors, Hi-Q mobile loading coil and turns counter.

L

LTA Industries Inc.
PO Box 92
Canfield,OH 44406
Phone: 216 533-0087
Tech: 216 565-1012
Established: 1989; *Employs* 3
Sells direct.
Major Lines: Monoband, HF Yagis

Lakeview Co. Inc.
3620-9A Whitehall Road
Anderson, SC 29624
Phone: 803 226-6990
FAX: 803 225-4565
Established: 1979; *Employs* 7
Sells direct and through dealers.
Major Lines: WD4BUM mobile antennas and mounts for HF, VHF and UHF. Fixed station ground plane antennas for 10M, UHF and VHF.

Larsen Antennas
3611 NE 112th Avenue
PO Box 1799
Vancouver, WA 98668
Phone: 206 944-7551; 800 426-1656
Established: 1965; *Employs* 100 +
Sells direct and through dealers.
Major Lines: Mobile, portable and base antennas from 27 MHz to 1.3 GHz and accessories.
Branch: Canadian Larsen Electronics Ltd.
149 West 6th Avenue
Vancouver, BC, Canada, V5Y 1K3
Phone: 604 872-8517; 800 426-1656

Lightning Bolt Antennas
RD #2, Rt. 19
Volant, PA 16156
Phone: 412 530-7396
Established: 1984; *Employs* 2
Sells direct.
Major Lines: Fiberglass quad antennas and parts, custom quads.

M

M2 Enterprises
7560 N. Del Mar Avenue
Fresno, CA 93711
Phone: 209 432-8873
FAX: 209 432-3059
Established: 1985; *Employs* 8
Sells direct and through dealers.
Major Lines: HF, VHF and UHF antennas, rotators, and antenna related products.

Metal & Cable Corp., Inc.
9241 Ravenna Rd., Unit C-10
PO Box 117
Twinsburg, OH 44087
Phone: 216 425-8455
Established: 1985; *Employs* 3
Sells direct and through dealers.
Major Lines: W3BMW Impossible Dream Whip HF Mag Mount; Copper Ground System Strap; Tubing and Rod —Aluminum 6061-T6 for masts and antennas.

Mirage/KLM
PO Box 1000
16890 Church St.
Morgan Hill, CA 95038
Phone: 408 779-7363
FAX: 408 779-8845
Established: 1979; *Employs* 40
Sells through dealers.
Major Lines: Amateur radio amplifiers and antennas.
Branch Office:
KLM Antennas, Inc.
14792 172nd Drive, SE, #1
Monroe, WA 98272
Phone: 206 794-2923
FAX: 206 794-0294

Mobile Mark, Inc.
3900-B River Road
Schiller Park, IL 60176
Phone: 708 671-6690
FAX: 708 671-6715
Established: 1948; *Employs* 50
Sells through distributors and dealers.
Major Lines: VHF & UHF antennas for amateur, commercial, CB, marine and cellular use along with a wide selection of accessories.

Mosley Electronics
1344 Baur Blvd.
St. Louis, MO 63132
Phone: 800 325-4016; 314 994-7872
Established: 1940
Sells direct.
Major Lines: Beam antennas, verticals, dipoles, and mobiles for HF, VHF, and UHF use.

N

N.C.G. Companies/Comet Antenna Distr.
1275 N. Grove Street
Anaheim, CA 92806-2114
Phone: 714 630-4541; 800 962-2611
FAX: 714 630-7024
Established: 1968; *Employs* 7
Sells through dealers.
Major Lines: US and Canadian distributor of the COMET Multi-Band Antenna Line. 900-MHz FM transceivers. Exclusive distributor for Comet Co. Ltd. antennas.

O

Orion Business International
360 W. Bedford Ave., Suite 111
Fresno, CA 93711
Phone: 209 432-4155
FAX: 209 261-0662
Established: 1985
Sells through dealers.
Major Lines: Rotators, HT antennas, roof towers, Tokyo Hi-Power, HF Handheld radio, VHF/UHF amplifiers, transverters, Orion Roof Towers, Orion Intermod Filters, Orion Toroid Filters.

Outbacker Antenna Sales
330 Cedar Glen Circle
Chattanooga, TN 37412
Phone: 615 899-3390
Sells direct.
Major Lines: Importers of mobile HF, multiband vertical antennas manufactured by Terlin Aerials of Australia.

P

Pro•Am (Div. of Valor Enterprises Inc.)
1711 N. Commerce Drive
Piqua, OH 45356
Phone: 513 778-0074
FAX: 513 778-0259
Established: 1974; *Employs* 180
Sells through dealers.
Major Lines: Two meter base/mobile, multi-band base/mobile, 450 portables, HF yagis, scanner mobile/base, two-meter portable, HF mobile antenna, cellular, commercial, marine antennas and accessories, RV antennas, UHF/VHF amplifiers.
Branch Office:
185 W. Hamilton Street
West Milton, OH 45383
Phone: 513 698-4194

ProComm
1372 Harmony Court
Thousand Oaks, CA 91362
Phone: 805 497-2397
Major Lines: Motorola transceivers, frequency counters, simplex repeaters, discone/HF antennas, preamps, ranger transceivers.

R

RAI Enterprises
4508 No. 48th Drive
Phoenix, AZ 85031
Phone: 602 848-9755
Established: 1989
Sells direct.
Major Lines: Raider™ Antennas, the Quickyagi, and EZ Log Plus (full function logging program).

R.F. Parts Co.
1320 Grand Avenue
San Marcos, CA 92069
Phone: 800 854-1927; 619 744-0728
Tech: 619 744-0720
Established: 1968; *Employs* 10
Sells direct.
Major Lines: Diamond Antennas VHF/ UHF antennas, duplexers, wattmeters, accessories, RF power transistors for transmitters, amplifiers.

The Radio Room
898 N. Broadway
N. Massapequa, NY 11758
Phone: 516 795-9371
Established: 1992; *Employs* 1
Sells direct and through dealers.
Major Lines: G5RV antennas and single band dipoles; imports Maldol Antennas and accessories.

Radio Shack
1500 One Tandy Center
Ft. Worth, TX 76102
Phone: 817 390-3011
Established: 1921; *Employs* 39,000
Over 7,000 stores in the U.S.
Major Lines: Computers, scanners, antennas, transceivers, coax, plugs, jacks, parts and supplies.

Radio Works, Inc.
PO Box 6159
Portsmouth, VA 23703
Phone: 804 484-0140
Established: 1984; Employs 4
Sells direct.
Major Lines: HF antennas, baluns, VHF base antennas, portable antennas.

Rutland Arrays
1703 Warren Street
New Cumberland, PA 17070
Phone: 717 774-3570
Orders Only: 800 536-3268
Established: 1986; *Employs* 4
Sells direct and through dealers.
Major Lines: VHF Yagi antennas designed by K1FO, power dividers, stacking frames.

S

SGC, Inc.
The SGC Building
13737 S.E. 26th St.
Bellevue, WA 98005
PO Box 3526
Bellevue, WA 98009
Phone: 206 746-6310
FAX: 206 746-6384
Established: 1972; *Employs* 100
Sells direct and through dealers.
Major Lines: Manufactures HF SSB radios, antenna couplers, power supplies, and antennas.

Sherwood Engineering
1268 South Ogden Street
Denver, CO 80210
Phone: 303 722-2257
Established: 1975; *Employs* 4
Sells direct.
Major Line: Mobile antennas.

Signal Engineering
2624 Fayette Drive
Mountain View, CA 94040
Phone: 415 948-3833
Tech: 415 948-3834
FAX: 415 949-5953
Established: 1973; *Employs* 8
Sells direct and through dealers.
Major Line: Antennas.

Smiley Antenna Co.
408 La Cresta Heights Road
El Cajon, CA 92021
Phone: 619 579-8916
FAX: 619 579-8598
Established: 1985; *Employs* 4
Sells through dealers.
Major Line: Antennas for handheld radios for amateur commercial and business band use.

Solorcon Corporation
7134 Railroad St., Box 176
Holland, OH 43611
Phone: 800 445-3991
FAX: 419 865-9449
Established: 1979; *Employs* 30
Sells through dealers.
Major Lines: Mobile and base antennas.

Sommer Antenna Systems
395 Osceola Road
PO Box 710
Geneva, FL 32732
Phone: 407 349-9114
FAX: 407 349-2485
Sells direct.
Major Line: HF & VHF antennas.

Spectrum International Inc.
PO Box 1084
Concord, MA 01742
Phone: 508 263-2145
FAX: 508 263-7008
Established: 1970
Sells direct and through dealers.
Major Lines: Antennas, filters, crystal filters, converters, pre-amps and weather satellite systems.

Spider Antenna
7131 Owensmouth Avenue, Suite 663
Canoga Park, CA 91303
Phone: 818 341-5460
Established: 1979
Sells direct.
Major Lines: Spider 4-band HF mobile antenna, maritimer antenna, 4-band dipole 10, 15, 20 & 40 meters, ideal for apartments, condominiums and CC&Rs.

Spi-Ro Manufacturing, Inc.
PO Box 5500
Lakeland, FL 33807
Phone: 813 646-7925
Established: 1970; *Employs* 6
Sells direct and through dealers.
Major Lines: Antennas, antenna traps, antenna connectors, insulators, transmission lines, antenna wire, antenna shorteners, limited space antennas, lightning-surge protectors, baluns, custom interconnect coax cables, multi-band & mono-band antennas.

Stewart Designs, H.
PO Box 643
Oregon City, OR 97045
Phone: 503 654-3350
Established: 1985
Sells direct.
Major Lines: Antennas: HF/VHF directionals, hidden base, concentric-feed vertical dipoles, J-poles, half-squares, and loops. Antenna accessories: DX Quickshift, DX MagCup, and DS MagCup mounts.

SUMMITEK
PO Box 520011
Salt Lake City, UT 84152
Phone: 801 277-4205
Tech: 801 278-2727
Established: 1980
Sells direct.
Major Line: VHF portable delta loop beams.

T

Telewave, Inc.
1155 Terra Bella
Mountain View, CA 94043
Phone: 415 968-4400; 800 331-3396
FAX: 415 968-1741
Sells through distributors.
Major Lines: Transmitter combining, duplexers, cavities, isolators, receive systems, antennas, wattmeters.

Telex Communications Inc.
Hy-Gain Division
9600 Aldrich Avenue South
Minneapolis, MN 55420
Phone: 612 887-5530
Tech: 402 467-5321
Established: 1936
Sells through dealers.
Major Lines: Multiband antennas, HF monobanders, vertical antennas, VHF/ UHF beam antennas,VHF/UHF omnidirectional antennas, rotators, crank-up towers.
Branch: Customer Service Parts
8601 E. Cornhusker Hwy.
Lincoln, NE 68505
Phone: 402 465-7021 (rotator parts);
402 465-7022 (antenna/tower parts)

Telrex
PO Box 879
Asbury Park, NJ 07712
Phone: 908 775-7252
Established: 1921; *Employs* 15
Sells direct.
Major Lines: HF, VHF & UHF antennas.

Ten-Tec, Inc.
1185 Dolly Parton Parkway
Sevierville, TN 37862
Phone: 615 453-7172
Tech: 615 428-0364
FAX: 615 428-4483
Established: 1968; *Employs* 120
Sells direct.
Major Lines: HF transceivers, mobile and base. HF amplifiers to 1500 watts. Mobile and base antenna tuners. Mobile antennas. Metal and plastic equipment enclosures. Custom tools and dies.

Texas Radio Products
5 East Upshaw
Temple, TX 76501
Phone: 817 771-1188
Major Lines: Bugcatcher mobile antennas, mobile antenna accessories, VHF/ UHF antennas.

U

Unadilla Antenna Manufacturing Co.
PO Box 4215
Andover, MA 01810-4215
Phone: 508 475-7831
FAX: 508 474-8949
Established: 1986
Sells through dealers and direct only for international and O.E.M. customers.
Major Lines: Baluns, antenna traps for 10-160 meters, remote coaxial switches, antenna kits for amateur, CAP and MARS antenna accessories, wire, end insulators and center insulators, mobile slot antennas, grounding systems.

V

Valor Enterprises Inc.
(See Pro•Am)

Van Gorden Engineering
PO Box 21305
S. Euclid, OH 44121
Phone: 216 481-6590
FAX: 216 481-8329
Established: 1964; *Employs* 7
Sells direct and through dealers.
Major Lines: Dipole antennas, shortened antennas, baluns, insulators, coils, traps, wire, feedline, and cable for amateur, SWL and commercial use.

W

W9INN Antennas
PO Box 393, 811 Cathy Lane
Mt. Prospect, IL 60056
Phone: 708 394-3414
Established: 1982; *Employs* 2
Sells direct.
Major Lines: Space-restricted antennas, HF multi-band dipoles, half and full slopers, MARS & marine wire antennas, multi-antenna systems, remotely-tuned antenna systems, and accessories .

Wallen USA, Les
19 Aero Drive
Amherst, NY 14225
Phone: 716 634-0634
FAX: 716 632-6304
Established: 1961; *Employs* 14
Sells direct and through dealers.
Major Lines: Antennas, voltage converters, zap traps.

Wilson Antenna, Inc.
1181 Grier Dr., Suite A
Las Vegas, NV 89119
Phone: 800 541-6116, 702 896-0399
FAX: 702 896-0409
Established: 1985
Sells through dealers.
Major Lines: Amateur and CB mobile antennas.

Wintenna,Inc.
911 Amity Road
Anderson, SC 29621-7097
Phone: 803 261-3965, 800 845-9724
FAX: 803 224-7920
Major Lines: Manufactures wide line of base and mobile antennas.

CANADA

Garantennas
721 River Street
Thunder Bay, ON P7A 357, Canada
Phone: 807 768-8164
FAX: 807 768-9838
Established: 1993; *Employs* 2
Major Lines: Amateur radio antennas.

Gem Quad
PO Box 291
Boissevain, Manitoba R0K 0E0, Canada
Phone: 204 534-6184
Established: 1968; *Employs* 4
Sells direct.
Major Line: Cubical quad antennas.

Interactive Image Technologies Ltd.
700 King St. West #815
Toronto, ON M5V 2Y6, Canada
Phone: 416 361 -0333
Sales: 800-263-5552
FAX: 416 368-5799
Established: 1982; *Employs* 24
Sells direct and through dealers.
Major Lines: Software circuit and test instrument simulation package.
Branch: 908 Niagara Falls Blvd.
North Tonawanda, NY 14120-2060
Phone: 416 361-0333

Sinclabs, Inc.
Division of Sinclair Radio Laboratories, Inc.
85 Mary Street
Aurora, ON L4G 3G9, Canada
Phone: 416 841-0624
FAX: 416 841-6255
Sells direct and through dealers.
Major Lines: VHF and UHF repeater duplexers and antennas, VHF and UHF mobile antennas, mobile diplexers, 12Vdc power supplies.

FOREIGN

Maldol Antennas
Hokushin Industry Co., Ltd.
1111-1 Nagasaku Cho;
Hanamigawa-ku
Chiba City, Chiba,-pref. Japan
Phone: 043-257-1581
FAX: 043-259-6000
Sells through dealers.
Major Lines: Mobile and base station antennas, mounting bases for mobile stations, duplexers, SWR meters, speaker microphones, extension speakers, roof towers.

Sagant Antenna
6-6, 2-chome, Kaisei
Saga-City 849 Japan

Manufacturer	Model	Band(s)	Gain	F/B	# Elements	Boom Length (ft.)	Price
AAE/ Bandmaster	Q-50-4	28	8.0	24.0	2	4.0	$200
Antenna Mart	AMQ-2-5-8**	10/12/ 15/17/20	7.0	19	2*	8.50	599
	AMQ-5-5-24**	10/12/ 15/17/20	9.3/10.2	26	5 -10, 12 m* 4 -15, 17, 20 m*	24.00	1030
	AMQ-5-5-31**	10/12/ 15/17/20	10.3/11.2	27	5 (10, 12 m)* 4 -15, 17, 20 m*	31.50	1445
	AMQ-4-30-40-48	30/40	10.2/10.7	25	4*	48.00	2995
	AMQ-6-6-12	6	13.8	30	6*	12.00	799
	AMQ-8-10-31	10	14.7	30	8*	31.00	1395
	AMQ-8-15-41	15	14.5	30	8*	41.00	1595
	AMQ-6-20-48	20	13.8	30	5*	48.00	1650
	AMQ-4-40-48	40	10.2	25	4*	48.00	2995
Butternut	HF5B 17/20	10/12/15/	3.0	20	2	6.00	333
	1011	10	5.0	15	2	4.00	147
Comet	CHA18	12	—	—	Dipole	—	96
	CHA24	17	—	—	Dipole	—	96
	H722	40/15/10	—	—	V-Dipole	—	249
Contest Radio	1712-3	12/17 11.5	5.4/4.4	15.5/	3	12.00	270
Creative Design	CY103	10	8.5	20	3	13.08	186
	CY10DX	10	13.0	22	6	30.50	414
	CY153	15	8.0	20	3	13.08	195
	CL15DX	15	13.5	22	6	40.67	779
	CY203	20	8.0	20	3	20.00	408
	AFA30	30	6.0	20	2	12.92	368
	AFA40	40	6.0	24	2	16.67	572
	318JR	10/15/20	8.0	18	3/3/3	13.00	426
	318	10/15/20/	8.5	22	3/3/3	16.37	512
	730V-1	10/15/20/40	—	—	V-Dipole	—	210
Cushcraft	TEN-3	10	7.8	25	3	8.00	140

Manufacturer	Model	Band(s)	Gain	F/B	# Elements	Boom Length (ft.)	Price
Cushcraft	10-3CD	10	8.0	30	3	12.00	217
	10-4CD	10	10.0	30	4	17.00	279
	15-3CD	15	8.0	30	3	14.00	284
	15-4CD	15	10.0	30	4	20.00	330
	20-3CD	20	8.0	30	3	18.00	409
	20-4CD	20	10.0	30	4	32.00	584
	D40	40	—	—	1	—	276
	40-2CD	40	5.5	20	2	23.00	584
	D3W	12/17/30	—	—	1	—	232
	D3	10/15/20	—	—	1	—	227
	D4	10/15/20/40	—	—	1	—	309
	A3S	10/15/20	8.0	25	3	14.00	474
	A4S	10/15/20	8.9	25	4	18.00	567
	A3WS	12/17	8.0	25	3	14.00	371
Delta Loop	DL202	20	7.0	20	2	9.00	397
	DL1520	15/20	7-7	20	2/2	9.00	597
	DL172	17	7.0	20	2	6.70	327
Force 12	N1012	10/12	11.4/10.7	20/14	7	15	297
	N1012X	10/12	13.8/11.3	20/14	10	24	495
	N1517	15/17	10.8/10.3	20/12	6	16	425
	N1517X	15/17	11.6/10.6	20/12	7	20	498
	N1517XL	15/17	14.0/12.1	20/14	9	36	685
	N1217	12/17	11.4/11.1	21/20	7	15	389
	EF-510	10	13.0	23	5	18	245
	EF-624	10	13.6	23	6	24	329
	EF-415	15	12.5	22	4	20	278
	EF-420	20	12.4	22	4	30	397
	EF-340	40	10.2	17	3	30	795
Force 12	308MAGNUM810	10	14.58	23	8	30	485
	357MAGNUM615	15	14.33	24	6	35.7	598
	357MAGNUM520	20	13.10	23	5	35.7	649
	44MAGNUM715	15	15.02	26	7	44	875
	44MAGNUM620	20	13.57	23	6	44	889
GAP Antenna	DXII	10/11	7.0	25	3	10.00	130
Gem Quad	2EL	10/15/20	7.0	25	2*	9.5(Ant.)	290
	3EL	10/15/20	8.9	30	3*	16.0(Ant.)	455
	4EL	10/15/20	10.0	30	4*	22.5(Ant.)	600
Ham Pro	H10-3	10	6.5	22	3	11.95	190
	H10-4	10	9.2	25	4	17.5	239
	H15-4	15	8.8	22	4	23.60	340
	H20-4	20	9.2	22	4	33.58	530
Hy-Gain	103BAS	10	8.5	25	3	8.00	148
	105BAS	10	12.0	34	5	24.00	283
	153BAS	15	8.0	25	3	12.10	205
	155CA	15	12.0	34	5	26.00	430
	203BAS	20	8.5	25	3	16.00	333
	204BAS	20	10.0	30	4	26.00	555
	205CA	20	12.0	35	5	34.00	762
	DISC7-1	30 or 40	—	35	1	2.70	303
	DISC7-2	40	4.7	15	2	22.60	680
	DISC7-3	40	7.0	26	1 Add-on Dir	35.00	428
	TH2MK3S	20/15/10	5.5	20	2	6.00	388
	TH3JRS	10/15/20	8.0	25	3	12.00	380
	EXP14S	10/15/20	8.9	27	4	14.10	605
	TH5MK2S	20/15/10	9.0	27	5	19.00	785
	TH7DXS	10/15/20	9.6	27	7	24.00	915
	TH11	10/12/15/17/20	8.5	25	12	24.00	TBA
	LP1007	20/17/15/12/10	14.0	12	—	26.50	By Quote
	LP1017	40/30/20/17/15/12/10	10.0	17	—	37.00	By Quote

Manufacturer	Model	Band(s)	Gain	F/B	# Elements	Boom Length (ft.)	Price
KLM/ Mirage	10M-4	10	7.7	25	4	10.00	223
	10M-6	10	11.0	30	6	27.50	351
	15M-4	15	7.7	25	4	14.00	244
	15M-6LD	15	10.5	30	6	36.00	431
	15M-6	15	11.0	30	6	36.00	574
	20M-4	20	7.7	25	4	21.00	459
	20M-5	20	9.7	30	5	42.00	710
	20M-6	20	11.0	30	6	57.00	1022
	40M-1	40	—	—	1	46.50	221
	40M-2A	40	4.9	12	2	16.00	542
	40M-3A	40	6.5	20	3	32.00	741
	40M-4	40	7.2	20	4	42.00	1028
	80M-1	80	—	—	1	45.00	837
	80M-2	80	4.0	12	2	36.00	2757
	80M-3	80	7.0	18	3	60.00	4564
	KT-31	10/15/20	—	—	1	24.40	269
	KT34A	10/15/20	8.2	20	4	16.00	533
	KT34XA	10/15/20	10.3	20	6	32.00	766
	12-17-30D	17	—	—	1	39.7	269
	12-17-30V	17	—	—	1	21.25	141
	17M-3	17	6.5	20	3	17.00	409
	10-30-7LPA	10-20MHz	7.0	15	7	30.00	1070
	20-30-6LPA	20-30MHz	7.0	20	6	24.00	365
	6-12-8LPA	6-12MHz	6.0	15	8	46.00	2299
	6-30—15LPA	6-30MHz	6.0	15	15	46.00	3802
	7.2/10-30LPA	7-30MHz	3/7	15	8	42.00	1262
LTA	LT310	10	8.4	30	3	11.50	138
	LT410	10	9.0	32	4	16.00	219
	LT610	10	10.1	34	6	31.00	389
	LT710	10	11.2	35	7	37.50	479
	LT810	10	11.6	38	8	40.00	699
	LT515L	15	10.4	32	5	31.00	499
	LT420HD	20	10.0	28	4	40.00	897
	LT520HDL	20	10.6	30	5	46.00	1219
	LT340	40	8.4	26	3	40.00	1795
Lightning Bolt	10MCQ	10	8.0	25	2*	6.00	90
	10MCQ-4	10	10.0	25	4*	16.00	170
	22MCQ	10/12/15	8.0	25	2*	8.00	99
	17MCQ	10/12/15/17	8.0	25	2*	9.00	225
	32MCQ	10/15/20	8.0	25	2*	12.00	265
	34MCQ	10/15/20	10.0	30	4*	24.00	675
	32MCQ/WB 17/20	10/12/15/	8.0	26	2*	10.00	290
	34MCQ/WB 17/20	10/12/15/	10.0	25	4*	24.00	726
	42MCQ	40	7.0	25	2	16.00	900
M^2	10M4	10	8.7	25	4	23.00	269
	10M7	10	10.3	25	7	45.00	499
	15M4	15	8.5	25	4	34	369
	15M6	15	9.4	25	6	45	499
	18M3	18	6.3	25	3	18.00	249
	20M4	20	8.7	25	4	45.00	649
	20M6	20	9.0	25	6	60.00	899
	10-30LP8	30/10	6 typ.	15 typ.	8	32.00	999
	7-10-30LP8	40, 30-10	6 typ.	15 typ.	8	30.00	1099
	40M1L	40	na	na	1	na	229
	40M2L	40	4.2	12	2	20.00	499
	40M3L	40	5.6	20	3	30.00	749
	40M4L	40	6.2	22	4	42	969
Mosley	TA-31	10/15/20	—	—	1	—	152
	TA-32	10/15/20	5.0	20	2	7.00	280
	TA-33	10/15/20	8.0	20	3	14.00	359
	CL-33	10/15/20	8.4	23	3	18.00	426
	TA-34	10/15/20	9.1	21	4	21.00	471
	CL-36	10/15/20	9.1	24	6	24.00	603
	PRO-57-A 17/20	10/12/15/	NA	20-25	7	24.00	661

Boom Manufacturer	Model	Band(s)	Gain	F/B	# Elements	Length (ft.)	Price
Mosley	PRO-67-A	10/12/15/ 17/20/40	NA	10-25	7	24.00	818
Sommer	XP403	10/15/20	6.0	20-25	4	7.90	450
	XP504	10/12/15/20	7.0	25	5	14.40	650
	XP507	10/12/15/17/ 20/30/40	1-7	0-25	5	14.40	933
	XP704	10/12/15/20	9.0	0	7	19.70	795
	XP707	10/12/15/17/ 20/30/40	1-9	0-28	7	19.70	1078
	XP804	10/12/15/20	0-10	0-30	11	23.00	1383
H. Stewart	II-DX	10	7.0	15-20	2	4.00	282
	II-DX	12	7.0	15-20	2	5.00	305
	Loop	10	7.0	15-20	2-4	varies	varies
	Loop	12	7.0	15-20	2-4	varies	varies
	H.S. Loop	10-40	varies	varies	1-3	varies	varies

* elements per band.
** UPS shippable models

Manufacturer	Model	Freq.	Gain	F/B	# Elements	Boom Length (ft.)	Price
AAE/ Bandmaster	Q-144-2	144	8.0	24.0	2	1.20	$35
	Q-144-3	144	9.0	24.0	3	2.50	50
	Q-144-4	144	10.0	24.0	4	3.30	60
	Q-144-6	144	12.0	24.0	6	5.00	80
	Q-220-6	220	12.0	24.0	6	3.30	70
	Q-440-6	440	12.0	24.0	6	2.00	60
	Q-50-4	50	10.0	24.0	4	8.5	170
AEA	430-16	430	14.8	20.0	16	10.00	119
Creative Design	CL6DX	50	13.0	22.0	6	19.00	161
	X209	144	11.5	16.0	9	12.08	155
	2X209	144	17.0	18.0	18(9X2)	12.17	285
	4X209	144	19.5	20.0	36(9X4)	12.17	769
	X713	430	16.0	18.0	13	7.58	113
	2X713	430	18.5	18.0	26(13X2)	7.58	277
	CLP130-1	50-1300	11.0	15.0	25	6.58	299
	CLP5130-2	105-1300	12.0	15.0	20	4.50	164
Comet	CY-1205	1280	11.0	na	5	na	41
	CYA-1216E	1260-1300	16.6	na	16	4.50	140
	PYA-913	900-930	15.8	na	13	na	145
Cushcraft	A50-3S	50	8.0	20.0	3	6.00	103
	A50-5S	50	10.5	24.0	5	12.00	170
	A50-6S	50	11.6	26.0	6	20.00	276
	617-6B	50	14.0	30.0	6	34.00	394
	A148-35	144	9.0	18.0	4	3.67	45
	A147-20T	144	12.2	20.0	20(2X10)	10.80	118
	124WB	144	10.2	24.0	4	4.00	69
	A144-10T	145	10.5	20.0	10	5.80	101
	A144-75	144	11.1	20.0	7	8.25	56
	A144-20T	145	12.2	20.0	20	10.80	145
	A148-105	144	13.5	20.0	11	12.00	80
	13B2	144	15.8	26.0	13	15.00	135
	A148-20	144	16.5	20.0	22(2X11)	12.00	220
	17B2	144	18.0	26.0	17	31.00	232
	26B2	144	18.8	26.0	26	15.00	382
	224WB	220	10.2	24.0	4	3.00	66
	225WB	220	15.5	24.0	15	10.00	140
	220B	220	17.2	30.0	17	19.00	181
	A449-6S	450	10.0	18.0	6	2.90	56
	416TB	435	12.5	20.0	16	6.70	114

Manufacturer	Model	Freq.	Gain	F/B	# Elements	Boom Length (ft.)	Price
	A449-11S	450	13.2	20.0	11	5.00	81
	A430-11S	430	13.2	20.0	11	4.70	81
	424B	430	18.2	30.0	24	17.00	155
Down East	3311LY	910	15.0	20.0	11	3.00	55
	3318LYARM	910	16.5	20.0	18	6.00	79
	3319LY	900	16.5	20.0	19	6.00	75
	3319LYA	910	16.5	20.0	19	6.00	75
	3333LY	900	18.5	20.0	33	12.00	89
	3333LYA	910	18.5	20.0	33	12.00	109
	3347LY	900	20.0	20.0	47	18.00	145
	2325LY	1296	18.0	20.0	25	6.00	69
	2324LYRM	1296	18.0	20.0	24	6.00	79
	2424LYRM	1296	18.0	20.0	25	6.00	79
	2345LY	1296	20.0	20.0	45	11.90	115
	2355LY	1296	21.0	20.0	55	15.00	129
	2445LY	1296	20.0	20.0	45	11.90	115
	1245LY	2300	20.0	20.0	45	6.75	93
	1345LY	2300	20.0	20.0	45	6.75	93
	1352LY	2300	21.0	20.0	52	8.00	99
	945LY	3300	20.0	20.0	45	4.50	93
Ham Pro	H6-6	50	10.4	30.0	6	15.42	200
	H144-5	144	9.1	25.0	5	6.00	74
	H144-15H	144	13.7	25.0	15	18.00	149
	H144-15V	144	13.7	25.0	15	18.00	149
	H220-5	220	9.0	25.0	5	4.75	65
	H220-17	220	13.5	25.0	17	19.30	149
	H430-5	430	9.3	25.0	5	2.91	65
	H432-24	430	16.1	25.0	24	17.00	149
	H915-ZZ	915	15.2	33.0	20	5.00	75
	H1296ZZ	1296	18.1	33.0	32	6.00	79
Hy-Gain	64DX	50	8.2	25.0	4	12.00	138
	66DX	50	10.3	25.0	6	24.50	262
	203FM	144	6.1	20.0	3	3.60	47
	205FM	144	9.1	20.0	5	6.25	58
	208FM	144	11.8	20.0	8	12.30	80
	214FM	144	13.0	20.0	14	15.50	90
	215DX	144	14.2	30.0	15	28.00	237
	216SAT	145	11.5	25.0	16	14.00	200
	215SAT	440	14.0	25.0	30	11.20	195
	218SAT	145/435	215SAT	AND	216SAT	Relays	472
	70-31DX	440	17.6	28.0	31	24.00	187
JayBeam	2XY-137-C	137	3.0	OMNI	2+2	3.75	95
	5XY-137-C	137	7.8	20.0	5+5	5.50	135
	10XY-2M	144	11.3	20.0	20	13.00	168
	70MBM48	430	14.0	20.0	48	6.00	115
	70MBM88	430	18.2	20.0	88	13.00	160
	1268-LY	1268	20.0	29 (loop)	8.00	60	
	1296LY	1296	20.0	20.0	29 (loop)	8.00	60
	1691LY (N)	1691	20.0	20.0	29 (loop)	6.00	99
KLM/ Mirage	6M-5	50	9.7	30.0	5	11.75	221
	6M-7LD	50	10.5	30.0	7	20.00	252
	6M-7LB	50	11.5	30.0	7	25.75	322
	6M-10	50	11.7	25.0	10	34.20	428
	6M-14	50	14.0	26.0	14	61.00	593
	2M-4X	144	8.5	20.0	4	4.20	69
	2M-8	144	10.3	30.0	8	7.25	108
	2M-14C	144	11.0	20.0	14	12.75	179
	2M-11X	144	12.5	20.0	11	15.30	92
	2M-22C	144	13.0	20.0	22	19.10	234
	2M-13LBA	144	13.3	20.0	13	21.50	105
	2M-16LBXM	144	14.5	20.0	16	28.00	214
	2M-20LBX	144	15.5	20.0	20	36.50	248
	220-7	220	8.8	20.0	7	4.75	83
	220-14X	220	13.5	20.0	14	14.67	120
	220-22LBX	220	15.6	20.0	22	29.75	151
	432-20LBX	430	15.3	20.0	20	12.30	160

Manufacturer	Model	Freq.	Gain	F/B	# Elements	Boom Length (ft.)	Price
	432-30LBX	430	17.3	20.0	30	21.90	188
	435-18C	435	12.0	20.0	18	7.30	235
	435-40CX	435	15.2	20.0	40	14.63	255
	440-10X	440	10.0	20.0	10	4.80	72
	440-16X	440	14.0	20.0	16	12.00	132
	440-6X	440	8.0	20.0	6	7.30	60
	1.2-1.5LBX	1260	13.6	39.0	15	3.50	100
	1.2-24LBX	1260	16.2	39.0	24	6.30	121
	1.2-44LBX	1260	18.2	39.0	44	12.30	169
LTA	LT806	50	13.5	38.0	8	37.00	399
Lightning Bolt	6MCQ	50	8.0	25.0	2	4.00	80
	6MCQ-4	50	10.0	26.0	4	12.00	135
	2MCQ-2	144	7.0	25.0	2	2.00	30
	2MCQ-4	144	10.0	25.0	4	4.00	40
	2MCQ-6	144	12.0	25.0	6	8.00	60
	70MCQ-4	440	9.0	25.0	4	—	30
	70MCQ-8	440	12.5	25.0	8	—	50
	270MCQ-4	144/440	7.5/9.0	25.0	2/4	—	50
	270MCQ-8	144/440	9.0/12.5	25.0	4/8	—	80
	OPP-1	145/435	2MCQ-4	AND	70MCQ-7	CrossBoom	$115
	OPP-2	145/435	2MCQ-6	AND	70MCQ-12	CrossBoom	$155
MFJ	MFJ-1763	144	6.9	17.0	3	2.75	40
M2	6M-5	50	9.4	12.0	5	15.70	149
	6M-7	50	10.5	23.0	7	26.00	229
	6M-2WL	50	12.3	25.0	9	39.50	379
	6M-2.5WL	50	13.0	22.0	11	50.30	449
	2M-CP14	144	10.0	20.0	14	9.80	150
	2M-CP22	144	12.1	25.0	22	18.00	225
	2M7	144	10.3	20.0	7	8.83	105
	2M12	144	13.0	25.0	12	19.50	129
	2M5-440P	144/430	9.0/12.0	15/20	5/10	4.92	149
	2M-5WL	144	15.0	22.0	17	33.00	169
	2M-18XXX	144	15.3	25.0	18	36.00	219
	2M-6WLD	144	16.0	22.0	20	41.30	379
	220-7WL	220	16.5	25.0	23.0	32.50	189
	420-50-11	420	11.3	20.0	11.0	5.00	99
	440-18	420	14.5	23.0	18.0	11.33	109
	436-30CP	430	14.5	22.0	30.0	9.75	229
	432-9WL	420	17.3	24.0	27.0	21.00	149
	432-13WL	430	18.0	22.0	39	30.70	229
Mosley	MY144-5	144	10.0	20.0	5	4.50	93
	A142	144	13.0	20.0	14	12.00	155
	MY144-9	144	14.0	20.0	9	9.00	135
	MY220-9	220	14.0	20.0	9	8.17	109
	A-2N6	50/144	11/9	11.0	5/4	14.00	155
Radio Room	HS-FOX2	144	9.5	18.0	3	3.71	TBA
	HS-FOX727	144/430	9.5/11.15	12.0	8	3.71	TBA
Rutland Arrays	RA4-50	50	10.3	22.0	4	12.33	140
	RA5-50	50	11.3	20.0	5	17.33	195
	RA7-50	50	12.6	25.0	7	26.50	280
	RA8-2UWB	144	13.3	22.0	8	11.75	92
	FO-12-144	144	14.7	22.0	12	17.30	143
	FO-15-144	144	15.9	21.0	15	24.67	193
	FO-12-147	147	14.7	22.0	12	17.30	143
	FO-16-222	220	14.0	22.0	16	17.25	130
	FO-33	432	19.9	23.0	33	23.30	224
	FO-25	432	18.6	25.0	25	17.00	135
	FO-22	432	17.9	22.0	22	14.00	115
	FO22-ATV	432	17.9	22.0	22	14.00	115
	FO-11	440	14.1	21.0	11	6.00	70

THE BIGGEST AMATEUR ANTENNAS IN THE WORLD

Most hams are satisfied with a triband Yagi and dipoles for the low bands. Some amateurs are driven to build much bigger antennas. This list of exceptionally large antennas was collected through an informal survey conducted during 1993. Photographs of some of these arrays appear elsewhere in the Almanac. Only antennas used exclusively for amateur radio are included. The 1000-foot radio astronomy dish at Arecibo, PR is occasionally used for amateur EME, but is not considered an amateur antenna.

If you have (or know of) any antennas larger than those listed here, please forward a detailed description and a photograph to Almanac Editor, CQ Communications, 76 N. Broadway, Hicksville, NY 11801. They will be included in this listing in the 1995 Almanac.

Since many of these stations are using arrays of stacked Yagis, the nomenclature "N/N/N/N" will be used where appropriate and is interpreted as a stacked array of 4 N-element Yagis.

AA6TT, Tiffany, CO:

160M
Four-square Vertical array, elevated radial system
80M
Four-square Vertical array, elevated radial system
40M
4/4, 72-foot booms 200/100 feet, lower fixed on Europe
20M
6/6/6, 60-foot booms at 66/133/200 feet on 200 foot tower
15M
8/8/8/8, 60-foot booms at 50/100/150/200 feet on 200 foot tower
10M
8/8/8/8, 48-foot booms at 40/80/120/160 on 160 foot tower
6M
10/10/10/10/10/10/10/10 (no, this is not a misprint!), 48-foot booms on 180 foot tower (dismantled summer '93)

Spotting Antennas
KT34 at 35 feet
13-element log periodic yagis at 70/125 feet, offset 120 degrees on rotating tower

WØUN, La Salle, CO:

160M
Four-square array of quarter-wave verticals constructed of 150 foot Rohn 25G towers with insulator sections at about 30 feet.
Sloping Dipole from 170 Feet
14 Beverage receiving antennas from 900 to 2000 feet long

80M
Inverted Vee at 160 ft
40M
4/4 at 80/160 feet
20M
6/6 at 80/160 feet
15M
7/7/7/7 at 40/80/120/160 ft Rotating tower (48 ft booms)
8/8 at 40/80 fixed on JA (60 ft booms)
8 element Yagi, 60 foot boom, at 56 ft on wooden pole
15M
7/7/7/7 (48' booms)
8/8 60' booms and
Single 8 element Yagi
10M
8/8/8/8 at 40/80/120/160 feet
8 element Yagi at 50 ft
8 element Yagi at 56 ft

WØAIH/9, Eau Claire, WI:

160M
3 element wire Yagi at 100 feet
4 element vertical beam
Full wave Loop
Extended Double Zepp
Sloping dipole
Dipole
Elevated 1/4-wave vertical
7 1040-foot Beverage receiving antennas, 1 2200-foot Beverage
80M
Bi-square
4 element inverted-V beam at 160 feet
5-element vertical beam
4 520-foot Beverage receiving antennas
40M
3/3 at 70/190 feet
3 element Yagi at 70 feet
20M
6/6 at 150/90 feet
5 element Yagi at 105 feet
4 element Yagi at 60 feet
4/4/4/4 at 195/160/120/80 feet on rotating tower
4/4 at 70/35 feet fixed Southeast
4-wavelength Rhombic on Europe
15M
4/4/4/4 at 199/170/140/110 feet
5/5 at 110/70 feet
5 element Yagi at 180 feet
4 element Yagi at 40 feet
3 element Yagi at 35 feet
6-wavelength Rhombic on Europe
6-wavelength Rhombic on Japan
10M
5/5/5/5 at 160/125/90/55 feet on rotating tower
3/3/3/3 at 160/140/120/100 feet
5 element at Yagi at 195 feet
4 element Yagi at 80 feet
3 element Yagi at 30 Feet
8-wavelength Rhombic on Japan
Also: 5 element 20/15M Yagi at 45 feet, 6-element 20/15/10M Yagi at 75 feet 19 towers total, 153 Yagi elements on 36 booms (40-10 Meters)

K5XI, Houston, TX:

20M
5/5/5/5 @ 35', 105', 175', 255'
15M
5/5/5/5 @ 70', 117', 164', 205'
10M
8 elements at 240'
Also: three more towers for 40, 10 and a smaller 20-15 stack.

N5AU, Rockwall, TX

160M
3 half-wave sloping dipoles from the 180' level of a 190' tower (NE, SE, & W)
80M
3 element delta loop; top at 160' bottom at 90', fixed on Europe
E-W broadside dipole @ 170'
N-S broadside dipole @ 150'
NE-SE broadside dipole @ 130'
NW-SE bobtail curtain
NE-SW bobtail curtain
40M
3 el 46' boom Yagi @ 120'
2/2 40-2cds @ 190'/ 120'
4 element quad 80' top, 40' bottom fixed on EU
20M
5 element Yagi 46' boom @ 190'
5 element Yagi 46' boom @ 100'
4 element quad @ 80'
4 element Yagi @ 70'
4 element Yagi fixed on SA @ 50'
4/4 @ 140'/ 70' fixed on EU
15M
5 element Yagi 32' boom @ 175'
5/5 @ 135'/ 90' fixed on EU

5/5 @ 70'/70' (70' apart side by side fixed on JA)
5 element Yagi @ 60'
4/4 @ 90'/45' fixed on South America
4 element Yagi fixed on South Pacific @ 135'

10M
6 element Yagi @ 120'
6 element Yagi @ 80'
4/4 @ 80'/50' fixed on Europe
4/4 @ 90'/60' fixed on JA
5 element Yagi @ 50'

OH6RM, Istunmaki, Finland

80M
4 element full-size monoband Yagi.
Boomlength: 98.5 feet (30meters).
Longest element: 151 feet (46 meters).
Height: 147 feet high (45 meters).
Weight: 882 lbs (400 kg) , excluding tower

The tower is a telescoping type having two 78 foot sections. OH6RM also built a 3-element version of this antenna which was installed at PJ9W on Curacao.

OH6RM also designed, constructed, and installed a full-size 3-element 160-Meter delta loop on a 180-foot crankup tower at PJ9W in October 1991.

TI4CF, Costa Rica

80M

Four 4-element quad loops (diamond configuration) with tops of loops at 160'—pointed NE, NW, SE, SW.

3-element rotary Yagi at 240'. All antennas tuned for SSB.

DIPOLE LENGTHS

Table of Half-Wave Dipole Lengths for Wire Antennas
(assuming 5% correction for wire diameter & end effect)

Band	Freq. kHz	Length Feet	Inches	Meters
160 Meters	1750	267	1.0	81.43
	1775	263	3.9	80.28
	1800	259	8.0	79.17
	1825	256	1.3	78.08
	1850	252	7.8	77.03
	1875	249	3.4	76.00
	1900	246	0.0	75.00
	1925	242	9.7	74.03
	1950	239	8.3	73.08
	1975	236	7.9	72.15
	2000	233	8.4	71.25
	2025	230	9.8	70.37
	2050	228	0.0	69.51
80 Meters	3450	135	5.7	41.30
	3475	134	6.0	41.01
	3500	133	6.5	40.71
	3525	132	7.1	40.43
	3550	131	7.9	40.14
	3575	130	8.9	39.86
	3600	129	10.0	39.58
	3625	128	11.3	39.31
	3650	128	0.7	39.04
	3675	127	2.2	38.78
	3700	126	3.9	38.51
	3725	125	5.7	38.26
	3750	124	7.7	38.00
	3775	123	9.8	37.75
	3800	123	0.0	37.50
	3825	122	2.4	37.25
	3850	121	4.8	37.01
	3875	120	7.4	36.77
	3900	119	10.2	36.54
	3925	119	1.0	36.31
	3950	118	3.9	36.08
	3975	117	7.0	35.85
	4000	116	10.2	35.63
	4025	116	1.5	35.40
	4050	115	4.9	35.19
40 Meters	6950	67	3.0	20.50
	6975	67	0.1	20.43
	7000	66	9.3	20.36
	7025	66	6.4	20.28
	7050	66	3.6	20.21
	7075	66	0.8	20.14
	7100	65	10.0	20.07
	7125	65	7.2	20.00
	7150	65	4.4	19.93
	7175	65	1.7	19.86
	7200	64	11.0	19.79
	7225	64	8.3	19.72
	7250	64	5.6	19.66
	7275	64	3.0	19.59
	7300	64	0.3	19.52
	7325	63	9.7	19.45
	7350	63	7.1	19.39

Band	Freq. kHz	Length Feet	Inches	Meters
30 Meters	10050	46	6.1	14.18
	10075	46	4.7	14.14
	10100	46	3.3	14.11
	10125	46	2.0	14.07
	10150	46	0.6	14.04
	10175	45	11.2	14.00
	10200	45	9.9	13.97
20 Meters	13950	33	6.1	10.22
	14000	33	4.6	10.18
	14050	33	3.2	10.14
	14100	33	1.8	10.11
	14150	33	0.4	10.07
	14200	32	11.0	10.04
	14250	32	9.6	10.00
	14300	32	8.2	9.97
	14350	32	6.9	9.93
	14400	32	5.5	9.90
17 Meters	18018	25	11.3	7.91
	18068	25	10.4	7.89
	18118	25	9.6	7.87
	18168	25	8.7	7.84
	18218	25	7.9	7.82
15 Meters	20950	22	3.7	6.80
	21000	22	3.1	6.79
	21050	22	2.5	6.77
	21100	22	1.8	6.75
	21150	22	1.2	6.74
	21200	22	0.6	6.72
	21250	21	11.9	6.71
	21300	21	11.3	6.69
	21350	21	10.7	6.67
	21400	21	10.1	6.66
	21450	21	9.5	6.64
	21500	21	8.9	6.63
12 Meters	24840	18	9.8	5.74
	24890	18	9.3	5.73
	24940	18	8.9	5.71
	24990	18	8.4	5.70
	25040	18	8.0	5.69
10 Meters	27800	16	9.8	5.13
	28000	16	8.3	5.09
	28200	16	6.9	5.05
	28400	16	5.5	5.02
	28600	16	4.1	4.98
	28800	16	2.8	4.95
	29000	16	1.4	4.91
	29200	16	0.1	4.88
	29400	15	10.8	4.85
	29600	15	9.5	4.81
	29800	15	8.2	4.78
	30000	15	7.0	4.75

1994 SCHEDULE

* = ARRL Conventions
+ = ARRL Hamfests
x = Other

January 8–9	+	Ft. Myers ARC, Ft. Myers, FL Jerry Deutscher, 802 Elinor Way, Sanibel, FL 33957
January 15	+	Green Hills, Missouri Valley & Ray-Clay RCs, Cameron, MO Gaylen Pearson, WBØW, 1210 Midyett Rd., St. Joseph, MO 64506
January 22	+	Sky High ARC, Crystal River, FL Larry Weaver, KB9V, 8061 N. Golfview Dr., Citrus Springs, FL 34434
January 30	+	Tusco ARC, Dover, OH Charles McEamemey, 428 Seneca Dr., Dover, OH 44622
January 30	+	Maryland Mobileers ARC, Odenton, MD Jim Botluk, KD3SI, 10 Tiburon Ct., Annapolis, MD 21403
February 5–6	*	Florida State Convention, Miami, FL Evelyn Gauzens, W4WYR, 2780 N W 3rd St., Miami, FL 33125
February 18–20	*	Southeastern Division Convention, Orlando, FL John Lenkerd, W4DNY, 1046 Turner Rd. Winter Park, FL 32789
February 26	+	Pensacola Area Hams Assn., Pensacola, FL Bill Behrends, WA4YRN, 1050 W. Carlton Rd., Pensacola, FL 32534
February 26–27	*	Great Lakes Division Convention, Cincinnati, OH Stan Cohen, WD8QDQ, 2301 Royal Oak Ct., Cincinnati, OH 45237
March 12-13	x	Charlotte Hamfest, NC Robert Starling, N4GVF, 7021 Holly Hill Rd., Charlotte, NC 28227
March 18–20	*	Nebraska Section Convention, Norfolk, NE Don Hoehne, KFØRE, PO Box 632, Stanton, NE 68779
March 20	+	Toledo Mobile Radio Assn., Maumee, OH Chuck Krukowski, KB8FXJ, 9408 Salisbury, Monclova, OH 43542-9700
March 26–27	*	Maryland State Convention, Timonium, MD Jim Green, WB3DJU, 36 Sunnyview Dr., Phoenix, MD 21131
April 8–9	*	Arkansas State Convention, N. Little Rock, AR ob Hancock, KB5IDB, 116 Nicole Dr., Little Rock, AR 72118
April 9	+	Lawton Ft. Sill ARC, Lawton, OK Bob Morford, KA5YED, 3111 Brent Circle, Lawton, OK 73505
April 17	*	North Carolina State Convention, Raleigh, NC Chuck Littlewood, K4HF, 2005 Quail Ridge Rd., Raleigh, NC 27609
April 29–May 1	x	Dayton Hamvention, OH Dayton Amateur Radio Association, P.O. Box 964, Dayton, OH 45401-0964
May 13–14	*	Nebraska State Convention, S. Sioux City, NE Dick Pitner, WØFZO, 2931 Pierce St., Sioux City, IA 51104
May 15	+	Warminster ARC, Wrightstown, PA William Gorodetzer, K3MFI, 25 Fawn Dr., Holland, PA 18966
May 15	+	Triple States RAC, Wheeling, WV Ralph McDonough, K8AN, RD 1, Box 240, Adena, OH 43901
May 20-22	x	Rochester Hamfest, NY Harold Smith, K2HC, 300 White Spruce Blvd., Rochester, NY 14623
May 21	+	PHD Kansas City Midwest, Kansas City, KS Peggy Gnegy, KAØKSI, P O Box 11, Liberty, MO 64068

June 10–12	*	ARRL National Convention, Arlington, TX John Fleet, WA5OHG, Box 25028, Dallas, TX 75225
June 17–18	*	Georgia State Convention, Albany, GA John Crosby, K4XA, 308 Residence Ave., Albany, GA 31701
June 18	*	Tennessee State Convention, Nashville, TN Willie Porter, KB4BLL, 4907 Idaho, Nashville, TN 37209
July 10	+	Genesee Radio Amateurs, Alexander, NY Don Partis, WA2AIV, 8786 Broadlawn Ave., Batavia, NY 14020
July 23-24	x	Atlanta Hamfest, GA Verne Fowler, W8BLA, 4343 Shallowford Rd., #E6, Marietta, GA 30062
July 24	+	DuPage ARC, Stickney, IL Ed Weinstein, WD9AYR, 7511 Walnut Ave., Woodridge, IL 60517
July 24	x	Manchester Hamfest, NH Warren Rothberg, WB1HBB, PO Box 573, Derry NH 03038
August 20-21	x	Huntsville Hamfest, AL Art Davis, WB4KKA, 2804 S. Memorial Pkwy., Huntsville, AL 35801
August 21	+	Greater Cincinnati ARA, Cincinnati, OH John Haungs, WA8STX, 10615 Thornview Dr., Cincinnati, OH 45241
August 26–28	*	Southwestern Division Convention, San Diego, CA Fried Heyn, WA6WZO, 962 Cheyenne St., Costa Mesa, CA 92626
September 3-4	x	Shelby ARC Hamfest, NC Barbara Elliot, PO Box 2206, Shelby, NC 28150
September 10	+	Statesboro ARC, Statesboro, GA Richard Franks, N4XTP, PO Box 402, Brooklet, GA 30415-0402
September 17–18	+	Peoria Area ARC, Peoria, IL Ronald Morgan, KB9NW, 114 Herman St., East Peoria, IL 61611-4420
September 17-18	x	Virginia Beach Hamfest, VA Lewis Steingold, W4BLO, 3449 Dickens Dr., Virginia Beach, VA 23452
October 1–2	*	New England Division Convention, Boxboro, MA Gene Hastings, W1VRK, 18 Churchill Rd., Marblehead, MA 01945
October 8–9	*	Tennessee State Convention, Memphis, TN Henry Leggette, WD4Q, 1555 Galveston St., Memphis, TN 38114
October 14–16	*	Midwest Division Convention, Omaha, NE Todd LeMense, NØPHF, 3603 S. 89th St., Omaha, NE 68124

INTRODUCTION TO AWARDS HUNTING

One of the best features of Amateur Radio is the number of ways there are to enjoy this hobby. Ragchewing, experimentation, VHF/UHF, Packet, Traffic Handling, DX, Contests and Awards Hunting. Old timers will remember Clif Evans, K6BX, and his Certificate Hunters Club which was formed in the early 1960s and continued until about 1980. Clif published an Awards Directory listing the requirements for fascinating and sometimes obscure awards.

Most countries are divided into smaller political areas, similar to our states and counties here in the U.S. Best of all, there are many awards for working them. These were to be even a tougher challenge than WAS. Many DX cards have this location information printed on them. Oblasts, Laens and DOKs slowly become familiar old friends to Award Hunters. K6BX died a few years ago leaving a void which was only sporadically filled by a few others who published directories for a short time and then disappeared.

In 1981, K1BV started to collect information about some of the lesser known awards. This became a minor passion. Award information was gathered from DX newsletters, DX columns in several magazines and even info from the backs of QSL cards where the rules were either printed or were attached to a gossamer piece of paper glued to the back. In late 1986, the scope of the data collection was broadened to start gathering data from the national organizations and known major sponsors all around the world.

The Scope of Ham DX Awards

The first tier of awards includes the major international awards like DXCC (DX Century Club), WAZ (Worked All Zones). In addition, the national organizations of most larger countries seem to have an awards series emphasizing the geographical or political organization of their country. These awards form the core of the well known ones: WAS and WACA from the U.S., DUF from France, CCC from England, R-150 from Russia. If you have earned DXCC, you have a fine start in meeting the requirements for more than several dozen colorful DX awards.

Next down the chain come local and regional awards. They may require the contacting of specific numbers of stations in stated areas of their country. Examples include WAGM for Scotland, WAPY for Brazil, etc. The DXer will need a bigger card collection for most of these. It's very likely that you have earned many of these right now!

Club and individual awards form the third category. They almost always require the hunter to contact certain numbers of members or even one station a number of times. Some clubs have tens of thousands of easy-to-find members, like the 10-X International Club. Others, like the Freebooters Club (of Hassleholm, Sweden), have somewhat fewer members (but the Freebooter Statuette is one of the nicer Awards in Amateur Radio). In most cases, though, the farther away you are from them, the fewer contacts are needed. Even so, your DX card collection will haveto be fairly extensive, or you will have to do some hunting. The odds are that you've got some of these earned right now and don't know it. In this category, sponsors will often make lists of members available.

Some Awards Tips From The K1BV DX Awards Directory

The newcomer to awards hunting should read this section to keep his or her expenses down and success ratio high. Your submissions should follow these general guidelines.

Applications:

Most major awards require that their specific application forms be used. The second and third-tier awards usually accept home-made applications, as long as they contain all required information. A sample form that K1BV has used to apply with great success follows this section. It includes all the data generally required by Award Sponsors. Rubber stamp or print your name and address in the top section and add more pages as required. You should write in advance for less known awards and ask the sponsor if it is still offered. Enclose a SASE/IRC as necessary. There is a fairly high mortality rate for awards, and if you don't get a reply in 3-4 months, it's probable that the award is defunct.

Don't forget to get the necessary signatures if the General Certification Rule (see below) is acceptable by the sponsor (99% allow GCR).

Include the fee as indicated. If money has to be sent, a piece of carbon paper folded around currency may prevent tampering. In some countries, mail which may contain money is always a target for pilfering. If you live in a large city, check the International Department of a bank for availability of foriegn currency. It may be a whole lot less expensive than IRCs.

IRCs are an almost universal medium of currency among awards hunters. Many awards specify 10-15 IRCs as the fee. The U.S. Post Office charges $.95 each. You can get them for about half that price from DX QSL managers. Keep an eye out in the various DX newsletters for notices. IRCs change "editions" every few years, so don't hoard large quantities. Always send valid ones of the current edition which are postmarked on the LEFT side.

GCR (General Certification Rule)

Most award sponsors allow GCR in lieu of actually wanting to see your cards. You need to have the cards! GCR usually means getting the signatures of two witnesses who certify that you possess the cards and that the information you state on the application is correct. If the award rules specify club officials, you should make sure their title follows their signature; include the name of the club just to make sure.

Levels

If the award is issued in several different levels, always specify the one you are seeking. If you have the basic level, indicate the serial number, if any, of the basic award and the correct designation of the one now being applied for. If all your contacts for a particular award are SSB and you don't say you want a special mode endorsement, you probably won't get it.

Number of Amateur Radio Awards Listed in K1BV Directory of DX Awards

(Not including awards offered for a single year)

Year	Number	Year	Number
1987	680	1990	1380
1988	830	1991	1729
1989	1055	1992	1980
		1993	2240

The K1BV Directory of DX Awards is issued annually as a service to amateur radio awards hunters throughout the world. All correspondence and inquiries should be directed to: Ted Melinosky K1BV HCR 10 © Box 837A Spofford, New Hampshire 03462 U.S.A. (SASE Appreciated).

Contributed by Ted Melinosky, K1BV.

List of Countries Offering Amateur Radio Awards

Alaska
Andorra
Anguilla
Argentina
Aruba
Ascension Isl.
Australia
Austria
Azores Isl.
Balearic Isl.
Belgium
Bermuda
Bolivia
Brazil
Brunei
Bulgaria
Byelorussia
Canada
Canary Isl.
Chile
Colombia
Corsica
Costa Rica
Cuba
Cyprus
Cyprus (UK Bases)
Czechoslovakia
Denmark
Djibouti
Dominican Rep.
Ecuador
England
Estonia
Faroe Isl.
Finland
France
French Guiana
Gabon
Germany
Gibraltar
Greece
Greenland
Guadeloupe
Guam
Guantanamo Bay
Guernsey
Honduras
Hong Kong
Hungary
Iceland
India
Indonesia
Ireland
Isle of Man
Israel
Italy
Japan
Jersey
Jordan
Kaliningrad
Kazakhstan
Kirghizia
Korea, South
Kuwait
Kwajalein Isl.
Latvia
Lebanon
Liechtenstein
Lithuania
Lord Howe Isl.
Luxembourg
Malaysia
Malta
Man, Isle of
Martinique
Mexico
Monaco
Mongolia
Morocco
Netherlands
New Caledonia
New Zealand
Nigeria
Norfolk Isl.
Northern Ireland
Norway
Oman
Panama
Papua New Guinea
Paraguay
Peru
Philippines
Poland
Portugal
Puerto Rico
Rhodes
Romania
Sardinia
Scotland
Senegal
Singapore
Solomon Isl.
South Africa
Spain
Sri Lanka
St. Pierre & M.
Sweden
Switzerland
Tahiti
Thailand
Turkoman
Ukraine
Uruguay
USA
USSR/COIS
Vanuatu
Venezuela
Vietnam
Wales
Yugoslavia
Zambia
Zimbabwe

Sample Awards Application Form

From:____

Date: ____

To:____

Application for:____

Awards fee enclosed: ____

The information and/or the QSLs required for this award have been checked and are certified to be correct by the following radio amateurs: ____

Signature ______________________________ Call____________________

Signature ______________________________ Call____________________

"I declare that all the necessary credits for this award have been obtained in accordance with the rules or the award, as well as the rules and regulations for radio amateurs in my country. Please accept this information and send the award to my QTH as listed above."

Applicant's Signature: ______________________________ Date:____________________

No.	Call	Date	Time	Band	Mode	RST	Other Information
1							
2							
3							
4							
5							
6							
7							
8							
9							
10							
11							
12							
13							
14							
15							
16							
17							
18							
19							
20							
21							
22							
23							
24							
25							

DX CENTURY CLUB RULES
June 1993 Edition
Current Countries Total: 327

The DXCC rules below were adopted by the ARRL DX Advisory Committee and approved for implementation by the ARRL Board of Directors on January 23, 1988, and modified on January 18, 1991.

Introduction

"...the number of countries worked is increasingly becoming the criterion of excellence among outstanding DX stations."—Clinton B. DeSoto, W1CBD, October 1935 "

From its simple beginnings, culminating in the announcement of the new DX award, The DX Century Club, in September 1937 *QST* (which was itself based on the "ARRL List of Countries" published in January 1937 *QST*), membership in the ARRL DX Century Club (DXCC) has been the mark of distinction among radio amateurs the world over. That it is regarded with such prestige by DXers is a testament to its integrity and level of achievement. The high standards of DXCC are intensely defended and supported by its membership. The rules established by the founders of DXCC were consistent with the art of Amateur Radio as it existed at the time. As technology improved the ability to communicate, the rules were progressively changed to maintain a competitive environment and complement the gaining popularity of DXCC.

Because of the vast changes in the international scene brought about by World War II, it logically followed that DXCC needed to be recast, as indicated in December 1945 *QST*. Ultimately, after a great deal of study, the first postwar DXCC Countries List emerged as published in February 1947 *QST*. The new DXCC Rules appeared in March 1947 *QST*. Contacts were valid from November 15, 1945, the date U.S. amateurs were authorized by the FCC to return to the air.

The DXCC rules today represent the aggregate of experience gained from administering postwar DXCC. Some countries on the DXCC Countries List do not, of course, meet the present criteria. This includes countries "grandfathered" from the WWII era or those that met the criteria as it existed at the time and are not subject to deletion (see Section III for the appropriate grounds for deletion). Changes are announced under DXCC Notes in *QST*.

Section I. Basis Rules

1) The DX Century Club Award, with certificate and lapel pin (there is a nominal fee of $3 for the DXCC lapel pin) is available to Amateur Radio operators throughout the world (see #15 below for the DXCC Award Fee Schedule). ARRL membership is required for DXCC applicants in the U.S. and possessions, and Puerto Rico. ARRL membership is not required for foreign applicants.

All DXCCs are endorsable (see Rule 5). There are 12 separate DXCC awards available, plus the DXCC Honor Roll:

(a) Mixed (general type): Contacts may be made using any mode since November 15, 1945.

(b) Phone: Contacts must be made using radiotelephone since November 15, 1945. Confirmations for cross-mode contacts for this award must be dated September 30, 1981, or earlier.

(c) CW: Contacts must be made using CW since January 1, 1975. Confirmations for cross-mode contacts for this award must be dated September 30, 1981, or earlier.

(d) RTTY: Contacts must be made using radioteletype since November 15, 1945. (Baudot, ASCII, AMTOR and packet count as RTTY.) Confirmations for cross-mode contacts for this award must be dated September 30, 1981, or earlier.

(e) 160 Meter: Contacts must be made on 160 meters since November 15, 1945.

(f) 80 Meter: Contacts must be made on 80 meters since November 15, 1945.

(g) 40 Meter: Contacts must be made on 40 meters since November 15, 1945.

(h) 10 Meter: Contacts must be made on 10 meters since November 15, 1945.

(i) 6 Meter: Contacts must be made on 6 meters since November 15, 1945

(j) 2 Meter: Contacts must be made on 2 meters since November 15, 1945.

(k) Satellite: Contacts must be made using satellites sinc March 1, 1965. Confirmations must indicate satellite QSO.

(l) Five-Band DXCC (5BDXCC): The 5BDXCC certificate is available for working and confirming 100 current DXCC countries (deleted countries don't count for this award) on each of the following five bands: 80, 40, 20, 15, and 10 Meters. Contacts are valid from November 15, 1945.

The 5BDXCC is endorsable for these additional bands: 160, 17, 12, 6, and 2 meters. 5BDXCC qualifiers are eligible for an individually engraved plaque (at a charge of $25.00 US).

(m) Honor Roll: Attaining the DXCC Honor Roll represents the pinnacle of DX achievement:

*Mixed—To qualify, you must have a total confirmed country count that places you among the numerical top ten DXCC countries total on the current DXCC Countries List (example: if there are 327 current DXCC countries, you must have at least 318 countries confirmed).

*Phone—same as Mixed.

*CW—same as Mixed.

To establish the number of DXCC country credits needed to qualify for the Honor Roll, the maximum possible number of current countries available for credit is published monthly in *QST*. First-time Honor Roll members are recognized monthly in *QST*. Complete Honor Roll standings are published annually in *QST*, usually in the July issue. See DXCC notes in *QST* for specific information on qualifying for this Honor Roll standings list. Once recognized on this list or in a subsequent monthly update of new members, you retain your Honor Roll standing until the next standings list is published. In addition, Honor Roll members are recognized in the DXCC Annual List (usually published in the January issue of *QST*) for those who have been listed in the previous Honor Roll listings or have gained Honor Roll status in a subsequent monthly listing. Honor Roll qualifiers receive an Honor Roll endorsement sticker for their DXCC certificate and are eligible for an Honor Roll lapel pin ($2) and an Honor Roll plaque ($25 plus shipping). Write the DXCC Desk for details.

#1 Honor Roll: To qualify for a Mixed, Phone or CW Number One plaque, you must have worked every country on the current DXCC Countries List. Write the DXCC Desk for details.

2) Written proof (confirmations, i.e., QSL cards) of having made two-way communication must be submitted directly to ARRL Headquarters for all DXCC countries claimed. Electronically transmitted confirmations (including, but not limited to, FAX, telex and telegram) are not acceptable for DXCC purposes. Applicants for their first DXCC award may have the cards checked by ARRL DXCC Field Representatives-see Section V for details. The use of the official DXCC application forms or an approved facsimile (e.g., produced by a computer program) is required. Complete application materials are available from ARRL Headquarters. Confirmations for a total of 100 or more countries must be included with your first application. By ARRL Board of Directors action, 10-MHz confirmations are creditable to the Mixed, CW and RTTY awards only.

3) The ARRL DXCC Countries List criteria will be used in determining what constitutes a DXCC country.

4) Confirmation data for two-way communications (i.e., contacts) must include the call signs of both stations, the country, mode, and date, time and frequency band.

5) Endorsement stickers for affixing to certificates or pins will be awarded as additional DXCC credits are granted. For the Mixed, Phone, CW, RTTY and 10-Meter DXCC, these stickers are in exact multiples of 25, i.e., 125, 150, etc., between 100 and 250 DXCC countries; in multiples of 10 between 250 and 300, and in multiples of 5 above 300 DXCC countries. For 160-Meter, 80-Meter, 40-Meter, 6-Meter, 2-Meter and Satellite DXCC, the stickers are in exact multiples of 10 starting at 100 and multiples of 5 above 200. Confirmations for DXCC countries may be submitted for credits in any increment. (See #15 for applicable fees, if any.)

6) All contacts must be made with amateur stations working in the authorized amateur bands or with other stations licensed or authorized to work amateurs. Contacts made through "repeater" devices or any other power relay method (aside from Satellite DXCC) are invalid for DXCC credit.

7) In countries where amateurs are licensed in the normal man-

ner, credit may be claimed only for stations using regular government-assigned call signs or portable call signs where reciprocal agreements exist or the host government has so authorized portable operation. No credit may be claimed for contacts with stations in any country that has temporarily or permanently closed down Amateur Radio operations by special government edict where amateur licenses were formerly issued in the normal manner. Some countries, in spite of such prohibitions, issue authorizations which are acceptable.

8) All stations contacted must be "land stations." Contacts with ships and boats, anchored or under way, and airborne aircraft, cannot be counted.

9) All stations must be contacted from the same DXCC country.

10) All contacts must be made by the same station licensee. However, contacts may have been made under different call signs in the same country if the licensee for all was the same. That is, you may simultaneously feed one DXCC from several call signs held, as long as the provisions of Rule 9 are met.

11) Any altered, forged, or otherwise invalid confirmations submitted by an applicant for DXCC credit may result in disqualification of the applicant. Any holder of a DXCC award submitting altered, forged or otherwise invalid confirmations may forfeit the right to continued DXCC membership. The ARRL Awards Committee shall rule in these matters and may also determine the eligibility of any DXCC applicant who was ever barred from DXCC to reapply and the conditions of such application.

12) Operations Ethics:

(a) Fair play and good sportsmanship in operating are required of all DXCC members. In the event of specific objections relative to continued poor operating ethics, an individual may be disqualified from DXCC by action on the ARRL Awards Committee.

(b) Credit for contacts with individuals who have displayed continued poor operating ethics may be disallowed by action of the ARRL Awards Committee.

(c) For (a) and (b) above, "operating" includes confirmation procedures and/or documentation submitted for DXCC accreditation.

13) Each DXCC applicant must stipulate that he/she has observed all DXCC rules as well as all pertinent governmental regulations established for Amateur Radio in the country or countries concerned, and agrees to be bound by the decisions of the ARRL Awards Committee. Decisions of the ARRL Awards Committee regarding interpretations of the rules here printed or later amended shall be final.

14) All DXCC applications (both new and endorsements) must include sufficient funds to cover the cost of returning all confirmations (QSL cards) via the method chosen. Funds must be in US dollars, utilizing US currency, check or money order made payable to the ARRL, or International Reply Coupons (IRCs). A chart showing the various return postage rates is available from the DXCC Desk. Address all correspondence and inquiries relating to the various DXCC awards and all applications to: ARRL Headquarters, DXCC Desk, 225 Main St, Newington, CT 06111, USA.

15) Effective October 1, 1990, amateurs applying for their very first DXCC Award (both members and non-members alike) will be charged a one-time Registration Fee of $10.00. Once registered, subsequent submissions will be handled as outlined in sections b, c, d, below.

(a) Participants who are DXCC members as of the implementation date are exempt from this fee.

(b) Each ARRL member will be allowed one submission per calendar year at no cost (except the usual postage charges). This annual submission may include any number of QSL cards, may involve any number of DXCC awards, and any combination of new and endorsement applications.

(c) Foreign non-members will be allowed the same annual submission as League members, however, they will be charged a $10.00 DXCC Award fee, in addition to return postage charges.

(d) DXCC participants who wish to submit more than once per year will be charged a DXCC Award fee for each additional submission made during the remainder of the calendar year. As always, the applicant must pay for return postage costs. The fee is dependent upon membership status:

ARRL Members: $10.00; Foreign non-members: $20.00

16) The ARRL DX Advisory Committee (DXAC) requests your comments and suggestions for improving DXCC. Address correspondence, including petitions for new country consideration, to ARRL Headquarters, DXAC, 225 Main St, Newington, CT 06111, USA.

Section II. Countries List Criteria

The ARRL DXCC Countries List is the result of progressive changes in DXing since 1945. The full list will not necessarily conform completely with current criteria since some of the listings were recognized from pre-WWII or were accredited from earlier versions of the criteria. While the general policy has remained the same, specific mileages in Point 2(a) and Point 3, mentioned in the following criteria, have been used in considerations made April 1960 and after. The specific mileage in Point 2(b) has been used in considerations made April 1963 and after.

When an area in question meets at least one of the following three points, it is eligible as a separate country listing for the DXCC Countries List. These criteria address considerations by virtue of Government [Point 1] or geographical separation [Points 2 and 3], while Point 4 addresses ineligible areas. All distances are given in statute miles.

Point 1, Government

An independent country or nation-state having sovereignty (that is, a body politic or society united together, occupying a definite territory and having a definite population, politically organized and controlled under one exclusive regime, and engaging in foreign relations-including the capacity to carry out obligations of international law and applicable international agreements) constitutes a separate DXCC country by reason of Government. This may be indicated by membership in the United Nations (UN). However, some nations that possess the attributes of sovereignty are not members of the UN, although these nations may have been recognized by a number of UN-member nations. Recognition is the formal act of one nation committing itself to treat an entity as a sovereign state. There are some entities that have been admitted to the UN that lack the requisite attributes of sovereignty and, as a result, are not recognized by a number of UN-member nations.

Other entities which are not totally independent may also be considered for separate DXCC country status by reason of Government. Included are Territories, Protectorates, Dependencies, Associated States, and so on. Such an entity may delegate to another country or international organization a measure of its authority (such as the conduct of its foreign relations in whole or in part, or other functions such as customs, communications or diplomatic protection) without surrendering its sovereign status. DXCC country status for such an entity is individually considered, based on all the available facts in the particular case. In making a reasonable determination as to whether a sufficient degree of sovereignty exists for DXCC purposes, the following characteristics (list not necessarily all-inclusive) are taken into consideration:

(a) Membership in specialized agencies of the UN, such as the International Telecommunications Union (ITU).

(b) Authorized use of ITU-assigned call sign prefixes.

(c) Diplomatic relations (entering into international agreements and/or supporting embassies and consulates), and maintaining a standing army.

(d) Regulation of foreign trade and commerce, customs, immigration and licensing (including landing and operating permits), and the issuance of currency and stamps.

An entity that qualifies under Point 1, but consists of two or more separate land areas, will be considered a single DXCC country (since none of these areas alone retains an independent capacity to carry out the obligations of sovereignty), unless the areas can qualify under Points 2 or 3.

Point 2, Separation by Water

An island or a group of islands which is part of a DXCC country established by reason of Government, Point 1, is considered as a separate DXCC country under the following conditions:

(a) The island or islands are situated off shore, geographically separated by a minimum of 225 miles of open water from a continent, another island or group of islands that make up any part of the "parent" DXCC country.

For any additional island or islands to qualify as an additional separate DXCC country or countries, such must qualify under Point 2(b).

(b) This point applies to the "second" island or island grouping geographically separated from the "first" DXCC country created under Point 2(a). For the second island or island grouping to qualify, at least a 500-mile separation of open water from the first is required, as well as meeting the 225-mile requirement of (a) from the "parent". For any subsequent island(s) to qualify, the 500-mile separation would again have to be met. This precludes, for example, using the 225-mile measurement for each of several islands from the parent country to make several DXCC countries.

Point 3, Separation by Another DXCC Country

(a) Where a Point 1 DXCC country, composed of one or more continental land areas or of continental land areas and islands, is totally separated by an intervening DXCC country into two land areas which are at least 75 miles apart, two DXCC countries result. This distance is measured along the great circle between the two closest points of the two areas divided. The measured distance may include inland lakes and seas which are part of the intervening DXCC country. The test for total separation into two areas requires that a great circle cannot be drawn from any point on the continental land and/or islands of one area to any point on the continental land and/or islands of the other area without intersecting any land of the intervening DXCC country.

(b) Where a Point 1 DXCC country, composed entirely of islands, is totally separated by an intervening DXCC country into two areas, then two DXCC countries result. No minimal distance is required for the separation. The test for total separation into two areas requires that a great circle cannot be drawn from any point on any island of one area to any point on any island of the other area without intersecting any land of the intervening DXCC country.

Point 4, Ineligible Areas

(a) Any area which is unclaimed or unowned by any recognized government does not count as a separate DXCC country.

(b) Any area which is classified as a Demilitarized Zone, Neutral Zone or Buffer Zone does not count as a separate DXCC country.

(c) The following do not count as a separate DXCC country from the host country: Embassies, consulates and extra-territorial legal entities of any nature, including, but not limited to, monuments, offices of the United Nations agencies or related organizations, other inter-governmental organizations or diplomatic missions.

Section III. Deletion Criteria

A DXCC country is subject to deletion from the ARRL DXCC Countries List if political change causes it to cease to meet Point 1 of the Countries List Criteria (a derivative of such change may cause it to cease to meet Points 2 or 3) or if it falls into Point 4 of the criteria. Additions to and deletions from the DXCC Countries List come about as a result of a myriad of such political changes. Reviewing the nature of the changes which have occurred since 1945 as they affect DXCC, these changes can be grouped into categories as follows:

(a) Annexation. When an area that has been recognized as a separate country under Point 1 is annexed or absorbed by an adjacent Point 1 country, the annexed area becomes a deleted country. Examples: India annexed Sikkim (AC3); China annexed Tibet (AC4); Indonesia annexed Portuguese Timor (CR8).

(b) Unification. When two or more entities that have been separate DXCC countries under Point 1 unite or combine into a single entity under a common administration, one new DXCC country is created and two or more DXCC countries have been deleted. Example: Italian Somaliland (I5) plus British Somaliland (VQ6) became Somalia (6O/T5).

(c) Partition. When one country is divided or partitioned into two or more countries, one DXCC country is deleted and two or more DXCC countries are created. Example: French Equatorial Africa (FQ) was deleted and replaced by Central Africa (TL), Congo (TN), Gabon (TR) and Chad (TT). The partition category is not employed when the original political entity continues in some form. That is, if part of country A splits off to form country B, the original DXCC country (A) is retained and one new DXCC country (B) is added. Examples: the British Sovereign Bases on Cyprus (ZC4); Aruba (P4).

(d) Independence. Mere independence does not result in a Countries List deletion. Examples: the Tonga Islands, then a British protectorate (VR5), is the same country as the present listing of the Kingdom of Tonga (A3). Further, an entity already recognized as a separate DXCC country is not deleted because of a change in its independent status. Bangladesh (S2) is the same listing as East Pakistan (AP), which was already separate from West Pakistan by virtue of Point 3. Also, a country that merely changes its name (such as when Upper Volta became Burkina Faso) does not change its basic status as a DXCC country on the DXCC Countries List.

Section IV. Accreditation Criteria

1) The many vagaries of how each nation manages its telecommunications matters does not lend itself to a hard set of rules that can be applied across the board in accrediting all Amateur Radio DX operations. However, during the course of more than 40 years of DXCC administration, basic standards have evolved in determining whether a DX operation meets the test of legitimate operation. The intent is to assure that DXCC credit is given only for contacts with operations that are conducted appropriately in two respects: (1) proper licensing; and (2) physical presence in the country to be credited.

2) The following points should be of particular interest to those seeking accreditation for a DX operation:

(a) The vast majority of operations are accredited routinely without any requirement for submitting authenticating documentation.

(b) In countries where Amateur Radio operation has not been permitted or has been suspended or where some reluctance to license amateur stations has been evidenced, authenticating documents may be required prior to accrediting an operation.

(c) Some DXCC countries, even though part of a country with no Amateur Radio restrictions, nevertheless require the permission of a governmental agency or private party prior to conducting Amateur Radio operations on territory within their jurisdiction. Examples: Desecheo I. (KP5); Palmyra I. (KH5); Kingman Reef (KH5K).

3) In those cases where supporting documentation is required, the following should be used as a guide as to what information may be necessary to make a reasonable determination of the validity of the operation:

(a) Photocopy of license or operating authorization.

(b) Photocopy of passport entry and exit stamps.

(c) For islands, a landing permit and/or signed statement of the transporting ship's, boat's, or aircraft's captain, showing all pertinent data, such as date, place of landing, etc.

(d) For some locations where special permission is known to be required to gain access, evidence of this permission having been given is required.

4) These accreditation requirements are intended to preserve the DXCC program's integrity and to ensure that the program does not encourage amateurs to "bend the rules" in their enthusiasm, thus jeopardizing the future development of Amateur Radio. Every effort will be made to apply these criteria in a uniform manner in conformity with these objectives.

Section V. Field Checking of QSL Cards

QSL cards for new DXCC awards may be checked by two DXCC Field Representatives. This program applies only to the first DXCC award for an individual or station. Specifically excluded from this program are additional new DXCC awards and endorsements of existing awards. Also excluded are 5BDXCC, 6 meter, 2 meter and Satellite DXCC.

1) Countries Eligible for Field Checking:

(a) Eligible countries will be indicated in the ARRL DXCC Countries List, and are subject to change. Only cards from these eligible countries may be checked by DXCC Field Representatives. QSLs for other DXCC countries must be submitted directly to ARRL Headquarters.

(b) The ARRL Awards Committee determines which countries are eligible for Field Checking.

2) DXCC Field Representatives:

(a) DXCC Field Representatives must be ARRL members who have DXCC award endorsed for at least 300 countries.

(b) To become a DXCC Field Representative, a person must be nominated by a DX club. (A DX club is an ARRL affiliated club with at least 25 members who are DXCC members and which has, as its primary interest, DX. If there are any questions regarding the validity of a DX club, the issue shall be determined by the Division Director where the DX club is located.) A person does not have to be a member to be nominated by a DX club.

(c) DXCC Field Representatives are approved by the Director of the ARRL Division in which they reside and appointed by the President of the ARRL.

(d) DXCC Field Representative appointments must be renewed annually.

3) Card Checking Process:

(a) Only cards from the list of eligible countries can be checked by DXCC Field Representatives. An application shall contain a minimum of 100 QSL confirmations from the list and shall not contain any QSLs from countries that are not on the list of eligible countries. The application may contain the maximum number of countries that appear on the list of eligible countries. That is, if there are 245 countries on the list, the initial application for a field-checked DXCC award could contain 245 countries.

(b) It is the applicant's responsibility to get cards to and from the DXCC Field Representatives.

(c) Field Representatives may, at their own discretion, handle members' cards by mail.

(d) The ARRL is not responsible for cards handled by DXCC Field Representatives and will not honor any claims.

(e) The QSL cards must be checked by two DXCC Field Representatives.

(f) The applicant and both DXCC Field Representatives must sign the application form. (See Section I no. 11 regarding altered, forged or otherwise invalid confirmations.)

(g) The applicant shall provide a stamped no. 10 envelope (business size) addressed to ARRL HQ to the DXCC Field Representatives. The applicant shall also provide the application fee (check or money order payable to ARRL—no cash) for the initial DXCC award.

(h) The DXCC Field Representatives will forward completed applications and appropriate fee(s) to ARRL HQ.

4) ARRL HQ involvement in the card checking process:

(a) ARRL HQ staff will receive field-checked applications, enter application data into DXCC records and issue DXCC credits and awards as appropriate.

(b) ARRL HQ staff will perform random audits of applications. Applicants or members may be requested to forward cards to HQ for checking before or after credit is issued.

(c) The applicant and both DXCC Field Representatives will be advised of any errors or discrepancies encountered by ARRL staff.

(d) ARRL HQ staff provides instructions and guidelines to DXCC Field Representatives.

5) Applicants and DXCC members may send cards to ARRL Headquarters at any time for review or recheck if the individual feels that an incorrect determination has been made.

Courtesy of the ARRL

CHANGES TO THE DXCC LIST IN 1993

Added Croatia 9A as of June 26, 1991
Added Slovenia S5 as of June 26, 1991
Added Bosnia-Hercegovina T9 as of October 15, 1991
Added Republic of Macedonia Z3 as of September 8, 1991
Note: Yugoslavia continues to hold the YT-YU, 4N-4O ITU allocations.

OK Czechoslovakia Deleted December 31,1992
Added OK, OL Czech Republic as of January 1,1993
Added OM Slovakia as of January 1,1993

A15 Abu Ail Deleted 1993

In July 1993, the DXAC voted 6 yes and 10 no on the question of adding band or mode-specific Honor Rolls to the DXCC program. Those voting against the proposal were concerned about a proliferation of awards.

In another matter, the DXAC voted unanimously against a proposal that would have changed the Countries List Criteria Point 2, Separation by Water. Under the failed proposal, distances would have changed from 225 2(a) and 500-mile 2(b) separations to 100 miles 2(a) and 100 miles 2(b). Committee members felt there was insufficient support for the proposed change.

In mid-1993, a tentative date was announced for Namibia's takeover of both Walvis Bay (ZS9) and the Penguin Islands (ZSØ) as 28 February 1994. The announcement pointed out that many details remain to be worked out, and that this date should be considered as a target date. It is possible that the DXCC list may be changed sometime after that date.

On September 30, 1993, the ARRL Awards Committee voted unanimously to accept a recommendation of the DXAC to reinstate Eritrea (E3) as a DXCC Country. The Awards Committee in a 4 to 3 vote made reinstatement effective May 24, 1991. Those who have credit for deleted Eritrea (ET2) need not resubmit cards.

DXCC COUNTRY LIST

The ARRL DXCC Countries List is also available (in full-page format) from the ARRL Publication Sales Department for $2. In addition to the Countries List, that version includes the DXCC rules, DXCC Award Application, ARRL DXCC Field Representatives, Incoming and Outgoing QSL Bureau information and more.

NOTES:

@ Indicates eligible for field checking.

* Indicates current list of countries for which QSLs may be forwarded by the ARRL membership outgoing QSL service.

#Indicates countries with which U.S. amateurs may legally handle third-party message traffic.

& Indicates third-party traffic permitted with special-events stations in the United Kingdom having the prefix GB only, with the exception that GB3 stations are not included in this agreement.

Prefix	Country	Cont.	Zone ITU	Zone CQ
1AØ(1)	Sov. Mil. Order of Malta	EU	28	15
1S(1)	Spratly Is.	AS	50	26
@3A*	Monaco	EU	27	14
3B6,7*	Agalega & St. Brandon	AF	53	39
@3B8*	Mauritius	AF	53	39
@3B9*	Rodriguez I.	AF	53	39
@3C	Equatorial Guinea	AF	47	36
3CØ	Pagalu I.	AF	52	36
@3D2*	Fiji	OC	56	32
@3D2*	Conway Reef	OC	56	32
@3D2*	Rotuma I.	OC	56	32
@3DA#*	Swaziland	AF	57	38
3V	Tunisia	AF	37	33
3W,XV	Vietnam	AS	49	26
3X	Guinea	AF	46	35
3Y*	Bouvet	AF	67	38
3Y*	Peter I I.	AN	72	12
4J1F*	Malyj Vysotskij I.	EU	29	16
@4K2,UA1*	Franz Josef Land	EU	75	40
4N4,4O4, YU5(2)*	Macedonia	EU	28	15
@4P-4S*	Sri Lanka	AS	41	22
@4U#*	ITUHQ	EU	28	14
@4U*	United Nations HQ	NA	08	05
@4X,4Z#*	Israel	AS	39	20
5A	Libya	AF	38	34
@5B*	Cyprus	AS	39	20
@5H-5I	Tanzania	AF	53	37
@5N-5O*	Nigeria	AF	46	35
5R-5S	Madagascar	AF	53	39
@5T(3)	Mauritania	AF	46	35
5U(4)	Niger	AF	46	35
@5V*	Togo	AF	46	35

@5W*	Western Samoa	OC	62	32
5X	Uganda	AF	48	37
@5Y-5Z*	Kenya	AF	48	37
@6V-6W(5)*	Senegal	AF	46	35
@6Y#*	Jamaica	NA	11	08
7O(6)	Yemen	AS	39	21
@7P*	Lesotho	AF	57	38
@7Q	Malawi	AF	53	37
@7T-7Y*	Algeria	AF	37	33
@8P*	Barbados	NA	11	08
@8Q	Maldives	AS/AF	41	22
@8R#*	Guyana	SA	12	09
9A,YU2(7)*	Croatia	EU	28	15
9G(8)#	Ghana	AF	46	35
@9H*	Malta	EU	28	15
@9I-9J*	Zambia	AF	53	36
@9K*	Kuwait	AS	39	21
@9L#*	Sierra Leone	AF	46	35
@9M2,4(9)*	West Malaysia	AS	54	28
@9M6,8(9)*	East Malaysia	OC	54	28
@9N	Nepal	AS	42	22
@9Q-9T	Zaire	AF	52	36
9U(10)	Burundi	AF	52	36
@9V(11)	Singapore	AS	54	28
@9X(12)	Rwanda	AF	52	36
@9Y-9Z#*	Trinidad & Tobago	SA	11	09
@A2*	Botswana	AF	57	38
@A3*	Tonga	OC	62	32
@A4*	Oman	AS	39	21
A5	Bhutan	AS	41	22
@A6	United Arab Emirates	AS	39	21
@A7	Qatar	AS	39	21
@A9*	Bahrain	AS	39	21
@AP-AS*	Pakistan	AS	41	21
@BV*	Taiwan	AS	44	24
@BY,BT*	China	AS	(A)	23,24
@C2*	Nauru	OC	65	31
@C3*	Andorra	EU	27	14
@C5#*	The Gambia	AF	46	35
@C6*	Bahamas	NA	11	08
C8-9	Mozambique	AF	53	37
@CA-CE#*	Chile	SA	14,16	12
@CEØ#*	Easter I.	SA	63	12
@CEØ#*	Juan Fernandez Is.	SA	14	12
CEØ#*	San Felix & San Ambrosio	SA	14	12
@CE9/KC4^*	Antarctica	AN	(B)	(C)
@CM,CO#*	Cuba	NA	11	08
@CN*	Morocco	AF	37	33
@CP#*	Bolivia	SA	12,14	10
@CT*	Portugal	EU	37	14
@CT3*	Madeira Is.	AF	36	33
@CU*	Azores	EU	36	14
@CV-CX#*	Uruguay	SA	14	13
@CY*	Sable I.	NA	09	05
@CY*	St. Paul I.	NA	09	05
D2-3	Angola	AF	52	36
@D4*	Cape Verde	AF	46	35
@D6#(12)*	Comoros	AF	53	39
@DA-DL, Y2-Y9(13)*	Fed. Rep. of Germany	EU	28	14
@DU-DZ#*	Philippines	OC	50	27
@EA-EH*	Spain	EU	37	14
@EA6-EH6*	Balearic Is.	EU	37	14
@EA8-EH8*	Canary Is.	AF	36	33
@EA9-EH9*	Ceuta & Melilla	AF	37	33
@EI-EJ*	Ireland	EU	27	14
@EL#*	Liberia	AF	46	35
EP-EQ	Iran	AS	40	21
@ES*	Estonia	EU	29	15
ET	Ethiopia	AF	48	37
@F*	France	EU	27	14
@FG*	Guadeloupe	NA	11	08
@FJ,FS(1)*	Saint Martin	NA	11	08
@FH(12)*	Mayotte	AF	53	39

@FK*	New Caledonia	OC	56	32
@FM*	Martinique	NA	11	08
FO*	Clipperton I.	NA	10	07
@FO*	French Polynesia	OC	63	32
@FP*	St. Pierre & Miquelon	NA	09	05
FR/G(14)*	Glorioso Is.	AF	53	39
FR/J,E(14)*	Juande Nova, Europa	AF	53	39
@FR*	Reunion	AF	53	39
FR/T*	Tromelin I.	AF	53	39
@FT8W*	Crozet I.	AF	68	39
@FT8X*	Kerguelen Is.	AF	68	39
@FT8Z*	Amsterdam & St. Paul Is.	AF	68	39
@FW*	Wallis & Futuna Is.	OC	62	32
@FY*	French Guiana	SA	12	09
@G,GX*&	England	EU	27	14
@GD,GT*	Isle of Man	EU	27	14
@GI,GN*	Northern Ireland	EU	27	14
@GJ,GH*	Jersey	EU	27	14
@GM,GS*	Scotland	EU	27	14
@GU,GP*	Guernsey	EU	27	14
@GW,GC*	Wales	EU	27	14
@H4*	Solomon Is.	OC	51	28
@HA,HG*	Hungary	EU	28	15
@HB*	Switzerland	EU	28	14
@HB*	Liechtenstein	EU	28	14
@HC-HD#*	Ecuador	SA	12	10
@HC8-HD8#*	Galapagos Is.	SA	12	10
@HH#*	Haiti	NA	11	08
@HI#*	Dominican Republic	NA	11	08
@HJ-HK#*	Colombia	SA	12	09
@HKØ#*	Malpelo I.	SA	12	09
@HKØ#*	San Andres & Providencia	NA	11	07
@HL*	South Korea	AS	44	25
@HO-HP#*	Panama	NA	11	07
@HQ-HR#*	Honduras	NA	11	07
@HS*	Thailand	AS	49	26
@HV*	Vatican	EU	28	15
@HZ*	Saudi Arabia	AS	39	21
@I*	Italy	EU	28,33	15
@IS,IM*	Sardinia	EU	28	15
@J2*	Djibouti	AF	48	37
@J3#*	Grenada	NA	11	08
@J5	Guinea-Bissau	AF	46	35
@J6#*	St. Lucia	NA	11	08
@J7#*	Dominica	NA	11	08
@J8#*	St. Vincent	NA	11	08
@JA-JS*	Japan	AS	45	25
@JD1(15)*	Minami Torishima	OC	90	27
@JD1(16)*	Ogasawara	AS	45	27
@JT-JV*	Mongolia	AS	32,33	23
@JW*	Svalbard	EU	18	40
@JX*	Jan Mayen	EU	18	40
@JY#*	Jordan	AS	39	20
@K,W,N, AA-AK#	United States of America	NA	6,7,8	3,4,5
@KC6(17)	Belau (W. Caroline Is.)	OC	64	27
@KG4#*	Guantanamo Bay	NA	11	08
@KH0#	Mariana Is.	OC	64	27
KH1#	Baker & Howland Is.	OC	61,62	31
@KH2#*	Guam	OC	64	27
@KH3#*	Johnston I.	OC	61	31
@KH4#	Midway I.	OC	61	31
KH5#	Palmyra & Jarvis Is.	OC	61	31
KH5K#	Kingman Reef	OC	61	31
@KH6#*	Hawaii	OC	61	31
@KH7#	Kure I.	OC	61	31
@KH8#	American Samoa	OC	62	32
@KH9#	Wake I.	OC	65	31
@KL7#*	Alaska	NA	1,2	1
KP1#	Navassa I.	NA	11	08
@KP2#*	Virgin Is.	NA	11	08
@KP4#*	Puerto Rico	NA	11	08
KP5(18)#	Desecheo I.	NA	11	08
@LA-LN*	Norway	EU	18	14

@LO-LW#*	Argentina	SA	14,16	13
@LX*	Luxembourg	EU	27	14
@LY,UP*	Lithuania	EU	29	15
@LZ*	Bulgaria	EU	28	20
@OA-OC#*	Peru	SA	12	10
@OD	Lebanon	AS	39	20
@OE*	Austria	EU	28	15
@OF-OI*	Finland	EU	18	15
@OHØ*	Aland Is.	EU	18	15
@OJØ*	Market Reef	EU	18	15
OK-OL(19)*	Czech Republic	EU	28	15
OM(19)*	Slovak Republic	EU	28	15
@ON-OT*	Belgium	EU	27	14
@OX*	Greenland	NA	5,7,5	40
@OY*	Faroe Is.	EU	18	14
@OZ*	Denmark	EU	18	14
@P2(20)*	Papua New Guinea	OC	51	28
@P4(21)*	Aruba	SA	11	09
@PA-PI*	Netherlands	EU	27	14
@PJ2,4,9*	Bonaire, Curacao (Neth. Antilles)	SA	11	09
@PJ5-8*	St. Maarten, Saba, St. Eustatius	NA	11	08
@PP-PY#*	Brazil	SA	(D)	11
@PPØ-PYØ#	Fernandode Noronha	SA	13	11
PPØ-PYØ#*	St. Peter & St. Paul Rocks	SA	13	11
@PPØ-PYØ#*	Trindade & Martim Vaz Is.	SA	15	11
@PZ*	Suriname	SA	12	09
SØ(1),(22)*	Western Sahara	AF	37	33
S2	Bangladesh	AS	41	22
S5,YU3(7)*	Slovenia	EU	28	15
@S7	Seychelles	AF	53	39
@S9*	Sao Tome & Principe	AF	47	36
@SA-SM*	Sweden	EU	18	14
@SN-SR*	Poland	EU	28	15
@ST*	Sudan	AF	48	34
@STØ*	Southern Sudan	AF	47,48	34
@SU*	Egypt	AF	38	34
@SV-SZ*	Greece	EU	28	20
SV/A*	Mount Athos	EU	28	20
@SV5*	Dodecanese	EU	28	20
@SV9*	Crete	EU	28	20
@T2(23)	Tuvalu	OC	65	31
@T3Ø	W. Kiribati (Gilbert Is.)	OC	65	31
@T31	C. Kiribati (Brit. Phoenix Is.)	OC	62	31
@T32	E. Kiribati (Line Is.)	OC	61,63	31
@T33	Banaba I.(Ocean I.)	OC	65	31
T5	Somalia	AF	48	37
@T7*	San Marino	EU	28	15
T9,4N4 4O4,YU4(24)*	Bosnia-Herzegovina	EU	28	15
@TA-TC*	Turkey	EU/AS	39	20
@TF*	Iceland	EU	17	40
@TG,TD#*	Guatemala	NA	11	07
@TI,TE#*	Costa Rica	NA	11	07
@TI9#*	Cocos I.	NA	11	07
@TJ	Cameroon	AF	47	36
@TK*	Corsica	EU	28	15
@TL(25)	Central Africa	AF	47	36
TN(26)	Congo	AF	52	36
@TR(27)*	Gabon	AF	52	36
TT(28)	Chad	AF	47	36
@TU(29)*	Ivory Coast	AF	46	35
@TY(30)	Benin	AF	46	35
@TZ(31)	Mali	AF	46	35
UA1,3,4,6*	European Russia	EU	(E)	16
UA2*	Kaliningrad	EU	29	15
UA8,9,Ø*	Asiatic Russia	AS	(F)	(G)
UB,UT,UY*	Ukraine	EU	29	16
UC*	Belarus	EU	29	16
UD*	Azerbaijan	AS	29	21
UF*	Georgia	AS	29	21
UG*	Armenia	AS	29	21
UH*	Turkmenistan	AS	30	17
UI*	Uzbekistan	AS	30	17
UJ*	Tajikistan	AS	30	17
UL*	Kazakhstan	AS	29-31	17
UM*	Kyrgyzstan	AS	30,31	17
UO*	Moldova	EU	29	16
@V2#*	Antigua & Barbuda	NA	11	08
@V3#	Belize	NA	11	07
@V4(32)#	St. Kitts & Nevis	NA	11	08
@V5*	Namibia	AF	57	38
@V6(33)	Micronesia (E. Caroline Is.)	OC	65	27
@V7#*	Marshall Is.	OC	65	31
@V8*	Brunei	OC	54	28
@VE,VO,VY#*	Canada	NA	(H)	1-5
@VK#*	Australia	OC	(I)	29,30
VKØ#*	Heard I.	AF	68	39
@VKØ#*	Macquarie I.	OC	60	30
@VK9C#*	Cocos-Keeling Is.	OC	54	29
@VK9L#*	Lord Howe I.	OC	60	30
@VK9M#*	Mellish Reef	OC	56	30
@VK9N#*	Norfolk I.	OC	60	32
@VK9W#*	Willis I.	OC	55	30
@VK9X#*	Christmas I.	OC	54	29
@VP2E(32)	Anguilla	NA	11	08
@VP2M(32)	Montserrat	NA	11	08
@VP2V(32)*	British Virgin Is.	NA	11	08
@VP5*	Turks & Caicos Is.	NA	11	08
@VP8*	Falkland Is.	SA	16	13
@VP8,LU*	South Georgia I.	SA	73	13
@VP8,LU*	South Orkney Is.	SA	73	13
@VP8,LU*	South Sandwich Is.	SA	73	13
@VP8,LU, CE9,HFØ,4K1*	South Shetland Is.	SA	73	13
@VP9*	Bermuda	NA	11	05
@VQ9*	Chagos Is.	AF	41	39
@VR6#	Pitcairn I.	OC	63	32
@VS6,VR2*	Hong Kong	AS	44	24
@VU*	India	AS	41	22
@VU*	Andaman & Nicobar Is.	AS	49	26
@VU*	Laccadive Is.	AS	41	22
@XA-XI#*	Mexico	NA	10	06
XA4-XI4#*	Revilla Gigedo	NA	10	06
@XT(34)	Burkina Faso	AF	46	35
XU	Cambodia	AS	49	26
XW	Laos	AS	49	26
@XX9	Macao	AS	44	24
XY-XZ	Myanmar	AS	49	26
YA	Afghanistan	AS	40	21
@YB-YH(33)*	Indonesia	OC	51,54	28
YI	Iraq	AS	39	21
@YJ*	Vanuatu	OC	56	32
YK*	Syria	AS	39	20
@YL,UQ*	Latvia	EU	29	15
@YN#*	Nicaragua	NA	11	07
@YO-YR*	Romania	EU	28	20
@YS#*	El Salvador	NA	11	07
@YT-YU,YZ*	Yugoslavia	EU	28	15
@YV-YY#*	Venezuela	SA	12	09
YVØ#*	Aves I.	NA	11	08
@Z2*	Zimbabwe	AF	53	38
ZA*	Albania	EU	28	15
@ZB2*	Gibraltar	EU	37	14
@ZC4(36)*	UK Sov. Base Areas on Cyprus	AS	39	20
@ZD7	St. Helena	AF	66	36
@ZD8*	Ascension I.	AF	66	36
@ZD9	Tristanda Cunha & Gough I.	AF	66	38
@ZF*	Cayman Is.	NA	11	08
ZK1*	N. Cook Is.	OC	62	32
@ZK1*	S. Cook Is.	OC	62	32
@ZK2*	Niue	OC	62	32
ZK3	Tokelau Is.	OC	62	31
@ZL-ZM*	New Zealand	OC	60	32
@ZL7*	Chatham Is.	OC	60	32

ZL8*	Kermadec Is.	OC	60	32
ZL9*	Auckland & Campbell Is.	OC	60	32
@ZP#*	Paraguay	SA	14	11
@ZR-ZU*	South Africa	AF	57	38
ZSØ,1*	Penguin Is.	AF	57	38
@ZS8*	Prince Edward & Marion Is.	AF	57	38
ZS9(37)*	Walvis Bay	AF	57	38

NOTES:

1. Unofficial prefix.
2. (4N5, YU5) Only contacts made Septemer 8, 1991, and after, count for this country.
3. (5T) Only contacts made June 20, 1960, and after, count for this country.
4. (5U) Only contacts made August 3, 1960, and after, count for this country.
5. (6W) Only contact made June 20, 1960, and after, count for this country.
6. (70) Only contacts made May 22, 1990, and after, count for this country.
7. (9A, YU2, S5, YU3) Only contacts made June 26, 1991, and after, count for this country.
8. (9G) Only contacts made March 5, 1957, and after, count for this country.
9. (9M2, 4, 6, 8) Only contacts made September 16, 1963, and after count for this country.
10. (9U, 9X) Only contacts made July 1, 1962, and after, count for this country.
11. (9V) Contacts made from September 16, 1963 to August 8, 1965, count for West Malaysia.
12. (D6, FH8) Only contacts made July 15, 1975, and after, count for this country.
13. (DA-DL, Y2-Y9) Only contacts made with DA-DL stations September 17, 1973, and after, and contacts made with Y2-Y9 stations October 3, 1990 and after, count for this country.
14. (FR) Only contacts made June 25, 1960, and after, count for this country.
15. (JD) Formerly Marcus Island.
16. (KC6) Formerly Bonin and Volcano Islands
17. (KC6) Includes Yap Islands December 31, 1980, and before.
18. (KP5, KP4) Only contacts made March 1, 1979, and after, count for this country.
19. (OK-OL, OM) Only contacts made January 1, 1993, and after, count for this country.
20. (P2) Only contacts made September 16, 1975, and after, count for this country.
21. (P4) Only contacts made January 1, 1986, and after, count for this country.
22. (SØ) Contacts with Rio de Oro (Spanish Sahara), EA9, also count for this country.
23. (T2) Only contacts made January 1, 1976, and after, count for this country.
24. (T9, 4N4, 4O4, YU4) Only contacts made October 15, 1991, and after, count for this country.
25. (TL) Only contacts made August 13, 1960, and after, count for this country.
26. (TN) Only contacts made August 15, 1960, and after, count for this country.
27. (TR) Only contacts made August 17, 1960, and after, count for this country.
28. (TT) Only contacts made August 11, 1960, and after, count for this country.
29. (TU) Only contacts made August 7, 1960, and after, count for this country.
30. (TY) Only contacts made August 1, 1960, and after, count for this country.
31. (TZ) Only contacts made June 20, 1960, and after, count for this country.
32. (V4, VP2) For DXCC credit for contacts made May 31, 1958, and before, see page 97, June 1958 *QST*.
33. (V6, KC6) Includes Yap Islands January 1, 1981, and after.
34. (XT) Only contacts made August 16, 1960, and after, count for this country.
35. (YB) Only contacts made May 1, 1963, and after, count for this country.
36. (ZC4) Only contacts made August 16, 1960, and after, count for this country.
37. (ZS9) Only contacts made September 1, 1977, and after, count for this country.

^ Also 3Y, 4K1, 8J1, ATØ, DPØ, FT8Y, LU, OR4, VKØ, VP8, ZL5, ZS1, ZXØ, etc. QSL via country under whose auspices the particular station is operating. The availability of a third- party traffic agreement and a QSL Bureau applies to the country under whose auspices the particular station is operating.

Deleted Countries (Total: 56)

Credit for any of these countries can be given if the date of contact in question agrees with the date(s) shown in the corresponding footnote.

Prefix	Country	Cont.	Zone ITU	Zone CQ
(2)	Blenheim Reef	AF	41	39
(3)	Geyser Reef	AF	53	39
(4)	Abu Ail Is.	AS	39	21
1M(1), (5)	Minerva Reef	OC	62	32
4W(6)	Yemen Arab Rep.	AS	39	21
7J1(7)	Okino Tori-shima	AS	45	27
8Z4(8)	Saudi Arabia/ Iraq Neut. Zone	AS	39	21
8Z5,9K3(9)	Kuwait/Saudi Arabia Neut. Zone	AS	39	21
9S4(10)	Saar	EU	28	14
9U5(11)	Ruanda-Urundi	AF	52	36
AC3(1),(12)	Sikkim	AS	41	22
AC4(1),(13)	Tibet	AS	41	23
C9(14)	Manchuria	AS	33	24
CN2(15)	Tangier	AF	37	33
CR8(16)	Damao, Diu	AS	41	22
CR8(16)	Goa	AS	41	22
CR8, CRØ(17)	Portuguese Timor	OC	54	28
DA-DM(18)	Germany	EU	28	14
DM,Y2-9(19)	German Dem. Rep.	EU	28	14
EA9(20)	Ifni	AF	37	33
ET2(21)	Eritrea	AF	48	37
FF(22)	French West Africa	AF	46	35
FH,FB8(23)	Comoros	AF	53	39
FI8(24)	French Indo-China	AS	49	26
FN8(25)	French India	AS	41	22
FQ8(26)	Fr. Equatorial Africa	AF	47,52	36
HKØ(27)	Bajo Nuevo	NA	11	08
HKØ,KP3, KS4(27)	Serrana Bank & Roncador Cay	NA	11	07
I1(28)	Trieste	EU	28	15
I5(29)	Italian Somaliland	AF	48	37
JZ0(30)	Netherlands N. Guinea	OC	51	28
KR6,8,JR6, KA6(31)	Okinawa (Ryukyu Is.)	AS	45	25
KS4(32)	Swan Is.	NA	11	07
KZ5(33)	Canal Zone	NA	11	07
OK-OM(34)	Checkoslovakia	EU	28	15
P2,VK9(35)	Papua Territory	OC	51	28
P2,VK9(35)	Terr. New Guinea	OC	51	28
PK1-3(36)	Java	OC	54	28
PK4(36)	Sumatra	OC	54	28
PK5(36)	Netherlands Borneo	OC	54	28
PK6(36)	Celebe & Molucca Is.	OC	54	28
UN1(37)	Karelo-Finnish Rep.	EU	19	16
VO(38)	Newfoundland, Labrador	NA	09	02,05
VQ1,5H1(39)	Zanzibar	AF	53	37
VQ6(40)	British Somaliland	AF	48	37
VQ9(41)	Aldabra	AF	53	39
VQ9(41)	Desroches	AF	53	39
VQ9(41)	Farquhar	AF	53	39
VS2,9M2(42)	Malaya	AS	54	28
VS4(42)	Sarawak	OC	54	28

VS9A,P,S(43)	People's Dem. Rep of Yemen	AS	39	21
VS9H(44)	Kuria Muria I.	AS	39	21
VS9K(45)	Kamaran Is.	AS	39	21
ZC5(42)	British North Borneo	OC	54	28
ZC6,4X1(46)	Palestine	AS	39	20
ZD4(47)	Gold Coast, Togoland	AF	46	35

NOTES:

1. Unofficial prefix.
2. (Blenheim Reef) Only contacts made from May 4, 1967, to June 30, 1975, count for this country. Contacts made July 1, 1975, and after, count as Chagos (VQ9).
3. (Geysey Reef) Only contacts made from May 4, 1967, to February 28, 1978, count for this country.
4. (Abu Ail Is.) Only contacts made March 30, 1991, and before, count for this country.
5. (1M) Only contacts made from July 15, 1972, and before, count for this country. Contacts made July 16, 1972, and after, count as Tonga (A3).
6. (4W) Only contacts made before May 21, 1990, and before, count for this country.
7. (7J1) Only contacts made May 30, 1976, to November 30, 1980, count for this country. Contacts made December 1, 1980, and after country as Ogasawara (JD1).
8. (8Z4) Only contacts made December 25, 1981, and before, count for this country.
9. (8Z5,9K3) Only contacts made December 14, 1969, and before, count for this country.
10. (9S4) Only contacts made March 31, 1957, and before, count for this country.
11. (9U5) Only contacts made from July, 1960, to June 30, 1962, count for this country. Contact made July 1, 1962, and after, count as Burundi (9U) or Rwanda (9X).
12. (AC3) Only contacts made April 30, 1975, and before, count for this country. Contacts made May 1, 1975, and after, count as India (VU).
13. (AC4) Only contacts made May 30, 1974, and before, count for this country. Contact made May 31, 1974, and after, count as China (BY).
14. (C9) Only contacts made September 16, 1963, and before, count for this country. Contact made September 16, 1963, and after, count as China (BY).
15. (CN2) Only contacts made June 30, 1960, and before, count for this country. Contact made July 1, 1960, and after, count as Morocco (CN).
16. (CR8)Only contacts made December 31, 1961, and before, count for this country.
17. (CR8, CRØ) Only contacts made September 14, 1976, and before, count for this country.
18. (DA-DM) Only contacts made September 16, 1973, and before, count for this country. Contacts made September 17, 1973, and after, count as either FRG (DA-DL) or GDR (Y2-Y9).
19. (DM, Y2-Y9) Only contacts made from September 17, 1973, to October 2, 1990 count for this country. On October 3, 1990 the GDR became part of the FRG.
20. (EA9) Only contacts made May 13, 1969, and before, count for this country.
21. (ET2) Only contacts made November 14, 1962, and before, count for this country. Contacts made November 15, 1962, and after, count as Ethiopia (ET).
22. (FF) Only contacts made August 6, 1960, and before, count for this country.
23. (FH, FB8) Only contacts made July 5, 1975, and before, count for this country. Contacts made July 6, 1975, and after, count as Comoros (D6) or Mayotte (FH).
24. (FI8) Only contacts made December 20, 1950, and before, count for this country.
25. (FN8) Only contacts made October 31, 1954, and before, count for this country.
26. (FQ8) Only contacts made August 16, 1960, and before count for this country.
27. (HK, KP3, KS4) Only contacts made September 16, 1981, and before, count for this country. Contacts made September 17, 1981, and after, count as San Andres (HK).
28. (I1) Only contacts made March 31, 1957, and before, count for this country.
29. (I5) Only contacts made June 30, 1960, and before, count for this country.
30. (JZ) Only contacts made April 30, 1963, and before, count for this country.
31. (KR6, 8, JR6, KA6) Only contacts made May 14, 1972, and before, count for this country. Contacts made May 15, 1972, and after, count as Japan (JA).
32. (KS4) Only contacts made August 31, 1972, and before, count for this country. Contacts made September 1, 1972, and after, count as Honduras (HR).
33. (KZ5) Only contacts made September 30, 1979, and before, count for this country.
34. (OK-OM) Only contacts made December 31, 1992, and before, count for this country.
35. (P2, VK9) Only contacts made September 15, 1975, and before, count for this country. Contacts made September 16, 1975, and after, count as Papua new Guinea (P2).
36. (PK1-6) Only contacts made April 30, 1963, and before, count for this country. Contact made May 1, 1963, and after, count as Indonesia.
37. (UN1) Only contacts made June 30, 1960, and before, count for this country. Contacts made July 1, 1960, and after count as European RSFSR (UA).
38. (VO) Only contacts made March 31, 1949, and before, count for this country. Contacts made April 1, 1949, and after, count as Canada (VE).
39. (VQ1, 5H1) Only contacts made May 31, 1974, and before, count for this country. Contacts made June 1, 1974, and after, count as Tanzania (5H).
40. (VQ6) Only contacts made June 30, 1960, and before, count for this country.
41. (VQ9) Only contacts made June 28, 1976, and before, count for this country. Contacts made June 29, 1976, and after, count as Seychelles (S7).
42. (VS2, VS4, ZC5, 9M2) Only contacts made September 15, 1963, and before, count for this country. Contacts made September 16, 1963, and after, count as West malaysia (9M2) or East Malaysia (9M6, 8).
43. (VS9A, P, S) Only contacts made before May 22, 1990, and before, count for this country.
44. (VS9H) Only contacts made November 29, 1967, and before, count for this country.
45. (VS9K) Only contacts made on March 10, 1982, and before, count for this country.
46. (ZC6, 4X1) Only contacts made June 30, 1968, and before, count for this country. Contacts made July 1, 1968, and after, count as Israel (4X).
47. (ZD4) Only contacts made March 5, 1957, and before, count for this country.

Courtesy of the ARRL

THE 1993 *DX MAGAZINE* 100 MOST-WANTED COUNTRIES SURVEY

Each year since the late 1960s, The *DX Magazine* has surveyed its subscribers to determine which DXCC countries are most needed. This information is used by DXpedition organizers to plan major operations. The 1993 survey results are shown below:

1993 Rank	Country	Prefix	1992 Rank	1980 Rank	CW % Need	SSB % Need	% Need
1	Peter 1 Island	3Y1	1	-	62.1	69.2	69.6
2	Bhutan	A5	2	55	62.6	65.8	62.6
3	Libya	5A	3	22	56.8	70.3	59.5
4	Andaman	VU4	4	10	57.6	61.1	59.4
5	Heard Island	VKØ	6	62	57.6	59.2	58.2

1993 Rank	Country	Prefix	1992 Rank	1980 Rank	CW % Need	SSB % Need	% Need
6	Tunisia	3V	7	71	45.7	53.9	50.4
7	Yemen	7O	11	-	64.6	46.7	50.4
8	Tromelin	FR/T	13	38	58.0	40.0	45.6
9	Macquarie Island	VKØ	21	52	64.6	38.6	45.0
10	Mount Athos	SV/A	20	45	46.9	45.3	44.5
11	Kermadec I.	ZL8	23	44	46.9	45.8	43.1
12	Burma	XZ	24	3	43.2	47.2	42.6
13	Laccadive Island	VU7	5	55	46.1	41.1	42.1
14	Mellish Reef	VK9M	26	50	35.0	43.1	41.1
15	Bouvet	3Y	30	12	36.6	40.8	39.2
16	Glorioso Island	FR/G	16	15	43.6	36.1	38.8
17	SMOM	1AØ	28	-	44.4	38.6	38.4
18	Juan de Nova	FR/J	25	14	45.7	37.2	37.7
19	Amsterdam	FT/Z	35	-	37.0	38.9	36.6
20	Auckland/Campbell	ZL9	33	58	34.6	41.9	36.0
21	Burundi	9U	37	16	38.3	38.1	35.1
22	Congo	TN	19	28	51.0	30.8	34.6
23	Agalega & St. Brandon Is	3B6	38	-	39.9	36.4	34.2
24	South Georgia Island	VP8G	22	53	48.6	27.8	33.6
25	Iran	EP	15	-	33.7	40.0	32.5
26	Marion Island	ZS8	34	74	49.0	29.2	32.3
27	Laos	XW	40	26	37.0	33.3	32.2
28	Crozet Island	FT/W	45	9	26.3	35.8	31.3
29	Chad	TT	41	33	44.4	24.7	31.1
30	Spratly Island	1S	9	53	31.7	33.1	30.5
31	Annobon Island	3CØ	46	39	30.0	31.9	30.1
32	Kerguelen	FT/X	51	80	36.2	32.5	30.0
33	Tristan da Cunha/Gough	ZD9	36	35	51.9	25.0	29.7
34	Iraq	YI	32	41	48.1	25.8	28.6
35	Christmas Island	VK9X	48	-	27.6	31.9	28.6
36	Cocos-Keeling Island	VK9C	43	52	30.5	31.9	28.5
37	Conway Reef	3D2	55	-	23.9	31.7	28.3
38	Malpelo Island	HKØ	53	18	28.4	31.1	28.1
39	St. Peter & Paul Rocks	PYØ S	52	36	32.9	26.1	27.6
40	Kampuchea	XU	42	81	25.9	30.6	27.4
41	Ethiopia	ET	27	-	35.8	28.1	26.9
42	Syria	YK	47	-	41.2	26.1	26.9
43	South Sandwich Islands	VP8S	31	48	27.2	27.2	25.9
44	South Sudan	STØ	54	57	38.3	23.9	25.8
45	Madagascar	5R	10	31	25.5	26.1	25.6
46	Vietnam	3W	58	17	24.3	29.2	25.6
47	Kingman Reef	KH5K	17	-	26.3	27.5	25.4
48	Maldives	8Q	103	-	23.5	31.1	25.4
49	Banaba (Ocean Island)	T33	68	-	23.0	28.1	25.3
50	Nepal	9N	64	-	39.9	22.8	24.9
51	Bangladesh	S2	14	49	23.0	27.5	24.5
52	Willis Island	VK9W	44	37	28.4	25.6	24.5
53	Afghanistan	YA	57	19	19.3	30.6	24.3
54	United Arab Emirates	A6	56	30	37.4	20.3	24.2
55	Benin	TY	61	34	33.3	22.8	23.2
56	Western Sahara	SØ	50	-	32.5	19.7	22.8
57	Cocos I.	TI9	60	-	31.3	20.0	22.4
58	Rodriguez I.	3B9	74	82	28.0	20.8	22.3
59	Penguin Is.	ZS1	65	-	18.5	25.0	20.9
60	Equatorial Guinea	3C	102	-	21.0	20.6	20.4
61	Trindade	PYØ T	29	62	24.7	21.7	20.2
62	Ghana	9G	12	-	23.0	22.2	20.0
63	Minami Torishima	JD1	80	93	31.3	17.5	19.4
64	Tokelau Island	ZK3	72	29	23.5	21.7	19.3
65	Bahrain	A9	110	65	34.6	16.1	19.3
66	Central Kiribati	T31	82	-	19.3	22.5	19.0
67	Uganda	5X	8	23	17.7	21.4	18.9
68	UK Sovereign Bases	ZC4	66	-	21.4	21.1	18.9
69	Qatar	A7	39	-	21.4	18.9	18.8
70	St. Paul I.	CY9	71	-	20.2	20.6	18.1

1993 Rank	Country	Prefix	1992 Rank	1980 Rank	CW % Need	SSB % Need	% Need
71	Nauru	C2	75	-	28.8	18.6	17.9
72	Aves Island	YVØ	63	70	16.9	21.4	17.5
73	Comoros Is.	D6	85	43	13.6	21.1	17.4
74	Somalia	T5	49	21	18.5	18.6	17.3
75	Juan Fernandez	CEØ	79	40	21.4	17.8	17.2
76	Cameroon	TJ	101	68	23.9	18.3	17.2
77	Midway I.	KH4	86	-	16.5	23.6	16.9
78	Baker, Howland Islands	KH1	18	-	15.6	20.3	16.7
79	Burkino Faso	XT	76	88	21.8	19.2	16.6
80	Egypt	SU	77	-	17.7	17.8	16.5
81	Palmyra Island	KH5	69	-	7.3	20.8	16.4
82	Togo	5V	88	45	22.6	16.7	16.4
83	Rwanda	9X	81	-	18.9	17.5	16.1
84	Sable I.	CY	62	-	17.7	17.8	16.0
85	Jan Mayen	JX	67	77	18.5	18.6	15.9
86	Sao Tome	S9	70	72	20.2	13.6	15.5
87	Mauritania	5T	90	-	21.0	13.9	15.2
88	South Orkney Islands	VP8O	78	-	30.0	13.3	14.7
89	Belau	KC6	83	83	13.6	18.6	14.7
90	Market Reef	OJØ	73	-	16.5	17.8	13.6
91	Djibouti	J2	111	-	17.7	14.2	13.6
92	Malyj Vystoskij Island	4J	92	-	11.1	16.4	13.1
93	North Cook Is.	ZK1	89	-	15.6	14.2	12.6
94	Guinea-Bissau	J5	87	61	16.0	15.3	12.3
95	Mali	TZ	104	59	28.8	8.6	12.3
96	St. Helena I.	ZD7	105	-	29.6	10.3	12.3
97	Clipperton Island	FO/X	94	64	13.6	13.6	12.1
98	Guinea	3X	109	13	14.0	11.7	11.6
99	Niger	5U	84	66	14.0	11.9	10.9
100	Angola	D2	59	-	18.9	8.3	9.9

A complete analysis of this data is provided in the November 1993 issue of *The DX Magazine*.

HOLDERS OF THE TOP TEN DXCC COUNTRY TOTALS
(based on total countries, including deleted countries)

(* Indicates DXCC Honor Roll Member)

Mixed

377
*W1GKK
375
*ZL1HY
*W2AGW
*W2BXA
*K6ZO
*W7MB
374
*LU6DJX
*W1BIH
*W4AIT
*W6HX
*W7KH
*W9ZM
373
*W1AX
*W3EVW
*W4BQY
*K6OJ
*W0BW
372
*G3AAE
*KH6CD
*W3MP
*N4SU
*K5UC
*W5IO
*W8JBI
*WØMLY
371
*DL1KB
*4X4JU
*W2AG
*W3VT
*W6ZO
*WØCM
370
*GW3AHN
*W2LV
*W4EX
*W6KUT
*W8AH
*W9FKC
369
*OH2NB
*W1DK
*W1FZ
*W1HX
*W2QHH
*K4SM
*W8RT
*KØLUZ
*WØELA
368
*DL3RK
*IØAMU
*KH6IJ
*4X4DK
*W1NU
*W2OKM
*K4PDV
*W4LYV
*W4YJ
*W6BZE
*W6RT
*W6TZD
*W7OF
*W8LKH
*W9GIL
*W9WHM
367
*DJ2BW
*DL1BO
*G3FKM
*G3FXB
*G4CP
*HB9TL
*ON4DM
*SM3BIZ
*W1AXA
*W1JR
*K2FL
*W2GW
*W2HTI
*W2SSC
*W3CWG
*K4EZ
*K4KQ
*W4DR
*K5DX
*W5KGX
*W6BS
*W6YK
*W7CG
*W7GN
*W8KPL
*W8ZCQ
*WØPGI

Phone

373
*ZL1HY
*W2BXA
372
*TI2HP
*VK6RU
*W6GVM
371
*VK5MS
368
*W5IO
*W9WHM
*WØCM
367
*GW3AHN
*IØAMU
*ON4DM
*4X4DK
*W2OKM
366
*HB9TL
*ON4DH
*SM3BIX
*ZP5CF
*4X4JU
*W1GKK
*W8AH
*WØBW
365
*W3CWG
*W4EEE
364
*DJ2YI
*LU4DMG
*PAØHBO
*W4YJ
*W9RNX
363
*W1FZ
*W2HTI
*W4DR
*W4SKO
*W5KGX
*WØMLY
362
*DL9OH
*ON4SZ
*ZS6LW
*K5UC
*W9YSX
W9ZM

CW

334
*W9KNI
333
*N4WW
332
*DJ2BW
331
*JA1ELY
*JA1JRK
*JA3FYC
*W8AH
330
*JA8EAT
*JF1PJK
*ON5NT
*SMØAJU
*K2FL
*K3FN
*K4PI
*N4RJ
*K5UR
*W8RSW
*K9MM
3]29
*G3KMA
*JA1GTF
*JA3BQE
*JH3CXL
*OZ1LO
*SM3EVR
*W2FP
*N4MM
*N4VZ
*W7LR
*K8MFO
*K9AJ
*K9QVB
*W9ZM
*NØRR
328
*DL1PM
*DL8AN
*JR1FYS
*JA1BK
*JA6BSM
*JE1JKL
*VE3CKF
*VE3ICR
*K1MEM
*NR1R
*W1NG
*K2TQC
*W2SM
*W3AP
*AA4KT
*K5KLA
*K5VT
*WA6LTA
*WB6RSE
*W6GO
*W6PT
*W8UVZ
*W9DWQ
*W9XX
*W9ZR
327
*F3AT
*JA1UQP
*JA3DY
*JH1EDB
*OZ3Y
*PY2TM
*PY7ZZ
*SM6CST
*K1MM
*K1RH
*W1JR
*K2UO
*N2KW
*K3UA
*N4KG
*W4VQ
*W4WJ
*N5JR
*K6GA
*NS7J
*K8ZH
326
*DL6EN
*JA1FNA
*JA1IFP
*JA1MDK
*OZ7BW
*SM5AKT
*K1ST
*W1GL
*W2MIG
*K4XO
*K5AS
*K5YY
*K6DT
*N6JV
*W6TC
*AA7A
*W8RT
*K9BG
*W9TY
*WØSR
325
*EA4MY
*I3OBO
*JA3CSZ
*JA3MNP
*OK1MP
*W1FZ
*N2LT
*W2YY
*KU4J
*K4SE
*K5NW
*WB6ZUC
*K8PYD
*WØIZ

The CQ DX Awards Program

1. The CQ DX Award is issued in three categories. The CQ DX CW Award is issued to an amateur radio station submitting proof of contact with 100 or more countries. The CQ DX SSB Award is issued to an amateur radio station submitting proof of contact with 100 or more countries. The CQ DX RTTY Award is issued to an amateur radio station submitting proof of contact with 100 countries using two-way RTTY. Applications should be submitted on the official CQ DX Award application (form 1067B). Reasonable facsimiles or computer printouts are also acceptable.

2. All contacts must be two-way in the mode for which the application is made. Cross-mode or one-way contacts are not valid. QSLs must be listed in alphanumeric order (A to Z and 1 to Ø) by prefix. All contacts must have been made after November 15, 1945. Deleted countries do not count. Only currently active countries are acceptable.

3. QSL cards must be verified by one of the authorized check points for the CQ DX Awards, or must be included with the application. Return postage must be included.

4. Country endorsement stickers are issued for 150, 200, 250, 275, 300, 310, and 320 active countries. A fee of $1.00 per sticker (where stickers are issued) is charged.

5. Special endorsements, as follows, are available for a fee of $1.00 each:

(a) 28 MHz endorsement—for 100 or more countries confirmed in the 10 meter band.

(b) 3.5/7 MHz endorsement—for 100 or more countries confirmed using any combination of the 40 and 80 meter bands.

(c) 1.8 MHz endorsement—for 50 or more countries confirmed using the 160 meter band.

(d) QRPp endorsement—for 50 or more countries confirmed using 5 watts output or less.

(e) Mobile endorsement—for 50 or more countries confirmed with the applicant operating mobile.

(f) Slow Scan TV endorsement—for 50 or more countries confirmed using two-way SSTV.

(g) OSCAR endorsement—for 50 or more countries confirmed via amateur satellite.

6. Any altered or forged confirmations will result in permanent disqualification of the applicant.

7. Fair play and good sportsmanship in operating are required for all amateurs working toward CQ DX Awards. Continued use of poor ethics will result in disqualification of the applicant.

8. A fee of $4.00 is required for *CQ* subscribers applying for a CQ DX Award certificate. The latest *CQ* mailing label must be attached for the subscriber discount. For non-subscribers the certificate fee is $10.00. IRCs are acceptable in lieu of check or cash.

9. Normally the ARRL DXCC country list constitutes the basis for CQ DX Award country status. Deleted countries are *not* valid for the CQ DX Award. As a country is deleted, country totals of applicants are automatically adjusted accordingly.

10. All contacts must be with land-based amateur stations working within authorized amateur bands. Contacts with ships and aircraft are not acceptable.

11. Decisions of the CQ DX Awards Manager shall be final.

CQ DX Honor Roll

12. The CQ DX Honor Roll lists all stations with a total of 275 or more active countries.

13. Separate Honor Rolls are maintained for SSB and CW. To remain on the Honor Roll, a station must update his or her totals at least once per year. Updates indicating "no change" are acceptable to meet this requirement.

14. An audit sheet showing countries needed by an Honor Roll member is available for $3.00 plus an SASE for each mode. These are available from the CQ DX Award Manager.

15. All checks must be made payable to B.F. Williams. Applications should be sent to Billy Williams, N4UF, CQ DX Award Manager, P.O. Box 9673, Jacksonville, FL 32208.

THE CQ WAZ AWARDS PROGRAM

The CQ Worked All Zones (WAZ) Award and its variations are issued to any licensed amateur station presenting proof of contact with the appropriate number of CQ zones of the world. This proof consists of proper QSL cards which in many cases may be checked by any of the authorized check points or sent directly to the WAZ Award Manager, Jim Dionne, K1MEM, 31 DeMarco Road, Sudbury, MA 01776. Many of the major DX clubs in the USA and Canada and most national amateur radio societies are authorized CQ check points. If in doubt, consult the WAZ Award Manager. Any legal type of emission may be used, providing communication was established after November 14, 1945.

1. The Official CQ WAZ Zone Map and the printed zone list which follows these rules are used to determine the zone in which a station is located.

2. Confirmations must be accompanied by a list of claimed zones, using CQ form 1479 or a facsimile, showing the callsign of the station contacted within each zone, with the date, time, band, and mode of each contact. The list must also clearly show the applicant's name, callsign, and complete mailing address. The applicant must show the type of award for which he or she is applying, such as Mixed Mode, All SSB, or All CW (see #7 below). A hand-written list may be submitted and will be accepted for processing, provided that the above information is shown.

3. All contacts must be made with licensed, land-based, amateur service stations operating in authorized (on the date of contact) amateur bands. Contacts with non-land-based stations, such as ships at sea, aeronautical mobile, or polar ice stations are not acceptable. Awards obtained by any mobile station will be endorsed as such, as will awards obtained by QRP stations, providing that the QSL cards submitted specify these modifiers.

4. All contacts submitted by the applicant must be made from within the same DXCC country. It is recommended that each submitted QSL clearly show the contacted station's zone number, if possible. When the applicant submits cards made out to different callsigns, evidence should be provided to show that he or she also holds or has held those callsigns at the time of the contact.

5. Any altered or forged confirmations submitted by an applicant for WAZ credit may result in permanent disqualification. The WAZ Manager may request the resubmission of certain confirmations as required. While a QSL card is normally accepted as proof of a contact, the final proof is an entry in the DX station's logbook for the listed QSO. Failure to resubmit QSLs in a timely manner when request- ed by the WAZ Manager may result in the recall of the award in question. Submission of an application for any WAZ award acknowledges consent to abide by the decisions of the CQ WAZ Manager and the CQ Awards Committee.

6. An application must be accompanied by the processing fee (subscribers must include a recent CQ mailing label or copy with the application fee of $4.00; non-subscribers $10.00) and a self-addressed envelope with sufficient postage or International Reply Coupons (IRCs) to return the QSL cards by the class of mail desired and indicated. International Reply Coupons equal in redemption value to the processing fee are acceptable. The 1993 redemption value of IRCs is $.50 each. Checks should be made out to the name of the WAZ Award Manager.

7. In addition to the basic certificate for which any and all HF bands may be used, specially endorsed and numbered certificates are available for Phone (including AM), Single Sideband, and CW operation. The Phone certificate requires that all contacts be Two-Way Phone, the SSB certificate requires that all contact be Two-Way SSB, and the CW certificate requires that all contacts be Two-Way CW.[1]

8. If at the time of the original application a note is made stating the possibility of a subsequent application for an endorsement or special certificate, only the missing confirmations required for that endorsement need be submitted with the later application, providing a copy of the original authorization signed by the WAZ Manager is enclosed.

9. Decisions of the CQ DX Advisory Committee on any matter pertaining to the administration of this award are final.

10. All applications should be sent to the WAZ Award Manager after the QSL cards have been checked by an authorized CQ check point. If the application is for 160 meters or the 5 Band WAZ, all QSL cards must be checked by the WAZ Award Manager. Photocopies are not acceptable.

11. Zone maps, printed rules, and application forms are available from the WAZ Award Manager. Send a large self-addressed envelope with 2 units of postage, or $1.00 and an address label.

For DX stations, send an address label and 2 IRCs.

The following list of zones is presented as a guide. Any questions will be decided by the CQ Zone Map. For rulings on borderline areas, consult the WAZ Award Manager.

Zone 1. Northwestern Zone of North America: KL7, VY1/VE8 Yukon, the Northwest Territories west of 102 degrees. (Includes the islands of Victoria, Banks, Melville, and Prince Patrick.)

Zone 2. Northeastern Zone of North America: VO2 Labrador, the portion of VE2 Quebec north of the 50th parallel, the VE8 Northwest Territories east of 102 degrees. (Includes the islands of King Christian, King William, Prince of Wales, Somerset, Bathurst, Devon, Ellesmere, Baffin, and the Melville and Boothia Peninsulas, excluding Akimiski Island.)

Zone 3. Western Zone of North America: VE7, W6, and the W7 states of Arizona, Idaho, Nevada, Oregon, Utah, and Washington.

Zone 4. Central Zone of North America: VE3, VE4, VE5, VE6, VE8 Akimiski Island, and W7 states of Montana and Wyoming. WØ, W9, W8 (except West Virginia), W5, and the W4 states of Alabama, Tennessee, and Kentucky.

Zone 5. Eastern Zone of North America: 4U1UN, CY9, CYØ, FP, VE1/VY2, VO1, the portion of VE2 Quebec south of the 50th parallel, VP9, W1, W2, W3, and the W4 states of Florida, Georgia, South Carolina, North Carolina, Virginia, and the W8 state of West Virginia.

Zone 6. Southern Zone of North America: XE/XF, XF4 (Revilla Gigedo).

Zone 7. Central American Zone: FO (Clipperton), HKØ (San Andres), HP, HR, TG, TI, TI9, V3, YN, and YS.

Zone 8. West Indies Zone: C6, CO, FG, FJ, FM, FS, HH, HI, J3, J6, J7, J8, KG4 (Guantanamo), KP1, KP2, KP4, KP5, PJ (Saba, St. Maarten, St. Eustatius), V2, V4, VP2, VP5, YVØ (Aves Is.), ZF, 6Y, and 8P.

Zone 9. Northern Zone of South America: FY, HK, HKØ (Malpelo), P4, PJ (Bonaire, Curacao), PZ, YV, 8R, and 9Y.

Zone 10. Western Zone of South America: CP, HC, HC8, and OA.

Zone 11. Central Zone of South America: PY, PYØ, and ZP.

Zone 12. Southwest Zone of South America: 3Y (Peter I), CE, CEØ (Easter Is., Juan Fernandez Is., San Felix Is.), and some Antarctic stations.[2]

Zone 13. Southeast Zone of South America: CX, LU, VP8 Islands, and some Antarctic stations.[2]

Zone 14. Western Zone of Europe: C3, CT, CU, DL, EA, EA6, EI, F, G, GD, GI, GJ, GM, GU, GW, HB, HBØ, LA, LX, ON, OY, OZ, PA, SM, ZB, 3A, and 4U1ITU.

Zone 15. Central European Zone: ES (UR), HA, HV, I, ISØ, LY (UP), OE, OH, OHØ, OJØ, OK, OM, S5, SP, T7, T9, TK, UA2, YL (UQ), YU, ZA, 1AØ, Z3, 9A, 9H.

Zone 16. Eastern Zone of Europe: UA1, UA3, UA4, UA6, UA9 (S,W), UB, UC, UO, and 4J1 (M.V. Island).

Zone 17. Western Zone of Siberia: UA9 (A, C, F, G, J, K, L, M, Q, X) and UH, UI, UJ, UL, and UM.

Zone 18. Central Siberian Zone: UA8 (T,V), UA9 (H, O, U, V, Y, Z), and UAØ (A, B, H, S, U, W).

Zone 19. Eastern Siberian Zone: UAØ (C, D, F, I, J, K, L, Q, X, Z).

Zone 20. Balkan Zone: JY, LZ, OD, SV, TA, YK, YO, ZC4, 4X, and 5B.

Zone 21. Southwestern Zone of Asia: A4, A6, A7, A9, AP, EP, HZ, UD, UF, UG, YA, YI, 4W, 7O, and 9K.

Zone 22. Southern Zone of Asia: A5, S2, VU, VU (Laccadive Is.), 4S, 8Q, and 9N.

Zone 23. Central Zone of Asia: JT, UAØY, BY3G-L, BY9A-L, BY9T-Z, and BYØ.

Zone 24. Eastern Zone of Asia: BV, BY1, BY2, BY3A-F, BY3M-S, BY3T-Z, BY4, BY5, BY6, BY7, BY8, BY9M-S, VS6, and XX.

Zone 25. Japanese Zone: HL and JA.

Zone 26. Southeastern Zone of Asia: HS, VU (Andaman and Nicobar Islands), XV, XU, XW, XZ, and 1S (Spratly Islands).

Zone 27. Philippine Zone: DU (Philippines), JD1 (Minami Torishima), JD1 (Ogasawara), KC6 (Republic of Belau), KH2 (Guam), KHØ (Marianas Is.), V6 (Fed. States of Micronesia).

Zone 28. Indonesian Zone: H4, P2, V8, YB, 9M, and 9V.

Zone 29. Western Zone of Australia: VK6, VK8, VK9X (Christmas Is.), VK9Y (Cocos-Keeling Is.), and some Antarctic stations.[2]

Zone 30. Eastern Zone of Australia: VK1, VK5, VK7, VK9L (Lord Howe Is.), VK9 (Willis Is.), VK9 (Mellish Reef), VKØ (Macquarie Is.), and some Antarctic stations.[2]

Zone 31. Central Pacific Zone: C2, FO (Marquises), KH1, KH3, KH4, KH5, KH6, KH7, KH9, T2, T3, V7, and ZK3.

Zone 32. New Zealand Zone: A3, FK, FO (except Marquises and Clipperton), FW, KH8, VK9 (Norfolk Is.), VR6, YJ, ZK1, ZK2, ZL, 3D2, 5W, and some Antarctic stations.[2]

Zone 33. Northwestern Zone of Africa: CN, CT3, EA8, EA9, IG9, IH9 (Pantelleria Is.), SØ, 3V, and 7X.

Zone 34. Northeastern Zone of Africa: ST, STØ, SU, and 5A.

Zone 35. Central Zone of Africa: C5, D4, EL, J5, TU, TY, TZ, XT, 3X, 5N, 5T, 5U, 5V, 6W, 9G, and 9L.

Zone 36. Equatorial Zone of Africa: D2, TJ, TL, TN, S9, TR, TT, ZD7, ZD8, 3C, 9J, 9Q, 9U, and 9X.

Zone 37. Eastern Zone of Africa: C9, ET, E3, J2, T5, 5H, 5X, 5Z, and 7Q.

Zone 38. South African Zone: A2, ZD9, Z2, ZS1-9, 3DAØ, 3Y (Bouvet Is.), 7P, and some Antarctic stations.[2]

Zone 39. Madagascar Zone: D6, FT-W, FT-X, FT-Z, FH, FR, S7, VKØ (Heard Is.), VQ9, 3B6/7, 3B8, 3B9, 5R8, and some Antarctic stations.[2]

Zone 40. North Atlantic Zone: JW, JX, OX, TF, and 4K2 (Franz Josef Land).

[1]Previously all Mixed WAZ Awards were numbered consecutively, with ALL CW noted. This will continue for mixed mode applications. As of January 1, 1991, the ALL CW WAZ Award is issued. To qualify, the QSL card from each zone must be dated after January 1, 1991.

[2]Antarctic notes. The boundries of CQ zones 12, 13, 29, 30, 32, 38, and 39 coverage at the South Pole. Stations KC4AAA and KC4USN are at the South Pole, ansd will count for any one of the listed zones. Most Antarctic stations indicate their zone on the QSL card. A few stations and their zones are: 4K1A 39, 4K1B 29, 4K1C 29, 4K1D 38, 4K1E 29, 4K1F 13, 4K1G 30, 4K1H 32, 4K1J 13, 8J1RL 39, CE9 13, DPØ 38, FT-Y 30, HFØPOL 13, HL5BDS 13, KC4AAC 13, KC4AAD 13, KC4AAE 29, KC4USB 32, KC4USV 30, LU-Z 13, VKØGM 29, VP8ME 38, Y38ANT 38, AND ZL5AA 30. This list changes frequently. Questions regarding the zone location of a particular Antarctic station should be directed to the WAZ Award Manager.

Single Band WAZ

Awards will be issued to amateur radio stations presenting proof of contact with the 40 zones of the world on one of the bands: 80, 40, 20, 15, 10. Contacts for a single band WAZ must have been made after January 1, 1973. Single band certificates will be awarded for ALL SSB or for ALL CW only.

5 Band WAZ

Applicants who succeed in presenting proof of contact with the 40 zones of the world on the 80, 40, 20, 15, and 10 meter bands (for a total of 200) receive a special certificate in recognition of this achievement. A prerequisite for 5 Band WAZ is that the applicant must already be a holder of any 40-zone WAZ.

The 5 Band WAZ Award is offered for any combination of CW, SSB, RTTY, or other mode contact, MIXED MODE only. Separate awards will not be offered for the different modes. Contacts must have been made after 0000Z January 1, 1979. Proof of contact shall consist only of QSL cards checked by the WAZ Manager, and all provisions of Rule 5 of the WAZ rules are strictly enforced. The first plateau is a total of 150 zones on a combination of 5 bands. Applicants should use a separate sheet for each band, using CQ form 1479 or a facsimile. See rule 6 for fee and postage information.

After the 150 zone point, each 10 zones requires the submission of the QSL cards and a $1.00 fee. At the 200 zone point the

HOLDERS OF THE CQ 5-BAND WORKED-ALL-ZONES AWARD
(All 200 Zones Worked and Confirmed)

The First Ten

1. ON4UN
2. K4MQG
3. SM4CAN
4. AA6AA
5. W8AH
6. W6KUT
7. EA8AK
8. LA7JO
9. EA3SF
10. OH1XX

Alphabetical List of All Holders

4N7ZZ	EA8QL	I6FLD	K1MM	N4VZ	RB7GG	VK6HD
4Z4DX	EA8XS	I8IGS	K1VKO	N4WJ	RT4UA	VK9NS
5B4TI	EA9IE	I8SAT	K2TQC	N5CB	RT5UN	WØJLC
A71AD	F5VU	IKØAGU	K3TW	N6AR	RT5UO	WØMLY
A92BE	F6BEE	IKØIOL	K4CEB	N6DX	RT5UY	WØSD
AA4LU	F6BKI	IK4ALM	K4MQG	NR1R	S59VM	WØZV
AA4V	F6BLP	IK4GME	K5TSQ	NS7Z	SMØAJU	W1NG
AA6AA	F6DZU	IT9TQH	K5UC	NW5K	SMØBZH	W1NW
CT1BH	F6EXV	IT9ZGY	K5UR	OA4OS	SMØDJZ	W3AP
CT1FL	FM5WD	IV3PRK	K6SIK	OE1ZJ	SM3EVR	W3GG
CT1TM	G3GIQ	IV3YYK	K6SSS	OE2VEL	SM3GSK	W3UM
CT2AK	G3MCS	JAØCWZ	K7EJ	OE3WWB	SM4CAN	W4DR
CT3BM	G3TJW	JAØDAI	K8EJ	OE6IMD	SM4CTT	W4VQ
CT4BD	G3UML	JA1BWA	K8NA	OH1XX	SM5AKT	W6GO
CT4NH	G3XTT	JA1ELY	K9AJ	OH2EE	SM5AQD	W6KUT
DF3GY	G4BUE	JA1FNA	K9EL	OH3JF	SM5CLE	W7OM
DF6CY	G4BWP	JA1GTF	K9FD	OH3RF	SM6BGG	W8AH
DF7NM	G4GED	JA1GV	K9JF	OH3TQ	SM6CST	W8UVZ
DF9ZP	G4GIR	JA1IFP	K9RHY	OH3YI	SM6CTQ	W9ZR
DJ2YA	G4IUF	JA1SVP	K9UWA	OH6JW	SM6CVX	WA1AER
DJ4PI	G4LJF	JA1UQP	KBØG	OH7KI	SM6DYK	WA2TMP/7
DJ5JH	GW4OFQ	JA2AAQ	KBØU	OH8SR	SM7BYP	WB2P
DJ6RX	HAØDU	JA2BL	KB8DB	OK1ADM	SM7CRW	WB9Z
DJ7RD	HAØMM	JA2DSY	KC7EM	OK1AWZ	SM7DZZ	WS9V
DJ8NK	HA3NU	JA2ODS	KD7P/KH2	OK1DDS	SM7FIG	XE1J
DJ9RQ	HA5WA	JA3CSZ	KG4W	OK1MG	SP3BQD	XE1OX
DJ9ZB	HA8XX	JA3DY	KM1H	OK1MP	SP3IBS	XE1VIC
DK2OY	HA9RE	JA3EMU	KS1L	OK1RD	SP5AA	Y22JD
DK5AD	HB9AHL	JA3FYC	LA1VFA	OK2DB	SP7KTE	YBØWR
DK7PE	HB9AMO	JA3MNP	LA2GV	OK3CGP	SP8EMO	YO3AC
DL1YD	HB9ATA	JA4IKD	LA4HW	OK3CSC	SV1ADG	YO3CD
DL3RK	HB9CIP	JA4MRL	LA5YJ	OK3DG	SV1JA	YT3AA
DL4YAH	HB9RG	JA4VUQ	LA6OT	OK3TCA	SV1JG	YT7DX
DL6EN	HC5EA	JA5DQH	LA7JO	ON4ACG	TG9NX	YU1EXY
DL6WD	HG19HB	JA6JPS	LA7ZO	ON4ADZ	TG9VT	YU2AA
DL7AA	HK3DDD	JA6LCJ	LA9GV	ON4QX	UA3TT	YU2CBM
DL7AFV	HL1IUA	JA6VU	LU8DPM	ON4UN	UA4RZ	YU2HDE
DL7HZ	IØRIZ	JA7FS	LU9FFA	ON5NT	UA6JD	YU2TW
DL7XS	I1APQ	JA7FWR	LZ1GC	ON5WQ	UA6JWW	YU2WV
DL8AN	I1BSN	JA7GLB	LZ1HA	ON6HE	UA9CBO	YU3AN
DL8MAG	I1HAG	JA7HMZ	LZ1NG	ON6OS	UK2RDX	YU7DX
EA1OD	I1JQJ	JA7IL	LZ2CC	ON7EM	UP1BZZ	ZL1BIL
EA2IA	I1ZEU	JA7JWF	LZ2DF	ON7PQ	UQ1GXX	ZL1BOQ
EA3AD	I2JQ	JA8EAT	LZ2JF	OZ3PZ	UQ2MU	ZL1BQD
EA3SF	I2UIY	JH1XYR	LZ2KK	OZ7OP	UR2QD	ZL3GQ
EA4BVE	I2ZGC	JH7FMJ	NØXA	OZ7YY	UWØMF	ZL4BO
EA4DO	I3MAU	JR3HZW	N2MF	PAØCLN	UZ2FWA	ZP5JCY
EA5SP	I4EAT	JR3IIR	N4CC	PAØLVB	VE1NG	ZS5BK
EA6ET	I4EWH	JR6PGB	N4JJ	PAØXPQ	VE3EJ	ZS5LB
EA6NB	I4RYC	JT1BG	N4KE	PAØZH	VE3ICR	ZS5MY
EA8AK	I4USC	KØZZ	N4KG	PY1APS	VE7IG	ZS6BCR
EA8OZ	I4YNO	K1MEM	N4RR	PY1OL	VK3QI	

applicant will be awarded a gold sticker for the certificate and the opportunity to purchase a hand-engraved plaque to commemorate the achievement.

All applications should be sent to the WAZ Award Manager. The 5 Band Award is governed by the same rules as the regular WAZ Award and uses the same boundaries.

WARC Bands WAZ

Effective January 1, 1991 single band WAZ Awards will be issued to amateur radio stations presenting proof of contact with the 40 zones of the world on any one of the WARC bands: 30, 17, or 12 meters. (Each band constitutes a separate award, and each may be applied for separately.) This award is available for MIXED MODE, ALL SSB, ALL CW, or ALL RTTY. Contacts for each one of these WARC WAZ Awards must have been made after each station involved in the contact had permission from its licensing authority to operate on the band and mode.

RTTY WAZ

Special WAZ Awards are issued to amateur radio stations presenting proof of contact with the 40 zones of the world using RTTY. For the mixed band award QSL cards must show a date of November 15, 1945 or later. The RTTY WAZ is also available with a single band endorsement. For a single band endorsement for 80, 40, 20, 15, or 10 meters the QSL cards must show a date of January 1, 1973 or later.

WAZ AWARDS

Worked-All-Zones Awards Issued from September 1, 1992 through August 31, 1993

Mixed

7266	KN7N	7295	KN4UB	7324	JA2ACI	7353	CT1EEB
7267	AB4PY	7296	N1IR	7325	JA2NOQ	7354	JA1QND
7268	IV3ZAC	7297	K7KBN	7326 CW	W3OOU	7355	DL3EO
7269 CW	N4WP	7298	JA1QVR	7327 CW	WG8M	7356	G4XPG
7270 CW	W5EHM	7299	WK9Z	7328	AA4UF	7357 CW	K4SB
7271 CW	K3ANS	7300	N7DBA	7329	IT9BCC	7358	W3FTG
7272	K3ANS	7301	OZ1IWE	7330	SP3NYG	7359	JA9KKD
7273	W1YIF	7302 CW	OH6MHN	7331 CW	SP3FAR	7360	ZL2BRQ
7274	K6ZTQ	7303 CW	FE1JUD	7332 CW	IK8FUN	7361 CW	NX1Q
7275	N4ZR	7304	AA5ZX	7333 CW	HA8DE	7362 CW	IK2MMF
7276	HB9BHY	7305	NZ9Z	7334	N4XMX	7363	AD8C
7277	VE7CV	7306	SP6RYB	7335	WG9L	7364	IK7SUE
7278 CW	JP1PCK	7307	K6ASB	7336 CW	F6DRA	7365	KØOST
7279 CW	WA2YEX	7308	NA2Q	7337	HB9US	7366 CW	UA4OZ
7280	JAØOIK	7309	DKØEE	7338	ZL1AK	7367	WZ2H
7281 CW	HA7PF	7310	WW8N	7339	KS4Q	7368 CW	DL2AXI
7282	VE6LB	7311	IK6FTZ	7340 CW	OH2RL	7369 CW	WA6JCD
7283	JH1BAM	7312	DL4MDU	7341	WA9YSD	7370 CW	N3RW
7284	WY2E	7313 CW	KB3X	7342	ON8DX	7371	K4PY
7285CW	SMØKRN	7314	SM6PRX	7343 CW	WB2WBU	7372	SP8HKT
7286	OE2BZL	7315	ZS4TX	7344	KI6X	7373	GM4AGS
7287	DJ7BP	7316 CW	I8IYW	7345	VE3CE	7374 CW	WB6MBF
7288 CW	IK2MRZ	7317	JL1HDH	7346 CW	IK5NTK	7375	WB7NXY
7289 CW	CT4AH	7318	IKØQBI	7347	N5HH	7376	F5OZK
7290	PA3CJS	7319	I1SLI	7348	W4WKQ	7377	S52TU
7291 CW	OK1FPG	7320 CW	HB9BHV	7349	IT9POD	7378 CW	ON4SW
7292	SP2DX	7321 CW	NZ7W	7350	F6CBH		
7293 CW	JA1AVV/QRP	7322 CW	DL5HBS	7351	AA7AN		
7294	PT2NP	7323 CW	HP1AC	7352	VE7DK		

Phone

613	K3ANS	615	I4MFA	617	CT1EEB	619	WA8YQR
614	LA1ZE	616	EA3CWK	618	K7TED		

SSB

3995	DL4MEH	4025	KE2UV	4055	IK8FUN	4085	SP5AUB
3996	K3ANS	4026	IK5IIU	4056	LW1DHI	4086	WA4DRU
3997	SM6DHU	4027	KD1CT	4057	IK7IJP	4087	EA3KB
3998	IK7NXO	4028	KA4RAW	4058	JA3SHL	4088	EA1BCK
3999	VE7CV	4029	N5AHS	4059	K3IXD	4089	IV3NZN
4000	N1CPC	4030	W4DMT	4060	JA9BFN	4090	4X1EL
4001	HB9BGV	4031	K4LRX	4061	W1VXV	4091	IT9JOF
4002	HC4L	4032	KC4PCX	4062	JL2EZB	4092	JE6KYA
4003	WB3D	4033	NY3T	4063	IK7NXM	4093	KM6YX
4004	K6ONE	4034	DF5CT/A	4064	ZL1AK	4094	GØFTA
4005	EA6MQ	4035	DK6WF	4065	JH7XVB	4095	K4SB
4006	EA2BOT	4036	KB3X	4066	DK8UH	4096	KT1H
4007	WB2NQT	4037	WB5EUC	4067	KA8JHD	4097	ZP5YW
4008	NB6G	4038	N4VRR	4068	OH1KF	4098	DX1DBT
4009	YV5DEH	4039	VE1UK	4069	GM4XLU	4099	K7TED
4010	IK2CFH	4040	NX5C	4070	JA8KJR	4100	HK6DOS
4011	OE7XMH	4041	EA3CWK	4071	NØHCH	4101	JA6IVR
4012	JH1AFD	4042	EA5ZR	4072	W5GVP	4102	IK7MXB
4013	IK7CSA	4043	KD7GQ	4073	WD4AFY	4103	IK7OKB
4014	CE5BTS	4044	YV5IVB	4074	WD8LTM	4104	WA6JCD
4015	I8JJB	4045	IK4HPU	4075	KD6ZM	4105	W9AGH
4016	LA9MC	4046	OH1BV	4076	N4XMX	4106	EA1AYN
4017	WA6EZV	4047	VY2VT	4077	WB2WBU	4107	DL1ZBB
4018	DL1XE	4048	N4LLC	4078	KA9WON	4108	KB5MRT
4019	KK4TR	4049	IK3ITX	4079	DL3NAT	4109	K6UV
4020	WA3KKO	4050	IK8LWA	4080	KD1HN	4110	VU2JJQ
4021	PY3JZ	4051	WG8M	4081	N6DUR	4111	K2ZFW
4022	YV5MRR	4052	WA9FXH	4082	CT3FF	4112	ON6TD
4023	WBØYQT	4053	JF1MBA	4083	AC4NJ	4113	ON4SW
4024	IK7CNX	4054	JJ1JGI	4084	FE1JSK		

CW

18	WD4JHY	23	AB5EU	28	WS1F	33	WQ3E
19	NW8F	24	G4BWP	29	AA6WJ	34	F3SG
20	WD8HIW	25	F6HMJ	30	N1IR		
21	HB9BGY	26	FE1PBM	31	N4OT		
22	W4DMT	27	AA5BT	32	LX2KQ		

RTTY WAZ

Mixed

72	JA1BYL	77	WA4MCZ
73	AB4PY	78	ZL3GQ
74	W9RY	79	WA7BPI
75	IK1HSR	80	KB5GL
76	AA4M/6		

20M

41	WA4MCZ

Satellite

1	KL7GRF
2	VE6LQ
3	KD6PY
4	OH5LK
5	AA6PJ

WNZ

Mixed

8	KB4ZMR	28 ZONES
9	WB4UMQ	31 ZONES

10 SSB

52	KB2NEK	26 Zones
53	N6ZWC	29 Zones
54	KA5OER	25 Zones

Single-Band/Mode WAZ

10M

SSB

440	JA2DLM	449	HB9RB	458	JR7CDL
441	DL8MEJ	450	K2EEK	459	WB2WBU
442	PA3FGI	451	KA2ANF	460	EA3EJI
443	UB3IDX	452	XE1VIC	461	IT9JOF
444	WA6APQ	453	JH1FSF	462	IK4PMA
445	IV3JVJ	454	OH3MFP	463	ON6DP
446	K9ZXG	455	KA6PUW	464	OE6CLD
447	DL3NCA	456	JE4WOK	465	HB9ATM
448	YC3OSE	457	KE5PO	466	EA2KL

CW

134	WB5MTV
135	WØSR
136	WB2WBU
137	OH4OJ
138	WA3CGE

12M

Mixed

10	K2ENT
11	OH3MEP
12	I2EOW

CW

9	N4MM

SSB

6	JR2KDN
7	OZ1ING

15M

SSB

432	JAØLFV	442	IK2HSW
433	WA4APM	443	ZL1AK
434	K9ZXG	444	JA1JMF
435	JR1WCT	445	WB6JMS
436	JG2CMJ	446	WB2WBU
437	EA3CWK	447	KAØZFX
438	WA6YOD	448	HB9ATM
439	JR9OPJ	449	WB2NQT
440	JH7HJL	450	7L1WII
441	W3OOU	451	EA2KL

CW

235	JF6TEI	245	WB2WBU
236	K9ZXG	246	JR2SHA
237	SM6DHU	247	OE3EMN
238	K2LFL	248	JF2WXS
239	WF9K	249	ON4ACG
240	KA1CLV	250	JJ1BMB
241	BV2TA	251	WA3CGE
242	JG1DUN	252	HB9BGV
243	JK1AJX		
244	FE1JNA		

17M

Mixed

16	KB4SA	20	ON4ACG
17	LX2KQ	21	K3UA
18	N5CB	22	K2ENT
19	N4CC		

CW

6	SM6EVR
7	K8MFO
8	N4MM
9	K3UA

20M

SSB				CW			
902	K3ANS	918	KØJPM	407	EA7AZA	423	HB9BMU
903	PY6WT	919	IK2GOT	408	K4IQJ	424	W5EW
904	OH3OJ	920	JA1SHE	409	SP8JMA	425	K3ANS
905	WA4APM	921	N5HSF	410	W4CKD	426	SP6CPF
906	K9ZXG	922	KF7VC	411	SM6DHU	427	ND6G
907	WT3W	923	W8KZM	412	HB9DDZ	428	K9ZXG
908	WB2RAJ	924	WA2WBU	413	WS4E	429	UC2WAZ
909	N4KW	925	KO4XM	414	I2VRF	430	DL6UNF
910	KG6VI	926	UA4CX	415	KA1CLV	431	OE3EMN
911	KAØZFX	927	WB2NQT	416	DK7SU	432	WB9CIF
912	JR1DUP	928	ON6DP	417	JN3SAC	433	WB2WBU
913	N7MLN	929	K2AJY	418	DK2UR	434	WZ3Q
914	OE1KW	930	NR3Y	419	JA3VOV	435	K4SB
915	NV8Z	931	HB9BGV	420	BV2TA	436	W8JCC
916	EA2KL	932	OH3OJ	421	WA4JTI	437	W8IQ
917	W3OOU			422	I6DQE	438	K5FUV

40M

SSB				CW	
157	K3UA	164	W1WAI	79	EA2KL
158	JE1GWO	165	ON4ACG		
159	K4IQJ	166	WB2WBU		
160	WB8ZRL	167	OE3EMN		
161	JA7BT	168	NQ1W		
162	K5PC	169	K5FUV		
163	JA6VU	170	WA3CGE		

80M

SSB		CW					
61	JR2KDN	34	ON5NT	36	JA6VU	38	K9EL
		35	W1MK	37	ON7PQ		

160M

71	WB9Z	37 ZONES	72	SM4CAN	40 ZONES	73	ON4ACG	30 ZONES

50th Anniversary WAZ

126	WB2WBU	127	I1POR

WNZ

WNZ stands for "Worked Novice Zones" and is available only to holders of a U.S. Novice or Technician class license. Proof of contact with at least 25 of the 40 CQ zones as defined by the WAZ rules is required. All contacts must be made using the 80, 40, 15, and 10 meter Novice bands. All contacts must be made while holding a Novice or Technician class license, although the application may be submitted at a later date. Contacts must be made prior to receiving authorization to operate with higher class privileges. The WNZ is available as a MIXED MODE, CW ONLY, or SSB ONLY award. It may also be endorsed for a single band. The WNZ Award may be used to fulfill part of the application requirement for the WAZ Award when all 40 zones are confirmed.

1. The basic award may be secured by submitting QSL cards for 25 zones. The processing fee is $5.00 for all applicants.

2. All QSL cards must show a date of January 1, 1952 or later.

3. Use CQ Form 1479 or a facsimile to make application for this award.

160 Meter WAZ

The WAZ Award for 160 Meters requires that the applicant submit directly to the WAZ Manager QSL cards from at least 30 zones. All QSL cards must be dated January 1, 1975 or later, and a $5.00 application fee must accompany all applications. The 160 WAZ is a mixed mode award only. The basic 160 WAZ Award may be secured by submitting QSL cards from 30 zones. Stickers for 35, 36, 37, 38, 39, and 40 zones may be secured from the WAZ Manager upon the submission of the QSL cards and $2.00 for each sticker.

Satellite WAZ

The Satellite WAZ Award is issued to amateur radio stations submitting proof of contact with all 40 CQ zones through any amateur radio satellite. The award is available for MIXED MODE only. All QSL cards must show a date of January 1, 1989 or later.

THE CQ WPX AWARDS PROGRAM

The CQ WPX Award recognizes the accomplishments of confirmed QSOs with the many prefixes used by amateurs throughout the world. Separate, distinctively marked certificates are available for 2× SSB, CW, and MIXED (CW and SSB/Phone) modes, as well as the VPX Award for shortwave listeners and the WPNX Award for Novices.

1. Applications

A. All applications for WPX certificates (and endorsements) must be submitted on the official application form (CQ 1051A). This form can be obtained by sending a self-addressed, stamped, business-size (4 × 9 inch) envelope to the WPX Award Manager, Norm Koch, K6ZDL, P.O. Box 593, Clovis, NM 88101.

B. All QSOs must be made from the same country.

C. All call letters must be in strict alphabetical order and the entire call letters must be shown.

D. All entries must be clearly legible.

E. Certificates are issued for HF (160–10) for the following modes and number of prefixes (VHF contacts do not count for the WPX Award program). Cross-mode QSOs are not valid for the CW or 2× SSB certificates. Mixed (CW and SSB/Phone only): 400 prefixes confirmed. CW: 300 prefixes confirmed. 2× SSB: 300 prefixes confirmed. Separate applications are required for each mode.

F. Cards need not be sent, but they must be in the possession of the applicant. Any and all cards may be requested by the WPX Award Manager or by the CQ DX Committee.

G. The application fee for each certificate is $4.00 for *CQ* subscribers (subscribers must include a recent *CQ* mailing label, or a photocopy of it) and $10.00 for non-subscribers, or the equivalent in IRCs.

H. All applications and endorsement requests should be sent to the WPX Award Manager.

2. Endorsements

A. Prefix endorsements are issued for each 50 additional prefixes submitted. Minimum submission at any one time is 50 prefixes.

B. Band endorsements are available for working the following numbers of prefixes on the various bands: 1.8 MHz—50, 3.5 MHz—175, 7 MHz—250, 14 MHz—300, 21 MHz—300, 28 MHz—300.

C. Continental endorsements are given for working the following numbers of prefixes in the respective continents: North America 160, South America 95, Europe 160, Africa 90, Asia 75, and Oceania 60.

D. Endorsement applications must be submitted on CQ form 1051A. Use a separate application for each mode of your endorsement application.

E. For prefix endorsements list only additional call letters confirmed since the last endorsement application.

F. A self-addressed, stamped envelope or proper IRCs for surface or airmail return is required, and $1.00 or 5 IRCs for *each* endorsement sticker.

3. Prefixes

A. The letter/numeral combinations which form the first part of the amateur call will be considered the prefix. Examples: K6, N6, Y22, Y23, WD4, HG1, HG19, WB2, WB2ØØ, KC2, KC2ØØ, OE2, OE25, U3, GB75, ZS66, NG84, etc. Any difference in the numbering, lettering, or order of same shall constitute a separate prefix.

B. Any prefix will be considered legitimate if its use was licensed or permitted by the governing authority in the country of operation after November 15, 1945.

C. In cases of portable operation in another country or call area, the portable designator would then become the prefix. Example: K6ZDL/7 would count as K7, J6/K6ZDL would count as J6, KH6/K6ZDL would count as KH6, etc. Portable designators without numbers will be assigned a zero (Ø) at the end of the designator to form the prefix. Example: LX/K6ZDL would count as LXØ. When claiming a prefix which has been sent as K6ZDL/XV5, for example, and you are claiming the XV5 for credit, it is requested that the *claimed prefix* be listed in the proper alphabetical position, such as XV5/K6ZDL, if for XV5; or K6ZDL/XV5 if for K6. The portable prefix must be an authorized prefix of the country/area of operation. Maritime mobile, mobile, /A, /E, /J, /P, or interim license class identifiers do not count as prefixes.

D. All calls without numbers will be assigned a zero (Ø) plus the first two letters to form a prefix. Examples: XEFTJW would count as XEØ, RAEM would count as RAØ, AIR as AIØ, etc.

VPX

The VPX (Verified Prefixes) Award may be earned by shortwave listeners (SWLs) who possess QSL cards confirming reception of at least 300 different amateur prefixes. No mode endorsements are available. Applications must be submitted to the WPX Award Manager in accordance with the WPX rules.

WPNX

The WPNX Award can be earned by USA Novices who work 100 different prefixes prior to receiving a higher class license. The application may be submitted after receiving the higher license, providing the actual contacts were made as a Novice. Prefixes worked for the WPNX Award may be used later for credit toward the WPX Award.

The rules for the WPNX Award are the same as for the WPX Award except that only 100 prefixes must be confirmed. Applications are to be sent to the WPX Award Manager.

WPX Honor Roll

The WPX Honor Roll recognizes the operators and stations that maintain a high standing in confirmed, current prefixes. The rules, therefore, reflect the belief that Honor Roll membership should be accessible to all active radio amateurs and not be unduly advantageous to the "old timers." With the exceptions listed below, all general rules for WPX apply toward Honor Roll credit.

A minimum of 600 prefixes is required to be eligible for the WPX Honor Roll. No certificates are issued, but a listing of members appears in *CQ* every other month.

A. Only current prefixes will be counted toward the WPX Honor Roll standings. A list of prefixes to be deleted from the Honor Roll is published annually in *CQ* and is available from the WPX Award Manager. Prefixes will be deleted from the Honor Roll listing two years after they are no longer authorized for use by the governing authority or by the ITU.

B. Special-issue prefixes (i.e., OF, OS, 4A, etc.) will be considered current for as long as they are assigned to a particular country and deducted as credit for Honor Roll standings after cessation of their use or assignment.

C. Honor Roll applicants must submit their list of current prefixes (entire call required) separate from their regular WPX applications. Use regular form 1051 and indicate "Honor Roll" at the top of the form. Forms may be obtained by sending a business-size, self-addressed, stamped envelope or 1 IRC (foreign stations send extra postage or IRC if airmail is desired) to the WPX Award Manager. A separate application must be made for each mode. Lifetime Honor Roll fee *for each mode* is $4.00. A computer printout of your individual Honor Roll file may be obtained from the WPX Award Manager for $5.00.

D. Endorsements for the Honor Roll may be made for 10 or more prefixes. An SASE or IRC should be included. For prefixes by countries see the *Callbook* listings.

WPX Award of Excellence

This is the ultimate award for the prefix DXer. The requirements are 1000 prefixes Mixed mode, 600 prefixes SSB, 600 prefixes CW, all 6 continental endorsements, and the 5 band endorsements 80–10 meters. A special 160 meter endorsement bar is also available.

The WPX Award of Excellence plaque fee is $60.00. The 160 meter bar is $5.25.

Only plaque holders will be listed in the WPX program in *CQ* magazine.

WORKED ALL CONTINENTS (WAC) AWARD RULES

In recognition of international two-way amateur radio communication, the International Amateur Radio Union (IARU) issues Worked-All-Continents certificates to amateur radio stations of the world.

Qualification for the WAC award is based on an examination by the International Secretariat, or a member-society, of the IARU of QSL cards that the applicant has received from other amateur stations in each of the six continental areas of the world. All contacts must be made from the same country or separate territory within the same continental area of the world. All QSL cards (no photocopies) must show the mode and/or band for any endorsement applied for.

Contacts made on 10/18/24 MHz or via satellites are void for the 5-band certificate and 6-band sticker. All contacts for the QRP sticker must be made on or after January 1, 1985 while running a maximum power of 5 watts output or 10 watts input.

The following information should be helpful in determining the continental area of a station located adjacent to a continental boundary. North America includes Greenland (OX) and Panama (HP). South America includes Trinidad & Tobago (9Y), Aruba (P4), Curacao & Bonaire (PJ2-4) and Easter Island (CEØ). Oceania includes Minami Tori-shima (JD1), Philippines (DU), East Malaysia (9M6-8) and Indonesia (YB). Asia includes Ogasawara Islands (JD1), Maldives (8Q), Socotra Island (7O), Abu Ail Island (J2/A), Cyprus (5B, ZC4), Eastern Turkey (TA2-8) and Georgia

(UF). Europe includes the fourth and sixth call areas of RSFSR (UA4-6), Istanbul (TA1), all Italian islands(I) and Azores (CU). Africa includes Ceuta & Melilla (EA9), Madeira (CT3), Gan Island (VS9M), French Austral Territory (FT) and Heard Island (VKØ).

For amateurs in the United States or countries without IARU representation, applications should be directed to the below address. After verification, the cards will be returned and the award sent soon afterward. There is no application fee. However, sufficient return postage for the cards, in the form of a self-addressed stamped enveloped, or IRCs, is required. US amateurs must have current ARRL membership.

(For other amateurs)—Applicants must be members of their national amateur radio societies affiliated with IARU, apply through the society.

International Amateur Radio Union, P.O. Box AAA, Newington, CT 06111, U.S.A.

CQ USA-CA AWARD PROGRAM

The United States of America Counties Award sponsored by *CQ* is issued for confirmed two-way radio contacts with specified numbers of U.S. counties under rules and conditions hereafter stated.

A. Award Classes

The USA-CA Award is issued in seven different classes, each a separate achievement as endorsed on the basic certificate by use of special seals for higher class. Also, special endorsements are made for all one band or mode operations subject to the rules.

Class	Counties Required	States Required
USA-500	500	any
USA-1000	1000	25
USA-1500	1500	45
USA-2000	2000	50
USA-2500	2500	50
USA-3000	3000	50

USA 3076-CA for ALL counties and Special Honors Plaque $50.00

B. Conditions

1. USA-CA is available to all licensed amateurs everywhere in the world and is issued to them as individuals for all county contacts made, regardless of calls held, operating QTHs, or dates.

Special USA-CA Awards are also available to SWLs on a heard basis.

2. All contacts must be confirmed by QSL, and such QSLs must be in the applicant's possession for identification by certification officials.

3. Any QSL card found to be altered in any way disqualifies the applicant.

4. QSOs via repeaters, satellites, moon bounce, and phone patches are **not** valid for USA-CA.

5. So-called "team" contacts, wherein one person acknowledges a signal report and another returns a signal report, while both amateur callsigns are logged, are **not** valid for USA-CA. Acceptable contact may be made with only one station at a time.

C. County Identity

1. Unless otherwise indicated on QSL cards, the QTH printed on cards will determine county identity.

2. The National Zip Code & Directory of Post Offices will be helpful in some cases in determining the identity of counties of contact as ascertained by name or nearest municipality. Publication No. 65 is available from the Superintendent of Documents, U.S. Government Printing Office, Washington, D.C. 20402, Stock No. 039-000-00264-7, shipped one, to U.S.A. or Canada.

3. For mobile and portable operations the postmark shall identify the county unless information stated on QSL cards makes other positive identity.

4. In the case of cities, parks, or reservations not within counties proper, applicants may claim any one of the adjoining counties for credit (once).

5. QSOs via repeaters, satellites, moon bounce, and phone patches are *not* valid for USA-CA.

D. Administration of USA-CA Program

1. The USA-CA program is administered by a *CQ* staff member acting as USA-CA Custodian, and all applications and related correspondence should be sent directly to this person's QTH.

2. Decisions of the Custodian in administering these rules and their interpretation, including future amendments, are final.

E. Record Book and Bookkeeping

1. The scope of the USA-CA Award makes it mandatory that special Record Books be used for application. For this purpose, *CQ* has provided a 64-page 4 1/4" x 11" Record Book which contains application and certification forms and provides record-log space meeting the conditions of any class award and/or endorsement requested.

2. A completed USA-CA Record Book constitutes the medium of basic application and becomes the property of *CQ* for record purposes. On subsequent applications for either higher classes or for special endorsements, the applicant may use additional Record Books to list required data, or he or she may make up alphabetical lists conforming to requirements.

3. Record Books are to be obtained directly from CQ, 76 North Broadway, Hicksville, NY 11801, for $2.00 each. We recommend that two be obtained—one for application use and one for a personal file copy.

F. Application

1. Make Record Book entries necessary for county identity and enter other log data necessary to satisfy any special endorsements (band/mode) requested.

2. Have the certification form provided signed by two licensed amateurs (General Class or higher) or an official of a national-level radio organization or affiliated club verifying that QSL cards for all contacts as listed have been seen. The USA-CA Custodian reserves the right to request any specific cards to satisfy any doubt whatsoever. In such cases the applicant should send sufficient postage for the return of cards by registered mail.

3. Send the *original* completed Record Book (*not* a copy) and certification forms and handling fee. Fee for *CQ* subscribers is $4.00 or 12 IRCs (subscribers must include a recent *CQ* mailing label), and for non-subscribers it is $10.00 or 40 IRCs. Send to Norm Van Raay, WA3RTY, Box 76, Pleasant Mount, PA 18453-0076. For later applications for higher class seals, send Record Book or self-prepared list per rules and $1.25 or 6 IRCs handling charge. For application for later special endorsements (band/mode) where certificates must be returned for endorsement, send certificate and $1.50 or 8 IRCs for handling charges. *Note:* At the time any USA-CA Award certificate is being processed, there are no charges other than the basic fee, regardless of the number of endorsements or seals; likewise, one may skip lower classes of USA-CA and get higher classes without losing any lower awards credits or paying any fee for them. *Also note:* IRCs are *not* accepted from U.S. stations.

UNITED STATES COUNTIES

ALASKA
First
Second
Third
Fourth

ALABAMA
Autauga
Baldwin
Barbour
Bibb
Blount
Bullock
Butler
Calhoun
Chambers
Cherokee
Chilton
Choctaw
Clarke
Clay
Cleburne
Coffee
Colbert
Conecuh
Coosa
Covington
Crenshaw
Cullman
Dale
Dallas
DeKalb
Elmore
Escambia
Etowah
Fayette
Franklin
Geneva
Greene
Hale
Henry
Houston
Jackson
Jefferson
Lamar
Lauderdale
Lawrence
Lee
Limestone
Lowndes
Macon
Madison
Marengo
Marion
Marshall
Mobile
Monroe
Montgomery
Morgan
Perry
Pickens
Pike
Randolph
Russell
SaintClair
Shelby
Sumter
Talladega
Tallapoosa

Tuscaloosa
Walker
Washington
Wilcox
Winston

ARKANSAS

Arkansas
Ashley
Baxter
Benton
Boone
Bradley
Calhoun
Carroll
Chicot
Clark
Clay
Cleburne
Cleveland
Columbia
Conway
Craighead
Crawford
Crittenden
Cross
Dallas
Desha
Drew
Faulkner
Franklin
Fulton
Garland
Grant
Greene
Hempstead
HotSpring
Howard
Independence
Izard
Jackson
Jefferson
Johnson
Lafayette
Lawrence
Lee
Lincoln
LittleRiver
Logan
Lonoke
Madison
Marion
Miller
Mississippi
Monroe
Montgomery
Nevada
Newton
Ouachita
Perry
Phillips
Pike
Poinsett
Polk
Pope
Prairie
Pulaski
Randolph
Saline
Scott
Searcy
Sebastian
Sevier
Sharp
St.Francis
Stone
Union
VanBuren
Washington
White
Woodruff
Yell

ARIZONA

Apache
Cochise
Coconino
Gila
Graham
Greenlee
LaPaz
Maricopa
Mohave
Navajo
Pima
Pinal
SantaCruz
Yavapai
Yuma

CALIFORNIA

Alameda
Alpine
Amador
Butte
Calaveras
Colusa
ContraCosta
DelNorte
ElDorado
Fresno
Glenn
Humboldt
Imperial
Inyo
Kern
Kings
Lake
Lassen
LosAngeles
Madera
Marin
Mariposa
Mendocino
Merced
Modoc
Mono
Monterey
Napa
Nevada
Orange
Placer
Plumas
Riverside
Sacramento
SanBenito
SanBernadino
SanDiego
SanFrancisco
SanJoaquin
SanLuisObispo
SanMateo
SantaBarbara
SantaClara
SantaCruz
Shasta
Sierra
Siskiyou
Solano
Sonoma
Stanislaus
Sutter
Tehama
Trinity
Tulare
Tuolumne
Ventura
Yolo
Yuba

COLORADO

Adams
Alamosa
Arapahoe
Archuleta
Baca
Bent
Boulder
Chaffee
Cheyenne
ClearCreek
Conejos
Costilla
Crowley
Custer
Delta
Denver
Dolores
Douglas
Eagle
ElPaso
Elbert
Fremont
Garfield
Gilpin
Grand
Gunnison
Hinsdale
Huerfano
Jackson
Jefferson
Kiowa
KitCarson
LaPlata
Lake
Larimer
LasAnimas
Lincoln
Logan
Mesa
Mineral
Moffat
Montezuma
Montrose
Morgan
Otero
Ouray
Park
Phillips
Pitkin
Prowers
Pueblo
RioBlanco
RioGrande
Routt
Saguache
SanJuan
SanMiguel
Sedgwick
Summit
Teller
Washington
Weld
Yuma

CONNECTICUT

Fairfield
Hartford
Litchfield
Middlesex
NewHaven
NewLondon
Tolland
Windham

DELAWARE

Kent
NewCastle
Sussex

FLORIDA

Alachua
Baker
Bay
Bradford
Brevard
Broward
Calhoun
Charlotte
Citrus
Clay
Collier
Columbia
Dade
DeSoto
Dixie
Duval
Escambia
Flagler
Franklin
Gadsden
Gilchrist
Glades
Gulf
Hamilton
Hardee
Hendry
Hernando
Highlands
Hillsborough
Holmes
IndianRiver
Jackson
Jefferson
Lafayette
Lake
Lee
Leon
Levy
Liberty
Madison
Manatee
Marion
Martin
Monroe
Nassau
Okaloosa
Okeechobee
Orange
Osceola
PalmBeach
Pasco
Pinellas
Polk
Putnam
SantaRosa
Sarasota
Seminole
St.Johns
St.Lucie
Sumter
Suwannee
Taylor
Union
Volusia
Wakulla
Walton
Washington

GEORGIA

Appling
Atkinson
Bacon
Baker
Baldwin
Banks
Barrow
Bartow
BenHill
Berrien
Bibb
Bleckley
Brantley
Brooks
Bryan
Bulloch
Burke
Butts
Calhoun
Camden
Candler
Carroll
Catoosa
Charlton
Chatham
Chattahoochee
Chattooga
Cherokee
Clarke
Clay
Clayton
Clinch
Cobb
Coffee
Colquitt
Columbia
Cook
Coweta
Crawford
Crisp
Dade
Dawson
DeKalb
Decatur
Dodge
Dooly
Dougherty
Douglas
Early
Echols
Effingham
Elbert
Emanuel
Evans
Fannin
Fayette
Floyd
Forsyth
Franklin
Fulton
Gilmer
Glascock
Glynn
Gordon
Grady
Greene
Gwinnett
Habersham
Hall
Hancock
Haralson
Harris
Hart
Heard
Henry
Houston
Irwin
Jackson
Jasper
JeffDavis
Jefferson
Jenkins
Johnson
Jones
Lamar
Lanier
Laurens
Lee
Liberty
Lincoln
Long
Lowndes
Lumpkin
Macon
Madison
Marion
McDuffie
McIntosh
Meriwether
Miller
Mitchell
Monroe
Montgomery
Morgan
Murray
Muscogee
Newton
Oconee
Oglethorpe
Paulding
Peach
Pickens
Pierce
Pike
Polk
Pulaski
Putnam
Quitman
Rabun
Randolph
Richmond
Rockdale
Schley
Screven
Seminole
Spalding
Stephens
Stewart
Sumter
Talbot
Taliaferro
Tattnall
Taylor
Telfair
Terrell
Thomas
Tift
Toombs
Towns
Treutlen
Troup
Turner
Twiggs
Union
Upson
Walker
Walton
Ware
Warren
Washington
Wayne
Webster

Wheeler
White
Whitfield
Wilcox
Wilkes
Wilkinson
Worth

HAWAII
Hawaii
Honolulu
Kalawao
Kauai
Maui

IOWA
Adair
Adams
Allamakee
Appanoose
Audubon
Benton
BlackHawk
Boone
Bremer
Buchanan
BuenaVista
Butler
Calhoun
Carroll
Cass
Cedar
CerroGordo
Cherokee
Chickasaw
Clarke
Clay
Clayton
Clinton
Crawford
Dallas
Davis
Decatur
Delaware
DesMoines
Dickinson
Dubuque
Emmet
Fayette
Floyd
Franklin
Fremont
Greene
Grundy
Guthrie
Hamilton
Hancock
Hardin
Harrison
Henry
Howard
Humboldt
Ida
Iowa
Jackson
Jasper
Jefferson
Johnson
Jones
Keokuk
Kossuth
Lee
Linn
Louisa
Lucas
Lyon
Madison
Mahaska
Marion
Marshall
Mills
Mitchell
Monona
Monroe
Montgomery
Muscatine
O'Brien
Osceola
Page
PaloAlto
Plymouth
Pocahontas
Polk
Pottawattamie
Poweshiek
Ringgold
Sac
Scott
Shelby
Sioux
Story
Tama
Taylor
Union
VanBuren
Wapello
Warren
Washington
Wayne
Webster
Winnebago
Winneshiek
Woodbury
Worth
Wright

IDAHO
Ada
Adams
Bannock
BearLake
Benewah
Bingham
Blaine
Boise
Bonner
Bonneville
Boundary
Butte
Camas
Canyon
Caribou
Cassia
Clark
Clearwater
Custer
Elmore
Franklin
Fremont
Gem
Gooding
Idaho
Jefferson
Jerome
Kootenai
Latah
Lemhi
Lewis
Lincoln
Madison
Minidoka
NezPerce
Oneida
Owyhee
Payette
Power
Shoshone
Teton
TwinFalls
Valley
Washington

ILLINOIS
Adams
Alexander
Bond
Boone
Brown
Bureau
Calhoun
Carroll
Cass
Champaign
Christian
Clark
Clay
Clinton
Coles
Cook
Crawford
Cumberland
DeKalb
DeWitt
Douglas
DuPage
Edgar
Edwards
Effingham
Fayette
Ford
Franklin
Fulton
Gallatin
Greene
Grundy
Hamilton
Hancock
Hardin
Henderson
Henry
Iroquois
Jackson
Jasper
Jefferson
Jersey
JoDaviess
Johnson
Kane
Kankakee
Kendall
Knox
LaSalle
Lake
Lawrence
Lee
Livingston
Logan
Macon
Macoupin
Madison
Marion
Marshall
Mason
Massac
McDonough
McHenry
McLean
Menard
Mercer
Monroe
Montgomery
Morgan
Moultrie
Ogle
Peoria
Perry
Piatt
Pike
Pope
Pulaski
Putnam
Randolph
Richland
RockIsland
Saline
Sangamon
Schuyler
Scott
Shelby
St.Clair
Stark
Stephenson
Tazewell
Union
Vermilion
Wabash
Warren
Washington
Wayne
White
Whiteside
Will
Williamson
Winnebago
Woodford

INDIANA
Adams
Allen
Bartholomew
Benton
Blackford
Boone
Brown
Carroll
Cass
Clark
Clay
Clinton
Crawford
Daviess
DeKalb
Dearborn
Decatur
Delaware
Dubois
Elkhart
Fayette
Floyd
Fountain
Franklin
Fulton
Gibson
Grant
Greene
Hamilton
Hancock
Harrison
Hendricks
Henry
Howard
Huntington
Jackson
Jasper
Jay
Jefferson
Jennings
Johnson
Knox
Kosciusko
LaPorte
Lagrange
Lake
Lawrence
Madison
Marion
Marshall
Martin
Miami
Monroe
Montgomery
Morgan
Newton
Noble
Ohio
Orange
Owen
Parke
Perry
Pike
Porter
Posey
Pulaski
Putnam
Randolph
Ripley
Rush
Scott
Shelby
Spencer
St.Joseph
Starke
Steuben
Sullivan
Switzerland
Tippecanoe
Tipton
Union
Vanderburgh
Vermillion
Vigo
Wabash
Warren
Warrick
Washington
Wayne
Wells
White
Whitley

KANSAS
Allen
Anderson
Atchison
Barber
Barton
Bourbon
Brown
Butler
Chase
Chautauqua
Cherokee
Cheyenne
Clark
Clay
Cloud
Coffey
Comanche
Cowley
Crawford
Decatur
Dickinson
Doniphan
Douglas
Edwards
Elk
Ellis
Ellsworth
Finney
Ford
Franklin
Geary
Gove
Graham
Grant
Gray
Greeley
Greenwood
Hamilton
Harper
Harvey
Haskell
Hodgeman
Jackson
Jefferson
Jewell
Johnson
Kearny
Kingman
Kiowa
Labette
Lane
Leavenworth
Lincoln
Linn
Logan
Lyon
Marion
Marshall
McPherson
Meade
Miami
Mitchell
Montgomery
Morris
Morton
Nemaha
Neosho
Ness
Norton
Osage
Osborne
Ottawa
Pawnee
Phillips
Pottawatomie
Pratt
Rawlins
Reno
Republic
Rice
Riley
Rooks
Rush
Russell
Saline
Scott
Sedgwick
Seward
Shawnee
Sheridan
Sherman
Smith
Stafford
Stanton
Stevens
Sumner
Thomas
Trego
Wabaunsee
Wallace
Washington

Wichita
Wilson
Woodson
Wyandotte

KENTUCKY
Adair
Allen
Anderson
Ballard
Barren
Bath
Bell
Boone
Bourbon
Boyd
Boyle
Bracken
Breathitt
Breckenridge
Bullitt
Butler
Caldwell
Calloway
Campbell
Carlisle
Carroll
Carter
Casey
Christian
Clark
Clay
Clinton
Crittenden
Cumberland
Daviess
Edmonson
Elliott
Estill
Fayette
Fleming
Floyd
Franklin
Fulton
Gallatin
Garrard
Grant
Graves
Grayson
Green
Greenup
Hancock
Hardin
Harlan
Harrison
Hart
Henderson
Henry
Hickman
Hopkins
Jackson
Jefferson
Jessamine
Johnson
Kenton
Knott
Knox
Larue
Laurel
Lawrence
Lee
Leslie
Letcher
Lewis
Lincoln
Livingston
Logan
Lyon
Madison
Magoffin
Marion
Marshall
Martin
Mason
McCracken
McCreary
McLean
Meade
Menifee
Mercer
Metcalfe
Monroe
Montgomery
Morgan
Muhlenberg
Nelson
Nicholas
Ohio
Oldham
Owen
Owsley
Pendleton
Perry
Pike
Powell
Pulaski
Robertson
Rockcastle
Rowan
Russell
Scott
Shelby
Simpson
Spencer
Taylor
Todd
Trigg
Trimble
Union
Warren
Washington
Wayne
Webster
Whitley
Wolfe
Woodford

LOUISIANA
Acadia
Allen
Ascension
Assumption
Avoyelles
Beauregard
Bienville
Bossier
Caddo
Calcasieu
Caldwell
Cameron
Catahoula
Claiborne
Concordia
DeSoto
E.BatonRouge
EastCarroll
EastFeliciana
Evangeline
Franklin
Grant
Iberia
Iberville
Jackson
Jefferson
JeffersonDavis
LaSalle
Lafayette
Lafourche
Lincoln
Livingston
Madison
Morehouse
Natchitoches
Orleans
Ouachita
Plaquemines
PointeCoupee
Rapides
RedRiver
Richland
Sabine
St.Bernard
St.Charles
St.Helena
St.James
St.JohntheBts
St.Landry
St.Martin
St.Mary
St.Tammany
Tangipahoa
Tensas
Terrebonne
Union
Vermilion
Vernon
W.BatonRouge
Washington
Webster
WestCarroll
WestFeliciana
Winn

MASSACHUSETTS
Barnstable
Berkshire
Bristol
Dukes
Essex
Franklin
Hampden
Hampshire
Middlesex
Nantucket
Norfolk
Plymouth
Suffolk
Worcester

MARYLAND
Allegany
AnneArundel
Baltimore
BaltimoreCity
Calvert
Caroline
Carroll
Cecil
Charles
Dorchester
Frederick
Garrett
Harford
Howard
Kent
Montgomery
PrinceGeorges
QueenAnnes
Somerset
St.Marys
Talbot
Washington
Wicomico
Worcester

MAINE
Androscoggin
Aroostook
Cumberland
Franklin
Hancock
Kennebec
Knox
Lincoln
Oxford
Penobscot
Piscataquis
Sagadahoc
Somerset
Waldo
Washington
York

MICHIGAN
Alcona
Alger
Allegan
Alpena
Antrim
Arenac
Baraga
Barry
Bay
Benzie
Berrien
Branch
Calhoun
Cass
Charlevoix
Cheboygan
Chippewa
Clare
Clinton
Crawford
Delta
Dickinson
Eaton
Emmet
Genesee
Gladwin
Gogebic
GrandTraverse
Gratiot
Hillsdale
Houghton
Huron
Ingham
Ionia
Iosco
Iron
Isabella
Jackson
Kalamazoo
Kalkaska
Kent
Keweenaw
Lake
Lapeer
Leelanau
Lenawee
Livingston
Luce
Mackinac
Macomb
Manistee
Marquette
Mason
Mecosta
Menominee
Midland
Missaukee
Monroe
Montcalm
Montmorency
Muskegon
Newaygo
Oakland
Oceana
Ogemaw
Ontonagon
Osceola
Oscoda
Otsego
Ottawa
PresqueIsle
Roscommon
Saginaw
Sanilac
Schoolcraft
Shiawassee
St.Clair
St.Joseph
Tuscola
VanBuren
Washtenaw
Wayne
Wexford

MINNESOTA
Aitkin
Anoka
Becker
Beltrami
Benton
BigStone
BlueEarth
Brown
Carlton
Carver
Cass
Chippewa
Chisago
Clay
Clearwater
Cook
Cottonwood
CrowWing
Dakota
Dodge
Douglas
Faribault
Fillmore
Freeborn
Goodhue
Grant
Hennepin
Houston
Hubbard
Isanti
Itasca
Jackson
Kanabec
Kandiyohi
Kittson
Koochiching
L.oftheWoods
LacQuiParle
Lake
LeSueur
Lincoln
Lyon
Mahnomen
Marshall
Martin
McLeod
Meeker
MilleLacs
Morrison
Mower
Murray
Nicollet
Nobles
Norman
Olmsted
OtterTail
Pennington
Pine
Pipestone
Polk
Pope
Ramsey
RedLake
Redwood
Renville
Rice
Rock
Roseau
Scott
Sherburne
Sibley
St.Louis
Stearns
Steele
Stevens
Swift
Todd
Traverse
Wabasha
Wadena
Waseca
Washington
Watonwan
Wilkin
Winona
Wright
YellowMedicine

MISSOURI
Adair
Andrew
Atchison
Audrain
Barry
Barton
Bates
Benton
Bollinger
Boone
Buchanan
Butler
Caldwell
Callaway
Camden
CapeGirardeau
Carroll
Carter
Cass
Cedar
Chariton
Christian
Clark
Clay
Clinton
Cole
Cooper
Crawford
Dade
Dallas
Daviess
DeKalb
Dent
Douglas

Dunklin
Franklin
Gasconade
Gentry
Greene
Grundy
Harrison
Henry
Hickory
Holt
Howard
Howell
Iron
Jackson
Jasper
Jefferson
Johnson
Knox
Laclede
Lafayette
Lawrence
Lewis
Lincoln
Linn
Livingston
Macon
Madison
Maries
Marion
McDonald
Mercer
Miller
Mississippi
Moniteau
Monroe
Montgomery
Morgan
NewMadrid
Newton
Nodaway
Oregon
Osage
Ozark
Pemiscot
Perry
Pettis
Phelps
Pike
Platte
Polk
Pulaski
Putnam
Ralls
Randolph
Ray
Reynolds
Ripley
Saline
Schuyler
Scotland
Scott
Shannon
Shelby
St.Charles
St.Clair
St.Francois
St.Louis
St.LouisCity
Ste.Genevieve
Stoddard
Stone
Sullivan
Taney
Texas
Vernon
Warren
Washington
Wayne
Webster
Worth
Wright

MISSISSIPPI

Adams
Alcorn
Amite
Attala
Benton
Bolivar
Calhoun
Carroll
Chickasaw
Choctaw
Claiborne
Clarke
Clay
Coahoma
Copiah
Covington
DeSoto
Forrest
Franklin
George
Greene
Grenada
Hancock
Harrison
Hinds
Holmes
Humphreys
Issaquena
Itawamba
Jackson
Jasper
Jefferson
JeffersonDavis
Jones
Kemper
Lafayette
Lamar
Lauderdale
Lawrence
Leake
Lee
Leflore
Lincoln
Lowndes
Madison
Marion
Marshall
Monroe
Montgomery
Neshoba
Newton
Noxubee
Oktibbeha
Panola
PearlRiver
Perry
Pike
Pontotoc
Prentiss
Quitman
Rankin
Scott
Sharkey
Simpson
Smith
Stone
Sunflower
Tallahatchie
Tate
Tippah
Tishomingo
Tunica
Union
Walthall
Warren
Washington
Wayne
Webster
Wilkinson
Winston
Yalobusha
Yazoo

MONTANA

Beaverhead
BigHorn
Blaine
Broadwater
Carbon
Carter
Cascade
Chouteau
Custer
Daniels
Dawson
DeerLodge
Fallon
Fergus
Flathead
Gallatin
Garfield
Glacier
GoldenValley
Granite
Hill
Jefferson
JudithBasin
Lake
LewisandClark
Liberty
Lincoln
Madison
McCone
Meagher
Mineral
Missoula
Musselshell
Park
Petroleum
Phillips
Pondera
PowderRiver
Powell
Prairie
Ravalli
Richland
Roosevelt
Rosebud
Sanders
Sheridan
SilverBow
Stillwater
SweetGrass
Teton
Toole
Treasure
Valley
Wheatland
Wibaux
Yellowstone

NORTH CAROLINA

Alamance
Alexander
Alleghany
Anson
Ashe
Avery
Beaufort
Bertie
Bladen
Brunswick
Buncombe
Burke
Cabarrus
Caldwell
Camden
Carteret
Caswell
Catawba
Chatham
Cherokee
Chowan
Clay
Cleveland
Columbus
Craven
Cumberland
Currituck
Dare
Davidson
Davie
Duplin
Durham
Edgecombe
Forsyth
Franklin
Gaston
Gates
Graham
Granville
Greene
Guilford
Halifax
Harnett
Haywood
Henderson
Hertford
Hoke
Hyde
Iredell
Jackson
Johnston
Jones
Lee
Lenoir
Lincoln
Macon
Madison
Martin
McDowell
Mecklenburg
Mitchell
Montgomery
Moore
Nash
NewHanover
Northampton
Onslow
Orange
Pamlico
Pasquotank
Pender
Perquimans
Person
Pitt
Polk
Randolph
Richmond
Robeson
Rockingham
Rowan
Rutherford
Sampson
Scotland
Stanly
Stokes
Surry
Swain
Transylvania
Tyrrell
Union
Vance
Wake
Warren
Washington
Watauga
Wayne
Wilkes
Wilson
Yadkin
Yancy

NORTH DAKOTA

Adams
Barnes
Benson
Billings
Bottineau
Bowman
Burke
Burleigh
Cass
Cavalier
Dickey
Divide
Dunn
Eddy
Emmons
Foster
GoldenValley
GrandForks
Grant
Griggs
Hettinger
Kidder
LaMoure
Logan
McHenry
McIntosh
McKenzie
McLean
Mercer
Morton
Mountrail
Nelson
Oliver
Pembina
Pierce
Ramsey
Ransom
Renville
Richland
Rolette
Sargent
Sheridan
Sioux
Slope
Stark
Steele
Stutsman
Towner
Traill
Walsh
Ward
Wells
Williams

NEBRASKA

Adams
Antelope
Arthur
Banner
Blaine
Boone
BoxButte
Boyd
Brown
Buffalo
Burt
Butler
Cass
Cedar
Chase
Cherry
Cheyenne
Clay
Colfax
Cuming
Custer
Dakota
Dawes
Dawson
Deuel
Dixon
Dodge
Douglas
Dundy
Fillmore
Franklin
Frontier
Furnas
Gage
Garden
Garfield
Gosper
Grant
Greeley
Hall
Hamilton
Harlan
Hayes
Hitchcock
Holt
Hooker
Howard
Jefferson
Johnson
Kearney
Keith
KeyaPaha
Kimball
Knox
Lancaster
Lincoln
Logan
Loup
Madison
McPherson
Merrick
Morrill
Nance
Nemaha
Nuckolls
Otoe
Pawnee
Perkins
Phelps
Pierce
Platte
Polk
RedWillow
Richardson
Rock
Saline
Sarpy
Saunders

ScottsBluff
Seward
Sheridan
Sherman
Sioux
Stanton
Thayer
Thomas
Thurston
Valley
Washington
Wayne
Webster
Wheeler
York

NEW HAMPSHIRE

Belknap
Carroll
Cheshire
Coos
Grafton
Hillsboro
Merrimack
Rockingham
Strafford
Sullivan

NEW JERSEY

Atlantic
Bergen
Burlington
Camden
CapeMay
Cumberland
Essex
Gloucester
Hudson
Hunterdon
Mercer
Middlesex
Monmouth
Morris
Ocean
Passaic
Salem
Somerset
Sussex
Union
Warren

NEW MEXICO

Bernalillo
Catron
Chaves
Cibola
Colfax
Curry
DeBaca
DonaAna
Eddy
Grant
Guadalupe
Harding
Hidalgo
Lea
Lincoln
LosAlamos
Luna
McKinley
Mora
Otero
Quay
RioArriba
Roosevelt
SanJuan
SanMiguel
Sandoval
SantaFe
Sierra
Socorro
Taos
Torrance
Union
Valencia

NEVADA

Churchill
Clark
Douglas
Elko
Esmeralda
Eureka
Humboldt
Lander
Lincoln
Lyon
Mineral
Nye
Pershing
Storey
Washoe
WhitePine

NEW YORK

Albany
Allegany
Bronx
Broome
Cattaraugus
Cayuga
Chautauqua
Chemung
Chenango
Clinton
Columbia
Cortland
Delaware
Dutchess
Erie
Essex
Franklin
Fulton
Genesee
Greene
Hamilton
Herkimer
Jefferson
Kings
Lewis
Livingston
Madison
Monroe
Montgomery
Nassau
NewYork
Niagara
Oneida
Onondaga
Ontario
Orange
Orleans
Oswego
Otsego
Putnam
Queens
Rensselaer
Rockland
Saratoga
Schenectady
Schoharie
Schuyler
Seneca
St.Lawrence
StatenIsland
Steuben
Suffolk
Sullivan
Tioga
Tompkins
Ulster
Warren
Washington
Wayne
Westchester
Wyoming
Yates

OHIO

Adams
Allen
Ashland
Ashtabula
Athens
Auglaize
Belmont
Brown
Butler
Carroll
Champaign
Clark
Clermont
Clinton
Columbiana
Coshocton
Crawford
Cuyahoga
Darke
Defiance
Delaware
Erie
Fairfield
Fayette
Franklin
Fulton
Gallia
Geauga
Greene
Guernsey
Hamilton
Hancock
Hardin
Harrison
Henry
Highland
Hocking
Holmes
Huron
Jackson
Jefferson
Knox
Lake
Lawrence
Licking
Logan
Lorain
Lucas
Madison
Mahoning
Marion
Medina
Meigs
Mercer
Miami
Monroe
Montgomery
Morgan
Morrow
Muskingum
Noble
Ottawa
Paulding
Perry
Pickaway
Pike
Portage
Preble
Putnam
Richland
Ross
Sandusky
Scioto
Seneca
Shelby
Stark
Summit
Trumbull
Tuscarawas
Union
VanWert
Vinton
Warren
Washington
Wayne
Williams
Wood
Wyandot

OKLAHOMA

Adair
Alfalfa
Atoka
Beaver
Beckham
Blaine
Bryan
Caddo
Canadian
Carter
Cherokee
Choctaw
Cimarron
Cleveland
Coal
Comanche
Cotton
Craig
Creek
Custer
Delaware
Dewey
Ellis
Garfield
Garvin
Grady
Grant
Greer
Harmon
Harper
Haskell
Hughes
Jackson
Jefferson
Johnston
Kay
Kingfisher
Kiowa
Latimer
LeFlore
Lincoln
Logan
Love
Major
Marshall
Mayes
McClain
McCurtain
McIntosh
Murray
Muskogee
Noble
Nowata
Okfuskee
Oklahoma
Okmulgee
Osage
Ottawa
Pawnee
Payne
Pittsburg
Pontotoc
Pottawatomie
Pushmataha
RogerMills
Rogers
Seminole
Sequoyah
Stephens
Texas
Tillman
Tulsa
Wagoner
Washington
Washita
Woods
Woodward

OREGON

Baker
Benton
Clackamas
Clatsop
Columbia
Coos
Crook
Curry
Deschutes
Douglas
Gilliam
Grant
Harney
HoodRiver
Jackson
Jefferson
Josephine
Klamath
Lake
Lane
Lincoln
Linn
Malheur
Marion
Morrow
Multnomah
Polk
Sherman
Tillamook
Umatilla
Union
Wallowa
Wasco
Washington
Wheeler
Yamhill

PENNSYLVANIA

Adams
Allegheny
Armstrong
Beaver
Bedford
Berks
Blair
Bradford
Bucks
Butler
Cambria
Cameron
Carbon
Centre
Chester
Clarion
Clearfield
Clinton
Columbia
Crawford
Cumberland
Dauphin
Delaware
Elk
Erie
Fayette
Forest
Franklin
Fulton
Greene
Huntingdon
Indiana
Jefferson
Juniata
Lackawanna
Lancaster
Lawrence
Lebanon
Lehigh
Luzerne
Lycoming
McKean
Mercer
Mifflin
Monroe
Montgomery
Montour
Northampton
Northumberland
Perry
Philadelphia
Pike
Potter
Schuylkill
Snyder
Somerset
Sullivan
Susquehanna
Tioga
Union
Venango
Warren
Washington
Wayne
Westmoreland
Wyoming
York

RHODE ISLAND

Bristol
Kent
Newport
Providence
Washington

SOUTH CAROLINA

Abbeville
Aiken
Allendale
Anderson
Bamberg
Barnwell
Beaufort

Berkeley
Calhoun
Charleston
Cherokee
Chester
Chesterfield
Clarendon
Colleton
Darlington
Dillon
Dorchester
Edgefield
Fairfield
Florence
Georgetown
Greenville
Greenwood
Hampton
Horry
Jasper
Kershaw
Lancaster
Laurens
Lee
Lexington
Marion
Marlboro
McCormick
Newberry
Oconee
Orangeburg
Pickens
Richland
Saluda
Spartanburg
Sumter
Union
Williamsburg
York

SOUTH DAKOTA

Aurora
Beadle
Bennett
BonHomme
Brookings
Brown
Brule
Buffalo
Butte
Campbell
CharlesMix
Clark
Clay
Codington
Corson
Custer
Davison
Day
Deuel
Dewey
Douglas
Edmunds
FallRiver
Faulk
Grant
Gregory
Haakon
Hamlin
Hand
Hanson
Harding
Hughes
Hutchinson
Hyde
Jackson
Jerauld
Jones
Kingsbury
Lake
Lawrence
Lincoln
Lyman
Marshall
McCook
McPherson
Meade
Mellette
Miner
Minnehaha
Moody
Pennington
Perkins
Potter
Roberts
Sanborn
Shannon
Spink
Stanley
Sully
Todd
Tripp
Turner
Union
Walworth
Yankton
Ziebach

TENNESSEE

Anderson
Bedford
Benton
Bledsoe
Blount
Bradley
Tampbell
Tannon
Tarroll
Tarter
Theatham
Thester
Tlaiborne
Tlay
Tocke
Toffee
Trockett
Tumberland
Davidson
DeKalb
Decatur
Dickson
Dyer
Fayette
Fentress
Franklin
Gibson
Giles
Grainger
Greene
Grundy
Hamblen
Hamilton
Hancock
Hardeman
Hardin
Hawkins
Haywood
Henderson
Henry
Hickman
Houston
Humphreys
Jackson
Jefferson
Johnson
Knox
Lake
Lauderdale
Lawrence
Lewis
Lincoln
Loudon
Macon
Madison
Marion
Marshall
Maury
McMinn
McNairy
Meigs
Monroe
Montgomery
Moore
Morgan
Obion
Overton
Perry
Pickett
Polk
Putnam
Rhea
Roane
Robertson
Rutherford
Scott
Sequatchie
Sevier
Shelby
Smith
Stewart
Sullivan
Sumner
Tipton
Trousdale
Unicoi
Union
VanBuren
Warren
Washington
Wayne
Weakley
White
Williamson
Wilson

TEXAS

Anderson
Andrews
Angelina
Aransas
Archer
Armstrong
Atascosa
Austin
Bailey
Bandera
Bastrop
Baylor
Bee
Bell
Bexar
Blanco
Borden
Bosque
Bowie
Brazoria
Brazos
Brewster
Briscoe
Brooks
Brown
Burleson
Burnet
Caldwell
Calhoun
Callahan
Cameron
Camp
Carson
Cass
Castro
Chambers
Cherokee
Childress
Clay
Cochran
Coke
Coleman
Collin
Collingsworth
Colorado
Comal
Comanche
Concho
Cooke
Coryell
Cottle
Crane
Crockett
Crosby
Culberson
Dallam
Dallas
Dawson
DeWitt
DeafSmith
Delta
Denton
Dickens
Dimmit
Donley
Duval
Eastland
Ector
Edwards
ElPaso
Ellis
Erath
Falls
Fannin
Fayette
Fisher
Floyd
Foard
FortBend
Franklin
Freestone
Frio
Gaines
Galveston
Garza
Gillespie
Glasscock
Goliad
Gonzales
Gray
Grayson
Gregg
Grimes
Guadalupe
Hale
Hall
Hamilton
Hansford
Hardeman
Hardin
Harris
Harrison
Hartley
Haskell
Hays
Hemphill
Henderson
Hidalgo
Hill
Hockley
Hood
Hopkins
Houston
Howard
Hudspeth
Hunt
Hutchinson
Irion
Jack
Jackson
Jasper
JeffDavis
Jefferson
JimHogg
JimWells
Johnson
Jones
Karnes
Kaufman
Kendall
Kenedy
Kent
Kerr
Kimble
King
Kinney
Kleberg
Knox
LaSalle
Lamar
Lamb
Lampasas
Lavaca
Lee
Leon
Liberty
Limestone
Lipscomb
LiveOak
Llano
Loving
Lubbock
Lynn
Madison
Marion
Martin
Mason
Matagorda
Maverick
McCulloch
McLennan
McMullen
Medina
Menard
Midland
Milam
Mills
Mitchell
Montague
Montgomery
Moore
Morris
Motley
Nacogdoches
Navarro
Newton
Nolan
Nueces
Ochiltree
Oldham
Orange
PaloPinto
Panola
Parker
Parmer
Pecos
Polk
Potter
Presidio
Rains
Randall
Reagan
Real
RedRiver
Reeves
Refugio
Roberts
Robertson
Rockwall
Runnels
Rusk
Sabine
SanAugustine
SanJacinto
SanPatricio
SanSaba
Schleicher
Scurry
Shackelford
Shelby
Sherman
Smith
Somervell
Starr
Stephens
Sterling
Stonewall
Sutton
Swisher
Tarrant
Taylor
Terrell
Terry
Throckmorton
Titus
TomGreen
Travis
Trinity
Tyler
Upshur
Upton
Uvalde
ValVerde
VanZandt
Victoria
Walker
Waller
Ward
Washington
Webb
Wharton
Wheeler
Wichita
Wilbarger
Willacy
Williamson
Wilson
Winkler
Wise
Wood
Yoakum
Young
Zapata
Zavala

UTAH
Beaver
BoxElder
Cache
Carbon
Daggett
Davis
Duchesne
Emery
Garfield
Grand
Iron
Juab
Kane
Millard
Morgan
Piute
Rich
SaltLake
SanJuan
Sanpete
Sevier
Summit
Tooele
Uintah
Utah
Wasatch
Washington
Wayne
Weber

VIRGINIA
Accomack
Albemarle
Alleghany
Amelia
Amherst
Appomattox
Arlington
Augusta
Bath
Bedford
Bland
Botetourt
Brunswick
Buchanan
Buckingham
Campbell
Caroline
Carroll
CharlesCity
Charlotte
Chesterfield
Clarke
Craig
Culpeper
Cumberland
Dickenson
Dinwiddie
Essex
Fairfax
Fauquier
Floyd
Fluvanna
Franklin
Frederick
Giles
Gloucester
Goochland
Grayson
Greene
Greensville
Halifax
Hanover
Henrico
Henry
Highland
IsleofWight
JamesCity
KingandQueen
KingGeorge
KingWilliam
Lancaster
Lee
Loudoun
Louisa
Lunenburg
Madison
Mathews
Mecklenburg
Middlesex
Montgomery
Nelson
NewKent
Northampton
Northumberland
Nottoway
Orange
Page
Patrick
Pittsylvania
Powhatan
PrinceEdward
PrinceGeorge
PrinceWilliam
Pulaski
Rappahannock
Richmond
Roanoke
Rockbridge
Rockingham
Russell
Scott
Shenandoah
Smyth
Southampton
Spotsylvania
Stafford
Surry
Sussex
Tazewell
Warren
Washington
Westmoreland
Wise
Wythe
York

VERMONT
Addison
Bennington
Caledonia
Chittendon
Essex
Franklin
GrandIsle
Lamoille
Orange
Orleans
Rutland
Washington
Windham
Windsor

WASHINGTON
Adams
Asotin
Benton
Chelan
Clallam
Clark
Columbia
Cowlitz
Douglas
Ferry
Franklin
Garfield
Grant
GraysHarbor
Island
Jefferson
King
Kitsap
Kittitas
Klickitat
Lewis
Lincoln
Mason
Okanogan
Pacific
PendOreille
Pierce
SanJuan
Skagit
Skamania
Snohomish
Spokane
Stevens
Thurston
Wahkiakum
WallaWalla
Whatcom
Whitman
Yakima

WISCONSiN
Adams
Ashland
Barron
Bayfield
Brown
Buffalo
Burnett
Calumet
Chippewa
Clark
Columbia
Crawford
Dane
Dodge
Door
Douglas
Dunn
EauClaire
Florence
FondduLac
Forest
Grant
Green
GreenLake
Iowa
Iron
Jackson
Jefferson
Juneau
Kenosha
Kewaunee
LaCrosse
Lafayette
Langlade
Lincoln
Manitowoc
Marathon
Marinette
Marquette
Menominee
Milwaukee
Monroe
Oconto
Oneida
Outagamie
Ozaukee
Pepin
Pierce
Polk
Portage
Price
Racine
Richland
Rock
Rusk
Sauk
Sawyer
Shawano
Sheboygan
St.Croix
Taylor
Trempealeau
Vernon
Vilas
Walworth
Washburn
Washington
Waukesha
Waupaca
Waushara
Winnebago
Wood

WEST VIRGINIA
Barbour
Berkeley
Boone
Braxton
Brooke
Cabell
Calhoun
Clay
Doddridge
Fayette
Gilmer
Grant
Greenbrier
Hampshire
Hancock
Hardy
Harrison
Jackson
Jefferson
Kanawha
Lewis
Lincoln
Logan
Marion
Marshall
Mason
McDowell
Mercer
Mineral
Mingo
Monongalia
Monroe
Morgan
Nicholas
Ohio
Pendleton
Pleasants
Pocahontas
Preston
Putnam
Raleigh
Randolph
Ritchie
Roane
Summers
Taylor
Tucker
Tyler
Upshur
Wayne
Webster
Wetzel
Wirt
Wood
Wyoming

WYOMING
Albany
BigHorn
Campbell
Carbon
Converse
Crook
Fremont
Goshen
HotSprings
Johnson
Laramie
Lincoln
Natrona
Niobrara
Park
Platte
Sheridan
Sublette
Sweetwater
Teton
Uinta
Washakie
Weston

List Courtesy of N6OQZ

HOLDERS OF THE CQ USA-CA WORKED ALL U.S.A. COUNTIES AWARD (All 3076 Counties)

Number	Callsign	Number	Callsign	Number	Callsign	Number	Callsign
1	K9EAB	14	W8UMR	29	WA7IRD	44	W7KBC
1	KFØLZ	15	N4PN	30	W4NXD	45	K5KDG
2	WØBK	16	W7KOI	31	K7WQJ	46	K4ISE
3	K8CIR	17	K1CXP	32	WØSJE	47	WA8NDL
4	W2QHH	18	K5DRF	33	NJØC	48	W4GGU
5	WØBL	19	WA4BMC	34	WB2SJQ	49	W5VD
6	WØGYM	20	K4AUL	35	W6DIX	50	K1WQU
7	K1QZV	21	WA3HGV	36	K7ZJP	51	W6JHV
8	K8IWI	22	W6HVU	37	N4XE	52	ZL1KG
9	K8KOM	23	W1EQ	38	W2OST	53	NFØN
10	NS9Y	24	K8BHG	39	W5TQE	54	K7NN
11	WAØEVO	25	W8DCD	40	N4GLV	55	WAØSBR
12	W2JWK	26	W8DCH	41	WA4YQC	56	K2OO
13	K4LSP	27	WØKZZ	42	WAØSHE	57	W4LXI
		28	W7LUQ	43	W4KA	58	K5RPC

59 W9UZC
60 W8MJG
61 WAØJRZ
62 N2BL
63 WA9FZR
64 W3JZY
65 WØAYL
66 WA1RAN
67 WAØWOB
68 WA1CXE
69 W9DRL
70 N2CW
71 WA4LMR
72 N4YY
73 N5DGQ
74 WB6CPE
75 W4HA
76 W6TCD
77 WAØLRQ
78 K3LXN
79 WAØGZA
80 W2KXL
81 K1OAZ
82 W7OK
83 VE3CBY
84 W4IZR
85 K5BTM
86 K9DCJ
87 WB4FBS
88 WDX6ETT
89 K7JWZ
90 WA4MGC
91 WB6EXT
92 W8WT
93 K8ODY
94 W3FNT
95 WB5DVT
96 WPE9ETT
97 WA9OFF
98 K8IQB
99 W6UNP
100 K8DCR
101 W4LK
102 WA4LSU
103 WB6RMZ
104 K9HRC
105 W8UOQ
106 KØAYO
107 K7SQD
108 WA3GLJ
109 W5HDK
110 W1AQE
111 K4ELK
112 K5VYT
113 W3LDD
114 K9UTI
115 W8WUT
116 WA6OTV
117 K5HKG
118 G4JZ
119 KØARS
120 N6UW
121 AC2O
122 W5VPV
123 WAØCEL
124 WA4WQG
125 KØEQY
126 W9ZD
127 W1DIT
128 WA6MAR
129 WA5YSC
130 K9QGR
131 W5UUM
132 K1QFD
133 VE7ATI
134 N7SU
135 WB5AKI
136 W9CRN
137 WA2GPT
138 GW3NWV
139 W7WVD
140 WØGV
141 W6CCM
142 K8EUX
143 VE4QZ
144 WA7GMX
145 WAØUPL
146 W7PXA
147 W8ZCV
148 W9ABM
149 WAØKQQ
150 WØGQR
151 K5JBC
152 W6QPF
153 K1IK
154 W2CUC
155 KB4IF
156 WA3TUC
157 VE4EL
158 W8CXS
159 W4JVN
160 W8RSW
161 WA9CNV
162 K8NQP
163 W1LQQ
164 KBØKS
164 WAØYJL
165 AB5C
166 W6HDV
167 WØFBB
168 KW3F
169 W5AWT
170 WA6ZUD
171 W2QKJ
172 W4YWV
173 K1UNM
174 W9CNG
175 AK4N
176 WB9DCZ
177 AE5B
178 WB6EGQ
179 WA1UVX
180 W2MCY
181 WA2WCW
182 WBØCQO
183 NI7B
184 WB5C
185 W7GHT
186 KØITP
187 K2PBU
188 W9JR
189 KØPFV
190 VE1RQ
191 N7TT
192 W2CUE
193 W4SWW
194 WB2NHP
195 WA9ZRP
196 WB4TNY
197 K7CLO
198 WAØBPE
199 WG9A
200 WØKMH
201 K4IUO
202 VE1DI
203 W5LXG
204 K2LFG
205 W2UP
206 K7LQI
207 W4SSU
208 WN5MBS
209 WB4AIL
210 W7CUJ
211 W4OWY
212 KØMT
213 WB4UPW
214 K8WXJ
215 W5FS
216 AD8W
217 WB6VRR
218 K9DZG
219 WO4L
220 WB9SPD
221 W7CB
222 WØUM
223 WA9GOH
224 VE4XN
225 WØHNV
226 KC9A
227 K1KPS
228 K3LK
229 W8NJC
230 WB9OOE
231 K5GC
232 WA9OBR
233 WØIU
234 KB5KM
235 WD4HRN
236 WØDG
237 WAØUHC
238 KK6DU
238 WA6JJC
239 N6QS
240 K7WUR
241 KC4AE
242 W9LMT
243 WA6LBO
244 W4ISF
245 NFØX
246 WB8SNO
247 WA2GLU
248 KD9Q
249 WØRP
250 K9GTQ
251 W7NXZ
252 VE3IR
253 WA6AQR
254 WB4RVW
255 WA3QVJ
256 WB9TKR
257 W1UYL
258 KD6PP
259 K2QK
260 W7DXN
261 KØDJC
262 K7TM
263 KD6HZ
264 K7GNC
265 VE3RN
266 W1FAB
267 K3GOO
268 AC2J
269 KØXT
270 N4ANV
271 WØLRH
272 W1ORV
273 K7JJ
274 K7SE
275 K5IW
276 WA4UNS
277 W5VDW
278 SM4EAC
279 KE9O
280 WA9WGJ
281 W4JUJ
282 K4ZT
283 W6NAT
284 WB2NFB
285 K2UVG
286 N9ER
287 KC7EI
288 K6RLR
289 WØDSY
290 W5VNW
291 WB4ZXP
292 WA3ZTY
293 KBØXB
294 WAØRJJ
295 W7ULC
296 W5UMD
297 W4EHN
298 WB7AYN
299 KE6RN
300 KL7MF
301 WA3ZMY
302 K9DAF
303 N2RT
304 WDØEMS
305 W2MEI
306 N7CLA
307 VE4ZX
308 WA2JFL
309 WD9BCG
310 VE3BFJ
311 K4ZA
312 WA6GQY
313 WD4HVZ
314 AH6IP
315 WB5YDH
316 W8UPH
317 W5QEM
318 KCØUJ
319 WA3UQR
320 WB9RCY
321 WA5ZDZ
322 WBØAXN
323 W4LQF
324 K6XZ
325 W4XT
326 W7LQT
327 WB7OHB
328 WB7WBZ
329 K9CSL
330 WA5DTK
331 6Y5RS
332 WA4AUL
333 NZØA
334 WA2TJL
335 W9FD
336 W9VPE
337 AC8F
338 K1NWE
339 WD8AYN
340 WB9ELH
341 WB6SRK
342 K1YRP
343 WB9YZE
344 WB5KEA
345 WW1N
346 K9EHP
347 NGØT
348 WB5UJO
349 WD7N
349 WBØGRN
350 KA5A
351 WBØMNE
352 N9ATA
353 N8BNI
354 W5RBO
355 WN4M
356 W1VJ
357 N5QQ
358 VE3GCO
358 VE3XN
359 KB7W
360 W1III
361 KC9DD
362 NØBHO

No.	Call
363	WAØYFQ
364	KDØU
365	WA2AKJ
366	WAØSGJ
367	AG9S
368	KI4W
369	K1VSJ
370	W4ARH
371	N7AKG
372	N9CHU
373	K7GTK
374	WØGOR
375	N7BKW
376	K9BX
377	K4QFK
378	N4CCJ
379	W1WHQ
380	W1SXX
381	KS5A
382	K5MOF
383	WB6ALC
384	KB7QO
385	WB6GMM
386	KKØV
387	AI5P
388	WA3HMJ
389	K5WQM
390	WBØLOU
391	KK5P
392	KM4W
393	W5PWG
394	WAØLKL
395	WB5CWI
396	WA9IWM
397	KD4PY
398	W8ILC
399	N8BLO
400	VE3BHZ
401	N8BGF
402	KU9G
403	W1JR
404	W4KFA
405	KCØMB
406	W1APU
407	KN5I
408	KD6PY
409	VE4SK
410	N7AKT
411	KF5F
412	WA3QNT
413	WD9GBH
414	WB2WZE
415	W8GZF
416	N9TN
417	ON4UN
418	NØCKN
419	W5EHY
420	VE7ATH
421	W2XQ
422	N8AIL
424	KD4DJ
425	WAØMQM
426	K7XN
427	W5QLD
428	K2HVN
429	WA6UFY
430	WØRSR
431	WDØCFZ
432	KS7T
432	WV5S
433	KKØL
434	N1GMU
434	N1GMU
435	K5CKQ
436	KX2W
437	N5BDY
438	AB4HR
439	KCØJG
440	KCØVB
441	WBØTVL
442	NØCOL
443	KC2RS
444	W3ARK
445	N5DUQ
446	W6KAW
447	KC5UO
448	W1CRL
449	K8MW
450	WØEWH
451	K2YIY
452	WA2JTY
453	W2IN
454	VE7AIO
455	KB3SN
456	KA2K
457	AI1Q
458	KB5DM
459	WØBXM
460	W7EFO
461	WD9ITF
462	W1EKZ
463	KT4U
464	AA4FF
465	K2POA
466	KU7F
467	WA9EZT
468	KB4XK
469	WB3DWH
470	WA4PGM
471	K6HZI
472	N7CYQ
473	WBØJYB
474	N3ANX
475	WA7NNH
476	WBØODS
477	N8GEQ
478	KC4IF
479	KCØVA
480	K8OOK
481	W3HQU
482	KZ2P
483	N8CIJ
484	WA7YID
485	WB2ZSO
486	KG5J
487	K4CCW
488	K4BZV
489	NØCKC
490	W7ULA
491	W2CC
492	NØAKC
493	KØIFL
494	WDX9DCJ
495	WB9YCO
496	WDX4KEF
497	WA9QNI
498	N9DEH
499	WA1KPJ
500	WA6VJP
501	W4RKV
502	WB3IQJ
503	N9CLZ
504	WAØLMK
505	VE7OR
506	K5HT
507	W3XE
508	KA1CKX
509	K5OUK
510	W2DWO
511	N9BDM
512	KB5FU
513	KX1A
514	KC4OV
515	W2CUK
516	AI9Y
517	KA4SAX
518	WA1JYO
519	W3NB
520	WA4CHI
521	NG9L
522	G2AFQ
523	KF6CN
524	AK8A
525	W4IGW
526	N9AUV
527	N4EED
528	NØDPX
529	KD4ON
530	WA4WIN
531	W7IEU
532	N4IWY
533	W4WXJ
534	YV5AGD
535	WD4RAF
536	G4KHG
537	KA1NX
538	KC3X
539	K8CW
540	K2UPD
541	WB7VIZ
542	WØGOQ
543	W5ILR
544	KC5CV
545	WBØVNN
546	W2PDM
547	WA9ROU
548	N9DR
549	K1ZIT
550	K8OHC
551	KA2CNG
552	WØFF
553	W5UJO
554	W1TEE
555	N4FSZ
556	KØGSV
557	W4LHP
558	4X4JU
559	KD8GL
560	WØNNH
561	KC7JC
562	WB6FJU
563	KYØE
564	N6EBU
565	WA5INV
566	N3AHA
567	W4UYC
568	W1WLW
569	WB2RCJ
570	KC3AD
571	N8EMV
572	K6SLP
573	WB6TJW
574	K1CGI
575	K3GWA
576	W6TKV
577	W6PXE
578	W2FXA
579	W7GQK
580	KY9Y
581	NB8R
582	NF8G
583	K7EQ
584	WBØDPD
585	W6YMV
586	NK8P
587	N9CVP
587	N8CVP
588	W2EZ
589	W6NNV
590	KAØHJR
591	WA2VQW
592	K9KKX
593	K5UTH
594	K9MGF
595	WØMHK
596	DJ3OE
597	K2CTJ
598	WA6OCI
599	KJ4EJ
600	KC3YT
601	KA5RNH
602	WØIZV
603	W8DZL
604	WA6CQW
605	KF5HY
606	KA6BTU
607	W9ET
608	W7BKM
609	KF9FU
610	N8ESR
611	N4OA
612	NT7R
613	WD9GSU
614	W7HRD
615	ZL2ACP
616	NF9A
617	WA1YZV
618	W7HZL
619	K8DTO
620	W7KEU
621	KD4ZJ
622	WB2ABD
623	KF5AT
624	N3DRO
625	WØOWY
626	WT4S
627	AG2K
628	K8IXU
629	ZL2BCX
630	WB2HXZ
631	N5KGY
631	K5KGY
632	N4KE
633	KJ5W
634	HB9AFI
635	WPE6YL
636	KB9ER
637	NØCYB
638	N5JRH
639	NV4Z
640	VE2MS
641	KB1GN
642	KD9KK
643	AK2H
644	VE3OEE
645	W5RJH
646	K1QPV
647	KD9ZF
648	KF4BU
649	WA6MUK
650	KD8HA
651	WA4NBC
652	WB9STT
653	WAØZBK
654	WA8RSQ
655	WA4KER
656	WD7X
657	KA9ZRW
658	WB4UHN
659	I2PHN
660	WB7QID
661	K5IID
662	KA4IFF
663	WB9NUL
664	K9ETB
665	KA9JOL
666	CT1TZ
667	W9MYY

668	KØGEN
669	N4UMR
670	NT9V
671	W2RPZ
672	K7OQZ
673	KØOJG
674	N6QA
675	K2POF
676	N2CWG
677	KA1LSD
678	W2EMW
679	WU4S
680	KC5P
681	K9ZWH
682	N8HAM
683	KAØNVT
684	KX8Z
685	K5XY
686	N5AWE
687	KD2NN
688	W9DC
689	AB4OI
690	K8MDU
691	W7GVF
692	W3SQA
693	K7IOO
694	KG8I
695	AA4LY
696	K8BXT
697	NU9M
698	WA6KHK
699	WDØEAM
700	K8GPC
701	KW3H
702	KCØZU
703	OE2EGL
704	NV6L
705	NA5F
706	KF4FP
707	VE2YM
708	WI9C
709	K8KIR
710	KB3WN
711	W3RWJ
712	W5MW
713	KA3DRO
714	NZ8Q
715	K1BM
716	KD9OT
717	WA4IMC
718	KA5VWD
719	W5UGD
720	KJ4LG
721	N6ERM
722	K4JFI
723	ND1H
724	KQ1Z
725	WØAWP
726	WB9QNX
727	W4HSA
728	VE1GU
729	W6TMD
730	N6PLQ
731	VK5AQZ
732	N9HRX
733	W5RIT
734	WØWYJ
735	K5TVC
736	VE3FNM
737	KC4DUP
738	KA5ZXF
739	N8AJC
740	KC4SF
741	VE1AIT
742	K4BBF
743	KJ4JC
744	WD8AGC
745	KA1JPR
746	KF7RU
747	WA1FNS
748	W9OP
749	K9AGB
750	KE9CA
751	HR1KAS
752	K5AAY
753	NWØF
754	WD9HEB
755	AC4MP
756	K2NJ
757	KN4Y
758	G5PQ
759	KB3GN
760	WD9HAW
761	WA5OPO
762	N8ELQ
763	N4IXV
764	WØWYX
765	N6OKX
766	I6FLD
767	WB4CCT
768	WM9F
769	N7POK
770	AA2AV
771	KD8HB
772	W8PN
773	WV2B
774	KK6BB
775	KN4JR
776	K6PQA
777	SM4BNZ
778	AA4LB
779	NW1O
780	N9AC
781	NC2O
782	N4SMH
783	WD4NEG
784	W3DYA
785	KD2Q
786	KM8U
787	N8FEB
788	AA9CW
789	WA2CNJ
790	N7LWX
791	HB9RG
792	KS3I
793	NV6I
794	WA4HXG
795	NØLDT
796	N2JNE
797	AA4HD
798	WA8KIW
799	N6HJY
800	AB4QD
801	KO4QZ
802	KI6YX
803	KA5PVB
804	NO2W

(Courtesy N6OQZ)

WORKED ALL STATES (WAS) AWARD RULES

1. The WAS (Worked All States) award is available to all amateurs worldwide who submit proof with written confirmation of having contacted each of the 50 states of the United States of America. The WAS awards program includes 10 different and separately numbered awards as listed below. In addition, ENDORSEMENT stickers are available as listed below.

2. Two-way communications must be established on amateur bands with each state. Specialty awards and endorsements must be two-way (2X) on that band and/or mode. There is no minimum signal report required. Any or all bands may be used for general WAS. The District of Columbia may be counted for Maryland.

3. Contacts must all be made from the same location, or from locations no two of which are more than 50 miles apart which is affirmed by signature of the applicant on the application. Club station applicants, please include clearly the club name and callsign of the club station (or trustee).

4. Contacts may be made over any period or years. Contacts must be confirmed in writing, preferably in the form of QSL cards. Written confirmations must be submitted (no photocopies). Confirmations must show your call and indicate that two-way communications was established. Applications for SPECIALTY awards or ENDORSEMENTS must submit confirmations that clearly confirm two-way contact on the specialty mode/band. Contacts made with Alaska must be dated January 3, 1959 or later and with Hawaii date August 21, 1959, or after.

5. Specialty awards (numbered separately) are available for OSCAR satellite, SSTV, RTTY, 432 MHz., 220 MHz., 144 MHz., 50 MHz., and 160- meters. In addition, the "75-Meter, 2-letter Extra Class" award is available to any Extra Class amateur who has worked all states consisting of 1X2, 2X1, or 2X2 callsigns on the Extra Class portion of 75-meters. Acceptable callsigns for the "75-Meter 2-letter Extra Class" specialty award include one of the following:

a. All 1X2s

b. All 2X1s

c. 2X2s with AA through AL prefixes only in all districts (including AH6 and AL7 in Alaska and Hawaii)

d. 2X2s with KH6 and KL7 prefixes only

ENDORSEMENT stickers for the basic mixed mode/band award and any of the SPECIALTY awards are available for SSB, CW, Novices, QRP, Packet, EME, and any Single Band. The Novice endorsement is available for the applicant who has worked all states as a Novice licensee. QRP is defined as 10 watts input (or 5 watts output) of the applicant only and is affirmed by signature of the applicant on the application.

6. Contacts made through "repeater" devices or any other power relay method cannot be used for WAS confirmation. A separate WAS is available for OSCAR contacts. All stations contacted must be "land stations." Contact with ships, anchored or otherwise, and aircraft, cannot be counted.

7. A W/VE applicant must be an ARRL member to participate in the WAS program. DX stations are exempt from this requirement.

8. Hq. reserves the right to spot call for inspection of cards (at ARRL expense) of applications verified by an HF Awards Manager. The purpose of this is not to call into question the integrity of any individual, but rather to ensure the overall integrity of the program. More difficult-to-attain specialty awards (such as 220 MHz WAS for example) are more likely to be so called. Failure of the applicant to respond to such spot check will result in non-issuance of the WAS certificate.

9. DISQUALIFICATION. False statements on this application or submission of forged or altered cards may result in disqualification. ARRL does not submit any marked over cards. The decision of the ARRL Awards Committee in such cases is final.

10. APPLICATION PROCEDURE (Please follow carefully):

(a) Confirmations (QSLs) and applications for (MCS-217) may be submitted to an approved ARRL Special Service Club HF Awards Manager. ARRL Special Service Clubs appoint HF Awards Managers whose names are on file at Hq. If you do not know of HF Awards Managers in your local area, call a club officer to see if one has bee appointed. If you can have your application so verified locally, you need not submit your cards to HQ., as indicated on the application form.

(b) Be sure that when cards are presented for verification (either locally or to Hq.) sort them alphabetically by state, as listed on the back of the application form, MCS-217.

(c) All QSL cards sent to Hq. must be accompanied by sufficient postage for their safe return.

Courtesy of the ARRL

W1JR AND HIS AWARDS

W1JR, Joseph H. Reisert Jr., Amherst, NH. Born 1936 - Extra Class

His first WAS award was issued on July 15, 1975 as #25083. Next he qualified for the Bicentential W.A.S. in 1976.

5 Band Worked-All-States was # 505 issued in February 1979.
6 Meter WAS, #374 in February 1980.
2 Meter WAS, #26 in August 1980.
160 Meter WAS, #139 in March 1981.
432 Mhz WAS, #6 in April 1982.
Oscar satellite WAS, #82 in December 1982.
12 Meter Endorsement of his 5 Band WAS, in November 1987.
E.M.E. (Moonbounce) Endorsement in October 1988.
17 Meter Endorsement of his 5 Band WAS in March 1989.

Joe has completed his 30 Meter WAS but, no awards are issued for that band. Joe also has 47 states confimed on 220 MHz!

Presently, Joe has been Awarded WAS on 11 Bands plus Oscar and E.M.E !

Bill Kennamer, K5FUV, has confirmed that Joe has completed the DXCC requirements on 160M, 80M, 40M, 20M, 17M, 15 M, 12M, 10M, 6 M. That's 9 Band DXCC. Additionally, Joe has completed 30M, for which there is no award offered.

Joe has completed the Worked-All-Continents requirements on 160M, 80M, 40M, 20M, 17M, 15M, 12M, 10M, 6M, 2M, and 432 MHz. Additionally, Joe has completed the requirements for 30M WAC but this award is not offered.

Joe's callsign is listed with the other operators who are waiting to work their last ones for 5 Band WAZ. He has 199 Band Zones submitted out of the 200 and has yet to work Zone #23 on 80M.

Joe is also a member of the Yankee Clipper Contest Club.

(See Photo Section for picture of W1JR)

W.A.E. COUNTRIES LIST

Prefix	Country
CT1,4-8,Ø	Portugal
CU	Azores
C3	Andorra
DA-DL	Germany
EA1-5,7,Ø	Spain
EA6	Balearic Island
EI	Ireland
ES	Estonia
F,TP	France
G	England
GD	Isle of Man
GI	N. Ireland
GJ	Jersey
GM	Scotland
GM	Shetland Islands
GU	Guernsey (along with Aldernesy, Brechou, Great Sark, Herm, Jethou, Lihou, and Little Sark.)
GW	Wales
HA,HG	Hungary
HB4,9	Switzerland
HBØ	Liechtenstein
HV	Vatican City
I	Italy
IS,IM,IWØ	Sardinia
IT,IW9	Sicily
JW	Spitzbergen
JW/B	Bear Island
JX	Jan Mayen
LA	Norway
LX	Luxembourg
LY	Lithuania
LZ	Bulgaria
OE	Austria
OH1-9	Finland
OHØ	Aland Island
OJØ	Market Reef
OK,OL	Czech Republic
OM	Slovakia
ON	Belgium
OY	Faroes Islands
OZ	Denmark
PA	Netherlands
SM	Sweden
SP	Poland
SV1-4,6-8	Greece
SV5	Dodecanese
SV9	Crete
SY	Mount Athos
S5	Slovenia
TA1	Turkey (European)
TF	Iceland
TK	Corsica
T7	San Marino
T9	Bosnia and Herzegovina
R,UA-UI1,3,4,6	Russian Federation
R,UA-UI1N	Karelin
R,UA-UI-UA2F	Kaliningrad
UR-UZ,EM-EO	Ukraine
EU-EW	Belarus
ER	Moldavia
YL	Latvia
YO	Romania
YT,YU,YZ,4N,4O	Yugoslavia
ZA	Albania
ZB	Gibraltar
Z3	Macedonia
1A	Sovereign Military Order of Malta
3A	Monaco
4J1	Malyj Vysotskij Island
4K2	Franz Josef-land
4U1ITU	International Telecommunications Union HQ Station
4U1VIC	Vienna International Center
9A	Croatia
9H	Malta

73 Countries

Provided by DL2DN and D.A.R.C.

CQ CONTEST HALL OF FAME

Inductee	Date Inducted
1. Hazzard "Buzz" Reeves, K2GL	Sept 1986
2. Katashi Nose, KH6IJ	Apr 1987
3. Al J. Slater, G3FXB	Apr 1988
4. Martti Laine, OH2BH	Apr 1989
5. Bernie W. Welch, W8IMZ	Jun 1989
6. Lenord Chertok, W3GRF	Dec 1991
7. W. Gerry Mathis, W3GM	Dec 1991
8. Frank Anzalone, W1WY	Apr 1993
9. Jim Lawson, W2PV	Apr 1993
10. Ed Bissell, W3AU	Apr 1993
11. Fred Laun, K3ZO	Apr 1993
12. Vic Clark, W4KFC	Apr 1993
13. Rush Drake, W7RM	Apr 1993

CQ DX HALL OF FAME

Inductee	Date Inducted
1. Gus M. Browing, W4BPD	Nov 1967
2. John M. Cummings, W2CTN	Mar 1968
3. Stewart S. Perry, W1BB	Aug 1968
4. Richard C. Spenceley, KV4AA	Mar 1969
5. Danny Weil, VP2VB	Sep 1969
6. H. Dale Strieter, W4DQS	May 1970
7. Stuart Meyer, W2GHK	Oct 1970
8. Martti Laine, OH2BH	Jan 1972
9. Ted Thorpe, ZL2AWJ	Aug 1972
10. Chuck Swain, K7LMU	Aug 1972
11. C. J. (Joe) Hiller, W4OPM	Mar 1973
12. Ernst Krenkel, RAEM	Apr 1974
13. Frank Anzalone, W1WY	Jun 1976
14. Lloyd Colvin, W6KG	Nov 1976
15. Iris Colvin, W6QL	Nov 1976
16. Geoff Watts, Editor and Publisher	Jun 1977
17. Don C. Wallace, W6AM	1978
18. Joe Arcure, Jr., W3HNK	Dec 1979
19. Hugh Cassidy, WA6AUD	Apr 1980
20. Eric A. Sjolund, SMØAGD	Apr 1981
21. Franz Langner, DJ9ZB	1982
22. Dr. Sanford E. Hutson, K5YY	Jan 1983
23. Rodney H. Newkirk, W9BRD	Feb 1984
24. Ronald W. Wright, ZL1AMO	Apr 1985
25. Herb Becker, W6QD	Apr 1985
26. Jim Smith, P29JS/VK9NS	Apr 1986
27. Kan Mizoguchi, JA1BK	Apr 1987
28. John Troster, W6ISQ	Apr 1988

RECIPIENTS OF SCHOLARSHIP AWARDS OF THE ARRL FOUNDATION SCHOLARSHIP PROGRAM

1980–81

James M. Zambik, WB2QYG—Long Island Scholarship—$250

Gregory D. Jay, WA2EDY—Long Island Scholarship—$250

Larry E. Smith, Jr., WB9UKE—YL ISSB Memorial Scholarship—$300

1982–83

Paul M. Silverman, KA2DSP—Long Island Scholarship—$250

Larry E. Smith, WB9UKE—YL ISSB Memorial Scholarship—$709

1983–84

Pamela S. Hayward, WBØMUS—Paul & Helen L. Grauer Scholarship—$500

1985

John Allcorn, KAAØEWS—Paul and Helen L. Grauer Scholarship—$500

David J. Schmocker, KJ9I—Perry F. Hadlock Memorial Scholarship—$500

1986

William J. Hulka, KA9AKI—The ARRL Scholarship to Honor Barry Goldwater—$5000

John Allcorn, KAØEWS—Paul and Helen L. Grauer Scholarship—$500

Michael R. Dargel, N1AMR—Perry F. Hadlock Memorial Scholarship—$500

1987

William H. Sands, IV, KA3FXX—The ARRL Scholarship to Honor Barry Goldwater—$5000

Raymond J. Gomez, Jr., NØGNA—Paul and Helen L. Grauer Scholarship—$500

Peter S. Jaworski, KC2KK—Perry F. Hadlock Memorial Scholarship—$500

Stephanie A. Dougherty, N8FIT—You've Got A Friend In Pennsylvania Scholarship—$500

Robert S. Hulka, Jr., KA9AKJ—Edmond A. Metzger Scholarship—$500

1988

Shawn A. Wakefield, WK5P—The ARRL Scholarship to Honor Barry Goldwater—$5000

Raymond J. Gomez, Jr., NØGNA—Paul and Helen L. Grauer Scholarship—$500

Robert N. Keenan, WU6L—Perry F. Hadlock Memorial Scholarship—$500

Douglas N. Benish, N3CXB—You've Got A Friend In Pennsylvania Scholarship—$500

Raymond P. Klump, KA9WFR—Edmond A. Metzger Scholarship—$500

Paul W. Hoffman, NK3M—L. Phil and Alice J. Wicker Scholarship—$500

David A. Clemons, K1VUT—Dr. James A. Lawson Memorial Scholarship—$500

Stephanie A. Dougherty, N8FIT—Edward D. Jaikins Memorial Scholarship—$500

1989

David A. Clemons, K1VUT—The ARRL Scholarship to Honor Barry Goldwater—$5000

Cary E. Watkins, KA5YRK—Paul and Helen L. Grauer Scholarship—$500 (1)

Robert N. Keenan, WU6L—Paul and Helen L. Grauer Scholarship—$500 (2)

William A. Kjontvedt, NØHZB—Perry F. Hadlock Memorial Scholarship—$1000

Jonathan J. Vidal, N3GUI—You've Got A Friend In Pennsylvania—$1000

David A. Hulka, KD9UA—Edmond A. Metzger Scholarship—$500

Andrew J. Jackson, N4FUF—L. Phil and Alice J. Wicker Scholarship—$1000

David A. Stein, KD2ZE—Dr. James A. Lawson Memorial Scholarship—$500

Troy A. Campbell, N7KWY—Edward A. Jaikins Memorial Scholarship—$500

1990

Kurt D. Schwehr, N6XWB—ARRL Scholarship to Honor Barry Goldwater—$5000

Michelle M. Lehman, KBØFNE—Paul and Helen L. Grauer Scholarship—$500 (1)

Christopher N. Haddan, NØGXB—Paul and Helen L. Grauer Scholarship—$500(2)

Daniel C. Lawry, KA1PNC—Perry F. Hadlock Memorial Scholarship—$1000

Douglas M. Benish, N3CXB—You've Got A Friend In Pennsylvania—$1000

Scott L. Young, N9FZS—Edmond A. Metzger Scholarship—$500

Christopher C. Peters, KB4MRH—L. Phil and Alice J. Wicker Scholarship—$1000

Gregory H. Laufman, N6GPA—Dr. James L. Lawson Memorial Scholarship—$500

Dennis P. Ward, KI8X—Edward D. Jaikins Memorial Scholarship—$500

Robert J. Inderbitzen, NQ1R—New England FEMARA Scholarship—$600

1991

James R. Harper, KB5CTQ—ARRL Scholarship to Honor Barry Goldwater—$5000

Jason N. Efken, NØKOQ—Paul and Helen L. Grauer Scholarship—$1000

Daniel C. Lawry, KA1PNE—Perry F. Hadlock Memorial Scholarships—$1000

George P. Gumbrell, KA3RLZ—You've Got A Friend In Pennsylvania—$1000

Michael W. Barton, KB9AQR—Edmond A. Metzger Scholarship—$500
John T. Crago, KB8DAN—L. Phil and Alice J. Wicker Scholarship—$1000
Michael D. Ambrose, KC1UK—Dr. James L. Lawson Memorial Scholarship—$500
Dennis P. Ward, KT8X—Edward D. Jaikins Memorial Scholarship—$500
Jeffrey A. Brower, N6XZX—Charles N. Fisher Memorial Scholarship—$1000
William G. Rubin, N1HWC—Irving W. Cook, WAØCGS Scholarship—$500
Christos N. Conner, N5MZD—Mississippi Scholarship—$500
Michael T. Decerbo, N1FYO—New England FEMARA Scholarship—$600
Jason G. Lovett, N1EJD—New England FEMARA Scholarship—$600
Joel F. Kluender, NF9G—New England FEMARA Scholarship—$600
Frederick J. Darling, Jr.—New England FEMARA Scholarship—$600
John R. Labenski, KA1KRL—New England FEMARA Scholarship—$600

1992

Harry Litaker, Jr., AC4BO—ARRL Scholarship to Honor Barry Goldwater—$5000
Kristin Poduska, WOØH—Paul and Helen L. Grauer Scholarship—$1000
Daniel Lawry, KA1PNE—Perry F. Hadlock Memorial Scholarship—$1000
John Smertneck, KA3SFX—You've Got A Friend In Pennsylvania—$1000
James P. Harper, KB5CTQ—General Fund Scholarship—$1000 (1)
Dennis Washington, N4YFL—General Fund Scholarship—$1000 (2)
Andrew Ross, KC6OHS—Charles N. Fisher Memorial Scholarship—$1000
Brian J. Kuebert, N4UEZ—L. Phil and Alice J. Wicker Scholarship—$1000
Stephen Byrd, N5WGE—Mississippi Scholarship—$500
Rachel Fremmer, KB2GOT—Dr. James L. Lawson Memorial Scholarship—$500
Robert Goemans, N9HAD—Edmond A. Metzger Scholarship—$500
Chad Seuser, KBØCTL—Irving W. Cook, WAØCGS Scholarship—$500
Richard E. McLaughlin, Jr.—Edward D. Jaikins Memorial Scholarship—$500
Mark Gilbert, N5MG/1—New England FEMARA Scholarship—$600
Laurie Mann, KA1KXP—New England FEMARA Scholarship—$600
Deborah Stein, KB2BM—New England FEMARA Scholarship—$600
David Perrin, Jr., KC1TS—New England FEMARA Scholarship—$600
Allan Hallberg, N1KBE—New England FEMARA Scholarship—$600

1993

Phillip Rowe, KA3TOK—ARRL Scholarship to Honor Barry Goldwater—$5000
Grant Kesselring, NØICI—Paul and Helen L. Grauer Scholarship—$1000
Ravi Hariprasad, AA2CR—Perry F. Hadlock Memorial Scholarship—$1000
Melissa L. Benish, N3FAC—You've Got A Friend In Pennsylvania—$1000
Brian J. Kuebert, N4UEZ—L. Phil and Alice J. Wicker Scholarship—$1000
Peter C. Laing, N7TXI—Charles N. Fisher Memorial Scholarship—$1000
Craig E. Flavin, AAØFF—K2TEO Martin J. Green, Sr. Memorial Scholarship—$1000
Vern J. Wirka, WBØGQM—General Fund Scholarship—$1000
Steven D. Kraft, KE9RW—General Fund Scholarship—$1000
John C. Evanson, WJ1U—New England FEMARA Scholarship—$600
Scott H. Ledder, KA1RLT—New England FEMARA Scholarship—$600
David B. Perrin, Jr., KC1TS—New England FEMARA Scholarship—$600
Michael T. Decerbo, N1FYO—New England FEMARA Scholarship—$600
Cristofor M. Cataudella, N1FWC—New England FEMARA Scholarship—$600
Elizabeth A. Skolaut, KAØYSP—PHD Scholarship—$500
Michael B. Madden, N9OHW—Edmond A. Metzger Scholarship—$500
Matthew J. Minney, N8PGI—Edward D. Jaikins Memorial Scholarship—$500
Michael D. Ambrose, KC1UK—Dr. James L. Lawson Memorial Scholarship—$500
Martin L. Kollman, Jr., NØRQP—Irving W. Cook, WAØCGS Scholarship—$500
Mansel P. Bell, KB5HVV—Mississippi Scholarship—$500

DAYTON HAMS OF THE YEAR

1955	William C. Jenney, W8FYW; Westlake, Ohio Benjamin S. Zieg, W9EHU, K4OQK; Atlanta, Georgia
1956	Edmund C. Ryan, W8LRR; Mansfield, Ohio
1957	Ralph Crammer, W8VHO; Columbus, Ohio
1958	Rev. C. Lynn White, K4CC; Tavarres, Florida
1959	Harlow Lucas, W8QQ; Columbus, Ohio
1960	Paul Wolfe, W8IVE; Cincinnati, Ohio
1961	Ed Bonnet, W8OVG; Dayton, Ohio
1962	Dana Cartwright, W8UPB; Cincinnati, Ohio
1963	Chester Funk, K8EUF; Phoenix, Arizona
1964	H. Ruble, W8PTF; Dayton, Ohio
1965	Carl B. Snyder, W8ARW; Greenville, Ohio
1966	Robert K. Caskey, W9DNQ; Indianapolis, Indiana
1967	Jack Gray, W8JDV; Mason, Ohio
1968	Elmer Schubert, W8ALW; Cincinnati, Ohio
1969	Wayne Walters, W9DOG; Plainfield, Indiana
1970	Kay Anderson, W8DUV; Huntington, West Virginia
1971	Al Michel, W8WC; Cincinnati, Ohio
1972	Don C. Miller, W9NTP; Waldron, Indiana
1973	Ray E. Myers, W6MLZ; San Gabriel, California
1974	Barry Goldwater, K7UGA; Scottsdale, Arizona
1975	Richard A. Daniels, WA4DGU; Arlington, Virginia
1976	Joseph M. Hertzberg, N3EA; Bryn Mawr, Pennsylvania
1977	Rafael M. Estevez, WA4ZZG; Hialeah, Florida
1978	Frank Schwab, W8OK; Dayton, Ohio
1979	George B. Batterson, W2GB; Rochester, New York
1980	Wayne Overbeck, N6NB; Woodland Hills, California
1981	Eric C. Shalkhauser, W9CI; Washington, Illinois
1982	Robert G. Heil, Jr., K9EID; Marissa, Illinois
1983	Katashi Nose, KH6IJ; Honolulu, Hawaii
1984	Dave L. Bell, W6AQ; Los Angeles, California
1985	John J. Willig, W8ACE; Sarasota, Florida
1986	Roy Neal, K6DUE; Woodlawn Hill, California
1987	Carole Perry, WB2MGP; Staten Island, New York
1988	Bill Bennett, W7PHO; Seattle, Washington
1989	Bill Pasternak, WA6ITF; Saugus, California
1990	Stephen Mendelsohn; WA2DHF; Dumont, New Jersey
1991	John B. Johnston, W3BE; Derwood, Maryland
1992	Richard Baldwin, W1RU; Waldoboro, Maine

QSL CARDS

"The final courtesy of a QSO is a QSL"—one of the oldest quotes in amateur radio. A QSL card is a reminder, souvenir , or proof of a contact. Many of the awards pursued by amateurs require submission of QSL cards as proof of contact.

Hams take pride in their own QSLs and their collections. QSL card contests are held at many hamfests, with prizes for the most original design. Many clubs offer their members the opportunity to purchase club QSL cards, and awards are available for obtaining a number of QSLs from club members.

Exchanging QSL cards can often be a challenge, particularly when dealing with stations in remote locations where postal service is unreliable. It is also a great expense for stations who make large numbers of contacts to verify every contact directly. To simplify things, QSL bureaus and QSL managers are often used by the more active stations.

QSL Bureaus

QSL Bureaus serve as "clearinghouses" for QSL cards for hams in a particular geographic area. In the United States, each call area has a QSL bureau for incoming cards. Cards are sorted and distributed by volunteers to individual hams, usually by means of envelopes provided to the bureau. These bureaus are listed below.

The ARRL Incoming QSL Bureau System

Purpose

Within the U.S. and Canada, the ARRL DX QSL Bureau System is made up of numerous call area bureaus that act as central clearing houses for QSLs arriving from foreign countries. These "incoming" bureaus are staffed by volunteers. The service is free and ARRL membership is not required.

How it Works

A majority of the DX QSLs are shipped directly to the individual incoming bureaus where volunteers sort the incoming QSLs by the first letter of the call sign suffix. One individual may be assigned the responsibility of handling from one or more letters of the alphabet. Operating costs are funded from ARRL membership dues.

Claiming your QSLs

Send a 5 x 7-1/2 or 6 x 9 inch self-addressed, stamped envelope (SASE) to the bureau serving your callsign district. Neatly print your call-sign in the upper left corner of the envelope. A suggested way to send envelopes is to affix a first class stamp and clip extra postage to the envelope. Then, if you receive more than 1 oz. of cards, they can be sent in the single package.

Some incoming bureaus sell envelopes or postage credits in addition to the normal SASE handling. They provide the proper envelope and postage upon the prepayment of a certain fee. The exact arrangements can be obtained by sending your inquiry with a SASE to your area bureau. A list of bureaus appears later in this section.

Helpful Hints

Good cooperation between the DXer and the bureau is important to ensure a smooth flow of cards. Remember that the people who work in the area bureaus are volunteers. They are providing you with a valuable service. With that thought in mind, please pay close attention to the following DOs and DON'Ts.

DOs

• DO keep self-addressed 5 x 7-1/2 or 6 x 9 inch envelopes on file at your bureau, with your call in the upper left corner, and affix at least one unit of first-class postage.

• DO send the bureau enough postage to cover SASEs on file and enough to take care of possible postage rate increases.

• DO respond quickly to any bureau request for SASEs, stamps or money. Unclaimed card backlogs are the bureau's biggest problem.

• DO notify the bureau of your new call as you upgrade. Please send SASEs with new call, in addition to SASEs with old call.

• DO include a SASE with any information request to the bureau.

• DO notify the bureau in writing if you don't want your cards.

DON'Ts

• DON'T send domestic U.S. to U.S. cards to your call-area bureau.

• DON'T expect DX cards to arrive for several months after the QSO. Overseas delivery is very slow. Many cards coming from overseas bureaus are over a year old.

• DON'T send your outgoing DX cards to your call-area bureau.

• DON'T send SASEs to your "portable" bureau. For example, AA2Z/1 sends SASEs to the W2 bureau, not the W1 bureau.

• DON'T send SASEs to the ARRL Outgoing QSL Service.

ARRL INCOMING DX QSL BUREAU ADDRESSES

First Call Area: All calls*—W1 QSL Bureau, Y.C.C.C., Box 80216, Springfield, MA 01138-0216

Second Call Area: All calls*—ARRL 2nd District QSL Bureau, N.J.D.X.A., P.O. Box 99, Morris Plains, NJ 07950.

Third Call Area: All calls—C-CARS, P.O. Box 448, New Kingstown, PA 17072 - 0448

Fourth Call Area: All single-letter prefixes (K4, N4, W4)—Mecklenburg Amateur Radio Club, P.O. Box DX, Charlotte NC 28220

Fourth Call Area: All two-letter prefixes (AA4, KB4, NC4, WD4, etc.)—Sterling Park Amateur Radio Club, Call Box 599, Sterling, VA 20167

Fifth Call Area: All calls*—ARRL W5 Incoming QSL Bureau, P.O. Box 50625, Midland, TX 79710

Sixth Call Area: All calls*—ARRL Sixth (6th) District DX QSL Bureau, P.O. Box 1460, Sun Valley, CA 91352

Seventh Call Area: All calls—Willamette Valley DX Club, Inc., P.O. Box 555, Portland, OR 97207

Eighth Call Area: All calls—8th Area QSL Bureau, P.O. Box 182165, Columbus, OH 43218-2165

Ninth Call Area: All calls*—Northern Illinois DX Assn., Box 519, Elmhurst, IL 60126

Zero Call Area: All calls*—WØ QSL Bureau, P.O. Box 4798, Overland Park, KS 66204

Puerto Rico: All calls*—KP4 QSL Bureau, P.O. Box 1061, San Juan, PR 00902

U.S. Virgin Islands: All calls—Virgin Islands ARC, GPO Box 11360, Charlotte Amalie, Virgin Islands 00801

Hawaiian Islands: All calls*—Wayne Jones, NH6GJ, P.O. Box 788, Wahiawa, HI 96786

Alaska: All calls*—Alaska QSL Bureau, 4304 Garfield St., Anchorage, AK 99503

Guam: MARC—Box 445, Agana, Guam 96910

SWL: Mike Witkowski—4206 Nebel St., Stevens Point, WI 54481

QSL Cards for Canada may be sent to:

RAC Incoming QSL Bureau, PO Box 51, St. John, NB E2L 3X1

QSL cards may also be sent to the individual bureaus:

VE1,VEØ*,VY2—James Wade, PO Box 141, Petitcodiac, NB EØA 2HØ

VE1DH, VE2—A.G. Daemen, VE2IJ, 2960 Douglas Ave., Montreal, QB H3R 2E3

VE3—Garry Hammond, VE2IJ, 5 McLaren Ave., 26 Morrison St., Listowel, ON N4W 3K1

VE4—Adam Romanchuk, VE4SN, 26 Morrison St., Winnipeg, MB R2V 3B4

VE5*—Bj. Madsen, VE5FX, 739 Washington Dr., Weyburn SK S4H 2S4

VE6*—Norm Waltho, VE6VW, PO Box 1890, Morinville AB T0G 1P0

VE7*—Dennis Livesey, VE7DK, 8309 112th St., Delta, B.C. V4C 4W7

VE8*—Rolf Ziemann, VE8RZ, 2 Taylor Road, Yellowknife, NWT X1A 2K9

VY1—W.L. Champagne, VY1AU, PO Box 4597, Whitehorse, YU Y1A 2RB

VO1, VO2—Roland Peddle, VO1BD, PO Box 6, St. John's, NF A1C 5H5

** These bureaus sell envelopes or postage credits. Send a SASE to the bureau for further information.*

THE ARRL OUTGOING QSL SERVICE

Note: The ARRL QSL Service should not be used to exchange QSL cards within the 48 contiguous states.

One of the greatest bargains of ARRL membership is being able to use the ARRL Outgoing QSL Service to conveniently send your DX QSL cards overseas to foreign QSL Bureaus. Your ticket for using this service is your *QST* address label and just $2.00 per pound. For those not quite so DX active (sending 10 cards or less), enclose $1.00. You can't even get a deal like that at your local warehouse supermarket! And the potential savings over the substantial cost of individual QSLing is equal to many times the price of your annual dues. Your cards are sorted promptly by the Outgoing Service staff, and cards are on their way overseas usually within a week of arrival at ARRL Hq. Approximately two million cards are handled by the Service each year!

QSL cards are shipped to QSL Bureaus throughout the world, which are typically maintained by the national Amateur Radio Society of each county. While no cards are sent to individuals or individual QSL managers, keep in mind that what you might lose in speed is more than made up in the convenience and savings of not having to address and mail QSL cards separately. (In the case of DXpeditions and/or active DX stations that use U.S. QSL managers, a better approach is to QSL directly to the QSL manager. The various DX newsletters, the W6GO QSL manager directory, and other publications, are good sources of up-to-date QSL manager information.)

As postage costs become increasingly prohibitive, don't go broke before you're even halfway towards making DXCC. There's a better and cheaper way—"QSL VIA BURO" through the ARRL Outgoing QSL Service!

1) Presort your DX QSLs alphabetically by parent call-sign prefix (AP, C6, CE, DL, ES, F, G, JA, LY, PY, U, 5N, 9Y and so on). NOTE: Some countries have a parent prefix and use additional prefixes, i.e., CE (parent prefix) = XQ, 3G,.... When sorting countries that have multiple prefixes, keep that country's prefixes grouped together in your alphabetical stack. Addresses are not required. DO NOT separate the country prefix by use of paper clips, rubber bands, slips of paper or envelopes.

2) Enclose the address label from your current copy of ^. The label shows that you are a current ARRL member.

3) Enclose payment of $2.00 per each pound of cards—approximately 150 cards weigh one pound. A package of ten (10) cards or fewer costs only $1.00. Please pay by check (or money order) and write your callsign on the check. Send "green stamps" (cash) at your own risk. DON'T send postage stamps or I.R.C.s.

4) Include only the cards, address label and check in the package. Wrap the package securely and address it to the ARRL Outgoing QSL Service, 225 Main Street, Newington CT 06111.

5) Family members may also use the service by enclosing their QSLs with those of the primary member. Include the appropriate fee with each individual's cards and indicate "family membership" on the primary member's *QST* address label.

6) Blind members who do not receive *QST* need only include the appropriate fee along with a note indicating the cards are from a blind member.

7) ARRL affiliated-club stations may use the service when submitting club QSLs by indicating the club name. Club secretaries should check affiliation papers to ensure that affiliation is current. In addition to sending club station QSLs through this service, affiliated clubs may also "pool" their members' individual QSL cards to effect an even greater savings. Each club member using this service must also be a League member. Cards should be sorted "en masse" by prefix, and a *QST* label enclosed for each ARRL member.

Recommended QSL Card Dimensions

The efficient operation of the worldwide system of QSL Bureau requires that cards be easy to handle and sort. Cards of unusual dimensions, either much larger or much smaller than normal, slow the work of the Bureaus, most of which is done by unpaid volunteers. A review of the cards received by the ARRL Outgoing QSL Service indicates that most fall in the following range: Height = 2-3/4 to 4-1/4 in. (70 to 110 mm), Width = 4-3/4 to 6-1/4 in. (120 to 160 mm). Cards in this range can be easily sorted, stacked and packaged. Cards outside this range create problems; in particular, the larger cards often cannot be handled without folding or otherwise damaging them. In the interest of efficient operation of the worldwide QSL Bureau system, it is recommended that cards entering the system be limited to the range of dimensions given. [Note: IARU Region 2 has suggested the following dimensions as optimum: Height 3 1/2 in. (90 mm), Width 5 1/2 in. (140 mm).]

Countries Not Served By The Outgoing QSL Service

Approximately 260 DXCC countries are served by the ARRL Outgoing QSL Service, as detailed in the ARRL DXCC Countries List. This includes nearly every active country. As noted previously, cards are forwarded from the ARRL Outgoing Service to a counterpart Bureau in each of these countries. In some cases, there is no Incoming Bureau in a particular country, and cards therefore cannot be forwarded. However, QSL cards can be forwarded to a QSL manager, i.e.; 3C1MB via (EA7KF). The ARRL Outgoing Service cannot forward cards to the following countries:

A5	Bhutan
A6	United Arab Emirates
C9	Mozambique
D2	Angola
EP	Iran
ET	Ethiopia
J5	Guinea-Bissau
KC4	U.S. bases in Antarctica
KC6	Belau
KHØ	Mariana Is.
KH1	Baker and Howland Is.
KH4	Midway I.
KH5	Palmyra and Jarvis Is.
KH7	Kure I.
KH8	Am. Samoa
KH9	Wake I.
KP1	Navassa I.
KP5	Desecheo I.
OD	Lebanon
P5	North Korea
S2	Bangladesh
S7	Seychelles
T2	Tuvalu
T3	Kiribati
T5	Somalia
TJ	Cameroon
TL	Central African Republic
TN	Congo
TT	Chad
TY	Benin
TZ	Mali
V4	St. Kitts & Nevis
V6 (KC6)	Micronesia
VP2E	Anguilla
VP2M	Montserrat
VR6	Pitcairn Island
XT	Burkina Faso
XU	Kampuchea
XW	Laos
XX9	Macao
XZ (1Z)	Myanmar (Burma)
YA	Afghanistan
YI	Iraq
ZD7	St. Helena
ZD9	Tristan da Cunha
ZK3	Tokelau

3CØ	Pagalu I.
3C	Equatorial Guinea
3V	Tunisia
3W, XV	Vietnam
3X	Guinea
5A	Libya
5H	Tanzania
5R	Madagascar
5T	Mauritania
5U	Niger
5X	Uganda
70,4W	Yemen
7Q	Malawi
8Q	Maldives
9G	Ghana
9N	Nepal
9Q	Zaire
9U	Burundi
9X	Rwanda

NOTE: SWL cards can be forwarded through the QSL Service.

NOTE: We no longer hold cards for countries with no Incoming Bureau. Only cards indicating a QSL manager for a station in these particular countries will be forwarded.

(Courtesy of ARRL)

IARU LIST OF WORLDWIDE BUREAUS; VERSION : 26 JULY 1993

3A	MONACO: Association des Radio-Amateurs de Monaco, Box 2, MC-98001 Monaco Cedex
3B	MAURITIUS: Mauritius Amateur Radio Society, Box 467, Port Louis
3D2	FIJI: Fiji Association of Radio Amateurs, Box 184, Suva
3DA	SWAZILAND: Radio Society of Swaziland, Box 1649, Matsadha
4P-4S	SRI LANKA: Radio Society of Sri Lanka, Box 907, Colombo
4X,4Z	ISRAEL: IARC QSL Bureau, Box 3500, Haifa 31034
5B	CYPRUS: Cyprus Amateur Radio Society, Box 1267, Limassol
5N-5O	NIGERIA: Nigerian Amateur Radio Society, Box 2873, GPO, Marina, Lagos
5W	WESTERN SAMOA: WSARC QSL Bureau, Box 1069, Apia
5Y-5Z	KENYA: Radio Society of Kenya, Box 45681, Nairobi
6V-6W	SENEGAL: Association des Radio-Amateurs du Senegal, Box 971, Dakar
6Y	JAMAICA: Jamaica Amateur Radio Association, 75 Arnold Rd., Kingston 5
7P	LESOTHO: Lesotho Amateur Radio Society, Box 949, Maseru 100
7T-7Y	ALGERIA: Amateurs Radio Algeriens, Box 2, Alger Gare
8P	BARBADOS: Amateur Radio Society of Barbados, Box 814E, Bridgetown
8R:	GUYANA: c/o S. D'Ornellas, 8R1B, 110 Barrack St., Kingston, Georgetown
9A	CROATIA: Hrvatski Radio-Amaterski Savez, Box 564, HR-41000 Zagreb
9G	GHANA: Ghana Amateur Radio Society
9H	MALTA: Malta Amateur Radio League, Box 575, Valletta
9I-9J	ZAMBIA: Radio Society of Zambia, Box 20332, Kitwe
9K	KUWAIT: Kuwait Amateur Radio Society, Box 5240, Safat 13053
9L	SIERRA LEONE: Sierra Leone Amateur Radio Society, Box 10, Freetown
9M	MALAYSIA: Malaysian Amateur Radio Transmitters' Society, Box 10777, 50724 Kuala Lumpur
9O-9T	ZAIRE: Union Zairoise des Radio-Amateurs (closed)
9V	SINGAPORE: Singapore Amateur Radio Transmitting Society, Box 2728, GPO, Singapore 9047
9Y-9Z	TRINIDAD AND TOBAGO: Trinidad and Tobago Amateur Radio Society, Box 1167, Port of Spain
A2,8O	BOTSWANA: Botswana Amateur Radio Society, Box 10148, Gaborone
A3	TONGA: Amateur Radio Club of Tonga, Box 1553, Nuku'alofa
A4	OMAN: Royal Omani Amateur Radio Society, Box 981, Muscat
A9	BAHRAIN: ARAB QSL Bureau, Box 25425, Awali
AP-AS	PAKISTAN: Pakistan Amateur Radio Society, Box 1450, Islamabad 44000
BA-BZ	CHINA: Chinese Radio Sports Association, Box 6106, Beijing
BV	TAIWAN: Chinese Taipei Amateur Radio League, Box 93, Taipei
C3	ANDORRA: Unio de Radioaficionats Andorrans, Box 150, La Vella
C5	GAMBIA: Radio Society of The Gambia, c/o J.-M. Voinot, PMB 120, Banjul
C6	BAHAMAS: Bahamas Amateur Radio Society, Box SS-6004, Nassau NP
C8-C9	MOZAMBIQUE: Liga dos Radio Emissores de Moambique, Box 25, Maputo
CA-CE, XQ-XR	CHILE: Radio Club de Chile, Box 13630, Santiago 21
CM,CO,T4	CUBA: Federacion de Radioaficionados de Cuba, Box 1, Havana 10100
CN	MOROCCO: Association Royale des Radio-Amateurs du Maroc, Box 299, Rabat
CP	BOLIVIA: Radio Club Boliviano, Box 2800, Cochabamba
CQ-CU	PORTUGAL: Rede dos Emissores Portugueses, Rua D. Pedro V 7-4, P-1200 Lisboa
CV-CX	URUGUAY: Radio Club Uruguayo, Box 37, Montevideo
D2-D3	ANGOLA: Liga dos Amadores de Radio de Angola (closed)
DA-DR	GERMANY: Deutscher Amateur-Radio-Club, Box 1155, W-3507 Baunatal
DU-DZ, 4D-4I	PHILIPPINES: Philippine Amateur Radio Association, Box 4083, Manila
EA-EH, AM-AO	SPAIN: Union de Radioaficionados Espanoles, Box 220, E-28080 Madrid
EI-EJ	IRELAND: Irish Radio Tramsmitters Society, Box 462, Dublin 9
EL,5L-5M	LIBERIA: Liberia Radio Amateur Association, Box 10-1477, 1000 Monrovia 10
ES	ESTONIA: Eesti Raadioamatooride Uhing, Box 125, EE-0090 Tallinn
F,HW-HY,TK TM, TO-TQ	FRANCE: Reseau des Emetteurs Francais, Box 2129, F-37021 Tours Cedex
FO	FRENCH POLYNESIA: CORA QSL Bureau, Box 5006, Pirae, Tahiti
G,2A-2Z	UNITED KINGDOM:
G	RSGB QSL Bureau, Box 1773, Potters Bar EN6 3EP, England
GD	c/o G.W. Ripley, GD3AHV, "Corea Bungalow," Ronague Rd., Ballasalla, Isle of Man
GI	c/o E. Barr, GI7FFF, "Ed-Mar," 1 Onslow Dr., New Gransha Rd., Bangor BT19 7HQ, Northern Ireland
GJ	c/o H.J. Chater, GJ2LU, 106 Rouge Bouillon, St. Helier, Jersey

GM	c/o G.E. Bell, GM4LKJ, 21 Saint Andrew Crescent, Dumbarton G82 3ER, Scotland
GU	c/o S.T. Henry, GU4GNS, The Hermitage, L'Ancresse, Vale, Guernsey
GW	c/o K. Hudspeth, GW0ARK, 67 Bloomfield Rd., Blackwood, Gwent NP2 1LX, Wales
H4	SOLOMON ISLANDS: Solomon Islands Radio Society, Box 418, Honiara
HA,HG	HUNGARY: MRASZ QSL Bureau, Box 214, H-1368 Budapest 5
HB,HE	SWITZERLAND: USKA QSL Service, Box 15, CH-4705 Wangen an der Aare
HB0	LIECHTENSTEIN: AFVL QSL Bureau, Box 27, FL-9486 Schaanwald
HC-HD	ECQUADOR: Guayaquil Radio Club, Box 5757, Guayaquil
HH,4V	HAITI: Radio Club d'Haiti, Box 501, Port-au-Prince
HI	DOMINICANA: Radio Club Dominicana, Box 1157, Santo Domingo
HJ-HK, 5J-5K	COLOMBIA: Liga Colombiana de Radioaficionados, Box 584, Bogota
HL	KOREA (Republic of): Korean Amateur Radio League, Box 162, CPO, Seoul 100-601
HO-HP,H3	PANAMA: Liga Paname a de Radioaficionados, Box 175, Panama 9A
HQ-HR	HONDURAS: Radio Club de Honduras, Box 273, San Pedro Sula
HS,E2	THAILAND: RAST QSL Bureau, Box 2008, GPO, Bangkok 10501
I	ITALY: ARI QSL Bureau, Box 6, I-28024 Gozzano
J2	DJIBOUTI: Association des Radioamateurs de Djibouti, Box 1076, Djibouti
J3	GRENADA: Grenada Amateur Radio Club, Box 737, St. George's
J7	DOMINICA: Dominica Amateur Radio Club, Box 389, Roseau
JA-JS, 7J-7N,8J-8N	JAPAN: Japan Amateur Radio League, 1-14-2 Sugamo, Toshima, Tokyo 170
JT-JV	MONGOLIA: Mongolian Radio Sports Federation, Box 639, Ulaan Baatar 13
JY	JORDAN: Royal Jordanian Radio Amateur Society, Box 2353, Amman
LA-LN, JW-JX,3Y	NORWAY: Norsk Radio Relae Liga, Box 21, Refstad, N-0513 Oslo 5
LO-LW,AY-AZ,L2-L9	ARGENTINA: Radio Club Argentino, Box 97, 1000 Buenos Aires
LX	LUXEMBOURG: c/o A. Rischette, LX1AR, 25 Rue A. Munchen, L-2172 Luxembourg
LY	LITHUANIA: Lietuvos Radijo Megeju Draugija, Box 1000, 2001 Vilnius
LZ	BULGARIA: Bulgarian Federation of Radio Amateurs, Box 830, 1000 Sofia
OA-OC,4T	PERU: Radio Club Peruano, Box 538, Lima 100
OD	LEBANON: Association des Radio-Amateurs Libanais, Box 118888, Beirut
OE	AUSTRIA: Oesterreichischer Versuchssenderverband, Theresiengasse 11, A-1180 Vienna
OF-OJ	FINLAND: SRAL QSL Bureau, Box 30, SF-00381 Helsinki
ON-OT	BELGIUM: UBA QSL Bureau, Box 400, B-8400 Ostend WV
OU-OZ	DENMARK: c/o B.W. Nielsen, OZ7BW, Solbjerghedevej 76, DK-8355 Ny Solbjerg
OY	FAROE ISLANDS: FRA QSL Bureau, Box 1358, FR-110 Torshavn
P2-P3	PAPUA NEW GUINEA: PNGARS QSL Bureau, Box 141, Port Moresby
P4	ARUBA: Aruba Amateur Radio Club, Box 2273, San Nicolas
PA-PI	NETHERLANDS: Dutch QSL Bureau, Box 330, NL-6800 AH Arnhem
PJ	NETHERLANDS ANTILLES: Vereniging voor Experimenteel Radio, Onderzoek in Nederlandse Antillen, Box 3383, Curacao
PP-PY, ZV-ZZ	BRAZIL: Liga de Amadores Brasileiros de Radio Emissao, Box 07-0004, 70.359 Brasilia DF
PZ	SURINAME: VRAS QSL Bureau, Box 566, Paramaribo
S2-S3	BANGLADESH: Bangladesh Amateur Radio League, Box 3512, GPO, Dhaka
S5	SLOVENIA: Zveza Radioamaterjev Slovenije, Box 180, 61001 Ljubljana
SA-SM,7S, 8S	SWEDEN: Foreningen Sveriges Sandareamatorer, Ostmarksgatan 43, S-12342 Farsta
SN-SR,HF, 3Z	POLAND: PZK QSL Bureau, Box 320, PL-00950 Warszawa 1
SU	EGYPT: EARS QSL Bureau, c/o Wireless Officers Club, Ramsis Bldg. Floor 13 Flat 10, No. 6 Ramsis Sq., Cairo 11111
SV-SZ,J4	GREECE: Radio Amateur Association of Greece, Box 3564, GR-10210 Athens
T7	SAN MARINO: Associazione Radioamatori della Repubblica di San Marino, Box 77, RSM-47031 San Marino
TA-TC,YM	TURKEY: Telsiz Radyo Amatorleri Cemiyeti, Box 109, Istanbul
TF	ICELAND: Islenzkir Radioamatorar, Box 1058, IS-121 Reykjavik
TG,TD	GUATEMALA: Club de Radioaficionados de Guatemala, Box 115, Guatemala City
TI,TE	COSTA RICA: Radio Club de Costa Rica, Box 2412, San Jose 1000
TR	GABON: Association Gabonaise des Radio-Amateurs, Box 1826, Libreville
TU	IVORY COAST: Association des Radio-Amateurs Ivoiriens, Box 2946, Abidjan 01
V2	ANTIGUA AND BARBUDA: Antigua and Barbuda Amateur Radio Society, Box 1111, St. John's
V3	BELIZE: c/o B. Leonard, V31HK, Box 168, Belmopan
V5:	NAMIBIA Namibian Amateur Radio League, Box 1100, Windhoek 9000
V8	BRUNEI: Negara Brunei Darussalam Amateur Radio Association, Box 73, Gadong, Bandar Seri Begawan 3100
VA-VG,VO, VX-VY,CF-CK,CY-CZ, XJ-XO	CANADA: Kennebcasis Valley A.R.C., Box 51, St. John, NB E2L 3X1
VE,VO,VY	
VE0-1,VY2	c/o J. Wade, VE1DH, Box 141, Petitcodiac, NB E0A 2H0
VE2	c/o A.G. Daemen, VE2IJ, 2960 Douglas Ave., Montreal, PQ H3R 2E3
VE3	c/o G. Hammond, VE3XN, 5 McLaren Ave., Listowel, ON N4W 3K1
VE4	c/o A. Romanchuk, VE4SN, 26 Morrison St., Winnipeg, MB R2V 3B4
VE5	c/o Bj. Madsen, VE5FX, 739 Washington Dr., Weyburn, SK S4H 3C7
VE6	c/o N.F. Waltho, VE6VW, Box 1890, Morinvile, AB T0G 1P0
VE7	c/o D. Livesay, VE7DK, 8309 112th St., Delta, BC V4C 4W7
VE8	c/o R. Ziemann, VE8RZ, 2 Taylor Rd., Yellowknife, NT X1A 2K9
VO	c/o R. Peddle, VO1BD, Box 6, St. John's, NF A1C 5H5
VY1	c/o W. Champagne, VY1AU, Box 4597, Whitehorse, YT Y1A 2R8

VH-VN,AX AUSTRALIA:
VK1 Box E46, Queen Victoria Terrace, ACT 2600
VK2 Box 73, Teralba, NSW 2284
VK3 Box 757G, GPO, Melbourne, Victoria 3001
VK4 Box 638, GPO, Brisbane, QLD 4001
VK5 Box 10092, Gouger Street, Adelaide, SA 5000
VK6 c/o J. Rumble, VK6RU, Box F319, GPO, Perth, WA 6001
VK7 Box 371D, GPO, Hobart, TAS 7001
VK8 c/o H.G. Andersson, VK8HA, Box 619, Humpty Doo, NT 0836
VK9-0 c/o N. Penfold, VK6NE, 2 Moss Court, Kingsley, WA 6026

VP2M MONTSERRAT: Montserrat Amateur Radio Society, Box 448, Plymouth
VP2V BRITISH VIRGIN ISLANDS: British Virgin I Islands Radio League, Box 653, Road Town, Tortola
VP5 TURKS AND CAICOS ISLANDS: Turks and Caicos Amateur Radio Society, c/o J. Millspaugh, VP5JM, Box 218, Providenciales
VP9 BERMUDA: Radio Society of Bermuda, Box HM 275, Hamilton HM AX
VS6 HONG KONG: Hong Kong Amateur Radio Transmitting Society, Box 541, Hong Kong
VT-VW INDIA: Amateur Radio Society of India, Box 6143, Madras 600017

W,AA-AL, K,N U.S.A.:
W1 Box 80216, Springfield, MA 01138-0216
W2 North Jersey DX Association, Box 599, Morris Plains, NJ 07950
W3 Cumberland County Amateur Radio Service, Box 448, New Kingstown, PA 17072-0448
K4,N4,W4 Mecklenburg Amateur Radio Society, Box DX, Charlotte, NC 28220
AA-AK4,KA-KZ4,NA-NZ4,WA-WZ4 Sterling Park Amateur Radio Club, Call Box 599, Sterling, VA 20167
W5 Box 50625, Midland, TX 79710
W6 Box 1460, Sun Valley, CA 91352
W7 Willamette Valley DX Club, Box 555, Portland, OR 97207
W8 Box 182165, Columbus, OH 43218-2165
W9 Northern Illinois DX Association, Box 519, Elmhurst, IL 60126
W0 Box 4798, Overland Park, KS 66204
KA2-5**, KA7-9** Far East Amateur Radio League: c/o D. Arthur, KA8DA, or J. Arthur, KA8JA, 6920 ESG, PSC, Box 2253, APO, AP 93319-2253
KA6** Radio Club of Okinawa, Box 217, Torii Station, APO AP 96331
KG4** Guantanamo Amateur Radio Club, Box 73, FPO, AE 09593
KH2 Marianas Amateur Radio Club, Box 445, Agana, GU 96910
KH3 Box 73, APO, AP 96558
KH4 U.S. Naval Air Facility, FPO, AP 96614
KH6 Box 788, Wahiawa, HI 96786
KH0 Box 7388, Saipan, CM 96950
KL7 4304 Garfield St., Anchorage, AK 99503
KP2 Virgin Islands Amateur Radio Club, Box 11360, GPO, Charlotte Amalie, VI 00801
KP4 Radio Club de Puerto Rico, Box 1061, San Juan, PR 00902
SWL c/o M. Witkowski, 4206 Nebel St., Stevens Point, WI 54481

XA-XI,4A-4C,6D-6J MEXICO: Federacion Mexicana de Radio Experimentadores, Box 907, 06000 Mexico D.F.
XY-XZ MYANMAR: Burma Amateur Radio Transmitting Society (closed)
YB-YE,8A-8I INDONESIA: ORARI QSL Bureau, Box 96, Jakarta 10002
YJ VANUATU: Vanuatu Amateur Radio Society, Box 665, Port Villa
YK,6C SYRIA: Technical Institute of Radio, Box 245, Damascus
YN,HT NICARAGUA: Club de Radioexperimentadores de Nicaragua, Box 925, Managua
YO-YR ROMANIA: Federatia Romana de Radioamatorism, Box 22-50, R-71100 Bucuresti
YS El SALVADOR: Club de Radio Aficionados de El Salvador, Box 517, San Salvador
YT-YU,YZ, 4N-4O YUGOSLAVIA: Savez Radio-Amatera Jugoslavije, Box 48, YU-11001 Beograd
YV-YY,4M VENEZUELA: Radio Club Venezolano, Box 2285, Caracas 1010A
Z2 ZIMBABWE: Zimbabwe Amateur Radio Society, Box 2377, Harare
Z3 FORMER YUGOSLAV REPUBLIC OF MACEDONIA: Association of Amateur Radio Operators of Macedonia, Box 14, 91000 Skopje
ZA ALBANIA: Albanian Amateur Radio Association, Box 66, Tirana
ZB2 GILBRALTAR: Gibraltar Amateur Radio Society, Box 292, Gibraltar
ZF CAYMAN ISLANDS: Cayman Amateur Radio Society, Box 1029, Grand Cayman
ZL-ZM NEW ZEALAND: NZART QSL Bureau, Box 857 Wanganui 5000
ZP PARAGUAY: Radio Club Paraguayo, Box 512, Asuncion
ZR-ZU SOUTH AFRICA: South African Radio League, Box 807, Houghton 2041

In addition to those listed above, the following QSL bureaus are in operation in countries or territories where there is no IARU member-society. This listing, however, neither confirms nor denies the possibility of their being affiliated with the IARU in the future.

4U1ITU SWITZERLAND: International Amateur Radio Club: Box 6, CH-1211 Geneva 20,
A7 QATAR: Qatar Amateur Radio Society, Box 22122, Doha
ET ETHIOPIA: Ethiopian Amateur Radio Society, Box 7447, Addis Ababa
FK NEW CALEDONIA: Association des Radio-Amateurs de Nouvelle-Caledonie, Box 3956, Noumea
HL9 US PERSONNEL IN THE REPUBLIC OF KOREA: American Amateur Radio Club of Korea, Dependent Mail Section, Box 153, APO, AP 96206
OK-OL CZECH REPUBLIC: Czech Radio Club, Box 69, 11327 Praha 1
OM SLOVAKIA: Slovak Amateur Radio Association, Box 1, 85299 Bratislava
R,UA-UI,EX RUSSIA: Krenkel Central Radio Club, Box 88, Moscow D-362
UR-UZ, EM-EO UKRAINE: URL, Box 56, 252001 Kiev 1
EU-EW BELARUS: Box 469, 220050 Minsk
UN-UQ KAZAKHSTAN: Kazakhstan Amateur Radio Union, Box 112, 470055 Karaganda
V7 MARSHALL ISLANDS: Kwajalein Amateur Radio Club, Box 444, APO, AP 96555, USA
VP2E ANGUILLA: Anguilla Amateur Radio Society, Box DX, The Valley

VP8 FALKLAND ISLANDS: Falkland Islands Radio Club, Box 260, Mount Pleasant Airport
VQ9 BRITISH INDIAN OCEAN TERRITORY: c/o R. Shaw, VQ9RS/KA0MXI, NSF, Box 16, FPO, AP 96464, USA
ZC4 BRITISH FORCES CYPRUS: Joint Signal Board Hq., BFC, BFPO 53, London GPO, UNITED KINGDOM
ZD8 ASCENSION ISLAND: Ascension Amateur Radio Relay League, Box 4127, Patrick AFB, FL 32925-0127, USA

(Reprinted courtesy of IARU)

QSL MANAGERS

A QSL manager is an individual who volunteers to handle the QSL chores for a DX station, freeing the rare DX to operate more and spend less time filling out cards. The DX station sends a copy of his log periodically to his manager, who takes care of answering cards and mailing replies. Usually, DX operators will announce their manager during a contact, but sometimes a pileup's volume may make it difficult for the DX station to announce his manager to every station he works.

Several QSL Manager Lists have been compiled over the years to assist DXers in obtaining the cards they need for various awards. Managers are also routinely listed in the DX columns of the major amateur magazines, on-line databases, and PacketCluster (tm) systems.

The best-known QSL manager list is published by W6GO, in both paper and electronic formats. An interesting database has been compiled over the last few years on the Copenhagen DX Cluster (OZ2DXC). It contains more than 80,000 QSL references. The input sources come from all known DX magazines, packet worldwide DX files and from DX Spots on the DX clusters in Europe. The incoming rate is about 500-700 new entries per month.

Some QSL managers handle QSLs for several stations. A select few managers provide QSL services for so many stations that their calls are almost synonymous with QSL Manager. According to the Copenhagen list, the following are the Top Ten QSL managers, in terms of number of calls for which they manage cards for.

1. W3HNK: 492
2. F6FNU: 365
3. W2CTN: 369
4. YASME: 225
5. W2GHK: 223
6. WA3HUP: 199
7. DJ9ZB: 167
8. IØWDX: 121
9. KA6V: 114
10. W4FRU: 105

(Compiled by OZ1CTK)

QSL CARD PRINTERS

There are many sources of QSL cards. Most ham magazines contain advertisements every month. Many will provide a few samples of their work and a price list for a self-addressed stamped envelope (SASE). Some of the QSL card printers who advertise regularly are listed below:

WX9X, 161 W. Lincolnway, Valparaiso,I N 46383, Phone: (219)465-7128, Fax: (219)464-7333
QSLs by W4MPY, Wayne Carroll, W4MPY, 682 Mt. Pleasant Road, Monetts, SC 29105, Fax: (803) 685-7117
Shell Printing, KD9KW, Box 50, Rockton, IL 61072, Phone: (815) 629-2193
Colorful QSLs, WA7LNW, P.O. Box 5358, Glendale, AZ 85312-5358
Marcum's QSLs, KA6GND, 4645 Pine Street, Riverside, CA 92501
KD6EUT Perryprints, 12812 Shadowline Drive, Poway, CA 92064, Phone/FAX: (619) 748-8315
Mac's Shop, P.O. Box 43175, Seven Points, TX 75143
Harry A. Hamlen, K2QFL, P.O. Box 1, Stewartsville, NJ 08886, Fax:1-(800)-AIR-FAXX
Olde Press, WB9MPP, Box 1252, Kankakee, IL 60901
Mahre & Sons Print Shop, 2095 Prosperity Avenue, Maplewood, MN 55109-3621
WordWise Services, 16 Kent Drive, Foxmeadow, Hockessin, DE 19707
Little Print Shop, Box 1160, Pflugerville, TX 78660, Phone: (512) 990-1192
Jerry Fitz-Randolph, K5KRN, P.O. Box 3473 , Jackson, TN 38303
Brownies QSL Cards, 3035 Lehigh Street, Allentown, PA 18103
Charlie Hansen , NØTT, RR 1, Box 108-B, Napolean, MO 64074
Samcards, 48 Monte Carlo Drive, Pittsburgh, PA 15239
Visual Conception, Vi-Con International, P.O. Box 10013, Kansas City, MO 64111, Phone:1 (800) 869-7527, Phone: (816) 531-3939
K-K-Labels, Box 412 , Troy, NY 12181-0412
K2MK QSLs, 551 Norwood Road, Mt. Laurel, NJ 08054
Bud Smith, Box 1262, Points Roberts, WA 98281
Spangler X-Pressions, P.O. Box 6262, Kansas City, MO 66106, Phone:1 (800) 466-1616
W5YI Group (QSLs), Box 565101, Dallas, TX 75356, Phone: (817) 461-6443
Chester QSLs, 310 Commercial, Emphoria, KS 66801, Phone: (316) 342-8792, Fax: (316) 342-4705
Raum's, 8617 Orchard Road, Coopersburg, PA 18036, Phone/Fax: 1 (215) 679-7238
Ebbert Graphics D-3, Box 70, Westerville, OH 43081
New Dimension QSLs, 6600 Lucia Lane, Minneapolis, MN 55432, Phone: (612) 571-5881
Network QSLs, Phone:1 (800) 354-0830, Phone: (318) 443-7261
Bert P. van der Berg, N6ID, BVE Professional Printing, 2023 Chicago Ave #b13, Riverside, CA 92507, Phone: (714) 781-0283
Pro-Print, WA5LKS, 5301 Junction Road, Norman, OK 73701, Phone: 1 (405) 364-6676
Rusprint, 26037 220th Terr., Spring Hill, KS 66083
Gazebo Press, 4148 Mimosa Lane , La Plata, MD 20646
M. Smith, VE7FI, 18610 62nd Avenue, Surrey, B.C. CANADA , V3S 7P1

THE WORLD'S BIGGEST QSL CARD COLLECTION

The biggest collection of QSL cards in the world is believed to be that of the YASME Foundation. "Yasme" is a Japanese word meaning "good luck," and was the name of a boat sailed around the world by Danny Weil, VP2VB, who activated many rare island groups in the 1960s. The YASME Foundation was formed in 1961 by KV4AA and VP2VB. Lloyd and Iris Colvin, W6KG and W6QL, joined in 1965.

Lloyd and Iris, married over 50 years, may be the most-traveled DXers in the world. They have visited over 200 DXCC countries and operated from over half of them, including 14 of the 15 Republics of the former U.S.S.R. The QSL cards from the many hams who have sent their "QSL via YASME" total close to a million, all neatly stored in organized file drawers.

The YASME address has become one of the best-known addresses in the world among DXers: YASME Foundation, Box 2025, Castro Valley, CA 94546.

Postal Rates

Hams in search of QSL cards from overseas stations need to know the latest postal rates. The following information is from *Publication 51* - International Postal Rates and Fees, April 1993 Edition, published by the United States Postal Service. This publication is a condensed version of general information included in the *International Mail Manual.* The international Mail Manual is the definitive reference book on international mailing. A copy of the IMM may be ordered from:

Superintendent of Documents, P.O. BOX 371954, Pittsburgh, PA 15250-7954

The postal rates listed here were in effect at press time and are subject to change. If rates have changed, details should be available from your local post office

SOURCES OF FOREIGN POSTAGE

DX QSL Associates, 434 Blair Road NW, Vienna, VA 22180
Mackey DX Postage, 187 Ridgewood Road / Box 270569, West Hartford, CT 06107
Plum DX Supplies, 12 Glenn Road, Flemington, NJ 08822

Postcards/Postal Cards	
Canada	$0.30
Mexico	$0.30
All other—surface	$0.35
All other—air	$0.40

Letters and Letter Packages—Airmail Rates
Countries other than Canada & Mexico

Weight not over	Rate	Weight not over	Rate	Weight not over	Rate
0.5 ozs.	$0.50	16.5 ozs.	$13.04	33 ozs.	$25.52
1.0	0.95	17.0	13.43	34	25.91
1.5	1.34	17.5	13.82	35	26.30
2.0	1.73	18.0	14.21	36	26.69
2.5	2.12	18.5	14.60	37	27.08
3.0	2.51	19.0	14.99	38	27.47
3.5	2.90	19.5	15.38	39	27.86
4.0	3.29	20.0	15.77	40	28.25
4.5	3.68	20.5	16.16	41	28.64
5.0	4.07	21.0	16.55	42	29.03
5.5	4.46	21.5	16.94	43	29.42
6.0	4.85	22.0	17.33	44	29.81
6.5	5.24	22.5	17.72	45	30.20
7.0	5.63	23.0	18.11	46	30.59
7.5	6.02	23.5	18.50	47	30.98
8.0	6.41	24.0	18.89	48	31.37
8.5	6.80	24.5	19.28	49	31.76
9.0	7.19	25.0	19.67	50	32.15
9.5	7.58	25.5	20.06	51	32.54
10.0	7.97	26.0	20.45	52	32.93
10.5	8.36	26.5	20.84	53	33.32
11.0	8.75	27.0	21.23	54	33.71
11.5	9.14	27.5	21.62	55	34.10
12.0	9.53	28.0	22.01	56	34.49
12.5	9.92	28.5	22.40	57	34.88
13.0	10.31	29.0	22.79	58	35.27
13.5	10.70	29.5	23.18	59	35.66
14.0	11.09	30.0	23.57	60	36.05
14.5	11.48	30.5	23.96	61	36.44
15.0	11.87	31.0	24.35	62	36.83
15.5	12.26	31.5	24.74	63	37.22
16.0	12.65	32.0	25.13	64	37.61

Weight limit: 64 ozs. (4 lbs.)

Letters and Letter Packages

Weight not over		Canada	Mexico	Weight not over		Canada	Mexico
0 lbs.	.5 ozs	$0.40	$0.35	0 lbs.	10 ozs.	$2.47	$2.65
0	1.0	.40	.45	0	11	2.70	2.90
0	1.5	.63	.55	0	12	2.93	3.15
0	2	.63	.65	1	0	3.25	4.15
0	3	.86	.90	1	8	3.85	6.15
0	4	1.09	1.15	2	0	4.45	8.15
0	5	1.32	1.40	2	8	5.38	10.15
0	6	1.55	1.65	3	0	6.31	12.15
0	7	1.78	1.90	3	8	7.24	14.15
0	8	2.01	2.15	4	0	8.17	16.15
0	9	2.24	2.40				

4 lb. maximum except registered items to CANADA may weigh up to 66 lbs.
Over 4 lbs. – $1.86 per lb. up to 66 lbs. limit.
Note: Mail paid at this rate receives First-Class service in the U.S. and airmail service in Canada and Mexico.

International Reply Coupons— The REAL Story

International Reply Coupons (IRCs) provide a mechanism for sending return postage to a person in another country. They are often sent by hams with their QSL cards as a courtesy when requesting a QSL card from a rare station. They are exchangeable in any country of the Universal Postal Union (which includes most countries) for the minimum postage for a foreign letter. The minimum postage varies from country to country. In the U.S., for example, the "first unit" is a half-ounce letter. In other countries, the minimum varies from a quarter-ounce to an ounce.

IRCs are issued by the UPU, and sold on request to the various postal administrations in the member countries, who then resell them to their customers. When a customer presents an IRC to the local post office for exchange, that customer is entitled to stamps equal to the cost of the first unit of airmail postage. The local post office forwards the exchanged IRC to the national postal administration, and at the end of the year, all exchanged coupons are sent to the UPU office in Bern, Switzerland for compensation.

Historically, IRCs have been exchangeable for the first unit of surface postage. However, in 1989, the UPU member countries met in Washington, DC to discuss and update numerous international mail regulations, including IRCs. It was decided that since surface mail is rarely used for letters, that IRCs should be upgraded to be exchangeable for airmail postage, effective February 1991. All post-1975 IRCs are now exchangeable for airmail postage, regardless of what is printed on them. IRCs printed after 1991 indicate that they are valid for airmail postage in the last few word of the French text on the front of the coupon ("...par voie aerienne"). IRCs printed between 1975 and 1991 refer to surface-mail validity at the end of the text ("...par voie de surface").

Many amateurs purchase IRCs from other amateurs (especially active DXers who receive them frequently). Many hams are confused about the difference between the airmail and surface IRCs — the fact is that there is no difference! Both are equally valid for airmail postage. If you bring a valid IRC originally purchased in another country to a U.S. Post office, you are entitled to exchange it for 50 cents worth of stamps (postal rates in effect as of September 1993). If you buy an IRC in the U.S. and decide to cash it in at a later date, you are entitled to 94 cents worth of stamps (for an IRC purchased for 95 cents).

Amateurs who have tried to exchange IRCs at their local post office have often been frustrated by postal employees who have never seen IRCs before. Most smaller post offices don't stock them, and don't know how to exchange them for postage. The revised rules make it even more difficult to convince a postal employee that an IRC marked "surface" is actually valid for airmail postage.

If this happens to you, refer the postal employee to the International Mail Manual, Section 392. In Issue 9 of the International Mail Manual, dated 2-3-91, the relevant text appears on page 69, and is reproduced here in its entirety:

International Reply Coupons

Description

a. The sender of a letter may prepay a reply by purchasing reply coupons which are sold and exchangeable for postage stamps at post offices in member countries of the Universal Postal Union. The period of exchange of international reply coupons issued by the Universal Postal Union on or after January 1, 1975, is unlimited.

b. International reply coupons (in French, Coupons-Reponse Internationaux) are printed in blue ink on paper which has the letters UPU in large characters in the watermark. The front of each coupon is printed in French. The reverse side of the coupon shows the text relating to its use in German, English, Arabic, Chinese, Spanish, and Russian.

c. Coupons sold in the United States have the selling price printed on them, while coupons in other countries may not.

Availability

Reply coupons may be requisitioned by post offices in the same manner as postage stamps. The coupons should be stocked at post offices which have a demand for them.

Selling Price and Rate of Exchange

a. The selling price of a reply coupon in the United States is 95 cents. One coupon is exchangeable in any other member country for a stamp or stamps representing the minimum postage on an unregistered air letter. Unused U.S. coupons (that is, those with the U.S. selling price stamped on them) may be exchanged only for United States postage stamps by the original purchaser at a discount of 1 cent below the purchase price.

b. International reply coupons purchased in foreign countries are exchangeable in U.S. post offices toward the purchase of postage stamps, postage meter stamps, and embossed stamped envelopes (including aerogrammes) at the rate of 50 cents per coupon, irrespective of the country where it was purchased.

392.4 Processing Requirements

a. U.S. post offices must postmark coupons in the lower left circle at the time of sale. Coupons issued by foreign countries will contain a control stamp of the country of origin.

b. A post office redeeming an unused U.S. coupon must postmark it in the right circle. Post offices must not accept foreign coupons which already bear a USPS postmark.

c. Reply coupons issued by foreign countries prior to January 1, 1975, are no longer redeemable at U.S. post offices. These old-style coupons are distinguishable from the newer coupons printed by the International Bureau of the Universal Postal Union, because the name of the country of origin is always present on the old-style coupons. Customers processing pre-1975 coupons should be advised to return them to their correspondents in the country of origin for replacement or redemption through the selling post office.

d. Reply coupons formerly issued by the Postal Union of the Americas and Spain are no longer valid. These coupons are printed in green ink and bear the caption Cupons Respuesta America-Espanol. Customers possessing any of these coupons should return them to their correspondents in the country of issue for redemption through the selling post office.

e. Postmasters must process exchanged foreign and redeemed U.S. coupons as prescribed in 458 International Reply Coupons (IRCs) Handbook F-1, Post Office Accounting Procedures.

Comparison of Surface and Airmail IRCs

(Both were purchased for 150 yen in Japan in 1991, and both are currently valid for airmail postage!)

INTERNATIONAL AMATEUR RADIO UNION
List of Member Societies (Version: 26 July 1993)

ALBANIA
Albanian Amateur Radio Association [AARA]
Address: P.O. Box 66, Tirana
ALGERIA
Amateurs Radio Algeriens [ARA]
Address: P.O. Box 2, Alger Gare
Location: 7 Square Port Said, Alger
Telephone: +213 (2) 644432
ANDORRA
Unio de Radioaficionats Andorrans [URA]
Address: P.O. Box 150, La Vella
Telephone: +33 (628) 25380
Telefax: +33 (628) 25380
ANGOLA
Liga dos Amadores de Radio de Angola [LARA]
ANGUILLA
Anguilla Amateur Radio Society [AARS]
* Proposed for membership in Calendar No. 162
Voting to be completed on 16 September 1993
Address: P.O. Box DX, The Valley
Telephone: +1 (809) 497-2150
ANTIGUA & BARBUDA
Antigua and Barbuda Amateur Radio Society [ABARS]
Address: P.O. Box 1111, St. John's
ARGENTINA
Radio Club Argentino [RCA]
Address: P.O. Box 97, 1000 Buenos Aires
Location: Carlos Calvo 1420/24, 1102 Buenos Aires
Telephone: +54 (1) 304-0555 & 26-0505
Telefax: +54 (1) 304-0555
Telex: 18506 MILIA
ARUBA
Aruba Amateur Radio Club [AARC]
Address: P.O. Box 2273, San Nicolas
AUSTRALIA
Wirelesss Institute of Australia [WIA]
Address: P.O. Box 300, South Caulfield, Victoria 3162
Location: 3/105 Hawthorn Rd., North Caulfield, Vic. 3161
Telephone: +61 (3) 528-5962
Telefax: +61 (3) 523-8191
AUSTRIA
Oesterreichischer Versuchssenderverband [OEVSV]
Address: Theresiengasse 11, A-1180 Vienna
Telephone: +43 (1) 4085535
Telefax: +43 (1) 4031830
BAHAMAS
Bahamas Amateur Radio Society [BARS]
Address: P.O. Box SS-6004, Nassau, N.P.
BAHRAIN
Amateur Radio Association Bahrain [ARAB]
Address: P.O. Box 22381, Muharraq
BANGLADESH
Bangladesh Amateur Radio League [BARL]
Address: G.P.O. Box 3512, Dhaka
BARBADOS
Amateur Radio Society of Barbados [ARSB]
Address: P.O. Box 814E, Bridgetown
Telephone: +1 (809) 426-2502
BELGIUM
]Union Belge des Amateurs-Emetteurs
Unie van de Belgische Amateur-Zenders [UBA]
Union der Belgischen Amateurfunker
Address: c/o Etienne David, ON5IA
A. Vermeylenstraat 49, B-8400 Oostende
BELIZE
Belize Amateur Radio Club [BARC]
BERMUDA
Radio Society of Bermuda [RSB]
Address: P.O. Box HM 275, Hamilton HM AX
BOLIVIA
Radio Club Boliviano [RCB]
Address: P.O. Box 2800, Cochabamba
Telephone: +591 (42) 31469
Telefax: +591 (42) 29905
Telex: 4442 VIMAC
BOSNIA AND HERZEGOVINA
Savez Radioamatera Bosne i Hercegovine [SRABiH]
* Proposed for membership in Calendar No. 163
Voting to be completed on 27 December 1993
Address: P.O. Box 61, 71001 Sarajevo
(via 58000 Split, Croatia)
Location: Daniela Ozme 7, 71000 Sarajevo
BOTSWANA
Botswana Amateur Radio Society [BARS]
Address: P.O. Box 10148, Gaborone
BRAZIL
Liga de Amadores Brasileiros de Radio Emissao [LABRE]
Address: P.O. Box 07-0004, 70.359 Brasilia D.F.
Location: Setor de Clubes Esportivos Sul, Trecho 04
Lote 1/A, 70.200 Brasilia, D.F.
Telephone: +55 (61) 223-1157
Telefax: +55 (61) 223-1157
BRITISH VIRGIN ISLANDS
British Virgin Islands Radio League [BVIRL]
Address: P.O. Box 4, West End, Tortola
BRUNEI
Brunei Darussalam Amateur Radio Association [BDARA]
Address: P.O. Box 73, Gadong, Bandar Seri Begawan 3100
BULGARIA
Bulgarian Federation of Radio Amateurs [BFRA]
Address: P.O. Box 830, 1000 Sofia
Location: Arso Pandurski St. No. 1, 1722 Sofia
Telephone: +359 (2) 623022 X216
Telefax: +359 (2) 467553
Telex: 23741 COMPTR
CANADA
Radio Amateurs of Canada [RAC]
Address: P.O. Box 356, Kingston, Ontario K7L 4W2
Location: 370 King St., Kingston, Ontario K7 4W2
Telephone: +1 (613) 545-9100
CAYMAN ISLANDS
Cayman Amateur Radio Society [CARS]
Address: P.O. Box 1029, Grand Cayman
CHILE
Radio Club de Chile [RCCH]
Address: P.O. Box 13630, Santiago 21
Location: Nataniel Cox 1054, Santiago
Telephone: +56 (2) 696-4707
Telefax: +56 (2) 672-2623
CHINA
Chinese Radio Sports Association [CRSA]
Address: 9 Tiyuguan Road, Beijing
Telephone: +86 (1) 701-1177
Telefax: +86 (1) 701-5858
Telex: 22323 CHOC
COLOMBIA
Liga Colombiana de Radioaficionados [LCRA]
Address: P.O. Box 584, Bogota
Location: Carrera 32 No. 94-67, Bogota
Telephone: +57 (1) 610-8499
Telefax: +57 (1) 610-9877
COSTA RICA
Radio Club de Costa Rica [RCCR]
Address: P.O. Box 2412, San Jose 1000
Telephone: +506 216903
CROATIA
Hrvatski Radio-Amaterski Savez [HRS]
Address: P.O. Box 564, HR-41000 Zagreb
Location: Dalmatinska 12, HR-41000 Zagreb
Telephone: +38 (41) 433025
Telefax: +38 (41) 274391

CUBA
Federacion de Radioaficionados de Cuba [FRC]
Address: P.O. Box 1, Habana 10100
Location: Paseo #611 e/ 25 y 27, Vidado, Habana 10400
Telephone: +53 (7) 34811
CYPRUS
Cyprus Amateur Radio Society [CARS]
Address: P.O. Box 1267, Limassol
CZECH REPUBLIC
Cesky Radioklub [CRK]
* Proposed for membership in Calendar No. 162
Voting to be completed on 16 September 1993
Address: P.O. Box 69, 11327 Praha 1
Location: U. Pergamenky 3, 17000 Praha 7
Telephone: +42 (2) 876989
Telefax: +42 (2) 809587
DENMARK
Eksperimenterende Danske Radioamatorer [EDR]
Address: P.O. Box 172, DK-5100 Odense C
Telephone: +45 (66) 137700
DJIBOUTI
Association des Radioamateurs de Djibouti [ARAD]
Address: P.O. Box 1076, Djibouti
DOMINICA
Dominica Amateur Radio Club [DARC]
Address: P.O. Box 389, Roseau
Location: 69 Cork Street, Roseau
Telephone: +1 (809) 448-8533
Telex: 8625
DOMINICAN REPUBLIC
Radio Club Dominicano [RCD]
Address: P.O. Box 1157, Santo Domingo
Telephone: +1 (809) 533-2211
ECUADOR
Guayaquil Radio Club [GRC]
Address: P.O. Box 5757, Guayaquil
Telephone: +593 (4) 392671
EGYPT
Egypt Amateur Radio Society [EARS]
Address: c/o E.S. Ramadan, Box 78, Heliopolis, Cairo 11341
EL SALVADOR
Club de Radio Aficionados de El Salvador [CRAS]
Address: P.O. Box 517, San Salvaodr
Location: Centro Comercial El Rosal, Local 12 Pte.
Calle Progreso 2823, San Salvador
Telephone: +503 246714/245975
ESTONIA
Eesti Raadioamatooride Uhing [ERAU]
Address: P.O. Box 125, EE-0090 Tallinn
Telephone: +372 449312
FAROE ISLANDS
Foroyskir Radioamatorar [FRA]
Address: P.O. Box 343, FR-110 Torshavn
Telephone: 009-298-10644
FIJI
Fiji Association of Radio Amateurs [FARA]
Address: P.O. Box 184, Suva
FINLAND
Suomen Radioamatooriliitto [SRAL]
Address: P.O. Box 44, SF-00441 Helsinki
Location: Kaupinmaenpolku 9, SF-00440 Helsinki
Telephone: +358 (0) 562-5973
Telefax: +358 (0) 562-3987
FORMER YUGOSLAV REPUBLIC OF MACEDONIA
Association of Amateur Radio Operators of Macedonia [AAROM]
Address: P.O. Box 14, 91000 Skopje
Location: Gradski zid blok 5, 91000 Skopje
Telephone: +38 (91) 237371
Telefax: +38 (91) 221917
FRANCE
Reseau des Emetteurs Francais [REF]
Address: P.O. Box 2129, F-37021 Tours Cedex
Telephone: +33 (47) 418873
Telefax: +33 (47) 418888
FRENCH POLYNESIA
Club Oceanien de Radio et d'Astronomie [CORA]
Address: P.O. Box 2139, Papeete, Tahiti
Telefax: +689 435230
GABON
Association Gabonaise des Radio-Amateurs [AGRA]
Address: P.O. Box 1826, Libreville
GAMBIA
Radio Society of The Gambia [RSTG]
Address: c/o Jean-Michel Voinot, C53GB, P.M.B. 120, Banjul
GERMANY
Deutscher Amateur-Radio-Club [DARC]
Address: P.O. Box 1155, W-3507 Baunatal
Location: Lindenallee 6, W-3507 Baunatal 1
Telephone: +49 (561) 949880
Telefax: +49 (561) 9498850
GHANA
Ghana Amateur Radio Society [GARS]
Address: c/o Kofi A. Jackson, 9G1AJ, P.O. Box M 144, Accra
GIBRALTAR
Gibraltar Amateur Radio Society [GARS]
Address: P.O. Box 292, Gibraltar
Location: 3 Hargreaves Court, Gibraltar
GREECE
Radio Amateur Association of Greece [RAAG]
Address: P.O. Box 3564, GR-10210 Athens
Location: 2 Lenorman Street, Athens
Telephone: +30 (1) 522-6516
Telefax: +30 (1) 522-6505
GRENADA
Grenada Amateur Radio Club [GARC]
Address: P.O. Box 737, St. George's
GUATEMALA
Club de Radioaficionados de Guatemala [CRAG]
Address: P.O. Box 115, Guatemala City 01901
Location: 5o. Nivel, Local 517, 12 Calle 2-04
Zona 9, Guatemala City
Telephone: +502 (2) 314683
GUYANA:
Guyana Amateur Radio Association [GARA]
HAITI
Radio Club d'Haiti [RCH]
HONDURAS
Radio Club de Honduras [RCH]
Address: P.O. Box 273, San Pedro Sula
Location: Colonia El Altiplano, San Pedro Sula
Telephone: +504 532035
HONG KONG
Hong Kong Amateur Radio Transmitting Society [HARTS]
Address: G.P.O. Box 541, Hong Kong
HUNGARY
Magyar Radioamator Szovetseg [MRASZ]
Address: P.O. Box 11, H-1400 Budapest
Location: Zoltan U.16 III 315-316, Budapest 5
Telephone: +36 (1) 112-1616
Telefax: +36 (1) 111-6204
ICELAND
Islenzkir Radioamatorar [IRA]
Address: P.O. Box 1058, IS-121 Reykjavik
INDIA
Amateur Radio Society of India [ARSI]
Address: P.O. Box 6143, Madras 600017
INDONESIA
Organisasi Amatir Radio Indonesia [ORARI]
Address: P.O. Box 6797 JKSRB, Jakarta 12067
Location: Jl. Danau Tondano T 10, Pejompongan Jakarta 10210
Telephone: +62 (21) 582226
IRELAND
Irish Radio Transmitters Society [IRTS]
Address: P.O. Box 462, Dublin 9

ISRAEL
Israel Amateur Radio Club [IARC]
Address: P.O. Box 4099, Tel-Aviv 61040
ITALY
Associazione Radioamatori Italiani [ARI]
Address: Via Scarlatti 31, I-20124 Milano
Telephone: +39 (2) 6692192
Telefax: +39 (2) 6692894
IVORY COAST
Association des Radio-Amateurs Ivoiriens [ARAI]
Address: P.O. Box 2946, Abidjan 01
JAMAICA
Jamaica Amateur Radio Association [JARA]
Address: 76 Arnold Road, Kingston 5
JAPAN
Japan Amateur Radio League [JARL]
Address: 1-14-2 Sugamo, Toshima, Tokyo 170
Telephone: +81 (3) 5395-3106
Telefax: +81 (3) 3943-8282
Telex: 23868 JAPRETAR
JORDAN
Royal Jordanian Radio Amateur Society [RJRAS]
Address: P.O. Box 2353, Amman
Telephone: +962 (6) 666235
KENYA
Radio Society of Kenya [RSK]
Address: P.O. Box 45681, Nairobi
REPUBLIC OF KOREA
Korean Amateur Radio League [KARL]
Address: C.P.O. Box 162, Seoul 100-601
Telephone: +82 (2) 817-7493
Telefax: +82 (2) 817-7494
Telex: 22065
KUWAIT
Kuwait Amateur Radio Society [KARS]
Address: P.O. Box 5240, Safat 13053
Location: House No. 2, Subst. No. 12
St. No. 1, Block No. 2, Al Surra
Telephone: +965 533-3762
Telefax: +965 531-1188
Telex: 23357 KALIFCO
LEBANON
Association des Radio-Amateurs Libanais [RAL]
Address: P.O. Box 8888, Beirut
Telephone: +961 (9) 911223
LESOTHO
Lesotho Amateur Radio Society [LARS]
Address: P.O. Box 949, Maseru 100
LIBERIA: Liberia Radio Amateur Association [LRAA]
Address: P.O. Box 10-1477, 1000 Monrovia 10
Telephone: +231 225855
Telefax: +231 224153
LIECHTENSTEIN
Amateurfunk Verein Liechtenstein [AFVL]
Address: P.O. Box 629, FL-9495 Triesen
Telephone: +41 (75) 392-1665
Telefax: +41 (75) 373-5960
LITHUANIA
Lietuvos Radijo Megeju Draugija [LRMD]
Address: P.O. Box 1000, Vilnius 2001
LUXEMBOURG
Reseau Luxembourgeois des Amateurs d'Ondes Courtes [RL]
Address: c/o J. Kirsch, LX1DK
23 Route de Noertzange, L-3530 Dudelange
Telephone: +352 511133
MALAYSIA
Malaysian Amateur Radio Transmitters' Society [MARTS]
Address: P.O. Box 10777, 50724 Kuala Lumpur
MALTA
Malta Amateur Radio League [MARL]
Address: P.O. Box 575, Valletta
MAURITIUS
Mauritius Amateur Radio Society [MARS]
Address: P.O. Box 467, Port Louis
MEXICO
Federacion Mexicana de Radio Experimentadores [FMRE]
Address: P.O. Box 907, 06000 Mexico, D.F.
Location: Av. Molinos 51, Desp. 307/308, Mexico 19, D.F.
MONACO
Association des Radio-Amateurs de Monaco [ARM]
Address: P.O. Box 2, MC-98001 Monaco Cedex
MONGOLIA
Mongolian Radio Sports Federation [MRSF]
Address: P.O. Box 639, Ulaanbaatar 13
Telephone: 20058
MONTSERRAT
Montserrat Amateur Radio Society [MARS]
Address: P.O. Box 448, Plymouth
MOROCCO
Association Royale des Radio-Amateurs du Maroc [ARRAM]
Address: P.O. Box 299, Rabat
Location: 12 Rue Ahmed Arabi, Agdal, Rabat
Telephone: +212 (7) 73703
MOZAMBIQUE
Liga dos Radio Emissores de Mocambique [LREM]
Address: P.O. Box 25, Maputo
MYANMAR
Burma Amateur Radio Transmitting Society [BARTS]
NAMIBIA
Namibian Amateur Radio League [NARL]
Address: P.O. Box 1100, Windhoek 9000
NETHERLANDS
Vereniging voor Experimenteel Radio Onderzoek in Nederland [VERON]
Address: P.O. Box 1166, NL-6801 BD Arnhem
Telephone: + 31 (85) 426760
NETHERLANDS ANTILLES
Vereniging voor Experimenteel Radio Onderzoek in de
Nederlandse
Antillen [VERONA]
Address: P.O. Box 3383, Curacao
NEW ZEALAND
New Zealand Association of Radio Transmitters [NZART]
Address: P.O. Box 40-525, Upper Hutt
Location: Astral Tower Bldg. 6F
88-90 Main St., Upper Hutt
Telephone: +64 (4) 528-2170
Telefax: +64 (4) 528-2170
NICARAGUA
Club de Radioexperimentadores de Nicaragua [CREN]
Address: P.O. Box 925, Managua
Telephone: +505 (2) 71274
NIGERIA
Nigeria Amateur Radio Society [NARS]
Address: P.O. Box 2873, G.P.O. Marina, Lagos
Location: 13 Orimolade Rd. (off Aina St.)
Egbe (Alimosho Local Government), Lagos State
Telephone: +234 (1) 884145/860974/964912
NORWAY
Norsk Radio Relae Liga [NRRL]
Address: P.O. Box 21, Refstad, N-0513 Oslo 5
Location: Nedre Rommen 5 E, N-0988 Oslo 9
Telephone: +47 (2) 213790
Telefax: +47 (2) 213791
OMAN
Royal Omani Amateur Radio Society [ROARS]
Address: P.O. Box 981, Muscat
Telephone: +968 600407
Telefax: +968 696670
Telex: 5556 POSTAL
PAKISTAN
Pakistan Amateur Radio Society [PARS]
Address: P.O. Box 1450, Islamabad 44000

PANAMA
Liga Panamena de Radioaficionados [LPRA]
Address: P.O. Box 9A-175, Panama
Telephone: +507 26-3160
PAPUA NEW GUINEA
Papua New Guinea Amateur Radio Society [PNGARS]
Address: P.O. Box 204, Port Moresby, N.C.D.
PARAGUAY
Radio Club Paraguayo [RCP]
Address: P.O. Box 512, Asuncion
Location: Humaita 1057, Asuncion
Telephone: +595 (21) 446124
Telefax: +595 (21) 440762
PERU
Radio Club Peruano [RCP]
Address: P.O. Box 538, Lima 100
Telephone: +51 (14) 414837
PHILIPPINES
Philippine Amateur Radio Association [PARA]
Address: P.O. Box 4083, Manila
Location: Room 207, Remedios Bldg.
#55 A. Rices Ave., Quezon City
Telephone: +63 (2) 964069
Telefax: +63 (2) 964069
POLAND
Polski Zwiazek Krotkofalowcow [PZK]
Address: P.O. Box 61, PL-64100 Leszno 1
Telephone: +48 (65) 200276
Telefax: +48 (65) 209529
PORTUGAL
Rede dos Emissores Portugueses [REP]
Address: Rua D. Pedro V 7-4, P-1200 Lisboa
Telephone: +351 (1) 361186
QATAR
Qatar Amateur Radio Society [QARS]
* Proposed for membership in Calendar No. 163
Voting to be completed on 27 December 1993
Address: P.O. Box 22122, Doha
Location: 82 Suhaim Bin Hamad Rd., Doha
Telephone: +974 439191
Telefax: +974 439595
ROMANIA
Federatia Romana de Radioamatorism [FRR]
Address: P.O. Box 22-50, R-71100 Bucuresti
Location: Str. N. Beloianis 27, R-70166 Bucuresti
Telephone: +40 (90) 119787
Telex: 11180 SPORTROM
SAN MARINO
Associazione Radioamatori della Repubblica di San Marino [ARRSM]
Address: P.O. Box 77, RSM-47031 San Marino
SENEGAL
Association des Radio-Amateurs du Senegal [ARAS]
Address: P.O. Box 971, Dakar
Location: Immeuble des Colis Postaux
Avenue El-Hadj Malick Sy, Dakar
Telefax: +221 217830
SIERRA LEONE
Sierra Leone Amateur Radio Society [SLARS]
Address: P.O. Box 10, Freetown
Telephone: +232 223335
SINGAPORE
Singapore Amateur Radio Transmitting Society [SARTS]
Address: G.P.O. Box 2728, Singapore 9047
Telephone: +65 281-9227
Telefax: +65 281-5898
SLOVAKIA
Slovensky Zvaz Radioamaterov [SZR]
Slovak Amateur Radio Association [SARA]
* Proposed for membership in Calendar No. 162
Voting to be completed on 16 September 1993
Address: P.O. Box 1, 85299 Bratislava 5
Location: Wolkrova 4, 85101 Bratislava
Telephone: +42 (7) 847501
Telefax: +42 (7) 845138
SLOVENIA
Zveza Radioamaterjev Slovenije [ZRS]
Address: Lepi Pot 6, 61000 Ljubljana
Telephone: +38 (61) 222459
SOLOMON ISLANDS
Solomon Islands Radio Society [SIRS]
Address: P.O. Box 418, Honiara
SOUTH AFRICA
South African Radio League [SARL]
Address: P.O. Box 807, Houghton 2041
Location: Cor. Duff Rd. & Louis Botha Ave., Houghton 2198
Telephone: +27 (11) 484-2830
Telefax: +27 (11) 484-2831
SPAIN
Union de Radioaficionados Espanoles [URE]
Address: P.O. Box 220, E-28080 Madrid
Location: Monte Igueldo 102, E-28018 Madrid
Telephone: +34 (1) 477-1413, (41) 24-4045 <EA1QF>
Telefax: +34 (1) 477-2071, (41) 24-4045 <EA1QF>
SRI LANKA
Radio Society of Sri Lanka [RSSL]
Address: P.O. Box 907, Colombo
Telephone: +94 (1) 505420
SURINAME
Vereniging van Radio Amateurs in Suriname [VRAS]
Address: P.O. Box 1153, Paramaribo
SWAZILAND
Radio Society of Swaziland [RSS]
Address: P.O. Box 1649, Matsadha
SWEDEN
Foreningen Sveriges Sandareamatorer [SSA]
Address: Ostmarksgatan 43, S-12342 Farsta
Telephone: +46 (8) 604-4006
SWITZERLAND
Union Schweizerischer Kurzwellen-Amateure [USKA]
Address: P.O. Box 9, CH-4539 Rumisberg
SYRIA
Technical Institute of Radio [TIR]
Address: P.O. Box 245, Damascus
TAIWAN
Chinese Taipei Amateur Radio League [CTARL]
Address: P.O. Box 93, Taipei
Location: 4F, #19 Lane 312, Sec. 2, Pa Teh Rd., Taipei
Telephone: +886 (2) 711-4652
Telefax: +886 (2) 777-3107
THAILAND
Radio Amateur Society of Thailand [RAST]
Address: G.P.O. Box 155, Bangkok 10501
Telephone: +66 (2) 277-9453
Telefax: +66 (2) 275-7288
TONGA
Amateur Radio Club of Tonga [ARCOT]
Address: P.O. Box 1553, Nuku'alofa
TRINIDAD AND TOBAGO
Trinidad and Tobago Amateur Radio Society [TTARS]
Address: P.O. Box 1167, Port of Spain
TURKEY
Telsiz Radyo Amatorleri Cemiyeti [TRAC]
Address: P.O. Box 109, Istanbul
Telephone: +90 (1) 571-1651
TURKS AND CAICOS ISLANDS
Turks and Caicos Amateur Radio Society [TCARS]
Address: c/o Jody Millspaugh, P.O. Box 350567
Ft. Lauderdale, FL 33335, U.S.A.
Telephone: +1 (809) 946-4680
Telefax: +1 (809) 946-4998
U.S.S.R.
* The U.S.S.R. ceased to exist towards the end of 1991.
Organizational changes are underway to reflect this fact.
Radio Sport Federation of the Russian Federation [RSF]
Address: P.O. Box 88, Moscow D-362, Russia
Telephone: +7 (95) 491-8661
Telefax: +7 (95) 200-2216 or 2217
Telex: 411852 TANTL

UNITED KINGDOM:
Radio Society of Great Britain [RSGB]
Address: Lambda House, Cranborne Rd.
Potters Bar, Herts. EN6 3JE
Telephone: +44 (707) 659015
Telefax: +44 (707) 645105
Telex: 9312-130923 RSGB

U.S.A.
American Radio Relay League [ARRL]
Address: 225 Main Street, Newington, CT 06111
Telephone: +1 (203) 666-1541
Telefax: +1 (203) 665-7531
Telex: 650215-5052 MCI

URUGUAY
Radio Club Uruguayo [RCU]
Address: P.O. Box 37, Montevideo
Location: Simon Blivar 1195, Montevideo
Telephone: +598 (2) 787523/787879

VANUATU
Vanuatu Amateur Radio Society [VARS]
Address: P.O. Box 665, Port Vila

VENEZUELA
Radio Club Venezolano [RCV]
Address: P.O. Box 2285, Caracas 1010-A
Location: Av. Lima, con Av. La Salle, Los Caboros, Caracas
Telephone: +58 (2) 781-7754
Telefax: +58 (2) 793-6883

WESTERN SAMOA
Western Samoa Amateur Radio Club [WSARC]
Address: P.O. Box 2015, Apia

YUGOSLAVIA
Savez Radio-Amatera Jugoslavije [SRJ]
Address: P.O. Box 48, YU-11001 Beograd
Telephone: +38 (11) 332216
Telex: 12405 UPRAD <M.S. Mandrino, Int'l Affairs Sec.>

ZAIRE
Union Zairoise des Radio-Amateurs [UZRA]

ZAMBIA
Radio Society of Zambia [RSZ]
Address: P.O. Box 20332, Kitwe

ZIMBABWE
Zimbabwe Amateur Radio Society [ZARS]
Address: P.O. Box 2377, Harare

Administrative Council

Richard L. Baldwin, W1RU - President, IARU
Michael J. Owen, VK3KI - Vice President, IARU
Larry E. Price, W4RA - Secretary IARU
L.v.d. Nadort, PA0LOU - Chairman, IARU Region 1
John Allaway, G3FKM - Secretary, IARU Region 1
Alberto Shaio, HK3DEU - President, IARU Region 2
Pedro Seidemann, YV5BPG - Secretary, IARU Region 2
David Rankin, 9V1RH - Chairman, IARU Region 3
Fred Johnson, ZL2AMJ - Director, IARU Region 3

International Secretariat

Address: P.O. Box 310905, Newington, CT 06131-0905, U.S.A.
Location: 225 Main Street, Newington, CT 06111-1494, U.S.A.
Telephone: +1 (203) 666-1541
Telefax: +1 (203) 665-7531
Telex: 650215-5052 MCI

President Emeritus
Noel B. Eaton - VE3CJ

Regional Organizations

IARU Region 1
Address: 10 Knightlow Road, Birmingham B17 8QB, UK
Telephone: +44 (21) 429-3200
Telefax: +44 (21) 429-4800
Cable: AMRAD BIRMINGHAM

IARU Region 2
Address: P.O. Box 2253, Caracas 1010A, Venezuela
Telephone: +58 (2) 986-8759
Telefax: +58 (2) 986-8759

IARU Region 3
Address: P.O. Box 73, Toshima, Tokyo 170-91, Japan
Location: Matsuoka Bldg. No. 2, 1-14-5 Sugamo, Toshima, Tokyo 170, JPN
Telephone: +81 (3) 3944-3322
Telefax: +81 (3) 3943-8282
Telex: 23868 JAPRETAR

Coordinators

Beacon Project: John G. Troster, W6ISQ,
82 Belbrook Way
Atherton, CA 94025, U.S.A.

CISPR: Tom Sprenger, PA3AVV, Dolomietenlaan 3
NL-5691 JP Son, The Netherlands

Monitoring System:
International—R.E. Knowles, ZL1BAD, Onewhero, R.D. 2
Tuakau, New Zealand

Region 1—Ronald Roden, G4GKO, 27 Wilmington Close, Hassocks
West Sussex BN6 8QB, United Kingdom
Region 2—Mark S. Allen, WJ7X, P.O. Box 451, Chanhassen MN 55317, U.S.A.
Region 3—R.M. Wahrlich, ZL1CVK,
Whangamarino Road, R.D. 2
Te Kauwhata, New Zealand

Satellite: Freddy De Guchteneire, ON6UG, Olmstr.18
B-9910 Gent OV, Belgium

(Courtesy of IARU)

ARRL DIVISION DIRECTORS AND VICE DIRECTORS (As Of September 1993)

Atlantic Division:
Hugh A. Trumbull, W3ABC
Vice Director—Kay C. Craigie, WT3P

Central Division:
Edmond A. Metzger, W9PRN
Vice Director—Howard S. Hunitington, K9KM

Dakota Division:
Rick Whiting, WØTN
Vice Director—Vacant

Delta Division:
Joel M. Harrison, WB5IGF
Rick Roderick, K5UR

Great Lakes Division:
Allan L. Severson, AB8P
Vice Director—George E. Race, WB8BGY

Hudson Division:
Stephen A. Mendelsohn, WA2DHF
Vice Director—Paul Vydareny, WB2VUK

Midwest Division:
Bill McGrannahan, KØORB
Vice Director—Larry Staples, WØAIB

New England Division:
William Burden, WB1BRE
Vice Director—Warren Rothberg, WB1HBB

Northwestern Division:
Mary Lewis, W7QGP
Vice Director—Mary Lou Brown, NM7N

Pacific Division:
Charles P. McConnell, W6DPD
Vice Director—Brad Wyatt, K6WR

Roanoke Division:
John C. Kanode, N4MM
Vice Director—Dennis Bodson, W4PWF

Rocky Mountain Division:
Marshall Quiat, AGØX
Vice Director—Bob Scupp, WB5YYX

Southeastern Division:
Frank M. Butler, W4RH
Vice Director—Evelyn Gauzens, W4WYR

Southwestern Division:
Fried Heyn, WA6WZO
Vice Director—Art Goddard, W6XD

Western Gulf Division:
Tom Comstock, N5TC
Vice Director—Sam C. Sitton KV5X

ARRL Section Managers

Atlantic Division:
Delaware—Randall K. Carlson, WBØJJX
Eastern Pennsylvania—Bob Stanhope, KB3YS
Maryland-D.C.—William Howard, WB3V
Southern New Jersey—Bruce Eichmann, KE2OP
Western New York—William Thompson, W2MTA
Western Pennsylvania—Bernie Fuller, N3EFN

Central Division:
Illinois—Sharon Harlan, WB9SFT
Indiana—Peggy Coulter, W9JUJ
Wisconsin—Roland R. Regent, K9GDF

Dakota Division:
Minnesota—Randy "Max" Wendel, NØFKU
North Dakota—Roger "Bill" Kurtti, WCØM
South Dakota—Roland Cory, WØYMB

Delta Division:
Arkansas—Bob Ideker, WB5VUH
Louisiana—Lionel A. "Al" Oubre, K5DPG
Mississippi—Richard Reed, KA5WRX
Tennessee—O.D. Keaton, WA4GLS

Great Lakes Division:
Kentucky—Steve Morgan, WB4NHO
Michigan—Dale Williams, WA8EFK
Ohio—David Kersten, N8AUH

Hudson Division:
Eastern New York—Paul S. Vydarney, WB2VUK
New York City-Long Island—Richard Ramhap, N2GQR
Northern New Jersey—Richard S. Moseson, NW2L

Midwest Division:
Iowa— Jack Duncan, KØCNM
Kansas—Robert M. Summers, KØBXF
Missouri—Roger Volk, KØGOB
Nebraska—Vern J. Wirka, WBØGQM

New England:
Connecticut—Betsey Doane, K1EIC
Eastern Massachusetts—David Crocker, W1TMO
Maine—Michelle Emmons, WM1C
New Hampshire—Alan Shuman, N1FIK
Rhode Island—Rick Fairweather, K1KYI
Vermont—Mitchell Stern, WB2JSJ
Western Massachusetts—Bill Voedisch, W1UD

Northwestern Division:
Alaska—Merle Beller, AL7LD
Eastern Washington—Kyle Pugh, KA7CSP
Idaho—Don Clower, KA7T
Montana—Darrell Thomas, N7KOR
Oregon—Randy Stimson, KZ7T
Western Washington—Harry Lewis, W7JWJ

Pacific Division:
East Bay—Bob Vaillo, W6RGG
Nevada—Joe Lambert, W8IXD
Pacific—Robert Schneider, AH6J
Sacramento Valley—Jettie Hill, W6RFF
San Francisco—John Wallack, W6TLK
San Joaquin Valley—Mike Siegel, KI6PR
Santa Clara Valley—Steve Wilson, KA6S

Roanoke Division:
North Carlonia—W. Reed Whitten, AB4W
South Carolina—Charles E. Moeller, N4FVU
Virginia—Edward Dingler, N4KSO
West Virginia—Karl S. Thompson, K8KT

Rocky Mountain Division:
Colorado—Tim Armagost, WBØTUB
New Mexico—Joe Knight, W5PDY
Utah—Richard Fisher, NS7K
Wyoming—Warren "Rev" Morton, WS7W

Southeastern Division:
Alabama—Ken McGlaughn, KM4JD
Georgia—Jim Altman, N4UCK
Nothern Florida—Rudy Hubbard, WA4PUP

Southern Florida—Richard D. Hill, WA4PFK
Puerto Rico—Tele Figeroa, KP4P
Virgin Islands—Ronald Hall, Sr., KP2N

Southwestern Division:
Arizona—Clifford Hauser, KD6XH
Los Angeles—Phineas J. Icenbice Jr.,W6BF
Orange—Joe H. Brown, W6UBQ
San Diego—Harry A. Hodges, WA6YOO
Santa Barbara—Thomas I. Geiger, W2KVA

West Gulf Division:
North Texas—Robert Adler, NZ2T
Oklahoma—Joseph Lynch, N6CL
South Texas—Alan Cross, WA5UZB
West Texas—Amelia "Milly" Wise, W5OVH

ARRL ADVISORY COMMITTEES

Contest Advisory Committee (As of May 16, 1993)

Atlantic: Dave Hallidy, KD5RO
8747 Tabors Corners Road, Wayland, NY 14572

Central: Joe Sego, KJ9D
5336 Elmwood Ave., Indianapolis, IN 46203

Dakota: Hans Brakob, KØHB
1610 N Weston Lane, Plymouth, MN 55447

Delta: Bill Rayburn, K4CXY
289 Taraview, Collierville, TN 38107

Great Lakes: John Tymensky, N8CXX
12333 Sandy Bottom Drive S., South Lyon, MI 48178

Hudson: J.P. Kleinhaus, AA2DU
11 Cotswold Way, Scarsdale, NY 10583

Midwest: Richard Barnett, KBØU
PO Box 4798, Overland Park, KS 66204

New England: Kurt Pauer, W1PH
PO Box 754, Amherst, NH 03031

Northwestern: Dan Eskenazi, K7SS
4821 51st SW, Seattle, WA 98116

Pacific: John Hultquist, K6GSS
188 Noe Street, Kihei, Maui, HI 96753

Roanoke: David Siddall, K3ZJ
9700 Darlene Lane, Great Falls, VA 22066-3803

Rocky Mountain: CHAIR Walt Stinson, WØCP
4150 East Quincy Avenue, Englewood, CO 80110-5051

Southeastern: Steve McElroy, K4JPD
5587 Five Notch Trail, Dougliasville, GA 30135

Southwestern: Mark Beckwith, WA6OTU
PO Box 4, Sierra Madre, CA 91024

West Gulf: James Eppright, K5RX
3123 Tower Trail, Dallas, TX 75229

RAC: Tim Ellam, VE6SH
107 Strathearn Rise SW, Calgary, Alberta T3H 1R5

Board Liaison: Brad Waytt, K6WR
18400-5 Overlook Road, Los Gatos, CA 95030

Staff Liaison: Billy Lunt,
225 Main Street, Newington, CT 06111

DX Advisory Committee (As of May 17, 1993)

Atlantic: Tony Gargano, N2SS
26 Winchester Drive, Sewell, NJ 08080

Central: Steve Lamb, W9NUF
27 Keswick Court, Lincolnshire, IL 60069

Dakota: Vernon Veenhuis, KUØS
207 N. O'Day Street, St. Paul, MN 55119

Delta: Rick Roderick, K5UR
PO Box 1463, Little Rock, AR 72203

Great Lakes: Theodore Mirgliotta, KB8NW
16806 W 130th Street, Strongville, OH 44136

Hudson: Bill Hellman, NA2M
3713 Valleyview Street, Mohegan Lake, NY 10547

Midwest: James Spencer, WØSR
3712 Tanager Drive NE, Cedar Rapids, IA 52402

New England: Bill Shipp, KC1AG
1195 Hill Road, Suffield, CT 06078

Northwestern: David Norton, AB9O
2612 NW 18th Avenue, Camas, WA 98607

Pacific: James Maxwell, W6CF
PO Box 473, Redwood Estates, CA 95044

Roanoke: Gary Dixon, K4MQG
1606 Crescent Ridge, Fort Mill, SC 29715

Rocky Mountain: Charlie Summers, KYØA
6392 S Yellowstone Way, Aurora, CO 80016

Southeastern: CHAIR Robert R. Beatty III, W4VQ
11 Heritage Cove Court, Casselberry, FL 32707

Southwestern: Bill E. Mauzey, Jr., W6RT
1631 Comstock Avenue, Los Angeles, CA 90024

West Gulf: Jim Lane, N5DC
1602 Chestnut Ridge Road, Kingwood, TX 77339

RAC: Garth Hamilton, VE3HO, 1309 Pelham St.,
Box 1156, Fonthill, Ontario L0S 1E0
OR PO Box 2641, Niagra Falls, NY 14302

Board Liaision: Rick Roderick, K5UR
PO Box 1463, Little Rock, AR 72203

Staff Liaison: Chuck Hutchinson, K8CH
225 Main Street, Newington, CT 06111

Public Service Advisory Committee (as of May 16, 1993)

Atlantic: Bob Josuweit, WA3PZO
3341 Sheffield Ave. Philadelphia PA 19136

Central: Richard (Rich) R. Regent, K9GDF
5003 S. 26th St., Milwaukee, WI 53221

Dakota: R. H. Munger, KAØARP
8386 Pequaywan Lk. Rd., Duluth, MN 55803

Delta: Jim Leist: KB5W
2632 Valley Wood Drive, Gautier, MS 39553

Great Lakes: David L. Kersten, N8AUH
2197 McKinley Avenue, Lakewood, OH 44107-5432

Hudson: Joe Schimmel, W2HPM
41 Midvale Ave., Farmingville, NY 11738

Midwest: Laurance (Larry) S. Staples, Jr., WØAIB
7862 Howe Circle, Shawnee Mission KS 66208-4260

New England: Bob Salow, WA1IDA
Box 3773, Natick, MA 01760-0030

Northwestern: John White, K7RUN
P. O. Box 13274, Portland, OR 97213

Pacific: Steve Wilson KA6S
813 Berryessa St., Milpitas, CA 95035

Roanoke: Charles (Ned) E. Moeller, N4FVU
116 Willow Winds Drive, Columbia, SC 29210-4454

Rocky Mtn.: Joe T. Knight: W5PDY
10408 Snow Heights, NE, Albuquerque, NM 87112-3057

Southeastern: Joel I. Kandel, KI4T
5463 SW 92nd Ave., Miami, FL 33165

West Gulf: CHAIR, Tom Anderson, WW5L
3505 Cliffwood Dr., Bedford, TX 76021-2043

RAC: Bill Hardie, VE3EFX
755 Johnston Crescent, Kincardine, Ontario, Canada N2Z 1S5

BOD Liaison: Art Goddard, W6XD
2901 Palau Pl., Costa Mesa, CA 92626

Southwestern: Ron Boan, AK6Y
PO Box 50351, Parks, AZ 86018

ARRL HQ Staff Liaison: Luck Hurder, KY1T, Field Services Dept.
ARRL, 225 Main St., Newington, CT 06111
TEL: 203-666-1541; FAX: 203-665-7531

ARRL VHF Repeater Advisory Committee

Atlantic: William Van Aller, K3CZ
Central: George Isley, WD9GIG
Dakota: Reuben Ruen, WBØBWL
Delta: Nita Wofford, N4DON
Great Lakes: David Prestal, W8AJR
Hudson: Chris Packham, WG2W
Midwest: Wayne L. Fowler, KAØE
New England: Mitch Stern, WB2JSJ
Northwest: Clay Freinwald, K7CR
Pacific: Bob Watson, W6IEW, Chairman
Roanoke: Herman Cone, WB4DBB
Rocky Mountain: Mike Barnell, WDØFVV
Southeastern: David L. Shiplett, AC4MU
Southwestern: Karl Pagel, N6BVU
West Gulf: Joe Jarrett, K5FOG
RAC: Dr. David Toth, VE3GYQ
Board Liason: George Race, WB8BGY
Staff Liason: Jay Mabey, NUØX

ARRL VHF/UHF Advisory Committee

Atlantic: Robert Bennett, W3WCQ, Chairman
Central: Joseph Schoder, W9JUV
Dakota: Edward Grey, WØSD
Delta: R.A. "Bob" Taylor, WB5LBT
Great Lakes: David Smith, W8YZ
Hudson: Gordon Beattie, N2DSY
Midwest: Larry Lambert, NØLL
New England: Thomas Kirby, W1EJ
Northwestern: Merle Cox, W7YOZ
Pacific: Charles Swedblom, WA6EXV
Roanoke: Thomas Gooding, K4LHB
Rocky Mountain: Lauren Libby, KXØO
Southeastern: Ronald E. Monk, W4ODW
Southwestern: David Guitierrez, WA6PMX
West Gulf: Kent Britain, WA5VJB
RAC: Dana A. Shtun, VE3DSS
Board Liason: Warren Rothberg, WB1HBB
Staff Liason: Zack Lau, KH6CP

AMERICAN RADIO RELAY LEAGUE FIELD ORGANIZATION

The United States is divided into 15 ARRL Divisions. Every two years, the ARRL full members in each of these divisions elect a director and a vice director to represent them on the League's Board of Directors. The Board determines the policies of the League, which are carried out by the Headquarters staff. A director's function is principally policymaking at the highest level, but the Board of Directors is all-powerful in the conduct of League affairs.

The 15 divisions are further broken down into 69 sections and the ARRL full members in each section elect a Section Manager (SM). The SM is the senior elected ARRL official in the section, and in cooperation with the director, fosters and encourages all ARRL activities within the section. A breakdown of sections within each division (and counties within each split-state section) follows:

Atlantic Division:

Delaware;
Eastern Pennsylvania;
(Adams, Berks, Bucks, Carbon, Chester, Columbia, Cumberland, Dauphin, Delaware, Juniata, Lackawanna, Lancaster, Lebanon, Lehigh, Luzerne, Lycoming, Monroe, Montgomery, Montour, Northampton, Northumberland, Perry, Philadelphia, Pike, Schuylkill, Snyder, Sullivan, Susquehanna, Tioga, Union, Wayne, Wyoming, York.)
Maryland-D.C.;
Southern New Jersey;
(Atlantic, Burlington, Camden, Cape May, Cumberland, Gloucester, Mercer, Ocean, Salem.)
Western New York;
(Allegany, Broome, Cattaraugus, Cayuga, Chautauqua, Chemung, Chenango, Clinton, Cortland, Delaware, Erie, Essex, Franklin, Fulton, Genesee, Hamilton, Herkimer, Jefferson, Lewis, Livingston, Madison, Monroe, Montgomery, Niagara, Oneida, Onondaga, Ontario, Orleans, Oswego, Otsego, St. Lawrence, Schoharie, Schuyler, Seneca, Steuben, Tioga, Tompkins, Wayne, Wyoming, Yates.)
Western Pennsylvania;
(Those counties not listed under Eastern Pennsylvania.)

Central Division:

Illinois;
Indiana;
Wisconsin.

Dakota Division:

Minnesota;
North Dakota;
South Dakota.

Delta Division:

Arkansas;
Louisiana;
Mississippi;
Tennessee.

Great Lakes Division:

Kentucky;
Michigan;
Ohio.

Hudson Division:
Eastern New York;
(Albany, Columbia, Dutchess, Greene, Orange, Putnam, Rensselaer, Rockland, Saratoga, Schenectady, Sullivan, Ulster, Warren, Washington, Westchester.)
New York City, Long Island;
(Bronx, Kings, Nassau, New York, Queens, Staten Island, Suffolk.)
Northern New Jersey;
(Bergen, Essex, Hudson, Hunterdon, Middlesex, Monmouth, Morris, Passaic, Somerset, Sussex, Union, Warren.)

Midwest Division:
Iowa;
Kansas;
Missouri;
Nebraska.

New England Division:
Connecticut;
Maine;
Eastern Massachusetts;
(Barnstable, Bristol, Essex, Middlesex, Nantucket, Norfolk, Plymouth, Suffolk.)
New Hampshire;
Rhode Island;
Vermont;
Western Massachusetts;
(Those counties not listed under Eastern Massachusetts.)

Northwestern Division:
Alaska;
Idaho;
Montana;
Oregon;
Eastern Washington;
(Okanogan, Chelan, Douglas, Kittitas, Yakima, Klickitat, Benton, Franklin, Walla Walla, Adams, Grant, Lincoln, Ferry, Stevens, Pend Oreille, Spokane, Whitman, Columbia, Garfield, Asotin.)
Western Washington;
(Those counties not listed under Eastern Washington.)

Pacific Division:
East Bay;
(Alameda, Contra Costa, Napa, Solano.)
Nevada;
Pacific;
(Hawaii and U.S. possessions in the Pacific.)
Sacramento Valley;
(Alpine, Amador, Butte, Colusa, El Dorado, Glenn, Lassen, Modoc, Nevada, Placer, Plumas, Sacramento, Shasta, Sierra, Siskiyou, Sutter, Tehama, Trinity, Yolo, Yuba.)
San Francisco;
(Del Norte, Humboldt, Lake, Marin, Mendocino, San Francisco, Sonoma.)
San Joaquin Valley;
(Calaveras, Fresno, Kern, Kings, Madera, Mariposa, Merced, Mono, San Joaquin, Stanislaus, Tulare, Tuolumne.)
Santa Clara Valley;
(Monterey, San Benito, San Mateo, Santa Clara, Santa Cruz.)

Roanoke Division:
North Carolina;
South Carolina;
Virginia;
West Virginia.

Rocky Mountain Division:
Colorado;
Utah;
New Mexico;
Wyoming.

Southeastern Division:
Alabama;
Georgia;
Northern Florida;
(Alachua, Baker, Bay, Bradford, Calhoun, Citrus, Clay, Columbia, Dixie, Duval, Escambia, Flagler, Franklin, Gadsden, Gilchrist, Gulf, Hamilton, Hernando, Holmes, Jackson, Jefferson, Lafayette, Lake, Leon, Levy, Liberty, Madison, Marion, Nassau, Okaloosa, Orange, Pasco, Putnam, Santa Rosa, Seminole, St. Johns, Sumter, Suwanee, Taylor, Union, Volusia, Wakulla, Walton, Washington.)
South Florida;
(Those counties not listed under Northern Florida.)
Puerto Rico;
U.S. Virgin Islands;
(including Guantanamo Bay.)

Western Gulf Division:
Northern Texas;
(Anderson, Archer, Baylor, Bell, Bosque, Bowie, Brown, Camp, Cass, Cherokee, Clay, Collin, Comanche, Cooke, Coryell, Dallas, Delta, Denton, Eastland, Ellis, Erath, Falls, Fannin, Franklin, Freestone, Grayson, Gregg, Hamilton, Harrison, Henderson, Hill, Hood, Hopkins, Hunt, Jack, Johnson, Kaufman, Lamar, Lampasas, Limestone, Mc Lennan, Marion, Mills, Maontague, Morris, Nacogdoches, Navarro, Palo Pinto, Panola, Parker, Rains, Red River, Rockwall, Rusk, Shelby, Smith, Somervell, Stephens, Tarrant, Throckmorton, Titus, Upshur, Van Zandt, Wichita, Wilbarger, Wise, Wood, Young.)

Oklahoma;
Southern Texas;
(Angelina, Aransas, Atacosa, Austin, Bandera, Bastrop, Bee, Bexar, Blanco, Brazoria, Brazos, Brooks, Burlseon, Burnet, Caldwell, Calhoun, Cameron, Chambers, Colorado, Comal, Concho, DeWitt, Dimmitt, Duval, Edwards, Fayette, Fort Bend, Frio, Galveston, Gillespie, Goliad, Gonzales, Grimes, Guadalupe, Hardin, Harris, Hays, Hidalgo, Houston, Jackson, Jasper, Jefferson, Jim Hogg, Jim Wells, Karnes, Kendall, Kenedy, Kerr, Kimble, Kinney, Kleberg, LaSalle, Lavaca, Lee, Leon, Liberty, Live Oak, Llano, Madison, Mason, Matagorda, Maverick, McCulloch, McMullen, Medina, Menard, Milam, Montgomery, Newton, Nueces, Orange, Polk, Real, Refugio, Robertson, Sabine, San Augustine, San Jacinto, San Patricio, Victoria, Walker, Waller, Washington, Webb, Wharton, Willacy, Williamson, Wilson, Zapata, Zavala.)

Western Texas;
(Those Counties not already listed under Northern and Southern Texas.)

The following entities were formerly part of the Canadian Division of the ARRL, and are often used along with the sections as multipliers in contests such as the ARRL November Sweepstakes:

Alberta;
British Columbia;
Manitoba;
Maritime;
(Nova Scotia, New Brunswick, Prince Edward Island, Labrador, Newfoundland.)
Northwest Territories;
(and Yukon.)
Ontario;
Quebec;
Saskatchewan

(Courtesy of ARRL)

HAM ASTRONAUTS IN SPACE

Name	Callsign
Jay Apt	N5QWL
Sergei Avdeyev	RV3DW
Ellen S. Baker	KB5SIX
Alexander Balandin	U7MIR
John David F. Bartoe	W4NYZ
Kenneth "Ken" D. Cameron	KB5AWP
Kenneth "Ken" D. Cockrell	KB5UAH
Brian Duffy	N5WQW
Anthony "Tony" W. England	WØORE
Martin Fettman	KC5AXA
Klau-Dietrich Flade	DPØMIR
Colin "Mike" M. Foale	KB5UAC
Dirk D. Frimount	ON1AFD
Reinhard Furrer	DD6CF/DPØSL
Owen K. Garriott	W5LFL
Linda M. Godwin	N5RAX
Alexander Kaleri	U8MIR
Sergei Krikalev	U5MIR
Dave C. Leetsma	N5WQC
Bill McArthur	KC5ACR
Musa Manarov	RV3AM/U2MIR
Ernst Messerschmid	DG2KM/DPØSL
Mamoru Mohri	7L2NJY
Steven "Steve" R. Nagel	N5RAW
Ellen Ochoa	KB5TZZ
Wubbo Ockels	PE1LFO/DPØSL
Steve Oswald	KB5YSR
Ronald "Ron" A. Parise	WA4SIR
Valery Polyakov	U3MIR
Charles Precourt	KB5YSQ
Richard "Dick" N. Richards	KB5SIW
Jerry L. Ross	N5SCW
Hans-Wilhelm Schlegel	DG1KIH
Helen Sharman	GB1MIR
Anatoly Solovov	U6MIR
Kathryn "Kathy" D. Sullivan	N5YYV
Vladimir Titov	U1MIR
Michael Tognini	F5MIR
Alexander Viktorenko	U9MIR
Alexander Volkov	U4MIR
Janice Voss	KC5BTK
Ulrich Walter	DG1KIM

* It has long been rumored that Yuri Gagarin was at some point licensed as a Radio Amateur. This has been determined to be false.

Space Center Callsigns

These groups provide Shuttle Audio re-transmission on various frequencies during missions.

WA3NAN: Goddard Space Center, Goddard A.R.C., Maryland (3.86, 7.185, 14.295, 21.395, 28.650, 147.45 MHz).
W5RRR: Johnson Space Center, J.S.C. A.R.C., Texas (3.85, 7.227, 14.280, 21.350, 28.400, 146.64 MHz).
W6VIO: Jet Propulsion Labrotory, J.P.L.A.R.C., Pasadena, California (14.270, 21.340, 224.04 Mhz).
K6MF: Los Altos,California (3.84, 7.165, 145.585 MHz).

AMATEUR RADIO SATELLITES

Satellite	Launch	Status
OSCAR-1	DEC12-61	Functioned for 21 days—battery exhausted.
OSCAR-2	JUN02-62	Functioned for 19 days—battery exhausted.
OSCAR-3	MAR09-65	Functioned for 18 days—battery exhausted/first with solar cells.
OSCAR-4	DEC21-65	Functioned for 85 days-fully solar powered-bad orbit.
Australis/OSCAR-5	JAN23-70	Functioned for 52 days-contained beacon only-battery exhausted.
PHASE-2a/OSCAR-6	OCT15-72	Functioned for 4 1/2 yrs/first transponder/solar cells + batteries.
PHASE-2b/OSCAR-7	NOV15-74	Functioned for 6 1/2 yrs/two transponders.
PHASE-2c/OSCAR-8	MAR05-78	Functioned for 5 1/2 yrs/two transponders.
RS-1	OCT26-78	Functioned for several months/one transponder.
RS-2	OCT26-78	Functioned for 3 yrs/one transponder.
Phase-3a/OSCAR-10	MAY23-80	launch failure.
ISKRA-1	JUL10-81	Functioned 89 days.
UO-9	OCT06-81	Functioned 8 yrs/first with camera.
RS-3	DEC17-81	Functioned for several months/batteries exhausted.
RS-4	DEC17-81	Functioned for several months/batteries exhausted.
RS-5	DEC17-81	Functioned 7 yrs/batteries exhausted.
RS-6	DEC17-81	Functioned for several yrs/batteries exhausted.
RS-7	DEC17-81	Functioned for 8 yrs/batteries exhausted.
RS-8	DEC17-81	Functioned for several yrs/batteries exhausted.
ISKRA-2	MAY17-82	Functioned for 53 days/launced by hand from SALYUT-7.
ISKRA-3	NOV18-82	Functioned for 28 days/launched by hand from SALYUT-7.
PHASE-3B/AO-10	JUN16-83	Presently functioning/bad orbit.
UoSAT-B/UO-11	MAR02-84	Failed SEPT09-93/reloading program—up soon.
NUSAT-1	APR29-85	Functioned 2 yrs/shuttle launched/commercial-amateur built.
JAS-1a/FO-12	AUG12-86	Functioned for 3 yrs/electrical failure.
RS-10/11	JUN23-87	Presently operating.

Satellite	Launch	Status
PHASE-3C/AO-13	JUN15-88	Presently operating.
UoSAT-D/UO-14	JAN22-90	Presently operating.
UoSAT-E/UO-15	JAN22-90	Failed immediately after launch.
PACSAT/AO-16	JAN22-90	Presently functioning.
DOVE/DO-17	JAN22-90	Presently functioning.
NUSAT-2/WEBERSAT/WO-18	JAN22-90	Presently functioning-camera.
LUSAT/LO-19	JAN22-90	Presently functioning.
JAS-1b/FO-20	FEB07-90	Presently functioning.
BADR-A	JUL16-90	Functioned for 145 days.
AO-21/RS-14	JAN29-91	Presently functioning.
RS-12/13	FEB05-91	Presently functioning.
MICROSAT-1>7	JUL17-91	Functioned for 6 months/bad orbit/non-amateur.
UoSAT-5-F/UO-22	JUL17-91	Presently functioning.
KITSAT-A/KO-23	AUG10-92	Presently functioning.
ARSENE/AO-24	MAY13-93	No telemetry since SEP09-93.
ITAMSAT-1/IO-26	SEP26-93	Just launched.
KITSAT-B/KO-25	SEP26-93	Just launched.
POSAT-A	SEP26-93	Just launched.
EYESAT-1/AO-27	SEP26-93	Just launched.

O.S.C.A.R—Orbital Satellite Carrying Amateur Radio.

R.S.—Radiosputnik

AMATEUR RADIO SATELLITES PROPOSED OR WAITING TO LAUNCH

Satellite	Planned Launch	Satellite	Planned Launch
UMAMSAT-1	1993/94	SEDSAT-1	Unknown
POSAT-B	1993/94	SUNSAT	Unknown
RS-15	1993/94	NANOSAT	Unknown
TECHSAT	1993/94	SOLAR SAIL MOON RACER	Unknown

AMATEUR RADIO SATELLITES FREQUENCY/MODES

Satellite	Beacon/Mode	Uplink Frequency	Downlink Frequency	Modes Used
AO-10				
	145.810 CARRIER			Do not use satellite if beacon is FMing.
	B	435.050-435.155	145.850-145.955	CW,SSB-INVERTING
UO-11				
	145.825 AFSK/FM			
	435.025 AFSK/FM			
	2401.500 AFSK/FM			
RS-10				
	29.357 CW BEACON			
	29.403 CW BEACON			
	145.857 CW BEACON			
	145.903 CW BEACON			
	A	145.860-145.900	29.360-29.400	CW,SSB
	K	21.260-21.200	29.360-29.400	CW,SSB
	T	21.160-21.200	145.860-145.900	CW,SSB
	KA	21.160-21.200	145.860-145-900 AND 29.360-29.400	CW,SSB
	KT	21.160-21.200	145.860-145.900 AND 29.360-29.400	CW,SSB
	A-ROBOT	145.820	29.357 OR 29.403	CW
	K-ROBOT	21.120	29.357 OR 29.403	CW
	T-ROBOT	21.120	145.857 OR 145.903	CW
RS-11				
	29.453 CW BEACON			
	29.407 CW BEACON			
	145.907 CW BEACON			
	145.953 CW BEACON			
	A	145.910-145.950	29.410-29.450	CW,SSB
	K	21.210-21.250	29.410-29.450	CW,SSB
	T	21.210-21.250	145.910-145.950	CW,SSB
	KA	21.210-21.250 AND 145.910-145.950	29.410-29.450	CW,SSB
	KT	21.210-21.250	29.410-29.450 AND 145.910-145.950	CW,SSB

Satellite	Beacon/Mode	Uplink Frequency	Downlink Frequency	Modes Used
	A-ROBOT	145.830	29.453 OR 29.407	CW
	K-ROBOT	21.130	29.453 OR 29.407	CW
	T-ROBOT	21.130	145.907 OR 145.953	CW
AO-13				
	145.812 B BEACON			
	145.985 B Eng. BEACON			
	435.651 J OR L BEACON			
	2400.325 S BEACON			
	B	435.420-435.570	145.825-145.975	CW,SSB-INVERTING
	J	144.425-144.475	435.940-435.990	CW,SSB-INVERTING
	L	1269.330-1269.620	435.715-436.005	CW,SSB-INVERTING
	JL	Both Modes in Operation Simultaneously		
	S	435.601-435.637	2400.711-2400.747	CW,SSB,FM-INVERTING
	RUDAK		Inoperative	
PACSAT/UO-14				
		Operating in Non-Amateur Modes at present		
AO-16				
	J	145.90/.92/.94/.96		1200 BPS AFSK(FM)
	J	437.035		1200 BPS PSK(SSB) AX.25
	J	437.050		1200 BPS RAISED COSINE AX.25
	S	2401.143		200 BPS PSK(SSB) AX.25
DOVE/DO-17				
	145.825 BEACON			FM DIGITAL VOICE-or- 1200 BPS AFSK(FM) AX.25
	2401.221 BEACON			FM DIGITAL VOICE-or- 1200 BPS AFSK(FM) AX.25
WEBERSAT/WO-18				
	437.125 BEACON			12 W.P.M. CW TELEMETRY

Satellite	Beacon/Mode	Uplink Frequency	Downlink Frequency	Modes Used
	L	1265.0		NTSC AM ATV
	J	437.075		1200 BPS PSK(SSB) AX.25
	J	437.126		1200 BPS RAISED COSINE (SSB) AX.25
	J	144.3-144.5		DIGITAL
LUSAT/LO-19				
	437.125 BEACON			12 W.P.M. CW TELEMETRY
	J	145.84/.86/.88/.90		1200 BPS AFSK(FM) Manchester
	J	437.153		1200 BPS PSK(SSB) AX.25
	J	437.125		1200 BPS RAISED COSINE (SSB) AX.25
FUJI/FO-20				
	435.795 BEACON			CW
	435.91 BEACON			DIGITAL TELEMETRY
	JA	145.900-146.000	435.800-435.900	CW,SSB,ANOLOG-INVERTING-WEDNES-DAYS-UTC.
	JD	145.85/.87/.89/.91	435.910	1200 BPS AFSK(FM) AX.25-EVERY DAY BUT WEDNESDAY-UTC.
AO-21/RS-14				
	145.822 BEACON			CW
	145.952 BEACON			PSK(FM)
	145.983 BEACON			PSK(SSB)
	145.948 BEACON			CW
	145.838 BEACON			PSK(FM)
	145.800 BEACON			PSK(FM)
	B-PRIMARY	435.022-435.102	145.852-145.932	LINEAR,CW,SSB-INVERTING

Satellite	Beacon/Mode	Uplink Frequency	Downlink Frequency	Modes Used
	B-SECONDARY	435.043-435.123	145.866-145.946	CW,SSB-INVERTING
	RUDAK-2 RX-1	435.016		1200 BPS AFSK(FM) +VOICE
	RUDAK-2 RX-2	435.155		2400 BPS PSK(FM)
	RUDAK-2 RX-3a	435.193	145.983	4800 BPS PSK(FM)
	RUDAK-2 RX-3b	435.193		9600 BPS PSK(FM)
	RUDAK-2 RX-4	435.043		MANY MODES+DSP
	RUDAK-2		145.987	300, 1200, 2400, 4800,9600 BPS
	L-RUDAK	1269.675	435.675	PSK(FM)+CW,RTTY, SSTV,FAX,DSP
RS-12	29.408 CW BEACON			
	29.454 CW BEACON			
	145.912 CW BEACON			
	145.958 CW BEACON			
	A	145.910-145.950	29.410-29.450	CW,SSB
	K	21.210-21.250	29.410-29.450	CW,SSB
	T	21.210-21.250 950	145.910-145..950	CW,SSB
	KA	21.210-21.250	145.910-145-950-AND-29.410-29.450	CW,SSB
	KT	21.210-21.250	145.910-145.950-AND-29.410-29.450	CW,SSB
	A-ROBOT	145.830	29.408-or-29.454	CW
	K-ROBOT	21.129	29.408-or-29.454	CW
	T-ROBOT	21.129	145.912-or-145.958	CW
RS-13	29.458 CW BEACON			
	29.504 CW BEACON			
	145.862 CW BEACON			
	145.908 CW BEACON			
	A	145.960-146.000	29.460-29.500	CW,SSB
	K	21.260-21.300	29.460-29.500	CW,SSB
	T	21.260-21.300	145.960-146.000	CW,SSB
	KA	21.260-21.300-AND-145.960-146.000	29.460-29.500	CW,SSB
	KT	21.260-21.300	29.460-29.500-AND-145.960-146.000	CW,SSB
	A-ROBOT	145.840	29.458-or-29.504	CW
	K-ROBOT	21.138	29.458-or-29.504	CW

Satellite	Beacon/Mode	Uplink Frequency	Downlink Frequency	Modes Used
	T-ROBOT	21.138	145.862-or-145.908	CW
UO-22	B	145.900-or-145.975	435.120	9600 BPS FSK(FM)
KISAT-A/KO-23	J	145.900-or-145.850	435.167	9600 BPS FSK(FM)+DSP+CAMERA
ARSENE/AO-24		NO TELEMETRY SINCE SEP09-93		
	B	435.050,435.100,435.150	145.975	1200 BPS PSK(FM) AX.25
	S	435.110	2446.540	LINEAR
ITAMSAT-1/IO-26	J	145.875,145.900		1200/4800 BPS
	J	145.925,145.950		1200/9600 BPS
	J	435.867		1200 BPS
	J	435.822		1200 PSK(FM) AFSK(FM) 9600BPS(G3RUH)
KITSAT-B/KO-25	J	145.870,145.980	435.175,436.500	9600 BPS FSK PACKET+DSP+CAMERAS
POSAT-A	J	145.925,145.975	435.250,435.275	9600 BPS
EYESAT-1/AO-27	J	145.850	436.800	300-9600 BPS

AMATEUR RADIO-RELATED TELEPHONE BULLETIN-BOARD SYSTEMS

Listing criteria: Significant HAM interest section, General open public access, Non-Commercial
(Sorted by telephone Area Code)

Board Name	Number/State	SYSOP	FidoNET
The DX Connection	201-692-3705 NJ		
BFWK BBS	201-941-3302 NJ	KB2JXK	
Info-Link	203-295-8384 CT		Fido 1:320/73
Windsor Amateur Radio Union	203-298-9989 CT	WB1CBY	Fido 1:142/100
Trumbull-Mini	203-261-6434 CT	WA1QKS	Fido 1:141/370
The Planet Earth BBS	203-335-7742 CT	WA1UCQ	Fido 1:141/455
The Dark Side BBS	203-438-4721 CT		Fido 1:141/745
Gemstone BBS	203-449-8747 CT	N1GZA	Fido 1:320/157
Rod's Maximus	203-621-9936 CT	N1FNE	Fido 1:141/1840
ARRL BBS	203-666-0578 CT	W1AW	
Teletalk	203-799-7454 CT		Fido 1:141/328
Bill VE4UB	204-785-8518 MB		
The Data Connection	205-601-0917 AL	N4SZO	Fido 1:3625/465
The Bulletin Board BBS	205-758-5017 AL	W4WYP WD4DAT	
Bears BBS	206-237-3472 WA	WM7O	
The AA6ED Packet Gateway	206-271-4657 WA	AA6ED	
Boone's Farm	206-282-2851 WA		
The Precedent	206-355-1295 WA	N7NIP	Fido 1:343/9
KA1SVC BBS	207-247-6225 ME	KA1VSC	
Cobra BBS	207-725-0899 ME	N1MQY	
The Rebel BBS	208-997-3937 ID		
WCPB	209-661-5355 CA	KM6HK	Fido 1:10/45
The Ninety 6 Quarts of Gin	209-625-0618 CA	N6QOG	
Communication Specialties	212-645-8673 NY	KF2JO	Fido 1:278/712
Kenwood Factory BBS	213-761-8284 CA		
COM Port One	214-226-1181 TX	WA5EHA	Fido 1:124/7009
The One Stop BBS	214-240-2069 TX	N5NMA	
Datalink BBS AMSAT	214-394-7438 TX	N5ITU	
Smoked Armadillos	214-669-9645 TX	AA5SA	Fido 1:124/5118
The 5th Dimension	215-827-7689 PA	K3DSM	Fido 1:273/304
Better Amateur Radio	216-237-8208 OH	KB8NW	
Bill	216-526-9482 OH		
The Radio Room BBS	216-686-8800 OH	KD8GC	Fido 1:157/607.0
Cleveland Hamnet	216-942-7516 OH	WB8APD	
	216-942 6382 OH	WB8APD	
Radio Daze	219-256-2255 IN		
PC-HAM	301-593 9067 MD	G3ZCZ	
3 WINKS BBS	301-590-9629 MD	W3INK	Fido 1:109/418
Around and About	301-621-9669 MD	WA3TKW	
Diamond Jims	301-645-7964 MD		
WJ3P Ham Exchange BBS	301-831-5954 MD	WJ3P	
First Due BBS	301-949-1927 MD	WA3ZKE	
WB3IKP BBS	302-798-8186 DE	WB3IKP	Fido 1:150/220.0
Mile High	303-431-1404 CO	NØRSE	Fido 1:104/223
The S.T.A.R BBS	305-238-8851 FL		Fido 1:135/17
The Right Connections BBS	305-382-6687 FL	N4LDG	Fido 1:135/63
The Bashful Pervert	305-472-7715 FL	N4BP	
Telcom Central	305-828-7909 FL	KD4BBM	Fido 1:135/23
FTW	307-328-1923 WY	N7PQZ	
TP PACKET BBS(Twisted pair)	309-822-8781 IL	WD9HYY	
PC Haven	310-374-7929 CA	AB6GA	Fido 1:102/137
GFRN BBS	310-541-2503 CA	WB6YMH	
Air Studio	313-546-7045 MI	KA8NCR	Fido 1:120/216
The M.A.R.C. BBS	313-669-4279 MI	N8NSX	
Arthur BBS	313-879-2318 MI	KB8IQW	Fido 1:120/120
The Black Hole BBS	313-879-7387 MI	N8MAX	Fido 1:120/36

Fun City USA	314-893-9166 MO	NØIWK	Fido 1:289/18
Dots-N-Dashes BBS	315-642-1220 NY		Fido 1:2609/811
Ham-Net BBS	315-682-1824 IN	N2PMM	Fido 1:260/375
N2JEU BBS	315-697-5123 NY	N2JEU	Fido 1:260/304
Southside BBS	317-535-9097 IN	KB9BVN	Fido 1:231/30
American Silver Dollar BBS	318-443-0271 LA	WB5ASD	
Tri-State Data Exchange	319-583-6462 IA		Fido 1:283/610
The Roadrunner BBS	401-821-1457 RI		
Aksarben ARC BBS	402-289-4658 NE	WB0QPP	
The Cameo BBS	403-295-7088 AB	VE6TAK	Fido 1:134/63
Alta Packet Info Net	403-464-5069 AB		Fido 1:342/7
Terraplex	403-743-4696 AB	VE6CYR	Fido 1:3402/4
Thunder Bay Trading PosT	404-516-1282 GA	WA3ZLB	
WA4BRO'S Ham Board BBS	404-552-0868 GA	WA4BRO	
Top of the Rock BBS	404-921-8687 GA	KB4ZTN	
Retriever's Retreat	405-359-1540 OK	KB5WIF	Fido 1:147/2001
N7GXP Hamshack	406-458-9379 MT		
HAM BYTES	407-575-9680 FL	KD4VBS	
Pclogic	407-879-4823 FL	W4NVC	
Atlanta Amateur Radio Club	404-393-3083 GA		
Lockheed Arc BBS	404-949-0687 GA		
Mt. Retreat	408-335-4595 CA		Fido 1:216/506.0
The House of Ill Compute	408-338-6860 CA		Fido 1:216/21
Saratoga Clone	408-395-1402 CA	WA6LYZ/WD5ICZ	
CSI Online	409-321-3198 TX		
The Amateur Radio BBS	410-661-2475 MD	WB3FFV	
	410-661-2598 MD	WB3FFV	
	410-661-2648 MD	WB3FFV	
NB3P BBS	410-750-6403 MD	NB3P	
Allegheny-Kiski	412-226-7357 PA	KA3NVP	
Beaver Valley Ara BBS	412-775-7536 PA	KA3CYW	
Joe's Garage	414-453-5145 WI	N9JR	Fido 1:154/222
Milwaukee Heath Users Grp	414-548-9866 WI	KA9TGN	
No-Name RBBS	415-481-0252 CA	N6MON RBBS	
BBS-JC	415-961-7250 CA	K6LLK	
The Black Hole BBS	419-228-7236 OH	KB8BMQ	Fido 1:234/16
The Ether Net	501-455-0628 AR	WDØGRC	
Freedom One HST	501-932-7932 AR	KB5SEJ	Fido 1:389/6
Deckman's Exchange	502-267-7422 KY	N4VEH	
The Rose	503-286-3855 OR		Fido 1:105/7
MacHam	503-656-0510 OR	KI7FG	
The Wireless BBS	503-692-7097 OR	WB7VHB	
Helpnet of Baton Rouge	504-273-3116 LA	W5KGG	Fido 1:396/101
The Digital Cottage	504-897-6614 LA	K8VDU	Fido 1:396/65
Salt Air	508-385-3427 MA	KQ1K	
The Cul-de-Sac BBS	508-429-8385 MA	WA1YDL	Fido 1:322:360
Waystar BBS	508-481-7147 MA		
Ham Shack BBS	508-949-3590 MA		
Secret BBS	508-998-6434 MA		Fido 1:101/873
Think Tank II	509-244-6446 WA		Fido 1:346/8
Time & Eternity	510-886-5467 CA	KB2NSX	Fido 1:215/17
USS Pegasus - Austin Node	512-335-5403 TX	KB5NFN	Fido 1:382/47.0
The Antenna Farm BBS	512-444-1052 TX		
Hams on Health-Link	512-444-9908 TX	KB5IN	Fido 1:382/5
The Thirst for Knowledge	512-454-8065 TX	K5ARS	Fido 1:382/74
The 128 P.C.	512-827-1025 TX		Fido 1:387/1101
The Armadillo BBS	512-837-2003 TX	N5OWD	Fido 1:382/32
Computer Data Services	512-887-0787 TX		
The Electronic Avenue	512-979-0469 TX	KA5THB	Fido 1:387/306
The Listening Post	513-474-3719 OH		
Light in the Darke BBS	513-547-3313 OH	WA8RUO	Fido 1:108/210
KIC-BBS	513-762-1115 OH	N8KTW	Fido 1:108/89
VE2MMM Amateur Radio BBS	514-624-5651 QU		Fido 1:167/230
TTGCITN Super BBS	515-265-0164 IA	NØPBS	Fido 1:290/10
The Ham Tech BBS	515-981-9116 IA	NØEPU	

The Long Island AR BBS	516-368-4979 NY	N2MCS	
Amateur Radio Selling Post	516-581-1896 NY		
No Frills Plus Ham BBS	516-661-3643 NY		
Your Software Resource	516-736-6662 NY	N2HAA	
Datalink BBS	516-862-8764 NY	KB2KUR	Fido 1:107/241
AA8ES Amateur Radio BBS	517-939-0169 MI	AA8ES	Fido 1:239/1020
RADIO FREQS	518-782-0507 NY		Fido 1:267/103
Kitchner-Waterloo AR BBS	519-578-9314 ON	VE3MTS	Fido 1:221/177
The Voice of Windsor	519-969-0747 ON	VE3TIZ	Fido 1:246/36
Neighborhood Net	602-495-1797 AZ	KB7DJE	Fido 1:114/24
The Pembroke Connection	603-485-8549 NH	N1MEN	Fido 1:132/169
The Legal Beagle	603-883-4466 NH	K1TCD	Fido 1:132/115
Fantasy Lights Software	604-583-3919 BC	VE7HTP	Fido 1:153/919
The Grapevine BBS	604-764-4672 BC		Fido 1:353/220
Pics Online(sm)	609-654-0999 NJ	N2LQH	Fido 1:266/21
The Radio Wave BBS	609-764-0812 NJ		
Pinelands RBBS	609-859-1910 NJ	W2XQ	Fido 1:266/32
Jersey Devil Citadel	609-893-2152 NJ	K2NE	Fido 1:266/33
Ham>Link<	612-HAM-0000 MN	KØTG	Fido 1:282/100
The Enterprise Board	612-571-3290 MN	N0JVD	Fido 1:282/60
	612-571-6280 MN		
The Lion's Den BBS	613-392-8294 ON	VE3JFD	Fido 1:249/303
Drl BBS	613-548-3691 ON		Fido 1:249/124
CHANNEL-23 BBS	613-830-5391 ON	VE3CUZ	Fido 1:243/23
South Parking Lot	614-351-2274 OH		Fido 1:226/330
Cross-Fire BBS	614-294-5336 OH		Fido 1:226/170
Ham BBS	614-895-2553 OH	N8EMR	
The Sounding Board	615-281-2104 TN	WB4HQN	
Lebanon Link	615-443-2237 TN	N4SCT	Fido 1:116/26
The Paragon Data Serv. BBS	615-892-1031 TN	WA8GKH	Fido 1:362/575
Pet Finders System	616-765-3372 MI	KC8RO	
	616-765-3372 MI		
De Shop	617-233-0297 MA		
M.V.A.R.G.	617-391-2827 MA	N1GKE	
The Garden Spot	617-545-6239 MA	NS1N	
Baystate BBS	617-598-6646 MA		
Tom's BBS	617-698-8649 MA	KA1TOX	Fido 1:101/470
Also Cheers BBS	617-770-9451 MA		Fido 1:101/2306
Radio Sport BBS	619-279-3921 CA	WB6BDY	
Lakeside Wildcat! BBS	619-390-7328 CA	N6CQW	Fido 1:135/63
Ham/Shortwave BBS	702-368-0846 NV		Fido 1:209/730
Frequency Forum	703-207-9622 VA	N4ULS	
The Capitol Connection	703-280-5490 VA	KB4ZSS	
	703-280-5423 VA	KB4ZSS	
Jack's Emporium	703-373-8215 VA	W4VQX	Fido 1:274/30
The Technicians Exchange BBS	703-387-1780 VA	KA4YUY	
Max's Doghouse	703-548-7849 VA		Fido 1:109/136
KC3OL BBS	703-689-7156 VA	KC3OL	
AMRAD BBS	703-734-1387 VA		
Das Spitzen Sparken Board	703-791-6198 VA	WD4AZG	
N7IJI	704-372-8925 NC		
NC EMS BBS	704-637-6906 NC	W4HG	Fido 1:379/308
Radio Hobby Online	708-238-1901 IL		Fido 1:115/747
The Precision Board	708-391-8773 IL	N9MHT	Fido 1:115/410
Micro Overflow	708-355-6942 IL	AF9M	
Samson BBS	708-394-0071 IL	KB9DIP	Fido 1:115/108
Elk Grove Repeater	708-529-1586 IL		
The Far Point Relay	713-463-8324 TX		Fido 1:106/8324
USS Pegasus - Houston node	713-777-0821 TX	KB5NFN	Fido 1:106/9636.0
Cell Bio BBS	713-798-4955 TX	K2TNO	Fido 1:106/9636.1
Acom II	713-879-1448 TX		
The Comport	713-947-9866 TX	KE5WJ	Fido 1:106/18
InterFlex Systems Design	714-497-5860 CA	WB6UUT	
T.E.L. Net Systems #2	714-597-7858 CA	KC6ZOL	Fido 1:207/107

F.O.G.	714-638-2298 CA	N6GIS	Fido 1:103/100
	714-683-8353 CA	N6GIS	Fido 1:103/122
The Shack Too	716-288-5848 NY	WD4SGU	Fido 1:260/232
Vector Board	716-544-1863 NY		
NF2G Online	716-663-8478 NY	NF2G	Fido 1:260/218
Highland BBS	716-761-6460 NY	N2JYG	
Vaccumn Valley BBS	717-323-1645 PA	N3DQC	
Tec-Board	717-561-8145 PA	KA3ADU	
KB7UV Roserver/PRMBS	718-956-7133 NY	KB7UV	
The Mav Plus BBS	801-634-3655 UT	KB4YHB	Fido 1:15/10
The HAM Connection	802-868-5274 VT	KA2UZC	
WV4B	803-223-5185 NC		
KC4YJC	803-269-7899 NC		
The Byte Bucket BBS	803-871-3076 SC	N4PGN	
Ben & Cheryl BBS	804-261-1819 VA		Fido 1:264/166.6
The Computer Forum BBS	804-471-3360 VA	KF4GL	
HamdiNet BBS	804-496-3320 VA		Fido 1:275/429
HamBones Fish House	804-665-7906 VA	KD4NFI	
The Listening Post	804-850-8586 VA	KD4IEW	Fido 1:271/263
Believers Bounty BBS	804-855-8421 VA	KD4GJH	Fido 1:275/40
CVACC	805-499-5699 CA	KD6AEJ	Fido 1:102/1002
Simi Valley Am. Radio BBS	805-583-2282 CA	N6VDV	
The Barn	809-781-9805 PR	WP4KVF	
Indiana On-Line	812-332-7227 IN	WB9LWQ/KC9HI	
KA9LQM's Ham Shack BBS	812 428-3352 IN	KA9LQM	
The Roy Hobbs BBS	813-626-8982 FL	N2UTO	Fido 1:377/73
The Cat House	813-796-2486 FL	KA3DBK	Fido 1:3603/110
Pac-Comm, Inc. BBS	813-874-3078 FL		
Solomon's Portico	813-954-5139 FL		Fido 1:137/19
KCATVG Support BBS	816-459-9752 MO	NØOXV	Fido 1:280/12
THe Archive BBS	817-447-1969 TX	AA5MM	Fido 1:130/22
Revelstone HST	817-732-1767 TX	N5SUV	Fido 1:130/402.0
N6MBR BBS	818-597-0641 CA	N6MBR	Fido 1:102/1004
Anime Lane BBS	818-762-3695 CA	KC6VMP	Fido 1:102/833
R&D BBS	819-772-2952 QU		Fido 1:163/506
Database of Tenn. BBS	901-749-5256 TN	KD4PYN	
	901-749-5224 TN	KD4PYN	
Marty's Place	903-753-0485 TX	N5KBP	Fido 1:19/62
The Hot Muddy Duck BBS	904-651-8684 FL	N4HMD	
Ancient City Wireless	904-823-3513 FL	KC4TDS	Fido 1:3620/9
Discovery Software BBS	907-248-8130 AK	NL7EL	
The Micro Room	908-245-6614 NJ	WA2BFW	Fido 1:107/919
Planet Shadowstar TBBS	908-494-3417 NJ	N2HGY	Fido 1:107/344
Microphone TBBS	908-494 3649 NJ	K2SHY	
Albany Amateur Radio Club	912-435-9466 GA	W4MM	Fido 1:3617/6
Namu BBS	913-273-1550 KS	WVØS	
The Boarding House BBS	913-827-0744 KS	KØFPC	
Coynet Amateur Radio BBS	914-485-3393 NY	WB2COY	
Joe Brown's BBS	914-667-9385 NY	KB2NBN	Fido 1:272/39
Hamnet BBS	915-653-9077 TX	N5JZZ	Fido 1:383/4
The CD-Rom BBS	915-673-8014 TX	AA5WF	Fido 1:392/6
Tele-Port	915-944-1436 TX	N5OZX	Fido 1:383/8
Galatic Crossroads BBS	916-334-5641 CA	KC6IRK	Fido 1:203/57
WA6RDH	916-678-1535 CA	WA6RDH	
QST	916-920-1288 CA	WA6AXZ	Fido 1:203/730
DX-BBS	916-992-0923 CA	W6GO	
The Ham Radio Emporium	918-272-4327 OK	WA4BFE	Fido 1:170/801
Dark Oak BBS	919-380-7194 NC	WD4DKT	
Raleigh ARS BBS	919-676-8469 NC		
SweDX	+46 40-973280 Sweden		Fido 2:200/110
COOL WORLD	+61 3 4320716 Australia	VK3KBL	

(list compiled by W3INK; 6 August 1993 version)

AMATEUR RADIO AND THE INTERNET

Since the beginning of the hobby, radio amateurs have been fascinated by all forms of electronic communications. A new computer communication and information medium is emerging that many hams have discovered. It is called the Internet.

"The Internet is a loose amalgam of thousands of computer networks, linking millions of people around the world." So begins an excellent book on the topic, *The Internet Companion,* by Tracy LaQuey (Addison-Wesley, ISBN 0-201-62224-6, $10.95). The Internet evolved from several different large computer networks, including ARPANET, NSFNET, MILNET, and USENET. Over time, these networks became interconnected, and standards and protocols were established to enable other networks to connect. Most commercial service providers like Compuserve and MCIMail provide electronic mail service connections to the Internet. Other providers offer live connections, which are more powerful. A good deal of the material in this book was located and downloaded using the Internet.

Through Internet, you have access to an astounding amount of information. This information can be retrieved, and instantly downloaded to your computer instantly. In addition to a huge assortment of databases, there are hundreds of "newsgroups," on topics from astrology to zoology. It is no surprise that a technology-oriented communication medium would attract radio amateurs, and eventually the hams found each other electronically. The following message, downloaded from the INFO-HAMS News Digest service on the Internet (and reprinted with permission of the author) is a helpful introduction to "where the hams are" on the Internet.

Guide to the Usenet Amateur Radio Newsgroups

This message describes the rec.radio.amateur.*, rec.radio.cb, rec.radio.info, and rec.radio.swap newsgroups. It is intended to serve as a guide for the new reader on what to find where. Questions and comments may be directed to the author, Jay Maynard, K5ZC, by Internet electronic mail at jmaynard@oac.hsc.uth.tmc.edu. This message was last changed on 30 June 1993 to add the groups created during the latest reorganization vote and the description of the cs.utexas.edu gateway.

History

Way back when, before there was a Usenet, the Internet hosted a mailing list for hams, called (appropriately enough) INFO-HAMS. Ham radio discussions were held on the mailing list, and sent to the mailboxes of those who had signed up for it. When the Usenet software was created, and net news as we now know it was developed, a newsgroup was created for hams: net.ham-radio. The mailing list and the newsgroup were gatewayed together, eventually.

As the net grew, and as packet radio came into vogue, packet discussion began to dominate other topics in the group and on the list. This resulted in the logical solution: a group was created to hold the packet discussion, and another corresponding mailing list was created as well: net.ham-radio.packet and PACKET-RADIO, respectively.

These two groups served for several years, and went through Usenet's Great Renaming essentially unchanged, moving from net.ham-radio[.packet] to rec.ham-radio[.packet]. Readership and volume grew with the rest of the network.

The INFO-HAMS mailing list was originally run from a US Army computer at White Sands Missile Range, SIMTEL20. There were few problems with this arrangement, but one was that the system was not supposed to be used for commercial purposes. Since one of hams' favorite pastimes is swapping gear, it was natural for hams to post messages about equipment for sale to INFO-HAMS/rec.ham-radio. This ran afoul of SIMTEL20's no-commercial-use restriction, and after some argument, a group was created specifically for messages like that: rec.ham-radio.swap. This group wasn't gatewayed to a mailing list, thus avoiding problems.

While all this was happening, other folks wanted to discuss other aspects of the world of radio than the personal communications services. Those folks created the rec.radio.shortwave and rec.radio.noncomm newsgroups, and established the precedent of the rec.radio.* hierarchy, which in turn reflected Usenet's overall trend toward a hierarchical name structure.

The debate between proponents of a no-code ham radio license and its opponents grew fierce and voluminous in late 1989 and 1990. Eventually, both sides grew weary of the debate, and those who had not been involved even more so. A proposal for a newsgroup dedicated to licensing issues failed. A later proposal was made for a group that would cover the many recurring legal issues discussions. During discussion of the latter proposal, it became clear that it would be desirable to fit the ham radio groups under the rec.radio.* hierarchy. A full-blown reorganization was passed by Usenet voters in January 1991, leading to the overall structure we now use.

After the reorganization, more and more regular information postings began to appear, and were spread out across the various groups in rec.radio.*. Taking the successful example of the news.answers group, where informational postings from across the net are sent, the group rec.radio.info was created in December, 1992, with Mark Salyzyn, VE6MGS, initially serving as moderator.

In January, 1993, many users started complaining about the volume in rec.radio.amateur.misc. This led to a discussion about a second reorganization, which sparked the creation of a mailing list by Ian Kluft, KD6EUI. This list, which was eventually joined by many of the most prolific posters to the ham radio groups, came up with a proposal to add 11 groups to the rec.radio.amateur hierarchy in April 1993. The subsequent vote, held in May and early June, approved the creation of five groups: rec.radio.amateur.digital.misc (to replace .packet), .equipment, .homebrew, .antenna, and .space.

The Current Groups

I can hear you asking, "OK, so this is all neat history, but what does it have to do with me now?" The answer is that the history of each group has a direct bearing on what the group is used for, and what's considered appropriate where.

The easy one is rec.radio.amateur.misc. It is what rec.ham-radio was renamed to during the reorganization. Any message that's not more appropriate in one of the other groups belongs here, from contesting to DX to ragchewing on VHF to information on becoming a ham.

The group rec.radio.amateur.digital.misc is for discussions related to (surprise!) digital amateur radio. This doesn't have to be the common two-meter AX.25 variety of packet radio, either; some of the most knowledgeable folks in radio digital communications can be found here, and anything in the general area is welcome. The name was changed to emphasize this, and to encourage discussion not only of other text-based digital modes, such as AMTOR, RTTY, and Clover, but things like digital voice and video as well. The former group, rec.radio.amateur.packet, has not been removed as of this writing, but it is obsolete, and you should use .digital.misc instead. The group has the .misc as part of the name to allow further specialization if the users wish it, such as .digital.tcp-ip.

The swap group is now rec.radio.swap. This recognizes a fact that became evident shortly after the original group was formed: Hams don't just swap ham radio gear, and other folks besides hams swap ham equipment. If you have radio equipment, or test gear, or computer stuff that hams would be interested in, here's the place. Equipment wanted postings belong here too. Discussions about the equipment generally don't; if you wish to discuss a particular posting with the buyer, email is a much better way to do it, and the other groups, especially .equipment and .homebrew, are the place for public discussions. There is now a regular posting with information on how to go about buying and selling items in rec.radio.swap; please refer to it before you post there.

The first reorganization added two groups to the list, one of which is rec.radio.amateur.policy. This group was created as a place for all the discussions that seem to drag on interminably about the many rules, regulations, legalities, and policies that surround amateur radio, both existing and proposed. The neverending no-code debate goes here, as does the New Jersey scanner law, the legality of ordering a pizza on the autopatch, what a bunch of rotten no-goodniks the local frequency coordinating body is, and so on.

The other added group is rec.radio.cb. This is the place for all discussion about the Citizens' Band radio service. Such discussions have been very inflammatory in rec.ham-radio in the past;

please do not cross-post to both rec.radio.cb and rec.radio.amateur.* unless the topic is genuinely of interest to both hams and CBers—and very few topics are.

The rec.radio.info group is just what its name implies: it's the place where informational messages from across rec.radio.* may be found, regardless of where else they're posted. As of this writing, information posted to the group includes Cary Oler's daily solar progagation bulletins, ARRL bulletins, the Frequently-Asked Questions files for the various groups, and radio modification instructions. This group is moderated, so you cannot post to it directly; if you try, even if your message is crossposted to one of the other groups, your message will be mailed to the moderator, who is currently Mark Salyzyn, VE6MGS. The email address for submissions to the group is rec-radio-info@ve6mgs.ampr.ab.ca. Inquires and other administrivia should be directed to rec-radio-request@ve6mgs.ampr.ab.ca. For more information about rec.radio.info, consult the introduction and posting guidelines that are regularly posted to that newsgroup.

The groups rec.radio.amateur.antenna, .equipment, .homebrew, and .space are for more specialized areas of ham radio: discussions about antennas, commercially-made equipment, homebrewing, and amateur radio space operations. The .equipment group is not the place for buying or selling equipment; that's what rec.radio.swap is for. Similarly, the .space group is specifically about amateur radio in space, such as the OSCAR program and SAREX, the Shuttle Amateur Radio EXperiment; other groups cover other aspects of satellites and space. Homebrewing isn't about making your own alcoholic beverages at home (that's rec.crafts.brewing), but rather construction of radio and electronic equipment by the amateur experimenter.

The rec.radio.amateur.misc, .packet, and .policy groups, and the rec.radio.info group, are available by Internet electronic mail in digest format; send a mail message containing "help" on a line by itself to listserv@ucsd.edu for instructions on how to use the mail server. The rec.radio.swap group is not available for reading by electronic mail. At this writing, the most recently added groups are also not available for reading by electronic mail, although that may change.

All of the groups can be posted to by electronic mail, though, by using a gateway at the University of Texas at Austin. To post a message this way, change the name of the group you wish to post to by replacing all of the '.'s with '-'s - for example, rec.radio.swap becomes rec-radio-swap - and send to that name@cs.utexas.edu (rec-radio-swap@cs.utexas.edu, for example). You may crosspost by including multiple addresses as Cc: entries (but see below). This gateway's continued availability is at the pleasure of the admins at UT-Austin, and is subject to going away at any time—and especially if forgeries and other net.abuses become a problem. You have been warned.

A Few Words on Crossposting

Please do not crosspost messages to two or more groups unless there is genuine interest in both groups in the topic being discussed, and when you do, please include a header line of the form "Followup-To: group.name" in your article's headers (before the first blank line). This will cause followups to your article to go to the group listed in the Followup-To: line. If you wish to have replies to go to you by email, rather than be posted, use the word "poster" instead of the name of a group. Such a line appears in the headers of this article.

One of the few examples of productive cross-posting is with the rec.radio.info newsgroup. To provide a filtered presentation of information articles, while still maintaining visibility in their home newsgroups, the moderator strongly encourages cross-posting. All information articles should be submitted to the rec.radio.info moderator so that he may simultaneously cross-post your information to the appropriate newsgroups. Most newsreaders will only present the article once, and network bandwidth is conserved since only one article is propagated. If you make regular informational postings, and have made arrangements with the moderator to post directly to the group, please cross-post as appropriate.

There are many questions that appear frequently in the various Internet amateur radio newsgroups. To alleviate repeating the same questions and answers over and over, a series of Frequently-Asked Questions (FAQ, in Internet parlance) and their answers have been made available.

HOW TO FIND THE REC.RADIO.AMATEUR. MISC FREQUENTLY-ASKED QUESTIONS LIST.

This article will tell you how to find the answers to frequently-asked Questions (FAQ) from rec.radio.amateur.misc. The FAQ articles are posted on the 7th of each month. This article is posted on the 14th, 21st, and 28th of every month as a reminder of where to find the FAQ.

The FAQ articles are intended to summarize some common questions on the rec.radio.amateur.misc newsgroup and Info-Hams mail list as well as to help beginners get started.

Besides the monthly posting, the FAQ is always available via anonymous FTP and from e-mail servers. This article contains instructions for obtaining a copy of the FAQ. It also contains the table of contents from the FAQ so that you know which questions are covered by it.

Please provide a copy of the FAQ to any new or soon-to-be Hams you know.

Regular FAQ postings can help save network bandwidth and maintain a good signal-to-noise ratio in the newsgroup. However, they can't do it alone—you, the reader, have to use them. If you are a new user, please print and review the FAQ articles and look at the instructions in the news.newusers newsgroup before posting any articles. If you are an experienced user, please help by refraining from answering frequently-asked questions on the newsgroup if they are already answered by the FAQ articles. Instead, send e-mail to the user who asked the question. (It will be helpful if you include the part of the FAQ that answers their question, but not the whole thing.)

How to Obtain a Current Copy of the FAQ

There are 3 ways to obtain a copy of the FAQ.

1) NetNews
2) Anonymous FTP
3) An Electronic Mail Server

Option #1: NetNews

If you are familiar enough with NetNews to look through previous articles on your system, Option #1 above may be the easiest for you. The FAQ is posted so that it should not expire from your site's news spool until the next one is posted. Unfortunately, some news administrators do not honor the expiration dates meant to preserve the FAQ.

Look in rec.radio.amateur.misc, rec.radio.info, rec.answers, or news.answers. If the FAQ has expired at your site, try Option #2 (and ask your news administrator to honor expiration dates for articles cross-posted to news.answers if he/she can.)

The following sites have copies of the FAQ:

site name & address	path to FAQ articles	comments
ftp.amdahl.com	pub/radio/amateur/faq._1-3.Z	located in western USA, updated daily when changes occur
ftp.cs.buffalo.edu	pub/ham-radio/faq_ham__1-3	located in eastern USA, updated monthly
rtfm.mit.edu	pub/usenet/news.answers/ham-radio-faq/part*	located in eastern USA, updated monthly contains news.answers archive - most UseNet AQs are here
grivel.une.edu.au	pub/ham-radio/buffalo/ham-radio/faq_ham__1-3	located in Australia, updated monthly (mirror of Buffalo)
nic.funet.fi	pub/ham/info/faq_ham__1-3	located in Finland, updated monthly

Remember, when connecting to the remote system, use the login name of "anonymous" and, as a courtesy to the site administrators, your e-mail address for the password.

Option #2: Anonymous FTP

Anonymous FTP uses the File Transfer Protocol. It is only available to sites which are directly connected to the Internet. If you don't know how to use FTP and can't find a friend to help you, continue to Option #3. If your site is not connected to the Internet, you should also continue to Option #3.

Option #3: Electronic Mail Server

If you can't use Options 1 or 2, your only remaining option is electronic mail. You can retrieve a copy of the FAQ by sending a message to:

mail-server@rtfm.mit.edu

The body of your mail will contain a command for the mail server software. To get all of the FAQ (consisting of 70K of e-mail in 3 parts), place the following in the first line of your message:

send usenet/news.answers/radio/ham-radio/faq/*

Leave out the subject of your message because the mail server will ignore it.

```
---- begin sample mail message ----
   To: mail-server@rtfm.mit.edu
   From: me@here.org
   Date: Mon Aug 14 22:27:33 PDT 1995

   send usenet/news.answers/radio/ham-radio/faq/*
---- end sample mail message ----
```

THE USENET REC.RADIO.AMATEUR.MISC FREQUENTLY-ASKED QUESTIONS LIST

Table of Contents

Dates indicate last modification.

Part 1—Introduction to the FAQ and Amateur Radio

** Table of Contents (6/93)
** Introduction to the FAQ (11/92)
* How to Contribute to the FAQ Articles (6/93)
* Acknowledgments (6/93)
* Notes on "Netiquette" (1/93)
** What is Amateur Radio? (11/92)
** Who can become a ham? (6/93)
** Where can I locate information and books on Amateur Radio? (4/92)
** How much does it cost? (4/92)
** Where can I take the tests? (pre-4/92)
** What are the tests like? (6/93)
** What can I do with a ham radio license? (5/92)
** What can't I do with an Amateur Radio license? (pre-4/92)
** I'm interested, who will help me? (11/92)
** Should I build my own equipment or antenna? (11/92)

Part 2 - Amateur Radio Organizations, Services, and Information Sources

** Where can I find Ham Radio information with a computer? (11/92)
* The rec.radio.* newsgroups (6/93)
* The ARRL e-mail server (1/93)
* The Internet File Transfer Protocol (FTP) (6/93)
* Access to FTP archives via electronic mail (1/93)
* The Info-Hams mail list: rec.radio.amateur.misc by mail (1/93)
* Telephone BBSs with Ham-related information (11/92)
* Callsign servers and geographical name servers (11/92)
* FTP access to FCC Part 97 and FCC Amateur Radio question pools (11/92)
* Lists of radio modifications and extensions (11/92)
** Can I send ARRL or W5YI electronic mail? (11/92)
** "Why doesn't the ARRL do...?" (11/92)
** What magazines are available for Ham Radio? (pre-4/92)
** How do I use the incoming and outgoing QSL bureau? (11/92)
** Are there any news groups for CAP? (11/92)
** What's the name of the QRP club that issues QRP numbers? (pre-4/92)
** How do I become a 10-10 member? (pre-4/92)
** How do I join MARS? (1/93)
** How do I join RACES? (pre-4/92)
** What organizations are available to help handicapped hams? (pre-4/92)
** I am looking for a specific ham, can anyone help me find him? (6/93)
** Can I post my neat new ham related program on rec.radio.amateur.misc? (pre-4/92)
** Where can I get ham radio software for my computer? (4/92)
** Are there Dialup News services or BBSs for Amateur Radio? (4/92)
** Where can I find VE sessions in my local area? (6/92)
** Why isn't XXX available electronically? (4/92)

Part 3 - Amateur Radio Advanced and Technical Questions

** What are the different US amateur classes and what can each of them do? (pre-4/92)
** What is the best way to learn Morse Code? (10/92)
** What is the standard for measuring Morse code speed? (pre-4/92)
** I'm confused. What do all those abbreviations mean??? (6/93)
** What do all those "tones" mean? (pre-4/92)
** Where can I learn more about Amateur Radio if I live outside the US? (6/93)
** How can I get a "reciprocal license" if I am a licensed ham from another country or if I am a FCC licensed ham who wants to operate in another country (on vacation)? (11/92)
** My apartment or housing complex does not allow outdoor antennas, now what do I do? (6/93)
** I got TVI...HELP!!! (pre-4/92)
** Did you know that you can get college credit for being a ham? (pre-4/92)
** On what frequencies do JPL and GSFC retransmit the shuttle audio? (10/92)
** Can I take my HT on an airplane and operate it if I get the permission of the captain? (4/92)
** How do I modify my current Amateur license? (4/92)
** I'm confused about XXX, should I ask the FCC? (4/92)
** Is there any information on antique radios? (pre-4/92)
** Where can I buy vacuum tubes? (pre-4/92)
** What do I need to get started in packet radio? (5/92)
** What do I need to get started in satellite communications? (pre-4/92)
** What is available to get started in ATV, SSTV and WEFAX? (5/92)
** What are these contests I sometimes hear, and how do I participate? (7/92)

Submitting changes for the FAQ

If you have comments or updates for the FAQ, send e-mail to
hamradio-faq@amdahl.com

This will send mail to all the people on the FAQ editorial review group.

THE INTERNET AMATEUR RADIO ELMERS LIST

This administrivia file and the companion Amateur Radio Elmers Resource Directory are intended for non-commercial distribution via Usenet. Reproduction here is done with the permission of the author, Paul Schleck, KD3FU.

A Brief Historical Overview

If there is any one constant in the changing state of the communications art, it is that "Hams" (Amateur Radio Operators) have always been on the forefront of it. Rumors abound where the term "Ham" came from. Some of the more amusing are described at the end of this article.

Regardless of origin of the name, a "Ham" is universally recognizable as one who experiments in radio and communications.

Whether it be constructing a low-power CW radio with vacuum tubes, or designing TCP/IP packet networks, such experimentation has historically spilled over into the mainstream such as was the case with Edwin Armstrong, who developed the regenerative oscillator and FM radio, or General Curtis LeMay (W6EZV) who was instrumental in making Single- Sideband the communications standard for the Strategic Air Command (1947-1992, now reorganized into a joint command called StratComm) and eventually the U.S. Air Force. Although packet-switching techniques originated from DARPA (Defense Advanced Research Projects Agency) and the ARPANet, no one can deny the tremendous influence that amateurs have had in demonstrating the viability of TCP/IP and AX.25 communications via radio links. The efforts of AMSAT (the Amateur Satellite Corporation), including the development of many ham satellites and the low-orbiting Microsats (communications satellites no bigger than a breadbox that use store-and forward packet techniques), have certainly advanced the state-of-the-art in communications, one of the defined purposes of the Amateur Radio Service, as recognized by international treaty.

Since in many cases hams are writing "the book," there is often no "book" or other established reference for a beginner to refer to. Traditionally, information has been passed on from ham to ham via word- of-mouth. Like many of the traditional crafts, a variation of the Master-Apprentice system has emerged, the Elmer-Novice relationship. Called "Elmers" because they are usually older and wiser, having the benefit of many years in the hobby, including several failed projects, and an electric shock or two, they have traditionally been the mainstay of amateur radio, and the source of many new hams, particularly those interested in working on emerging technologies.

Even more importantly, Elmers provided an outlet for the impatient newcomer who wanted "to know everything, and right away." Faced with such a request, a good Elmer will smile and proceed to lead the novice through some project or operating experience. Several hours, days, or weeks later, the novice would have his answers, but would have earned them. Even better, the sense of accomplishment would boost the novice's confidence and nudge him or her down the road to being a model, experienced ham operator.

Many present hams feel that such an experience is missing today. In today's hustle-bustle world, the response to such natural curiosity and desire to learn is, more often than not, "I'm too busy" or "RTFM." As a result, the quality of new hams declines and the knowledge and operating habits they develop in their first formative months and years leave much to be desired. And the very same hams who claim that they "can't understand the new generation" also, in almost the same breath, lament about the "decline of amateur radio."

What is an Elmer Today?

An Elmer today is of any age, male or female, who has some expertise and is willing to share it with beginners. Elmers don't even need to be licensed amateurs, just people with knowledge in some area of electronics or communications technology.

What is a Usenet Elmer?

With the ever-widening scope of the Internet, and the amateur radio newsgroups on Usenet, the potential for Elmers to share their knowledge to a wide audience has never been greater. To that end, I have started to maintain a list of such Elmers. Volunteers need only send me their name, E-mail address, and area of expertise. I have set up an administrivia mailbox for this purpose (elmers-request@ unomaha.edu, the default Reply-To: of this message).

Those desiring a more extensive list, or who need more specific assistance, are encouraged to contact Rosalie White, WA1STO, Educational Services Manager at the American Radio Relay League, 225 Main St., Newington, CT 06111 or via electronic mail addressed to rwhite@arrl.org.

How May I Obtain the Latest Copy of the Elmers List?

There are currently 4 ways of obtaining the Elmers List. Any site at least reachable by Internet E-mail can use options 3 or 4:

1. Usenet News: The latest copy of the list can be found in the companion posting to this message, "Amateur Radio Elmers Resource Directory." Since the list is cross-posted to rec.radio.amateur.misc, rec.radio.info, rec.answers, and news.answers on the 1st of each month, with an expiration date 6 weeks into the future, there should always be a copy available at most news sites. Check your newsreader documentation for information about reading previously-read articles.

2. Anonymous FTP: If your site is directly connected to the Internet, you may retrieve the latest copy via File Transfer Protocol (FTP) from the following sites:

    ftp.cs.buffalo.edu /pub/ham-radio/elmers*
    rtfm.mit.edu /pub/usenet/news.answers/radio/ham-radio/elmers/*

3. Mailing-List: Since the list is cross-posted to rec.radio.info, the latest copy may be obtained from the mailing-list gateway for that newsgroup (along with many other informational articles about radio) when it is published each month. To subscribe, send E-mail to:

    listserv@ucsd.edu

and in the BODY (not the Subject) of the message, write:

    subscribe radio-info

The server may not be able to determine your return address. In that case write:

    subscribe radio-info (your E-mail address)

You should get an acknowledgment very shortly.

4. Mail-Server: If you don't want to read through the entire gateway of rec.radio.info, or want a copy of the list right away, send E-mail to:

    mail-server@rtfm.mit.edu

and in the BODY (not the Subject) of the message, write:

    send usenet/news.answers/radio/ham-radio/elmers/admin
    send usenet/news.answers/radio/ham-radio/elmers/list
    send usenet/news.answers/radio/ham-radio/elmers/diff

and the latest copy of the list should be sent to you E-mail within 24 hours (the mail-server uses batch priority to reduce system demand).

How May I Contribute to the Elmers List?

By using this resource, you are benefiting the net by obtaining assistance in the fastest and most efficient way possible. By volunteering to appear on this list, you are contributing to the good reputation of the radio-related newsgroups.

Thanks to all the volunteer Elmers, as well as courteous list users, for making this service a success.

73, Paul W. Schleck, KD3FU

pschleck@unomaha.edu (personal mail)
elmers-request@unomaha.edu (Elmers List administrivia)

OTHER INTERNET SERVICES FOR HAMS

The American Radio Relay League (ARRL) has a useful Internet service—the ARRL Automated Electronic Mail Server. This server lets you access many information files, containing information about various facets of Amateur Radio. You can retrieve any or all of these files by sending an email message containing valid commands to info@arrl.org here at ARRL HQ. Each file you request is then electronically mailed to you automatically, usually within a few hours.

To use it, mail messages to:

    info@arrl.org

The subject line is ignored. Each line of the message should contain a command as shown below. You may place as many commands in a message as you want. Each file you request will be sent to you in a separate message. Only ASCII text files are supported at present.

Valid INFO commands:

help	Sends this help file
index	Sends an index of the files available from INFO
send FILENAME	Sends "FILENAME" example: send ARRL-EMAIL-ADR
quit	Terminates the transaction (use this if you have a signature or other text at the end of the message.)
reply <address>	Sends the response to the specified address. Put this at the BEGINNING of your message if your From: address is not a valid Internet address.

Note: your message will *not* be read by a human! Do not include any requests or questions except by way of the above commands. Retrieve the "ARRL-EMAIL-ADR" file for a list of addresses of ARRL HQ staff.

#Note: If you are not yet an Amateur Radio operator retrieve the #file PROSPECT (send PROSPECT) for information on how to easily get #started in this fun hobby.

SAMPLE OF FILES AVAILABLE FROM INFO@ARRL.ORG

FILE NAME	SIZE	DATE	DESCRIPTION
PROSPECT	2k	930514	How to get your Amateur Radio license
EXAM-SCHEDULE	52k	930629	Current exam schedule info—updated bi-weekly
EXAM-INFO	9k	921020	Examinations—what to bring—requirements
ARRL-EMAIL-ADR	6k	930119	List of HQ Email addresses
ARRL-CATALOG	39k	930709	Catalog of ARRL Publications—commercial content
ARRL-JOIN	2k	930621	How become an ARRL member
ARRL-SERVICES	5k	930621	A condensed list of ARRL membership services
ARRL-TOUR	28k	930621	An electronic tour of ARRL Headquarters
VISIT-HQ	5k	930310	Visiting ARRL HQ—directions and tour information
BANDS-HF	7k	921203	Breakdown of users of HF spectrum
Q-SIGNALS	1k	921203	ARRL list of Amateur Radio Q-signals
W1AW-SCHEDULE	2k	930120	W1AW schedule of transmissions and operation
BEST-RIG-1	12k	930227	Which rig is best? Part 1 - QST Lab Notes
BEST-RIG-2	22k	930227	Which rig is best? Part 2 - QST Lab Notes
EMI-GEN	37k	930120	How to solve an EMI/RFI problem - QST Lab Notes
EMI-SOURCE	13k	930607	Where to buy filters - EMI-proof telephones etc.
ADDRESSES	16k	930318	Lots and lots of ham/electronic company addresses
KITS	6k	930430	List of companies that sell kits
BBS	12k	930601	List of ham-radio land-line bulletin boards
FAQ-1	25k	930707	Introduction to the FAQ and Amateur Radio
FAQ-2	45k	930707	Amateur Radio Orgs, Services and Info Sources
FAQ-3	32k	930707	Amateur Radio Advanced and Technical Questions

Please direct comments or suggestions to ehare@arrl.org. Many other files are also available.

Internet Contest/DX Mailing Lists

CQ-CONTEST@TGV.COM is an electronic mail reflector dedicated to hams interested in all types of amateur radio contesting. This is a good place for score reports, expedition rumors, and other contest-related discussion or announcements. This forum is more like the NCJ than QST; INFO-HAMS@UCSD.EDU and rec.radio.amateur.misc are good places to look for a more rounded discussion of the hobby.

Each message you send to CQ-CONTEST@TGV.COM will be sent out to all the other subscribers, like a two meter repeater that has a coverage radius of 12,000 miles or so. This is a good place for score reports, expedition rumors, and other contest-related discussion or announcements.

CQ-CONTEST-REQUEST@TGV.COM is where you should send requests to change your CQ-CONTEST subscription. Send a message to CQ-CONTEST-REQUEST@TGV.COM with the word HELP in the body of the message.

Although there is an overlap between contesters and DXers, CQ-CONTEST is not a DX-oriented group. DX@UNBC.EDU is an electronic mail mailing list dedicated to the discussion of DXing. To "get on the list" for the DXing discussion, send mail to DX-REQUEST@UNBC.EDU.

DX bulletins distributed by the Ohio-Penn DX Association are archived by the organizer of the DX mailing list.

To access the archives, FTP to unbc.edu, log in as 'anonymous' and use your e-mail address (*not* callsign) as your password. Once logged in, cd to ampr/bulletins/opdx and help yourself.

DX PACKETCLUSTER™ NODES

Abbreviations

FRC	Frankford Radio Club
GLPS	Great Lakes PacketCluster System
INWDXN	Inland NorthWest DX Network
LIDXA	Long Island DX Association
NCC	North Coast Contesters
NCN	Northeast Cluster Network
NFIDXA	Niagara Frontier International DX Assoc.
NJDXA	North Jersey DX Association
NWDXSN	Northwest DX Spotting Network
PVDXSN	Potomac Valley DX Spotting Network
PVRC	Potomac Valley Radio Club
TSCN	Tristate Cluster Network
YCCC	Yankee Clipper Contest Club

Alabama

Birmingham	K4FHQ-1	BHMDX	144.930 (Network node)
Birmingham	K4FHQ-2	HAMDX	145.790 (Network node)
Ft. Payne	W4BRE-1	FTPDX1	448.400 (Network node)
Ft. Payne	W4BRE-2	FTPDX2	145.750 (2400 baud network node)
Hoover	W4AXO	———	145.750
Huntsville	K4CEF	———	144.930
Huntsville	K4CEF-1	HSVDX	144.930 (Network node)

Huntsville	K4CEF-4	HSVDX4	448.400 (Network node)
Jacksonville	N4QLB-2	JAXDX	144.930 (Network node)
Loachapoka	KA4PKB	———	144.910
Tuscumbia	WB4VKW-1	TUSDX	144.930 (Network node)

Arizona

Carefree	K5VT	K5VT	145.030
Chandler	K7NO	CADXA	145.090
Phoenix (NW)	N7CIX	CADXA	144.930
Tucson	N7BXX	SADXA	144.930

Arkansas

Batesville	K5EJ		145.010

California (Northern)

Network Node alias shown in brackets, i.e. [DX3]

Clovis	N6IXX		144.950 (Fresno)
	N6IXX	[DX6]	144.950 (Bear Mountain)
Los Gatos	N6ST		146.580 (Santa Cruz Mtns, Monterey Bay)
	N6ST	[DXF]	146.580 (Santa Cruz/Los Gatos)
Mountain View	K6LLK		144.950 (Mtn View, Ntwk Node and Hub)
Oakdale	K6AYA		146.580 (Modesto area)
Redwood City	W6OAT		145.770 (Redwood City North & East Bay)
	W6OAT	[DX5]	145.770 (Mt. Diablo)
Reno, Nevada	KI3V		144.950 (441.500 & 51.7)
	KI3V	[PCDX]	144.950 (Virginia City, NV)
Rio Linda	W6GO		144.950 (Sacramento, Woodland, Davis)
	W6GO	[DX3]	144.950 (Pine Grove - Stockton area)
	W6GO	[DXC]	144.950 (Cohasset Ridge - Chico, Redding)
San Francisco	W6OTC		146.580 (East Bay and North)
	W6OTC	[DX4]	146.580 (Sugarloaf Mt.- Napa)
Santa Rosa	WB2CHO		144.950
Milpitas	KJ6NN	[DXFMT]	1299.90 (San Jose - Fremont area)

California (Southern)

Chino	NN6U		145.660 (Inland Empire West)
El Segundo	W6PQS		144.490 & 145.690 (South Bay, Central LA, San Gabriel Vly)
Fullerton	KK6BB		145.680 (Orange County)
Oxnard/Ventura	N6VR		144.915
Palmdale	K6GXO		145.660 (Antelope Valley)
Ramona	KD6HRO		145.050 (Limited Cluster)
San Diego	K6JYO		144.950 (San Marcos)
San Diego	KM6K		144.950 (Kearney Mesa)
San Diego	KD6XM		144.690 (Fallbrook)
San Diego	N6ND		144.360 (Pt. Loma)
San Fernando Vly	WB6EXC		144.490 & 145.670
San Fernando Vly	N6BIC		145.670
Santa Ana	N6HVZ		145.605 (Serving West Orange Co)
Santa Maria	N6MB		144.950

Colorado

Aurora	KYØA		144.950
Boulder	KE6LT		144.930
Englewood	WØCP		144.970
Fort Smith	AB5K		144.910

Connecticut

Burlington	W1RM		144.950
Dayville	KB1H		144.930

——> Also see YCCC

Delaware

Middletown	N3FDL-1	DEFRC	144.950 (KANODE to WB2YOF)

——> Also see FRC

District of Columbia

——> See PVDXSN

Florida

Apopka	N4WW		144.950
Boca Raton	N4TL	SFDXA	145.590
Bradenton	WB4FNH		144.970
Ft Lauderdale	WA4YLD		145.590
Ft Walton Beach	WD4HDT	NWFDG	144.970
Jacksonville	NO4J	NFDXA	144.950 & 145.690
Melbourne	K3ARV		144.950 & 145.590
Orlando	N4WW		144.950
Palm Harbor	N4UYO		145.510
St. Leo	AB4PY		145.510
St. Petersburg	KO4J		144.950

Georgia

Augusta	N4JA		145.610
Atlanta	W8ZF		145.630 (2400 baud)
Atlanta	N4UCK		145.650
Atlanta		ATL	145.750 (2400 baud network node)
Atlanta		ATL1	145.750 (2400 baud network node)
Atlanta		ATL2	145.750 (2400 baud network node)
Douglasville	K4KG		145.910 (2400 baud)
Lawrenceville	KK4JF		145.710
		COMDX	145.710
		COMDX2	145.710 (2400 baud)
		COMDX3	440.750 (9600 baud)
Newnan	W1UA		145.610 (2400 baud)

Iowa

Bettendorf	G3WJN		144.910
Ely	WB8ZRL		144.910 223.420 (Cedar Rapids)
Mitchelville	NCØP		144.910 147.510 (Des Moines)
Sioux City	AAØDQ		144.910

Idaho

Boise, ID	NK7U		145.15 BOIDX Digi

Illinois

Crete	K9AJ		144.910 & 223.420
Elk Grove	KU9Z		223.440 (Chicago Northwest Metro area)
Godfrey	K9SD		Freq Unknown
Lockport	N9AOL		144.910 & 223.420 (Chicago South Metro Area)
Remote	K9RHY		223.420 (Chicago North Metro Area)
Roscoe	KA9LTR		144.910
Sterling	N4RR		144.910
Urbana	K9CW		144.910 & 223.440
Vermont	W9OER		Freq Unknown

Indiana

Crown Point	KE9I		147.435 & 223.420
Fort Wayne	KA9A		144.910
Indianapolis	KJ9D		145.510
Indianapolis	KJ9D		223.440 (W9FAM2:DX or K9CW-3:DX3)
Valparaiso	WX9X		223.420
West Lafayette	K9FN		144.950

Kansas

Olathe	WBØISW		144.950 (Kansas City, KS & MO and suburbs)

Kentucky

Bowling Green		BGNDX	145.750 (Network node)
Elsmere	N4DBR		145.590
Georgetown	N4TY		144.910

Louisville	KC4MK		145.590
Paducah	N4FFO		147.495 (Linked to KB4HU Nashville, TN)

Louisiana

Baton Rouge	WB5TDD		144.950
Lafayette	N5JUW		Frequency Unknown
Lafayette	N7JUW		144.950
New Orleans	K5NV		144.950
Shreveport	N5OCD		145.050 & 144.930

Maine

Windham	K1OT		144.930 (KANODE to NK1K)

Maryland

Frederick	K3NA		145.630 (HBG220 or HBURG, then Elkton)
Glenwood	W3LPL		145.590
Glenwood	W3LPL		144.950 (Digi to DEFRC KANODE/FRC)
Lothian	N2FB		145.570

——>Also see PVDXSN

Massachusetts

Bolton	AK1A		145.570
Groton	NO1A		144.990 & 145.650
Harvard	K1EA		144.950
Peru	KY1H		145.690
Roslindale	WA1G		145.690
Spencer	W1BIM		145.030 & 145.090

——> Also see YCCC

Michigan

Adrian	K8AQM		144.970
Clarkston	W8WD		145.710
East Detroit	WI8L		145.690
Fraser	K8NLD		144.950
Galesburg	AB8Y		144.950
Grand Blanc	KB8S		145.710
Ada	WJ8R		144.910
Jackson	KD8B		147.540
Port Huron	K8DD		144.970
Toledo	W8HHF		144.970
Southfield	K8NLD		144.950
Ypsilanti	K8CC		144.910

Minnesota

Bemidji	WAØPUJ	(PCBJI)	144.910, 145.010
Duluth	NØBIL	(PCDLH)	144.910, 145.070
Minneapolis	NJØM	(PCMSP)	144.950
Plymouth	NØAT	(PCPLY)	144.970
Rochester	WØMXW	(PCRST)	144.970
St. Cloud	KØIR	(PCSTC)	144.910
St. Paul	NØRC	(PCSTP)	144.930
Virginia	WBØQXM	(PCVIR)	144.970

Missouri

Godfrey, Il	K9SD		Freq unknown (St. Louis, MO area)

North Carolina

Charlotte	KD4IL		145.090
Elizabethy City	W4CVX		144.970
Greensboro	WB4WOR-3	DXGSO	145.630 (1200 Link Node to DXBVDS)
Hickory		HKYDX	144.930 (1200 baud link to N4ZC)
New Port	K4DHZ		144.950 (1200 baud)
Raliegh	NOØT-1	DXRNC	144.930 (2400 Baud Link to DXVIR:DXBVDS)
Raliegh	NOØT-2	SWAN	147.570 (1200 Baud, HDWRD to DXRNC)
Raliegh	W4DW		147.570

Rocky Mount	KO4PE		144.970 (Connected thru W4DW)
Salisbury	W4HG-4	DXSAL	144.930 (1200 Link Node to N4ZC)
Stanley	N4ZC		144.930
Winston-Salem	W4NC-2	DXINT	145.630 (1200 Link Node to DXBVDS)
Winston-Salem	KC4LWI-3	DXNC	145.750 (2400 Link From DXRKE TO DXSAL)

NOTES
145.75 is Cluster Link/BackBone Freq Only
145.63 is Cluster Users Freq.
147.57 is Raleigh Users Freq to Connect to DXBVDS

Nebraska

Fremont	AJØI	144.910
Omaha	KNØL	144.910

New Hampshire

Exeter	NK1K	144.930
Hollis	K1GQ	144.970
Rindge	K1XX	145.710

———> Also see YCCC

New Jersey

Moorestown	WB2YOF	144.950
Parsippany	W2JT	144.930

———> Also see FRC

New Mexico

Corrales	KN5D	Freq unknown
Santa Fe	W7LHO	Freq unknown

New York

Altamont	K2TR	145.690
Buffalo	KD2YP	144.930
Cottekill	K5NA	145.670
E. Fishkill	K2EK	145.750
Hamburg	KB2YJ-3	144.930
Huntington	W2HAP-2	144.930 (Digi to KB2XL)
Johnson City	KK4L	144.910, 145.630, 147.435, 443.0125(+)
Pleasantville	KE2AY	Freq unknown
Port Jefferson Sta.	KB2XL	144.930
Rochester	NG2P	144.910
Utica	WA2TVE	145.050
Vista	N1DVS	144.990
Woodside	K2GX	145.690

———> Also see LIDXA & YCCC

Nevada

Reno	KI3V	144.950 & 51.700

———> Also see CA listings

Ohio

Akron	WØCG	145.590* 222.060**
Chesterland	K8AZ	144.930*** 222.060**
Cincinnati	K4ZLE	145.670* 221.110**
Columbus	N8HTT	145.090* 223.420* 445.500**
Columbus	KC8MK	144.950* 445.500** 447.000*
Dayton	N8BJQ	145.030* 221.110**
Findlay	N8ET	144.95
Mentor	KQ8M	144.910*** 144.930*** 145.590* 222.030**
Parma	K8MR	144.910*** 144.930*** 145.590* 222.060**
Toledo	W8HHF	Freq Unknown
Westerville	KC8MK	144.950* 145.590* 446.975* 445.500**
Youngstown	N8IZR	144.910* 144.930**

NOTE: * = Users Only; ** = Node Connects Only; *** = Node & User Connects

Oklahoma			
Claremore	N5OK		144.970 & 145.010
Oklahoma City	AD1S		144.950
Poteau	N5JKN		145.010

Oregon			
Baker	NK7U		145.15 BKEDX Digi, See INWDXN
Veneta	KO7N		145.69 (Eugene area)
N. Portland	NØJO		145.71
E. Portland	WR7D		145.69
Salem	N7AVK		145.67 (Mid-Willamette Valley)
West Portland	WR7D-4		145.73 (Buckmaster database server)

——> Also see NWDXSN

Pennsylvania			
Camp Hill	NE3H		145.770
Erie	K3TUP		144.930
Mt Cobb	W3IQS		145.690
Perkasie	K3WW		144.950
Phoenixville	W3FRY		144.930
Pittsburgh	AD8J		144.930
Williamsport	KD3CR		145.010

——> Also see FRC & PVDXSN

Puerto Rico			
San Juan	WP4K		145.030

Rhode Island			
Cranston	KC1CE		145.090
Johnston	NE1R		144.970

——> Also see YCCC

South Carolina			
Bennettsville	K4QO		147.420
Catawba	W4UNP-5 CAT		145.750 (2400 baud network node)
Columbia	K4AVU		144.970
Columbia	KO4BR		144.610
Ft. Mill	KD4IL		145.090
Greenville	AC4TN		145.650

South Dakota			
Sioux Falls	NØGIB		145.070, 145.010, 442.100

Tennessee			
Athens	W4RJC-1	ATHDX	144.910
Chattanooga	K4JAF		144.990
Cleveland	AG4M-2	WOM2	147.730 (Network node)
Cleveland	AG4M-4	WOM4	448.400 (Network node)
Elora		SMTNDX	145.730 (Network node)
Juliet	AA4DO		147.495
Knoxville	AG4M-3	ETDXA	147.585
Nashville	KB4HU		144.970
Nashville	KB4HU		145.585
Nashville	KB4HU		145.750
Memphis	KN4F		144.950, 446.050
Murfreesboro	KB4HU-2	NASDX	145.750 (Network node)
Murfreesboro	KB4HU-1	NASDX1	144.930 (Network node)
Oak Ridge	AG4M		144.910
Oak Ridge	AG4M		147.585
Ridgetop	K4UVH-4	NASDX4	

Texas			
Abilene	N5HRG		144.910 *
Amarillo	WA4NXI		145.010 & 145.050 *
Austin	KG5ND		144.950 (AUSDXC) *

Carrollton	WA5YKO		144.970
Cibolo	WB5DDP		145.010 & 223.580 & 446.100 (CIBDXC) *
Dickinson	AB5A		145.030 & 7089.0 (DKNDX) ** #
Edinburg	K5TSQ		144.910 *
El Paso	WA5PIE		145.010 ELP ELP2
Ft. Worth	WC5P		144.950
Haslet	K9MK		144.910 MK
Hempstead	KE5IV		144.910 & 144.990 (HMPDXC) * **
Houston	K5DX		144.970 TDXS97 **
Irving	W5AH		145.730 & 441.125
Kingsville	KA5SWC		145.070 *
La Marque	KC5SC		144.930 & 144.970 (LMQDXC) **
Lubbock	KA5EJX		145.010 & 145.050 *
Midland	WF5E		144.910 (MAFDXC) *
Rockwall	W5XJ		144.930 *
San Antonio	KA5IAU		144.970
Tyler	KD5GD		144.990

(******) Running Multi-port G8BPQ Switch with PacketCluster.
* PacketClusters are connected via TexNet System
** PacketClusters may be accessed by TCAPS System in greater Houston area, AB5A and KE5IV are linked via the 19.2kbps backbone.
# AB5A, WU3V, and K5NV have 9.6kbps backbone system.

Utah

Salt Lake City	K7CU		144.950

Vermont

Westford	KD1R		145.030

Virginia

Chesapeake	WY7C		145.010 DX PacketCluster node (SEVA)
Chesapeake	WY7C		145.070 DX PacketCluster node
Culpeper	AB4N-6	DXCULP	Planned 145.630 (Network node)
Dale City	N4WYH-2	#VADX1	221.010 (Network node link: DCA1 to DXWOOD)
Dale City	N4WYH-6	DXWOOD	145.630 (Network node to K3NA)
Elliston	KC4DY		Connects to N4SR & WB8CQV DX nodes
Elliston	KC4DY	POOR	145.090 DX PacketCluster Node
Elliston	KC4DY		145.650 DX PacketCluster Node
Elliston	KC4DY	DXPOOR	147.510 DX PacketCluster Node
Fair Port	WD4EBY-6	DXFAIR	Planned (Network node)
Great Falls	WØYVA		145.510 DX PacketCluster node
Hampton	WA4OHX		145.010 DX PacketCluster node (SEVA)
Hampton	WA4OHX		145.070 DX PacketCluster node
Lexington	N4FHL-3	DXLEX	145.630 (1200 Baud, Node to DXBVDS)
Lorton	N4SR		145.530 DX PacketCluster node
Richmond	WU4G		145.530 (Link port to N4SR)
Richmond	WU4G	CVCC	145.070 (DX PacketCluster node LAN)
Roanoke	N4MGQ	POOR	145.090 (Network Node to KC4DY)
Roanoke	KC4DY-1	DXSWVA	145.530 (Link Port to N4SR Back Bone Only)
Roanoke	KC4DY-3	DXPOOR	147.510 (Network Node to KC4DY)
Roanoke	KC4LWI		145.050
Roanoke	KC4LWI		145.750 (2400 Baud, Link Freq Only)
Roanoke	KC4LWI-1	DXBVDS	145.630 (Cahos Mtn, Link to KC4LWI Node)
Roanoke	KC4LWI-4	DXRKE	145.750 (2400 Link Node to DXNC)
Warrenton	WA6YOU-6	DXWARR	145.630 (Network node to K3NA)
Waynesboro	KC4DY-2	DXBRDN	145.530 (Link Node to N4SR Back Bone Only)

——-> Also see PVDXSN

Washington

N. Seattle	NV6Z		145.730 (Linked to N7FSW & WY7I)
S. Seattle	N7FSW		145.770
Marysville	WY7I		145.750
Tacoma	K7JF		145.710 (Linked to NV6Z)
Spokane	WS7I		144.930 & EWARG Digi 144.930

——-> Also see NWDXSN

City	Call	Node	Frequency
Beverly	NY7T		145.030 (BVEDX)
Pasco	NY7T		145.030 (EWDXA)
Spokane	WV7Y		144.930 DataBase Server
Spokane	WS7I		144.930 (EWARG) & 145.01 & 223.46 & 10.018

——> Also see INWDXN

West Virginia

City	Call	Node	Frequency
Charleston	WB8CQV		145.090 446.500

Wisconsin

City	Call	Node	Frequency
Delafield	NB9C		223.460 (backbone frequency)
Fox Lake		FOX	223.460 (KA-Node)
Freedom	AA9A		223.440 (Near Green Bay, WI)
Madison		MSNDX	223.440 (KA-Node)
McFarland	WI9L		223.440
North Freedom		NFDX	223.420 (KA-Node)
Oshkosh		OSHDX	144.970 (KA-Node)
Plymouth		NF9R-2	223.460 (KA-Node)
Racine	KS9K		223.480
Sheboygan	KR9S		223.420
Stevens Point		WISTE2	223.440 (KA-Node)

Wyoming

City	Call	Node	Frequency
Jackson	N7NG		145.010

Canada

City	Call	Node	Frequency
Comox, BC	VE7GCE		7.101, 145.010, 145.710, 147.56
Fredricton, NB	VE1NH		145.010
Halifax, NS	VE1DXC		145.010
Middleport, ON	VE3CDX		145.710
Montreal, PQ	VE2PWI		145.010
Orillia, ON	VE3FJB		145.070
Ottawa, ON	VE3XDX		145.110
Toronto, ON	VE3TDX		144.970
Toronto, ON	VE3ZRB		145.770
Vancouver, BC	VE7CQD		145.710, 144.930 +600, 145.070 +600

AFRICA

Zaire

City	Call	Node	Frequency
Kinshasa	9Q5XO		145.775
Kinshasa	9Q5XO-7		28.103 (KAnode/Gateway to 9Q5XO)

South Africa

City	Call	Node	Frequency
Pretoria	ZS6AI-2		28.103

(BPQ Switch - Issue Command: C 2 9Q5XO-7, then X 9Q5XO to Connect to the 9Q5XO Node)

EUROPE

Germany

City	Call	Node	Frequency
Munchen	DBØBCC		Freq unknown
Gau Bischofsheim	DJØRX		Freq unknown

England

City	Call	Node	Frequency
Cheltenham	GB7DXC		Freq unknown
Wokingham	GB7DXI		Freq Unknown

Finland

City	Call	Node	Frequency
Hanko	OH2RBG		Freq unknown

Sweden

City	Call	Node	Frequency
Skovde	SK6EI-2		144.625
	SK6EI-7		443.650
	SL6AL-1		145.350
City unknown	SK3BG-6		Freq Unknown
City unknown	SM3SJN-1		28.103 (KAnode/gateway to SK3BG-6)

Belgium

City	Call	Node	Frequency
Tielt	ON1CED-5		144.650 & 433.650 (connect via ON1ABT only)

ASIA

Korea

Seoul	HL9OB	Freq unknown

Japan

JA1, JA2		
Kawasaki/Kanagawa	JH1ORA	No user port
Toshimaku/Tokyo	JR1CTA	431.36
Koganei/Tokyo	JH1GTV	431.08/431.28/52.60
Oyama/Tochigi	JA1PEJ	431.26/431.44
Yokohama/Kanagawa	JR1MLU	431.30
Yokohama/Kanagawa	JE1GMM	431.22
Hanno/Saitama	JR1MAF	431.38/14.105
Kawaguchi/Saitama	JH1ROJ	431.44/438.44
Setagaya/Tokyo	JA1SQD	438.42/21.123
Amagi/Shizuoka	JG2ZCG	431.24/52.66
Nagaoka/Shizuoka	JH2TIP	431.38
Abiko/Chiba	JR2BNF/1	431.16
Omiya/Saitama	JK1FVP	438.44
Odawara/Kanagawa	JK1GOK	431.14
JA3		
Kusatsu	JA3YIH	—
Kyoto	JA3ZDX	1293.240
Osaka	JJ3ZKD	1293.260
Shiga	\JA3YIH	—
Toyanaka	JJ3ZKD	1293.260
All Node Links are on 431.080		
JA7		
Akita	JA7XRO	431.020
Iwate	JA7RHJ	431.260
Miyagi	JA7MYQ	438.980
Morioka	JA7RHJ	431.260
Sendai	JA7MYQ	438.980
Yokote	JA7XRO	431.020

U.S. PACKETCLUSTER™ NETWORKS

FRC (Frankford Radio Club)

Nodecall	QRG	QTH
W3FRY	144.930	Phoenixville, PA
WB2YOF	144.950	Moorestown, NJ
K3WW	145.530	Perkasie, PA
K2TW	145.570	Flemmington, NJ
KD3CN	—	Strasburg, PA

In addition, we have six feeder NETROMs/TheNets:

Nodecall	QRG	QTH	Type
DEFRC (N3FDL-1)	144.930	Middletown, DE	NETROM
NAR (KA3PIT-1)	144.930	Narvon, PA	TheNet
RDG (K3NW-1)	144.930	Reading, PA	TheNet
LANCO (N3BNA-1)	144.930	Lititz, PA	NETROM
FRCNET (K3RL-1)	145.540	Coopersburg, PA	TheNet
NNJ (K2SG-1)	145.540	White Plains, NJ	TheNet

INWDXN (Inland NorthWest DX Network)

Nodecall	QRG	QTH
NK7U (BKEDX)	145.150	Baker, OR
NY7T (BEVDX) Digi to NY7T	145.150	Beverly, WA
NK7U (BOIDX) Digi to NK7U	145.150	Boise, ID
NY7T (EWADX)	145.030	Pasco, WA
WV7Y DataBase Server	144.930	Spokane, WA
WS7I (EWARG) Note 1	144.930	Spokane, WA

NOTE 1 - WS7I Linked to VE3CDX, N7NG, KE7X, K7CU on a frequent basis.

GLPS (Great Lakes PacketCluster System)

Nodecall	QRG	QTH
AB8Y	145.950	Galesburg, MI
KD8B	147.540	Jackson, MI
WJ8R	144.910	Ada, MI
K8AQM	144.970	Adrian, MI
K8CC	144.910	Ypsilanti, MI
W8HHF	144.970	Toledo, OH
K8NLD	144.950	Fraser, MI
W8WD	145.710	Clarkston, MI
KB8S	145.710	Grand Blanc, MI
WI8L	145.690	E. Detroit, MI
K8DD	144.970	Port Huron, MI

LIDXA (Long Island DX Association)

Nodecall	QRG	QTH
KB2XL	144.930	Port Jefferson Station, NY

NCC (North Coast Contesters)

Nodecall	QRG	QTH
AD8J	144.930	Pittsburgh, PA
K3TUP	144.930	Erie, PA
K8AZ	144.930	Chesterland, OH
KQ8M	145.590	Mentor, OH
N8IZR	144.930	Youngstown, OH
WØCG	145.590	Akron/Canton, OH
VE3CDX	147.480	Middleport, ON
VE3CDX	145.670	Middleport, ON

NCN (Northeast Cluster Network)

Nodecall	QRG	QTH
KB1H	144.930	Dayville, CT
AK1A	145.570	Bolton, MA
K1GQ	144.970	Hollis, NH
KY1H***	145.690	Peru, MA
W1RM	144.950	Burlington, CT
NO1A	144.990	Groton, MA
NO1A	145.650	Groton, MA
NG2P	144.910	Rochester, NY
K2TR**	144.970	Altamont, NY
KD2YP	144.930	Tonawanda, NY
KC8PE	145.710	Cheshire, CT
K2EK	145.750	E. Fishkill, NY
KD3CR	145.010	Williamsport, PA
K1EA	144.950	Harvard, MA
K5NA	145.670	Cottekill, NY
NK1K	144.930	Exeter, NH
W1BIM	145.030	Spencer, MA
W1BIM	145.090	Spencer, MA
KD1R	145.030	Westford, VT
K1XX	145.710	Rindge, NH
WA1G	145.690	Roslindale, MA
WA2TVE*	145.050	Utica, NY
W3IQS	145.690	Mt. Cobb, PA
KK4L	144.910	Johnson City, NY

*WA2TVE also on 147.42 for local connects. Connect to UTICA2 then DXCLUS, UTICA2 is LAN for Utica. On NEDA network just connect to 'DXCLUS' to get WA2TVE. 'UTICA' is local NEDA node in that area of WA2TVE.
**'KNOX' is local neda node for K2TR. If you connect to KNOX then you can connect to DXKNOX, then to K2TR.
*** KY1H reachable from node 'WMA220.'
+ KK4L also on 145.63, 147.435, 443.0125(+)

NCXDA (National Capital DX Association)
(——> See PVDXSN)

NFIDXA (Niagara Frontier International DX Assoc.)

Nodecall	QRG	QTH
K3TUP	144.930	Erie, PA
KD2YP	144.930	Buffalo, NY
KE6LT	144.930	Boulder, CO
KN4F	144.950	Memphis TN
KQ8M	144.950	Mentor, OH
NØBIL	144.910	Duluth, MN
N4WW	144.950	Apopka, FL
NG2P	144.970	Rochester, NY
VE2PWI	145.010	Montreal, QUE
VE3CDX	145.710	Middleport, ONT
VE3FJB	145.070	Orillia, ONT
VE3TDX	144.970	Toronto, ONT
VE3XDX	144.930	Ottawa, ONT
VE3ZRB	145.770	Toronto, ONT
WAØPUJ	145.010	Bemidji, MN
K3ARV	144.950	Melbourne, FL
KD2YP	144.930	Tonawanda, NY
VE1DXC	145.010	Halifax, NS

NJDXA (North Jersey DX Association)

Nodecall	QRG	QTH
W2JT	144.930	Parsippany, NJ

NWDXSN (Northwest DX Spotting Network)

Nodecall	QRG	QTH
N7FSW	145.770	Burien, WA
NV6Z	145.730	Kenmore, WA (N. Seattle)
WY7I	145.750	Marysville, WA
K7JF	145.710	Tacoma, WA
NK7U	145.150	Baker, OR
KO7N	145.690	Veneta, OR (Eugene area)
NØJO	145.710	N. Portland, OR
WR7D	145.690	E. Portland, OR
N7AVK	145.670	Salem, OR (Mid-Willamette Valley)
WR7D-4	145.730	W. Portland, OR
VE7CQD	145.710	Vancouver, BC

PVDXSN (Potomac Valley DX Spotting Network)

Nodecall	QRG	QTH	NOTES
K3NA	145.630	Frederick, MD	HBURG or HBG220, then Elkton
W3LPL	145.590	Glenwood, MD	
W3LPL	144.950	Glenwood, MD	Digi to DEFRC KANODE/FRC
N2FB	145.570	Lothian, MD	
NE3H	145.770	Camp Hill, PA	
WY7C	145.010	Chesapeake, VA	SEVA
WY7C	145.070	Chesapeake, VA	
AB4N-6	145.630	Culpeper, VA	
N4WYH-2	221.010	Dale City, VA	Node link to DCA1 to DXWOOD
N4WYH-6	145.630	Dale City, VA	Node to K3NA
WØYVA	145.510	Great Falls, VA	
WA4OHX	145.010	Hampton, VA	SEVA
WA4OHX	145.070	Hampton, VA	DX PacketCluster Node
N4SR	145.530	Lorton, VA	
WU4G	145.530	Richmond, VA	Link port ot N4SR
WU4G	145.070	Richmond, VA	DX PacketCluster Node
N4LSP-3	145.530	Sumerduck, VA	KANODE linking N4SR & N4EHJ
WA6YOU-6	145.630	Warrenton, VA	Network Node to K3NA

PVRC (Potomac Valley Radio Club)

——> See PVDXSN

TSCN (Tristate Cluster Network)

Nodecall	QRG	QTH
K2GX	145.690	Queens, NY
K2SG	145.530	Morris plains, NJ
KB2XL	144.930	Pt. Jefferson Station, NY
KE2AY	144.950	Pleasantville, NY
KE2CG	144.990	Piscataway, NJ
N1DVS	144.990	Vista, NY
W2JT	144.930	Parsippany, NJ
WB2KXA	145.590	Allentown, NJ
K2RW	File server	
N2INX	File server	
WA2UEC	Tri-state routing	

YCCC (Yankee Clipper Contest Club)

Nodecall	QRG	QTH
K2TR	144.970	Altamont, NY
AK1A	144.950	Bolton, MA
W1RM	145.950	Burlington, Ct
K5NA	145.670	Cottekill, NY
KB1H	144.930	Dayville, CT
NK1K	144.930	Exeter, NH
NO1A	144.990	Groton, MA
NO1A	145.650	Groton, MA
K1EA	144.950	Harvard, MA
K1GQ	144.970	Hollis, NH
NE1R	144.970	North Scituate, RI
W2JT	144.930	Parsippany, NJ
KY1H	145.690	Peru, MA
KE2AY	145.950	Pleasantville, NY
KB2XL	144.930	Port Jefferson Station, NY
K2GX	145.690	Queens (NYC), NY
K1XX	145.710	Rindge, NH
WA1G	145.690	Roslindale, MA
W1BIM	145.030/090	Spencer, MA
N1DVS	144.990	Vista, NY
YCCCWF	147.430	West Falmouth, MA See Note 1.
KD1R	145.030	Westford, VT

Note 1: KA-NODE - After connecting, use command "XC NE1R"

DX PacketCluster DXNODES database contributed by Ron Rueter, NV6Z, 2113 108th St. S.E., Everett, WA 98208-5108

Please send updates, corrections or comments, to the above address or to NV6Z via: CompuServe 72200,1347—OR—PacketCluster DXPSN Node:W6GO—OR—DX-BBS (916) 992-0923

CENSUS OF US AMATEURS BY ZIP CODE, AS OF AUGUST 1, 1993
(Note that most large cities comprise several ZIP codes)

00601	105	00676	15	00764	37	00929	25	01057	19	01257	6
00602	157	00677	13	00765	10	00930	2	01059	2	01258	3
00603	234	00678	5	00766	11	00931	8	01060	54	01259	3
00604	35	00680	27	00767	46	00934	1	01061	1	01260	1
00605	151	00681	16	00768	41	00936	80	01066	3	01262	5
00606	1	00683	14	00769	5	00937	4	01068	9	01264	1
00607	40	00685	23	00771	15	00940	5	01069	17	01266	6
00608	4	00686	1	00772	4	00949	65	01070	2	01267	27
00609	26	00687	1	00773	10	00950	56	01071	1	01270	5
00610	35	00688	2	00775	4	00951	7	01072	10	01301	40
00612	125	00690	4	00777	22	00952	2	01073	14	01330	2
00613	64	00692	36	00778	9	00953	7	01075	34	01331	47
00615	5	00693	21	00779	1	00954	2	01077	40	01337	3
00616	30	00694	8	00780	1	00956	28	01079	1	01339	3
00617	29	00698	13	00782	1	00957	32	01080	5	01340	10
00618	22	00701	106	00783	5	00958	5	01081	1	01341	2
00619	346	00702	2	00784	15	00959	21	01082	11	01342	5
00620	65	00703	1	00785	12	00960	15	01083	12	01343	1
00621	44	00704	2	00791	15	00961	6	01085	83	01344	3
00622	11	00705	7	00792	3	00962	6	01086	4	01346	1
00623	77	00706	2	00794	2	00963	3	01088	3	01349	3
00624	3	00707	11	00795	5	00966	5	01089	40	01351	6
00625	370	00708	192	00796	1	00968	1	01090	6	01355	3
00626	218	00709	103	00801	67	00969	16	01092	1	01360	15
00627	107	00714	1	00802	43	00970	6	01093	1	01362	1
00628	44	00715	10	00803	29	00971	3	01094	2	01364	25
00629	70	00716	106	00804	5	00972	2	01095	36	01366	5
00630	207	00717	21	00820	61	00976	15	01096	5	01368	4
00631	3	00718	83	00821	6	00977	6	01098	6	01370	9
00632	43	00719	42	00822	8	00978	4	01101	5	01373	7
00633	48	00720	15	00823	9	00979	4	01103	1	01375	9
00634	17	00721	10	00824	21	00982	9	01104	22	01376	15
00635	31	00723	29	00830	18	00983	10	01105	4	01379	3
00636	2	00724	12	00831	4	00984	4	01106	33	01400	1
00637	3	00725	35	00836	1	00985	26	01107	10	01420	74
00638	50	00726	19	00840	19	00986	1	01108	29	01430	18
00639	38	00728	1	00841	1	00987	4	01109	24	01431	9
00640	27	00729	15	00850	12	01001	22	01118	21	01432	24
00641	9	00731	239	00851	16	01002	79	01119	26	01433	37
00642	9	00732	45	00859	1	01003	2	01128	12	01436	6
00643	28	00733	10	00875	1	01004	4	01129	19	01437	5
00644	5	00735	15	00901	4	01005	16	01139	2	01438	5
00645	5	00737	2	00902	14	01007	37	01151	11	01440	40
00646	50	00738	34	00903	5	01008	3	01152	1	01450	60
00648	93	00739	9	00904	4	01009	2	01159	1	01451	59
00649	1	00740	14	00905	5	01010	8	01173	1	01452	8
00650	20	00741	19	00906	4	01011	1	01201	163	01453	100
00651	1	00742	36	00907	33	01012	1	01202	2	01460	39
00652	1	00743	36	00908	10	01013	41	01220	25	01462	25
00653	3	00744	23	00909	9	01020	76	01222	2	01463	54
00654	42	00745	32	00910	13	01022	5	01223	7	01464	28
00655	21	00746	1	00911	13	01026	4	01224	1	01466	2
00656	22	00747	41	00912	6	01027	48	01225	10	01468	18
00657	132	00748	10	00913	24	01028	44	01226	38	01469	36
00658	57	00749	10	00914	8	01030	40	01230	19	01472	2
00659	33	00750	10	00915	46	01033	15	01235	11	01473	20
00660	24	00751	25	00916	3	01034	8	01236	1	01474	6
00661	192	00752	24	00917	41	01035	14	01237	16	01475	19
00662	113	00753	48	00918	29	01036	27	01238	11	01501	29
00664	25	00754	39	00919	36	01037	8	01240	20	01503	12
00665	30	00755	111	00920	46	01038	1	01242	2	01504	14
00666	50	00756	2	00921	87	01039	3	01243	1	01505	17
00667	64	00757	24	00922	26	01040	54	01244	1	01506	4
00669	61	00758	30	00923	42	01041	1	01245	1	01507	8
00670	8	00759	56	00924	111	01050	5	01247	42	01508	2
00671	63	00760	35	00925	14	01051	1	01253	1	01509	2
00672	12	00761	46	00926	225	01053	3	01254	4	01510	28
00673	43	00762	125	00927	52	01054	2	01255	1	01515	6
00674	42	00763	75	00928	43	01056	32	01256	8	01516	14

01518	8	01749	87	01944	23	02128	20	02334	1	02646	8
01519	14	01752	148	01945	87	02129	17	02338	17	02647	1
01520	42	01754	50	01949	18	02130	32	02339	29	02648	24
01521	2	01756	19	01950	52	02131	31	02341	19	02649	22
01522	7	01757	50	01951	4	02132	43	02343	26	02650	4
01523	17	01760	117	01952	9	02134	12	02345	8	02651	95
01524	16	01770	25	01960	129	02135	35	02346	38	02652	2
01525	1	01772	19	01961	1	02136	30	02347	12	02653	48
01526	2	01773	35	01965	2	02137	2	02351	37	02655	15
01527	23	01775	51	01966	27	02138	67	02356	26	02657	12
01529	4	01776	125	01969	24	02139	76	02358	2	02659	4
01530	1	01778	67	01970	72	02140	22	02359	34	02660	22
01531	1	01784	2	01971	2	02141	13	02360	120	02661	1
01532	46	01799	1	01982	23	02142	6	02361	4	02662	9
01534	11	01801	63	01983	30	02143	34	02362	3	02663	6
01535	9	01803	73	01984	10	02144	45	02364	38	02664	32
01536	18	01805	1	01985	18	02145	14	02366	4	02665	1
01537	1	01810	132	02019	47	02146	77	02367	5	02666	5
01538	2	01821	89	02020	4	02148	69	02368	71	02667	7
01539	1	01824	150	02021	29	02149	50	02370	25	02668	6
01540	28	01826	42	02025	21	02150	24	02374	1	02669	5
01541	12	01827	8	02026	44	02151	58	02375	20	02670	3
01542	2	01830	96	02030	19	02152	29	02379	17	02671	3
01543	9	01831	1	02032	7	02154	117	02381	4	02672	1
01545	69	01832	12	02033	1	02155	105	02382	29	02673	26
01549	1	01833	23	02035	46	02158	35	02401	60	02675	31
01550	37	01834	14	02038	57	02159	59	02402	52	02691	1
01560	8	01835	10	02040	3	02160	26	02403	5	02702	13
01561	7	01841	33	02041	1	02161	21	02405	1	02703	94
01562	43	01842	2	02042	1	02162	8	02410	1	02714	1
01564	10	01843	9	02043	49	02163	1	02532	28	02715	9
01565	5	01844	86	02045	26	02164	6	02534	4	02717	15
01566	16	01845	69	02048	40	02165	40	02535	2	02718	7
01568	15	01850	22	02050	32	02166	23	02536	72	02719	49
01569	25	01851	40	02051	8	02167	48	02537	18	02720	48
01570	51	01852	29	02052	27	02168	23	02538	9	02721	25
01571	7	01853	4	02053	43	02169	56	02539	13	02722	1
01581	54	01854	31	02054	37	02170	23	02540	44	02723	22
01583	19	01858	1	02055	2	02171	19	02541	3	02724	13
01585	14	01860	14	02056	26	02172	51	02542	10	02725	2
01586	1	01862	35	02060	4	02173	160	02543	28	02726	42
01587	3	01863	29	02061	23	02174	124	02552	2	02728	1
01588	11	01864	48	02062	72	02176	67	02553	7	02738	15
01590	11	01865	3	02065	5	02178	69	02554	24	02739	13
01601	1	01866	9	02066	42	02179	2	02556	28	02740	75
01602	39	01867	72	02067	69	02180	54	02557	10	02742	1
01603	21	01871	1	02070	2	02181	76	02558	3	02743	22
01604	34	01876	94	02071	7	02184	72	02559	16	02744	20
01605	23	01879	36	02072	61	02185	1	02561	2	02745	55
01606	49	01880	81	02081	33	02186	38	02562	4	02746	19
01607	12	01885	1	02090	49	02187	5	02563	18	02747	54
01608	1	01886	124	02093	35	02188	24	02564	1	02748	39
01609	34	01887	71	02101	4	02189	28	02568	17	02760	70
01610	17	01890	65	02102	1	02190	33	02571	18	02762	16
01611	7	01901	1	02103	1	02191	28	02574	12	02763	4
01612	23	01902	43	02105	1	02192	86	02576	2	02764	6
01613	5	01903	6	02106	1	02193	40	02581	1	02766	39
01640	1	01904	37	02108	4	02194	25	02584	2	02767	33
01652	1	01905	43	02109	2	02199	5	02593	1	02768	3
01687	1	01906	60	02110	1	02205	1	02601	24	02769	25
01701	244	01907	55	02111	1	02215	9	02630	7	02770	12
01718	4	01908	12	02113	3	02238	6	02631	36	02771	38
01719	21	01913	26	02114	21	02254	1	02632	29	02777	35
01720	128	01915	93	02115	11	02258	2	02633	15	02779	5
01721	40	01920	1	02116	16	02260	1	02635	12	02780	77
01730	78	01921	29	02118	6	02269	1	02636	1	02783	1
01731	4	01922	6	02119	8	02272	3	02637	2	02790	32
01740	24	01923	96	02120	4	02322	12	02638	9	02801	2
01741	55	01929	11	02121	7	02324	38	02639	11	02802	1
01742	87	01930	88	02122	12	02327	9	02641	18	02804	11
01745	1	01932	1	02124	20	02330	21	02642	118	02806	59
01746	67	01936	3	02125	16	02331	13	02643	9	02807	7
01747	22	01938	40	02126	6	02332	38	02644	10	02808	14
01748	49	01940	45	02127	22	02333	30	02645	34	02809	50

02812	5	02925	1	03245	3	03585	2	03850	2	04057	6
02813	18	02940	1	03246	93	03590	3	03851	7	04058	2
02814	21	03013	1	03247	5	03592	11	03853	1	04061	6
02816	119	03031	80	03251	2	03595	1	03854	4	04062	25
02817	6	03032	13	03252	1	03598	12	03855	3	04063	1
02818	63	03033	24	03253	27	03601	1	03856	2	04064	28
02821	1	03034	10	03254	4	03602	7	03857	20	04066	6
02822	15	03035	1	03255	4	03603	6	03858	11	04068	3
02823	2	03036	21	03256	1	03605	13	03859	2	04069	11
02824	2	03037	18	03257	16	03606	5	03860	7	04070	1
02825	28	03038	154	03259	2	03608	10	03862	10	04071	15
02826	2	03040	2	03260	2	03670	1	03864	10	04072	37
02827	5	03041	4	03261	13	03740	1	03865	25	04073	28
02828	21	03042	16	03262	1	03741	12	03867	76	04074	47
02829	4	03043	9	03263	20	03743	52	03868	7	04075	13
02830	10	03044	13	03264	23	03745	5	03870	9	04076	3
02831	13	03045	37	03266	7	03746	2	03871	1	04078	5
02832	7	03047	9	03268	3	03748	8	03872	16	04079	4
02833	1	03048	32	03269	1	03750	7	03873	10	04080	2
02835	23	03049	48	03273	1	03751	2	03874	28	04081	5
02837	11	03050	2	03275	39	03752	14	03875	2	04082	3
02838	3	03051	120	03276	15	03753	4	03878	17	04083	6
02839	1	03053	109	03278	8	03754	1	03883	2	04084	4
02840	129	03054	117	03279	2	03755	18	03884	5	04085	9
02841	4	03055	55	03280	8	03765	2	03885	16	04086	33
02842	1	03057	17	03281	17	03766	21	03887	10	04087	12
02852	56	03060	177	03282	2	03768	2	03890	2	04088	2
02857	24	03061	8	03284	1	03769	1	03894	19	04090	13
02859	17	03062	131	03286	1	03770	1	03896	4	04091	2
02860	44	03063	63	03289	2	03771	3	03901	18	04092	54
02861	56	03070	24	03290	3	03772	1	03902	1	04093	11
02862	2	03071	21	03291	1	03773	27	03903	27	04094	4
02863	8	03073	7	03293	1	03774	2	03904	41	04095	3
02864	83	03076	37	03301	142	03777	1	03905	11	04096	95
02865	47	03077	34	03302	2	03779	2	03906	9	04097	1
02871	97	03079	99	03303	32	03780	3	03907	6	04098	1
02874	10	03082	4	03304	11	03781	1	03908	10	04101	11
02875	3	03084	7	03357	1	03782	6	03909	14	04102	29
02876	6	03086	18	03431	72	03784	7	03910	2	04103	55
02877	3	03087	55	03440	10	03785	8	03911	2	04104	7
02878	61	03101	2	03441	1	03801	73	04001	1	04105	37
02879	41	03102	109	03442	3	03802	2	04002	14	04106	55
02881	7	03103	116	03443	3	03809	7	04003	5	04107	36
02882	28	03104	81	03444	12	03810	5	04005	44	04108	5
02883	11	03105	8	03445	4	03811	35	04008	10	04110	3
02885	23	03106	24	03446	5	03812	2	04009	36	04162	1
02886	109	03108	9	03447	11	03813	2	04010	2	04174	1
02887	2	03109	1	03448	1	03814	3	04011	68	04210	55
02888	60	03110	20	03449	12	03815	1	04014	4	04212	1
02889	58	03215	1	03450	2	03816	1	04015	8	04217	11
02891	53	03216	1	03451	15	03817	1	04017	1	04219	4
02892	8	03217	1	03452	15	03818	13	04020	4	04220	5
02893	68	03218	1	03455	7	03819	5	04021	18	04221	6
02894	2	03220	15	03456	7	03820	73	04022	8	04222	1
02895	93	03221	7	03457	6	03824	31	04024	2	04224	6
02898	2	03222	13	03458	35	03825	26	04027	11	04225	7
02901	1	03223	4	03461	25	03826	16	04029	2	04226	1
02903	7	03224	5	03462	7	03827	16	04030	4	04227	1
02904	35	03225	4	03464	4	03830	3	04031	1	04231	2
02905	27	03226	21	03465	9	03832	1	04032	29	04234	1
02906	35	03227	5	03466	2	03833	41	04037	4	04235	1
02907	16	03229	27	03467	6	03835	30	04038	29	04236	3
02908	46	03230	2	03469	13	03836	2	04039	13	04237	1
02909	30	03231	3	03470	15	03837	6	04040	19	04238	4
02910	47	03232	1	03561	31	03838	2	04041	2	04239	3
02911	36	03233	1	03570	11	03840	11	04042	7	04240	47
02912	3	03234	14	03574	4	03841	27	04043	39	04241	2
02914	48	03235	15	03576	11	03842	43	04046	17	04250	14
02915	50	03237	6	03579	2	03844	8	04047	5	04251	1
02916	23	03240	8	03580	8	03845	2	04048	17	04252	22
02917	26	03241	1	03581	8	03846	8	04049	6	04253	2
02919	73	03242	16	03582	2	03847	1	04054	8	04254	3
02920	98	03243	6	03583	3	03848	15	04055	19	04255	1
02921	6	03244	28	03584	7	03849	5	04056	2	04256	12

04257	3	04442	1	04634	6	04843	22	04986	2	05260	2
04258	1	04443	8	04638	2	04846	1	04987	2	05261	15
04259	6	04444	23	04640	10	04848	8	04988	2	05262	11
04260	11	04448	1	04641	1	04849	8	04989	5	05301	29
04263	6	04449	1	04643	5	04851	1	04990	1	05303	1
04265	1	04450	5	04648	2	04853	2	04992	2	05340	2
04267	4	04451	4	04649	1	04854	5	05001	21	05341	1
04268	18	04453	4	04652	9	04855	1	05030	4	05342	1
04270	9	04455	3	04654	25	04856	10	05031	2	05343	1
04271	1	04456	7	04655	3	04857	1	05032	7	05344	4
04273	2	04457	18	04656	5	04858	6	05033	6	05345	2
04274	3	04458	5	04658	3	04859	5	05035	1	05346	24
04276	15	04459	2	04660	9	04860	2	05036	11	05351	3
04278	1	04460	4	04662	5	04861	8	05037	1	05352	2
04279	1	04461	3	04664	2	04862	24	05038	2	05353	4
04280	7	04462	18	04666	4	04863	7	05039	2	05354	7
04281	27	04463	6	04667	2	04864	6	05040	3	05356	2
04282	7	04464	3	04668	7	04865	2	05042	2	05357	2
04284	5	04465	1	04669	1	04869	1	05043	5	05359	2
04285	4	04468	26	04671	1	04901	58	05044	1	05363	9
04289	7	04469	2	04674	1	04902	3	05045	4	05401	101
04290	4	04472	1	04675	2	04910	3	05046	3	05402	2
04292	1	04473	21	04676	3	04911	5	05047	2	05403	39
04294	6	04474	21	04677	2	04912	1	05048	3	05404	9
04330	89	04475	4	04679	5	04915	26	05051	1	05407	1
04332	3	04476	4	04680	1	04918	5	05052	1	05439	1
04341	6	04479	3	04681	5	04920	1	05055	15	05440	4
04342	4	04487	3	04684	4	04921	7	05056	1	05443	24
04343	2	04488	2	04685	1	04922	2	05058	2	05444	6
04344	7	04489	5	04689	3	04923	3	05059	2	05445	16
04345	52	04496	10	04690	1	04924	1	05060	19	05446	45
04346	3	04509	1	04691	7	04926	1	05061	7	05447	5
04347	14	04530	57	04692	1	04927	3	05062	3	05450	7
04348	8	04537	4	04693	15	04928	3	05065	6	05451	5
04349	4	04538	7	04694	17	04929	2	05068	5	05452	100
04350	8	04539	4	04730	28	04930	17	05069	1	05453	2
04351	4	04543	11	04732	4	04932	3	05070	1	05454	13
04352	6	04544	2	04735	1	04935	4	05071	2	05456	4
04353	4	04547	4	04736	14	04937	24	05072	2	05457	2
04354	4	04548	3	04738	6	04938	30	05075	6	05458	4
04355	3	04551	2	04740	4	04939	5	05076	1	05459	5
04357	18	04553	7	04741	1	04940	1	05077	4	05461	9
04358	6	04554	4	04742	8	04941	6	05079	1	05462	6
04359	3	04555	11	04743	15	04942	2	05080	1	05464	13
04360	1	04556	6	04744	1	04943	1	05081	2	05465	27
04361	1	04558	1	04745	1	04945	2	05084	1	05466	4
04362	1	04562	2	04746	2	04947	10	05085	1	05468	42
04363	9	04563	2	04747	4	04949	2	05086	1	05469	1
04364	34	04564	3	04749	1	04950	5	05088	5	05472	3
04401	117	04565	1	04750	10	04951	3	05089	20	05473	1
04402	1	04568	3	04751	16	04952	2	05091	7	05474	2
04406	5	04571	2	04756	16	04953	16	05101	24	05476	5
04411	2	04572	24	04757	5	04954	1	05142	4	05477	14
04412	39	04574	3	04758	3	04955	8	05143	17	05478	22
04414	2	04576	6	04760	4	04956	6	05146	2	05481	1
04415	3	04578	24	04761	3	04957	26	05149	1	05482	30
04416	11	04579	3	04762	3	04958	2	05150	2	05483	1
04419	15	04605	42	04763	3	04962	7	05151	3	05485	1
04420	1	04606	2	04764	1	04963	14	05152	2	05486	7
04421	3	04607	9	04765	6	04964	1	05153	1	05487	4
04422	5	04609	18	04768	1	04966	1	05154	7	05488	20
04423	2	04612	1	04769	51	04967	16	05156	29	05489	24
04424	1	04613	1	04770	1	04969	2	05158	1	05490	4
04426	15	04614	22	04772	1	04970	2	05159	5	05491	19
04427	6	04615	2	04773	1	04971	4	05161	3	05492	3
04428	4	04617	7	04774	3	04972	1	05201	54	05494	14
04429	14	04619	19	04779	3	04974	16	05202	1	05495	34
04430	5	04622	4	04780	2	04976	40	05250	14	05601	2
04431	3	04623	5	04783	1	04978	1	05251	7	05602	54
04433	1	04627	10	04784	3	04979	6	05252	2	05641	37
04434	1	04628	1	04785	1	04981	13	05253	2	05647	3
04435	1	04629	1	04786	6	04982	1	05254	3	05648	4
04438	4	04630	15	04787	3	04983	1	05255	10	05649	1
04441	5	04631	9	04841	33	04984	2	05257	5	05650	2

05651	5	05850	1	06094	1	06359	11	06492	133	06805	9
05654	6	05851	8	06095	78	06360	90	06496	1	06807	12
05655	2	05853	1	06096	28	06365	4	06497	112	06810	80
05656	2	05855	16	06098	74	06370	26	06498	27	06811	49
05657	1	05857	1	06103	2	06371	40	06502	2	06812	36
05658	5	05859	6	06105	20	06372	2	06505	1	06813	2
05660	3	05862	1	06106	27	06374	13	06510	3	06820	43
05661	14	05867	6	06107	57	06375	17	06511	29	06829	3
05663	22	05873	3	06108	44	06377	4	06512	46	06830	54
05667	12	05874	3	06109	83	06378	23	06513	21	06831	14
05669	3	05875	1	06110	33	06379	18	06514	58	06836	4
05672	10	05906	1	06111	141	06380	3	06515	19	06840	48
05673	3	05907	1	06112	10	06382	39	06516	116	06848	1
05674	4	06001	36	06114	25	06384	12	06517	34	06850	36
05675	4	06002	52	06116	1	06385	76	06518	35	06851	82
05676	13	06010	185	06117	64	06388	2	06519	4	06852	1
05677	2	06011	5	06118	47	06390	2	06520	5	06853	6
05679	8	06013	41	06119	32	06401	42	06524	3	06854	43
05680	2	06016	14	06120	2	06403	12	06525	40	06855	17
05681	1	06018	7	06131	8	06404	1	06530	1	06856	3
05682	7	06019	16	06137	1	06405	45	06533	1	06870	16
05699	1	06021	2	06141	1	06410	90	06601	3	06875	1
05701	56	06022	14	06153	1	06412	19	06602	1	06876	2
05702	2	06023	1	06226	30	06413	43	06604	38	06877	75
05730	2	06025	1	06231	12	06414	1	06605	19	06878	21
05731	1	06026	24	06232	16	06415	37	06606	54	06880	73
05732	1	06027	7	06233	1	06416	36	06607	8	06881	2
05733	8	06028	1	06234	12	06417	39	06608	23	06883	24
05735	6	06029	29	06235	3	06418	19	06610	28	06896	20
05736	1	06031	3	06237	17	06419	6	06611	120	06897	37
05737	2	06032	55	06238	38	06420	6	06612	21	06901	2
05738	3	06033	59	06239	15	06422	35	06702	1	06902	71
05739	2	06035	30	06240	1	06423	14	06704	23	06903	50
05742	1	06037	55	06241	11	06424	24	06705	21	06904	1
05743	7	06039	12	06242	3	06425	1	06706	15	06905	51
05744	3	06040	119	06243	1	06426	13	06708	46	06906	12
05750	1	06041	1	06245	1	06430	113	06710	8	06907	16
05751	5	06043	8	06247	5	06432	17	06712	20	06959	1
05753	21	06050	2	06248	18	06436	2	06716	42	06987	1
05757	5	06051	33	06249	13	06437	71	06720	1	07001	28
05758	1	06052	14	06250	15	06438	7	06750	3	07002	75
05759	8	06053	47	06251	2	06439	4	06751	9	07003	81
05760	1	06057	23	06254	2	06441	22	06752	10	07004	2
05761	1	06058	1	06255	9	06442	8	06753	3	07005	68
05763	14	06059	4	06256	6	06443	51	06754	6	07006	96
05764	2	06060	11	06259	8	06444	4	06755	1	07007	2
05765	2	06062	46	06260	19	06447	21	06756	8	07008	30
05766	1	06063	6	06263	1	06450	168	06757	4	07009	46
05767	5	06065	7	06264	2	06451	1	06758	2	07010	21
05769	5	06066	79	06267	5	06454	1	06759	22	07011	43
05770	3	06067	51	06268	28	06455	5	06761	1	07012	42
05773	5	06068	1	06273	1	06456	1	06762	17	07013	74
05774	7	06069	18	06277	10	06457	78	06763	5	07014	16
05775	1	06070	48	06278	9	06460	173	06770	57	07015	2
05777	10	06071	27	06279	17	06467	2	06776	53	07016	60
05778	1	06072	1	06280	6	06468	41	06777	15	07017	15
05819	14	06073	7	06281	13	06469	2	06778	2	07018	8
05820	2	06074	59	06282	1	06470	47	06779	12	07020	6
05821	2	06075	1	06320	51	06471	21	06781	4	07021	8
05822	1	06076	24	06330	7	06472	28	06782	12	07022	15
05824	3	06077	1	06331	6	06473	37	06783	10	07023	15
05827	1	06078	26	06332	2	06475	34	06784	7	07024	43
05828	6	06079	3	06333	19	06477	56	06785	1	07026	36
05829	6	06081	8	06334	8	06478	5	06786	25	07027	7
05830	4	06082	110	06335	43	06479	30	06787	19	07028	16
05832	2	06083	2	06336	1	06480	28	06790	103	07029	14
05836	4	06084	48	06337	2	06481	2	06791	31	07030	18
05839	5	06085	21	06339	44	06482	31	06793	2	07031	5
05841	3	06088	10	06340	121	06483	45	06794	3	07032	74
05842	1	06089	5	06349	6	06484	113	06795	32	07033	16
05843	6	06090	1	06351	31	06487	3	06796	5	07034	25
05845	2	06091	1	06354	7	06488	66	06798	22	07035	22
05846	15	06092	21	06355	55	06489	112	06801	423	07036	62
05849	5	06093	21	06357	38	06490	15	06804	38	07039	75

07040	32	07401	12	07632	45	07826	23	08009	30	08095	1
07041	6	07403	29	07634	1	07827	10	08010	18	08096	80
07042	32	07405	54	07640	10	07828	25	08012	63	08097	11
07043	28	07407	37	07641	10	07829	1	08015	51	08098	13
07044	32	07410	96	07642	41	07830	27	08016	39	08102	3
07045	14	07416	6	07643	24	07832	6	08018	2	08103	6
07046	11	07417	55	07644	43	07834	62	08019	8	08104	10
07047	67	07418	4	07645	26	07836	30	08020	8	08105	24
07050	9	07419	19	07646	41	07838	8	08021	72	08106	25
07052	76	07420	12	07647	5	07840	46	08022	13	08107	29
07054	63	07421	20	07648	9	07843	39	08023	3	08108	63
07055	65	07422	15	07649	26	07845	3	08025	2	08109	54
07056	1	07423	14	07650	12	07846	1	08026	9	08110	36
07057	7	07424	55	07652	67	07847	4	08027	8	08201	61
07058	11	07425	1	07653	1	07848	10	08028	29	08202	8
07059	8	07428	7	07656	44	07849	18	08029	12	08203	16
07060	105	07430	29	07657	32	07850	27	08030	28	08204	54
07061	1	07431	1	07660	21	07852	1	08031	37	08210	18
07062	21	07432	18	07661	32	07853	41	08032	1	08212	2
07063	10	07435	7	07662	56	07856	11	08033	80	08213	2
07064	7	07436	46	07664	1	07857	5	08034	85	08214	2
07065	37	07437	1	07666	80	07860	72	08035	38	08215	36
07066	46	07438	23	07670	38	07861	1	08036	2	08217	1
07067	49	07439	7	07675	132	07863	8	08037	38	08219	3
07068	10	07440	13	07701	101	07865	16	08038	2	08220	3
07070	37	07442	19	07702	6	07866	58	08039	1	08221	41
07071	27	07444	25	07703	1	07869	49	08042	6	08223	6
07072	13	07446	35	07704	9	07870	2	08043	49	08224	2
07073	6	07450	64	07710	1	07871	58	08044	1	08225	23
07074	4	07451	2	07711	5	07874	38	08045	2	08226	37
07075	18	07452	25	07712	93	07876	42	08046	75	08230	9
07076	48	07456	52	07716	15	07878	5	08048	5	08232	71
07077	10	07457	6	07717	3	07879	1	08049	18	08240	5
07078	26	07458	43	07718	21	07882	32	08050	47	08241	4
07079	15	07460	24	07719	39	07885	16	08051	12	08242	4
07080	43	07461	52	07720	8	07901	45	08052	40	08243	3
07081	43	07462	24	07721	4	07902	1	08053	77	08244	21
07082	14	07463	32	07722	35	07915	1	08054	81	08245	1
07083	94	07465	11	07723	9	07920	48	08055	86	08246	4
07087	76	07470	146	07724	94	07921	11	08056	6	08247	6
07088	5	07474	5	07726	74	07922	38	08057	88	08250	3
07090	91	07480	29	07727	16	07924	16	08059	8	08251	22
07092	17	07481	86	07728	106	07926	5	08060	76	08260	28
07093	47	07501	10	07730	40	07927	11	08061	2	08270	10
07094	26	07502	8	07731	69	07928	91	08062	5	08302	53
07095	33	07503	10	07732	16	07930	28	08063	1	08310	4
07096	2	07504	9	07733	48	07931	9	08065	21	08311	9
07101	3	07505	1	07734	34	07932	25	08066	12	08312	10
07103	6	07506	47	07735	45	07933	18	08067	2	08316	2
07104	22	07507	3	07737	10	07934	1	08068	9	08317	6
07105	28	07508	41	07738	28	07935	2	08069	24	08318	21
07106	17	07509	6	07739	28	07936	14	08070	29	08319	2
07107	15	07512	12	07740	52	07940	51	08071	46	08320	3
07108	6	07513	4	07746	36	07945	22	08072	3	08322	21
07109	39	07514	12	07747	90	07946	17	08074	4	08323	2
07110	55	07522	3	07748	81	07950	52	08075	53	08326	3
07111	23	07524	5	07750	10	07960	72	08077	73	08328	4
07112	5	07580	1	07751	23	07961	10	08078	21	08329	2
07114	9	07601	46	07752	1	07970	3	08079	29	08330	84
07201	26	07603	17	07753	86	07974	38	08080	44	08332	100
07202	28	07604	25	07755	30	07976	1	08081	36	08338	1
07203	25	07605	22	07756	11	07977	1	08082	1	08340	3
07204	24	07606	2	07757	13	07978	2	08083	22	08341	2
07205	41	07607	40	07758	13	07979	2	08084	23	08343	15
07206	14	07616	1	07760	37	07980	5	08085	7	08344	20
07207	2	07620	2	07762	29	07981	24	08086	9	08345	6
07208	28	07621	61	07763	2	08001	10	08087	51	08349	3
07302	16	07624	39	07764	23	08002	66	08088	74	08350	1
07304	17	07625	1	07801	55	08003	130	08089	11	08352	1
07305	34	07626	18	07820	1	08004	19	08090	26	08353	1
07306	28	07627	17	07821	21	08005	53	08091	8	08360	107
07307	41	07628	47	07822	10	08006	3	08092	17	08365	1
07309	1	07630	21	07823	23	08007	21	08093	18	08401	21
07310	3	07631	45	07825	12	08008	48	08094	47	08402	22

08403	2	08742	60	08887	5	09182	2	09567	1	10031	29
08404	1	08750	8	08889	20	09183	1	09570	1	10032	27
08405	2	08751	3	08901	21	09185	5	09571	3	10033	53
08406	16	08752	6	08902	49	09189	4	09578	1	10034	31
08501	10	08753	176	08903	1	09192	4	09586	1	10035	6
08502	42	08754	2	08904	30	09193	4	09587	1	10036	7
08504	2	08755	19	09007	1	09210	16	09588	1	10037	4
08505	21	08756	2	09009	10	09213	3	09590	2	10038	11
08510	2	08757	93	09011	1	09216	1	09593	4	10039	10
08511	1	08758	24	09012	19	09220	2	09596	1	10040	27
08512	46	08759	46	09019	2	09221	3	09613	1	10044	6
08514	7	08760	1	09021	7	09223	1	09616	1	10101	1
08515	4	08801	28	09025	3	09224	3	09622	1	10113	2
08518	4	08802	15	09026	4	09226	1	09633	16	10116	3
08520	65	08803	1	09028	2	09227	5	09644	1	10128	40
08525	24	08804	8	09031	2	09238	1	09645	1	10150	1
08527	73	08805	20	09033	1	09240	4	09659	1	10152	1
08528	5	08807	110	09034	4	09242	2	09662	1	10156	1
08530	16	08808	1	09035	8	09245	1	09667	2	10159	2
08533	9	08809	8	09036	1	09252	1	09669	1	10162	1
08534	27	08810	6	09037	1	09253	3	09672	3	10163	6
08535	4	08812	17	09038	4	09264	1	09675	5	10166	2
08536	25	08816	98	09039	1	09279	2	09690	1	10169	1
08540	83	08817	91	09046	2	09281	2	09694	1	10185	3
08542	2	08818	3	09052	4	09283	1	09696	5	10203	1
08543	2	08820	56	09055	2	09284	4	09697	1	10235	1
08550	18	08822	73	09056	6	09289	1	09701	1	10268	1
08551	14	08823	9	09057	19	09291	3	09705	1	10274	1
08553	2	08824	22	09059	3	09292	2	09718	2	10280	7
08554	5	08825	18	09061	1	09293	3	09720	2	10301	45
08555	4	08826	17	09063	2	09305	2	09728	1	10302	42
08556	1	08827	13	09066	4	09325	2	09742	9	10303	66
08558	9	08828	4	09068	1	09326	1	09755	2	10304	43
08559	14	08829	9	09074	1	09330	2	09757	6	10305	45
08560	15	08830	26	09077	1	09333	2	09777	1	10306	99
08561	2	08831	26	09078	1	09352	1	09794	2	10307	11
08562	12	08832	2	09079	3	09360	1	09801	2	10308	48
08608	1	08833	17	09080	5	09378	2	09803	1	10309	12
08609	8	08834	2	09081	1	09406	2	09810	1	10310	36
08610	60	08835	17	09086	9	09407	1	09812	2	10312	62
08611	15	08836	13	09088	1	09455	2	09839	1	10314	1059
08618	47	08837	14	09091	1	09456	1	09842	2	10316	1
08619	55	08840	43	09094	1	09457	4	09846	1	10421	1
08620	30	08846	26	09098	10	09458	2	09852	1	10451	15
08628	27	08848	23	09102	7	09459	1	09860	6	10452	22
08629	14	08850	23	09105	1	09464	2	10001	14	10453	11
08638	43	08851	1	09107	2	09465	5	10002	66	10454	11
08640	7	08852	14	09108	2	09468	13	10003	39	10455	20
08641	11	08853	40	09109	8	09501	2	10004	15	10456	18
08648	59	08854	104	09114	6	09503	1	10005	1	10457	15
08650	2	08855	1	09123	13	09508	2	10006	1	10458	36
08652	1	08857	54	09125	1	09510	2	10007	2	10459	12
08653	1	08858	1	09127	5	09511	1	10008	4	10460	28
08690	52	08859	32	09128	2	09517	1	10009	59	10461	45
08691	18	08860	1	09130	6	09518	2	10010	22	10462	44
08701	120	08861	79	09131	4	09521	2	10011	50	10463	54
08702	1	08862	13	09132	14	09523	11	10012	27	10464	12
08714	1	08863	33	09139	4	09524	2	10013	12	10465	73
08721	47	08865	67	09146	4	09525	1	10014	30	10466	40
08722	32	08867	20	09150	1	09532	2	10016	40	10467	51
08723	98	08868	2	09154	6	09537	1	10017	18	10468	27
08724	43	08869	13	09155	4	09539	3	10018	4	10469	34
08729	1	08870	2	09156	1	09540	4	10019	33	10470	11
08730	9	08872	19	09157	1	09542	1	10020	3	10471	31
08731	57	08873	58	09159	1	09544	1	10021	87	10472	32
08732	6	08875	1	09161	1	09546	1	10022	30	10473	32
08733	43	08876	96	09164	2	09548	1	10023	57	10474	1
08734	21	08877	1	09165	4	09549	2	10024	50	10475	29
08735	7	08879	59	09169	3	09551	2	10025	73	10501	4
08736	30	08880	7	09175	1	09557	1	10026	4	10502	16
08738	7	08882	27	09176	4	09560	2	10027	30	10503	2
08739	2	08884	21	09178	3	09561	1	10028	48	10504	17
08740	2	08885	1	09179	6	09562	1	10029	49	10505	1
08741	8	08886	4	09180	1	09565	3	10030	2	10506	10

10507	12	10802	3	11050	84	11378	51	11680	1	11789	19
10509	37	10803	20	11091	1	11379	35	11691	34	11790	86
10510	26	10804	36	11101	11	11385	64	11692	10	11791	80
10511	4	10805	30	11102	17	11395	1	11693	8	11792	22
10512	51	10835	1	11103	32	11411	42	11694	53	11793	87
10514	43	10901	41	11104	22	11412	28	11696	4	11794	2
10516	13	10912	1	11105	31	11413	30	11697	8	11795	67
10517	3	10913	13	11106	23	11414	51	11701	39	11796	9
10518	1	10914	4	11201	50	11415	29	11702	45	11797	19
10519	2	10916	6	11202	4	11416	14	11703	61	11798	14
10520	29	10917	4	11203	39	11417	22	11704	53	11801	89
10522	20	10918	13	11204	54	11418	42	11705	18	11802	6
10523	6	10919	7	11205	11	11419	53	11706	119	11803	100
10524	4	10920	20	11206	26	11420	46	11709	10	11804	23
10526	6	10921	9	11207	25	11421	42	11710	72	11901	39
10528	18	10923	20	11208	26	11422	30	11713	19	11907	1
10530	29	10924	21	11209	73	11423	19	11714	49	11930	5
10532	10	10925	14	11210	60	11424	1	11715	13	11931	3
10533	7	10926	10	11211	28	11426	35	11716	17	11932	4
10535	4	10927	9	11212	15	11427	23	11717	64	11933	10
10536	19	10928	1	11213	26	11428	18	11718	13	11934	17
10537	8	10930	22	11214	82	11429	14	11719	10	11935	13
10538	48	10931	1	11215	55	11430	5	11720	86	11937	30
10540	2	10932	1	11216	18	11431	3	11721	31	11939	6
10541	45	10933	1	11217	21	11432	59	11722	40	11940	13
10543	31	10940	79	11218	62	11433	9	11724	8	11941	4
10545	4	10950	42	11219	40	11434	38	11725	88	11942	21
10546	5	10952	62	11220	46	11435	45	11726	33	11944	8
10547	14	10953	1	11221	16	11436	7	11727	47	11946	38
10548	11	10954	29	11222	24	11439	1	11729	60	11947	2
10549	28	10956	80	11223	56	11470	1	11730	29	11948	1
10550	33	10958	4	11224	41	11501	36	11731	116	11949	10
10552	37	10960	12	11225	22	11507	25	11732	3	11950	35
10553	11	10961	1	11226	38	11509	6	11733	79	11951	23
10560	1	10962	13	11227	4	11510	69	11735	61	11952	9
10562	41	10963	2	11228	53	11514	6	11738	43	11953	25
10566	73	10964	5	11229	108	11516	16	11739	3	11954	8
10570	35	10965	36	11230	83	11518	23	11740	33	11955	10
10573	37	10967	1	11231	20	11520	70	11741	48	11956	1
10576	29	10968	4	11232	11	11530	63	11742	29	11957	3
10577	4	10969	2	11233	9	11536	1	11743	165	11959	3
10578	3	10970	37	11234	85	11538	1	11746	181	11960	2
10579	28	10972	1	11235	72	11542	47	11747	34	11961	28
10580	31	10973	8	11236	116	11545	33	11750	1	11963	23
10583	79	10974	7	11237	10	11547	1	11751	23	11964	11
10587	2	10976	3	11238	17	11548	1	11752	21	11965	9
10588	6	10977	83	11239	9	11550	43	11753	18	11967	43
10589	15	10979	2	11275	1	11551	1	11754	46	11968	31
10590	16	10980	26	11278	1	11552	63	11755	21	11970	1
10591	30	10982	3	11314	1	11553	39	11756	108	11971	16
10594	13	10983	13	11317	1	11554	80	11757	115	11972	4
10595	16	10984	6	11352	11	11557	17	11758	155	11973	7
10596	7	10986	4	11354	39	11558	14	11762	60	11975	1
10597	2	10987	5	11355	109	11559	20	11763	79	11976	7
10598	88	10989	14	11356	28	11560	7	11764	32	11977	2
10601	4	10990	43	11357	66	11561	35	11765	2	11978	11
10602	3	10992	14	11358	40	11563	33	11766	21	11980	12
10603	25	10993	7	11360	35	11565	15	11767	27	12007	1
10604	12	10994	6	11361	36	11566	112	11768	76	12008	5
10605	30	10996	15	11362	21	11567	1	11769	22	12009	24
10606	10	10997	8	11363	9	11568	4	11770	1	12010	51
10607	12	10998	1	11364	49	11569	3	11771	36	12015	4
10656	1	11001	65	11365	65	11570	44	11772	84	12018	25
10701	38	11003	56	11366	16	11572	59	11776	51	12019	59
10702	1	11004	31	11367	56	11575	12	11777	36	12020	84
10703	27	11005	5	11368	39	11576	33	11778	44	12023	3
10704	69	11010	43	11369	18	11577	30	11779	64	12024	1
10705	47	11020	17	11370	20	11579	17	11780	39	12025	16
10706	13	11021	43	11371	1	11580	68	11782	46	12027	25
10707	37	11023	34	11372	54	11581	42	11783	37	12028	1
10708	31	11024	16	11373	57	11590	66	11784	61	12029	1
10709	14	11030	37	11374	38	11596	27	11786	18	12032	8
10710	54	11040	98	11375	82	11598	45	11787	119	12033	31
10801	27	11046	1	11377	56	11638	1	11788	28	12034	1

12035	3	12155	5	12423	6	12529	9	12771	28	12926	1
12037	14	12156	4	12424	2	12531	11	12775	3	12927	3
12041	1	12157	6	12426	1	12533	73	12776	4	12928	6
12042	4	12158	12	12428	6	12534	38	12777	2	12929	7
12043	17	12159	10	12429	1	12537	4	12779	2	12930	2
12046	2	12160	5	12430	2	12538	43	12780	1	12932	7
12047	54	12161	2	12431	2	12540	24	12783	3	12935	1
12050	3	12162	1	12433	3	12541	2	12784	2	12936	1
12051	4	12164	6	12434	3	12542	11	12785	1	12937	2
12052	2	12165	1	12435	3	12543	7	12787	3	12939	1
12053	15	12166	3	12436	1	12544	2	12788	2	12941	1
12054	63	12167	8	12440	2	12545	13	12789	4	12942	3
12056	4	12168	15	12442	6	12546	4	12790	18	12943	3
12057	2	12169	3	12443	10	12547	5	12791	1	12944	5
12058	3	12170	11	12444	1	12548	3	12801	82	12945	6
12059	4	12173	4	12446	11	12549	20	12803	9	12946	15
12060	7	12174	1	12447	1	12550	108	12804	19	12950	4
12061	15	12175	10	12448	1	12553	9	12809	4	12952	2
12062	1	12176	6	12449	12	12554	1	12814	12	12953	37
12063	2	12177	1	12450	1	12561	35	12815	1	12957	3
12064	1	12180	101	12451	3	12563	14	12816	8	12958	3
12065	107	12182	30	12455	16	12564	20	12817	2	12962	23
12066	6	12183	4	12457	2	12565	11	12821	1	12966	8
12067	2	12184	27	12458	17	12566	21	12822	16	12967	1
12068	6	12185	6	12459	1	12567	4	12824	2	12970	1
12069	1	12186	22	12460	1	12568	1	12827	13	12972	14
12070	6	12187	4	12461	2	12569	48	12828	17	12974	4
12072	5	12188	19	12463	2	12570	9	12831	30	12975	1
12073	1	12189	30	12465	1	12571	37	12832	5	12977	1
12074	8	12190	1	12466	6	12572	26	12833	8	12978	1
12075	11	12191	1	12468	4	12575	6	12834	19	12979	4
12076	2	12192	3	12469	1	12577	1	12835	5	12980	3
12077	16	12193	9	12470	1	12578	11	12836	3	12981	6
12078	49	12194	1	12471	9	12580	12	12837	1	12983	17
12082	3	12195	2	12472	1	12581	6	12838	2	12985	1
12083	9	12196	9	12473	2	12582	15	12839	24	12986	40
12084	5	12197	6	12474	2	12583	2	12842	6	12989	2
12085	1	12198	4	12477	51	12584	1	12845	19	12990	1
12086	10	12201	1	12480	1	12585	3	12846	6	12992	7
12087	5	12202	7	12481	7	12586	19	12847	1	12993	7
12090	19	12203	51	12482	1	12588	1	12849	1	12996	4
12092	1	12204	6	12484	15	12589	31	12850	15	12997	3
12093	5	12205	67	12485	1	12590	137	12852	2	13020	1
12094	4	12206	20	12486	5	12592	4	12853	4	13021	107
12095	77	12208	40	12487	13	12594	3	12855	1	13026	14
12099	1	12209	20	12489	4	12601	69	12856	1	13027	76
12106	3	12210	7	12491	18	12603	189	12857	1	13028	1
12107	1	12211	22	12493	4	12607	1	12859	1	13029	19
12108	2	12212	3	12494	3	12701	9	12861	1	13030	23
12110	36	12222	1	12496	4	12719	3	12863	2	13031	42
12115	1	12224	1	12498	36	12721	15	12865	6	13032	35
12116	6	12250	1	12501	5	12722	1	12866	78	13033	4
12117	4	12279	1	12502	5	12723	3	12870	2	13034	5
12118	22	12301	2	12503	1	12724	2	12871	10	13035	19
12121	2	12302	125	12507	1	12726	6	12873	1	13036	21
12122	19	12303	77	12508	31	12732	2	12874	1	13037	21
12123	24	12304	51	12509	1	12734	9	12883	13	13039	12
12124	1	12305	7	12510	1	12737	1	12884	2	13040	1
12125	5	12306	75	12512	2	12739	3	12885	11	13041	39
12130	8	12307	11	12513	7	12740	18	12887	4	13042	5
12134	7	12308	33	12514	7	12742	2	12901	90	13044	11
12136	3	12309	127	12515	2	12746	4	12903	10	13045	63
12137	4	12401	91	12516	2	12748	2	12907	1	13050	2
12138	9	12404	6	12517	3	12750	1	12910	3	13052	2
12140	6	12405	5	12518	12	12752	3	12912	2	13053	15
12141	2	12406	2	12520	13	12754	19	12913	3	13054	12
12143	13	12407	1	12521	3	12758	5	12914	1	13055	4
12144	50	12409	5	12522	7	12759	2	12916	3	13057	48
12147	1	12412	5	12523	8	12760	1	12917	1	13060	10
12148	21	12413	10	12524	52	12763	3	12918	5	13061	3
12149	6	12414	21	12525	4	12764	4	12919	9	13062	4
12150	4	12415	1	12526	6	12765	7	12920	7	13063	3
12153	3	12418	2	12527	2	12768	1	12921	5	13064	3
12154	3	12419	4	12528	33	12770	1	12923	4	13066	42

13068	20	13212	88	13441	4	13668	9	13815	40	14082	1
13069	64	13214	39	13452	10	13669	40	13820	53	14083	1
13071	5	13215	43	13454	4	13670	5	13825	20	14085	10
13072	4	13217	2	13456	15	13671	1	13826	1	14086	68
13073	16	13219	52	13459	2	13672	1	13827	71	14091	5
13074	11	13220	3	13460	10	13673	3	13830	17	14092	33
13076	4	13224	29	13461	13	13676	40	13832	1	14094	156
13077	22	13244	1	13464	4	13678	1	13833	13	14095	1
13078	20	13250	1	13466	1	13679	4	13835	5	14097	1
13080	6	13303	8	13468	1	13684	2	13838	17	14098	5
13081	3	13304	2	13469	4	13685	4	13839	5	14101	5
13082	17	13305	3	13470	4	13687	1	13841	2	14102	5
13083	3	13308	9	13471	6	13688	1	13843	6	14103	34
13084	9	13309	17	13472	2	13690	3	13844	2	14105	10
13087	1	13312	3	13473	4	13691	4	13845	1	14108	16
13088	90	13315	5	13476	9	13693	8	13849	17	14111	1
13090	76	13316	11	13477	2	13694	3	13850	108	14113	1
13092	9	13317	10	13478	32	13695	2	13856	13	14120	109
13093	1	13318	4	13479	1	13696	1	13861	1	14125	4
13101	4	13320	5	13480	19	13697	2	13862	13	14126	4
13102	3	13321	5	13482	1	13699	3	13864	3	14127	71
13103	1	13322	9	13486	3	13705	1	13865	23	14129	4
13104	39	13323	34	13488	1	13730	8	13901	70	14131	7
13108	17	13324	11	13489	1	13731	1	13902	9	14132	10
13110	5	13326	22	13490	9	13732	49	13903	78	14134	1
13111	10	13327	1	13491	14	13733	14	13904	24	14136	14
13112	4	13328	2	13492	48	13734	3	13905	82	14138	4
13114	18	13329	12	13493	7	13736	8	14001	22	14139	6
13115	5	13332	5	13495	5	13739	1	14004	25	14140	3
13116	26	13333	2	13501	72	13740	5	14005	6	14141	28
13117	1	13334	2	13502	98	13742	1	14006	20	14143	6
13118	21	13335	8	13503	2	13743	7	14008	2	14145	2
13120	7	13337	2	13504	1	13744	9	14009	24	14150	168
13122	2	13338	2	13562	1	13745	3	14011	11	14167	5
13126	74	13339	10	13601	87	13746	10	14012	9	14168	1
13129	1	13340	22	13602	3	13748	10	14013	3	14170	7
13131	7	13341	2	13603	3	13750	2	14020	93	14171	4
13132	11	13342	5	13605	12	13751	1	14024	2	14172	10
13135	26	13343	6	13606	2	13752	2	14025	9	14173	3
13136	2	13346	9	13607	9	13753	6	14026	3	14174	19
13138	6	13348	5	13612	8	13754	3	14027	1	14201	8
13140	5	13350	33	13613	4	13755	4	14028	7	14202	4
13142	16	13353	2	13615	2	13756	1	14030	2	14203	3
13143	4	13354	21	13616	4	13757	1	14031	17	14205	2
13145	2	13357	30	13617	22	13760	176	14032	10	14206	25
13146	7	13360	1	13618	7	13761	1	14033	5	14207	29
13147	2	13361	2	13619	11	13763	1	14034	7	14208	3
13148	31	13363	15	13620	4	13775	4	14036	12	14209	3
13150	1	13364	1	13622	8	13776	1	14037	2	14210	18
13152	32	13365	24	13624	7	13777	2	14039	1	14211	16
13153	2	13367	24	13625	11	13778	19	14040	5	14212	13
13156	5	13368	4	13630	3	13779	1	14041	1	14213	17
13157	4	13401	2	13634	8	13780	6	14042	4	14214	34
13158	3	13402	11	13635	8	13783	2	14043	42	14215	39
13159	15	13403	11	13637	3	13786	1	14047	17	14216	31
13160	13	13407	25	13639	2	13787	7	14048	22	14217	65
13161	1	13408	7	13642	29	13788	1	14051	29	14218	31
13162	3	13409	1	13643	1	13790	46	14052	73	14219	25
13163	5	13410	1	13645	3	13795	11	14054	7	14220	36
13164	6	13411	11	13646	7	13796	3	14055	1	14221	124
13165	26	13413	63	13647	5	13797	5	14057	19	14222	11
13166	12	13416	5	13648	7	13798	1	14058	8	14223	74
13167	13	13417	6	13650	5	13801	3	14059	53	14224	95
13190	1	13420	7	13652	6	13802	11	14062	8	14225	92
13202	4	13421	48	13654	3	13803	22	14063	42	14226	89
13203	28	13424	11	13656	6	13804	1	14065	5	14227	34
13204	18	13425	7	13658	6	13806	2	14067	23	14228	14
13205	31	13428	3	13659	2	13807	4	14068	11	14231	1
13206	28	13431	6	13660	8	13808	2	14069	2	14260	1
13207	38	13436	1	13661	1	13809	3	14070	15	14301	9
13208	30	13437	1	13662	26	13810	1	14072	58	14302	1
13209	37	13438	11	13664	1	13811	29	14075	110	14303	11
13210	41	13439	13	13665	1	13812	12	14080	17	14304	56
13211	27	13440	169	13667	6	13813	8	14081	7	14305	27

14411	29	14541	3	14729	1	14858	2	15060	1	15227	73
14414	12	14542	1	14730	2	14859	5	15061	47	15228	44
14415	1	14543	19	14731	2	14860	8	15062	18	15229	25
14416	10	14544	4	14733	8	14861	6	15063	32	15230	1
14418	6	14545	1	14735	6	14864	5	15064	1	15232	12
14420	54	14546	24	14736	1	14865	11	15065	27	15233	2
14422	5	14548	6	14737	8	14867	23	15066	53	15234	21
14423	20	14549	2	14738	11	14868	1	15067	9	15235	85
14424	61	14550	1	14739	12	14870	24	15068	80	15236	85
14425	28	14551	9	14740	6	14871	18	15071	18	15237	99
14426	1	14554	1	14741	8	14872	5	15074	32	15238	36
14427	6	14555	4	14742	1	14873	10	15075	1	15239	40
14428	31	14557	1	14743	6	14877	2	15078	1	15240	3
14429	1	14559	34	14744	10	14878	2	15081	1	15241	52
14431	1	14560	3	14747	9	14879	6	15084	12	15242	1
14432	14	14561	13	14748	1	14880	2	15085	25	15243	33
14433	6	14564	40	14749	1	14881	4	15086	1	15244	2
14435	7	14568	31	14750	12	14882	15	15087	1	15260	3
14437	16	14569	18	14753	3	14883	20	15088	2	15265	1
14441	2	14572	7	14754	3	14885	2	15089	17	15275	1
14443	3	14580	147	14755	6	14886	18	15090	29	15301	89
14445	25	14584	1	14756	4	14888	1	15101	58	15311	2
14449	2	14585	2	14757	22	14889	6	15102	80	15312	2
14450	161	14586	28	14760	38	14890	1	15104	7	15313	1
14453	2	14588	1	14767	3	14891	12	15106	32	15314	2
14454	7	14589	29	14769	3	14892	26	15108	119	15315	4
14456	40	14590	12	14770	5	14894	3	15110	6	15317	70
14461	2	14591	4	14772	8	14895	22	15112	3	15320	14
14464	19	14602	1	14775	11	14896	2	15116	37	15321	3
14466	6	14604	4	14776	1	14898	1	15120	36	15322	2
14467	59	14605	4	14777	2	14901	30	15122	45	15323	4
14468	68	14606	49	14779	9	14902	3	15126	14	15327	4
14469	24	14607	17	14781	4	14903	38	15127	3	15329	3
14470	16	14608	10	14782	2	14904	52	15129	14	15330	23
14471	14	14609	82	14784	6	14905	26	15131	25	15332	18
14472	38	14610	53	14787	22	15001	114	15132	34	15333	3
14475	1	14611	13	14801	8	15002	1	15133	9	15337	1
14476	7	14612	91	14802	5	15003	33	15135	11	15338	4
14477	2	14613	25	14803	3	15005	29	15136	32	15339	2
14478	6	14614	1	14804	2	15006	2	15137	21	15340	3
14479	1	14615	48	14805	3	15009	82	15139	8	15342	5
14480	1	14616	113	14806	7	15010	105	15140	4	15344	1
14481	2	14617	80	14807	6	15012	51	15143	46	15345	2
14482	19	14618	96	14809	5	15014	6	15144	14	15346	2
14485	6	14619	27	14810	28	15015	6	15145	8	15347	5
14487	10	14620	51	14812	13	15017	27	15146	81	15349	5
14489	21	14621	26	14813	3	15018	4	15147	37	15350	1
14502	35	14622	55	14814	5	15019	9	15148	8	15351	4
14504	1	14623	80	14815	1	15020	2	15201	9	15352	2
14505	16	14624	87	14816	8	15021	13	15202	37	15357	2
14506	3	14625	47	14817	7	15022	21	15203	11	15358	1
14507	5	14626	83	14818	3	15024	25	15204	16	15360	1
14508	1	14627	5	14819	3	15025	26	15205	47	15362	2
14510	8	14650	2	14821	3	15026	8	15206	29	15363	2
14511	3	14676	2	14822	2	15027	14	15207	24	15364	2
14512	15	14689	1	14823	19	15030	2	15208	14	15365	1
14513	24	14692	8	14824	3	15032	3	15209	26	15367	12
14514	8	14701	97	14825	1	15033	10	15210	34	15368	1
14515	1	14702	1	14826	1	15034	6	15211	22	15370	7
14516	10	14706	7	14830	39	15035	7	15212	35	15376	5
14517	12	14709	2	14837	10	15037	21	15213	30	15401	66
14519	37	14710	14	14838	7	15038	3	15214	26	15411	1
14521	5	14711	1	14839	4	15042	26	15215	9	15412	1
14522	33	14712	13	14840	21	15043	3	15216	42	15417	10
14525	7	14715	2	14841	1	15044	50	15217	75	15419	4
14526	78	14716	7	14842	5	15045	3	15218	31	15421	3
14527	35	14717	1	14843	27	15046	1	15219	9	15423	3
14528	1	14718	4	14845	69	15047	1	15220	26	15424	3
14530	19	14719	2	14847	12	15050	15	15221	68	15425	55
14532	12	14720	2	14850	170	15052	17	15222	1	15427	3
14533	2	14721	1	14851	5	15055	3	15223	6	15428	8
14534	135	14722	4	14853	5	15056	3	15224	8	15431	7
14538	4	14723	4	14854	1	15057	11	15225	2	15432	1
14540	1	14727	8	14856	1	15059	12	15226	25	15434	1

15436	1	15658	16	15870	3	16120	3	16354	25	16661	4
15437	3	15661	1	15901	2	16121	6	16360	2	16662	5
15438	6	15663	4	15902	16	16123	6	16362	1	16666	5
15440	1	15665	2	15904	50	16124	4	16364	1	16668	6
15442	7	15666	43	15905	47	16125	42	16365	55	16669	4
15444	3	15668	55	15906	32	16127	39	16370	1	16670	1
15445	7	15670	3	15907	1	16130	4	16371	5	16673	10
15446	5	15671	1	15909	9	16131	3	16373	2	16674	1
15450	1	15672	7	15920	5	16133	6	16374	1	16678	2
15451	1	15675	2	15921	1	16134	13	16401	12	16683	2
15458	3	15678	2	15923	3	16136	1	16402	1	16684	1
15459	2	15679	4	15924	1	16137	24	16403	14	16686	27
15461	9	15681	8	15926	3	16140	3	16404	2	16689	1
15463	1	15683	16	15928	2	16141	2	16405	1	16693	7
15464	4	15684	4	15930	2	16142	12	16406	5	16695	1
15466	5	15686	3	15931	10	16143	4	16407	26	16701	46
15468	1	15690	12	15935	1	16145	8	16410	10	16725	3
15470	1	15691	1	15936	1	16146	56	16411	5	16727	1
15473	11	15695	1	15937	2	16148	19	16412	16	16731	4
15474	7	15696	4	15938	1	16150	34	16413	1	16732	2
15475	8	15697	6	15940	1	16151	1	16415	20	16734	2
15478	13	15698	1	15942	3	16153	4	16417	20	16735	22
15479	4	15701	71	15943	1	16154	10	16420	2	16738	8
15480	2	15710	4	15944	7	16156	6	16421	4	16740	1
15483	4	15711	1	15946	15	16157	8	16423	5	16743	10
15485	1	15714	10	15948	1	16159	17	16424	8	16746	1
15486	2	15715	4	15951	2	16160	1	16426	10	16748	5
15490	1	15716	1	15954	8	16201	20	16428	31	16749	9
15501	31	15717	12	15955	5	16210	2	16433	13	16750	1
15522	32	15722	3	15956	2	16214	16	16434	5	16801	102
15530	7	15724	8	15957	2	16218	2	16435	2	16802	4
15533	2	15725	7	15958	2	16222	3	16436	1	16803	57
15535	6	15727	1	15959	3	16226	12	16438	24	16804	3
15536	1	15728	10	15961	3	16229	13	16440	1	16805	3
15537	12	15729	1	15963	16	16232	11	16441	24	16822	1
15538	3	15731	3	16001	152	16233	4	16442	3	16823	38
15541	4	15732	2	16022	1	16235	2	16443	9	16824	1
15542	2	15739	1	16023	7	16236	1	16501	3	16825	1
15544	1	15745	3	16024	1	16239	5	16502	21	16827	15
15545	10	15747	1	16025	12	16240	1	16503	15	16828	6
15550	1	15748	16	16027	3	16242	2	16504	41	16829	1
15551	3	15753	3	16028	3	16248	4	16505	52	16830	30
15552	13	15754	1	16029	2	16249	3	16506	58	16832	1
15554	1	15757	6	16033	21	16254	4	16507	12	16833	9
15557	6	15759	5	16034	4	16255	4	16508	41	16834	1
15558	1	15762	4	16036	1	16256	1	16509	76	16838	4
15559	1	15765	8	16037	11	16258	5	16510	56	16841	1
15560	1	15767	48	16038	6	16259	4	16511	30	16843	2
15563	4	15771	7	16040	2	16260	2	16512	6	16844	1
15601	89	15772	3	16041	3	16262	7	16514	1	16845	1
15604	1	15775	2	16046	31	16301	45	16516	1	16848	1
15610	6	15780	1	16049	8	16311	2	16601	57	16851	7
15611	1	15801	41	16050	3	16313	3	16602	53	16852	1
15613	40	15822	1	16051	10	16314	9	16603	2	16853	3
15615	1	15823	2	16052	12	16316	16	16611	6	16858	1
15618	4	15824	10	16053	5	16317	8	16617	9	16865	15
15621	1	15825	27	16054	1	16319	4	16622	1	16866	8
15623	1	15829	5	16055	14	16323	47	16623	2	16868	4
15624	2	15832	2	16056	11	16326	2	16625	10	16870	12
15626	14	15834	18	16057	15	16327	6	16627	2	16872	1
15627	9	15840	5	16059	16	16329	2	16630	10	16874	2
15628	1	15845	4	16061	4	16331	1	16635	32	16875	2
15629	2	15846	3	16063	30	16333	1	16636	1	16876	1
15630	1	15847	1	16101	77	16334	4	16637	7	16901	58
15632	23	15849	3	16102	7	16335	99	16641	1	16911	1
15634	1	15851	16	16103	1	16341	4	16646	1	16912	5
15637	5	15853	18	16105	33	16342	4	16647	3	16914	7
15639	7	15856	3	16111	2	16344	2	16648	21	16915	13
15641	1	15857	16	16112	9	16345	13	16650	4	16917	4
15642	102	15860	14	16113	1	16346	16	16652	50	16918	2
15644	24	15861	2	16114	2	16347	2	16653	1	16920	3
15650	38	15864	7	16115	8	16350	5	16655	5	16921	1
15655	2	15866	2	16116	6	16351	1	16656	1	16922	8
15656	25	15868	2	16117	29	16353	8	16657	2	16925	14

16926	3	17078	24	17342	1	17581	2	17877	2	18071	12
16927	1	17082	10	17343	2	17582	7	17878	5	18072	11
16928	5	17084	9	17344	2	17584	19	17881	3	18073	18
16929	7	17087	3	17345	14	17601	113	17884	1	18074	9
16930	2	17088	3	17347	8	17602	47	17886	1	18076	7
16931	3	17090	7	17349	24	17603	102	17888	1	18077	4
16933	22	17093	4	17350	13	17604	3	17889	4	18078	8
16935	5	17094	6	17353	5	17606	1	17901	49	18079	1
16936	6	17097	1	17355	1	17622	1	17920	2	18080	22
16938	4	17098	4	17356	32	17701	143	17921	5	18083	2
16940	2	17099	3	17358	1	17720	2	17922	8	18085	4
16942	3	17101	1	17360	11	17721	2	17923	1	18087	1
16943	1	17102	5	17361	15	17722	1	17929	2	18088	11
16946	5	17103	13	17362	14	17723	1	17931	18	18091	12
16947	11	17104	20	17363	13	17724	12	17935	2	18092	8
16948	4	17105	2	17364	5	17726	1	17936	2	18101	3
16950	6	17108	1	17365	1	17728	13	17938	4	18102	60
17003	23	17109	65	17366	8	17729	1	17945	1	18103	118
17004	2	17110	28	17367	1	17731	1	17948	5	18104	79
17005	1	17111	48	17368	14	17735	1	17949	1	18105	4
17007	8	17112	66	17370	8	17737	6	17952	1	18106	16
17009	2	17113	17	17371	2	17740	18	17954	5	18107	1
17010	2	17127	1	17372	7	17744	9	17959	5	18164	1
17011	91	17201	48	17401	1	17745	11	17960	6	18201	63
17013	92	17211	1	17402	103	17747	3	17961	18	18210	6
17017	1	17214	7	17403	81	17751	5	17963	20	18211	1
17018	7	17215	2	17404	98	17752	5	17965	3	18214	7
17019	24	17222	13	17405	3	17754	32	17967	2	18216	2
17020	8	17224	2	17406	16	17756	17	17970	6	18218	4
17022	53	17225	18	17407	6	17758	1	17972	23	18219	2
17023	6	17229	1	17501	19	17763	1	17974	1	18221	3
17024	1	17233	1	17502	6	17767	1	17976	11	18222	11
17025	17	17236	10	17506	1	17769	1	17979	1	18224	6
17026	4	17238	3	17507	2	17771	4	17980	6	18227	1
17028	5	17240	1	17509	2	17772	1	17981	5	18229	15
17029	1	17241	11	17512	23	17774	1	17983	1	18231	3
17030	4	17243	2	17516	9	17776	1	18010	2	18232	6
17032	10	17244	1	17517	23	17777	6	18011	7	18235	25
17033	27	17249	1	17519	8	17779	3	18013	48	18237	10
17034	3	17250	1	17520	17	17801	28	18014	15	18242	2
17035	1	17252	1	17521	1	17810	1	18015	48	18247	6
17036	50	17257	21	17522	57	17813	4	18016	1	18249	12
17037	1	17260	2	17524	1	17814	15	18017	102	18250	9
17038	21	17264	8	17527	6	17815	63	18018	70	18252	38
17040	4	17265	2	17529	2	17820	14	18031	9	18254	2
17041	2	17266	1	17532	4	17821	47	18032	14	18255	13
17042	101	17267	5	17533	2	17823	3	18034	13	18266	1
17043	12	17268	50	17535	1	17824	11	18035	1	18301	48
17044	33	17272	1	17536	1	17829	1	18036	46	18321	3
17045	5	17301	11	17537	3	17830	3	18037	7	18322	10
17047	2	17302	14	17538	17	17831	1	18038	8	18324	12
17048	7	17304	3	17540	20	17832	1	18040	1	18325	6
17049	2	17306	1	17543	63	17834	5	18041	12	18326	9
17051	2	17307	9	17545	29	17837	15	18042	121	18327	3
17052	4	17309	4	17547	7	17841	9	18043	2	18328	9
17053	4	17311	3	17550	1	17842	6	18044	4	18330	9
17055	121	17313	18	17551	11	17844	17	18049	34	18331	2
17056	1	17314	17	17552	28	17845	1	18051	3	18332	4
17057	34	17315	46	17554	15	17846	2	18052	36	18333	8
17058	3	17316	6	17555	10	17847	18	18053	1	18334	1
17059	16	17318	6	17557	21	17851	7	18054	10	18335	6
17060	5	17319	21	17560	4	17853	3	18055	8	18336	15
17061	5	17320	22	17562	5	17855	1	18056	1	18337	17
17062	8	17321	2	17563	1	17856	6	18058	6	18340	2
17063	4	17322	11	17565	5	17857	14	18059	1	18341	2
17064	5	17323	2	17566	19	17858	1	18062	22	18343	7
17065	7	17324	4	17567	1	17859	9	18063	1	18344	9
17066	10	17325	49	17569	3	17860	3	18064	32	18346	8
17067	36	17327	17	17570	1	17862	1	18065	1	18347	7
17068	7	17329	6	17572	3	17866	1	18066	3	18350	4
17070	34	17331	116	17577	1	17868	2	18067	19	18351	5
17073	6	17334	1	17578	9	17870	18	18068	1	18352	4
17074	8	17339	15	17579	10	17872	39	18069	7	18353	23
17077	1	17340	14	17580	1	17876	2	18070	1	18354	3

18355	2	18640	18	18942	11	19065	2	19203	1	19473	19
18356	1	18641	12	18943	3	19066	13	19249	1	19474	7
18360	51	18642	10	18944	53	19067	105	19301	32	19475	15
18403	11	18643	13	18947	17	19070	46	19310	6	19477	1
18405	2	18644	15	18951	64	19072	32	19311	5	19478	4
18407	19	18651	26	18954	42	19073	75	19312	41	19480	1
18411	77	18655	14	18955	2	19074	14	19314	1	19481	11
18414	15	18656	10	18956	1	19075	30	19317	28	19486	1
18415	7	18657	49	18957	3	19076	11	19319	1	19490	4
18417	3	18660	14	18960	21	19078	93	19320	56	19491	1
18419	8	18661	15	18962	3	19079	12	19330	7	19492	6
18421	9	18701	2	18963	4	19081	43	19331	1	19501	2
18424	14	18702	72	18964	21	19082	48	19333	14	19503	1
18425	3	18703	6	18966	160	19083	104	19335	72	19504	3
18426	10	18704	73	18968	2	19084	1	19341	34	19505	4
18427	2	18705	30	18969	37	19085	15	19342	44	19506	9
18428	14	18706	8	18971	1	19086	31	19343	17	19507	8
18430	1	18707	22	18972	8	19087	81	19344	26	19508	23
18431	30	18708	17	18974	135	19090	60	19347	1	19510	6
18433	16	18709	3	18976	49	19094	30	19348	44	19511	1
18434	4	18711	1	18977	16	19095	21	19350	18	19512	21
18436	17	18801	38	18979	2	19096	20	19352	5	19518	12
18438	2	18810	7	18980	6	19101	2	19355	89	19519	2
18443	1	18812	14	18981	1	19102	6	19357	1	19520	22
18444	34	18816	4	19000	1	19103	12	19360	2	19522	23
18445	5	18817	1	19001	49	19104	32	19362	7	19523	4
18446	8	18818	6	19002	71	19105	5	19363	22	19525	15
18447	9	18821	4	19003	25	19106	15	19365	10	19526	18
18451	1	18822	12	19004	17	19107	4	19366	1	19529	4
18452	15	18824	3	19006	55	19111	97	19369	6	19530	13
18453	5	18825	1	19007	45	19112	6	19372	2	19533	8
18455	1	18826	4	19008	72	19113	2	19373	5	19534	6
18456	1	18827	2	19009	2	19114	32	19374	1	19535	2
18458	11	18829	5	19010	63	19115	46	19375	3	19539	6
18461	1	18830	3	19012	20	19116	60	19380	126	19540	28
18462	3	18831	2	19013	50	19117	44	19381	3	19541	5
18463	1	18832	5	19014	51	19118	37	19382	71	19542	3
18464	5	18833	6	19015	28	19119	27	19390	12	19543	10
18465	4	18834	11	19018	64	19120	70	19395	6	19547	3
18466	12	18837	19	19020	114	19121	3	19399	2	19548	1
18469	5	18840	19	19021	4	19122	4	19401	76	19550	1
18470	4	18843	2	19022	8	19123	4	19403	89	19551	11
18472	9	18844	8	19023	35	19124	50	19405	8	19555	8
18501	2	18846	1	19025	15	19125	9	19406	70	19560	13
18504	21	18847	21	19026	88	19126	16	19407	1	19562	4
18505	25	18848	26	19028	2	19127	5	19408	5	19564	2
18507	4	18850	10	19029	6	19128	49	19409	2	19565	12
18508	25	18851	3	19030	25	19129	11	19421	2	19567	5
18509	13	18853	10	19031	13	19130	18	19422	32	19601	22
18510	30	18854	7	19032	17	19131	44	19423	2	19602	17
18512	31	18901	75	19033	53	19132	11	19425	12	19603	1
18517	7	18910	2	19034	20	19133	12	19426	45	19604	30
18518	11	18911	2	19035	9	19134	48	19428	25	19605	42
18519	10	18912	1	19036	15	19135	43	19430	1	19606	68
18561	1	18914	45	19037	5	19136	26	19431	1	19607	36
18601	1	18915	3	19038	51	19137	2	19435	1	19608	31
18602	1	18916	2	19040	93	19138	15	19436	2	19609	23
18603	65	18917	5	19041	14	19139	15	19437	7	19610	31
18610	5	18920	3	19043	10	19140	26	19438	46	19611	11
18612	26	18921	1	19044	49	19141	20	19440	56	19612	2
18615	6	18923	1	19046	35	19142	26	19442	1	19701	26
18617	8	18925	10	19047	105	19143	38	19443	2	19702	49
18618	5	18926	1	19048	1	19144	23	19444	17	19703	29
18621	13	18927	2	19050	44	19145	45	19446	137	19706	3
18622	1	18928	1	19052	1	19146	3	19452	1	19707	37
18623	4	18929	17	19053	23	19147	31	19453	3	19709	20
18626	3	18930	8	19054	35	19148	34	19454	61	19710	3
18628	2	18931	1	19055	29	19149	63	19457	2	19711	88
18629	6	18932	4	19056	48	19150	21	19460	50	19713	67
18630	5	18934	1	19057	38	19151	50	19462	13	19714	1
18631	1	18935	1	19058	1	19152	57	19464	112	19715	3
18632	2	18936	1	19061	45	19153	6	19466	1	19720	68
18634	35	18938	17	19063	90	19154	43	19468	39	19730	1
18635	9	18940	71	19064	73	19156	1	19470	1	19732	1

19733	1	20026	1	20676	9	20794	21	21028	9	21204	83
19734	8	20027	3	20677	5	20795	15	21029	27	21205	7
19736	2	20028	6	20678	7	20801	17	21030	49	21206	55
19801	4	20031	13	20680	5	20810	9	21032	33	21207	71
19802	21	20032	7	20684	2	20811	7	21034	4	21208	60
19803	82	20034	19	20685	12	20812	2	21035	25	21209	37
19804	37	20036	16	20686	4	20814	81	21036	4	21210	17
19805	49	20037	9	20687	2	20815	51	21037	59	21211	24
19806	20	20039	1	20688	8	20816	41	21040	32	21212	59
19807	23	20041	1	20689	5	20817	114	21042	30	21213	19
19808	94	20044	5	20690	3	20818	7	21043	149	21214	30
19809	46	20050	2	20692	3	20820	1	21044	113	21215	49
19810	75	20052	1	20695	13	20825	3	21045	118	21216	15
19850	1	20064	1	20701	4	20827	1	21046	65	21217	14
19896	1	20074	2	20702	1	20830	2	21047	32	21218	42
19899	1	20091	1	20703	1	20832	57	21048	32	21219	9
19901	90	20148	1	20704	2	20833	13	21050	23	21220	62
19902	5	20154	1	20705	61	20834	1	21051	1	21221	48
19903	3	20157	1	20706	70	20837	11	21053	9	21222	53
19913	1	20164	7	20707	115	20838	1	21054	44	21223	8
19931	1	20165	7	20708	70	20840	7	21055	1	21224	34
19933	5	20317	10	20710	9	20841	6	21056	4	21225	20
19934	21	20331	7	20711	8	20842	1	21057	21	21226	7
19938	2	20335	15	20712	7	20847	1	21060	29	21227	82
19939	9	20336	12	20714	3	20850	82	21061	186	21228	108
19940	11	20350	1	20715	131	20851	43	21071	3	21229	38
19941	1	20377	1	20716	52	20852	84	21074	27	21230	18
19943	18	20390	1	20717	2	20853	118	21076	26	21231	10
19945	7	20510	1	20720	11	20854	147	21077	4	21234	126
19946	7	20520	20	20721	5	20855	58	21078	34	21236	43
19947	21	20521	8	20722	14	20856	1	21082	3	21237	41
19950	6	20547	2	20723	23	20860	3	21084	19	21239	44
19951	1	20581	1	20724	18	20861	3	21085	34	21240	1
19952	11	20593	1	20726	1	20862	5	21087	9	21244	4
19953	15	20601	68	20730	2	20863	2	21088	1	21284	1
19954	4	20602	16	20731	1	20866	31	21090	29	21286	3
19956	17	20603	16	20732	13	20868	2	21093	115	21401	222
19958	33	20604	1	20733	8	20870	10	21095	1	21402	7
19960	8	20606	1	20734	1	20871	17	21102	24	21403	138
19962	6	20607	14	20735	68	20872	53	21104	7	21408	1
19963	33	20609	5	20736	11	20874	90	21106	4	21412	3
19964	4	20610	1	20737	18	20875	2	21107	4	21449	1
19966	20	20611	1	20740	68	20876	10	21108	71	21502	119
19967	2	20612	2	20742	5	20877	44	21111	6	21505	1
19968	12	20613	23	20743	13	20878	113	21113	30	21521	1
19970	11	20616	7	20744	91	20879	144	21114	48	21523	1
19971	22	20617	6	20745	23	20880	4	21117	44	21529	4
19973	49	20619	32	20746	13	20882	14	21120	16	21530	2
19975	13	20620	1	20747	18	20884	2	21122	164	21531	2
19977	10	20621	5	20748	63	20895	52	21128	17	21532	25
20001	6	20622	5	20749	1	20896	1	21131	24	21536	1
20002	11	20623	4	20750	11	20898	2	21132	6	21538	1
20003	23	20627	1	20751	12	20901	107	21133	39	21539	2
20004	1	20629	1	20754	18	20902	110	21136	67	21541	5
20005	6	20632	2	20755	44	20903	35	21139	1	21542	3
20006	5	20634	12	20758	2	20904	179	21140	11	21545	6
20007	33	20635	1	20759	6	20905	18	21144	72	21550	40
20008	50	20636	39	20760	15	20906	147	21146	119	21555	4
20009	25	20637	7	20763	13	20910	63	21150	2	21556	2
20010	10	20639	13	20764	4	20912	45	21152	7	21557	8
20011	28	20640	15	20765	5	20915	1	21153	4	21561	6
20012	25	20646	26	20766	2	20950	1	21154	13	21562	7
20013	18	20650	24	20767	3	20961	1	21155	6	21601	61
20014	16	20653	69	20769	12	21001	42	21156	2	21610	2
20015	59	20656	1	20770	47	21005	1	21157	102	21612	1
20016	48	20657	38	20772	79	21009	15	21158	9	21613	17
20017	14	20658	3	20776	10	21012	92	21160	5	21617	5
20018	9	20659	38	20777	13	21013	12	21161	16	21619	6
20019	11	20662	1	20778	5	21014	85	21162	4	21620	35
20020	18	20664	1	20781	19	21015	8	21163	6	21622	1
20021	7	20667	2	20782	40	21017	5	21164	1	21625	4
20022	6	20670	9	20783	49	21021	4	21201	10	21629	14
20023	5	20674	1	20784	43	21022	4	21202	2	21631	4
20024	25	20675	4	20785	34	21027	1	21203	4	21632	9

21634	1	21794	7	22039	44	22301	21	22620	8	22901	142
21636	1	21795	10	22040	1	22302	32	22622	1	22902	9
21638	6	21797	18	22041	54	22303	39	22623	1	22903	32
21639	11	21798	3	22042	70	22304	67	22624	2	22904	1
21643	4	21801	106	22043	46	22305	19	22625	11	22906	5
21645	3	21803	1	22044	26	22306	53	22627	3	22908	1
21646	1	21807	1	22046	49	22307	27	22630	56	22920	2
21649	1	21810	1	22060	16	22308	71	22637	1	22922	1
21650	1	21811	29	22065	27	22309	69	22639	1	22923	11
21651	7	21813	4	22066	59	22310	100	22640	2	22932	11
21652	1	21814	1	22068	11	22311	21	22641	1	22935	1
21654	9	21817	13	22069	23	22312	51	22642	6	22936	32
21655	11	21821	1	22070	110	22313	3	22644	1	22939	6
21657	1	21822	2	22071	75	22314	31	22645	10	22940	6
21658	11	21826	7	22075	73	22401	62	22650	3	22942	14
21659	1	21829	1	22076	1	22402	2	22651	1	22943	3
21660	10	21830	6	22079	29	22403	1	22652	1	22945	3
21661	7	21835	3	22080	16	22404	2	22653	2	22947	3
21662	3	21837	3	22090	35	22405	67	22655	39	22949	1
21663	17	21838	2	22091	117	22406	8	22656	11	22952	4
21666	40	21841	2	22094	13	22407	30	22657	9	22957	1
21667	1	21842	22	22101	124	22408	10	22660	2	22958	3
21668	3	21849	6	22102	49	22427	7	22664	12	22959	4
21669	2	21850	2	22103	1	22432	5	22701	61	22960	24
21671	2	21851	18	22106	4	22433	1	22709	2	22963	13
21672	1	21853	10	22110	188	22435	11	22712	15	22964	1
21673	4	21856	1	22111	82	22438	3	22713	2	22967	1
21678	7	21861	3	22115	13	22443	12	22714	1	22968	8
21701	169	21863	10	22116	4	22446	1	22716	2	22971	2
21702	27	21864	2	22117	9	22448	16	22718	1	22972	1
21710	4	21865	5	22121	3	22454	3	22719	1	22973	7
21713	8	21870	2	22122	2	22460	1	22720	2	22974	5
21714	3	21871	2	22123	29	22463	1	22724	4	22980	83
21716	10	21874	5	22124	62	22469	2	22727	1	22990	1
21719	7	21875	15	22125	3	22471	1	22728	7	23001	1
21720	1	21901	26	22128	1	22472	1	22730	1	23002	17
21722	5	21902	3	22129	1	22473	7	22731	1	23003	1
21723	1	21903	11	22131	2	22475	2	22733	1	23005	37
21727	7	21904	8	22132	13	22480	7	22734	8	23009	3
21733	2	21911	15	22134	7	22481	1	22735	5	23011	3
21734	3	21912	1	22141	13	22482	13	22737	5	23012	1
21737	6	21914	3	22147	1	22485	36	22738	3	23015	14
21738	11	21915	3	22150	53	22501	2	22739	4	23018	2
21740	136	21917	10	22151	69	22503	11	22740	1	23024	3
21742	21	21918	8	22152	106	22507	2	22742	2	23027	2
21750	1	21919	10	22153	80	22508	13	22743	1	23030	3
21754	19	21920	2	22157	1	22511	3	22747	4	23035	4
21755	13	21921	52	22170	163	22513	5	22801	107	23038	2
21756	4	21930	1	22171	2	22514	2	22805	1	23039	3
21757	6	22001	2	22172	11	22517	2	22810	4	23040	6
21758	9	22002	9	22176	1	22520	12	22811	1	23042	1
21760	1	22003	181	22180	245	22524	1	22812	12	23043	13
21765	1	22005	1	22181	18	22534	5	22815	11	23047	4
21766	1	22010	1	22182	24	22539	7	22821	11	23058	2
21767	2	22011	22	22183	2	22542	2	22824	5	23060	44
21768	1	22012	8	22186	101	22546	12	22827	6	23061	34
21769	30	22013	1	22190	3	22553	32	22830	2	23062	23
21770	23	22014	10	22191	65	22554	113	22831	1	23063	2
21771	92	22015	114	22192	119	22555	2	22832	1	23064	2
21773	18	22016	1	22193	172	22560	14	22834	2	23065	7
21774	3	22017	1	22194	2	22565	3	22835	18	23066	2
21776	13	22018	2	22201	37	22567	10	22840	5	23070	2
21777	6	22019	10	22202	40	22568	6	22841	9	23071	4
21778	5	22020	94	22203	48	22572	11	22842	3	23072	28
21780	2	22021	34	22204	67	22576	7	22843	3	23075	19
21781	1	22024	28	22205	55	22577	1	22844	5	23076	1
21782	3	22025	5	22206	33	22578	3	22846	9	23080	1
21783	19	22026	36	22207	98	22579	2	22847	1	23084	3
21784	76	22027	5	22209	19	22580	3	22848	1	23086	1
21787	11	22030	133	22210	2	22601	113	22849	16	23089	5
21788	14	22031	63	22213	15	22602	19	22850	1	23090	3
21790	1	22032	96	22214	1	22603	14	22851	3	23092	2
21791	16	22033	48	22215	1	22604	2	22853	8	23093	17
21793	27	22038	2	22216	1	22611	14	22874	1	23103	6

23109	9	23316	1	23593	10	23947	9	24143	1	24352	1
23111	72	23320	130	23601	65	23952	1	24147	1	24354	30
23112	41	23321	69	23602	182	23957	1	24148	14	24360	32
23113	86	23322	34	23603	5	23958	4	24149	8	24361	5
23114	1	23323	39	23604	6	23960	3	24150	5	24363	1
23117	14	23324	24	23605	13	23962	1	24151	14	24366	5
23119	2	23325	41	23606	58	23964	5	24153	83	24368	10
23120	3	23336	9	23607	14	23970	11	24165	3	24370	9
23123	3	23337	5	23609	4	23974	3	24167	1	24374	3
23124	4	23347	3	23633	1	24012	65	24168	1	24375	5
23127	4	23350	4	23651	2	24013	3	24171	11	24380	4
23128	3	23354	2	23661	13	24014	42	24174	5	24381	9
23129	3	23356	3	23662	47	24015	49	24175	24	24382	53
23130	1	23359	3	23663	23	24016	6	24176	3	24401	75
23131	1	23361	1	23664	31	24017	37	24179	37	24416	20
23133	1	23369	1	23665	15	24018	131	24184	5	24421	9
23138	4	23389	1	23666	96	24019	65	24185	1	24422	14
23139	33	23397	1	23669	85	24025	1	24201	76	24426	54
23140	2	23401	1	23670	3	24030	3	24203	2	24430	1
23141	5	23403	1	23690	10	24036	1	24210	40	24431	10
23142	1	23405	1	23692	59	24037	2	24216	3	24433	1
23146	5	23408	1	23693	9	24053	4	24217	1	24435	6
23148	3	23410	11	23696	19	24054	1	24219	7	24437	1
23149	2	23413	1	23701	29	24055	16	24224	9	24440	4
23150	23	23414	5	23702	22	24059	2	24225	10	24441	5
23153	1	23415	1	23703	60	24060	88	24228	18	24445	11
23156	2	23416	1	23704	13	24061	1	24230	37	24448	2
23157	1	23417	19	23707	27	24062	2	24236	2	24450	46
23168	7	23418	7	23709	1	24063	2	24237	5	24457	1
23169	1	23420	2	23801	3	24064	15	24243	1	24459	4
23170	1	23421	19	23803	33	24065	15	24244	8	24460	5
23175	4	23422	3	23805	14	24066	8	24245	3	24464	1
23176	2	23423	1	23824	3	24067	1	24248	6	24465	5
23178	1	23426	1	23831	58	24068	1	24250	3	24467	1
23180	1	23427	2	23832	52	24069	3	24251	38	24469	2
23181	8	23430	15	23833	1	24070	4	24256	5	24471	8
23183	3	23432	3	23834	29	24072	1	24258	5	24472	5
23184	1	23433	4	23837	2	24073	48	24260	8	24473	1
23185	110	23434	25	23840	3	24076	1	24263	20	24474	1
23187	5	23435	17	23841	2	24077	1	24266	26	24477	22
23188	14	23437	5	23842	8	24078	19	24269	3	24479	7
23192	6	23438	2	23847	1	24079	1	24271	1	24482	4
23201	2	23442	7	23850	1	24083	12	24273	16	24484	3
23209	1	23451	51	23851	6	24084	25	24277	19	24486	6
23219	2	23452	176	23856	2	24085	7	24279	3	24501	59
23220	21	23454	113	23860	47	24086	2	24280	1	24502	163
23221	18	23455	93	23866	4	24087	9	24281	4	24503	83
23222	11	23456	91	23867	3	24088	2	24282	1	24504	15
23223	8	23457	3	23868	2	24089	2	24283	3	24506	2
23224	29	23460	2	23872	1	24090	9	24290	1	24517	11
23225	58	23461	1	23875	19	24091	32	24292	1	24520	5
23226	45	23462	113	23876	1	24093	1	24293	17	24521	13
23227	33	23464	173	23879	1	24095	4	24297	1	24522	20
23228	78	23467	1	23881	1	24101	10	24301	28	24523	67
23229	123	23480	3	23882	3	24104	9	24302	1	24525	1
23230	13	23481	1	23883	1	24109	1	24311	1	24526	5
23231	36	23483	1	23890	2	24111	1	24312	2	24527	5
23233	91	23486	1	23898	4	24112	60	24313	2	24528	8
23234	66	23487	2	23899	1	24113	1	24314	1	24529	6
23235	111	23488	1	23901	25	24115	3	24315	7	24531	6
23236	51	23502	20	23917	6	24120	1	24317	7	24533	1
23237	24	23503	82	23920	1	24121	27	24318	5	24534	5
23261	1	23504	4	23921	3	24122	2	24319	9	24538	6
23287	1	23505	57	23922	1	24124	11	24324	6	24540	50
23294	10	23507	11	23923	3	24126	1	24325	2	24541	77
23298	1	23508	22	23924	12	24127	5	24326	5	24543	4
23301	10	23509	29	23927	21	24128	4	24327	5	24549	10
23303	2	23510	5	23930	11	24133	7	24328	2	24550	12
23306	5	23511	7	23936	1	24134	12	24330	6	24551	62
23307	1	23513	37	23937	2	24136	6	24333	51	24552	1
23308	6	23517	8	23941	1	24137	2	24340	8	24553	1
23310	3	23518	84	23942	1	24138	4	24343	22	24554	7
23314	10	23521	3	23943	6	24139	1	24347	1	24555	3
23315	1	23523	2	23944	1	24141	49	24348	9	24556	14

24557	11	24825	2	25039	3	25265	3	25564	1	25854	5
24558	11	24827	1	25040	3	25271	22	25565	1	25857	2
24562	1	24828	4	25043	4	25275	3	25567	3	25862	3
24563	16	24832	2	25044	2	25276	19	25570	18	25865	3
24566	2	24836	4	25045	10	25279	2	25571	6	25866	3
24570	1	24842	4	25048	3	25280	2	25601	42	25867	1
24571	4	24844	24	25053	20	25286	1	25606	8	25868	1
24572	35	24846	2	25054	1	25301	4	25607	5	25870	1
24574	14	24849	5	25057	1	25302	45	25617	14	25871	2
24576	1	24850	5	25059	1	25303	34	25618	1	25873	6
24577	12	24852	1	25060	1	25304	18	25619	2	25874	1
24578	3	24853	1	25063	1	25306	11	25621	5	25878	1
24586	9	24856	1	25064	35	25309	57	25625	5	25880	10
24588	27	24857	1	25067	1	25311	15	25628	9	25882	20
24589	4	24860	2	25070	3	25312	28	25630	2	25901	41
24590	12	24861	5	25071	16	25313	29	25631	3	25902	4
24592	42	24862	3	25075	1	25314	42	25632	1	25908	4
24593	4	24868	2	25079	2	25315	4	25633	3	25917	4
24594	4	24870	15	25081	4	25320	7	25634	3	25918	10
24595	1	24871	3	25082	2	25321	1	25635	4	25919	1
24597	4	24872	11	25084	1	25324	2	25636	11	25921	11
24598	3	24873	8	25085	1	25327	1	25638	5	25922	1
24602	3	24874	8	25086	3	25332	1	25639	12	25938	3
24604	1	24877	3	25093	1	25362	1	25642	1	25951	41
24605	47	24878	1	25095	1	25364	1	25643	1	25958	1
24606	1	24881	7	25102	1	25365	1	25645	2	25962	7
24607	4	24884	1	25103	1	25401	64	25646	4	25969	3
24609	19	24886	3	25108	2	25402	1	25647	4	25971	1
24612	1	24887	1	25110	1	25410	1	25652	4	25976	1
24613	7	24892	4	25111	3	25411	31	25661	21	25978	1
24614	12	24894	1	25112	4	25413	14	25665	1	25979	3
24618	1	24895	4	25119	1	25414	13	25667	3	25981	1
24619	1	24897	2	25121	6	25419	6	25669	2	25984	6
24622	1	24899	1	25123	6	25420	3	25670	14	25988	1
24624	2	24901	26	25124	6	25422	6	25672	2	26003	139
24630	11	24910	7	25125	3	25425	22	25674	3	26016	1
24631	1	24915	2	25130	15	25427	13	25676	2	26030	2
24632	1	24916	3	25132	2	25428	17	25678	6	26031	7
24635	4	24918	2	25136	14	25430	11	25685	1	26032	3
24637	6	24919	2	25139	1	25434	4	25688	2	26033	6
24639	5	24924	2	25140	4	25438	3	25692	3	26034	14
24640	1	24925	1	25143	15	25440	1	25696	3	26035	8
24641	16	24928	9	25148	1	25442	2	25701	53	26037	14
24646	2	24933	1	25149	1	25443	11	25702	20	26038	22
24649	1	24934	3	25154	1	25501	2	25703	5	26039	12
24651	19	24938	4	25156	1	25503	1	25704	65	26040	10
24656	3	24944	2	25159	14	25504	34	25705	85	26041	59
24657	1	24945	1	25162	5	25506	7	25706	3	26047	18
24701	112	24946	2	25165	2	25507	3	25708	1	26050	1
24712	13	24951	2	25168	3	25508	20	25714	2	26055	21
24715	3	24954	4	25173	2	25510	9	25718	1	26056	5
24716	1	24961	1	25177	105	25511	2	25778	1	26059	4
24719	4	24963	4	25181	4	25512	2	25801	93	26060	3
24720	1	24966	2	25186	1	25514	9	25802	2	26062	56
24724	1	24970	9	25187	1	25515	2	25810	3	26070	20
24726	1	24976	1	25201	1	25517	2	25812	7	26074	5
24730	1	24981	6	25202	3	25520	3	25813	10	26101	121
24733	6	24983	1	25209	3	25521	1	25816	1	26102	1
24736	2	24985	1	25213	11	25523	8	25817	1	26103	3
24737	4	24986	5	25214	2	25524	3	25818	4	26104	22
24740	114	24991	1	25234	1	25526	59	25820	1	26105	36
24747	3	24993	1	25239	5	25530	18	25823	14	26107	1
24770	1	25002	1	25241	4	25534	1	25825	2	26133	1
24801	20	25003	1	25243	2	25535	8	25826	2	26134	4
24808	6	25007	2	25245	2	25537	5	25827	16	26135	2
24811	7	25009	1	25248	2	25540	1	25831	2	26136	1
24813	3	25013	1	25253	2	25541	10	25832	12	26137	4
24815	1	25015	10	25255	1	25544	1	25833	1	26138	3
24816	2	25019	1	25256	1	25545	8	25836	3	26142	12
24817	5	25024	1	25257	1	25547	1	25839	3	26143	15
24818	1	25026	3	25259	1	25550	12	25840	20	26144	1
24819	1	25031	1	25260	9	25557	1	25843	4	26145	1
24820	1	25033	2	25261	1	25559	4	25846	1	26146	3
24822	2	25035	2	25262	5	25560	33	25847	10	26147	20

26149	8	26423	4	26750	2	27203	80	27371	5	27574	1
26150	12	26424	5	26753	14	27204	3	27374	3	27576	13
26155	65	26425	3	26757	17	27207	1	27375	1	27577	29
26159	16	26426	4	26762	1	27209	1	27376	13	27582	1
26162	1	26431	17	26763	2	27210	1	27377	5	27583	3
26164	23	26435	1	26764	17	27212	4	27379	7	27587	50
26167	6	26438	3	26767	1	27214	11	27392	1	27588	2
26169	4	26439	1	26801	1	27215	116	27401	9	27589	5
26170	22	26440	2	26802	8	27216	1	27402	1	27591	39
26173	1	26444	5	26806	5	27217	12	27403	59	27592	6
26175	7	26447	3	26807	29	27229	2	27404	4	27596	24
26179	2	26448	1	26808	2	27230	1	27405	82	27597	18
26180	8	26451	2	26810	1	27231	3	27406	87	27599	1
26181	28	26452	61	26811	2	27233	2	27407	84	27601	2
26184	2	26456	6	26813	4	27235	12	27408	82	27602	2
26187	13	26462	3	26814	1	27239	6	27409	16	27603	63
26201	71	26502	1	26815	2	27242	1	27410	91	27604	116
26202	14	26504	2	26816	1	27243	3	27415	5	27605	8
26205	13	26505	178	26833	4	27244	14	27416	1	27606	88
26206	3	26506	1	26836	9	27248	9	27419	1	27607	67
26208	1	26507	7	26845	2	27249	19	27420	2	27608	34
26218	3	26525	10	26847	11	27252	1	27435	1	27609	196
26222	1	26527	2	26851	1	27253	52	27455	2	27610	36
26229	2	26529	2	26855	1	27258	5	27460	1	27611	1
26234	4	26531	1	26866	23	27259	1	27501	7	27612	135
26241	41	26534	2	26879	1	27260	102	27502	85	27613	36
26250	9	26537	17	27006	22	27261	3	27503	8	27614	45
26253	10	26542	3	27007	2	27262	34	27504	12	27615	89
26257	1	26544	4	27010	1	27263	46	27505	2	27619	3
26260	2	26545	1	27011	6	27265	29	27506	9	27620	1
26261	15	26547	5	27012	46	27278	46	27507	1	27622	1
26273	1	26554	96	27013	10	27280	1	27509	12	27623	1
26276	1	26555	2	27014	10	27282	22	27510	23	27624	2
26280	2	26559	1	27017	9	27283	11	27511	190	27627	3
26283	2	26562	2	27018	14	27284	84	27512	5	27650	2
26287	6	26563	1	27019	7	27285	4	27513	66	27658	2
26288	7	26566	2	27020	12	27288	66	27514	109	27661	1
26292	9	26568	3	27021	21	27292	121	27515	4	27687	1
26293	3	26571	3	27022	1	27293	7	27516	31	27695	1
26298	1	26574	2	27023	20	27298	22	27520	34	27701	16
26301	101	26576	1	27024	4	27299	4	27521	10	27702	3
26302	1	26581	1	27025	18	27301	14	27522	4	27703	30
26320	1	26582	13	27027	12	27302	38	27524	6	27704	34
26321	2	26587	1	27028	20	27305	1	27525	9	27705	58
26323	4	26588	3	27030	56	27306	5	27526	29	27706	2
26330	48	26591	2	27040	38	27310	6	27529	58	27707	55
26332	5	26601	14	27041	11	27311	2	27530	83	27709	7
26335	1	26610	2	27043	3	27312	27	27531	1	27712	55
26337	4	26611	3	27045	28	27313	23	27532	4	27713	69
26338	3	26619	1	27046	2	27315	5	27533	2	27722	2
26344	1	26621	1	27047	2	27316	2	27534	32	27801	28
26346	3	26623	2	27048	15	27317	16	27536	23	27802	4
26347	5	26624	8	27050	9	27320	67	27540	4	27803	12
26351	13	26629	1	27051	13	27323	3	27541	6	27804	33
26352	1	26631	1	27052	9	27325	8	27542	3	27805	3
26354	28	26638	2	27053	1	27326	4	27543	1	27806	3
26362	13	26651	22	27054	3	27330	53	27545	27	27807	4
26374	2	26656	1	27055	28	27331	3	27546	9	27808	7
26376	2	26662	1	27064	1	27340	2	27549	10	27809	3
26377	1	26672	1	27101	30	27341	2	27552	1	27810	5
26378	7	26674	1	27102	1	27342	3	27553	1	27812	2
26383	1	26676	4	27103	87	27343	2	27555	1	27814	1
26384	1	26678	6	27104	93	27344	22	27557	5	27817	6
26385	15	26679	5	27105	50	27349	4	27559	2	27820	2
26386	6	26681	4	27106	107	27350	11	27560	9	27822	17
26401	1	26704	4	27107	89	27351	6	27562	5	27826	1
26405	1	26705	4	27108	4	27355	2	27563	3	27828	22
26408	8	26707	1	27113	1	27356	1	27564	1	27829	4
26410	2	26710	3	27116	1	27357	3	27565	34	27831	2
26411	1	26711	3	27127	23	27358	15	27568	2	27832	1
26415	4	26719	7	27130	1	27359	2	27569	9	27834	127
26416	16	26722	1	27150	1	27360	61	27571	1	27835	4
26419	4	26726	37	27201	3	27361	3	27572	6	27836	4
26422	2	26743	1	27202	1	27370	34	27573	14	27837	11

27839	5	28002	1	28136	4	28327	8	28456	2	28603	10
27842	2	28006	1	28137	7	28328	25	28457	7	28604	8
27845	2	28009	4	28138	14	28331	2	28458	5	28605	5
27846	5	28012	34	28139	36	28333	7	28459	28	28606	2
27850	8	28016	21	28144	106	28334	17	28460	5	28607	35
27851	1	28017	13	28145	2	28337	8	28461	40	28609	21
27852	1	28018	17	28146	27	28338	5	28462	11	28610	14
27855	3	28019	1	28150	146	28339	5	28463	2	28612	13
27856	14	28020	1	28151	1	28340	7	28465	14	28613	25
27857	1	28021	27	28152	22	28341	1	28466	6	28615	3
27858	78	28023	30	28159	5	28342	1	28467	4	28616	3
27860	4	28024	4	28160	10	28344	1	28469	1	28617	2
27861	1	28025	112	28163	14	28345	20	28470	2	28618	1
27863	3	28026	1	28164	12	28348	33	28471	4	28619	8
27864	7	28027	11	28166	8	28349	2	28472	23	28621	37
27866	1	28031	1	28167	7	28352	32	28479	2	28622	1
27869	1	28032	1	28168	10	28353	1	28480	10	28623	1
27870	28	28033	2	28170	19	28356	2	28491	1	28626	2
27871	7	28034	22	28173	113	28357	1	28501	69	28627	4
27874	8	28036	15	28174	4	28358	48	28502	4	28628	2
27878	1	28037	22	28179	1	28359	2	28508	1	28629	5
27879	1	28038	1	28183	1	28363	5	28509	1	28630	32
27880	2	28040	7	28202	4	28364	3	28510	8	28631	1
27882	1	28041	3	28203	10	28365	6	28511	1	28634	3
27884	1	28042	9	28204	11	28366	2	28512	23	28635	4
27886	23	28043	48	28205	62	28367	1	28513	15	28636	7
27888	4	28045	1	28206	1	28371	2	28516	20	28637	4
27889	63	28052	90	28207	19	28373	3	28518	6	28638	11
27891	1	28053	1	28208	23	28374	25	28519	4	28640	9
27892	23	28054	71	28209	48	28376	24	28521	1	28641	1
27893	56	28055	1	28210	96	28377	6	28523	3	28642	11
27894	2	28056	17	28211	104	28379	41	28525	5	28643	5
27895	2	28071	5	28212	102	28382	3	28526	4	28645	90
27897	2	28072	4	28213	45	28383	3	28528	2	28646	3
27907	1	28073	9	28214	25	28384	8	28530	14	28647	1
27909	67	28075	20	28215	52	28387	20	28531	1	28649	2
27910	13	28076	7	28216	9	28388	1	28532	36	28650	21
27916	1	28078	31	28217	17	28389	4	28533	4	28651	6
27919	8	28079	12	28218	3	28390	31	28539	17	28653	1
27920	6	28080	8	28219	2	28391	5	28540	85	28654	4
27921	14	28081	53	28220	2	28392	1	28541	2	28655	95
27923	1	28083	9	28221	2	28393	1	28542	20	28657	18
27924	1	28086	52	28222	1	28394	8	28543	2	28658	35
27925	6	28088	9	28224	2	28395	2	28544	11	28659	36
27927	3	28089	3	28225	1	28396	3	28545	1	28662	7
27929	2	28090	12	28226	80	28398	5	28546	16	28665	1
27932	16	28091	2	28227	38	28401	32	28551	24	28666	1
27935	2	28092	45	28231	2	28402	2	28552	1	28667	2
27936	2	28093	1	28235	1	28403	98	28553	2	28668	1
27937	2	28097	7	28256	2	28405	75	28555	4	28669	4
27938	1	28098	6	28262	6	28406	3	28556	3	28670	5
27939	3	28101	4	28269	6	28407	1	28557	45	28671	5
27944	8	28103	5	28270	19	28409	27	28560	106	28673	9
27948	18	28105	116	28273	5	28412	12	28561	3	28675	25
27949	8	28106	4	28277	11	28421	1	28562	42	28676	8
27950	1	28107	12	28278	3	28422	6	28564	1	28677	81
27954	22	28108	1	28299	1	28425	14	28570	41	28678	4
27958	7	28110	51	28301	56	28428	13	28571	19	28679	1
27959	4	28111	3	28302	4	28429	11	28572	13	28680	3
27960	3	28112	11	28303	81	28430	1	28573	3	28681	19
27962	16	28114	14	28304	111	28431	2	28574	15	28682	6
27964	1	28115	60	28305	10	28432	1	28577	2	28683	5
27965	2	28120	23	28306	41	28433	10	28578	2	28684	1
27966	5	28123	2	28307	144	28435	1	28580	6	28690	40
27968	1	28124	12	28308	2	28436	2	28581	1	28692	3
27972	2	28125	1	28309	3	28443	24	28582	2	28693	2
27973	5	28126	4	28311	51	28444	3	28584	29	28694	14
27974	4	28127	10	28314	58	28445	8	28585	5	28697	19
27976	1	28128	9	28315	6	28447	2	28586	2	28699	1
27979	1	28129	3	28318	2	28449	1	28587	1	28701	6
27981	6	28130	3	28320	10	28450	5	28590	20	28703	1
27983	6	28133	5	28323	2	28451	9	28594	5	28704	38
27986	4	28134	18	28325	1	28452	1	28601	140	28705	13
28001	36	28135	4	28326	4	28455	1	28602	29	28709	3

28710	4	28804	60	29138	9	29379	26	29556	4	29667	4
28711	38	28805	47	29142	2	29384	3	29560	6	29669	16
28712	71	28806	122	29148	8	29388	16	29563	1	29670	10
28713	12	28807	1	29150	110	29401	8	29565	5	29671	49
28714	54	28813	2	29151	1	29402	3	29566	15	29673	29
28715	70	28814	8	29152	16	29403	5	29569	8	29675	1
28716	42	28815	5	29153	3	29404	2	29571	10	29676	17
28717	4	28816	12	29154	52	29405	29	29572	2	29677	4
28718	2	28850	1	29160	7	29406	45	29574	7	29678	66
28719	4	28901	12	29161	3	29407	100	29575	19	29679	1
28721	24	28902	5	29162	4	29408	12	29576	33	29681	86
28722	21	28904	16	29164	4	29409	3	29577	82	29682	2
28723	17	28905	6	29166	1	29410	3	29578	4	29684	4
28724	3	28906	49	29168	3	29411	1	29581	1	29685	1
28725	1	28909	2	29169	93	29412	63	29582	23	29686	3
28726	2	28950	1	29170	9	29414	12	29583	3	29687	86
28727	2	29001	1	29171	1	29417	2	29584	1	29688	3
28728	5	29002	2	29172	1	29418	66	29585	8	29689	4
28729	11	29003	18	29177	2	29420	7	29587	4	29690	29
28730	26	29006	11	29178	2	29429	2	29591	1	29691	15
28731	17	29009	6	29180	6	29430	1	29592	1	29692	2
28732	39	29010	17	29201	6	29431	6	29596	2	29693	19
28734	85	29015	3	29202	7	29432	2	29597	2	29696	6
28735	1	29016	12	29203	18	29435	5	29598	1	29697	19
28736	1	29018	5	29204	25	29436	4	29601	8	29699	1
28738	3	29020	23	29205	48	29437	6	29602	2	29702	14
28739	158	29030	3	29206	54	29438	3	29603	1	29704	6
28740	6	29032	2	29209	54	29439	8	29605	40	29706	25
28741	12	29033	34	29210	92	29440	19	29606	4	29709	9
28742	19	29036	14	29211	3	29442	4	29607	75	29710	34
28743	4	29037	1	29212	39	29445	72	29608	1	29714	5
28745	2	29038	4	29221	1	29448	8	29609	75	29715	72
28746	3	29039	1	29223	47	29449	2	29611	61	29716	1
28747	5	29040	10	29224	1	29451	17	29612	1	29718	1
28748	27	29042	5	29225	1	29455	25	29614	3	29720	74
28749	4	29044	7	29230	2	29456	43	29615	78	29721	1
28750	2	29045	11	29233	1	29457	3	29616	1	29726	1
28751	9	29047	2	29250	6	29458	1	29620	15	29727	2
28752	85	29048	1	29260	1	29461	38	29621	92	29728	2
28753	22	29053	9	29290	1	29464	67	29622	8	29729	4
28754	20	29054	10	29301	71	29469	1	29623	3	29730	113
28755	7	29055	4	29302	63	29470	1	29624	30	29731	6
28756	4	29058	3	29303	42	29472	9	29625	25	29732	28
28757	5	29059	4	29304	7	29474	1	29627	25	29741	1
28758	5	29061	14	29305	1	29475	1	29628	2	29742	3
28760	5	29063	37	29306	1	29477	8	29630	12	29743	2
28761	13	29067	18	29307	1	29479	6	29631	25	29744	2
28762	31	29069	3	29316	1	29481	3	29633	4	29745	26
28763	8	29070	26	29320	1	29482	5	29634	1	29801	91
28766	3	29071	3	29321	6	29483	114	29638	3	29802	3
28768	23	29072	70	29322	8	29484	4	29639	7	29803	21
28771	24	29073	25	29323	15	29485	16	29640	67	29807	1
28772	2	29075	6	29325	13	29487	4	29641	8	29809	1
28773	3	29078	4	29329	1	29488	19	29642	17	29810	4
28774	1	29080	1	29330	11	29501	91	29643	6	29812	15
28775	3	29101	5	29332	1	29502	1	29644	16	29816	1
28776	3	29102	8	29334	5	29503	1	29645	11	29817	3
28777	38	29104	2	29335	6	29504	1	29646	82	29819	1
28778	19	29105	4	29336	1	29505	15	29648	1	29821	3
28779	35	29107	4	29340	39	29510	1	29649	15	29822	2
28781	5	29108	24	29341	2	29511	4	29650	18	29824	6
28782	19	29112	3	29342	2	29512	9	29651	60	29826	2
28783	5	29115	53	29348	1	29520	30	29652	2	29827	5
28784	2	29116	3	29349	39	29525	1	29653	7	29828	3
28786	55	29123	7	29351	2	29526	28	29654	8	29829	6
28787	38	29124	2	29356	8	29527	3	29655	5	29831	9
28788	2	29126	1	29360	30	29532	19	29656	1	29832	3
28789	7	29127	7	29365	17	29536	11	29657	13	29834	2
28790	1	29128	3	29369	13	29541	2	29658	1	29835	1
28792	8	29129	5	29370	1	29544	3	29659	1	29838	2
28793	8	29130	2	29372	3	29550	18	29661	3	29841	72
28801	16	29132	1	29374	5	29551	1	29662	25	29845	1
28802	4	29135	13	29375	1	29554	4	29664	6	29848	1
28803	56	29137	4	29376	7	29555	3	29666	10	29851	2

29853	7	30107	8	30235	2	30332	12	30531	26	30677	30
29901	3	30108	14	30236	85	30333	1	30533	26	30680	35
29902	45	30110	11	30237	3	30336	2	30534	22	30683	15
29903	2	30113	3	30239	1	30337	19	30535	7	30701	44
29904	1	30114	54	30240	64	30338	99	30537	6	30703	4
29910	3	30117	76	30241	9	30339	28	30538	8	30705	33
29918	1	30120	56	30243	53	30340	73	30539	3	30707	21
29920	11	30123	1	30244	62	30341	68	30540	17	30710	6
29921	1	30124	5	30245	136	30342	48	30541	2	30711	2
29924	5	30125	36	30246	7	30343	1	30542	27	30720	68
29925	1	30130	102	30247	191	30344	52	30543	2	30721	32
29926	10	30131	5	30248	5	30345	68	30544	1	30724	4
29927	5	30132	77	30249	38	30346	2	30545	3	30725	5
29928	35	30133	3	30251	3	30347	2	30546	27	30728	44
29935	3	30134	31	30252	2	30348	1	30547	3	30730	4
29936	4	30135	117	30253	33	30349	37	30548	10	30731	6
29938	5	30136	115	30255	2	30350	30	30549	9	30732	1
29940	3	30139	5	30256	2	30354	10	30552	7	30735	4
29944	2	30140	1	30257	5	30355	5	30553	22	30736	63
29945	2	30141	18	30258	3	30356	2	30554	9	30738	10
29956	1	30142	5	30259	6	30357	3	30557	11	30739	8
30001	67	30143	22	30260	37	30358	5	30558	3	30740	30
30002	16	30144	133	30262	2	30359	2	30559	5	30741	49
30007	2	30145	2	30263	92	30360	35	30560	5	30742	11
30020	1	30146	1	30264	15	30362	3	30562	2	30747	25
30021	25	30147	9	30265	7	30366	2	30563	8	30750	4
30027	10	30149	1	30266	3	30401	11	30564	1	30752	8
30030	91	30150	1	30267	13	30411	1	30565	1	30753	11
30031	3	30153	33	30268	10	30413	1	30566	28	30755	14
30032	39	30161	111	30269	71	30415	5	30567	2	30756	1
30033	89	30165	5	30273	23	30417	8	30568	3	30757	10
30034	24	30170	4	30274	44	30421	3	30571	10	30801	1
30035	11	30173	17	30275	1	30426	1	30572	4	30802	6
30038	6	30174	47	30276	16	30427	2	30573	1	30805	6
30040	1	30175	3	30277	25	30428	2	30575	3	30808	4
30049	24	30176	4	30278	99	30434	4	30577	88	30809	24
30050	33	30177	2	30279	6	30436	4	30580	1	30813	24
30054	1	30178	7	30281	61	30439	13	30581	1	30814	13
30057	42	30179	5	30285	1	30441	1	30582	10	30815	50
30058	97	30180	16	30286	40	30442	2	30598	3	30816	2
30059	74	30182	7	30289	1	30445	2	30601	12	30817	6
30060	111	30183	6	30290	6	30452	1	30603	3	30820	1
30061	3	30184	2	30291	12	30453	3	30604	3	30822	2
30062	179	30185	3	30292	8	30454	1	30605	56	30823	1
30064	84	30187	12	30293	6	30456	3	30606	51	30824	19
30065	2	30188	107	30295	4	30457	1	30607	3	30828	5
30066	148	30193	1	30296	27	30458	47	30620	5	30830	19
30067	123	30201	90	30301	1	30467	12	30621	3	30833	4
30068	42	30202	27	30302	1	30470	3	30622	15	30901	8
30069	1	30203	12	30303	2	30471	2	30623	2	30903	1
30071	54	30204	19	30305	37	30473	2	30624	3	30904	50
30072	1	30205	5	30306	51	30474	12	30625	8	30905	23
30073	52	30206	8	30307	23	30477	3	30627	2	30906	85
30074	1	30207	62	30308	13	30501	84	30628	2	30907	95
30075	129	30208	71	30309	22	30502	1	30629	9	30909	56
30076	72	30209	62	30310	16	30503	3	30630	2	30914	2
30077	8	30210	1	30311	20	30504	5	30633	8	30917	1
30080	128	30211	24	30312	13	30506	63	30634	2	30919	3
30081	6	30212	1	30313	4	30507	8	30635	26	31001	1
30082	16	30213	21	30314	6	30510	12	30639	4	31002	1
30083	128	30214	114	30315	12	30511	4	30641	1	31004	1
30084	103	30216	1	30316	18	30512	30	30642	7	31005	33
30085	1	30217	4	30317	4	30513	8	30643	37	31006	3
30086	5	30218	2	30318	37	30516	2	30646	8	31008	20
30087	115	30220	6	30319	93	30517	3	30647	1	31009	3
30088	38	30221	14	30320	1	30518	61	30648	4	31014	18
30091	5	30222	3	30322	3	30520	4	30650	38	31015	21
30092	66	30223	102	30324	24	30521	2	30655	14	31016	3
30093	71	30224	3	30325	1	30522	4	30662	5	31017	1
30094	1	30226	1	30326	3	30523	19	30663	11	31018	1
30101	114	30228	19	30327	58	30525	11	30666	7	31019	2
30102	7	30230	5	30328	73	30527	2	30668	1	31020	3
30103	14	30233	13	30329	33	30528	30	30669	1	31021	58
30104	5	30234	1	30331	18	30529	11	30673	10	31022	1

31023	15	31327	1	31702	1	31830	2	32081	2	32210	157
31024	30	31328	7	31704	5	31831	2	32082	44	32211	142
31025	1	31329	4	31705	53	31833	7	32083	2	32212	3
31028	12	31331	4	31707	102	31901	5	32084	115	32215	2
31029	11	31332	1	31709	29	31902	2	32085	16	32216	137
31030	9	31401	9	31713	1	31903	18	32086	77	32217	74
31031	6	31402	3	31714	5	31904	53	32087	4	32218	58
31032	20	31403	1	31716	1	31905	10	32088	2	32219	13
31034	4	31404	37	31717	5	31906	30	32089	8	32220	15
31036	3	31405	50	31719	1	31907	50	32090	1	32221	54
31040	2	31406	77	31720	1	31908	1	32091	13	32222	14
31041	1	31407	1	31723	7	31909	23	32092	10	32223	64
31042	3	31408	7	31726	3	32002	3	32093	7	32224	18
31044	2	31409	2	31728	9	32004	3	32094	4	32225	65
31046	3	31410	45	31729	1	32007	2	32095	24	32226	24
31047	9	31411	14	31730	7	32008	4	32096	1	32227	6
31049	1	31414	4	31732	1	32009	6	32097	13	32228	1
31050	3	31416	3	31733	1	32010	10	32102	1	32229	1
31052	20	31418	4	31738	1	32011	17	32110	2	32233	66
31054	1	31419	64	31740	2	32012	11	32111	1	32234	5
31055	10	31501	42	31742	10	32014	49	32112	1	32236	3
31057	5	31502	6	31744	3	32015	3	32113	3	32238	6
31061	62	31503	4	31745	9	32016	1	32114	22	32239	4
31063	4	31510	8	31746	1	32017	43	32115	1	32240	2
31064	8	31513	10	31749	1	32018	42	32117	17	32241	3
31065	1	31516	7	31750	8	32019	124	32118	15	32244	54
31066	2	31519	2	31751	2	32020	1	32119	41	32246	8
31069	33	31520	64	31754	5	32021	1	32120	3	32247	5
31071	1	31521	1	31759	2	32023	1	32121	1	32250	69
31075	2	31522	57	31762	1	32028	9	32122	1	32252	1
31076	6	31525	10	31763	35	32029	1	32124	9	32256	15
31079	5	31527	1	31764	1	32030	9	32127	34	32257	36
31082	12	31533	14	31766	1	32031	6	32129	3	32258	9
31085	1	31537	14	31768	27	32032	40	32130	12	32259	10
31087	7	31539	8	31770	4	32033	5	32131	8	32264	1
31088	77	31543	1	31771	1	32034	47	32132	11	32266	8
31090	1	31545	32	31773	4	32035	7	32134	7	32267	2
31091	1	31546	1	31774	6	32036	17	32135	6	32268	1
31092	4	31547	1	31775	3	32037	36	32136	8	32275	1
31093	123	31548	9	31776	2	32038	11	32137	25	32301	74
31094	1	31550	1	31778	2	32039	2	32140	4	32302	9
31095	2	31553	2	31779	8	32040	6	32141	33	32303	106
31096	8	31554	2	31780	2	32043	49	32144	1	32304	36
31097	3	31555	3	31781	1	32044	5	32145	1	32308	98
31098	20	31558	32	31782	2	32045	1	32147	1	32310	15
31099	9	31560	11	31784	2	32046	19	32148	13	32311	19
31119	1	31561	4	31785	3	32047	3	32158	1	32312	54
31139	3	31565	2	31786	1	32048	15	32159	36	32314	1
31201	34	31566	1	31790	6	32050	1	32168	13	32315	5
31203	1	31567	1	31791	12	32052	6	32169	14	32316	2
31204	47	31569	8	31792	48	32054	2	32170	1	32317	6
31205	3	31601	36	31793	3	32055	47	32174	43	32320	12
31206	69	31602	46	31794	26	32056	4	32175	1	32321	3
31208	5	31603	4	31795	1	32057	2	32176	11	32322	2
31209	2	31604	1	31799	6	32058	5	32177	27	32323	3
31210	87	31620	5	31801	5	32059	7	32178	6	32324	5
31211	31	31622	1	31803	1	32060	34	32179	21	32327	34
31212	1	31624	1	31804	8	32062	5	32180	1	32328	1
31263	1	31626	3	31805	1	32063	13	32181	2	32329	1
31301	4	31631	1	31806	1	32065	48	32185	1	32331	2
31302	7	31632	6	31807	4	32066	4	32187	3	32333	10
31303	1	31634	2	31808	9	32067	3	32189	9	32334	1
31305	3	31635	7	31811	6	32068	59	32192	2	32336	1
31307	5	31636	10	31815	2	32069	44	32193	6	32340	23
31308	5	31639	9	31816	14	32070	3	32195	2	32344	10
31312	8	31641	1	31820	4	32071	3	32201	8	32346	4
31313	54	31642	2	31821	1	32072	1	32202	1	32347	33
31314	2	31643	8	31822	3	32073	179	32203	1	32350	1
31320	12	31645	2	31823	1	32074	129	32204	13	32351	14
31321	9	31646	2	31824	8	32076	1	32205	89	32355	2
31322	6	31647	1	31825	1	32077	25	32206	9	32358	3
31323	1	31650	1	31826	4	32078	4	32207	92	32359	13
31324	13	31699	2	31828	1	32079	3	32208	56	32361	1
31326	9	31701	15	31829	4	32080	3	32209	8	32362	2

32401	86	32562	2	32670	71	32760	1	32856	8	33024	183
32402	4	32564	6	32671	84	32761	9	32857	3	33025	35
32403	3	32565	3	32672	25	32762	3	32858	4	33026	57
32404	90	32566	15	32673	10	32763	33	32859	1	33027	15
32405	84	32567	5	32674	22	32764	5	32860	3	33029	6
32406	2	32568	1	32675	26	32765	57	32861	1	33030	92
32407	35	32569	52	32676	42	32766	12	32862	2	33031	15
32408	21	32570	83	32678	5	32767	10	32867	3	33032	46
32409	4	32571	28	32679	9	32769	44	32869	1	33033	55
32410	5	32572	9	32680	21	32770	1	32870	1	33034	17
32411	6	32577	2	32681	1	32771	75	32901	138	33035	4
32413	4	32578	103	32682	2	32772	7	32902	13	33036	16
32420	3	32579	57	32684	9	32773	25	32903	99	33037	73
32421	9	32580	28	32686	3	32774	3	32904	91	33039	16
32423	2	32583	10	32687	2	32775	4	32905	127	33040	76
32424	8	32586	1	32688	19	32776	23	32906	13	33041	4
32425	15	32588	1	32690	1	32778	75	32907	145	33042	23
32427	2	32590	2	32691	32	32779	86	32908	13	33043	38
32428	20	32591	1	32692	3	32780	186	32909	35	33044	2
32431	6	32592	2	32693	16	32781	12	32920	43	33045	4
32432	2	32593	1	32694	9	32782	4	32922	68	33050	90
32433	27	32596	1	32695	5	32783	5	32923	6	33051	1
32434	3	32598	1	32696	12	32784	38	32924	4	33052	11
32438	5	32601	63	32697	1	32785	31	32925	9	33054	30
32439	6	32602	7	32698	5	32786	20	32926	63	33055	121
32440	5	32603	9	32701	89	32787	20	32927	58	33056	8
32442	4	32604	10	32702	8	32788	35	32931	122	33060	52
32443	3	32605	98	32703	60	32789	79	32932	4	33061	5
32444	43	32606	60	32704	4	32790	12	32934	28	33062	70
32445	3	32607	49	32705	3	32791	5	32935	245	33063	96
32446	60	32608	44	32707	97	32792	124	32936	11	33064	154
32447	1	32609	27	32708	95	32793	2	32937	199	33065	91
32454	2	32610	1	32709	9	32794	1	32940	25	33066	66
32455	2	32611	1	32710	2	32795	1	32941	1	33067	27
32456	27	32612	2	32711	29	32796	106	32948	4	33068	102
32459	13	32613	1	32712	41	32797	2	32950	6	33069	16
32460	6	32614	2	32713	38	32798	6	32951	59	33070	31
32461	2	32615	16	32714	59	32801	19	32952	189	33071	42
32462	3	32617	2	32716	1	32802	3	32953	64	33072	2
32463	2	32618	14	32720	90	32803	78	32954	7	33073	14
32464	5	32619	3	32721	2	32804	82	32955	103	33074	1
32465	6	32620	33	32722	2	32805	23	32956	1	33075	1
32466	11	32621	11	32723	3	32806	103	32957	6	33076	7
32501	18	32624	2	32724	62	32807	97	32958	70	33081	6
32503	108	32625	2	32725	126	32808	85	32959	4	33083	1
32504	116	32626	24	32726	75	32809	88	32960	85	33084	6
32505	82	32627	5	32727	3	32810	51	32961	6	33090	7
32506	178	32628	17	32728	3	32811	45	32962	41	33100	1
32507	95	32629	52	32729	2	32812	48	32963	27	33101	9
32508	7	32630	78	32730	20	32813	1	32964	5	33113	1
32511	4	32631	2	32731	17	32814	4	32965	5	33114	8
32512	1	32634	2	32732	15	32815	1	32966	14	33115	1
32513	1	32636	31	32733	2	32817	93	32967	4	33116	22
32514	121	32637	11	32734	1	32818	33	32968	14	33119	4
32516	5	32640	26	32735	12	32819	52	32971	1	33122	2
32522	3	32642	29	32736	9	32820	14	32976	5	33123	1
32524	1	32643	8	32737	4	32821	44	32978	2	33124	1
32526	31	32646	47	32738	59	32822	68	33001	3	33125	119
32531	5	32647	18	32741	45	32824	12	33004	25	33126	96
32533	113	32648	1	32742	3	32825	31	33008	1	33127	20
32534	20	32649	2	32743	40	32826	30	33009	57	33128	4
32535	9	32650	79	32744	10	32827	3	33010	111	33129	24
32536	71	32651	3	32746	31	32828	7	33011	12	33130	38
32537	2	32652	25	32747	3	32829	6	33012	311	33131	8
32538	1	32656	28	32748	45	32830	2	33013	137	33132	1
32540	1	32658	1	32749	3	32832	1	33014	115	33133	104
32541	30	32659	14	32750	96	32833	6	33015	86	33134	119
32542	28	32661	21	32751	78	32835	14	33016	90	33135	82
32544	2	32664	2	32752	3	32836	3	33017	2	33136	16
32547	20	32665	44	32754	35	32837	8	33019	24	33137	36
32548	183	32666	21	32756	2	32839	8	33020	58	33138	42
32549	13	32667	5	32757	50	32853	2	33021	141	33139	68
32560	4	32668	2	32758	9	32854	4	33022	7	33140	30
32561	102	32669	8	32759	6	32855	1	33023	160	33141	52

33142	64	33313	79	33454	2	33543	57	33624	48	33843	9
33143	101	33314	63	33455	60	33544	46	33625	32	33844	32
33144	94	33315	51	33456	5	33545	2	33626	5	33846	2
33145	112	33316	69	33457	41	33546	30	33629	47	33848	3
33146	29	33317	134	33458	95	33547	5	33634	21	33849	2
33147	48	33318	8	33460	67	33548	8	33635	6	33850	12
33148	1	33319	103	33461	69	33549	78	33637	13	33851	1
33149	26	33320	2	33462	69	33550	2	33643	1	33852	81
33150	14	33321	101	33463	80	33551	2	33647	7	33853	72
33152	11	33322	105	33464	1	33552	78	33657	1	33854	1
33153	1	33323	38	33465	2	33553	9	33673	1	33855	3
33154	27	33324	64	33466	8	33554	1	33674	3	33856	4
33155	176	33325	49	33467	59	33555	15	33675	1	33857	7
33156	114	33326	22	33468	2	33556	31	33679	1	33858	3
33157	155	33328	55	33469	20	33557	13	33681	3	33859	6
33158	29	33329	5	33470	26	33558	1	33682	3	33860	19
33159	6	33330	36	33471	12	33559	12	33684	1	33864	6
33160	48	33331	20	33472	22	33560	1	33685	4	33865	2
33161	92	33332	9	33473	1	33561	25	33687	4	33868	10
33162	96	33334	81	33474	17	33562	11	33688	2	33870	103
33163	1	33335	12	33475	13	33563	74	33689	1	33871	4
33164	7	33338	2	33476	6	33564	5	33690	1	33872	32
33165	268	33339	3	33477	29	33565	81	33695	1	33873	11
33166	103	33340	10	33478	17	33566	53	33697	1	33877	4
33167	26	33343	1	33480	19	33567	50	33701	39	33880	83
33168	73	33349	1	33482	19	33568	36	33702	100	33881	38
33169	57	33351	40	33483	21	33569	40	33703	86	33882	4
33170	7	33401	19	33484	30	33570	97	33704	43	33883	1
33172	77	33402	9	33485	3	33572	35	33705	42	33884	25
33173	127	33403	20	33486	56	33573	59	33706	56	33890	4
33174	106	33404	48	33487	31	33575	31	33707	82	33901	59
33175	174	33405	43	33490	12	33576	3	33708	62	33902	13
33176	139	33406	88	33492	6	33577	29	33709	88	33903	111
33177	48	33407	33	33494	67	33578	15	33710	144	33904	137
33178	5	33408	75	33496	22	33579	35	33711	26	33905	57
33179	58	33409	52	33497	27	33580	40	33712	33	33906	3
33180	30	33410	76	33498	20	33581	53	33713	77	33907	71
33181	52	33411	95	33503	1	33582	41	33714	39	33908	53
33182	6	33412	1	33504	5	33583	32	33715	24	33909	17
33183	96	33413	11	33505	43	33584	49	33716	5	33910	1
33184	73	33414	55	33506	3	33585	2	33731	6	33912	25
33185	14	33415	51	33507	47	33589	24	33733	9	33913	1
33186	115	33416	12	33508	21	33590	38	33734	5	33914	26
33187	38	33417	27	33509	3	33591	1	33736	4	33915	4
33189	27	33418	26	33510	33	33592	20	33738	5	33916	2
33190	8	33419	2	33511	105	33593	1	33740	2	33917	49
33193	35	33420	3	33512	52	33594	79	33742	2	33918	7
33195	1	33422	2	33513	27	33595	71	33743	6	33919	43
33196	21	33425	1	33514	1	33596	16	33752	1	33920	12
33197	4	33426	10	33515	86	33597	11	33769	1	33921	6
33233	10	33427	3	33516	82	33598	9	33779	1	33922	17
33237	1	33428	76	33517	4	33599	15	33790	1	33923	50
33238	1	33429	8	33518	1	33601	2	33801	97	33924	2
33245	9	33430	24	33519	37	33602	9	33802	8	33925	1
33255	1	33431	101	33520	16	33603	26	33803	105	33928	10
33256	5	33432	107	33521	3	33604	67	33804	2	33929	6
33257	2	33433	92	33523	3	33605	9	33805	47	33930	1
33261	5	33434	70	33525	84	33606	20	33806	3	33931	33
33265	5	33435	78	33526	88	33607	25	33807	4	33933	2
33266	2	33436	45	33527	5	33608	2	33809	55	33934	5
33269	1	33437	40	33528	65	33609	62	33811	19	33935	17
33281	1	33438	3	33529	30	33610	26	33813	30	33936	49
33301	64	33440	15	33530	2	33611	65	33821	61	33937	27
33302	16	33441	74	33531	1	33612	92	33823	35	33939	4
33303	8	33442	21	33532	13	33613	34	33825	47	33940	92
33304	36	33443	4	33533	55	33614	103	33827	6	33941	7
33305	39	33444	49	33534	12	33615	106	33830	38	33942	78
33306	12	33445	92	33535	9	33616	25	33834	6	33943	3
33307	3	33446	24	33536	1	33617	83	33837	20	33944	1
33308	73	33449	6	33538	13	33618	41	33838	3	33945	1
33309	82	33450	44	33539	10	33619	21	33839	8	33946	5
33310	6	33451	10	33540	112	33621	4	33840	3	33947	11
33311	34	33452	63	33541	93	33622	2	33841	6	33948	40
33312	133	33453	2	33542	82	33623	3	33842	4	33949	6

33950	142	34233	23	34481	8	34736	2	35045	37	35206	65
33951	5	34234	16	34482	5	34737	3	35051	8	35207	3
33952	160	34235	11	34484	1	34741	26	35052	1	35208	24
33953	7	34236	20	34488	9	34742	5	35053	3	35209	83
33954	8	34237	15	34489	2	34743	13	35054	8	35210	54
33955	14	34238	15	34491	6	34744	21	35055	50	35211	18
33956	30	34239	20	34498	2	34746	24	35060	2	35212	14
33957	25	34240	21	34567	1	34748	37	35062	18	35213	50
33959	6	34241	26	34594	1	34755	6	35063	3	35214	38
33960	1	34242	27	34601	70	34756	8	35064	21	35215	185
33961	13	34243	43	34602	19	34758	10	35068	14	35216	104
33962	68	34248	46	34606	59	34759	3	35070	2	35217	31
33963	41	34249	16	34607	16	34760	2	35071	29	35218	15
33964	26	34251	1	34608	38	34761	10	35072	11	35219	3
33970	1	34253	1	34609	42	34762	1	35073	4	35220	2
33971	4	34254	1	34610	27	34769	18	35077	9	35222	38
33980	33	34256	2	34613	36	34770	6	35078	2	35223	45
33981	20	34261	2	34614	7	34771	8	35079	8	35224	21
33982	14	34263	1	34615	30	34772	15	35080	29	35226	125
33983	39	34264	2	34616	37	34773	2	35083	6	35228	26
33990	45	34266	2	34617	3	34777	1	35085	3	35229	3
33991	11	34274	1	34618	3	34785	9	35089	1	35232	2
33999	42	34275	27	34619	19	34786	7	35091	3	35234	2
34001	7	34276	1	34620	14	34787	19	35094	32	35235	69
34002	29	34277	3	34621	29	34788	42	35096	12	35237	1
34003	2	34280	1	34622	10	34797	2	35098	1	35242	29
34004	13	34281	4	34623	24	34924	1	35111	10	35243	75
34005	17	34282	1	34624	51	34944	1	35112	1	35244	42
34006	1	34283	3	34625	20	34946	9	35114	8	35253	4
34008	6	34284	3	34630	16	34947	4	35115	29	35255	1
34020	1	34285	18	34635	12	34949	14	35116	8	35259	2
34022	2	34287	33	34639	22	34950	14	35117	15	35345	1
34023	2	34289	2	34640	42	34951	26	35118	9	35401	38
34024	1	34290	2	34641	34	34952	61	35119	1	35402	2
34030	2	34291	1	34642	50	34953	30	35120	14	35403	1
34035	1	34292	23	34643	29	34954	5	35121	16	35404	44
34036	2	34293	49	34644	32	34956	7	35123	2	35405	48
34037	1	34294	2	34646	30	34957	50	35124	42	35406	27
34039	6	34295	3	34647	31	34972	25	35125	37	35440	1
34051	5	34296	2	34648	38	34973	6	35126	54	35441	1
34053	3	34297	1	34649	5	34974	30	35127	31	35444	2
34054	1	34299	1	34652	59	34981	5	35130	5	35446	3
34058	3	34332	1	34653	58	34982	40	35131	5	35447	4
34060	2	34420	4	34654	33	34983	55	35133	4	35452	6
34061	3	34421	4	34655	32	34984	13	35135	2	35453	18
34078	2	34428	7	34656	4	34985	7	35136	3	35456	3
34080	1	34429	4	34660	1	34986	3	35137	1	35460	1
34090	1	34430	4	34661	1	34987	1	35143	7	35461	6
34091	2	34431	7	34664	4	34988	2	35146	18	35462	5
34093	4	34432	4	34665	24	34990	57	35147	3	35463	1
34099	3	34433	2	34666	25	34992	1	35148	4	35466	4
34202	19	34434	11	34667	79	34994	27	35149	1	35470	7
34203	31	34436	3	34668	133	34995	7	35150	32	35474	1
34205	44	34442	10	34669	29	34996	15	35152	1	35476	64
34206	2	34446	7	34673	3	34997	52	35156	1	35478	1
34207	43	34447	1	34674	4	35004	6	35160	57	35481	4
34208	24	34448	3	34677	16	35005	26	35171	14	35486	6
34209	65	34449	6	34680	3	35006	3	35172	4	35487	2
34210	24	34450	7	34681	2	35007	55	35173	63	35501	79
34215	2	34451	1	34682	3	35010	31	35175	16	35540	1
34216	3	34452	7	34683	51	35014	5	35176	2	35541	6
34217	11	34453	2	34684	33	35016	34	35178	2	35542	3
34218	1	34460	2	34685	5	35019	4	35179	14	35544	1
34219	8	34461	1	34688	3	35020	84	35180	27	35546	4
34220	2	34465	5	34689	29	35021	1	35181	1	35548	1
34221	33	34470	17	34690	29	35023	123	35184	8	35549	5
34222	19	34471	17	34691	27	35031	31	35185	1	35550	13
34223	41	34472	10	34695	23	35032	1	35186	13	35553	2
34224	43	34474	7	34697	3	35033	1	35188	4	35555	21
34228	13	34476	17	34698	55	35034	5	35201	5	35563	9
34229	10	34477	1	34705	3	35040	6	35202	3	35564	2
34230	32	34478	3	34711	24	35042	13	35203	1	35565	20
34231	42	34479	10	34712	4	35043	12	35204	6	35570	17
34232	41	34480	7	34731	13	35044	6	35205	23	35571	2

35574	1	35801	179	36052	1	36323	6	36559	3	36849	1
35576	2	35802	195	36054	32	36330	68	36561	15	36853	8
35578	4	35803	199	36064	2	36331	1	36562	2	36854	13
35579	2	35804	2	36066	11	36340	7	36564	3	36855	1
35580	9	35805	84	36067	38	36344	9	36567	17	36861	7
35581	3	35806	60	36069	1	36345	11	36568	1	36862	1
35582	5	35807	9	36075	2	36346	10	36569	1	36863	15
35583	1	35808	4	36078	6	36349	1	36571	23	36864	4
35585	1	35810	122	36080	2	36350	6	36572	4	36865	1
35586	3	35811	64	36081	29	36351	12	36574	3	36866	5
35587	1	35812	1	36083	6	36352	6	36575	25	36867	33
35592	5	35814	2	36087	1	36360	47	36576	9	36868	1
35593	1	35815	6	36088	7	36361	7	36578	1	36869	6
35594	26	35816	37	36089	1	36362	5	36579	2	36872	1
35601	90	35824	7	36091	3	36370	1	36580	2	36874	8
35602	9	35901	124	36092	24	36371	3	36581	1	36875	2
35603	65	35902	1	36102	1	36374	3	36582	52	36876	1
35611	110	35903	62	36103	1	36375	6	36584	1	36877	9
35615	1	35904	36	36104	7	36376	4	36585	1	36879	1
35616	10	35905	9	36105	20	36401	4	36587	4	36904	1
35617	1	35906	11	36106	24	36404	1	36590	1	36925	3
35618	1	35950	46	36107	20	36409	1	36601	2	37010	2
35619	9	35952	4	36108	16	36420	26	36602	3	37012	1
35620	11	35953	11	36109	86	36426	19	36603	2	37013	59
35621	4	35954	20	36110	26	36429	1	36604	11	37014	2
35622	7	35957	39	36111	41	36432	3	36605	53	37015	11
35630	131	35958	8	36113	5	36436	1	36606	40	37018	2
35631	3	35959	4	36115	2	36441	6	36607	12	37022	6
35632	1	35960	11	36116	67	36442	5	36608	86	37024	2
35633	20	35961	3	36117	37	36444	4	36609	119	37025	3
35636	1	35962	1	36121	1	36445	7	36610	1	37026	3
35640	36	35963	4	36201	94	36451	6	36611	9	37027	70
35645	43	35966	1	36202	4	36456	2	36612	1	37028	2
35646	12	35967	37	36203	32	36458	2	36613	23	37029	13
35648	5	35971	10	36204	1	36460	17	36616	2	37030	12
35649	1	35972	2	36205	2	36461	4	36617	3	37031	3
35650	27	35973	2	36206	23	36467	21	36618	55	37032	4
35651	7	35974	3	36226	1	36475	1	36619	37	37033	8
35652	18	35976	27	36250	16	36476	1	36633	2	37034	3
35653	26	35978	4	36251	7	36477	2	36660	3	37035	3
35660	50	35979	2	36253	4	36480	10	36671	1	37036	5
35661	21	35980	4	36255	1	36482	2	36679	1	37037	7
35662	1	35981	5	36256	1	36502	8	36685	1	37040	50
35670	15	35983	4	36258	1	36504	1	36688	2	37042	41
35671	2	35984	5	36260	5	36505	3	36689	2	37043	31
35672	3	35986	6	36264	14	36507	18	36691	1	37046	6
35673	11	35987	6	36265	45	36509	3	36693	31	37047	2
35674	52	35988	6	36266	10	36511	2	36695	34	37048	9
35677	1	35989	3	36268	12	36518	2	36701	128	37049	4
35739	4	35990	2	36270	1	36521	2	36702	1	37050	2
35740	3	36003	1	36271	13	36522	2	36725	2	37051	1
35741	17	36006	3	36272	15	36523	5	36731	2	37055	35
35742	1	36010	2	36273	3	36524	2	36732	18	37057	1
35744	1	36016	5	36274	21	36525	3	36738	1	37058	4
35746	1	36020	2	36276	2	36526	37	36742	3	37060	2
35747	9	36022	12	36277	16	36527	8	36744	8	37061	7
35748	7	36023	2	36278	3	36528	2	36748	5	37062	12
35749	21	36024	3	36279	3	36529	1	36749	1	37064	92
35750	27	36025	5	36280	4	36530	22	36752	2	37065	2
35752	3	36026	2	36301	128	36532	44	36754	1	37066	70
35754	27	36027	22	36302	4	36533	8	36756	5	37067	1
35758	174	36028	4	36303	59	36535	24	36759	2	37070	2
35759	18	36032	8	36304	2	36536	5	36769	2	37072	46
35760	8	36033	9	36310	6	36541	16	36778	1	37073	23
35761	12	36034	1	36311	4	36542	12	36782	5	37074	2
35763	12	36035	2	36312	3	36543	1	36783	5	37075	105
35764	2	36036	2	36314	2	36544	5	36784	1	37076	56
35765	7	36037	22	36316	2	36545	10	36785	1	37077	3
35766	1	36042	1	36317	1	36547	1	36786	2	37079	7
35768	43	36043	5	36318	1	36549	22	36793	1	37080	10
35771	4	36047	1	36319	4	36551	6	36801	59	37082	5
35772	7	36048	1	36320	6	36553	1	36803	6	37083	8
35773	27	36049	3	36321	2	36555	3	36830	80	37085	3
35776	5	36051	2	36322	10	36556	1	36831	5	37086	17

37087	83	37228	3	37402	1	37742	6	37881	1	38083	1
37088	2	37229	2	37404	20	37743	113	37882	4	38087	1
37091	40	37301	3	37405	28	37744	2	37885	3	38101	3
37095	1	37302	5	37406	10	37748	88	37886	8	38104	48
37096	11	37303	53	37407	9	37752	10	37887	42	38105	3
37097	1	37304	1	37409	9	37753	1	37888	1	38106	10
37098	2	37305	2	37411	32	37754	18	37890	16	38107	15
37101	7	37306	1	37412	69	37755	7	37891	3	38108	27
37110	39	37307	21	37415	71	37756	2	37892	4	38109	32
37115	61	37308	3	37416	50	37757	32	37901	2	38111	111
37116	2	37309	8	37419	7	37760	14	37909	25	38112	20
37118	1	37310	13	37421	138	37762	4	37912	55	38114	22
37121	1	37311	200	37422	1	37763	83	37914	56	38115	104
37122	63	37312	47	37601	156	37764	9	37915	8	38116	51
37129	44	37313	2	37602	2	37765	1	37916	9	38117	149
37130	88	37315	71	37603	2	37766	106	37917	51	38118	127
37132	1	37317	2	37604	67	37767	1	37918	145	38119	65
37133	2	37318	1	37605	3	37769	15	37919	102	38120	12
37134	3	37319	1	37614	6	37770	1	37920	104	38122	71
37135	7	37320	9	37615	36	37771	89	37921	67	38124	1
37137	1	37321	44	37616	19	37774	43	37922	140	38125	31
37138	52	37322	12	37617	44	37777	27	37923	86	38126	1
37143	8	37323	35	37618	37	37779	2	37924	34	38127	96
37144	1	37324	9	37620	111	37801	149	37927	1	38128	90
37145	13	37325	10	37621	5	37802	7	37928	6	38130	3
37146	2	37327	13	37625	2	37803	1	37930	2	38133	16
37147	1	37328	1	37640	3	37804	28	37931	69	38134	205
37148	13	37329	7	37641	14	37806	3	37932	40	38135	31
37149	1	37330	16	37642	28	37807	11	37933	2	38137	1
37150	1	37331	31	37643	100	37809	2	37937	1	38138	130
37152	1	37332	3	37644	6	37810	8	37938	36	38139	17
37153	1	37334	50	37645	3	37811	2	37939	2	38141	24
37155	1	37335	5	37650	24	37813	25	37940	1	38174	2
37158	1	37336	5	37656	3	37814	107	37950	4	38175	1
37160	57	37337	2	37657	2	37815	2	37996	4	38177	2
37166	11	37338	1	37658	6	37816	2	37998	6	38181	2
37167	38	37339	2	37659	49	37818	7	38001	5	38184	1
37171	1	37341	49	37660	89	37820	16	38002	17	38187	2
37172	58	37342	3	37662	1	37821	44	38004	13	38201	10
37174	2	37343	137	37663	52	37825	10	38006	6	38220	1
37178	1	37345	3	37664	120	37826	14	38008	7	38221	4
37179	4	37347	25	37665	18	37828	13	38011	12	38222	14
37180	1	37348	3	37680	3	37829	8	38012	17	38224	3
37181	1	37350	16	37681	7	37830	261	38017	69	38225	3
37183	8	37352	3	37682	4	37831	10	38018	71	38226	1
37184	25	37353	25	37683	12	37840	52	38019	20	38229	8
37185	9	37354	21	37684	2	37841	4	38024	35	38230	4
37186	7	37355	61	37686	13	37843	4	38027	1	38231	2
37187	15	37356	4	37687	8	37845	15	38028	24	38232	8
37188	8	37359	2	37690	6	37846	6	38029	1	38233	5
37189	6	37360	4	37692	9	37847	3	38033	1	38237	25
37190	7	37361	1	37694	9	37849	76	38034	2	38240	5
37191	3	37362	7	37701	20	37852	2	38037	1	38241	4
37201	1	37363	63	37705	7	37853	7	38039	2	38242	47
37202	5	37364	1	37708	9	37854	52	38042	2	38251	11
37203	5	37367	11	37710	2	37857	24	38043	1	38253	1
37204	21	37370	16	37711	5	37860	2	38044	1	38255	1
37205	66	37371	2	37713	1	37861	9	38049	2	38256	10
37206	28	37372	1	37714	13	37862	67	38052	4	38257	4
37207	40	37373	4	37716	88	37863	7	38053	67	38258	6
37208	7	37374	1	37717	1	37864	7	38054	6	38259	1
37209	48	37375	3	37719	2	37865	41	38057	4	38260	5
37210	17	37377	64	37720	8	37866	2	38058	7	38261	27
37211	92	37379	39	37721	31	37867	3	38059	6	38280	1
37212	15	37380	11	37722	9	37868	2	38060	7	38301	71
37214	68	37381	17	37723	1	37869	1	38061	1	38302	3
37215	52	37385	4	37724	8	37870	8	38063	4	38303	1
37216	53	37387	2	37725	26	37871	9	38066	1	38305	58
37217	64	37388	79	37726	4	37872	4	38067	1	38310	2
37218	10	37391	1	37728	2	37873	1	38068	4	38313	6
37220	31	37395	2	37729	2	37874	29	38069	3	38314	2
37221	39	37397	12	37731	1	37877	19	38075	1	38315	7
37222	3	37398	26	37737	15	37879	9	38079	5	38316	10
37225	1	37401	2	37738	10	37880	9	38080	1	38317	7

38318	2	38551	5	38753	2	39058	1	39282	2	39502	1
38320	20	38553	2	38754	1	39059	15	39284	1	39503	66
38321	2	38555	67	38756	10	39060	1	39286	3	39505	2
38327	1	38556	29	38759	1	39062	1	39288	5	39506	2
38329	4	38557	1	38771	2	39063	2	39301	54	39507	26
38330	5	38559	3	38773	1	39066	4	39302	3	39520	53
38332	2	38560	2	38778	1	39067	4	39304	1	39521	3
38333	2	38562	11	38801	62	39071	3	39305	56	39522	1
38337	1	38563	2	38802	2	39073	29	39307	5	39525	1
38338	1	38564	1	38820	2	39074	15	39311	1	39529	1
38339	1	38568	2	38821	40	39077	1	39320	1	39530	22
38340	36	38569	2	38824	13	39078	1	39323	3	39531	73
38341	2	38570	12	38825	1	39079	4	39325	8	39532	93
38343	42	38572	1	38826	4	39082	2	39327	1	39533	7
38344	11	38574	7	38827	4	39083	5	39328	1	39534	16
38345	2	38577	1	38828	7	39090	13	39330	5	39535	1
38351	16	38578	2	38829	46	39092	3	39332	2	39551	1
38355	5	38579	1	38833	6	39094	3	39335	6	39552	2
38356	4	38580	1	38834	74	39095	3	39336	1	39553	43
38357	4	38581	2	38835	1	39108	1	39337	4	39556	2
38358	20	38582	4	38841	1	39110	15	39339	25	39558	3
38361	2	38583	26	38843	14	39111	15	39341	1	39560	55
38362	6	38585	6	38846	4	39114	8	39342	3	39563	16
38363	9	38587	4	38847	2	39116	4	39345	11	39564	108
38365	2	38588	2	38849	9	39117	11	39346	5	39567	67
38366	5	38601	1	38851	15	39119	1	39350	20	39571	28
38367	7	38603	4	38852	29	39120	49	39355	3	39572	5
38368	1	38606	5	38855	2	39121	1	39356	1	39573	11
38369	2	38610	2	38856	1	39130	2	39358	4	39574	15
38370	1	38611	14	38857	5	39140	1	39360	4	39576	20
38372	28	38614	14	38858	11	39143	1	39363	1	39577	7
38375	24	38617	1	38859	1	39145	9	39364	3	39581	13
38379	1	38618	13	38862	1	39146	2	39365	29	39601	13
38382	40	38619	2	38863	25	39149	2	39367	15	39629	4
38392	3	38626	1	38865	10	39150	7	39401	108	39630	1
38401	71	38629	1	38866	15	39153	2	39402	47	39631	5
38402	2	38632	30	38868	8	39154	17	39403	1	39638	11
38410	1	38633	1	38869	1	39157	19	39404	1	39641	1
38425	2	38635	4	38870	5	39158	1	39406	1	39645	1
38449	7	38637	19	38871	5	39159	21	39421	2	39647	2
38451	6	38641	2	38873	14	39160	2	39422	8	39648	26
38452	1	38642	1	38879	5	39163	1	39423	5	39652	5
38453	1	38643	1	38880	1	39168	4	39425	2	39653	2
38456	3	38646	5	38901	23	39169	1	39426	22	39654	10
38457	1	38647	4	38915	5	39170	7	39427	1	39657	3
38459	3	38650	6	38916	1	39175	5	39428	6	39661	1
38460	7	38651	12	38917	1	39176	1	39429	23	39663	2
38461	4	38652	26	38918	1	39180	139	39437	33	39664	5
38462	4	38654	28	38921	4	39181	1	39439	3	39665	2
38463	1	38655	15	38922	4	39182	3	39440	79	39666	11
38464	28	38659	2	38923	1	39189	3	39441	5	39667	11
38468	2	38663	21	38925	4	39190	3	39442	3	39668	2
38469	3	38666	2	38926	1	39191	7	39450	1	39669	1
38472	3	38668	13	38930	19	39192	1	39451	3	39701	41
38473	2	38671	45	38941	2	39193	1	39452	67	39702	15
38474	10	38676	2	38943	1	39194	8	39455	13	39703	1
38477	4	38677	2	38946	1	39201	2	39459	10	39730	13
38478	32	38680	18	38957	2	39202	8	39463	1	39735	17
38481	1	38683	1	38959	1	39203	1	39464	1	39736	1
38482	2	38685	1	38961	1	39204	26	39465	24	39737	4
38483	6	38701	38	38965	13	39205	1	39466	45	39740	3
38485	9	38702	1	38966	1	39206	26	39470	33	39741	2
38486	4	38703	3	38967	8	39207	4	39474	12	39744	7
38488	6	38721	6	39011	1	39208	43	39475	11	39745	2
38501	111	38722	2	39038	2	39209	23	39476	4	39746	5
38502	2	38725	1	39039	2	39211	73	39477	1	39747	2
38503	4	38732	24	39040	1	39212	68	39478	4	39750	4
38504	1	38733	3	39041	2	39213	6	39479	6	39752	2
38505	7	38736	1	39042	71	39215	2	39480	3	39754	1
38541	1	38737	1	39044	6	39216	9	39481	1	39755	1
38543	1	38739	1	39046	13	39218	5	39482	20	39756	3
38544	7	38744	1	39051	1	39225	1	39483	3	39759	83
38547	1	38748	4	39056	63	39226	1	39484	1	39762	13
38549	3	38751	18	39057	2	39236	2	39501	77	39766	4

39772	2	40213	39	40444	16	40977	28	41214	1	41614	2
39773	16	40214	99	40447	4	41001	25	41216	2	41615	2
39904	1	40215	38	40456	9	41002	12	41219	4	41616	1
39922	1	40216	90	40460	1	41003	4	41222	3	41626	1
39937	1	40217	28	40461	4	41005	21	41224	7	41629	2
39951	1	40218	41	40464	3	41006	4	41228	1	41630	3
40003	3	40219	97	40468	2	41007	3	41230	18	41631	12
40004	135	40220	82	40472	8	41008	9	41232	2	41635	7
40006	2	40222	86	40475	57	41010	1	41238	2	41637	2
40008	4	40223	61	40484	7	41011	27	41240	17	41640	4
40009	3	40228	33	40489	3	41014	7	41250	1	41642	8
40010	2	40229	40	40501	1	41015	45	41256	3	41645	3
40013	6	40232	1	40502	123	41016	10	41258	1	41647	1
40014	37	40233	2	40503	148	41017	79	41262	1	41649	8
40019	3	40241	17	40504	65	41018	40	41264	3	41650	5
40020	1	40242	6	40505	105	41030	7	41265	4	41651	1
40022	2	40243	36	40507	3	41031	6	41269	1	41653	33
40023	5	40245	7	40508	14	41033	3	41270	1	41659	4
40026	15	40252	1	40509	16	41034	3	41271	1	41660	4
40031	39	40258	49	40510	1	41035	3	41274	1	41667	1
40033	10	40259	3	40511	15	41036	1	41301	6	41668	8
40042	1	40269	1	40512	1	41039	2	41311	1	41701	19
40045	3	40272	74	40513	21	41040	3	41314	5	41702	1
40047	22	40280	2	40514	6	41041	3	41332	4	41712	1
40048	1	40291	77	40515	37	41042	67	41339	12	41720	2
40050	1	40292	1	40516	1	41043	2	41348	1	41722	3
40051	3	40299	69	40517	45	41044	3	41352	1	41725	3
40054	1	40306	1	40523	1	41048	3	41360	1	41727	1
40055	3	40310	3	40524	2	41049	1	41365	1	41731	1
40056	8	40311	2	40544	2	41051	27	41378	1	41739	1
40057	5	40312	9	40555	4	41056	43	41385	2	41745	3
40059	11	40313	5	40579	1	41059	1	41426	1	41746	1
40061	1	40316	1	40601	83	41063	6	41465	4	41749	3
40065	23	40324	40	40603	1	41064	2	41472	8	41751	1
40067	3	40330	24	40701	50	41071	20	41501	90	41774	4
40068	4	40336	22	40702	2	41072	1	41502	9	41810	1
40069	4	40337	9	40732	1	41073	15	41503	3	41812	1
40071	6	40340	2	40734	6	41074	19	41512	2	41815	2
40076	3	40342	39	40737	3	41075	36	41513	1	41822	2
40077	1	40345	2	40740	4	41076	25	41514	2	41823	1
40104	1	40346	2	40741	72	41077	1	41519	3	41826	3
40107	4	40347	3	40743	1	41080	4	41522	1	41829	3
40108	16	40351	23	40759	3	41085	1	41524	1	41830	1
40109	8	40353	33	40763	1	41091	19	41527	2	41831	1
40110	1	40356	84	40769	33	41092	2	41528	1	41837	2
40111	1	40357	2	40771	1	41093	2	41536	1	41840	6
40118	21	40358	5	40774	1	41094	13	41537	7	41849	1
40119	1	40359	4	40806	16	41095	2	41538	1	41851	1
40121	13	40360	16	40810	2	41097	4	41539	1	41855	2
40143	2	40361	15	40813	1	41101	120	41542	1	41858	14
40144	5	40366	1	40823	10	41102	17	41543	1	42001	105
40145	1	40370	6	40826	3	41105	5	41544	7	42002	10
40146	7	40371	2	40828	6	41121	2	41545	1	42003	31
40150	5	40372	7	40829	2	41129	43	41547	3	42006	1
40152	2	40374	2	40831	12	41132	2	41548	1	42020	8
40155	5	40376	1	40840	1	41139	43	41553	11	42023	5
40157	2	40379	2	40845	2	41141	1	41554	2	42024	4
40160	56	40380	7	40854	7	41143	41	41557	5	42025	71
40162	3	40383	52	40855	2	41144	13	41558	2	42027	4
40165	57	40385	9	40858	1	41146	3	41560	6	42028	2
40175	24	40387	3	40862	1	41157	2	41562	3	42029	15
40176	7	40390	11	40865	1	41159	1	41563	1	42031	4
40201	2	40391	78	40873	3	41163	1	41564	1	42034	1
40202	3	40392	2	40902	2	41164	17	41566	2	42035	2
40203	8	40402	1	40903	2	41168	7	41569	1	42036	3
40204	23	40403	21	40906	14	41169	24	41571	1	42037	1
40205	52	40404	3	40927	1	41171	5	41572	7	42038	8
40206	45	40405	1	40940	3	41174	1	41601	8	42039	1
40207	70	40409	1	40941	2	41175	6	41602	4	42040	4
40208	17	40422	31	40949	1	41179	6	41603	5	42041	8
40209	9	40423	2	40958	2	41180	4	41604	2	42044	16
40210	8	40434	3	40962	17	41183	9	41605	6	42045	5
40211	5	40437	3	40965	48	41189	4	41607	2	42046	2
40212	13	40440	1	40972	3	41203	1	41612	3	42048	4

42049	2	42327	7	42713	1	43080	6	43240	1	43502	10
42050	5	42328	2	42714	1	43081	171	43301	1	43504	1
42051	6	42330	21	42717	3	43083	2	43302	146	43505	1
42053	4	42332	1	42718	31	43084	1	43310	9	43506	37
42054	1	42333	1	42720	1	43085	122	43311	59	43511	6
42055	4	42337	3	42721	2	43086	1	43314	13	43512	72
42056	4	42339	1	42722	1	43101	1	43315	16	43515	32
42058	7	42340	1	42723	1	43102	12	43316	8	43516	3
42060	1	42345	22	42724	9	43103	20	43318	7	43517	8
42064	17	42347	11	42726	11	43104	1	43319	4	43518	5
42066	22	42348	14	42728	10	43105	8	43320	11	43521	5
42069	1	42350	4	42732	4	43106	5	43322	1	43522	5
42070	1	42351	17	42733	1	43107	1	43324	20	43524	5
42071	74	42352	8	42736	2	43110	40	43325	1	43525	1
42076	5	42354	1	42743	13	43112	7	43326	33	43526	12
42078	9	42355	5	42746	5	43113	47	43331	21	43527	7
42079	1	42361	1	42748	12	43116	2	43332	10	43528	29
42081	8	42364	2	42749	5	43119	39	43333	2	43530	1
42082	6	42366	17	42753	1	43123	72	43334	6	43532	8
42083	1	42369	1	42754	27	43125	21	43335	1	43533	2
42086	4	42372	1	42757	3	43128	8	43337	2	43534	5
42087	2	42374	4	42764	1	43130	149	43338	29	43535	1
42101	101	42376	11	42765	4	43135	12	43340	3	43537	86
42102	4	42378	4	42768	1	43136	1	43341	3	43540	2
42103	18	42404	11	42776	2	43137	7	43342	4	43542	11
42104	19	42406	1	42784	2	43138	29	43343	7	43543	10
42122	9	42408	15	43001	9	43140	30	43344	11	43545	23
42123	1	42409	11	43002	4	43143	7	43345	5	43548	2
42127	11	42410	2	43003	5	43144	1	43347	5	43549	3
42129	3	42411	9	43004	10	43145	3	43348	9	43550	1
42133	1	42413	7	43005	1	43146	15	43351	17	43551	105
42134	7	42420	94	43008	11	43147	70	43356	3	43553	3
42140	1	42431	74	43009	3	43148	4	43357	19	43554	5
42141	77	42436	4	43011	16	43149	3	43358	13	43555	3
42142	1	42437	6	43013	2	43150	4	43359	1	43556	3
42144	1	42440	1	43014	1	43152	2	43360	1	43557	7
42152	3	42441	3	43015	130	43153	1	43402	73	43558	31
42154	3	42442	5	43017	67	43154	3	43403	1	43560	78
42159	2	42445	31	43018	1	43155	2	43406	1	43565	2
42160	4	42450	13	43019	15	43157	1	43408	1	43566	18
42164	9	42451	3	43021	29	43158	1	43410	34	43567	41
42166	6	42452	2	43022	6	43160	59	43412	17	43569	9
42167	7	42455	2	43023	39	43162	13	43413	3	43570	4
42170	1	42456	2	43025	15	43164	1	43416	12	43571	14
42171	3	42457	1	43026	50	43167	1	43420	56	43603	1
42202	2	42459	11	43028	5	43201	34	43421	1	43604	3
42204	1	42460	1	43029	1	43202	39	43429	1	43605	75
42206	6	42461	3	43031	21	43203	2	43430	10	43606	41
42210	4	42463	1	43032	1	43204	64	43431	5	43607	24
42211	8	42464	3	43035	1	43205	3	43432	3	43608	34
42214	2	42501	64	43040	46	43206	29	43435	2	43609	53
42217	7	42502	1	43044	7	43207	53	43437	2	43610	5
42220	2	42518	1	43045	6	43209	57	43439	2	43611	53
42223	18	42519	4	43046	7	43210	7	43440	17	43612	65
42234	2	42528	1	43050	51	43211	19	43441	1	43613	91
42236	4	42533	5	43054	22	43212	43	43442	6	43614	91
42240	66	42539	10	43055	202	43213	90	43443	6	43615	79
42254	1	42544	2	43056	31	43214	88	43445	1	43616	58
42256	5	42553	4	43060	1	43215	13	43446	1	43617	22
42261	3	42555	1	43061	7	43216	3	43447	10	43618	7
42262	3	42566	1	43062	39	43217	2	43449	15	43619	22
42266	2	42567	2	43064	23	43219	19	43450	9	43620	3
42274	5	42602	7	43065	50	43220	101	43451	3	43623	56
42275	4	42629	3	43066	1	43221	83	43452	40	43695	1
42276	11	42631	1	43067	4	43222	4	43456	3	43699	1
42284	1	42633	12	43068	116	43223	27	43457	5	43701	137
42285	2	42635	4	43070	2	43224	73	43458	2	43713	20
42301	112	42642	9	43071	4	43227	75	43460	10	43717	1
42302	2	42647	3	43072	18	43228	71	43462	4	43718	2
42303	32	42649	1	43073	2	43229	135	43463	1	43719	6
42320	13	42653	3	43074	16	43230	109	43464	1	43722	1
42323	2	42701	67	43076	16	43231	13	43465	14	43723	6
42325	3	42702	4	43077	2	43232	50	43466	4	43724	13
42326	2	42712	2	43078	55	43235	38	43469	5	43725	59

43727	1	43940	9	44085	6	44233	29	44438	12	44651	2
43730	2	43942	6	44086	13	44234	9	44440	4	44653	1
43731	8	43943	7	44087	28	44235	1	44441	4	44654	36
43732	2	43944	11	44088	1	44236	86	44442	11	44656	2
43733	1	43945	5	44089	51	44240	173	44443	8	44657	16
43734	5	43946	7	44090	36	44241	22	44444	46	44661	1
43735	1	43947	19	44092	57	44246	1	44445	13	44662	23
43739	3	43948	1	44093	2	44250	5	44446	42	44663	49
43740	1	43950	60	44094	154	44251	1	44449	1	44666	1
43742	1	43951	5	44095	37	44253	10	44450	4	44667	44
43746	7	43952	85	44101	5	44254	17	44451	4	44669	5
43747	9	43962	1	44102	32	44255	31	44452	5	44672	7
43748	4	43964	45	44103	10	44256	112	44453	1	44675	6
43749	9	43968	16	44104	5	44260	37	44454	2	44676	3
43754	3	43972	1	44105	29	44262	16	44455	7	44677	15
43755	3	43973	3	44106	31	44264	9	44460	90	44678	1
43756	10	43974	1	44107	95	44265	2	44470	13	44680	7
43758	5	43976	3	44108	9	44266	77	44471	26	44681	10
43759	2	43977	8	44109	80	44270	23	44473	21	44682	3
43760	2	43981	3	44110	16	44272	8	44481	26	44683	18
43762	18	43983	5	44111	71	44273	16	44482	3	44685	68
43764	13	43986	2	44112	8	44275	4	44483	51	44688	3
43766	1	43988	3	44113	9	44276	1	44484	57	44691	111
43767	6	44001	81	44114	3	44278	57	44485	44	44695	9
43768	1	44003	7	44116	62	44280	8	44490	3	44698	3
43771	1	44004	77	44117	27	44281	65	44491	11	44699	15
43772	1	44010	8	44118	87	44286	27	44493	2	44701	1
43773	12	44011	37	44119	22	44287	11	44501	4	44703	19
43777	10	44012	44	44120	37	44288	11	44502	24	44704	5
43778	5	44017	60	44121	86	44301	56	44504	7	44705	32
43780	4	44021	12	44122	72	44302	6	44505	25	44706	65
43783	6	44022	107	44123	45	44303	16	44506	3	44707	21
43787	3	44023	2	44124	114	44304	10	44507	15	44708	69
43788	1	44024	57	44125	48	44305	45	44509	33	44709	52
43793	20	44026	67	44126	53	44306	30	44510	1	44710	28
43804	7	44028	31	44127	10	44307	10	44511	43	44711	2
43812	54	44030	72	44128	20	44308	2	44512	80	44714	17
43821	8	44032	3	44129	84	44310	35	44514	60	44718	32
43822	4	44033	1	44130	129	44311	15	44515	83	44720	131
43824	5	44035	212	44131	59	44312	87	44516	1	44721	36
43828	1	44036	1	44132	38	44313	112	44601	77	44724	1
43830	8	44039	116	44133	58	44314	54	44606	24	44730	13
43832	26	44040	8	44134	108	44316	1	44608	5	44735	1
43836	2	44041	20	44135	67	44317	1	44609	16	44802	2
43837	4	44044	61	44136	94	44319	87	44610	2	44804	3
43840	6	44045	2	44137	54	44320	27	44611	5	44805	89
43842	2	44046	5	44138	57	44321	50	44612	13	44807	6
43843	2	44047	21	44139	54	44333	37	44613	1	44809	1
43844	9	44048	8	44140	54	44401	12	44614	38	44811	36
43845	16	44049	2	44141	51	44402	8	44615	15	44813	21
43885	1	44050	19	44142	55	44403	16	44618	22	44814	11
43901	3	44052	81	44143	54	44404	2	44619	1	44815	3
43902	1	44053	57	44144	59	44405	13	44620	3	44817	6
43903	4	44054	37	44145	74	44406	44	44621	12	44818	3
43905	1	44055	30	44146	108	44408	31	44622	63	44819	1
43906	34	44056	35	44147	44	44410	38	44624	2	44820	36
43907	23	44057	52	44164	1	44411	5	44625	1	44822	6
43908	10	44060	214	44181	1	44412	8	44626	7	44824	9
43909	1	44061	2	44199	1	44413	57	44627	5	44826	4
43910	5	44062	12	44201	25	44417	6	44628	4	44827	14
43912	19	44064	10	44202	43	44418	3	44629	14	44828	2
43913	3	44065	9	44203	143	44420	56	44632	20	44830	37
43915	3	44066	1	44210	2	44422	2	44633	3	44833	63
43916	2	44067	32	44211	3	44423	5	44634	3	44836	1
43917	5	44068	2	44212	102	44425	37	44636	1	44837	8
43920	80	44069	1	44214	2	44427	1	44637	3	44838	1
43930	4	44070	127	44215	7	44428	5	44638	5	44839	59
43931	2	44072	21	44216	41	44429	8	44639	1	44840	3
43932	4	44074	42	44217	3	44430	7	44641	46	44841	2
43933	4	44076	15	44221	93	44431	9	44643	7	44842	15
43934	1	44077	112	44223	46	44432	34	44644	16	44843	8
43935	36	44081	12	44224	127	44434	1	44645	4	44844	1
43938	22	44082	6	44230	33	44436	12	44646	138	44846	17
43939	2	44084	7	44231	8	44437	10	44647	7	44847	4

44848	2	45121	15	45255	39	45404	13	45673	1	45830	17
44849	3	45122	46	45262	2	45405	56	45674	3	45831	7
44851	8	45123	17	45263	1	45406	47	45677	1	45832	8
44853	2	45130	9	45267	1	45407	8	45678	2	45833	36
44854	2	45133	86	45301	1	45408	2	45679	8	45836	5
44855	4	45135	12	45302	5	45409	30	45680	32	45839	1
44857	39	45140	133	45303	5	45410	42	45681	8	45840	158
44861	1	45142	10	45304	25	45413	1	45684	5	45841	2
44864	4	45144	22	45305	41	45414	82	45685	2	45843	13
44865	5	45145	2	45306	1	45415	52	45686	5	45844	2
44866	7	45146	4	45307	4	45416	18	45689	1	45845	4
44867	4	45147	5	45308	17	45417	8	45690	27	45846	4
44870	77	45150	102	45309	44	45418	20	45692	11	45848	1
44871	1	45152	20	45311	33	45419	58	45693	18	45849	6
44875	46	45153	3	45312	10	45420	75	45694	25	45850	7
44878	1	45154	15	45314	13	45424	195	45695	1	45853	2
44880	7	45157	28	45315	7	45426	60	45696	1	45854	2
44882	5	45159	9	45316	2	45427	14	45697	4	45855	3
44883	68	45160	4	45317	6	45429	135	45701	70	45856	10
44887	3	45162	12	45318	20	45430	46	45710	6	45858	8
44889	8	45167	4	45320	52	45431	109	45711	1	45862	12
44890	25	45168	2	45321	2	45432	78	45714	46	45863	2
44895	1	45169	20	45322	63	45433	22	45715	7	45864	1
44902	3	45171	6	45323	38	45434	18	45719	4	45865	2
44903	97	45174	7	45324	146	45437	1	45721	1	45867	5
44904	49	45176	14	45325	16	45439	38	45723	10	45868	3
44905	41	45177	79	45326	2	45440	88	45724	3	45869	10
44906	52	45201	2	45327	46	45449	72	45726	1	45871	8
44907	65	45202	9	45328	2	45458	35	45727	1	45872	13
45001	2	45203	2	45329	1	45459	163	45730	1	45874	3
45002	30	45204	7	45330	1	45462	1	45732	18	45875	18
45003	4	45205	25	45331	100	45469	2	45735	3	45876	2
45004	1	45206	8	45332	1	45502	45	45738	2	45877	6
45005	120	45207	11	45333	4	45503	76	45742	15	45879	30
45011	147	45208	56	45334	5	45504	51	45743	1	45880	4
45012	2	45209	14	45335	11	45505	47	45744	7	45881	6
45013	235	45210	17	45337	5	45506	25	45745	1	45882	7
45014	134	45211	118	45338	8	45521	1	45750	95	45883	3
45015	33	45212	39	45339	8	45523	1	45760	12	45885	26
45030	33	45213	39	45340	3	45601	137	45761	7	45887	10
45032	2	45214	12	45341	16	45612	4	45764	21	45889	3
45033	1	45215	99	45342	136	45613	6	45766	1	45890	1
45036	61	45216	16	45344	75	45614	6	45767	8	45891	63
45039	27	45217	18	45345	18	45616	2	45768	3	45893	1
45040	89	45218	24	45346	2	45619	13	45769	24	45894	2
45041	1	45219	30	45347	9	45620	3	45771	1	45895	26
45042	120	45220	40	45349	6	45621	1	45772	4	45896	2
45044	88	45222	1	45352	4	45623	7	45773	2	45898	3
45050	19	45223	10	45354	5	45628	9	45776	4	45899	3
45052	8	45224	73	45356	83	45629	3	45778	1	45901	1
45053	5	45225	4	45358	4	45630	3	45779	2	45924	1
45054	5	45226	8	45359	4	45631	39	45780	10	45929	2
45056	79	45227	42	45362	3	45634	2	45781	2	45985	1
45061	2	45229	17	45363	1	45636	2	45783	2	46001	39
45062	5	45230	133	45365	66	45638	51	45784	4	46011	66
45064	15	45231	136	45368	8	45640	40	45786	5	46012	69
45065	3	45232	3	45369	7	45644	5	45788	5	46013	52
45066	50	45233	23	45370	24	45645	1	45801	65	46014	22
45067	33	45236	92	45371	72	45647	1	45802	1	46015	2
45068	39	45237	35	45373	120	45648	21	45804	37	46016	11
45069	113	45238	157	45377	73	45651	7	45805	49	46017	13
45070	1	45239	134	45378	6	45652	7	45806	56	46018	2
45089	1	45240	86	45380	6	45653	5	45807	32	46030	9
45101	8	45241	88	45381	17	45656	13	45809	5	46031	4
45102	26	45242	77	45382	8	45657	6	45810	14	46032	122
45103	60	45243	64	45383	30	45658	1	45812	4	46033	10
45106	29	45244	86	45384	4	45659	1	45813	1	46034	13
45107	23	45245	43	45385	186	45660	32	45814	10	46035	4
45110	1	45246	37	45387	35	45661	4	45817	16	46036	35
45111	1	45247	63	45388	1	45662	108	45820	1	46038	34
45113	6	45248	48	45390	4	45663	5	45821	4	46039	3
45118	10	45249	15	45401	2	45669	22	45822	29	46040	29
45119	3	45251	20	45402	2	45671	1	45827	2	46041	53
45120	8	45252	5	45403	25	45672	3	45828	5	46044	16

46047	1	46184	20	46374	4	46619	31	46816	38	47024	4
46049	3	46186	1	46375	28	46624	1	46818	33	47025	29
46050	8	46201	47	46377	1	46625	3	46819	31	47030	2
46051	7	46202	14	46379	1	46628	43	46825	88	47031	20
46052	49	46203	66	46382	1	46635	12	46835	73	47032	4
46055	16	46204	2	46383	146	46637	37	46845	19	47034	1
46056	9	46205	30	46384	3	46656	1	46850	1	47036	2
46057	4	46206	6	46390	4	46701	20	46851	1	47037	22
46058	1	46208	63	46391	16	46702	16	46856	1	47038	1
46060	89	46214	25	46392	16	46703	45	46862	2	47039	1
46063	1	46216	3	46393	1	46704	1	46863	1	47040	4
46064	20	46217	41	46394	26	46705	1	46885	3	47041	11
46065	6	46218	34	46401	3	46706	60	46896	1	47042	24
46068	14	46219	124	46402	1	46710	5	46898	2	47043	8
46069	16	46220	123	46403	11	46711	21	46901	181	47060	15
46070	16	46221	9	46404	6	46713	1	46902	171	47102	4
46071	10	46222	50	46405	27	46714	28	46904	1	47105	1
46072	19	46223	1	46406	6	46721	13	46910	4	47106	6
46074	21	46224	90	46407	5	46723	25	46911	5	47108	5
46075	3	46225	8	46408	33	46725	84	46913	5	47111	18
46076	14	46226	110	46409	10	46730	1	46914	7	47112	19
46077	47	46227	126	46410	65	46731	1	46915	1	47115	4
46102	1	46229	50	46419	1	46732	6	46916	1	47117	9
46104	4	46231	13	46421	1	46733	44	46917	7	47118	4
46105	2	46234	41	46501	9	46737	17	46919	11	47119	20
46106	5	46236	62	46502	1	46738	16	46920	4	47120	2
46107	25	46237	39	46504	1	46740	8	46923	7	47122	16
46110	1	46239	35	46506	36	46741	7	46926	3	47125	3
46112	52	46240	70	46507	7	46742	7	46928	23	47126	9
46113	14	46241	71	46508	1	46743	2	46929	5	47129	10
46115	5	46244	1	46510	2	46745	5	46930	2	47130	104
46116	1	46247	1	46511	21	46746	3	46932	13	47135	1
46118	9	46250	48	46514	106	46747	4	46933	15	47136	10
46120	13	46251	3	46515	4	46748	15	46936	30	47138	5
46121	4	46253	1	46516	49	46750	118	46937	2	47140	5
46122	31	46254	47	46517	48	46755	21	46938	6	47143	7
46124	13	46256	71	46524	6	46759	1	46939	4	47145	8
46125	1	46259	13	46526	110	46760	2	46940	10	47147	2
46126	8	46260	77	46530	38	46761	11	46941	3	47150	84
46127	4	46268	40	46531	4	46763	3	46947	72	47151	1
46128	4	46276	1	46532	4	46764	4	46951	1	47161	4
46130	9	46277	1	46534	25	46765	22	46952	84	47164	4
46131	49	46278	13	46536	6	46766	4	46953	50	47165	11
46133	1	46280	24	46538	11	46767	10	46957	2	47167	49
46135	30	46284	1	46539	4	46770	5	46958	1	47170	14
46140	99	46302	1	46540	11	46773	7	46960	4	47172	21
46142	88	46303	15	46542	9	46774	47	46962	12	47175	1
46143	35	46304	63	46543	4	46776	3	46967	2	47177	3
46144	1	46307	68	46544	94	46777	16	46970	54	47201	84
46147	1	46310	20	46545	34	46779	8	46971	4	47202	3
46148	15	46311	43	46550	31	46780	1	46974	1	47203	38
46149	9	46312	11	46552	37	46781	2	46975	32	47220	1
46150	2	46319	35	46553	10	46783	14	46977	1	47223	3
46151	96	46320	20	46554	16	46784	2	46978	5	47224	1
46154	1	46321	66	46555	5	46785	7	46979	25	47229	3
46156	1	46322	46	46556	2	46787	12	46982	12	47230	3
46157	11	46323	52	46561	32	46788	6	46984	1	47231	2
46158	40	46324	53	46562	20	46791	2	46985	4	47232	8
46160	9	46325	1	46563	45	46792	5	46986	7	47234	5
46161	6	46327	24	46565	7	46793	7	46987	2	47240	32
46162	3	46340	1	46567	18	46794	3	46988	1	47241	1
46163	22	46341	26	46570	1	46795	17	46989	10	47243	18
46164	13	46342	46	46571	6	46797	11	46990	2	47246	11
46165	2	46346	1	46573	9	46798	1	46991	2	47250	39
46166	3	46347	5	46574	19	46799	1	46992	29	47260	3
46167	7	46349	4	46580	105	46802	7	46994	14	47265	15
46168	79	46350	113	46581	2	46803	16	46995	2	47270	1
46172	1	46356	22	46590	23	46804	99	46996	14	47272	3
46173	36	46360	105	46601	2	46805	73	47001	19	47273	1
46175	1	46365	6	46613	19	46806	74	47006	13	47274	42
46176	72	46366	11	46614	84	46807	58	47012	23	47280	4
46180	1	46368	72	46615	57	46808	57	47018	12	47281	1
46181	10	46371	13	46616	16	46809	42	47022	4	47283	15
46182	9	46373	14	46617	26	46815	166	47023	2	47302	77

47303	55	47452	12	47708	1	47948	3	48046	2	48131	11
47304	89	47453	3	47710	45	47949	5	48047	33	48133	10
47305	8	47454	21	47711	99	47950	1	48048	6	48134	36
47306	1	47459	8	47712	64	47951	2	48049	6	48135	81
47307	1	47460	21	47713	9	47952	3	48050	35	48137	12
47312	1	47462	7	47714	67	47954	5	48051	19	48138	25
47320	7	47467	1	47715	56	47955	5	48053	13	48139	4
47324	1	47468	4	47719	2	47957	2	48054	35	48140	6
47326	2	47469	4	47720	10	47959	5	48055	22	48141	18
47327	7	47470	3	47724	1	47960	33	48056	3	48142	1
47329	1	47471	6	47731	1	47963	1	48057	9	48144	26
47330	15	47501	23	47732	1	47965	3	48058	8	48145	6
47331	95	47512	15	47802	77	47967	1	48059	18	48146	53
47334	15	47513	3	47803	61	47968	2	48060	127	48150	76
47335	2	47516	9	47804	25	47969	1	48061	1	48151	4
47336	19	47520	7	47805	50	47970	2	48062	20	48152	77
47338	10	47522	3	47807	17	47971	3	48063	79	48154	147
47340	7	47523	7	47808	7	47974	7	48064	25	48157	1
47341	9	47528	2	47830	2	47975	1	48065	35	48158	17
47342	6	47529	7	47831	1	47977	2	48066	77	48159	9
47345	8	47532	2	47832	4	47978	8	48067	65	48160	27
47346	14	47537	2	47833	2	47980	3	48068	4	48161	121
47348	17	47542	15	47834	43	47981	4	48069	4	48164	9
47352	3	47545	2	47837	2	47982	3	48070	32	48165	10
47353	12	47546	23	47838	3	47986	2	48071	45	48166	14
47354	2	47550	1	47840	1	47987	12	48072	59	48167	67
47355	11	47553	9	47841	7	47989	1	48073	83	48169	42
47356	25	47557	2	47842	15	47990	7	48074	11	48170	118
47357	5	47558	2	47846	6	47991	2	48075	38	48173	30
47358	2	47559	1	47848	10	47992	3	48076	71	48174	37
47359	5	47561	5	47849	1	47993	2	48077	66	48175	3
47360	1	47562	4	47850	8	47994	1	48078	62	48176	56
47362	81	47564	1	47851	1	47995	2	48079	30	48177	1
47363	1	47567	33	47852	1	47997	1	48080	48	48178	56
47366	4	47568	1	47853	1	48001	23	48081	40	48179	6
47368	11	47573	2	47854	1	48002	6	48082	47	48180	96
47369	2	47574	1	47855	1	48003	13	48083	43	48182	49
47371	32	47575	2	47857	1	48004	2	48084	39	48183	110
47373	4	47577	1	47861	3	48005	12	48085	32	48184	23
47374	136	47579	2	47862	3	48006	6	48087	63	48185	146
47375	3	47581	32	47863	1	48008	7	48088	30	48187	87
47380	6	47585	4	47866	2	48009	52	48089	46	48188	34
47382	2	47586	14	47868	8	48010	47	48090	1	48189	37
47383	1	47591	95	47871	1	48013	51	48091	39	48190	2
47384	2	47597	6	47872	8	48014	4	48092	47	48191	6
47385	7	47598	12	47874	5	48015	13	48093	107	48192	81
47386	1	47601	27	47875	3	48016	40	48094	21	48194	1
47387	2	47610	21	47876	3	48017	31	48095	30	48195	53
47388	1	47611	2	47877	1	48018	108	48096	10	48197	94
47390	7	47613	4	47878	1	48019	13	48097	15	48198	49
47393	4	47615	1	47879	3	48020	21	48098	76	48201	6
47394	23	47616	1	47882	18	48021	57	48099	5	48202	9
47396	26	47617	2	47885	33	48022	4	48101	60	48203	15
47401	164	47619	2	47901	8	48023	7	48103	130	48204	8
47402	8	47620	23	47902	4	48024	54	48104	82	48205	45
47403	24	47630	72	47904	33	48025	19	48105	89	48206	7
47404	16	47631	1	47905	136	48026	28	48106	5	48207	3
47406	3	47633	2	47906	132	48027	15	48107	3	48208	2
47407	2	47634	15	47907	3	48029	10	48108	18	48209	24
47408	14	47635	27	47917	1	48030	33	48109	4	48210	15
47421	78	47637	6	47918	7	48031	29	48111	62	48211	1
47424	28	47638	13	47920	10	48032	7	48116	80	48212	14
47429	13	47639	5	47921	2	48033	76	48117	26	48213	8
47431	5	47640	1	47923	5	48034	60	48118	29	48214	14
47432	4	47648	4	47925	1	48035	51	48120	5	48215	2
47433	7	47649	14	47926	1	48036	10	48121	1	48217	2
47436	6	47654	1	47928	4	48038	5	48122	19	48218	7
47438	11	47660	14	47932	21	48039	11	48123	2	48219	52
47441	25	47665	8	47933	90	48040	25	48124	96	48220	47
47443	3	47666	2	47940	13	48041	4	48125	46	48221	16
47446	28	47670	39	47941	1	48042	58	48126	47	48223	32
47448	16	47676	1	47942	1	48043	81	48127	85	48224	56
47449	2	47683	1	47944	6	48044	45	48128	38	48225	28
47451	6	47706	2	47946	1	48045	75	48130	29	48226	3

48227	13	48415	8	48615	7	48759	2	48889	6	49076	4
48228	50	48416	5	48616	5	48761	5	48890	4	49077	4
48229	6	48417	3	48617	10	48762	4	48891	6	49078	19
48230	58	48418	14	48618	11	48763	17	48892	7	49079	46
48234	15	48419	8	48619	2	48766	3	48893	12	49080	28
48235	24	48420	42	48621	5	48767	1	48895	24	49081	22
48236	94	48421	9	48622	15	48768	17	48897	3	49082	18
48237	50	48422	12	48623	10	48770	5	48901	3	49083	27
48238	10	48423	82	48624	53	48801	40	48906	61	49084	1
48239	82	48426	1	48625	23	48804	1	48907	1	49085	120
48240	49	48427	13	48626	12	48805	4	48910	88	49087	5
48242	1	48428	7	48627	2	48806	4	48911	38	49088	6
48260	1	48429	28	48628	3	48807	1	48912	24	49090	45
48301	13	48430	80	48629	19	48808	7	48915	7	49091	43
48302	13	48432	3	48630	3	48809	28	48917	60	49093	38
48303	2	48433	81	48631	8	48811	3	48933	5	49094	6
48304	15	48434	4	48632	12	48812	1	49001	101	49095	2
48306	13	48435	6	48633	3	48813	47	49002	84	49096	2
48307	23	48436	10	48634	11	48815	1	49003	2	49097	19
48308	2	48438	8	48635	3	48817	8	49004	30	49098	20
48309	29	48439	118	48636	2	48818	9	49005	3	49099	15
48310	46	48440	2	48637	4	48819	1	49006	10	49101	10
48312	24	48441	6	48640	194	48820	22	49007	68	49102	5
48313	15	48442	49	48642	22	48821	26	49008	39	49103	64
48314	12	48444	13	48647	20	48822	6	49009	63	49104	4
48315	8	48446	46	48649	1	48823	73	49010	39	49106	10
48316	19	48449	16	48650	21	48825	4	49011	3	49107	19
48317	20	48450	9	48651	12	48826	2	49012	11	49111	8
48318	2	48451	25	48652	1	48827	37	49013	34	49112	31
48322	33	48453	7	48653	34	48829	6	49014	1	49113	2
48323	14	48454	1	48654	6	48831	6	49015	88	49117	12
48324	7	48455	18	48655	10	48832	2	49016	5	49120	100
48326	6	48456	1	48656	10	48834	1	49017	176	49125	3
48327	17	48457	17	48657	24	48835	1	49020	3	49126	2
48328	19	48458	43	48658	9	48836	21	49021	11	49127	50
48329	26	48460	6	48659	2	48837	40	49022	58	49128	7
48331	14	48461	14	48661	22	48838	46	49026	2	49129	2
48333	1	48462	19	48662	3	48840	21	49028	26	49130	6
48334	7	48463	13	48686	2	48841	2	49029	3	49201	99
48335	10	48464	3	48701	4	48842	43	49030	9	49202	38
48336	16	48466	1	48703	7	48843	92	49031	17	49203	103
48340	4	48467	6	48705	1	48844	2	49032	5	49204	4
48341	6	48468	2	48706	85	48845	3	49033	3	49220	3
48342	2	48471	10	48708	25	48846	16	49034	14	49221	138
48343	1	48472	3	48718	1	48847	13	49035	2	49224	22
48346	24	48473	76	48720	2	48848	16	49036	53	49227	2
48347	4	48474	1	48722	6	48849	4	49038	14	49228	12
48348	11	48475	2	48723	14	48850	11	49040	6	49229	8
48350	11	48476	1	48725	6	48851	6	49041	1	49230	19
48353	4	48477	1	48726	9	48853	1	49042	9	49232	2
48356	8	48501	2	48727	1	48854	37	49043	3	49233	3
48357	20	48502	1	48730	14	48856	2	49045	10	49234	10
48359	2	48503	62	48731	4	48857	4	49046	21	49235	8
48360	6	48504	89	48732	18	48858	39	49047	21	49236	6
48362	8	48505	23	48733	2	48859	1	49050	3	49237	6
48363	5	48506	72	48734	14	48860	2	49051	6	49238	2
48370	1	48507	91	48737	7	48861	5	49052	3	49240	14
48371	8	48509	27	48738	1	48864	47	49053	11	49241	9
48374	2	48519	26	48739	8	48865	5	49055	20	49242	17
48375	9	48529	19	48740	5	48866	14	49056	8	49245	8
48377	3	48532	23	48741	9	48867	61	49057	7	49246	8
48380	17	48552	2	48742	1	48871	2	49058	25	49247	9
48381	17	48554	1	48743	1	48872	13	49060	10	49248	4
48382	23	48601	30	48744	5	48875	19	49061	2	49249	8
48383	15	48602	72	48745	1	48876	8	49062	1	49250	13
48386	17	48603	108	48746	11	48877	3	49064	17	49251	14
48387	9	48604	22	48747	1	48879	19	49065	16	49252	7
48390	14	48607	1	48748	5	48880	13	49066	3	49253	9
48393	8	48609	4	48749	1	48881	7	49067	5	49254	8
48401	5	48610	12	48750	16	48883	11	49068	30	49255	3
48407	1	48611	7	48753	3	48884	8	49070	8	49256	10
48412	8	48612	20	48755	8	48885	3	49071	14	49259	3
48413	33	48613	3	48756	9	48886	5	49072	3	49261	1
48414	5	48614	1	48757	1	48888	12	49073	13	49263	1

49264	4	49412	24	49633	6	49746	3	49891	2	50054	3
49265	10	49415	5	49634	1	49747	2	49892	6	50055	1
49266	3	49416	1	49635	6	49749	10	49894	4	50058	9
49267	7	49417	86	49636	3	49751	4	49895	4	50060	4
49268	1	49418	51	49637	9	49753	1	49896	1	50061	4
49269	8	49419	12	49638	1	49755	4	49901	2	50062	2
49270	15	49420	6	49639	3	49756	7	49902	2	50063	4
49271	1	49421	18	49640	3	49757	1	49903	1	50064	1
49272	12	49423	119	49642	1	49759	6	49905	5	50065	3
49274	7	49424	36	49643	11	49761	1	49908	3	50068	2
49275	1	49425	10	49644	4	49762	3	49911	4	50069	3
49276	3	49426	32	49645	3	49764	2	49912	1	50070	4
49277	20	49428	62	49646	19	49765	2	49913	62	50072	7
49278	1	49429	1	49647	2	49766	6	49915	1	50073	1
49279	4	49431	60	49648	5	49768	1	49916	8	50074	1
49281	1	49434	1	49649	5	49769	7	49918	3	50075	3
49283	7	49435	10	49650	2	49770	32	49919	1	50076	2
49284	9	49436	5	49651	20	49774	3	49920	19	50101	1
49285	10	49437	17	49653	6	49776	1	49921	4	50105	2
49286	39	49440	2	49654	4	49777	2	49922	9	50106	4
49287	3	49441	101	49655	2	49778	1	49925	1	50107	9
49288	4	49442	61	49656	5	49779	13	49927	4	50109	1
49301	28	49444	46	49657	1	49780	4	49929	1	50110	1
49302	14	49445	45	49659	13	49781	8	49930	27	50111	6
49303	2	49446	3	49660	27	49782	3	49931	33	50112	22
49304	4	49447	1	49663	8	49783	41	49934	5	50115	5
49305	4	49448	6	49664	4	49788	2	49935	21	50118	5
49306	21	49449	15	49665	6	49790	1	49938	14	50119	1
49307	41	49450	6	49667	3	49791	1	49942	5	50122	1
49309	1	49451	1	49668	7	49793	2	49943	1	50123	1
49310	6	49452	1	49670	8	49795	11	49945	9	50124	2
49314	1	49453	6	49674	3	49797	1	49946	12	50125	33
49315	13	49454	8	49675	1	49799	3	49947	2	50126	2
49316	24	49455	12	49676	7	49801	60	49948	1	50128	2
49318	4	49456	55	49677	10	49806	1	49950	3	50129	6
49319	25	49457	13	49679	3	49807	8	49953	14	50130	6
49320	2	49459	1	49680	1	49810	1	49955	5	50131	8
49321	31	49460	7	49682	5	49812	1	49958	4	50132	1
49322	2	49461	33	49683	5	49814	1	49959	3	50134	2
49323	12	49464	34	49684	210	49815	1	49961	2	50135	1
49325	5	49501	4	49685	1	49816	3	49963	1	50136	1
49326	14	49503	25	49688	9	49817	1	49964	7	50138	21
49327	6	49504	120	49689	3	49821	1	49965	3	50140	10
49328	7	49505	122	49690	19	49825	2	49967	1	50141	6
49329	4	49506	78	49701	12	49827	6	49968	2	50144	4
49330	11	49507	46	49705	1	49829	55	49969	3	50148	3
49331	32	49508	151	49706	10	49833	1	49970	4	50149	3
49332	3	49509	139	49707	45	49835	7	49971	2	50151	5
49333	25	49510	1	49709	18	49836	1	50003	3	50152	1
49335	1	49512	7	49710	1	49837	50	50005	3	50153	1
49336	5	49516	1	49711	1	49839	3	50006	2	50155	1
49337	49	49518	1	49712	12	49840	2	50007	1	50156	11
49338	3	49528	1	49715	9	49841	20	50009	16	50158	99
49339	1	49546	18	49716	2	49843	24	50010	137	50160	3
49340	7	49548	26	49717	1	49847	2	50011	2	50161	1
49341	68	49601	37	49718	2	49849	52	50013	5	50162	1
49342	4	49612	4	49719	3	49851	3	50020	4	50163	3
49343	7	49613	2	49720	28	49853	4	50021	61	50164	1
49344	7	49614	3	49721	24	49854	18	50022	23	50167	1
49345	25	49615	13	49722	1	49855	103	50025	9	50168	2
49346	12	49616	4	49724	1	49858	29	50026	3	50169	7
49347	3	49617	1	49725	5	49862	10	50028	1	50170	4
49348	22	49618	1	49726	4	49866	24	50029	3	50171	7
49349	19	49619	2	49727	11	49868	19	50030	1	50172	1
49355	1	49620	2	49728	2	49870	5	50032	1	50173	2
49401	22	49621	7	49729	7	49871	3	50035	3	50174	2
49402	2	49622	11	49730	3	49873	1	50036	50	50201	11
49403	1	49625	5	49733	3	49876	1	50039	2	50207	5
49404	17	49626	1	49735	63	49878	17	50042	1	50208	27
49405	3	49628	3	49736	1	49879	2	50044	1	50210	3
49408	19	49629	8	49738	36	49883	2	50047	11	50211	18
49409	2	49630	2	49740	21	49885	2	50049	36	50212	13
49410	9	49631	4	49743	3	49887	5	50050	1	50213	5
49411	6	49632	1	49745	1	49889	4	50051	1	50216	4

50217	1	50448	1	50612	1	51007	1	51364	1	52032	1
50219	28	50450	10	50613	87	51008	1	51365	1	52033	5
50220	14	50453	2	50616	18	51010	4	51366	4	52037	1
50222	1	50456	3	50617	1	51011	1	51401	12	52039	1
50225	2	50458	4	50621	6	51012	19	51436	2	52040	1
50226	5	50459	11	50622	8	51016	8	51439	1	52041	1
50228	2	50461	8	50624	1	51019	1	51440	1	52042	1
50229	2	50464	1	50625	2	51023	6	51442	12	52045	4
50230	1	50466	2	50627	6	51024	11	51443	1	52049	1
50231	1	50468	2	50628	3	51025	5	51445	2	52052	6
50232	2	50469	4	50629	2	51026	4	51446	1	52057	9
50233	1	50470	4	50630	4	51027	1	51448	1	52060	13
50234	3	50471	2	50631	1	51030	4	51450	2	52062	1
50235	1	50472	2	50632	3	51031	17	51453	4	52064	2
50236	4	50476	1	50635	3	51033	1	51454	1	52068	3
50237	1	50478	2	50636	2	51034	5	51455	6	52069	2
50238	2	50479	1	50637	2	51035	1	51458	4	52070	2
50240	3	50480	2	50638	5	51036	1	51461	3	52073	5
50242	1	50484	1	50641	5	51037	1	51462	1	52076	3
50243	1	50501	61	50643	4	51038	1	51463	1	52077	1
50244	2	50510	2	50644	19	51039	7	51465	2	52078	1
50247	5	50511	8	50645	8	51040	2	51466	2	52101	12
50248	8	50514	3	50647	2	51041	8	51467	1	52133	1
50249	6	50515	5	50648	8	51046	3	51501	93	52134	4
50250	3	50516	3	50650	3	51049	1	51503	41	52136	27
50252	2	50517	3	50651	11	51050	4	51510	3	52141	3
50254	1	50520	4	50653	3	51052	3	51521	3	52146	2
50256	1	50522	2	50654	1	51054	8	51525	1	52151	3
50257	2	50523	3	50658	9	51055	1	51526	2	52155	2
50258	1	50524	1	50659	8	51057	1	51527	1	52156	1
50259	1	50525	9	50660	1	51058	2	51529	1	52157	2
50261	5	50528	2	50662	16	51061	1	51530	1	52159	3
50263	7	50529	4	50665	3	51062	2	51533	1	52161	2
50265	58	50530	3	50666	1	51063	2	51534	17	52162	4
50268	1	50532	4	50667	5	51101	1	51535	10	52170	1
50272	2	50533	8	50668	2	51102	3	51537	5	52172	9
50273	17	50535	1	50669	4	51103	36	51540	5	52175	2
50274	3	50536	12	50670	6	51104	67	51541	1	52201	1
50276	4	50538	1	50671	1	51105	12	51542	1	52203	1
50277	1	50540	1	50672	1	51106	77	51546	3	52205	27
50278	1	50541	4	50674	2	51107	1	51548	1	52206	6
50302	1	50542	4	50675	3	51108	13	51551	4	52208	9
50306	3	50543	3	50677	14	51109	5	51553	3	52209	1
50309	8	50544	1	50681	1	51110	1	51555	9	52210	2
50310	95	50545	2	50682	4	51201	11	51556	4	52211	1
50311	42	50546	1	50701	69	51235	2	51557	2	52212	1
50312	32	50548	38	50702	30	51237	5	51558	5	52213	10
50313	37	50554	3	50703	15	51238	1	51559	2	52214	3
50314	6	50557	4	50706	1	51239	1	51560	9	52215	1
50315	61	50560	3	50707	12	51241	1	51561	4	52216	2
50316	20	50563	9	50801	22	51245	5	51563	1	52218	3
50317	73	50566	2	50830	4	51246	7	51566	9	52222	1
50320	12	50568	4	50833	12	51247	1	51570	3	52223	3
50321	8	50569	2	50834	3	51248	4	51571	1	52224	5
50322	74	50571	1	50835	2	51249	7	51573	3	52225	1
50323	1	50573	1	50836	2	51250	3	51575	1	52227	6
50325	3	50576	1	50837	1	51301	55	51576	4	52228	6
50393	1	50579	5	50841	7	51330	1	51577	1	52229	1
50394	1	50581	1	50846	1	51331	3	51579	6	52233	20
50401	76	50582	2	50847	1	51333	1	51601	25	52237	1
50421	4	50583	10	50849	16	51334	18	51631	4	52240	83
50423	2	50585	1	50851	4	51338	3	51632	28	52241	25
50424	1	50588	28	50853	2	51342	2	51636	1	52244	4
50428	21	50590	2	50854	5	51345	1	51638	2	52245	19
50430	1	50591	2	50858	1	51346	4	51640	1	52246	11
50432	4	50595	29	50859	6	51347	6	51645	1	52247	10
50434	1	50597	5	50860	1	51349	2	51647	3	52248	2
50435	1	50598	1	50864	5	51350	2	51652	1	52249	2
50436	10	50601	5	50875	1	51351	22	51653	1	52253	5
50438	7	50602	1	51001	10	51354	2	51654	5	52254	2
50440	2	50604	2	51002	6	51355	1	52001	105	52255	2
50441	5	50605	2	51003	2	51357	2	52002	5	52257	1
50444	2	50608	1	51004	1	51358	1	52003	9	52300	1
50447	1	50609	1	51006	1	51360	22	52004	1	52301	6

52302	182	52575	2	52807	18	53101	1	53219	64	53580	1
52305	3	52577	22	52808	2	53103	16	53220	50	53581	16
52306	2	52580	2	52809	4	53104	8	53221	80	53582	1
52307	1	52585	1	52866	1	53105	36	53222	53	53583	10
52308	1	52588	1	53002	6	53108	8	53223	62	53585	2
52310	9	52590	2	53004	1	53110	20	53224	26	53586	2
52312	2	52591	2	53005	113	53114	5	53225	34	53588	2
52313	2	52594	1	53006	3	53115	32	53226	40	53589	23
52314	14	52595	6	53007	8	53118	15	53227	53	53590	40
52315	4	52601	226	53010	4	53119	6	53228	33	53593	30
52316	3	52619	1	53011	4	53120	9	53233	9	53594	4
52317	10	52620	1	53012	73	53121	24	53295	1	53597	18
52318	2	52621	2	53013	3	53122	18	53312	1	53598	3
52320	4	52623	8	53014	6	53125	7	53401	1	53629	1
52322	1	52625	4	53015	5	53126	18	53402	76	53701	4
52323	3	52626	1	53016	1	53127	1	53403	49	53703	17
52324	8	52627	54	53017	12	53128	4	53404	22	53704	87
52327	5	52630	1	53018	10	53129	39	53405	58	53705	93
52328	14	52632	28	53019	3	53130	30	53406	44	53706	7
52330	3	52637	4	53020	8	53132	39	53429	1	53711	148
52332	6	52638	12	53021	5	53137	1	53502	4	53713	40
52333	16	52639	3	53022	24	53139	3	53503	3	53714	40
52336	7	52640	1	53023	1	53140	56	53506	1	53715	20
52337	2	52641	45	53024	57	53141	4	53507	2	53716	46
52338	3	52644	4	53027	21	53142	71	53508	2	53717	11
52339	11	52645	6	53029	25	53143	8	53510	2	53719	14
52341	8	52647	2	53032	11	53144	10	53511	87	53801	2
52342	13	52649	3	53033	8	53146	7	53515	3	53803	2
52343	1	52653	7	53035	4	53147	25	53516	2	53804	1
52344	2	52654	2	53036	2	53149	22	53517	5	53805	1
52345	2	52655	24	53037	6	53150	31	53518	3	53806	3
52346	1	52656	3	53038	2	53151	81	53520	7	53807	2
52349	29	52658	4	53039	9	53153	1	53521	5	53809	5
52350	1	52659	2	53040	4	53154	35	53522	1	53810	1
52352	3	52660	2	53042	4	53156	4	53523	7	53813	7
52353	8	52720	4	53044	6	53157	1	53525	8	53818	19
52356	4	52721	2	53045	4	53159	3	53527	11	53820	1
52357	2	52722	76	53046	1	53168	17	53528	16	53821	3
52358	6	52726	12	53048	2	53170	4	53530	1	53824	1
52361	6	52727	1	53050	7	53171	1	53531	6	53826	1
52401	34	52728	3	53051	64	53172	60	53532	13	53901	24
52402	244	52730	7	53052	1	53177	11	53533	1	53910	4
52403	97	52732	116	53056	1	53178	4	53534	10	53911	6
52404	50	52738	3	53057	3	53179	4	53536	8	53913	40
52405	91	52739	1	53058	7	53181	5	53537	3	53916	43
52406	3	52742	16	53059	4	53182	8	53538	37	53919	4
52407	1	52746	3	53060	2	53183	7	53540	1	53922	4
52408	1	52747	1	53061	11	53184	8	53541	1	53924	1
52501	104	52748	24	53063	2	53185	19	53544	2	53925	8
52530	1	52749	1	53064	1	53186	125	53545	77	53929	1
52531	8	52750	1	53065	2	53187	1	53546	15	53930	2
52533	7	52751	3	53066	42	53188	70	53547	1	53931	1
52535	5	52752	2	53069	1	53190	11	53549	7	53932	1
52537	18	52753	12	53070	9	53191	2	53550	3	53933	6
52540	3	52755	1	53072	22	53192	1	53551	16	53934	17
52544	12	52756	5	53073	14	53193	2	53553	2	53936	3
52548	2	52757	1	53074	26	53201	7	53555	23	53941	1
52550	3	52759	1	53075	2	53202	17	53557	1	53942	1
52551	4	52760	6	53076	8	53203	1	53558	23	53943	1
52552	2	52761	86	53078	5	53204	16	53559	18	53944	2
52553	1	52766	2	53079	1	53205	2	53560	3	53946	10
52554	5	52767	1	53080	16	53206	13	53561	2	53947	1
52556	53	52768	7	53081	81	53207	86	53562	54	53948	18
52557	1	52769	2	53083	22	53208	26	53563	23	53949	6
52561	3	52772	10	53085	26	53209	58	53565	5	53950	8
52563	3	52773	7	53086	7	53210	29	53566	19	53951	1
52565	1	52776	3	53089	24	53211	51	53570	3	53952	11
52567	1	52777	3	53091	3	53212	16	53572	18	53954	14
52568	1	52778	6	53092	67	53213	68	53573	2	53955	15
52569	1	52801	1	53093	2	53214	68	53574	6	53956	8
52570	1	52802	18	53094	41	53215	43	53575	25	53959	13
52571	5	52803	58	53095	68	53216	31	53576	3	53960	6
52572	1	52804	67	53099	1	53217	87	53578	4	53963	20
52574	3	52806	77	53100	1	53218	58	53579	3	53964	5

53965	14	54201	6	54459	4	54619	3	54770	7	54947	1
53968	2	54202	4	54460	1	54621	2	54771	7	54949	4
53969	1	54205	1	54462	1	54622	1	54773	9	54950	1
54001	9	54206	2	54463	1	54623	2	54786	1	54952	40
54002	9	54208	3	54466	11	54624	1	54801	13	54956	61
54003	2	54209	2	54467	19	54625	1	54805	1	54960	1
54004	2	54210	2	54468	1	54626	2	54806	28	54961	9
54005	2	54211	3	54469	5	54627	3	54808	1	54962	5
54006	3	54212	4	54470	1	54628	1	54810	4	54963	9
54009	3	54213	1	54471	2	54629	2	54812	6	54964	1
54011	6	54215	2	54473	4	54630	1	54814	13	54965	3
54012	1	54216	15	54474	12	54631	3	54817	4	54966	2
54013	4	54217	2	54475	5	54634	9	54819	1	54968	5
54014	5	54220	85	54476	36	54635	4	54820	1	54970	6
54016	53	54221	1	54479	4	54636	12	54821	7	54971	14
54017	10	54227	2	54480	1	54639	1	54822	5	54974	3
54020	3	54228	3	54481	106	54642	2	54826	1	54977	3
54021	2	54234	5	54484	5	54645	1	54827	2	54979	4
54022	39	54235	50	54485	4	54646	8	54828	2	54981	33
54023	11	54240	1	54486	2	54648	1	54829	7	54982	11
54024	16	54241	30	54487	64	54650	51	54830	4	54983	1
54025	5	54245	1	54490	2	54651	2	54835	1	54984	7
54026	4	54246	7	54493	1	54653	2	54836	2	54985	1
54027	1	54247	1	54494	91	54655	2	54837	5	54986	7
54028	2	54301	63	54495	1	54656	17	54838	5	55001	12
54082	6	54302	43	54498	1	54658	5	54840	6	55002	1
54101	1	54303	55	54499	5	54660	26	54843	22	55003	4
54102	4	54304	59	54501	90	54661	4	54845	1	55005	7
54103	1	54305	2	54512	3	54664	1	54847	3	55006	3
54104	7	54306	1	54513	1	54665	5	54848	12	55007	6
54106	5	54307	1	54514	8	54666	2	54849	7	55008	19
54107	6	54311	12	54517	1	54667	1	54850	2	55009	20
54110	5	54313	26	54519	3	54669	6	54854	1	55010	2
54111	5	54401	142	54520	4	54670	2	54855	1	55011	15
54112	1	54402	2	54521	30	54701	106	54856	2	55012	2
54113	4	54404	1	54524	2	54702	3	54858	1	55013	7
54114	6	54405	5	54526	2	54703	63	54859	7	55014	37
54115	34	54406	1	54527	5	54705	1	54864	2	55016	56
54120	1	54407	3	54529	6	54720	17	54868	20	55017	1
54121	8	54408	2	54531	2	54721	2	54870	3	55019	1
54124	8	54409	34	54533	1	54722	5	54871	5	55020	1
54125	1	54410	5	54534	4	54723	1	54872	3	55021	33
54126	5	54411	2	54538	8	54724	12	54873	6	55024	21
54128	1	54412	5	54539	9	54725	7	54874	10	55025	51
54129	6	54414	4	54540	2	54727	1	54876	3	55026	2
54130	32	54416	3	54541	1	54728	20	54880	87	55027	4
54135	4	54418	6	54542	1	54729	135	54888	6	55030	1
54136	5	54420	2	54545	1	54730	13	54890	1	55031	5
54138	1	54421	6	54547	3	54731	2	54891	4	55032	1
54139	2	54422	1	54548	18	54732	3	54893	10	55033	34
54140	11	54423	9	54550	3	54736	5	54894	1	55037	4
54141	3	54424	8	54552	28	54738	11	54896	2	55038	16
54143	38	54425	7	54554	2	54739	3	54901	118	55040	10
54149	5	54426	3	54555	13	54740	2	54903	1	55041	11
54151	10	54427	2	54556	1	54741	2	54904	9	55042	12
54153	15	54432	1	54557	1	54742	4	54909	2	55043	6
54154	2	54433	4	54558	5	54744	2	54911	65	55044	32
54155	5	54435	3	54559	1	54745	4	54913	1	55045	7
54156	2	54436	1	54560	1	54748	12	54914	32	55046	2
54157	5	54437	2	54561	1	54749	5	54915	85	55047	6
54159	7	54440	1	54562	7	54750	2	54921	4	55051	33
54161	2	54441	1	54564	6	54751	64	54922	1	55052	1
54162	5	54442	3	54566	2	54754	1	54923	15	55053	1
54165	9	54443	9	54567	1	54755	8	54927	2	55055	8
54166	43	54446	5	54568	10	54756	2	54929	13	55056	15
54169	1	54447	4	54601	78	54757	4	54930	2	55057	28
54170	5	54448	1	54602	1	54758	4	54934	1	55060	53
54171	2	54449	59	54603	10	54759	3	54935	105	55063	7
54173	2	54451	18	54610	3	54760	2	54937	7	55065	3
54174	2	54452	39	54612	2	54762	1	54940	2	55066	21
54175	2	54454	1	54613	1	54763	2	54941	5	55068	34
54177	4	54455	22	54614	3	54766	6	54942	1	55069	7
54180	3	54456	7	54615	9	54767	1	54944	5	55070	8
54182	1	54457	17	54618	5	54768	4	54945	10	55071	10

55072	2	55338	1	55431	85	55767	15	55972	5	56115	2
55073	8	55339	2	55432	94	55768	10	55974	1	56116	1
55074	1	55340	10	55433	117	55769	6	55975	13	56119	1
55075	79	55342	5	55434	60	55771	4	55976	10	56125	2
55076	4	55343	141	55435	39	55772	1	55979	2	56127	1
55077	7	55344	58	55436	40	55773	3	55981	8	56128	2
55079	14	55345	58	55437	69	55775	7	55987	96	56129	2
55080	3	55346	22	55438	39	55779	11	55988	1	56130	1
55081	1	55347	19	55439	5	55781	2	55992	8	56131	1
55082	49	55349	1	55441	41	55782	1	56001	125	56133	1
55084	2	55350	13	55442	32	55783	2	56002	1	56134	5
55086	1	55352	11	55443	42	55784	1	56003	5	56138	2
55088	3	55353	1	55444	38	55786	1	56007	43	56139	2
55090	1	55354	1	55445	16	55790	13	56009	1	56142	5
55092	8	55355	17	55446	7	55792	19	56010	3	56143	6
55101	21	55356	24	55447	40	55793	3	56011	3	56144	1
55102	27	55357	3	55448	8	55796	1	56013	8	56145	1
55103	15	55358	4	55449	5	55797	1	56016	1	56149	1
55104	84	55359	10	55454	4	55801	2	56017	4	56150	4
55105	77	55360	1	55455	2	55802	8	56023	2	56151	1
55106	63	55362	14	55458	1	55803	55	56024	1	56155	1
55107	12	55364	38	55601	1	55804	45	56025	1	56156	5
55108	39	55368	2	55602	1	55805	24	56026	3	56157	2
55109	85	55369	86	55603	3	55806	26	56028	1	56158	2
55110	134	55370	2	55604	11	55807	20	56029	3	56159	5
55111	3	55371	14	55606	1	55808	16	56031	21	56162	1
55112	149	55372	33	55609	2	55810	24	56034	2	56164	6
55113	131	55373	4	55612	1	55811	89	56035	1	56168	3
55115	14	55374	17	55614	9	55812	22	56036	7	56169	1
55116	61	55375	2	55615	1	55816	3	56037	5	56171	1
55117	67	55376	10	55616	15	55820	1	56039	1	56172	3
55118	59	55378	18	55701	3	55901	209	56041	1	56173	1
55119	76	55379	23	55702	1	55902	51	56043	2	56175	7
55120	11	55382	5	55703	4	55903	5	56044	1	56178	6
55121	14	55384	1	55704	2	55904	75	56045	1	56179	2
55122	61	55387	9	55705	9	55906	23	56048	5	56180	1
55123	40	55388	2	55706	7	55909	1	56050	5	56181	2
55124	119	55389	2	55707	5	55910	1	56051	1	56187	38
55125	60	55390	2	55708	1	55912	55	56052	1	56201	59
55126	50	55391	44	55709	2	55917	2	56054	1	56208	3
55127	23	55395	2	55710	2	55918	2	56055	4	56209	10
55128	23	55396	1	55711	1	55920	14	56057	1	56211	3
55175	3	55397	4	55712	5	55921	5	56058	10	56215	11
55218	1	55398	9	55713	5	55923	1	56060	3	56218	1
55246	1	55401	6	55718	5	55924	5	56062	4	56219	1
55302	6	55402	3	55719	15	55925	1	56063	4	56220	4
55303	86	55403	15	55720	35	55926	2	56065	1	56221	2
55304	36	55404	14	55721	6	55927	5	56068	1	56222	1
55305	4	55405	30	55722	2	55929	3	56069	7	56223	1
55307	4	55406	71	55723	6	55932	3	56071	12	56225	1
55308	2	55407	39	55724	2	55934	5	56072	2	56228	2
55309	17	55408	25	55725	2	55936	1	56073	28	56229	2
55310	1	55409	34	55731	23	55939	2	56075	1	56231	1
55311	1	55410	48	55732	17	55940	1	56077	1	56232	2
55313	15	55411	21	55733	13	55941	4	56078	1	56233	4
55315	2	55412	29	55734	16	55942	1	56079	1	56240	2
55316	39	55413	13	55735	4	55943	6	56080	3	56241	5
55317	19	55414	29	55736	3	55944	7	56081	2	56244	1
55318	42	55415	1	55741	10	55946	1	56082	21	56249	1
55319	6	55416	70	55742	1	55947	15	56085	5	56250	2
55320	1	55417	76	55744	58	55951	8	56087	1	56251	3
55321	3	55418	59	55746	54	55952	2	56088	3	56252	9
55322	9	55419	43	55748	2	55955	1	56089	1	56253	3
55323	1	55420	92	55749	3	55956	3	56090	2	56256	3
55327	6	55421	61	55750	11	55957	2	56092	1	56257	1
55328	8	55422	70	55751	8	55959	4	56093	59	56258	42
55329	2	55423	111	55752	2	55960	25	56094	1	56264	10
55330	43	55424	19	55753	1	55961	1	56096	6	56265	9
55331	51	55425	13	55757	2	55963	9	56097	6	56266	2
55332	3	55426	56	55758	1	55964	2	56098	1	56267	4
55334	2	55427	72	55760	3	55965	4	56101	11	56270	1
55335	1	55428	55	55763	1	55967	1	56110	1	56271	3
55336	5	55429	62	55764	1	55969	2	56111	1	56273	6
55337	131	55430	49	55765	1	55971	4	56113	6	56274	1

56277	1	56452	5	56628	2	57033	4	57317	1	57633	1
56278	4	56453	1	56629	1	57036	1	57325	8	57639	1
56283	11	56458	2	56630	6	57038	6	57328	2	57642	3
56284	2	56461	4	56631	1	57039	9	57330	2	57652	1
56285	1	56464	10	56633	7	57040	2	57331	1	57653	1
56288	14	56465	6	56634	1	57042	11	57332	1	57701	124
56289	1	56466	3	56636	7	57043	3	57338	3	57702	47
56291	2	56467	9	56639	1	57045	1	57340	1	57706	10
56293	2	56468	10	56644	1	57046	2	57341	2	57707	1
56301	51	56469	2	56646	2	57049	2	57345	4	57709	11
56302	1	56470	32	56649	48	57051	1	57348	2	57717	6
56303	16	56472	15	56650	2	57054	1	57349	1	57718	12
56304	15	56473	3	56653	7	57057	1	57350	36	57719	8
56307	2	56474	8	56655	6	57058	4	57353	1	57720	2
56308	63	56477	4	56659	1	57059	1	57355	4	57722	1
56309	3	56479	9	56660	3	57061	1	57359	1	57730	10
56310	3	56481	5	56661	3	57062	4	57362	3	57732	7
56315	4	56482	7	56662	1	57064	2	57363	9	57735	3
56316	5	56484	16	56664	4	57065	1	57365	1	57741	2
56318	2	56485	1	56668	3	57066	3	57366	2	57744	2
56319	6	56501	28	56669	3	57067	2	57367	1	57745	8
56320	8	56510	5	56671	1	57068	2	57368	1	57747	69
56321	3	56511	1	56673	4	57069	34	57369	2	57751	3
56327	5	56514	5	56676	2	57070	2	57370	1	57754	11
56329	10	56515	7	56679	5	57071	7	57374	1	57759	1
56331	1	56517	1	56682	1	57075	1	57376	3	57762	1
56332	3	56520	17	56683	4	57076	1	57379	3	57763	1
56334	9	56522	1	56701	27	57078	30	57380	1	57764	1
56336	4	56524	4	56712	1	57101	4	57382	1	57766	1
56338	3	56528	3	56713	3	57102	1	57384	3	57769	6
56339	2	56529	8	56714	2	57103	45	57385	1	57783	13
56340	2	56531	10	56716	18	57104	22	57401	82	57785	18
56342	8	56534	2	56721	20	57105	57	57402	1	57793	4
56343	2	56535	2	56723	3	57106	42	57430	3	58001	6
56345	16	56537	72	56725	2	57107	6	57439	1	58004	2
56347	7	56538	1	56728	4	57197	1	57440	1	58006	1
56352	4	56540	7	56731	1	57201	72	57441	1	58008	1
56353	4	56542	5	56732	10	57212	3	57442	2	58011	1
56354	3	56544	5	56733	1	57213	2	57445	1	58012	2
56355	1	56547	1	56736	3	57216	2	57451	2	58015	1
56357	2	56549	3	56737	1	57218	1	57452	1	58017	1
56358	4	56551	5	56740	1	57221	1	57454	1	58018	1
56359	6	56552	5	56741	1	57223	6	57456	3	58021	1
56360	3	56553	1	56744	1	57224	6	57461	5	58022	1
56361	11	56554	5	56750	5	57225	9	57462	1	58027	2
56362	7	56556	2	56751	20	57226	7	57468	2	58032	1
56367	12	56560	84	56754	1	57231	2	57469	16	58038	2
56368	3	56567	4	56756	1	57234	5	57471	1	58041	1
56369	1	56568	1	56757	2	57236	3	57472	3	58042	14
56371	1	56569	1	56760	1	57237	5	57473	1	58047	6
56374	5	56570	3	56761	5	57239	1	57475	1	58049	3
56375	1	56571	5	56762	2	57241	3	57479	2	58051	5
56377	5	56572	15	56763	17	57243	2	57501	48	58052	2
56378	10	56573	4	57001	3	57248	2	57528	4	58053	1
56379	52	56574	1	57002	3	57251	3	57532	4	58054	6
56381	3	56575	1	57003	1	57252	13	57533	2	58060	5
56382	2	56576	3	57004	2	57255	1	57536	1	58062	1
56385	1	56578	1	57005	9	57257	1	57541	2	58063	3
56386	3	56579	2	57006	50	57262	8	57543	1	58068	1
56387	11	56580	2	57010	4	57263	1	57544	2	58072	14
56401	53	56581	1	57012	2	57266	2	57551	3	58075	18
56431	16	56584	2	57013	18	57268	1	57555	1	58078	20
56433	9	56585	2	57014	3	57272	6	57559	2	58081	2
56435	6	56586	2	57016	1	57273	1	57564	2	58102	119
56436	1	56588	2	57017	5	57274	9	57567	5	58103	95
56438	1	56589	1	57018	2	57276	5	57569	2	58104	5
56440	1	56592	2	57022	2	57278	1	57572	1	58105	3
56441	6	56593	2	57025	5	57279	10	57580	2	58107	3
56442	12	56594	3	57026	2	57301	26	57585	1	58108	2
56443	4	56601	86	57028	3	57310	1	57601	16	58109	1
56444	11	56621	3	57029	10	57311	4	57620	1	58201	81
56447	3	56623	11	57030	2	57313	1	57623	1	58202	1
56449	2	56626	1	57031	1	57314	4	57625	2	58203	17
56450	2	56627	3	57032	11	57315	2	57626	1	58204	10

58205	7	58429	1	58705	2	59104	3	59482	2	59840	45
58206	3	58431	1	58718	2	59105	36	59484	1	59841	4
58207	3	58433	5	58721	4	59106	20	59485	4	59844	3
58212	4	58436	9	58722	1	59107	1	59486	1	59846	2
58213	4	58438	2	58723	1	59108	1	59501	57	59847	14
58214	5	58440	2	58725	3	59201	32	59520	3	59851	2
58215	3	58443	1	58730	2	59217	2	59522	13	59854	2
58216	2	58448	1	58736	2	59218	1	59523	3	59855	1
58218	3	58455	2	58737	2	59221	1	59527	1	59858	2
58220	7	58456	1	58740	1	59222	1	59528	1	59859	5
58225	2	58458	1	58746	1	59223	3	59532	2	59860	16
58228	2	58460	6	58760	1	59225	1	59537	1	59864	10
58230	2	58461	2	58761	2	59226	2	59538	2	59865	2
58237	12	58463	2	58763	1	59230	13	59540	1	59867	1
58238	1	58464	2	58770	3	59231	1	59544	1	59868	2
58240	4	58466	1	58772	2	59240	1	59601	119	59870	20
58241	1	58468	1	58773	2	59247	4	59604	6	59872	5
58243	1	58471	1	58778	3	59248	4	59607	1	59873	4
58244	1	58474	1	58779	1	59250	1	59624	2	59874	6
58249	1	58478	3	58781	1	59252	1	59631	1	59875	7
58250	2	58479	1	58783	1	59253	1	59632	8	59901	84
58251	5	58483	1	58784	5	59254	10	59633	2	59903	5
58254	1	58488	1	58785	3	59255	2	59634	12	59910	6
58256	1	58492	4	58789	1	59258	2	59635	22	59911	17
58257	14	58496	1	58790	4	59259	2	59639	3	59912	24
58261	1	58497	1	58793	1	59261	4	59644	6	59913	1
58266	1	58501	168	58801	24	59262	8	59648	2	59917	7
58267	4	58502	7	58802	3	59263	4	59701	108	59918	2
58270	8	58504	25	58830	2	59270	25	59702	6	59919	2
58274	5	58505	1	58831	1	59274	1	59703	3	59920	3
58275	2	58523	5	58835	1	59276	3	59710	1	59922	6
58276	1	58529	1	58838	3	59301	41	59711	28	59923	40
58277	2	58530	6	58843	1	59313	10	59714	19	59926	1
58278	1	58532	2	58844	1	59317	2	59715	181	59928	1
58282	9	58533	1	58852	1	59323	29	59716	1	59930	1
58301	29	58535	4	58854	2	59327	24	59721	2	59931	1
58310	1	58538	1	58856	1	59330	33	59722	6	59932	7
58317	1	58540	4	59001	8	59336	1	59725	13	59934	4
58318	7	58545	3	59002	1	59349	4	59728	2	59935	6
58323	1	58547	1	59003	3	59351	2	59729	7	59936	3
58324	5	58552	5	59014	1	59353	4	59735	1	59937	22
58327	2	58554	30	59015	2	59401	51	59740	1	60001	1
58328	1	58558	2	59019	5	59402	5	59741	9	60002	25
58329	2	58561	4	59021	9	59403	8	59749	4	60004	196
58341	3	58563	9	59022	1	59404	48	59750	1	60005	71
58344	3	58565	1	59024	1	59405	75	59752	3	60006	1
58345	1	58570	1	59026	1	59406	4	59756	1	60007	108
58346	1	58577	1	59027	7	59412	5	59758	2	60008	61
58348	12	58579	1	59028	2	59414	3	59759	8	60009	1
58351	1	58580	2	59030	2	59416	4	59761	1	60010	109
58352	2	58581	1	59034	12	59417	2	59762	1	60011	2
58353	1	58601	85	59035	5	59418	1	59771	11	60012	8
58356	4	58602	2	59036	2	59420	2	59772	7	60013	74
58357	1	58621	3	59037	3	59421	2	59801	93	60014	99
58360	1	58622	2	59038	2	59422	2	59802	43	60015	95
58365	6	58623	15	59041	4	59425	9	59803	28	60016	133
58366	1	58626	1	59042	1	59427	12	59805	1	60017	3
58367	1	58627	2	59044	18	59430	1	59806	11	60018	69
58368	7	58630	1	59047	45	59434	3	59807	4	60020	8
58370	2	58631	1	59056	1	59436	3	59820	4	60021	12
58374	1	58634	1	59061	2	59440	2	59821	1	60022	21
58380	3	58636	1	59063	1	59442	7	59823	2	60025	125
58384	2	58639	5	59068	9	59443	2	59824	3	60026	1
58385	1	58643	1	59069	4	59446	1	59825	5	60029	1
58401	45	58645	2	59070	2	59447	3	59826	1	60030	36
58402	4	58646	2	59071	2	59450	2	59827	4	60031	50
58416	9	58647	2	59072	1	59452	1	59828	5	60033	17
58417	2	58650	2	59074	4	59454	2	59829	6	60034	2
58421	3	58651	3	59079	2	59456	2	59831	3	60035	89
58422	1	58652	5	59080	1	59457	21	59832	2	60037	3
58424	2	58653	5	59088	4	59472	2	59833	10	60039	4
58425	7	58701	104	59101	78	59474	9	59834	8	60040	7
58426	1	58702	3	59102	96	59479	3	59836	1	60041	23
58427	1	58704	23	59103	6	59480	1	59837	1	60042	10

60043	8	60142	12	60429	29	60536	1	60647	48	61036	6
60044	22	60143	24	60430	70	60537	1	60648	67	61037	1
60045	48	60144	1	60432	10	60538	35	60649	19	61041	3
60046	70	60145	7	60433	12	60539	1	60650	63	61042	2
60047	89	60146	10	60434	3	60540	184	60651	16	61043	1
60048	90	60147	2	60435	109	60541	5	60652	49	61044	1
60050	116	60148	143	60436	27	60542	27	60653	6	61046	8
60053	85	60150	3	60438	67	60543	32	60654	1	61047	3
60056	126	60151	10	60439	129	60544	39	60655	48	61048	2
60057	1	60152	28	60440	36	60545	17	60656	73	61049	2
60060	82	60153	61	60441	95	60546	47	60657	38	61051	1
60061	33	60154	16	60442	9	60548	19	60658	16	61052	1
60062	114	60157	10	60443	26	60549	2	60659	44	61053	13
60064	13	60159	1	60444	4	60550	4	60660	34	61054	13
60065	3	60160	20	60445	42	60551	6	60667	1	61060	1
60066	1	60161	1	60447	27	60552	6	60680	4	61061	16
60067	163	60162	27	60448	33	60554	9	60690	5	61062	1
60068	109	60163	8	60449	14	60555	35	60705	1	61063	5
60069	11	60164	35	60450	34	60556	6	60714	11	61064	13
60070	73	60165	6	60451	44	60558	28	60723	1	61065	7
60071	9	60168	3	60452	52	60559	113	60901	57	61067	1
60072	1	60171	30	60453	102	60560	16	60904	1	61068	22
60073	57	60172	64	60454	1	60561	4	60913	7	61071	51
60074	21	60173	8	60455	25	60563	34	60914	31	61072	15
60076	130	60174	118	60456	17	60564	9	60915	20	61073	39
60077	74	60175	19	60457	24	60565	92	60918	4	61074	17
60078	1	60176	28	60458	16	60566	1	60924	1	61075	1
60079	2	60177	24	60459	53	60567	1	60927	6	61076	1
60080	1	60178	51	60460	4	60590	1	60928	2	61077	1
60081	4	60180	9	60461	9	60601	12	60935	2	61078	3
60082	2	60181	106	60462	101	60602	1	60936	11	61080	7
60083	2	60183	2	60463	15	60604	1	60938	2	61081	97
60084	35	60184	7	60464	24	60605	2	60940	5	61084	6
60085	65	60185	75	60465	32	60606	6	60941	1	61085	2
60087	46	60187	204	60466	47	60607	10	60942	8	61087	1
60088	14	60188	82	60468	6	60608	28	60946	2	61088	13
60089	80	60189	4	60469	6	60609	26	60948	8	61089	1
60090	102	60190	31	60470	1	60610	37	60949	1	61101	7
60091	95	60191	28	60471	19	60611	27	60950	10	61102	25
60093	50	60193	138	60472	2	60612	14	60951	1	61103	70
60096	34	60194	101	60473	46	60613	24	60953	2	61104	11
60097	24	60195	105	60474	2	60614	59	60954	6	61107	71
60098	69	60196	2	60475	15	60615	26	60957	17	61108	120
60099	126	60198	1	60476	5	60616	14	60959	2	61109	82
60101	79	60199	1	60477	88	60617	42	60960	2	61111	127
60102	63	60201	51	60478	5	60618	89	60961	4	61114	1
60103	156	60202	63	60480	7	60619	33	60963	1	61115	3
60104	13	60203	18	60481	15	60620	38	60964	2	61125	1
60106	31	60204	1	60482	27	60621	7	60966	4	61126	1
60107	69	60208	2	60499	1	60622	12	60968	1	61132	1
60108	39	60301	1	60501	8	60623	24	60970	11	61174	1
60109	1	60302	77	60504	33	60624	2	61001	2	61201	64
60110	56	60303	2	60505	74	60625	64	61006	3	61204	1
60111	1	60304	52	60506	124	60626	43	61007	1	61230	2
60112	6	60305	26	60507	1	60627	25	61008	49	61231	13
60115	72	60401	9	60510	74	60628	24	61010	4	61232	2
60117	1	60402	104	60511	4	60629	71	61011	1	61233	1
60118	43	60406	32	60512	2	60630	99	61012	2	61234	1
60119	22	60407	3	60513	58	60631	53	61013	3	61236	3
60120	109	60408	10	60514	46	60632	48	61014	3	61238	2
60121	2	60409	43	60515	129	60633	15	61015	2	61240	20
60123	78	60410	11	60516	72	60634	94	61016	19	61241	21
60126	151	60411	61	60517	32	60635	55	61017	1	61242	2
60129	2	60415	10	60518	4	60636	8	61018	1	61244	48
60130	40	60416	14	60519	1	60637	21	61019	3	61250	1
60131	32	60417	26	60520	6	60638	60	61020	2	61252	10
60134	45	60419	41	60521	119	60639	44	61021	71	61254	28
60135	13	60420	18	60522	2	60640	47	61024	6	61256	5
60136	7	60421	10	60523	1	60641	79	61025	5	61257	5
60137	146	60422	23	60525	120	60642	42	61026	1	61259	2
60138	1	60423	28	60530	1	60643	57	61028	1	61260	2
60139	43	60424	5	60531	3	60644	8	61030	8	61261	1
60140	26	60425	24	60532	71	60645	86	61031	7	61262	2
60141	2	60426	41	60534	18	60646	104	61032	66	61264	28

61265	99	61430	2	61606	13	61843	2	62033	37	62253	5
61270	30	61434	9	61607	35	61844	1	62034	11	62254	17
61272	9	61439	1	61611	80	61845	2	62035	77	62255	1
61273	12	61440	1	61614	133	61846	11	62036	2	62257	14
61274	1	61442	5	61615	57	61847	2	62037	2	62258	26
61275	9	61443	15	61701	144	61849	4	62040	113	62260	11
61276	1	61447	2	61702	6	61850	1	62044	1	62262	7
61277	8	61448	7	61703	1	61851	2	62046	4	62263	3
61279	1	61450	4	61704	41	61853	28	62047	1	62264	4
61281	7	61453	1	61721	6	61854	7	62048	1	62265	7
61282	16	61455	55	61722	2	61855	2	62049	37	62266	1
61283	2	61458	4	61723	9	61856	31	62052	19	62268	1
61284	7	61459	1	61724	2	61858	3	62054	2	62269	54
61285	3	61460	2	61725	3	61859	4	62056	35	62271	4
61301	17	61462	27	61726	7	61862	2	62058	1	62272	3
61310	10	61467	2	61727	38	61863	1	62059	1	62274	13
61314	2	61469	6	61728	1	61864	3	62060	5	62275	2
61315	2	61470	3	61729	5	61865	4	62061	4	62278	7
61318	1	61472	3	61730	1	61866	36	62062	1	62281	1
61320	1	61473	3	61732	1	61868	1	62063	1	62282	1
61325	2	61475	1	61733	1	61870	5	62065	1	62283	2
61326	6	61476	7	61734	5	61872	2	62067	6	62284	2
61327	14	61477	4	61735	3	61873	11	62069	7	62285	1
61329	2	61479	2	61736	6	61874	3	62074	3	62286	8
61330	2	61480	2	61737	1	61875	2	62075	4	62288	4
61333	1	61483	11	61738	8	61876	3	62077	1	62292	5
61334	3	61484	13	61739	4	61877	3	62079	1	62293	12
61335	3	61486	3	61740	3	61878	4	62080	14	62294	33
61336	1	61488	2	61741	3	61880	5	62081	1	62296	1
61338	1	61489	1	61742	5	61883	15	62082	4	62297	1
61339	1	61490	1	61744	4	61884	6	62083	2	62298	13
61340	3	61501	1	61745	10	61892	1	62084	3	62301	174
61341	20	61517	9	61747	4	61910	6	62086	3	62305	2
61342	8	61520	47	61748	7	61911	11	62087	1	62306	2
61345	2	61523	27	61749	1	61912	6	62088	3	62307	1
61346	1	61524	1	61750	2	61913	5	62089	1	62311	3
61348	8	61525	22	61752	5	61914	1	62092	2	62312	9
61349	7	61526	12	61753	3	61917	3	62094	2	62313	1
61350	38	61528	5	61754	9	61920	32	62095	21	62314	2
61353	4	61529	5	61755	4	61924	7	62097	4	62316	3
61354	20	61530	20	61756	4	61925	2	62201	7	62318	2
61356	30	61531	8	61758	1	61928	4	62203	4	62320	6
61358	5	61532	3	61759	6	61929	7	62204	4	62321	17
61360	6	61533	4	61760	5	61931	1	62205	3	62324	2
61361	3	61534	3	61761	97	61932	1	62206	24	62325	3
61362	9	61535	4	61764	21	61936	4	62207	2	62326	7
61363	1	61536	4	61769	2	61937	3	62208	46	62330	10
61364	63	61537	7	61770	5	61938	32	62214	2	62336	1
61367	9	61540	1	61772	1	61942	1	62215	1	62338	1
61368	1	61542	7	61774	3	61943	2	62216	3	62339	1
61369	2	61544	2	61776	5	61944	36	62217	3	62340	2
61370	3	61545	2	61778	1	61951	21	62218	1	62341	3
61373	1	61546	15	61801	113	61953	10	62219	2	62344	2
61375	2	61547	5	61810	1	61956	4	62220	25	62347	12
61376	8	61548	27	61811	3	61957	9	62221	113	62348	1
61377	6	61550	77	61813	12	62001	5	62222	4	62349	2
61378	2	61552	3	61814	3	62002	79	62223	77	62351	5
61379	1	61554	109	61815	1	62006	1	62225	27	62352	1
61401	108	61555	3	61817	3	62009	3	62230	2	62353	8
61402	2	61559	5	61818	2	62010	19	62231	13	62354	4
61410	7	61560	1	61820	73	62011	1	62232	16	62357	1
61411	1	61561	7	61821	96	62012	17	62233	4	62358	1
61412	3	61562	4	61822	1	62014	17	62234	85	62359	1
61413	2	61564	3	61824	1	62015	1	62236	12	62360	6
61414	3	61565	8	61825	1	62016	6	62237	4	62363	13
61415	4	61567	3	61826	2	62017	4	62239	12	62365	1
61418	2	61568	12	61830	1	62018	8	62240	6	62366	2
61420	7	61569	3	61832	126	62019	1	62241	1	62367	8
61421	1	61570	1	61833	3	62021	1	62242	4	62370	1
61422	6	61571	61	61837	1	62022	2	62243	13	62374	1
61423	2	61572	4	61839	3	62024	40	62246	63	62376	2
61425	3	61603	26	61840	3	62025	75	62248	1	62378	5
61427	4	61604	49	61841	3	62028	13	62249	20	62379	4
61428	3	61605	12	61842	4	62032	2	62250	2	62380	3

62401	46	62543	2	62708	5	62913	1	63040	5	63302	3
62410	8	62544	2	62791	3	62914	18	63042	53	63303	118
62411	10	62545	1	62794	1	62915	1	63043	66	63304	19
62413	3	62546	7	62801	89	62917	3	63044	54	63332	1
62414	6	62548	8	62803	4	62918	15	63046	1	63333	1
62417	6	62549	15	62806	8	62920	4	63048	3	63334	6
62418	2	62550	4	62807	3	62921	1	63049	31	63336	1
62419	1	62551	1	62808	3	62922	8	63050	27	63338	1
62420	19	62552	3	62810	2	62923	2	63051	30	63341	5
62421	4	62554	9	62812	20	62924	6	63052	27	63342	2
62422	2	62555	1	62814	4	62926	2	63055	5	63343	12
62423	1	62556	2	62816	4	62930	13	63057	1	63344	4
62424	2	62557	13	62817	3	62931	1	63060	5	63347	6
62425	1	62558	10	62819	1	62932	8	63068	4	63348	10
62426	8	62560	4	62821	25	62933	2	63069	21	63349	1
62427	1	62561	11	62822	3	62934	3	63070	2	63350	3
62428	6	62563	19	62823	1	62938	8	63072	8	63351	4
62431	2	62565	17	62828	3	62939	7	63073	1	63352	4
62432	2	62568	52	62830	2	62940	1	63074	36	63353	13
62433	6	62570	5	62832	21	62942	2	63077	14	63357	8
62434	1	62571	1	62833	2	62946	25	63080	31	63361	5
62439	10	62573	1	62835	5	62948	31	63084	24	63362	3
62440	3	62601	2	62837	15	62949	1	63087	1	63364	1
62441	12	62610	1	62838	2	62951	17	63088	5	63366	58
62442	8	62611	1	62839	8	62952	18	63089	10	63367	16
62443	8	62612	4	62844	10	62957	1	63090	38	63369	4
62445	2	62613	7	62848	1	62958	5	63091	1	63373	2
62446	1	62615	9	62849	3	62959	61	63101	1	63374	1
62447	8	62618	13	62850	2	62960	31	63102	2	63376	122
62448	13	62624	3	62851	1	62964	5	63103	3	63377	3
62449	10	62625	5	62852	1	62966	36	63104	8	63379	43
62450	23	62626	24	62853	1	62967	3	63105	25	63383	17
62451	5	62628	1	62854	9	62970	2	63106	3	63384	3
62452	1	62629	19	62855	1	62974	1	63107	1	63385	17
62454	33	62630	2	62856	1	62979	1	63108	22	63388	3
62458	9	62631	1	62858	2	62982	2	63109	50	63389	11
62459	1	62633	1	62859	35	62983	1	63110	25	63390	11
62460	4	62638	2	62863	30	62984	1	63111	21	63401	85
62461	1	62639	2	62864	69	62985	4	63112	7	63430	1
62463	6	62640	11	62865	3	62987	3	63113	1	63435	5
62466	7	62641	1	62867	1	62988	2	63114	87	63436	3
62467	1	62642	3	62868	6	62990	2	63115	9	63437	2
62468	13	62644	12	62869	6	62992	1	63116	61	63438	1
62469	1	62650	55	62870	4	62994	2	63117	20	63440	2
62471	10	62656	29	62871	2	62995	10	63118	33	63443	4
62473	2	62661	3	62872	1	62996	4	63119	100	63445	4
62474	3	62664	5	62874	1	62997	3	63120	2	63448	1
62475	1	62665	2	62875	3	62999	3	63121	29	63451	2
62476	1	62666	2	62877	1	63001	1	63122	105	63452	1
62477	13	62668	4	62878	2	63005	9	63123	134	63454	1
62478	1	62670	14	62880	2	63007	1	63124	35	63456	5
62479	1	62671	2	62881	32	63010	57	63125	64	63457	1
62480	2	62674	2	62882	8	63011	133	63126	59	63459	13
62501	1	62675	9	62883	1	63012	11	63127	12	63461	10
62510	3	62676	1	62884	24	63013	2	63128	78	63462	3
62513	2	62677	9	62885	1	63014	2	63129	63	63463	2
62514	2	62681	25	62888	2	63015	4	63130	40	63465	1
62515	2	62682	2	62889	1	63016	15	63131	57	63468	3
62517	1	62684	8	62890	2	63017	104	63132	28	63471	5
62520	5	62685	5	62891	4	63019	12	63133	5	63501	32
62521	102	62688	2	62893	2	63020	30	63134	21	63530	1
62522	41	62689	1	62894	3	63021	73	63135	54	63532	3
62523	3	62690	7	62895	8	63023	7	63136	43	63533	2
62526	85	62691	10	62896	30	63025	6	63137	33	63534	1
62530	5	62692	2	62898	3	63026	97	63138	47	63536	2
62531	3	62693	2	62899	2	63028	42	63139	32	63537	3
62532	1	62694	4	62901	68	63031	124	63141	75	63538	1
62534	7	62695	2	62902	2	63032	1	63143	32	63543	2
62535	1	62701	2	62903	2	63033	109	63144	27	63544	2
62536	1	62702	69	62905	2	63034	26	63145	1	63546	1
62537	3	62703	62	62906	13	63036	4	63146	65	63548	6
62538	1	62704	100	62907	6	63037	2	63147	7	63549	5
62539	3	62705	5	62910	2	63038	7	63156	1	63551	1
62540	2	62707	50	62912	1	63039	6	63301	150	63552	52

63555	1	63931	2	64089	22	64470	1	64756	1	65068	3
63556	2	63934	2	64090	3	64471	2	64759	11	65072	8
63559	3	63935	7	64091	1	64474	3	64761	1	65074	1
63560	1	63936	2	64092	1	64477	5	64763	4	65075	1
63565	3	63937	4	64093	39	64479	2	64770	2	65078	4
63601	24	63939	2	64097	2	64482	2	64772	28	65079	11
63621	2	63940	1	64098	10	64484	2	64776	11	65080	1
63624	13	63941	2	64106	5	64485	16	64779	2	65081	1
63628	37	63942	1	64108	2	64486	1	64780	2	65084	9
63629	5	63943	6	64109	7	64487	1	64784	1	65085	1
63630	3	63944	2	64110	19	64489	2	64785	1	65101	106
63631	1	63945	1	64111	15	64490	5	64788	3	65102	2
63637	1	63947	2	64112	18	64492	4	64801	107	65109	43
63638	1	63953	1	64113	34	64493	1	64802	5	65110	1
63639	5	63954	1	64114	58	64494	3	64803	3	65141	1
63640	28	63957	8	64116	44	64498	1	64804	69	65201	66
63645	17	63960	8	64117	35	64499	1	64820	1	65202	58
63650	7	63961	4	64118	138	64501	9	64830	1	65203	44
63655	2	63963	1	64119	88	64503	32	64831	9	65205	3
63656	1	63964	2	64123	22	64504	21	64832	1	65206	2
63660	1	63965	2	64124	8	64505	24	64834	13	65230	2
63662	1	63966	7	64125	4	64506	45	64835	2	65231	4
63663	1	63967	3	64126	18	64507	35	64836	53	65232	1
63664	9	64011	6	64127	19	64520	1	64840	6	65233	11
63666	2	64012	56	64128	8	64601	14	64841	1	65237	1
63670	15	64013	1	64129	26	64623	1	64842	3	65240	16
63673	1	64014	18	64130	12	64625	2	64843	1	65243	2
63701	80	64015	75	64131	43	64628	14	64844	4	65246	2
63702	1	64016	2	64132	8	64631	2	64846	1	65247	5
63730	6	64018	2	64133	123	64633	12	64848	1	65248	11
63735	1	64019	2	64134	64	64635	2	64850	50	65250	3
63736	4	64020	9	64137	37	64637	1	64854	6	65251	27
63740	7	64021	3	64138	73	64640	9	64855	3	65255	9
63747	1	64024	30	64141	4	64642	1	64856	2	65256	4
63748	1	64026	1	64142	2	64644	11	64857	1	65257	4
63751	1	64029	10	64145	11	64645	1	64858	2	65258	2
63754	1	64030	67	64146	4	64646	1	64859	1	65259	6
63755	26	64034	12	64150	7	64648	2	64862	7	65260	2
63762	1	64035	2	64151	53	64649	1	64863	1	65261	3
63764	10	64037	16	64152	75	64651	1	64864	1	65262	1
63767	2	64040	5	64153	3	64652	1	64865	22	65263	1
63768	1	64048	17	64154	14	64653	2	64866	1	65265	39
63775	21	64050	81	64155	44	64658	8	64867	2	65270	57
63776	1	64051	7	64156	3	64660	1	64870	28	65274	4
63779	1	64052	78	64161	1	64664	2	64873	2	65275	10
63780	26	64053	15	64163	1	64668	1	65004	1	65276	5
63783	4	64054	13	64166	1	64670	2	65010	11	65279	5
63801	28	64055	125	64168	1	64671	1	65013	2	65281	9
63822	6	64056	39	64169	1	64673	7	65017	1	65283	3
63825	8	64057	24	64401	3	64674	2	65018	11	65284	5
63827	2	64058	22	64402	4	64679	1	65020	29	65285	3
63830	7	64060	25	64421	5	64681	1	65023	2	65286	1
63833	1	64061	8	64424	6	64682	2	65025	1	65301	56
63834	3	64062	5	64426	3	64683	14	65026	20	65302	3
63841	21	64063	153	64428	1	64688	1	65032	4	65305	3
63845	1	64064	7	64429	11	64689	3	65035	3	65322	1
63846	2	64067	8	64430	5	64701	26	65037	7	65323	10
63848	3	64068	89	64432	2	64720	3	65039	5	65324	3
63851	2	64070	6	64433	1	64724	6	65040	3	65325	5
63852	1	64071	1	64436	2	64725	6	65041	9	65326	10
63855	1	64072	3	64439	1	64728	4	65043	19	65332	2
63857	24	64074	1	64443	1	64730	10	65046	1	65334	5
63862	1	64075	22	64444	2	64733	2	65047	1	65336	5
63863	10	64076	14	64448	1	64734	10	65049	11	65338	9
63867	1	64077	9	64454	10	64735	53	65051	5	65340	38
63869	13	64078	23	64455	1	64738	2	65052	9	65344	2
63870	1	64079	18	64456	12	64739	2	65053	1	65345	4
63871	1	64080	14	64459	1	64742	7	65054	2	65348	4
63873	9	64081	18	64461	5	64744	29	65058	1	65349	5
63876	3	64082	11	64463	2	64746	10	65061	2	65350	3
63877	1	64083	22	64465	10	64747	5	65063	10	65351	3
63882	1	64084	6	64466	2	64748	4	65064	2	65355	33
63901	84	64085	15	64468	15	64752	1	65065	14	65360	10
63928	1	64088	4	64469	3	64755	3	65066	5	65401	100

65438	3	65655	7	65804	120	66101	5	66526	2	66834	3
65440	2	65656	19	65806	15	66102	51	66527	2	66835	3
65441	11	65658	9	65807	125	66103	23	66528	4	66838	1
65443	1	65661	5	65808	3	66104	40	66531	2	66839	25
65444	1	65663	3	65809	14	66105	2	66532	1	66840	2
65452	5	65667	3	65810	10	66106	51	66533	5	66845	1
65453	13	65668	19	65973	1	66109	48	66534	2	66846	10
65457	1	65669	5	66002	33	66111	16	66535	7	66848	1
65459	13	65672	17	66006	8	66112	22	66536	17	66854	2
65462	2	65674	7	66007	6	66201	1	66537	1	66856	3
65463	1	65676	4	66008	1	66202	37	66538	11	66857	2
65464	1	65679	6	66010	1	66203	68	66539	16	66860	2
65468	1	65680	1	66012	20	66204	79	66540	2	66861	5
65470	1	65681	8	66013	6	66205	54	66542	8	66865	1
65473	4	65682	3	66014	1	66206	37	66543	9	66866	2
65483	14	65683	1	66015	5	66207	72	66546	1	66868	2
65486	4	65684	1	66016	1	66208	83	66547	32	66869	1
65507	1	65685	1	66018	16	66209	27	66548	5	66871	4
65529	1	65686	28	66019	2	66210	21	66549	2	66901	26
65532	2	65689	6	66020	7	66211	4	66550	1	66930	4
65534	1	65692	1	66021	2	66212	120	66551	1	66931	2
65535	5	65704	9	66024	4	66213	13	66554	4	66933	2
65536	59	65705	11	66025	6	66214	35	66600	1	66935	9
65540	3	65706	23	66026	2	66215	63	66601	4	66936	1
65542	4	65707	5	66027	3	66216	57	66603	7	66937	1
65543	2	65708	22	66030	20	66217	6	66604	65	66938	2
65548	11	65709	1	66031	1	66218	4	66605	67	66939	3
65550	10	65710	1	66032	13	66219	10	66606	37	66940	1
65552	9	65711	21	66035	2	66221	4	66607	14	66941	2
65555	3	65712	12	66038	1	66223	4	66608	12	66943	3
65556	9	65713	3	66039	1	66224	4	66609	22	66944	1
65559	12	65714	26	66040	11	66226	3	66610	10	66948	2
65560	42	65717	4	66041	2	66227	5	66611	35	66951	5
65565	7	65721	24	66043	29	66402	9	66612	3	66953	2
65566	6	65722	7	66044	93	66403	5	66614	78	66956	4
65567	2	65723	6	66045	1	66406	2	66615	3	66960	1
65571	5	65724	7	66046	49	66407	1	66616	12	66961	2
65578	1	65725	6	66047	8	66409	12	66617	26	66964	2
65582	7	65726	2	66048	139	66411	7	66618	18	66966	1
65583	34	65729	2	66049	11	66412	1	66619	10	66967	13
65588	1	65732	4	66050	4	66413	7	66701	28	66968	3
65589	1	65733	2	66052	4	66414	4	66710	3	67002	11
65590	2	65734	2	66053	8	66416	2	66712	1	67003	22
65604	12	65737	23	66054	11	66419	1	66713	14	67004	2
65605	34	65738	17	66056	12	66422	3	66714	1	67005	33
65606	4	65740	5	66058	1	66423	2	66717	3	67008	1
65608	15	65742	12	66060	2	66427	4	66720	35	67009	2
65610	4	65745	4	66061	88	66429	2	66724	4	67010	49
65611	9	65746	18	66062	102	66431	3	66725	7	67013	12
65612	2	65747	33	66063	1	66433	2	66733	6	67016	3
65613	43	65753	2	66064	25	66434	18	66736	9	67017	7
65616	56	65757	17	66066	6	66436	11	66739	13	67018	2
65617	3	65759	1	66067	29	66438	2	66740	4	67019	3
65619	11	65760	3	66070	14	66439	7	66743	8	67020	3
65622	17	65761	5	66071	25	66440	7	66746	1	67022	5
65624	2	65764	2	66072	7	66441	66	66748	6	67025	3
65625	23	65767	2	66073	3	66442	23	66749	19	67026	16
65626	1	65769	4	66075	4	66449	2	66753	1	67029	7
65627	3	65770	5	66076	6	66451	10	66756	6	67030	1
65631	3	65772	2	66077	1	66501	1	66757	3	67031	4
65632	4	65774	2	66078	3	66502	125	66758	2	67032	1
65633	9	65775	18	66079	2	66506	6	66762	67	67035	1
65635	1	65779	4	66080	5	66507	3	66766	1	67036	2
65637	1	65781	22	66083	19	66508	15	66769	1	67037	70
65638	1	65785	38	66085	21	66512	9	66770	1	67038	1
65640	2	65786	5	66086	11	66514	3	66771	2	67039	6
65641	9	65788	2	66087	1	66515	1	66772	2	67041	1
65644	3	65789	5	66088	4	66516	2	66773	1	67042	28
65646	4	65790	3	66090	5	66517	1	66779	2	67045	8
65647	6	65791	20	66091	1	66520	1	66780	1	67047	3
65648	16	65793	31	66092	7	66521	5	66781	6	67050	2
65650	1	65801	9	66093	1	66522	1	66783	4	67051	1
65652	5	65802	78	66094	1	66523	12	66793	1	67052	13
65653	18	65803	75	66095	1	66524	8	66801	59	67053	3

67054	4	67345	1	67550	6	67853	2	68118	5	68434	20
67056	8	67346	1	67552	2	67854	2	68122	4	68439	1
67057	1	67349	4	67554	12	67855	9	68123	67	68441	3
67058	13	67351	5	67560	7	67860	3	68124	51	68442	3
67059	2	67352	2	67561	3	67861	6	68127	36	68443	2
67060	14	67354	3	67564	2	67863	1	68128	31	68446	4
67061	1	67355	1	67565	2	67864	4	68130	15	68447	1
67062	64	67356	2	67566	3	67865	1	68131	16	68450	2
67063	18	67357	44	67567	2	67867	1	68132	32	68454	1
67067	4	67360	1	67568	1	67868	1	68133	6	68455	7
67068	4	67361	7	67569	1	67869	8	68134	66	68456	3
67070	6	67401	151	67570	4	67870	2	68135	5	68457	1
67074	2	67402	1	67574	2	67871	27	68137	51	68460	4
67101	4	67410	20	67576	5	67876	1	68138	19	68461	3
67104	5	67416	1	67578	6	67877	2	68142	3	68462	8
67106	3	67418	4	67579	6	67878	11	68144	48	68464	6
67107	5	67420	10	67581	1	67879	4	68147	22	68465	6
67108	9	67422	5	67582	1	67880	15	68152	27	68466	1
67109	2	67423	2	67584	1	67901	24	68154	29	68467	17
67110	19	67425	4	67601	57	67950	5	68157	10	68501	4
67111	2	67427	3	67622	4	67951	8	68164	38	68502	69
67112	1	67428	2	67623	6	67952	1	68178	1	68503	36
67114	69	67430	8	67631	1	68002	1	68301	4	68504	38
67117	5	67431	6	67635	1	68003	7	68304	3	68505	66
67120	5	67432	21	67636	1	68005	79	68305	8	68506	116
67123	2	67436	3	67637	5	68007	3	68307	2	68507	53
67124	16	67437	14	67639	1	68008	25	68310	23	68508	13
67133	20	67438	1	67642	2	68015	3	68313	4	68510	57
67134	1	67439	10	67645	3	68016	2	68316	4	68512	28
67135	8	67441	5	67646	1	68017	7	68317	2	68516	68
67137	3	67443	2	67648	1	68018	3	68319	1	68517	1
67144	6	67445	4	67649	5	68019	2	68320	3	68520	1
67146	2	67446	1	67654	14	68022	13	68321	1	68521	39
67147	19	67448	2	67659	1	68023	3	68323	4	68522	6
67149	2	67449	13	67661	19	68025	114	68324	2	68524	13
67152	35	67450	1	67663	8	68028	9	68331	1	68527	3
67154	4	67451	5	67665	8	68029	2	68333	20	68528	11
67156	80	67455	19	67667	1	68031	5	68335	2	68531	1
67201	4	67456	4	67669	2	68033	4	68336	2	68570	1
67202	4	67460	35	67670	2	68036	3	68337	1	68571	1
67203	66	67463	1	67671	2	68038	2	68339	1	68601	51
67204	55	67464	4	67672	10	68040	1	68340	2	68615	1
67205	4	67465	1	67673	1	68041	2	68341	3	68620	22
67206	29	67466	7	67675	4	68042	1	68342	2	68621	5
67207	57	67467	5	67676	1	68043	1	68347	3	68624	1
67208	54	67470	2	67701	26	68044	2	68349	3	68626	2
67209	28	67473	13	67732	4	68045	8	68352	17	68627	1
67210	9	67474	4	67734	1	68046	27	68355	19	68628	3
67211	46	67475	1	67735	13	68047	1	68360	2	68629	8
67212	97	67479	2	67737	1	68048	34	68361	2	68631	2
67213	47	67481	1	67740	7	68050	2	68366	2	68632	7
67214	14	67484	1	67743	1	68059	4	68370	1	68633	1
67215	3	67485	5	67744	1	68061	1	68371	2	68634	1
67216	54	67487	1	67745	2	68063	1	68372	4	68635	1
67217	76	67490	8	67747	1	68064	5	68376	1	68636	8
67218	68	67501	78	67748	1	68066	6	68377	2	68638	5
67219	17	67502	31	67749	7	68067	1	68378	3	68640	3
67220	26	67504	5	67751	1	68068	2	68402	2	68641	1
67221	1	67505	3	67752	4	68069	5	68403	1	68643	1
67226	25	67510	1	67756	2	68072	1	68404	3	68649	5
67230	25	67511	2	67757	2	68073	5	68405	5	68651	7
67232	1	67512	3	67758	1	68101	1	68409	5	68652	1
67233	15	67514	2	67761	2	68102	5	68410	25	68659	1
67235	10	67516	2	67762	1	68104	65	68413	1	68660	3
67277	3	67522	4	67764	1	68105	32	68415	1	68661	19
67278	1	67525	4	67801	27	68106	41	68418	1	68663	1
67301	65	67526	5	67830	1	68107	24	68419	1	68665	1
67330	10	67530	71	67834	1	68108	16	68420	3	68666	5
67333	12	67543	6	67835	4	68110	12	68421	1	68667	3
67335	5	67544	3	67838	4	68111	23	68422	1	68669	1
67336	4	67545	1	67839	5	68112	34	68428	5	68701	79
67337	69	67546	3	67843	1	68113	9	68430	5	68702	1
67340	2	67547	4	67844	2	68114	39	68431	1	68710	2
67342	6	67548	2	67846	42	68117	12	68433	2	68713	3

68714	6	68853	5	69127	1	70053	38	70358	2	70526	13
68718	1	68854	3	69129	1	70054	3	70359	2	70527	4
68723	2	68856	5	69130	15	70055	2	70360	46	70528	2
68724	1	68862	3	69131	2	70056	61	70361	6	70529	4
68725	5	68863	3	69133	1	70057	2	70363	18	70531	3
68726	2	68865	3	69138	7	70058	50	70364	29	70532	5
68727	1	68868	1	69140	3	70059	4	70372	2	70533	6
68729	8	68870	5	69143	5	70062	63	70373	3	70535	12
68730	5	68871	1	69144	1	70064	2	70374	4	70537	1
68731	9	68873	2	69145	11	70065	75	70377	2	70538	10
68732	1	68874	4	69147	1	70067	1	70380	30	70543	1
68733	1	68876	4	69149	4	70068	24	70381	1	70544	7
68735	3	68879	3	69151	1	70069	2	70390	1	70546	16
68739	1	68883	5	69152	2	70070	25	70392	22	70548	8
68740	7	68901	54	69153	27	70071	2	70394	17	70549	4
68741	1	68920	5	69154	2	70072	53	70395	1	70550	2
68742	6	68922	3	69155	2	70073	1	70397	2	70552	2
68744	1	68924	5	69156	5	70075	16	70401	27	70554	1
68746	1	68925	1	69161	1	70079	8	70402	1	70555	9
68747	1	68926	3	69162	31	70080	1	70403	19	70558	1
68748	1	68928	3	69163	2	70083	3	70404	3	70559	1
68756	18	68929	1	69165	2	70084	3	70420	5	70560	80
68757	2	68930	1	69166	2	70085	8	70422	7	70562	5
68758	2	68932	1	69170	1	70087	7	70426	12	70569	1
68759	2	68933	3	69201	13	70090	5	70427	38	70570	24
68761	8	68934	3	69210	7	70091	1	70431	3	70571	2
68763	16	68935	2	69211	6	70092	5	70432	1	70577	2
68764	2	68936	3	69217	1	70094	35	70433	60	70578	4
68766	3	68937	4	69218	3	70112	1	70434	4	70582	24
68767	1	68938	5	69301	16	70114	56	70437	9	70583	12
68768	1	68939	2	69331	1	70115	48	70438	26	70584	6
68769	2	68940	3	69333	1	70116	6	70443	5	70586	10
68770	2	68944	1	69334	4	70117	11	70444	12	70589	2
68771	1	68945	3	69336	10	70118	33	70445	36	70592	3
68776	22	68947	2	69337	36	70119	24	70446	4	70593	2
68777	1	68948	1	69339	5	70121	23	70447	8	70601	34
68778	1	68949	15	69341	19	70122	68	70448	49	70602	2
68779	20	68950	4	69343	5	70123	71	70449	1	70603	1
68780	1	68952	1	69345	1	70124	74	70450	2	70605	85
68783	2	68955	4	69347	1	70125	21	70451	3	70609	1
68785	2	68956	1	69348	8	70126	23	70452	36	70611	13
68787	3	68957	1	69352	1	70127	29	70453	1	70612	1
68788	3	68958	2	69354	1	70128	5	70454	24	70616	1
68789	1	68959	4	69355	1	70129	14	70455	2	70633	6
68790	1	68961	1	69356	4	70130	7	70456	1	70634	30
68791	3	68966	3	69357	7	70131	35	70457	2	70638	5
68801	69	68967	17	69358	4	70143	1	70458	166	70639	2
68802	3	68969	1	69360	5	70150	4	70459	8	70643	1
68803	38	68970	1	69361	32	70151	2	70460	43	70645	2
68807	1	68971	4	69363	2	70152	1	70461	54	70647	7
68810	1	68976	1	69367	1	70153	1	70462	4	70648	3
68812	1	68977	1	69377	1	70157	1	70463	5	70651	1
68813	5	68978	7	70001	81	70174	3	70465	1	70653	4
68815	1	68979	5	70002	49	70178	1	70466	2	70655	1
68816	1	68982	3	70003	105	70179	1	70469	1	70656	5
68818	17	69001	38	70004	3	70181	1	70470	2	70657	3
68820	1	69021	4	70005	84	70182	3	70481	1	70658	2
68822	13	69022	13	70006	36	70184	4	70501	22	70659	4
68823	10	69024	3	70009	2	70185	1	70502	3	70661	7
68824	2	69025	4	70010	1	70187	1	70503	68	70663	42
68825	1	69033	1	70030	2	70189	1	70504	6	70664	1
68826	8	69034	4	70031	1	70190	2	70505	3	70668	9
68827	1	69036	1	70032	23	70301	25	70506	51	70669	18
68829	1	69037	1	70033	3	70302	2	70507	17	70704	3
68831	4	69038	2	70037	22	70339	2	70508	25	70705	1
68832	4	69039	1	70039	4	70340	3	70509	2	70707	5
68835	1	69040	2	70040	4	70342	14	70510	19	70710	7
68836	2	69044	3	70041	1	70343	1	70517	17	70711	3
68840	5	69045	1	70043	63	70344	2	70518	21	70712	1
68842	1	69046	5	70044	4	70345	3	70519	3	70714	49
68847	59	69101	110	70046	1	70346	3	70520	16	70719	5
68848	1	69103	1	70047	13	70354	2	70521	2	70722	5
68849	1	69120	1	70051	2	70356	1	70523	2	70726	81
68850	12	69123	1	70052	5	70357	3	70525	2	70727	3

70728	1	71027	4	71238	9	71432	2	71833	1	72055	1
70729	1	71033	7	71239	1	71433	4	71834	1	72057	1
70730	6	71037	33	71241	10	71434	1	71835	1	72058	28
70733	2	71038	6	71247	5	71435	8	71837	4	72060	2
70734	6	71039	4	71251	24	71438	1	71839	1	72063	1
70737	34	71040	7	71253	2	71439	3	71841	2	72064	8
70739	40	71043	5	71254	1	71440	2	71842	4	72065	2
70740	8	71044	1	71259	3	71441	1	71845	5	72067	13
70744	1	71045	1	71260	2	71446	39	71846	1	72069	3
70747	1	71047	20	71263	9	71447	1	71852	22	72073	3
70748	7	71049	6	71266	1	71449	37	71857	11	72076	80
70750	3	71051	3	71268	4	71450	3	71858	1	72079	1
70752	1	71052	19	71269	17	71451	1	71859	2	72080	1
70754	8	71055	33	71270	68	71454	1	71860	4	72081	6
70757	18	71058	5	71272	2	71457	23	71861	4	72082	1
70759	1	71059	2	71273	2	71459	17	71865	2	72083	2
70760	15	71060	9	71275	1	71461	5	71866	2	72084	3
70761	4	71061	5	71279	1	71462	1	71901	104	72086	12
70762	2	71064	7	71280	2	71463	5	71902	5	72087	1
70764	12	71065	2	71281	2	71465	8	71909	37	72088	8
70765	6	71066	1	71282	4	71467	15	71913	90	72101	5
70767	14	71068	4	71291	91	71469	4	71914	2	72102	3
70769	25	71069	1	71292	16	71473	2	71921	3	72103	19
70770	6	71070	2	71295	25	71474	6	71923	45	72104	79
70772	7	71071	9	71301	75	71475	1	71929	9	72106	9
70773	2	71072	6	71302	14	71477	2	71933	1	72110	14
70774	13	71073	2	71303	35	71483	22	71937	6	72112	7
70775	23	71075	55	71306	4	71485	6	71940	3	72113	5
70776	3	71078	5	71307	2	71486	4	71941	20	72114	8
70777	3	71082	12	71309	2	71496	4	71943	6	72115	3
70778	2	71087	1	71315	2	71523	1	71945	9	72116	108
70782	1	71101	8	71322	4	71601	16	71950	2	72117	14
70783	8	71103	7	71325	1	71602	32	71953	48	72118	63
70784	1	71104	31	71327	1	71603	48	71956	1	72120	28
70785	32	71105	110	71328	8	71613	2	71957	7	72121	4
70791	28	71106	54	71334	8	71635	28	71958	5	72125	1
70801	1	71107	73	71336	2	71638	4	71960	2	72126	9
70802	12	71108	38	71340	3	71639	3	71961	1	72128	6
70805	40	71109	22	71341	5	71640	4	71964	17	72129	6
70806	55	71110	7	71342	14	71646	2	71966	3	72131	6
70807	11	71111	50	71343	3	71647	1	71968	11	72132	5
70808	100	71112	47	71346	1	71653	2	71969	1	72135	8
70809	49	71113	1	71348	2	71654	7	71971	1	72136	2
70810	66	71115	25	71350	1	71655	11	71973	4	72137	2
70811	19	71116	1	71351	1	71665	6	72002	30	72141	2
70812	7	71118	70	71353	8	71666	1	72003	1	72142	6
70813	1	71119	32	71355	4	71667	10	72006	5	72143	56
70814	43	71129	18	71357	4	71671	5	72007	6	72149	3
70815	115	71133	1	71358	1	71676	1	72011	7	72150	10
70816	93	71134	1	71360	79	71701	29	72012	7	72153	9
70817	44	71135	1	71361	3	71720	1	72013	4	72156	1
70818	21	71137	1	71366	5	71724	1	72015	113	72160	5
70819	15	71148	1	71367	2	71726	1	72016	5	72167	2
70820	7	71161	1	71368	1	71730	71	72017	1	72170	1
70821	6	71163	1	71369	2	71740	13	72020	1	72173	8
70828	15	71171	6	71371	1	71742	4	72021	2	72176	6
70879	3	71172	1	71373	8	71743	10	72022	13	72178	1
70893	7	71201	46	71375	1	71747	6	72023	41	72179	1
70894	1	71202	11	71378	3	71750	2	72024	7	72180	1
70895	5	71203	72	71403	7	71752	1	72025	6	72181	2
70896	2	71207	4	71404	3	71753	29	72027	2	72183	1
71001	2	71211	2	71405	4	71758	1	72028	1	72201	4
71004	1	71219	3	71407	2	71759	1	72031	38	72202	9
71006	12	71220	30	71409	11	71762	4	72032	116	72203	3
71007	4	71221	3	71411	3	71763	2	72033	1	72204	66
71008	3	71222	5	71415	6	71764	1	72039	5	72205	62
71009	5	71225	5	71417	1	71765	2	72040	1	72206	34
71010	3	71226	2	71418	12	71766	1	72042	4	72207	87
71016	3	71227	1	71419	1	71770	1	72043	1	72208	2
71018	9	71230	1	71422	7	71801	12	72044	3	72209	85
71019	9	71232	4	71423	10	71822	14	72045	3	72210	13
71021	3	71234	5	71425	3	71823	2	72046	2	72211	32
71023	8	71235	6	71429	3	71825	2	72047	1	72212	46
71024	3	71237	2	71430	3	71832	21	72051	8	72215	2

72217	2	72482	1	72687	25	72921	14	73070	29	73169	1
72219	4	72501	61	72701	89	72923	13	73071	103	73170	30
72231	2	72503	5	72702	4	72927	24	73072	66	73177	2
72301	61	72512	4	72703	54	72928	1	73074	1	73179	2
72303	2	72513	2	72712	33	72932	7	73075	18	73189	1
72311	1	72519	13	72714	29	72933	14	73077	4	73401	70
72315	37	72521	14	72718	1	72934	1	73078	18	73402	5
72324	10	72524	3	72719	1	72935	3	73080	14	73403	1
72326	1	72525	6	72722	6	72936	22	73081	1	73430	8
72327	1	72527	1	72723	1	72937	2	73082	4	73438	6
72331	1	72529	5	72724	1	72938	4	73083	9	73439	16
72333	1	72530	3	72727	3	72940	4	73084	8	73441	4
72335	22	72531	1	72728	5	72941	4	73086	20	73443	3
72339	2	72532	3	72730	7	72943	8	73089	29	73446	9
72342	12	72534	4	72732	5	72944	2	73091	2	73447	1
72346	2	72537	3	72734	8	72946	11	73093	6	73448	4
72347	1	72542	19	72735	2	72947	4	73095	5	73449	7
72348	6	72543	24	72736	7	72948	1	73096	18	73453	4
72351	1	72546	1	72738	2	72949	9	73097	1	73456	2
72354	2	72548	2	72739	12	72950	3	73098	10	73458	1
72358	1	72550	3	72740	16	72952	2	73099	88	73460	5
72360	3	72554	7	72742	1	72956	47	73101	5	73461	1
72364	36	72555	2	72744	4	72958	5	73102	3	73463	7
72365	1	72556	11	72745	13	72959	4	73103	6	73501	70
72366	1	72560	15	72751	4	73005	21	73104	1	73502	7
72370	10	72561	1	72753	24	73006	4	73105	5	73503	10
72373	3	72562	4	72756	110	73007	6	73106	14	73505	117
72376	1	72565	3	72757	6	73008	105	73107	52	73506	1
72384	2	72568	5	72761	38	73009	4	73108	22	73507	29
72386	2	72575	2	72762	9	73010	33	73109	33	73520	1
72390	13	72576	4	72764	95	73011	1	73110	104	73521	80
72394	4	72579	2	72765	8	73013	47	73111	5	73522	2
72395	6	72581	2	72766	2	73014	12	73112	92	73523	1
72396	14	72583	1	72769	1	73015	2	73113	4	73526	1
72401	152	72584	1	72770	3	73016	5	73114	26	73527	10
72402	1	72601	106	72773	11	73017	4	73115	68	73529	11
72403	4	72602	1	72774	14	73018	30	73116	32	73530	2
72411	7	72610	1	72775	2	73020	41	73117	1	73533	78
72412	2	72611	2	72801	122	73023	3	73118	34	73534	3
72415	4	72613	3	72807	1	73024	3	73119	58	73537	4
72416	9	72615	2	72811	1	73025	1	73120	74	73538	7
72417	5	72616	18	72821	3	73028	3	73121	8	73541	6
72420	1	72618	1	72823	14	73029	3	73122	58	73542	10
72421	2	72619	5	72824	4	73030	14	73123	5	73543	2
72422	2	72624	1	72829	2	73031	1	73125	1	73544	1
72429	1	72626	3	72830	27	73032	1	73126	1	73546	1
72430	1	72628	1	72832	1	73034	186	73127	54	73547	3
72432	9	72629	1	72833	12	73035	3	73128	3	73549	1
72433	12	72630	1	72834	13	73036	56	73129	25	73550	3
72434	3	72632	38	72835	4	73038	1	73130	53	73552	6
72435	1	72633	8	72837	21	73039	1	73131	5	73554	9
72436	3	72634	8	72840	6	73040	4	73132	92	73556	3
72437	7	72635	7	72842	5	73041	1	73134	2	73558	1
72438	3	72636	1	72843	4	73042	2	73135	38	73559	2
72442	2	72638	6	72845	4	73044	32	73136	1	73565	3
72443	7	72641	3	72846	3	73045	22	73139	42	73566	2
72444	1	72642	18	72847	12	73047	2	73140	5	73567	2
72447	2	72644	4	72853	23	73048	1	73141	3	73568	7
72449	2	72645	5	72854	2	73049	11	73142	17	73570	8
72450	121	72650	6	72855	3	73051	17	73143	2	73572	6
72451	3	72651	10	72856	1	73052	7	73144	6	73573	2
72454	6	72653	117	72857	5	73053	1	73145	9	73575	2
72455	13	72655	3	72858	9	73054	15	73146	1	73601	11
72459	2	72658	5	72863	1	73055	31	73147	3	73620	2
72460	1	72662	6	72865	1	73057	5	73149	5	73624	7
72461	8	72666	1	72901	48	73059	4	73150	8	73626	4
72466	7	72668	2	72902	4	73062	1	73153	6	73627	5
72467	2	72672	6	72903	81	73063	3	73154	4	73628	4
72469	2	72675	1	72904	39	73064	40	73156	4	73632	8
72470	1	72677	3	72906	2	73065	14	73157	1	73639	1
72472	22	72679	1	72913	1	73066	3	73159	70	73642	1
72473	2	72680	2	72914	2	73067	3	73160	113	73644	22
72476	24	72683	2	72916	4	73068	18	73162	30	73645	3
72479	1	72686	4	72917	1	73069	108	73165	16	73646	1

ZIP	Count	ZIP	Count	ZIP	Count	ZIP	Count	ZIP	Count	ZIP	Count
73650	5	73950	2	74126	8	74447	59	74764	2	75018	1
73651	11	74002	2	74127	20	74450	2	74801	82	75019	58
73655	3	74003	86	74128	43	74451	9	74802	1	75020	94
73658	2	74004	1	74129	65	74454	2	74820	46	75021	3
73660	1	74005	5	74130	4	74455	3	74824	5	75023	193
73662	5	74006	106	74131	7	74461	1	74827	2	75024	11
73663	2	74008	29	74132	13	74462	23	74831	4	75025	28
73666	1	74010	13	74133	70	74464	36	74832	3	75026	2
73667	3	74011	52	74134	40	74465	1	74833	2	75028	57
73669	2	74012	116	74135	80	74467	14	74834	10	75029	2
73673	1	74013	9	74136	71	74469	6	74839	2	75031	5
73701	88	74014	59	74137	37	74470	4	74840	6	75034	24
73702	5	74015	17	74138	1	74471	1	74842	2	75038	22
73703	47	74016	8	74145	89	74477	1	74843	1	75039	2
73706	1	74017	72	74146	41	74501	72	74844	2	75040	156
73717	9	74018	4	74150	3	74502	4	74848	13	75041	87
73718	1	74020	23	74152	2	74506	1	74851	12	75042	205
73720	1	74021	23	74157	1	74523	10	74854	1	75043	114
73723	3	74022	6	74158	5	74524	1	74855	12	75044	47
73724	22	74023	12	74159	6	74525	28	74856	1	75045	1
73725	1	74026	1	74169	3	74528	1	74857	14	75046	16
73728	6	74027	4	74170	3	74533	2	74859	8	75047	2
73729	3	74028	1	74171	3	74535	1	74860	6	75048	11
73730	3	74029	8	74301	48	74538	12	74864	6	75049	1
73734	8	74030	2	74330	5	74546	2	74865	4	75050	67
73735	2	74032	6	74331	12	74547	7	74867	3	75051	88
73737	24	74033	13	74332	5	74552	1	74868	21	75052	53
73738	1	74035	7	74337	15	74553	5	74869	5	75053	4
73742	12	74036	11	74338	6	74554	7	74871	1	75056	70
73747	1	74037	26	74339	1	74555	2	74872	1	75057	4
73750	14	74038	3	74340	1	74557	1	74873	18	75058	4
73753	4	74039	11	74342	4	74561	2	74875	2	75059	7
73754	5	74041	1	74343	7	74563	4	74878	5	75060	67
73755	4	74044	7	74344	28	74565	1	74880	2	75061	84
73759	4	74047	14	74346	6	74569	1	74881	14	75062	121
73760	1	74048	9	74347	5	74571	6	74883	4	75063	13
73761	1	74050	6	74349	2	74573	1	74884	12	75064	6
73762	10	74053	3	74350	1	74578	2	74901	4	75065	8
73763	3	74054	3	74352	3	74601	72	74902	3	75067	166
73766	4	74055	69	74353	1	74602	2	74932	2	75068	16
73768	2	74056	19	74354	48	74604	18	74937	5	75069	105
73770	1	74058	6	74355	4	74630	2	74939	4	75070	18
73771	1	74059	5	74358	1	74631	21	74940	3	75071	2
73772	15	74060	1	74360	3	74632	1	74941	2	75072	1
73773	3	74061	3	74361	14	74633	1	74943	1	75073	5
73801	32	74062	4	74362	6	74637	3	74947	1	75074	169
73802	2	74063	63	74363	8	74641	5	74948	14	75075	191
73832	1	74066	72	74364	1	74643	4	74949	2	75076	20
73834	3	74067	1	74365	4	74644	2	74951	2	75077	25
73840	1	74070	24	74366	7	74647	6	74953	12	75078	4
73841	6	74072	3	74367	1	74651	1	74954	10	75080	240
73843	5	74073	10	74368	1	74652	1	74955	19	75081	187
73848	6	74074	57	74369	2	74653	6	74956	2	75082	16
73849	1	74075	33	74370	6	74701	58	74957	1	75083	13
73852	18	74076	5	74401	49	74702	1	74959	9	75085	4
73853	1	74077	1	74403	37	74723	1	74960	1	75086	2
73855	2	74079	11	74421	5	74725	1	74962	3	75087	57
73858	6	74080	4	74422	10	74726	3	74963	2	75088	68
73859	7	74083	2	74423	1	74727	4	74965	9	75089	14
73920	1	74085	3	74425	2	74728	4	74966	2	75090	118
73930	2	74101	6	74426	16	74729	4	75001	4	75091	1
73931	4	74103	2	74427	6	74730	7	75002	127	75093	20
73932	5	74104	33	74428	2	74731	2	75003	9	75094	9
73933	3	74105	81	74429	16	74733	7	75004	4	75095	9
73935	1	74106	5	74430	2	74735	2	75005	4	75098	58
73937	2	74107	28	74431	1	74740	2	75006	109	75101	1
73938	2	74108	18	74432	33	74741	5	75007	133	75102	4
73939	2	74110	18	74434	12	74743	23	75009	6	75103	13
73942	24	74112	78	74435	4	74745	10	75010	5	75104	54
73944	2	74114	57	74436	8	74747	1	75011	8	75110	68
73945	4	74115	67	74437	27	74748	1	75012	1	75115	78
73946	1	74116	15	74441	1	74750	2	75014	1	75116	74
73947	1	74119	9	74445	15	74753	1	75015	3	75117	8
73949	3	74120	10	74446	1	74756	1	75016	4	75119	24

75120	2	75241	9	75478	1	75686	21	75929	5	76053	111
75124	9	75243	93	75479	9	75688	2	75930	1	76054	42
75125	6	75244	35	75480	4	75691	1	75931	6	76055	5
75126	18	75246	3	75482	26	75692	3	75932	3	76056	9
75127	4	75248	106	75486	12	75693	14	75933	4	76058	31
75134	16	75249	14	75488	5	75694	1	75935	6	76059	23
75135	1	75251	2	75489	4	75701	94	75938	3	76060	3
75137	48	75252	55	75490	10	75702	18	75939	2	76061	3
75138	1	75253	18	75491	3	75703	93	75941	7	76063	28
75140	12	75261	4	75494	17	75704	13	75943	4	76065	28
75141	4	75266	3	75495	4	75705	2	75944	5	76066	13
75142	24	75275	5	75496	10	75706	5	75946	5	76067	56
75143	29	75287	33	75497	5	75707	12	75948	14	76071	7
75144	1	75354	1	75501	56	75708	5	75949	10	76072	1
75146	21	75355	2	75502	35	75709	8	75951	25	76073	9
75147	72	75371	2	75503	30	75710	3	75954	3	76075	2
75148	16	75374	4	75504	4	75711	3	75956	12	76076	3
75149	97	75376	1	75505	3	75712	2	75959	2	76078	10
75150	135	75378	1	75550	1	75713	4	75960	1	76079	1
75152	7	75379	3	75551	26	75737	1	75961	62	76082	16
75154	44	75380	2	75554	8	75750	12	75962	5	76083	1
75155	4	75381	1	75555	3	75751	68	75963	3	76084	10
75158	7	75382	1	75556	1	75754	3	75966	1	76086	98
75159	12	75401	106	75558	4	75755	11	75968	2	76087	25
75160	39	75402	4	75559	10	75756	4	75969	8	76092	28
75163	17	75403	3	75560	6	75757	16	75970	1	76093	5
75165	69	75407	9	75561	11	75758	20	75972	8	76094	4
75166	2	75409	1	75562	1	75760	1	75973	3	76095	4
75169	22	75410	5	75563	8	75762	12	75974	2	76101	5
75172	8	75411	2	75566	2	75763	13	75975	3	76102	4
75173	4	75412	1	75567	2	75765	11	75979	14	76103	35
75180	20	75414	2	75568	27	75766	51	75980	3	76104	6
75181	11	75416	2	75569	2	75770	3	76003	3	76105	10
75182	9	75417	2	75570	48	75771	35	76004	2	76106	15
75185	3	75418	29	75571	8	75773	16	76005	1	76107	43
75189	2	75421	2	75572	8	75778	3	76006	30	76108	103
75197	1	75422	5	75573	4	75779	2	76007	1	76109	68
75201	2	75423	6	75574	5	75782	1	76008	20	76110	39
75202	1	75424	3	75579	1	75783	13	76009	40	76111	37
75203	5	75426	9	75601	80	75784	2	76010	104	76112	95
75204	9	75428	25	75602	22	75785	26	76011	42	76114	62
75205	65	75429	2	75603	8	75789	17	76012	78	76115	20
75206	31	75431	1	75604	40	75790	1	76013	126	76116	146
75208	25	75432	8	75605	16	75791	28	76014	69	76117	79
75209	21	75433	5	75606	11	75792	4	76015	43	76118	85
75211	47	75434	1	75607	11	75801	94	76016	111	76119	50
75212	2	75435	1	75608	3	75802	3	76017	107	76120	9
75213	1	75436	1	75630	6	75831	19	76018	43	76121	3
75214	80	75437	3	75631	5	75833	2	76019	1	76122	2
75215	1	75438	4	75633	49	75835	13	76020	60	76123	20
75216	23	75439	3	75638	14	75839	8	76021	106	76124	2
75217	73	75440	5	75639	7	75840	21	76022	36	76126	63
75218	91	75442	5	75640	7	75844	4	76023	20	76127	2
75219	12	75444	5	75643	9	75845	7	76024	8	76129	2
75220	51	75446	26	75644	27	75846	4	76026	18	76131	9
75221	6	75447	2	75647	17	75847	3	76028	116	76132	45
75222	3	75448	1	75650	14	75849	1	76030	7	76133	174
75223	10	75449	2	75651	6	75850	4	76031	105	76134	62
75224	32	75452	6	75652	58	75851	2	76033	3	76135	45
75225	55	75453	10	75653	2	75852	2	76034	39	76136	3
75226	1	75454	3	75656	12	75853	3	76035	2	76137	43
75227	64	75455	35	75657	14	75855	5	76036	45	76140	28
75228	150	75456	1	75658	1	75858	1	76037	1	76146	1
75229	140	75457	8	75660	1	75859	6	76039	73	76148	69
75230	75	75459	2	75661	5	75860	13	76040	23	76155	3
75231	44	75460	70	75662	40	75861	4	76043	5	76161	1
75232	34	75461	3	75666	1	75862	16	76044	6	76162	1
75233	21	75462	2	75667	1	75901	97	76045	4	76163	3
75234	99	75469	3	75668	9	75902	1	76046	33	76179	50
75235	12	75471	2	75669	1	75903	5	76048	89	76180	121
75236	20	75472	6	75670	41	75905	1	76049	16	76182	1
75237	2	75473	9	75681	6	75915	1	76050	10	76185	2
75238	102	75474	46	75683	7	75925	9	76051	77	76193	1
75240	78	75476	4	75684	7	75926	1	76052	10	76201	155

76202	5	76457	11	76649	2	76906	2	77064	22	77275	1
76203	3	76458	2	76651	4	76908	2	77065	25	77277	7
76204	1	76460	1	76652	3	76909	2	77066	34	77280	4
76205	48	76464	2	76653	2	76933	1	77067	18	77284	1
76206	3	76468	1	76654	1	76934	1	77068	26	77287	1
76207	1	76470	11	76655	15	76936	4	77069	35	77289	3
76208	2	76471	2	76656	5	76941	1	77070	73	77290	3
76225	4	76472	1	76657	12	76943	11	77071	46	77301	18
76226	18	76474	1	76660	1	76945	3	77072	75	77302	28
76227	13	76475	1	76661	10	76950	2	77073	11	77303	39
76228	5	76476	1	76664	9	76951	3	77074	49	77304	14
76230	43	76485	4	76665	6	76957	1	77075	44	77305	7
76233	5	76501	67	76667	13	77001	1	77076	43	77325	3
76234	16	76502	59	76670	1	77002	11	77077	79	77326	1
76239	2	76503	4	76673	4	77003	1	77078	9	77327	77
76240	54	76504	17	76678	1	77004	8	77079	90	77328	6
76244	1	76505	6	76679	12	77005	45	77080	72	77331	9
76245	6	76511	2	76681	2	77006	19	77081	22	77332	1
76246	1	76513	79	76682	2	77007	18	77082	29	77335	5
76247	9	76518	4	76686	1	77008	49	77083	51	77336	15
76248	54	76520	13	76687	3	77009	31	77084	80	77338	46
76249	15	76522	48	76689	14	77011	1	77085	11	77339	71
76250	2	76524	10	76690	5	77012	7	77086	22	77340	53
76251	1	76526	1	76691	6	77013	7	77087	36	77341	1
76252	2	76527	7	76692	25	77014	9	77088	60	77342	2
76255	4	76528	35	76693	3	77015	62	77089	109	77345	17
76258	3	76530	4	76701	1	77016	13	77090	26	77346	29
76259	5	76531	6	76702	2	77017	39	77091	15	77347	3
76262	36	76534	3	76704	1	77018	63	77092	47	77348	1
76264	2	76537	1	76705	44	77019	17	77093	34	77351	90
76265	1	76538	2	76706	34	77020	3	77094	2	77355	53
76266	45	76539	17	76707	21	77021	3	77095	43	77356	25
76268	2	76541	44	76708	29	77022	18	77096	125	77357	49
76270	4	76542	25	76710	101	77023	24	77098	16	77358	9
76272	7	76543	25	76711	16	77024	81	77099	59	77360	6
76273	15	76544	14	76712	39	77025	65	77205	3	77362	7
76301	43	76545	2	76714	3	77026	1	77207	2	77363	4
76302	23	76546	1	76715	1	77027	15	77208	3	77365	22
76303	2	76547	1	76748	1	77028	7	77210	2	77367	3
76304	2	76550	18	76801	56	77029	11	77215	1	77368	1
76305	26	76554	3	76803	1	77030	15	77217	1	77371	12
76306	18	76557	2	76804	2	77031	28	77218	3	77372	8
76308	77	76558	1	76820	2	77032	11	77219	2	77373	80
76309	46	76559	2	76821	4	77033	13	77220	1	77374	1
76310	48	76561	4	76823	3	77034	61	77221	1	77375	62
76311	3	76563	1	76825	17	77035	61	77222	1	77377	2
76351	3	76567	18	76827	3	77036	63	77223	1	77378	36
76354	40	76569	2	76828	1	77037	34	77224	1	77379	95
76357	1	76570	7	76834	14	77038	23	77225	2	77380	34
76360	8	76571	6	76837	1	77039	35	77227	7	77381	29
76365	31	76574	25	76844	14	77040	63	77231	4	77383	6
76366	5	76577	4	76848	1	77041	14	77234	3	77384	3
76367	31	76578	2	76849	6	77042	64	77237	1	77385	23
76369	1	76579	8	76854	1	77043	45	77240	1	77386	21
76371	1	76621	1	76856	2	77044	10	77241	1	77387	1
76372	4	76622	1	76857	4	77045	7	77242	2	77388	42
76374	13	76624	1	76858	2	77046	2	77244	3	77389	27
76380	6	76626	6	76861	2	77047	10	77245	1	77391	2
76384	28	76627	1	76862	1	77048	5	77249	1	77396	14
76389	1	76629	1	76864	2	77049	20	77253	4	77401	60
76401	40	76630	1	76865	1	77050	3	77254	2	77402	2
76429	1	76632	3	76866	1	77051	2	77255	1	77411	2
76430	6	76633	7	76870	1	77052	1	77256	3	77413	1
76432	2	76634	21	76871	2	77053	16	77258	3	77414	42
76437	10	76636	4	76875	2	77054	9	77259	1	77415	4
76442	17	76637	1	76877	1	77055	54	77261	1	77417	1
76443	6	76638	4	76878	1	77056	30	77262	1	77418	19
76444	5	76639	5	76886	2	77057	44	77265	1	77419	2
76446	13	76640	5	76890	3	77058	69	77266	1	77422	20
76448	15	76641	5	76901	84	77059	41	77267	1	77423	9
76450	18	76642	3	76902	8	77060	24	77269	2	77426	4
76453	1	76643	25	76903	44	77061	33	77270	3	77429	56
76454	2	76645	14	76904	81	77062	134	77272	6	77430	1
76455	5	76648	5	76905	19	77063	44	77274	3	77434	2

77435	5	77554	7	77840	127	78054	1	78228	87	78387	4
77437	15	77559	1	77841	7	78055	2	78229	50	78390	8
77441	3	77560	2	77842	1	78056	1	78230	91	78393	6
77442	1	77561	3	77843	3	78057	1	78231	32	78401	6
77444	1	77562	21	77844	9	78058	2	78232	66	78402	4
77445	12	77563	9	77845	24	78059	4	78233	88	78403	5
77447	15	77564	2	77853	1	78061	10	78234	11	78404	32
77449	50	77565	54	77856	5	78063	14	78235	5	78405	2
77450	69	77566	106	77857	3	78064	12	78236	1	78407	7
77456	2	77568	33	77859	8	78065	10	78237	11	78408	10
77457	2	77571	49	77861	3	78069	1	78238	69	78409	1
77458	1	77572	2	77864	11	78070	8	78239	82	78410	25
77459	54	77573	113	77865	3	78071	1	78240	114	78411	108
77461	4	77575	5	77866	1	78072	2	78241	2	78412	94
77464	2	77577	4	77868	8	78073	5	78242	38	78413	60
77465	15	77578	23	77871	10	78074	1	78243	4	78414	13
77469	80	77580	3	77872	6	78076	24	78244	20	78415	40
77470	3	77581	107	77875	2	78101	10	78245	73	78416	7
77471	25	77582	1	77876	1	78102	31	78247	63	78417	1
77473	1	77583	18	77878	1	78103	1	78248	6	78418	68
77474	13	77584	39	77879	6	78104	13	78249	57	78419	2
77475	1	77586	97	77880	2	78108	9	78250	129	78420	1
77476	4	77587	26	77881	1	78109	17	78251	39	78426	1
77477	40	77588	6	77890	1	78112	4	78252	2	78427	1
77478	77	77590	76	77901	112	78114	16	78253	15	78463	1
77479	22	77591	12	77902	2	78118	4	78254	5	78465	1
77480	12	77597	2	77903	4	78119	6	78255	25	78466	3
77481	2	77598	48	77904	43	78121	6	78256	4	78467	1
77482	3	77611	17	77905	1	78123	9	78257	5	78468	1
77483	4	77612	20	77935	1	78124	7	78258	11	78472	4
77484	9	77614	2	77951	1	78130	80	78259	7	78501	56
77485	3	77615	1	77954	11	78131	5	78260	10	78502	7
77486	22	77616	2	77957	13	78132	12	78261	4	78503	2
77487	4	77619	71	77962	2	78133	21	78263	6	78504	30
77488	25	77624	1	77963	4	78140	2	78265	8	78510	1
77489	20	77625	20	77964	12	78147	2	78266	1	78516	24
77491	4	77626	4	77967	3	78148	48	78268	1	78520	42
77492	3	77627	62	77968	3	78151	2	78269	1	78521	52
77493	4	77629	1	77978	10	78152	1	78270	2	78523	2
77494	5	77630	104	77979	54	78154	31	78279	2	78535	3
77501	4	77639	2	77982	4	78155	53	78280	4	78537	11
77502	82	77640	57	77983	6	78156	1	78284	2	78538	1
77503	45	77642	40	77984	1	78159	1	78293	2	78539	26
77504	31	77643	1	77987	2	78160	2	78297	2	78540	2
77505	23	77650	3	77989	1	78161	2	78299	2	78543	3
77506	30	77651	47	77991	2	78163	19	78330	1	78545	1
77508	3	77656	51	77993	1	78164	4	78332	12	78550	62
77510	35	77659	12	77995	11	78189	1	78333	1	78552	37
77511	102	77662	48	78001	1	78201	59	78336	21	78559	19
77512	8	77663	6	78002	4	78202	1	78340	1	78560	1
77514	9	77664	6	78003	16	78203	3	78343	3	78563	1
77515	56	77665	6	78005	1	78204	7	78344	2	78566	17
77516	1	77670	2	78006	63	78205	1	78355	2	78568	1
77517	15	77673	1	78009	9	78207	10	78356	1	78569	5
77518	10	77701	13	78010	13	78208	1	78357	5	78570	9
77520	71	77702	2	78011	1	78209	83	78358	3	78572	88
77521	54	77703	17	78013	7	78210	39	78359	2	78573	1
77522	7	77704	2	78014	4	78211	4	78361	9	78575	2
77530	27	77705	44	78016	8	78212	36	78362	16	78576	1
77531	32	77706	74	78017	1	78213	125	78363	34	78577	25
77532	43	77707	38	78022	2	78214	16	78364	1	78578	20
77534	1	77708	29	78023	21	78215	3	78368	8	78580	9
77535	47	77711	11	78024	4	78216	79	78369	2	78582	8
77536	56	77713	2	78025	18	78217	70	78370	3	78583	2
77538	1	77801	50	78026	5	78218	74	78372	3	78586	25
77539	70	77802	58	78028	129	78219	14	78373	8	78589	6
77541	30	77803	21	78029	6	78220	17	78374	39	78593	3
77545	1	77805	5	78039	3	78221	60	78375	1	78594	1
77546	129	77806	2	78040	41	78222	21	78376	1	78595	1
77547	7	77830	1	78041	44	78223	71	78377	28	78596	39
77550	47	77833	43	78043	12	78224	9	78380	11	78597	6
77551	20	77835	4	78044	9	78225	5	78381	1	78598	4
77552	1	77836	9	78051	1	78226	8	78382	53	78599	1
77553	1	77837	1	78052	7	78227	84	78383	7	78602	35

78604	1	78721	2	78935	4	79114	3	79424	61	79764	18
78605	4	78722	7	78941	4	79116	5	79453	1	79765	9
78606	15	78723	37	78942	14	79117	2	79464	4	79766	2
78607	2	78724	4	78944	1	79118	9	79489	1	79768	4
78609	5	78726	5	78945	31	79119	5	79490	2	79772	9
78610	15	78727	46	78946	1	79120	1	79499	2	79782	5
78611	14	78728	10	78947	6	79121	13	79501	5	79785	2
78612	9	78729	46	78948	1	79124	6	79502	3	79788	2
78613	39	78730	4	78949	1	79130	1	79503	1	79821	4
78614	1	78731	99	78950	2	79133	1	79504	20	79830	32
78615	1	78732	3	78952	1	79159	2	79505	1	79831	22
78616	6	78733	17	78953	3	79201	21	79506	1	79835	5
78617	11	78734	20	78956	7	79221	1	79510	18	79836	8
78618	1	78735	12	78957	39	79225	2	79511	3	79838	2
78619	3	78736	24	78959	1	79226	7	79512	5	79839	1
78620	15	78737	24	78962	5	79227	7	79516	1	79842	1
78621	15	78738	2	78964	1	79232	2	79517	2	79843	9
78623	6	78739	6	79002	2	79235	5	79520	5	79845	2
78624	50	78741	30	79005	12	79241	1	79521	14	79847	3
78626	38	78742	2	79007	35	79244	1	79525	4	79849	3
78627	8	78744	32	79008	2	79245	8	79526	2	79851	2
78628	60	78745	120	79009	1	79248	1	79529	5	79852	2
78629	10	78746	84	79010	2	79250	1	79530	1	79855	6
78631	3	78747	11	79011	1	79252	6	79536	9	79901	2
78632	3	78748	32	79014	4	79255	1	79543	1	79902	34
78634	5	78749	29	79015	27	79257	6	79545	2	79903	24
78636	2	78750	102	79016	2	79311	11	79546	1	79904	75
78638	8	78751	31	79018	[illegible]	79313	1	79548	1	79905	14
78639	27	78752	21	79019	4	79316	25	79549	30	79906	12
78640	12	78753	70	79022	8	79322	2	79553	8	79907	26
78641	44	78754	7	79027	5	79323	5	79556	34	79908	2
78642	14	78755	1	79029	18	79325	2	79562	5	79912	111
78643	17	78756	19	79033	1	79329	3	79567	2	79913	7
78644	15	78757	50	79034	1	79330	1	79601	74	79914	3
78645	10	78758	111	79036	15	79331	27	79602	41	79915	22
78648	6	78759	151	79039	1	79336	41	79603	59	79916	5
78650	3	78760	8	79040	1	79338	1	79604	7	79919	1
78652	21	78761	3	79041	6	79339	11	79605	93	79922	16
78653	9	78762	1	79043	2	79343	2	79606	38	79923	2
78654	38	78763	7	79045	14	79345	1	79607	7	79924	179
78655	2	78764	7	79046	2	79346	1	79608	1	79925	102
78656	1	78765	2	79051	1	79347	9	79624	1	79927	21
78659	5	78766	1	79052	1	79351	13	79665	1	79930	46
78660	48	78767	3	79053	1	79356	3	79699	2	79931	2
78661	1	78768	1	79054	2	79357	2	79701	73	79932	20
78662	3	78784	1	79057	5	79359	5	79702	14	79934	9
78663	2	78785	1	79059	3	79360	23	79703	87	79935	41
78664	71	78801	39	79065	47	79363	5	79704	6	79936	84
78665	1	78802	10	79068	5	79364	18	79705	64	79937	6
78666	36	78828	2	79070	22	79366	2	79707	47	79952	1
78667	3	78832	12	79071	1	79367	3	79708	3	79993	1
78669	9	78833	3	79072	49	79370	1	79710	1	80001	6
78670	1	78834	1	79073	3	79371	3	79713	1	80002	34
78671	2	78838	1	79078	3	79372	8	79714	19	80003	85
78672	4	78839	1	79079	5	79373	3	79718	1	80004	121
78674	1	78840	61	79081	8	79376	2	79719	2	80005	46
78676	19	78841	9	79083	13	79377	6	79720	51	80010	73
78680	3	78842	3	79088	13	79382	8	79721	3	80011	96
78681	63	78843	2	79091	1	79401	12	79731	5	80012	116
78701	5	78852	32	79095	2	79403	13	79733	1	80013	132
78702	11	78853	4	79096	3	79404	5	79734	7	80014	75
78703	41	78861	12	79097	3	79405	1	79735	56	80015	87
78704	65	78867	1	79098	1	79406	1	79739	1	80016	11
78705	23	78870	5	79101	5	79407	28	79743	2	80017	57
78709	3	78871	1	79102	12	79408	5	79744	2	80020	124
78711	2	78872	1	79103	9	79409	3	79745	15	80021	18
78712	1	78873	3	79104	3	79410	29	79749	1	80022	28
78713	6	78879	1	79105	9	79411	8	79752	5	80024	3
78714	2	78880	2	79106	63	79412	37	79756	21	80025	1
78716	3	78881	1	79107	34	79413	68	79758	5	80026	54
78717	4	78883	3	79108	17	79414	49	79760	3	80027	50
78718	2	78884	1	79109	88	79415	9	79761	28	80029	1
78719	4	78932	3	79110	46	79416	52	79762	85	80030	79
78720	5	78934	11	79111	1	79423	40	79763	53	80033	52

80034	6	80237	39	80523	1	80818	6	81058	1	81430	2
80037	6	80238	1	80524	82	80819	5	81059	1	81432	3
80038	3	80239	40	80525	132	80820	3	81062	3	81435	4
80040	4	80241	24	80526	116	80821	9	81067	2	81501	72
80041	4	80249	2	80527	1	80824	1	81069	6	81502	14
80044	1	80250	2	80532	4	80825	1	81070	1	81503	74
80045	4	80253	1	80533	3	80827	2	81071	1	81504	40
80047	3	80301	79	80534	6	80828	1	81073	6	81505	9
80101	3	80302	175	80535	5	80829	11	81076	3	81506	18
80102	10	80303	233	80536	8	80831	22	81080	1	81511	1
80103	4	80304	33	80537	176	80840	12	81082	7	81520	13
80104	39	80306	32	80538	83	80841	9	81084	2	81521	15
80105	2	80307	5	80539	6	80860	2	81089	13	81523	2
80106	16	80308	4	80540	15	80863	47	81090	4	81524	3
80107	14	80401	117	80541	5	80864	1	81091	2	81525	2
80110	97	80402	6	80543	3	80866	47	81092	6	81526	10
80111	68	80403	73	80544	5	80901	4	81101	19	81527	2
80112	65	80418	1	80545	1	80902	1	81120	1	81546	1
80113	1	80421	27	80547	2	80903	25	81121	1	81601	34
80116	7	80422	5	80549	7	80904	79	81122	10	81602	13
80117	1	80424	11	80550	13	80905	4	81125	3	81611	12
80118	12	80425	2	80601	27	80906	108	81130	3	81612	17
80120	80	80427	4	80610	3	80907	102	81131	3	81615	2
80121	72	80428	2	80611	1	80908	73	81133	3	81620	6
80122	117	80432	3	80615	3	80909	147	81135	1	81621	4
80123	198	80433	36	80620	8	80910	47	81137	11	81623	20
80124	25	80435	6	80621	6	80911	71	81140	1	81624	2
80125	10	80436	1	80623	1	80913	4	81141	4	81625	33
80126	33	80438	7	80631	90	80914	1	81144	5	81626	2
80127	66	80439	73	80632	3	80915	60	81146	1	81628	1
80132	54	80441	1	80634	31	80916	65	81147	20	81631	7
80133	7	80442	2	80640	7	80917	90	81154	2	81632	6
80134	92	80443	5	80642	3	80918	158	81157	6	81635	6
80135	12	80444	1	80643	3	80919	83	81201	23	81637	5
80136	6	80446	62	80644	1	80920	54	81210	1	81639	1
80151	1	80447	6	80645	9	80921	18	81211	30	81641	5
80155	3	80448	1	80648	2	80922	2	81212	94	81643	4
80160	1	80451	9	80650	2	80925	1	81215	5	81647	5
80161	2	80452	13	80651	6	80926	3	81220	2	81648	4
80162	5	80454	5	80654	1	80929	1	81221	2	81650	9
80201	4	80455	2	80701	25	80930	1	81222	2	81652	6
80202	6	80456	3	80720	5	80932	4	81223	3	81654	2
80203	21	80457	2	80721	1	80933	7	81224	1	81657	9
80204	18	80459	5	80722	4	80934	4	81226	18	81658	4
80205	15	80461	17	80723	7	80935	6	81230	22	82001	135
80206	34	80465	34	80727	1	80936	3	81233	6	82003	17
80207	28	80466	20	80728	3	80937	3	81235	2	82005	2
80209	29	80468	2	80729	1	80949	4	81236	6	82007	26
80210	82	80470	11	80731	1	80960	1	81240	6	82009	69
80211	24	80471	1	80734	10	80962	5	81243	1	82050	1
80212	24	80474	6	80736	1	81001	72	81244	2	82052	1
80213	1	80475	1	80737	4	81002	3	81250	1	82053	2
80214	27	80477	23	80741	5	81003	27	81252	11	82054	2
80215	72	80478	5	80743	1	81004	61	81301	105	82063	1
80216	1	80480	1	80744	2	81005	69	81302	17	82070	112
80217	2	80481	4	80745	1	81006	44	81321	21	82071	6
80218	18	80482	4	80749	2	81007	18	81323	7	82083	2
80219	70	80483	4	80750	1	81008	17	81326	1	82122	1
80220	61	80487	3	80751	99	81019	5	81327	1	82190	4
80221	113	80488	5	80755	1	81022	4	81328	6	82201	16
80222	65	80501	231	80757	2	81023	6	81329	1	82213	3
80223	19	80502	8	80758	7	81025	2	81401	79	82221	8
80224	41	80503	43	80759	6	81028	3	81402	9	82223	3
80226	98	80504	4	80801	1	81029	2	81410	1	82225	9
80227	75	80510	4	80804	2	81036	1	81413	11	82240	52
80228	106	80512	8	80807	3	81038	1	81415	1	82301	41
80229	62	80513	15	80808	13	81039	2	81416	15	82310	1
80230	4	80514	7	80809	4	81041	1	81418	6	82321	1
80231	72	80515	4	80810	8	81044	2	81419	1	82325	3
80232	20	80516	16	80813	3	81047	5	81423	3	82327	2
80233	100	80517	66	80814	14	81050	39	81424	8	82331	4
80234	29	80520	7	80815	2	81052	12	81425	8	82334	7
80235	6	80521	80	80816	13	81054	10	81427	4	82336	1
80236	32	80522	4	80817	17	81055	2	81428	3	82401	17

82410	6	83201	84	83434	7	83680	1	84022	16	84123	50
82411	2	83202	34	83435	1	83686	41	84023	4	84124	65
82414	31	83204	13	83436	1	83687	14	84025	31	84147	2
82422	2	83205	1	83440	58	83701	6	84027	1	84150	3
82426	5	83206	2	83442	36	83702	61	84029	4	84151	3
82428	1	83209	1	83443	1	83703	40	84032	15	84157	2
82432	2	83210	7	83445	16	83704	181	84033	1	84158	1
82433	1	83211	5	83448	3	83705	108	84035	1	84165	1
82435	12	83213	2	83451	5	83706	77	84036	1	84170	1
82442	3	83221	44	83452	3	83707	5	84037	95	84210	1
82443	9	83226	1	83454	2	83709	146	84039	3	84218	1
82450	3	83227	3	83455	1	83711	3	84040	27	84301	1
82501	44	83234	4	83462	2	83712	22	84041	103	84302	59
82513	9	83236	5	83463	2	83714	6	84042	7	84305	2
82516	4	83239	1	83467	12	83715	4	84043	29	84307	4
82520	24	83244	2	83501	73	83724	1	84044	34	84310	8
82523	1	83250	1	83520	1	83801	14	84046	3	84311	1
82601	94	83252	4	83522	2	83803	1	84047	42	84312	6
82602	7	83254	4	83523	4	83804	1	84049	10	84313	1
82604	54	83255	1	83524	1	83805	22	84050	17	84315	18
82609	53	83256	1	83530	15	83809	4	84051	2	84317	3
82633	13	83260	2	83535	2	83810	3	84052	3	84318	14
82636	5	83261	2	83536	19	83811	3	84053	1	84319	27
82637	8	83262	1	83537	5	83813	2	84054	22	84320	11
82643	1	83263	22	83539	15	83814	145	84056	8	84321	161
82644	6	83274	22	83540	2	83822	1	84057	266	84322	3
82646	1	83276	4	83543	1	83823	3	84058	119	84323	1
82649	1	83278	5	83544	31	83825	1	84059	3	84324	4
82701	4	83286	1	83545	2	83827	1	84060	28	84325	2
82711	1	83287	1	83546	2	83830	3	84061	1	84326	12
82712	2	83301	60	83548	1	83832	2	84062	56	84327	4
82716	65	83303	2	83549	4	83833	3	84065	46	84328	6
82717	7	83309	1	83555	1	83835	40	84066	69	84329	2
82720	6	83311	1	83605	72	83836	2	84067	68	84331	1
82721	1	83313	4	83606	2	83837	9	84068	4	84332	17
82727	1	83316	14	83610	3	83839	3	84069	2	84333	1
82729	6	83318	18	83611	2	83840	3	84070	98	84335	27
82730	2	83320	2	83612	3	83841	1	84072	1	84337	11
82732	1	83321	2	83615	5	83843	81	84074	41	84339	7
82801	80	83323	1	83616	22	83845	6	84075	6	84340	3
82833	3	83327	2	83617	33	83846	4	84076	9	84355	1
82834	11	83328	9	83619	18	83847	4	84078	38	84390	1
82835	1	83329	1	83620	1	83849	7	84080	1	84400	1
82836	2	83330	10	83622	2	83850	16	84082	1	84401	51
82839	4	83332	1	83623	6	83853	2	84083	1	84403	65
82842	4	83333	7	83624	2	83854	66	84084	96	84404	107
82901	39	83334	1	83627	2	83855	6	84086	2	84405	32
82902	14	83335	1	83628	10	83856	19	84087	19	84408	1
82911	1	83336	2	83629	2	83857	3	84088	25	84409	3
82923	1	83338	19	83630	1	83858	22	84091	3	84414	23
82926	1	83340	11	83631	3	83860	12	84092	104	84470	1
82929	1	83341	8	83632	1	83861	16	84093	32	84501	49
82930	33	83344	2	83634	16	83864	51	84094	22	84503	1
82931	3	83346	2	83635	1	83867	4	84098	1	84511	3
82933	1	83347	1	83638	12	83868	2	84101	5	84513	13
82935	54	83349	1	83639	3	83869	11	84102	28	84516	1
82937	6	83350	14	83641	2	83870	2	84103	51	84520	2
82941	7	83352	2	83642	83	83871	9	84104	18	84521	2
83001	27	83353	3	83644	7	83872	2	84105	52	84522	1
83011	2	83355	5	83645	1	83873	3	84106	72	84523	5
83012	1	83401	157	83647	47	83876	4	84107	78	84526	10
83013	2	83402	65	83648	18	84001	7	84108	144	84528	2
83014	1	83403	1	83651	110	84003	110	84109	98	84530	1
83023	1	83404	40	83652	1	84004	6	84110	7	84532	30
83025	1	83405	1	83653	3	84006	1	84111	15	84535	6
83101	18	83406	20	83654	4	84007	4	84112	2	84536	2
83110	8	83420	8	83655	7	84010	136	84113	1	84537	4
83111	1	83421	1	83656	2	84013	1	84115	36	84542	2
83113	4	83422	3	83660	10	84014	43	84116	36	84544	1
83114	4	83423	1	83661	16	84015	80	84117	93	84601	129
83116	2	83427	2	83669	3	84017	3	84118	122	84602	3
83118	3	83428	1	83672	17	84018	1	84119	73	84603	12
83121	3	83429	1	83676	10	84020	12	84120	89	84604	145
83128	1	83433	1	83677	2	84021	17	84121	110	84606	31

84620	7	85003	8	85226	65	85339	14	85622	5	85937	23
84622	3	85004	11	85228	29	85340	30	85623	8	85938	3
84624	17	85006	35	85230	2	85342	5	85624	5	85939	5
84627	3	85007	17	85231	4	85343	1	85625	14	85942	2
84629	4	85008	97	85232	20	85344	22	85628	2	86001	121
84630	2	85009	31	85234	110	85345	113	85629	12	86002	15
84631	5	85010	1	85236	11	85346	15	85630	10	86003	10
84632	1	85011	3	85237	4	85347	2	85631	7	86004	55
84633	1	85012	18	85238	2	85348	8	85632	2	86017	7
84634	8	85013	49	85239	11	85349	1	85634	1	86018	6
84635	7	85014	63	85240	1	85350	3	85635	222	86021	5
84636	6	85015	68	85242	13	85351	184	85636	26	86022	3
84637	1	85016	91	85244	3	85352	1	85637	11	86023	4
84642	18	85017	70	85245	1	85353	10	85638	4	86024	3
84643	1	85018	127	85248	39	85354	3	85640	1	86025	29
84645	2	85019	56	85249	5	85355	6	85641	7	86029	2
84647	3	85020	98	85250	23	85356	4	85643	14	86031	1
84648	9	85021	172	85251	110	85357	1	85644	3	86032	1
84649	1	85022	96	85252	15	85358	25	85645	3	86033	4
84651	70	85023	194	85253	133	85359	4	85646	5	86039	6
84652	4	85024	38	85254	170	85361	7	85648	4	86040	58
84653	14	85027	129	85255	11	85362	8	85652	3	86042	2
84654	8	85028	103	85256	8	85363	12	85653	14	86045	1
84655	14	85029	182	85257	119	85364	153	85701	4	86046	10
84660	88	85031	63	85258	60	85365	112	85703	6	86047	34
84662	6	85032	151	85259	28	85366	6	85704	136	86052	1
84663	45	85033	116	85260	74	85372	3	85705	115	86301	175
84664	5	85034	1	85261	5	85373	55	85706	87	86302	16
84665	1	85035	44	85262	2	85374	8	85707	1	86303	45
84668	1	85036	2	85267	1	85375	144	85708	8	86304	5
84701	15	85037	42	85268	48	85377	20	85710	213	86312	28
84711	2	85038	1	85269	3	85380	1	85711	133	86313	2
84713	1	85039	18	85271	1	85381	18	85712	79	86314	50
84715	1	85040	52	85272	1	85382	14	85713	63	86316	1
84718	2	85041	15	85273	4	85390	4	85714	20	86320	4
84720	100	85043	21	85275	1	85444	2	85715	140	86321	3
84721	4	85044	100	85277	1	85501	38	85716	58	86322	40
84722	3	85046	5	85278	5	85502	3	85717	6	86323	35
84723	3	85051	96	85280	3	85530	1	85718	100	86324	9
84724	5	85057	1	85281	104	85531	1	85719	86	86325	5
84725	5	85060	4	85282	181	85532	8	85720	2	86326	83
84728	1	85061	4	85283	132	85533	4	85722	1	86327	25
84729	2	85063	7	85284	53	85534	20	85726	15	86331	3
84734	1	85064	7	85285	13	85535	3	85728	1	86332	7
84737	16	85067	5	85287	1	85536	5	85730	85	86333	19
84738	11	85068	9	85291	4	85539	5	85731	12	86334	7
84739	1	85069	4	85292	5	85540	4	85732	10	86335	8
84741	28	85071	3	85301	101	85541	108	85733	3	86336	62
84745	7	85075	1	85302	105	85543	11	85734	3	86337	3
84746	1	85076	3	85303	35	85544	18	85735	6	86338	2
84747	1	85078	2	85304	117	85545	3	85736	7	86339	1
84751	4	85079	1	85305	3	85546	42	85737	43	86340	8
84753	2	85080	7	85306	96	85547	14	85738	8	86341	1
84754	14	85082	3	85307	5	85550	1	85740	7	86342	7
84758	1	85201	83	85308	119	85551	2	85741	128	86401	157
84759	3	85202	145	85310	16	85552	14	85743	24	86402	14
84760	1	85203	139	85311	10	85553	4	85745	50	86403	144
84761	6	85204	143	85312	8	85554	11	85746	74	86405	6
84762	1	85205	199	85316	1	85601	9	85747	15	86412	3
84765	10	85206	68	85321	22	85602	55	85748	46	86427	8
84767	3	85207	59	85322	1	85603	21	85749	109	86430	31
84770	121	85208	109	85323	15	85606	4	85751	10	86431	2
84771	3	85210	40	85324	7	85607	40	85833	1	86432	1
84772	2	85211	4	85325	3	85608	4	85901	57	86433	2
84774	3	85213	58	85326	22	85609	1	85912	2	86436	8
84775	1	85214	4	85328	1	85610	5	85920	4	86438	1
84779	2	85216	2	85329	3	85611	6	85922	3	86440	18
84780	11	85217	10	85331	46	85613	25	85924	2	86441	16
84782	1	85219	62	85332	4	85614	97	85925	11	86442	53
84783	1	85220	78	85334	2	85615	23	85928	7	86444	10
84784	2	85222	32	85335	2	85616	13	85929	23	86461	1
84925	1	85223	8	85336	1	85617	11	85933	5	86503	2
85001	2	85224	174	85337	1	85618	4	85935	22	86504	4
85002	4	85225	27	85338	13	85621	24	85936	33	86509	2

86510	1	87323	1	87937	7	88316	1	89125	7	89570	3
86512	4	87325	1	87941	1	88317	12	89126	8	89701	131
86515	13	87326	1	87942	1	88318	1	89127	3	89702	16
86556	1	87327	4	88001	231	88325	9	89128	53	89703	16
87002	36	87328	2	88002	9	88330	9	89129	25	89704	10
87004	4	87401	81	88003	7	88337	19	89130	14	89705	7
87008	14	87402	4	88004	15	88339	3	89131	6	89706	33
87010	2	87410	11	88005	119	88340	1	89132	1	89707	1
87013	1	87412	1	88006	8	88341	2	89133	1	89721	2
87015	21	87413	3	88008	4	88345	17	89134	11	89801	52
87016	2	87415	4	88009	1	88346	2	89160	4	89803	2
87020	11	87417	11	88020	2	88349	5	89170	4	89820	13
87022	2	87418	1	88021	33	88350	2	89180	3	89822	3
87023	2	87420	2	88023	1	88352	15	89185	2	89824	1
87025	7	87421	2	88026	1	88353	1	89191	3	89825	2
87031	39	87499	9	88027	1	88401	15	89193	7	89828	1
87032	1	87501	91	88029	7	88415	4	89205	1	89830	1
87035	13	87502	10	88030	87	88416	4	89301	10	89831	1
87036	2	87504	8	88031	30	88426	1	89302	1	89835	2
87041	2	87505	46	88032	2	88434	1	89310	1	90001	34
87042	1	87506	2	88033	4	88624	1	89315	1	90002	14
87043	12	87510	2	88038	1	89001	2	89316	6	90003	27
87046	1	87511	2	88039	1	89003	4	89317	3	90004	133
87047	32	87517	1	88040	1	89004	4	89318	1	90005	59
87048	22	87520	1	88041	3	89005	109	89402	11	90006	62
87053	1	87522	2	88042	1	89006	3	89403	35	90007	27
87059	40	87529	2	88043	6	89008	1	89404	1	90008	43
87062	1	87531	1	88044	4	89009	11	89406	31	90009	22
87068	7	87532	12	88045	6	89010	5	89407	1	90010	5
87071	1	87533	4	88046	3	89013	2	89408	25	90011	23
87102	8	87535	2	88047	15	89014	47	89410	59	90012	14
87104	15	87537	2	88048	3	89015	110	89411	10	90013	4
87105	57	87543	2	88049	7	89019	3	89412	1	90014	5
87106	43	87544	281	88051	2	89020	4	89413	4	90015	14
87107	58	87545	1	88052	10	89021	8	89415	8	90016	59
87108	82	87546	1	88053	4	89023	2	89416	1	90017	5
87109	128	87548	1	88054	1	89028	1	89418	2	90018	34
87110	180	87550	2	88055	1	89029	15	89419	3	90019	65
87111	196	87552	2	88056	1	89030	49	89422	2	90020	78
87112	179	87556	1	88057	1	89031	6	89423	57	90021	5
87113	10	87557	4	88061	80	89039	4	89427	1	90022	27
87114	56	87558	2	88062	35	89040	9	89428	6	90023	23
87115	1	87563	1	88063	3	89041	87	89429	16	90024	100
87116	6	87564	2	88065	10	89042	5	89431	141	90025	104
87117	1	87566	1	88101	93	89043	2	89432	38	90026	114
87118	2	87567	4	88102	1	89044	1	89433	40	90027	67
87119	1	87571	13	88103	1	89045	3	89434	21	90028	37
87120	66	87574	2	88112	2	89046	12	89436	13	90029	41
87121	10	87575	1	88116	3	89049	15	89438	1	90030	2
87122	44	87577	3	88119	2	89056	1	89439	6	90031	30
87123	124	87579	2	88124	2	89057	1	89440	3	90032	37
87124	105	87581	2	88130	13	89101	43	89442	1	90033	26
87125	2	87611	1	88134	1	89102	70	89444	11	90034	144
87154	9	87701	23	88135	2	89103	70	89445	26	90035	61
87174	6	87709	1	88201	138	89104	53	89446	2	90036	73
87176	1	87710	4	88202	2	89105	4	89447	21	90037	20
87184	1	87732	1	88210	30	89106	21	89448	13	90038	43
87185	3	87740	8	88211	1	89107	86	89449	19	90039	80
87190	1	87743	2	88213	1	89108	102	89450	31	90040	15
87191	2	87745	3	88220	58	89109	41	89451	6	90041	110
87192	5	87747	1	88221	3	89110	98	89501	4	90042	125
87194	2	87801	58	88230	9	89111	1	89502	78	90043	50
87195	1	87821	2	88231	1	89112	6	89503	69	90044	33
87196	1	87823	1	88232	1	89114	6	89504	14	90045	222
87198	2	87825	1	88240	99	89115	99	89505	6	90046	90
87199	2	87828	1	88241	1	89116	7	89506	94	90047	41
87209	1	87829	3	88252	5	89117	55	89507	12	90048	38
87233	1	87830	1	88254	5	89118	18	89509	117	90049	167
87301	18	87832	1	88255	1	89119	52	89510	28	90050	4
87305	1	87901	24	88256	2	89120	43	89511	67	90051	2
87312	1	87930	1	88260	25	89121	105	89512	32	90053	7
87313	5	87931	1	88267	1	89122	48	89513	2	90054	1
87319	1	87932	1	88310	161	89123	20	89515	9	90056	26
87321	5	87935	13	88311	11	89124	5	89523	23	90057	28

90058	4	90296	1	90714	7	91116	1	91367	149	91744	118
90059	6	90301	42	90715	47	91117	4	91372	1	91745	125
90060	2	90302	39	90716	14	91118	1	91376	4	91746	30
90061	12	90303	25	90717	106	91125	7	91380	6	91747	2
90062	12	90304	17	90720	143	91126	3	91381	8	91748	93
90063	28	90305	27	90723	60	91128	1	91384	29	91750	137
90064	111	90307	1	90731	167	91129	3	91385	2	91752	71
90065	92	90308	3	90732	129	91154	1	91386	5	91754	124
90066	323	90310	1	90733	24	91201	52	91392	6	91759	7
90067	12	90312	1	90734	4	91202	73	91394	2	91760	86
90068	99	90316	1	90740	214	91203	14	91401	95	91761	118
90069	50	90360	1	90742	22	91204	30	91402	132	91762	117
90070	1	90366	1	90743	4	91205	68	91403	80	91763	69
90071	3	90371	1	90744	125	91206	134	91405	93	91764	82
90072	4	90401	25	90745	362	91207	29	91406	124	91765	166
90073	3	90402	82	90746	91	91208	69	91407	1	91766	73
90075	2	90403	87	90747	1	91209	12	91409	12	91767	98
90077	52	90404	72	90748	16	91214	141	91411	48	91768	53
90078	7	90405	121	90749	5	91221	2	91412	3	91769	4
90083	3	90406	10	90782	1	91224	3	91413	6	91770	90
90086	2	90408	1	90801	22	91226	1	91416	1	91773	113
90091	1	90409	3	90802	57	91230	1	91423	78	91775	78
90093	2	90433	1	90803	282	91244	1	91424	1	91776	65
90104	1	90452	1	90804	69	91256	1	91426	1	91780	145
90125	1	90501	128	90805	159	91265	1	91436	68	91785	4
90131	1	90502	49	90806	82	91280	1	91501	46	91786	260
90175	1	90503	195	90807	138	91301	168	91502	20	91788	3
90201	71	90504	126	90808	228	91302	52	91503	4	91789	132
90206	1	90505	193	90809	3	91303	45	91504	101	91790	170
90207	2	90508	2	90810	91	91304	160	91505	122	91791	102
90210	93	90509	2	90813	31	91305	1	91506	70	91792	72
90211	36	90510	8	90814	54	91306	144	91507	5	91793	6
90212	38	90520	1	90815	209	91307	105	91510	12	91801	103
90213	14	90562	1	90822	4	91308	1	91511	1	91802	5
90216	1	90568	1	90832	3	91309	2	91521	1	91803	76
90217	1	90600	1	90853	7	91310	8	91523	1	91810	1
90220	41	90601	102	90901	1	91311	143	91560	1	91879	1
90221	23	90602	46	90940	1	91313	6	91570	1	91901	14
90222	13	90603	98	91001	144	91316	116	91601	65	91902	21
90223	1	90604	107	91003	1	91319	3	91602	42	91903	3
90224	2	90605	92	91006	220	91320	172	91603	3	91905	2
90227	1	90606	59	91007	30	91321	102	91604	88	91906	2
90230	185	90607	2	91010	75	91322	5	91605	96	91908	3
90231	8	90608	3	91011	173	91324	78	91606	96	91909	1
90232	52	90609	7	91012	4	91325	129	91607	73	91910	50
90240	104	90610	1	91016	137	91326	150	91608	6	91911	45
90241	157	90617	1	91017	2	91328	5	91610	3	91912	6
90242	72	90620	190	91020	32	91331	98	91615	2	91913	9
90245	96	90621	61	91023	5	91332	1	91617	3	91915	1
90247	99	90622	2	91024	76	91334	1	91660	1	91916	1
90248	35	90623	94	91025	4	91335	182	91701	225	91919	1
90249	87	90630	206	91026	1	91337	2	91702	99	91932	23
90250	212	90631	259	91030	82	91340	30	91704	1	91933	3
90251	9	90632	1	91031	5	91341	1	91706	114	91935	14
90254	77	90633	1	91033	1	91342	183	91708	10	91941	45
90255	65	90637	6	91040	94	91343	139	91709	97	91942	29
90260	85	90638	175	91042	124	91344	267	91710	172	91944	2
90262	49	90640	113	91043	2	91345	46	91711	159	91945	19
90263	1	90650	227	91046	3	91346	3	91718	7	91946	4
90265	158	90660	78	91050	1	91350	161	91719	103	91947	1
90266	201	90669	1	91066	5	91351	228	91720	207	91948	1
90270	14	90670	27	91070	1	91352	100	91722	117	91950	16
90272	137	90680	51	91077	1	91353	4	91723	47	91952	1
90274	517	90688	1	91101	45	91354	21	91724	115	91962	3
90275	1	90701	290	91102	3	91355	128	91728	1	91977	35
90277	170	90702	4	91103	29	91356	95	91729	10	91978	5
90278	179	90703	2	91104	124	91357	3	91730	126	91979	1
90280	113	90704	25	91105	45	91358	2	91731	17	91982	1
90290	34	90706	144	91106	75	91359	12	91732	71	92001	41
90291	156	90707	2	91107	164	91360	239	91733	44	92002	35
90292	153	90710	74	91108	58	91361	85	91734	8	92003	4
90293	51	90711	4	91109	7	91362	75	91737	25	92004	30
90294	6	90712	159	91114	2	91364	154	91739	21	92005	4
90295	42	90713	112	91115	1	91365	7	91740	196	92006	13

92007	46	92104	78	92230	7	92339	9	92433	1	92633	177
92008	132	92105	78	92231	5	92340	1	92500	1	92634	7
92009	49	92106	314	92234	67	92341	1	92501	37	92635	118
92010	128	92107	175	92235	3	92342	10	92502	3	92636	1
92011	105	92108	17	92236	5	92343	170	92503	202	92639	1
92012	11	92109	150	92239	8	92344	65	92504	190	92640	162
92013	2	92110	84	92240	80	92345	205	92505	135	92641	123
92014	71	92111	162	92242	11	92346	120	92506	163	92642	9
92016	8	92112	13	92243	39	92347	3	92507	70	92643	84
92018	2	92113	12	92244	9	92348	10	92508	40	92644	74
92019	57	92114	126	92250	20	92349	20	92509	182	92645	109
92020	167	92115	152	92251	6	92350	1	92513	11	92646	414
92021	199	92116	79	92252	67	92351	1	92514	2	92647	321
92022	10	92117	262	92253	26	92352	17	92515	8	92648	162
92023	2	92118	128	92254	3	92353	1	92516	5	92649	219
92024	135	92119	131	92255	2	92354	165	92517	12	92650	1
92025	171	92120	156	92256	9	92355	7	92518	3	92651	90
92026	116	92121	13	92257	17	92356	28	92519	2	92652	8
92027	116	92122	165	92258	6	92357	1	92530	39	92653	187
92028	137	92123	119	92259	3	92358	13	92532	10	92654	5
92029	22	92124	108	92260	99	92359	22	92536	8	92655	36
92030	2	92126	194	92261	10	92360	15	92539	47	92656	28
92032	29	92127	39	92262	62	92361	6	92543	32	92658	9
92033	3	92128	96	92263	6	92362	36	92544	78	92659	13
92034	3	92129	148	92264	36	92363	24	92545	37	92660	205
92035	26	92130	28	92266	1	92364	1	92546	1	92661	47
92036	23	92131	86	92268	6	92365	13	92548	8	92662	46
92037	183	92132	1	92269	1	92367	17	92549	38	92663	193
92038	19	92135	3	92270	33	92369	1	92552	1	92664	2
92039	1	92136	1	92273	4	92370	93	92553	63	92665	88
92040	124	92137	4	92274	6	92371	85	92554	1	92666	55
92041	147	92138	45	92275	4	92372	28	92555	9	92667	211
92042	17	92139	68	92276	13	92373	182	92556	2	92668	66
92044	2	92142	1	92277	120	92374	94	92557	37	92669	116
92045	59	92143	3	92278	20	92375	1	92561	14	92670	199
92046	4	92145	3	92281	3	92376	179	92562	16	92671	1
92049	1	92150	1	92282	1	92377	2	92563	10	92672	136
92050	44	92152	2	92283	6	92378	1	92564	2	92673	1
92053	2	92154	120	92284	158	92379	1	92567	6	92674	3
92054	121	92155	3	92285	6	92380	22	92570	29	92675	109
92055	6	92159	2	92286	15	92381	67	92571	11	92676	13
92056	121	92160	3	92301	36	92382	34	92572	2	92677	154
92057	26	92162	2	92302	17	92383	25	92582	7	92678	3
92059	1	92163	2	92303	1	92384	1	92583	12	92679	27
92060	10	92164	2	92305	29	92385	4	92584	10	92680	173
92061	12	92166	20	92306	25	92386	10	92585	6	92681	10
92062	9	92167	2	92307	160	92387	36	92586	31	92682	3
92063	5	92168	1	92308	69	92388	151	92587	20	92683	388
92064	220	92169	1	92309	1	92389	1	92590	4	92684	7
92065	150	92172	2	92310	12	92390	52	92591	7	92686	210
92066	9	92173	2	92311	169	92391	6	92592	15	92687	23
92067	46	92174	1	92312	5	92392	172	92593	1	92688	23
92068	4	92175	1	92313	1	92393	7	92595	16	92690	9
92069	110	92176	2	92314	62	92394	4	92596	2	92691	201
92070	2	92177	2	92315	75	92395	22	92601	3	92692	126
92071	207	92178	4	92316	37	92396	6	92604	1	92693	4
92072	4	92186	4	92317	9	92397	34	92605	3	92697	1
92073	12	92190	3	92318	4	92398	15	92607	2	92701	85
92074	2	92192	1	92320	48	92399	205	92608	1	92702	1
92075	44	92193	1	92321	13	92401	7	92610	4	92703	57
92077	115	92194	1	92322	4	92402	5	92613	5	92704	155
92078	14	92195	1	92324	155	92404	153	92615	3	92705	165
92079	1	92196	2	92325	64	92405	77	92621	132	92706	84
92082	46	92197	1	92326	1	92406	5	92622	5	92707	117
92083	183	92198	2	92327	9	92407	64	92623	1	92708	425
92084	92	92201	49	92328	2	92408	31	92624	31	92709	5
92085	7	92202	5	92329	3	92409	5	92625	90	92710	2
92086	5	92210	10	92330	103	92410	55	92626	349	92711	4
92088	3	92220	57	92331	3	92411	8	92627	250	92712	2
92092	2	92222	1	92333	6	92412	9	92628	13	92713	16
92093	1	92223	58	92334	1	92413	2	92629	86	92714	290
92101	35	92225	26	92335	243	92414	1	92630	203	92715	130
92102	40	92226	7	92336	49	92415	1	92631	138	92716	8
92103	113	92227	24	92337	1	92427	1	92632	59	92718	2

92720	91	93111	119	93312	41	93527	33	93657	24	94019	63
92728	6	93116	15	93313	14	93528	1	93660	1	94020	27
92767	1	93117	158	93351	1	93529	10	93662	22	94021	2
92799	8	93118	1	93380	2	93532	10	93664	6	94022	351
92801	135	93120	12	93384	1	93534	185	93665	1	94023	5
92802	113	93121	6	93387	1	93535	172	93666	1	94024	50
92803	7	93130	5	93388	1	93536	119	93667	3	94025	257
92804	215	93140	5	93389	5	93539	14	93668	2	94026	10
92805	105	93150	6	93401	117	93541	2	93675	5	94027	8
92806	121	93160	3	93402	85	93543	53	93701	3	94028	13
92807	197	93190	2	93403	2	93544	10	93702	44	94030	55
92808	31	93202	18	93405	25	93545	10	93703	60	94035	9
92812	5	93203	5	93406	13	93546	26	93704	61	94037	12
92814	2	93204	5	93408	1	93549	2	93705	67	94038	17
92815	1	93205	24	93409	1	93550	242	93706	23	94039	5
92816	1	93206	1	93410	1	93551	60	93707	1	94040	172
92817	4	93207	1	93412	6	93552	12	93708	1	94041	48
92825	3	93210	36	93420	100	93553	11	93710	91	94042	9
92826	1	93212	8	93422	72	93554	2	93711	84	94043	114
92841	1	93215	51	93423	12	93555	328	93714	2	94044	110
92866	1	93219	1	93424	3	93556	13	93720	16	94045	1
92868	2	93221	24	93426	7	93558	1	93721	1	94050	1
92901	1	93222	6	93427	22	93560	44	93722	41	94055	1
92932	1	93223	2	93428	28	93561	97	93725	21	94060	11
92952	1	93224	1	93430	14	93562	5	93726	88	94061	122
93001	130	93225	34	93431	3	93563	2	93727	127	94062	130
93002	11	93226	3	93432	4	93576	1	93728	18	94063	75
93003	200	93230	159	93433	28	93581	4	93729	1	94064	20
93004	48	93232	5	93434	4	93582	4	93736	1	94065	16
93006	7	93235	2	93435	1	93584	2	93744	2	94066	110
93007	1	93238	17	93436	226	93586	1	93747	1	94067	1
93008	1	93240	43	93437	16	93590	6	93755	3	94070	148
93010	240	93241	6	93438	8	93591	5	93774	2	94075	1
93011	15	93242	5	93440	1	93592	1	93775	1	94080	114
93012	55	93243	7	93441	10	93596	1	93791	1	94083	2
93013	39	93244	1	93442	51	93601	7	93792	1	94086	298
93014	2	93245	212	93443	2	93602	26	93821	1	94087	361
93015	19	93246	3	93444	54	93604	7	93840	1	94088	15
93016	3	93247	23	93445	17	93605	2	93901	50	94089	66
93017	34	93250	5	93446	110	93609	6	93905	32	94101	4
93020	2	93251	3	93447	16	93610	8	93906	62	94102	16
93021	79	93252	5	93448	4	93611	6	93907	56	94103	17
93022	21	93255	5	93449	26	93612	155	93908	29	94104	4
93023	90	93257	94	93451	9	93613	9	93912	4	94105	9
93030	149	93258	5	93452	3	93614	24	93915	2	94107	22
93031	10	93260	2	93453	6	93615	1	93920	5	94108	13
93033	118	93263	18	93454	156	93616	3	93921	28	94109	51
93034	2	93265	16	93455	166	93618	23	93922	8	94110	53
93035	72	93266	10	93456	8	93620	8	93923	30	94111	9
93040	1	93267	10	93457	1	93621	1	93924	28	94112	67
93041	60	93268	41	93460	26	93622	9	93926	1	94114	37
93042	8	93270	18	93461	4	93625	5	93927	4	94115	22
93043	3	93271	5	93463	29	93626	2	93930	11	94116	95
93044	7	93274	62	93464	4	93628	1	93932	3	94117	46
93045	2	93275	2	93465	13	93630	8	93933	29	94118	40
93055	1	93277	152	93466	1	93631	24	93940	99	94119	6
93060	64	93278	7	93483	2	93635	18	93941	22	94121	54
93061	2	93279	3	93501	16	93637	63	93942	7	94122	79
93062	8	93280	3	93502	1	93638	62	93943	4	94123	31
93063	229	93283	16	93504	2	93639	7	93944	2	94124	13
93065	232	93285	21	93505	20	93640	3	93950	59	94126	1
93066	14	93286	10	93509	1	93641	2	93953	26	94127	54
93067	5	93290	1	93510	32	93643	19	93955	48	94128	8
93093	3	93291	52	93512	1	93644	61	93960	2	94129	10
93101	53	93292	4	93513	8	93645	2	93962	1	94130	11
93102	4	93301	23	93514	81	93646	15	94002	131	94131	53
93103	39	93302	1	93515	4	93647	5	94005	14	94132	32
93104	1	93304	59	93516	4	93648	5	94007	1	94133	29
93105	142	93305	37	93517	1	93649	2	94010	124	94134	36
93106	3	93306	108	93518	4	93650	5	94011	4	94140	1
93107	4	93307	43	93519	1	93651	6	94014	74	94141	1
93108	65	93308	97	93522	2	93653	5	94015	114	94142	4
93109	54	93309	132	93523	19	93654	28	94017	2	94159	2
93110	82	93311	17	93526	2	93656	5	94018	27	94162	1

94164	2	94574	27	94924	5	95051	240	95204	70	95347	4
94188	2	94575	1	94925	34	95052	3	95205	56	95348	22
94301	81	94576	11	94927	1	95053	1	95206	26	95350	89
94302	3	94577	98	94928	95	95054	33	95207	122	95351	94
94303	161	94578	63	94930	26	95055	10	95208	4	95352	7
94304	11	94579	41	94931	12	95056	2	95209	71	95353	3
94305	34	94580	75	94933	2	95060	196	95210	51	95354	29
94306	157	94581	7	94934	1	95061	12	95211	1	95355	72
94309	15	94583	88	94935	1	95062	187	95212	29	95356	39
94321	1	94585	96	94937	6	95063	19	95213	3	95357	5
94401	43	94586	4	94938	1	95064	6	95215	11	95358	4
94402	73	94587	138	94939	17	95065	54	95219	8	95360	5
94403	110	94588	25	94940	1	95066	99	95220	9	95361	72
94404	79	94589	99	94941	88	95068	1	95221	12	95363	11
94501	198	94590	121	94942	3	95070	252	95222	18	95364	2
94506	13	94591	98	94945	22	95071	13	95223	36	95365	1
94507	21	94592	6	94946	2	95073	55	95224	8	95366	19
94508	58	94595	72	94947	117	95075	3	95225	1	95367	12
94509	115	94596	125	94948	5	95076	149	95227	3	95368	3
94510	73	94597	2	94949	33	95077	8	95228	5	95369	5
94511	14	94598	88	94950	1	95096	1	95231	11	95370	104
94513	29	94599	9	94951	18	95104	1	95232	4	95372	12
94514	29	94601	36	94952	139	95106	2	95233	4	95373	5
94515	16	94602	70	94953	8	95108	1	95234	1	95375	2
94516	2	94603	8	94954	26	95109	5	95236	10	95376	129
94517	22	94604	9	94956	12	95110	11	95237	7	95378	6
94518	76	94605	47	94957	11	95111	99	95240	96	95379	11
94519	51	94606	20	94960	52	95112	60	95241	8	95380	127
94520	74	94607	8	94963	1	95114	1	95242	16	95381	4
94521	101	94608	16	94964	1	95116	38	95245	7	95383	26
94522	4	94609	17	94965	46	95117	74	95246	12	95384	1
94523	122	94610	49	94966	25	95118	105	95247	25	95386	7
94524	6	94611	105	94970	2	95119	47	95248	1	95388	18
94525	8	94612	16	94971	5	95120	180	95249	13	95389	7
94526	105	94618	40	94973	2	95121	68	95251	1	95401	140
94527	4	94619	51	94975	1	95122	64	95252	23	95402	14
94528	5	94621	4	94979	1	95123	216	95255	8	95403	55
94530	78	94623	1	95001	2	95124	177	95257	2	95404	115
94533	177	94624	1	95002	5	95125	159	95258	3	95405	113
94535	11	94627	1	95003	116	95126	56	95269	1	95406	7
94536	204	94661	1	95004	8	95127	130	95301	49	95407	37
94537	7	94701	4	95005	55	95128	98	95303	1	95409	45
94538	170	94702	32	95006	49	95129	192	95304	4	95410	3
94539	128	94703	32	95007	6	95130	62	95306	3	95412	2
94540	8	94704	50	95008	164	95131	69	95307	47	95414	2
94541	112	94705	44	95009	4	95132	134	95309	2	95415	5
94542	27	94706	61	95010	62	95133	45	95310	10	95416	2
94544	85	94707	71	95011	2	95134	14	95311	6	95418	2
94545	56	94708	50	95012	5	95135	52	95315	14	95421	2
94546	141	94709	40	95013	2	95136	96	95316	17	95422	38
94547	70	94710	10	95014	300	95137	1	95317	1	95423	20
94548	1	94715	1	95015	8	95138	9	95318	2	95424	6
94549	116	94720	8	95017	2	95139	34	95319	5	95425	16
94550	288	94801	19	95018	60	95140	10	95320	30	95426	12
94551	4	94802	3	95019	15	95143	1	95321	22	95427	2
94552	18	94803	66	95020	90	95148	118	95322	7	95428	7
94553	136	94804	58	95021	4	95150	13	95323	1	95430	1
94555	75	94805	47	95023	76	95151	2	95324	10	95433	6
94556	38	94806	94	95024	1	95152	5	95326	8	95434	1
94558	174	94807	3	95030	286	95153	8	95327	16	95435	2
94559	35	94820	1	95031	22	95154	6	95328	3	95436	20
94560	121	94838	1	95032	43	95155	1	95329	2	95437	42
94561	30	94858	1	95035	169	95156	1	95330	9	95438	1
94563	93	94901	100	95036	2	95157	6	95333	4	95439	2
94564	51	94903	91	95037	118	95159	5	95334	3	95440	13
94565	106	94904	24	95038	2	95160	1	95335	1	95441	2
94566	192	94907	1	95039	10	95161	4	95336	107	95442	32
94567	6	94912	7	95041	12	95164	1	95338	71	95443	3
94568	60	94913	3	95042	1	95170	3	95340	70	95444	3
94569	1	94914	2	95043	3	95171	2	95341	3	95445	31
94570	1	94915	5	95044	6	95185	1	95342	2	95446	15
94571	8	94920	50	95045	14	95201	2	95344	3	95448	42
94572	17	94921	1	95046	19	95202	1	95345	5	95450	4
94573	2	94923	6	95050	105	95203	11	95346	35	95451	35

95452	9	95606	1	95690	4	95835	2	95993	21	96110	2
95453	38	95607	2	95691	51	95837	5	96001	87	96111	2
95454	13	95608	179	95692	8	95838	38	96002	71	96113	2
95456	5	95609	5	95693	24	95841	54	96003	62	96114	15
95457	21	95610	147	95694	16	95842	94	96007	48	96115	3
95458	16	95611	13	95695	102	95852	2	96008	7	96117	2
95459	1	95612	5	95696	8	95856	1	96010	16	96118	1
95460	14	95613	1	95697	1	95860	3	96013	44	96119	1
95461	18	95614	11	95698	1	95864	86	96014	1	96120	3
95462	5	95615	1	95699	1	95865	7	96015	2	96121	2
95464	16	95616	146	95701	3	95866	1	96016	2	96122	22
95465	10	95617	7	95702	8	95876	1	96017	2	96123	1
95466	5	95618	6	95703	9	95901	76	96019	13	96124	1
95467	3	95619	32	95705	6	95903	18	96020	19	96125	1
95468	2	95620	55	95706	6	95913	1	96021	23	96126	2
95469	9	95621	113	95708	6	95914	6	96022	30	96130	32
95470	18	95622	1	95709	36	95916	12	96024	8	96133	1
95472	99	95623	9	95711	3	95917	5	96025	9	96134	12
95473	1	95624	60	95712	7	95918	1	96027	10	96135	2
95476	92	95625	3	95713	27	95919	13	96028	6	96137	25
95480	2	95626	15	95714	2	95920	1	96031	4	96140	6
95482	88	95627	6	95715	1	95922	1	96032	19	96142	1
95484	1	95628	173	95718	1	95923	2	96033	1	96143	8
95485	6	95629	12	95719	2	95924	11	96034	2	96145	7
95487	2	95630	122	95720	1	95925	1	96035	6	96146	2
95488	2	95631	42	95722	33	95926	188	96037	2	96148	10
95489	7	95632	31	95723	2	95927	16	96038	4	96150	2
95490	83	95633	6	95726	59	95928	47	96039	9	96151	5
95492	26	95634	16	95727	1	95932	9	96040	1	96152	2
95493	2	95635	1	95728	2	95934	1	96041	14	96155	1
95495	2	95636	7	95729	5	95935	5	96042	4	96157	1
95497	12	95638	2	95730	20	95936	2	96044	11	96158	3
95501	122	95640	18	95731	17	95937	3	96046	3	96160	4
95502	13	95641	9	95732	2	95938	16	96047	6	96161	5
95503	18	95642	26	95733	1	95941	3	96048	1	96162	5
95504	1	95643	2	95734	11	95942	10	96049	10	96204	5
95521	75	95645	6	95736	20	95944	1	96051	9	96205	4
95524	6	95647	1	95737	3	95945	129	96052	7	96213	4
95525	3	95648	28	95741	4	95946	49	96054	1	96214	2
95526	4	95650	53	95742	1	95947	13	96055	14	96224	1
95527	1	95651	1	95743	1	95948	18	96056	5	96228	1
95528	7	95652	3	95746	11	95949	70	96057	8	96230	9
95531	113	95653	3	95747	4	95951	1	96058	9	96246	1
95534	3	95655	8	95758	29	95952	1	96059	6	96248	1
95536	3	95656	7	95759	2	95953	25	96061	1	96251	2
95538	2	95658	25	95761	2	95954	76	96062	3	96254	1
95540	52	95659	1	95762	7	95955	2	96063	1	96258	1
95542	2	95660	127	95765	1	95956	2	96064	24	96259	1
95543	2	95661	59	95776	1	95957	2	96065	1	96260	4
95547	4	95662	97	95801	1	95959	93	96067	53	96264	2
95549	3	95663	15	95807	1	95960	3	96069	1	96266	5
95551	5	95664	14	95812	1	95961	16	96073	13	96270	1
95552	2	95665	37	95813	1	95962	3	96074	1	96271	4
95553	4	95666	41	95814	22	95963	11	96076	2	96274	1
95554	1	95667	167	95815	58	95965	77	96079	4	96286	10
95555	1	95668	4	95816	37	95966	60	96080	88	96289	1
95556	1	95669	14	95817	22	95967	7	96084	2	96293	5
95558	2	95670	110	95818	29	95968	6	96085	1	96298	2
95559	1	95671	1	95819	56	95969	176	96086	3	96301	22
95560	8	95672	21	95820	69	95971	15	96087	3	96302	1
95562	5	95673	47	95821	120	95974	1	96088	33	96305	1
95563	6	95675	1	95822	101	95975	9	96089	2	96311	4
95564	1	95677	54	95823	104	95976	1	96091	5	96324	1
95565	4	95678	105	95824	30	95977	2	96093	35	96325	2
95567	3	95680	1	95825	110	95978	2	96094	31	96326	9
95569	1	95681	2	95826	135	95979	1	96096	1	96328	3
95570	9	95682	108	95827	54	95982	17	96097	36	96331	5
95571	2	95683	5	95828	125	95983	1	96099	12	96334	14
95573	2	95684	14	95829	15	95984	3	96101	14	96337	3
95585	2	95685	18	95830	2	95986	1	96103	3	96343	5
95602	8	95686	2	95831	65	95987	1	96104	2	96346	7
95603	143	95687	61	95832	22	95988	13	96105	1	96349	7
95604	19	95688	126	95833	57	95991	118	96106	1	96356	5
95605	11	95689	13	95834	11	95992	6	96107	2	96362	2

96364	9	96699	1	96794	1	97009	53	97127	3	97321	156
96366	14	96701	102	96795	17	97010	1	97128	75	97324	3
96367	12	96703	1	96796	18	97011	4	97130	3	97325	15
96368	1	96704	19	96797	64	97013	63	97131	7	97326	2
96369	5	96705	11	96799	32	97014	5	97132	79	97327	9
96370	1	96706	72	96801	1	97015	58	97133	3	97329	2
96372	1	96707	42	96803	1	97016	29	97134	1	97330	179
96373	1	96708	10	96804	1	97017	8	97135	5	97331	5
96376	4	96710	2	96805	1	97018	5	97136	8	97333	49
96377	5	96712	27	96806	1	97019	9	97137	3	97338	47
96379	1	96713	7	96807	1	97020	3	97138	48	97339	17
96408	2	96714	6	96808	2	97021	5	97140	43	97341	10
96410	1	96715	2	96809	2	97022	18	97141	51	97343	1
96432	2	96716	20	96810	3	97023	42	97143	1	97344	2
96440	3	96717	12	96812	3	97024	3	97145	4	97345	1
96451	2	96719	3	96813	43	97026	1	97146	22	97346	1
96461	1	96720	164	96814	39	97027	33	97147	6	97347	2
96464	3	96721	16	96815	92	97028	1	97148	9	97348	9
96505	7	96722	4	96816	143	97029	5	97149	2	97350	1
96506	7	96725	7	96817	104	97030	121	97164	1	97351	13
96512	1	96727	1	96818	153	97031	69	97201	79	97352	12
96516	1	96728	1	96819	71	97032	11	97202	90	97355	99
96519	11	96729	1	96820	24	97034	83	97203	41	97357	1
96528	3	96731	1	96821	51	97035	38	97204	1	97358	2
96534	1	96732	40	96822	142	97036	1	97205	8	97359	1
96537	1	96734	130	96823	3	97037	2	97206	129	97360	8
96540	2	96739	3	96825	75	97038	28	97207	7	97361	22
96543	1	96740	53	96826	71	97039	1	97208	8	97362	9
96548	4	96741	37	96827	2	97040	2	97209	7	97365	40
96550	1	96743	16	96828	2	97041	7	97210	26	97366	13
96555	38	96744	132	96830	23	97042	12	97211	51	97367	39
96557	2	96745	25	96834	1	97045	120	97212	47	97368	13
96558	2	96746	29	96835	2	97048	27	97213	82	97369	4
96601	8	96747	6	96836	8	97049	7	97214	42	97370	28
96602	1	96748	19	96837	2	97050	1	97215	52	97371	5
96603	2	96749	36	96848	1	97051	24	97216	36	97374	10
96604	2	96750	15	96854	2	97053	7	97217	88	97375	5
96614	1	96751	2	96857	2	97054	4	97218	34	97376	14
96618	2	96752	26	96858	1	97055	55	97219	143	97377	2
96622	1	96753	26	96859	1	97056	32	97220	74	97378	11
96624	1	96754	10	96860	5	97058	60	97221	55	97380	5
96629	5	96755	9	96862	2	97060	45	97222	119	97381	34
96630	20	96756	18	96863	2	97062	32	97223	124	97383	16
96634	4	96757	3	96893	1	97063	2	97224	48	97384	1
96635	2	96759	2	96897	1	97064	32	97225	96	97385	5
96637	1	96760	5	96898	4	97065	1	97227	2	97386	40
96641	3	96761	16	96910	48	97067	9	97228	1	97388	9
96643	1	96762	16	96911	78	97068	69	97229	143	97389	4
96646	1	96764	1	96912	28	97070	29	97230	139	97390	4
96648	1	96765	14	96913	19	97071	49	97231	25	97391	17
96651	14	96766	31	96914	5	97075	11	97232	21	97392	11
96652	1	96767	5	96915	10	97077	1	97233	85	97394	27
96654	4	96768	16	96916	3	97080	75	97236	89	97396	3
96656	2	96769	5	96917	14	97101	11	97238	3	97401	113
96658	1	96771	6	96919	2	97102	2	97240	1	97402	112
96661	2	96772	9	96921	148	97103	99	97242	3	97403	20
96662	4	96773	3	96922	3	97106	14	97266	82	97404	124
96665	1	96776	4	96923	4	97107	9	97267	65	97405	138
96666	1	96777	1	96925	2	97108	4	97268	1	97406	1
96667	3	96778	26	96926	4	97110	7	97280	1	97410	2
96671	1	96779	12	96928	10	97111	7	97281	1	97411	29
96672	1	96781	5	96929	4	97112	7	97283	2	97412	8
96673	1	96782	117	96930	3	97113	57	97286	2	97413	5
96674	3	96783	4	96931	11	97114	9	97290	2	97415	82
96675	1	96784	3	96950	71	97115	16	97291	1	97416	3
96677	3	96785	11	96951	1	97116	60	97301	112	97417	4
96678	2	96786	85	96999	1	97117	3	97302	129	97419	8
96679	2	96787	2	97001	2	97118	3	97303	123	97420	111
96680	3	96788	7	97002	19	97119	17	97304	68	97423	33
96683	2	96789	84	97003	1	97121	2	97305	40	97424	35
96685	6	96790	22	97004	27	97122	4	97306	46	97426	12
96692	2	96791	14	97005	201	97123	131	97308	3	97427	4
96697	1	96792	71	97006	150	97124	87	97309	5	97429	8
96698	2	96793	38	97007	190	97125	2	97310	1	97430	4

97431	9	97536	4	97848	1	98059	27	98231	1	98331	7
97432	1	97537	34	97850	62	98061	2	98232	9	98332	10
97434	1	97538	9	97856	1	98062	3	98233	35	98333	25
97435	8	97539	4	97857	1	98063	6	98234	1	98334	1
97436	5	97540	23	97859	4	98064	14	98235	19	98335	208
97437	19	97541	4	97862	59	98065	11	98236	25	98336	4
97438	3	97543	3	97865	1	98070	62	98237	9	98338	54
97439	88	97544	13	97867	1	98071	6	98238	1	98339	10
97440	27	97575	1	97868	4	98072	128	98239	55	98340	24
97441	2	97601	192	97869	1	98073	12	98240	17	98342	4
97442	3	97602	3	97873	1	98083	11	98241	7	98343	1
97443	7	97603	156	97875	7	98093	1	98243	9	98344	1
97444	23	97607	1	97876	5	98101	33	98244	11	98345	13
97446	8	97608	1	97880	1	98102	52	98245	14	98346	40
97447	1	97621	1	97882	10	98103	150	98247	17	98349	30
97448	31	97622	3	97883	5	98104	19	98248	60	98351	6
97449	13	97623	17	97884	1	98105	86	98249	29	98353	5
97450	8	97624	19	97886	7	98106	49	98250	72	98354	13
97451	2	97625	1	97901	2	98107	82	98251	8	98355	2
97452	1	97627	29	97907	2	98108	29	98252	24	98356	7
97453	5	97630	19	97910	1	98109	68	98253	17	98357	3
97454	7	97632	3	97913	4	98110	92	98255	9	98358	14
97455	12	97633	10	97914	35	98111	9	98256	5	98359	25
97456	16	97634	2	97918	1	98112	61	98257	38	98360	27
97457	13	97635	2	98000	1	98113	1	98258	74	98361	6
97458	12	97636	2	98001	70	98114	1	98259	1	98362	161
97459	61	97638	1	98002	191	98115	200	98260	25	98365	62
97461	3	97639	1	98003	116	98116	63	98261	21	98366	241
97462	13	97641	2	98004	121	98117	137	98262	6	98368	93
97463	10	97701	119	98005	70	98118	59	98263	2	98370	124
97464	1	97702	85	98006	154	98119	60	98264	37	98371	91
97465	12	97707	20	98007	66	98120	1	98266	4	98372	34
97467	20	97708	8	98008	125	98121	12	98267	1	98373	91
97469	3	97709	2	98009	19	98122	29	98268	1	98374	68
97470	176	97720	16	98010	5	98124	5	98270	172	98376	13
97473	2	97730	2	98011	178	98125	126	98271	14	98377	3
97476	7	97731	1	98012	90	98126	60	98272	37	98378	1
97477	112	97733	3	98013	5	98127	1	98273	113	98380	7
97478	54	97734	5	98014	21	98133	160	98275	52	98381	2
97479	22	97735	1	98019	23	98134	1	98276	5	98382	130
97480	1	97737	3	98020	199	98136	83	98277	164	98383	71
97481	2	97738	9	98021	59	98138	2	98278	4	98384	1
97484	7	97739	42	98022	86	98144	23	98279	9	98385	4
97486	4	97741	34	98023	97	98145	11	98280	11	98386	1
97487	26	97750	2	98024	21	98146	101	98281	3	98387	69
97488	7	97753	9	98025	4	98148	45	98283	4	98388	27
97489	6	97754	28	98026	26	98155	165	98284	237	98390	163
97490	2	97756	56	98027	189	98165	1	98286	3	98392	9
97491	1	97759	20	98028	5	98166	142	98288	1	98393	4
97493	8	97760	13	98031	208	98168	107	98290	179	98394	19
97495	5	97761	2	98032	93	98177	101	98292	141	98395	5
97496	19	97786	1	98033	132	98178	86	98294	22	98401	6
97497	7	97801	115	98034	130	98188	120	98295	11	98402	7
97498	19	97810	3	98035	2	98189	1	98296	1	98403	17
97499	6	97813	8	98036	158	98195	2	98297	3	98404	74
97501	174	97814	50	98037	99	98198	56	98303	5	98405	53
97502	68	97818	6	98038	49	98199	94	98304	2	98406	76
97503	37	97820	2	98039	3	98201	66	98305	1	98407	75
97504	108	97824	2	98040	117	98203	140	98310	231	98408	82
97506	1	97825	2	98041	6	98204	134	98312	147	98409	46
97508	1	97826	4	98042	103	98205	53	98314	4	98411	9
97520	85	97827	12	98043	76	98206	31	98315	22	98416	1
97521	1	97828	4	98045	39	98207	1	98319	1	98421	1
97522	7	97830	2	98046	8	98208	109	98320	6	98422	43
97523	29	97833	3	98047	13	98209	1	98321	39	98424	16
97524	29	97834	2	98050	2	98220	2	98322	6	98425	1
97525	26	97835	2	98051	8	98221	136	98323	1	98431	1
97526	180	97836	5	98052	193	98222	3	98324	3	98433	44
97527	116	97838	66	98053	114	98223	73	98325	2	98438	1
97530	30	97841	2	98054	4	98224	1	98326	2	98439	11
97531	1	97843	1	98055	145	98225	154	98327	3	98441	1
97532	16	97844	6	98056	136	98226	110	98328	28	98442	4
97533	3	97845	2	98057	4	98227	26	98329	17	98443	22
97535	24	97846	16	98058	118	98230	38	98330	2	98444	62

98445	46	98612	6	98814	1	99022	17	99212	54	99576	12
98446	31	98613	2	98815	9	99023	3	99213	1	99577	100
98457	1	98614	2	98816	16	99024	1	99214	5	99581	4
98465	19	98617	5	98821	3	99025	11	99216	77	99584	1
98466	83	98620	35	98822	4	99026	19	99218	39	99587	5
98467	31	98621	3	98823	81	99027	18	99220	2	99588	13
98497	2	98623	1	98826	38	99029	3	99223	47	99589	1
98498	87	98624	9	98828	8	99030	3	99258	4	99590	1
98499	65	98625	17	98829	4	99031	10	99301	106	99598	1
98501	121	98626	78	98830	2	99032	4	99302	7	99603	28
98502	180	98629	24	98831	8	99033	3	99303	1	99605	2
98503	178	98631	17	98834	4	99034	2	99307	1	99606	2
98506	90	98632	196	98836	1	99036	5	99320	17	99610	5
98507	18	98635	5	98837	39	99037	46	99322	1	99611	38
98509	1	98637	2	98840	7	99101	6	99324	112	99612	1
98512	6	98638	4	98841	31	99102	2	99326	7	99613	1
98513	6	98639	1	98843	3	99103	5	99328	15	99614	1
98516	4	98640	29	98844	7	99109	20	99329	3	99615	43
98520	85	98641	6	98846	9	99110	9	99330	4	99619	11
98524	7	98642	46	98847	2	99111	15	99335	1	99623	2
98526	1	98644	1	98848	14	99113	7	99336	116	99624	1
98527	1	98645	10	98849	1	99114	40	99337	79	99627	1
98528	40	98647	1	98851	12	99115	5	99341	2	99631	1
98530	2	98648	6	98852	3	99116	3	99342	1	99633	7
98531	45	98649	9	98855	13	99117	2	99343	3	99635	11
98532	62	98650	1	98856	8	99119	4	99344	16	99637	1
98535	1	98651	1	98857	3	99122	9	99346	1	99642	1
98537	7	98660	20	98858	9	99123	11	99347	13	99643	1
98540	1	98661	87	98859	4	99124	1	99348	3	99645	60
98541	27	98662	89	98862	3	99128	1	99350	20	99647	1
98542	4	98663	35	98901	48	99129	2	99352	237	99652	14
98546	10	98664	80	98902	108	99130	1	99357	1	99653	1
98547	9	98665	80	98903	45	99131	1	99360	4	99654	13
98548	14	98666	6	98904	1	99133	13	99361	5	99657	2
98550	40	98668	12	98907	9	99134	5	99362	179	99658	3
98555	1	98671	37	98908	98	99135	2	99371	1	99660	2
98556	4	98672	23	98909	5	99138	6	99402	4	99664	15
98557	9	98673	3	98922	10	99139	8	99403	47	99667	3
98558	4	98674	20	98923	3	99141	8	99501	44	99668	3
98560	1	98675	12	98925	4	99144	1	99502	53	99669	57
98562	3	98682	41	98926	103	99148	21	99503	69	99671	1
98563	33	98684	78	98930	8	99149	3	99504	151	99672	14
98564	8	98685	50	98932	4	99150	2	99505	13	99674	2
98569	27	98686	30	98933	10	99155	1	99506	23	99676	5
98570	12	98702	1	98934	3	99156	114	99507	70	99677	1
98571	3	98703	1	98935	6	99157	1	99508	83	99681	1
98575	1	98704	1	98936	13	99158	4	99509	12	99683	23
98576	3	98707	1	98937	24	99159	2	99510	24	99684	1
98577	23	98723	2	98938	3	99160	1	99511	21	99685	2
98579	10	98733	7	98940	3	99161	4	99513	2	99686	17
98580	28	98736	5	98941	1	99163	87	99514	7	99687	83
98581	5	98760	1	98942	56	99165	6	99515	58	99688	14
98582	4	98762	7	98944	27	99166	7	99516	99	99692	1
98584	94	98764	4	98946	3	99167	5	99517	45	99693	1
98585	2	98765	1	98947	2	99168	1	99518	22	99694	1
98586	8	98766	3	98948	12	99169	9	99519	5	99695	1
98588	1	98767	2	98951	13	99170	1	99520	6	99701	121
98589	17	98768	1	98952	4	99171	12	99521	10	99702	17
98590	3	98769	1	98953	12	99173	2	99522	3	99703	13
98591	35	98772	1	98961	1	99176	2	99523	6	99704	6
98592	6	98773	2	99001	9	99180	5	99524	7	99705	87
98593	4	98774	4	99003	19	99181	9	99549	1	99706	21
98595	6	98775	1	99004	40	99185	4	99550	2	99707	49
98596	14	98777	8	99005	13	99196	1	99552	1	99708	87
98597	33	98778	1	99006	22	99201	14	99556	6	99709	102
98601	9	98780	2	99008	1	99202	40	99557	1	99710	15
98604	76	98791	9	99009	5	99203	102	99559	74	99711	8
98605	7	98799	7	99011	15	99204	64	99567	50	99712	42
98606	34	98801	136	99012	3	99205	134	99568	2	99714	10
98607	53	98802	47	99014	3	99206	161	99569	1	99716	1
98608	1	98803	1	99016	26	99207	132	99571	1	99721	1
98609	2	98807	2	99017	2	99208	130	99572	9	99723	12
98610	3	98812	14	99019	20	99210	5	99573	6	99725	5
98611	48	98813	15	99021	16	99211	3	99574	10	99729	3

99730	1	99751	1	99775	4	99803	21	99833	29	99925	3
99737	22	99752	5	99777	3	99805	1	99835	43	99926	2
99738	11	99755	3	99779	1	99806	1	99836	1	99927	3
99741	3	99756	11	99780	14	99821	19	99840	2	99928	4
99742	2	99757	4	99782	1	99824	14	99850	1	Source:	
99743	4	99759	1	99784	1	99826	3	99901	49	Buckmaster	
99744	1	99760	10	99791	3	99827	14	99903	1	Publishing	
99747	2	99762	13	99801	87	99829	4	99919	1		
99750	1	99766	1	99802	29	99832	3	99924	1		

TOP 25 HAM-POPULATED ZIP CODES IN THE U.S.

(As of August 1, 1993)

	ZIP	Hams	City, State
1.	10314	1059	Staten Island, NY
2.	90274	517	Palos Verdes Estates, CA
3.	92708	425	Fountain Valley, CA
4.	06801	423	Bethel, CT
5.	92646	414	Huntington Beach, CA
6.	92683	388	Westminster, CA
7.	00625	370	Caguas, Puerto Rico
8.	90745	362	Carson, CA
9.	94087	361	Sunnyvale, CA
10.	94022	351	Los Altos, CA
11.	92626	349	Costa Mesa, CA
12.	00619	346	Bayamon, Puerto Rico
13.	93555	328	Ridgecrest, CA
14.	90066	323	Los Angeles, CA
15.	92647	321	Huntington Beach, CA
16.	92106	314	San Diego, CA
17.	33012	311	Hialeah, FL
18.	95014	300	Cupertino, CA
19.	94086	298	Sunnyvale, CA
20.	90701	290	Cerritos, CA
21.	92714	290	Irvine, CA
22.	94550	288	Livermore, CA
23.	95030	286	Los Gatos, CA
24.	90803	282	Long Beach, CA
25.	87544	281	Los Alamos, NM

Source: Buckmaster Publishing

TOP 10 HAM-POPULATED ZIP CODES BY STATE /TERRITORY

(As of August 1, 1993)

Alabama

35803 199 (Huntsville)
35802 195 (Huntsville)
35215 185 (Center Point)
35801 179 (Huntsville)
35758 174 (Madison)
35630 131 (Florence)
36301 128 (Dothan)
36701 128 (Selma)
35226 125 (Birmingham)
35901 124 (Gadsden)

Alaska

99504 151 (Anchorage)
99701 121 (Fairbanks)
99709 102 (Fairbanks)
99577 100 (Eagle River)
99516 99 (Anchorage)
99705 87 (Fairbanks)
99708 87 (Fairbanks)
99801 87 (Juneau)
99508 83 (Anchorage)
99687 83 (Wasilla)

Arizona

85635 222 (Sierra Vista)
85710 213 (Tucson)
85205 199 (Scottsdale)
85023 194 (Phoenix)
85351 184 (Sun City)
85029 182 (Phoenix)
85282 181 (Tempe)
86301 175 (Prescott)
85224 174 (Chandler)
85021 172 (Phoenix)

Arkansas

72401 152 (Jonesboro)
72801 122 (Russellville)
72450 121 (Paragould)
72653 117 (Mountain Home)
72032 116 (Conway)
72015 113 (Benton)
72756 110 (Rogers)
72116 108 (North Little Rock)
72601 106 (Harrison)
71901 104 (Hot Springs National Park)

California

90274 517 (Palos Verdes Estates)
92708 425 (Fountain Valley)
92646 414 (Huntington Beach)
92683 388 (Westminster)
90745 362 (Carson)
94087 361 (Sunnyvale)
94022 351 (Los Altos)
92626 349 (Costa Mesa)
93555 328 (Ridgecrest)
90066 323 (Los Angeles)
92647 321 (Huntington Beach)
92106 314 (San Diego)
95014 300 (Cupertino)
94086 298 (Sunnyvale)
90701 290 (Cerritos)
92714 290 (Irvine)
94550 288 (Livermore)
95030 286 (Los Gatos)
90803 282 (Long Beach)
91344 267 (Granada Hills)

Colorado

80303 233 (Boulder)
80501 231 (Longmont)
80123 198 (Littleton)
80537 176 (Loveland)
80302 175 (Boulder)
80918 158 (Colorado Springs)
80909 147 (Colorado Springs)
80013 132 (Aurora)
80525 132 (Fort Collins)
80020 124 (Broomfield)

Connecticut

06801 423 (Bethel)
06010 185 (Bristol)
06460 173 (Milford)
06450 168 (Meriden)
06111 141 (Newington)
06492 133 (Wallingford)
06340 121 (Groton)
06611 120 (Trumbull)
06040 119 (Manchester)
06516 116 (West Haven)

Delaware

19808 94 (Wilmington)
19901 90 (Dover)
19711 88 (Newark)
19803 82 (Wilmington)

19810 75 (Wilmington)
19720 68 (New Castle)
19713 67 (Newark)
19702 49 (Newark)
19805 49 (Wilmington)
19973 49 (Seaford)

District of Columbia

20015 59 (Washington)
20008 50 (Washington)
20016 48 (Washington)
20007 33 (Washington)
20011 28 (Washington)
20009 25 (Washington)
20012 25 (Washington)
20024 25 (Washington)
20003 23 (Washington)
20520 20 (State Department)

Florida

33012 311 (Hialeah)
33165 268 (Miami)
32935 245 (Melbourne)
32937 199 (Satellite Beach)
32952 189 (Merritt Island)
32780 186 (Titusville)
32548 183 (Fort Walton Beach)
33024 183 (Hollywood)
32073 179 (Orange Park)
32506 178 (Pensacola)

Georgia

30247 191 (Lilburn)
30062 179 (Marietta)
30066 148 (Marietta)
30245 136 (Lawrenceville)
30144 133 (Kennesaw)
30075 129 (Roswell)
30080 128 (Smyrna)
30083 128 (Stone Mountain)
30067 123 (Marietta)
31093 123 (Warner Robins)

Hawaii

96720 164 (Hilo)
96818 153 (Honolulu)
96816 143 (Honolulu)
96822 142 (Honolulu)
96744 132 (Kaneohe)
96734 130 (Kailua)
96782 117 (Pearl City)
96817 104 (Honolulu)
96701 102 (Aiea)
96815 92 (Honolulu)

Idaho

83704 181 (Boise)
83401 157 (Idaho Falls)
83709 146 (Boise)
83814 145 (Coeur d'Alene)
83651 110 (Nampa)
83705 108 (Boise)
83201 84 (Pocatello)
83642 83 (Meridian)
83843 81 (Moscow)
83706 77 (Boise)

Illinois

60187 204 (Wheaton)
60004 196 (Arlington Heights)
60540 184 (Naperville)
62301 174 (Quincy)
60067 163 (Palatine)
60103 156 (Bartlett)
60126 151 (Elmhurst)
60137 146 (Glen Ellyn)
61701 144 (Bloomington)
60148 143 (Lombard)

Indiana

46901 181 (Kokomo)
46902 171 (Kokomo)
46815 166 (Fort Wayne)
47401 164 (Bloomington)
46383 146 (Valparaiso)
47374 136 (Richmond)
47905 136 (Lafayette)
47906 132 (West Lafayette)
46227 126 (Indianapolis)
46219 124 (Indianapolis)

Iowa

52402 244 (Cedar Rapids)
52601 226 (Burlington)
52302 182 (Marion)
50010 137 (Ames)
52732 116 (Clinton)
52001 105 (Dubuque)
52501 104 (Ottumwa)
50158 99 (Marshalltown)
52403 97 (Cedar Rapids)
50310 95 (Des Moines)

Kansas

67401 151 (Salina)
66048 139 (Leavenworth)
66502 125 (Manhattan)
66212 120 (Shawnee Mission)
66062 102 (Olathe)
67212 97 (Wichita)
66044 93 (Lawrence)
66061 88 (Olathe)
66208 83 (Shawnee Mission)
67156 80 (Winfield)

Kentucky

40503 148 (Lexington)
40004 135 (Bardstown)
40502 123 (Lexington)
41101 120 (Ashland)
42301 112 (Owensboro)
40505 105 (Lexington)
42001 105 (Paducah)
42101 101 (Bowling Green)
40214 99 (Louisville)
40219 97 (Louisville)

Louisiana

70458 166 (Slidell)
70815 115 (Baton Rouge)
71105 110 (Shreveport)
70003 105 (Metairie)
70808 100 (Baton Rouge)
70816 93 (Baton Rouge)
71291 91 (West Monroe)
70605 85 (Lake Charles)
70005 84 (Metairie)
70001 81 (Metairie)
70726 81 (Denham Springs)

Maine

04401 117 (Bangor)
04096 95 (Yarmouth)
04330 89 (Augusta)
04011 68 (Brunswick)
04901 58 (Waterville)
04530 57 (Bath)
04103 55 (Portland)
04106 55 (South Portland)
04210 55 (Auburn)
04092 54 (Westbrook)

Maryland

21401 222 (Annapolis)
21061 186 (Glen Burnie)
20904 179 (Silver Spring)
21701 169 (Frederick)
21122 164 (Baltimore)
21043 149 (Ellicott City)
20854 147 (Rockville)
20906 147 (Silver Spring)

20879 144 (Gaithersburg)
21403 138 (Annapolis)

Massachusetts

01701 244 (Framingham)
01201 163 (Pittsfield)
02173 160 (Lexington)
01824 150 (Chelmsford)
01752 148 (Marlborough)
01810 132 (Andover)
01960 129 (Peabody)
01720 128 (Acton)
01776 125 (Sudbury)
01886 124 (Westford)
02174 124 (Arlington)(tie)

Michigan

49684 210 (Traverse City)
48640 194 (Midland)
49017 176 (Battle Creek)
49508 151 (Grand Rapids)
48154 147 (Livonia)
48185 146 (Westland)
49509 139 (Grand Rapids)
49221 138 (Adrian)
48103 130 (Ann Arbor)
48060 127 (Port Huron)

Minnesota

55901 209 (Rochester)
55112 149 (Saint Paul)
55343 141 (Hopkins)
55110 134 (Saint Paul)
55113 131 (Saint Paul)
55337 131 (Burnsville)
56001 125 (Mankato)
55124 119 (Saint Paul)
55433 117 (Minneapolis)
55423 111 (Minneapolis)

Mississippi

39180 139 (Vicksburg)
39401 108 (Hattiesburg)
39564 108 (Ocean Springs)
39532 93 (Biloxi)
39759 83 (Starkville)
39440 79 (Laurel)
39501 77 (Gulfport)
38834 74 (Corinth)
39211 73 (Jackson)
39531 73 (Biloxi)

Missouri

64063 153 (Lees Summit)
63301 150 (Saint Charles)
64118 138 (Kansas City)
63123 134 (Saint Louis)
63011 133 (Ballwin)
64055 125 (Independence)
65807 125 (Springfield)
63031 124 (Florissant)
64133 123 (Kansas City)
63376 122 (Saint Peters)

Montana

59715 181 (Bozeman)
59601 119 (Helena)
59701 108 (Butte)
59102 96 (Billings)
59801 93 (Missoula)
59901 84 (Kalispell)
59101 78 (Billings)
59405 75 (Great Falls)
59501 57 (Havre)
59401 51 (Great Falls)

Nebraska

68506 116 (Lincoln)
68025 114 (Fremont)
69101 110 (North Platte)
68005 79 (Bellevue)
68701 79 (Norfolk)
68502 69 (Lincoln)
68801 69 (Grand Island)
68516 68 (Lincoln)
68123 67 (Omaha)
68134 66 (Omaha)
68505 66 (Lincoln)

Nevada

89431 141 (Sparks)
89701 131 (Carson City)
89509 117 (Reno)
89015 110 (Henderson)
89005 109 (Boulder City)
89121 105 (Las Vegas)
89108 102 (Las Vegas)
89115 99 (Las Vegas)
89110 98 (Las Vegas)
89506 94 (Reno)

New Hampshire

03060 177 (Nashua)
03038 154 (Derry)
03301 142 (Concord)
03062 131 (Nashua)
03051 120 (Hudson)
03054 117 (Merrimack)
03103 116 (Manchester)
03053 109 (Londonderry)
03102 109 (Manchester)
03079 99 (Salem)

New Jersey

08753 176 (Toms River)
07470 146 (Wayne)
07675 132 (Westwood)
08003 130 (Cherry Hill)
08701 120 (Lakewood)
08807 110 (Bridgewater)
08360 107 (Vineland)
07728 106 (Freehold)
07060 105 (Plainfield)
08854 104 (Piscataway)

New Mexico

87544 281 (Los Alamos)
88001 231 (Las Cruces)
87111 196 (Albuquerque)
87110 180 (Albuquerque)
87112 179 (Albuquerque)
88310 161 (Alamogordo)
88201 138 (Roswell)
87109 128 (Albuquerque)
87123 124 (Albuquerque)
88005 119 (Las Cruces)

New York

10314 1059 (Staten Island)
12603 189 (Poughkeepsie)
11746 181 (Huntington Station)
13760 176 (Endicott)
14850 170 (Ithaca)
13440 169 (Rome)
14150 168 (Tonawanda)
11743 165 (Huntington)
14450 161 (Fairport)
14094 156 (Lockport)

North Carolina

27609 196 (Raleigh)
27511 190 (Cary)
28739 158 (Hendersonville)
28150 146 (Shelby)
28307 144 (Fort Bragg)
28601 140 (Hickory)
27612 135 (Raleigh)
27834 127 (Greenville)
28806 122 (Asheville)
27292 121 (Lexington)

North Dakota
58501 168 (Bismarck)
58102 119 (Fargo)
58701 104 (Minot)
58103 95 (Fargo)
58601 85 (Dickinson)
58201 81 (Grand Forks)
58401 45 (Jamestown)
58554 30 (Mandan)
58301 29 (Devils Lake)
58504 25 (Bismarck)

Ohio
45013 235 (Hamilton)
44060 214 (Mentor)
44035 212 (Elyria)
43055 202 (Newark)
45424 195 (Dayton)
45385 186 (Xenia)
44240 173 (Kent)
43081 171 (Westerville)
45459 163 (Dayton)
45840 158 (Findlay)

Oklahoma
73034 186 (Edmond)
73505 117 (Lawton)
74012 116 (Broken Arrow)
73160 113 (Oklahoma City)
73069 108 (Norman)
74006 106 (Bartlesville)
73008 105 (Bethany)
73110 104 (Oklahoma City)
73071 103 (Norman)
73112 92 (Oklahoma City)
73132 92 (Oklahoma City)

Oregon
97005 201 (Beaverton)
97601 192 (Klamath Falls)
97007 190 (Beaverton)
97526 180 (Grants Pass)
97330 179 (Corvallis)
97470 176 (Roseburg)
97501 174 (Medford)
97321 156 (Albany)
97603 156 (Klamath Falls)
97006 150 (Beaverton)

Pennsylvania
18966 160 (Southampton)
16001 152 (Butler)
17701 143 (Williamsport)
19446 137 (Lansdale)
18974 135 (Warminster)
19380 126 (West Chester)
17055 121 (Mechanicsburg)
18042 121 (Easton)
15108 119 (Coraopolis)
18103 118 (Allentown)

Rhode Island
02840 129 (Newport)
02816 119 (Coventry)
02886 109 (Warwick)
02920 98 (Garden City)
02871 97 (Portsmouth)
02895 93 (Woonsocket)
02864 83 (Cumberland)
02919 73 (Johnston)
02893 68 (West Warwick)
02818 63 (East Greenwich)

South Carolina
29483 114 (Summerville)
29730 113 (Rock Hill)
29150 110 (Sumter)
29407 100 (Charleston)
29169 93 (West Columbia)
29210 92 (Columbia)
29621 92 (Anderson)
29501 91 (Florence)
29801 91 (Aiken)
29681 86 (Simpsonville)
29687 86 (Taylors)

South Dakota
57701 124 (Rapid City)
57401 82 (Aberdeen)
57201 72 (Watertown)
57747 69 (Hot Springs)
57105 57 (Sioux Falls)
57006 50 (Brookings)
57501 48 (Pierre)
57702 47 (Rapid City)
57103 45 (Sioux Falls)
57106 42 (Sioux Falls)

Tennessee
37830 261 (Oak Ridge)
38134 205 (Memphis)
37311 200 (Cleveland)
37601 156 (Johnson City)
37801 149 (Maryville)
38117 149 (Memphis)
37918 145 (Knoxville)
37922 140 (Knoxville)
37421 138 (Chattanooga)
37343 137 (Hixson)

Texas
75080 240 (Richardson)
75042 205 (Garland)
75023 193 (Plano)
75075 191 (Plano)
75081 187 (Richardson)
79924 179 (El Paso)
76133 174 (Fort Worth)
75074 169 (Plano)
75067 166 (Lewisville)
75040 156 (Garland)

Utah
84057 266 (Orem)
84321 161 (Logan)
84604 145 (Provo)
84108 144 (Salt Lake City)
84010 136 (Bountiful)
84601 129 (Provo)
84118 122 (Salt Lake City)
84770 121 (St. George)
84058 119 (Orem)
84003 110 (American Fork)
84121 110 (Salt Lake City)

Vermont
05401 101 (Burlington)
05452 100 (Essex Junction)
05701 56 (Rutland)
05201 54 (Bennington)
05602 54 (Montpelier)
05446 45 (Colchester)
05468 42 (Milton)
05403 39 (South Burlington)
05641 37 (Barre)
05495 34 (Williston)

Virginia
22180 245 (Vienna)
22110 188 (Manassas)
23602 182 (Newport News)
22003 181 (Annandale)
23452 176 (Virginia Beach)
23464 173 (Virginia Beach)
22193 172 (Woodbridge)
22170 163 (Sterling)
24502 163 (Lynchburg)
22901 142 (Charlottesville)

Washington

98366 241 (Port Orchard)
98284 237 (Sedro Woolley)
99352 237 (Richland)
98310 231 (Bremerton)
98031 208 (Kent)
98335 208 (Gig Harbor)
98115 200 (Seattle)
98020 199 (Edmonds)
98632 196 (Longview)
98052 193 (Redmond)

West Virginia

26505 178 (Morgantown)
26003 139 (Wheeling)
26101 121 (Parkersburg)
24740 114 (Princeton)
24701 112 (Bluefield)
25177 105 (Saint Albans)
26301 101 (Clarksburg)
26554 96 (Fairmont)
25801 93 (Beckley)
25705 85 (Huntington)

Wisconsin

53711 148 (Madison)
54401 142 (Wausau)
54729 135 (Chippewa Falls)
53186 125 (Waukesha)
54901 118 (Oshkosh)
53005 113 (Brookfield)
54481 106 (Stevens Point)
54701 106 (Eau Claire)
54935 105 (Fond du Lac)
53705 93 (Madison)

Wyoming

82001 135 (Cheyenne)
82070 112 (Laramie)
82601 94 (Casper)
82801 80 (Sheridan)
82009 69 (Cheyenne)
82716 65 (Gillette)
82604 54 (Casper)
82935 54 (Green River)
82609 53 (Casper)
82240 52 (Torrington)

U.S. Territories and Possessions

Guam

96921 148 (Barrigada)
96911 78 (Tamuning)
96950 71 (Saipan)
96910 48 (Agana)
96912 28 (Dededo)

Puerto Rico

00625 370 (Caguas)
00619 346 (Bayamon)
00731 239 (Ponce)
00603 234 (Aguadilla)
00926 225 (San Juan)
00626 218 (Caguas)
00630 207 (Carolina)
00661 192 (Humacao)
00708 192 (Mayaguez)
00602 157 (Aguada)

U.S. Virgin Islands

00801 67 (Charlotte Amalie)
00820 61 (Christiansted)
00802 43 (Charlotte Amalie)
00803 29 (Charlotte Amalie)
00824 21 (Christiansted)

HAM TALLY BY STATE (As of September 1993)

State	Extra	Advanced	General	Technician	Novice	Total
AK	297	543	646	788	465	2739
AL	961	1627	1723	3648	1039	8998
AR	594	963	1006	2144	628	5335
AS	6	5	12	14	9	46
AZ	1252	2399	2476	4846	1257	12230
CA	7845	15801	16558	35735	17743	93682
CO	1082	1982	2134	3422	1352	9972
CT	1045	1556	1929	2446	1729	8705
DC	85	98	129	104	85	501
DE	183	232	284	435	214	1348
FL	3795	7417	8753	11243	6967	38175
GA	1336	2377	2524	4551	1563	12351
GU	45	45	53	93	172	408
HI	298	516	582	929	696	3021
IA	664	1437	1495	1826	1082	6504
ID	274	554	688	1121	417	3054
IL	2387	4089	4859	7608	3674	22617
IN	1356	2348	2759	5144	2133	13740
KS	680	1116	1546	2188	1060	6590
KY	741	1158	1390	2760	1262	7311
LA	762	1333	1422	2314	934	6765
MA	1917	2745	3315	4693	2338	15008
MD	1391	2233	2249	3399	1575	10847
ME	439	672	1002	1187	587	3887
MI	1966	3563	4243	6745	2725	19242
MN	1044	1956	2319	3024	1341	9684
MO	1237	2162	2601	3634	1576	11210
MS	422	789	834	1484	569	4098
MT	281	416	569	735	370	2371
NC	1502	2702	2900	5298	1992	14394

ND	145	238	379	444	267	1473
NE	349	776	990	1098	506	3719
NH	581	725	948	1408	596	4258
NJ	2037	3184	3449	5149	2776	16595
NM	523	891	872	1464	395	4145
NV	342	616	784	1205	363	3310
NY	3507	5769	6822	10818	7251	34167
OH	2828	4870	5554	11008	4259	28519
OK	815	1465	1459	2973	1143	7855
OR	1096	2041	2586	3638	1670	11031
PA	2737	4381	5074	7417	3756	23365
PR	238	537	669	2365	4497	8306
RI	287	350	525	786	442	2390
SC	596	1027	1299	1916	703	5541
SD	149	319	378	394	188	1428
TN	1285	2235	2212	4644	1566	11942
TX	4131	7152	7588	13063	4483	36417
UT	410	751	724	2674	812	5371
VA	1825	2917	3056	4844	2113	14755
VI	43	51	82	100	43	319
VT	216	301	410	646	236	1809
WA	2057	3582	4359	7432	3176	20606
WI	1017	1777	2165	3084	1336	9379
WV	480	695	908	2039	906	5028
TOTAL	63638	111527	126338	214364	101076	616943

SOURCE: BUCKMASTER PUBLISHING

NUMBER OF U.S. AMATEUR LICENSES BY YEAR
(excluding RACES licenses, as of 1 September in each year)

Year	Number	Year	Number
1993	628,142	1988	438,688
1992	580,291	1987	431,776
1991	531,860	1986	423,401
1990	493,848	1985	414,012
1989	465,349	1984	412,695
		1983	412,870

SOURCE: FCC, GETTYSBURG

Note: While it is true that the number of amateurs has been growing in recent years, some of the statistics above reflect the change in January 1984 from 5-year license terms to 10-year license terms. Thus, licenses that would normally have expired and not been renewed after a five-year term have stayed in effect for an additional five years. The first 10-year licenses began expiring in January 1994.

MOST RECENT U.S. CALLSIGNS
by Month, September 1992 - September 1993

"++" indicates that all call signs in this group have been issued in this area.

September 1, 1992

District	Group A Extra	Group B Advanced	Group C Tech/Gen	Group D Novice
Ø	AAØJZ	KGØAN	NØUAK	KBØKRB
1	AA1DW	KD1KG	N1NKE	KB1AJI
2	AA2KW	KF2KH	N2SIT	KB2PKB
3	AA3BY	KE3EP	N3NHH	KB3AHZ
4	AC4UW	KQ4FC	++	KD4SNJ
5	AB5HU	KJ5EI	++	KB5VAR
6	AB6OB	KN6AA	++	KD6NDD
7	AA7RE	KI7GK	++	KB7PVX
8	AA8IO	KF8WZ	N8VNZ	KB8OGQ
9	AA9EZ	KF9LJ	N9QXR	KB9IDJ
Hawaii	++	AH6MC	WH6IV	WH6CPX
Alaska	++	AL7OK	WL7GC	WL7CGD
Puerto Rico	++	KP4UG	++	WP4LKR

October 1, 1992

District	Group A	Group B	Group C	Group D
	Extra	Advanced	Tech/Gen	Novice
Ø	AAØKI	KGØBF	NØUGS	KBØKSR
1	AA1EE	KD1KS	N1NOE	KB1AKO
2	AA2LK	KF2KT	N2SPQ	KB2PLW
3	AA3CF	KE3EY	N3NLN	KB3AIR
4	AC4WF	KQ4GU	++	KD4TJB
5	AB5IK	KJ5FI	++	KB5VMX
6	AB6OQ	KN6BD	++	KD6OAB
7	AA7RT	KI7HG	++	KB7QGM
8	AA8IX	KF8XK	N8VUN	KB8OIC
9	AA9FE	KF9LR	N9RDV	KB9IEK
Hawaii	++	AH6MD	WH6JI	WH6CPZ
Alaska	++	AL7OM	WL7GG	WL7CGE
Puerto Rico	++	KP4UH	++	WP4LLW

November 1, 1992

District	Group A	Group B	Group C	Group D
	Extra	Advanced	Tech/Gen	Novice
Ø	AAØKO	KGØBQ	NØUMM	KBØKTT
1	AA1EJ	KD1LA	N1NRO	KB1ALH
2	AA2LL	KF2LA	N2STS	KB2PNP
3	AA3CH	KE3FK	N3NOO	KB3AJL
4	AC4WU	KQ4IG	++	KD4TWT
5	AB5IY	KJ5GB	++	KB5VWB
6	AB6OV	KN6CN	++	KD6OSU
7	AA7SE	KI7HQ	++	KB7QNG
8	AA8JC	KF8XP	N8VZO	KB8OJC
9	AA9FG	KF9MA	N9RIE	KB9IFD
Hawaii	++	AH6ME	WH6JN	WH6CQA
Alaska	++	AL7ON	WL7GN	WL7CGF
Puerto Rico	++	KP4UK	++	WP4LND

December 1, 1992

District	Group A	Group B	Group C	Group D
	Extra	Advanced	Tech/Gen	Novice
Ø	AAØKS	KGØBY	NØUPN	KBØKUW
1	AA1EM	KD1LK	N1NUA	KB1AMB
2	AA2LN	KF2LH	N2SXD	KB2PPA
3	AA3CK	KE3FN	N3NQE	KB3AKE
4	AC4XF	KQ4JF	++	KD4UHQ
5	AB5JD	KJ5GJ	++	KB5WCU
6	AB6PC	KN6DF	++	KD6PFZ
7	AA7SL	KI7IA	++	KB7QWZ
8	AA8JG	KF8XY	N8WEJ	KB8OKK
9	AA9FG	KF9MI	N9RLL	KB9IFW
Hawaii	++	AH6ME	WH6JQ	WH6CQA
Alaska	++	AL7ON	WL7GN	WL7CGF
Puerto Rico	++	KP4UL	++	WP4LOF

January 1, 1993

District	Group A	Group B	Group C	Group D
	Extra	Advanced	Tech/Gen	Novice
Ø	AAØKZ	KGØCI	NØUXC	KBØKVV
1	AA1EW	KD1LZ	N1NZA	KB1ANK
2	AA2MB	KF2MC	N2TFP	KB2PRF
3	AA3CU	KE3GE	N3NVF	KB3ALG
4	AC4YL	KQ4KY	++	KD4VFC
5	AB5JS	KJ5HK	++	KB5WQW
6	AB6PR	KN6EY	++	KD6QIP
7	AA7SX	KI7IV	++	KB7RLT
8	AA8JP	KF8YK	N8WMC	KB8OLY
9	AA9FP	KF9MQ	N9RSZ	KB9IGV
Hawaii	++	AH6MH	WH6KD	WH6CQB
Alaska	++	AL7ON	WL7HL	WL7CGJ
Puerto Rico	++	KP4UO	++	WP4LQC

February 1, 1993

District	Group A Extra	Group B Advanced	Group C Tech/Gen	Group D Novice
Ø	AAØLH	KGØDI	NØVHH	KBØKYS
1	AA1FD	KD1MU	N1OFW	KB1AQS
2	AA2MK	KF2MW	N2TPL	KB2PVW
3	AA3DE	KE3GQ	N3OCP	KB3AOG
4	AC4ZT	KQ4NA	++	KD4WLX
5	AB5KI	KJ5HW	++	KB5YJN
6	AB6QH	KN6GJ	++	KD6RVS
7	AA7TO	KI7JT	++	KB7SGY
8	AA8JU	KF8YV	N8WXO	KB8OQD
9	AA9FT	KF9NF	N9SDT	KB9IJP
Hawaii	++	AH6MH	WH6KL	WH6CQE
Alaska	++	AL7OO	WL7IK	WL7CGP
Puerto Rico	++	KP4UQ	++	WP4LTF

March 1, 1993

District	Group A Extra	Group B Advanced	Group C Tech/Gen	Group D Novice
Ø	AAØLX	KGØDS	NØVRS	KBØLAU
1	AA1FM	KD1NI	N1ONN	KB1ASR
2	AA2MV	KF2NG	N2TZR	KB2PZS
3	AA3DP	KE3HF	N3OJS	KB3APW
4	AD4AS	KQ4PC	++	KD4YME
5	AB5LE	KJ5IW	++	KB5YWC
6	AB6RE	KN6HQ	++	KD6SYN
7	AA7UK	KI7KY	++	KB7SXK
8	AA8KH	KF8ZG	N8XKP	KB8ORZ
9	AA9GA	KF9NP	N9SMB	KB9ILH
Hawaii	++	AH6MI	WH6KV	WH6CQF
Alaska	++	AL7OR	WL7IV	WL7CGQ
Puerto Rico	++	KP4UX	++	WP4LUV

April 1, 1993

District	Group A Extra	Group B Advanced	Group C Tech/Gen	Group D Novice
Ø	AAØMJ	KGØES	NØWFK	KBØLCI
1	AA1FY	KD1NZ	N1OUI	KB1ATW
2	AA2NG	KF2NZ	N2UKS	KB2QBQ
3	AA3DX	KE3HQ	N3OSA	KB3AQQ
4	AD4CK	KQ4RI	++	KD4ZSA
5	AB5MC	KJ5KE	++	KB5ZOK
6	AB6SI	KN6JQ	++	KD6TZG
7	AA7VC	KI7LZ	++	KB7TOM
8	AA8KP	KG8AA	N8XWJ	KB8OTL
9	AA9GM	KF9OM	N9SZR	KB9IML
Hawaii	++	AH6MK	WH6LT	WH6CQI
Alaska	++	AL7OV	WL7JV	WL7CGT
Puerto Rico	++	KP4UZ	++	WP4LWH

May 1, 1993

District	Group A Extra	Group B Advanced	Group C Tech/Gen	Group D Novice
Ø	AAØMR	KGØFH	NØWMS	KBØLFG
1	AA1GE	KD1ON	N1OZA	KB1AVV
2	AA2NM	KF2OJ	N2UQC	KB2QDW
3	AA3EI	KE3HV	N3OXE	KB3ASK
4	AD4DH	KQ4TB	++	KE4AQU
5	AB5MO	KJ5KY	++	KC5ACP
6	AB6SY	KN6KS	++	KD6UUI
7	AA7VR	KI7MP	++	KB7UEE
8	AA8KV	KG8AR	N8YGD	KB8OXC
9	AA9GY	KF9PA	N9TGL	KB9IOG
Hawaii	++	AH6MO	WH6MC	WH6CQJ
Alaska	++	AL7OV	WL7KE	WL7CGY
Puerto Rico	++	KP4VG	++	WP4LYI

June 1, 1993

District	Group A Extra	Group B Advanced	Group C Tech/Gen	Group D Novice
Ø	AAØNG	KGØGE	NØXCO	KBØLGZ
1	AA1GS	KD1PE	N1PGU	KB1AXJ
2	AA2NZ	KF2PE	N2VAX	KB2QGL
3	AA3ER	KE3II	N3PEV	KB3AUP
4	AD4ES	KQ4VO	++	KE4BWU
5	AB5NQ	KJ5MN	++	KC5AWV
6	AB6TV	KN6MM	++	KD6WHW
7	AA7WF	KI7NO	++	KB7VBN
8	AA8LI	KG8BM	N8YVY	KB8OZJ
9	AA9HG	KF9PN	N9TRQ	KB9IQE
Hawaii	++	AH6MS	WH6MR	WH6CQN
Alaska	++	AL7OY	WL7KU	WL7CHB
Puerto Rico	++	KP4VI	++	WP4MAP

July 1, 1993

District	Group A Extra	Group B Advanced	Group C Tech/Gen	Group D Novice
Ø	AAØOE	KGØHD	NØXRX	KBØLJZ
1	AA1GY	KD1PZ	N1PRM	KB1AZO
2	AA2OQ	KF2QE	N2VRQ	KB2QKK
3	AA3FD	KE3JF	N3PQT	KB3AWR
4	AD4GZ	KQ4YF	++	KE4DMW
5	AB5OK	KJ5NZ	++	KC5BPS
6	AB6UR	KN6OB	++	KD6YUR
7	AA7XE	KI7OU	++	KB7WCK
8	AA8LT	KG8CL	N8ZPJ	KB8PCH
9	AA9HR	KF9QI	N9UFS	KB9ISZ
Hawaii	++	AH6MX	WH6NR	WH6CQQ
Alaska	++	AL7PD	WL7LZ	WL7CHE
Puerto Rico	++	KP4VL	++	WP4MEH

August 1, 1993

District	Group A Extra	Group B Advanced	Group C Tech/Gen	Group D Novice
Ø	AAØOI	KGØHJ	NØXYO	KBØLKT
1	AA1HA	KD1QE	N1PUO	KB1BCO
2	AA2OW	KF2QK	N2VVX	KB2QNJ
3	AA3FE	KE3JJ	N3PTK	KB3AXR
4	AD4HV	KQ4ZF	++	KE4EAC
5	AB5OQ	KJ5OP	++	KC5BYC
6	AB6VF	KN6OS	++	KD6ZMC
7	AA7XP	KI7PL	++	KB7WKF
8	AA8LZ	KG8CS	N8ZUK	KB8PDB
9	AA9HT	KF9QO	N9UIZ	KB9ITU
Hawaii	++	AH6MY	WH6NX	WH6CQT
Alaska	++	AL7PE	WL7LZ	WL7CHF
Puerto Rico	++	KP4VN	++	WP4MHO

September 1, 1993

District	Group A Extra	Group B Advanced	Group C Tech/Gen	Group D Novice
Ø	AAØOR	KGØHW	NØYJG	KBØLLM
1	AA1HG	KD1QU	N1QBM	KB1BDK
2	AA2PI	KF2QV	N2WEQ	KB2QOE
3	AA3FS	KE3JR	N3QAO	KB3AYE
4	AD4JB	KR4BL	++	KE4FBE
5	AB5PD	KJ5PJ	++	KC5CNE
6	AB6VY	KN6QI	++	KE6AOT
7	AA7YG	KI7QS	++	KB7YBV
8	AA8MD	KG8DQ	++	KB8PKS
9	AA9ID	KF9RF	N9URQ	KB9IUZ
Hawaii	++	AH6NC	WH6OQ	WH6CQV
Alaska	++	AL7PF	WL7MO	WL7AHU
Puerto Rico	++	KP4VQ	++	WP4MJF

U.S. HAM TALLY BY BIRTH YEAR

Year	Number	Year	Number	Year	Number	Year	Number
1889	5	1914	4676	1939	10971	1964	7087
1890	4	1915	5289	1940	12093	1965	5924
1891	11	1916	5653	1941	13049	1966	5413
1892	12	1917	6560	1942	15310	1967	4902
1893	19	1918	7416	1943	15136	1968	4722
1894	27	1919	7249	1944	13646	1969	4599
1895	39	1920	8529	1945	13090	1970	4544
1896	65	1921	9290	1946	15549	1971	4342
1897	102	1922	9067	1947	17312	1972	4125
1898	119	1923	9109	1948	14743	1973	3863
1899	170	1924	9588	1949	14372	1974	3898
1900	250	1925	9562	1950	13454	1975	3541
1901	353	1926	9259	1951	13561	1976	3391
1902	447	1927	9137	1952	13584	1977	3052
1903	673	1928	8955	1953	13309	1978	2497
1904	900	1929	8548	1954	12867	1979	2093
1905	1297	1930	9066	1955	12261	1980	1369
1906	1711	1931	8897	1956	11446	1981	869
1907	2081	1932	8709	1957	10913	1982	394
1908	2371	1933	8249	1958	9979	1983	185
1909	2391	1934	8485	1959	9668	1984	68
1910	2698	1935	8800	1960	9385	1985	17
1911	2871	1936	9027	1961	9400	1986	7
1912	3368	1937	9710	1962	8674	1987	10
1913	3960	1938	10841	1963	8041	1988	1

SOURCE: BUCKMASTER PUBLISHING

WELL-KNOWN PERSONALITIES HOLDING AMATEUR RADIO LICENSES

This list includes widely-known personalities who are (or were) public figures and who would be recognized by an average person. Many prominent businessmen, local radio/TV personalities, and mid-ranking government officials are also licensed amateurs, but they are not listed here, in the interest of protecting their privacy.

Several lists have propagated through the amateur community from time to time, often with errors. For example, some lists claim N6KGB was actor Jimmy Stewart, when the call was really held by another well-known actor: Stewart Granger (whose real name was James Stewart and who became a Silent Key in 1993). Many lists claim that Russian cosmonaut Yuri Gagarin was a ham (some lists even claim his call was UA1LO); there is no hard evidence that he was ever licensed. Another rumor insists that musician Jon Bon Jovi is a ham. He is *not* licensed but his cousin, record producer Tony Bongiovi, is KX2Z. Other lists indicate that musician Jose Feliciano is a ham; WP4CO's name is definitely Jose Feliciano, but he's not the famous musician. Donny Osmond was once licensed as KA7EVD, but his license has expired—another Donald Osmond holds the call WD4SKT, but it's not the same person. KD6OY insists that his name is really Garry Shankling, not Shandling, even though he lives in Los Angeles. And WA7WYV's name is indeed Andy Griffith, but he's never played either Andy of Mayberry or Matlock on television.

Royalty

Juan Carlos I de Borbon y Borbon, EAØJC, (1938-), King, Spain
Bhumiphol Adulayadej, HS1A, (1927-), King, Thailand
Hussein I, JY1, (1935-), King, Hashemite Kingdom of Jordan

Political and Religious Leaders

Francesco Cossiga, IØFCG, (1929-), President, Italy
Barry Goldwater, K7UGA, (1909-), former U. S. Senator (R-AZ)
Carlos Saul Menem, LU1SM, (1930-), President, Argentina
Rajiv Gandhi, VU2RG, (1944-1991), former Prime Minister, Republic of India
General Curtis LeMay, W6EZV, (1906-1991), Vice-Presidential Candidate (with George Wallace), 1968
General Anastasio Somoza Debayle, YN1AS, (1925-1980), former President, Republic of Nicaragua
Roger Cardinal Mahony, W6QYI, (1936-), Cardinal of the Roman Catholic Archdiocese of Los Angeles

Entertainers/Musicians

Marlon Brando, FO5GJ, (1924-), Actor
Arthur Godfrey, K4LIB, (1903-1983), Entertainer
Burl Ives, KA6HVK, (1909-1991), Singer
Donny Osmond, ex-KA7EVD (expired), (1957-), Entertainer
Patty Loveless (born Patricia Ramey), KD4WUJ, (1957-), Musician
Stu Gilliam, KI6M, (1933-), Comedian
Larry Junstrom, KN4UB, (1957-), Rock Musician (".38 Special")
Stewart Granger (born James Stewart), N6KGB, (1918-1993), Actor
Priscilla Presley, N6YOS, (1945-), Actress
Alvino Rey, W6UK, (1908-), Musician/Bandleader
Chet Atkins, WA4CZD (1924-), Musician
Ronnie Milsap, WB4KCG, (1943-), Musician
Joe Walsh, WB6ACU, (1947-), Rock Musician ("Eagles," "James Gang")
Andy Devine, WB6RER, (1905-1977), Actor

Writers/Authors

Jean Shepherd, K2ORS, (1921-), Writer/Humorist
Roy Neal, K6DUE, (1921-), Network Science Reporter, NBC (retired)
Walter Cronkite, KB2GSD, (1916-), Network News Anchorman, CBS (retired)
David French, N4KET, (1938-), former Network News Anchorman, CNN
David Ruben, M.D., TI2DR, (1933-), Author (*Everything You Always Wanted to Know About Sex - But Were Afraid to Ask*)
Dr. Alexander Comfort, KA6UXR, (1920-), Author (*The Joy of Sex*)

Others

Joe Rudi, NK7U (1946-), Major League Baseball Player (retired)
Dick Rutan, KB6LQS, (1938-), pilot of Voyager airplane non-stop around the world
Dr. Joseph Taylor, Jr., K1JT (1941-), winner 1958 VHF SS Contest and 1993 Nobel Prize in Physics
Jeana Yeager, KB6LQR, (1952-), co-pilot of Voyager airplane non-stop around the world

Numerous astronauts and cosmonauts also hold amateur licenses. A list appears in the "Amateur Radio in Space" section.

MAJOR DXPEDITIONS OF 1992-93

The year's events included many definitive DXpeditions that will surely change the TOP 100 Most Wanted Countries for next year! With six Major Pacific DXpeditions, the continued works of Romeo Stepanenko and the return of Eritrea to the Active Country List, as well as the additions from the Yugoslavian changes, it has been a good and busy year for DXing!

The 5AØRR operation was one of the most awaited DXpeditions of 1993. On June 16, 1993, 5AØRR appeared on 20 Meter SSB. Transmitting on 14.195, he announced his listening frequency as "14.200 to 14.300," and the ensuing pileup covered up most of the U.S. 20 Meter phone band. Romeo operated for approximately three hours, then moved to other bands for a few short periods, then abruptly disapperead for several days. After about two months and several dozen rumors as to Romeo's whereabouts, the following press release from Romeo was received by Ed, NT2X, who did the Russian/English translation and released the news to various amateur radio news outlets.

LIBYAN DXPEDITION

Originally, plans called for the use of six amateur radio operators for 5A. Due to the lack of funding we had to limit ourselves to three operators: Said, who currently holds the callsign 5AØRR, Danny, LZ2UU, and myself.

During the operation, which lasted five days, we worked over 11,000 stations.

This DXpedition coincided with the International Arab Summit being held in Cairo. With mounting pressure from the world-wide ham community, we were focused on commencement of the operation and gave very little consideration to the Arab Summit. National security throughout the region was at a fever pitch.The DXpedition was terminated when Danny and I were accused by Libyan counter-intelligence and Egyptian police of planning to assassinate both President Mubarek and Libyan Leader Quaddafy. To make matters worse and even more bizarre, they said we were using ham radio as a cover for illegal drug trafficking by communicating with Turkish ships in the ports of Benghazi and Alexendria. Of course, these charges were absurd and insanely ridiculous. We were both arrested and placed in the Libyan prison system. We spent many weeks in prison and were held incommunicado. Our constant requests to speak with consular officials from Russia and Bulgaria were met with insults and abuse. This unpleasant experience, the details of which I will not go into at this time, has caused my health to deteriorate greatly and I am currently under doctor's care and receiving medical treatment. Fortunately, events unfolded resulting in our release, which was nothing short of miraculous. Perhaps, in time, this story will be told.

Said, 5AØRR, will continue to operate from Libya under this call sign which is in effect for two years. We left him an FT-990, a FL-7000 amp and a Mosley antenna. He is an outstanding CW operator but might be limited in his SSB operating since we didn't have the opportunity to train him in this mode.

Copies of the 5AØRR logs are in Bulgaria. QSL's are being sent.

If my medical condition permits, I hope to travel to theUnited States soon. At that time I will present the documentation for the 5A-Libyan operation to the American Radio Relay League. I also have in my possession the additional documentation requested by the ARRL for the P5-North Korean DXpedition.

The unwarranted and undeserved criticisms, along with false charges, leveled in my direction from the amateur radio community (some of which were anonymous) have disturbed me a great deal. I was disappointed to see how few hams supported me or rallied to my defense. Truly, it is this experience above all else which gives me great cause to consider discontinuing my efforts to put the very rarest countries on the air.

To those of you world-wide who throughout the years have always shown your friendship, support and encouragement, THANK YOU VERY MUCH! I will always cherish our relationship as well as all the great moments and memories.

Warmest regards.

73,

Romeo,
3W3RR/AHØM/RV7RR/EKØRR/XYØRR/1SØRR/9DØRR/YAØRR/5AØRR and forty-five other call signs.

9DØRR, August 1992
QTH: IRAN, near Meshked, approximately 100 miles from C.I.S.

Band	QSOs
1.8	172
3.5	306
7.0	1558
14.0	6205
21.0	6890
28.0	762
RTTY	307
WARC	4890
	21,090 Total QSOs

*QSL via: NT2X
*Ops:4K2OT/UB1KA, 3W3RR/AHØM, UH8EA.
*Acknowledgements and/or Sponsors: JA1BK, W8BLA, NCDXF, *JA-CQ Ham Radio Magazine*, INDEXA.
(Information provided by Ed Kritsky, NT2X)

VK9WW/VK9NL/W, October 1992
QTH: Willis Island

*Over 18,000 QSOs reported.
*QSL via: VK9NS
*Ops: VK9NL,VK2BEX,VK9NS
*Acknowledgements and/or Sponsors: H.I.DX A., VK4CRR, JA1BK, JA1ACB, N6HVZ, NØIMH, NCDXF, CDXC, *JA-CQ Ham Radio Magazine*, *JA-59 Magazine*. Special thanks to G4YDO of the *R.S.G.B Newsletter* for coordination in Europe—DK8OK, G3VXJ, G4SJX.

ET3BC/ET3YL, October 1992
QTH: Addis-Ababa, Ethiopia

*Over 7,000 Total QSOs
*QSL: ET3YL via K4PHE
*QSL: ET3BC via N4NX
*Ops: WN4FVU,WB4ZNH.
*Acknowledgements: Mr. Atto Ghetnet of the Ethiopian Telecommunications Authority, Delta Airlines and our QSL managers.
(Information provided by Martha and Carl Henson)

9ER1TA/9ER1TB, October 1992
QTH: Asmara, Eritrea

*Over 7,000 Total QSOs.
*QSL 9ER1TA via N4NX
*QSL 9ER1TB via K4PHE
*Ops: WN4FVU,WB4ZNH.
*Acknowledgements: The Provisional Government of Eritrea, the Telecommunications Authority of Eritrea, Delta Airlines and our QSL managers.

(Information provided by Martha and Carl Henson)

4J1FM/4J1FW, October 1992
QTH: Malyj-Vysotskij Island

4J1FW-CQ WW SSB

Band	QSOs
1.8	211
3.5	578
7.0	671
14.0	1380
21.0	1206
28.0	1648
	5694 Total Contest QSOs.

*Over 12,000 Total QSOs reported.
*QSL via: OH2LVG
*Ops: OH8PF, OH6EI, OH6LK, OH6LI, AA7FM/OH2LVG, 3W3RR, UA3AB, XE1VIC, NT2X, UY5XE.
*Acknowledgements and/or Sponsors: OH5NZ, INDEXA, NCDXF, SRAL, RF Electronic of Finland, HRO-Phoenix, OH2BH, WA7LNW, K5VT, W7ZMD, KE7LZ, N2KK, OH2VR, WB2JZK, WB2ZHB, XE2GV, RW3AH, RC2AR/AA3BG, UA3AF, KZ3H, AA2MF, UW3AX, UT5JDA, UA1FA, OH8AA, OH6NVI, OH6MRA, K8CH, K7ES/OH2ZE, Battle Creek Special antenna (W8UVZ, WØCD, K8GG).

*Ed, NT2X, hopes that he has not forgotten anyone.

(Information provided by Ed Kritsky, NT2X)

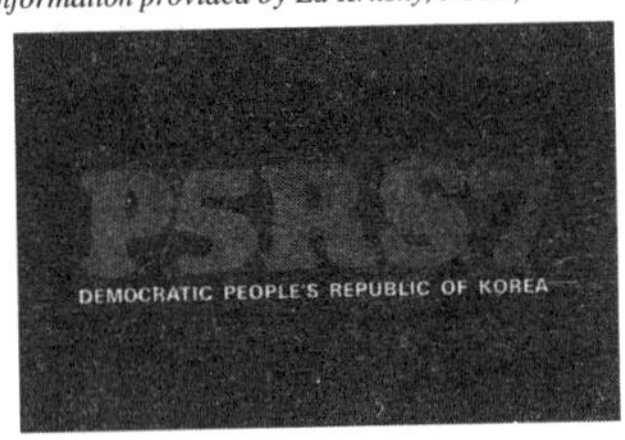

P5RS7, December 1992
QTH: North Korea

Band	QSOs
1.8	950
3.5	3900
7.0	4800
14.0	14,200
21.0	9,700
28.0	1,850
50.0	5
	35,405 Total QSOs.

*QSL via: JA1HGY
*Ops: 3W3RR,UT3UY,UB4JDM,UW0MF,and Oleg.
*Acknowledgements and/or Sponsors: *JA-CQ Ham Radio Magazine*, JA1BK, JA1FTI, JA1HGY, UJ8JLT, Kenwood Corp., UA6HZ, RB7GG, RT5UL, UV3DCX, UL7IDX, UAØNL, UA3AB, UT3UX, RW3AH, 4K2OT, UY5XE, LZ2PO, LZ2UU, JI1DLZ, JK1KRS, BZ1AA, *BZ1WX, LA9UX, KD7P. Ed, NT2X, hopes that he has not forgotten anyone.

(Information provided by Ed Kritsky, NT2X)

NØTG/KP5, January 1993
QTH: Desecheo Island

QSOs	Mode
15,640	SSB
6,760	C.W.
600	RTTY
200	1.8 MHz
	23,000 Total QSOs.

*QSL via: NØTG
*Ops: NØTG, KW2P, WØRJU, AA4VK, WA4DAN.
*Acknowledgements and/or Sponsors: KP2A, VP2ML, W5KNE, RADIO WORKS CO., N1DX, WA8LOW, W6PQS, N4YIC, KP4RF, U.S. Department of the Interior, KP4PQ, JA1ELY, JA1DM, Lewis and Clark R.C., Lone Star DX Assn., RTTY DX Assn., Members of the 2500 Club, and a very special appreciation to the following for their help with QLSing and computer work: KD5ZD, N5WNG, N5ORT.

(Information provided by Randy Rowe, NØTG)

AH1A, February 1993
QTH: Howland Island

Bands	QSOs
1.8	1049
3.5	3581
7.0	6200
10.1	2046
14.0	14236
18.0	3353
21.0	13717
24.9	2877
28.0	4683
50.0	88
	51,830 Total QSOs

*QSL via: Mile High DX Association, P.O.Box 1, Franktown, CO 80116 USA.
*Ops: F6EXV, G4LJF, I8ULL, K4UEE, K9AJ, KØEU, ON6TT, PA3DUU, W9IXX, WØCP, WØRLX. Beth Flint, Ph.D.,U.S.F&W, Dave Woodside, U.S.F&W.
*Acknowledgements and/or Sponsors: Alpha/ETO, Butternut, Cushcraft, Kenwood, W6EL propagation software, WF1B

RTTY software, AH6FS, AH6IO, Battle Creek Special antenna (provided by K8GG,W8UVZ,WØCD), AH9B (Oklahoma Comm Center), K9AY, KGØE, NH6UY, WH6BC, W9KNI (Logikeyer), N6AMG Memorial Group (K6MYC & K6QXY-6 meter gear), W9SU (ICE Filters), Panamax, K9EID (Heil mics), Casio, IDXF, Duane K. McDermond-Refuge Mgr. U.S.F&W, K1MM, JA1BK, W8KKF, WA2MOE, K1ER, N2IC/Ø, K4DLI, K4UPL, KH6DD, KH6GDR, WØUN, WYØJ, ON4WW, Chiltern DX Club, Clipperton DX Club of France, INDEXA, European DX Foundation, JG2BRI & Friends, Mile High DX Assn., Northern California DX Foundation, LYNX DX Group, Reseau des Emmeteurs Francais, Southeastern DX Club, Union de Radioaficianados Espanoles, Apple Computer Benelux, Birmingham (AL) ARC, Danish DX Group, Northern Illinois DX Assn. (& N9US), 890 Satellite Fund, F6AML, F6CYD, F6FYD, KJ4VH, N4LIS, N. Jersey DX Assn., Flanders DX Club, W8BLA, KH6LJ, KH6OR, T30MT, N3SL, Captian Bill Austin & the crew of the MACHIAS, and for tolerance and loving support to our wives, families and friends.

(Information provided by Walt Stinson, WØCP)

N9NS/KH5K, March 1993
QTH: Kingman Island

Bands	QSOs
1.8	1
3.5	500
7.0	1834
10.1	843
14.0	6124
18.0	2400
21.0	3102
24.9	2802
28.0	3894
SAT	83
RTTY	277
	22,785 QSOs reported.

*QSL via: N9NS
*Ops: N9NS, NØAFW, PAØERA, PA3DZN, OZ1LGF, VE5RA, G3KHZ, GØLMX, W7KNT, NH6UY, HB9AEE, HB9AHL.

(Information provided by Doug Renwick, VE5RA, and Mike Goode, N9NS)

NØAFW/KH5, March 1993
QTH: Palmyra Island

Bands	QSOs
7.0	279
14.0	3,229
18.0	1 (FK8CP)
21.0	2,560
24.9	1 (FK8CP)
28.0	2,053
Sat.	79
	8,202 Total QSOs.

*QSL via: WA2FIJ
*Ops: N9NS, NØAFW, PAØERA, PA3DZN, OZ1LGF, VE5RA, G3KHZ, GØLMX, W7KNT, NH6UY, HB9AEE, HB9AHL.
*Acknowledgements and/or Sponsors: ICOM America, NCDXF, Oklahoma Comm Center, So. Cal. DX Club, National Wire & Cable Co., ICE Filters, Hoosier Contesters, Cushcraft, Danish DX Group, Flanders DX Group, Clipperton DX Club, Nagara Antennas, 256 DX Group, EUDXF, IRDXA Chiltern DX Group, WA2FIJ, N7QQ, AH9B, K8JP, N6RJ, DL1SDN, WT8S, KD6AYV, WB6UDI, W1PNR, WA6PJR, W6PQS, K9AJ, WØRLX, and especially KH6HH, KH6DD, KH6IFN.

(Information provided by Peter Meyer, NØAFW, and Jay Kobelin, WA2FIJ)

9G1AA, March 1993
QTH: Ghana, Dormaa Hospital

Band	QSOs
1.8	54
	Over 38,000 Total QSOs reported.

*QSL via: PA3AWW
*Ops: PA3AWW, PA3DEW, PA3ERA, PA3FUE, PAØTUK.
*Acknowledgements and/or Sponsors: Schaart (Yaesu Importer), GB (for beams), Johnson & Johnson, Siemens Netherlands, Agfa Gevaert, PI4DEC, Merwede Hospital Dordrecht, Tulip Computers Netherlands, Mr. Jackson, 9G1AJ, Dorma Hospital-Ghana, DAGOE Foundation, PAØMRG, PA3FFJ, PA3DDG, AC4NJ.

(Information provided by Willem, PA3DDG, and Cliff, AC4NJ)

9MØS, May 1993
QTH: Layang-Layang (Swallow Reef), Spratley Group, South China Sea

*QSOs: Over 37,000 Total QSOs
*QSL via: W4FRU
*Ops: OH2BH, JA5DQH, AB6NJ, WA6AUE, 9M2FK, 9M6TC, 9V1YW, N7NG, OH1NYP, OH2MAK.
*Acknowledgements and/or Sponsors: Mr. Mohd Elliza Bin Haji Hashim, Commander on Layang-Layang, Malasian Amateur Radio Society (9M2), Sabah Amateur Radio Society (9M6).

(Information from OH2BH, International Press Release)

E35X, June 1993
QTH: Asmara, Eritrea

*Over 20,000 Total QSOs reported.
*QSL via: LA6ZH
*Ops: LA6VM, LA9DL, LA7XK/KK6ZS, LA1EE, JF1IST.
*Acknowledgements and/or Sponsors: Ham Radio Outlet, ICOM America, INDEXA, NCDXF, plus many others which were unavailable at Press time.

(Information from May 24,1993 Press Release)

5AØRR
QTH: Libya

*Over 11,000 QSOs reported.
*QSL: Box 812, Sofia, Bulgaria
*Ops: Romeo, 3W3RR, Danny, LZ2UU, Said, 5AØRR.

*Acknowledgements and/or Sponsors: This list was not available at press time.

(Information from NT2X translation of Romeo's Press Release)

E31A, August 1993
QTH: Asmara, Eritrea

*QSL via: JH1AJT
*Ops: JH1AJT, DJ9ZB, K5VT.
*Acknowledgements and/or Sponsors: This list was unavailable at press time.

KH9, September 1993
QTH: Wake Island

Band	QSOs
1.8	201
3.5	2185
7.0	1983
10.1	558
14.0	8787
18.1	2565
21.0	2207
24.9	1085
28.0	507
Sat (AO-13)	613
	20,691 Total QSOs.

*QSL via: OKDXA
*Ops: KC6CEX, AH6MM, AH9B, AB6EV, AH6ML, NH6UY.
*Acknowledgements and/or Sponsors: Cal-Poly A.R.C., U.S. Air Force and Air Mobility Command, NCDXF, EUDXF, Oklahoma DX Assn., KWAJALEIN ARC, V73C, AD1S, KH6HH, and the Oklahoma Comm Center.

(Information provided by George Adkins, AD1S, and Craig Boyer, AH9B)

VK9MM, late September 1993
QTH: Mellish Reef

*QSL via:VK4CRR
*QSOs: Approximately 40,000 reported.
*Ops: VK4CRR, VK2BEX, V73C, K5VT, VK2BJL, G3WGV, P29DX, WA4DAN.
*Acknowledgements and/or Sponsors: This list was unavailable at press time.

Jim Reisert, AD1C, helped compile the above data.

DXPEDITIONS APPROVED IN 1992-1993

Documentation has been received and approved for the following operations:

4S7/NZ9Z	Operations beginning 13 January 1993
5R8DC	Operations beginning 13 October 1992
5R8DD	Operations beginning 14 October 1992
5R8DE	Operations beginning 4 September 1992
5R8DF	Operations beginning 4 September 1992
5R8DH	Operations beginning 4 November 1992
5R8DI	Operations beginning 4 November 1992
5R8DJ	Operations beginning 24 November, 1992
5R8DL	Operations beginning 9 November 1992
5R8DM	Operations beginning 5 November 1992
5X1A	Operations beginning 4 March, 1993
5X1B	Operations beginning 12 March, 1993
5X1C	Operations beginning 29 April,1993
5X1XT	Operations beginning 26 April, 1993
6O/G3KOX	Operations beginning 14 December, 1992
6Y5/DF5UL	Operations beginning 25 April 1993
6Y5/DL2FAI	Operations beginning 25 April 1993
6Y5/DL4ZBI	Operations beginning 25 April 1993
6Y5/VE1AI	Operations beginning 23 March 1993
7Q7CE	Operations beginning 20 July 1993
8Q7AF	Operations beginning 17 March 1993
9F2CW	Operations beginning 15 December, 1992
9G1AA	Operations beginning 24 March, 1993
AH1A	Operations beginning 25 January 1993
D2/AA4HU	Operations beginning 26 January, 1993
D2/KC6HUE	Operations beginning 26 January, 1993
D2/N6QHO	Operations beginning 26 January, 1993
D2BG	Operations beginning 17 February, 1993
D2SA	Operations beginning 18 March 1993
D68CA	Operations beginning 9 August 1993
ET3DX	Operations beginning 11 April, 1993
ET3JR	Operations beginning 15 October, 1992
ET3RA	Operations beginning 22 November, 1992
ET3YU	Operations beginning 26 February, 1993
FH/I4ALU	Operations beginning 21 August 1993
FJ/I4UFH	Operations beginning 9 August 1993
KP1/W5IJU et al	Operations beginning 23 March 1993
S21ZG	Operations beginning 6 December,1992
S21ZH	Operations beginning 6 March, 1993
S21ZJ	Operations beginning 6 March, 1993
S21ZK	Operations beginning 6 March, 1993
S21ZM	Operations beginning 7 March, 1993
S75S	Operations beginning 28 December 1993
T5/DF5UX	Operations beginning 1 March 1993
T5/DL1VJ	Operations beginning 1 March 1993
T5/DL8YR	Operations beginning 20 April 1993
T5/K3OQF	Operations beginning 21 February, 1993
T5/KF6BL	Operations beginning 26 December, 1992
T5/KJ6QO	Operations beginning 11 March 1993
T53UN	Operations beginning 20 March, 1992
T55FO	Operations beginning 6 January, 1993
T5CB	Operations beginning 31 January, 1993
T5HLL	Operations beginning 15 March 1993
T5THW	Operations beginning 1 March 1993
TT8AKX	Operations beginning 16 January 1993
TU4EA	Operations beginning 14 April 1992
TY8OBO	Operations beginning 14 August 1993
VP5/W2IQ	Operations beginning 1 January 1993
XU7VK	Operations beginning 1 December 1992
YI9CW	Operations beginning July, 1992
ZB2JL	Operations beginning 8 January 1993

The DXCC Desk requested that cards for the 9F2CW/A operation of 26 January through 4 February, 1993 be held pending the DXAC's disposition of the petition for new country status for Eritrea. Their action may affect the way this operation is credited.

Courtesy of ARRL.

A BRIEF HISTORY OF THE CQ WW CONTEST

Since the basis of much of the contest revolves around the concept of the WAZ Zones, it may be useful for the reader to review the history of the WAZ Award (see the Awards chapter in this *Almanac*).

The CQ World Wide DX Contest started in 1948, three years after *CQ* magazine was first published. But the very first "Worldwide DX Contest" grew out of an idea developed by Herb Becker, W6QD, the DX contributing editor for *Radio* magazine in 1939.

In the October 1939 issue, Herb announced the first *Radio* magazine World-Wide DX Contest. In Herb's words,

> The World-Wide Contest which should be a break for the working man and those in schools, will be over two weekends, with 48 hours each. The starting time will be 0200 GMT November 25 and December 2. The competition will be divided into two divisions, CW. and phone. Each of these two divisions will be divided into two sections—the one-operator section and the more-than-one-operator section. CW. stations must work CW. stations, and phone stations must work phone stations. Competitors in the one-operator section may use one transmitter only, and competitors in the more-than-one-operator section may use any number of transmitters. Any number of receivers may be used by all competitors. Remember that the 7, 14, and 28 MHz bands are the only ones used in the contest.

This first WW DX contest was held in 1939 and reported in the June 1940 issue of *Radio*. It was in June of that same year that the US government suspended amateur radio activity due to World War II. Accordingly, W6QD reported in the July issue of *Radio* that the 1940 contest was canceled. WW II prevented the "World Wide Contest" from taking hold.

The thrust of *Radio* magazine shifted more and more towards the engineering side of radio, and in 1945, Radio Magazines, Inc. founded *CQ* to take up the needs of amateurs. *Radio* magazine itself continued until 1947 when it was renamed *Audio Engineering* and continues to this day as *Audio* magazine.

After the War, *CQ* showed up with a familiar layout—the old pre-war *Radio* layout. W6QD showed up as the DX and overseas editor for the new *CQ* magazine. Hams were back on the air in the summer of 1946 and, in January 1947, *CQ* announced the CQ WAZ award. The WAZ map was the same as first published in 1936. In the October 1948 issue of *CQ*, the announcement was made of "CQ's World-Wide DX Contest" to be held on October 29 to 31 (phone) and the CW contest on November 5 to 7. The rules read just like the earlier *Radio* magazine World-Wide DX Contest. The contest period was again from 0200 GMT Saturday to 0200 GMT Monday. Only the 7, 14, and 27/28 MHz bands were to be used. The competition was not separated into single or multi-operator and there was only an all-band category. The results were reported in the June, 1949 issue. It was reported that in that first contest that all 40 zones were active! In the write-up, all the scores were listed by zone. Under each zone the call area or country was listed. Both single operator and multi-operator were competing against one another! Only the point score was given with no further breakdown.

In the second year of the contest (1949), single and multi-operator stations now competed for separate awards. Another improvement was the single-band category. There were about 1,450 logs submitted in the second year of the CQWW. There was such an unexpected outpouring of interest in this contest that it caught *CQ* by surprise. The results actually had to be published over two months!

By the time the third CQ WW contest occurred in 1950, participation had grown to about 1,600 entrants. The scores were listed for the first time by country instead of by zone. Single-band scores were listed for the first time. The contest continued to be the last full weekend of October and the first weekend of November. The phone and CW sections were now reported in separate issues.

In the 1951 results, Herb had the assistance of his friend W6ENV in reporting the scores. He sums up the essence of the contest saying,

It seems that what you [DX/Contesters] want is a contest where there is DX...Every now and again a few of the boys think that too much publicity is given the high point men. There are a couple of ways of looking at it. In all hobbies, the man who scores the highest number of points or comes out ahead attracts the most attention. We would be sadly neglectful if we did not recognize it.

In 1952, W6QD was back as the sole author for the contest results. This was to be Herb's last year as the DX overseas editor for *CQ*. The DX column was handed over to Dick Spenceley, KV4AA. Dick was living in the Virgin Islands, and he could not take on the logistical problem of having contest logs mailed to him and then back to *CQ* in New York.

So in 1953, under the guidance of Larry LeKashman, W9IOP, *CQ* turned sponsorship over to a group in Indiana and Michigan. The contest was now sponsored by the International DX Club and they promptly renamed it the "International DX Contest," even saying that it was formerly known as the World-Wide CQ DX Contest. The International DX Club issued their own certificates for the contest. A picture of one of these certificates appears along with the 1953 results in August 1954 *CQ*. The International DX Club could not find the time to check the logs so they turned the checking process over to the Potomac Valley Radio Club of suburban Washington, D.C. The reporting was back to the early days. In the write-up, only the entrant's category and score were listed. In addition, only the top scores were listed. Full results were available for an SASE.

In 1954, the rules for the International DX Contest had the phone weekend occurring on October 23 and the CW weekend on October 30. The 1954 rules make the first mention of a club competition. When the contest results were reported by W9IOP, it was apparent that something was wrong. The International DX Club was not capable of fully checking the results. Only calls and scores were listed under each category—nothing else. As *CQ* was searching for what to do with the contest, Bill Leonard, W2SKE, wrote an article in the December 1955 issue which summarized briefly the 1955 CQ WW Contest that had just occurred, encouraging hams to enter the 1956 contest. It was at this time that *CQ* took back the contest. W9IOP rewrote the rules and *CQ* Editor Wayne Green, W2NSD, recruited Frank Anzalone, W1WY, to check the 1955 results.

The 1955 CQ World Wide DX Contest, as it was now renamed, was reported by Frank, W1WY, in the May issue. Up until 1955, there were no power categories in the CQ WW. Starting in 1955 there were five power categories! A: up to 30 W; B: up to 125 W; C: up to 500 W and D: over 500 W. With W1WY at the helm, the format of the modern CQ WW reporting took on its familiar style. The *CQ* contest committee was now located in the New York area and the checking of logs took on a serious nature.

When the 1956 results were reported, there was a new department on the *CQ* masthead: The Contest Calendar, edited by W1WY. Contesters now had their own column and a concerned patron. The 1956 rules changed the power category of two of the power groups: 30 now became 35 W and 125 W became 150 W.

From 1955 to 1973, Frank worked to bring the CQ WW up to its present level. The 1959 rules indicated a change in the country multiplier list. As always, the DXCC list was used, but now the WAE country list was added. This year also saw the elimination of the novice category, which had been initiated in 1955 to give new hams a chance to compete among themselves. It was now realized that novice power limitation and frequency privileges were very different all over the world. There was no way to make the category a fair one. The rules of 1959 saw the multi-operator category divided into two categories. Due mainly to K2GL's station and his enthusiasm, there was now a multi-single and a multi-multi category for competitors.

The next significant rule changes occurred in the 1962 contest. Up to 1961, all the CQ WW contests began at 0200 UTC Saturday morning and ended at 0200 UTC Monday morning, convenient times for West Coast U.S. operators. In 1962, the contest now began and ended at 0000 UTC, a logical time to start a world wide event. This year also saw the elimination of the power categories. Lastly, 1962 was when the North American two-point rule came into existence. With this rule, it was hoped that more activity would occur in the Caribbean and Central American countries. All these changes were brought into the rules by Frank, W1WY.

From the middle 60s to the early 70s the new multi-multi category flourished. All over the U.S., big stations such as K2GL, W3MSK (W3AU), W6RW, W6VSS (K6UA), W7RM and W4BVV were assembled. The operators of these stations were enlisted to help in checking the logs. Between 1970 and 1975, K3EST, N2AA (K2KUR), WB2SQN (K2SS), N6AA, WA6EPQ (N6AR), K6NA and N6TJ all joined the *CQ* Contest Committee. Being in New York, K2GL contributed first to the contest committee with Fred, W2IWC (now K6SSS). Fred was an operator at K2GL and had volunteered to help Frank in checking the logs. After the results were reported for the 1973 contest, Frank asked Fred to take over as CQ WW contest director while he remained as overall contest chairman. Fred took over and reported the 1974 and 1975 results. It was under Fred's leadership that the contest committee took on its present profile—that is representative of both U.S. coasts. He invited several well known W6s who were contesters and DXers to join the committee. The contest was now being run from Southern California were it began some 35 years earlier.

After two years, Fred resigned as director and suggested WA6EPQ (now N6AR) as his replacement. Frank, W1WY, wanted more balance and they agreed to name two directors from the ranks of the Contest Committee. In 1976, K3EST and N6AR took over at the helm of the contest.

In 1978, the QRP category was initiated and the assisted category began in 1987. In the early 1980s, K3EST brought DX advisors onto the committee. These advisors helped resolve local problems and help the directors understand the ideas of their particular country.

In the early 1980s, the Contest Committee and top competitors realized that a more thorough checking of top scores was necessary in order to certify winners. Committee member K2SS developed a computer log checking procedure which, with a few variations and enhancements added by N6TR, remains the method used to check logs today.

So there you have the history of the CQ WW in brief. As you can see, the contest has a long tradition, beginning with the first *Radio* magazine World-Wide DX Contest in 1939. The *CQ* Contest Committee, with the help of amateurs all over the world, retains the original enthusiasm of W6QD.

This brief history is from The CQ World Wide Contest Handbook, *by K3EST, available from R2R International, 1816 Poplar Ln, Davis, CA 95616, USA.*

(In the following sections, parentheses indicate operator callsign, brackets indicate operator's current callsign.)

DX WINNERS OF CQ WORLD WIDE DX PHONE CONTEST BY YEAR/CATEGORY

YEAR	S/O	S/O/Asst	QRP	M/S	M/M	160	80	40	20	15	10
1992	HC8A(N6KT)	WM5G(KR0Y)	AA2U	VP2EC	PJ1B	9A1HCD	TI1C(TI2CF)	PJ9E(OH5BM)	PJ9P(OH6MW)	ZV5A(PY5	EG)ZW5B(N5FA)
1991	CR3A(OH2MM)	N4RJ(KM9P)	4M1G(YV1CLM)	PJ1B	VP9AD	IV3PRK	GW4OFQ	ZF2JR(N6RJ)	YW1A(YV1AVO)	ZX9A(PY5CC)	ZV5A(PY5EG)
1990	CT3BH(OH2BH)	K1ZM	KR2Q	IQ4A	PJ1B	UG6GAW	HA8IE	ZF2JR(N6RJ)	YV3A(YV5IVB)	P4ØR(K4UEE)	ZPØY(ZP5JCY)
1989	EA8RCT(N6KT)	YT3AA	YU2TY	P4ØV	PJ1B	IH9/IV3PRK	HK3MAE	DJ4PT	YW1A(YV1AVO)	EL2CX(K3RV)	P4ØR(K4UEE)
1988	CT9BZ(OH2BH)	*#A*	ZY5EG(PY5CC)	EA8AGD	P4ØV	YU3MM	IK5BAF	TI1W(TI2KD)	TF3CW	ZP5Y(ZP5JCY)	VP2ET(K5RX)
1987	9Y4TT(NQ4I)		PJ2FR(K7SS)	KP2A	PJ1B	UG7GWO	P4ØR(K4UEE)	EA8RCT(OH2MM)	P4ØSS(K2SS)	PY5EG	ZY5EG(PY5CC)
1986	8R1X(NQ4I)		WP4G	VP2EC	PJ1B	LZ2CJ	NP4A	ZY5EG	OH8PF	ZZ5EG(N5FA)	LU1E(LU3AJW)
1985	PJ2FR(N6KT)		WP4G	P44B	HC8X	LZ2CJ	VE3BMV	VP2ET(K5RX)	YZ9A(YT3AA?)	TI2CF	TI2KD
1984	PJ2FR(N6KT)		UP2BIM	4V2C	TI1C	LZ2CJ	YV3AZC	EA8AK	KØGU/8R1	HC1OT	CE6EZ
1983	PJ2FR(N6KT)		AA2Z/1	9Y4W	TI1C	UP2BBT/U6V	YV3AZC	YV2AMM	ZM1BIL	KD7P/KH2	CE6EZ
1982	9Y4VT(N6AA)		TG9GI	9Y4W	OHØW	EA8AK	4M3AZC	YV3BRF	YS1X	AHØAB(JA3ODC)	YV2AMM
1981	9Y4VT(N6AA)		I5NSR	VP2MFW	P41C	UP2BAW	YV3AZC	ZL1BIL	VP2KAA(N4PN)	VP2KAC(N4RJ)	ZZ5EG
1980	EA8AK		G4BUE	I4RYC	PJ2CC	YU3EF	4M3AZC	SP3DOI	I5NPH	NP4A	KH6XX
1979	9Y4VT(N6AA)		W6PQZ	HI8XWP	VP2KC	PA5ØHIP	CT3BZ(OH2BH)	I5NPH	UA6HZ	H31LR(HP1XOJ)	OH2MM/CT3
1978	9Y4VT(N6AA)		VP9AD	FY7BC	PJ9JR	GM3ZSP	W1CF	I3MAU	KV4FZ	YU3ZV	CW3BR
1977	PJ9CG(K1JX)		*#Q*	FMØFC	EA8CR	DJ8WLA	KP4RF	KX6LA	YV2AMM	YU3ZV	PY1MAG
1976	PJ9CG(K1JX)			VP2G	VP5M	KY4F2	EA8CR	CX4CR	FY7AK	CW3BR	CE6EZ
1975	FY7AK(F5QQ)			VP2M	DLØPG	XJ3BMV	KV4FZ	OH5NW	CW3BR	G3WJN	CV4CR
1974	ZD3X(OH2BH)			PY2CAB	PJ9JR	PAØHIP	EIØREI	EA8CR	CR6WW	CR6OZ	CR6NO
1973	ZD3Z(OH2MM)			VP2M	PJ9GIW	ZF1GS/VP7	KV4FZ	KP4AST	CV4C	G3HCT	CR6CN
1972	4M4UA[N6TJ]			PJ1AA	ZD3X	KV4FZ	YV4AGP	HR1RF	CR6IK	G3HCT	KG6SL
1971	6D1AA[KØDQ]			UK9ABA	4M1A	GM3YCB	VE3MR/4X	HR1RF	KV4FZ	CX1JM	XX7IK
1970	KV4FZ			PA9AF	OH5SM	GM3YCB	LAØAD	YV1BI	YV1LA	CW4CR	KP4AST
1969	9Y4AA[N6TJ]			ON4UN	PJØDX	VE3BS	CT2AT	SM5BPJ	PY4OD	CWØAA	4X4JU
1968	ZD8Z[N6TJ]			DLØWR	OH2AM	W8GDO	W1FZJ/KP4	YV4UA	YV5ANF	CX2CO	YV1LA
1967	VK2ADY/9(W9WNV)			I4GAD	OF2AM	DL9KRA	OK1WGW	K2GXI	G5AAM	DL6EN	LU1DAB
1966	VQ9AA/D(W9WNV)			CX2CO	YV9AA	——	YV5BTS	DJ5BV	YV5BIG	DL6EN	LU1DAB
1965	CX2CO			ET3USA	YV9AA	GW3PMR	ON4UN	OX3JV	FY7BL	DL6EN	LU1DAB
1964	YV5BIG			YV9AA	YV5AKU	——	GI3CDF	DJ2YA	CX2CO	WA2SFP[W29V]	LU1DAB
1963	ZD7BW			DL1KB	CX2CO	——	4X4DK	W3PHL	HL9KH (W9WNY)	W1IRIL	LU1DAB
1962	XT2Z(9G1DP)			CX2CO	DLØWW	——	ON4UN	W3PHL	MP4BBW	G3FXB	LU1DAB
1961	CX2CO			VQ4RF	DJ3OU	——	I1AIM	4X4DK	ZS7P	ZB1HC	LU1DAB
1960	VQ4DT			4X4GB	ET2US	——	——	YO9CN	CX2CO	VQ4RF	LU1DAB
1959	4X4GB			HZ1AB	KA2RB	——	G5MP	——	CO2ZS	CE3DY	CX1AK
1958	F8PI			DJ3VM	*#MM*	——	G5MP	SP3PL	CE2CC	CO2ZS	OH5NW
1957	F8CH			ON4SZ		——	W1ZBT	JA1EF	OD5BZ	CE3DY	DL4AAP
1956	4X4DK			I1BDV		——	OK2KOD	JA1EF	CO2OZ	HC1ES	VQ4RF
1955	CX2CO			ON4SZ		——	OZ8KR	JA1VP	W3JNN	VQ4RF	LU1BK
1954	CN8MM			F7BM		——	I1CSP	JA1GV	KA2CR	OQ5RU	LU4ARR
1953	CT1FT			TA3AA		——	DL1LH	W8JIN	OD5AD	ZS6DW	CX3BT
1952	CE3CZ			TA3AA		——	W9EDC	PAØEEM	ZS6BW	——	CE1AJ
1951	PY2CK			MI3US		——	W8UKS	ZL1HY	DL4WC	——	CE1AJ
1950	HC2JR			CN8ET		——	——	——	CN8EX	——	VP2GG
1949	PY2AC			HC2JR		——	——	ZS5U	ZS6JS	——	VQ4IMS
1948	PY2AC			W6SA							
#1940											
1939	CE3AG			——							

Footnote # 1991. The Single Operator Low Power class was added beginningwith the 1991 event. Output power limited to 100 watts.

Footnote # A. The Single Operator Assisted Class was added beginning with the 1989 event. Rules permitted single operators to utilize any form "of DXspotting nets or DX alerting assistance."

Footnote # 1987. The 1987 RESULTS were the first time European TOP Scores were listed.

Footnote # Q. QRPp Single Operator was added to the 1978 event. Output power limited to 5 watts.

Footnote # MM. Multi-Operator Multi-Transmitter added to the 1959 event.

Footnote # 1948. CQ's original rules: 0200z start time for 48 hours. Fouth full weekend of October for Phone and first full weekend of November for CW, 80m, 40m, 20m and 27-29 MHz. Single-Operator and Multi-Operator. No limit to the number of transmitters and receivers but you must observe all the rules of your license. Exchange RS(T) and CQ W.A.Z. Zone number. One point per contact multiplied by the sum of zones per band and countries per band. (August 1948 *CQ*)

Footnote # 1940. The July, 1940 issue of *RADIO* magazine carried the rules and announcement for the Second Annual RADIO World-Wide DXContest. The changes included one weekend for CW, which was to begin 2300z October 4 to 0800z October 7, 1940 and one for Phone which was to begin 2300z October 11 to 0800z October 14, 1940. Log Deadline was November 4th! The available classes were changed: "Competitors will not be limited in the number of operators, or in equiptment." **After the issue had been prepared, the FCC banned all amateur communications with foreign stations. Besides adding a Full Page Contest Cancellation, there were several boxes throughout the issue stating that the WWDX Contest had been cancelled.

U.S.A. WINNERS OF CQ WORLD-WIDE DX PHONE CONTEST BY YEAR/CATEGORY

YEAR	S/O	S/O/Asst	QRP	M/S	M/M	160	80	40	20	15	10
1992	K1AR	WM5G(KRØY)	AA2U	K1DG	N2RM	WB9Z	K1ZM	W7XR(W7WA)	K4XS	K5MR	N4RJ(KM9P)
1991	K1AR	N4RJ(KM9P)	WA2UUK	K3LR	N2RM	AB4RU	K1UO	KC7EM	KS1L	K3RV/4	NR5M
1990	WM5G(KRØY)	K1ZM/2	KR2Q	K1AR	N2RM	K5UR	W6RJ	KVØQ	W1RR	NG2X	NR5M
1989	N2NT	K1ZM/2	KD2TT	KS9K	W3LPL	K5UR	K4HJJ	WQ2M	W1RR	W7WA	K5GA
1988	KC1F	*#A*	KR2Q	N2RM	W3LPL	K5UR	W6RJ	K5RR(WD5K)	KV4P	K3RV/4	WØZV
1987	KC1F		N3RS	K1AR	W3LPL	WB9HAD[WB9Z]	WB8JBM(NZ4K)	KVØQ	K2VV	K3RV/4	K6SVL
1986	K2TR		K3WS	KX4S	N5AU	K5UR	K7SS	KØRF	K2EK	K3RV/4	K4JRB
1985	K1AR		K3WS	KX4S	N2AA	AA1K/3	W6RJ	W7RM(W7WA)	K1OX	K2EK	KG1E
1984	K1AR		K7SS	K2BU	N2AA	K5UR	W6RJ	KJ9D	W2YV(KQ2M)	K2EK	NU4Y
1983	AI6V(WA6VEF)		AA2Z/1	KX4S	N2AA	WA2SPL	W1ZM(K1ZM)	N7DD	K1UO	W6YA(N6NI)	NU4Y
1982	W1ZM(K1ZM)		K8IA	W4QAW	N2AA	W8LRL	K1JX	KØGU	K1KI	WØZV	W6YA(N6NI)
1981	K1AR		WB2ULI	K3LR	W2PV	WB3GCG	W7IVX	KØRF	K2HFX	N7DD	WØZV
1980	K7RI		AI6V	KØUK	N2AA	K5UR	N4KE	KM4K	K2HFX	KM6B	N7DD
1979	N7DD		W6PQZ	K4VX	N2AA	W8LRL	WØMJ	K4JRB	KØKX	K1RM	WA2SPL
1978	W4DR(WA8ZDT)		WA4IAR	K5GA	N2AA	K1PBW	W1CF	KØRF	K9DX	WA6EKL	K6OQ
1977	W3WJD(WA3LRO)		*#Q**	K5JA	W2PV	N4EA	W2VP	W7KW	K2HFX	WA6EKL	WB6PXP[AE6E]
1976	W1ZM([K1ZM)]			W6ONV	W7RM	K1PBW	W7KW	AA6EPQ[N4AR]	WBØLLR	K4YYL	AB5HIH
1975	W7RM([K7JA])			W6ONV	W2PV	W8LRL	W1EBC[K1EB]	W3PHL	K9PPY	K1JHX[K1RM]	WB5HIH
1974	W6RR			W3WJD	W2PV	WB8APH	W1EBC[K1EB]	W3PHL	K2KUR/2[N2AA]	K6SDR[N6CW]	K4JRB
1973	K6AHV			W7SFA	W2PV	WB8APH	W5SZ	W4QCW[W4DR]	K2KUR[N2AA]	W4WSF[N4MM]	WB4UYD
1972	W6RR			W7SFA	W3WJD	WA4SGF	K6ERT	W3PHL	WB2OEU[K2TR]	W2AH	K4YYL
1971	W2PV			WB2SQN	W7RM	K1PBW	W4CRW	W3PHL	W2ONV	K1VTM	W6QJW
1970	W6RR			WB2SQN	W3AU	WA4SGF	K3UZE	K2GXI	W4AXE	W1RIL	W2YT
1969	K1KTH[N6JL]			W4AXE	WA2ZAA	K1PBW	K3UZE	W2DXL[W2IB]	WA3GUL[K3OO]	W4YHD[W4RX]	K3HPG
1968	W2PV			W2CP/2	W3MSK	W8GDO	W4AXE	K2GXI	W2ONV	W6GHM/5	W2SKE
1967	W4AXE			WA6ZQU	K2GL	W8GDQ	K2RBT	K2GXI	K8YBU[K8RK]	W1HQV	W2BXA
1966	WA2SFP[W2PV]			WA6EPQ	K2GL	—	K8YWG	W3PHL	W3JNN	WA8CZH	W2OKM
1965	WA2SFP[W2PV]			K2HLB	W3MSK	—	W1AQH	K2GXI	—	WA4PXP	WA4SUR
1964	W3MSK([N4RV)]			K2IEG	K2GL	—	W1BU	K2GXI	K2HWL	WA2SFP[W2PV]	K6CT
1963	K2HLB(W2VCZ)			W3TMZ	K2GL	—	—	W3PHL	K2HFX	W1RIL	W2TVR
1962	K5MDX			WA6EPQ	W3MSK	—	W1BU	W3PHL	K2HFX	K9ECE	K5ORH
1961	K5MDX			W4HXC	K2GL	—	W1BU	K2GXI	K2IEG	W2WZ	W9PWU
1960	W6GHM			K6EVR	K2GL	—	—	K2DGT	W1ONK	W9ZTD	W5LGG
1959	W1ONK			K6EVR	W8HGO	—	W1ZBT	—	W2HTI	W3AOH	W2VCZ
1958	W9EWC			K2GL	*#MM*	—	—	W6UED	W7HQC	W4NQM	K8AEK
1957	W6YY			K2GL	—		W1ZBT	—	W6LTY	W2GFO	W1ONK
1956	K2AAA			K2GL	—	—	—	W3ECR	W6VSS	W4NQM	W3JTK
1955	W6YY			W2HJR	—		W7JLU	W8FXG	W4KFC	W2WZ	W3MDE
1954	W1ATE			W6AM	—		—	W7JLU	W3LOE	K6CZY	W4NQM
1953	W1ATE			W7DL	—		W9MEM	W8JIN	W6HNX	W2JDE	W4NQM
1952	W1ATE			W6AM	—		W9EDC	—	W6PWR	—	WØGEK
1951	W4ESK			W6RRG	—		W8UKS	—	W6UYX	—	W4QBK
1950	W1ATE			W6AM	—		—	—	W1AFZ	—	W4VB
1949	W1ATE			W6SA	—		—	—	W6DI	—	W1BEQ
1948	W8KML			W6SA							
#1940											
1939	W6OCH	—									

Footnote #1991. The Single Operator Low Power class was added beginning with the 1991 event. Output power limited to 100 watts.
Footnote #A. The Single Operator Assisted Class was added beginning with the 1989 event. Rules permitted Single operators to utilize any form "of DX spotting nets or DX alerting assistance."
Footnote #1987. The 1987 RESULTS were the first time European TOP Scores were listed.
Footnote #Q. QRPp Single Operator was added to the 1978 event. Output power limited to 5 watts.
Footnote #MM. Multi-Operator Multi-Transmitter added to the 1959 event.
Footnote #1948. CQ's original rules: 0200z start time for 48 hours. Fouth full weekend of October for Phone and first full weekend of November for CW, 80m, 40m, 20m and 27-29 MHz. Single-Operator and Multi-Operator. No limit to the number of transmitters and receivers but you must observe all the rules of your license. Exchange RS(T) and CQ W.A.Z. Zone number. One point per contact multiplied by the sum of zones per band and countries per band. (August 1948 *CQ*)
Footnote #1940. The July, 1940 issue of *RADIO* magazine carried the rules and announcement for the Second Annual RADIO World-Wide DX Contest. The changes included one weekend for CW, which was to begin 2300z October 4 to 0800z October 7, 1940 and one for Phone which was to begin 2300z October 11 to 0800z October 14, 1940. Log Deadline was November 4th! The available classes were changed: "Competitors will not limited in the number of operators, or in equiptment." **After preparing the issue, the FCC banned all amateur communications with foreign stations. Besides adding a Full Page Contest Cancellation, there were several boxes throughout the issue stating that the WW DX Contest had been cancelled.

WORLD WINNERS OF CQ WORLDWIDE DX CW CONTEST BY YEAR/CATEGORY

YEAR	S/O	S/OQRP	S/O/Ast	M/S	M/M	160	80	40	20	15	10
1991	EA8EA(OH2MM)	HI8A(JA5DQH)	N4RJ(KM9P)	EA9EA	PJ9A	4X4NJ	ZB2X(OH2KI)	C42A(YU4OO)	P4ØV(N7NG)	ZW5B(LU8DQ)	ZS6BCR[ZS6EZ]
1990	CT3M(OH7JT)	HI8A(JA5DQH)	K3WW	TA5KA	PJ9A	UG6GAW	EA9EU	P4ØJ(WX4G)	ED9ED(EA5BRA)	C56/OH7XM	CXØCW(CX8BBH)
1989	P4ØGD(W2GD)	W2TZ	K1DG	EA9EA	CT3M	LY2BTA	TA2BK	YW1A(YV1DIG)	4Z8DX	N7DF/NH2	ZPØY(LU8DQ)
1988	FY5YE(OH2MM)	YU3BC	-#A-	VP2MW	PJ1B	TA2BK	NP4A(K1ZM)	YX5A(YV5ANT)	ZS6BCR[ZS6EZ]	CW8B(CX8BBH)	4M7A(YV7QP)
1987	FY5YE(OH2MM)	VE7DX(K7SS)		EA8AGD	KP2A	UP2NK/UF	ZC4DX(4Z4DX)	YW1O(YV1DIG)	EA8ID(DK3GI)	LO8WW(LU8DQ)	4M7A(YV7QP)
1986	9Y4VT(N6AA)	LZ1BB		KP4BZ	KP2N	HB9AMO	P4ØR(K4UEE)	UP3BA/UF	P40N(N4PN)	PY5CA(N5FA)	4M7A(YV7QP)
1985	EA9IE(N6AA)	YU3BC		V3A	RF3V	YV3AGT	EA2IA	KP4FI	YX5A(YV5ANT)	CX5AO	ZS6P
1984	9Y4VT(N6AA)	K8IA		FYØGA	EA9CE	LZ1KDP	UP2NK/UF	YX5A(YV5ANT)	LU8DQ	9Y4W(?)	4M7QP(YV7QP)
1983	9Y4VT(N6AA)	UB5UCJ		HH2VP	RW9A	UP2BBT/U6V	VP2KAC(N4RJ)	VP2KAA(N4PN)	YW5R	YX5A	C53T
1982	9Y4VT(N6AA)	UP2BIM		NP4A	P42E	EA8AK	EA2IA	KV4FZ	VE3BMV	CX7CO(CX8BBH)	V3TV
1981	9Y4VT(N6AA)	AC2U		P41E	W2PV	EA8AK	I4IND	UA1DZ	OH8SR	LU8DQ	YJ8RW
1980	9Y4VT(N6AA)	YU3BC		RG6G	NP4A	OK3KFF(OK3CQW)	WB2FZO(KQ2M)	KØRF	VP2KAA(N4PN)	HDØE(K7CA)	KG6DX
1979	EA8AK(OH6DX)	G4BUE		NP4A	PJ2CC	G3S2A	EA2OP	YU2CDS(YU2RRX)	YU3ZV	VP2MEE(N8BM)	LU8DQ
1978	CT3BZ(OH2BH)	OA8V		RF6F	EA8CR	VR3AH	UI8LAG	AH6Z	KV4FZ	LU8DQ	FY7BC
1977	9Y4VT(N6AA)	-#Q-		4L6M	KP4EAJ	K1PBW	CT3/OH1TV	KV4F2	2W4OD	KX6LA	LU1DZ
1976	KP4AST			PJ9MM	UK9AAN	KV4FZ	VR3AH	W5WIQ	CW3BR(CX1EK)	5Z4NI	YV4CB
1975	EA8CR			FY7AK	W3AU	YV1OB	KV4FZ	ZP5GS	CX4CR	ZE8JN	LU6EF
1974	KH6RS(K1GQ)			OD5IQ	PJ9JT	PAØHIP	YU3DBC	ZL1AMO	CR6IK	CR6OZ	WB4KSE/KW6
1973	ZD3X(OH2BH)			PJ1AA	W3AU	KV4FZ	UB5CI	KP4AST	CV8B	CV1B	CX9BT
1972	ZD3Z(OH2MM)			PJ2VD	CW3AA	ZF1GS	DL7AV	K6EBB	CR6IK	CW9BT	ZE8JN
1971	KH6RS(K1GQ)			UK9ABA	PJ9JT	KG4CS	W3MFW	KV4FZ	PY4AP	VK6HD	7Q7AA
1970	ZS3AW			4M5ANT	PJØFC	DL1CF	SM5BPJ	W6ISA	KV4FZ	TJ1AW	CX1AAC
1969	9Y4AA(N6TJ)			UA9KAX	PJØCW	HB9NL	OZ5DX	SM5BLA	CR6GO	VQ8CR	CR6IK
1968	KV4FZ			DLØKF	PJØCC	DL1CF	OM1BY	LZ1KPG	PY4OD	CR6GO	K1JGD
1967	ZD8J			4L3A	PJ3CC	ZC4RB	OK1ALW	4X4RD	PY2BGL	G3HCT	PY2SO
1966	ZD8J			4L7A	K2GL	VO1FB	SM6MX	OK1ZQ	1G5A(W9WNV)	CX1AAC	9J2BC
1965	VR2EW(W9WNV)			ET3USA	K2GL	W1BB/1	DJ3KR	KZ5TW	PY2SO	W8WZ	WA4WIP
1964	PY4OD			YV9AA	K2GL	OK1ZC	4X4DH	5A1TW[N2AA]	CX2CO	ZS6IW	——
1963	5A1TW()			VK5NO	CX2CO	DJ3KR	UB5MZ	4X4DH	VP8GQ	ZS6IW	HK7ZI
1962	HL9KH(W9WNV)			CX2CO	4X9HQ	DJ2KS	OK1MG	VK3AZZ	PY4OD	ZS6IW	HK7ZT
1961	7G1A			VK5NQ	DJ3JZ	OK1ADX	OK3DG	W9WNV	UA9DN	PY4GA	K2HWL
1960	UA9DN			UB5KAB	W3AOH	OK1WT	SP2DX	K2DGT	CX2CO	DL6EN	4X4LC
1959	CN8JX			W1BIH	DJ3JZ	DL1FF	OK1AWJ	K2DGT	CE3AG	KH6DLF	OQ5IG
1958	CN8JX			K2GL	-#MM-	OK2NRO	K1MG	W8FGX	W2AIW	W4YHD	K8AEK
1957	W4KFC			W6RW	——	——	SP5IA	W3BVN	G2LB	CX2CO	DL4AAP
1956	4X4BX			KH6CBP	——	——	DL1FF	W3BVN	W4VZQ	W8BKP	JA1CO
1955	W2HJR			HA5KBA	——	——	G5MP	W8FXG	W4KFC	W2WZ	W3MDE
1954	4X4DX			W4KVX	——	——	G3HWF	OK1JX	W3LOE	LU3EX	——
1953	4X4RE			ET2US	——	——	DL1FF	KH6ER	G2LB	DL3RM	——
1952	4X4RE			TA3AA	——	——	DL1FF	5A3TR	5A3TU	VK4FJ	G2BW
1951	4X4BX			ZC4XP	——	——	G5MP	ZL3LL	GW3ZV	-N/A-	VE7YR
1950	4X4RE			CN8EG	——	——	——	KH6ZG	W3JTC	-N/A-	PY1AJ
1949	PAØUN			W6SZY	——	——	——	W4BRB	G2LB	-N/A-	G3DCU
1948	GI6TK			ZL4GA							
#1940											
1939	K6CGK[KH6IJ]	——									

Footnote #1991. The Single Operator Low Power class was added beginning with the 1991 event. Output power limited to 100 watts.
Footnote #A. The Single Operator Assisted Class was added beginning with the 1989 event. Rules permitted Single operators to utilize any form "of DX spotting nets or DX alerting assistance."
Footnote #1987. The 1987 RESULTS were the first time European TOP Scores were listed.
Footnote #Q. QRPp Single Operator was added to the 1978 event. Output power limited to 5 watts.
Footnote #MM. Multi-Operator Multi-Transmitter added to the 1959 event.
Footnote #1948. CQ's original rules: 0200z start time for 48 hours. Fouth full weekend of October for Phone and first full weekend of November for CW, 80m, 40m, 20m and 27-29 MHz. Single-Operator and Multi-Operator. No limit to the number of transmitters and receivers but you must observe all the rules of your license. Exchange RS(T) and CQ W.A.Z. Zone number. One point per contact multiplied by the sum of zones per band and countries per band (August 1948 CQ).
Footnote #1940. The July,1940 issue of RADIO magazine carried the rules and announcement for the Second Annual RADIO World-Wide DX Contest. The changes included one weekend for CW, which was to begin 2300z October 4 to 0800z October 7, 1940 and one for Phone which was to begin 2300z October 11 to 0800z October 14, 1940. Log Deadline was November 4th! The available classes were changed: "Competitors will not limited in the number of operators, or in equiptment." After the issue was prepared, the FCC banned all amateur communications with foreign stations. Besides adding a Full Page Contest Cancellation, there were several boxes throughout the issue stating that the WW DX Contest had been cancelled.

U.S.A. WINNERS OF CQ WORLDWIDE DX CW CONTEST BY YEAR/CATEGORY

YEAR	S/O	S/O/Ast	QRP	M/S	M/M	160	80	40	20	15	10
1992	N4RJ(KM9P)	K8AZ	AA2U	N3RS	K1AR	K2EK	K1ZM	K8PO/1	K2VV	K2SS/1	KA5W
1991	KM1H(KQ2M)	N4RJ(KM9P)	AA2U	K5NA/2	N2RM	N6SS/7	W1FV	WØZV	K4XS(WC4E)	K1RM	WØUN(N2IC)
1990	K1CC	K3WW	AA2U	N3RS	N2RM	K5UR	W1FV	K1ZM	WY7I	KE3Q	WØZV
1989	K3TUP(K5ZD)	K1DG	W2TZ	K1AR	W3LPL	K5UR	W1FV	K1NA	K2EK	W7WA	K1ZM
1988	W1KM	**#A**	WA2HZR	K1AR	W3LPL	K5UR	W1FV	K2EK	N5CR	K3RV/4	K1ZZ
1987	K1EA		W8VSK	K1GQ	W3LPL	K5UR	W1FV	W6YA	K3RV/4	K5GO	N4EJW
1986	W1KM		K1CGP	N4WW	N2AA	W1CF(WA2SPL)	W1FV	N6QR	W2YV(KQ2M)	K3RV/4	N6BFM/4
1985	K1AR		K3WS	K1KI	N2AA	K5UR	W1FV	K1OX(KC1F)	K2VV	K1RM	WA3CGE
1984	N2LT		K8IA	K5RC	N2AA	K5UR	W1FV	N5JJ	N5CR	K2EK	W8WPC(N9AG)
1983	W1KM		N3RS	K1GQ	N2AA	K1ZM	W1FV	W6AM(N6AW)	WØZV	NA5R(KN5H)	KZ5M
1982	K1AR		K8IA	K5RC	N2AA	AE6U	K1PT	K1XM	K1KI	W1RM	N4WW
1981	K1GQ		AC2U	N4AR	W2PV	W8LRL	W1ZM(K1ZM)	KØRF	W8UVZ	K6EWL	N4ZNC
1980	K1AR		WØKEA	N4AR	N2AA	W8LRL	WB2FZO(KQ2M)	KØRF	N7UA	W1RM	WØZV
1979	K1AR		WA4LOF	K5RC	N2AA	K1PBW	WB3AVN	W5UN	K8ZH	W1RM	N4WW
1978	W3RJ		W5YZ	N3RS	N2AA	K1PBW	K5NU	W5UN	W6VPH	N6CW	K8MFO
1977	W3LPL		*#Q*	N4AR	W2PV	K1PBW	WB3AVN	W5UN	K1OX(KC1F)	N4RJ	W5MYA
1976	W3LPL			AA5LES	W3WJD	K1PBW	W1MX(WA8WNU)	W5WZQ[W5UN]	K3MBF	W4WSF[N4MM]	K5FVA[K5LM]
1975	W3LPL			W6OUN	W3AU	K1PBW	W1MX(WA8WNU)	W5WZQ[W5UN]	K8IDE[W8TA]	W2HBT[N2RM]	W8WPC
1974	W1BGD/2[W1RM]			K4GSU	W3AU	K1PBW	W3MFW	WB5DTX(W5BJA)	K6SDR[N6CW]	W4KFC	WA5RTG[K5GO]
1973	W3LPL			K6EBB	W3AU	WB8APH	W3MFW	W5WZQ[W5UN]	W4AAV	W4KFC	K1LWI
1972	W3WJD[N3RS]			K1DIR	W3AU	WA4SGF	W1MX	K6EBB	WA1JUY	K8WWU	W4KFC
1971	W1FBY[W1XT]			K6EBB	W4BVV	K1PBW	W3MFW	K6ERT	WB9FJX	W5WMU/5	K5ABV
1970	K1KTH [N6JL]			W3WJD	W4BVV	W1HGT	W3MFW	W6ISA	K8MMM	WA8LYF[K8LX]	K1LWI
1969	W4YHD[W4RX]			W9EXE	W4BVV	K1PBW	W8LT	K6NA	W7VY	K1NOL[K1NA]	W8VSK
1968	W3GRF			K1DIR	W3MSK	W1BB	W1SWX[W1NH]	W2LXK	W4AXE	W1MDO[N1XX]	K1JGD
1967	K1DIR			W3WJD	W3MSK	W1BB/1	K2RBT	W2LXK	K9ECO	W2MEL	K1LWI
1966	W3GRF			W3MVB	K2GL	——	W8NBK	W4BGO	W2AIW	W4KFC	K1IMP
1965	W4KFC			W2PCJ	K2GL	W1BB/1	W8NBK	W8FGX	W7YGN	W8WZ	WA4WIP
1964	W3GRF			WA6SBO	K2GL	W1BG/1	K6BPR	W6AM(W9WWNV)	W4KFC	K1NOL[K1NA]	——
1963	W3GRF			W6RW	W3MSK	W2EQS	K2DGT	W8FGX	W4KFC	W1WY	W6ID
1962	W3GRF			W1BIH	W3MSK	W2FYT	W2BU	K2DGT	W4KFC	W2HTI	K2YFE
1961	W3GRF			W9YT	W3MSK	K7EKD	K6EIV	W9WNV	W1BIH	W2WZ	K2HWL
1960	W4YHD[W4RX]			W6GHM/6	W3AOH	——	W9PNE	K2DGT	W4KFC	W2WZ	W3LSG
1959	W3GRF			W1BIH	W3AOH	W1BB	W1BU	K2DGT	W8QFR	W8UPN	W3LSG
1958	W8JIN			K2GL	*#MM*	W7ZVY	W1BU	W8FGX	W2AIW	W4YHD[W4RX]	K8AEK
1957	W4KFC			W6RW		——	W3EIS	W3BVN	W8DUY	W2WZ	W8WZ
1956	W4KVX			W6DFY		——	W9PNE	W3BVN	W4VZQ	W8BKP	K4CTU
1955	W2HJR			W6AM		——	W3EIS	W8FXG	W4KFC	W2WZ	W3MDE
1954	W4KFC			W4KVX		——	W4HQN	W3MSK[W3AU]	W3LOE	W8JIN	W6ITA
1953	W4KFC			W6AM		——	W8KIA	K2EDL	W6BAX	W8BHW	——
1952	W8JIN			W8WZ		——	W6ZAT	W6RW	W6BAX	W3AYS	W5LFG
1951	W4KFC			W6AM		——	WØNWX	W1RWP	W6BAX	——	W8CCJ
1950	W4KFC			W6GAL		——	——	W4BRB	W3JTC	——	W4EEO
1949	W4KFC			W6SZY		——	——	W4BRB	W9DUY	——	W3JKO
1948	W4KFC			W2IQG							
#1940											
**#1939*											
1939	W6QD	W6GRL									

Footnote #1991. The Single Operator Low Power class was added beginning with the 1991 event. Output power limited to 100 watts.

Footnote #A. The Single Operator Assisted Class was added beginning with the 1989 event. Rules permitted Single operators to utilize any form "of DX spotting nets or DX alerting assistance."

Footnote #1987. The 1987 RESULTS were the first time European TOP Scores were listed.

Footnote #Q. QRPp Single Operator was added to the 1978 event. Output power limited to 5 watts.

Footnote #MM. Multi-Operator Multi-Transmitter added to the 1959 event.

Footnote #1948. CQ's original rules: 0200z start time for 48 hours. Fouth full weekend of October for Phone and first full weekend of November for CW, 80m, 40m, 20m and 27-29 MHz. Single-Operator and Multi-Operator. No limit to the number of transmitters and receivers but you must observe all the rules of your license. Exchange RS(T) and CQ W.A.Z. Zone number. One point per contact multiplied by the sum of zones per band and countries per band (August 1948 CQ).

Footnote #1940. The July,1940 issue of RADIO magazine carried the rules and announcement for the Second Annual RADIO World-Wide DX Contest. The changes included one weekend for CW, which was to begin 2300z October 4 to 0800z October 7, 1940 and one for Phone which was to begin 2300z October 11 to 0800z October 14, 1940. Log Deadline was November 4th! The available classes were changed: "Competitors will not limited in the number of operators, or in equiptment." After the issue was prepared, the FCC banned all amateur communications with foreign stations. Besides adding a Full Page Contest Cancellation, there were several boxes throughout the issue stating that the WW DX Contest had been cancelled.

CQ WW DX Contest

Phone World Records

	Call	Year	Score
Single-Op All-Band (No Packet)			
AF	CT3BH (OH2BH)	90	14,892,102
AS	EX6F (UF6FFF?)	84	6,362,000
EU	ZB2X (OH2KI)	91	7,128,646
NA	FG5R (W7EJ)	90	12,192,368
OC	YJ1A (OH1RY)	90	9,516,731
SA	HC8A (N6KT)	92	16,316,568
Single-Op Low Power (No Packet)			
AF	TJ1GG (I2VXJ)	92	5,925,760
AS	ZC4BS	91	5,244,877
EU	LY3BX	91	2,107,140
NA	VP2MBA	92	2,509,821
OC	KH8/WB7RFA	92	4,301,640
SA	PX1Z	91	1,810,710
Single-Band Low-Power			
160	SM5AQD	92	34,782
80	S59ZA	92	70,240
40	TG9AJR	92	395,488
20	YO4NF	92	541,960
15	CT3BD	92	920,080
10	Z21HQ	91	1,118,611
Single-Op QRP <5 W (No Packet)			
AF	No Entry		
AS	JA6VZB	91	267,729
EU	YU2TY	89	758,523
NA	KR2Q	90	1,248,207
OC	AH6EK	84	168,198
SA	PJ2FR (K7SS)	87	3,171,166
Single-Band QRP			
160	UP2BKF	82	12,516
80	UB5IRN	88	15,704
40	UA4LC	90	76,131
20	YU1NR	85	114,912
15	UG/UB4WZZ	87	219,744
10	N6BFM/4	90	327,928
S/O 28 MHz			
AF	ZD8Z (N6TJ)	91	2,341,866
AS	JH1AJT	88	1,421,070
EU	YU3ZV	88	1,541,603
NA	VP2ET (K5RX)	88	2,432,880
OC	KD7P/NH2	88	2,309,304
SA	ZV5A (PY5EG)	91	2,984,166
S/O 21 MHz			
AF	EL2CX (K3RV)	89	2,242,968
AS	JHØJHA	92	1,430,856
EU	CQ4A (CT1BOP)	90	1,757,780
NA	FM6A (F6HMQ)	91	1,934,659
OC	AH0AB(JA3DOC)	82	1,923,840
SA	P40R (K4UEE)	90	2,719,336
S/O 14 MHz			
AF	5Z4BI	92	1,478,932
AS	RFØFWW (UF6FFF)	87	1,447,128
EU	OH2BH (OH2IW)	92	1,870,170
NA	VP2KAA (N4PN)	81	2,011,185
OC	ZM1BIL	83	1,334,232
SA	PJ9P (OH6MW)	92	1,875,300
S/O 7 MHz			
AF	EA8RCT (OH2MM)	87	859,362
AS	JA8IXM	90	469,012
EU	S59UN	92	875,875
NA	ZF2JR (N6RJ)	92	917,316
OC	V7MHZ	92	680,720
SA	PJ9E (OH5BM)	92	992,068
S/O 3.5 MHz			
AF	CT3BZ	79	235,113
AS	UW9AF	83	222,192
EU	HA8IE	90	361,343
NA	TI1C (TI2CF)	92	498,037
OC	T32AF	85	222,768
SA	P4ØR (K4UEE)	87	552,786
S/O 1.8 MHz			
AF	IH9/IV3PRK	89	81,344
AS	UG7GWO	87	255,852
EU	LZ2CJ	84	107,818
NA	VE3BMV	86	52,240
OC	KH6CC	85	45,984
SA	YV2IF	84	18,291
Single-Op WITH Packet			
AF	ZS6STU	92	412,560
AS	JA8RWU	92	3,865,056
EU	YT3AA	89	5,756,932
NA	WM5G (KRØY)	92	6,631,513
OC	NY6M/KH2	89	2,108,408
SA	PT5W (PY5AA)	92	38,130
Multi-Op Single Transmitter			
AF	EA8AGD	88	17,172,672
AS	YM5KA	90	15,056,664
EU	IQ4A	90	17,255,700
NA	VP2EC	92	16,287,152
OC	KH2S	91	11,095,392
SA	PJ1B	91	21,214,809
Multi-Op Multi-Transmitter			
AF	EA8CR	77	21,351,898
AS	EW6V	82	18,746,136
EU	LX7A	89	26,578,978
NA	VP2KC	79	37,770,012
OC	KHØAM	90	35,730,600
SA	PJ1B	90	57,610,400

USA/VE Phone Records

Call Area	Call	Year	Score
Single-Op All-Band (No Packet)			
W1	K1AR	92	7,810,446
W2	N2LT	89	5,403,200
W3	K3TUP (K3LR)	88	6,004,683
W4	N4RJ (KM9P)	90	4,683,448
W5	WM5G (KRØY)	90	6,308,064
W6	K6NA	88	3,642,240
W7	N7DD	79	3,113,788
W8	NA8V	89	2,837,423
W9	W9RE	90	4,525,010
WØ	N2IC/Ø	88	3,656,100
VE	VB3XN	88	5,373,693
Single-Op. Low Power (No Packet)			
W1	KG1D	92	1,160,764
W2	WA2UUK	92	1,154,136
W3	W3UJ	91	603,630
W4	KØEJ/4	92	1,207,288
W5	K5RX	91	993,806
W6	WB6JPY	92	754,974
W7	K7RI	91	1,286,946
W8	N8II	92	1,864,747
W9	WB9IQI	92	900,015
WØ	KX5Z/Ø	91	842,898
VE	VY2SS	92	2,035,230

Single-Op QRP<5 W (No Packet)			
W1	KN1M	90	606,816
W2	KR2Q	90	1,248,207
W3	K3ZR	81	434,720
W4	WR4K	88	575,200
W5	K5RX	90	1,103,513
W6	AI6V	80	194,040
W7	K7RI	92	860,560
W8	K8IA	82	337,666
W9	N9AW	92	112,344
WØ	WØUO	89	297,591
VE	VE1CBF	87	588,555

S/O 28 MHz			
W1	KS1L	88	955,632
W2	WA2SPL	79	735,528
W3	WE3C	90	729,289
W4	K4XS	88	955,344
W5	NR5M	90	1,116,390
W6	W6NV (WB6SHD)	90	877,389
W7	K7RI	85	973,947
W8	K3ZJ/8	88	1,026,684
W9	WØAIH (N0BSH)	89	793,507
WØ	WØZV	88	1,145,368
VE	VO1SA	91	1,381,913

S/O 21 MHz			
W1	K1RM	79	870,237
W2	K2VV	88	1,172,760
W3	K3EST	83	380,540
W4	K3RV/4	88	1,270,478
W5	K5MR	92	1,168,044
W6	W6QHS	92	877,401
W7	N7DD	81	923,945
W8	K3ZJ/8	92	748,328
W9	K9DX	80	690,228
WØ	WØUN(WØUA)	92	1,094,052
VE	VD7SV	92	1,662,660

S/O 14 MHz			
W1	K1OX (KC1F)	85	1,131,328
W2	K2VV	91	939,624
W3	K3IPK	87	368,816
W4	K4XS	92	941,192
W5	W5WMU	82	305,660
W6	W6QHS	86	510,510
W7	W7WA	87	649,250
W8	KW8N (WD8IXE)	87	563,313
W9	K9BN	85	467,390
WØ	WOØG [WX3N]	90	734,290
VE	VE2ZP	88	1,254,282

S/O 7 MHz			
W1	K1UO	92	264,922
W2	K5NA/2	92	147,735
W3	W3PHL	75	110,799
W4	N4ZC	92	135,314
W5	K5RR (WD5K)	88	177,280
W6	N6RJ	83	197,820
W7	W7XR (W7WA)	92	363,900
W8	K8MJZ	90	102,368
W9	KJ9D	84	103,362
WØ	KØGU	82	195,624
VE	XN3BMV	85	546,615

S/O 3.5 MHz			
W1	W1ZM	83	177,862
W2	K1ZM/2	92	229,295
W3	WE3C	92	125,440
W4	WA4SVO	87	77,559
W5	WØMJ/5	84	91,952
W6	W6RJ	92	140,595
W7	K7SS	86	217,038
W8	WB8JBM (NZ4K)	87	105,138
W9	AI9J	82	67,068
WØ	KØRF	76	54,096
VE	VE3BMV	85	383,040

S/O 1.8 MHz			
W1	K1ZM	85	20,502
W2	WA2SPL	83	18,483
W3	AA1K/3	85	24,663
W4	W4DR	86	11,648
W5	K5UR	86	19,044
W6	AE6U	82	5,005
W7	K7IDX	87	7,080
W8	W8LRL	82	16,191
W9	WB9HAD [WB9Z]	87	27,181
WØ	WØZV	87	12,204
VE	VE3BMV	86	54,478

S/Op WITH Packet (Since 1989)			
W1	W1PH	92	4,290,198
W2	K1ZM/2	90	4,405,350
W3	K3WW	92	5,228,249
W4	N4RJ (KM9P)	91	4,005,762
W5	WM5G (KRØY)	92	6,631,513
W6	WK6V	90	1,168,458
W7	KI3V/7	90	2,299,142
W8	K8MR	90	2,853,600
W9	KK9V	90	1,943,470
WØ	K0RF	92	3,715,920
VE	VE3VET	90	531,810

Multi-Op Single Transmitter			
W1	K1AR	90	11,193,606
W2	N2RM	88	6,923,136
W3	N3RS	90	7,752,168
W4	K4ISV	92	6,098,814
W5	W5WMU	88	6,056,298
W6	W6GO	92	4,852,386
W7	KO7N	88	4,079,140
W8	K8AZ	92	6,039,200
W9	KS9K	90	7,190,746
WØ	K4VX/Ø	88	6,227,259
VE	XM1DX	90	11,159,888

Multi-Op Multi-Transmitter			
W1	NX1H	92	12,347,656
W2	N2RM	92	19,603,032
W3	W3LPL	90	16,517,214
W4	N4RJ	88	9,655,415
W5	N5AU	90	16,736,436
W6	N6ND	90	8,483,628
W7	W7XR	90	12,232,124
W8	K8CC	90	9,785,580
W9	WØAIH/9	92	6,700,464
WØ	AA6TT/Ø	92	11,891,552
VE	VC1DX	91	15,458,874

CQ WW DX Contest

CW World Records

	Call	Year	Score
Single-Op All-Band (No Packet)			
AF	EA8EA (OH2MM)	91	13,225,295
AS	JY8VJ (DL1VJ)	92	8,031,168
EU	ZB2X (OH2KI)	91	5,450,761
NA	PJ7A (K1TO)	91	8,357,236
OC	AH3C	90	6,789,363
SA	HC8N (WN4KKN)	92	10,773,628
Single-Op Low Power (No Packet)			
AF	7Q7XX (JH1ORL)	92	3,257,128
AS	9V1YC	92	2,679,948
EU	OG6GIO	92	2,296,625
NA	N8II	92	2,008,982

OC	9M8DX (VK2DXI)	91	2,388,719
SA	OA4ZV	92	1,945,555

Single-Band Low-Meters

160	T32AF(KH6UR)	92	49,210
80	UV3WU	92	91,605
40	VK6LW	92	533,696
20	4M5X (WM2C)	92	1,145,087
15	LU1ICX	91	545,034
10	C56/G4ODV	91	902,967

Single-Op QRP <5W. (No Packet)

AF	ED8BIE	86	45,441
AS	7J6CAM	89	574,938
EU	DK3GI	91	1,359,280
NA	HI8A (JA5DQH)	91	3,316,768
OC	P29DK	91	272,630
SA	YV2BE	86	114,062

Single-Band QRP

160	UC2WAF	92	27,280
80	SP4GFG	92	33,150
40	UA4PMW	84	91,698
20	UW1BI	88	230,528
15	4Z4NUT	85	189,306
10	CX7CO	90	178,364

S/O 28 MHz

AF	D68GA (N6ZV)	92	1,281,656
AS	4Z5DX	90	826,759
EU	9H1EL	92	794,846
NA	J79DX (AA5DX)	89	859,360
OC	KD7P/NH2	88	1,037,608
SA	CXØCW (CX8BBH)	90	1,890,607

S/O 21 MHz

AF	CR3W (DF5UL)	92	1,652,170
AS	4Z4T (4Z4UT)	91	939,900
EU	OH6MCW	89	775,620
NA	V29W (KD6WW)	90	1,110,512
OC	N7DF/NH2	89	1,205,776
SA	ZW5B (LU8DQ)	91	1,864,372

S/O 14 MHz

AF	ED9ED	90	1,444,436
AS	7L1GVE	92	1,181,937
EU	OH2BH (OH6UM)	90	915,136
NA	VP2KAA (N4PN)	80	1,244,782
OC	ZL3GQ	91	1,148,418
SA	P4ØV (N7NG)	91	1,883,700

S/O 7 MHz

AF	OH7JT/CT9	88	904,038
AS	C42A (YU4OO)	91	980,490
EU	S59UN	92	971,049
NA	ZF2TG (WQ5W)	92	1,087,862
OC	VK6LW	92	533,696
SA	PJ9U (OH1VR)	92	1,171,864

S/O 3.5 MHz

AF	EA8XS (OH5XT)	88	516,390
AS	ZC4DX (4Z4DX)	87	430,560
EU	ZB2X (OH2KI)	91	435,456
NA	NP4A (K1ZM)	88	808,640
OC	VR3AH	76	178,560
SA	P4ØR (K4UEE)	86	576,725

S/O 1.8 MHz

AF	EA8AK	82	75,768
AS	UG6GAW	90	164,430
EU	ON4UN	90	118,776
NA	K5UR	85	47,005
OC	KH6CC	90	60,352
SA	YV3AGT	85	147,588

Single-Op WITH Packet (Since 1989)

AF	No Entry		
AS	JA1YFG (JJ3OLZ)	91	874,725
EU	OK1ALW	90	4,502,748
NA	K1DG	89	5,048,802
OC	No Entry		
SA	No Entry		

Multi-Op Single Transmitter

AF	EA9EA	91	13,096,080
AS	TA5KA	90	13,915,044
EU	LZ9A	89	9,962,386
NA	NP4A	82	11,648,565
OC	KH2S	92	7,249,952
SA	PJ2X	88	8,948,660

Multi-Op Multi-Transmitter

AF	CN5N	90	33,659,256
AS	VS6WV	92	17,799,960
EU	LX7A	89	20,497,632
NA	KP2A	88	32,325,150
OC	KHØAM	92	23,951,385
SA	PJ1B	88	38,415,760

Club Score	Frankford Radio Club	92	389,564,535

CQ WW DX CONTEST

U.S.A./VE CW Records

Call Area	Call	Year	Score
Single-Op All-Band (No Packet)			
W1	KM1H (KQ2M)	92	5,675,756
W2	N2NT	92	5,705,000
W3	K3TUP (K5ZD)	89	5,564,556
W4	N4RJ KM9P)	92	5,851,152
W5	N5AU (WN4KKN)	89	4,395,825
W6	N6UR (KR6X)	92	3,729,600
W7	K5MM/7	89	2,898,266
W8	KN8Z	92	5,436,795
W9	W9RE (WA8YVR)	90	4,755,206
WØ	WØZV	89	3,534,810
VE	VE3EJ	92	5,011,815
S-Op Low Power (No Packet)			
W1	KM1X	92	1,266,515
W2	W2TZ	92	1,986,240
W3	KX3Y	92	1,019,151
W4	K7SV/4	92	1,335,780
W5	N8RR/5	92	1,185,845
W6	W6JTI	91	912,216
W7	WAØRJY/7	91	423,073
W8	N8II	92	2,008,982
W9	K9QVB	91	814,484
WØ	NSØW	92	482,202
VE	VD2ZP	92	2,346,096
Single-Op QRP <5 W (No Packet)			
W1	K1CGJ	90	701,838
W2	AA2U	92	1,188,000
W3	N3RS	81	577,205
W4	N4KG	90	748,410
W5	K5RX	90	756,952
W6	WB6JMS	92	248,196
W7	NX7K	90	709,665
W8	K8IA	82	400,064
W9	W9KNI	82	345,417
WØ	WØUO	90	675,840
VE	VE7DX (K7SS)	87	687,690
S/O 28 MHz			
W1	K1ZZ	88	537,568
W2	K1ZM/2	89	732,564
W3	K3UA	89	453,055

W4	K4XS	89	604,035
W5	KA5W	92	446,439
W6	W6YA	89	454,358
W7	KT7O	89	352,674
W8	N8CXX	89	653,868
W9	W9SU	89	550,565
WØ	WØZV	90	506,989
VE	CZ7SZ (WA6VEF)	90	530,208

S/O 21 MHz

W1	W1RM	90	698,257
W2	KR2Q	91	509,250
W3	KE3Q	90	753,660
W4	AA4NC	90	614,376
W5	W5VX	92	511,187
W6	N6RO (K3EST)	89	677,292
W7	W7WA	89	777,146
W8	K8MFO	92	519,750
W9	K9BG	89	534,240
WØ	WØUN (WØUA)	92	647,168
VE	VE7SZ (WA6VEF)	89	802,032

S/O 14 MHz

W1	W1RR	89	718,550
W2	K2VV	92	943,920
W3	N3RS	84	314,505
W4	K3RV/4	85	634,293
W5	N5CR	89	700,135
W6	W6VPH	78	468,312
W7	WY7I	90	637,208
W8	KW8N (NZ4K)	92	815,948
W9	KC9T	90	573,501
WØ	NQØI	92	424,461
VE	VE2ZP	89	807,234

S/O 7 MHz

W1	K8PO	92	821,473
W2	K1ZM	90	839,520
W3	W2UP/3	92	521,076
W4	K4XS	92	683,459
W5	K5GO	90	542,108
W6	N6RO	92	392,515
W7	W7XR (K7SS)	92	794,992
W8	KV8H	90	319,501
W9	WA8YVR/9	85	256,080
WØ	WØZV	92	440,316
VE	XN3BMV	84	436,100

S/O 3.5 MHz

W1	K1IU	92	315,826
W2	K1ZM/2	92	416,160
W3	WE3C	92	153,930
W4	KT3Y/4	92	205,683
W5	K5RX	87	116,584
W6	W6RJ	86	106,600
W7	K9JF/7	85	45,056
W8	K7EG/8 (NZ4K)	90	122,943
W9	K9RX	85	58,696
WØ	KØRF	92	139,072
VE	VE2HQ	85	176,180

S/O 1.8 MHz

W1	W1CF (WA2SPL)	86	43,460
W2	K2EK	92	34,522
W3	AA1K/3	85	24,120
W4	N4IN	86	22,200
W5	K5UR	85	47,005
W6	K6DDO	85	8,534
W7	N6SS/7	92	13,112
W8	W8LRL	90	20,000
W9	WB9HAD [WB9Z]	87	24,382
WØ	WØZV	87	18,054
VE	CG3MFA	85	33,276

Single Operator WITH Packet (Since 1989)

W1	K1DG	89	5,048,802
W2	K5NA/2	92	4,363,824
W3	K3WW	90	4,979,475
W4	N4RJ (KM9P)	91	4,481,038
W5	KA5W (KS1G)	90	2,642,640
W6	WZ6Z	90	1,738,110
W7	NK7U (KY7M)	90	2,556,400
W8	K8AZ	92	4,740,060
W9	KK9V	90	2,204,494
WØ	N2IC/Ø	90	3,728,264
VE	VD7DX (N6HR)	92	1,309,459

Multi-Op Single Transmitter

W1	K1AR	89	9,383,458
W2	N2RM	89	8,512,840
W3	N3RS	92	8,585,380
W4	N4RJ	89	7,811,622
W5	W5WMU	92	5,361,675
W6	W6GO	92	5,252,702
W7	KO7N	88	3,405,324
W8	K8AZ	90	5,880,834
W9	K9UWA	90	3,356,796
WØ	KØRF	89	5,544,000
VE	XN3EJ	91	6,955,345

Multi-Op Multi-Transmitter

W1	K1AR	92	19,473,615
W2	N2RM	92	18,408,663
W3	W3LPL	91	17,108,280
W4	K4JPD	88	7,853,620
W5	NR5M	89	12,302,131
W6	K6UA	90	9,265,088
W7	KO7N	89	7,752,240
W8	K8LX	80	7,601,825
W9	WØAIH/9	90	10,029,830
WØ	K4VX/Ø	89	11,988,957
VE	VE2CSI	92	8,184,910

CQ WORLD-WIDE MISCELLANEOUS DATA

PHONE WINNERS BY CONTINENT

Single-Op Continental Wins:

South America: 24
Africa: 14
Europe: 3
North America: 2
Asia: 2
Oceania: 1

Multi-Single Continental Wins:

Europe: 12
South America: 12
North America: 10
Africa: 6
Asia: 5
Oceania: 0

Multi-Multi Continental Wins

South America: 18
Europe: 7
North America: 5
Africa: 3
Asia: 1
Oceania: 0

CW WINNERS BY CONTINENT

Single-Op Continental Wins

Africa: 16
South America: 12
Asia: 8
North America: 4
Oceania: 3
Europe: 2

Multi-Single Continental Wins:

North America: 11
Asia: 11
South America: 9
Africa: 6
Europe: 4
Oceania: 4

Multi-Multi Continental Wins

South America: 13
North America: 11
Asia: 4
Africa: 4
Europe: 2
Oceania: 0

CQWW Phone Contest (USA WINNERS)

Single-Ops

K1AR: 5
W1ATE: 5
WA2SFP[W2PV]: 4
W6RR: 3
KC1F: 2
K1ZM: 2
K5MDX: 2
W6YY: 2
Each of the following have one win:
K1KTH, W1ONK, K2AAA, K1HLB, N2NT, K2TR, W3LPL, W3MSK[W3AU], W3WJD[N3RS], W4AXE, W4DR, W4ESK[W7RM], WA6VEF, K6AHV, W6GHM, K7RI, W8KML, W9EWC, KRØY.

Multi-Single

W2HJR[K2GL]: 4
KX4S: 3
W6AM: 3
K1AR: 2
WB2SQN/K2SS: 2
K3LR: 2
K6EVR: 2
WA6EPQ[N6AR]: 2
W7SFA: 2
Each of the following have one win:
K1DG, K2BU, W2CP/2, K2HLB, K2IEG, N2RM, W3TMZ, W3WJD/N3RS, K4VX, W4ATE, W4HXC, W4QAW, K5GA, K5JA, W6OUN, W6ONV, W6RRG, WA6ZQU, W7DL, KS9K, KØUK.

Multi-Multi

K2GL/N2AA: 14
W3MSK/W3AU: 5
W2PV: 4
N2RM: 3
W3LPL: 3
W7RM: 2
W3WJD[N3RS]: 1
N5AU: 1
W8NGO: 1

CQWW DX CW Contest (USA Winners)

Single-Ops

W4KFC: 9
W3GRF: 6
K1AR: 4
W3LPL: 4
W1KM: 3
W4YHD: 2
W8JIN: 2
Each of the following have one S/O win:
K1CC, K1DIR, K1EA, K1GQ, K1KTH[N6JL], W1FBY[W1XT], W1BGD/2[W1RM], W2HJR[K2GL], N2LT, KQ2M, W3RJ, W3WJD/N3RS, W4KVX, K5ZD, KM9P.

Multi-Single

W3WJD[N3RS]: 5
K4GSU[N4AR]: 4
AA5LES[K5RC]: 4
W6AM: 3
K1AR: 2
K1DIR: 2
K1GQ: 2
W1BIH: 2
K6EBB: 2
W6RW: 2
Each of the following have one M/S win:
K1KI, K1GL, W2IQG, W2PCF, W3MVB, N4WW, W4KVX, K5NA, W6DFY, W6GAL, W6GHM/6, W6OUN, W6SZY, WA6SBO, W8WZ, W9EXE, W9YT.

Multi-Multi

K2GL[N2AA]: 11
W3MSK[W3AU]: 9
W3LPL: 3
W4BVV: 3
N2RM: 2
W2PV: 2
W3AOH: 2
K1AR: 1
W3WJD/N3RS: 1

Single-Band WAZ During CQWW Contest

Callsign	Year	Category	Mode	Band
W6RW	1957	M/O	CW	20
K6EIV	1960	SO/SB	CW	20
W3MSK[W3AU]	1966	M/O	CW	20
W2ONV	1966	SO/SB	SSB	20
K2KUR	1968	SO/SB	SSB	20
K8MMM	1968	SO/SB	SSB	20
VE3LZ	1968	SO/SB	SSB	20
OH2AM	1968	M/O	SSB	20
W3MSK[W3AU]	1968	M/O	SSB	20
W4ETO	1968	M/O	SSB	20
OH2AM	1968	M/O	CW	20
W4BVV	1969	M/O	CW	20
WA2ZAA	1969	M/O	CW	20
W3MSK[W3AU]	1969	M/O	CW	20
K3AFO	1972	SO/SB	SSB	20
W4WSF	1972	SO/SB	SSB	20
W8JGU	1972	SO/SB	SSB	20
UW1AR	1972	SO/SB	SSB	20
G3RRS	1978	SO/SB	SSB	20
EX9A	1978	M/O	SSB	20
N2AA	1979	M/O	SSB	20
N2AA	1979	M/O	SSB	15
SK2KW	1979	M/O	SSB	10
YU3EY	1979	M/O	SSB	20

N2AA	1979	M/O	CW	20
WA2RLQ	1980	SO/SB	SSB	20
6D7LCH	1980	SO/SB	SSB	20
OH8SR	1980	SO/SB	SSB	20
N2AA	1980	M/O	SSB	20
K8LX	1980	M/O	SSB	20
K3WW	1980	M/O	SSB	20
SK2KW	1980	M/O	SSB	20
LZ7A	1980	M/O	SSB	10
YU3TU	1981	SO/SB	SSB	15
OH1AA	1981	M/O	SSB	20
K3KG/4	1982	SO/SB	SSB	20
YU3TWT	1982	SO/SB	SSB	20
YT3L	1982	SO/SB	SSB	20
OHØW	1982	M/O	SSB	20
OHØW	1982	M/O	SSB	15
WØZV	1983	SO/SB	SSB	20
YT3M	1984	SO/SB	SSB	20
K2HFX	1986	SO/SB	SSB	20
N2ME	1986	SO/SB	SSB	20
KX4S	1986	SO/SB	SSB	20
N4ZC	1986	SO/SB	SSB	20
RFØFWW	1987	SO/SB	SSB	20
IK8ETA	1987	SO/SB	SSB	20
IO1ZEU	1987	SO/SB	SSB	20
JAØQNJ	1987	SO/SB	SSB	20
JH8JWF	1987	SO/SB	SSB	20
4N7N	1987	SO/SB	SSB	20
JA7MHZ	1987	SO/SB	CW	40
YC2UKM	1988	SO/SB	SSB	15
IR4LCK	1988	M/O	SSB	10
VE2ZP	1988	S/O/S/B	CW	20
K1TO	1988	SO/AB	CW	20
N6GG	1988	SO/SB	CW	20
ZS6BCR	1988	SO/SB	CW	20
JA5DQH	1988	SO/SB	CW	15
JA7FTR	1988	SO/SB	CW	20
G3TXF	1988	SO/SB	CW	20
IT9GSF	1988	SO/SB	CW	20
UR2RDO	1988	SO/SB	CW	20
CW8B	1988	SO/SB	CW	15
K1AR	1988	M/O	CW	20
N3RS	1988	M/O	CW	20
K8AZ	1988	M/O	CW	20
K5NA/2	1988	M/O	CW	20
WM5G	1988	M/O	CW	20
W3LPL	1988	M/O	CW	20
NR5M	1988	M/O	CW	20
K1ST	1988	M/O	CW	20
K4JPD	1988	M/O	CW	20
K4VX/Ø	1988	M/O	CW	20
PJ1B	1988	M/O	CW	20
KP2A	1988	M/O	CW	15
EA9EA	1988	M/O	CW	20
OL8A	1988	M/O	CW	20
UL8LYA	1988	M/O	CW	20
HG5A	1988	M/O	CW	20
HG5A	1988	M/O	CW	15
LZ9A	1988	M/O	CW	20
LZ9A	1988	M/O	CW	15
JA7SGV	1989	SO/SB	SSB	20
DF8XC	1989	SO/SB	SSB	20
N3RS	1989	M/O	SSB	20
KS9K	1989	M/O	SSB	15
W3LPL	1989	M/O	SSB	20
NB1H	1989	M/O	SSB	20
K5NA/2	1989	M/O	SSB	20
PJ1B	1989	M/O	SSB	20
ZW5B	1989	M/O	SSB	20
ZW5B	1989	M/O	SSB	15
VP9AD	1989	M/O	SSB	20
LZ9A	1989	M/O	CW	15
NX7K	1990	SO/SB	SSB	20
N2RM	1990	M/O	SSB	20
N5AU	1990	M/O	SSB	20
KY1H	1990	M/O	SSB	20
KY1H	1990	M/O	SSB	15
LZ9A	1990	M/O	CW	10
ZAØRS	1991	M/M	SSB	15
ZW5B(LU8DQ)	1991	S/O/S/B	CW	15
ZD8Z(N6TJ)	1992	S/OAB	SSB	20
IR4T(I4JMY)	1992	SO/SB	SSB	20
LY5A(LY2BN)	1992	SO/SB	SSB	20
PJ1B	1992	M/M	SSB	20
K1RU	1992	SO/SB	SSB	20
N2RM	1992	M/M	SSB	20
N3RS	1992	M/S	SSB	20
W3LPL	1992	M/M	SSB	20
W5FO	1992	M/M	SSB	20
N2RM	1992	M/M	SSB	15
IT9A(IT9GSF)	1992	SO/SB	SSB	10
YL2KL	1992	SO/SB	CW	40
IQ4A	1992	M/S	CW	40
HG73DX	1992	M/M	CW	40
K2VV	1992	SO/SB	CW	20
7L1GVE	1992	SO/SB	CW	20
W8UVZ	1992	S/O/AS/B	CW	20
UB4HO	1992	SO/SB	CW	15
S59AA	1992	SO/SB	CW	10

122 have achieved SB WAZ during CQ WW Contest!

66-N.A.	20-YRS	49CW	6-10M
56-DX		74PH	17-15M
			96-20M
			4-40M

*N2AA (Ex. K2KUR) has achieved 5 WAZ in CQ WW Contest: K2KUR (1968 CW), WA2ZAA (1969 CW), N2AA (1979 PH+CW, 1980 PH) all on 20M!

*LZ9A/LZ7A M/S entries have achieved five WAZ and LZ2CC and LZ2DF have been on each of those teams!

*K1TO is only S/O CW All-Bander to achieve CQWW WAZ!

*ZD8Z (N6TJ) IS ONLY S/O SSB ALL BANDER TO ACHIEVE CQWW WAZ!

*IT9GSF has achieved two WAZ under two different callsigns: IT9GSF, 1988 CW 20M and IT9A, 1992 SSB 10M!

Stations with three CQWW WAZ (year third WAZ achieved indicated in parentheses):

W3MSK [W3AU] (1969), ZW5B (1991), PJ1B, N2RM, N3RS, W3LPL (1992).

Stations with two CQWW WAZ:
OH2AM, OHØW, HG5A, K1ST/NB1H, K5NA, KY1H, IT9GSF.

CQWW THEORETICAL MAXIMUM SCORES

Although presented in the October 1989 CQ as part of K1AR's Contest column, surely many a contest operator has reviewed the final contest results to find interesting facts, trends and achievement. This is a compilation of the maximum achieved in each area: QSOs, zones and countries worked.

1992 CQWW DX SSB Contest Maximum

Band	QSOs	Zones	Countries
160	672-9A1HCD	16-VP2EC	65-9A1HCD
80	1695-TI1C(TI2CF)	31-TI1C(TI2CF)	108-TI1C(TI2CF)
40	2737-9A1A	38-G0KPW	137-G0KPW
20	4118-PJ1B	40-MANY(6)	178-N2RM, W3LPL
15	4381-PJ1B	40-N2RM	178-N2RM
10	4735-ZW5B (N5FA)	40-IT9A (IT9GSF)	170-N2RM
Total	18,338	205	836
	@ 2.93 Pts/QSO = 55,932,930		

***PJ1B Accomplishes 5 Band DXCC!

	M/M World	M/M USA	M/S World	M/S USA
QSOs	PJ1B-15,554	N2RM-7010	VP9AD-8138	K1DG-3396
Zones	HG73DX- 187	N2RM- 185	VP2EC- 183	K4ISV-175
Countries	IQ4A- 774	N2RM- 793	VP2EC- 685	K1DG- 701
Max. Score	= 43.79M	= 20.08M	= 20.69M	= 8.71M
Actual Score	PJ1B = 43.15M	N2RM = 19.60M	VP2EC = 16.28M	K1DG = 8.44M

1992 CQWW DX CW Contest Maximum

Band	QSOs	Zones	Countries	
160	893-ON4UN	23-AA6TT	76-ON4UN	
80	1856-OE3GSA	31-LZ9A	107-K1AR	
40	2985-ZF2TG(WQ5W)	40-SEVERAL!	144-W3LPL	
20	3042-KHØAM	40-SEVERAL!	156-K1AR	
15	3092-CR3W(DF5UL)	40-UB4HO	154-K1AR	ZD8LII(GØLII)
10	2746-P4ØX(N6BT)	40-S59AA	139-N2RM	
Total	14,614	214	776	
	@ 2.93 Pts/QSO = 42,390,810			

***K1AR Accomplishes 5 Band DXCC!

	M/M World	M/M USA	M/S World	M/S USA
QSOs	EA9EA-12,305	K1AR- 7,127	ZC4Z-5,537	N3RS-3,478
Zones	UX1A- 211	N2RM,W3LPL-195	LZ9A- 194	N3RS- 186
Countries	UX1A- 718	K1AR- 753	IQ4A- 678	N3RS- 674
Max Score	= 33.49M	= 19.79M	= 14.14M	= 8.76M
Actual Score	EA9EA = 30.03M	K1AR = 19.47M	ZC4Z = 11.09M	N3RS = 8.58M

1991 CQ WWDX SSB Contest Maximum

Band	QSOs	Zones	Countries
160	559-VP9AD	18-K2TR	57-EA3ALD
80	1270-HG73DX	28-W7XR	96-HG73DX
40	2290-HG73DX	34-W7XR	128-IQ4A
20	4110-ZAØRS	39-MANY!	171-K2TR
15	4535-FM6A(F6HMQ)	40-ZAØRS	169-N2RM
10	5154-ZV5A(PY5EG)	38-FR5DX	162-N2RM
TOTAL	17,918	197	783
	@ 2.93 Pts/QSO = 51,449,020		

World Maximums

	M/M World	M/M USA	M/S World	M/S USA
QSOs	VP9AD-15,029	N2RM- 5465	PJ1B-9460	K3LR-2598
Zones	ZAØRS- 179	W3LPL- 181	LZ9A- 185	K3LR- 166
Countries	ZAØRS- 727	W3LPL- 703	IQ4A- 753	N3RS- 605
Max. Score	= 39.89M	= 14.00M	= 25.99M	= 5.80M
Actual High	VP9AD=28.08M	N2RM =12.88M	PJ1B=21.21M	K3LR=5.51M

1991 CQ WWDX CW Contest Maximum

Band	QSOs	Zones	Countries
160	620-J6DX	18-J6DX	63-HG73DX
80	1500-CT3M	33-RZ1A	102-RZ1A
40	2577-C42A(YU4OO)	39-K5NA	133-HG73DX
20	4036-PJ9A	39-SEVERAL!	145-K1AR
15	3951-J6DX	40-ZW5B(LU8DQ)	138-ZW5B(LU8DQ)
10	3534-PJ9A	38-IQ4A	133-W3LPL
Total	16,218	207	713
	@ 2.93 Pts/QSO = 43,716,560		

*** RZ1A Accomplishes 5 Band DXCC!

	M/M World	M/M USA	M/S World	M/S USA
QSOs	PJ9A-14,991	N2RM-5072	EA9EA-5854	K5NA-2960
Zones	HG73DX-191	N2RM- 187	RZ1A- 193	N3RS- 183

Countries	HG73DX- 664	W3LPL-663	RZ1A- 642	N3RS- 633
Max Score	= 37.55M	= 12.63	= 14.32M	= 7.07M
Actual Score	PJ9A = 35.32M	N2RM=12.37M	EA9EA=13.09M	K5NA=6.71M

1990 CQ WW DX SSB CONTEST MAXIMUM

Band	QSOs	Zones	Countries
160	805-UG6GAW	20-VE1ZZ	56-IQ4A
80	1455-HA8IE	35-HA8IE	116-HA8IE
40	2275-PJ9W	37-IQ3A,IK5BAF	126-IQ3A
20	4925-PJ9W	40-SEVERAL(3)	179-PJ1B
15	5395-PJ1B	40-KY1H	176-PJ1B
10	5430-PJ1B	39-MANY!	182-PJ1B
Total	20,285	212	835
	@ 2.93 Pts/QSO = 62,228,445!		

	M/M World	M/M USA	M/S World	M/S USA
QSOs	PJ1B-19,655	N2RM-7321	6D2X-8169	K1AR-4437
Zones	PJ1B- 189	N5AU- 187	LZ9A- 202	KS9K- 177
Countries	PJ1B- 803	N2RM- 716	OM5W- 624	K1AR- 703
Max. Score	= 57.12M	= 19.36M	= 19.77M	= 11.44M
Actual Score	PJ1B=57.61M	N2RM=18.14M	IQ4A=17.25M	K1AR=11.19M

1990 CQ WWDX CW Contest Maximums

Band	QSOs	Zones	Countries
160	936-ON4UN	21-V73AZ(NZ8B)	68-ON4UN
80	1873-PJ9A	28-W3LPL	99-PJ9A
40	2598-PJ9A	37-LZ9A	125-K1ZM
20	3936-CN5N	39-SEVERAL(4)	149-K1AR,N2RM,CN5N
15	3689-PJ9A	39-SEVERAL(3)	142-CN5N
10	3795-CXØCW(CX8BBH)	40-LZ9A	137-W3LPL
Total	16,827	204	720
	@ 2.93 Pts/QSO = 45,555,972		

	M/M World	M/M USA	M/S World	M/S USA
QSOs	PJ9A-15,242	N2RM-7018	TA5KA-7201	N3RS-3532
Zones	PA6DX- 185	N2RM- 189	LZ9A- 191	K5NA- 182
Countries	PJ9A- 659	K1AR- 683	LZ9A- 618	K5NA- 609
Max. Score	= 37.69M	= 17.93M	= 17.06M	= 8.18M
Actual Score	PJ9A=34.93M	N2RM=17.28M	TA5KA=13.91M	N3RS=8.024M

1989 CQWW DX SSB Contest Maximums

Band	QSOs	Zones	Countries
160	1527-RB8M	14-VP9AD	57-VP9AD
80	1884-LX7A	25-HK3MAE	94-HK3MAE
40	2409-LX7A	35-LZ9A	121-PJ1B,LX7A
20	5420-VP9AD	40-MANY!	186-PJ1B
15	4445-EL2CX(K3RV)	40-ZW5B,KS9K	178-ZW5B
10	5714-PJ1B	39-ZW5B	178-PJ1B
Total	21,399	193	814
	@ 2.93 Pts/QSO = 63,137,893		

	M/M World	M/M USA	M/S World	M/S USA
QSOs	PJ1B-18,175	W3LPL-6061	PJ9W-9265	KS9K-2883
Zones	ZW5B- 189	W3LPL- 172	LZ9A- 180	KS9K- 167
Countries	PJ1B- 764	W3LPL- 706	LZ9A- 665	N3RS- 595
Max. Score	= 50.74M	= 15.59M	= 22.93M	= 6.43M
Actual Score	PJ1B=48.98M	W3LPL=15.02M	P40V=18.52M	KS9K=6.04M

1989 CQWW DX CW Contest Maximums

Band	QSOs	Zones	Countries
160	882-LY2BTA	21-K5UR	68-LY2BTA
80	1859-LX7A	31-RB8M	100-LX7A
40	2720-4U0ITU	37-LZ9A,K5NA	125-LX7A
20	4253-CT3M	39-SEVERAL(3)	148-LX7A
15	3652-NL7G	40-LZ9A	133-LX7A
10	3495-ZP0Y(LU8DQ)	39-LZ9A	140-W3LPL
Total	16,861	207	714
	@ 2.93 Pts/QSO = 45,499,242		

	M/M World	M/M USA	M/S World	M/S USA
QSOs	CT3M-14,473	W3LPL-6866	EA9EA-5923	K1AR-4101
Zones	RB8M- 199	W3LPL- 190	LZ9A- 200	K1AR- 190
Countries	LX7A- 705	W3LPL- 619	LZ9A- 626	N2RM- 605
Max. Score	= 38.33M	= 16.27M	= 14.33M	= 9.55M
Actual Score	CT3M=32.03M	W3LPL=16.22M	EA9EA=11.75M	K1AR=9.38M

1988 CQWW DX SSB Contest Maximum

Band	QSOs	Zones	Countries
160	738-UP8A	20-K5UR	56-IV3PRK
80	1504-P4ØV	27-IK5BAF	97-P4ØV
40	2063-P4ØV	38-IR4LCK	125-P4ØV
20	4884-P4ØV	39-MANY!	166-P4ØV
15	4878-KP2A	40-YC2UKM	161-N5AU
10	5137-VP2ET	40-IR4LCK	163-JH1AJT
Total	19,204	204	768
	@ 2.93 Pts/QSO = 54,692,223 !		

	M/M World	M/M USA	M/S World	M/S USA
QSOs	P40V-18,065	W3LPL-6477	EA8AGD-8203	N2RM-3378
Zones	P40V- 189	N5AU- 185	LZ9A- 193	K4VX- 170
Countries	P40V- 745	N5AU- 685	IR4LCK- 678	K8CC, K4VX-549
Max. Score	= 49.43M	= 16.50M	= 20.93M	= 7.11M
Actual Score	P40V = 49.29M	W3LPL=16.09M	EA8AGD=17.17M	N2RM=6.92M

1988 CQWW DX CW Contest Maximums

Band	QSOs	Zones	Countries
160	1008-SP3BQ	22-K5UR	75-HB9AMO
80	2243-NP4A	31-NP4A	102-NP4A
40	3119-PJ1B	38-OL8A	133-PJ1B
20	3791-PJ1B	40-MANY!	147-NR5M
15	3743-KP2A	40-SEVERAL!	142-P40V
10	3169-HD8EX	39-OL8A	130-P40V
Total	17,073	210	729
	@ 2.93 Pts/QSO = 46,971,597 !		

	M/M World	M/M USA	M/S World	M/S USA
QSOs	KP2A-15,198	W3LPL-5387	VP2MW-5968	K1AR-3324
Zones	UP8A-207	W3LPL-194	LZ9A-193	K1AR-185
Countries	LX8A- 687	W3LPL- 624	LZ9A-591	K1AR-576
Max. Score	= 39.80M	= 12.91M	= 13.70M	= 7.41M
Actual Score	PJ1B=38.41M	W3LPL=12.80M	VP2MW=9.04M	K1AR=7.37M

ALL-TIME MAXIMUM ACHIEVEMENTS DURING CQ WW DX PHONE AND CW

Maximum CQ WW DX Phone (results through 1992)

Band	QSOs	Zones	Countries
160	1527-RB8M-'89	20-VE1ZZ-'90 K5UR-'88	65-9A1HCD-'92
80	1884-LX7A-'89	35-HA8IE-'90	116-HA8IE-'90
40	2737-9A1A-'92	38-GØKPW-'92 IR4LCK-'88 JA5BJC-'84	137-G0KPW-'92
20	5420-VP9AD-'89	40-MANY!	186-PJ1B-'89
15	5417-VP2KC-'79	40-MANY!	178-N2RM-'92 ZW5B-'89
10	5714-PJ1B-'89	40-SEVERAL!	182-PJ1B-'90
Total	22,699	213	864
	@ 2.93 Pts/QSO = 71,629,116 !!!!		

All-time Category Theorectical Maximums

	M/M World	M/M USA	M/S World	M/S USA
QSOs	19,655-PJ1B-'90	7,321-N2RM-'90	9,460-PJ1B-'91	4,437-K1AR'90
Zones	189-Three	187-N5AU-'90	202-LZ9A-'90	177-KS9K-'90
Countries	803-PJ1B-'90	793-N2RM-'92	753-IQ4A-'91	703-K1AR-'90
Max Score	= 57.12 M	= 21.02 M	= 26.46 M	= 11.44 M

Maximum CQWW DX CW (through 1992 results)

Band	QSOs	Zones	Countries
160	1008-SP3BQ-'88	26-K5UR-'87	76-ON4UN-'92
80	2243-NP4A (K1ZM)-'88	34-SP3GEM-'86	107-K1AR'92
40	3119-PJ1B-'88	40-SEVERAL!	144-W3LPL-'92
20	4253-CT3M-'89	40-MANY!	156-K1AR-'92
15	3951-J6DX-'91	40-MANY!	154-K1AR-'92
10	3795-CX0CW-'90 (CX8BBH)	40-S59AA-'92 LZ9A-'90	140-W3LPL-'89
Total	18,369	220	777
	@ 2.93 Pts/QSO = 53,659,537		

All-time Category Theorectical Maximums

	M/M World	M/M USA	M/S World	M/S USA
QSOs	15,242-PJ9A-'90	7,127-K1AR-'92	7,201-TA5KA-'90	4,101-K1AR-'89
Zones	211-UX1A-'92	195-N2RM, W3LPL-'92	200-LZ9A-'89	90-K1AR-'89
Countries	718-UX1A-'92	753-K1AR-'92	678-IQ4A-'92	674-N3RS-'92
Max. Score	= 41.48 M	= 19.79 M	= 18.52 M	= 10.38 M

WINNERS OF NOVEMBER SWEEPSTAKES CW

Year	SS#	S/O-HI	S/O-LOW-POWER	S/O-QRP	MULTI-OP	#Sweeps	Club-Unlimited-Medium-Local
1992	#59	N4RJ(KM9P)	N5RZ	W9UP(KA9FOX)	AA5B	209	N.C.C.C.-N.Tx.C.C.-N.M. Big River C.C.
1991	#58	N5AU(WN4KKN/5)	N5RZ	NF7P	W6GO	127	FRC-N.Tx.C.C.-River City C.
1990	#57	N5AU(WN4KKN/5)	N5RZ	K7SS	WXØB	5	Mn.W.A.-N.Tx.C.C.-River City C.
1989	#56	N5AU(WN4KKN/5)	KØEU	KØSCM	K5LZO	7	S.M.C.-Mn.W.A.-Rubber Circle C.C.
1988	#55	KØRF(WØUA)	KØEU	KVØI	N4RJ	60	———N.Tx.C.C.-River City C.
1987	#54	W5WMU(K5GA)	NF7P	N2IC	AA5B	73	Murphy's-N.Tx.C.C.-River City C.
1986	#53	NP4A(K5ZD)	K3RR	*#5*	K5CM	134	S.M.C.-Mad River R.C.-Rubber Circle C.C.
1985	#52	K6LL	K4JPD(N4ZZ)	AA5B		108	S.M.C.-N.Tx.C.C.-Rubber Circle C.C.
1984	#51	N5AU(K5ZD)	K7JA	N6BT		100	N.C.C.C.-Tx.DX.S.-Rubber Circle C.C.
1983	#50	N5AU(K5ZD)	NØNO	K5CM		219	P.V.R.C.-N.Tx.C.C.-Colorado Contest Conspiracy
1982	#49	N5AU(K5ZD)	N6IG	WB8JBM		47	P.V.R.C.-Tx.DX.S.-Lincoln ARC
1981	#48	N5AU(K5ZD)	W2TZ	N5DKG		55	P.V.R.C.-N.C.C.C.-Alburquerque DX Assn.
1980	#47	KØRF(WØUA)	W1ZT	K1VTM		29	N.C.C.C.-Tx.DX.S.-Willamette Valley (Ore) DXC.
1979	#46	KP2A(K2TR)	VE4VV	K6RLY		145	N.C.C.C.-Y.C.C.C.-South Jersey Contest Coalition
1978	#45	W2GD	AA7A	WA2ECA		86	N.C.C.C.-Murphy's-Cascades ARC (Mi)
1977	#44	KP4RF(KP4EAJ)	K5LZO	W4BVV		27	N.C.C.C.-*# CL*-*****
1976	#43	KV4FZ(K7VPF)[K7JA]	AC8CQN[W8FJ]	WØZLN		17	N.C.C.C.
1975	#42	WA5LES[K5RC]	WA5VDH[K5UR]	W6YRA		0	N.C.C.C.
1974	#41	W6RR(W6RTT)[AH3C]	W8CQN[W8FJ]	KH6RS		62	PVRC
1973	#40	W7RM(K7VPF)[K7JA]	WB2RJJ[N2OO]	WA1KID[W6XR]		25	MM
1972	#39	W7RM(K7VPF)[K7JA]	WBØDLE	W7SFA[W7FU]		16	PVRC
1971	#38	W7RM(K7VPF)[K7JA]	WA3DSZ	K4SXD[N4RG]		29	Mad River R.C.
1970	#37	W6HX(WB6OLD)[N6NT]	K5RHZ	WB6WIT		14	PVRC
1969	#36	W6RW(W6DQX)[N6ZZ]	WA3DSZ	K5LZO		22	PVRC
#LP							
1968	#35	KV4FZ			W6RW	18	PVRC
1967	#34	W9YT(K9ZMS)[K6NA]			K4VDL	38	PVRC
1966	#33	W6CUF[W6CF]			K5LZO	17	PVRC
1965	#32	W4KFC			K5LZO	3	PVRC
1964	#31	W4KFC			W3MWC	17	PVRC
#24							
1963	#30	W9IOP			WB2APG	24	FRC
#CK,CM							
1962	#29	W5WZQ[W5UN]			W3GQF	93	PVRC
1961	#28	W5WZQ[W5UN]			W3GQF	77	PVRC
1960	#27	W9IOP			W9WBY	69	FRC
1959	#26	W9IOP			W3FYS	93	PVRC
1958	#25	W4KFC			W3FYS	104	FRC
1957	#24	W2IOP			W3FYS	59	FRC
1956	#23	W4KVX			W9OCB	27	PVRC
1955	#22	W7KVU			W9OCB	36	PVRC
1954	#21	W4KVX			W3FRY[K3WW]	37	PVRC

1953	#20	W9IOP	W3CTJ	17	PVRC
1952	#19	W4KFC	W3LTW	32	PVRC
1951	#18	W6BJU(W6CUF[W6CF])	W6EFW	9	PVRC
1950	#17	W4KFC	W3KT	8	PVRC
1949	#16	W2IOP		5	PVRC
1948	#15	W2IOP	W3CPV	3	PVRC
1947	#14	W4KFC	VE7ACS	2	FRC
1946	#13	W4FUH	*#YB*	1	FRC
#ZF					
1941	#12	W9FS	W4WE	0	FRC
1940	#11	W3BES	W8YX	0	FRC
1939	#10	W2IOP	W1AQ	6	FRC
1938	#9	W3BES	W8ADV	0	FRC
1937	#8	W6MVK	W8ADV	1	FRC*[W6MVK FIRST CW SWEEP!]
1936	#7	W1EZ	K5AC	0	FRC
1935	#6	W8JIN	W4IB	0	
1934	#5	W9HKC	W6BIP	0	
1933	#4	W9AUH	W9GDH	0	
1932	#3	W8ER	W5WF	0	
1931	#2	1ST-W8CHC-305Qx54; 2ND-W5WF-(4OPS)-?Qx58!,3RD-W7AAT-265x55; *276 Entrants some phone work reported.			
1930	#1	1ST-W1ADW-153Qx43; 2ND-W9DEX-142x43,3RD-W2BAI-155x390; **#ZZ**116 Entrants			

Footnotes to Sweepstakes

Footnote #1-The "P.I.N.S. (Participation IN Sweepstakes)" Program began with the 1990 event. CURRENT
Footnote #2-The WASHINGTON state section was split into the EAST Washington section and the WEST Washington section beginning with the 1989 event. (Total sections = 77). CURRENT
Footnote #3-The WEST INDIES section was split into the Puerto Rico section and the Virgin Is. section beginning with the 1988 event. (Total sections = 76).
Footnote #4-The WEST TEXAS section was created beginning with the 1987 event. (Total sections = 75).
Footnote #5-QRP Single Operator class was added beginning with the 1987 event. CURRENT
Footnote #CL-The Club Competition rules were changed to accommodate Large-Unlimited clubs, Medium clubs and Small,Local clubs. CURRENT
Footnote #LP-The Low Power (150 watts or less) category power multiplier was eliminated after the 1968 event. CURRENT
Footnote #24-The 1964 S.S. was the first 24Hour, Single Mode Event. CURRENT
Footnote #CK-Beginning with the 1963 event, The year you were first licensed became your message check number. CURRENT
Footnote #CM-In 1963, the Maryland-Delaware Section, MDD was split into the Maryland, D.C., MDC section and the Delaware, DEL section.
Footnote #YB-The full scores listings for the 13TH Sweepstakes were never published. There was a mailing to each entrant.
Footnote #ZF-A.R.R.L. November Sweepstakes was QRT for WWII from 1942 to 1945.
Footnote #ZZ-There were two classes: Above and Below 100 watts. A 9 day, mixed mode event in which operators were permitted up to 90 hours of operation, exchanging actual messages.

WINNERS OF NOVEMBER SWEEPSTAKES PHONE

YEAR	SS#	S/OHI	S/OLOW POWER	S/OQRP	MULTI-OP	#Sweeps	Club-Unclub-Medclub-Local
1992	#59	WM5G(KRØY)	VE4GV	WE9V	K7SS	458	N.C.C.C.-N.Tx.C.C.-N.M. Big River C.C.
1991	#58	N5RZ	K4XS	K7SS	K9RS	214	FRC-N.Tx.C.C.-River City C.
1990	#57	W6GO(N6IG)	K7QQ	K7SS	AA5B	215	Mn.W.A.-N.Tx.C.C.-River CityC.
1989	#56	W7XR(W7WA)	KØEU	K7SS	AI7B	141	S.M.C.-Mn.W.A.-Rubber CircleC.C.
1988	#55	KP2A(N2IC)	AA5B	WØLSD	W7EJ	177	———N.Tx.C.C.-River CityC.
1987	#54	W7WA	K4XU	KE7X	KØUK	128	Murphy's-N.Tx.C.C.-River City C.
1986	#53	N6BV	KE5CV	*#5*	K5LZO	143	S.M.C.-Mad River CC-Rubber Circle C.C.
1985	#52	WA7NIN(W6OAT)	KE5CV		AA5B	146	S.M.C.-N.Tx.C.C.-Rubber Circle C.C.
1984	#51	KP4BZ	K4XS		KN6M	87	N.C.C.C.-T.DX.S.-Rubber Circle C.C.
1983	#50	KP4BZ	K7RI(K7SS)		N4WW	198	P.V.R.C.-N.Tx.C.C.-Colorado C.C.
1982	#49	NP4A(K1ZM)	KØUK		N6BT	160	P.V.R.C.-T.DX.S.-Lincoln ARC
1981	#48	KV4FZ(WA6VEF)	W5MYA		KØWA	323	P.V.R.C.-Colorado.C.C.-Albuquerque DXA.
1980	#47	N7DD(K7JA)	K7SS		W7ZR	175	N.C.C.C.-T.DX.S.-Willamette Valley (Or) DX Club
1979	#46	KP4Q(K2TR)	W7XN		AF3P	333	N.C.C.C.-Y.C.C.C.-South Jersey Contest Coalition
1978	#45	KP4RF[AH3C]	N5DX(K8CC)		K1GZL	269	N.C.C.C.-Murphy's-Cascades ARC (Mi)
1977	#44	KP4RF	N4MM		W2SZ	168	N.C.C.C.
1976	#43	WØTR([WØUA]	WBØMIV		W4BVV	109	N.C.C.C.
1975	#42	W7RM([K7JA])	WA5VDH[K5UR]		W5GAD	24	N.C.C.C.
1974	#41	W6HX([N6NT])	WB5FMJ		W5LUJ[W5XJ	56	PVRC
1973	#40	W7RM([K7JA])	K7JCA/6[K7SS]		W6ONV	75	Murphy's Marauders
1972	#39	W7RM([K7JA])	WBØDSP		WB5DTX[N5DD	102	PVRC
1971	#38	W7RM([K7JA])	K1EUF		WA7ORM	125	MAD RIVER OHIO
1970	#37	K7VPF/7[K7JA]	K5RHZ		W1FBY[W1XT]	80	PVRC
1969	#36	K9LBQ/7	K4WAR		K5LZO	38	PVRC
#LP							
1968	#35	KV4FZ			K5LZO	26	PVRC
1967	#34	K4WJT			WAØCHH	21	PVRC
1966	#33	W7ESK[W7RM]			WAØCHH	9	PVRC
1965	#32	W4KFC			K5IIS	13	PVRC
1964	#31	K6EVR(W9WNV)			W3MWC	2	PVRC
#24							
1963	#30	K5MDX			K3KLQ	2	FRC
#CK,CM							
1962	#29	K6EVR			W0EEE	11	PVRC
1961	#28	W7ESK[W7RM]			WA2LPF	3	PVRC
1960	#27	K6EVR			WØYQ	6	FRC
1959	#26	K5MDX			WØYQ	15	PVRC
1958	#25	K6EVR			W1KBN	18	FRC
1957	#24	WØEDX			WØYQ	13	FRC
1956	#23	W6AM			K5EAT/	5 8	PVRC
1955	#22	K2AAA			W5ZED	3	PVRC
1954	#21	W6AM(W6FRW)			W9WHN	6	PVRC
1953	#20	W9NDA			W4TEW/4	2	PVRC
1952	#19	WØEDX			W9HHX	3	PVRC

1951	#18	W6QEU	——		7	PVRC	
1950	#17	W6QEU		W6YX	3	PVRC	
1949	#16	W6QEU			0	PVRC	
1948	#15	W6QEU		VE7AKY	5	PVRC	
1947	#14	W6MLY		W4MOE	2	FRC	
1946	#13	W6ITH	*#yb*		1	FRC	
1941	#12	W9RBI	——		0	FRC	
1940	#11	1ST-W6ITH,2ND-W9YQN,3RD-W5BB	——		1	FRC	274-OTHER PHONE SCORES REPORTED.
1939	#10	1ST-W6ITH,2ND-W6OCH,3RD-W9RBI		W1AW	2	FRC	307-OTHER PHONE SCORES REPORTED.
1938	#9	1ST-W6ITH,2ND-W6OCH,3RD-VE5VO		W4EQK	0	FRC	110-OTHER PHONE SCORES REPORTED.
1937	#8	1ST-W6ITH,2ND-W9PWU,3RD-VE9AL(VE3BC)		W2JSE	0	FRC	99-OTHER PHONE SCORES REPORTED.
1936	#7	1ST-W6ITH,2ND-W9ATP,3RD-W9PWU	——		1	FRC	13-OTHER PHONE SCORES REPORTED.*[W6ITH FIRST S. S. PHONE SWEEP!]
1935	#6	1ST-VE3ER,2ND-W4BZA,3RD-W4DGS	——		0	—	3-OTHER PHONE SCORES NOTED.
1934	#5	1ST-W9GAF,2ND-W8DML,3RD-W9KBT	——		0	—	13-OTHER PHONE SCORES NOTED.
1933	#4	1ST-W6AHP,2ND-W9ACU,3RD-W8EMP	——		0	—	22-OTHER PHONE SCORES NOTED.W6AHP PLACED 8TH OVERALL!
1932	#3	1ST-W8ALC,2ND-W1APK,3RD-W9CUK	——		0	—	No OTHER PHONE SCORES NOTED OR LISTED.
1931	#2	PHONE OPERATION NOTED BUT NOT REPORTED.	——		0	—	
1930	#1	ALL C.W. ——	0	—			

Footnotes to Sweepstakes

Footnote#1 -The 'P.I.N.S. (ParticipationIN Sweepstakes) Program' began with the 1990 event. CURRENT

Footnote#2-The WASHINGTON state section was split into the EAST Washington section and the WEST Washington section beginning with the 1989 event. (Total sections = 77). CURRENT

Footnote#3-The WEST INDIES section was split into the Peurto Rico section and the Virgin Is. section beginning with the 1988 event. (Total sections = 76).

Footnote#4-The WEST TEXAS section was created beginning with the 1987 event. (Total sections = 75).

Footnote#5-QRP Single Operator (NoPacket) class was added beginning with the 1987 event. CURRENT

Footnote#CL-The Club Competition rules were changed to accommodate Large-Unlimited clubs, Medium clubs and Small,Local clubs. CURRENT

Footnote#LP-The Low Power (150 watts or less) category power multiplier was eliminated after the 1968 event. CURRENT

Footnote#24-The 1964 S.S. was the first 24Hour, Single Mode Event. CURRENT

Footnote#CK-Beginning with the 1963 event, The year you were first licensed becams your message check number. CURRENT

Footnote#CM-In 1963, the Maryland-Delaware Section, MDD was split into the Maryland, D.C. (MDC) section and the Delaware (DEL) section.

Footnote#YB-The full Scores listings for the 13TH Sweepstakes were never published. There was a mailing to each entrant.

Footnote#ZF-A.R.R.L. November Sweepstakes was QRT for WWII from 1942 to 1945.

Footnote#ZZ-There were two classes: Above and Below 100 watts. A 9 day, mixed mode event in which operators were permitted up to 90 hours of operation, exchanging actual messages. Although 'Phone operations occurred, they were but a small percentage of the total activity; 3 ops in 1932, 25 ops in 1933.

ARRL NOVEMBER SWEEPSTAKES CW SECTION RECORDS

Single-Operator, High Power

Section	Call	Year	Score
CT	K1TO	92	195,320
EMA	K1AR	78	171,000
ME	N1SW	79	147,822
NH	K1DG(WZ1R)	92	177,716
RI	K1IU	89	147,896
VT	WB1GQR (WB2JSJ)	92	156,002
WMA	W2SC	92	166,288
ENY	K1ZM	90	180,950
NLI	NQ2D	90	167,092
NNJ	W2RQ	92	184,030
SNJ	KZ2S	92	191,268
WNY	K2KIR	92	167,090
DE	W3XU	81	157,176
EPA	W3RJ	77	165,020
MDC	KE3Q	92	188,496
WPA	K3LR	91	207,746
ALA	WZ4F	88	168,112
GA	N4RJ(KM9P)	92	220,836
KY	N4AR	92	174,020
NC	AA4NC	91	174,944
NFL	K4XS	91	183,568
PR	NP4A (K5ZD)	86	195,656
SC	KØEJ/4	88	121,500
SFL	N4RR	78	175,346
TN	N4ZZ	92	173,588
VA	K4VX([KT3Y])	78	168,900
VI	KP2N	92	60,350
ARK	K5GO	92	182,182
LA	W5WMU(K5GA)	92	209,440
MS	W5XX	92	180,026
NM	AA5B	91	188,650
NTX	N5AU(WN4KKN)	92	215,600
OK	WM4Z	91	160,776
STX	K5GN	92	196,042
WTX	WF5E	87	113,880
EB	N6RO	91	185,570
LAX	W6AM(N6TJ)	77	182,646
ORG	K6RR([AH3C])	78	176,712
PAC	AH3C	90	178,800
SBR	N6TR	83	183,076
SCV	W6XX	92	180,576
SDG	N6ND(NI6W)	92	190,190
SF	W6NUT[K6BB]	74	153,750
SJV	N6UR(KR6X)	92	196,042
SV	W6GO(N6IG)	90	184,650
AK	AL7CQ	90	158,250
AZ	K6LL	91	199,430
EWA	WA7EGA	91	132,088
ID	K7NHV	83	172,568
MT	KØPP/7	92	148,918
NV	KI3V/7	92	194,040
OR	N6TR/7	92	208,054
UT	W7CFL	91	159,544
WWA	W7WA	92	190,456
WYO	N7NG(AH3C)	92	193,648
MI	K8CC	91	182,490
OH	KW8N(WD8IXE)	92	180,334
WV	N8II(KC8C)	86	154,906
IL	AG9A	91	176,022
IN	W9RE	92	185,878
WI	WØAIH(KØFVF)	92	158,928
CO	KØRF(WØUA)	91	204,358
IA	NCØP(AG9A)	92	196,504
KS	NØXA(KØVBU)	92	170,940
MN	NØAT	91	187,110
MO	K4VX/Ø([WX3N])	91	197,890
ND	WBØO	87	166,204
NE	KØUP	78	133,298
SD	KØZZ	78	171,828
MAR	VE1QST(AK4L)	80	139,870
PQ	VE2FU	91	115,808
ONT	VE3EJ(K5ZD)	92	206,822
MB	VE4OY	78	135,648
SK	VE5DX	81	161,024
AL	VE6UX	91	125,048
BC	VE7SZ	92	202,048
NWT/YUK	NØTT/VE8	83	97,382

Dead Records for "Deleted Sections"

Section	Call	Year	Score
C.Z.	KZ5FR	78	138,262
EFL	WA4NGO	63	235,875
WFL	W4JJ(K4VFY)	63	140,799
W.I.	KP4RF([AH3C])	77	193,732
WA	K7RI([KC1F])	78	169,608

Single-Operator Low-Power

Section	Call	Year	Score
CT	K1CC	87	145,928
EMA	K1EA	82	129,204
ME	NX1T	91	97,532
NH	W1PH	92	152,304
RI	K1IU	92	156,772
VT	N4DW	91	137,522
WMA	W1ZT	80	139,392
ENY	WA2STM	92	139,688
NLI	NQ2D	91	127,224
NNJ	W2GD	92	160,776
SNJ	N2MM	90	130,950
WNY	W2TZ	92	164,312
DE	K3WUW	84	114,108
EPA	K3NW	92	135,432
MDC	KN5H	92	127,224
WPA	WA3FYJ	83	115,884
ALA	KC4ZV	89	114,912
GA	KM9P/4	90	155,040
KY	N4QS	92	120,992
NC	N4AA	92	145,838
NFL	WC4E	92	157,388
PR	NP4Z	92	166,744
SC	KØEJ	91	132,088
SFL	N4BP	77	149,850
TN	N4ZZ	92	173,558
VA	N4DW	78	137,850
VI	N6OP/NP2	92	170,696
ARK	K5UR	77	137,970
LA	K5MC	90	104,932
MS	W5XX	89	114,700
NM	KT5X	92	141,208
NTX	N5RZ	90	167,700
OK	KM5H	87	122,840
STX	K5LZO	77	153,180
WTX	N5RZ	91	187,264
EB	N6IG	82	136,802
LAX	N6HC	91	143,220
ORG	K7JA	83	144,004
PAC	KH6HKM	72	91,542
SBR	WA6FGV	91	119,550
SCV	N6PN	92	138,150
SDG	K6UA(AA5DX)	91	160,006
SF	W6JTI	89	121,360
SJV	W9NQ/6	92	120,992
SV	W1FEA	92	154,000
AK	AA6DX	91	91,048
AZ	KY7M	92	159,236
EWA	K7MM	92	137,100
ID	WO7Y	91	131,276
MT	KE7X	87	120,304
NV	NF7P	87	152,400
OR	KQ7I	92	152,400
UT	N7DF	79	150,234

WWA	K7QQ	91	151,544
WYO	K7MM	88	128,464
MI	W8CQN[W8FJ]	74	137,492
OH	K8CX	92	153,846
WV	KD8G	82	115,778
IL	K4XU/9	90	151,950
IN	AJ9C	92	141,680
WI	WB9YXY(N0BSH)	91	137,224
CO	KØEU	92	172,326
IA	KØLUZ	79	130,378
KS	NØXA(KØVBU)	91	133,989
MN	NØAT	92	156,712
MO	K4VX([WX3N])	88	144,900
ND	WBØO	92	148,918
NE	KVØI	90	135,864
SD	WDØT	91	159,450
MAR	VY2SS	92	117,800
PQ	VE2UJ	92	77,404
ONT	VE3AKG	78	121,656
MB	VE4VV	79	155,198
SK	VE5MX	92	135,982
AL	VE6OU[VE3EJ]	83	98,420
BC	VE7ARQ	88	98,988
NWT/YUK	VY1JA	92	44,608

Multi-Operator

Section	Call	Year	Score
CT	K1VTM	80	147,744
EMA	WA1JUY	72	111,672
ME	K1RQ	92	150,300
NH	KM1C	82	124,040
RI	K1AD	77	111,148
VT	WA8RGJ/1	72	52,608
WMA	W1PUO	74	99,012
ENY	K2TR	77	143,226
NLI	WA2CXY	72	37,476
NNJ	W2VJN	81	148,336
SNJ	N2NU	91	148,456
WNY	K2ZJ	92	165,550
DE	NX3A	91	40,194
EPA	K3WW	92	163,394
MDC	K1DQV	91	141,988
WPA	K3UA	92	186,340
ALA	N4KG	85	140,896
GA	W4AQL	92	180,424
KY	N4TY	92	154,000
NC	W4BFB	81	67,864
NFL	N4EEB	88	130,950
PR	WP4BDS	81	46,944
SC	WB4VJK	72	30,380
SFL	WA4LZR (K4XS)	77	98,420
TN	KI4UZ	91	141,834
VA	W4BVV	77	159,840
VI	No Entry		
ARK	WC5N	88	105,228
LA	K5MC	91	160,160
MS	W5TV	78	27,938
NM	AA5B	92	203,434
NTX	K5OJI	92	165,088
OK	WM4Z	92	172,368
STX	K5LZO	89	167,808
WTX	WF5E	92	166,012
EB	K6ZM	84	113,664
LAX	W6UE	87	150,750
ORG	N6PE	87	106,142
PAC	KH6RS	74	151,950
SBR	N6VR	92	165,088
SCV	N6BT	84	165,316
SDG	KT6V	91	103,600
SF	W6BIP	91	139,370
SJV	K6AYA	78	125,208
SV	W6GO	92	193,424
AK	AL7CQ	91	131,024
AZ	N7CSC	81	86,664
EWA	K7WUW	90	32,240
ID	W7UQ	79	109,668
MT	K7QA	80	130,640
NV	KI3V	91	170,324
OR	KQ7I	91	143,700
UT	W7MR	90	129,940
WWA	K7LXC	85	143,708
WYO	K7MM	90	153,772
MI	K8AQM	87	162,504
OH	WB8JBM	83	161,616
WV	KB8FJ	90	42,228
IL	KS9O	92	154,616
IN	KJ9D	85	161,468
WI	WØAIH/9	85	145,336
CO	KØRF	87	170,940
IA	K9LUW/Ø	92	119,320
KS	KØWA	92	165,376
MN	AAØFY	91	143,220
MO	WØZLN	76	147,168
ND	NJ9C	88	93,388
NE	KØGND	90	160,468
SD	WDØT	92	185,262
MAR	VE1NH	92	79,310
PQ	VE2UN	82	68,340
ONT	VE3ART	87	141,408
MB	VE4RRC	78	43,560
SK	VE5BBQ	79	16,932
AL	VE6AO	90	60,582
BC	VE7YU	91	90,244
NWT/YUK	No Entry		

Single-Operator

Section	Call (Since 1987)	Year	Score
CT	KH6CP/1	92	80,864
EMA	K1CGJ	91	77,390
ME	W1KX	91	26,280
NH	K1TR	92	106,552
RI	No Entry		
VT	WA1GUV	92	96,096
WMA	KB1W	87	66,640
ENY	KR2V	92	18,960
NLI	KK2E	92	47,080
NNJ	W2GD	91	114,730
SNJ	K2YY	91	84,150
WNY	NM2L	88	89,668
DE	NY3C	92	18,308
EPA	K3WW	87	63,072
MDC	K3TM	92	96,000
WPA	AG3H	90	36,570
ALA	N4KG (NB9P)	91	89,850
GA	KB4GID	91	88,396
KY	KJ4VH	89	54,020
NC	K3PI	92	73,584
NFL	KØLUZ	92	68,856
PR	KP4DDB	92	41,172
SC	KØEJ	92	100,320
SFL	K4MF	89	74,444
TN	K5MK	91	61,124
VA	W4MYA	88	78,292
VI	NP2E	92	10,120
ARK	W9OBF	90	53,480
LA	NO5W	89	39,900
MS	K4VFY/5 (N4EVS)	88	89,644
NM	K5IID	91	81,400
NTX	AA5KK	91	76,320
OK	WA5RES	92	50,544
STX	AC5K	89	79,032
WTX	W5VGX	87	44,460

EB	No Entry		
LAX	WB6JJE	90	60,088
ORG	WB9AJZ/6	90	27,720
PAC	No Entry		
SBR	N6NMH	89	44,162
SCV	W6IO	89	88,200
SDG	K6ZH	92	72,072
SF	W6JTI	91	93,324
SJV	WB6ITM	87	14,364
SV	WA6AUE	89	35,108
AK	NL7DU	87	9,840
AZ	N7IR	92	88,800
EWA	AA7HG	91	45,890
ID	KK7A	88	61,320
MT	KE7X	88	90,150
NV	NF7P	91	121,352
ORE	K7DBV	90	34,706
UT	K6EIL	91	56,880
WWA	K7LR	91	103,796
WYO	K7SS	90	113,344
MI	WK8V	92	51,830
OH	WA8RJF	92	82,950
WV	W8DL	92	62,320
IL	K9ZO	92	95,000
IN	KA4IQD/9	92	51,322
WI	W9UP (KA9FOX)	92	117,348
CO	N3SL/Ø	92	110,264
IA	WBØB	90	10,058
KS	NWØF	92	56,800
MN	N9CIQ	92	95,400
MO	KYØB	92	41,814
ND	WBØO	90	104,832
NE	KØSCM	92	112,480
SD	WAØZPT	91	66,816
MAR	No Entry		
PQ	VE2BLX	92	11,300
ONT	VE3OOL	88	44,588
MB	No Entry		
SK	VE5VA	92	24,600
AL	VE6BIR	91	43,776
BC	VE7YU	90	69,840
NWT/YUK	No Entry		

ARRL SWEEPSTAKES PHONE SECTION RECORDS

Single-Operator High Power

Section	Call	Year	Score
CT	K1KI	92	273,966
EMA	N6BV/1	88	258,704
ME	K1RQ (NJ1F)	92	204,050
NH	N6BV/1	92	272,888
RI	WA1TFF	78	196,200
VT	WB1GQR (WB2JSJ)	92	284,900
WMA	WA1ABW [K1BW]	76	214,500
ENY	K2TR	78	276,150
NLI	KD2RD	90	206,100
NNJ	WB2K	91	252,252
SNJ	K2PS	91	228,228
WNY	W2HPF	91	242,242
DE	K3WUW	90	216,062
EPA	K3ZA	92	239,316
MDC	K3ZO	92	260,414
WPA	K3LR (WR3G)	91	268,268
ALA	WZ4F	91	245,938
GA	K4JPD (WA4OZT)	77	229,200
KY	ND4Y	91	246,554
NC	KQ1Y/4	90	201,586
NFL	K4XS	90	341,880
	WJ2O/KP4	92	193,800
SC	KØEJ	92	235,774
SFL	KC4VA	81	233,162
TN	N4ZZ	89	255,332
VA	W4MYA	91	271,194
VI	KP2A (N2IC)	88	398,088
ARK	WA5RTG [K5GO]	75	222,300
LA	W5WMU	90	339,416
MS	W5VSZ	90	261,338
NM	K5TA	91	334,026
NTX	WM5G (KRØY)	92	374,682
OK	KM5H	92	239,316
STX	NR5M	90	340,032
WTX	N5RZ	91	374,374
EB	N6IG	88	320,720
LAX	W6HX (N6NT)	78	290,250
ORG	K6RR (N6IN)	79	243,756
PAC	K7SS/KH6	79	285,048
SBR	KB6I (N6TR)	81	280,608
SCV	W6QHS (WN4KKN)	91	324,324
SDG	K6JYO	90	310,464
SF	N6BV	78	246,300
SJV	WC6H	90	304,304
SV	W6GO (N6IG)	90	378,532
AK	AL7CQ	88	274,500
AZ	K6LL	89	363,286
EWA	K7FR	90	239,470
ID	W7ZRC	91	262,262
MT	KØPP/7	92	272,580
NV	WA7NIN (N6KT)	91	373,912
OR	W7NI (AI7B)	90	326,172
UT	W7CFL	91	301,224
WWA	W7XR (W7WA)	90	363,440
WYO	K7MM	90	311,696
MI	K8MJZ	91	239,008
OH	K8AZ (K8NZ)	91	238,700
WV	N8II	81	217,686
IL	AG9A	90	273,042
IN	W9RE	79	226,884
WI	W9UP (NØBSH)	92	255,948
CO	KØRF (WØUA)	91	318,010
IA	WØEJ	91	245,168
KS	K5JZN/Ø	79	222,592
MN	KØKX	79	243,162
MO	K4VX/Ø ([WX3N])	91	296,604
ND	WBØO	90	337,722
NE	KØSCM	79	213,416
SD	KØDD	88	319,808
MAR	VE1YX (AA2Z)	81	250,860
PQ	VA2UN ([K3RV])	71	148,296
ONT	VE3RM	92	203,896
MB	VE4RM	79	241,684
SK	VE5DX	78	289,050
AL	KS6H/VE6	91	175,098
BC	VE7SZ	92	300,608
NWT/YUK	VY1JA	92	121,352

Records for “Delected Sections”

C.Z.	KZ5NO (K1MM)	78	163,950
EFL	K4KXX	59	156,449
WFL	W4JLW	63	111,754
WA	K7SS	77	286,950
W.I.	KP4RF ([AH3C])	78	333,600

Single-Operator High Power

Section	Call	Year	Score
CT	KC1SJ	91	159,544
EMA	WA1UZH	79	145,632
ME	K1BZ (N1ATN)	89	119,776
NH	KM1C (WB8BTH)	82	184,836
RI	WA1TAQ	90	169,400
VT	WB2JSJ/1	77	116,772
WMA	KZ1M	92	195,118
ENY	WA2STM	92	186,802
NLI	KD2RD	91	161,100
NNJ	KY2P	85	159,248

SNJ	W2KI (K2PO)	78	151,900
WNY	W2TZ	89	148,500
DE	K3WUW	84	133,776
EPA	K3MQH	91	161,424
MDC	K3TM	80	125,504
WPA	K5ZD	91	190,190
ALA	KC4ZV	88	135,280
GA	KB4I (K2PO)	81	176,660
KY	AA4RX	92	207,130
NC	AA4S (WQ4V)	92	165,088
NFL	K4XS	91	290,598
PR	KØOO/KP4	80	98,124
SC	KØEJ	87	133,200
SFL	WD4AHZ	92	158,004
TN	N4ZZ	90	237,468
VA	W4MYA	92	204,358
VI	NP2I	92	157,542
ARK	N5DX (K8CC)	78	197,100
LA	N5PST	92	174,344
MS	W5XX	90	197,120
NM	AA5B	88	254,904
NTX	KN6M/5	91	267,036
OK	KM5H	91	214,522
STX	KE5FI	92	218,218
WTX	N5DO	90	161,084
EB	WA6DIL	81	191,660
LAX	N6HC	89	196,042
ORG	N6RJ (N6PEQ)	92	202,818
PAC	K6GSS/KH6	89	177,870
SBR	WA6FGV	91	188,188
SCV	N6NF	92	201,740
SDG	W6UQF	91	182,028
SF	WA8LLY	89	132,450
SJV	W9NQ/6	90	189,882
SV	W1FEA/6	90	237,930
AK	KL7IVX	79	142,376
AZ	KY7M	92	219,296
EWA	K7IOO	91	131,838
ID	WO7Y	89	206,400
MT	W7GKF	77	148,200
NV	ND7M	88	175,864
OR	W7XN	79	180,264
UT	W7CFL	92	202,972
WWA	K7QQ	90	278,124
WYO	K7MM	87	154,808
MI	AA8AV	92	186,494
OH	K8BL	92	148,610
WV	KC8JH	87	102,666
IL	AG9A	91	230,538
IN	AJ9C	92	233,618
WI	WØAIH (KA9FOX)	92	189,574
CO	KØEU	91	265,034
IA	WDØEWD	81	175,972
KS	NOØY	92	182,336
MN	KØHB	92	200,970
MO	NØCDH	87	125,850
ND	WDØECS	79	109,056
NE	KØSCM	92	215,840
SD	KA3DRR/Ø	90	178,044
MAR	VO1AA (K6ZH)	79	89,838
PQ	VE2MS	89	66,880
ONT	VE3GP	81	89,644
MB	VE4GV	92	254,870
SK	VE5MX	92	226,380
AL	VE6ATT	89	157,916
BC	VE7IN	92	119,504
NWT/YUK	VY1CC	82	57,084

Multi-Operator

Section	Callsign	Year	Score
CT	N1MM	78	219,600
EMA	W1AF	91	208,824
ME	N1SD	79	146,584
NH	K1GZL	78	231,150
RI	K1NG	90	262,108
VT	K1IK	80	208,236
WMA	K1KDP [W1BR]	76	153,900
ENY	WA2UKP	92	223,916
NLI	N2MG	88	176,850
NNJ	KZ2S	88	205,200
SNJ	AB2Y	83	135,196
WNY	WA2ECA	78	209,850
DE	AC3T	83	132,568
EPA	K3WW	92	258,874
MDC	K1DQV	91	244,244
WPA	AF3P	79	233,692
ALA	K4BFT	92	173,250
GA	W4AQL	92	231,154
KY	N4TY	92	248,402
NC	AA4NC	88	213,408
NFL	N4WW	83	268,472
PR	WA3FET/KP4	77	196,692
SC	N4QWL	90	168,014
SFL	AC4CT	91	251,790
TN	N4ZZ	92	267,652
VA	W4QAW	81	222,740
VI	KP2N	92	224,224
ARK	WA5TCL	82	192,992
LA	N5WA	92	198,660
MS	K5TYP	91	250,712
NM	AA5B	90	376,684
NTX	KW5P	90	260,106
OK	NJ1V	92	285,054
STX	K5LZO	86	267,288
WTX	KD5SP	92	246,862
EB	K6OYE	79	230,732
LAX	W6UE	92	281,358
ORG	KF6OG	91	314,776
PAC	N7NR/KH6	91	273,042
SBR	N6NB	77	188,352
SCV	N6BT	82	245,134
SDG	N6AWF	91	230,400
SF	W6BIP	81	206,904
SJV	N6EE	77	173,100
SV	W6GO	92	336,490
AK	AL7CQ	91	231,462
AZ	N7EDV	83	179,524
EWA	WA7EGA	92	240,397
ID	W7LQT	80	178,044
MT	KB7SE	81	191,698
NV	NF7P	91	289,366
OR	K7SS	92	367,906
UT	W7MR	91	241,780
WWA	W7XR	88	282,872
WYO	K7MM	88	228,760
MI	K8CC	87	214,500
OH	KW8N	92	304,766
WV	K8KT	78	154,906
IL	WB9GCS [N9SS]	76	200,736
IN	K9RS	89	242,242
WI	W9XT	90	285,054
CO	KØUK	87	281,550
IA	NØICI	90	196,812
KS	WØCEM	91	266,304
MN	NØAT	92	259,028
MO	WØRR	87	183,300
ND	AKØT	80	218,448
NE	KØDG	80	198,024
SD	WDØT	90	285,054
MAR	VE1NH	92	64,970
PQ	K2IQ/VE2	82	88,750
ONT	VE3XD	92	250,404
MB	NJØC/VE4	87	176,700
SK	VE5FN	88	183,768
AL	VE6AO	90	101,520
BC	VE7DV	92	89,166
NWT/YUK	N7DF/VY1	81	132,904

Single-Operator QRP (Category began 1987)

Section	Call	Year	Score
CT	KH6CP/1	88	58,380
EMA	WB1EHL	90	18,762
ME	N1AFC	88	27,300
NH	WA1LNP	92	71,148
RI	KA1NJW	89	27,560
VT	WA1GUV	90	33,000
WMA	K1KNQ	88	59,472
ENY	WV2V	90	48,384
NLI	KD2TT	90	71,250
NNJ	AA2U	92	81,158
SNJ	K2YY	92	87,764
WNY	WA2UUK	92	70,984
DE	K3WUW	87	61,200
EPA	N3KAQ	91	64,540
MDC	K3DI	90	64,380
WPA	W3SMX	91	31,892
ALA	N4UQD/T	89	14,592
GA	KB4GID	90	67,144
KY	AA4RX	89	102,718
NC	AA4NC	91	51,300
NFL	K4VFY(N4EVS)	88	44,400
PR	KP4DDB	92	24,090
SC	KJ4KB	90	31,008
SFL	K4VFY(N4EVS)	87	22,420
TN	N4TG	91	92,400
VA	WA4PGM	92	83,622
VI	NP2E	92	44,548
ARK	W9OBF	90	54,864
LA	K5KLA	88	36,984
MS	WB5KYK	88	9,400
NM	K5IID	91	145,992
NTX	KF5QR	92	66,682
OK	W5PAA(WC5D)	88	66,120
STX	N5NMX	92	100,100
WTX	W5VGX	88	79,804
EB	AA6GM	90	850
LAX	WB2ODH/6	91	83,250
ORG	WB9AJZ/6	90	7,740
PAC	NH6WH	90	12,540
SBR	K6VMN	92	91,250
SCV	KD6PY	87	72,854
SDG	K6ZH	89	43,632
SF	WA8LLY	91	16,740
SJV	W9NQ	92	117,648
SV	N6WMF	92	51,456
AK	AL7MK	91	4,810
AZ	N7IR	91	39,858
EWA	N7RWH	92	45,150
ID	KK7A	92	45,158
MT	KE7X	87	113,120
NV	KB7GAP	92	11,024
OR	K7SS	87	103,200
UT	WA7TUX	89	23,302
WY	K7MM	91	125,100
WWA	K7SS	91	169,400
MI	KB8DLH	89	43,216
OH	W8ILC	92	64,064
WV	NQ8Y	90	26,026
IL	K9ZO	91	117,040
IN	N9DHX	89	53,808
WI	WE9V	92	128,288
CO	KØFRP	91	137,676
IA	WAØVBW	88	72,200
KS	NOØY	91	39,520
MN	KBØZQ	88	61,350
MO	NØEID	92	36,920
ND	No Entry		
NE	WVØP	91	59,214
SD	No Entry		
MAR	No Entry		
PQ	No Entry		
ONT	VE3POS	92	58,368
MB	VE4VV	92	115,654
SK	No Entry		
AL	VE6SH	92	52,822
BC	VE7EKS	88	8,256
NWT/YUK	No Entry		

ARRL DX COMPETITION CW DX WINNERS BY YEAR/CATEGORY.

YEAR	Single-Op	QRP	Asst	M/S	M2	M/M	160	80	40	20	15	1Ø
1993	VP5F(KRØY)	V73C	ON4WW	P49V	ZL3GQ	9A1A	NO9M/KP4	YV1OB	T32AF(KH6UR)	OH8LQ	VP5U(N4MO)	ZD8LII(GØLII)
1992	V27T(YU1RL)	G4BUE	JJ3YBB(JI3ERV)	ZF2KE	UZ2FWA	HI8A	NO9M/KP4	G3LNS	ON4UN	OG1AA	LX/DL1VJ	FFØXX(FB1MUX)
1991	HKØ/N3JT	YU2TY	HI8A(JA5DQH)	XE2FU	JA8YBY	YT2R	VP2EXX	CU2AK	IO4IKW	YT1BB	9Y4VU	N6OP/NP2
1990	TGØAA(OH2BH)	K7SS/KH6	JA7YAB	ZF2KE	JA1YDU	YT2R	YV1OB	OK3CBU	KØGVB/C6A	IA8A	G3FXB	N6OP/NP2
1989	P4ØGD(W2GD)	YU2TY	*#2*	KP2A	6Y5L	I3JSS	YV1OB	KØGVB/C6A	I2VXJ	AI6V/VP9	KV4FZ(N6OP)	HC2G(HC2SL)
1988	P4ØGD(W2GD)	NP4Z		ZF2KE	JA1YXP	I3FIY	YV1OB	K8WW/VP9	KV4FZ(N6OP)	G3FXB	PY5ZBA	VP2ERA
1987	P4ØGD(W2GD)	YX3A		ZF2KE	XE2FU	KH6XX	K8WW/VP9	EA8RL	KP4FI	LU8DQ	HK1KYR	HK3MAE
1986	9Y4AA(N6TJ)	YV3AGT P4ØM		GB4DX	IO3FIY	V3DA	NP4Z	IØJX	K7SS/KH6	ZP5XDW	PAØVDV/PJ2	
1985	VP2MGD(W2GD)	C6AAA(KF1V)		KV4FZ	WH6W	KH6XX	VP5GEX	EA8RL	KP4FI	VP2EAG(KJØD)	ZF2AY(K9LA)	LU5DVO
1984	HR1DAP(K8CC)	K7SS/KH6		N5RM/C6A	HH2B	XE2FU	YV1OB	W9NXD/HR2	4M7QP	KP4EQF	YT3L(YU3EV)	ZP5XDW(N4PW)
1983	8P6J(N6TJ)	JA1MCU		AH6BK	VP5FUX	YU1EXY	F8VJ	CT2AK	9Y4VU	OH8AV(OH8PF)	ZY5XFR	LU5DVO
1982	V3MS(WØCP)	YV2BE		VP2E	*#4**	V2AMK	JA5DQH	DL1KB	IØJX	YU4GD	LU8DQ	XE2BC(N6OP)
1981	HH2VP	G4BUE		JA7YAA		NL7M	OK3CPL	EA8RL	KP4EQF	OH5TQ	TF3YH	G4GIR
1980	VP2ML(K1ZZ)	G4BUE		DKØTU		JA7YAA	G3SZA	UP2NK	I2XXG	YU3TU	YU7BCD	LU8DQ
1979	VP2MOC(K2YY)	*#Q*		XE2FU		JA7YAA	LowBand:	WA4UAZ/HC1	HighBand:	YU1KV		
1978	KP4EAJ			DKØTU		JA7YAA	LowBand:	IØJX	HighBand:	KP4USN(K5PM)		
1977	KP4EAJ			KP4EAS		YU1BCD	LowBand:	YV2OB	HighBand:	G3UJE		
1976	KP4EAJ			ZF1AL		JA1YXP	LowBand:	AJ4EAS(KP4EAS)	HighBand:	YU1BCD		
1975	PJ2VD	—	—	KH6GKD		VP2A	Low Band	KP4EAS	High Band	KH6IGC		

YEAR	World High S/O	M/S	M/M	S/O AF	S/O AS	S/O EU	S/O NA	S/O OC	S/O SA
1975	PJ2VD	KH6GKD	VP2A	5T5CJ	JA2JW	CT2BN	KV4IO	KH6RS(K1GQ)	PJ2VD
1974	LU5HFI[K3ZO]	KZ5NG	ZF1AL	CR6AI	JA1BRK	EA2IA	OX3YY	KH6RS(K1GQ)	LU5HFI(K3ZO)
1973	KH6RS(K1GQ)	6Y5EE	JH1YVW	5T5CJ	JA1CWZ	EA2IA	KV4HW(W6OAT)	KH6RS(K1GQ)	PJ2VD
1972	XE1IIJ(KØDQ)	YU3CV	OH1AD	5T5CJ	KR6AY	OZ1LO	XE1IIJ	KH6RS(K1GQ)	4M5KL
1971	KH6RS(K1GQ)	LU2ES	K6AB	EL2CB	JA1CG	G3FXB	HR2GK	KH6RS(K1GQ)	YV5KL
1970	PJ2VD	SK6AB	*#MM*	EL2CB	JA1AEA	LAØAD	OX3WQ	KH6IJ	PJ2VD
1969	ZD8Z[N6TJ])	SK6AB		ZD8Z[N6TJ]	JA1AEA	DJ4ZR	XEØGEN	KH6GPQ	PJ2VD
1968	ZD8J	LU8DQ		ZD8J	KA7AB	GI3OQR	VP2VL	KH6IJ	HK3RQ
1967	HI8XAL([K3ZO])	OH2AM		ZD8J	JA1CWZ	GI3ØQR	HI8XAL	KH6IJ	PY2BGL
1966	CO2BO	PJ5ME		7G1A	JA1IBX	GI3OQR	CO2BO	VK2EO	HK3RQ
1965	HP1IE	EL2AE		5A3TX	JA1VX	HB9JG	HP1IE	VK5ZP	YV1DP
1964	HP1IE	KZ5FC		CN8FW	JA1BRK	G4CP	HP1IE	KG6AAY	YV1DP
1963	HC1DC	PJ5ME		5A1TW[N2AA]	JA1VX	G4CP	KV4CF	W6ZDF/KM6	HC1DC
1962	HC1AGI	DL4QF		5N2JKO	KR6AR	G4CP	KP4CC	VK2GW	HC1AGI
1961	KV4AQ	KH6ECD		EL4A	JA1VX	F8VJ	KV4AQ	VK2GW	CE1AD
1960	VP1JH(WØNWX)	KS4AZ		ST2AR	JA1VX	G4CP	VP1JH(WØNWX)	VK2GW	VP3YG
1959	VP7BT	UR2KAA		CN8JE	JA1VX	SVØWP	VP7BT	KH6IJ	CE3AG
1958	KH6IJ	KG6FAE		CN8GU	JA1VX	SVØWP(W3JTC)	XE2FA	KH6IJ	CE3AG
1957	XF1A(XE1A)	KH6AYG		CR6AI	JA1VX	OK1MB	XF1A(XE1A)	KH6CBP	PJ2AV
1956	KV4AA	KH6AYG		CR6AI	KR6LJ	PAØUN	KV4AA	KH6IJ	VP3YG
1955	KH6MG	OE13USA		EL2X	JA1CJ	DJ1BZ	VP7NM	KH6MG	HK4DP
1954	KV4AA	KG4AT		EL2X	JA3AF	EA4CH	KV4AA	KH6IJ	LU3EX
1953	KG4AF	VP9BDA		ZE3JP	TA3AA	EA4CN	KG4AT	KH6MG	CE3AG
1952	KV4AA	CN8EX		ZS6OW	JA2IM	GW3ZV	KV4AA	KH6IJ	PY1ADA
1951	KV4AA	KP4KB		EK1AO	4X4RE	GW3ZV	KV4AA	KH6DK	LU1DH
1950	XF1A(XE1A)	——		EK1AO	JA2CK	GW3ZV	XF1A(XE1A)	KH6IJ	CE3DZ

1949	XF1A(XE1A)	KZ5ER	EL3A	JA3AA	OK1FF	XF1A(XE1A)	KH6IJ	PY2AC
1948	XF1A(XE1A)	HC1JB	ZS2A	J3AAD	HB9CX	XF1A(XE1A)	KH6IJ	CE3AG
1947	XE1A	——	ZS2AL	XU6GRL	HB9AW	XE1A	KH6DD	LU2FC
1940	XF1A(XE1A)	*NONE*	OQ5AB	XU8WS	*NONE*	XF1A(XE1A)	K6SCB	LU7AZ
1939	XE2N(XE1A)	*NONE*	ZS2AL	J2JJ	EI4J	XE2N(XE1A)	ZL1MR	LU5AN
1938	XE1AG	I6TK	ZS1AH	J3FJ	OK1BC	XE1A	K6CGK[KH6IJ]	LU7AZ
1937	K5AY EI8B	ZS2A	J4CT	F8EO	K5AY	K6CGK[KH6IJ]	OA4J	
1936	XE2N(XE1A)	——	EA8AO	J2LO	EA4AO	XE2N(XE1A)	ZL2KK	OA4J
1935	HC1FG(YL)	——	FM8BG	J2GX	ON4AU	X1AY	K6HLP	HC1FG
1934	NY1AB	CM2OP	ZS2A	J2GX	EA5BE	NY1AB	ZL4AI	HC1LC
1933	EAR185	G5BY	FM5IH	J1EC	EAR185	K4AAN	VK3ML	HC1FG
1929	*#ZY*							
1928	eg5BY[G]	*#ZZ*						

Footnote#1-There has not been a DX LowPower TopTen Box or Plaque/Trophy.
Footnote#2-Single Operator Assisted added for 1990 event. Single operator with Packet, with only ONE H.F. signal at a time. NO 10 minute rule.
Footnote#3-Changed format of event from 96 Hours during two weekends for each mode (Total of 192 hours) to 48 hours for one weekend for each mode (Total of 96 hours) beginning with the 1979 event.
Footnote#4-Added the Multi-Operator-TWO Transmitter class to the 1983 event. Each TX permitted only one signal and each must observe the 10 minute rule.
Footnote#Q-Added the QRPp Single Operator Class to the 1980 Event.
Footnote#1975-Added the Hi-Band and Lo-Band Single Operator Categories. These categories were only active from 1975-1979.
Footnote#MM-Added the Multi-Operator Single-Transmitter Class beginning with the 1971 event.
Footnote#1947- A stack of DX Phone logs was "lost, strayed or stolen". No awards will be issued until the affected amateurs have had a chance to resubmit copies of their 1947 DX Contest logs. Deadline was Feb 1,1948. Only 75 DX scores were included in the Nov 1947 Write-up. In the Nov 1948 issue of QST, after the final results of the 1948 DX contest, was an Addendum to the 1947 DX Contest. Resubmissions arrived from: OQ5AR, VQ4ERR, J3GNX, F8SI, G2PU, D4AEP, LA6J, LA7Y, GM8MN, TG9RC, ZL1MQ, LU5CK, PY2CK, PY2AJ, CE3AG, CE1AU.
Footnote#1937-Original ARRL DX Phone Competition Rules: March 20-28, 1937. 90 hours of operation MAXIMUM. Exchange RS(T) and a message number.
Footnote#1934-A gap was discovered in QST 1934 September Issue containing the final score listings of the Sixth International Relay Competition Results. The lapse begins after the score of EUROPEAN, AUSTRIA, OE1ER thru to NORTH AMERICAN, MEXICO, X1BC. Missing results were taken from write-up.
Footnote#ZY-The Hiram Percy Maxim 60th Birthday Relay. Planning for this event actually began during late 1927, early 1928 when the ARRL Board of Directors decided to celebrate H.P.M.'s 60th birthday with a Birthday Relay.When it was discovered that H.P.M. would not be 60 years old until September 2, 1929 the Birthday Relay was put on hold and kept secret for over a year ! The event began August 31, a Saturday, at 6 P.M. E.S.T. until Monday, September 2nd at 6P.M. E.S.T. During August of 1929, relay announcements were mailed to ARRL Official Relay Stations, Affiliated Clubs, Section Comm. Managers, and Route Managers throughout the U.S. and Canada. During the ten days prior to the Birthday Relay, ARRL Official Broadcast Stations were broadcasting the details of the event. (Luckily, H.P.M. never tuned in !) H.Q. station W1MK was manned by F.Edward Handy, R.P. and E.V. for the full 48 Hrs ! They received 356 messages on 3575kcs and 7150kcs. The first station worked had one message for H.P.M. . The second station to contact W1MK had 10 messages for H.P.M. !! One station actually transmitted 40 messages to W1MK ! It was reported that 'hardly two messages had the same wording.'
Footnote#ZZ-The 1928 International Relay Party results were reported in August 1928 QST by Louis R Huber. Prizes were offered and were listed in Feb 1928 QST as well as late additions in August 1928 QST. In the write-up it's called 'TheInternationalRelay CONTEST of1928'. (Possibly the FIRST reference of radio competition as a CONTEST.) Disqualifications included: 1BW, 5KC, 1ALR, 2AVB, 2BFQ, 3AFW, 4EC, 9DPW and 9AMN. The winner was proclaimed to be 1ASR with 305 points. But British station 5BY had 573 points, Belgian 4AU had 486 points, from Puerto Rico, 4SA had 405 points, followed by Australian 7CW at 369 points and NewZealander 3AR at 328. The USA TopTen: 1ASR-305, 2ALU-295, 2TP-259, 8GZ-253, 1CMP-241, 4FU-223, 9DNG-213, 1BHS-209, 5WZ-202, 8AHC-201. 6AM[W6AM] had 156 points and placed 15th.

ARRL DX COMPETITION CW USA WINNERS BY YEAR/CATEGORY.

YEAR	Single-Op	Low-Power	QRP	SOA	M/S	M2	M/M
1993	K1ZM	W1PH	AA2U	K3WW	K3LR	K1AR	W3LPL
1992	WM5G(KRØY)	W1PH	AA2U	WB2Q	W3BGN	K1AR	N2RM
1991	KM1H(KQ2M)	KM9P	W2TZ	WB2Q	W3BGN	K1AR	W3LPL
1990	K1AR	W1PH	KR2Q	AA1K	W3BGN	N3RS	W3LPL
1989	KM1H(KQ2M)	VO1MP	KR2Q	*#2*	W3BGN	K1AR	W3LPL
1988	KM1H(KQ2M)	VO1MP	W8VSK		K3WW	N3RS	W3LPL
1987	KM1H(KQ2M)	VO1MP	NN4Q		K3KG	NR5M	W3LPL
1986	W3GRF(KØDQ)	VO1MP	NN4Q		N4WW	W2REH	W3LPL
1985	K1AR	VO1MP	K1UO		N4WW	K2TR	W3LPL
1984	K1AR	N8II	K3WS		W3BGN	W3GM	KN3O
1983	N2LT	N5AW	AA4AK		W3BGN	K5RC	N2AA
1982	K1GQ	K1JX	AC2U		K1ZZ	*#4*	K2UA
1981	W2PV(N2NT)	N5AW/1	N2AA		K5RC		K2UA
1980	K1PR	N4HI	N4BP		K5RC		W4BVV
1979	K1GQ	N5AW	*#Q*		W3AU		N2AA
1978	W3LPL	N4HI			N3RD		W4BVV
1977	W3LPL	WA1SSH[W1NG]			WA1NRF[K1PR]		N3RS
1976	W3LPL	WA1SSH[W1NG]			W2YD		W3WJD[N3RS]

1975	Single-Op	Low Power	Multi-Single	Multi-Multi	Club
1975	W7RM	WA1SSH[W1NG]	WA5LES[K5RC]	W3AU	FRC
1974	W3LPL	WA1SSH[W1NG]	K4VX	W3AU	MM
1973	K1NOL[K1NA]	K2MFY	K1ZND[K1ZZ]	W3AU	FRC
1972	K1ZND[K1ZZ]	WA1ABW[K1BW]	WA8JUN[K8MD]	W3AU	PVRC
1971	W1BGD/2[W1RM]	W4CRW	K6EBB	W3AU	FRC
1970	K1DIR	K5ABV	W4BVV	*#MM*	PVRC
1969	W1BPW[W1UU]	W8QXQ[N8AA]	W3MSK[W3AU]		PVRC
1968	W9WNV/2	W4BRB	W3TMZ[W3OZ]		PVRC
1967	K1DIR	K1ZND[K1ZZ]	W4BVV		PVRC
1966	W4KFC	VE2NV	W3MSK[W3AU]		FRC
1965	K2HLB	K1ZND[K1ZZ]	W3MSK[W3AU]		PVRC
1964	W3GRF	K1LPL[W3LPL]	W3MSK[W3AU]		FRC
1963	W3GRF	K4TEA	W6RW		FRC

	Single-Op	Multi-Single	Club
1962	W4KFC	W3MSK[W3AU]	PVRC
1961	W3ECR	W3MSK[W3AU]	FRC
1960	W3ECR(W3MFW)	W3AOH	FRC
1959	W3ECR(W3MFW)	W6RW	FRC
1958	W3LOE	W3AOH	PVRC
1957	W4KFC	W3CTJ	PVRC
1956	W3DGM/3VE4RO	W6RW	SouthernCaliforniaDXClub
1955	W2SAI([W3GM])	W3CTJ	FRC
1954	W3CTJ(W3NOH)	W2SAI	FRC
1953	W2SAI([W3GM])	W3MSK[W3AU]	FRC
1952	W5ENE	W3BES[W3GM]	FRC
1951	W3LOE	W3KT	FRC
1950	W3LOE	W6EOG	SouthernCaliforniaDXClub
1949	W8BHW	W2IQG	FRC
1948	W2GWE	W6LHN	FRC
1947	W2GWE	——	FRC
1940	W6GRL	——	SouthBayAmateursAssoc.ofL.A.,Ca.
1939	W3CHE	W4YC	SouthBayAmateursAssoc.ofL.A.,Ca.
1938	W2UK	W3HIL	SouthBayAmateursAssoc.ofL.A.,Ca.
1937	W2UK	W1TW	Tri-CountyAmateurRadioAssoc.ofPlainfield,N.J.
1936	W4DHZ	W6GRL	**ClubWinnerNotAnnounced**
1935	W3SI	W6GRL	**ClubWinnerNotAnnounced**
1934	W3ZJ	W4CBY	**ClubWinnerNotAnnounced**
1933	W3ZD	W1SZ	**ClubWinnerNotAnnounced**
1929	HPM Birthday Relay: W1MK-356,W1AOX-151,W8CHC-134		
1928	1ASF		

Footnote#1-There has not been a DX Low Power Top Ten Box or Plaque/Trophy.

Footnote#2-Single Operator Assisted added for 1990 event. Single operator with Packet, with only ONE H.F. signal at a time. No 10 minute rule.

Footnote#3-Changed format of event from 96 Hours during two weekends for each mode (Total of 192 hours) to 48 hours for one weekend for each mode (Total of 96 hours) beginning with the 1979 event.

Footnote#4-Added the Multi-Operator-TWO Transmitter class to the 1983 event. Each TX permitted only one signal and each must observe the 10 minute rule.

Footnote#Q-Added the QRPp Single Operator Class to the 1980 Event.

Footnote#1980-DX-to DX QSOs were permitted in the 1980 event as an experiments. This was rescinded for 1981, reverting back to the previous form: "The world working the U.S." *(Ed.—Things were chaotic that next year too!)*

Footnote#1975-Added the Hi-Band and Lo-Band Single Operator Categories. These categories were only active from 1975-1979.

Footnote#MM-Added the Multi-Operator Single-Transmitter Class beginning with the 1971 event.

Footnote#1963-Added the Low Power Single Operator Class.

Footnote#1947- A stack of DX Phone logs was "lost, strayed or stolen". No awards will be issued until the affected amateurs have had a chance to resubmit copies of their 1947 DX Contest logs. Deadline was Feb 1,1948. Only 75 DX scores were included in the Nov 1947 Write-up. In the Nov 1948 issue of QST, after the final results of the 1948 DX contest, was an Addendum to the 1947 DX Contest. Resubmissions arrived from: OQ5AR, VQ4ERR, J3GNX, F8SI, G2PU, D4AEP, LA6J, LA7Y, GM8MN, TG9RC, ZL1MQ, LU5CK, PY2CK, PY2AJ, CE3AG, CE1AU.

Footnote#1937-Original ARRL DX Phone Competition Rules: March 20-28, 1937. 90 hours of operation MAXIMUM. Exchange RS(T) and a message number.

160	80	40	20	15	10	Club-Unlimited-Med-Local
W1FJH(AD8V)	W1FV	W6XX	KT3Y	KØLUZ/4	K5MR	FRC-Mad River-River City C.
K5UR	WE3C	K8PO	K1TO	K2VV	WOUN	FRC-NCC-RiverCityC.
W1NG	W1FV	K1ZM	W1RR	K4VX/Ø(WO0G)	WM5G(KR0Y)	FRC-NCC-C.Va.C.C.
W1NG	W1FV	WOØG	K4VX(W9WI)	WN4KKN/5	K1ZM	FRC-SMC-Overlook Mtn.
K1ZM	W1FV	KBØG	N2AA	K2VV	K1RM	FRC-NTCC-Overlook Mtn.
K1ZM	W6RJ	K2EK	K2VV	K1RM	N4BP	YCCC-PVRC-Overlook Mtn.
K1ZM	W1FV	K4XS	K1RM	W5VX	K9LA/5	YCCC-PVRC-Overlook Mtn.
K5UR	W1FV	N6QR	K2VV	K3RV	KR1R	FRC-PVRC-Overlook Mtn.
W1RR		W1FV	N4PN	N2AA	N2EK	WA7KLKFRC-PVRC-CentralVaCC
W1RR	W1FV	W2YV(KQ2M)	K3UA	WB4TDH	W1WEF	FRC-PVRC-CentralVaCC
W8LRL	K1PT	NA5R(N5EA)	K8NA	WØZV	WB4TDH	FRC-N.Tx.C.C.-CentralVaCC
N4WW	W1ZM(K1ZM)	W6XX	K1KI	K6LL/7	N4ZZ	FRC-Murphy's-ILLWINDC.
N4IN	W1ZM(K1ZM)	W5UN	K5IY(KA5CHW)	K1RM	W0ZV	FRC-Murphy's-ILLWINDC.
W8LRL	N4AR	W5UN	K3TW	K6LL/7	N4WW	FRC-Murphy's-CentralVaCC
LowBand:	K7UR	HighBand:	AE2A			FRC-Murphy's-CentralVaCC.
LowBand:	K3ZO	HighBand:	N2OO			FRC
LowBand:	N4PN	HighBand:	K1NOL[K1NA]			PVRC
LowBand:	K1NOL[K1NA]	HighBand:	W2DXL[W2IB]			FRC

Footnote#1934-A gap was discovered in *QST* 1934 September Issue containing the final score listings of the Sixth International Relay Competition Results. The lapse begins after the score of EUROPEAN, AUSTRIA, OE1ER through to NORTH AMERICAN, MEXICO, X1BC. Missing results were taken from the write-up.

Footnote#ZY-The Hiram Percy Maxim 60th Birthday Relay. Planning for this event actually began during late 1927, early 1928 when the ARRL Board of Directors decided to celebrate H.P.M.'s 60th birthday with a Birthday Relay. This was put on hold when it was discovered that H.P.M. would not be 60 years old until September 2, 1929 ! The Birthday Relay was put on hold and kept secret for over a year ! The event began August 31, a Saturday, at 6 P.M. EST until Monday, September 2nd at 6 P.M.. EST. During August of 1929, relay announcements were mailed to ARRL Official Relay Stations, Affiliated Clubs, Section Comm. Managers, and Route Managers throughout the U.S. and Canada. During the ten days prior to the Birthday Relay, ARRL Official Broadcast Stations were broadcasting the details of the event. (Luckily, H.P.M. never tuned in!) H.Q. station W1MK was manned by F. Edward Handy, R.P. and E.V. for the full 48 Hrs! They received 356 messages on 3575kcs and 7150kcs. The first station worked had one message for H.P.M. The second station to contact W1MK had 10 messages for H.P.M.!! One station actually transmitted 40 messages to W1MK! It was reported that "hardly two messages had the same wording."

Footnote#ZZ-The 1928 International Relay Party results were reported in August 1928 *QST* by Louis R Huber. Prizes were offered and were listed in Feb 1928 *QST* as well as late additions in August 1928 *QST*. In the write-up it's called "The International Relay CONTEST of 1928." (Possibly the FIRST reference of radio competition as a CONTEST.) DQs included: 1BW, 5KC, 1ALR, 2AVB, 2BFQ, 3AFW, 4EC, 9DPW and 9AMN. The winner was proclaimed to be 1ASR with 305 points. But British station 5BY had 573 points, Belgian 4AU had 486 points, from Puerto Rico, 4SA had 405 points , followed by Australian 7CW at 369 points and New Zealander 3AR at 328. The USA Top Ten: 1ASR-305, 2ALU-295, 2TP-259, 8GZ-253, 1CMP-241, 4FU-223, 9DNG-213, 1BHS-209, 5WZ-202, 8AHC-201. 6AM[W6AM] had 156 points and placed 15th.

ARRL DX COMPETITION PHONE DX WINNERS BY YEAR/CATEGORY

YEAR	Single-Op	QRP	Asst	M/S	M2	M/M
1993	HC8A(N6KT)	V7A(V73C)	PYØFM	PJØB	6D2X	I3MAU
1992	TI1C(N6KT)	NH6T	EA3NY	PJØB	UZ2FWA	XE21
1991	EA8RCT(OHØXX)	TG9GI	HI8A	8P9X	XE2FU	I3MAU
1990	P4ØV(AI6V)	HB9ADD	SP2UUU	VP2E	K6GSS/KH6	4B2A
1989	V31C(KE5CV)	JA2JSF	*#2*	VP2MU	XE2FU	6D2DX
1988	PJ2FR(N6KT)	TG9GI		VP2MU	KP4BZ	I3MAU
1987	V31CV(KE5CV)	YX3A		NP4CC	K2SS/VP2V	VP9AD
1986	LU1BR	K7SS/KH6		ZF2HI	V47M	I3EVK
1985	ZF2FL(N6RJ)	AH6EK		HH2CQ	J87J	JA9YBA
1984	ZF2FL(N6RJ)	OK3CGP		ZF2HM	K9GL/VP2V	XE2FU
1983	ZF2FL(N6RJ)	TG9GI		KP4BZ	VP5KMX	VK2WU
1982	ZF2FL(N6RJ)	TG9GI		VP2E	*#4**	J3AVT
1981	VP2MP(K2YY)	I5NSR		VP2E		G4ANT
1980	VP2ML(WB2CHO)	TG9GI		VP1A		GB4ANT
1979	XE1OW(N5AU)	*#Q*		FY7AK		K1CO/PJ7
1978	KH6IJ			KH6DL		SK6JA
1977	KP4EAS			KH6GQW		PJ8CO
1976	KP4AST			WØNAR/6Y5		PJ8CO
1975	KZ5BC			OA4O		YU3DBC
1975	KZ5BC			OA4O		YU3DBC
1974	HR1RF			YV4AGP		KP4AXM
1973	6J9AA(KØDQ)			G4ANT		DL5AY
1972	XE1IIJ(KØDQ)			KZ5ZZ		KH6HCM
1971	XE1KS			HC1ARE		OH2BO
1970	KP4AST			KH6SP		*#MM*
1969	KV4FZ			6YØA		
1968	KH6IJ			XE2PTBC		
1967	HI8XAL			KS6BV		
1966	KP4CKU			ZF1BP		
1965	HK3RQ			I1RB		
1964	YV5BIG			YV5AHG		
1963	XE1CCB			I1CWN		
1962	XE1CV			CO8RA		
1961	KP4AVQ			KH6ECD		
1960	VP2DX			GB2SM		
1959	KH6IJ			CN8JE		
1958	KH6IJ			KX6AF		
1957	KH6IJ			KH6CBP		
1956	TG9AD			KH6AYG		
1955	KH6IJ			ZB2A		
1954	KH6IJ			KH6AWM		
1953	KV4BB			VP9BDA		
1952	KH6IJ			XE1QB		
1951	VP6SD			MI3US		
1950	XF1A(XE1A)			OA1E		
1949	KP4ES			G3DFC		
1948	XF1A(XE1A)			VQ3HGE		
1947	XE1A	***#1947*		——		
1940	K4FKC			——		
1939	CO2WM			——		
1938	K4SA			——		
1937	XE2N(X1EA)			F8KW		

Although phone was in use long before 1937 and phone use in Sweepstakes was reported as early as 1932, the ARRL DX Competition did not report any phone work until the 1937 event, when March 6-14,1937 was for CW and March 20-28 was for phone.

Footnote#1-There has not been a DX Low Power Top Ten Box or Plaque/Trophy.
Footnote#2-Single Operator Assisted added for 1990 event. Single operator with Packet, with only ONE H.F. signal at a time. No 10 minute rule.
Footnote#3-Changed format of event from 96 Hours during two weekends for each mode (Total of 192 hours) to 48 hours for one weekend for each mode (Total of 96 hours) beginning with the 1979 event.
Footnote#4-Added the Multi-Operator-TWO Transmitter class to the 1983 event. Each TX permitted only one signal and each must observe the 10 minute rule.
Footnote#Q-Added the QRPp Single Operator Class to the 1980 Event.
Footnote#1980-DX-to DX QSOs were permitted in the 1980 event as an experiments. This was rescinded for 1981, reverting back to the previous form: "The world working the U.S." *(Ed.—Things were chaotic that next year too!)*
Footnote#1975-Added the Hi-Band and Lo-Band Single Operator Categories. These categories were only active from 1975-1979.
Footnote#MM-Added the Multi-Operator Single-Transmitter Class beginning with the 1971 event.
Footnote#1963-Added the Low Power Single Operator Class.
Footnote#1947- A stack of DX Phone logs was "lost, strayed or stolen". No awards will be issued until the affected amateurs have had a chance to resubmit copies of their 1947 DX Contest logs. Deadline was Feb 1,1948. Only 75 DX scores were included in the Nov 1947 Write-up. In the Nov 1948 issue of QST, after the final results of the 1948 DX contest, was an Addendum to the 1947 DX Contest. Resubmissions arrived from: OQ5AR, VQ4ERR, J3GNX, F8SI, G2PU, D4AEP, LA6J, LA7Y, GM8MN, TG9RC, ZL1MQ, LU5CK, PY2CK, PY2AJ, CE3AG, CE1AU.

160	80	40	20	15	10
CY2CE	4M3X	ZF2ND	IR4T(I4UFH)HC1OT	LU6ETB	
KV4FZ	ZF2ND	ON4UN(ON4WW)	IR4T(I4UFH)	9Y4VU	PJ9M(OH6RM)
CT1AOZ	YV1EQW	IO4VEQ	YT1BB	FM/F6HMQ	CT1BOP
YV1DRK	T32AF	4M5T(YV5JBI)	G3FXB	NP4CC	PJ9M(OH6RM)
HK3DFT	TE1L	ZF2MV	T32AF(KH6UR)	NP4CC	P4ØT(KB2HZ)
4U1UN(K2GM)	TI2LTA	XE2NQ(AA5B)	HC1HC	PT9ZZ(PY5CC)	CE6EZ
CT1AOZ	CU2AK	9Y4AA(N6TJ)	KK9A/VP2V	PY5IW	LU1E(LU3AJW)
IV3PRK	4U1UN(K2GM)	HC5EA	KP4FI	HK3MAE	LU1E(LU3AJW)
VP5SBX(AK8A)	KK9A/PJ7	T32AF(KH6UR)	HC1HC	ZV9ZZ(PY5IW)	LU6ETB
AH6BK	HI8LC	JA2BAY	KP4EQF	KK9A/V2A	HC1HC
T32AF(KH6UR)	FM7WS	FM7CD	YT3A(YU3SO)	VP2MKD(K9MK)	CP6EL
——	YV1CD	HC1HC	F2SI	IØWDX	G4GIR
HI8JAG	HI8PGG	FMØFJE	OH2MM	YU3TU	FGØFOO/FS(N6RA)
G3SZA	CT2AK	PJ2FR	OH5LF	OH2FQ(OH2BH)	H31LR(HP1XOJ)
LowBand:	HI8JAG	HighBand:	OA4ASX(K1MM)		
LowBand:	KP4WI	HighBand:	HC1BU		
LowBand:	G3TJW	HighBand:	HC1BU		
LowBand:	W4EV/VP9	HighBand:	YN1RWG		
LowBand:	EA4LH	HighBand:	HC1BU		

S/O AF	S/O AS	S/O EU	S/O NA	S/O OC	S/O SA
GW8DY	JA2JW	I3MAU	KZ5BC	KH6IJ	YV4YC
CR6NO	JA1BRK	CT2BG	HR1RF	KH6IJ	CE6EZ
ZS6DW	JA2IYJ	CT1BH	6J9AA	KH6IJ	4M4AGP
ZS6DW	JA2JW	CT1BH	XE1IIJ	KH6RS(K1GQ)	HC1RF
EL2CB	JH1CJQ	LAØAD	XE1KS	KH6RS(K1GQ)	YV5CVE
ZS6DW	JA1AEA	CT2AT	KP4AST	KH6IJ	HC1TH
ZD8Z([N6TJ)	JA1AEA	I1BAF	KV4FZ	KH6GPQ[K1GQ]	HC1TH
ZS6DW	KA7AB	EA3JE	YS1XEE	KH6IJ	HK3RQ
ZS6DW	KA7AB	DJ6QT	HI8XAL	KH6IJ	HK3RQ
ET3AC	JA1IBX	I1BAF	KP4CKU	VR1Z	HK4KL
ZD8HL	JA1CG	EA4GD	FG7XL	VK2APK	HK3RQ
6O6BW	JA1BRK	DL1KB	KP4AOO	KX6BU	YV5BIG
ET3USN	HL9KH(W9WNV)	EI4KA	XE2CCB	VR30	HC1DC
VQ2AT	KA2MA	OE1RZ	XE1CV	KW6DG	YV5AGD
EL8D	JA1BWA	OE1RZ	KP4AVQ	KW6DG	HC1KA
EL8D	JA3IS	ON4OC	VP2DX	ZL1MQ	VP3HAG
5A5TO	KA2UJ	DJ1BZ	VP9L	KH6IJ	VP3HAG
ZS6UR	KA2RB	F8PI	VP9L	KH6IJ	VP3HAG
ZS5JY	KA2FQ	F8PI	VP9L	KH6IJ	HC2BH
ZS6DW	JA3BB	EA4DL	TG9AD	KH6IJ	HC1ES
EL2X	KA2OJ	CT1SQ	VP7NX	KH6IJ	PJ2AF
ZS6DW	TA3AA(W1VQG)	G2PU	HP3FL	KH6IJ	PJ2AF
ZS6DW	TA3AA	CT1BS	KV4BB	KH6MG	PJ2AA
ZS6DW	JA8AB	I1BDV	VP6SD	KH6IJ	PY2CK
ZS6DW	TA3GVU	I1US	VP6SD	ZL1MQ	HC2OS
ZS6DW	XZ2SY	G2PU	XF1A(XE1A)	KH6IJ	CE2CC
ZS6DW	JA3AA	G2PU	KP4ES	KH6IJ	HC1KP
EL5A	J3GNX	G2PU	XF1A(XE1A)	KG6AW/VK9	PY2AC
ZS6DW	J3GNX	G2PU	XE1A	KH6IJ	OA4M
OQ5AB	XU8AM	——	K4FKC	K6PLZ	LU5AN
ZS6DW	J3FZ	GM6RG	VP7NS	——	——
ZS6DW	J2MI	G6LK	K4SA	VK2IQ	LU9BV
ZU6P	XU8HW	G6LK	XE2N(XE1A)	K6MVV	LU9BV

Footnote#1937-Original ARRL DX Phone Competition Rules: March 20-28, 1937. 90 hours of operation MAXIMUM. Exchange RS(T) and a message number.

Footnote#1934-A gap was discovered in *QST* 1934 September Issue containing the final score listings of the Sixth International Relay Competition Results. The lapse begins after the score of EUROPEAN, AUSTRIA, OE1ER through to NORTH AMERICAN, MEXICO, X1BC. Missing results were taken from the write-up.

Footnote#ZY-The Hiram Percy Maxim 60th Birthday Relay. Planning for this event actually began during late 1927, early 1928 when the ARRL Board of Directors decided to celebrate H.P.M.'s 60th birthday with a Birthday Relay. This was put on hold when it was discovered that H.P.M. would not be 60 years old until September 2, 1929 ! The Birthday Relay was put on hold and kept secret for over a year ! The event began August 31, a Saturday, at 6 P.M. EST until Monday, September 2nd at 6 P.M.. EST. During August of 1929, relay announcements were mailed to ARRL Official Relay Stations, Affiliated Clubs, Section Comm. Managers, and Route Managers throughout the U.S. and Canada. During the ten days prior to the Birthday Relay, ARRL Official Broadcast Stations were broadcasting the details of the event. (Luckily, H.P.M. never tuned in!) H.Q. station W1MK was manned by F. Edward Handy, R.P. and E.V. for the full 48 Hrs! They received 356 messages on 3575kcs and 7150kcs. The first station worked had one message for H.P.M. The second station to contact W1MK had 10 messages for H.P.M.!! One station actually transmitted 40 messages to W1MK! It was reported that "hardly two messages had the same wording."

Footnote#ZZ-The 1928 International Relay Party results were reported in August 1928 *QST* by Louis R Huber. Prizes were offered and were listed in Feb 1928 *QST* as well as late additions in August 1928 *QST*. In the write-up it's called "The International Relay CONTEST of 1928." (Possibly the FIRST reference of radio competition as a CONTEST.) DQs included: 1BW, 5KC, 1ALR, 2AVB, 2BFQ, 3AFW, 4EC, 9DPW and 9AMN. The winner was proclaimed to be 1ASR with 305 points. But British station 5BY had 573 points, Belgian 4AU had 486 points, from Puerto Rico, 4SA had 405 points , followed by Australian 7CW at 369 points and New Zealander 3AR at 328. The USA Top Ten: 1ASR-305, 2ALU-295, 2TP-259, 8GZ-253, 1CMP-241, 4FU-223, 9DNG-213, 1BHS-209, 5WZ-202, 8AHC-201. 6AM[W6AM] had 156 points and placed 15th.

ARRL DX COMPETITION PHONE USA WINNERS BY YEAR/CATEGORY.

YEAR	Single-Op	Low Power	QRP	Asst	M/S	M2	M/M
1993	K1DG	N8II	AA2U	N4RJ(KM9P)	K8AZ	K1AR	N2RM
1992	KM1H(KQ2M)	W1PH	AA2U	NZ7E(KI3V)	NQ4I	N2NT	W3LPL
1991	WM5G(KRØY)	K7RI	K5RX	K1AR	W3BGN	K2TR	W3LPL
1990	K1RU	W1PH	N4KG	WM5G(KRØY)	W3BGN	K2TR	W3LPL
1989	K3TUP(K3LR)	W2HPF	KR2Q	*#2*	AA1K	KC1F	W3LPL
1988	K3TUP(K3LR)	W2TZ	N6OJ		W3BGN	K2TR	W3LPL
1987	K1AR	W2TZ	K3WS		K3TUP	K5RX	KX4S
1986	K1KI	VE1NG	K3WS		K3TUP	KX4S	W3LPL
1985	K1RX	VE1NG	W8VSK		K4VX/Ø	K2TR	W3LPL
1984	W1ZM	WA4PFN/2	K4JRB		K2BU	K2TR	KN3O
1983	AI6V(N6KT)	W2TZ	WB4BBH		W3BGN	W4QAW	N2AA
1982	W1ZM(K1ZM)	K1JX	KA1VQ		K1OX	*#4*	W3LPL
1981	K1VTM(K1JX)	W2TZ	N2AA		KØRF		W2PV
1980	K1VTM	VO2CW	VE3KKB		K4VX		N2AA
1979	K1PR	KB9ET	*#Q*		K5JA		W2PV
1978	W1ZM(K1ZM)	WB2SJG[KQ2M]			W1ZA		W2PV
1977	W2HMH[K2BU]	WA1SSH[W1NG]			W5TMN[K5JA]		W7RM
1976	W6HX	WA1SSH[W1NG]			WA1KID[W6XR]		AC2PV
1975	W3WJD[N3RS]	WA1SSH[W1NG]			W6ONV		W2PV
1975	***1975***						
1974	W6OAT	WA1SSH[W1NG]			WA1NRV		W3AU
1973	W7RM(K7VPF)	W4WRY			W1FBY[W1XT]		W3AU
1972	W7RM(K7VPF)	W8ECA			W4FDA		W3AU
1971	WA3HGV	WAØYAW			W5RER		W3AU
1970	W6RR	WA1DJG[K1CC]			W3ZKH/3[N4RV]		*#MM*
1969	W6RR	WA1DJG[K1CC]			W3MSK[W3AU]		
1968	K1DIR	WA1DJG[K1CC]			W3ZKH/3[N4RV]		
1967	K8DOC	W8ECA			W3MSK[W3AU]		
1966	WA4PXP	W8LXU			W3MSK[W3AU]		
1965	W4KFC	WA5ALB			W3MSK[W3AU]		
1964	K2HLB	WA2OOO			W3MSK[W3AU]		
1963	K5MDX	K9ECE			W3MSK[W3AU]		
1962	K2GXI	**#1963**			W3MSK[W3AU]		
1961	K2GXI				W1ETF		
1960	W1ONK				W8NWO		
1959	W3DHM				W3ECR		
1958	W8BKP				W3AOH		
1957	W2ATE				W3DHM		
1956	W2SKE/2				W6AM		
1955	W1ATE				W2SAI		
1954	W1ATE				W2SAI		
1953	W4ESK[W7RM]				W3LVF		
1952	W4ESK[W7RM]				W3BES		
1951	W4DCQ				W6AM		
1950	W1ATE				W1QDE		
1949	W2SAI				WØUQV		
1948	W2AFQ				W3BES		
1947	W2SAI				W5MLX		
1940	W6OCH				——		
1939	W3EMM				W4YC		
1938	W3EMM				W6GRL		
1937	W9ARA				W9PV		

Although phone was in use long before 1937 and phone use in Sweepstakes was reported as early as 1932, the ARRL DX Competition did not report any phone work until the 1937 event, when March 6-14,1937 was for CW and March 20-28 was for phone.

Footnote#1-There has not been a DX Low Power Top Ten Box or Plaque/Trophy.

Footnote#2-Single Operator Assisted added for 1990 event. Single operator with Packet, with only ONE H.F. signal at a time. No 10 minute rule.

Footnote#3-Changed format of event from 96 Hours during two weekends for each mode (Total of 192 hours) to 48 hours for one weekend for each mode (Total of 96 hours) beginning with the 1979 event.

Footnote#4-Added the Multi-Operator-TWO Transmitter class to the 1983 event. Each TX permitted only one signal and each must observe the 10 minute rule.

Footnote#Q-Added the QRPp Single Operator Class to the 1980 Event.

Footnote#1980-DX-to DX QSOs were permitted in the 1980 event as an experiments. This was rescinded for 1981, reverting back to the previous form: "The world working the U.S." *(Ed.—Things were chaotic that next year too!)*

Footnote#1975-Added the Hi-Band and Lo-Band Single Operator Categories. These categories were only active from 1975-1979.

Footnote#MM-Added the Multi-Operator Single-Transmitter Class beginning with the 1971 event.

Footnote#1963-Added the Low Power Single Operator Class.

Footnote#1947- A stack of DX Phone logs was "lost, strayed or stolen". No awards will be issued until the affected amateurs have had a chance to resubmit copies of their 1947 DX Contest logs. Deadline was Feb 1,1948. Only 75 DX scores were included in the Nov 1947 Write-up. In the Nov 1948 issue of QST, after the final results of the 1948 DX contest, was an Addendum to the 1947 DX Contest. Resubmissions arrived from: OQ5AR, VQ4ERR, J3GNX, F8SI, G2PU, D4AEP, LA6J, LA7Y, GM8MN, TG9RC, ZL1MQ, LU5CK, PY2CK, PY2AJ, CE3AG, CE1AU.

160	80	40	20	15	10
WB9Z	WE3C	K1UO	K5MR	WØUN(WØUA)	K4XS
K1ZM	K1UO	KC7EM	KK9A	K2SS/1	WØUN(WØUA)
K1ZM	K8UR/1	WOØG	KS1L	W7WA	N1GLG
K1ZM	KA1XN	K4XS	WØZV	W7WA	K3ZJ
K1ZM	K4HJJ	KVØQ	AI7B	W7EJ	K4XS
WA4SVO	N2NT	K6NA	KS1L	K4XS(WC4E)	K5UR
K5UR	W5WMU	W6AQ(WA6OTU)	VO1SA	K6SVL	KE5FI
K1ZM	K2EK	NZ5I	K2VV	K3RV	K4JRB
K1ZM	WØMJ	KM6B	KS8S(KU8E)	W5XZ	WA3EEE
VE1YX	W1FC	K8NN/9	K1UO	WØZV	WA6DBC
VE1YX	KR2N	N6BV	N2PP	WØZV	WA6DBC
WA2SPL	K1PT	N5JJ	K1KI	W7RM(W7WA)	WØZV
W8LRL	W1CF(K8UR)	K7UR	K3KG	K7RI(W7WA)	K1UO
W4PZV	WA4SVO	WA7ZLC(N4EA)	K9DX	N7XX(WA1KKM)	VE6WQ
Low Band:	W1FC	High Band:	K9DX		
Low Band:	K3ZO	High Band:	N2LT		
Low Band:	K4YFQ[N4WW]	High Band:	N4MM		
Low Band:	WA8ZDF	High Band:	WB6PXP[AE6E]		
Low Band:	WA8ZDF	High Band:	K6SVL		

Footnote#1937-Original ARRL DX Phone Competition Rules: March 20-28, 1937. 90 hours of operation MAXIMUM. Exchange RS(T) and a message number.

Footnote#1934-A gap was discovered in *QST* 1934 September Issue containing the final score listings of the Sixth International Relay Competition Results. The lapse begins after the score of EUROPEAN, AUSTRIA, OE1ER through to NORTH AMERICAN, MEXICO, X1BC. Missing results were taken from the write-up.

Footnote#ZY-The Hiram Percy Maxim 60th Birthday Relay. Planning for this event actually began during late 1927, early 1928 when the ARRL Board of Directors decided to celebrate H.P.M.'s 60th birthday with a Birthday Relay. This was put on hold when it was discovered that H.P.M. would not be 60 years old until September 2, 1929 ! The Birthday Relay was put on hold and kept secret for over a year ! The event began August 31, a Saturday, at 6 P.M. EST until Monday, September 2nd at 6 P.M.. EST. During August of 1929, relay announcements were mailed to ARRL Official Relay Stations, Affiliated Clubs, Section Comm. Managers, and Route Managers throughout the U.S. and Canada. During the ten days prior to the Birthday Relay, ARRL Official Broadcast Stations were broadcasting the details of the event. (Luckily, H.P.M. never tuned in!) H.Q. station W1MK was manned by F. Edward Handy, R.P. and E.V. for the full 48 Hrs! They received 356 messages on 3575kcs and 7150kcs. The first station worked had one message for H.P.M. The second station to contact W1MK had 10 messages for H.P.M.!! One station actually transmitted 40 messages to W1MK! It was reported that "hardly two messages had the same wording."

Footnote#ZZ-The 1928 International Relay Party results were reported in August 1928 *QST* by Louis R Huber. Prizes were offered and were listed in Feb 1928 *QST* as well as late additions in August 1928 *QST*. In the write-up it's called "The International Relay CONTEST of 1928." (Possibly the FIRST reference of radio competition as a CONTEST.) DQs included: 1BW, 5KC, 1ALR, 2AVB, 2BFQ, 3AFW, 4EC, 9DPW and 9AMN. The winner was proclaimed to be 1ASR with 305 points. But British station 5BY had 573 points, Belgian 4AU had 486 points, from Puerto Rico, 4SA had 405 points , followed by Australian 7CW at 369 points and New Zealander 3AR at 328. The USA Top Ten: 1ASR-305, 2ALU-295, 2TP-259, 8GZ-253, 1CMP-241, 4FU-223, 9DNG-213, 1BHS-209, 5WZ-202, 8AHC-201. 6AM[W6AM] had 156 points and placed 15th.

ARRL DX CONTEST

Continental CW Records

Continent	Call	Year	Score
Single-Op All-Band (NoPacket)			
AF	EA8EA(OH2MM)	93	4,730,226
AS	JA7FWR	89	1,748,682
EU	CR7M(CT1BOH)	93	3,468,867
NA	VP5F(KRØY)	93	6,489,216
OC	NH6T(WØZZ)	92	3,119,364
SA	P4ØGD(W2GD)	88	6,031,005
Single-Op QRP (NoPacket)			
AF	EA8BIE	87	72,891
AS	JA9RPU	92	231,840
EU	G4BUE	92	513,240
NA	NP4Z	88	1,480,290
OC	K7SS/KH6	90	1,394,271
SA	YV3AGT	86	769,986
Single-Op Low Power			
AF	EA8/DL2HBX	93	2,189,796
AS	JR7OMD/2	93	577,404
EU	TM5GG(F6FGZ)	93	1,188,414
NA	TE5T(TI4SU)	93	1,785,240
OC	VK2APK	93	1,074,708
SA	PY2OU	93	496,353
S/O - 28 MHz			
AF	ZD8LII(GØLII)	93	378,000
AS	JHØKHR	89	215,655
EU	FFØXX(FB1MUX)	92	281,961
NA	N6OP/NP2	90	380,475
OC	VE7QO/AH6	89	247,800
SA	HC2G	89	306,900
S/O-21 MHz			
AF	ZD8LII(GØLII)	91	255,303
AS	7L1GVE(JAØJCJ)	91	217,674
EU	TF3YH	81	317,520
NA	VP5U(N4MO)	93	320,208
OC	KG6DX	89	187,587
SA	PY5ZBA	88	312,852
S/O-14 MHz			
AF	EA8QE	83	135,099
AS	RZ9UA	92	254,520
EU	OG1AA	92	315,945
NA	AI6V/VP9	89	342,684
OC	K7SS/KH6	85	258,042
SA	LU8DQ	86	293,538
S/O-7 MHz			
AF	EA9EU	82	113,679
AS	JAØJHA	89	108,528
EU	ON4UN	92	221,613
NA	KP4FI	86	353,115
OC	T32AF(KH6UR)	93	227,244
SA	4M7QP	83	223,776
S/O-3.5 MHz			
AF	EA8RL	84	129,426
AS	JA3YKC	90	36,972
EU	CU2AK	91	111,456
NA	K8WW/VP9	88	184,800
OC	W7AW/KH6	88	26,532
SA	YV1OB	93	114,348
S/O-1.8MHz			
AF	No Entry		
AS	JA1GTF	84	3,024
EU	CT1AOZ	88	34,440
NA	K8WW/VP9	86	87,363
OC	K9VV/KH6	93	8,064
SA	YV1OB	88	66,144
Single Op. WITH Packet (Since1990)			
AF	No Entry		
AS	JJ3YBB(JI3ERV)	92	1,229,256
EU	HG3DXC(HA4XT)	91	1,934,640
NA	HI8A(JA5DQH)	91	3,718,728
OC	No Entry		
SA	No Entry		
Multi-Op Single Transmitter			
AF	EA4KR/EA8	93	3,270,939
AS	JA7YAA	81	2,729,124
EU	UX1A	92	4,422,888
NA	ZF2KE	90	5,980,590
OC	NH6T	93	4,633,263
SA	PJ9J	88	5,521,473
Multi-Op Two Transmitter			
AF	5H3XX	93	598,764
AS	JA8YBY	91	2,374,392
EU	UZ2FWA	92	4,097,184
NA	HH2B	83	6,668,004
OC	ZL3GQ	93	3,524,148
SA	HK3MAE	89	155,868
Multi-Op Multi-Transmitter			
AF	No Entry		
AS	JA8YBY	89	2,484,720
EU	9A1A	93	4,057,371
NA	XE2FU	83	8,064,153
OC	KH6XX	86	4,275,177
SA	No Entry		

ARRL DX CONTEST

U.S.A./Canada CW Records

Section	Call	Year	Score
Single-Op All-Band (No Packet)			
W1	KM1H(KQ2M)	91	4,001,790
W2	K1ZM	92	3,736,665
W3	K3TUP(K5ZD)	91	3,632,820
W4	N4RJ(KM9P)	89	2,591,730
W5	WM5G(KRØY)	92	3,954,411
W6	N6TV	91	1,694,628
W7	WA7NIN(N6TV)	92	2,415,969
W8	KW8N(WD8IXE)	92	2,919,168
W9	W9RE	91	2,737,788
WØ	KØRF(WØUA)	91	3,047,154
VE	VE3EJ	93	2,351,700
Single-Op Low Power (NoPacket) Since 1983			
W1	W1PH	91	1,631,817
W2	KZ2S	89	1,464,120
W3	W3UJ	91	732,450
W4	KM9P/4	91	1,826,181
W5	N5AW	89	1,080,108
W6	W6JTI	89	897,408
W7	W7YAQ	89	905,360
W8	N8II	84	981,360
W9	K9QVB	91	1,008,267
WØ	K3GWA	92	472,320
VE	VO1MP	89	1,601,538
Single-Op QRP<5 W (NoPacket)			
W1	KN1M	91	579,852
W2	AA2U	92	836,964
W3	W3EWL	91	496,701
W4	N4KG	91	685,482
W5	K5RX	91	659,178
W6	W6JTI	91	325,740

W7	NØAX	92	543,585
W8	W8VSK	89	389,340
W9	KS9U	89	227,835
WØ	WØUO	91	589,344
VE	VE1NH	89	124,146

S/O-28 MHz

W1	K1XA	92	487,740
W2	N2KW	89	196,056
W3	KA3SIO	89	305,025
W4	K4XS(WC4E)	92	470,250
W5	WM5G(KRØY)	91	423,000
W6	W6YA	89	286,794
W7	W7WA	89	294,570
W8	N8DCJ	89	422,718
W9	K9QVB	92	312,708
WØ	WØUN(WØUA)	92	539,235
VE	VC4VV	92	216,384

S/O-21 MHz

W1	K1TO	89	504,495
W2	K2VV	89	557,235
W3	KE3Q	89	510,600
W4	K3RV/4	88	682,362
W5	W5WMU	92	404,040
W6	WN4KKN/6	91	389,367
W7	K6LL/7	91	375,768
W8	KW8N	88	509,878
W9	K9QVB	81	241,230
WØ	K4VX/Ø(WOØG)	91	478,332
VE	VE7SZ(WA6VEF)	91	375,900

S/O-14 MHz

W1	K1TO	92	609,504
W2	N2AA	89	600,696
W3	KE3Q	91	365,400
W4	KT3Y	93	495,405
W5	K5MR	92	450,780
W6	NI6W	89	365,904
W7	WA7RKJ	89	302,160
W8	W8TA	81	339,810
W9	K9QVB	89	281,340
WØ	K4VX/Ø(W9WI)	90	335,400
VE	VO1QU	88	270,354

S/O-7 MHz

W1	K8PO	92	339,660
W2	K1ZM/2	91	401,472
W3	W3GH	93	193,617
W4	K4JPD	92	320,985
W5	K5GW	91	259,515
W6	W6XX	93	307,146
W7	K7QQ	93	205,884
W8	K8LX	92	178,533
W9	WB9Z	89	165,438
WØ	WOØG[WX3N]	90	229,890
VE	VE2FU	89	172,992

S/O-3.5 MHz

W1	W1FV	93	172,326
W2	K2EK	90	123,360
W3	WE3C	93	95,064
W4	N4ZC	87	112,860
W5	K5UR	81	34,953
W6	W6RJ	88	70,584
W7	KC7EM	90	33,276
W8	K7EG	91	93,507
W9	WB9Z	90	32,712
WØ	WØZV	90	48,675
VE	VE1AXT	81	14,784

S/O-1.8 MHz

W1	W1RR	85	25,020
W2	K1ZM/2	88	21,960
W3	AA1K/3	85	22,134
W4	N4IN	88	15,741
W5	K5UR	85	19,902
W6	K6DDO	86	4,392
W7	N6TR/7	86	2,054
W8	W8LRL	83	6,300
W9	WB9Z	93	7,371
WØ	WØZV	85	13,818
VE	VE3DO	91	7,437

Single Operator WITH Packet

W1	AA2Z	92	2,885,325
W2	WB2Q	92	4,604,574
W3	K3WW	92	4,158,168
W4	N4RJ(KM9P)	92	4,421,520
W5	N5GM	90	708,624
W6	N6ZZ	93	925,344
W7	NZ7E(KI3V)	92	2,845,248
W8	WR3G/8	92	2,842,800
W9	KK9V	91	1,720,950
WØ	NØAT	91	1,580,796
VE	NoEntry		

Multi-Op Single Transmitter

W1	K1VR	92	3,678,096
W2	WW2Y	92	3,284,310
W3	K3LR	93	3,906,720
W4	N4RJ	93	3,389,463
W5	K5RC	81	3,142,191
W6	W6QHS	91	2,517,318
W7	N7NG	89	1,745,100
W8	K8CC	92	2,903,040
W9	NA9J	89	1,810,215
WØ	KØRF	89	2,600,631
VE	VE6OU[VE3EJ]	81	1,462,500

Multi-Op Two Transmitter

W1	K1AR	92	8,295,039
W2	N2NT	93	6,968,592
W3	N3RS	91	7,145,100
W4	N4AR	92	5,051,811
W5	WM5G	89	4,831,083
W6	N6RO	89	4,561,716
W7	KO7N	89	3,249,900
W8	K8AZ	91	6,114,051
W9	WØAIH/9	83	738,204
WØ	K4VX/Ø	89	5,496,942
VE	VE1CR	83	43,281

Multi-Op Multi-Transmitter

W1	K1ST	91	9,939,822
W2	N2RM	92	10,756,002
W3	W3LPL	92	10,555,032
W4	W4BVV	79	5,778,663
W5	NR5M	89	7,370,745
W6	N6RO	90	4,516,740
W7	W7FU	79	4,115,286
W8	K8CC	93	5,037,210
W9	WØAIH/9	92	7,433,289
WØ	K4VX/Ø	93	5,710,944
VE	No Entry		

Club Score	FRC	92	202,360,257

ARRL DX CONTEST

Continental PHONE Records

Continent	Call	Year	Score
Single-Op All-Band (NoPacket)			
AF	EA4KR/EA8	93	4,643,001
AS	JH7DNO	92	2,125,416

EU	Y24UK	92	3,310,704
NA	TI1C(N6KT)	92	9,619,584
OC	KH6/WR6R	93	5,329,242
SA	HC8A(N6KT)	88	10,114,020
Single-Op QRP (NoPacket)			
AF	A22AA	89	39,600
AS	JA2JSF	91	131,670
EU	GØPAM(G4BUE)	92	335,943
NA	TG9GI	88	1,169,280
OC	V7A(V73C)	93	2,016,333
SA	4M1G	93	1,223,388
S/O-28MHz			
AF	ZD8LII(GØLII)	93	516,309
AS	JAØJHA	90	376,362
EU	CT1BOP	91	583,965
NA	AL7CQ	92	586,401
OC	WR6R/KH6	89	469,104
SA	P4ØT(KB2HZ)	89	887,301
S/O-21MHz			
AF	EA9UK	92	342,084
AS	7L1GVE	92	386,460
EU	IØWDX	82	495,432
NA	NP4CC	89	606,879
OC	AH6GQ	88	433,608
SA	PT9ZZ	88	637,188
S/O-14MHz			
AF	TR8SA	88	208,620
AS	RZ9UA	93	276,834
EU	IR4T(I4UFH)	92	567,180
NA	KK9A/VP2V	86	614,916
OC	T32AF(KB2HZ)	89	420,831
SA	HC1HC	88	486,330
S/O-7MHz			
AF	EA1AK/EA8	93	87,840
AS	JA2BAY	92	99,372
EU	OT3T(ON4WW)	93	240,096
NA	ZF2ND	93	365,859
OC	T32AF(KH6UR)	84	201,135
SA	9Y4AA(N6TJ)	86	364,008
S/O-3.5MHz			
AF	CQ3B(CT3EE)	93	67,680
AS	JH1HGC	92	19,200
EU	CT2CB	84	145,530
NA	KK9A/PJ7	84	403,389
OC	T32AF	90	141,075
SA	4M3X	93	170,316
S/O-1.8MHz			
AF	NoEntry		
AS	NoEntry		
EU	CT1AOZ	88	34,515
NA	4U1UN(K2GM)	88	191,352
OC	AH6BK	83	13,392
SA	YV2IF	88	61,308
Single Operator WITH Packet			
AF	NoEntry		
AS	JJ3YBB(JI3ERV)	92	1,229,256
EU	EA3NY	92	2,449,842
NA	HI8A(JA5DQH)	91	3,983,175
OC	NoEntry		
SA	PYØFM(PY5CC)	93	4,644,252
Multi-Op SingleTransmitter			
AF	EL9A	81	2,694,435
AS	JA8YBY	92	2,122,926
EU	TM5C	92	5,469,690
NA	VP2E	90	9,764,490
OC	KH6XX	82	4,834,392
SA	PJØB	90	8,692,464
Multi-Op TwoTransmitter			
AF	CT3M	92	3,120,351
AS	JA8YBY	90	2,283,147
EU	UZ2FWA	92	5,664,375
NA	6D2X	93	14,466,708
OC	K6GSS/KH6	90	4,481,583
SA	PJØB	85	6,936,393
Multi-Op Multi-Transmitter			
AF	EA9IE	81	86,838
AS	JE2YRD	91	3,173,904
EU	I3MAU	91	6,092,406
NA	K1CO/PJ7	79	11,547,432
OC	KH6XX	86	6,062,463
SA	PP4Y	93	2,424,744

ARRL DX CONTEST

U.S.A./Canada Phone Records

Area	Call	Year	Score
Single-Op All-Band (No Packet)			
W1	KM1H(KQ2M)	92	4,932,396
W2	N2LT	93	3,238,497
W3	K3OO	92	3,868,368
W4	K4XS	92	3,914,295
W5	WM5G(KRØY)	91	4,628,835
W6	AI6V	83	1,998,975
W7	N7TT	90	1,718,556
W8	NA8V	90	3,332,220
W9	W9RE	92	3,600,030
WØ	KØRF(WØUA)	91	2,721,510
VE	VE3EJ(K5ZD)	92	4,496,832
S-Op. Low Power (No Packet)			
W1	W1PH	92	1,596,456
W2	W2TZ	93	1,055,610
W3	KQ3V	92	1,115,400
W4	KM9P/4	90	751,308
W5	K5RX	92	1,351,920
W6	K6SIK	89	729,195
W7	K7RI	91	1,716,075
W8	N8II	93	1,375,998
W9	KS9B(KB9BIB)	93	795,108
WØ	WD5COV/Ø	91	830,532
VE	VE3RM	93	1,156,680
Single-Op QRP<5 W (No Packet)			
W1	KA1VQ	82	457,305
W2	AA2U	92	716,496
W3	W3EWL	91	529,842
W4	N4KG	91	628,056
W5	K5RX	91	653,760
W6	N6OJ	88	135,000
W7	KB7VD	93	168,480
W8	KN8P	82	428,028
W9	N9AW	92	304,704
WØ	WØUO	90	322,599
VE	VE3KKB	81	162,060
S/O-28 MHz			
W1	NX1H	92	816,660
W2	KE2C	82	355,740
W3	K3ZJ	90	726,516
W4	K4XS	89	806,577
W5	W5WMU(KE5FI)	89	587,250
W6	N6TU	91	529,758
W7	AI7B	91	562,590
W8	N8CXX	90	631,158
W9	K9MDO	91	516,186

WØ	WØUN(WØUA)	92	871,125
VE	VE6WQ	80	650,268

S/O-21 MHz

W1	K2SS/1	92	907,200
W2	N2WT	82	584,052
W3	K3LR	82	689,040
W4	K3RV/4	92	866,502
W5	W5WMU(KZ5D)	93	645,795
W6	K3EST/6	92	832,866
W7	W7WA	91	808,860
W8	WB8JBM(N8DCJ)	88	354,594
W9	AI9J	82	500,502
WØ	WØUN(WØUA)	93	879,396
VE	VE7IN	81	491,892

S/O-14 MHz

W1	K1KI	89	656,124
W2	K2VV	86	625,485
W3	K3ZJ	92	526,350
W4	K3KG/4	81	338,742
W5	K5MR	93	359,910
W6	W6QHS	88	262,680
W7	W7WA	87	451,572
W8	WB8JBM(N8DCJ)	87	490,776
W9	KK9A	92	657,951
WØ	WØZV	90	544,236
VE	VO1SA	87	643,560

S/O-7 MHz

W1	K1UO	93	147,882
W2	KM2P	90	85,779
W3	W3GH	93	117,030
W4	K4XS	90	129,774
W5	W5KFT	93	114,750
W6	K6NA	88	124,806
W7	KC7EM	92	145,314
W8	W8JGU	93	42,864
W9	WB9Z	91	106,677
WØ	WOØG[WX3N]	91	117,096
VE	VE7WJ	80	55,266

S/O-3.5 MHz

W1	K8UR/1	91	66,960
W2	N2NT	88	78,210
W3	WE3C	93	73,125
W4	WX4G	85	50,076
W5	WØMJ/5	85	78,039
W6	W6RJ	93	62,016
W7	WB7EWC	92	7,296
W8	KW8N	88	72,420
W9	KS9K	87	14,841
WØ	KMØJ	93	27,450
VE	VE3POS	93	16,362

S/O-1.8 MHz

W1	W1RR	85	11,376
W2	K1ZM/2	85	11,592
W3	AA1K/3	84	5,832
W4	WA4SVO	88	17,658
W5	K5UR	87	14,310
W6	N6LL(WA6CDR)	88	1,176
W7	K7IDX	87	3,000
W8	N8ATR	87	3,600
W9	WB9HAD[WB9Z]	87	12,126
WØ	WØZV	87	4,896
VE	VE1YX	84	12,696

S/O WITH Packet [Since 1990]

W1	K1AR	90	3,831,828
W2	W2GD	91	2,315,640
W3	K3WW	93	3,415,464
W4	N4RJ(KM9P)	93	4,534,068
W5	WM5G(KRØY)	90	3,902,892
W6	N3AHA	93	2,052,648
W7	NZ7E(KI3V)	92	4,050,954
W8	WB3KKX[WR3G]	91	2,678,775
W9	KK9V	91	2,147,769
WØ	KØSCM	91	1,091,664
VE	VE3VET	91	434,808

Multi-Op Single Transmitter

W1	K1RU	91	4,237,038
W2	N2RM	91	4,505,814
W3	W3BGN	91	4,768,248
W4	NQ4I	92	4,412,880
W5	K5GA	81	3,758,637
W6	N6RO	90	2,590,199
W7	K7SP	81	2,537,115
W8	K8AZ	93	4,130,820
W9	KS9K	93	3,779,787
WØ	KØRF	81	3,878,175
VE	VE7ON	91	2,487,024

Multi-Op TwoTransmitter

W1	K1AR	93	9,851,358
W2	N2NT	92	8,668,605
W3	N3RS	92	8,496,798
W4	W4QAW	84	4,332,076
W5	N5AU	89	5,354,538
W6	N6RO	89	4,696,314
W7	NI7T	92	3,695,760
W8	K8CC	92	4,346,424
W9	KS9K	92	6,914,916
WØ	AA6TT/Ø	92	7,665,075
VE	VG3GCB	92	708,867

Multi-Op Multi-Transmitter

W1	KY1H	91	9,657,606
W2	N2RM	93	13,024,950
W3	W3LPL	92	12,412,320
W4	W4MYA	92	7,327,704
W5	N5AU	92	9,329,688
W6	N6RO	82	5,250,015
W7	NK7U	93	4,522,425
W8	K8CC	91	6,780,972
W9	WØAIH/9	92	7,133,049
WØ	KØRF	79	4,033,155
VE	No Entry		

Club	Frankford Radio Club 1992	202,360,257

ARRL DX CW, USA WINNERS

Single-Operator 1928–1992

KM1H(KQ2M op)	4
W3LPL	4
K1AR	3
W3ECR(W3MFW)	3
W3LOE	3
W4KFC	3
K1DIR	2
K1GQ	2
W2GWE	2
W2UK	2
W2SAI(W3BES op)[W3GM]	2

Each of the following have achieved one win:

1ASF, W1BGD/2[W1RM], W1BPW[W1UU], K1NOL[K1NA], K1PR, K1ZM, K1ZND[K1ZZ], K2HLB, N2LT, W2PV(N2NT op), W3CHE, W3CTJ, W3DGM/3, W3GRF, W3GRF(KØDQ op), W3SI, W3ZD, W3ZJ, W4DHZ, W5ENE, WM5G(KRØY op), W6GRL, W7RM, W8BHW, W9WNV/2.

Single Operator Low Power 1964–1992

VO1MP	5	1985–1989
WA1SSH[W1NG]	4	1974-1977
W1PH	3	
N5AW	3	
K1ZND[K1ZZ]	2	
N4HI	2	

Each of the following have achieved one win:
WA1ABW[K1BW], K1JX, K1LPL[W3LPL], K2MFY, W4BRB, W4CRW, K5ABV, N8II, W8QXQ[N8AA], KM9P, VE2NV.

Multi-Operator Single Transmitter 1933–1992

W3MSK[W3AU]	8	
W3BGN	6	4-IN-A-ROW(1989–1992)
WA5LES/K5RC	3	
K1ZND/K1ZZ	2	
W3AOH	2	
W3CTJ	2	
W4BVV	2	
N4WW	2	
W6GRL	2	
W6RW	2	

Each of the following have achieved one win:
WA1NRF[K1PR], W1SZ, W1TX, W2IQG, W2SAI, W2YD, W3BES[W3GM], W3HIL, K3KG, K3LR, W3KT, N3RD, W3TMZ[W3OZ], K3WW, W4CBY, K4VX, W4YC, K6EBB, W6EOG, W6HLN, WA8JUN[K8MD].

Multi-Operator TWO Transmitter 1983–1992

K1AR	4
N3RS	2

Each of the following have achieved one win:
W2REH, K2TR, W3GM, NR5M, K5RC.

Multi-Operator Multi-Transmitter 1971–1992

W3LPL	8	IN-A-ROW! (1985–1991)
W3AU	5	IN-A-ROW! (1971–1975)
W4BVV	2	
N2AA	2	
K2UA	2	
W3WJD/N3RS	2	

Each of the following have achieved one win:
N2RM, KN3O.

USA PHONE WINNERS ARRL DX BY CATEGORY

Single Operator

W1ATE	4
K1VTM	2
W1ZM(K1ZM)	2
K2GXI	2
W2SAI	2
W3EMM	2
K3TUP(K3LR)	2
W4ESK[W7RM]	2
W6RR	2
W7RM[K7JA]	2

Each of the following have achieved one win:
K1AR, K1DIR, K1DG, KM1H(KQ2M op), K1KI, W1ONK, K1PR, K1RU, K1RX, W2AFQ, K2HLB, W2HMH[K2BU], W2SKE/2 W3DHM, WA3HGV, W3WJD[N3RS], W4DCQ, W4KFC, WA4PXP, WM5G(KRØY op), W6HX, W6OAT, W6OCH, AI6V(N6KT op), W8BKP, K8DOC, W9ARE.

Single-Operator Low Power 1964-1992

WA1SSH[W1NG]	4	1974-1977!
W2TZ	4	
WA1DJG[K1CC]	3	1968-1970!
W1PH	3	
W8ECA	2	
VE1NG	2	

Each of the following have achieved one win:
K1JX, W2HPF, WA2OOO, WB2SJG[KQ2M], W4WRY, WA4PFN/2, WA5ALB, K7RI, W8LXU, KB9ET, WAØYAW, VO2CW.

Multi-Operator Single Transmitter 1937-1992

W3MSK[W3AU]	6
W3BGN	4
W2SAI	2
W3BES[W3GM]	2
K3TUP	2
W3ZKH//3[N4RV]	2
K4VX	2
W5TMN/K5JA	2

Each of the following have acheived one win:
W1ETF, W1FBY[W1XT], AA1K, WA1KID[W6XR], WA1NRV, K1OX, W1QDE, W1ZA, K2BU, W3AOH, W3DHM, W3ECR, W3LVF, NQ4I, W4FDA, W4YC, W5MLX, W5RER, W6AM, W6GRL, W6ONV, K8AZ, W8NWO, W9PV, KØRF, WØUQV.

Multi-Operator TWO Transmitter 1983-1992

K2TR	5

Each of the following have achieved one win:
K1AR, KC1F, N2NT, W4QAW, KX4S, K5RX.

Multi-Operator Multi-Transmitter 1971 - 1992

W3LPL	8
W2PV	5
W3AU	4
N2AA	2

Each of the following have one win:
N2RM, KN3O, KX4S, W7RM.

Continental Winners of W.A.E. CW THROUGH 1991

YEAR	SINGLE OPERATOR EU	AF	AS	NA	OC	SA	MULTI-OPERATOR SINGLE TX EU	AF	AS	NA	SA	MULTI MULTI EU	AF	AS	NA	OC	SA
1991	UT4UZ	EA8AB	5B4ADA	K4XS	VK2DXI/9M8	LU1ICX	LY2WW	CN5A	UZ9CWA	N3RS		LY2ZO					
1990	LY2BTA	5H3TW	UA9SA	N6AR	YB2FRR	PX5A	LY2WW	CN2DX	UL8LYA	K4XS	ZW5B						
1989	Y24UK	EA8AB	H27T(YU1RL)	K1EA	ZL3GQ	LU1EWL	LZ9A		UZ9FYR	N5RZ	CE3AYZ						
1988	Y24UK	EA5BS/EA8	P37T(YU1RL)	K1EA	ZL3GQ	OA4ZV	UP1BZZ	EA8RCT	UZ9WWH	N3BNA	PY5ZBA			**MM**			
1987	Y24UK	5L2GA	5B4OA	K1EA	VK2APK	LU8DQ	UP1BZZ	ZS1CT	UZ9WWH	W3GG	CX5AO						
1986	Y24UK	EA8ABR	5B4TI	K1ZM	VK2APK	LU8DQ	DL6FBL	ZS1CT	UZ9WWH	K1IU							
1985	YZ9A		UH8EA	K1ZM	VK2APK	LU8DQ	DL6FBL	EA9CE	RF0FWW	K1AR	CX8BBH						
1984	YU3EY	5Z4MX	UA9SA	W2YV(KQ2M)	VK2APK	LU1EWL	HG5A	VQ9CI	UZ9CWW	KQ3S/8							
1983	YU3EY	ZS1CT	4X6FR	KC1F	VK2APK	LU8DQ	UK2PCR		UK9FER	K1AR	PY2BW						
1982	DK3GI	TU2IE	UF6CR	W1ZM	VK2APK	LU9EIE	UK2BAS		UK9AAN	VE2HQ	PY2BW						
1981	Y24UK	DL2VK/ST3	UM8MAO	K1GQ	VK2APK	LU8DQ	UK2BBB	TU2FZ	UK9FER	W1IHN							
1980	Y24UK	EA8EY	UA9TS	K1VTM(K1JX)	VK3AEW	PY1BOA	UK2BBB		UK7LAH	K3EST							
1979	UB5JGR	C5AJ	4X4VE	K1PR	5W1BZ	PY1BOA	UK2BBB	EA9EO	UK9CAE	N1NA							
1978	DT2TUK	5Z4ZW	UA9ACN	K1GQ	KH6IJ	LU8DQ		UK2PCR		UK6FAA	CG3BMV						
1977	UB5JIM	CT3BQ	UF6VAZ	N3RD	ZL3GQ	PY2BW	UK2BBB		UK9CAE	CY3IXE							
1976	YU3EY	D2AAI	UV9AX	W3LPL[WA3HRV]	ZL3GQ	PJ2VD	UK2BAS		UK9AAN	WA1ABV/1							
1975	G3FXB	C9MIZ	4X4VE	WA1KID[K1ZZ]	KG6JAR	CX9BT	UK2BAS		UK9SAY	K3EST	LU1DZ						
1974	DJ8SW	CR7IZ	UW9WL	K4VX(K4PQL)	9M2CX	LU1DZ	UK3AAO		UK9AAN	W3AU	CX3BH						
1973	DJ8SW	ZS3AK	UA9ACN	WA1ABV[K1RX]	KH6RS[K1GQ]	LU5HFI(K3ZO)	**MS**										
1972	YU3EY		4X4VE	K1JHX[K1RM]													
1971	DJ8SW	TJ1AW	UV9CU	W1BPW[W1UU]													
1970	DL7AV	TJ1AW	UA9WS	W3AU		PJ2VD											
1969	DL7AV	CR6GO	UA9WS	W1BPW[W1UU]													
1968	DJ8SW	CR6GO	EP2BQ	W1BPW[W1UU]													
1967	SM2BJI	CR6CK	UA9WS	WB2CKS[K2LE]													
1966	SM2BJI	CR6GO	4X4HF	WØGTA		CP5EZ											
1965	DJ3KR	CR6AI	UA9DN	W3GRF													
1964	DJ3KR	CN8GB	EP2RC	W2JAE[W5VQ]													
1963	DJ3KR	6O1ND	UA9DN	W2JAE[W5VQ]		HC1DC											
1962	DJ3KR	ZS6IW	UA9DN	WA2WBH		HC1DC											
1961	DJ3KR	5A3TQ	EP2BK	W3GRF													
1960	DJ3KR		UA3DN	K2DGT													
1959	DL1KB	CR6AI	FA9UO	K2DGT		PY1ADA											
1958	DL1KB	CR6AI	4X4KK	W2EQS													
1957	DL1DX			W3GRF		CE3AG											
1956	DL1DX																
1955	OK1FF	CR6AI	4X4FS	W2WZ													

CONTINENTAL WINNERS OF W.A.E. SSB THROUGH 1991

	SINGLE OPERATOR						MULTI-OPERATOR SINGLE TX						MULTI MULTI				
YEAR	EU	AF	AS	NA	OC	SA	EU	AF	AS	NA	OC	SA	EU	AS	NA	OC	SA
1991	Y33UL	FR5DX	UA9CDT	K4XS	YB2FRR	PX5A	LZ9A		5B4ES	N5KEA		YW1A	LY2ZO	JE2YRD	W3FV	DX1DBF	LU1CF
1990	YT9ØA	EA8/DL6FBL	RHØE	KM3T	VK2APK	HC1OT	R6L		UL8LYA	K4XS		ZW5B	LZ9A	JE2YRD			
1989	OK1RI	EA9IE	UA9SN	K1ZM	YB2FRR	PY5EG	Y34K		5B4ES	N5KEA		AY6D	UP1BZZ	UL8LYA	LU1CF		
1988	YT3T	EA9IE	UL7OB	K4YKZ		LU3F	UP1BZZ		UL8LYA	NAØK		YV1AVO					
1987	YU3EO	EA9RM	UL7OB	KM1H	VK2FOC	ZY5EG	Y34K		UL8LYA	8P6AW		YV1AVO					
1986	DK9IP	EA9IE	UW9CO	K1ZM	YB4FW	LU6ETB	LZ2KTS		RL8PYL	WB3JRU		YW1A					
1985	YZ9A	EA9LZ	UH8EA	K1ZM	YB4FW	ZZ5EG	LZ2KTS		RL8PYL	N1AU		YV1TO					
1984	Y23EK	EA9KF	UF6CR	W2YV	VK3EZ	PY5EG	LZ4ØKTS	ZS6TUK	RFØFWW	K6OKW		YV1AVO					
1983	PA2TMS	CT3BM	UA9CKC	KC1F	VK6AJW	ZY5EG	Y34K	ED9EA	N2BZQ/4X	K9MWMØ	VK3FY						
1982	YU3MY	5N8ARY	UF6CR	K1KI	VK6AJW	ZY5EG	Y24UK	EA9IE	UK9AAN	N5AU		PY2BW					
1981	YU3EY	9G1JX	UF6DZ	W1ZM	VK6AJW	PP2ZDD	Y24UK		UK9AAN	K1AR		PY5EG					
1980	I4VEQ	EA8LS	4X4VE	W2YV(N2NT)	VK6AJW	ZZ5EG	UK2BBB		UK7PAL	KØUK		PY1BQK					
1979	DM2DUK	EA8LS	UL7MAR	VP2ML	ZL2ACP	DL2RL/YV6	UK2BBB	3V8ONU	UK9CAE	W1RR		YX1DIG					
1978	G3FXB	9G1JW	UL7EAJ	W1ZM	VK6CT	DL2RL/YV6	YU1BCD		UK6FAF	K2SS		YV1TO					
1977	DK2BI	9G1JX	4Z4MQ	W1ZM(K1ZM)	VK2APK	PJ2FR	YU1BCD	9GØARS	UK9ABA	WA4PYF		YV1AVO					
1976	DK1FW	9G1JX	4Z4MQ	W1ZM[WA2CLQ]	YBØACH	LU8AJG	YU1BCD		UK9AAN	K2IGW		PY1ZBJ					
1975	DK1FW	5L7F	4X4NJ	W1ZM[WA2CLQ]	VK6CT	YV4YC	G3WYX		UK9CAE	WA2MBM		PY1EMM					
1974	DK1FW	EA8CR	UW9AF	WB2OEU[K2TR]	VK4VU	PY4KL	YU1BCD	CR6OZ	4Z4HF	W9YT	9M2CJ	PY1EMM					
1973	DK4TP	EA8CR	UA9BE	WA2BVU	VK4AK	CE8AO	******										
1972	DJ4LK	IH9JT	UW9WR	W3AU	DU1FH												
1971	DJ4LK	9E3USA	JY8BI	WA2BVU													
1970	OH2BH	CR6GA	UW9AF	WB2SQN[K2SS]	DU1FH	CX9CO											
1969	ON8CT	CR6GO	EP2BQ	W3GM													
1968	DJ2YA	CR6FY	OD5BZ		VK2DKZ	PY3BXW											
1967	DJ6QT	7XØAH		W3GRF		PY1CAD											
1966	DJ6QT	5A2TF	OD5BZ	WØGTA													
1965	DJ6QT	EA8CR	OD5BZ	OX3JV													
1964	DJ6QT	EA8CR	VS1LP	W3WJD		OA4KY											
1963	F9RY	5N2JKO	VS9AAA	OX3JV		PZ1CE											
1962	DJ3KR	9G1YL	EP3RO	OX3AI		PY6MP											
1961																	
1960																	
1959																	
1958	DL1KB	VQ4RF	OD5BZ	TI2OE	VK2AOM	CE3HL											
1957	DL1KB																
1956	DL1KB																
1955	OE5CK	VQ4RF		W2SKE	KC6CG	PY2CK											

WAE DX CONTEST

Continental CW Records

Continent	Call	Year	Score
Single-Op All-Band (With Packet)			
AF	ZS1CT	83	1,278,238
AS	P37T (YU1RL)	88	2,142,476
EU	DK3GI	82	1,795,986
NA	K1GQ	81	1,128,330
OC	ZL3GQ	89	595,907
SA	LU1SM (LU8DQ)	90	1,299,060
Multi-Op Single Transmitter			
AF	EA9CE	85	1,526,742
AS	UK9AAN [(UZ9AYA)]	82	1,426,128
EU	UK2BAS [LY2ZZ]	82	2,886,296
NA	K4XS	90	1,151,781
OC	No Entry		
SA	ZW5B	90	1,102,469
Multi-Op Multi-Transmitter			
AF	No Entry		
AS	JE2YRD	89	1,045,384
EU	LY2ZO	91	1,353,604
NA	No Entry		
OC	No Entry		
SA	No Entry		

NOTE: As of 1991 ALL classes may use PacketClusters.

WAE DX CONTEST

Continental Phone Records

Continent	Call	Year	Score
Single-Op All-Band (With Packet)			
AF	EA9IE	86	1,977,872
AS	UF6CR	82	1,568,192
EU	YU3MY	82	2,742,961
NA	KM3T	90	1,711,668
OC	YB2FRR	91	347,095
SA	PY5EG	89	1,371,111
Multi-Op Single Transmitter			
AF	ED9EA	83	1,300,320
AS	RFØFWW	84	2,394,738
EU	Y24UK	82	5,094,720
NA	N4ZC	90	1,348,925
OC	VK3FY	83	59,112
SA	ZW5B	90	1,885,680
Multi-Op Multi-Transmitter			
AF	No Entry		
AS	JE2YRD	90	1,304,807
EU	LZ9A	90	2,524,158
NA	W3FV	91	167,668
OC	DX1DBF	91	87,016
SA	LU1CF	89	96,640

NOTE: As of 1991 all classes may use PacketClusters.

WAE DX CONTEST

U.S.A. Records

Call Area	Call	Year	Score
Single-Op All-Band (No Packet)			
W1	K1GQ	81	1,128,330
W2	W2YV (KQ2M)	84	936,240
W3	K3WW	90	732,096
W4	N6AR/4	90	958,848
W5	K5RC (K5ZD)	81	549,360
W6	N6AR	82	305,492
W7	W7IR	79	272,475
W8	WA8YVR	83	661,912
W9	W9RE	90	486,864
WØ	WØSF	79	229,840
VE	VE1FH	82	422,870
Multi-Op Single Transmitter			
W1	W1IHN	81	669,708
W2	NQ2D	90	1,103,925
W3	N3RS	91	998,034
W4	K4XS	90	1,151,871
W5	N5RZ	89	529,074
W6	N6AV	79	171,990
W7	WA7FAB	90	82,536
W8	W8LU	83	419,680
W9	No Entry		
WØ	NCØP	90	104,520
VE	VE2HQ	82	941,951
Multi-Op Multi-Transmitter			
W1	No Entry		
W2	No Entry		
W3	No Entry		
W4	No Entry		
W5	No Entry		
W6	No Entry		
W7	No Entry		
W8	No Entry		
W9	No Entry		
WØ	No Entry		
VE	No Entry		

NOTE: As of 1991 ALL classes may use PacketClusters.

WAE DX CONTEST

U.S.A. Records

Section	Call	Year	Score
Single-Op All-Band (No Packet)			
W1	KM3T	90	1,711,668
W2	W2YV (N2NT)	80	1,404,480
W3	NM3U	89	465,745
W4	K4XS	91	1,336,929
W5	K5KLA	81	215,912
W6	K6SVL	90	305,500
W7	WA7JYW	81	43,884
W8	AB8K	80	280,388
W9	KBØC/9	90	381,260
WØ	WAØTKJ	79	51,246
VE	VE2DU	79	458,118
Multi-Op Single Transmitter			
W1	W1RR	79	939,214
W2	K1ZM	90	1,025,398
W3	WB3CZK	80	54,696
W4	N4ZC	90	1,348,925
W5	N5KEA	89	450,016
W6	K6OKW	81	140,592
W7	No Entry		
W8	W8CCI	91	125,020
W9	W9UP	91	326,598
WØ	KØUK	80	161,684
VE	No Entry		
Multi-Op Multi-Transmitter			
W1	No Entry		
W2	No Entry		
W3	W3FV	91	167,668
W4	No Entry		
W5	No Entry		
W6	No Entry		
W7	No Entry		
W8	No Entry		
W9	No Entry		
W0	No Entry		
VE	No Entry		

NOTE: As of 1991 ALL classes may use PacketClusters.

CQ WW WPX PHONE DX WINNERS BY YEAR/CATEGORY

YEAR	S/O	QRP	M/S	M/M	160	80	40	20	15	10
1992	HC8A(N6KT)	HI5ØA(JA5DQH)	VP2EC	CT3M	EI7M	CT7N(CT4NH)	EA9LZ	ZV5A(PY5EG)	ZZ9A(PY5CC)	ZW5B(N5FA)
1991	ZW5B(N5FA)	VP2E	P4ØV	ED8ACH	UL7ACI	VA3EJ(VE3EJ)	YV5A(YV5ANF)	H2A(5B4SA)	ZX5C(PY5CC)	ZP5ØY(ZP5JCY)
1990	P4ØV(AI6V)	VP2EXX	LZ9A	YT2A	UL7ACI	CF6OU/3	IO4VEQ	ID1V(I1ZEU)	ZPØY(ZP5JCY)	ZX5C(PY5CC)
1989	KP2A(KW8N)	4X6IF	ZX5C	FKØAW	VP9AD	TI2CC	TE1L(TI2LTA)	CQ1BOP	FG5R(W7EJ)	ZPØY(ZP5JCY)
1988	P4ØV(AI6V)	4X6IF	TXØA	KH6XX	CT1AOZ	VE2ZP	HA9RE	ZZ5EG(PY5ZBA)	ZP5Y(ZP5JCY)	ZY5EG
1987	EA9AM(EA9IE)	TR8SA	PJ2FR	ZZ5EG	OH1RY/CT3	CT3DL	H24LP(5B4LP)	ZP5JCY	CE6EZ	LU1E(LU3AJW)
1986	PJ2FR(N6KT)	K7SS/WH6	NP4CC	KH6XX	LZ2CJ	VE3BMV	NP4A	ZY5EG	ZZ5EG(N5FA)	XQ3D(CE3DPD)
1985	EA9IE	4X6IF	KD7P/NH4	KH6XX	CG3MFA	OH1RY/CT3	CZ3BMV	VP2EC	LU2FDR	LU1E(LU3AJW)
1984	VK2WU	H44R	ZZ5EG	VP2EC	EA9KF	4M3AZC	T32AF	FO8JP	CX7BY	CE6EZ
1983	PJ2FR(N6KT)	G4GIR	VP2EC	YZ1EXY	LZ2RF	IO3MAU	FM7CD	ZY5EG	OHØBH(OH2BH)	CE6EZ
1982	Y24UK	W8ILC	VP2EC	NP4A	VE3BBN	YV3BQS	DJ4PT	KG6DX	AI7B	KB7IJ/KH2
1981	NP4A	N2AA	VP5FRS	KH6XX	VE3MFT	DJ4PT	4M3AZC	4N3ZV	HC9A(HC1MD)	ZZ5EG
1980	PJ2CC(N4RV)	TG9GI	9A1ONU	VE7WJ	VE3JAY	4M3AZC	I5NPH	YX2AMM	HDØE(K7CA)	LU8DQ(LU6EF)
1979	OI1VR	W8ILC	UK9AAN	CK7WJ	VE3BBN	HA9RU	I3MAU	VR3AH	9L1CA	KH6XX
1978	UA9ACN	4T8V	KP4RF	UK9AAN	VE3BBN	YU3DBC	CG3IXE	ON4UN	CG3BMV	CW3BR
1977	UA9BE	-#3-	4J9B	CJ3DCB	VE3BBN	I3MAU	CT4AT(K7ZZ)	OI2BA	PY5EG	N6EE
1976	VP2G(W5MYA)		UK9AAN	4J3A	XJ3FFA	YY4YC	W4BRB/C6A	YV4AGP	YV2AMM	CE6EZ
1975	UW9AF		UK9ADT	VP5B	DL8PC	I3MAU	YV4YC	PJØJR	PT2ZBS	K4HWW
1974	CQ6LF		PJ9JR	CV2T	——	YU4EBL	OH2KI	YU2CDS	CR6OZ	CQ6OR
1973	9Y4VU		PY7BDX	WA3HRV	——	YU3APR	DJ2YA	CQ6LF	XX7IK	CR6OZ
1972	XE1IIJ (KØDG)		W4IZ/KP4	4X4GV	——	OHØAM(OH3XZ)	K6ERT	FLØQQ(F5QQ)	PY2DSE	CR6LF
1971	PX3BXW		G3WYX	4X4NJ	——	4X4DK	WB6KBK	PJ9JR(W3ZKH)	W3AU(K3EST)	LU2DEK
1970	PJ9JR(W3ZKH)		UK9AAN	4Z4HF	——	YV5BTS	YV1BI	KV4FZ	YV1SA	KG6AQY
1969	KV4FZ		PR2CQ	CE6CA	——	LA5KG	G3NLY	PU7APS	VP2MF	PR2AHJ
1968	ET2FMA		KW6EJ	PJ5MM	——	YV5BTS	DJ4AX	JA1AEA	W4BVV	LU1DAB
1967	ZL1KG		I9RB	-#MM-	——	YV5BTS	G3NLY	JA1AEA	YV1LA	LU1DAB
1966	1M4A(W9WNV)		4U1ITU		——	ON4UN	DJ5BV	ET3AC	YV1LA	LU1DAB
1965	DL3LL		I1RB		——	GI3CDF	G3NLY	SM5BLA	4X4TP	HC1EW
1964	DL3LL		9A1ZG		——	GI3CDF	OH2TH	HC2JT	W4RLS	WA4SUR
1963	DL3LL		GB3RAF		——	4X4DK	K2GXI	HL9KH(W9WNV)	KP4BMA	——
1962	4X4DK									
1961	ZS5JY									
1960	CN8JF									
1959	HB9IE									
1958	CN8MM									
1957	CN8MM									

Footnote#1-Changed the maximum allowable operating time for Single Operators from 30 Hours(18 hours off) to 36 Hours (12 hours off) beginning with the 1992 event.

Footnote#2-Added the Single Operator Low Power category beginning with the 1992 event.

Footnote#3-Added a Club Competition in 1978(Phone Only), this would encompass both the Phone and C.W. events in 1979. The 1978 Club Competition Winner was The Western Washington DX Club. Added the S/O QRPp Class in 1978.

Footnote#MM-Added the Multi-Multi Category beginning with the 1968 event.

1994 CQ Amateur Radio Almanac Comment Card

The staff of the CQ Amateur Radio Almanac wants your comments.

1. What section(s) of the Almanac did you find the *most* interesting or useful?

2. What section(s) did you find the *least* interesting or useful?

3. Is there anything missing that you'd like to see us add in future editions? (and do you know where we can get it?)

4. Are there any errors that you'd like to bring to our attention so we can correct them in future editions? (Please provide a source for verification of any errors.)

Thank you for your help!

NAME ______________________________

CALLSIGN ______________________________

STREET ______________________________

CITY ______________ STATE/PROV ______________

ZIP CODE ______________ COUNTRY ______________

Place
Stamp
Here

Managing Editor
CQ Amateur Radio Almanac
76 North Broadway
Hicksville, NY 11801

CQ WW WPX PHONE USA WINNERS BY YEAR/CATEGORY

YEAR	S/O	QRP	M/S	M/M	160	80	40	20	15	10
1992	KM1H(KQ2M)	KR2Q	WC4E	WZ6Z	WT3Q	K1ZM	KC7EM	KK9A	WN4KKN/6	KO4QW
1991	KM1H(KQ2M)	AA2U	WC4E	WZ6Z	AA4MM	KQ3V	KVØQ	K2VV	WN4KKN/6	NX1H
1990	KQ2M	KR2Q	WC4E	WZ6Z	W2GD	KE5FI	WB9Z	KK9A	WB5VZL	
	WN4KKN/5									
1989	KM1H(KQ2M)	N1AFC	WC4E	WZ6Z	WA2IUO	K1ZM	WQ5W	N8BJQ	WB5VZL	WM5G
1988	KM1H(KQ2M)	WC7Q	WC4E	KC3EK	K5UR	NO2I	KVØQ	KM6B	WB5VZL	KY5N
1987	KM1H(KQ2M)	N8CQA	KI6P	N5AU	K5UR	KN8R	KM6B	K2VV	K6SVL	K5MK
1986	N4WW	WB9HRO	KRØY	N5AU	K5UR	KR2J	K5NW	KQ2M	W3BGN	KR9G
1985	KI6P	WD4NBX	KN6M/5	NF5I	K5UR	KQ2M	NI6W	KG1E	N4MM	N4EJV
1984	K2VV	KH6CP/3	N5AU	NG5X	WB3GCG	N7DF/Ø	KI6P(WA6VEF)	WAØTKJ	NA5R	KN5H
1983	K2VV	W8ILC	N5AU	NA8V	W8LRL	KI6P(N6RO)	KR2Q	AI7B	KC2X	
	A5R(K5GN)									
1982	ABØI(WA6DGX)	W8ILC	KJ9W	KN6M	W8LRL	KO6G(N6NE)	N6RO	K8NA	AI7B	
	N5AU(K5ZD)									
1981	N6CW	N2AA	K7RI	AI6V	W8LRL	WB2FZO[KR2N]	KM5X	K8NA	AI7B	
	N4ZC(N5TR)									
1980	K1AR	N2AA	N4WW	K3WW	W8LRL	K5UR	N4KE	K8NA	WA6EKL	
	N2RM(N2ME)									
1979	K7RI	W8ILC	K4VX	K5JA	W8LRL	K8KX	W6AXX/3	N4KE	N7XX	K6SVL
1978	K2SS	W8ILC	K4VX	——	W8LRL	N6VI	WA8LXJ	W3GG	N6CW	K5JA
1977	W3LPL	-#3-	K3RV	N7XX	W8LRL	W1CF(K1OME)	W5TMN[K5JA]	K8YZW	N6CW	N6EE
1976	AA9BWY[W9RE]		AC6YRA	AA4IVL	W8LRL	AC1CF[W1CF]	AC3USS(WA1FEO)		AC3CRE	
	AC4WSF[N4MM]	AB2CST								
1975	W2PV		——	K6BCE/6	WB8APH	W4BVV	K6JAN	K4VX	WA1NZT	K4HWW
1974	W2PV		WA6GLD	W5NOP/5	WB8APH	W7YTN[K7UR]	W6PAA[N6RO]	W3AU(K3EST)	K6SDR[N6CW]	K6SVL
1973	W2PV		W1YK	WA3HRV	——	K9CUY	K6JAN	W3SS	WB6EJV	W3AZD
1972	W5QQQ/7		WA3HRV	WB6GFJ/6	——	K5PFL[K5NA]	K6ERT	W1OKA	W6GFS	WA7PEZ
1971	W2SKE		W6HX	WB6GFJ	WA4PXP	K9CUY	WB6KBK[N6MG]	K7HTZ[K7CW]	W3AU(K3EST)	
	W3JSX[W3FV]									
1970	W5RER		W6HX	W3SS	——	WA3KEG	K6AHV[W6RJ]	WB2SQN[K2SS]	W3AZD	K5MDX
1969	W3MSK[W3AU]		W2SKE	——	——	WA2WMT[KØKE]	W8IHD	W4AXE	W3WJD[N3RS]	K8HYC
1968	W3JNN		W7SFA	——	——	WA5ALB	W5ODJ	K8YBU[K8RK]	W4BVV	WA3IJS
1967	WA2SFP[W2PV]		K6SEN/6	——	——	K8DOC	K2GXI	WA4PXP	W3AZD	K4YYL
1966	WA2SFP[W2PV]		WB2FOV	——	——	W2ZPO	WA4PXP	W3JNN	W2SKE/2	WA4WIP
1965	K2HLB		——	——	——	——	K6AHV	W3JNN	W5LGG	WA4SUR
1964	W6AM		W3MSK[W3AU]	——	——	——	K6AHV[W6RJ]	K2HWL	W4RLS	WA4SUR
1963	W2VCZ			——	——	W5AJY	K2GXI	W1ZFV	W1AOL	——
1962	W1ONK									
1961	W2VCZ									
1960	W2SKE/2									
1959	W2SKE/2									
1958	W9EWC									
1957	UNKNOWN									

Footnote#1-Changed the maximum allowable operating time for Single Operators from 30 Hours(18 hours off) to 36 Hours (12 hours off) beginning with the 1992 event.
Footnote#2-Added the Single Operator Low Power category beginning with the 1992 event.
Footnote#3-Added a Club Competition in 1978(Phone Only), this would encompass both the Phone and C.W. events in 1979. The 1978 Club Competition Winner was The Western Washington DX Club. Added the S/O QRPp Class in 1978.

CQWW WPX CW DX WINNERS BY YEAR/CATEGORY

YEAR	S/O	QRP	M/S	M/M	160	80	40	20	15	10	CLUB-WRLD-USA
1992	ZV5A(YU1RL)	W2GD	LU8DPM	HG73DX	4N2X(4N2LH)	GW8GT	AM9TY	LZ5W(LZ3ZZ)	TU4SR(OH8SR)	ZD8LII	NCCC-YCCC
1991	4M2BYT(YU1RL)	VP2MU(KJ4VH)	4JØQ	HG73DX	YL2GVW	4N1A(YU1EA)	LZ5W(LZ3ZZ)	YW1A(YV1DIS)	ZD8LII	ZS6BCR(ZS6EZ)	NCCC——
1990	ZW5B(OH2MM)	N3RS	YM3KA	HG73DX	OK5TOP	4N1A(YU1EA)	V73AS	PY2RN	4N3E(YT3AM)	YV3A(YV5ANT)	ARAUCARIA-NCCC
1989	V27T(YU1RL)	YU3BC	KP2A	Y34K	OK1DFP	YX3A(YV5ANT)	FS5R(W7EJ)	LZ5A(LZ1AX)	FS5T(AI7B)	CE3DNP	NCCC-NTCC
1988	NH6J/NHØ	4X1IF	RL1P	UP4A	UA2FF	I4AVG	IO4IND	YY5A(YV5ANT)	9Y3VU	ZY5ZBA(PY5CW)	NCCC-PVRC
1987	5L7T(YU1RL)	4X6IF	V31A	UP7A	UA2FF	UA9TS	YX5A(YV5ANT)	YT3AA	ZY4OD	4M7A(YV7QP)	NTCC-NCCC
1986	YU1AO	WP4F	LZ7A	IO3JSS	UB4FWC	CT5AT(K7ZZ)	VP2VCW(N6CW)	WC4E/KP4	ZY4OD	YW7A(YV7QP)	NCCC-YCCC
1985	YZ4GD	4X6IF	LZ2KTS	KH6XX	UP3BP/UF	UP2NK/UF	DF9ZP(DL6FBL)	YX5A(YV5ANT)	YT3L(YU3OH)	YO3KWJ	NCCC-NTCC
1984	UF6CR	NY4D(K4XS)	VP2EC	YZ1EXY	LZ2CJ(LZ2SC)	EA8RL	VE3BMV	KP4BZ(NP4Z)	4N2CQ	OK3LZ	NTCC-TDXS
1983	L8DQ(LU8DQ)	PAØPUR	UK6LAR	YZ1EXY	YU3EF	HA8KQX	I4IND	CY3BMV	KP4EQF	JH7UJU	YU-DX-C.-NTCC
1982	HK3A(K3ZO)	4X4UH	NP4A	YQØA	YU3EF	UA9AJO	OA4AWD	4N3DX	5Z4CS(JE1JKL)	PY1OBA	N.Oh.A.R.S.-NTCC
1981	YT2D	OA8V	UK2PCR	YTØR	YU3EF	4Z4DX	OA4AWD	YU4GD	LU8DQ	KG6DX	YUDXC-FRC
1980	KP2A(N6CW)	N3RS	UZ9A	K3WW	SP5IXI	AN2OP	4Z4DX	4N1U	HDØE	LU8DQ	FraserVal.-PVRC
1979	KG6SW(K7JA)	SMØGMG	4N4Y	HD1A	AE6U	UB5BAT	YT2D	ZW4OD	VE3BMV	JA1PIG/PZ	W.Wash.DXC-PVRC

Footnote#1-Changed the maximum allowable operating time for Single Operators from 30 Hours (18 hours off) to 36 Hours (12 hours off) beginning with the 1992 event.
Footnote#2-Added the Single Operator Low Power category beginning with the 1992 event.
Footnote#3-Added a Club Competition in 1978(Phone Only), this would encompass both the Phone and C.W. events in 1979. The 1978 Club Competition Winner was The Western Washington DX Club. Added the S/O QRPp Class in 1978.

CQWW WPX CW USA WINNER BY YEAR/CATEGORY

YEAR	S/O	QRP	LP	M/S	M/M	160	80	40	20	15	10
1992	KM1H(KQ2M)	W2GD	WR3G(K5ZD)	N4WW	WZ1R	WT3Q	N6SS	W3BGN	K2VV	KA2AEV	WE3C
1991	KM1H(KQ2M)	N3RS	——	N4WW	——	W4VJN	K1ZM	NQ2D	NI8L	NE8T	WE3C
1990	KT3Y	N3RS	——	N4WW	AC6T	K1ZM	——	NQ2D	K1TO	N3GB	K5RX
1989	KT3Y	KA2AEV	——	N4WW	WZ6Z	N6LL	WA6VNR	KVØQ	N2AA	K1XA	N5RZ
1988	KT3Y	W8VSK	——	N4WW	NSØZ	K5NA/2	NA3J	NM2Y/3	K2VV	K6LL/7	WA6FGV
1987	KT3Y	N3RS	——	N4WW	K3TUP	K5UR	N3AD	K1XA	K2VV	N4VZ	NU4Y
1986	K3ZO	W8VSK	——	KRØY	NM5M	WØZV	K5NA/2	KM3T	K2VV	WZ4Z	KE5CV
1985	KC1F	KA2AEV	——	NA5R	NM5M	K5UR	N2AU	N5RZ	N2AA	KA5W	KE5CV
1984	N5AU(N5RZ)	NY4D(K4XS)	——	N4WW	NM5M	KA1SR	KJ9D	N6CW	NA8V	KW8N(WD8LLD)	——
1983	KC1F	N3RS	——	NA5R	K0UK	W8LRL	NE6W	N6QR	N8II	KZ5M	KT4W
1982	KC1F	WD6EWG	——	N4WW	K4CG	W8LRL	N6PE	W6BIP	K5GA	WA6DBC	N4ZC
1981	KC1F	N3RS	——	N4WW	AI6V	W9CG	K5UR	K7RI	N2MM	K6LL/7	N4ZC
1980	K1GQ	N3RS	——	K3EST	K3WW	AE6U	K1MM	N6ND	W5FO	W3MM	K8WW
1979	AE4H	W9PNE	——	K3EST	N9MM	AE6U	K5UR	WA4DRU	K5GA	K1RM	K5RC(K5ZD)

Footnote#1-Changed the maximum allowable operating time for Single Operators from 30 Hours(18 hours off) to 36 Hours(12 hours off) beginning with the 1992 event.
Footnote#2-Added the Single Operator Low Power category for the 1992 event.
Footnote#3-Added a Club Competition in 1978(Phone Only), this would encompass both the Phone and C.W. events in 1979. The 1978 Club Competition Winner was The Western Washington DX Club. Added the S/O QRPp Class in 1978.

CQ WPX CONTEST

Continental Phone Records

Continent	Call	Year	Score
Single-Op All-Band (No Packet)			
AF	EA9AH	92	14,303,300
AS	7Z2AB	92	9,177,296
EU	YZ9A	91	8,518,112
NA	KP2A	90	15,056,886
OC	WR6R/KH6	92	8,394,030
SA	HC8A	92	24,809,300
Single-Op Lo-Power (No Packet) 100-Watt Output (Since 1992)			
AF	EA8BWW	92	3,387,412
AS	JF1SEK	92	2,779,975
EU	Y48PJ	92	1,599,430
NA	KG4DD	92	5,379,660
OC	NH6T	92	3,117,650
SA	8R1JV	92	2,109,970
Single-Op QRP < 5-W (No Packet)			
AF	TR8SA	87	1,041,112
AS	4X6IF	90	997,149
EU	YU2TY	90	770,450
NA	VP2EXX	90	6,727,444
OC	K7SS/WH6	86	2,078,490
SA	PQ2DX	90	4,902,525
S/O 28 MHz			
AF	FR5DX	91	7,543,818
AS	JH1AJT	89	4,848,480
EU	9H1EL	89	5,882,825
NA	J68AX	92	4,709,985
OC	P2ØA	92	5,184,625
SA	ZW5B (N5FA)	92	13,006,917
QRP	NP4CC	90	2,165,940
L.P.	JG1EGG	92	3,276,396
S/O 21 MHz			
AF	TR1G	90	6,788,925
AS	7L1GVE	92	6,848,136
EU	CT2A	92	6,029,559
NA	FG5R (W7EJ)	89	9,936,240
OC	AHØK	92	7,206,850
SA	ZPØY	90	12,070,245
QRP	RW9AB	92	638,392
L.P.	WP4CEL	92	1,497,792
S/O 14 MHz			
AF	TU4BR	86	3,483,480
AS	H2A (5B4SA)	91	6,297,464
EU	LZ5W	92	5,671,509
NA	TI2CC	87	5,491,290
OC	KG6DX	90	4,558,527
SA	ZZ5EG (PY5ZBA)	88	8,219,627
QRP	RV3E/JT1BY	90	675,990
L.P.	BY4BB	92	792,939
S/O 7 MHz			
AF	EA9LZ	92	4,721,924
AS	H24LP (5B4LP)	87	5,348,975
EU	IO4VEQ	90	3,878,928
NA	NP4A	86	6,668,184
OC	T32AF	90	3,345,864
SA	YV5A (YV5ANF)	91	3,460,900
QRP	LZ2QV	86	58,764
L.P.	OK1PFJ	92	89,095
S/O 3.5 MHz			
AF	OH1RY/CT3	85	2,816,754
AS	UF6VZ	90	835,584
EU	CT7N (CT4NH)	92	1,456,704
NA	VA3EJ	91	1,950,592
OC	AH6AZ	88	492,030
SA	YV3A (YV5IVB)	91	1,664,476
QRP	OK3CTT	86	65,968
L.P.	VG3LRL	92	401,478
S/O 1.8 MHz			
AF	OH1RY/CT3	87	290,140
AS	UL7ACI	91	331,008
EU	LZ2BE	84	261,504
NA	CG3MFA	85	319,140
OC	T32AF	83	16,872
SA	YV5JEA	84	40,320
QRP	UY5XE	84	25,110
L.P.	OZ3SK	92	55,968
Multi-Op Single Transmitter			
AF	5H1HK	90	13,980,480
AS	TA5/NØFYR	91	16,474,965
EU	LZ9A	89	14,399,625
NA	VP2EC	92	24,409,580
OC	AHØK	91	11,552,112
SA	P4ØV	91	26,987,142
Multi-Op Multi-Transmitter			
AF	ED8ACH	91	47,278,236
AS	JA9YBA	89	13,579,072
EU	HG73DX	91	30,664,095
NA	VP2EC	87	37,446,109
OC	FKØAW	89	26,538,972
SA	ZZ5EG	87	38,096,250
Club	Northern California Contest Club	92	97,527,906

CQ WPX CONTEST

U.S.A. Phone Records

Section	Call	Year	Score
Single-Op All-Band (No Packet)			
W1	KM1H (KQ2M)	92	7,854,840
W2	KQ2M	90	5,682,876
W3	NW3B	91	5,148,550
W4	W4NT (KM9P)	89	4,867,629
W5	N5RZ	90	4,317,060
W6	NU6S	92	4,667,208
W7	N7AVK	92	4,910,290
W8	KW8N	92	4,652,883
W9	W9RE (WA8YVR)	89	5,057,994
WØ	AA9AK/Ø	92	5,946,529
VE	VG3EJ	92	8,958,439
Single-Op Low Power (No Packet)			
W1	N1HOQ	92	1,195,110
W2	K2POF	92	1,079,884
W3	WW3S	92	173,520
W4	KJ4TI	92	615,750
W5	WB5NXH (WB5VZL)	92	2,423,284
W6	KG6AR	92	193,772
W7	WB7USJ	92	491,700
W8	KA8WEO	92	890,625
W9	NG9L	92	520,080
WØ	ACØW	92	795,586
VE	CY2C (VY2SS)	92	4,812,740
Single-Op QRP <5 W (No Packet)			
W1	N1AFC	91	781,664
W2	KR2Q	92	1,269,960
W3	WT3W	92	382,800
W4	WD4NBX	85	177,800
W5	KY5N	92	845,598
W6	WB6JMS	92	438,426
W7	WC7Q	88	414,462
W8	W8ILC	82	1,044,012
W9	W9UP	91	139,755
WØ	WAØVBW	87	47,250
VE	VE3KZ	79	507,210
S/O 28 MHz			
W1	NX1H	91	3,015,377
W2	KC2X	82	1,201,089
W3	KS3F	91	2,767,580
W4	KO4QW	92	2,828,120
W5	WM5G (KRØY)	89	4,213,127
W6	K6OYE	80	2,029,131
W7	NA7P (K7SS)	89	3,085,779
W8	N8II	81	1,440,285
W9	WØAIH/9 (NØBSH)	89	1,929,660
WØ	KØGU	81	1,260,441
VE	VG7NTT	92	4,105,570
S/O 21 MHz			
W1	K1VTM	79	2,293,110
W2	KA2AEV	92	4,278,888
W3	W3AU	79	1,739,410
W4	N4ZZ	89	2,230,452
W5	K5MR	92	4,443,048

W6	WN4KKN/6	92	4,538,050
W7	AI7B	82	4,151,232
W8	K3ZJ/8	92	3,063,720
W9	K9RX	81	1,095,252
WØ	KVØQ	83	1,675,242
VE	XL7SV	90	6,202,042
S/O 14 MHz			
W1	KG1E	85	2,906,676
W2	K2VV	87	3,546,294
W3	W3USS (K3ZJ)	87	1,975,725
W4	KC2X	91	1,549,561
W5	WD5N	90	2,005,291
W6	KM6B	88	1,319,830
W7	N7TT	87	1,479,075
W8	K8NA	82	2,252,688
W9	KK9A	92	3,389,568
WØ	KØRWL	85	1,003,220
VE	VE1NG	86	3,916,965
S/O 7 MHz			
W1	KA1DWX	91	164,352
W2	WQ2M	91	695,196
W3	KM3T	83	214,124
W4	WC4E (K4XS)	87	581,640
W5	N5RZ	92	1,043,316
W6	KM6B	87	1,164,800
W7	KC7EM	92	1,396,646
W8	K8NA	83	212,544
W9	WB9Z	90	594,176
WØ	KVØQ	91	1,068,144
VE	XL7SV	86	3,454,864
S/O 3.5MHz			
W1	NJ1F	89	318,204
W2	K1ZM	92	1,266,514
W3	WE3C	92	536,514
W4	N4BAA	81	213,428
W5	N5RZ	85	428,542
W6	KI6P	83	524,356
W7	K7GWK	85	133,952
W8	KN8R	86	392,128
W9	K9ZO	85	299,464
WØ	N7DF/Ø	84	148,930
VE	VA3EJ	91	1,950,592
S/O 1.8 MHz			
W1	KA1SR	85	37,204
W2	K5NA/2	87	46,746
W3	WB3GCG	84	43,368
W4	KG4W	85	74,112
W5	K5UR	85	122,664
W6	N6VI	86	18,300
W7	N6TR/7	86	24,926
W8	W8LRL	83	30,654
W9	WD9AHJ	82	3,564
WØ	N7DF/Ø	85	19,592
VE	CG3MFA	85	319,140
Multi-Op Single Transmitter			
W1	KI1G	89	6,644,360
W2	WT2S	92	3,522,534
W3	K3EST	80	3,781,888
W4	WC4E	92	11,611,929
W5	N5AU	84	6,301,977
W6	KI6P	87	5,825,328
W7	W7RM	84	5,800,090
W8	NE8T	92	6,333,020
W9	KJ9W [WX3N]	82	6,168,450
WØ	WOØG [WX3N]	89	7,900,395
VE	VG7SZ	92	10,313,226
Multi-Op Multi-Transmitter			
W1	NX1H	92	13,173,594
W2	KF2U	81	6,594,258
W3	K3WW	80	6,385,880
W4	WK4Y	92	11,226,946
W5	N5AU	86	9,733,248
W6	WZ6Z	89	18,737,170
W7	No Entry		
W8	KW8N	86	8,473,705
W9	W9ZRX	80	5,417,178
WØ	WOØG [WX3N]	90	10,682,362
VE	CZ7Z	92	20,228,367
Club	Northern California Contest Club	1992	97,527,906

CQ WPX CONTEST

Continental CW Records

Continent	Call	Year	Score
Single-Op All-Band (No Packet)			
AF	5L7T (YU1RL)	87	8,619,226
AS	P31A (5B4ADA)	92	10,293,858
EU	LZ3DX	91	4,713,706
NA	V27T (YU1RL)	89	9,408,672
OC	NH6J/NHØ(JE1JKL)	88	4,484,760
SA	ZV5A (YU1RL)	92	12,184,011
Single-Op Low Power (No Packet)			
AF	VQ9JT (K5DIY)	92	181,476
AS	7Z2AB (K2XR)	92	3,231,025
EU	RY8I(RB1IZ)	92	2,303,224
NA	C6A/KD6WW	92	4,142,112
OC	9M6HF	92	949,780
SA	FY5FY	92	3,317,918
Single-Op QRP <5W (No Packet)			
AF	5Y4FO	92	649,057
AS	4X4UH	82	1,028,904
EU	LZ2BE	91	1,137,488
NA	VP2MU (KJ4VH)	91	1,554,735
OC	FO8JP	86	572,131
SA	OA8V	81	441,768
S/O 28 MHz			
AF	ZS6BCR (ZS6EZ)	91	3,621,173
AS	4X4UH	81	1,081,262
EU	9H1EL	88	805,552
NA	HI8JKA	89	891,242
OC	KG6DX	81	1,238,806
SA	CE3DNP	89	2,857,038
QRP	ZLØAAH	89	256,665
L.P.	9M8DX (VK2DXI)	92	597,600
S/O 21 MHz			
AF	ZD8LII	91	5,118,527
AS	7L1GVE	91	2,811,478
EU	4N3E (YT3AM)	90	3,239,453
NA	FS5T (AI7B)	89	4,552,470
OC	N7DF/WH2	89	3,243,450
SA	LTØA (LU5UL)	91	4,290,988
QRP	4Z7U (4Z4UT)	91	1,031,400
L.P	LU4FD	92	707,629
S/O 14 MHz			
AF	9J2AL	90	1,333,724
AS	4Z6DX	91	4,614,030
EU	LZ5W (LZ3ZZ)	92	4,222,665
NA	WC4E/KP4	86	3,613,248
OC	ZL3GQ	89	2,775,744
SA	YW1A (YV1DIS)	91	4,617,456
QRP	W8VSK	89	376,648
L.P	H23W (5B4WN)	92	3,826,112
S/O 7 MHz			
AF	AM9TY	92	2,002,224
AS	UP2NK/UF	86	2,084,880
EU	DF9ZP	85	1,998,372
NA	VP2VCW	86	4,641,120
OC	V73AS	90	1,793,840
SA	YX5A (YV5ANT)	87	2,999,977
QRP	RA3DUU	84	157,430
L.P	DL1IAO	92	620,830
S/O 3.5 MHz			
AF	EA8RL	84	453,456
AS	UP2NK/UF	85	701,012
EU	GW8GT (G4FAM)	92	740,440
NA	HK3MAE/HKØ	87	456,280
OC	KX6DC (NZ8B)	89	258,258
SA	YX3A (YV5ANT)	89	1,004,060
QRP	4N7MOD	90	141,075
L.P	UB4QYA	92	222,554
S/O 1.8 MHz			
AF	ZS6BCR (ZS6EZ)	85	20
AS	UP3BP/UF	85	125,240
EU	UA2FF	87	117,424
NA	VE3BMV	86	43,428

OC	KX6DC (NZ8B)	88	12,240
SA	YV1OB	86	11,550
QRP	RA3AUU	87	39,600
L.P.	UA3LID	92	39,720
Multi-Op Single Transmitter			
AF	ZD8ØV	91	10,938,352
AS	YM5KA	90	13,098,790
EU	ZB2X	91	8,618,823
NA	KP2A	89	12,843,135
OC	AG9A/AH2	91	9,005,641
SA	P43GR	90	10,990,482
Multi-Op Multi-Transmitter			
AF	EA9CE	84	4,383,308
AS	JE2YRD	91	8,388,942
EU	HG73DX	91	16,468,480
NA	WL7E	88	12,397,316
OC	KH6XX	85	8,551,399
SA	LQ5A	89	8,290,016

CQ WPX CONTEST

U.S.A. CW Records

Call Area	Call	Year	Score
Single-Op All-Band (No Packet)			
W1	KM1H (KQ2M)	92	5,313,160
W2	KE2PF	91	3,537,675
W3	KT3Y	88	4,079,036
W4	N4WW	83	2,620,440
W5	N5AU (N5RZ)	84	2,659,590
W6	WN4KKN/6	92	3,240,068
W7	NN7L	88	2,301,026
W8	KW8N (WD8IXE)	91	2,569,432
W9	W9SU	88	2,157,600
WØ	KRØY	85	2,814,336
VE	VA8A (KQ8M)	92	5,962,176
S-Op Low Power (No Packet)			
W1	KQ1V	92	2,272
W2	K2SHL	92	286,058
W3	WR3G (K5ZD)	92	1,397,682
W4	N8LM	92	312,480
W5	K5RX	92	1,114,540
W6	WA6IET	92	424,380
W7	K7DBV	92	135,762
W8	KV8Q	92	703,392
W9	K9LJN	92	351,750
WØ	AJØI	92	110,700
VE	VE1ST	92	1,505,424
S-Op QRP <5 W (No Packet)			
W1	KN1M	89	498,960
W2	W2GD	92	741,802
W3	N3RS	91	828,808
W4	NY4D (K4XS)	84	484,575
W5	K5RX	91	463,710
W6	NA6A (W6REC)	88	415,712
W7	NX7K	89	436,044
W8	W8VSK	88	528,504
W9	WB9HRO	88	184,920
WØ	WØKEA	89	155,916
VE	VE3KP	91	159,120
S/O 28 MHz			
W1	K1TR	84	33,109
W2	K5NA/2	91	90,147
W3	WE3C	91	95,890
W4	N4ZC	89	153,081
W5	N5RZ	89	162,134
W6	WA6FGV	88	87,889
W7	WB7FDQ	86	4,148
W8	K8MFO	91	64,610
W9	KB9HG	81	16,200
WØ	WD9FTZ/Ø	89	15,566
VE	VE3BMV	80	113,412
S/O 21 MHz			
W1	K1XA	89	1,037,374
W2	KA2AEV	92	1,405,072
W3	N3RS	88	1,846,086
W4	K4BAI	88	1,255,626
W5	WM5K	88	890,568
W6	N6RO	81	1,184,612
W7	K6LL/7	88	2,163,388
W8	NE8T (K8JM)	91	1,848,300
W9	K9QVB	88	1,088,263
WØ	NØBSH	88	1,888,195
VE	VE3BMV	81	1,534,669
S/O 14 MHz			
W1	WS1M (YU3OH)	92	2,334,384
W2	K2VV	86	2,525,880
W3	N3RS	86	1,464,469
W4	K4JPD	91	1,606,826
W5	W5FO	88	1,640,745
W6	KI6P (WA6VEF)	83	1,417,565
W7	AI7B	86	1,278,011
W8	WD8IXE	86	1,713,162
W9	NØBSH/9	89	1,069,430
WØ	KØRWL	84	707,535
VE	XK1CYL	89	3,016,142
S/O 7 MHz			
W1	K1MM	85	1,390,720
W2	KR2Q	85	1,555,048
W3	KM3T	86	1,640,820
W4	K1ZZI	90	719,280
W5	N5RZ	85	1,754,664
W6	NI6W	85	1,048,775
W7	K7RI	81	535,464
W8	K8MFO	92	502,740
W9	K9ZO	85	278,460
WØ	KVØQ	89	498,550
VE	VE7SV	92	1,500,642
S/O 3.5 MHz			
W1	KA1DWX	86	21,216
W2	K1ZM	91	247,744
W3	N3AD	87	90,610
W4	N4ZC	91	208,964
W5	K5UR	83	13,176
W6	NE6W (N6IG)	83	105,672
W7	N6SS	92	68,376
W8	W8IMZ (WB8MRU)	87	11,050
W9	KJ9D (KK9V)	85	26,460
WØ	KMØL	86	52,800
VE	VE3BMV	85	311,080
S/O 1.8 MHz			
W1	KA1SR	85	884
W2	K5NA/2	88	8,052
W3	NA3J (WB2EKK)	88	13,392
W4	W4VJN	92	24
W5	K5UR	85	13,668
W6	N6LL (WA6CDR)	89	1,584
W7	KG7D	86	4,080
W8	W8LRL	83	1,482
W9	W9CG	79	266
WØ	WØZV	86	7,140
VE	VE3BMV	86	43,428
Multi-Op Single Transmitter			
W1	WF1B	91	3,784,880
W2	KU2Q	89	4,091,568
W3	WD3I	91	2,059,442
W4	N4WW	92	7,168,734
W5	NA5R	83	3,986,592
W6	KI6P	88	5,117,778
W7	KE7V	86	2,671,482
W8	KW8N	92	4,089,852
W9	KS9O	91	4,258,254
WØ	KRØY	86	4,516,974
VE	VE1DXA	83	3,728,256
Multi-Op Multi-Transmitter			
W1	WZ1R	92	6,824,800
W2	K3UA	81	392,840
W3	K3TUP	87	3,780,081
W4	K4CG	82	2,679,846
W5	WM5G	88	8,491,032
W6	AD6C	88	5,556,160
W7	No Entry		
W8	WD8LLD	92	3,071,900
W9	N9MM	79	2,124,150
WØ	NSØZ	88	10,870,380
VE	CY3PCA	83	4,977,817
Club Score	Northern California Contest Club	92	97,527,906

CLASSIC BOOKS ON AMATEUR RADIO

This is a short listing of books that are either classics, and should be in the well-stocked ham library, or books that are revised every year and should be replaced to keep your library current. You should check the advertisements in *CQ*, *QST*, or *73* or contact your local dealer for ordering information.

The Radio Amateur Callbook: The *Callbook* has been an institution in amateur radio since 1920! Published in two volumes (North American and International), it is the source for addresses of hams worldwide. With the growth in amateur radio, you really need to get a new set every year to keep current.

The Radio Amateur's Handbook: This mainstay of the ham's library includes sections on everything from semiconductor theory to Yagi construction, and everything in between. Written in a practical style without excessive math, it has served as an electronics reference book for hams and non-hams since the first edition was published in 1926. As the hobby has evolved, sections have been added to keep pace with the technology. If you haven't bought a *Handbook* in the last few years, you'll find a wealth of new material that you can use.

World Radio TV Handbook: Every SWL needs a current copy of this book. It includes schedules and frequencies for the world's short-wave broadcasters, and even listings of medium-wave, FM, and TV stations of the world. If you've got a general-coverage receiver, or a transceiver that tunes between the ham bands, you'll find this book an invaluable guide. Since broadcasters change their schedules, the WRTH is updated annually.

The ARRL Antenna Book: All hams need antennas, and most hams are interested in improving their antenna systems. *The ARRL Antenna Book* covers all types of antennas, from mobile whips to Yagis and loops. Recently updated to over 700 pages, it also includes information on transmission lines, antenna tuners, and more.

Radio Frequency Interference: Unfortunately, nearly every ham has to deal with RFI and TVI at some point in his life. This book is written by experts, and offers clear troubleshooting directions and suggestions on dealing with the diplomatic problems that come with TVI. It will definitely help you solve the problem.

The CQ Amateur Radio Almanac: This annual publication contains facts, figures, and data on amateur radio that you will be hard-pressed to find anywhere else. Much of the history of the hobby is captured, with a capsule history of the last year and complete listings of operating achievements. Reference tables, information on the number of hams by town in the U.S., and awards information is also found in this book. You'll want to get one every year.

NEW BOOKS, 1993-1994

The past year has been very exciting in the world of Amateur Radio publications. With the fast growth in the Technician Class Amateur license, there has been a wealth of books and publications published for the beginner. Antenna books continue to be most popular, with a number of new and re-released titles. Here's a brief overview of new books published in the last year.

For the Beginner

On July 1, 1993, the Technician Class license question pool was changed. Publishers scrambled to release a wealth of new study books and guides. Finding its roots in the successful publication, *Tune in The World,* first published in 1976, The ARRL's Technician class study guide *Now You're Talking* has been fully revised and updated with the new FCC question pool. NARA, W5YI, Gordon West, AMECO and other publishers have also released revised and up-to-date study guides for the Technician Class ticket.

The ARRL's *Understanding Basic Electronics*, by Larry Wolfgang, WR1B, is one of the best ever at teaching electronics theory as simply and painlessly as possible. Using a "building-block" approach, this book covers electronic math, AC and DC circuits, and includes simple easy-to-build circuits. Beginners will find this an invaluable tool; even experienced hams will find it a good "refresher" on subjects they haven't considered in years!

CQ's *Beginner's Guide to Amateur Radio* is chock-full of information newcomers will need to get licensed, to buy equipment, and to get on the air. It includes a listing of manufacturers and dealers of amateur radio related equipment and accessories.

The ARRL companion series, NARA's *Getting Started* series and a collaborative publication by both CQ and the ARRL, *Ham Radio Horizons,* have all been published to meet the beginner's needs. These books are written in simple, easy-to-understand terms. Illustrations and diagrams are used throughout to help the beginners understand the complex world of radio communications.

Video Programs

The ARRL release of a video training tape for the Technician Class license, produced by King Schools in California, was one of the highlights of this year's Dayton Hamvention. Long known in aviation circles for their video study programs for different FAA licenses, the Kings are also hams and the jump to amateur radio was very simple. This five-hour video covers all aspects of the Technician Class license using state-of-the-art graphics, charts, on-site demonstrations and more. The basic tape package sells for $98.95. A software study course is also available for $48.95, or $119 when purchased with the video.

CQ Communications released five video tapes by award winning television producer, Rich Moseson, NM2L. Rich worked at CBS for many years doing an number of different projects. His critically-acclaimed "Kids-Break" mini news features were a current event staple during CBS's Saturday morning children's programming for many years. The CQ tapes are written and produced to *show*, as well as tell you, about amateur radio. *Getting Started in DXing* tells you how to design and build a competitive station for DXing—from antennas to equipment. *Getting Started in Packet Radio* demystifies packet set-up and operation. You learn all about amateur satellites in *Getting Started in Satellites*. *Getting Started in Amateur Radio* is a beginner's guide to the fascinating hobby of ham radio. You'll find out how to get a license, what kind of equipment and antennas beginner's use and much more. Finally, *Ham Radio Horizons,* is a journey through the world of radio action. Rich shows you who hams are and what they do both in the hobby and as professionals. This tape is great for clubs looking for a way to introduce newcomers to amateur radio. CQ is also planning more tapes on other aspects of ham radio, including a soon to be released video on contesting.

Antenna Books

Antennas continue to be one of the most popular subjects for books, and there was a wealth of new books published last year. While not strictly an antenna book, PolyPhaser's *The Grounds for Lightning and EMP Protection* is a very important re-release. This book covers the mechanics of protecting your antenna, equipment, and home from the effects of lightning and EMP (electro-magnetic pulse). CQ published the long awaited *Cubical Quad* book by Bob Haviland, W4MB. First published as a series in *Ham Radio* and *Communications Quarterly* magazines, Bob's work is the most definitive ever on the cubical quad antenna. He covers just about every angel in design and installation of the quad.

The *ARRl's Antenna Compendium, Volume 3,* has been an instant best seller. *QST Magazine* receives far more articles than it can publish each year. The solution then, is to publish these articles in a book of their own. Chapters cover simple dipole designs to sophisticated four phased element receiving antennas. Joe Carr, K4IPV and Hi-Text published the *Receiving Antenna Handbook.* This collection of antenna ideas covers amateur and shortwave designs from small compact loops to long wires and Beverage designs.

After being out-of-print for quite some time, Radio Publications has just rereleased the very popular books by Bill Orr, W6SAI and Stu Cowan, W2LX: *All About Vertical Antennas, Simple Low Cost Wire Antennas, Beam Antenna Handbook, Interference Handbook, Cubical Quad Antennas, The Truth About CB Antennas,* and *The Antenna Handbook.* These books are full of tested designs, helpful ideas and tips that will make installing your antenna as simple and easy as possible. Bill has been around for many years as a *CQ* columnist and brings a unique insight to antenna design and application.

Kurt N. Sterba's first book *Aerials*, published by World Radio, was a sellout. In 1993, a second volume, *Aerials II,* was released. Taken from Kurt's World Radio column, this new collection takes a critical look at advertising claims, designs, and many of the myths and misconceptions that seem to live on in radio circles. World Radio has also published *40 years plus 5 of Mobileering,* by Don Johnson, W6AAQ. Don tells you what antennas to use, gives you ideas on how to eliminate interference and static, and lets you take advantage of his years of experience at mobile operation.

McGraw-Hill released a revised and updated third edition of *Antenna Engineering Handbook,* edited by Jasik and Johnson, priced at $119. One of the most comprehensive antenna books available, *Antenna Engineering Handbook* covers antennas from very low frequency application into the gigaHertz range. Fifteen new chapters cover new and state-of-the-art antenna technologies.

ARRL's *Low Profile Amateur Radio* covers more than hidden antenna designs and "stealth" operating techniques. Jim Kearman, KR1S, helps you find ways to operate from your apartment, home, or condo without disturbing the neighbors, landlord or restrictive deed covenants!

Wes Hayward, W7ZOI, wrote *Microsmith* as a helpful tool to use while designing circuits. This MS-DOS-based Smith Chart program takes advantage of the computer's "number crunching" powers and eliminates the drudgery of hand calculating and plotting impedance curves. Hayward's tutorial covers basic uses and shows you how to design L-networks, transmission lines, "Z" matching and more. The revised ARRL version is now available.

Digital Communications

Digital communication continues to be one of the fastest growing segments of amateur radio. Jon Mayo, KR3T, has just released a new book, *Digital Communication Handbook*, published by TAB. This book reflects the latest in digital communication technology and includes ROSE, TCP/IP, high-speed switches and data links, plus much more. Another new Packet book is Joe Kasser's, W3/G3ZCZ, *Basic Packet Radio.* This is more than a beginner's book though. It covers just about every nook and cranny that packet has.

Over a year ago, Buck Rogers,' K4ABT, packet primer, *Packet Notebook,* went out of print. In the spring of 1993, CQ released a new edition by Buck, *The Packet Users Notebook.* It's jam-packed with information on how to design and set-up a state-of-the-art packet station. Buck is one of the packet pioneers and knows his stuff. He is also able to communicate in a way that eliminates "techno-babble" and other jargon that confuses many! Buck's book includes wiring diagrams for the most popular TNC and radio to computer hookups.

For the beginner, three new books are available, NARA's *Getting Started in Packet Radio* was written by Dave Ingram, K4TWJ. Dave's easy-to-read conversational style eliminates many of the mysteries of packet radio and helps the beginner cut through the jargon and get his station on-the-air. The ARRL's *Packet Radio Companion* and *RTTY/AMTOR Companion*, both by Steve Ford, WB8IMY, are written to help the beginner get on the air as easily as possible. These companion books cover installation and operation of digital stations for packet and RTTY modes.

Directories

One of the biggest changes in 1993 has been the explosion of information available for the computer. Name and callsign directories are available in both CD-ROM and disk formats. Buckmaster's *HamCall CD-ROM* has listings for close to 1 million radio amateurs around the world. It also contains thousands of public domain and shareware programs for just about every application you can imagine. SAM and J-COM have both released directories that can be dumped on to your computer hard disk. These programs allow you to search based upon name, address, callsign, and just about every other combination you can imagine. This allows you to find hams in your town or long lost friends and helps ensure you've got the correct address for QSLing.

ARRL's *Repeater Directory* includes repeater and digipeater listings from around the world from 29 to above 1200 MHz. Artsci has taken the directory concept a step further with the *Repeater Map Book*. Adding state maps to indicate the most popular repeaters so you can see where a repeater is as you drive by, even at 65 MPH.

The *1994 Passport to Worldband Radio* is an updated listing of shortwave stations from around the world. It includes frequencies, times, programming notes, technical evaluations of equipment and accessories, and helpful information on shortwave listening.

General Interest Books

Bob Halprin, K1XA, has written two books for Tiare this year. *Ham Radio Contesting* is the first book to take a close look at the art of operating a contest station. Bob shares with you the secrets that K1EA, K1AR, and others use to consistently win contests. Antennas, accessories, radios, and amplifiers are all discussed. Bob's other book is a celebration on the art of CW operation, *The Code Book—Amateur Radio CW Operating*. Bob is a dedicated CW operator and he shows you how to master the code without driving yourself crazy.

McELROY, World's Champion Radio Telegrapher, by Tom French, W1IMQ, is a 150-page biography of T.R. McElroy who holds the world record for CW reception. Thousands of hours of research, including interviews with McElroy's family, friends, and employees provide a detailed history of this fascinating character. The book also includes photographs never before published and a complete reference for the Mac-Key products.

Many hams got their start on the air using Heath equipment. Heath has left the amateur equipment market, but the memories live on in *Heath Nostalgia*, by Terry Perdue, K8TP, a former Heath employee. This 124-page brief history and scrapbook includes information on many of the "Heathkits" that got generations of hams started.

PERIODICALS

The following list of publications contains a sampling of the most popular amateur radio bulletins and journals worldwide. Although every effort has been made to make it complete and useful, it's inevitable that some worthwhile ones will have been missed. Please send corrections to this list, as well as your suggestions for other publications to add to the list in the 1995 edition, to: Almanac Editor, c/o CQ Publishing, 76 North Broadway, Hicksville, NY 11801.

The most recent available pricing information is given for most, and unless stated otherwise, all prices are for full one-year subscriptions and are given in U.S. dollars. In some cases sample copies or trial subscriptions of less than one year are available, as are special rates for subscriptions of more than one year. Also, many publishers will now accept payment via credit cards, an especially convenient method of payment when subscriptions are quoted in foreign currency. A letter to the publisher asking for information on short- or long-term subscriptions or credit card payments will generally receive a swift response. In all cases, send along a self-addressed, stamped envelope or a self-addressed envelope with an IRC. Yes, publishers will usually respond without the help of SASEs and SAEs, but your response will generally appear more quickly if you make it easy for the publisher to answer. Good reading!

73 Amateur Radio Today: Amateur radio general coverage. Monthly. 1-year subscription: U.S.: $24.97. Canada: $34.21. Elsewhere: $43.97 surface mail, $66.97 via air. *73 Amateur Radio Today*, PO Box 50330, Boulder, CO 80321-0330.

Amateur Radio. Journal of the Wireless Institute of Australia: Monthly. Contact WIA for membership information. The Membership Secretary, Wireless Institute of Australia, PO Box 300, Caulfield South, Vic 3162, Australia.

The Amateur Radio Communicator: Journal of the National Amateur Radio Association. 1-year subscription: U.S. $10.00. National Amateur Radio Association, PO Box 598, Redmond, WA 98073-0598.

The AMSAT Journal: Amateur radio satellite communications. Bi-monthly. 1-year subscription: U.S.: $30.00. Canada: $36.00. All others $45.00. AMSAT, 850 Sligo Avenue, Suite 600, Silver Spring, MD 20910-4703.

Antique Radio Classified: Antique radio collecting and history. Monthly. 1-year subscription: U.S.: $29.95 by 2nd class mail, $44.95 by 1st class mail. Canada: $39.00 by 2nd class mail, $48.00 by air. Mexico: $47.00. All others $43.00 surface mail, $85.00 air. *Antique Radio Classified*, P.O. Box 2, Carlisle, MA 01741.

The Antique Radio Gazette: Antique radio collecting and history. Quarterly. 1-year subscription: U.S.: $12.00. Canada: $14.00. Elsewhere: $16.00. Antique Radio Club of America, c/o William H. Dawson, 300 Washington Trails, Washington, PA 15301.

The ARRL Letter: Newsletter covering amateur radio. Bi-weekly. 1-year subscription: U.S., Canada, Mexico: $19.50. All others $31.00 via air. Subscriptions are limited to ARRL members. American Radio Relay League, 225 Main St., Newington, CT 06111.

Break-In. Journal of the New Zealand Association of Radio Transmitters: Monthly. 1-year membership: New Zealand: $65.00 (New Zealand dollars). Overseas: $57.75 (New Zealand dollars.) NZART, PO Box 40-525, Upper Hutt, New Zealand.

The Canadian Amateur. Journal of the Radio Amateurs of Canada: Monthly. Canada: $28.00 (Canadian dollars). Elsewhere: $42.00 (U.S. dollars). Radio Amateurs of Canada, PO Box 356, Kingston, ON K7L 4W2, Canada.

Communications Quarterly: Amateur radio technical journal. Quarterly. 1-year subscription: U.S.: $29.95. CQ Communications, 76 North Broadway, Hicksville, NY 11801.

CQ-DL. Journal of the Deutscher Amateur-Radio-Club., e.V.: In German. Monthly. Contact publisher with SASE or SAE with IRC for latest rates. Deutscher Amateur-Radio-Club, e.V., Postfach 1155, D-3507 Baunatal 1, Germany.

CQ Ham Radio. Amateur radio general coverage; in Japanese. Monthly. 1-year subscription: Contact publisher for latest information. CQ Publishing Co., Ltd., 14-2 Sugamo, 1-chome, Toshima, Tokyo 170, Japan.

CQ Amateur Radio: Amateur radio general coverage. Monthly. 1-year subscription: U.S.: $22.95. Canada/Mexico: $25.00. Elsewhere: $27.00 surface, $80.00 via air. CQ Communications, Inc., 76 North Broadway, Hicksville, NY 11801.

Dots & Dashes: Historical Morse telegraphy. Quarterly. 1-year subscription: U.S.: $8.00. Morse Telegraph Club, Inc., 1101 Maplewood Dr., Normal, IL.

The DX Bulletin: Amateur radio DX information. Weekly. 1-year subscription: U.S.: $32.00 2nd class mail, $42.00 1st class (including Canada and Mexico). Elsewhere: $55.00 via air. *The DX Bulletin*, PO Box 50, Fulton, CA 95439-0050.

The DX Magazine: Amateur radio DX information. Bimonthly. 1-year subscription: U.S.: $15.00. Canada: $20.00. All others $25.00 by air. *The DX Magazine*, PO Box 50, Fulton, CA 95439.

DXMB: Amateur radio DX information; in German. Weekly. 1-year subscription: Contact publisher with SASE or SAE with IRC for latest rates. Bestellung DX-MB, DARC e. V., Postfach 11 55, W-3507 Baunatal, Germany.

The DX News Sheet: Amateur radio DX information. Weekly. 1-year subscription: Contact publisher with SASE or SAE with IRC for latest rates. Radio Society of Great Britain, Lambda House, Cranborne Road, Potters Bar EN6 3JE, England.

DXPress: Amateur radio DX information. Weekly. 1-year subscription: Contact publisher with SASE or SAE with IRC for latest rates. Central Bureau VERON, Box 1166, 6801 BD, Arnem, The Netherlands.

EA DX Bulletin: Amateur radio DX information; in Spanish. Weekly. 1-year subscription: Contact publisher with SASE or SAE with IRC for latest rates. Union de Radioaficionados Espanoles, Apartado Postal 220, 28080 Madrid, Spain.

Electric Radio: Collecting, restoring, and operating older tube-type equipment. Monthly. 1-year subscription: U.S.: $24.00 2nd class, $34.00 1st class. Canada: $35.00 by air. All other countries $60.00 by air. *Electric Radio*, PO Box 57, Hesperus, CO 81326.

Electronics Now: Hobby electronics. Monthly. 1-year subscription: U.S.: $19.97. Canada: $27.79. All other countries $28.97. *Electronics Now*, PO Box 51866, Boulder, CO 980321-1866.

Funk Amateur: Amateur radio, computers, hobby electronics; in German. 1-year subscription: Contact publisher with SASE or SAE with IRC for latest rates. Theuberger Verlag GmBH, Postfach 73, O-1020 Berlin, Germany.

ICOM Amateur Users' Exchange Group: Icom users' technical information. Bi-monthly. 1-year subscription: U.S. $12.00, 2nd class, $14.00 1st class. Mexico: $14.00 1st class. Canada: $15.00. Australia, Africa, New Zealand, Pacific Far East $19.50 via air. Elsewhere: $15.50 via air. International Radio and Computer, Inc., 3804 South U.S. 1, Fort Pierce, FL 34982. Inquire with publisher for special combined subscription rates with the Kenwood *Amateur Users' Exchange Group* bulletin.

I.R.T.S. Newsletter: Journal of the Irish Radio Transmitters Society. Monthly. Contact publisher with SASE or SAE with IRC for latest rates. I.R.T.S., PO Box 462, Dublin 9, Ireland.

Japan DX News: Amateur radio DX information; in Japanese. Weekly. Contact publisher with SASE or SAE with IRC for latest rates. Japan DX News, PO Box 42, Urawa-Cyuo, Saitama 336, Japan.

Kenwood Amateur Users' Exchange Group: Kenwood users' technical information. Bi-monthly. 1-year subscription: U.S. $12.00, 2nd class, $14.00 1st class. Mexico: $14.00 1st class. Canada: $15.00. Australia, Africa, New Zealand, Pacific Far East $19.50 via air. Elsewhere: $15.50 via air. International Radio and Computer, Inc., 3804 South U.S. 1, Fort Pierce, FL 34982. Inquire with publisher for special combined subscription rates with the *ICOM Amateur Users' Exchange Group* bulletin.

KH6BZF Reports: Propagation newsletter. Weekly. 1-year subscription: Contact publisher with SASE or SAE with IRC for latest rates. Lee Wical, KH6BZF, 45-601 Luluki Road, CRT #44-25, Kane'Ohe, O'Ahu, HI 96744-1845.

Les Nouvelles DX: Amateur radio DX information; in French. Weekly. 1-year subscription: Contact publisher with SASE or SAE with IRC for latest rates. Jacky Billaud, F6BBJ, 14 avenue Massena, F-78600 Maisons Lafitte, France.

The Long Island DX Bulletin: Amateur Radio DX information. Bi-Weekly. 1-year subscription: U.S.: $17.00. Elsewhere: Contact publisher with SASE or SAE with IRC for latest rates. The Long Island DX Bulletin, PO Box 173, Huntington, NY 11743-0173.

Long Skip, Journal of the Canadian DX Association: Monthly. 1-year subscription: U.S. $25.00. Canada, $25.00 Canadian. Other countries: $25.00. CANAD-X, PO Box 717, Station "Q," Toronto, ON M4T 2N7, Canada.

The Lowdown: Long wave radio. Monthly. 1-year subscription: U.S.: $18.00. Canada: $19.00. Elsewhere: $26.00 via air. Longwave Club of America, 45 Wildflower Road, Levittown, PA 19057.

Lynx DX Bulletin: Amateur radio DX information; in Spanish. Weekly. 1-year subscription: Contact publisher with SASE or SAE with IRC for latest rates. Lynx DX Group, Apartado 20053, 48080 Bilbao, Spain.

Monitoring Times: Shortwave listening, scanning, hobby radio. Monthly. 1-year subscription: U.S.: $19.95. Elsewhere: $28.50. *Monitoring Times*, PO Box 98, 140 Dog Branch Rd., Brasstown, NC 28902-0098.

Morsum Magnificat: Morse code lore. Bi-monthly. 1-year subscription: UK £12.00. Europe: £12.75. Rest of the world: £12.75 surface mail, £15.50 via air. G. C. Arnold Partners, 9 Wetherby Close, Broadstone, Dorset BH18 8JB, England. (U.S. subscribers may remit in U.S. dollars: $21.50 surface, $26.50 via air to Owl Worldwide Publications, 4314 West 238th St., Torrance, CA 90505-4509.)

NCJ, The National Contest Journal: Amateur radio contesting. Bi-monthly. 1-year subscription: U.S.: $10.00 2nd class, $19.00 first class. Canada and Mexico, $20.00 first class. Elsewhere, $20.00 surface mail, $28.00 via air. The American Radio Relay League, 225 Main St., Newington, CT 06111.

The Old Timer's Bulletin: Antique radio collecting and history. Quarterly. 1-year subscription: U.S.: $12.00. All other countries $15.00 by air. Antique Wireless Association, c/o Joyce Peckham (Secretary), Box E, Breesport, NY 14816.

Popular Communications: Shortwave listening, scanning, hobby radio. Monthly. 1-year subscription: U.S.: $19.95. Canada/Mexico: $22.00. Elsewhere: $24.00 surface, $77.00 via air.

CQ Communications, 76 North Broadway, Hicksville, NY 11801-2953.

Popular Electronics: Hobby electronics. Monthly. 1-year subscription: U.S.: $21.95. Canada: $28.84. Elsewhere: $29.45. Popular Electronics, Subscription Dept., PO Box 338, Mt. Morris, IL 61054-9935.

Practical Wireless: Amateur radio general coverage. Monthly. UK: £21.00. Europe: £23.00. U.S.: $45.00. Special rate for combined subscription with *Short Wave Magazine*. PW Publishing Ltd., Arrowsmith Ct., Station Approach, Bradstone, Dorset BH18 8PW, England.

QCWA Journal, Journal of the Quarter Century Wireless Association: Quarterly. Send SASE or SAE with IRC for latest membership information. Quarter Century Wireless Association, Inc., 159 E. 16th Ave., Eugene, OR 97401-4017.

QEX: Amateur radio experimenter's magazine. Monthly. U.S.: $12.00 for ARRL members, $24.00 for non-members, 3rd class mail. Elsewhere: $48.00 for ARRL members, $60.00 for ARRL non-members, via air. American Radio Relay League, 225 Main St., Newington, CT 06111.

QRZ DX: Amateur radio DX information. Weekly. 1-year subscription: U.S.: $36.00 1st class. Canada: $40.00 1st class. Mexico: $38.00. Other countries: $55.00 via air. QRZ-DX, PO Box 832205, Richardson, TX 75083.

QST, Journal of the American Radio Relay League: Monthly. 1-year membership: U.S.: $30.00. Elsewhere: $36.00. American Radio Relay League, 225 Main St., Newington, CT 06111.

Radio, Journal of the Reseau des Emetteurs Francais: in French. Monthly. 1-year membership: Contact publisher with SASE or SAE with IRC for latest rates. REF, Siege Social 2, Square Trudaine, F-75009 Paris, France.

Radio Byegones: Antique radio collecting and history. Bimonthly. 1-year subscription: UK £17.00. Europe: £18.00. Middle East, Africa, Southeast Asia, Central & South America, U.S.A & Canada: £22.00 via air. Australia, New Zealand, Far East & Pacific Regions: £23.00 via air. G. C. Arnold Partners, 9 Wetherby Close, Broadstone, Dorset BH18 8JB, England. (U.S. subscribers may remit in U.S. dollars: $31.00 surface, $37.50 via air to Owl Worldwide Publications, 4314 West 238th St., Torrance, CA 90505-4509.)

Radio Communication, Journal of the Radio Society of Great Britain: Monthly. 1-year membership: UK and overseas, £30.00, surface mail. Radio Society of Great Britain, Lambda House, Cranborne Road, Potters Bat, Herts EN63JE, England.

Radio Fun: Beginning amateur radio. Monthly. 1-year subscription: U.S.: $14.00. Canada: $22.00. Elsewhere: $26.00 surface, $46.00 via air. *Radio Fun*, PO Box 4926, Manchester, NH 03108-9839.

RadioRivista, Journal of the Associazione Radioamatori Italiani: in Italian. Monthly. 1-year membership: Contact publisher with SASE or SAE with IRC for latest rates. A.R.I., Ente Morale - via Domenico Scarlatti 31, I-20124 Milano MI, Italy.

Radio ZS, Journal of the South African Radio League: Monthly. Contact publisher with SASE or SAE with IRC for latest rates. South African Radio League, PO Box 807, Houghton, 2041, Republic of South Africa.

Revista Lynx: Amateur radio DX information. Monthly. 1-year subscription: Contact publisher with SASE or SAE with IRC for latest rates. Lynx DX Group, Apartado 20053, 48080 Bilbao, Spain.

RTTY Journal: Amateur radio digital communications. Monthly, except bi-monthly in May/June and July/August. 1-year subscription: U.S., Canada, Mexico: $16.00 2nd class, $19.00 1st class. Elsewhere $24.00 surface, $32.00 via air. RTTY Journal, 1904 Carolton Lane, Fallbrook, CA 92028-4614.

Shortwave Magazine: Shortwave listening, computing, hobby radio. Monthly. UK: £21.00. Europe: £23.00. U.S.: $45.00. Special rate for combined subscription with Practical Wireless. PW Publishing Ltd., Arrowsmith Ct., Station Approach, Bradstone, Dorset BH18 8PW, England.

The Vail Correspondent: Telegraph key collecting and history. Quarterly. 1-year subscription: U.S.: $10.00. Canada or Mexico: $12.00 by air. All other countries: $16.00 by air. *The Vail Correspondent*, Box 88, Maynard, MA 01754.

The W5YI Report: Newsletter covering amateur radio, personal computing, and emerging electronics. Twice monthly. 1-year subscription: U.S., Canada and Mexico $24.50. All other countries $39.50 by air. The W5YI Group, 2000 E. Randol Mill Rd. #608A, Arlington, TX 76011.

The W6GO/K6HHD List: QSLing information. Monthly. 1-year subscription: U.S.: $25.00. Canada and Mexico: $32.00. Overseas: $38.00 via air. The W6GO/K6HHD List, PO Box 700, Rio Linda, CA 95673. Europe/Mid East may also subscribe via Brian Russell, 163 Halton Rd., Runcorn, WA7 5RJ, Cheshire, England.

Westlink Report: Newsletter covering amateur radio. Weekly. 1-year subscription: U.S., Canada and Mexico: $24.50. Westlink International, 28221 Stanley Ct., Canyon Country, CA 91351-3818.

Worldradio: Amateur radio general coverage. Monthly. 1-year subscription: U.S. $14.00. All other countries $24.00 by surface mail. Worldradio, Inc., 520 Calvados Ave., Sacramento, CA 95815.

(Contributed by Craig Clark, NX1G)

OBITUARIES OF INTEREST TO RADIO AMATEURS (September 1, 1992 to August 31, 1993)

Hiram Hamilton Maxim (son of Hiram Percy Maxim)

The son of ARRL founder Hiram Percy Maxim has died. Hiram Hamilton Maxim, 92, died November 2, 1992 in Simsbury, Connecticut. "Ham," as he was called, was the widower of Alison Heminway Maxim, who died in 1990. He graduated from the Massachusetts Institute of Technology in 1921, returned home to work for his father, and took over the company, Maxim Silencer, when his father died in 1936.

Herbert Engelman, KD4OZY

Herbert Engelman, KD4OZY, of Lake Worth, Florida, was struck by lightning on August 30, 1992, in Homestead, Florida, while helping to unload relief supplies from an Army helicopter. He died three days later. A witness told the Palm Beach Post that Engelman was "using a hand held radio to relay information to a mobile ham radio operator" when he ran out to meet the helicopter during a thunderstorm. More than 120 people attended Engelman's funeral on September 4 in Lake Worth. He was 55 and taught adult and special education. He leaves a wife, mother, two daughters, and five grandchildren.

Al Slater, G3FXB

Al Slater, G3FXB, died Wednesday, November 11, 1992, at age 65, of a heart attack. He was known worldwide as a premier operator and an ambassador for Amateur Radio. His most recent honor was election to the CQ Contest Hall of Fame. According to his wife, Maud, Al had been out the night before his death cranking down his tower to protect his antennas in heavy winds. He had retired some years ago after suffering a mild heart attack.

G3FXB was one of the most active HF contest operators of the last two decades on both SSB and CW and was at the top of the Mixed DXCC Honor Roll. He also was a mainstay of the First Class CW Operators Club (FOC) and was a frequent visitor to the United States. He also had visited Australia and New Zealand in recent years, and had visited the Soviet Union as a private citizen soon after the glasnost and perestroika of Mikhail Gorbachev.

In addition to his wife, Al Slater leaves five children: sons John and Philip, and daughters Linda, Jackie, and Diane.

Robert E. Lee, former FCC Chairman

Former FCC Chairman Robert E. Lee died April 6, 1993, and was remembered by the Commission as its longest-serving commissioner. Lee, who was born in Chicago in 1912, was a commissioner from 1953 to 1981, having been appointed by President Eisenhower and reappointed by Presidents Johnson and Nixon. He served briefly as chairman of the Commission, from February 5 to May 18, 1981, in the initial days of the Reagan administration.

Before joining the FCC as an auditor, Lee was an FBI special agent, an administrative assistant to FBI Director J. Edgar Hoover, and a Director of Surveys and Investigations for the Appropriations Subcommittee of the House of Representatives.

Harold H. Beverage, inventor of Beverage antenna

Harold H. Beverage, ex-W2BML, died January 27, 1993 in Stony Brook, New York. He was 99 years old. Although not an active ham since the 1920s, his name is immortalized as the inventor of the Beverage receiving antenna (or, as he originally called it, the "Wave Antenna"). It was developed in 1917 to enhance communications between the U.S. and Europe during the First World War, and was described in QST in November, 1922.

Beverage said in 1980 that he considered his two greatest inventions (he received more than 40 patents) the Wave Antenna and diversity reception. A biography of Beverage, *Genius at Riverhead*, was written by Alberta I. Wallen and published by the North Haven (Maine) Historical Society in 1988.

Beverage was recognized with an obituary in the February 2 *New York Times*. The American Institute of Electrical Engineers awarded Beverage its Lamme Gold Medal in 1957, the Times said, and cited him "for his pioneering and outstanding achievements in the conception and application of principles basic to progress in national and worldwide radio communications."

Ron Henderson, VK1RH, President of the Wireless Institute of Australia

Ron Henderson, VK1RH, President of the Wireless Institute of Australia, died on April 26, 1993. An active amateur operator and adminstrative leader, Ron's untimely death was the result of cancer. He attended the full term of WARC-92 as a delegate from Australia and participated in the 1985 conference in Melbourne. He was a strong supporter of amateur radio and the ARRL.

Lenore Jensen, W6NAZ

Lenore Jensen, W6NAZ, died May 5, 1993, in Sherman Oaks, Calif. She was 79 years old, the widow of Robert Jensen, W6VGQ, and one of Amateur Radio's premier ambassadors.

She was first licensed as W9CHD in 1939, in Chicago, where she was a contract actress for NBC. She became W2NAZ upon moving to New York City in 1940, and then W6NAZ after the Second World War, when she and her husband, Joe, W2MSC, moved to Hollywood.

Most of her operating involved message handling and phone patching. She ran 68,000 Army MARS phone patches during the Vietnam War, according to a profile in *QST* for December, 1987.

Lenore Jensen was one of the 13 surviving founders of the Young Ladies Radio League, and the 1983 Dayton HamVention Special Achievement Award winner. She was especially important to amateur radio public relations, interviewing stars and celebrities for radio "spots."

Survivors include two stepchildren, Cindy Wall, KA7ITT, and Stephen Jensen, W6RHM.

Paul Grauer, WØFIR, ARRL Midwest Division Director

Paul Grauer, WØFIR, passed away June 5, 1993. Paul was ARRL Midwest Division Director from 1974 until three days before his death, when he resigned for health reasons. On June 3, the ARRL Board of Directors had elected him Honorary Vice President in recognition of his more than 21 years of service to the League as Vice Director and Director, and to the ARRL Foundation as President and Director.

Sako Hasegawa, JA1MP, Founder of Yaesu Musen Co.

Sako Hasegawa, JA1MP, Founder and Chairman of the Board of Yaesu Musen Co., died on June 12, 1993. Born in 1929, Mr. Hasegawa began building SSB equipment in Japan in 1956. He incorporated Yaesu Musen Company Ltd. in 1959. During the 1980s he co-founded and served as President of the Japan Amateur Industry Association.

JA1MP was an active operator, and won the first Japanese RTTY WAC award in 1971.

Shunsako Inoue, JA3ANC, President, Alinco Electronics

Shunsako Inoue, JA3ANC, President of Alinco Electronics died in June 1993. He was the son of Mr. Yoshizo Inoue, who founded the company in 1938.

Jim Rafferty, N6RJ, Vice-President, Ham Radio Outlet

Jim Rafferty, N6RJ, Vice-President of Ham Radio Outlet, died June 13, 1993 of cancer. Originally licensed as WA9UCE, he was known for the N6RJ "Second Op" and "Electronic Second Op" operating aids. Jim was also an active DXer and contest operator, and held numerous records operating as ZF2FL or ZF2JR. He was also a member of the 1974 KP6KR Kingman Reef DXpedition.

Len Chertok, W3GRF

Len Chertok, W3GRF, died June 24, 1993. Originally licensed in 1936, he was a well-known active contest operator and long-time member of the Potomac Valley Radio Club. When interviewed for the 1958 *Ham Register*, he was asked for information on hobbies other than Ham Radio. His succinct answer: none.

Francisco Velez, HKØBKX

Francisco Velez, HKØBKX, passed away August 1, 1993 following a stroke. He made HKØ, San Andres Island, available on all bands and modes for many years as the sole active operator.

Others (source: Silent Keys listings, *QST* Magazine)

U.S.

N1ACB
K1ADU
W1AFL
W1AGL
K1AIK
W1AOR
K1AOX
W1ASI
WA1AZP
KA1BH
N1BJP
W1BMX
K1BMU
WB1CDQ
W1CFU
W1COS
WB1CRR
K1CSY
K1CTV
K1CUF
KA1CYW
KA1DMO
WA1DPF
K1DVX
W1DYS
W1EGW
WB1ELP
W1EIY
W1EZG
AB1F
W1FAT
W1FBJ
WA1FCE
W1FEE
WA1FEU
N1FGI
W1FKC
WA1FQW
WB1FRQ
N1FS
WB1FTX
KA1GG
W1GIC
WB1GJI
W1GMN
WA1GOW
KA1GQU
W1GRT
W1GYI
N1HDK
W1HGI
N1HGO
W1HHF
WB1HIH
W1HKU
W1HOZ
KA1HPO
N1HRF
W1HRQ
KA1HXO
W1IDA
W1IDV
KA1ISK
W1JFH
KB1JJ
K1JRE
W1JZQ
W1KD
W1KEL
K1KFV
K1KGF
W1KID
K1KK
W1KKD
W1KYG
W1LAZ
W1LJK
KA1LPM
KA1LWN
W1LYN
W1MHC
N1MHS
W1MRC
KA1MRC
K1MRM
W1MXU
K1NFW
K1NPE
WA1NPM
WA1NQS
WA1NSC
KA1NUH
NS1O
WA1OBV
K1OJF
W1OK
W1OKB
W1OMC
W1OQK
AE1P
KA1PGM
K1PTV
KA1PUL
W1QAH
W1QB
W1QHG
W1QJI
W1QLL
K1QXF
KA1QY
W1QZR
W1RPW
W1RS
W1RVY
W1RZT
WO1S
KA1SBF
WA1SOC
W1SUQ
W1TBI
K1TGM
WA1TJC
WA1TKI
W1TUW
W1TVN
W1UK
WA1UKS
W1UNA
W1UQV
W1UWU
W1VOS
W1VWL
K1VYC
W1WAE
WA1WOT
W1YO
WA1ZHZ
W1ZJK
W1ZSH
KA1ZTA
NC2A
W2AAV
W2ABV
K2AMI
WA2ANH
K2ANR
N2ASN
W2AWF
N2AXP
W2AXX
WB2BFY
W2BKW
W2BMC
W2BUT
NJ2C
KB2CAB
W2CBB
KB2CCB
W2CCO
WB2CEX
WA2CKA
W2CUU
WA2CUV
W2CY
K2CYX
KB2D
W2DBW
K2DER
WA2DIG
W2DJX
KA2DKX
W2DOG
W2DSE
WA2DTY
K2DXK
KB2E
W2EBO
K2ECJ
N2EEA
W2EFU
WA2EIC
N2EKE
N2EKZ
N2ELQ
N2EOQ
N2EQQ
WB2ERK
KB2ERX
WA2EVK
KQ2F
KC2FA
KA2FKR
KA2FLC
N2FMG
W2FQF
N2FYQ
WB2FZB
WA2GBM
W2GGB
N2GIZ
W2GKE
W2GKH
W2GMJ
W2GP
KE2GR
N2GSH
W2GSJ
W2GSN
W2GZX
W2GZZ
NA2H
WA2HAO
WB2HDV
K2HEX
K2HFW
W2HH
N2HID
W2HIX
W2HMN
W2HOM
W2HPU
W2HZ
W2IBF
W2IDM
W2IER
WA2IFF
KC2IH
W2IMV
K2IN
W2IOO
WA2IPN
WA2ITU
K2JA
W2JCP
WA2JDZ
W2JE
W2JK
W2JLH
K2JWF
KS2K
W2KBH
WB2KIW
N2KJS
KA2KNZ
W2KOY
K2LFH
WA2LJG
WA2LJX
W2LLS
W2LMQ
KD2LR
KB2LRC
WB2LRN
N2LTT
K2LUG
W2LVD
WA2LVW
W2MLC
WB2MNT
W2MOP
W2MRG
W2MT
W2MXB
W2NCF
W2NCZ
N2NPP
W2NQO
W2NRQ
WA2NVU
W2NZS
W2OBM
WA2OES
W2OH
K2OV
N2OVA
KA2OXR
KA2PEQ
WA2PIL
KD2PY
W2PZU
W2QXE
K2RDS
W2RIB
W2RLP
W2RME
WA2RMN
W2RPO
KP2S
W2SCE
W2SHM
WA2SIH
W2SPB
KA2SSN
WA2SUQ
K2SXO
W2TDV
KA2TLA
WA2TMR
NM2U
K2UCQ
WA2UFF
W2UGM
WA2UGM
K2UIJ
KA2UJD
W2ULA
WA2UOM
WB2UTR
KA2UYY
WB2VGA
WB2VOL
W2VSC
KA2VSN
WB2VSX
KA2VUE
KA2VYV
W2VZT
W2WCC
W2WLO
WA2WWO
WA2WXU
KA2WYO
KB2XB
W2YLD
W2ZDB
KD2ZF
WA2ZPE
W2ZSJ
KB2ZR
KA3AHL
W3APF
W3APQ
W3ARK
WA3ATP
W3AVP
WA3AZZ
WB3BAP
W3BPO
W3BQP
W3BUR
W3BWU
N3CAK
K3CB
N3CCQ
W3CJS
W3CLQ
WB3CPW
W3CVT
KA3CYT
N3DAB
KB3DH
K3DHM
W3DNI
W3DZS
N3ECQ
W3EOM
WA3ESO
KA3EUJ
W3FBI
KB3FG
KA3FNJ
KA3FPE
W3FU
KV3G
K3GBN
K3GGA
N3GOE
KA3GTC
W3GTE
N3GYS
K3HBP
W3HET
WA3HLN
WB3HWU
W3HZS
K3IML
K3INV
N3JGS
N3JHB
KA3JJA
K3JKQ
KA3JUO
W3KDN
W3KHI
W3KHW
WB3KIW
W3KKY
WB3KLH
W3KMK
W3KOS
W3KOZ
W3KPV
WN3L
K3LAA
W3LEM
K3LK
K3LQQ
W3LST
KA3LVL
K3MZR
WA3NIL
WA3NPF
KB3NS
K3NYQ
W3OHX
KB3OQ
W3OVM
W3PVL
K3PZS
NB3Q
W3QHF
WA3REP
W3RFO
W3RMS
KA3SAE
W3SCB
W3SOB
W3SX
W3TNQ
W3TTV
W3TXN
KM3U
K3UGU
W3UN
K3UR
K3URP
W3UVK
W3VFL
K3VQI
K3VW
W3VXV

KA3WMC
W3WN
W3WR
W3WZC
KU3Y
W3ZD
K3ZVH
WD4ABZ
WD4ADG
W4AFH
W4AFR
WD4AGY
W4AHP
W4AHZ
N4AKZ
W4ANK
N4AO
KB4ARO
KA4AUZ
K4AVM
K4AVP
KB4AWR
KB4AWZ
K4AZS
KA4AZS
W4BA
WA4BAJ
W4BBP
W4BCL
K4BCZ
W4BEN
W4BEX
W4BGR
N4BGS
K4BHV
W4BIW
KB4BKU
KC4BME
KD4BNE
K4BNQ
KD4BRP
N4BUI
KD4BVU
W4BVU
W4BXD
N4BXX
WB4BZC
K4BZH
KC4CBZ
N4CE
WB4CGM
KJ4CH
W4CHI
KB4CKR
W4CM
K4CMK
K4CNP
W4CO
W4CRN
W4CRY
KB4CTI
K4CTZ
WA4CUC
WA4CVA
N4CXH
W4DA
WB4DAR
W4DCG
N4DDV
W4DFQ
W4DLT
W4DN
W4DPS
K4DVG

WA4DXW
KA4DYI
K4EB
KA4ECR
WB4EER
WA4EHH
W4EIV
KC4EQH
WB4ESH
N4ESN
WB4EWR
W4EYF
W4FAP
K4FCL
WB4FCL
W4FGH
KC4FKE
N4FKY
WD4FNX
W4FPO
K4FQ
KA4FSY
WB4FTN
K4GAG
WA4GBE
W4GCG
N4GCH
KD4GCW
KC4GHP
KC4GJ
W4GJO
W4GJZ
N4GLA
WB4GNL
W4GQS
WB4GPH
W4GWR
K4GX
KJ4GX
N4HAZ
W4HAZ
W4HFA
W4HKY
W4HON
W4HOT
W4HQ
WA4HTP
K4HV
W4HX
WA4HXI
W4HZL
KB4I
W4IBU
K4IBX
WD4ICF
KC4IHB
N4IHS
W4IJB
W4IKJ
WB4IKS
W4ILP
W4ILX
KK4IM
W4IQ
KB4IQP
KC4ISO
WB4IXA
K4IZT
K4JBI
W4JBP
WD4JDV
WA4JFC
K4JFJ
KB4JGZ

N4JJW
KA4JRH
K4JRF
KO4JU
K4JVT
W4KFG
K4KKP
N4KMM
K4KOM
W4KP
WB4KPU
N4KTY
WB4KVK
WA4KYC
W4LAI
K4LB
WB4LBD
WA4LBK
W4LCT
W4LCY
WB4LDN
W4LEP
N4LOC
K4LPQ
W4LQF
W4LRM
W4LTS
W4LUX
W4LWZ
N4LXA
W4LYN
WB4MDI
KD4MFG
WA4MLK
N4MOX
KB4MPQ
WD4MQM
WA4MSC
K4MUD
WA4MXZ
KF4NB
WA4NBE
KB4NC
N4NHV
K4NI
KB4NLR
W4NSK
W4NU
WA4OCL
KB4ODM
KC4OH
KC4OTW
KB4OU
KD4OW
WA4OZC
KB4PBS
W4PDL
KB4PE
WA4PET
N4PGA
W4PKT
WB4PLE
K4PLG
W4PMQ
W4PTH
W4PTR
W4PTT
KM4PZ
W4QA
K4QAT
N4QDG
K4QDM
N4QES
WB4QIC

WA4QLH
KB4QMG
K4QZ
NE4R
W4RD
W4REQ
KK4RR
WB4RSY
KC4RTL
WA4RWO
N4RXM
W4SBZ
K4SD
W4SIE
W4SGI
W4SK
KA4SKO
WD4SKS
KA4SLL
AA4SP
W4SUH
W4SZE
K4SZO
N4TBG
W4TGH
N4TJN
WB4TNY
KM4TO
N4TPJ
WA4TRM
W4TWO
K4UE
KA4UJP
K4UN
KJ4UN
KA4UOO
KA4UPQ
W4URM
W4UTR
KB4UWK
KC4UXL
W4VCN
WB4VFW
N4VIN
KJ4VU
W4VUI
W4WC
N4WD
KA4WDF
K4WI
N4WKB
WA4WKW
KC4WN
N4WPU
W4WQP
KB4WSB
KB4WUF
W4WX
N4XER
KF4Y
KB4YE
K4YK
W4YSJ
W4YTS
KE4YW
W4ZAW
W4ZBQ
W4ZFE
N4ZGV
WB4ZJP
W4ZKW
WA4ZLM
W4ZML
KB5ACL

W5ACS
WA5AET
W5ALL
W5AME
N5ARH
W5ASH
W5AT
K5AWI
W5AXD
W5BBS
N5BDK
N5BHF
W5BOW
KA5BSB
W5BX
W5BYY
WC5C
N5COD
KC5CS
N5CSY
K5CTJ
K5CUE
N5CUQ
WA5CYU
N5DBH
KB5DLW
KB5DUE
KD5E
W5ENI
WD5ERG
W5EXB
WD5EYU
W5EZP
W5FCG
WA5FDL
N5FPP
KB5FSU
WB5FUL
K5FXQ
W5GCJ
KB5GGE
N5GK
K5GKK
W5GNI
W5HD
K5HOB
W5HOY
W5HSE
KG5HQ
K5HUC
AB5HW
N5HWI
K5HZR
KA5IFA
WA5IFM
WB5IHC
W5IKH
KA5IUJ
KB5JFN
W5JHY
W5JJX
WB5JMH
N5JNA
W5JTR
W5JTZ
K5JVG
W5JYM
WB5JZL
W5KDB
K5KMA
W5KND
N5KQH
N5KQU
KE5KV

N5KZP
K5LCR
WA5LDG
W5LDN
WB5LIR
N5LJX
W5LN
K5LNI
W5LZP
W5MAW
WB5MBL
W5MCH
W5MI
W5MHP
KC5MM
N5MPN
WB5MQD
N5NIP
WB5NLG
KB5OAH
KC5OT
KA5OWE
W5PN
W5POH
W5PWX
WA5PZT
W5QEF
K5QHF
KB5QJ
W5QJG
WA5QLY
WA5QVP
WA5RDQ
KA5RHX
W5RFY
K5SDR
WB5SKM
K5SP
W5SXW
KA5SZD
KA5UMM
N5UYB
K5VKO
W5VNN
AA5WB
WB5WBE
KC5WL
NR5X
KB5XJ
KC5YA
K5YM
W5YV
WA5ZIF
K6AAL
K6ACN
N6ADQ
W6ANF
N6AT
WA6AVD
KH6BAF
WD6BAT
W6BAX
WB6BDE
KB6BEN
N6BFQ
N6BLG
W6BLI
KD6BLO
W6BLU
K6BMW
KH6BQG
W6BSR
W6BUO
AA6BW

KH6BX
N6CGB
N6COV
K6CWD
N6CZU
WB6DCG
WA6DDO
KA6DEN
W6DJI
K6DLD
W6DMB
WA6DOF
K6DOR
WD6DQC
W6DSV
KB6DSZ
W6DTD
W6DTQ
K6EC
W6EEY
WA6EFY
W6EYR
W6FBV
WD6FFM
KG6FG
KD6FHV
W6FKT
N6FMO
W6FNV
N6FOB
WA6FPB
WD6FPO
W6FSF
W6FST
N6FTD
W6FUZ
WD6FYF
W6GBE
WA6GJE
WB6GSP
W6GUE
WD6GVA
N6GY
K6HB
W6HCX
KD6HDP
KW6HF
W6HHD
KA6HOQ
N6HOR
KB6HOU
KE6HS
W6HTG
W6HWP
W6HWZ
N6HXN
K6ICK
KA6IDS
K6IE
KB6IFC
K6IGL
N6IJL
KH6ILU
WA6ION
KC6IRB
W6IRK
W6IZP
W6IZS
N6JDQ
KH6JG
KD6JKJ
W6JLM
W6JOE
WA6JQM
K6JRA
K6JRJ
KB6JSK
WA6JTM
N6JY
AA6K
KK6KA
N6KGH
W6KJA
K6KVD
WB6KWX
WA6LJU
W6LLF
W6LNE
W6LQA
N6LTV
W6LYJ
W6LXM
WA6MAR
WA6MAV
W6MBY
WA6MHO
W6MHZ
N6MIB
N6MJ
N6MO
W6MO
KA6MPH
W6MST
W6MUM
W6MV
W6NHW
W6NKD
W6NQJ
W6NQN
W6NSZ
W6ODQ
W6OE
KA6OEZ
K6OLM
W6OR
WB6ORR
W6OWQ
K6OYN
K6OZ
W6PCS
WA6PEX
NH6PH
W6PHE
W6PL
KC6QAD
WB6QGT
W6QJO
W6QMV
N6QPX
KG6QX
WA6QYV
N6QZ
WA6QZF
KB6RFD
WA6RLE
WB6RMA
K6RTZ
KB6RUJ
W6RYQ
KS6S
WX6S
K6SDD
W6SDF
KA6SDN
K6SIW
W6SJA
W6SMZ
W6SOF
WA6SOH
WB6SRZ
W6SSB
WB6TEE
WB6TJW
N6TKD
K6TL
W6TNV
W6TPS
K6TSB
W6TSI
W6TYC
W6TZI
W6TZM
WA6UBG
W6UCP
N6UKD
W6UR
N6UUP
WA6UWJ
W6UYF
WA6UZC
NX6V
KB6VMF
WA6VRP
K6VS
WA6VZO
W6WFE
N6WIR
WB6WNA
KF6WO
N6YDW
WA6YFV
WB6YPI
WA6YTT
KA6YXT
KA6YZQ
NK6Z
WA6ZJE
WB6ZKK
N6ZPQ
WB7ABU
WB7ACH
W7AFO
W7APS
N7AZA
WX7B
K7BEH
WB7BKF
W7BKV
W7BOC
W7BOZ
WB7BRK
N7BRU
N7BTA
W7BYR
K7CE
W7CMX
W7CRC
W7CX
K7CYZ
W7CZY
WD7D
WG7D
N7DDX
W7DGL
W7DGT
N7DHY
W7DTF
WB7DXE
W7DXQ
W7EBZ
N7EDZ
KB7ELG
KL7EN
N7ERF
KB7EV
N7EYN
KA7EZH
W7FES
W7FNE
W7FNJ
K7FO
WA7FFR
W7FTA
N7FXS
KD7GD
N7GEK
W7GFV
K7GOX
W7GRM
K7GUB
AA7GZ
W7HJY
KA7HKQ
W7HMJ
WA7HMP
WA7HSZ
W7HVT
W7IDA
W7IDZ
N7IGC
W7INZ
KS7J
KA7JHN
W7JHQ
KA7JLV
KC7JR
K7JYP
KA7KAX
N7KFN
W7KKY
WA7KMX
KA7KTN
W7KRP
W7KUG
KA7KWF
K7KWM
KB7LCU
KA7LDS
NL7LT
WA7LVD
W7LZA
KU7M
K7MC
W7MKF
WA7MOF
N7MOL
W7MPD
KB7MPK
WA7NLC
K7NMC
W7NPR
K7NUP
W7NX
K7OAK
W7OPH
K7OYK
NN7P
W7PD
W7PGY
KE7PZ
W7PZW
NX7Q
WS7Q
KC7QK
WB7QMH
K7RJD
WA7RMT
W7RXT
WB7SOT
W7SRM
KA7TPN
K7TV
W7TVL
WB7UBA
WB7UGO
WB7UUP
WA7VCC
WA7VEJ
W7VHY
K7VIN
WB7VWA
WA7WDJ
WA7WFC
KA7WFF
W7WI
WZ7X
W7YF
WA7YRC
WA7YUK
K7ZBN
WA7ZEE
K7ZHS
K7ZIQ
KD7ZK
KB7ZM
KE7ZY
KB8AAQ
K8AJJ
K8APV
WD8ASC
W8ATK
W8AUM
K8AXC
K8AXU
N8BC
W8BCR
W8BEK
K8BEL
W8BFO
W8BMK
N8BNJ
N8BOH
W8BTM
W8BTW
WB8BUD
W8CEY
K8CGW
K8CIQ
K8CKD
W8CMC
W8CYL
WB8CZH
N8DBO
WA8DEF
K8DGE
W8DLU
N8DMD
K8DNS
WD8DQP
W8DSC
W8DSF
WD8DVB
KA8DYB
WA8EAI
KB8EYP
KR8F
W8FCM
KB8FLW
W8FSU
KA8FUZ
W8FVC
W8FYA
W8FZR
AF8G
NC8G
K8GAE
N8GEA
WB8GEP
K8GFE
W8GRZ
WB8GTP
N8HDP
K8HRN
W8HT
W8IBO
W8IGK
W8IR
W8IRM
W8IY
WD8JCS
W8JHG
K8JVX
KF8KA
W8KFW
W8KHI
W8KPF
W8KS
W8KSS
W8KTR
KD8KU
K8KYS
W8LDD
W8LFS
W8LRZ
KA8LUE
K8LXF
W8LYD
W8LZE
AC8M
WD8MCQ
K8MDT
WB8MHI
W8MN
W8NWR
KA8MYA
W8MYG
W8NDX
K8OEL
W8OJN
WB8OSQ
W8OWP
W8OYV
N8OZI
WF8P
W8PGE
K8PNZ
WA8PQN
WB8PSS
W8PTI
K8QBM
W8QEQ
WD8QMT
K8RHC
KA8RFU
WA8RIV
WA8RLL
WA8RQX
W8RRR
W8RUU
WB8RWW
W8RWO
WB8RYA
KA8SCR
W8SOL

W8SON
WB8STJ
WA8SXA
AK8T
W8TEZ
K8TJN
WA8TRU
WA8TYQ
KD8UK
K8UZ
AF8V
KC8VJ
K8VUK
W8VZB
W8WCS
WA8WUT
K8WZX
K8YJQ
WB8YKF
WA8YLR
WA8YLW
W8YOU
WB8YZR
W8ZAU
W8ZCH
WA8ZTU
W8ZXN
W9AAY
K9ABG
W9ABI
N9AFH
W9AG
WA9AIH
W9AKR
N9ANW
W9ASN
K9AUF
W9AUO
WA9AVV
W9AYH
AD9B
W9BDP
W9BRX
K9BTR
W9BUM
W9BVE
W9BZA
KB9CDC
N9CGQ
KB9CNF
W9CP
WD9CSE
KA9DFY
W9DI
W9DPC
WD9DRL
KC9EA
W9EDG
KB9EFS
W9EGI
W9EGX
W9EJD
W9ERI
N9ERW
W9FAD
W9FEI
N9FGX
W9FJB
KB9FVJ
K9GEQ
W9GGG
KB9GK
W9GL
N9GQY
KA9GRW
W9GSA
W9GVC
KU9H
WD9HAK
W9HC
W9HDE
N9HFK
N9HFT
WA9HGA
KA9HHP
WD9HJN
K9HNA
W9HPS
W9HUX
W9HVF
WD9HZH
WB9HZI
NS9I
KA9IBR
W9IOH
W9IPH
W9IPQ
W9IW
WA9IWM
WW9J
K9JHQ
KA9JJB
N9JKB
W9JMW
N9JNZ
W9KAZ
KA9KMU
WB9KOS
W9KXG
W9KXR
W9KY
WB9LAB
W9LBE
W9LJA
K9LKA
N9LLH
K9LLT
WB9LTJ
W9LVB
W9LVE
K9LXI
W9LWH
AA9M
N9MFS
W9MG
W9MJ
N9MLS
W9MUL
W9MYG
WE9N
W9NJS
KA9NNW
N9NRZ
W9NZS
WZ9O
WØOEM
W9OO
WB9OWU
WU9P
WW9P
WA9PAI
N9PCQ
K9PL
W9PRC
WA9PUY
W9QXL
W9QYH
KA9R
KI9R
KC9RF
K9RO
W9SFK
WØSOY
KD9TB
KE9TG
W9TGB
W9TKW
WA9TNZ
KA9TRM
W9TSM
WA9UCX
K9UPV
W9USK
K9UUK
WA9UZY
W9VCL
KA9VIT
K9VRD
W9VW
K9VWQ
W9VZ
W9VZZ
WB9WDW
KA9WHK
WA9YET
W9YGG
WB9YMW
WT9Z
W9ZDB
W9ZGP
W9ZVE
NØAGE
NØAML
KØAPZ
NØASO
WBØBEA
WDØBGV
WAØBIE
WAØBJM
WDØBJV
WØBQL
WBØBTP
WØBZX
NØCAO
WØCF
KØCNQ
WØCSW
NØCWZ
WØCYM
NØCZT
AGØD
KAØDDY
WØDPT
WAØDOV
WØDR
NØDTV
WAØECH
WAØECK
WDØEFE
KBØEGM
NØEHX
WDØEIG
KØELC
KØENS
KØEWA
KAØEXM
WØEZI
WØFCO
NØFDB
KØFKJ
WØFIR
WØFWY
WDØG
KEØGB
WØGCJ
KBØGCR
NØGHU
WØGJM
NØGLD
WØGLS
KBØGN
KCØGP
KBØGVZ
WØHG
KCØHJ
KBØHOA
WDØHOF
WØHSL
WAØHTR
KØHVO
WØHYF
WØIER
NØIMC
WBØIQA
NKØJ
WØJDV
KFØJJ
KGØK
WØKHD
KØKKS
NØKMB
KØKOO
WØKUZ
WAØLLG
WØLNW
WØLO
WBØLTP
WØMA
WAØMES
WBØMPX
WØMUN
WØNEE
WØNIK
WØNLA
WØNMN
NØNWS
WØODL
WØOMG
WØOQH
NØPAK
KAØPBK
KAØPIW
NØPVY
WAØPZY
WBØQQV
NYØR
WAØRBJ
KAØRCQ
WØRJB
WØRND
KCØRZ
WØSOV
KDØSV
WBØTKT
WØTLA
WØTQL
WAØTTK
KØTYO
WGØU
KBØUC
WBØUEV
WØUSD
WØUU
WØVGA
WØVIP
WØVKP
WBØVNK
WAØVTZ
KBØXB
WØYNJ
WØYTL
WØYVI
NIØZ
WBØZFE
WØZOC
WBØZRA
WØZWN
WØZZZ

DX

AP2UR
EA1BMX
F8TH
G3GRJ
G3RKC/W1
GM4VDI
HB9BX
IK8DOI
LX1YZ
OH2BTU
PAØKZ
PY3AO
SMØAVK
SU1BA
TG9VT
VE3HD
VE3WT
VE4GB
VK6FM
VK6TS
VO1FN
VO1SV
VP5EMG
VP9L/W4
ZL2ANA
ZL2FT
ZS2GE